2023 Income Tax FUNDAMENTALS

GERALD E. WHITTENBURG

STEVEN L. GILL

San Diego State University

Australia • Brazil • Canada • Mexico • Singapore • United Kingdom • United States

***Income Tax Fundamentals*, 41st Edition**
Gerald E. Whittenburg and Steven L. Gill

Senior Vice President, Product: Erin Joyner

VP, Product: Thais Alencar

Portfolio Product Director: Joe Sabatino

Portfolio Product Manager: Jonathan Gross

Senior Content Manager: Tricia Hempel

Learning Designer: Kristen Meere

Product Assistant: Flannery Cowan

VP, Product Marketing: Jason Sakos

Product Marketing Manager: Colin Kramer

Digital Project Manager: Steven McMillian

Production Service: MPS Limited

Designer: Chris Doughman

Cover Images:
donatas1205/Shutterstock.com;
iStock.com/gerenme

Special page images:

Zhukov Oleg/Shutterstock.com;
ILYA AKINSHIN/Shutterstock.com

Intellectual Property

Content Acquisition Analyst: Nichole Nalenz
Project Manager: Anjali Kambli

Tax forms reproduced courtesy of the Internal Revenue Service (**www.irs.gov**).

Library of Congress Control Number: 2022919508

Student Edition:
ISBN: 978-0-357-71952-7

Loose-leaf Edition:
ISBN: 978-0-357-71954-1

Cengage
200 Pier 4 Boulevard
Boston, MA 02210
USA

Printed in the United States of America
Print Number: 01 Print Year: 2022

Concise, Current, & Practical!

Income Tax Fundamentals' Winning Forms Approach Is Time-Tested

Income Tax Fundamentals 2023 Edition is designed as a self-contained book for an introductory course in individual income taxation. We take pride in the concise, current, and practical coverage of the income tax return preparation process. *Income Tax Fundamentals* continues to be the **market-leading textbook** with a tax forms-based approach that is a reliable choice, with an experienced author team that offers a commitment to accuracy. The workbook format of the textbook presents materials in practical sections with multiple examples and review problems. The presentation of the material does not assume that the reader has taken a course in accounting, making it appropriate for use as a self-study guide to federal income tax. *Income Tax Fundamentals* adopters tell us:

> Great text. I have used it for years mostly because of its simple and straightforward approach to the basic income tax elements.
>
> — Jerold K. Braun, Daytona State College

> This text provides an excellent overview for community tax classes. The software gives these students good hands-on experience with the concepts.
>
> — Jay Wright, New River Community College

> I love this book with all its comprehensive problems that progress from easy to difficult.
>
> — LoAnn Nelson, PhD, CPA, Lake Region State College

> The layout of the chapters is well-thought out.
>
> — James Hromadka, San Jacinto College

> I enjoy using the Whittenburg text...it is the best I have found.
>
> — Jana Hosmer, Blue Ridge Community College

Whittenburg and Gill's hallmark "**Forms Approach**" allows students to practice filling out tax returns right in the book while also having the option to download tax forms online. *Income Tax Fundamentals* follows the Form 1040 and supporting Schedules 1 through 3 and A through E. Every attempt to align the concepts with the schedules has been made so students can follow from the detailed form or worksheet to the schedule and eventually to Form 1040.

ProConnect™ Tax

Each individual tax form required to complete the problems in the textbook is included within ***Income Tax Fundamentals*** and within the complimentary ProConnect Tax software. ProConnect Tax is an industry-leading tax preparation software that is hosted on the cloud and provides robust tax content and easy navigation. The ProConnect Tax website offers community and knowledge-based content, view alerts, and FAQ articles. All of the 2022 individual income tax return problems in the textbook may be solved using the ProConnect Tax software, or students may prepare the tax returns by hand.

eamesBot/Shutterstock.com

Income Tax Fundamentals

Evolves Each Year to Benefit You

New to This Edition

Many Changes to Tax Law

A number of changes that applied to tax year 2021 expired (child tax credit, child and dependent care credit, economic incentive payments, the recovery rebate credit, and virtually all COVID-related provisions). Most of these provisions returned to the 2017 Tax Cuts and Jobs Act versions that are scheduled to expire after 2025. The Inflation Reduction Act of 2022 impacted energy-related tax credits and brought back a form of the corporate alternative minimum tax to a limited number of very large corporations. All of these changes are included in this edition.

Introduction of Additional Real-life Source Documents

We continue to include commonly used source documents in the exercises and tax return problems, such as Form W-2, a myriad of forms 1099, Form 1095-A, payroll documents, and additional accounting schedules, such as trial balances and income statements, in an effort to replicate the tax return preparation process. Information that is extraneous to the problem is included to encourage students to use analytical and critical-thinking skills to deal with less-structured problems.

Additions to Content

This edition includes expanded coverage in a significant number of areas in an effort to create awareness of certain tax provisions:

- Head of household filing status requirements
- The electronic filing process
- A significant expansion of content surrounding fixed income investments such as bonds, including an overview of bond discount and premium
- The basis of property acquired by gift or inheritance
- Prepaid rent and deposits on rental properties
- Limitations applied to charitable contributions, including a new worksheet designed to assist students
- Overviews of divorced and separated taxpayers, amended returns, deceased taxpayers, foreign bank account reporting requirements, and taxpayers involved in farming
- Updates for the latests credits expanded or created by the Inflation Reduction Act of 2022
- Significant increase in the discussion of the "property regulations" that cover the decisions to capitalize or deduct expenditures
- Expanded content on Forms W-4, W-9, and the computation of estimated tax payments
- Added content related to tax preparer regulations, including substantial authority and Circular 230
- Tax treatment of virtual currencies such as Bitcoin

Updated Cumulative Software Problem

The cumulative software problem included as Group 5 questions at the end of Chapters 1–8 has been updated to include more source documents (Forms W-2, 1099, etc.) and extraneous information to encourage students to think more critically about the relevance of certain items when preparing tax returns.

A Complete Learning System—CNOWv2

CNOWv2 for Taxation takes students from motivation to mastery. It elevates thinking by providing superior content designed with the entire student workflow in mind. Students learn more efficiently with a variety of engaging assessments and learning tools. For instructors, CNOWv2 provides ultimate control and customization and a clear view into student performance that allows for the opportunity to tailor the learning experience to improve outcomes.

Motivation

Many instructors find that students come to class unmotivated and unprepared. To help with engagement and preparedness, CNOWv2 for Whittenburg offers the following feature:

Self-Study Questions based on the information presented in the textbook help students prepare for class lectures or review prior to an exam. Self-Study Questions provide ample practice for the students as they read the chapters, while providing them with valuable feedback and checks along the way, as the solutions are provided conveniently in Appendix E of the textbook.

Application

Students need to learn problem-solving skills in order to complete taxation problems on their own. However, as students try to work through homework problems, sometimes they become stuck and need guidance. To help reinforce concepts and keep students on the right track, CNOWv2 for Whittenburg offers the following:

- **End-of-chapter homework: Group 1 and 2 problems**
- **Algorithmic versions:** End-of-chapter homework is available for at least 10–15 problems per chapter.
- **Detailed feedback for each homework question:** Homework questions include enhanced, immediate feedback so students can learn as they go. Levels of feedback include an option for "check my work" prior to submission of an assignment. Then, after submitting an assignment, students receive even more extensive feedback explaining why their answers were incorrect. Instructors can decide how much feedback their students receive and when, including providing the full solution, if they wish.
- Built-in **Test Bank:** Provides online assessment.
- CNOWv2's **Adaptive Study Plan:** Complete with quizzes, an eBook, and more, it is designed to provide assistance for students who need additional support and prepare them for the exam.

Mastery

Finally, students need to make the leap from memorizing concepts to critical thinking. They need to be able to connect multiple topics and master the material. To help students grasp the big picture of taxation, tax return preparation, and achieve the end goal of mastery, CNOWv2 for Whittenburg offers the following:

- **Comprehensive Problems:** Allow students to complete the tax return problems by entering the relevant information on tax forms and schedules in the ProConnect Tax software or by manually preparing the tax forms and schedules provided in an online appendix.

Cengage Learning Testing Powered by Cognero®

Cognero® is a flexible, online system that allows instructors to:

- author, edit, and manage test bank content from multiple Cengage Learning solutions
- create multiple test versions in an instant
- deliver tests from your LMS, your classroom or wherever you want

Cognero® possesses the features necessary to make assessment fast, efficient, and effective:

- **Simplicity at every step:** A desktop-inspired interface features drop-down menus and familiar, intuitive tools.
- **Full-featured test generator:** Choose from various question types. Multi-language support, an equation editor, and unlimited metadata help ensure your tests are complete and compliant.
- **Cross-compatible capability:** Import and export content into other systems.

CL Testing Powered by Cognero® is accessible through the instructor companion site, **www.cengage.com/login.**

Key Terms

Key Terms with page references are located at the end of all of the chapters and reinforce the important tax terms introduced and discussed in each chapter.

Key Points

Following the Key Terms is a brief summary of the learning objective highlights for each chapter to allow students to focus quickly on the main points of each chapter.

Reliable Instructor Resources Are Convenient

Solutions Manual

The manual, located on the instructor companion website: **www.cengage.com/login**, contains detailed solutions to the end-of-chapter problems in the textbook.

Comprehensive Instructor Companion Website

This password-protected site contains instructor resources: the Solutions Manual, the Test Bank, Cognero® testing tools, Solutions to the Cumulative Tax Return Problems, ProConnect Tax software solutions and instructions, PowerPoints, and more: **www.cengage.com/login**.

As We Go to Press

To access tax law information after the publication of this textbook, please visit **www.cengage.com**. At the home page, input the ISBN of your textbook (from the back cover of your book). This will take you to the product page where free companion resources are located.

Step-by-Step Format Builds Student Confidence

The practical, step-by-step format in ***Income Tax Fundamentals 2023 Edition*** builds from simple to complex topics. The authors are careful to lead students down a path of understanding rather than overwhelming them with excessive detail and multiple Internal Revenue Code references.

- Helpful examples within each chapter provide realistic scenarios for students to consider.

EXAMPLE Ying and Michael are married filing jointly taxpayers with earned income and AGI of $23,200 in 2022. They have two children ages 3 and 5. All members of the family have Social Security numbers, are U.S. citizens, and lived together in the United States all year. Ying had $820 of tax withheld from her wages during the year. Michael did not work. Ying and Michael can claim the EIC as they meet all the tests for taxpayers with a qualifying child. Based ... me of $23,200 ... with two qualif...

- The short Learning Objective sections within each chapter offer numerous examples, supported by the "Self-Study Problems" throughout. The Self-Study Problems encourage students to answer a series of relevant questions in a short-answer format. The solutions to the Self-Study Problems are provided at the end of the textbook in Appendix E, offering immediate feedback to students to help build confidence.

- The Quick Tax Reference Guide on the inside of the back cover of the textbook includes the Tax Equation and federal tax rate schedule.

2022 Federal Tax Rate Schedule

If Taxable Income Is Over:	But Not Over:	The Tax Is:
SINGLE INDIVIDUAL		
$0	$10,275	10% of taxable income *
$10,275	$41,775	$1,027.50 + 12% of the excess over $10,275 *
$41,775	$89,075	$4,807.50 + 22% of the excess over $41,775 *
$89,075	$100,000	$15,213.50 + 24% of the excess over $89,075 *
$100,000	$170,050	$15,213.50 + 24% of the excess over $89,075
$170,050	$215,950	$34,647.50 + 32% of the excess over $170,050
$215,950	$539,900	$49,335.50 + 35% of the excess over $215,950
$539,900		$162,718.00 + 37% of the excess over $539,900
MARRIED FILING JOINTLY OR QUALIFYING WIDOW(ER)		
$0	$20,550	10% of taxable income *
$20,550	$83,550	$2,055.00 + 12% of the excess over $20,550 *
$83,550	$100,000	$9,615.00 + 22% of the excess over $83,550 *
$100,000		$9,615.00 + 22% of the excess over $83,550
$178,150		$30,427.00 + 24% of the excess over $178,150
...00		... 32% of the excess over $34...

LEARNING OBJECTIVES

After completing this chapter, you should be able to:

LO 5.1 Explain how Health Savings Accounts (HSAs) can be used for tax-advantaged medical care.

LO 5.2 Describe the self-employed health insurance deduction.

LO 5.3 Explain the treatment of Individual Retirement Accounts (IRAs), including Roth IRAs.

LO 5.4 Explain the general contribution rules for small business and self-employed retirement plans.

LO 5.5 Describe other ad... djusted gross income...

- Learning Objectives help organize information and are referenced in the end-of-chapter exercises.

Andrey_Popov/Shutterstock.com

Real-World Applications Keep Students Engaged

- The "Would You Sign This Tax Return?" feature places readers in the office of a tax preparer with interesting and sometimes humorous real-world tax ethics questions that will intrigue students. Many of these features are inspired by the authors' own experiences working with various clients in tax preparation. As part of each scenario, students decide if they would sign the tax return. The instructor can use the cases to spark group discussions on basic tax preparation ethics.

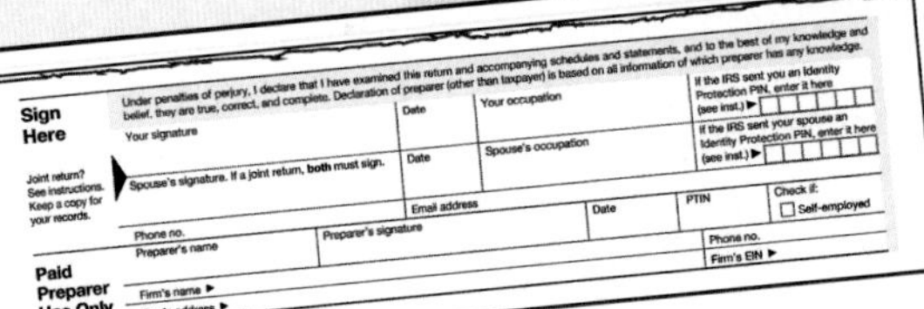

Sign Here

Joint return? See instructions. Keep a copy for your records.

Paid Preparer Use Only

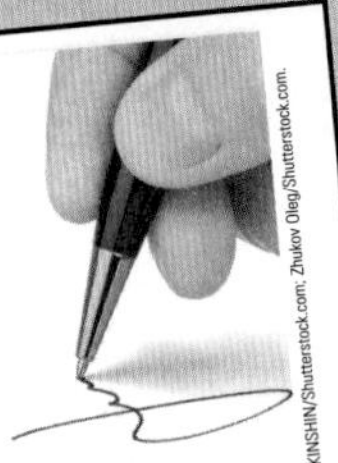

ILYA AKINSHIN/Shutterstock.com; Zhukov Oleg/Shutterstock.com

Would You Sign This Tax Return?

Your client, William Warrant, was hired for a management position at an Internet company planning to start a website called "indulgedanimals.com" for dogs, cats, and other pets. When he was hired, William was given an incentive stock option (ISO) worth $500,000, which he exercised during the year. Exercise of the ISO creates a tax preference item for alternative minimum tax (AMT) and causes him to have to pay substantial additional tax when combined with his other tax items for the year. He is livid about the extra tax and refuses to file the AMT Form 6251 with his tax return because the AMT tax is "unfair" and "un-American" according to him. Would you sign this tax return?

- Real-world examples within Tax Break segments provide actual, effective examples of tax-planning strategies that clearly illustrate the concepts discussed throughout the book and cover nearly every basic tax-planning technique used by tax preparers.

A gift of a contribution to a Roth IRA for a child or grandchild with a summer job can grow into a very large gift over time. The amount that may be contributed to a child's Roth IRA is the lesser of $6,000 or the child's earnings. A child with $6,000 in a Roth IRA at age 16 will have well over $100,000 at age 65 if the Roth IRA investment earns 7 percent annually.

TAX BREAK

- Interesting tax facts within "Would You Believe?" sections grab students' attention with interesting asides, including captivating facts and stories about tax laws and preparation.

Would You Believe?

A taxpayer from Oklahoma recently discovered that lying to the IRS can have consequences. In spite of the taxpayer initially reporting that he had one bank account, owned only his home and his body shop business property, and three cars, the IRS revenue agent eventually determined that the taxpayer had five bank accounts, three unreported rental properties, and had made payments on car loans for fifteen vehicles during the audit period. Amazingly, his taxable income for the same periods was $0, $0, and $114. The court affirmed the IRS assessment of a 75-percent fraud penalty. See *Clark v. Comm'r*, T.C. Memo 2021-114 in which the court provides a detailed discussion of the audit process undertaken.

- New Tax Law boxes throughout the textbook draw students' attention to specific areas affected by new tax legislation.

Not since 2011 has the IRS increased the standard mileage rate in the middle of a tax year but due to the high cost of fuel, the 2022 rate increased from 58.5 cents per mile for the first half of the year to 62.5 cents per mile starting July 1, 2022. The medical mileage rate also increased from 18 cents per mile to 22 cents per mile; however, the charity mileage rate is fixed by law at 14 cents per mile and did not change.

Income Tax Fundamentals

Delivers Proven End-of-Chapter Strengths

- The pages are perforated, allowing students to complete end-of-chapter problems and submit them for homework. Students can also tear out tax forms as needed.
- Several question types ensure a variety of assignment options:
  - Multiple-Choice Questions
  - Problems
  - Writing Assignments
  - Comprehensive Problems
  - The Cumulative Software Problem provided in Chapters 1–8 gives students the flexibility to use multiple resources, such as the tax forms within the book, ProConnect Tax or alternative tax preparation software. The problem evolves with each succeeding chapter's content, allowing students to build on their comprehension of various tax topics.
  - Additional Comprehensive Tax Return Problems are located in Appendix D.

Digital Tools Enhance Student Understanding

CNOWv2 is a powerful online homework tool. This online resource includes an interactive eBook, end-of-chapter homework, detailed student feedback and interactive quizzing, that covers the most challenging topics, a lab guide for using the ProConnect Tax software, and much more. The student companion website offers—*at no additional costs*—study resources for students. Go to **www.cengage.com**, and input the ISBN number of your textbook (from the back cover of your book). This will take you to the product page where free companion resources are located.

ProConnect™ Tax

ProConnect Tax access is included with each textbook. A detailed reference lab guide will help the student use the tax software for solving end-of-chapter problems.

For students who are new to the ProConnect Tax software product, we have placed tips throughout the textbook providing guidance to assist students with the transition from a paper form to using the tax software.

Marc Romanelli/Tetra images/Getty Images

Note to Students: Maximize Your Reading Experience

This textbook includes many examples to help illustrate learning objectives. After reading each section, including the examples, answer the corresponding Self-Study Problems. You can find the solutions to the Self-Study Problems at the end of the textbook in Appendix E to check your accuracy. Use your performance to measure your understanding, and re-read the Learning Objectives section if needed. Many key tax terms are defined in each chapter, which will help improve your overall comprehension.

USING TAX SOFTWARE

Numerous tax return problems in the textbook can be solved using either the online tax preparation software or hand preparation. The popular software, ProConnect Tax, is available with the textbook. Helpful tips for using ProConnect Tax have been placed throughout the book so that students can more easily train on the software and prepare the tax returns included in each of the first eleven chapters. A student guide to ProConnect Tax is provided at the companion website. Your college may offer additional tax preparation software, but remember that you can always prepare the solutions manually on the textbook-provided tax forms, schedules and worksheets located conveniently in one place in Appendix F which can be found online with student and instructor resources.

USING THE "WOULD YOU SIGN THIS TAX RETURN?" FEATURE

A practitioner who knows when to say "I cannot sign this tax return," even if it means losing a client, is exercising the most basic ethical wisdom. Most chapters contain a "Would You Sign This Tax Return?" case reflecting a common client issue. Each issue corresponds to an obvious concept illustrated in the previous section. However, the approach to advise the client is not always obvious nor easy. The art of explaining tax rules to a client who does not understand them, or, worse, wants to break them, requires not only a good understanding of the rules, but also good interpersonal skills and sometimes the gift of persuasion. The news in the last several years has shown reports of respected CPA firms with members who failed to say the simple words, "I cannot sign this tax return," demonstrating that simple ethical practice is not always easy. We hope instructors will use these cases to spark group discussions or contemplation, and, perhaps, add examples from their own experience.

USING THE CUMULATIVE SOFTWARE PROBLEM

The Cumulative Software Problem can be found at the end of Chapters 1–8. The case information provided in each chapter builds on the information presented in previous chapters, resulting in a lengthy and complex tax return by the conclusion of the problem in Chapter 8. Your instructor may have you work in groups to prepare each of the tax returns. The groups can follow the real-world accounting firm model using a preparer, a reviewer, and a firm owner who takes responsibility for the accuracy of the return and signs it. All of the issues in the problem are commonly seen by tax preparers and are covered in the textbook. The full return is difficult to prepare by hand, so tax software is recommended. If the problem is prepared using tax software, the data should be saved so the additional information in the succeeding chapters can be added without duplicating input from previous chapters.

About the Authors

Gerald E. Whittenburg In 2015, we unexpectedly lost our dear friend and co-author Gene Whittenburg. As the original author of *Income Tax Fundamentals*, Gene was critical in designing the forms-based approach that the book has used successfully for over two decades. Gene started his life in a small town in Texas, entered the Navy, served his country in Vietnam, earned a Bachelor's, Master's, and PhD degrees, and served as a distinguished faculty at San Diego State University for almost 40 years. We intend to continue to honor Gene by committing to uphold his standard of publishing excellence.

Steven L. Gill is an associate professor of accounting and taxation in the Charles W. Lamden School of Accountancy at San Diego State University. He also served as the Director of Graduate Programs at the Fowler College of Business at SDSU. Steve received a BS in Accounting from the University of Florida, an MS in Taxation from Northeastern University, and a PhD in Accounting from the University of Massachusetts. Prior to entering academia, he worked for almost 12 years in the field of tax and accounting, including roles in public accounting, internal audit, corporate accounting, and ultimately, vice president of finance. Although currently in inactive status, Steve holds a Certified Public Accountant designation. He has published a wide variety of articles in various academic and practitioner journals, and has taught at both the undergraduate and graduate levels, including taxation and financial and management accounting. Steven also serves as an author on Cengage's Federal Tax Research series.

Reviewers

Janice Akao, *Butler Community College*
Sandra Augustine, *Hilbert College*
George Barbi, *Lanier Technical College*
Lydia Botsford, *DeAnza College*
Mike Bowyer, *Montgomery Community College*
Jerold Braun, *Daytona State College*
Lindy Byrd, *Augusta Technical College*
Greg Carlton, *Davidson County Community College*
Diana Cescolini, *Chaffey College*
John Chappell, *Northland Community and Technical College*
Marilyn Ciolino, *Delgado Community College*
Diane Clugston, *Cambria-Rowe Business College*
Tonya Coates, *Western Piedmont Community College*
Thomas Confrey, *SUNY Orange*
Amy Conley, *Genesee Community College*
Eric DaGragnano, *Western Governors University*
Geoffrey Danzig, *Miami Dade College–Hialeah Campus*
Richard Davis, *Susquehanna University*
Susan Davis, *Green River Community College*
Vaun Day, *Central Arizona College*
Ken Dennis, *San Diego City College*
Kerry Dolan, *Great Falls College Montana State University*
Vicky C. Dominguez, *College of Southern Nevada*
Lisa Farnam, *College of Western Idaho*
John Fasler, *Whatcom Community College*
Brian Fink, *Danville Area Community College*
Brenda Fowler, *Central Carolina Community College*
George Frankel, *San Francisco State University*
Alan Fudge, *Linn-Benton Community College*
Gregory Gosman, *Keiser University*
Nancy Gromen, *Blue Mountain Community College*
Jeffery Haig, *Copper Mountain College*
Tracie Hayes, *Randolph Community College*
Michael Heath, *River Parishes Community College*
Cindy Hinz, *Jamestown Community College*
Rob Hochschild, *Ivy Tech Community College*
Japan Holmes, Jr., *Savannah Technical College*
Jana Hosmer, *Blue Ridge Community College*
James Hromadka, *San Jacinto College*
Carol Hughes, *Asheville Buncombe Technical Community College*
Norma Hunting, *Chabot College, Hayward, California*
Adrian Jarrell, *James Sprunt Community College*
Paul Johnson, *Mississippi Gulf Coast Community College*
Jessica Jones, *Mesa Community College*
Dieter Kiefer, *American River College*
Christopher Kinney, *Mount Wachusett Community College*
Angela Kirkendall, *South Puget Sound Community College*
Mark Klamrzynski, *Phoenix College*
Raymond Kreiner, *Piedmont College*
William Kryshak, *University Wisconsin-Stout*
Linda Lane, *Walla Walla Community College*

Christie Lee, *Lanier Technical College*
Anna Leyes, *Ivy Tech Community College*
Jeannie Liu, *Rio Hondo College*
Susan Logorda, *Lehigh Carbon Community College*
Heather Lynch, *Northeast Iowa Community College*
Diania McRae, *Western Carolina University*
Deanne Michaelson, *Pellissippi State Community College*
Jennifer Morton, *Ivy Tech Community College*
Sharon O'Reilly, *Gateway Technical College*
Mike Prockton, *Finger Lakes CC*
John Ribezzo, *Community College of Rhode Island*
Lance Rodrigues, *Ohlone College*
Hanna Sahebifard, *Golden West College*
Larry Sayler, *Greenville University*
James Shimko, *Jackson Community College*
Barry Siebert, *Concordia University – Saint Paul*
Kimberly Sipes, *Kentucky State University*
Amy Smith, *Pearl River Community College*
Thomas Snavely, *Yavapai College*
Joanie Sompayrc, *UT-Chattanooga*
Barbara Squires, *Corning Community College*
Todd Stowe, *Southwest Florida College*
Gracelyn Stuart-Tuggle, *Palm Beach State College*
Robert L. Taylor, *C.P.A., Lees-McRae College*
Teresa Thamer, *Brenau University*
Craig Vilhauer, *Merced College*
Stan Walker, *Georgia Northwestern Technical School*
Teresa Walker, *Greensboro College*
Joe Welker, *College of Western Idaho*
Jean Wells, *Howard University*
Mary Ann Whitehurst, *Southern Crescent Technical College*
Sharon Williams, *Sullivan University*
Douglas Woods, *Wayne College*
Patty Worsham, *Chaffey College*
Jay Wright, *New River Community College*
Douglas Yentsch, *South Central College*
James Zartman, *Elizabethtown PA College*
Jane Zlojutro, *Northwestern Michigan College*

Acknowledgments

The authors wish to thank all of the instructors who provided feedback for the 2023 edition via surveys as well as the following supplement authors and verifiers for their most valuable suggestions and support:

D. Elizabeth Stone Atkins—*High Point University, High Point, NC*
David Candelaria—*Mt. San Jacinto College, Menifee, CA*
Jim Clarkson—*San Jacinto College South, Houston, TX*
Pennie Eddy—*Appalachian Technical College, Jasper, GA*
Paul Shinal—*Cayga Community College, Auburn, NY*

The authors would like to thank Susan Gill, Doug Kelley, Jill Kelley, Nicole Doherty, and Tracy Tuong for their time and attention in reviewing chapters. We would also like to thank Tracy Newman and Wendy Shanker for their work of reviewing and verifying the content in CengageNOWv2, including the end-of-chapter items. We would also like to extend our thanks to the Tax Forms and Publications Division of the Internal Revenue Service for their assistance in obtaining draft forms each year.

We appreciate your continued support in advising us of any revisions or corrections you feel are appropriate.

Steve Gill

The Annotated 1040 Map

The annotated 1040 map is an expanded tax formula, illustrating where each piece of the tax formula is covered in the textbook. The 1040 map helps you understand how all of the elements of the textbook and the tax formula fit together. Use this as a reference and bookmark this page.

Form 1040 Department of the Treasury—Internal Revenue Service
U.S. Individual Income Tax Return **2022** OMB No. 1545-0074 IRS Use Only—Do not write or staple in this space.

Filing Status Check only one box. ☐ Single ☐ Married filing jointly ☐ Married filing separately (MFS) ☐ Head of household (HOH) ☐ Qualifying surviving spouse (QSS) LO 1.5

If you checked the MFS box, enter the name of your spouse. If you checked the HOH or QSS box, enter the child's name if the qualifying person is a child but not your dependent:

Your first name and middle initial	Last name	**Your social security number**
If joint return, spouse's first name and middle initial	Last name	**Spouse's social security number**

Home address (number and street). If you have a P.O. box, see instructions.		Apt. no.
City, town, or post office. If you have a foreign address, also complete spaces below.	State	ZIP code
Foreign country name	Foreign province/state/county	Foreign postal code

Presidential Election Campaign Check here if you, or your spouse if filing jointly, want $3 to go to this fund. Checking a box below will not change your tax or refund. ☐ You ☐ Spouse

Digital Assets At any time during 2022, did you: (a) receive (as a reward, award, or payment for property or services); or (b) sell, exchange, gift, or otherwise dispose of a digital asset (or a financial interest in a digital asset)? (See instructions.) ☐ Yes ☐ No LO 4.1

Standard Deduction **Someone can claim:** ☐ You as a dependent ☐ Your spouse as a dependent
☐ Spouse itemizes on a separate return or you were a dual-status alien LO 1.7

Age/Blindness **You:** ☐ Were born before January 2, 1958 ☐ Are blind **Spouse:** ☐ Was born before January 2, 1958 ☐ Is blind

Dependents (see instructions): If more than four dependents, see instructions and check here ☐

(1) First name Last name	(2) Social security number	(3) Relationship to you	(4) Child tax credit	(4) Credit for other dependents
LO 1.6			☐	☐
			☐ LO 1.6, 7.1	☐
			☐	☐
			☐	☐

Income

Attach Form(s) W-2 here. Also attach Forms W-2G and 1099-R if tax was withheld. If you did not get a Form W-2, see instructions.

1a	Total amount from Form(s) W-2, box 1 (see instructions)	1a	LO 2.2
b	Household employee wages not reported on Form(s) W-2	1b	LO 6.6
c	Tip income not reported on line 1a (see instructions)	1c	LO 9.1
d	Medicaid waiver payments not reported on Form(s) W-2 (see instructions)	1d	LO 2.1
e	Taxable dependent care benefits from Form 2441, line 26	1e	LO 2.5
f	Employer-provided adoption benefits from Form 8839, line 29	1f	LO 7.7
g	Wages from Form 8919, line 6	1g	LO 6.8
h	Other earned income (see instructions)	1h	
i	Nontaxable combat pay election (see instructions) 1i		
z	Add lines 1a through 1h	1z	
2a	Tax-exempt interest 2a LO 2.9 — b Taxable interest	2b	LO 2.9
3a	Qualified dividends 3a LO 2.10 — b Ordinary dividends	3b	LO 2.10
4a	IRA distributions 4a LO 5.3 — b Taxable amount	4b	LO 5.3
5a	Pensions and annuities 5a LO 2.7 — b Taxable amount	5b	LO 2.7
6a	Social security benefits 6a LO 2.16 — b Taxable amount	6b	LO 2.16
c	If you elect to use the lump-sum election method, check here (see instructions) ☐		
7	Capital gain or (loss). Attach Schedule D if required. If not required, check here ☐	7	LO 4.1 to 4.6
8	Other income from Schedule 1, line 10	8	Sch. 1
9	Add lines 1z, 2b, 3b, 4b, 5b, 6b, 7, and 8. This is your **total income**	9	
10	Adjustments to income from Schedule 1, line 26	10	Sch. 1
11	Subtract line 10 from line 9. This is your **adjusted gross income**	11	
12	**Standard deduction or itemized deductions** (from Schedule A)	12	LO 1.7, 5.6 to 5.10
13	Qualified business income deduction from Form 8995 or Form 8995-A	13	LO 4.11
14	Add lines 12 and 13	14	
15	Subtract line 14 from line 11. If zero or less, enter -0-. This is your **taxable income**	15	

Attach Sch. B if required.

Standard Deduction for—
- Single or Married filing separately, $12,950
- Married filing jointly or Qualifying surviving spouse, $25,900
- Head of household, $19,400
- If you checked any box under *Standard Deduction*, see instructions.

For Disclosure, Privacy Act, and Paperwork Reduction Act Notice, see separate instructions. Cat. No. 11320B Form **1040** (2022)

Form 1040 (2022) — Page **2**

Tax and Credits

Line	Description			Line	Amount
16	**Tax** (see instructions). Check if any from Form(s): 1 ☐ 8814 2 ☐ 4972 3 ☐ ______			16	LO 1.5, 2.10, 4.4, 6.4
17	Amount from Schedule 2, line 3			17	Sch. 2
18	Add lines 16 and 17			18	
19	Child tax credit or credit for other dependents from Schedule 8812			19	LO 7.1
20	Amount from Schedule 3, line 8			20	Sch. 3
21	Add lines 19 and 20			21	
22	Subtract line 21 from line 18. If zero or less, enter -0-			22	
23	Other taxes, including self-employment tax, from Schedule 2, line 21			23	Sch. 2
24	Add lines 22 and 23. This is your **total tax**			24	

Payments

If you have a qualifying child, attach Sch. EIC.

Line	Description	Line	Amount	Line	Amount
25	Federal income tax withheld from:				
a	Form(s) W-2	25a	LO 2.2, 9.1		
b	Form(s) 1099	25b	LO 9.1		
c	Other forms (see instructions)	25c			
d	Add lines 25a through 25c			25d	
26	2022 estimated tax payments and amount applied from 2021 return			26	LO 9.3
27	Earned income credit (EIC)	27	LO 7.2		
28	Additional child tax credit from Schedule 8812	28	LO 7.1		
29	American opportunity credit from Form 8863, line 8	29	LO 7.5		
30	Reserved for future use	30			
31	Amount from Schedule 3, line 15	31	Sch. 3		
32	Add lines 27, 28, 29, and 31. These are your **total other payments and refundable credits**			32	
33	Add lines 25d, 26, and 32. These are your **total payments**			33	

Refund

Direct deposit? See instructions.

Line	Description	Line	Amount	Line	Amount
34	If line 33 is more than line 24, subtract line 24 from line 33. This is the amount you **overpaid**			34	
35a	Amount of line 34 you want **refunded to you**. If Form 8888 is attached, check here ☐			35a	
b	Routing number ________ **c** Type: ☐ Checking ☐ Savings				
d	Account number ________				
36	Amount of line 34 you want **applied to your 2023 estimated tax**	36			

Amount You Owe

Line	Description	Line	Amount	Line	Amount
37	Subtract line 33 from line 24. This is the **amount you owe**. For details on how to pay, go to *www.irs.gov/Payments* or see instructions			37	
38	Estimated tax penalty (see instructions)	38			

Third Party Designee

Do you want to allow another person to discuss this return with the IRS? See instructions ☐ **Yes.** Complete below. ☐ **No**

Designee's name | Phone no. | Personal identification number (PIN)

Sign Here

Under penalties of perjury, I declare that I have examined this return and accompanying schedules and statements, and to the best of my knowledge and belief, they are true, correct, and complete. Declaration of preparer (other than taxpayer) is based on all information of which preparer has any knowledge.

Joint return? See instructions. Keep a copy for your records.

Your signature	Date	Your occupation	If the IRS sent you an Identity Protection PIN, enter it here (see inst.)
Spouse's signature. If a joint return, **both** must sign.	Date	Spouse's occupation	If the IRS sent your spouse an Identity Protection PIN, enter it here (see inst.)
Phone no.	Email address		

Paid Preparer Use Only

Preparer's name	Preparer's signature	Date	PTIN	Check if: ☐ Self-employed
Firm's name				Phone no.
Firm's address				Firm's EIN

Go to *www.irs.gov/Form1040* for instructions and the latest information. Form **1040** (2022)

SCHEDULE 1 (Form 1040)
Department of the Treasury Internal Revenue Service

Additional Income and Adjustments to Income

Attach to Form 1040, 1040-SR, or 1040-NR.
Go to *www.irs.gov/Form1040* for instructions and the latest information.

OMB No. 1545-0074
2022
Attachment Sequence No. 01

Name(s) shown on Form 1040, 1040-SR, or 1040-NR | **Your social security number**

Part I Additional Income

1	Taxable refunds, credits, or offsets of state and local income taxes			1	LO 5.7
2a	Alimony received			2a	LO 2.13
b	Date of original divorce or separation agreement (see instructions):				
3	Business income or (loss). Attach Schedule C			3	Chapter 3
4	Other gains or (losses). Attach Form 4797			4	LO 8.7, 8.8
5	Rental real estate, royalties, partnerships, S corporations, trusts, etc. Attach Schedule E			5	LO 4.7, 4.8
6	Farm income or (loss). Attach Schedule F			6	LO 6.8
7	Unemployment compensation			7	LO 2.15
8	Other income:				
a	Net operating loss	8a	(LO 4.9)		
b	Gambling	8b	LO 2.1, 2.6		
c	Cancellation of debt	8c	LO 2.18		
d	Foreign earned income exclusion from Form 2555	8d	(LO 7.6)		
e	Income from Form 8853	8e			
f	Income from Form 8889	8f			
g	Alaska Permanent Fund dividends	8g			
h	Jury duty pay	8h	LO 2.1		
i	Prizes and awards	8i	LO 2.6		
j	Activity not engaged in for profit income	8j	LO 3.12		
k	Stock options	8k	LO 2.1		
l	Income from the rental of personal property if you engaged in the rental for profit but were not in the business of renting such property	8l	LO 4.7		
m	Olympic and Paralympic medals and USOC prize money (see instructions)	8m	LO 2.6		
n	Section 951(a) inclusion (see instructions)	8n			
o	Section 951A(a) inclusion (see instructions)	8o			
p	Section 461(l) excess business loss adjustment	8p			
q	Taxable distributions from an ABLE account (see instructions)	8q			
r	Scholarship and fellowship grants not reported on Form W-2	8r	LO 2.12		
s	Nontaxable amount of Medicaid waiver payments included on Form 1040, line 1a or 1d	8s	( )		
t	Pension or annuity from a nonqualifed deferred compensation plan or a nongovernmental section 457 plan	8t			
u	Wages earned while incarcerated	8u			
z	Other income. List type and amount: Chapter 2	8z			
9	Total other income. Add lines 8a through 8z			9	
10	Combine lines 1 through 7 and 9. Enter here and on Form 1040, 1040-SR, or 1040-NR, line 8			10	

Schedule 1 (Form 1040) 2022 Page **2**

Part II Adjustments to Income

11	Educator expenses			11	LO 5.5
12	Certain business expenses of reservists, performing artists, and fee-basis government officials. Attach Form 2106			12	LO 5.5
13	Health savings account deduction. Attach Form 8889			13	LO 5.1
14	Moving expenses for members of the Armed Forces. Attach Form 3903			14	LO 5.5
15	Deductible part of self-employment tax. Attach Schedule SE			15	LO 4.10
16	Self-employed SEP, SIMPLE, and qualified plans			16	LO 5.4
17	Self-employed health insurance deduction			17	LO 5.2
18	Penalty on early withdrawal of savings			18	LO 2.9
19a	Alimony paid			19a	LO 2.13
b	Recipient's SSN				
c	Date of original divorce or separation agreement (see instructions):				
20	IRA deduction			20	LO 5.3
21	Student loan interest deduction			21	LO 5.8
22	Reserved for future use			22	
23	Archer MSA deduction			23	
24	Other adjustments:				
a	Jury duty pay (see instructions)	24a	LO 2.1		
b	Deductible expenses related to income reported on line 8l from the rental of personal property engaged in for profit	24b	LO 4.7		
c	Nontaxable amount of the value of Olympic and Paralympic medals and USOC prize money reported on line 8m	24c	LO 2.6		
d	Reforestation amortization and expenses	24d			
e	Repayment of supplemental unemployment benefits under the Trade Act of 1974	24e			
f	Contributions to section 501(c)(18)(D) pension plans	24f			
g	Contributions by certain chaplains to section 403(b) plans	24g			
h	Attorney fees and court costs for actions involving certain unlawful discrimination claims (see instructions)	24h			
i	Attorney fees and court costs you paid in connection with an award from the IRS for information you provided that helped the IRS detect tax law violations	24i			
j	Housing deduction from Form 2555	24j	LO 7.6		
k	Excess deductions of section 67(e) expenses from Schedule K-1 (Form 1041)	24k			
z	Other adjustments. List type and amount:	24z			
25	Total other adjustments. Add lines 24a through 24z			25	
26	Add lines 11 through 23 and 25. These are your **adjustments to income**. Enter here and on Form 1040 or 1040-SR, line 10, or Form 1040-NR, line 10a			26	

Schedule 1 (Form 1040) 2022

SCHEDULE 2 (Form 1040)

Department of the Treasury Internal Revenue Service

Additional Taxes

Attach to Form 1040, 1040-SR, or 1040-NR.

Go to *www.irs.gov/Form1040* for instructions and the latest information.

OMB No. 1545-0074

2022

Attachment Sequence No. **02**

Name(s) shown on Form 1040, 1040-SR, or 1040-NR | **Your social security number**

Part I Tax

1	Alternative minimum tax. Attach Form 6251	1	LO 6.5
2	Excess advance premium tax credit repayment. Attach Form 8962	2	LO 7.4
3	Add lines 1 and 2. Enter here and on Form 1040, 1040-SR, or 1040-NR, line 17	3	

Part II Other Taxes

4	Self-employment tax. Attach Schedule SE			4	LO 4.10
5	Social security and Medicare tax on unreported tip income. Attach Form 4137	5	LO 9.2		
6	Uncollected social security and Medicare tax on wages. Attach Form 8919	6	LO 9.2		
7	Total additional social security and Medicare tax. Add lines 5 and 6			7	
8	Additional tax on IRAs or other tax-favored accounts. Attach Form 5329 if required. If not required, check here ☐			8	LO 5.3
9	Household employment taxes. Attach Schedule H			9	LO 6.6
10	Repayment of first-time homebuyer credit. Attach Form 5405 if required			10	
11	Additional Medicare Tax. Attach Form 8959			11	LO 6.7
12	Net investment income tax. Attach Form 8960			12	LO 6.7
13	Uncollected social security and Medicare or RRTA tax on tips or group-term life insurance from Form W-2, box 12			13	
14	Interest on tax due on installment income from the sale of certain residential lots and timeshares			14	
15	Interest on the deferred tax on gain from certain installment sales with a sales price over $150,000			15	
16	Recapture of low-income housing credit. Attach Form 8611			16	

(continued on page 2)

For Paperwork Reduction Act Notice, see your tax return instructions. Cat. No. 71478U **Schedule 2 (Form 1040) 2022**

Schedule 2 (Form 1040) 2022 Page 2

Part II Other Taxes *(continued)*

17	Other additional taxes:		
a	Recapture of other credits. List type, form number, and amount: ____________	**17a**	
b	Recapture of federal mortgage subsidy, if you sold your home see instructions	**17b**	
c	Additional tax on HSA distributions. Attach Form 8889	**17c**	LO 5.1
d	Additional tax on an HSA because you didn't remain an eligible individual. Attach Form 8889	**17d**	
e	Additional tax on Archer MSA distributions. Attach Form 8853	**17e**	
f	Additional tax on Medicare Advantage MSA distributions. Attach Form 8853	**17f**	
g	Recapture of a charitable contribution deduction related to a fractional interest in tangible personal property	**17g**	
h	Income you received from a nonqualified deferred compensation plan that fails to meet the requirements of section 409A	**17h**	
i	Compensation you received from a nonqualified deferred compensation plan described in section 457A	**17i**	
j	Section 72(m)(5) excess benefits tax	**17j**	
k	Golden parachute payments	**17k**	
l	Tax on accumulation distribution of trusts	**17l**	
m	Excise tax on insider stock compensation from an expatriated corporation	**17m**	
n	Look-back interest under section 167(g) or 460(b) from Form 8697 or 8866	**17n**	
o	Tax on non-effectively connected income for any part of the year you were a nonresident alien from Form 1040-NR	**17o**	
p	Any interest from Form 8621, line 16f, relating to distributions from, and dispositions of, stock of a section 1291 fund	**17p**	
q	Any interest from Form 8621, line 24	**17q**	
z	Any other taxes. List type and amount: ____________	**17z**	
18	Total additional taxes. Add lines 17a through 17z		**18**
19	Reserved for future use		**19**
20	Section 965 net tax liability installment from Form 965-A	**20**	
21	Add lines 4, 7 through 16, and 18. These are your **total other taxes**. Enter here and on Form 1040 or 1040-SR, line 23, or Form 1040-NR, line 23b		**21**

SCHEDULE 3 (Form 1040)

Department of the Treasury Internal Revenue Service

Additional Credits and Payments

Attach to Form 1040, 1040-SR, or 1040-NR.

Go to *www.irs.gov/Form1040* for instructions and the latest information.

OMB No. 1545-0074

2022

Attachment Sequence No. **03**

Name(s) shown on Form 1040, 1040-SR, or 1040-NR

Your social security number

Part I Nonrefundable Credits

1	Foreign tax credit. Attach Form 1116 if required			1	LO 7.6
2	Credit for child and dependent care expenses from Form 2441, line 11. Attach Form 2441			2	LO 7.3
3	Education credits from Form 8863, line 19			3	LO 7.5
4	Retirement savings contributions credit. Attach Form 8880			4	LO 7.9
5	Residential energy credits. Attach Form 5695			5	LO 7.8
6	Other nonrefundable credits:				
a	General business credit. Attach Form 3800	6a			
b	Credit for prior year minimum tax. Attach Form 8801	6b			
c	Adoption credit. Attach Form 8839	6c	LO 7.7		
d	Credit for the elderly or disabled. Attach Schedule R	6d			
e	Alternative motor vehicle credit. Attach Form 8910	6e	LO 7.8		
f	Qualified plug-in motor vehicle credit. Attach Form 8936	6f	LO 7.8		
g	Mortgage interest credit. Attach Form 8396	6g			
h	District of Columbia first-time homebuyer credit. Attach Form 8859	6h			
i	Qualified electric vehicle credit. Attach Form 8834	6i	LO 7.8		
j	Reserved for future use	6j			
k	Credit to holders of tax credit bonds. Attach Form 8912	6k			
l	Amount on Form 8978, line 14. See instructions	6l			
z	Other nonrefundable credits. List type and amount:	6z			
7	Total other nonrefundable credits. Add lines 6a through 6z			7	
8	Add lines 1 through 5 and 7. Enter here and on Form 1040, 1040-SR, or 1040-NR, line 20			8	

(continued on page 2)

Schedule 3 (Form 1040) 2022 Page 2

Part II Other Payments and Refundable Credits

9	Net premium tax credit. Attach Form 8962			9	LO 7.4
10	Amount paid with request for extension to file (see instructions)			10	LO 9.3
11	Excess social security and tier 1 RRTA tax withheld			11	LO 9.2
12	Credit for federal tax on fuels. Attach Form 4136			12	
13	Other payments or refundable credits:				
a	Form 2439	13a			
b	Credit for qualified sick and family leave wages paid in 2022 from Schedule(s) H for leave taken before April 1, 2021	13b			
c	Reserved for future use	13c			
d	Credit for repayment of amounts included in income from earlier years	13d			
e	Reserved for future use	13e			
f	Deferred amount of net 965 tax liability (see instructions)	13f			
g	Reserved for future use	13g			
h	Credit for qualified sick and family leave wages paid in 2022 from Schedule(s) H for leave taken after March 31, 2021, and before October 1, 2021	13h			
z	Other payments or refundable credits. List type and amount:	13z			
14	Total other payments or refundable credits. Add lines 13a through 13z			14	
15	Add lines 9 through 12 and 14. Enter here and on Form 1040, 1040-SR, or 1040-NR, line 31			15	

Schedule 3 (Form 1040) 2022

TABLE OF CONTENTS

Worawee Meepian/Shutterstock.com

CHAPTER 7 Tax Credits

CHAPTER 8 Depreciation and Sale of Business Property

photosvit/Getty Images

CHAPTER 9 Employment Taxes, Estimated Payments, and Retirement Plans

CHAPTER 10 Partnership Taxation

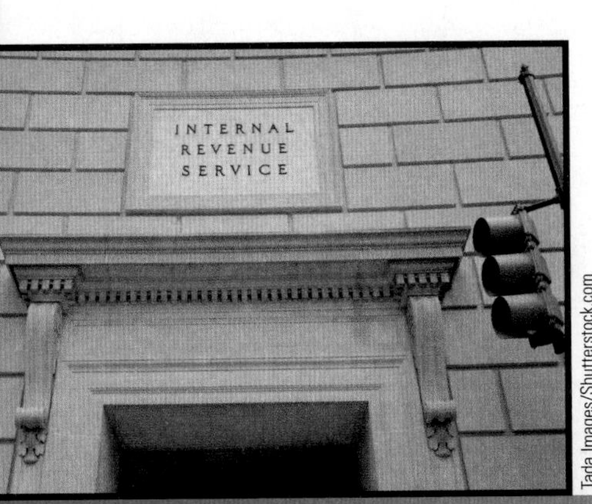

Tada Images/Shutterstock.com

QUESTIONS

Please contact the Cengage Learning Taxation publishing team if you have any questions:

Jonathan Gross, Portfolio Product Manager: jonathan.gross@cengage.com
Colin Kramer, Product Marketing Manager: colin.kramer@cengage.com
Tricia Hempel, Senior Content Manager: patricia.hempel@cengage.com

CHAPTER 1

The Individual Income Tax Return

The Congress shall have power to lay and collect taxes on incomes, from whatever source derived, without apportionment among the several States, and without regard to any census or enumeration.
– 16th Amendment, passed by Cogress July 2, 1909
Ratified February 3, 1913.

r.classen/Shutterstock.com

LEARNING OBJECTIVES

After completing this chapter, you should be able to:

- **LO 1.1** Explain the history and objectives of U.S. tax law.
- **LO 1.2** Describe the different entities subject to tax and reporting requirements.
- **LO 1.3** Apply the tax formula for individuals.
- **LO 1.4** Identify individuals who must file tax returns.
- **LO 1.5** Determine filing status and understand the calculation of tax according to filing status.
- **LO 1.6** Define qualifying dependents.
- **LO 1.7** Calculate the correct standard or itemized deduction amount for taxpayers.
- **LO 1.8** Compute basic capital gains and losses.
- **LO 1.9** Access and use various Internet tax resources.
- **LO 1.10** Describe the basics of electronic filing (e-filing).

OVERVIEW

This chapter introduces the U.S. individual income tax system. Important elements of the individual tax formula are covered, including the tax calculation, who must file, filing status, and the interaction of itemized deductions and the standard deduction. The chapter illustrates all of the steps required for completion of a basic Form 1040. There is also a discussion of reporting and taxable entities.

An introduction to capital gains and losses is included to provide a basic understanding of capital transactions prior to the detailed coverage in Chapter 4. An overview of tax information available at the Internal Revenue Service (IRS) website and other helpful tax websites is also provided. A discussion of the process for electronic filing (e-filing) of an individual tax return completes the chapter.

Learning Objective 1.1

Explain the history and objectives of U.S. tax law.

1-1 HISTORY AND OBJECTIVES OF THE TAX SYSTEM

1-1a Tax Law History and Objectives

The U.S. income tax was established on March 1, 1913, by the Sixteenth Amendment to the Constitution. Prior to the adoption of this amendment, the U.S. government had levied various income taxes for limited periods of time. For example, an income tax was used to help finance the Civil War. The finding by the courts that the income tax law enacted in 1894 was unconstitutional eventually led to the adoption of the Sixteenth Amendment. Since adoption of the amendment, the constitutionality of the income tax has not been questioned by the federal courts.

Many people inaccurately believe the sole purpose of the income tax is to raise sufficient revenue to operate the government. The tax law has many goals other than raising revenue. These goals fall into two general categories—economic goals and social goals—and it is often unclear which goal a specific tax provision was written to meet. Tax provisions have been used for such economic motives as reduction of unemployment, expansion of investment in productive (capital) assets, and control of inflation. Specific examples of economic tax provisions are the limited allowance for expensing of capital expenditures and the bonus depreciation provisions. In addition to pure economic goals, the tax law is used to encourage certain business activities and industries. For example, an income tax credit encourages businesses to engage in research and experimentation activities, the energy credits encourage investment in solar and wind energy businesses, and a special deduction for soil and water conservation expenditures related to farm land benefits farmers.

Social goals have also resulted in the adoption of many specific tax provisions. The child and dependent care credit, the earned income credit, and the charitable contributions deduction are examples of tax provisions designed to meet social goals. Social provisions may influence economic activities, but they are written primarily to encourage taxpayers to undertake activities to benefit themselves and society.

An example of a provision that has both economic and social objectives is the provision allowing the gain on the sale of a personal residence up to $250,000 ($500,000 if married) to be excluded from taxable income. From a social standpoint, this helps a family afford a new home, but it also helps achieve the economic goal of ensuring that the United States has a mobile workforce.

The use of the income tax as a tool to promote economic and social policies has increased in recent years. Keeping this in mind, the beginning tax student can better understand how and why the tax law has become so complex.

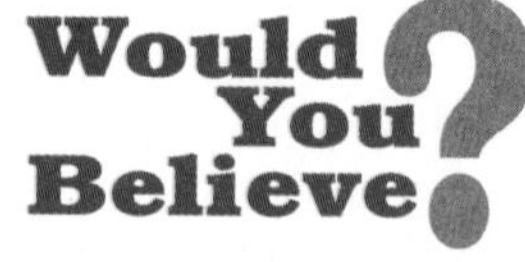

The United States tax law is often thought of as being complex. A count in 2014 puts the entire Internal Revenue Code at over 2,500 pages, and that is just the code itself. The regulations add an additional 9,000 pages. Jointly, the Code and regulations are well over two million words. To put this in context, the King James Bible has about 788,000 words and the entire Harry Potter book series has just over one million. In their 2020 Tax Complexity Index, taxcomplexity.org places the United States as the twentieth most complex tax law out of sixty-nine countries in the index. The top five most complex for that year: Croatia, Italy, Colombia, Belgium, and India. Among the least complex tax countries are Switzerland, Singapore, and Finland. See **www.taxcomplexity.org** for a complete list.

Self-Study Problem 1.1 *See Appendix E for Solutions to Self-Study Problems*

Which of the following is not a goal of the income tax system?

a. Raising revenue to operate the government.
b. Providing incentives for certain business and economic goals, such as higher employment rates, through business-favorable tax provisions.
c. Providing incentives for certain social goals, such as charitable giving, by allowing tax deductions, exclusions, or credits for selected activities.
d. All the above are goals of the income tax system.

1-2 REPORTING AND TAXABLE ENTITIES

1.2 Learning Objective

Describe the different entities subject to tax and reporting requirements.

Under U.S. tax law, there are five basic tax reporting entities: individuals, corporations, partnerships, estates, and trusts. The taxation of individuals is the major topic of this textbook; an overview of the taxation of partnerships and corporations is presented in Chapters 10 and 11, respectively. Taxation of estates and trusts is a specialized area not covered in this textbook.

1-2a The Individual

The most familiar taxable entity is the individual. Taxable income for individuals generally includes income from all sources such as wages, salaries, self-employment earnings, rents, interest, and dividends. Most individual taxpayers file either Form 1040, or for taxpayers ages 65 or older, Form 1040-SR. The Forms 1040 and 1040-SR are organized so that most taxpayers may only need to use that specific form. Items such as wages, certain interest and dividends, and common deductions and credits are reported directly on the Forms 1040 and 1040-SR. Less common items are reported on a series of supplemental schedules first and then totals from those schedules are carried to the Forms 1040 and 1040-SR.

Three supplemental schedules, Schedules 1, 2 and 3, are used for additional income and deductions, supplemental taxes, and other credits.

Schedule	*Primary Purpose*
1	Additional forms of income other than wages, interest, dividends, distributions from qualified retirement plans such as IRAs and pensions, Social Security benefits, and capital gains and losses, along with many of the deductions for adjusted gross income
2	Additional taxes beyond the basic income tax such as the alternative minimum tax, repayments of excess advance premium tax credit, self-employment taxes, and household employment taxes
3	Credits and payments other than withholding including education credits, the credit for child and dependent care expenses, residential energy credit, estimated tax payments, excess Social Security taxes withheld, and the net premium tax credit

In addition to Schedules 1–3, certain types of income and deductions must be reported on specific schedules that are included with the Forms 1040 or 1040-SR.

Schedule	*Primary Purpose*
A	Itemized deductions such as medical expenses, certain taxes, certain interest, charitable contributions, and other miscellaneous deductions
B	Interest income (over $1,500) or ordinary dividend income (over $1,500)
C	Net profit or loss from a sole proprietor trade or business, other than farm or ranch activities
D	Capital gains and losses
E	Rental, royalty, and pass-through income from partnerships, S corporations, estates, and trusts
F	Farm or ranch income

These tax forms and schedules and some less common forms are presented in this textbook.

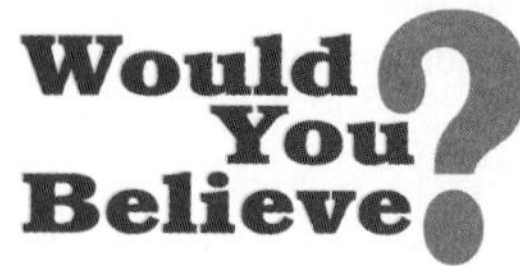

The origin of the Form 1040 has been rumored to be associated with the year 1040 B.C. when Samuel warned his people that if they demanded a king, the royal leader would be likely to require they pay taxes. However, in the early 1980s, the then-Commissioner of the IRS, Roscoe Eggers indicated that the number was simply the next one in the control numbering system for federal forms in 1914 when the form was issued for taxpayers for the tax year 1913. About 350,000 people filed a 1040 for 1913. All the returns were audited. In 2020, less than 1 percent of the approximately 150 million individual tax returns were audited.

1-2b The Corporation

Corporations are subject to the U.S. income tax and must report income annually on Form 1120. All corporations are taxed at a flat rate of 21 percent regardless of income level.

Some corporations may elect S corporation status. An S corporation does not generally pay regular corporate income taxes; instead, the corporation's income passes through to the shareholders and is included on their individual returns. S corporations must report tax information annually on Form 1120S. Chapter 11 covers the basics of corporate taxation, including a discussion of S corporations.

1-2c The Partnership

The partnership is not a taxable entity; instead it is a reporting entity. Generally, all income or loss of a partnership is included on the tax returns of the partners. However, a partnership must file Form 1065 annually to report the amount of the partnership's total income or loss and show the allocation of the income or loss to the partners. The partners, in turn, report their share of ordinary income or loss on their tax returns. Other special gains, losses, income, and deductions of the partnership are reported and allocated to the partners separately, since these items are given special tax treatment at the partner level. Capital gains and losses, for example, are reported and allocated separately, and the partners report their share on Schedule D of their income tax returns. See Chapter 10 for a discussion of partnerships, including limited partnerships and limited liability companies.

Summary of Major Tax Forms and Schedules

Form or Schedule	*Description*
1040	Individual income tax return
Schedule 1	Additional income and adjustments to income
Schedule 2	Additional taxes
Schedule 3	Additional credits and payments
Schedule A	Itemized deductions
Schedule B	Interest and dividend income
Schedule C	Profit or loss from business (sole proprietorship)
Schedule D	Capital gains and losses
Schedule E	Supplemental income and loss (rent, royalty, and pass-through income from Forms 1065, 1120S, and 1041)
Schedule F	Farm and ranch income
1041	Fiduciary (estates and trusts) tax return
1120	Corporate tax return
1120S	S corporation tax return
1065	Partnership information return
Schedule K-1 (Form 1065)	Partner's share of partnership results

All of the forms listed here, and more, are available at the IRS website (**www.irs.gov**).

Self-Study Problem 1.2 *See Appendix E for Solutions to Self-Study Problems*

Determine which is the most appropriate form or schedule(s) for each of the following items. Unless otherwise indicated in the problem, assume the taxpayer is an individual.

1. Bank interest income of $1,600 received by a taxpayer who itemizes deductions
2. Capital gain on the sale of Meta stock
3. Income from a farm
4. Estate income of $850
5. Partnership reporting of an individual partner's share of partnership income
6. Salary of $70,000 for a taxpayer under age 65 who itemizes deductions
7. Income from a sole proprietorship business
8. Income from rental property
9. Dividends of $2,000 received by a taxpayer who does not itemize deductions
10. Income of a corporation
11. Partnership's loss
12. Charitable contributions deduction for an individual who itemizes deductions
13. Single individual, age 67, with no dependents whose only income is $18,000 (all from Social Security) and who does not itemize deductions or have any credits

1-3 THE TAX FORMULA FOR INDIVIDUALS

1.3 Learning Objective

Apply the tax formula for individuals.

Individual taxpayers calculate their tax in accordance with a tax formula. Understanding the formula is important, since income tax determinations are based on the result. The formula is:

Gross Income
− Deductions for Adjusted Gross Income
= Adjusted Gross Income
− Greater of Itemized Deductions or the Standard Deduction
− Qualified Business Income Deduction
= Taxable Income
× Tax Rate (using appropriate tax tables or rate schedules)
= Gross Income Tax Liability and Additional Taxes
− Tax Credits and Prepayments
= Tax Due or Refund

According to the 2021 Comprehensive Taxpayer Attitude Survey, 88 percent of American taxpayers continue to say that it is "not at all" acceptable to cheat on taxes. Ninety-three percent agree that it is every American's civic duty to pay their fair share of taxes. However, only about 66 percent of taxpayers trust the IRS to fairly enforce the tax laws and to help taxpayers understand their tax obligations.

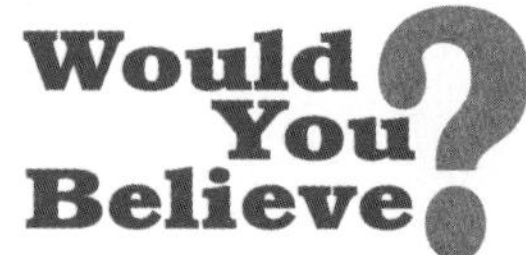

1-3a Gross Income

The calculation of taxable income begins with gross income. Gross income includes all income, unless the tax law provides for a specific exclusion. The exclusions from gross income are discussed in Chapter 2. Gross income from wages, interest, dividends, pensions, Social Security, and capital gains and losses are reported directly on Form 1040 (interest and dividends and capital gains and losses may first flow through Schedules B and D, respectively). All other forms of income are reported on Schedule 1.

The 2022 Forms 1040 and 1040-SR include 8 new lines (Lines 1b to 1i) that are designed to draw taxpayers' attention to report these items when applicable. The new lines include certain household wages, tip income, Medicare waiver payments, and other items.

1-3b Deductions for Adjusted Gross Income

The first category of deductions includes the deductions for adjusted gross income. These deductions include certain trade or business expenses, certain reimbursed employee business expenses paid under an accountable plan, pre-2019 alimony payments, student loan interest, the penalty on early withdrawal from savings, contributions to qualified retirement plans, and certain educator expenses. Later chapters explain these deductions in detail. Deductions for gross income are reported on Schedule 1.

1-3c Adjusted Gross Income (AGI)

The amount of adjusted gross income is sometimes referred to as the "magic line," since it is the basis for several deduction limitations, such as the limitation on medical expenses. A taxpayer's adjusted gross income is also used to determine limits on certain charitable contributions and contributions to certain individual retirement accounts.

1-3d Standard Deduction or Itemized Deductions

Itemized deductions are personal expense items that Congress has allowed as tax deductions. Included in this category are medical expenses, certain interest expenses, certain taxes, charitable contributions, certain casualty losses, and a small number of miscellaneous items. Taxpayers should itemize their deductions only if the total amount exceeds their standard deduction amount. The following table gives the standard deduction amounts for 2022.

Filing Status	*Standard Deduction*
Single	$ 12,950
Married, filing jointly	25,900
Married, filing separately	12,950
Head of household	19,400
Surviving spouse [qualified widow(er)]	25,900

Taxpayers who are 65 years of age or older or blind are entitled to an additional standard deduction amount. For 2022, the additional standard deduction amount is $1,750 for unmarried taxpayers and $1,400 for married taxpayers and surviving spouses. Taxpayers who are both 65 years of age or older and blind are entitled to two additional standard deduction amounts. A complete discussion of the basic and additional standard deduction amounts is found later in this chapter.

1-3e Exemptions

Prior to the TCJA, taxpayers received a deduction called an exemption for themselves, spouse (if married filing jointly), and dependents. Exemptions were suspended by the TCJA starting in 2018. The suspension is scheduled to expire at the end of 2025.

1-3f The Gross Tax Liability

A taxpayer's gross tax liability is calculated by referencing the tax table or by using a tax rate schedule. Tax credits and prepayments are subtracted from gross tax liability to calculate the net tax payable to the government or the refund to the taxpayer.

Taxpayers may provide information with their individual tax return authorizing the IRS to deposit refunds directly into their bank account. Taxpayers with a balance due may also pay their tax bill with a credit card, subject to a fee.

TAX BREAK

Self-Study Problem 1.3 *See Appendix E for Solutions to Self-Study Problems*

Bill is a single taxpayer, age 27. In 2022, his salary is $31,000 and he has interest income of $1,400. In addition, he has deductions for adjusted gross income of $2,000 and he has $6,500 of itemized deductions. Calculate the following amounts:

1. Gross income
2. Adjusted gross income
3. Standard deduction or itemized deduction amount
4. Taxable income

1-4 WHO MUST FILE

1.4 Learning Objective

Identify individuals who must file tax returns.

Several conditions must exist before a taxpayer is required to file a U.S. income tax return. These conditions primarily relate to the amount of the taxpayer's income and the taxpayer's filing status. Figures 1.1 through 1.3 summarize the filing requirements for taxpayers in 2022. If a taxpayer has any nontaxable income, the amount should be excluded in determining whether the taxpayer must file a return.

Taxpayers are also required to file a return if they have net earnings from self-employment of $400 or more, or owe taxes such as Social Security taxes on unreported tips. When a taxpayer is not required to file but is due a refund for overpayment of taxes, a return must be filed to obtain the refund.

A taxpayer who is required to file a return should electronically file the return or mail the return to the appropriate IRS Campus Processing Site listed on the IRS website (**www.irs.gov**). Generally, individual returns are due on the fifteenth day of the fourth month of the year following the close of the tax year. For a calendar year individual taxpayer, the return due date is generally April 15. If the fifteenth falls on a weekend or holiday, returns are due the next business day. However, there are two exceptions: (1) In Maine and Massachusetts, Patriots' Day is celebrated on the third Monday of April. When Patriots' Day is on April 15 or the first business day after April 15, the tax filing deadline is deferred for an additional

In an effort to avoid paying federal income taxes, a variety of schemes have been mounted over the years by "tax protestors." One of the more popular themes is that the Sixteenth Amendment was never ratified and therefore, the income tax is unconstitutional. In spite of numerous court cases that have debunked this "strategy," this claim remains popular. In a 1989 court case, *Miller v. U.S.*, the court noted, "As best we can surmise [Miller]...has followed the advice of those associated with the "tax protester movement." The leaders of this movement conduct seminars across the country in which they attempt to convince taxpayers that the Sixteenth Amendment and assorted enforcement provisions of the tax code are unconstitutional." The court continues, "We find it hard to understand why the long and unbroken line of cases upholding the constitutionality of the Sixteenth Amendment generally, *Brushaber v. Union Pacific Railroad Company*, 36 S. Ct. 236 (1916)...have not persuaded Miller and his compatriots to seek a more effective forum for airing their attack on the federal income tax structure." The IRS maintains a web page designed to address common tax protest myths at **www.irs.gov/businesses/small-businesses-self-employed/anti-tax-law-evasion-schemes**.

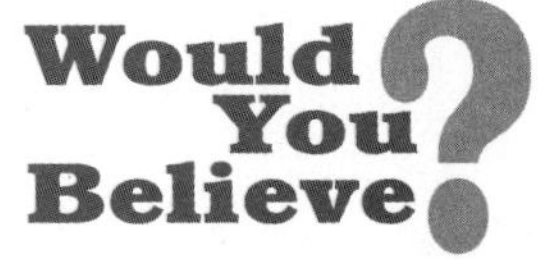

day for residents of Maine and Massachusetts. (2) The second exception is a result of Emancipation Day, a holiday observed in the District of Columbia. Emancipation Day is observed on April 16; however, when the sixteenth is a Saturday, the holiday is celebrated on the prior Friday and when the sixteenth is Sunday, the holiday is celebrated on the

FIGURE 1.1 WHO MUST FILE

Chart A—For Most People

IF your filing status is . . .	AND at the end of 2022 you were* . . .	THEN file a return if your gross income** was at least . . .
Single	under 65 65 or older	$12,950 14,700
Married filing jointly***	under 65 (both spouses) 65 or older (one spouse) 65 or older (both spouses)	$25,900 27,300 28,700
Married filing separately	any age	$5
Head of household	under 65 65 or older	$19,400 21,150
Qualifying widow(er)	under 65 65 or older	$25,900 27,300

**If you were born on January 1, 1958, you are considered to be age 65 at the end of 2022. (If your spouse died in 2022 or if you are preparing a return for someone who died in 2022, see Pub. 501.)*

*****Gross income** means all income you received in the form of money, goods, property, and services that isn't exempt from tax, including any income from sources outside the United States or from the sale of your main home (even if you can exclude part or all of it). Don't include any social security benefits unless (a) you are married filing a separate return and you lived with your spouse at any time in 2022, or (b) one-half of your social security benefits plus your other gross income and any tax-exempt interest is more than $25,000 ($32,000 if married filing jointly). If (a) or (b) applies, see the instructions for lines 6a and 6b to figure the taxable part of social security benefits you must include in gross income. Gross income includes gains, but not losses, reported on Form 8949 or Schedule D. Gross income from a business means, for example, the amount on Schedule C, line 7, or Schedule F, line 9. But, in figuring gross income, don't reduce your income by any losses, including any loss on Schedule C, line 7, or Schedule F, line 9.*

****If you didn't live with your spouse at the end of 2022 (or on the date your spouse died) and your gross income was at least $5, you must file a return regardless of your age.*

FIGURE 1.2

Chart B—For Children and Other Dependents (See *Who Qualifies as Your Dependent*, later.)

If your parent (or someone else) can claim you as a dependent, use this chart to see if you must file a return.
In this chart, **unearned income** includes taxable interest, ordinary dividends, and capital gain distributions. It also includes unemployment compensation, taxable social security benefits, pensions, annuities, and distributions of unearned income from a trust. **Earned income** includes salaries, wages, tips, professional fees, and taxable scholarship and fellowship grants. **Gross income** is the total of your unearned and earned income.

Single dependents. Were you **either** age 65 or older **or** blind?

☐ **No.** You must file a return if **any** of the following apply.
- Your unearned income was over $1,150.
- Your earned income was over $12,950.
- Your gross income was more than the **larger** of—
  - $1,150, or
  - Your earned income (up to $12,550) plus $400.

☐ **Yes.** You must file a return if **any** of the following apply.
- Your unearned income was over $2,900 ($4,650 if 65 or older **and** blind).
- Your earned income was over $14,700 ($16,450 if 65 or older **and** blind).
- Your gross income was more than the **larger** of—
  - $2,900 ($4,650 if 65 or older **and** blind), or
  - Your earned income (up to $12,550) plus $2,150 ($3,900 if 65 or older **and** blind).

Married dependents. Were you **either** age 65 or older **or** blind?

☐ **No.** You must file a return if **any** of the following apply.
- Your unearned income was over $1,150.
- Your earned income was over $12,950.
- Your gross income was at least $5 and your spouse files a separate return and itemizes deductions.
- Your gross income was more than the **larger** of—
  - $1,150, or
  - Your earned income (up to $12,550) plus $400.

☐ **Yes.** You must file a return if **any** of the following apply.
- Your unearned income was over $2,550 ($3,950 if 65 or older **and** blind).
- Your earned income was over $14,350 ($15,750 if 65 or older **and** blind).
- Your gross income was at least $5 and your spouse files a separate return and itemizes deductions.
- Your gross income was more than the **larger** of—
  - $2,550 ($3,950 if 65 or older **and** blind), or
  - Your earned income (up to $12,550) plus $1,800 ($3,200 if 65 or older **and** blind).

FIGURE 1.3

Chart C—Other Situations When You Must File

You must file a return if any of the seven conditions below apply for 2022.
1. You owe any special taxes, including any of the following. **a.** Alternative minimum tax. **b.** Additional tax on a qualified plan, including an individual retirement arrangement (IRA), or other tax-favored account. But if you are filing a return only because you owe this tax, you can file **Form 5329** by itself. **c.** Household employment taxes. But if you are filing a return only because you owe this tax, you can file **Schedule H** by itself. **d.** Social security and Medicare tax on tips you didn't report to your employer or on wages you received from an employer who didn't withhold these taxes. **e.** Write-in taxes, including uncollected social security and Medicare or RRTA tax on tips you reported to your employer or on group-term life insurance and additional taxes on health savings accounts. See the instructions for Schedule 2. **f.** Recapture taxes. See the instructions for line 16 and Schedule 2.
2. You (or your spouse, if filing jointly) received health savings account, Archer MSA, or Medicare Advantage MSA distributions.
3. You had net earnings from self-employment of at least $400.
4. You had wages of $108.28 or more from a church or qualified church-controlled organization that is exempt from employer social security and Medicare taxes.
5. Advance payments of the premium tax credit were made for you, your spouse, or a dependent who enrolled in coverage through the Marketplace. You or whoever enrolled you should have received Form(s) 1095-A showing the amount of the advance payments.
6. Advance payments of the health coverage tax credit were made for you, your spouse, or a dependent. You or whoever enrolled you should have received Form(s) 1099-H showing the amount of the advance payments.
7. You are required to include amounts in income under section 965 or you have a net tax liability under section 965 that you are paying in installments under section 965(h) or deferred by making an election under section 965(i).

following Monday. In 2023, April 15 is a Saturday, Patriots' Day is Monday, April 17, and Emancipation Day is Sunday, April 16, thus the filing deadline will be Tuesday, April 18.

A six-month extension of time to file may be requested on Form 4868 by the April due date. Regardless of the original filing deadline, the extension is until October 15 unless that day falls on a weekend or holiday, in which case the extended due date is the following business day. However, all tax due must be paid by the April due date or penalties and interest will apply.

Self-Study Problem 1.4

See Appendix E for Solutions to Self-Study Problems

Determine whether the following taxpayers are *required* to file a return for 2022 in each of the following independent situations:

1. Taxpayer (age 45) is single with income of $10,000.
2. Husband (age 67) and wife (age 64) have an income of $26,000 and file a joint return.
3. Taxpayer is a college student with a salary from a part-time job of $6,500. She is claimed as a dependent by her parents.
4. Taxpayer has net earnings from self-employment of $4,000.
5. Taxpayers are married with income of $15,900 and file a joint return. They expect a refund of $600 from excess withholding.
6. Taxpayer is a waiter and has unreported tips of $450.
7. Taxpayer is a surviving spouse (age 48) with a dependent son (age 18) and income of $24,800.

Learning Objective 1.5

Determine filing status and understand the calculation of tax according to filing status.

1-5 FILING STATUS AND TAX COMPUTATION

An important step in calculating the amount of a taxpayer's tax liability is the determination of the taxpayer's correct filing status. The tax law has five different filing statuses: single; married filing jointly; married filing separately; head of household; and surviving spouse. A tax table that must be used by most taxpayers, showing the tax liability for all five statuses, is provided in Appendix A. The tax table must be used unless the taxpayer's taxable income is $100,000 or more or the taxpayer is using a special method to calculate the tax liability. If taxpayers cannot use the tax table to determine their tax, a tax rate schedule is used. Each filing status has a separate tax rate schedule as presented in Appendix A.

1-5a Single Filing Status

A taxpayer who does not meet the definition of married, surviving spouse, or head of household status must file as single. This status must be used by any taxpayer who is unmarried or legally separated from his/her spouse by divorce or separate maintenance decree as of December 31 of the tax year. State law governs whether a taxpayer is married, divorced, or legally separated.

1-5b Married Filing Jointly

Taxpayers are considered married for tax purposes if they are married on December 31 of the tax year. Also, in the year of one spouse's death, the spouses are considered married for the full year. If a taxpayer remarries in the same year their spouse dies, they will be treated as married with the new spouse and the deceased spouse's tax return will be filed as married filing separately. In most situations, married taxpayers pay less tax by filing jointly than by filing separately. Married taxpayers may file a joint return even if they did not live together for the entire year.

Head of Household is a filing status that can be difficult to understand but comes with some substantial tax benefits if a taxpayer qualifies. Single parents should carefully analyze their situation since Head of Household provides lower tax rates and higher standard deductions than Single filing status. This benefit is not just limited to single parents. All unmarried taxpayers that maintain a household and provide support for another person should consider whether they qualify for this tax-advantageous status.

1-5c Married Filing Separately

Married taxpayers may file separate returns and should do so if it reduces their total tax liability. They may file separately if one or both had income during the year. If separate returns are filed, both taxpayers must compute their tax in the same manner. For example, if one spouse itemizes deductions, the other spouse must also itemize deductions. Each taxpayer reports his or her income, deductions, and credits and is responsible only for the tax due on their return. If the taxpayers live in a community property state, they must follow state law to determine community income and separate income. The community property states include Arizona, California, Idaho, Louisiana, Nevada, New Mexico, Texas, Washington, and Wisconsin. See Chapter 2 for additional discussion regarding income and losses from community property.

A legally married taxpayer may file as head of household (based on the general filing status rules) if he or she qualifies as an abandoned spouse. A taxpayer qualifies as an abandoned spouse only if *all* of the following requirements are met:

1. A separate return is filed,
2. The taxpayer paid more than half the cost (rent, utilities, etc.) to maintain their home during the year,
3. The spouse did not live with the taxpayer at any time in the last six months of the year, and
4. For over six months during the year the home was the principal residence for a dependent child, stepchild, or adopted child. Under certain conditions, a foster child may qualify as a dependent.

In certain circumstances, married couples may be able to reduce their total tax liability by filing separately. For instance, since some itemized deductions, such as medical expenses and casualty losses, are reduced by a percentage of adjusted gross income (discussed in Chapter 5), a spouse with a casualty loss and low separate adjusted gross income may benefit from filing separately.

1-5d **Head of Household**

If an unmarried taxpayer can meet special tests or if a married taxpayer qualifies as an abandoned spouse, they are allowed to file as head of household. Head of household tax rates are lower than rates for single or married filing separately. A taxpayer qualifies for head of household status if the following conditions exist:

1. The taxpayer was an unmarried or abandoned spouse as of December 31 of the tax year,
2. The taxpayer paid more than half of the cost of keeping a home for the year, and
3. A qualifying person lived with the taxpayer in the home for more than one-half of the year; however, if the qualifying person is a dependent parent, they are not required to live with the taxpayer.

The requirements to be a qualifying person are similar, but not identical to the requirements to be a dependent as either a qualifying child or qualifying relative (discussed in the next section).

Because head of household status provides tax benefits above those of a single taxpayer, tax preparers that complete an individual income tax return for a head of household taxpayer are required to complete Form 8867 Preparer's Due Diligence Checklist (see Pages 1-13 to 1-14). This same form is used if the taxpayer is claiming the earned income credit, the American Opportunities credit, the child tax credit, or the other dependent credit. For purposes of head of household due diligence, the emphasis is on inquiries surrounding the three above requirements and documenting what responses or information the taxpayer is able to provide related to the requirements. The Form 8867 is filed with the taxpayer's return like any other form.

Divorcing couples may save significant taxes if one or both of the spouses qualify as an "abandoned spouse" and can use the head of household filing status. The combination of head of household filing status for one spouse with married filing separately filing status for the other spouse is commonly seen in the year (or years) leading up to a divorce. In cases where each spouse has custody of a different child, the separated taxpayers may each claim head of household status.

1-5e **Surviving Spouse with Dependent Child**

A taxpayer may continue to benefit from the joint return rates for two years after the death of a spouse. To qualify to use the joint return rates, the surviving spouse or sometimes called qualifying widow(er), must pay over half the cost of maintaining a household where a dependent child, stepchild, adopted child, or foster child lives. After the two-year period, these taxpayers often qualify for the head of household filing status.

1-5f Tax Computation

For 2022, there are seven income tax brackets (10 percent, 12 percent, 22 percent, 24 percent, 32 percent, 35 percent, and 37 percent). Individuals with taxable income below $100,000 are required to use the tax tables presented in Appendix A. Taxpayers with income equal to or more than $100,000 use the tax rate schedules (also presented in Appendix A). An example of the single tax rate schedule is presented below. Certain high-income taxpayers are subject to additional taxes discussed in Chapter 6.

Single Tax Rate Schedule

If taxable income is over–	But not over–	The tax is:
$ 0	$10,275	10% of the taxable income
10,275	41,775	$1,027.50 + 12% of the excess over $10,275
41,775	89,075	$4,807.50 + 22% of the excess over $41,775
89,075	170,050	$15,213.50 + 24% of the excess over $89,075
170,050	215,950	$34,647.50 + 32% of the excess over $170,050
215,950	539,900	$49,335.50 + 35% of the excess over $215,950
539,900	---------	$162,718.00 + 37% of the excess over $539,900

The tax rates applicable to net long-term capital gains currently range from 0 percent to 31.8 percent depending on the taxpayer's tax bracket and the type of capital asset. The calculation of the tax on capital gains is discussed in detail in Chapter 4, and the applicable tax rates are discussed in this chapter.

The tax rates for qualifying dividends, discussed in detail in Chapter 2, range from 0 percent to 23.8 percent in 2022.

EXAMPLE Carol, a single taxpayer, has adjusted gross income of $120,000 and taxable income of $105,000 for 2022. Her tax is calculated using the 2022 tax rate schedule from Appendix A as follows:

$19,036.50 = $15,213.50 + [24% × ($105,000 − $89,075)] ♦

EXAMPLE Meg is a single taxpayer during 2022. Her taxable income for the year is $27,530. Using the tax table in Appendix A, her gross tax liability for the year is found to be $3,098. ♦

Taxpayers considering marriage may be able to save thousands of dollars by engaging in tax planning prior to setting a wedding date. If the couple would pay less in taxes by filing as married rather than as single (which will frequently happen if one spouse has low earnings for the year), they may prefer a December wedding. They can take advantage of the rule that requires taxpayers to file as married for the full year if they were married on the last day of the year. On the other hand, if filing a joint return would cause the couple to pay more in taxes (which frequently happens if both spouses have high incomes), they may prefer a January wedding.

Form **8867**

(Rev. November 2022)

Department of the Treasury
Internal Revenue Service

Paid Preparer's Due Diligence Checklist

Earned Income Credit (EIC), American Opportunity Tax Credit (AOTC), Child Tax Credit (CTC) (including the Additional Child Tax Credit (ACTC) and Credit for Other Dependents (ODC)), and Head of Household (HOH) Filing Status

To be completed by preparer and filed with Form 1040, 1040-SR, 1040-NR, 1040-PR, or 1040-SS.
Go to *www.irs.gov/Form8867* for instructions and the latest information.

OMB No. 1545-0074

For tax year 20 ____

Attachment Sequence No. **70**

Taxpayer name(s) shown on return | Taxpayer identification number

Preparer's name | Preparer tax identification number

Part I Due Diligence Requirements

Please check the appropriate box for the credit(s) and/or HOH filing status claimed on the return and complete the related Parts I–V for the benefit(s) claimed (check all that apply). ☐ EIC ☐ CTC/ACTC/ODC ☐ AOTC ☐ HOH

		Yes	No	N/A
1	Did you complete the return based on information for the applicable tax year provided by the taxpayer or reasonably obtained by you? (See instructions if relying on prior year earned income.)	☐	☐	
2	If credits are claimed on the return, did you complete the applicable EIC and/or CTC/ACTC/ODC worksheets found in the Form 1040, 1040-SR, 1040-NR, 1040-PR, 1040-SS, or Schedule 8812 (Form 1040) instructions, and/or the AOTC worksheet found in the Form 8863 instructions, or your own worksheet(s) that provides the same information, and all related forms and schedules for each credit claimed?	☐	☐	☐
3	Did you satisfy the knowledge requirement? To meet the knowledge requirement, you must do both of the following. • Interview the taxpayer, ask questions, and contemporaneously document the taxpayer's responses to determine that the taxpayer is eligible to claim the credit(s) and/or HOH filing status. • Review information to determine that the taxpayer is eligible to claim the credit(s) and/or HOH filing status and to figure the amount(s) of any credit(s)	☐	☐	
4	Did any information provided by the taxpayer or a third party for use in preparing the return, or information reasonably known to you, appear to be incorrect, incomplete, or inconsistent? (If "**Yes**," answer questions 4a and 4b. If "**No**," go to question 5.)	☐	☐	
a	Did you make reasonable inquiries to determine the correct, complete, and consistent information?	☐	☐	
b	Did you contemporaneously document your inquiries? (Documentation should include the questions you asked, whom you asked, when you asked, the information that was provided, and the impact the information had on your preparation of the return.)	☐	☐	
5	Did you satisfy the record retention requirement? To meet the record retention requirement, you must keep a copy of your documentation referenced in question 4b, a copy of this Form 8867, a copy of any applicable worksheet(s), a record of how, when, and from whom the information used to prepare Form 8867 and any applicable worksheet(s) was obtained, and a copy of any document(s) provided by the taxpayer that you relied on to determine eligibility for the credit(s) and/or HOH filing status or to figure the amount(s) of the credit(s)	☐	☐	
	List those documents provided by the taxpayer, if any, that you relied on: ____________________ ____________________ ____________________ ____________________			
6	Did you ask the taxpayer whether he/she could provide documentation to substantiate eligibility for the credit(s) and/or HOH filing status and the amount(s) of any credit(s) claimed on the return if his/her return is selected for audit?	☐	☐	
7	Did you ask the taxpayer if any of these credits were disallowed or reduced in a previous year? **(If credits were disallowed or reduced, go to question 7a; if not, go to question 8.)**	☐	☐	☐
a	Did you complete the required recertification Form 8862?	☐	☐	☐
8	If the taxpayer is reporting self-employment income, did you ask questions to prepare a complete and correct Schedule C (Form 1040)?	☐	☐	☐

For Paperwork Reduction Act Notice, see separate instructions. Cat. No. 26142H Form **8867** (Rev. 11-2022)

Form 8867 (Rev. 11-2022) Page **2**

Part II **Due Diligence Questions for Returns Claiming EIC** (If the return does not claim EIC, go to Part III.)

		Yes	No	N/A
9a	Have you determined that the taxpayer is eligible to claim the EIC for the number of qualifying children claimed, or is eligible to claim the EIC without a qualifying child? **(If the taxpayer is claiming the EIC and does not have a qualifying child, go to question 10.)**	☐	☐	
b	Did you ask the taxpayer if the child lived with the taxpayer for over half of the year, even if the taxpayer has supported the child the entire year?	☐	☐	
c	Did you explain to the taxpayer the rules about claiming the EIC when a child is the qualifying child of more than one person (tiebreaker rules)?	☐	☐	☐

Part III **Due Diligence Questions for Returns Claiming CTC/ACTC/ODC** (If the return does not claim CTC, ACTC, or ODC, go to Part IV.)

		Yes	No	N/A
10	Have you determined that each qualifying person for the CTC/ACTC/ODC is the taxpayer's dependent who is a citizen, national, or resident of the United States?	☐	☐	
11	Did you explain to the taxpayer that he/she may not claim the CTC/ACTC if the child has not lived with the taxpayer for over half of the year, even if the taxpayer has supported the child, unless the child's custodial parent has released a claim to exemption for the child?	☐	☐	☐
12	Did you explain to the taxpayer the rules about claiming the CTC/ACTC/ODC for a child of divorced or separated parents (or parents who live apart), including any requirement to attach a Form 8332 or similar statement to the return?	☐	☐	☐

Part IV **Due Diligence Questions for Returns Claiming AOTC** (If the return does not claim AOTC, go to Part V.)

		Yes	No
13	Did the taxpayer provide substantiation for the credit, such as a Form 1098-T and/or receipts for the qualified tuition and related expenses for the claimed AOTC?	☐	☐

Part V **Due Diligence Questions for Claiming HOH** (If the return does not claim HOH filing status, go to Part VI.)

		Yes	No
14	Have you determined that the taxpayer was unmarried or considered unmarried on the last day of the tax year and provided more than half of the cost of keeping up a home for the year for a qualifying person?	☐	☐

Part VI **Eligibility Certification**

You will have complied with all due diligence requirements for claiming the applicable credit(s) and/or HOH filing status on the return of the taxpayer identified above if you:

A. Interview the taxpayer, ask adequate questions, contemporaneously document the taxpayer's responses on the return or in your notes, review adequate information to determine if the taxpayer is eligible to claim the credit(s) and/or HOH filing status and to figure the amount(s) of the credit(s);

B. Complete this Form 8867 truthfully and accurately and complete the actions described in this checklist for any applicable credit(s) claimed and HOH filing status, if claimed;

C. Submit Form 8867 in the manner required; **and**

D. Keep all five of the following records for 3 years from the latest of the dates specified in the Form 8867 instructions under *Document Retention*.

1. A copy of this Form 8867.
2. The applicable worksheet(s) or your own worksheet(s) for any credit(s) claimed.
3. Copies of any documents provided by the taxpayer on which you relied to determine the taxpayer's eligibility for the credit(s) and/or HOH filing status and to figure the amount(s) of the credit(s).
4. A record of how, when, and from whom the information used to prepare this form and the applicable worksheet(s) was obtained.
5. A record of any additional information you relied upon, including questions you asked and the taxpayer's responses, to determine the taxpayer's eligibility for the credit(s) and/or HOH filing status and to figure the amount(s) of the credit(s).

If you have not complied with all due diligence requirements, you may have to pay a penalty for each failure to comply related to a claim of an applicable credit or HOH filing status (see instructions for more information).

		Yes	No
15	Do you certify that all of the answers on this Form 8867 are, to the best of your knowledge, true, correct, and complete?	☐	☐

Form **8867** (Rev. 11-2022)

Self-Study Problem 1.5 *See Appendix E for Solutions to Self-Study Problems*

Indicate the filing status (or statuses) in each of the following independent cases, using this legend:

A – Single
B – Married, filing a joint return
C – Married, filing separate returns
D – Head of household
E – Surviving spouse

1. The taxpayers are married on December 31 of the tax year.
2. The taxpayer is single, with a dependent child living in her home.
3. The taxpayer is unmarried and is living with his girlfriend.
4. The taxpayer is married and his spouse left midyear and has disappeared. The taxpayer has no dependents.
5. The unmarried taxpayer supports her dependent mother, who lives in her own home.
6. The taxpayer's wife died last year. His 15-year-old dependent son lives with him.

ProConnect™ Tax TIP

In ProConnect, much of the input is controlled by the left-hand margin. Filing status is part of Client Information under the General heading. By clicking on Filing Status, a dropdown appears in the main window to allow the preparer to select the taxpayer's filing status. For married filing jointly and separately statuses, the Live With Spouse box should be checked if it applies.

1-6 QUALIFYING DEPENDENTS

1.6 Learning Objective

Define qualifying dependents.

1-6a Dependents

Prior to 2018, taxpayers were able to deduct approximately $4,000 each for themselves, their spouse (if married filing jointly), and any dependents. The Tax Cuts and Jobs Act of 2017 (TCJA) eliminated the personal and dependency exemptions in lieu of a larger standard deduction; however, dependents remain important for other reasons. For example, head of household filing status, the child tax credit, and the earned income tax credit all require having a qualified dependent. Lastly, the suspension of personal and dependency exemptions is scheduled to expire after 2025 which means standard deduction amounts may be reduced and exemptions may yet return. A dependent is an individual who meets the tests discussed on the following pages to be considered either a *qualifying child* or a *qualifying relative.*

The IRS started requiring the disclosure of Social Security numbers for each dependent claimed by a taxpayer to stop dishonest taxpayers from claiming extra dependents or even claiming pets. Before this change, listing phony dependents was one of the most common forms of tax fraud. Reportedly, seven million dependents disappeared from the tax rolls after Congress required taxpayers to include dependents' Social Security numbers on tax returns.

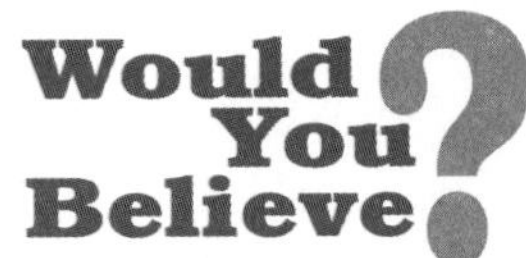

1-6b Qualifying Child

For a child to be a dependent, they must meet the following tests:

1. **Relationship Test**
The child must be the taxpayer's child, stepchild, or adopted child, or the taxpayer's brother or sister, half-brother or half-sister, or stepsibling, or a descendant of any of these. Under certain circumstances, a foster child can also qualify. The taxpayer must be older than the child unless the child is permanently disabled.
2. **Domicile Test**
The child must have the same principal place of abode as the taxpayer for more than half of the taxable year. In satisfying this requirement, temporary absences from the household due to special circumstances such as illness, education, and vacation are not considered.
3. **Age Test**
The child must be under age 19 or a full-time student under the age of 24. A child is considered a full-time student if enrolled full-time for at least five months of the year. Thus, a college senior graduating in May or June can qualify in the year of graduation.
4. **Joint Return Test**
The child must not file a joint return with his or her spouse. If neither the spouse nor the child is required to file, but they file a return merely to claim a refund of tax, they are not considered to have filed a return for purposes of this test.
5. **Citizenship Test**
The dependent must be a U.S. citizen, a tax resident of the United States, Canada, or Mexico, or an alien child adopted by and living with a U.S. citizen.
6. **Self-Support Test**
A child who provides more than one-half of his or her own support cannot be claimed as a dependent of someone else. Support includes expenditures for items such as food, lodging, clothes, medical and dental care, and education. To calculate support, the taxpayer uses the actual cost of the above items, except lodging. The value of lodging is calculated at its fair rental value. Funds received by students as scholarships are excluded from the support test.

In the event that a child satisfies the requirements of dependency for more than one taxpayer, the following tie-breaking rules apply:

- If one of the individuals eligible to claim the child is a parent, that person will be allowed to claim the dependent.
- If both parents qualify (separate returns are filed), then the parent with whom the child resides the longest during the year prevails. If the residence period is the same or is not ascertainable, then the parent with the highest AGI (Adjusted Gross Income) prevails.
- If no parents are involved, the taxpayer with the highest AGI prevails.

EXAMPLE Bill, age 12, lives in the same household with Irene, his mother, and Darlene, his aunt. Bill qualifies as a dependent of both Irene and Darlene. Since Irene is Bill's mother, she has the right to claim Bill as a dependent. The tie-breaking rules are not necessary if the taxpayer who can claim the dependent does not claim the dependent. Hence, Darlene can claim Bill as a dependent if Irene does not claim him. ♦

In the case of divorced or legally-separated parents with children, the ability to claim a qualifying child belongs to the parent with whom the child lived for more than six months out of the year. The opportunity to claim the child as a dependent can be shifted to the noncustodial parent if the custodial parent signs IRS Form 8332, and the form is attached to the noncustodial parent's tax return.

Figure 1.4 illustrates the interaction of the qualifying child dependency tests described above.

1-6c Qualifying Relative

A person who is not a qualifying child can be a qualifying relative if the following five-part test is met. A child of a taxpayer who does not meet the tests to be a qualifying child can still qualify as a dependent under the qualifying relative tests described below.

1. **Relationship or Member of Household Test**
   The individual must either be a relative of the taxpayer or a member of the household. The list of qualifying relatives is broad and includes parents, grandparents, children, grandchildren, siblings, aunts and uncles by blood, nephews and nieces, "in-laws," and adopted children. Foster children may also qualify in certain circumstances. If the potential dependent is a more distant relative, additional information is available at the IRS website (**www.irs.gov**). For example, cousins are not considered relatives for this purpose.

   In addition to the relatives listed, any person who lived in the taxpayer's home as a member of the household for the entire year meets the relationship test. A person is not considered a member of the household if at any time during the year the relationship between the taxpayer and the dependent was in violation of local law.

EXAMPLE Scott provides all of the support for an unrelated family friend who lives with him for the entire tax year. He also supports a cousin who lives in another state. The family friend can qualify as Scott's dependent, but the cousin cannot. The family friend meets the member of the household test. Even though the cousin is not considered a relative, he could have been a dependent if he met the member of the household part of the test. ♦

2. **Gross Income Test**
   The individual cannot have gross income equal to or above the exemption amount ($4,400 in 2022). Although exemptions are no longer deductible, the exemption amount will continue to be updated by the IRS. Gross income does not include any income exempt from tax (for example, tax-exempt interest or exempt Social Security benefits) but does include unemployment compensation and the taxable portion of Social Security benefits.
3. **Support Test**
   The dependent must receive over half of his or her support from the taxpayer or a group of taxpayers (see multiple support agreement below). Unlike the gross income test, income exempt from tax and earned by the potential dependent is considered for the support test.
4. **Joint Return Test**
   The dependent must not file a joint return unless it is only to claim a refund of taxes.
5. **Citizenship Test**
   The dependent must meet the citizenship test discussed above.

EXAMPLE A taxpayer has a 26-year-old son with gross income of less than the exemption amount and receives more than half of his support from his parents. The son fails the test to be a qualifying child based on his age, but passes the test to be a dependent based on the qualifying relative rules. ♦

Figure 1.5 illustrates the qualifying relative tests described above.

As long as the dependency tests are met, a person who was born or died during the year, such as a baby born before or on December 31, can be claimed as a dependent. Taxpayers must provide a Social Security number for all dependents.

If a dependent is supported by two or more taxpayers, a multiple support agreement may be filed. To file the agreement, the taxpayers (as a group) must provide over 50 percent of the support of the dependent. Assuming that all other dependency tests are met, the group may give the dependent to any member of the group who provided over 10 percent of the dependent's support.

FIGURE 1.4 **DEPENDENCY TESTS FLOW CHART FOR QUALIFYING CHILD**

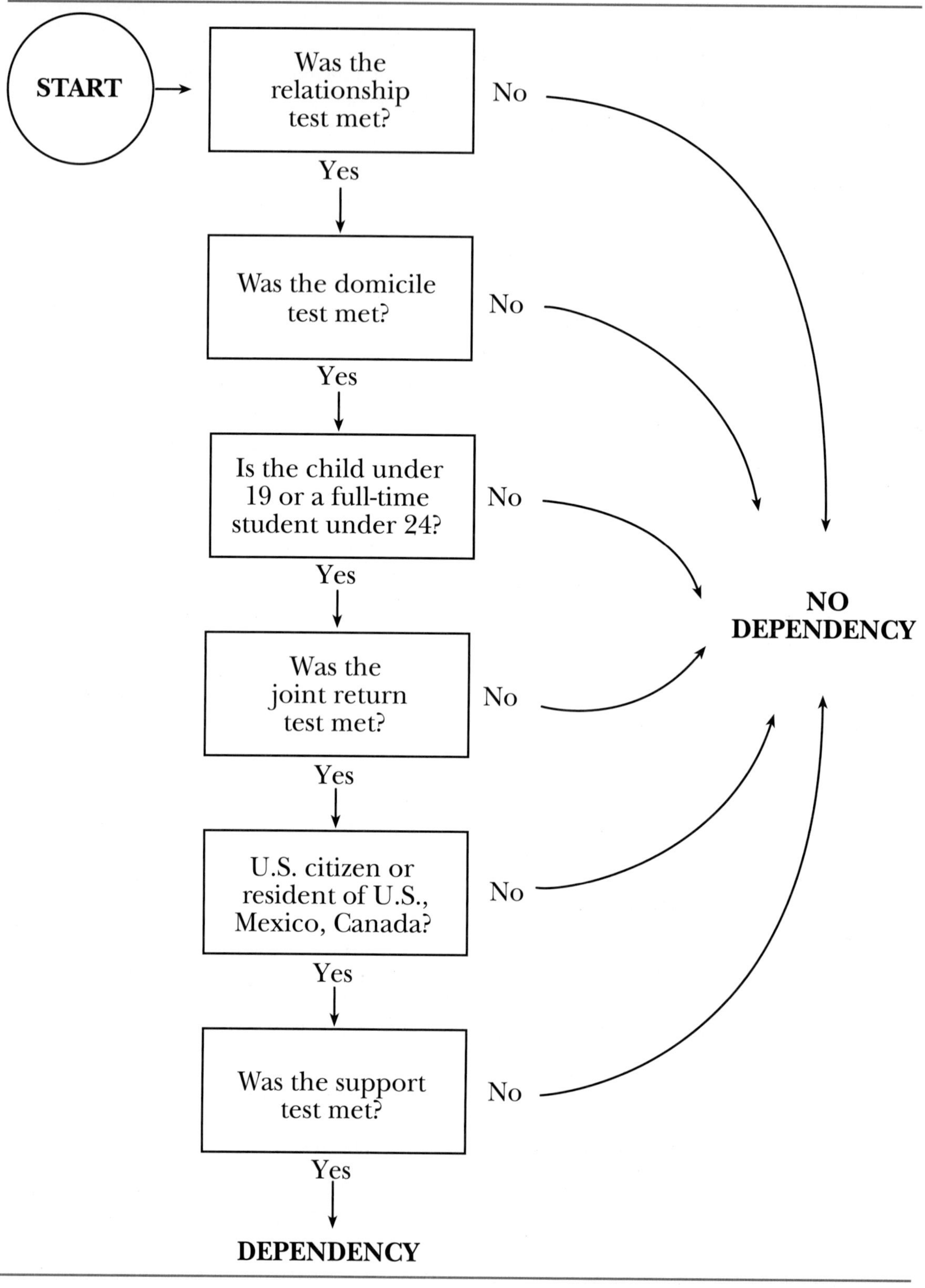

FIGURE 1.5 **DEPENDENCY TESTS FLOW CHART FOR QUALIFYING RELATIVE**

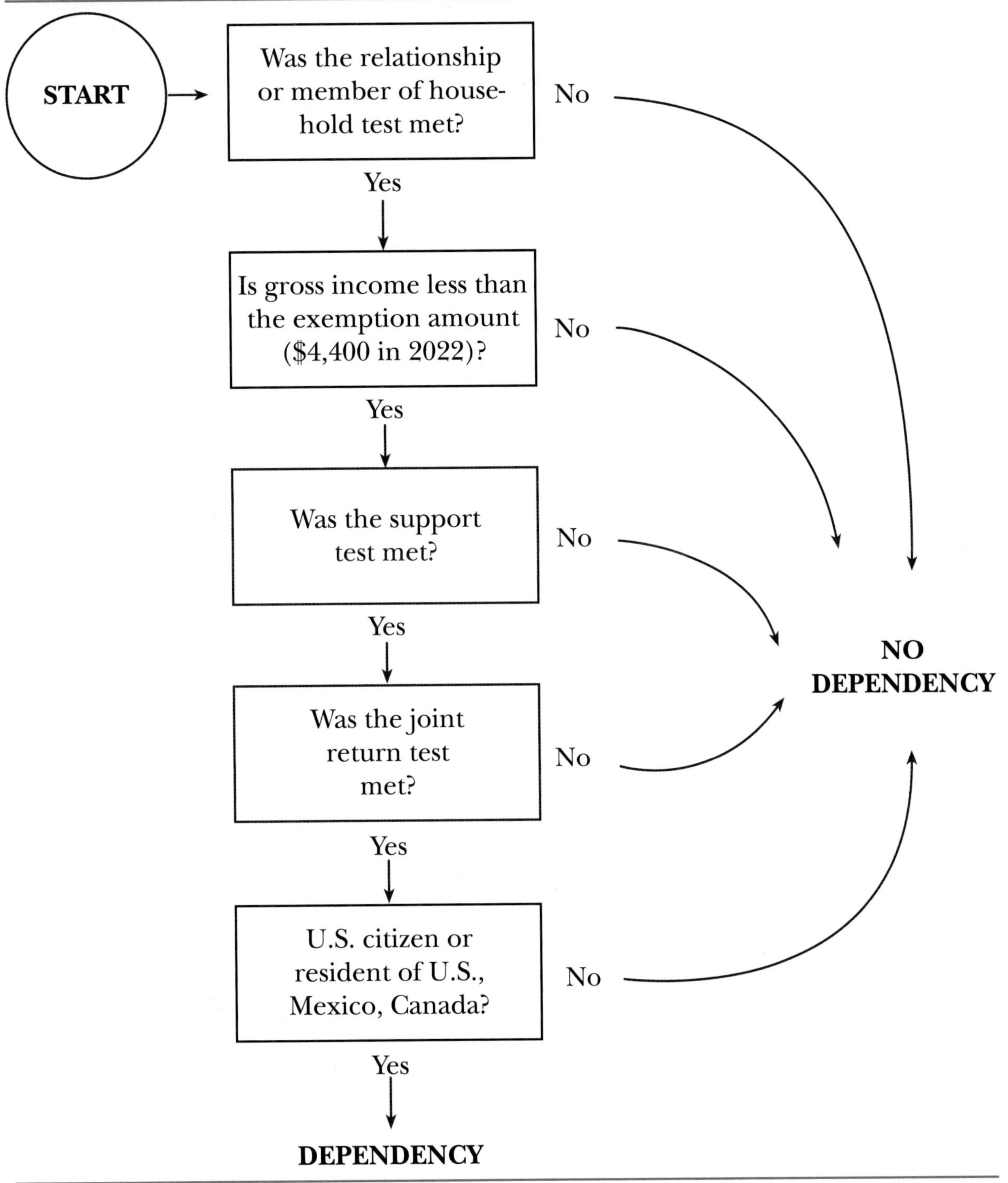

ProConnect™ Tax TIP

Spouse information is entered under Client Information and is just under Taxpayer Information on the left-hand margin. Dependents are a category under General. Be sure and input date of birth and other fields. Typically, the Child Tax Credit and the Earned Income Credit should be set to When Applicable to permit the software to make the correct determination based on input. New dependents can be added by clicking the [+] tab at the top of the main window for Dependents.

1-6d Qualifying Person for Head of Household

The rules to be a qualifying person and a dependent as a qualifying child or relative differ slightly. Figure 1.6 shows the differences for purposes of head of household filing status.

FIGURE 1.6

If the person is:	*Difference from Dependency Rules*
Qualifying child and single	Qualifying person rules do not require the qualifying child to meet the citizenship test
Qualifying child and married but unable to claim as a dependent	Qualifying person rules permit a non-dependent married qualifying child to be treated as a qualifying person if the only reason you cannot claim them as a dependent is if the taxpayer can be claimed as a dependent
Qualifying relative that is not a • child, stepchild, foster child, or decedent of any of them, • brother, sister, half brother, half sister, step brother, step sister • father, mother, grandparent or other direct ancestor • Stepfather, stepmother • Son or daughter of a brother or sister • Son or daughter of half-brother or half-sister • Brother or sister of your father or mother • Son-in-law, daughter-in-law, father-in-law, mother-in-law, brother-in-law, or sister-in-law And is only a qualifying relative because the person lived with the taxpayer all year under the household test	Does not meet the definition of a qualifying person

EXAMPLE Howard is a single taxpayer and lives with his girlfriend, Gloria. Gloria lives with Howard all year and meets all of the qualifying relative tests. Because she is not related to Howard in one of the ways presented in Figure 1.6, she is not a qualifying person. ♦

EXAMPLE Assuming the same facts as the previous example, Gloria has a 3-month-old child, Esther, for whom Howard is not the father. Esther lives with Howard and Gloria all year. Esther cannot be Howard's qualifying child because she does not meet the relationship test. Esther cannot be a qualifying relative because she is Gloria's qualifying child. Esther is a not a qualifying person. ♦

The rules that define qualifying persons are complex and thus the IRS makes available a number of different publications and aids to assist taxpayers and tax preparers with this decision. IRS Publication 501 describes qualifying child, relative, and person in detail with considerable examples. IRS Publication 4012, the resource guide for volunteers in the Volunteer Income Tax Assistance (VITA) program contains a decision tree, interview tips, and a chart to assist with determining head of household filing status. Lastly, the IRS website (**www.irs.gov/help/ita/what-is-my-filing-status**) offers an online Interactive Tax Assistant that uses interview question to assist in determining filing status. Tax preparers that use these aids responsibly should be able to meet the due diligence requirements of Form 8867.

1-6e Credits for Children and Other Dependents

Although deductions for personal exemptions are no longer permitted from 2018 through 2025, dependent status is important for claiming a number of individual tax credits such as the child tax credit, the credit for other dependents, and the earned income tax credit. Many of these tax credits are covered in Chapter 7; however, due to the relatively large number of taxpayers that are eligible for the child tax credit and the credit for other dependents, an overview is provided here.

A tax credit differs from a tax deduction. A tax deduction serves to lower the taxable income of the taxpayer.

EXAMPLE Emily's adjusted gross income is $50,175. She is eligible for a $12,950 standard deduction. This deduction lowers her taxable income to $37,225. If Emily is single, her 2022 tax liability is $4,262. ♦

A tax credit lowers the tax liability dollar for dollar. A credit is generally more advantageous than a deduction.

EXAMPLE Emily (from the previous example) is also eligible for a $500 tax credit. Rather than reduce her taxable income, the tax credit reduces the tax itself to $3,762 ($4,262 − $500). ♦

For 2022, the child tax credit is $2,000 for a child under 17 years of age. To qualify for the credit, this child must be a qualifying child and have a Social Security number at the time the tax return is filed.

The credit for other dependents is $500 per dependent. An "other dependent" need not be a child but must qualify as either a qualifying child or qualifying relative. Additional requirements are covered in Chapter 7.

EXAMPLE Bruce and Demi Mehr have two children, Anna (age 12) and Clark (age 18). Both Anna and Clark qualify as qualifying children under the dependent rules. Assuming all other requirements are met, the Mehrs may claim a $2,000 child tax credit for Anna and a $500 other dependent credit for Clark (as Clark is not under age 17). ♦

ProConnect™ Tax TIP

ProConnect is designed to automatically compute the child tax credit and other dependent credit based on the information input in the Dependent window. If no such credit is being shown, it could be due to missing information (for example, birthdate) or the credits were inadvertently suppressed in the Dependent window. The child tax credit and other dependent credit can be overridden under Credits/EIC, Residential Energy, Oth Credits in the left-hand margin, but overriding the system is generally not a good idea.

Self-Study Problem 1.6

See Appendix E for Solutions to Self-Study Problems

Indicate in each of the following situations whether the taxpayer has a dependent in 2022.

1. Betty and Bob, a married couple, had a new baby in December 2022.
2. Charlie, age 25, supports his 26-year-old brother, who is not a full-time student. His brother lives with Charlie all year. His brother's gross income is $4,500 from a part-time job.
3. Donna and her sister support their mother and provide 60 percent of her support. If Donna provides 25 percent of her mother's support and her sister signs a multiple support agreement, can Donna claim the mother as a dependent?
4. Frank is single and supports his son and his son's wife, both of whom lived with Frank for the entire year. The son (age 20) and his wife (age 19) file a joint return to get a refund, reporting $2,500 ($2,000 earned by the son) of gross income. Both the son and daughter-in-law are full-time students.
5. Gary is single and provides $5,000 toward his 19-year-old daughter's college expenses. The remainder of her support is provided by a tax-exempt $9,500 tuition scholarship. The daughter is a full-time student.
6. Helen is 50 years old and supports her 72-year-old mother, who is blind and has $5,000 of Social Security benefits that are not taxable.

Sign Here

Joint return? See instructions. Keep a copy for your records.

Under penalties of perjury, I declare that I have examined this return and accompanying schedules and statements, and to the best of my knowledge and belief, they are true, correct, and complete. Declaration of preparer (other than taxpayer) is based on all information of which preparer has any knowledge.

Your signature	Date	Your occupation	If the IRS sent you an Identity Protection PIN, enter it here (see inst.) ▶
Spouse's signature. If a joint return, **both** must sign.	Date	Spouse's occupation	If the IRS sent your spouse an Identity Protection PIN, enter it here (see inst.) ▶
Phone no.	Email address		

Paid Preparer Use Only

Preparer's name	Preparer's signature	Date	PTIN	Check if: ☐ Self-employed
Firm's name ▶			Phone no.	
Firm's address ▶			Firm's EIN ▶	

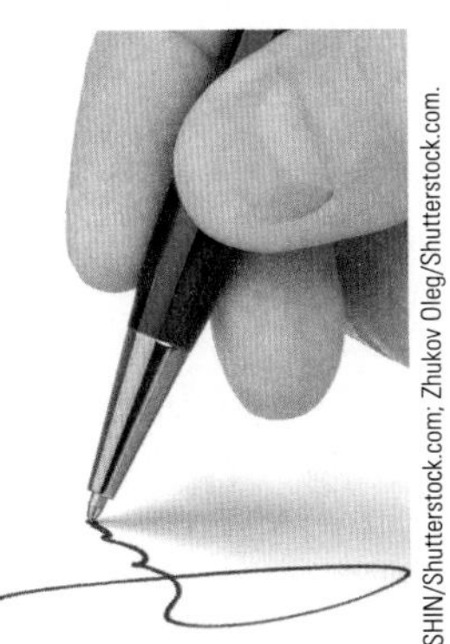

ILYA AKINSHIN/Shutterstock.com; Zhukov Oleg/Shutterstock.com.

Would You Sign This Tax Return?

Your clients, Adam and Amy Accrual, have a 21-year-old daughter named April. April is single and is a full-time student studying for her bachelor's degree in accounting at California Poly Academy (CPA) in Pismo Beach, California, where she lives with her roommates year-round. Last year, April worked at a local bar and restaurant four nights a week and made $18,000, which she used for tuition, fees, books, and living expenses. Her parents help April by sending her $300 each month to help with her expenses at college. This is all of the support given to April by her parents. When preparing Adam and Amy's tax return, you note that they claim April as a dependent for tax purposes. Adam is insistent that they can claim April because of the $300 per month support and the fact that they "have claimed her since she was born." He will not let you take April off his return as a dependent. Would you sign the Paid Preparer's declaration (see example above) on this return? Why or why not?

1-7 THE STANDARD DEDUCTION

1.7 Learning Objective

Calculate the correct standard or itemized deduction amount for taxpayers.

The standard deduction was placed in the tax law to provide relief for taxpayers with few itemized deductions. The amount of the standard deduction is subtracted from adjusted gross income by taxpayers who do not itemize their deductions. If a taxpayer's gross income is less than the standard deduction amount, the taxpayer has no taxable income. The 2022 standard deduction amounts are presented below:

Filing Status	*Standard Deduction*
Single	$ 12,950
Married, filing jointly	25,900
Married, filing separately	12,950
Head of household	19,400
Surviving spouse	25,900

The standard deduction amounts were increased significantly by the TCJA. The temporary increases are scheduled to expire after 2025.

In 2017, about 69 percent of individual taxpayers selected the standard deduction. After the expansion of the standard deduction amounts, the percentage jumped to over 88 percent. Recall that the expanded standard deduction is scheduled to expire at the end of 2025.

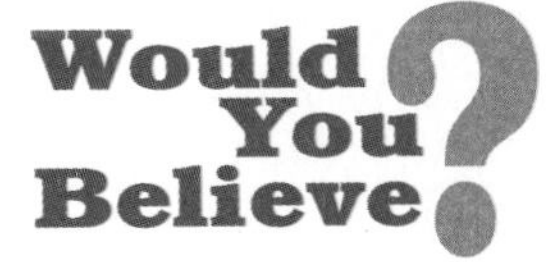

1-7a Additional Amounts for Old Age and Blindness

Taxpayers who are 65 years of age or older or blind are entitled to an additional standard deduction amount. For 2022, the additional standard deduction amount is $1,750 for unmarried taxpayers and $1,400 for married taxpayers and surviving spouses. Taxpayers who are both at least 65 years old and blind are entitled to two additional standard deduction amounts. The additional standard deduction amounts are also available for the taxpayer's spouse, but not for dependents. An individual is considered blind for purposes of receiving an additional standard deduction amount if:

1. Central visual acuity does not exceed 20/200 in the better eye with correcting lenses, or
2. Visual acuity is greater than 20/200 but is limited to a field of vision not greater than 20 degrees.

EXAMPLE John is single and 70 years old in 2022. His standard deduction is $14,700 ($12,950 plus an additional $1,750 for being 65 years of age or older). ♦

EXAMPLE Bob and Mary are married in 2022 and file a joint return. Bob is age 68, and Mary is 63 and meets the test for blindness. Their standard deduction is $28,700 ($25,900 plus $1,400 for Bob being 65 years or older and another $1,400 for Mary's blindness). ♦

1-7b Individuals Not Eligible for the Standard Deduction

The following taxpayers cannot use the standard deduction, but must itemize instead:

1. A married individual filing a separate return, whose spouse itemizes deductions
2. Most nonresident aliens
3. An individual filing a short-period tax return because of a change in the annual accounting period

EXAMPLE Ann and Ed are married individuals who file separate returns for 2022. Ann itemizes her deductions on her return. Ed's adjusted gross income is $12,000, and he has itemized deductions of $900. Ed's taxable income is calculated as follows:

Adjusted gross income	$ 12,000
Itemized deductions	(900)
Taxable income	$ 11,100

Since Ann and Ed file their taxes separately and Ann itemizes her deductions, Ed must also itemize deductions and is not entitled to use the standard deduction amount. ♦

1-7c Special Limitations for Dependents

The standard deduction is limited for the tax return of a dependent. The total standard deduction may not exceed the greater of $1,150 or the sum of $400 plus the dependent's earned income up to the basic standard deduction amount in total (e.g., $12,950 for single taxpayers), plus any additional standard deduction amount for old age or blindness. The standard deduction amount for old age and blindness is only allowed when a dependent files a tax return. It is not allowed to increase the standard deduction of the taxpayer claiming the dependent.

EXAMPLE Penzer, who is 8 years old, earned $17,000 as a child model during 2022. Penzer is claimed as a dependent by his parents on their tax return. Penzer is required to file a tax return, and his taxable income will be $4,050

($17,000 less $12,950, the standard deduction amount). If Penzer had earned only $9,000, his standard deduction would be $9,400 [the greater of $1,150 or $9,400 ($9,000 + $400)], and he would not owe any tax or be required to file a return. ♦

EXAMPLE Geoffrey, who is 4 years old and claimed as a dependent on his parents' tax return, earned $6,500 of interest income on a large bank account left to him by his grandmother. He had no earned income. His standard deduction is $1,150 (the greater of $1,150 or $400). His taxable income will be $5,350 ($6,500 less $1,150, the standard deduction amount). Dependent children may be taxed at their parents' tax rates when their taxable income is made up of unearned income, such as interest. The special "kiddie tax" calculations are covered in Chapter 6. ♦

Self-Study Problem 1.7 ***See Appendix E for Solutions to Self-Study Problems***

Indicate in each of the following independent situations the amount of the standard deduction the taxpayers should claim on their 2022 income tax returns.

1. Adam is 45 years old, in good health, and single.
2. Bill and Betty are married and file a joint return. Bill is 66 years old, and Betty is 60.
3. Charlie is 70, single, and blind.
4. Debbie qualifies for head of household filing status, is 35 years old, and is in good health.
5. Elizabeth is 9 years old, and her only income is $3,600 of interest on a savings account. She is claimed as a dependent on her parents' tax return.
6. Frank and Frieda are married with two dependent children. They file a joint return, are in good health, and both of them are under 65 years of age.

1-8 A BRIEF OVERVIEW OF CAPITAL GAINS AND LOSSES

1.8 Learning Objective

Compute basic capital gains and losses.

When a taxpayer sells an asset, there is normally a gain or loss on the transaction. Depending on the kind of asset sold, this gain or loss will have different tax consequences. Chapter 4 of this textbook has detailed coverage of the effect of gains and losses on a taxpayer's tax liability. Because of the importance of gains and losses to the understanding of the calculation of an individual's tax liability, a brief overview will be discussed here.

The amount of gain or loss realized by a taxpayer is determined by subtracting the *adjusted basis* of the asset from the *amount realized*. Generally, the adjusted basis of an asset is its cost less any depreciation (covered in Chapter 8) taken on the asset. The amount realized is generally what the taxpayer receives from the sale (e.g., the sales price less any cost of the sale). The formula for calculating the gain or loss can be stated as follows:

Gain (or loss) realized = Amount realized − Adjusted basis

Most gains and losses realized are also recognized for tax purposes. Recognized gains and losses are those that are included in the taxpayer's taxable income. The exceptions to this general tax recognition rule are discussed in Chapter 4.

EXAMPLE Lisa purchased a rental house a few years ago for $100,000. Total depreciation to date on the house is $25,000. In the current year she sells the house for $155,000 and receives $147,000 after paying selling expenses of $8,000. Her gain on the sale is $72,000, calculated as follows:

Amount realized ($155,000 – $8,000)	$ 147,000
Adjusted basis ($100,000 – $25,000)	(75,000)
Gain realized	$ 72,000

This gain realized will be recognized as a taxable gain. ♦

1-8a Capital Gains and Losses

Gains and losses can be either *ordinary* or *capital*. Ordinary gains and losses are treated for tax purposes just like other items of income such as salaries and interest, and they are taxed at ordinary rates. Capital gains and losses receive special tax treatment.

A capital gain or loss arises from the sale or exchange of a capital asset. In general, a capital asset is any property (either personal or investment) held by a taxpayer, with certain exceptions as listed in the tax law (see Chapter 4). Examples of capital assets held by individual taxpayers include stocks, bonds, land, cars, boats, and other items held as investments or for personal use. Typical assets that are not capital assets are inventory and accounts receivable.

The tax rates on long-term (held more than twelve months) capital gains are summarized as follows:

Income Level	2022 *Long-term capital gains rate**
Married filing jointly	
$0–$83,350	0%
$83,351–$517,200	15%
>$517,200	20%
Single	
$0–$41,675	0%
$41,676–$459,750	15%
>$459,750	20%
Head of household	
$0–$55,800	0%
$55,801–$488,500	15%
>$488,500	20%
Married filing separately	
$0–$41,675	0%
$41,676–$258,600	15%
>$258,600	20%

*Special higher rates for "high-income" taxpayers are covered in Chapter 6.

Gain from property held twelve months or less is deemed to be short-term capital gain and is taxed at ordinary income rates. Capital gains from the sale of assets that have been depreciated, or capital gains from "collectibles," may be taxed at higher rates as discussed in Chapter 4 and Chapter 8.

EXAMPLE In the current year, Chris, a single taxpayer, sells Meta stock for $25,000. He purchased the stock five years ago for $15,000, giving him an adjusted basis of $15,000 and a long-term gain of $10,000. Chris' taxable income without the sale of the stock is $140,000, which puts him in the 24 percent ordinary tax bracket. The tax due on the long-term capital gain would be $1,500 (15% × $10,000) instead of $2,400 (24% × $10,000) if the gain on the stock were treated as ordinary income. ♦

When calculating capital gain or loss, the taxpayer must net all capital asset transactions to determine the nature of the final gain or loss. If an individual taxpayer ends up with a net capital loss (short-term or long-term), up to $3,000 per year can be deducted against ordinary income. The net loss not used in the current year may be carried forward and used to reduce taxable income in future years. Losses from capital assets held for personal purposes, such as a nonbusiness auto or a personal residence, are not deductible, even though gains on personal assets are taxable.

EXAMPLE Amy purchased gold coins as an investment. She paid $50,000 for the coins. This year she sells the coins to a dealer for $35,000. As a result, Amy has a $15,000 capital loss. She may deduct $3,000 of the loss against her other income this year. The remaining unused loss of $12,000 ($15,000 − $3,000) is carried forward and may be deducted against other income in future years. Of course, the carryover is subject to the $3,000 annual limitation in future years. ♦

TAX BREAK

Volunteer Income Tax Assistance (VITA) Program

The Volunteer Income Tax Assistance (VITA) program offers free tax help to people who generally make $58,000 or less, persons with disabilities, the elderly, and limited English-speaking taxpayers who need assistance in preparing their own tax returns. IRS-certified volunteers provide free basic income tax return preparation with electronic filing to qualified individuals. VITA sites are generally located at community and neighborhood centers, libraries, schools, shopping malls, and other convenient locations across the country.

Many universities and colleges operate VITA sites in conjunction with their accounting programs. This is a small but vital part of the VITA program run by the IRS. The majority of the VITA sites are not run by schools, but rather by community groups, such as churches, senior groups (AARP), military bases, etc. If a student has a chance to participate in a VITA program, they should do so if at all possible. The experience provides valuable insight into preparing tax returns for others. Please see the IRS website **www.irs.gov** to locate the nearest VITA site and for more information.

Self-Study Problem 1.8 *See Appendix E for Solutions to Self-Study Problems*

Erin purchased stock in JKL Corporation several years ago for $8,750. In the current year, she sold the same stock for $12,800. She paid a $200 sales commission to her stockbroker.

1. What is Erin's amount realized?
2. What is Erin's adjusted basis?
3. What is Erin's *realized* gain or loss?
4. What is Erin's *recognized* gain or loss?
5. How is the gain or loss treated for tax purposes (if any)?

Learning Objective 1.9

Access and use various Internet tax resources.

1-9 TAX AND THE INTERNET

Taxpayers and tax practitioners can find a substantial amount of useful information on the Internet. Government agencies, businesses, organizations, and groups (e.g., the IRS, AICPA, and Cengage) maintain sites that contain information of interest to the public.

The information available on various websites is subject to rapid change. Discussed below are some current Internet sites that are of interest to taxpayers. Taxpayers should be aware that the locations and information provided on the Internet are subject to change by the site organizer without notice.

1-9a The IRS Website, www.irs.gov

One of the most useful websites containing tax information is the one maintained by the IRS. The IRS site has a search function to assist users in locating information. A number of common tasks are available at the home page such as refund status or making a tax payment. The Forms and Publications search function is particularly useful and allows the user to locate and download almost any tax form, instructions, or publication available from the IRS. A Help function is available to aid users of the IRS website. Online and telephone assistance from the IRS is provided for users who have questions or want to communicate with the IRS. The IRS also has a YouTube channel, a Twitter account, and a LinkedIn, Instagram, and Facebook page. The YouTube channel has numerous educational videos covering a number of tax-related topics, including how to check on a refund and how to file a tax return extension. The IRS offers various news feeds on Twitter, including @IRSnews, which are good sources of tax information. The IRS also offers IRS2GO—a mobile phone application.

A 2022 screenshot of the IRS website (**www.irs.gov**) is presented in Figure 1.7.

1-9b Intuit's ProConnect Tax Online

Intuit offers a line of tax preparation products such as ProConnect Tax, Lacerte, and the well-known Turbo Tax. Many of the Intuit products have training and support available online at no charge. You can find ProConnect help at **https://proconnect.intuit.com/community/support/**.

FIGURE 1.7 **IRS WEBSITE**

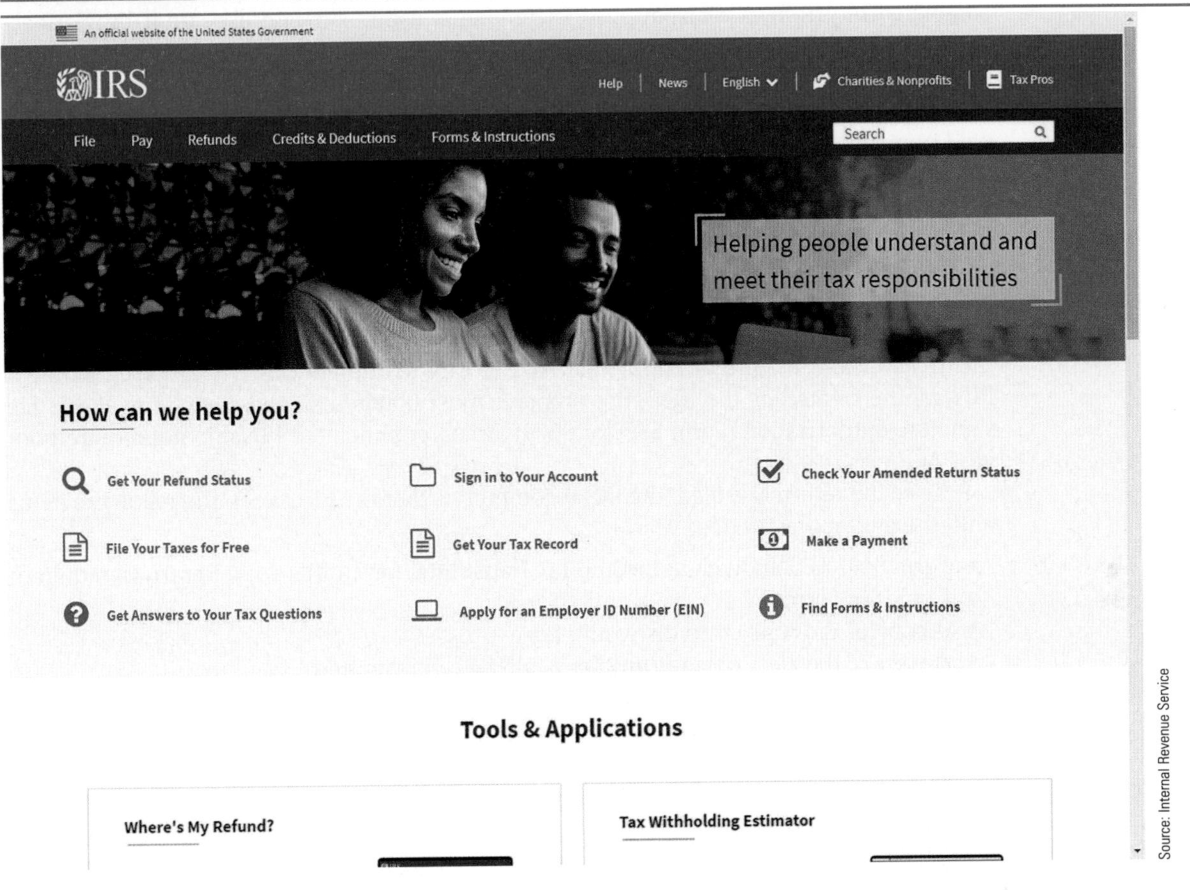

Source: Internal Revenue Service

Self-Study Problem 1.9 ***See Appendix E for Solutions to Self-Study Problems***

Indicate whether the following statements are true or false.

1. Taxpayers can download tax forms and IRS publications from the IRS website.
2. A help function is available to aid users of the IRS website.
3. The IRS has a mobile phone app.

1-10 ELECTRONIC FILING (E-FILING)

1.10 Learning Objective

Describe the basics of electronic filing (e-filing).

Electronic filing (e-filing) is the process of transmitting federal income tax return information to the IRS Service Center using a device with Internet access. For the taxpayer, electronic filing offers faster processing and generally a faster refund. The fastest refund can be obtained through a direct deposit to the taxpayer's bank account (however, the taxpayer may also choose to be paid by check). IRS statistics show an error rate of less than 1 percent on electronically-filed returns, compared with more than 20 percent on paper returns.

The e-filing process often involves a number of different parties starting with the Electronic Return Originator (ERO). The ERO either prepares the return or collects the completed return from a taxpayer. Most preparers using software like Intuit ProConnect will be EROs. When the return is prepared, the ERO either sends the electronic return to a Transmitter (that transmits the return to the IRS), acts as the Transmitter themselves, or uses an Intermediate Service Provider (ISP) to process the e-filing. EROs must identify the paid preparer's name, identifying number, and PTIN.

As with a paper-filed return, e-filed tax returns must be signed by the taxpayer. Taxpayers are also required to sign and date the Declaration of Taxpayer which authorizes the origination of the electronic submission to the IRS and includes the declaration under penalties of perjury that the return is true, correct, and complete. Tax returns are electronically signed through the use of a personal identification number or PIN. PINs can be either generated by the taxpayer or by the ERO. Self-selected PINs generated by the taxpayer also require the prior year AGI or PIN to authenticate the taxpayer. Before a PIN can be created by the ERO, the preparer must obtain a signed copy of an IRS E-file signature authorization (Form 8878 or 8879). Preparer-generated PINs do not require prior year AGI.

Once the return is e-filed, the IRS recommends that the ERO keep the following items until the end of the calendar year:

- Form 8453 U.S. Individual Income Tax Transmittal for an IRS e-file Return (if required)
- Copies of Forms W-2, W-2G, and 1099-R
- A copy of the consent to disclosure form
- A copy of the electronic return that could be retransmitted
- An acknowledgment file for IRS accepted return

Forms 8878 and 8879 must be kept for approximately three years.

A copy of the return must be provided to the taxpayer and can be in any media as long as acceptable to the taxpayer.

The IRS website contains detailed information on this process as the IRS is constantly working to make e-filing more user-friendly and widely available. The IRS provides free tax preparation and e-filing software to individuals with income below certain thresholds (see **https://apps.irs.gov/app/freeFile/**). Individuals with higher income may still e-file free, using IRS fill-in forms (see **https://www.irs.gov/e-file-providers/free-file-fillable-forms**). The fillable forms program performs calculations but will not provide the tax preparation guidance that standard tax software programs provide.

Electronic filing represents a significant growth area in computerized tax services. More than 90 percent of all individual taxpayers now e-file. Mandatory electronic filing is required for nearly the entire professional tax return preparation industry.

Self-Study Problem 1.10

See Appendix E for Solutions to Self-Study Problems

Indicate whether the following statements are true or false.

1. Compared to paper returns, electronic filings significantly reduce the error rate for tax returns filed.
2. Individuals must sign the tax return whether filing electronically or paper.
3. Taxpayers who e-file generally receive faster refunds.
4. Taxpayers who e-file can only request their refund in the form of a check.

KEY TERMS

individual, 1-3
Form 1040, 1-3
Form 1040-SR, 1-3
corporation, 1-4
partnership, 1-4
tax formula for individuals, 1-5
gross income, 1-6
adjusted gross income, 1-6
standard deduction, 1-6
itemized deductions, 1-6
exemptions, 1-6
single filing status, 1-10
married filing jointly, 1-10
married filing separately, 1-10
abandoned spouse, 1-11
head of household, 1-11
surviving spouse, 1-11
qualifying widow(er), 1-11
dependent, 1-15
qualifying child, 1-16
qualifying relative, 1-17
tax deduction, 1-21
tax credit, 1-21
adjusted basis, 1-25
amount realized, 1-25
ordinary gains and losses, 1-26
capital gains and losses, 1-26
capital assets, 1-26
e-filing, 1-29

KEY POINTS

Learning Objectives	Key Points
LO 1.1: Explain the history and objectives of U.S. tax law.	• The income tax was established on March 1, 1913 by the Sixteenth Amendment to the U.S. Constitution. • In addition to raising money to run the government's programs, the income tax is used as a tool for enacting economic and social policies. • Examples of economic tax provisions are the limited allowance for expensing capital expenditures and bonus depreciation provisions. The child and dependent care credit, earned income credit, and the charitable contributions deduction are examples of social tax provisions.
LO 1.2: Describe the different entities subject to tax and reporting requirements.	• Individual taxpayers file Form 1040 or 1040-SR (if age 65 or older) and any supplemental schedules required. • Corporations must report income annually on Form 1120 and pay taxes at a flat rate of 21 percent. • An S corporation generally does not pay regular corporate income taxes; instead, the corporation's income or loss passes through to its shareholders and is included in their individual tax returns. S corporations file on Form 1120S. • A partnership files Form 1065 to report the amount of partnership income or loss and to allocate the items of income, loss, deduction, and credit to the partners. Generally, all income or loss of a partnership is included in the tax returns of the partners.
LO 1.3: Apply the tax formula for individuals.	• AGI (adjusted gross income) is gross income less deductions for adjusted gross income. • AGI less the larger of itemized deductions or the standard deduction and less the qualified business income deduction equals taxable income. • Appropriate tax tables or rate schedules are applied to taxable income to calculate the gross tax liability. • The gross income tax liability plus additional taxes less credits and prepayments equals the tax due or refund.
LO 1.4: Identify individuals who must file tax returns.	• Conditions relating to the amount of the taxpayer's income must exist before a taxpayer is required to file a U.S. income tax return. • Taxpayers are also required to file a return if they have net earnings from self-employment of $400 or more, or owe taxes such as Social Security taxes on unreported tips.

LO 1.5: Determine filing status and understand the calculation of tax according to filing status.	• There are five filing statuses: single; married filing jointly; married filing separately; head of household; and surviving spouse [qualifying widow(er)]. • Tax is calculated using the appropriate tax table or tax rate schedule for the taxpayer's filing status.
LO 1.6: Define qualifying dependents.	• Personal and dependency exemptions were suspended by the TCJA for tax years 2018–2025. • Dependents are still important for determining filing status and certain credits. • A dependent is an individual who is either a qualifying child or qualifying relative.
LO 1.7: Calculate the correct standard or itemized deduction amount for taxpayers.	• The standard deduction was placed in the tax law to provide relief for taxpayers with few itemized deductions. • For 2022, the standard deduction amounts are: Single $12,950; Married, filing jointly $25,900; Married, filing separately $12,950; Head of household $19,400; Surviving spouse $25,900. • Taxpayers who are 65 years of age or older or blind are entitled to additional standard deduction amounts of $1,750 for unmarried taxpayers and $1,400 for married taxpayers and surviving spouses in 2022.
LO 1.8: Compute basic capital gains and losses.	• The amount of gain or loss realized by a taxpayer is determined by subtracting the adjusted basis of the asset from the amount realized. • Gains and losses can be either ordinary or capital. • Ordinary gains and losses are treated for tax purposes like other items such as salary and interest. • Capital gains and losses result from the sale or exchange of capital assets. • Common capital assets held by individual taxpayers include stocks, bonds, land, cars, boats, and other items held as investments. Typical assets that are not capital are inventory and accounts receivable. • Gain from property held twelve months or less is deemed to be short-term capital gain and is taxed at ordinary income tax rates. • Gain from property held more than twelve months is deemed to be long-term capital gain and is taxed at preferential income tax rates. • The long-term capital gain rates for 2022 vary between 0, 15, and 20 percent, depending on the taxpayer's income. • If an individual taxpayer ends up with a net capital loss (short-term or long-term), up to $3,000 per year can be deducted against ordinary income. Any excess capital loss is carried forward to subsequent tax years. Losses from personal-use assets are not deductible.
LO 1.9: Access and use various Internet tax resources.	• Taxpayers and tax practitioners can find a substantial amount of useful information on the Internet. • Useful websites containing tax information include the IRS (**www.irs.gov**) and the Intuit websites.
LO 1.10: Describe the basics of electronic filing (e-filing).	• Electronic filing (e-filing) is the process of transmitting federal income tax return information to the IRS Service Center using a device with Internet access. • Electronic filing offers a faster refund through a direct deposit to the taxpayer's bank account or the taxpayer can request the refund be sent by check.

QUESTIONS and PROBLEMS

GROUP 1: MULTIPLE CHOICE QUESTIONS

LO 1.1

1. The current income tax system is:
   a. Designed solely to raise money for the government
   b. Authorized by the founding fathers when the government was formed
   c. Not designed with social objectives in mind
   d. Used as a tool to promote social and economic policies as well as raise revenue
   e. None of the above

LO 1.1

2. The amendment to the United States Constitution that authorized the federal income tax is:
   a. Thirteenth Amendment in 1865
   b. Fourteenth Amendment in 1868
   c. Sixteenth Amendment in 1913
   d. Twenty-first Amendment in 1933

LO 1.2

3. Which of the following tax forms are used by individuals in 2022?
   a. 1040A
   b. 1040-EZ
   c. 1040-SR
   d. 1120

LO 1.2

4. Typically a partnership reports its taxable income or loss on:
   a. Form 1040
   b. Form 1120
   c. Form 1040X
   d. Form 1065

LO 1.2

5. On which of these would capital gain income be reported?
   a. Schedule 1
   b. Schedule 2
   c. Schedule 3
   d. Form 1040

LO 1.2

6. Which of the following entities is *not* likely to be a tax-paying entity?
   a. A single taxpayer over the age of 65
   b. A single taxpayer under the age of 65
   c. A corporation
   d. A partnership

LO 1.3

7. Which of the following is a deduction for adjusted gross income in 2022?
   a. Personal casualty losses
   b. Medical expenses
   c. Student loan interest
   d. Mortgage interest
   e. None of the above

LO 1.3

8. All of the following are itemized deductions in 2022 *except*:
   a. Charitable contributions
   b. Deductible IRA contributions
   c. State and local taxes
   d. Medical expenses
   e. All of the above are itemized deductions

LO 1.3

9. Ramon, a single taxpayer with no dependents, has adjusted gross income for 2022 of $98,000 and his itemized deductions total $13,000. What taxable income will Ramon show in 2022?
   a. $74,950
   b. $85,800
   c. $85,450
   d. $85,000
   e. $89,000

LO 1.3

10. To arrive at adjusted gross income (AGI), deduct ________ from gross income.
   a. from AGI deductions
   b. the greater of the standard deduction or itemized deductions
   c. The qualified business income deduction
   d. for AGI deductions

LO 1.3

11. Which of the following statements related to standard and itemized deductions is correct?
   a. A taxpayer may only deduct the lower of itemized deductions or the standard deduction.
   b. A taxpayer may deduct the greater of itemized deductions or the standard deduction.
   c. The standard deduction is the same for all tax filing statuses but itemized deductions may differ.
   d. Itemized deductions are only available to corporate taxpayers.

LO 1.3

12. Which of the following is *not* a from AGI deduction?
   a. The exclusion of an item of gross income
   b. Itemized deductions, if taken
   c. Standard deduction, if taken
   d. The qualified business income deduction

LO 1.4

13. The gross income threshold to require a federal income tax return for a single taxpayer is equal to:
   a. The sum of the taxpayer's itemized deductions.
   b. The same as the current year standard deduction ($12,950 in 2022).
   c. Any amount over zero.
   d. an amount that cannot be determined without knowing if any for AGI deductions will be claimed.

LO 1.4

14. Ben is a single taxpayer with no dependents and is 32 years old. What is the minimum amount of income that he must have to be required to file a tax return for 2022?
   a. $4,300
   b. $12,400
   c. $12,550
   d. $12,950
   e. None of the above

LO 1.4

15. Abed and Anahita are married filing jointly. Abed is 65 and Anahita is 63 and they also care for Anahita's mother and claim her as a dependent. What is the 2022 filing threshold for Abed and Anahita?
   a. $0
   b. $19,400
   c. $25,900
   d. $27,300
   e. $27,650

LO 1.4

16. Anahita is single, 82 years old, and blind. She is claimed as a dependent by her daughter and spouse, who file jointly. Anahita has no earned income but did receive $3,800 of investment (unearned) income in 2022. What is her filing threshold for the current year and is she required to file a tax return?
    a. $12,900 of earned income and thus not required to file
    b. $1,100 of unearned income and thus required to file
    c. $4,500 of unearned income and thus not required to file
    d. $400 of self-employment income and thus required to file

LO 1.5

17. Joan, who was divorced in 2022, had filed a joint tax return with her husband in 2021. During 2022, she did not remarry and continued to maintain her home in which her two dependent children lived. In the preparation of her tax return for 2022, Joan should file as:
    a. A single individual
    b. A surviving spouse
    c. Head of household
    d. Married, filing separately
    e. None of the above

LO 1.5

18. Glenda, a single taxpayer from Kansas, paid for more than one-half of the support for her mother, Dorothy. Dorothy did not live with Glenda in Kansas, but rather has lived in a nursing home in an adjacent state since Dorothy's husband died three years ago. Glenda's filing status should be:
    a. Single
    b. Married filing separately
    c. Surviving spouse
    d. Head of household
    e. Parental dependent

LO 1.5

19. Angela's spouse died in 2022. She has no dependent children, but she pays the entire cost to maintain her home. What is Angela's most advantageous filing status in the current year?
    a. Single
    b. Head of household
    c. Surviving spouse
    d. Married filing jointly

LO 1.5

20. Angela's spouse died in 2021. She has two dependent children, and she pays the entire cost to maintain her home. What is Angela's most advantageous filing status in the current year?
    a. Single
    b. Head of household
    c. Surviving spouse
    d. Married filing jointly

LO 1.6

21. Margaret and her sister support their mother and together provide 85 percent of their mother's support. If Margaret provides 40 percent of her mother's support:
    a. Her sister is the only one who can claim their mother as a dependent.
    b. Neither Margaret nor her sister may claim their mother as a dependent.
    c. Both Margaret and her sister may claim their mother as a dependent.
    d. Margaret and her sister may split the dependency exemption.
    e. Margaret may claim her mother as a dependent if her sister agrees in a multiple support agreement.

LO 1.6

22. Kardi, age 65, and Kanye, age 62, are married with a 23-year-old daughter who lives in their home. They provide over half of their daughter's support, and their daughter earned $4,600 this year from a part-time job. Their daughter is not a full-time student. With regard to their daughter's dependency status:
    a. She can be claimed because she lived in their household for twelve months.
    b. She can be claimed because she is a qualifying child.
    c. She can be claimed because she is a qualifying relative.
    d. She cannot be claimed because she fails the age and gross income test.

LO 1.6

23. Yasmine and her spouse Carlos, who file married filing jointly with 2022 AGI of $130,000, provide all the support for their 16-year-old son, Miguel. If Miguel qualifies as a qualifying child under the dependent rules, Yasmine and Carlos will be able to claim a 2022 child tax credit of:
    a. $0
    b. $500
    c. $1,000
    d. $2,000
    e. $3,000

LO 1.6

24. In 2022, Lakota and Dominique file married filing jointly and have a 13-year-old daughter. They also provide 25 percent of the support for Lakota's 82-year-old mother, who lives in a nursing home nearby. The amount of the combined child tax credit and other dependent credit for Lakota and Dominique is:
    a. $0
    b. $2,000
    c. $3,000
    d. $3,500
    e. $3,600

LO 1.6

25. In 2022, Alexandria is a single mother with a 17-year-old dependent child. Alexandria's adjusted gross income in 2022 is $78,000. What is the total amount of Alexandria's child tax credit and other dependent credit?
    a. $0
    b. $500
    c. $2,000
    d. $2,500

LO 1.7

26. Morgan is 65 years old and single. He supports his father, who is 90 years old, blind, and has no income. What is Morgan's standard deduction?
    a. $21,150
    b. $19,400
    c. $20,300
    d. $18,800
    e. $20,500

LO 1.7

27. Taxpayers who are 65 or older get the benefit of:
    a. An additional exemption
    b. An additional amount added to their standard deduction
    c. An additional amount added to their itemized deductions
    d. None of the above

LO 1.7

28. Taxpayers who are blind get the benefit of:
    a. An additional exemption
    b. An additional amount added to their standard deduction
    c. An additional amount added to their itemized deductions
    d. None of the above

LO 1.7

29. Marta, a single, 19-year-old, full-time student, is claimed as a dependent by her parents in 2022. She has earned income of $3,000 and unearned income of $130. What is Marta's 2022 standard deduction?
    a. $0
    b. $1,150
    c. $3,350
    d. $3,400
    e. $12,950

LO 1.7

30. Myrtle, a single, 19-year-old, full-time student, is claimed as a dependent by her parents in 2022. She has earned income of $13,000 and unearned income of $130. What is Myrtle's 2022 standard deduction?
    a. $0
    b. $1,150
    c. $3,350
    d. $13,400
    e. $12,950

LO 1.8

31. Which of the following is *not* a capital asset to an individual taxpayer?
    a. Stocks
    b. A 48-foot sailboat
    c. Raw land held as an investment
    d. Inventory in the taxpayer's business
    e. All of the above are capital assets

LO 1.8

32. Joyce purchased General Electric stock four years ago for $10,000. In the current year, she sells the stock for $25,000. What is Joyce's gain or loss?
    a. $15,000 long-term gain
    b. $15,000 short-term gain
    c. $15,000 ordinary loss
    d. $15,000 extraordinary gain
    e. No gain or loss is recognized on this transaction

LO 1.8

33. Alex purchased a rental house four years ago for $270,000. Her depreciation at the time of the sale is $40,000. Due to a decrease in real estate prices, she sells the house for only $240,000 in 2022. What is her gain or loss for tax purposes?
    a. $0
    b. $10,000 loss
    c. $10,000 gain
    d. $35,000 loss
    e. $25,000 gain

LO 1.8

34. Dorit, a single taxpayer, has a long-term capital loss of $7,000 on the sale of bonds in 2022 and no other capital gains or losses. Her taxable income without this transaction is $43,000. What is her taxable income considering this capital loss?
    a. $40,000
    b. $36,000
    c. $43,000
    d. $55,000
    e. Some other amount

LO 1.9

35. Access the Internet and go to **www.irs.gov** and select "Search Forms & Instructions." Enter "1040" into the search box. What is Line 7 of the 2022 Form 1040?
    a. Other income
    b. Multiply Line 6 by $500
    c. Capital gain or (loss)
    d. Earned income credit
    e. Your social security number

LO 1.10

36. If a tax preparer provides a PIN for the taxpayer:
    a. The taxpayer must also provide prior year AGI
    b. The tax preparer must obtain a signed Form 8878 or 8879
    c. The e-filing must go directly to the IRS
    d. Preparers may not provide PINs, only taxpayers.

LO 1.10

37. Electronically-filed tax returns:
    a. May not be transmitted from a taxpayer's home computer
    b. Constitute over 90 percent of the returns filed with the IRS
    c. Have error rates similar to paper returns
    d. Offer larger refunds than paper returns

GROUP 2: PROBLEMS

LO 1.1

1. List three major purposes of the tax system.

LO 1.2

2. Match each type of transaction with the form on which it is most likely reported

Transaction	Form
a. Wages and salaries	Schedule 1
b. Interest income over $1,500	Schedule 2
c. Capital gains from the sale of stock	Schedule 3
d. Deduction for charitable contributions	Schedule A
e. Self-employment taxes	Schedule B
f. Rental income	Schedule C
g. Credit for child and dependent care expenses	Schedule D
h. Net profit from sole proprietorship	Schedule E
i. Deductions for gross income	Form 1040

LO 1.3

3. Rahul and Ruby are married taxpayers. They are both under age 65 and in good health. For 2022, they have a total of $42,000 in wages and $300 in interest income. Rahul and Ruby's deductions for adjusted gross income amount to $6,000 and their itemized deductions equal $18,700. They have two children, ages 32 and 28, that are married and provide support for themselves.
    a. What is the amount of Rahul and Ruby's adjusted gross income?
    b. What is the amount of their itemized deductions or standard deduction?
    c. What is their taxable income?

LO 1.3

4. Xialu is a single taxpayer who is under age 65 and in good health. For 2022, she has a salary of $25,000 and itemized deductions of $7,000. Xialu allows her mother to live with her during the winter months (3–4 months per year), but her mother provides all of her own support otherwise.
    a. How much is Xialu's adjusted gross income?
    b. What amount of itemized or standard deduction(s) should she claim?
    c. What is the amount of Xialu's taxable income?

LO 1.3
LO 1.8

5. In 2022, Manon earns wages of $54,000. She also has dividend income of $2,800. Manon is single and has no dependents. During the year, Manon sold silver coins held as an investment for a $7,000 loss. Calculate the following amounts for Manon:
    a. Adjusted gross income
    b. Standard deduction
    c. Taxable income

LO 1.3
LO 1.5
LO 1.7

6. Diego, age 28, married Dolores, age 27, in 2022. Their salaries for the year amounted to $48,000. They had dividend income of $2,500. Diego and Dolores' deductions for adjusted gross income amounted to $3,000, their itemized deductions were $16,000, and they have no dependents.
   a. What is the amount of their adjusted gross income?
   b. What is the amount of their itemized deductions or standard deduction?
   c. What is the amount of their taxable income?
   d. Assuming no tax credits apply, what is their tax liability for 2022?

LO 1.3
LO 1.5
LO 1.7

7. Marco and Tatiana are married and file separate returns for 2022. Tatiana itemizes her deductions on her return. Marco's adjusted gross income was $18,000, his itemized deductions were $2,400. Neither have any dependents. Calculate Marco's income tax liability assuming the couple does not live in a community property state.

LO 1.3
LO 1.5
LO 1.7

8. Alicia, age 27, is a single, full-time college student. She earns $13,200 from a part-time job and has taxable interest income of $1,450. Her itemized deductions are $845. Calculate Alicia's taxable income for 2022.

LO 1.3
LO 1.5
LO 1.7

9. Jonathan is a 35-year-old single taxpayer with adjusted gross income in 2022 of $47,000. He uses the standard deduction and has no dependents.
   a. Calculate Jonathan's taxable income. Please show your work.
   b. When you calculate Jonathan's tax liability are you required to use the tax tables or the tax rate schedules, or does it matter?
   c. Assuming no tax credits, what is Jonathan's tax liability?

LO 1.3
LO 1.5
LO 1.7

10. Brock, age 50, and Erin, age 49, are married with three dependent children. They file a joint return for 2022. Their income from salaries totals $50,000, and they received $8,000 in taxable interest, $5,000 in royalties, and $3,000 in other ordinary income. Brock and Erin's deductions for adjusted gross income amount to $2,500, and they have itemized deductions totaling $27,000. Calculate the following amounts:
    a. Gross income
    b. Adjusted gross income
    c. Itemized deduction or standard deduction amount
    d. Taxable income
    e. Income tax liability (Do not consider the alternative minimum tax covered in Chapter 6 or any credits.)

LO 1.3
LO 1.5
LO 1.6
LO 1.7

11. Jackson, age 35, and Peggy, age 34, are married and file a joint income tax return for 2022. Their salaries for the year total $85,400 and they have dividend income of $4,000. They have no deductions for adjusted gross income. Their itemized deductions are $25,200. Jackson and Peggy do not have any dependents.
    a. What is the amount of their adjusted gross income?
    b. What is their deduction for personal exemptions?
    c. What is the amount of their taxable income?

LO 1.3
LO 1.5
LO 1.7

12. Wanda is a single 50-year-old taxpayer with no dependents. Her only 2022 income is $41,000 of wages. Calculate her taxable income and her tax liability assuming no tax credits. Please show your work.

LO 1.4

13. Griffin is a server at a California restaurant. Griffin received $1,200 in unreported tips during 2022 and owes Social Security and Medicare taxes on these tips. His total income for the year, including the tips, is $4,300. Is Griffin required to file an income tax return for 2022? Why or why not?

LO 1.4

14. For each of the following situations (none of the taxpayers claim dependents), indicate whether the taxpayer(s) is (are) required to file a tax return for 2022. Explain your answer.
    a. Helen is a head of household taxpayer with interest income of $14,000.
    b. Joan is a single college student who is claimed as a dependent by her parents. She earned $1,550 from a part-time job and has $1,200 in interest income.

c. Leslie, age 64, and Mark, age 66, are married and file a joint return. They received $26,000 in interest income from a savings account.
d. Ray, age 60, and Jean, age 57, are married and file a joint tax return. Their only income is $26,000 in interest income.
e. Harry, a 19-year-old single taxpayer, had net earnings from self-employment of $1,500.

LO 1.5

15. Each of the following taxpayers has 2022 taxable income before the standard deduction as shown. Determine the income tax liability (before any credits) for each taxpayer using the Tax Tables in Appendix A.

Taxpayer(s)	*Filing Status*	*Taxable Income Before the Standard Deduction*
a. Allen	Single	$34,600
b. Boyd	MFS	37,175
c. Caldwell	MFJ	62,710
d. Dell	H of H	49,513
e. Evans	Single	57,397

LO 1.5
LO 1.6

16. For each of the following taxpayers, indicate the filing status for the taxpayer(s) for 2022 using the following legend:

A—Single
B—Married filing a joint return
C—Married filing separate returns
D—Head of household
E—Surviving spouse [qualifying widow(er)]

a. Linda is single and she supports her mother (who has no income), including paying all the costs of her housing in an apartment across town.
b. Frank is single and claims his unrelated significant other as a qualifying relative as the significant other lives in the home Frank pays for and the significant other has no income.
c. Arthur is single and he supports his 30-year-old brother, who lives in his own home.
d. Leslie's spouse died in 2022. She has no dependents and did not remarry.
e. Lester's spouse dies in 2021. He has one 17-year-old dependent child that lives with him in the home Lester pays for.

LO 1.5

17. Melissa and Whitney are married taxpayers with taxable income of $106,000 and no dependents.
a. When you calculate their tax liability, are you required to use the tax tables or the tax rate schedules, or does it matter?
b. What is their 2022 pre-credit tax liability?

LO 1.5
LO 1.6

18. Karl is a single taxpayer and has listed his brother, Jonas, as a dependent (qualifying relative). Head of household filing status seems preferable for Karl. What questions should you ask Karl to confirm his filing status?

LO 1.5
LO 1.6

19. Maggie is single and supports her 85-year-old parents who have no income and live in a home rented for them by Maggie. What is Maggie's filing status and why?

LO 1.5

20. List each alternative filing status available to unmarried individual taxpayers and the circumstances under which the alternatives can be used.

LO 1.5
LO 1.6

21. Marquez is single and supports his 30-year-old son, who has income of $2,000 and lives in his own apartment.
a. Can Marquez claim his son as a dependent?
b. Can Marquez claim head of household filing status? Why or why not?

LO 1.6 22. In each of the following situations, determine whether the taxpayer(s) has/have a dependent and if so, the total amount of child tax credit and other dependent credit for 2022 (assuming no limitations apply).

a. Donna, a 20-year-old single taxpayer, supports her mother, who lives in her own home. Her mother has income of $1,350.
b. William, age 43, and Mary, age 45, are married and support William's 19-year-old sister, who is not a student. The sister's income from a part-time job is $4,400.
c. Devi was divorced in 2020 and receives child support of $250 per month from her ex-husband for the support of their 8-year-old son, John, who lives with her. Devi is 45 and provides more than half of her son's support.
d. Wendell, an 89-year-old single taxpayer, supports his son, who is 67 years old, lives with him, and earns no income.
e. Wilma, age 65, and Morris, age 66, are married. They file a joint return.

LO 1.6 23. What is the total dollar amount of personal and dependency exemptions a married couple with two children (ages 11 and 17, both of which are qualified children) and $80,000 of adjusted gross income would deduct in 2022? What is the total child and other dependent credit that could be claimed (before any advance payments or limitations)?

LO 1.6 24. If Charles, a 16-year-old child model, earns $50,000 a year and is completely self-supporting even though he lives with his parents, can his parents claim him as a dependent? Why or why not?

LO 1.6 25. Marc's brother, Phillip, who is a 20-year-old French citizen, lives in France for the full year. Marc supports Phillip while he attends college. Can Marc claim Phillip as a dependent? Why or why not?

LO 1.7 26. Describe the difference between the standard deduction and itemized deductions. How should a taxpayer decide whether to take the standard deduction or claim itemized deductions?

LO 1.7 27. Describe the three possible limits that can be used to compute the standard deduction for a taxpayer that can be claimed as a dependent.

LO 1.7 28. List the three types of individual taxpayers that are not eligible for the standard deduction.

LO 1.8 29. Compute the realized and recognized gain or loss for each of the following transactions and classify as short-term or long-term:

a. Marge, a single taxpayer, receives $8,000 for the sale of stock she purchased six years ago for $3,000.
b. Lisa, a single taxpayer, receives $3,000 for the sale of stock she purchased six months ago for $8,000.
c. Bart and Maggie, married filing jointly taxpayers, receive $3,000 for the sale of stock they purchased three years ago for $10,000.
d. Homer, a single taxpayer, receives $12,000 on the sale of his personal-use motorcycle. He purchased the motorcycle four months ago for $16,000.
e. Mo, a single taxpayer, receives $16,000 on the sale of his personal-use motorcycle. He purchased the motorcycle four years ago for $12,000.

LO 1.9 30. Go to the IRS website (**www.irs.gov/newsroom**) and note the name of the most recent news release.

LO 1.9 31. Go to the IRS website (**www.irs.gov**) and select the Forms & Instructions tab. Search for Form 8949 and provide the title of this form.

LO 1.9 32. Go to the Turbo Tax Blog (**http://blog.turbotax.intuit.com/**) and search the blog for an article on the deduction of student loan interest. What is the maximum deduction that can be taken in a year?

LO 1.10 33. Describe how a tax preparer can obtain a taxpayer signature on an electronically-filed tax return.

LO 1.10 34. List the documents the IRS recommends a tax preparer retain when electronically filing a taxpayer's return.

GROUP 3: WRITING ASSIGNMENTS

RESEARCH

1. Jerry, age 23, a full-time student and not disabled, lives with William and Sheila Carson. Jerry is William's older brother. Jerry is single, a U.S. citizen, and does not provide more than one-half of his own support. William and Sheila are both 21 and file a joint return. Can William and Sheila claim Jerry as a qualifying child?
Required: Go to the IRS website (**www.irs.gov**) and review Publication 501. Write a letter to William and Sheila stating if they can claim Jerry as a qualifying child.

ETHICS

2. Jason and Mary Wells, friends of yours, were married on December 30, 2022. They know you are studying taxes and have sent you an e-mail with a question concerning their filing status. Jason and Mary would each like to file single for tax year 2022. Jason has prepared their taxes both as single and married filing jointly, and he has realized that the couple will get a larger combined refund if they each file single. Jason argues "that it's not as if we were married for very long in 2022." Prepare an e-mail to respond to the couple's inquiry.

GROUP 4: COMPREHENSIVE PROBLEMS

Instructions for working all Group 4 Comprehensive Tax Return Problems in this textbook are as follows:

Birthdays: If using the tax software, create birthdates for taxpayers and dependents. Adult taxpayers should have ages between 25 and 64 unless a different age is specified.

Wages: Assume the wages subject to income tax in the problems are the same as Social Security wages and Medicare wages unless presented otherwise. Create employer names and other information which may be required by your tax software package.

Missing Data: Please make realistic assumptions about any missing data. Decide whether taxpayers contribute to the Presidential Election Campaign, which does not affect tax liability. No taxpayers will have traded digital assets unless specific details are provided. All taxpayers request a refund of any overpaid tax unless otherwise indicated.

Child and Dependent Credits: You are not required to complete Form 8812 unless instructed to do so. You may also assume no advance payments on the credit were received unless otherwise indicated.

Tax Forms: Tax forms to complete the problems are found in Appendix F. Additional copies can be found on the IRS website (**www.irs.gov**).

1A. Maria Tallchief is a single taxpayer (birthdate May 18, 1995) living at 543 Space Drive, Houston, TX 77099. Her Social Security number is 466-33-1234. For 2022, Maria has no dependents, and her W-2, from her job at a local restaurant where she is a cashier, contains the following information:

	a Employee's social security number 466-33-1234	OMB No. 1545-0008	Safe, accurate, FAST! Use IRS e-file	Visit the IRS website at www.irs.gov/efile
b Employer identification number (EIN) 33-1235672			1 Wages, tips, other compensation 22,114.40	2 Federal income tax withheld 1,198.75
c Employer's name, address, and ZIP code Burger Box 1234 Mountain Road Houston, TX 77099			3 Social security wages 22,114.40	4 Social security tax withheld 1,371.09
			5 Medicare wages and tips 22,114.40	6 Medicare tax withheld 320.66
			7 Social security tips	8 Allocated tips
d Control number			9	10 Dependent care benefits
e Employee's first name and initial Last name Suff. Maria Tallchief 543 Space Drive Houston, TX 77099			11 Nonqualified plans	12a See instructions for box 12
			13 Statutory employee ☐ Retirement plan ☐ Third-party sick pay ☐	12b
			14 Other	12c
f Employee's address and ZIP code				12d

15 State Employer's state ID number	16 State wages, tips, etc.	17 State income tax	18 Local wages, tips, etc.	19 Local income tax	20 Locality name
TX					

Form **W-2** Wage and Tax Statement 2022 Department of the Treasury—Internal Revenue Service
Copy B—To Be Filed With Employee's FEDERAL Tax Return.
This information is being furnished to the Internal Revenue Service.

These wages are Maria's only income for 2022.

Required: Complete Form 1040 for Maria Tallchief for the 2022 tax year.

1B. Using the information from Problem 1A, assume Maria's birthdate is May 18, 1955, and complete Form 1040-SR for Maria Tallchief for the 2022 tax year.

2A. Hardy and Dora Knox are married and file a joint return for 2022. Hardy's Social Security number is 466-47-3311 and her birthdate is January 4, 1976. Dora's Social Security number is 467-74-4451 and her birthday is July 7, 1977. They live at 143 Maple Street, Knoxville, TN 37932. For 2022, Hardy did not work, and Dora's W-2 from her teaching job showed the following:

	a Employee's social security number 467-74-4451	OMB No. 1545-0008	Safe, accurate, FAST! Use IRS e-file	Visit the IRS website at www.irs.gov/efile
b Employer identification number (EIN) 33-0711111			1 Wages, tips, other compensation 52,300.34	2 Federal income tax withheld 3,154.55
c Employer's name, address, and ZIP code Knoxville Unified School District 1700 Harding Valley Street Knoxville, TN 37932			3 Social security wages 52,300.34	4 Social security tax withheld 3,242.62
			5 Medicare wages and tips 52,300.34	6 Medicare tax withheld 758.35
			7 Social security tips	8 Allocated tips
d Control number			9	10 Dependent care benefits
e Employee's first name and initial Last name Suff. Dora Knox 143 Maple Street Knoxville, TN 37932			11 Nonqualified plans	12a See instructions for box 12
			13 Statutory employee ☐ Retirement plan ☐ Third-party sick pay ☐	12b
			14 Other	12c
f Employee's address and ZIP code				12d

15 State Employer's state ID number	16 State wages, tips, etc.	17 State income tax	18 Local wages, tips, etc.	19 Local income tax	20 Locality name
TN					

Form **W-2** Wage and Tax Statement 2022 Department of the Treasury—Internal Revenue Service
Copy B—To Be Filed With Employee's FEDERAL Tax Return.
This information is being furnished to the Internal Revenue Service.

Hardy and Dora have a son they provide more than half of the support for named Fort (birthdate December 21, 2002, Social Security number 552-52-5552), who is living with them, is not a full-time student, and generates $4,200 of gross income for himself. If Fort qualifies as a dependent, he will also qualify for the other dependent credit of $500.

Required: Complete Form 1040 for Hardy and Dora for the 2022 tax year. You are not required to complete a Form 8812 for this problem.

2B. Abigail (Abby) Boxer is a single mother (birthdate April 28, 1984) working as a civilian accountant for the U.S. Army. Her Social Security number is 676-73-3311 and she lives at 3456 S Career Avenue, Sioux Falls, SD 57107. Helen, Abby's 18-year-old daughter (Social Security number 676-73-3312 and birthdate April 16, 2004), is a dependent child living with her mother, and she does not qualify for the child tax credit due to her age but does qualify for the other dependent credit of $500. Abby's Form W-2 from the U.S. Department of Defense shows the following:

a Employee's social security number 676-73-3311	OMB No. 1545-0008	Safe, accurate, FAST! Use IRS e-file. Visit the IRS website at www.irs.gov/efile
b Employer identification number (EIN) 31-1575142	1 Wages, tips, other compensation 60,402.64	2 Federal income tax withheld 4,588.88
c Employer's name, address, and ZIP code DFAS Cleveland Center PO Box 998002 Cleveland, OH 44199	3 Social security wages 60,402.64	4 Social security tax withheld 3,744.96
	5 Medicare wages and tips 60,402.64	6 Medicare tax withheld 875.84
	7 Social security tips	8 Allocated tips
d Control number	9	10 Dependent care benefits
e Employee's first name and initial / Last name / Suff. Abigail Boxer 3456 S. Career Avenue Sioux Falls, SD 57107	11 Nonqualified plans	12a See instructions for box 12
	13 Statutory employee ☐ Retirement plan ☐ Third-party sick pay ☐	12b
	14 Other	12c
f Employee's address and ZIP code		12d

15 State Employer's state ID number	16 State wages, tips, etc.	17 State income tax	18 Local wages, tips, etc.	19 Local income tax	20 Locality name
SD					

Form **W-2** Wage and Tax Statement 2022 Department of the Treasury—Internal Revenue Service

Copy B—To Be Filed With Employee's FEDERAL Tax Return.
This information is being furnished to the Internal Revenue Service.

Abby also has taxable interest from Sioux Falls Savings and Loan of $250 and tax-exempt interest from bonds issued by the state of South Dakota of $140.

Required: Complete Form 1040 for Abigail for the 2022 tax year. You are not required to complete a Form 8812 for this problem.

GROUP 5:
CUMULATIVE SOFTWARE PROBLEM

1. Albert Gaytor and his wife Allison are married and file a joint return for 2022. The Gaytors live at 12340 Cocoshell Road, Coral Gables, FL 33134. Captain Albert Gaytor is a charter fishing boat captain but took six months off from his job in 2022 to train and study for his Masters Captain's License.

   In 2022, Albert received a Form W-2 from his employer, Coconut Grove Fishing Charters, Inc.:

a Employee's social security number	255-51-1966
OMB No. 1545-0008	Safe, accurate, FAST! Use IRS e-file. Visit the IRS website at www.irs.gov/efile
b Employer identification number (EIN)	60-3456789
c Employer's name, address, and ZIP code	Coconut Grove Fishing Charters, Inc. 2432 Bay Blvd. Coconut Grove, FL 33133
d Control number	
e Employee's first name and initial / Last name / Suff.	Albert T. Gaytor 12340 Cocoshell Road Coral Gables, FL 33134
f Employee's address and ZIP code	
1 Wages, tips, other compensation	67,917.71
2 Federal income tax withheld	5,478.87
3 Social security wages	67,917.71
4 Social security tax withheld	4,120.90
5 Medicare wages and tips	67,917.71
6 Medicare tax withheld	984.81
7 Social security tips	
8 Allocated tips	
9	
10 Dependent care benefits	
11 Nonqualified plans	
12a See instructions for box 12	
12b	
12c	
12d	
13 Statutory employee / Retirement plan / Third-party sick pay	☐ ☐ ☐
14 Other	

15 State Employer's state ID number	16 State wages, tips, etc.	17 State income tax	18 Local wages, tips, etc.	19 Local income tax	20 Locality name
FL					

Form **W-2** **Wage and Tax Statement** 2022 Department of the Treasury—Internal Revenue Service

Copy B—To Be Filed With Employee's FEDERAL Tax Return.
This information is being furnished to the Internal Revenue Service.

Name	*Social Security Number*	*Date of Birth*
Albert T. Gaytor	266-51-1966	09/22/1973
Allison A. Gaytor	266-34-1967	07/01/1974
Crocker Gaytor	261-55-1212	12/21/2004
Cayman Slacker	261-11-4444	03/13/2003
Sean Slacker	344-23-5656	05/01/2002

The Gaytors have an 18-year-old son, Crocker, who is a full-time freshman at Brickell State University. The Gaytors also have a 19-year-old daughter, Cayman, who is a part-time student at Dade County Community College (DCCC). Cayman is married to Sean Slacker, who is 20 years old and a part-time student at DCCC. Sean and Cayman have a 1-year-old child, Wanda Slacker (Social Security number 648-99-4306). Sean, Cayman, and Wanda all live in an apartment up the street from Albert and Allison during the entire current calendar year. Sean and Cayman both work for Sean's wealthy grandfather as apprentices in his business. Their wages for the year were a combined $50,000, which allowed them to pay all the personal expenses for themselves and their daughter. Albert's cousin, Jeff (everyone calls him Swampy) Gaytor is 25 years old (birthdate 4/16/1997, Social Security number 542-11-5562). Swampy lost his job and in 2022, received $3,200 of unemployment compensation. The remainder (well above 50 percent) of Swampy's support was provided by the Gaytors, including the rent on Swampy's apartment in Cutler Bay, FL, about 16 miles from the Gaytor's home.

Albert and Allison have a savings account and received the following Form 1099-INT for 2022:

☐ CORRECTED (if checked)

PAYER'S name, street address, city or town, state or province, country, ZIP or foreign postal code, and telephone no.		Payer's RTN (optional)	OMB No. 1545-0112	
Vizcaya National Bank 9871 Coral Way Miami, FL 33134		1 Interest income $ 354.11	Form **1099-INT** (Rev. January 2022) For calendar year 20 22	**Interest Income**
		2 Early withdrawal penalty $		**Copy B** **For Recipient**
PAYER'S TIN 60-7654321	RECIPIENT'S TIN 266-51-1966	3 Interest on U.S. Savings Bonds and Treasury obligations $		
RECIPIENT'S name Albert T. Gaytor		**4 Federal income tax withheld** $	5 Investment expenses $	This is important tax information and is being furnished to the IRS. If you are required to file a return, a negligence penalty or other sanction may be imposed on you if this income is taxable and the IRS determines that it has not been reported.
Street address (including apt. no.) 12340 Cocoshell Road		6 Foreign tax paid $	7 Foreign country or U.S. possession	
		8 Tax-exempt interest $	9 Specified private activity bond interest $	
City or town, state or province, country, and ZIP or foreign postal code Coral Gables, FL 33134		10 Market discount $	11 Bond premium $	
	FATCA filing requirement ☐	12 Bond premium on Treasury obligations $	13 Bond premium on tax-exempt bond $	
Account number (see instructions)		14 Tax-exempt and tax credit bond CUSIP no.	15 State / 16 State identification no.	17 State tax withheld $ $

Form **1099-INT** (Rev. 1-2022) (keep for your records) www.irs.gov/Form1099INT Department of the Treasury - Internal Revenue Service

Required: Use a computer software package such as Intuit ProConnect to complete Form 1040 for Albert and Allison Gaytor for 2022. Be sure to save your data input files since this case will be expanded with more tax information in later chapters. Make assumptions regarding any information not given.

CHAPTER 2

Gross Income and Exclusions

TSViPhoto/Shutterstock.com

LEARNING OBJECTIVES

After completing this chapter, you should be able to:

LO 2.1 Apply the definition of gross income.

LO 2.2 Describe salaries and wages income reporting and inclusion in gross income.

LO 2.3 Explain the general tax treatment of health insurance.

LO 2.4 Determine when meals and lodging may be excluded from taxable income.

LO 2.5 Identify the common employee fringe benefit income exclusions.

LO 2.6 Determine when prizes and awards are included in income.

LO 2.7 Calculate the taxable and nontaxable portions of annuity payments.

LO 2.8 Describe the tax treatment of life insurance proceeds.

LO 2.9 Identify the tax treatment of interest income.

LO 2.10 Identify the tax treatment of dividend income.

LO 2.11 Identify the general rules for the tax treatment of gifts and inheritances.

LO 2.12 Describe the elements of scholarship income that are excluded from tax.

LO 2.13 Describe the tax treatment of alimony and child support.

LO 2.14 Explain the tax implications of using educational savings vehicles.

LO 2.15 Describe the tax treatment of unemployment compensation.

LO 2.16 Apply the rules governing inclusion of Social Security benefits in gross income.

LO 2.17 Distinguish between the different rules for married taxpayers residing in community property states when filing separate returns.

LO 2.18 Describe the inclusion and exclusion of cancellation of debt income.

OVERVIEW

This chapter starts with the definition of gross income. Tables 2.1 and 2.2 list the common inclusions in and exclusions from gross income. Detailed coverage is provided for inclusions and exclusions that may present unique issues for taxpayers. The coverage includes the special tax treatment for interest and dividends, alimony, prizes and awards, annuities, life insurance proceeds, and gifts and inheritances. Coverage of exclusions from gross income includes scholarships, accident and health insurance benefits, certain meals and lodging, municipal bond interest, and the special treatment of Social Security benefits. The elements of gross income discussed here represent much of what is included in the first line of the individual tax formula.

Learning Objective 2.1

Apply the definition of gross income.

2-1 THE NATURE OF GROSS INCOME

Gross income is the starting point for calculating a taxpayer's tax liability. The tax law states that gross income is:

... all income from whatever source derived, including (but not limited to) the following items:

- Compensation for services, including fees, commissions, fringe benefits, and similar items
- Gross income derived from business
- Gains derived from dealings in property
- Interest
- Rents
- Royalties
- Dividends
- Annuities
- Income from life insurance and endowment contracts
- Pensions
- Income from discharge of indebtedness
- Distributive share of partnership gross income
- Income in respect of a decedent
- Income from an interest in an estate or trust

The definition of gross income as **"all income from whatever source derived"** is perhaps the most well-known definition in the tax law. Under this definition, unless there is an exception in the law, the U.S. government considers all income taxable. Therefore, prizes and awards, cash and noncash payments for goods and services, payments made in trade or *barter* (such as car repairs traded for tax preparation services), and illegal income not generally reported to the IRS are all still taxable income.

Table 2.1 provides an expanded list of items that are included in gross income. When in doubt, the general rule is that everything a taxpayer receives must be included in gross income unless specifically excluded. Any noncash items must be included in gross income at the fair market value of the items received.

The tax law provides that certain items of income are exempt from taxation; these items are referred to as *exclusions*. The exclusions include items such as life insurance proceeds, gifts, and veterans' benefits. A more complete list of exclusions from gross income is provided in Table 2.2.

TABLE 2.1 2022 INCLUSIONS IN GROSS INCOME—PARTIAL LIST

Accrued leave pay
Alimony (excluded after 2018)
Amounts recovered after being deducted in prior years
Annuities
Awards
Back pay
Bargain purchase from employer
Bonuses
Breach of contract damages
Business income
Clergy fees
Commissions
Compensation for services
Contributions received by members of the clergy
Damages for nonphysical personal injury
Death benefits
Debts forgiven
Differential wage payments
Directors' fees
Dividends
Embezzled funds
Employee awards (except certain service awards)
Employee benefits (except certain fringe benefits)
Employee bonuses
Employee stock options and stock appreciation rights
Estate and trust income
Farm income
Fees
Gains from illegal activities
Gains from sale of property
Gambling winnings
Group term life insurance premiums paid by employer for coverage over $50,000
Hobby income
Incentive awards
Income in respect of a decedent
Interest income
Jury duty fees
Living quarters, meals (unless furnished for employer's convenience, etc.)
Medicare waiver payments
Military pay (unless combat pay)
Notary fees
Outplacement services
Partnership income
Pensions
Prizes
Professional fees
Punitive damages
Rents
Retirement pay
Rewards
Royalties
Salaries
Scholarships (room and board)
Severance pay
Sick pay
Strike and lockout benefits
Supplemental unemployment benefits
Tips and gratuities
Unemployment compensation
Virtual currency (such as Bitcoin) paid for services
Wages

TABLE 2.2 2022 EXCLUSIONS FROM GROSS INCOME—PARTIAL LIST

Accident insurance proceeds
Alimony (excluded after 2018)
Annuities (to a limited extent)
Bequests
Casualty insurance proceeds
Child support payments
Damages for physical personal injury or sickness
Disability benefits (generally, but not always)
Gifts
Government cost-of-living allowances
Group term life insurance premiums paid by employer (coverage not over $50,000)
Health insurance proceeds
Inheritances
Insurance payments for living expenses after casualty loss to home
Life insurance proceeds
Meals and lodging (furnished for employer's convenience, etc.)
Military allowances (including G.I. bill benefits)
Minister's dwelling rental value allowance
Municipal bond interest
Olympic medals and cash awards given to athletes
Qualified Medicare waiver payments
Qualified retirement planning services paid by employer
Relocation payments
Scholarships (tuition and books)
Social Security benefits (with limits)
Veterans' benefits
Welfare payments
Workers' compensation

Self-Study Problem 2.1 *See Appendix E for Solutions to Self-Study Problems*

Determine whether each of the items listed below should be included in gross income or excluded from gross income in 2022.

1. Prizes and awards
2. Embezzled funds
3. Child support payments
4. Alimony from a 2021 divorce
5. Pensions
6. Inheritances
7. Welfare payments
8. Bequests
9. Jury duty fees
10. Royalties
11. Life insurance proceeds paid at death
12. Hobby income
13. Legal settlement related to physical injury
14. Partnership income
15. Casualty insurance proceeds
16. G.I. Bill benefits
17. Scholarships for room and board
18. Business income
19. Gifts

Learning Objective 2.2

Describe salaries and wages income reporting and inclusion in gross income.

2-2 SALARIES AND WAGES

Serving as an employee of a business is the most common way to earn income in the United States. More than 80 percent of all individual income tax returns include some amount of wage income, and wages represent approximately 70 percent of the adjusted gross income reported. Payments in almost any form, including salaries and wages, from an employer to an employee are considered income. The primary form of reporting wages to an employee is through Form W-2. An employee should receive a Form W-2 from an employer providing information about the wages paid to that employee during the year (the employer's responsibilities with Form W-2 are examined in Chapter 9). Figure 2.1 presents a Form W-2 for 2022.

Box 1 of Form W-2 is where employers should report taxable wages, salary, bonuses, awards, commissions, and almost every other type of taxable compensation. In most instances, the amount in Box 1 is reported directly on Line 1 of Form 1040, Wages, salaries, tips, etc. If a taxpayer receives more than one Form W-2 or is jointly filing with a spouse having their own Form W-2, the amounts in Box 1 are combined before entering on Line 1 of Form 1040.

FIGURE 2.1 FORM W-2

a Employee's social security number	791-51-4335
OMB No. 1545-0008	Safe, accurate, FAST! Use IRS e-file. Visit the IRS website at www.irs.gov/efile
b Employer identification number (EIN)	12-3456789
c Employer's name, address, and ZIP code	Ivy Technologies, Inc. 436 E. 35 Avenue Gary, IN 46409
d Control number	
e Employee's first name and initial / Last name / Suff.	Eric Hayes 555 E 81st Street Merrillville, IN 46410
f Employee's address and ZIP code	
1 Wages, tips, other compensation	140,804.00
2 Federal income tax withheld	16,167.34
3 Social security wages	147,000.00
4 Social security tax withheld	9,114.00
5 Medicare wages and tips	148,354.00
6 Medicare tax withheld	2,151.13
7 Social security tips	
8 Allocated tips	
9	
10 Dependent care benefits	5,000.00
11 Nonqualified plans	
12a See instructions for box 12	C 104.00
12b	D 7,550.00
12c	DD 12,108.43
12d	
13 Statutory employee / Retirement plan / Third-party sick pay	☐ / ☒ / ☐
14 Other	

15 State	Employer's state ID number	16 State wages, tips, etc.	17 State income tax	18 Local wages, tips, etc.	19 Local income tax	20 Locality name
IN	00122231001	140,804.00	5,051.23	140,804.00	1,002.00	LAKE

Form **W-2** Wage and Tax Statement 2022 Department of the Treasury—Internal Revenue Service

Copy B—To Be Filed With Employee's FEDERAL Tax Return.
This information is being furnished to the Internal Revenue Service.

EXAMPLE Bonnie and Clyde are married and file jointly. In 2022, Bonnie received two Forms W-2 from two separate employers reporting $34,000 of wages on one and $16,500 on the other. In addition, Clyde also received a Form W-2 reporting wages of $23,000 in Box 1. Bonnie and Clyde should report $73,500 ($34,000 + $16,500 + $23,000) on Line 1 of Form 1040 (or Form 1040-SR, if Bonnie or Clyde are age 65 or older). ♦

Box 2 of Form W-2 reports the amount of federal income tax withheld from the taxpayer's wages by the employer for the year. This amount is reported on Line 25a of Forms 1040 and 1040-SR.

Boxes 3 through 6 report information related to the amount of wages subject to Social Security and Medicare (employment) taxes and the related taxes withheld. The amounts generally do not impact the income tax reporting by a taxpayer, although as discussed in Chapter 9, when a taxpayer has multiple employers and the amount of Social Security tax withheld exceeds the annual limits of Social Security taxable wages, the excess is treated as an additional tax payment. Note that the amounts in Box 1 and Boxes 3 and 5 often agree but they are not always the same for all taxpayers. For example, if an employee contributes part of their salary to a qualified retirement plan such as a 401(k) plan, the contribution is not generally subject to income tax but is subject to employment taxes. The amount of taxable wages in Box 1 would be lower than the amounts reported in Boxes 3 and 5 by the retirement plan contribution amount. In addition, wages are subject to Social Security tax up to a limit ($147,000 in 2022) and therefore, Box 3 will not exceed the annual limit.

Box 8 reports allocated tips for amounts not included in Box 1 taxable wages. Box 10 is where flexible spending contributions to a dependent care program are reported (see LO 2.5 for more information). Box 12 is for reporting a variety of different forms of compensation such as reimbursed parking, health care premiums paid by the employer, and other fringe benefits. The type of compensation is identified by the code provided adjacent to the amount in Box 12, as described in the instructions to the Form W-2. Commonly used codes are:

Code	*Explanation*
C	Taxable group life insurance
D	Elective deferral into 401(k) plans
E	Elective deferral into 403(b) plans
G	Elective deferral into 457(b) plans
V	Income from nonstatutory stock options
W	Contributions to a health savings account
DD	Cost of employer-sponsored health care

The retirement plan box in Box 13 will be checked if the taxpayer is eligible to participate in a retirement plan [and thus may limit the amount of deductible IRA (individual retirement account) contributions]. Box 14 is designated to report other forms of compensation as needed.

State and local tax information is reported at the bottom of Form W-2 in Boxes 15 through 20. This includes the taxable wages for state tax purposes and the amount of state income tax withheld which is generally part of the state and local tax itemized deduction (see Chapter 5).

2-2a Employee versus Independent Contractor

Business owners are required to correctly determine whether the individuals providing services to their businesses are employees or independent contractors. Many taxpayers view this as a decision, when in fact, the classification is a function of law and not a choice on the part of either the employer or employee. Potential employees most often accept the choice made by the employer since attempting to negotiate this classification may prevent acquisition of the work. This classification makes a great deal of difference. Generally, an employer must withhold income taxes, withhold and pay Social Security and Medicare taxes, and pay unemployment tax on wages paid to an employee (see Chapter 9). A business does not generally have to withhold or pay any taxes on payments to independent contractors and will generally only have to provide an informational return such as the Form 1099-NEC (see Chapter 9). The differences extend beyond just payroll tax liability and processing. For example, employees are far more restricted in deducting employee-related business expenses. Independent contractors are generally not provided benefits and are required to pay self-employment taxes. Because the outcomes differ greatly and the guidance is less well understood, the subject of employee versus independent contractor also tends to be an area of tax controversy.

A potential source of confusion is that the tax code itself does not define employee in any meaningful way. Instead, regulations and court cases have over time congealed into a more-or-less acceptable common law definition that relies heavily on the degree of control and independence between the individual and the business. Characteristics that provide evidence of the degree of control and independence fall into three categories:

1. *Behavioral:* Does the business control or have the right to control what and how the worker does his or her job?
2. *Financial:* Are the business aspects of the worker's job controlled by the payer (how the worker is paid, whether expenses are reimbursed, who provides tools/supplies, etc.)?
3. *Relationship:* Are there written contracts or employee benefits (i.e. pension plan, insurance, vacation pay, etc.)? Will the relationship continue and is the work performed a key aspect of the business?

The IRS released a list of twenty factors to consider in classifying a worker as an employee or an independent contractor. The degree of importance for each factor can vary and no single factor is controlling.

Behavioral Factors

1. Instruction: Employees are more likely to be required to comply with when, where, and how the work is to be done.
2. Training: Employees are trained to perform the work.
3. Personally Rendered: Employees must generally perform the work themselves and cannot subcontract the work.
4. Hiring, Supervising and Paying Assistants: Independent contractors have the ability to hire, supervise, and pay assistants and are primarily responsible for the end result.
5. Continuing Relationship: Continuing relationships (even at infrequent intervals) are more common with employees.
6. Work Hours: Independent contractors are more likely to set their own work hours.
7. Time required: Employees work full-time for an employer.
8. Workplace: Employees are generally required to perform work on premises.
9. Sequence of Work: Employees follow the business entity sequence of work.
10. Reports: Employees will be required to submit regular reports whereas an independent contractor's main goal is to deliver results.

Financial Control Factors

11. Payment timing: Employees are paid by time period (hour, week, month). Contractors are paid based on project completion.
12. Travel/Business Expenses: Employees' travel and business expenses are controlled and covered by the employer.
13. Tool and Materials: Furnishing of tools, equipment, or an office indicates employee.
14. Investment: Contractors make a significant investment in the facilities where the work is performed.
15. Profit or loss: Employees generally bear no liability for loss.

Relationship Factors

16. Integration: Employees are more likely to be integrated into business operations.
17. Multiple Engagements: Contractors work for multiple unrelated businesses.
18. Availability of Services: Contractors make their services available to the general public.
19. Right to Discharge: Employees are subject to firing by the business.
20. Right to Quit: Employees can quit without breaching any agreements.

TAX BREAK

A tax law known as a Section 530 Safe Harbor can provide some protection to a taxpayer that may have classified workers as independent contractors in the past with some uncertainty. Section 530 was passed outside of the Internal Revenue Code and provides relief for possibly mistaken classifications under certain circumstances. To meet the safe harbor, one of the conditions is that the taxpayer must have a reasonable basis for not treating the worker as an employee. A reasonable basis exists if the treatment was based on (1) judicial precedent, published rulings, technical advice to the employer, or a letter ruling to the employer; (2) past examination of the employer by the IRS in which there was no assessment attributable to the treatment for employment tax purposes of individuals holding positions substantially similar to the position held by this individual; or (3) long-standing recognized practice of a significant segment of the industry in which the individual was engaged. The IRS also operates the Voluntary Classification Settlement Program (VCSP) for similar types of worker classification issues.

EXAMPLE Tabitha works at Pizza Cabana as a cashier. Her manager sets her schedule each week and she was trained by the company's Pizza Cabana University on her job duties and responsibilities. She is naturally expected to perform her role at the restaurant. Tabitha works at Pizza Cabana full time, is paid hourly, and participates in the company's retirement plan. This job is the primary source of Tabitha's income. She can quit at any time but is likely to provide a customary two-week notice. Tabitha appears to be under the behavioral, financial, and relationship control of Pizza Cabana and is classified as an employee. ♦

EXAMPLE Tracy drives her own vehicle for a number of different shared delivery services. She tends to drive for Flying Food on the weekends because they are connected to restaurants that have more customers during the weekends. She also delivers food for Snax Car and Mobile Munchies. She checks to see which service seems to have more demand at a particular date or time and logs on to work with that company. Tracy is paid per delivery, by miles driven, and through tips from customers. She only delivers when she feels like it or really needs the money. All the operating expenses, maintenance, and repairs on her vehicle are her costs to bear. Tracy has more of the characteristics associated with an independent contractor. ♦

The classification of a worker from a federal tax perspective has become more complex with the advent of certain states (for example, California) implementing labor laws designed to classify more workers as employees. Technically, these state-level laws would not control federal tax classification, but from a pragmatic perspective, most businesses would classify workers the same for state and federal purposes.

Self-Study Problem 2.2

See Appendix E for Solutions to Self-Study Problems

a Employee's social security number: 232-11-4444	OMB No. 1545-0008	Safe, accurate, FAST! Use IRS e-file. Visit the IRS website at www.irs.gov/efile
b Employer identification number (EIN): 12-9876543	1 Wages, tips, other compensation: 56,500.00	2 Federal income tax withheld: 3,509.12
c Employer's name, address, and ZIP code: QBI Company, 4512 Lake Drive, Grand Rapids, MI 49503	3 Social security wages: 61,500.00	4 Social security tax withheld: 3,813.00
	5 Medicare wages and tips: 61,500.00	6 Medicare tax withheld: 891.75
	7 Social security tips	8 Allocated tips
d Control number	9	10 Dependent care benefits
e Employee's first name and initial, Last name, Suff.: Summer Sandborne, 134 Bostwick Ave NE, Grand Rapids, MI 49503	11 Nonqualified plans	12a See instructions for box 12: D 5,000.00
	13 Statutory employee ☐ Retirement plan ☒ Third-party sick pay ☐	12b: DD 8,700.00
	14 Other	12c
f Employee's address and ZIP code		12d

15 State	Employer's state ID number	16 State wages, tips, etc.	17 State income tax	18 Local wages, tips, etc.	19 Local income tax	20 Locality name
MI		56,500.00	1,165.00			

Form **W-2** Wage and Tax Statement 2022 — Department of the Treasury—Internal Revenue Service

Copy B—To Be Filed With Employee's FEDERAL Tax Return.
This information is being furnished to the Internal Revenue Service.

Based on Summer's Form W-2, determine the following amounts:

a. Taxable wages to report on Line 1 of Form 1040
b. Federal tax payments withheld to report on Line 25a of Form 1040
c. The amount that Summer contributed to her company's 401k plan
d. The amount to report as state income taxes paid if Summer itemizes her deductions

ProConnect™ Tax TIP

Entering wages from a Form W-2 is one of the most common data entry points for a tax preparer. Predictably, wages are entered under the Income section, more specifically, under Wages, Salaries, Tips (W-2). When selecting the Wages subheading, the entire entry screen for the W-2 is presented in the main window. The subheadings on the left-hand margin slide the entry form up and down for easier entry. Any additional Forms W-2 can be added using the [+] tab at the top of the main window. Although the fictional textbook employers do not have import access, using ProConnect Tax, many Forms W-2 can be imported directly from an employer's payroll system. Enter the employer's identification number and click the circular arrow to import wages data.

2-3 ACCIDENT AND HEALTH INSURANCE

2.3 Learning Objective

Explain the general tax treatment of health insurance.

Many taxpayers are covered by accident and health insurance plans. These plans pay for the cost of medical care of the taxpayer and any dependents who are insured under the plan. The taxpayer may pay the total premiums of the plan, or their employer may pay part or all of the premiums. Taxpayers are allowed liberal exclusions for payments received from these accident and health plans. Generally, as long as the plan is nondiscriminatory, the taxpayer may exclude the total amount received for payment of medical care. This exclusion applies to any amount paid for the medical care of the taxpayer, their spouse, or dependents and can also apply to a retired employee, the surviving spouse of a deceased employee, or a former employee if the coverage is based on the employment relationship (for example, COBRA). The payment may be made to the doctor, the hospital, or the taxpayer as reimbursement for the payment of the expenses. In addition, any premiums paid by a taxpayer's employer are excluded from the taxpayer's income, and the premium payments may be deducted by the employer.

Most accident and health care policies also pay fixed amounts to the insured for loss of the use of a member or function of the body. These amounts may also be excluded from income. For example, a taxpayer who receives $25,000 because they are blinded in one eye may exclude the $25,000 from income.

EXAMPLE Bob is a married taxpayer. His employer pays a $750 per month premium on a policy covering Bob and his family. Jean, Bob's wife, is sick during the year and her medical bills amount to $6,500; the insurance company paid $6,000 for the bills. Bob and Jean may exclude from income the $750 per month premium paid by Bob's employer and the $6,000 paid by the insurance company. The $500 not paid by the insurance company is deductible on Bob and Jean's return, subject to the medical expense deduction limitations (see Chapter 5). ♦

Self-Study Problem 2.3 *See Appendix E for Solutions to Self-Study Problems*

Marjorie, a single taxpayer, is an employee of Big State Corporation. Big State Corporation pays premiums of $3,000 on her health insurance for the current year. Also, during the current year, Marjorie has an operation for which the insurance company pays $5,000 to her hospital and doctor. Of the above amounts, how much must Marjorie include in her gross income?

Learning Objective 2.4

Determine when meals and lodging may be excluded from taxable income.

2-4 MEALS AND LODGING

The value of meals provided to an employee may be excluded from the employee's gross income in two situations: (1) meals provided on the business premises and (2) de minimis meals. Meals provided on the business premises must be furnished to the employee on the business premises and must also be for the convenience of the employer. The term "for the convenience of the employer" is based on the facts and circumstances; however, the meals must be provided for a substantial noncompensatory business reason.

EXAMPLE Frank is a security guard at a casino. The casino furnishes his lunch at no charge in one of the casino restaurants to limit his lunch break to thirty minutes because the job requires that security watch the casino floor continuously to identify suspicious activity. The casino may exclude the value of the meals provided to Frank. ♦

If more than half of the employees are furnished meals for the convenience of the employer, the employer may treat all meals as furnished for the convenience of the employer. Meals furnished so employees can be available for emergency calls are considered for the employers' convenience.

EXAMPLE A hospital maintains a cafeteria and employees receive meals at no charge. Over half of the employees at the hospital at any time are on call to respond to emergencies, which the hospital can demonstrate have occurred. Although the hospital does not require employees to eat in the cafeteria, most do. Because the hospital provides meals to over half of the employees for the convenience of the hospital, the value of meals provided to all employees may be excluded. ♦

Meals furnished to food service employees during, immediately before, or immediately after the employee's working hours are considered for the convenience of the employer and may be excluded.

Meals are considered de minimis if provided occasionally and provide so little value that accounting for such value would be unreasonable or administratively impractical. Examples of de minimis meals might include:

- Coffee, doughnuts, and soft drinks
- Occasional overtime meals
- Occasional parties or picnics for employees

EXAMPLE Kerry provides bagels and doughnuts to all employees in the breakroom of her business every third Friday of the month. Kelly also hosts an employee holiday party in December each year and has food catered at a nearby park for employees and their families. The value of these meals would be considered de minimis and excludable from the employee's wages. ♦

The value of subsidized meals provided to employees at an on-premise employer-operated eating facility (i.e., a company cafeteria) are considered de minimis meals if the annual revenue of the facility exceeds the direct operating costs of the facility.

EXAMPLE Harper Company operates a company cafeteria for its employees. The employees are charged an amount for the meals that is equal to the cost of the meals to Harper (that is, the meals are subsidized). Because the facility is on the business premises and operates at break-even, the value of the meals may be excluded from the employees' income. ♦

As discussed in Chapter 3, the deductions for de minimis meals can be limited.

The value of lodging provided to an employee is excludable if it meets three requirements:

1. The lodging is furnished on the business premises,
2. The lodging is for the convenience of the employer, and
3. The lodging must be accepted as a condition of the employment

Lodging is a condition of employment if the employee must live on the business premises to be able to properly perform their duties.

EXAMPLE Harry Stamper works on an oil rig in the Gulf of Mexico 120 miles from the Louisiana coast. Due to the inaccessibility of the work site, lodging is provided by his employer on the rig. Harry is required to agree to lodging as a condition of his employment. Harry's employer may exclude the value of his lodging. ♦

EXAMPLE Pat Schneider works as the superintendent of a large apartment building in Indianapolis. In order to make emergency repairs and provide on-call service to the tenants of the building, Schneider is required to live in the building. Her employer provides an apartment to Schneider at no cost. The value of Schneider's lodging may be excluded. ♦

The exclusion for lodging also includes the value of utilities such as electricity, water, heat, gas, and similar items that make the lodging habitable. The value of meals or lodging provided by the employer in other situations, and cash allowances for meals or lodging, must be included in the employee's gross income.

EXAMPLE Greta receives an all-expenses paid trip to Cancun, Mexico, for achieving her sales quotas for the year. The cost of the airfare, lodging, and meals would be included in Greta's gross income. ♦

Self-Study Problem 2.4

See Appendix E for Solutions to Self-Study Problems

In each of the following independent cases, indicate whether the value of the meals or lodging should be included in or excluded from the taxpayer's income.

1. A waiter is required to eat lunch, furnished by his employer, on the premises during a busy lunch hour.
2. A police officer receives a cash allowance to pay for meals while on duty.
3. A worker receives lodging at a remote construction site in Alaska.
4. A taxpayer manages a motel and, although the owner does not require it, she lives at the motel rent free.
5. A bank teller is furnished meals on the premises to limit the time she is away during busy hours.

Learning Objective 2.5

Identify the common employee fringe benefit income exclusions.

2-5 EMPLOYEE FRINGE BENEFITS

The tax law provides that all fringe benefits must be included in the employee's gross income, unless specifically excluded by law. The primary types of fringe benefits that may be excluded from gross income are described below.

2-5a Flexible Spending Accounts (FSAs)

One way in which an employer may provide qualified nontaxable benefits to employees is the use of a cafeteria plan. A cafeteria plan is a written plan that permits employees to choose between two of more benefits consisting of cash or some qualified nontaxable benefit.

EXAMPLE Jersey Manufacturing Inc. operates a cafeteria plan that allows employees to choose between three options: (1) cash compensation, (2) health insurance for the employee and family, and (3) contributions to a 401(k) plan. As qualified benefits, payments for health insurance and 401(k) contributions will be excluded from the employees' gross income; whereas the cash payments are included. ♦

A popular form of cafeteria plan is to offer a flexible spending arrangement or flexible spending account (FSA) as part of the plan. FSAs permit employees to contribute pre-tax money to a special account from their wages to pay for health care, dependent care, or adoption expenses. If all the requirements of the plan are met, and the employee provides receipts for the expenses incurred, the full amount of expenses reimbursed out of the employee's account will be treated as a tax-free reduction in salary. These accounts may provide significant tax savings for employees, with only a small administrative cost to employers. The two most popular types of FSAs are those for health care costs and those for dependent care costs.

EXAMPLE In 2022, Dina has wage income of $43,000 and elects to defer $2,000 into a health care flexible spending account. She uses all $2,000 of the deferred funds for qualifying medical expenses in 2022. Dina's taxable wage income will be $41,000. The $2,000 is excluded from her income if she uses the funds for qualifying medical expenses. ♦

Health Care Flexible Spending Accounts

Employers may offer health care flexible spending accounts in which employees can set aside up to $2,850 (2022) from their salary to cover medical expenses that they anticipate incurring during the year. These expenses may include eyeglasses, laser-eye surgery, necessary dental work, and health insurance copayments. Amounts used from a health care FSA may not also be deducted as an itemized deduction for medical expenses (see Chapter 5). Health care FSAs should not be confused with Archer medical spending accounts (MSAs) or health savings accounts (HSAs) which are covered in Chapter 5.

Dependent Care Flexible Spending Accounts

Employers may offer dependent care flexible spending accounts (FSAs) in which employees may set aside up to $5,000 of their salary each year to cover the costs of caring for a dependent child or aging parent. Such costs may include day care, day camp, in-home care and preschool. A dependent care FSA is separate from dependent care assistance programs discussed later in this section.

Employees should be aware, however, of the "use-it-or-lose-it" rule for FSAs (e.g., any balance remaining in the employee's account at December 31 is lost). For health care flexible spending accounts, employers generally have the option to allow $570 (in 2022) of the unused medical spending account to carry over to 2023 or to offer a 2 ½-month grace period after year-end to incur additional medical expenses before the employee loses the balance in the account. The plan may not offer both types of relief from use-it-or-lose-it. A number of temporary COVID-related provisions were implemented for 2021. At the discretion of the plan:

- Any remaining medical FSA balances at the end of 2021 may be rolled forward to the next year.
- The grace period is extended to twelve months for year-end 2021.

EXAMPLE Allie contributed $2,700 in 2021 to her health FSA. Her employer typically allows a 2 ½-month grace period to pay expenses (through March 15, 2022). Due to COVID-19, Allie was unable to have her orthodontic work done in early 2022 and had to postpone the services until July 2022. Allie's employer is permitting employees a grace period through December 31, 2022; thus, Allie will have her costs paid in July covered by the FSA. ♦

2-5b **Transportation (Commuting) Benefits**

The value of transportation or commuting benefits can be excluded from an employee's gross income under two circumstances: (1) qualified transportation benefits and (2) de minimis transportation benefits.

Qualified transportation benefits often apply to parking but can also apply to use of a commuter highway vehicle (such as an employer-operated van pool) or a mass-transit pass (such as bus, rail, or ferry). Employees can exclude from gross income payments from employers of up to $280 per month in 2022 (the maximum exclusion is adjusted for inflation) to cover the cost of public transportation to, or parking for, work. However, employers *may not* deduct these payments to the extent they are excluded from the employee's income; thus, effectively limited the benefit from employer-paid transportation and parking.

EXAMPLE Portnoy Company provides parking for the executive management team at their headquarters building located in downtown. In 2022, the parking costs $300 per month for each parking space. Portnoy will be able to exclude $280 of the value of the provided parking from the employees' gross income. Portnoy will be unable to deduct the transportation costs when computing its own taxable income. ♦

A de minimis transportation benefit is any local transportation benefit provided to an employee that has little value (taking into account frequency) and accounting for it would be unreasonable or administratively impracticable. An occasional cab or ride-share fare provided to an employee for working overtime would likely qualify. Providing mass transit passes to employees at a discount is also a de minimis transportation benefit if the discount does not exceed $21 in any month.

Transportation costs can also be provided to employees under a compensation reduction agreement that operates in a fashion similar to FSAs. This type of program allows the employee to use pre-tax compensation to pay for a form of a qualified transportation benefit up to the monthly exclusion amount.

EXAMPLE Portnoy Company also provides a compensation reduction arrangement whereby non-executives may have anywhere from $80 to $280 (depending on the actual cost of the public transit pass) deducted from their pay each month to pay for a monthly transit pass to accommodate the employee's daily commute. Helen has $200 per month deducted from her pay to cover the cost of her light rail pass into downtown. Her wages subject to income tax will be reduced by $2,400 ($200 × 12) and thus she will use pre-tax dollars to pay for her commute. ♦

The bicycle commuter fringe is suspended until 2025.

2-5c Dependent Care Assistance Programs

Under a dependent care assistance program (DCAP), an employer may pay directly or indirectly up to $5,000 for dependent care services that allow the employee to work. The amount excluded cannot be more than the employee's earned income. The value of the dependent care assistance is reported in Box 10 of the Form W-2 of the employee. One method of offering a DCAP is through an FSA. The total amount of dependent care benefits may not exceed $5,000.

EXAMPLE Fizzy Bottling Company operates a dependent care assistance program for employees in which Fizzy pays for sudden or unexpected child care for employees at a nearby child care center. Charlie uses the child care center a number of times in 2022 when his regular day care was unavailable. The value of child care paid by Fizzy Bottling was $700. Charlie also participates in the dependent care FSA and had $4,500 withheld from his pay. Charlie's Form W-2 will reflect $5,200 ($4,500 + $700) of dependent care assistance and $200 will be included in his taxable wages. ♦

Dependent care expenses paid through an FSA may not also be used toward the child and dependent care credit (Chapter 7).

2-5d Group Term Life Insurance

Employers may pay for up to $50,000 of group term life insurance for employees as a tax-free fringe benefit. Providing group term life insurance to employees must not favor officers, shareholders, or highly-compensated personnel. Amounts paid for employee term life insurance coverage above $50,000 are subject to an income inclusion for the cost of the insurance above $50,000 based on costs provided by the IRS as shown in Table 2.3 below.

TABLE 2.3 COST PER $1,000 OF PROTECTION FOR 1 MONTH

Age	Cost
Under 25	$ 0.05
25 through 29	0.06
30 through 34	0.08
35 through 39	0.09
40 through 44	0.10
45 through 49	0.15
50 through 54	0.23
55 through 59	0.43
60 through 64	0.66
65 through 69	1.27
70 and older	2.06

Source: Adapted from IRS Publication 15-B.

EXAMPLE Terri's employer provides her with a $100,000 group term life insurance coverage. Terri is 45 and contributes $0 annually for the policy. Terri's employer will include $90 [($50,000 ÷ $1,000) × $0.15 × 12 months] of taxable income with her taxable wages and enter $90 and Code C in Box 12 of her Form W-2. ♦

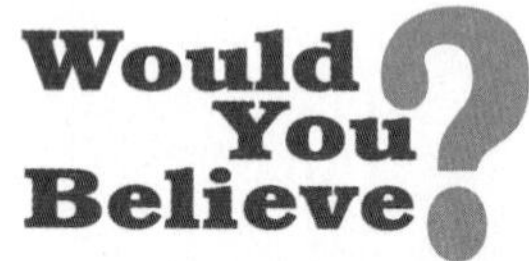

Internal Revenue Code §79 was first passed in 1964 and provided the exclusion of employer paid group term life insurance premiums up to $50,000. The $50,000 limit has not been adjusted since originally passed into law. In today's dollars, you would need over $475,000 to equal $50,000 in 1964. The National Funeral Directors Association estimated the median cost of a funeral in 1965 as $790 and over $7,800 in 2021.

2-5e Education Assistance Plans and Tuition Reduction

Employers may provide up to $5,250 of excludable annual tuition assistance under an educational assistance plan. The exclusion requires an employer to have a written plan and the educational assistance can be paid to an employee or former employee. Assistance over $5,250 is included in the taxpayer's wages unless otherwise excludable as a working condition benefit that would have been deductible as a business expense (see Chapter 3). Through 2025, payments from an education assistance plan can also be excluded if paid to an employee or lender if the payments are applied toward the employee's student loans.

EXAMPLE Ahmaud's employer offers an education plan that Ahmaud had been taking advantage of every year. Unfortunately, the cost of Ahmaud's college education exceeded $5,250 each year, and he was required to take out student loans. Ahmaud graduated in 2021. Before 2026, Ahmaud's employer may pay his student debt up to $5,250, and Ahmaud is not required to include the payment in his income. ♦

Employees of educational institutions may exclude from their income the value of a tuition reduction, if the plan is for an undergraduate education and available to all employees. The exclusion applies to the employees, their spouses, and their dependents. The value of a graduate education tuition reduction plan may only be excluded by graduate students of the institution who are teaching or doing research at that institution.

EXAMPLE Dale is a faculty affairs administrator for Vermont State University (VSU). One of the VSU benefits available to all VSU employees is a 50-percent discount on the tuition for any employee, spouse, or dependent. Dale's daughter, Pam, is a freshman at VSU and Dale saves $4,500 on her 2022 tuition and fees due to the employee discount. The discount is excluded from Dale's gross income. ♦

2-5f No-Additional-Cost Services and Qualified Employee Discounts

No-additional-cost services are services that are provided to employees and their families at little or no additional cost to the employer, and which would otherwise have remained unused. An airline employee who is allowed to fly at no cost on a standby basis is an example. The value of the airfare may be excluded from the employee's gross income.

Employees are only allowed to receive tax-free services in the major line of business in which they are employed. For example, if an airline company also owns a rental car agency, the employees working in the airline division would not be entitled to the tax-free use of rental cars. Different companies may enter into reciprocal agreements and provide no-additional-cost services to the other company's employees.

EXAMPLE BlueStar Airlines (BSA) permits employees and their spouses to fly for free on flights when seats are available. In addition, BSA has a written reciprocity agreement with TransAmerican Airlines (TAA) that allows flight crews to fly TAA and vice versa. In 2022, Yonah, a flight attendant for BSA, flies to Hawaii on BSA for free using available seats on the flight. On the return flight, BSA has no seats available so Yonah flies for free, on TAA's flight with open seats. The value of the flights is excludable from Yonah's income. ♦

A retired airline pilot attempted to exclude the value of airline tickets provided to a non-dependent relative as a no-additional-cost-service but was rebuffed by the Tax Court in 2022 (see *Mihalik*, TC Memo. 2022-36). Since the tax law permits the exclusion of such tickets provided to an "employee," the court focused on the definition of employee as provided in the regulations which defines an "employee" to include a retiree of the employer and the spouse and dependent children of a retiree. A "dependent child" is defined as any son, stepson, daughter, or stepdaughter who is a dependent of the employee, or both of whose parents are deceased and who has not attained age 25. Under the pilot's previous employer's retiree benefits, other relatives can "fly the friendly skies," but better be prepared to pay the accompanying tax, regardless of altitude.

The value of employee discounts may be excluded from gross income if the discounts are available on a nondiscriminatory basis. That is, the discounts must be available to substantially all full-time employees. The item being discounted must be from the line of business in which the employee is engaged. The discount exclusion also does not apply to discounts on real estate or personal property held for investment. For services provided at a discount, the exclusion is limited to 20 percent of the typical customer price. For merchandise, the exclusion is limited to the employer's gross markup on the goods.

EXAMPLE R.J. works for an auto parts store chain. R.J. purchases a new water pump for her car at the employee discounted price of $26. Normally, the part would be sold for $41. R.J.'s employer's cost for the part is $26. Because R.J.'s cost is not less than the cost of the part to her employer, the discount is within the exclusion and is not taxable to R.J. ♦

EXAMPLE Brendan is an administrative assistant at a law firm. In 2022, Brendan hires one of the lawyers at his firm to assist him with his personal divorce proceedings. The firms provides a 15-percent employee discount on legal services provided to employees. Brendan will exclude the value of the discount from his gross income. ♦

2-5g **Working Condition Fringe Benefits**

An employee may exclude the value of property or services provided by an employer to the extent that the cost of the property or services would be a deductible expense of the employee and the property or services are necessary for the employee to perform their job. Examples of this type of exclusion include the use of a company car for business (not personal) purposes and a subscription to a tax journal paid for by a CPA firm. The working condition fringe benefit rules also allow several expenses which would not be deductible if paid by the employee. These include the value of certain employer-provided education and certain use of demonstrator autos by automobile salespeople.

EXAMPLE Slick Tyre is a full-time salesperson for Lemon Autos, a local car dealer. Lemon provides Slick with a new model vehicle each year for customer test drives during Slick's business hours and personal use otherwise. Slick's use of the demonstrator car is considered a working condition fringe and the value of his personal use may be excluded from his gross income. ♦

2-5h **De Minimis Fringe Benefits**

The value of small fringe benefits may be excluded from an employee's gross income if the value of the item or service (taking into account the frequency) is small and accounting for it would be unreasonable or administratively impractical. Examples of this type of exclusion include occasional personal use of an office copy machine, personal letters typed by a company administrative assistant, small non-cash holiday gifts provided to employees (e.g., a holiday turkey), occasional tickets (not season tickets) for theatre or sporting events, and the de minimis meals described earlier in this section.

Cell phones provided to employees primarily for business purposes are considered tax-free de minimis fringe benefits. Examples of cell phones which qualify include those provided to allow employees to communicate with clients, or to allow employers to contact employees in the field or at home.

Cash and cash equivalent fringe benefits (gift certificates, gift cards, the use of a business credit card for personal expenses) are almost never de minimis regardless of how small the amount.

EXAMPLE Prestige Global provides each employee with a modest fruit basket on their birthday. One year, the normal supplier of fruit baskets was short of inventory and so Prestige gave employees a gift card to purchase a basket later. The employees that received the fruit baskets may exclude the value as a de minimis fringe; however, the employees that received the gift card will include the value of the card in their gross income. ♦

2-5i Athletic Facilities

Employees may exclude from gross income the value of the use of an athletic facility. The facility must be used primarily by employees, their spouses, and dependent children. The facility does not need to be on the business premises, but must be located on premises that the employer owns or leases and must be operated by the employer.

2-5j Retirement Planning Fringe Benefit

Qualified retirement planning services constitute a fringe benefit that is excluded from income. This change was made to encourage employers to provide retirement planning services for their employees to assist them in preparing for retirement. Qualified retirement planning services are any retirement planning services provided to an employee and his or her spouse by an employer maintaining a "qualified employer plan." The exclusion also applies to advice and information on retirement income planning for an individual and his or her spouse, including how the employer's plan fits into the individual's overall retirement income plan. The exclusion, however, does not apply to services that may be related to tax preparation, accounting, legal, or brokerage services.

EXAMPLE As part of its qualified plan, Linda's employer provides retirement planning services. Linda has a meeting with a financial planner to review her retirement plan. The cost of the meeting ($600) is paid for by her employer's qualified plan. The $600 is not income to Linda and is deductible to the employer. ♦

A summary of various fringe benefits is provided in Table 2.4.

2-5k Fringe Benefits and Eligibility

To be excluded from gross income, many fringe benefits must not discriminate in favor of highly-compensated employees. Fringe benefits that do not permit discrimination include accident and health insurance, dependent care assistance, education assistance programs, employee discounts, group term life insurance, de minimis meals offered at an employer-operated eating facility, no-additional-cost services, and retirement planning services.

TABLE 2.4 SUMMARY OF FRINGE BENEFITS

Type of Fringe	Summary of Treatment	Learning Objective
Accident and Health Benefits	Exempt except for long-term care provided through a flexible spending arrangement	2.3, 2.5
Achievement Awards	Exempt up to $1,600 for qualified plan awards ($400 for nonqualified)	2.6
Adoption Assistance	Exempt up to $14,890	7.7
Athletic Facilities	Exempt if substantially all use is by employees and families and operated on employer's premises	2.5
De Minimis Benefits	Exempt if property or service provided to employee has so little value that accounting for it would be unreasonable or administratively impracticable (never cash and cash equivalents)	2.5
Dependent Care Assistance	Exempt up to $5,000	2.5
Educational Assistance	Exempt up to $5,250	2.5
Employee Discounts	Exempt with certain limits	2.5
Employee Stock Options	Beyond scope of textbook	–
Employer-provided Cell Phones	Exempt if primarily for business purposes	2.5
Group term Life Insurance	Exempt up to $50,000	2.5
Health Savings Accounts (HSA)	Exempt up to certain limits	5.1
Lodging on Business Premises	Exempt if for convenience as a condition of employment	2.4
Meals	Exempt if furnished on premises for convenience or de minimis	2.4
Moving Expenses	Exempt if otherwise deductible and related to military service	5.5
No-additional-cost Services	Exempt	2.5
Retirement Planning Services	Exempt	2.5
Transportation (Commuting) Benefits	Exempt up to $280 per month for parking and transit passes and exempt if de minimis	2.5
Tuition Reduction	Exempt if undergraduate or if graduate and employee performs teaching or research	2.5
Working Condition Benefits	Exempt	2.5

Source: Adapted from IRS Publication 15-B.

Self-Study Problem 2.5 *See Appendix E for Solutions to Self-Study Problems*

Indicate in each of the following cases whether the value of the employee fringe benefit is included in or excluded from the employee's gross income.

1. An employee of a railroad receives a free train-trip pass.
2. An employee of a department store receives a 25 percent discount on a shirt. The department store's markup is 15 percent.
3. An employee attends a New Year's party paid for by her employer.
4. An employee of a stock brokerage firm receives a subscription to a financial newsletter paid for by his employer.
5. An employee's spouse regularly uses a company car to go shopping.
6. An employer sets aside $4,500 for an employee's dependent care costs.
7. An employee uses the company's employee fitness room.

Learning Objective 2.6

Determine when prizes and awards are included in income.

2-6 PRIZES AND AWARDS

Prizes and awards are taxable income to the recipient. Winnings from television or radio shows, door prizes, lotteries, and other contest winnings are income to taxpayers. In addition, most other awards are generally taxable, even if they are awards given for accomplishments and with no action on the part of the taxpayer. If the prize or award is received in tangible personal property instead of cash, the fair market value of the property is included in the taxpayer's income. For example, the gift bags given to the attendees at the Academy Awards include items such as expensive jewelry and vacations worth more than $200,000. The value of these gift bags is included in taxable income. Taxpayers may refuse a prize and exclude its value from income.

EXAMPLE Tanya has a streak of luck in 2022. She wins a radio quiz and is awarded tickets to a concert worth $250. She is also a contestant on the Press Your Fortune game show and wins cash and prizes worth $13,500. Tanya is required to include the $13,750 of prizes in her gross income. ♦

The popularity of fantasy sports has exploded in large part due to an exemption from the Unlawful Internet Gambling Enforcement Act of 2006 (UIGEA). Although technically not treated as online gambling under federal law, the IRS has issued clear guidance classifying daily fantasy sports games as wagering. Income generated from these activities would almost certainly be classified as gross income and by treating these activities as gambling, taxpayers are permitted to deduct their entry fees and other related costs as "losses" which are deductible as an itemized deduction that is not subject to the 2 percent of AGI floor.

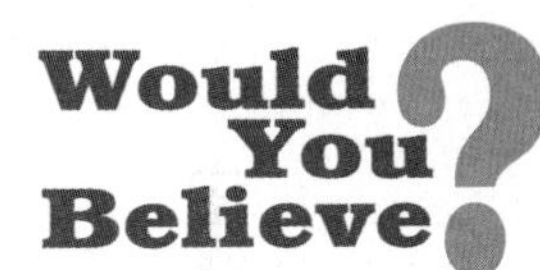

An exception is provided for certain employee achievement awards in the form of tangible personal property, such as a gold watch for 25 years of service. If the award is made in recognition of length of service or safety achievement, the value of the property may be excluded from income. Generally, the maximum amount excludable is $400. However, if the award is a "qualified plan award," the maximum exclusion is increased to $1,600. The definition of tangible personal property with respect to employee achievement awards excludes cash, cash equivalents, gift cards, gift coupons, gift certificates, vacations, meals, lodging, tickets to theater or sporting events, stocks, bonds, other securities, and other similar items.

EXAMPLE Van enters a drawing and wins a new automobile. The automobile has a sticker price of $20,200. The fair market value of the prize should be included in Van's gross income, but the fair market value is probably not the sticker price; instead, it is the price at which a similar car normally would be sold. ♦

There are two other awards or prizes that can be excluded from gross income under certain conditions. The first is an award received for accomplishment in religious, charitable, scientific, artistic, educational, literary, or civic fields (such as a Nobel or Pulitzer prize) which can be excluded only if:

- The taxpayer took no action to enter the contest,
- No substantial future services are required to be performed as a condition of the award, and
- The prize or award is transferred directly to a charitable organization or governmental unit.

The second excluded prize is a medal or prize money paid to Olympic or Paralympic athletes by the US Olympic Committee. The exclusion does not apply if the athlete's AGI exceeds $1 million.

Self-Study Problem 2.6 *See Appendix E for Solutions to Self-Study Problems*

For each of the following independent cases, indicate the amount of gross income that should be included on the taxpayer's return.

1. Helen enters a radio contest and wins $2,000.
2. Professor Deborah wins an award of $10,000 for a book on literature she published four years ago. The award was presented in recognition of her past literary achievements.
3. Bill is a professional baseball player. Because he has hit fifty home runs this season, he was given a new wrist watch worth $2,500.
4. John is an employee of Big Corporation. He is awarded $5,000 for a suggestion to improve the plant layout.
5. Martha received a desk clock worth $350 from her employer in recognition of her fifteen years of loyal service as an employee.

Learning Objective 2.7

Calculate the taxable and nontaxable portions of annuity payments.

2-7 ANNUITIES

An annuity is a type of investment in which the taxpayer purchases the right to receive periodic payments for the remainder of their life or for a fixed period of years. The amount of each periodic payment is based on the annuity purchase price, the life expectancy of the annuitant, or the life of the annuity contract. Qualified annuities are purchased as part of a qualified retirement plan [Individual Retirement Account (IRA), pension, 401k, 403(b), and 457 plans]. Nonqualified annuities are sold outside of a retirement plan. Life insurance companies are the primary seller of annuities. Annuities have two characteristics that make them attractive to potential buyers: (1) the opportunity to defer income taxes until distributed and (2) the ability to extend payments over an individual's lifetime providing income security. The number and types of annuities are extensive, but the taxation can be classified into annuities that use the simplified method and those that use the general method. Under both methods, the annuitant is entitled to receive a portion of their investment back tax-free. If the annuitant did not pay taxes on the contributions when originally made (such as in some qualified plans), the entire distribution may be taxable.

EXAMPLE Eugene retired from a manufacturing plant. While he was working at the plant, his employer withheld contributions from Eugene's pay to invest in the company pension fund. Eugene paid taxes on the amount contributed. At retirement, Eugene will receive a monthly pension payment from the fund for the rest of his life. Eugene will use the simplified or general method (depending on annuity starting date) to determine the tax-free part of monthly payments. If the contributions had been excluded from Eugene's gross income when earned, all of the payments in retirement would be taxable, since Eugene will have made no taxable investment in the annuity. ♦

2-7a The Simplified Method

Individual taxpayers generally must use the "simplified" method to calculate the taxable amount from a qualified annuity for annuities starting after November 18, 1996. Nonqualified plan annuities and certain annuitants age 75 or older must still use the general rule discussed below. Under the simplified method, standard mortality tables, based on the current age of the annuitant, are used to calculate the taxable annuity amount.

To calculate the excluded amount, the IRS provides the following worksheet.

Simplified Method Worksheet

1. Enter total amount received this year. 1. ____________
2. Enter cost in the plan at the annuity starting date. 2. ____________
3. Age at annuity starting date

	Enter
55 or under	360
56–60	310
61–65	260
66–70	210
71 or older	160

3. ____________

4. Divide line 2 by line 3. 4. ____________
5. Multiply line 4 by the number of monthly payments this year. If the annuity starting date was before 1987, also enter this amount on line 8, and skip lines 6 and 7. Otherwise, go to line 6. 5. ____________
6. Enter the amount, if any, recovered tax free in prior years. 6. ____________
7. Subtract line 6 from line 2. 7. ____________
8. Enter the smaller of line 5 or 7. 8. ____________
9. Taxable amount this year: Subtract line 8 from line 1. Do not enter less than zero. 9. ____________

Note 1: The denominators provided in step 3 above are effective for annuity starting dates after November 18, 1996. For annuity starting dates prior to November 18, 1996, see the IRS website.

Note 2: When annuity benefits with starting dates after 1997 are paid over two lives (joint and survivor annuities), a different set of denominators must be used in step 3.

Combined Age of Annuitants	Number of Payments
110 or under	410
111–120	360
121–130	310
131–140	260
141 or older	210

EXAMPLE Joey, age 67, began receiving benefits under a qualified joint and survivor annuity to be paid over the joint lives of himself and his wife Jody, who is 64. He received his first annuity payment in March of the current year. Joey contributed $38,000 after-tax to the annuity and he had no distributions from the plan before the current year. The monthly payment to Joey is $1,700.

Joey must use the simplified method to calculate his taxable amount. Using the worksheet, Joey's taxable amount for the current year would be:

SIMPLIFIED METHOD WORKSHEET

1. Enter total amount received this year. 1. *$17,000.00*
2. Enter cost in the plan at the annuity starting date. 2. *$38,000.00*
3. Combined age at annuity starting date

	Enter
110 or under	410
111–120	360
121–130	310
131–140	260
141 or older	210

3. *260*

4. Divide line 2 by line 3. 4. *$ 146.15*
5. Multiply line 4 by the number of monthly payments this year. 5. *$ 1,461.50*
6. Enter the amount, if any, recovered tax free in prior years. 6. *$ 0.00*
7. Subtract line 6 from line 2. 7. *$38,000.00*
8. Enter the smaller of line 5 or 7. 8. *$ 1,461.50*
9. Taxable amount this year: Subtract line 8 from line 1. Do not enter less than zero. ♦ 9. *$15,538.50*

The exclusion ratio (the result on line 4 of the Simplified Method Worksheet) is calculated at the start of the annuity and remains constant. For annuities starting after 1986, the maximum amount excludable is limited to the taxpayer's investment in the annuity. After the taxpayer's investment is recovered, all additional amounts received are fully taxable. If the taxpayer dies before the entire investment is recovered, any unrecovered amount is permitted as a miscellaneous itemized deduction (not subject to the 2 percent floor) at the time of the annuitant's death. For annuities starting before 1987, the exclusion ratio is used for the life of the annuitant, even after full recovery of the investment. For these earlier annuities, if the annuitant dies prior to recovering the entire investment, the unrecovered portion is lost.

2-7b The General Rule

Prior to implementation of the Simplified Method discussed above, the General Rule was used for most annuities and is still used for nonqualified annuities. Rather than use the denominators provided in Step 3 of the Simplified Method Worksheet, the life expectancy of the annuitant was determined based on mortality tables provided by the IRS. The excluded amount under the general rule can be calculated as follows:

$$\text{Amount Excluded} = \frac{\text{Investment in Contract}}{\text{Annual Payment} \times \text{Life Expectancy}} \times \text{Amount Received}$$

2-7c Reporting Annuities

Both annuities and pensions are reported to taxpayers on Form 1099-R. Much of the information necessary to compute the taxable portion of the annuity distribution will be reported on Form 1099-R including the total distributions made during the year (Box 1), the taxable portion if determined by the payor (Box 2a), and total annuitant contributions made to the annuity (Box 9b). As with other reporting forms, any tax withheld (Box 4) should be reported on the tax return. If the taxable portion is not included on the 1099-R then the simplified or general method must be employed to determine the taxable portion.

☐ CORRECTED (if checked)

PAYER'S name, street address, city or town, state or province, country, ZIP or foreign postal code, and telephone no.			1 Gross distribution $ 2a Taxable amount $	OMB No. 1545-0119 **2022** Form **1099-R**	**Distributions From Pensions, Annuities, Retirement or Profit-Sharing Plans, IRAs, Insurance Contracts, etc.**
			2b Taxable amount not determined ☐	Total distribution ☐	**Copy B**
PAYER'S TIN	RECIPIENT'S TIN		3 Capital gain (included in box 2a) $	4 Federal income tax withheld $	**Report this income on your federal tax return. If this form shows federal income tax withheld in box 4, attach this copy to your return.**
RECIPIENT'S name			5 Employee contributions/ Designated Roth contributions or insurance premiums $	6 Net unrealized appreciation in employer's securities $	
Street address (including apt. no.)			7 Distribution code(s) / IRA/ SEP/ SIMPLE ☐	8 Other $ %	This information is being furnished to the IRS.
City or town, state or province, country, and ZIP or foreign postal code			9a Your percentage of total distribution %	9b Total employee contributions $	
10 Amount allocable to IRR within 5 years $	11 1st year of desig. Roth contrib.	12 FATCA filing requirement ☐	14 State tax withheld $ $	15 State/Payer's state no.	16 State distribution $ $
Account number (see instructions)		13 Date of payment	17 Local tax withheld $ $	18 Name of locality	19 Local distribution $ $

Form **1099-R** www.irs.gov/Form1099R Department of the Treasury - Internal Revenue Service

Self-Study Problem 2.7

See Appendix E for Solutions to Self-Study Problems

Phil retired in January 2022 at age 63. His pension is $1,500 per month and this year he received eleven payments. Phil's remaining life expectancy is 21 years. He received the following 1099-R:

☐ CORRECTED (if checked)

PAYER'S name, street address, city or town, state or province, country, ZIP or foreign postal code, and telephone no. Pierce Corporation Pension Plan 6200 Winnetka Avenue Woodland Hills, CA 91371			1 Gross distribution $ 16,500.00 2a Taxable amount $	OMB No. 1545-0119 **2022** Form **1099-R**	**Distributions From Pensions, Annuities, Retirement or Profit-Sharing Plans, IRAs, Insurance Contracts, etc.**
			2b Taxable amount not determined ☒	Total distribution ☐	**Copy B**
PAYER'S TIN 24-7654567	RECIPIENT'S TIN 120-66-4377		3 Capital gain (included in box 2a) $	4 Federal income tax withheld $ 0.00	**Report this income on your federal tax return. If this form shows federal income tax withheld in box 4, attach this copy to your return.**
RECIPIENT'S name Phil Ventura			5 Employee contributions/ Designated Roth contributions or insurance premiums $	6 Net unrealized appreciation in employer's securities $	
Street address (including apt. no.) 1001 Chawareewong Blvd.			7 Distribution code(s) 7 / IRA/ SEP/ SIMPLE ☐	8 Other $ %	This information is being furnished to the IRS.
City or town, state or province, country, and ZIP or foreign postal code Sherman Oaks, CA 91403			9a Your percentage of total distribution %	9b Total employee contributions $ 42,500.00	
10 Amount allocable to IRR within 5 years $	11 1st year of desig. Roth contrib.	12 FATCA filing requirement ☐	14 State tax withheld $ $	15 State/Payer's state no.	16 State distribution $ $
Account number (see instructions)		13 Date of payment	17 Local tax withheld $ $	18 Name of locality	19 Local distribution $ $

Form **1099-R** www.irs.gov/Form1099R Department of the Treasury - Internal Revenue Service

a. Calculate Phil's taxable income from the annuity in the current year, using the general rule.
b. Calculate Phil's taxable income using the Simplified Method Worksheet found on Page 2-21.

Learning Objective 2.8

Describe the tax treatment of life insurance proceeds.

2-8 LIFE INSURANCE

A major exclusion from gross income is provided for life insurance proceeds. To be excluded, the proceeds must be paid to the beneficiary by reason of the death of the insured. If the proceeds are taken over several years instead of a lump sum, the insurance company pays interest on the unpaid proceeds. The interest is generally taxable income.

Early payouts of life insurance, also called accelerated death benefits or viatical settlements, are excluded from gross income for certain terminally or chronically ill taxpayers. The taxpayer may either collect an early payout from the insurance company or sell or assign the policy to a viatical settlement provider. A terminally ill individual must be certified by a medical doctor to have an illness which is reasonably expected to cause death within twenty-four months. A chronically ill individual must be certified by a medical doctor as unable to perform daily living activities without assistance. Chronically ill taxpayers may only exclude gain on accelerated death benefits to the extent proceeds are used for long-term care.

If an insurance policy is transferred to another person for valuable consideration, all or a portion of the proceeds from the life insurance policy may be taxable to the recipient. For example, taxable proceeds result when a policy is transferred to a creditor in payment of a debt. When a transfer for value occurs, the proceeds at the death of the insured are taxable to the extent they exceed the cash surrender value of the policy at the time it was transferred, plus the amount of the insurance premiums paid by the purchaser. There is an exception to the rule for policies transferred for valuable consideration resulting in taxable proceeds. Transfers to a partner of the insured, a partnership in which the insured is a partner, or a corporation in which the insured is an officer or a shareholder do not cause the policy proceeds to be taxable.

EXAMPLE Howard dies on January 15, 2019, and leaves Wanda, his wife, a $50,000 insurance policy, the proceeds of which she elects to receive as $10,000 per year plus interest for five years. In the current year, Wanda receives $10,500 ($10,000 + $500 interest). She must include the $500 of interest in income. ♦

EXAMPLE David owns a life insurance policy at the time he is diagnosed with a terminal illness. After his diagnosis, he sells the policy to Viatical Settlements, Inc., for $100,000. David is not required to include the gain on the sale of the insurance in his gross income. ♦

EXAMPLE Amy transfers to Bill an insurance policy with a face value of $40,000 and a cash surrender value of $10,000 for the cancellation of a debt owed to Bill. Bill continues to make payments, and after two years Bill has paid $2,000 in premiums. Amy dies and Bill collects the $40,000. Since the transfer was for valuable consideration, Bill must include $28,000 in taxable income, which is equal to the $40,000 total proceeds less $10,000 value at the time of transfer and $2,000 of premiums Bill paid. If Amy and Bill were partners in the same partnership, the entire proceeds ($40,000) would be tax free. ♦

Self-Study Problem 2.8 *See Appendix E for Solutions to Self-Study Problems*

On March 19, 2017, Karen dies and leaves Larry an insurance policy with a face value of $100,000. Karen is Larry's sister, and Larry elects to take the proceeds over 10 years ($10,000 plus interest each year). This year Larry receives $11,250 from the insurance company. How much income must Larry report for the current year?

2-9 INTEREST INCOME

2.9 Learning Objective

Identify the tax treatment of interest income.

Any interest a taxpayer receives or that is credited to his or her account is taxable income, unless it is specifically exempt from tax such as state or municipal bond interest. If the interest totals more than $1,500, the taxpayer is required to file Schedule B of Form 1040, which instructs the taxpayer to list the amounts and sources of the income.

The fair market value of gifts or services a taxpayer receives for making long-term deposits or opening accounts in savings institutions is also taxable interest income. Interest is reported in the year it is received by a cash-basis taxpayer.

TAX BREAK

Taxpayers may defer reporting interest income on a bank certificate of deposit (CD) if the CD has a maturity of one year or less and there is a substantial penalty for early withdrawal. For example, assume an investor purchases a six-month CD on September 1, 2021, which matures on March 1, 2022, and the bank charges a penalty equal to two months of interest in the event of early withdrawal. In this case, the four months of interest earned on the account during 2021 will not have to be reported until the investor's 2022 tax return is filed.

When a taxpayer withdraws funds early from a CD and must pay a penalty as described above, the full amount of the interest is reported as income and the penalty may be deducted on Form 1040 as a deduction for adjusted gross income.

2-9a U.S. Savings Bonds

The U.S. government issues three basic types of savings bonds to individuals: Series I Bonds, Series EE Bonds, and Series HH Bonds.

Series I Bonds can be purchased directly up to $10,000 per person or through an income tax refund for up to $5,000. I bonds are issued with a fixed interest rate component and an inflation-adjusted interest rate component that is reset every six months. In late 2022, I bonds were paying an interest rate of over 9 percent. I Bonds can be sold after five years with no penalty or after twelve months with a three-month interest penalty. Interest is paid to the I Bond holder when the bond is cashed.

EXAMPLE Zelda purchases $10,000 of I Bonds on January 1, 2022, when the rate is 6 percent. On July 1, 2022, the I Bond rate resets to 5 percent. She earns interest of $557.50 in 2022. Zelda elects to defer interest recognition and therefore has no taxable interest income from I Bonds in 2022. In 2028, Zelda sells the I Bonds and receives $13,946. She will recognize $3,946 of interest in 2028. ♦

Series EE Bonds, whether sold at a discount (before 2012) or at face value, increase in value over their life at a fixed rate of interest for the first twenty years of the bond's life. In late 2022, EE Bonds are paying 0.10 percent. After twenty years, the bond's value is doubled from the original purchase price with a one-time adjustment. EE Bonds pay interest when the bond is redeemed and have the same restrictions on redemptions as I bonds.

Cash-basis taxpayers report the increase in redemption value (interest) on an I or EE Bond using one of the following methods:

1. The interest may be reported in the year the bonds are cashed or in the year they mature, whichever is earlier (no election is required to use this method), or
2. The taxpayer may elect to report the increase in redemption value each year.

If the taxpayer wants to change from method (1) to method (2), he or she may do so without the permission of the IRS. In the year of change, all interest earned to date and not previously reported must be reported on all I and EE Bonds held by the taxpayer. Once method (2) is selected, the taxpayer must continue to use it for all EE Bonds currently held or acquired in the future. Taxpayers cannot change back to method (1) without permission of the IRS.

If the taxpayer uses the interest from I or EE Bonds to pay for higher education costs, the interest can be excluded from gross income. To exclude the savings bond interest under this provision, the I and EE bonds must have been redeemed in the same tax year as the payment of the higher education expenses for the taxpayer, spouse or dependent. The I or EE Bonds must have been purchased when the taxpayer was at least 24 years of age. Married filing separately taxpayers are not eligible for the exclusion. In 2022, the exclusion is phased out for taxpayers with adjusted gross income (excluding the bond interest and without a deduction for student loan interest) of over $128,650 for married filing jointly and $85,800 for all others. The phase-out range is $30,000 for married filing jointly and $15,000 for all others.

EXAMPLE Jorge, a married filing jointly taxpayer, cashes out Series EE Bonds that qualify for the higher education costs exclusion, for a value of $45,000 in 2022. He purchased the bonds for $37,000 and thus has $8,000 of potentially excludable interest. He pays $16,000 in qualified higher education expenses for his daughter to attend college. Jorge's 2022 AGI not including the bond interest or any student loan interest deduction is $136,000. Because Jorge's AGI exceeds the threshold, his exclusion is subject to a phase-out of $1,960 [($136,000 − $128,650)/$30,000 × $8,000]. Jorge may exclude $6,040 ($8,000 − $1,960) of the EE Bond interest. ♦

Form 8815 is used to report the higher education exclusion of interest from EE or I bonds.

Series HH Bonds were last issued in August 2004 and have a twenty-year maturity. HH Bonds were issued at face value and pay interest twice a year. Interest on Series HH Bonds is reported in the year received by a cash-basis taxpayer.

2-9b **Bond Interest**

A common source of interest income is from the ownership of bonds. The traditional definition of a bond is a fixed-income debt instrument that represents a loan made by an investor to a borrower. The return paid for the use of the money is interest and is generally gross income. Bonds are issued by a wide variety of sources including corporations and federal and state governments and related agencies.

U.S. Treasury Bills, Notes and Bonds

Treasury bills, notes, and bonds are direct debts of the United State government. Unlike municipal bonds, interest earned on U.S. government debt is subject to federal income tax but has the advantage of being exempt for individual state income taxes. Treasury bills (T-bills) are debt issued at a discount (a price lower than the face or par value) by the government typically in durations of one year or less. At maturity, the T-bill owner is paid the full par value. The difference between the purchase price and the maturity value is generally interest income. Treasury notes have a fixed rate for durations of two, three, five, seven, and ten years and pay interest every six months. Treasury bonds are similar to notes but have a thirty-year duration.

Corporate Bonds

Many large corporations issue bonds of varying maturities to provide capital to operate or expand their business. Corporate bonds generally pay interest every six months, although the terms of any specific bond can vary. Corporations can also issue zero coupon bonds at a deep discount and do not have any "coupon" interest rate. Instead, as the bond matures, interest is added to the principal value of the bond until reaching par value at maturity. As a result, these bonds pay no interest until maturity (much like T bills). The tax rules classify that discount as original issue discount or OID. The details of OID are outside the scope of this textbook but generally, a portion of OID is included in the bond holder's taxable income. OID is reported to the bond holder on Form 1099-OID.

State and Local Bonds (Municipals)

In 1913 when the Sixteenth Amendment was enacted, Congress questioned the constitutionality of taxing the interest earned on state and local government obligations. Congress provided an exclusion from taxpayers' income for the interest on such bonds. To qualify for the exclusion, the interest must be from an obligation of a state, territory, or possession of the United States, or a political subdivision of the foregoing or of the District of Columbia. For example, Puerto Rico bonds qualify for the exclusion. Federal obligations, such as treasury bills and treasury bonds, do not qualify.

The interest exclusion allows high-income taxpayers to lend money to state and local governments at lower interest rates (discounts).

EXAMPLE Rigby is considering two different bond investments. This first option is a corporate taxable bond that yields a pre-tax return of 8.4 percent. The second option is a tax-exempt municipal bond that yields 6.5 percent. If Rigby is in the 35 percent tax bracket, the after-tax return of the taxable bonds can be computed as:

$$\text{After-tax return} = \text{Pre-tax return} \times (1 - \text{tax rate})$$
$$5.46\% = 8.4\% \times (1 - 0.35)$$

Since the tax-exempt bond is not subject to tax, the after-tax return is 6.5 percent and thus is preferable. Using a re-arranged version of the same formula can determine what the equivalent yield on a taxable bond would need to be to make Rigby indifferent between the two bonds (all other terms being equal):

$$\text{After-tax return} = \text{Tax-free return} / (1 - \text{tax rate})$$
$$10.0\% = 6.5\%/(1 - 0.35)$$ ♦

Typically, interest rates on municipal bonds reflect the after-tax return that compensates for higher income tax rates (35 or 37 percent) and thus tax-exempt bonds will often have a lower after-tax yield than a taxable bond in the hands of a lower-income investor.

EXAMPLE Mordecai is also considering the same bonds as Rigby in the previous example; however, Mordecai is in the 22 percent tax bracket. The after-tax return on the corporate bond is 6.55 percent [8.4% × (1 − 0.22)]. In Mordecai's situation, the after-tax return on the taxable corporate bond is greater than the tax-exempt return of 6.5 percent on the municipal bond. ♦

TAX BREAK Taxpayers in low tax brackets are likely to find that they earn a higher overall return investing in taxable bonds rather than comparable tax-free municipal bonds. This is because the smaller tax benefit from the municipal bonds does not make up for the reduced interest rate paid on municipal bonds. Municipal bonds are also generally not appropriate investments for IRAs or other retirement accounts since income on these accounts is excluded from tax until withdrawn.

Bond Discount and Premium

For the most part, bonds of all types can be bought and sold on the secondary market at just about any time. This creates two challenges for taxpayers to consider: (1) the accrual of interest when bonds are purchased and sold between interest payment dates and (2) fluctuations in bond price creating market discount and premiums.

If a taxpayer sells a bond between interest payment dates, part of the sales price represents interest accrued to the date of sale. The interest portion of the sales price must be reported as interest income for the year of sale.

EXAMPLE Helga purchases at issuance a $10,000 bond that pays 5 percent annually on December 31. On January 31, she sells the bond for $10,042 to Hagar. The proceeds include $42 of interest accrued from the date of the last interest payment ($10,000 × 5% ÷ 365 × 31 days). Because on December 31, the holder of the bond is going to receive the entire coupon amount of $500 ($10,000 × 5%), Helga includes her share of the interest in her sales proceeds but treats the $42 as interest income, not as a gain on the sale of the bond. ♦

EXAMPLE Continued from the previous example, Hagar will receive $500 of interest on December 31st; however, he must deduct $42 to reflect only the interest he earned. The IRS recommends reporting the full $500 on Line 1 of Schedule B (if required) and then reporting the reduction as "Accrued Interest" on the last line above Line 2 of Schedule B. ♦

Bonds that are issued at a fixed rate of interest will often change in price when prevailing interest rates more broadly increase or decrease.

EXAMPLE Mabel owns a $10,000 30-year bond with a 4-percent annual interest rate, that matures in 28 years. Due to economic and market fluctuations, prevailing interest rates increase and thus bonds similar to Mabel's are now paying interest rates of 6-percent. If Mabel wishes to sell a 4-percent bond to investors that are seeking a 6-percent return, since the interest rate on the bond is fixed, Mabel will have to sell the bond at a discount (a price lower than the par value of the bond) for only $7,319. In this way, the purchaser will collect the 4-percent coupon rate as well as the increase in value to maturity of $2,681. ♦

The price of bonds has an inverse relationship with prevailing interest rates. If prevailing interest rates increase, bond prices decrease and if interest rates decrease bond prices increase. The resulting market discount and premium must be reflected as an addition to or a reduction of interest income by the bond holder. The mechanics of bond discount and premium are outside the scope of this textbook but in general, discount can be included in income each year or included at the sale or maturity of the bond. Market premium is generally amortized each year as a reduction of interest income and a commensurate reduction of basis in the bond. For tax-exempt state and local bonds, premium must be amortized. The rules for market discount and premium are complex. See IRS Publication 525 for additional details.

2-9c Below Market Loans

Individuals may often make smaller loans to one another with interest rates that are below prevailing market rates. Common below-market loans are between friends or family (gift loans), between a business and its employee, or between a business and an owner.

EXAMPLE Chuck loans his daughter, Elaine, $15,000 to help with the purchase of a new car. Out of affection for his daughter, Chuck charges no interest on the loan (the loan is a bona fide loan in all other respects). Elaine benefits from the use of $15,000 and is not required to compensate Chuck through the payment of interest. ♦

The tax law requires the lender in a gift loan to reflect foregone interest income that reflects the applicable federal rate of interest on similar loans. The applicable federal rates are issued by the IRS each month.

EXAMPLE Continuing with the previous example, the applicable federal rate for Chuck's loan to Elaine is 4 percent. If the balance of the loan is $15,000 for the entire year, Chuck will recognize deemed interest income of $600 ($15,000 × 4%). Since Chuck does not actually receive $600 from Elaine, he is treated as having gifted the $600 back to Elaine. ♦

The borrower in a gift loan is treated as having deemed interest expense based on the applicable federal rate. In many situations, the deemed interest expense is personal interest expense and not deductible by the borrower (see Chapter 5).

Below market gift loans and loans from an employer to an employee are not subject to the deemed interest rules if the loan amount is $10,000 or less.

EXAMPLE Jon loans his daughter Angelina $1,000 at a zero percent interest rate. The gift loan is not subject to the below market loan rules and Jon is not required to recognize deemed interest income. ♦

The rules that apply to below market loans between a business and its employees or owners are outside the scope of this textbook.

2-9d Reporting Interest Income

Generally, interest amounts greater than $10 must be reported by the payor to the recipient on a Form 1099-INT. On the Form 1099-INT, most taxable interest is reported in Box 1. The penalty for early withdrawal from a deposit account is reported in Box 2 and is generally deductible as a for adjusted gross income (AGI) or "above-the-line" deduction (see Chapter 5). Because states may not tax interest from U.S. government obligations such as Treasury Bills, Treasury Bonds, and U.S. savings bonds, interest from these items is reported in Box 3. Tax-exempt interest is reported in Box 8 and to the extent the payor withheld income tax, that amount is reported in Box 4 and should be included on Line 25b of Form 1040. Taxable interest from each payor is reported on Schedule B (shown on Page 2-31) if interest totals more than $1,500 or is simply totaled on Line 2b of Form 1040 if less than $1,500. Tax-exempt interest is reported on Line 2a of Form 1040 (but not on Schedule B). Payments on deposits held by cooperative banks, credit unions, domestic savings and loan associations, and federal savings and loan associations are often described as "dividends;" however, these payments represent interest and will generally be reported on a Form 1099-INT.

Self-Study Problem 2.9

See Appendix E for Solutions to Self-Study Problems

Christy and John Harris-Thomas received the following Forms 1099-INT during 2022:

☐ CORRECTED (if checked)

PAYER'S name, street address, city or town, state or province, country, ZIP or foreign postal code, and telephone no.	Lake Osbourne Savings and Loan 4400 S. Congressional Avenue Lake Worth, FL 33461
Payer's RTN (optional)	
OMB No. 1545-0112	Form **1099-INT** (Rev. January 2022) For calendar year 20 22
Interest Income	
1 Interest income	$ 1,356.19
2 Early withdrawal penalty	$
Copy B For Recipient	
PAYER'S TIN	13-2122333
RECIPIENT'S TIN	313-44-5454
3 Interest on U.S. Savings Bonds and Treasury obligations	$
RECIPIENT'S name	Christy Harris-Thomas
Street address (including apt. no.)	1112 Constitution Avenue, NW
City or town, state or province, country, and ZIP or foreign postal code	Washington, DC 20224
4 Federal income tax withheld	$
5 Investment expenses	$
6 Foreign tax paid	$
7 Foreign country or U.S. possession	
8 Tax-exempt interest	$
9 Specified private activity bond interest	$
10 Market discount	$
11 Bond premium	$
FATCA filing requirement	☐
12 Bond premium on Treasury obligations	$
13 Bond premium on tax-exempt bond	$
Account number (see instructions)	
14 Tax-exempt and tax credit bond CUSIP no.	
15 State	
16 State identification no.	
17 State tax withheld	$ $

This is important tax information and is being furnished to the IRS. If you are required to file a return, a negligence penalty or other sanction may be imposed on you if this income is taxable and the IRS determines that it has not been reported.

Form **1099-INT** (Rev. 1-2022) (keep for your records) www.irs.gov/Form1099INT Department of the Treasury - Internal Revenue Service

2022 Combined Forms 1099

This is important tax information and is being furnished to the IRS (except as indicated). If you are required to file a return, a negligence penalty or other sanction may be imposed on you if this income is taxable and the IRS determines that it has not been reported.

Copy B For Recipient
OMB No. 1545-0110

Friar Tuck Investments
38 Wall Street, 8th Floor
New York, NY 10005

John and Christy Harris-Thomas
1112 Constitution Ave., NW
Washington DC 20224

Account Number	Tax ID
3100987765	***-**-5454

Payer's Federal Tax ID: 33-1357246

Financial Adviser/Phone: Will Scarlett 888-555-1212

Form 1099-INT **Interest Income**

Box 1 Interest income	358.12
Box 2 Early withdrawal penalty	
Box 3 Interest on U.S. Savings Bonds and Treasury obligations	800.00
Box 4 Federal income tax withheld	
Box 5 Investment expenses	
Box 6 Foreign Tax Paid	
Box 7 Foreign country or U.S. possession	
Box 8 Tax-exempt interest	400.00
Box 9 Specified private activity bond interest	
Box 10 Market Discount	
Box 11 Bond Premium	
Box 12 Bond premium on Treasury obligations	
Box 13 Bond premium on tax-exempt bond	

According to John and Christy's records, they purchased US Treasury bonds between interest payments and paid accrued interest of $107.40 to the seller.

Complete Part I of Schedule B of Form 1040 on Page 2-31 for the Harris-Thomas' 2022 tax year.

Self-Study Problems 2.9 and 2.10

SCHEDULE B (Form 1040)
Department of the Treasury
Internal Revenue Service

Interest and Ordinary Dividends

Go to *www.irs.gov/ScheduleB* for instructions and the latest information.
Attach to Form 1040 or 1040-SR.

OMB No. 1545-0074
2022
Attachment Sequence No. **08**

Name(s) shown on return | **Your social security number**

Part I Interest

(See instructions and the Instructions for Form 1040, line 2b.)

Note: If you received a Form 1099-INT, Form 1099-OID, or substitute statement from a brokerage firm, list the firm's name as the payer and enter the total interest shown on that form.

			Amount
1	List name of payer. If any interest is from a seller-financed mortgage and the buyer used the property as a personal residence, see the instructions and list this interest first. Also, show that buyer's social security number and address:	1	
2	Add the amounts on line 1	2	
3	Excludable interest on series EE and I U.S. savings bonds issued after 1989. Attach Form 8815	3	
4	Subtract line 3 from line 2. Enter the result here and on Form 1040 or 1040-SR, line 2b	4	

Note: If line 4 is over $1,500, you must complete Part III.

Part II Ordinary Dividends

(See instructions and the Instructions for Form 1040, line 3b.)

Note: If you received a Form 1099-DIV or substitute statement from a brokerage firm, list the firm's name as the payer and enter the ordinary dividends shown on that form.

			Amount
5	List name of payer:	5	
6	Add the amounts on line 5. Enter the total here and on Form 1040 or 1040-SR, line 3b	6	

Note: If line 6 is over $1,500, you must complete Part III.

Part III Foreign Accounts and Trusts

Caution: If required, failure to file FinCEN Form 114 may result in substantial penalties. Additionally, you may be required to file Form 8938, Statement of Specified Foreign Financial Assets. See instructions.

You must complete this part if you (**a**) had over $1,500 of taxable interest or ordinary dividends; (**b**) had a foreign account; or (**c**) received a distribution from, or were a grantor of, or a transferor to, a foreign trust.

		Yes	No
7a	At any time during 2022, did you have a financial interest in or signature authority over a financial account (such as a bank account, securities account, or brokerage account) located in a foreign country? See instructions		
	If "Yes," are you required to file FinCEN Form 114, Report of Foreign Bank and Financial Accounts (FBAR), to report that financial interest or signature authority? See FinCEN Form 114 and its instructions for filing requirements and exceptions to those requirements		
b	If you are required to file FinCEN Form 114, list the name(s) of the foreign country(-ies) where the financial account(s) are located:		
8	During 2022, did you receive a distribution from, or were you the grantor of, or transferor to, a foreign trust? If "Yes," you may have to file Form 3520. See instructions		

Self-Study Problem 2.10

Qualified Dividends and Capital Gain Tax Worksheet—Line 16

Keep for Your Records 

Before you begin:
- √ See the earlier instructions for line 16 to see if you can use this worksheet to figure your tax.
- √ Before completing this worksheet, complete Form 1040 or 1040-SR through line 15.
- √ If you don't have to file Schedule D and you received capital gain distributions, be sure you checked the box on Form 1040 or 1040-SR, line 7.

1. Enter the amount from Form 1040 or 1040-SR, line 15. However, if you are filing Form 2555 (relating to foreign earned income), enter the amount from line 3 of the Foreign Earned Income Tax Worksheet . . . . . 1. ______
2. Enter the amount from Form 1040 or 1040-SR, line 3a* . . . . . 2. ______
3. Are you filing Schedule D?*
   - ☐ **Yes.** Enter the **smaller** of line 15 or 16 of Schedule D. If either line 15 or 16 is blank or a loss, enter -0-.
   - ☐ **No.** Enter the amount from Form 1040 or 1040-SR, line 7.

   3. ______
4. Add lines 2 and 3 . . . . . 4. ______
5. Subtract line 4 from line 1. If zero or less, enter -0- . . . . . 5. ______
6. Enter:
   $41,675 if single or married filing separately,
   $83,350 if married filing jointly or qualifying widow(er),
   $55,800 if head of household. . . . . 6. ______
7. Enter the smaller of line 1 or line 6 . . . . . 7. ______
8. Enter the smaller of line 5 or line 7 . . . . . 8. ______
9. Subtract line 8 from line 7. This amount is taxed at 0% . . . . . 9. ______
10. Enter the smaller of line 1 or line 4 . . . . . 10. ______
11. Enter the amount from line 9 . . . . . 11. ______
12. Subtract line 11 from line 10 . . . . . 12. ______
13. Enter:
    $459,750 if single,
    $258,600 if married filing separately,
    $517,200 if married filing jointly or qualifying widow(er),
    $488,500 if head of household. . . . . 13. ______
14. Enter the smaller of line 1 or line 13 . . . . . 14. ______
15. Add lines 5 and 9 . . . . . 15. ______
16. Subtract line 15 from line 14. If zero or less, enter -0- . . . . . 16. ______
17. Enter the smaller of line 12 or line 16 . . . . . 17. ______
18. Multiply line 17 by 15% (0.15) . . . . . 18. ______
19. Add lines 9 and 17 . . . . . 19. ______
20. Subtract line 19 from line 10 . . . . . 20. ______
21. Multiply line 20 by 20% (0.20) . . . . . 21. ______
22. Figure the tax on the amount on line 5. If the amount on line 5 is less than $100,000, use the Tax Table to figure the tax. If the amount on line 5 is $100,000 or more, use the Tax Computation Worksheet . . . . . 22. ______
23. Add lines 18, 21, and 22 . . . . . 23. ______
24. Figure the tax on the amount on line 1. If the amount on line 1 is less than $100,000, use the Tax Table to figure the tax. If the amount on line 1 is $100,000 or more, use the Tax Computation Worksheet . . . . . 24. ______
25. **Tax on all taxable income.** Enter the **smaller** of line 23 or 24. Also include this amount on the entry space on Form 1040 or 1040-SR, line 16. If you are filing Form 2555, don't enter this amount on the entry space on Form 1040 or 1040-SR, line 16. Instead, enter it on line 4 of the Foreign Earned Income Tax Worksheet . . . . . 25. ______

* *If you are filing Form 2555, see the footnote in the Foreign Earned Income Tax Worksheet before completing this line.*

This worksheet adapted from the 2021 worksheet.

2-10 DIVIDEND INCOME

2.10 Learning Objective

Identify the tax treatment of dividend income.

2-10a Dividends

Dividends are a type of distribution paid to a shareholder by a corporation. Taxpayers may receive the following types of distributions from a corporation or a mutual fund or similar investment that owns corporate stocks:

1. Ordinary and qualified dividends
2. Nontaxable distributions
3. Capital gain distributions

Ordinary dividends are by far the most common type of corporate distribution. They are paid from the earnings and profits of the corporation. Ordinary dividends are also qualifying dividends if the stock is held for a certain amount of time (generally sixty days) and the dividend is issued by a U.S. corporation. If the ordinary dividends are not qualifying dividends, then instead of being taxed at the lower long-term capital gains rate, they will be taxed at the ordinary income rate. Corporations issuing dividends and brokerage companies holding stock investments for taxpayers are required to classify and report the amount of qualifying dividends to investors.

Nontaxable distributions are a return of invested capital and are not paid from the earnings and profits of the corporation. They are considered a return of the taxpayer's investment in the corporation and are not included in the taxpayer's income. Instead, the taxpayer's basis in the stock is reduced by nontaxable distributions until the basis reaches zero.[1] After the stock has reached a zero basis, distributions that represent a return of capital are taxed as capital gains. Capital gain distributions are reported on Line 7 of Forms 1040 or 1040-SR or Schedule D, Line 13 (if required otherwise).

2-10b Current Tax Rates for Dividends

For years, experts have argued that corporate dividends are taxed twice, once when the corporation pays tax on profits, and once when the dividend is received by the shareholder. To provide some tax relief for individual taxpayers who receive corporate dividends, the tax rates on qualifying dividends are the same as long-term capital gains which are lower than the rates for ordinary income.

Income level	*Qualified dividends and long-term capital gains rates**
Married filing jointly	
\$0–\$83,350	0%
\$83,351–\$517,200	15%
>\$517,200	20%
Single	
\$0–\$41,675	0%
\$41,676–\$459,750	15%
>\$459,750	20%
Head of household	
\$0–\$55,800	0%
\$55,801–\$488,500	15%
>\$488,500	20%
Married filing separately	
\$0–\$41,675	0%
\$41,676–\$258,600	15%
>\$258,600	20%

*An additional 3.8 percent Medicare tax on net investment income, including qualifying dividends, applies to high-income taxpayers with income over certain thresholds. Please see Chapter 6 for further details.

[1]A taxpayer's basis in an investment is usually the cost of the investment. The basis is used to determine the gain or loss when the investment is sold.

Note that the break points between 0 and 15 percent for qualified dividends and long-term capital gains rates are similar to but not the same as the ordinary rate brackets for the same filing status. For example, the single ordinary income rate bracket breaks between 12 and 22 percent at $41,775; whereas the dividend/capital gain rate breaks at $41,675.

EXAMPLE Sandra is a single taxpayer with wage income of $42,000 and qualified dividends of $1,000 in 2022. Assume Sandra has no other deductions or income except the standard deduction. Sandra's taxable income is:

Wage income	$42,000
Qualified dividends	1,000
Standard deduction	(12,950)
Exemption (suspended by TCJA)	0
Taxable income	$30,050

Sandra's income now must be separated into the ordinary and qualified dividends portions:

Taxable income	$30,050
Qualified dividends	(1,000)
Ordinary income	$29,050

The 2022 tax on $29,050 of ordinary income is $3,284. As Sarah's taxable income of $30,050 including the qualified dividend is below $41,675, the threshold for 0 percent qualified dividend and long-term capital gains for a single taxpayer in 2022, her dividend tax rate is 0 percent and thus her total tax liability is $3,284. ♦

EXAMPLE Dee is a single taxpayer with wage income of $47,000 and qualified dividends of $8,000 in 2022. Assume Dee has no other deductions or income except the standard deduction. Dee's taxable income is

Wage income	$47,000
Qualified dividends	8,000
Standard deduction	(12,950)
Taxable income	$42,050

Dee's income now must be separated into the ordinary and qualified dividend and long-term capital gain portions:

Taxable income	$42,050
Qualified dividends	(8,000)
Ordinary income	$34,050

The 2022 tax on $34,050 of ordinary income is $3,884. Dee's taxable income without the qualified dividends is below the 15 percent threshold of $41,675 for a single taxpayer in 2022, but her taxable income with qualified dividends of $42,050 is above the threshold; thus a part of the qualified dividend will be taxed at 0 percent and a part at 15 percent. Of her $8,000 qualified dividends, $7,625 is below the $41,675 threshold and is taxed at 0 percent while $375 is above the $41,675 threshold and is taxed at 15 percent for an additional tax of $56.25 to bring Dee's total tax liability to $3,940. The treatment of Dee's ordinary and qualified dividend income is presented in Figure 2.2. ♦

FIGURE 2.2 TAX RATES FOR QUALIFIED DIVIDENDS AND LONG-TERM CAPITAL GAINS

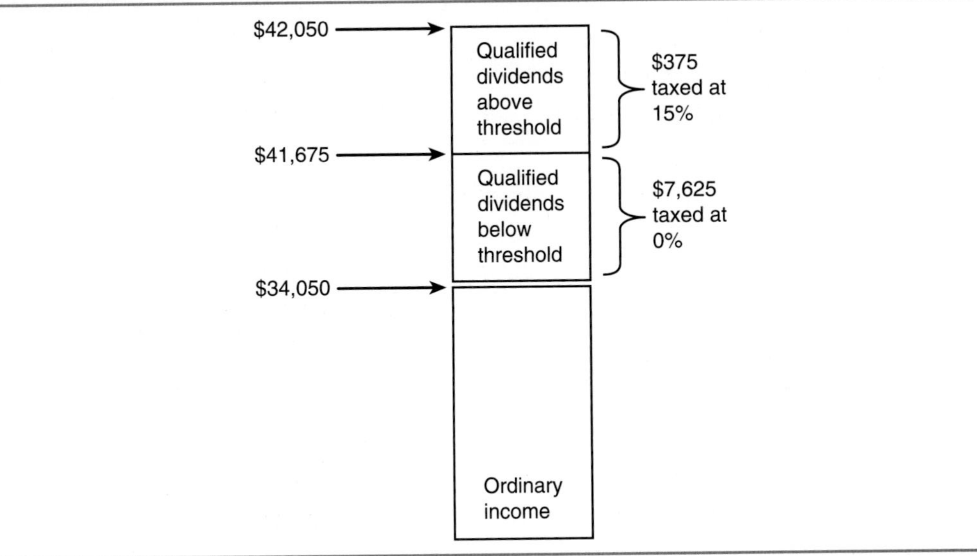

In order to assist with the calculation of preferential taxes on qualified dividends and long-term capital gains, the IRS provides the Qualified Dividends and Capital Gain Tax Worksheet as part of the Form 1040 instructions. This worksheet is presented on Page 2-32.

2-10c **Reporting Dividend Income**

Generally, dividend income in amounts greater than $10 must be reported by the payor to the recipient on a Form 1099-DIV. Form 1099-DIV reports total ordinary dividends in Box 1a. Box 1b reports the amount of qualified dividends included in Box 1a. These amounts are entered on Schedule B (if more than $1,500 in total) or directly on Lines 3a and 3b of Form 1040. Mutual fund investments, and to a lesser degree, corporate stock investments, can also pay capital gain dividends, which are reported in Box 2a of Form 1099-DIV. Unlike ordinary and qualified dividends which are reported by the taxpayer on Schedule B or Form 1040 as described above, capital gain dividends are reported on Schedule D of Form 1040 (see Chapter 4) or if a taxpayer has *only* capital gain distributions reported on Form 1099-DIV, the amount can be reported on Line 7 of Form 1040.

Self-Study Problem 2.10

See Appendix E for Solutions to Self-Study Problems

Christy and John Harris-Thomas received the following Forms 1099-DIV during 2022:

☐ CORRECTED (if checked)

PAYER'S name, street address, city or town, state or province, country, ZIP or foreign postal code, and telephone no.		1a Total ordinary dividends	OMB No. 1545-0110	
Tangerine Equity Fund PO Box 1001 Kansas City, MO 64108		$ 980.00	Form 1099-DIV (Rev. January 2022)	Dividends and Distributions
		1b Qualified dividends $ 980.00	For calendar year 20 22	
		2a Total capital gain distr. $	2b Unrecap. Sec. 1250 gain $	Copy B For Recipient
PAYER'S TIN 41-5982262	RECIPIENT'S TIN 513-17-7711	2c Section 1202 gain $	2d Collectibles (28%) gain $	
		2e Section 897 ordinary dividends $	2f Section 897 capital gain $	
RECIPIENT'S name John Harris-Thomas		3 Nondividend distributions $	4 Federal income tax withheld $	This is important tax information and is being furnished to the IRS. If you are required to file a return, a negligence penalty or other sanction may be imposed on you if this income is taxable and the IRS determines that it has not been reported.
Street address (including apt. no.) 1112 Constitution Ave., NW		5 Section 199A dividends $	6 Investment expenses $	
		7 Foreign tax paid $	8 Foreign country or U.S. possession	
City or town, state or province, country, and ZIP or foreign postal code Washington, DC 20224		9 Cash liquidation distributions $	10 Noncash liquidation distributions $	
	11 FATCA filing requirement ☐	12 Exempt-interest dividends $	13 Specified private activity bond interest dividends $	
Account number (see instructions)		14 State / 15 State identification no.	16 State tax withheld $ $	

Form 1099-DIV (Rev. 1-2022) (keep for your records) www.irs.gov/Form1099DIV Department of the Treasury - Internal Revenue Service

2022 Combined Forms 1099

This is important tax information and is being furnished to the IRS (except as indicated). If you are required to file a return, a negligence penalty or other sanction may be imposed on you if this income is taxable and the IRS determines that it has not been reported.

Copy B For Recipient
OMB No. 1545-0110

Friar Tuck Investments
38 Wall Street, 8th Floor
New York, NY 10005

John and Christy Harris-Thomas
1112 Constitution Ave., NW
Washington DC 20224

Account Number	Tax ID
3100987765	***-**-5454

Payer's Federal Tax ID
33-1357246
Financial Adviser/Phone
Will Scarlett 888-555-1212

Form 1099-DIV **Dividend Income**

Box 1a Total ordinary dividends	Box 1b Qualified dividends	Box 2a Total capital gain distr.
1,700.00	1,620.00	120.00
Box 2b Unrecap Sec 1250 gain	Box 2c Section 1202 gain	Box 2d Collectibles (28%) gain
Box 2e Section 897 ordinary dividends	Box 2f Section 897 capital gain	Box 3 Nondividend distributions
Box 4 Federal income tax withheld	Box 5 Section 199A dividends	Box 6 Investment expenses
Box 7 Foreign taxes paid	Box 8 Foreign country or possession	Box 9 Cash liquidation distributions

The Harris-Thomases file jointly, take the standard deduction, and have taxable income, including interest and dividends, of $85,000. Complete Part II of Schedule B of Form 1040 on Page 2-31. Using the information from this problem and Self-Study Problem 2-9, complete the Qualified Dividends and Capital Gains Tax Worksheet on Page 2-32 for the 2022 tax year.

ProConnect™ Tax TIP

Interest and dividends are both common forms of income in addition to wages. The way the two items are reported is slightly different and not always intuitive. Tax-exempt interest (which is entered on Line 2a of Form 1040) is not included as part of taxable interest (Line 2b). Qualified dividends (line 3a) however, are included as part of ordinary dividends (Line 3b). Interest and Dividends are both located in ProConnect Tax under Income and have a Quick Entry and a 1099 entry screen (with Box numbers presented) available. Quick Entry handles most Forms 1099-INT and Forms 1099-DIV; however, should one wish to use the detailed entry screens, they will appear in the left-hand margin when Quick Entry is open. One can always return to Quick Entry using the link at the top of the detail entry form (especially if there is a need to enter additional Forms 1099).

2-11 GIFTS AND INHERITANCES

2.11 Learning Objective

Identify the general rules for the tax treatment of gifts and inheritances.

Taxpayers are allowed to exclude from income the fair market value of gifts and inheritances received, but income received from the property after such a transfer is generally taxable. Normally, the gift tax or estate tax is paid by the donor or the decedent's estate; such property is, therefore, usually tax-free to the person receiving the gift or inheritance.

One tax problem that may arise concerning a gift is the definition of what constitutes a gift. The courts define a gift as a voluntary transfer of property without adequate consideration. Gifts made in a business setting are suspect since they may be disguised payments for goods or services. The courts are likely to rule that gifts in a business setting are taxable income, even if there was no obligation to make the payment. Also, if the recipient renders services for the gift, it will be presumed to be income for the services performed.

EXAMPLE In January of the current year, Richard inherits shares of Birch Corporation stock worth $22,000. After receiving the stock, he is paid $1,300 in dividends during the current year. His gross income from the inheritance in the current year would be $1,300. The $22,000 fair market value of the stock is excluded from gross income. ♦

TAX BREAK

Although the recipient of a gift generally excludes the value of the gift from income tax, the person that makes the gift might be subject to the unified transfer tax, more commonly known as the estate and gift tax. The lifetime exclusion amount increased to just over $12 million per person in 2022 (returns to $5 million after 2025) and thus most gifts will remain untaxed.

Self-Study Problem 2.11 *See Appendix E for Solutions to Self-Study Problems*

Don is an attorney who supplied a list of potential clients to a new attorney, Lori. This list aided in the success of Lori's practice. Lori was very pleased and decided to do something for Don. In the current year, Lori gives Don a new car worth $40,000. Lori was not obligated to give this gift to Don, and she did not expect Don to perform future services for the gift. How much income, if any, should Don report from this transaction? Explain your answer.

Learning Objective 2.12

Describe the elements of scholarship income that are excluded from tax.

2-12 SCHOLARSHIPS

A scholarship is an amount paid or awarded to, or for the benefit of, a student to aid in the pursuit of his or her studies. Scholarships granted to degree candidates are taxable income, with the exception of amounts spent for tuition, fees, books, and course-required supplies and equipment. Therefore, scholarship amounts received for items such as room and board are taxable to the recipient.

EXAMPLE In 2022, Diane receives a $5,000 scholarship to study accounting at Big State University. Diane's expenses for tuition and books amount to $3,200 during the fall semester; therefore, she would have taxable income of $1,800 ($5,000 − $3,200) from the scholarship. ♦

Payments received by students for part-time employment are not excludable; they are taxable as compensation. For example, students in work–study programs must include their compensation in gross income. Some scholarships will be reported on Form 1098-T. This form is discussed further in Chapter 7.

Self-Study Problem 2.12

See Appendix E for Solutions to Self-Study Problems

Indicate whether each item below would be included in or excluded from the income of the recipient in 2022.

1. A $2,000 National Merit Scholarship for tuition
2. A basketball scholarship for room and board
3. Payments under a work–study program
4. Salary for working at Beech Research Laboratory
5. A scholarship for $10,000 to cover qualified costs of $7,600.
6. Payment received from an employer while on leave working on a research project

Learning Objective 2.13

Describe the tax treatment of alimony and child support.

2-13 ALIMONY

The term alimony, for income tax purposes, includes separate maintenance payments or similar periodic payments made to a spouse or former spouse. Payments must meet certain requirements to be considered alimony.

1. The payments must be in cash and must be received by the spouse (or former spouse).
2. The payments must be made under a decree of divorce or separate maintenance or under a written instrument incident to the divorce.
3. The payor must have no liability to make payments for any period following the death of the spouse receiving the payments.
4. The payments must not be designated in the written agreement as anything other than alimony.
5. If the parties are divorced or legally separated, they must not be members of the same household at the time the payments are made.

Disguised child support payments may not be treated as alimony. Payments contingent on the status of a child, such as the age or marital status of the child, are not considered alimony.

EXAMPLE Under a 2016 divorce agreement, Sam has agreed to pay his former spouse, Silvia, $1,000 per month. The payments meet all the tests for classification as alimony, but they will be reduced to $600 per month when their child, in Silvia's custody, becomes 18 years of age. In this situation, $400 of each payment must be treated as nondeductible child support and cannot be considered alimony. ♦

Under previous tax law, alimony was deductible by the payer and includable in income by the recipient. However, the alimony provisions were repealed and these amounts are neither includable nor deductible for divorce and separation agreements entered into after December 31, 2018. For alimony paid pursuant to a divorce or separation instrument executed on or before December 31, 2018, alimony is deductible by the payor and included by the recipient unless the agreement is modified and the modification expressly provides that the new tax law applies to such modification.

EXAMPLE Brad and Jen were married in 2015. The relationship did not work out and they divorced in 2016. The divorce decree required Brad to pay Jen alimony of $1,000 per month. Because this divorce was effective prior to 2019, the alimony is deductible by Brad and is gross income to Jen. ♦

EXAMPLE Miley and Liam were married in 2017. The relationship did not work out and they divorced in 2022. Miley is required to pay Liam alimony of $1,000 per month. The alimony is neither deductible to Miley nor included in Liam's gross income. ♦

2-13a **Property Transfers**

A spouse who transfers property in settlement of a marital obligation is not required to recognize any gain as a result of the property's appreciation. Thus, if in a divorce settlement, a wife transfers property with a fair market value of $10,000 and a tax basis of $3,000 to her husband, she will not be required to recognize the gain of $7,000 ($10,000 − $3,000). Of course, the husband would be required to assume the wife's tax basis ($3,000) in the property. The transfer of property in settlement of a divorce is not considered alimony and there is no deduction by the spouse who transfers the property, nor is it income to the recipient.

2-13b **Child Support**

Payments made for child support are not deductible by the taxpayer making them, nor are they income to the recipient. However, they may be an important factor in determining which spouse is entitled to claim the dependent child (see Chapter 1). Child support payments must be up to date before any amount paid may be treated as alimony. That is, if a taxpayer is obligated to pay both child support and alimony, he or she must first meet the child support obligation before obtaining a deduction for alimony payments (for divorce agreements prior to 2019). Payments for child support include payments designated as such in the marital settlement agreement, plus any alimony payments that are contingent upon the status of a child.

EXAMPLE Jim is required under a 2015 divorce decree to pay $400 in alimony and $250 in child support per month. Since the decree separately states that $250 is child support, only $400 per month is deductible by Jim and counts as income to his ex-wife. ♦

ProConnect™ Tax TIP

Income from alimony, when applicable, is reported in the Income section under SS Benefits, Alimony, Misc. Income (SS Bene., Misc. Inc.). Once this heading is clicked, Alimony and Other Income will be presented as a subheading. Deductible alimony paid, when applicable, is reported under Deductions. Once Adjustments to Income is clicked, a series of subheadings is presented including Alimony Paid.

Self-Study Problem 2.13

See Appendix E for Solutions to Self-Study Problems

A taxpayer (payor ex-spouse) is required to pay an ex-spouse (recipient ex-spouse) alimony of $12,000 per year. Determine how much alimony is deductible by the payor ex-spouse and how much alimony is recognized as income by the recipient ex-spouse based on the following information:

a. The payments are made in 2022 as part of a divorce decree executed in 2018. The divorce decree is modified in 2021 to explicitly apply the provisions of the TCJA.
b. The payments are made in 2022 as part of a divorce decree executed in 2016.
c. The payments are made in 2022 as part of a divorce decree executed in 2021.

ILYA AKINSHIN/Shutterstock.com; Zhukov Oleg/Shutterstock.com.

Sign Here

Under penalties of perjury, I declare that I have examined this return and accompanying schedules and statements, and to the best of my knowledge and belief, they are true, correct, and complete. Declaration of preparer (other than taxpayer) is based on all information of which preparer has any knowledge.

Joint return? See instructions. Keep a copy for your records.

Your signature	Date	Your occupation	If the IRS sent you an Identity Protection PIN, enter it here (see inst.) ▶
Spouse's signature. If a joint return, **both** must sign.	Date	Spouse's occupation	If the IRS sent your spouse an Identity Protection PIN, enter it here (see inst.) ▶
Phone no.	Email address		

Paid Preparer Use Only

Preparer's name	Preparer's signature	Date	PTIN	Check if: ☐ Self-employed
Firm's name ▶			Phone no.	
Firm's address ▶			Firm's EIN ▶	

Would You Sign This Tax Return?

For the last 10 years, you prepared the joint tax returns for Dominic (husband; age 40) and Dulce (wife; age 35) Divorcio. In 2018, they divorced and remained as your separate tax clients. Under the dissolution decree, Dominic has to pay Dulce $2,500 per month alimony, which he does for the current year. You have completed Dominic's tax return for the current year, and you deducted the required alimony payments to Dulce on Dominic's Form 1040. Dulce came in to have you prepare her tax return and refused to report her alimony received as income. She stated, "I am not going to pay tax on the $30,000 from Dominic." She views the payments as "a gift for putting up with him for all those years of marriage." Dulce will not budge on excluding this alimony from income. Would you sign the Paid Preparer's declaration (see example above) on this return? Why or why not?

2-14 EDUCATIONAL INCENTIVES

2.14 Learning Objective

Explain the tax implications of using educational savings vehicles.

2-14a Qualified Tuition Programs (QTP)

A Qualified Tuition Program (more commonly referred to as a Section 529 tuition plan) allows taxpayers (1) to buy in-kind tuition credits or certificates for qualified higher education expenses (a prepaid tuition plan) or (2) to contribute to an account established to meet qualified higher education expenses (a savings-type plan). Such Section 529 plans may be sponsored by a state government or a private institution of higher learning. Section 529 plans permit tax-free distributions if the distribution is used for qualified higher education expenses. Qualified higher education expenses include tuition, fees, books, supplies, and equipment required for the enrollment or attendance at an eligible educational institution. In addition, reasonable room and board costs, subject to certain limitations, are also qualified expenses allowed to be paid from the Section 529 tuition plan. Qualified higher education expenses also include tuition in connection with enrollment or attendance at an elementary or secondary public, private, or religious school. The use of the specific term "tuition" excludes other types of qualifying education expenses such as books, supplies, and equipment for elementary or secondary students. The maximum exclusion for elementary or secondary education (i.e., K-12) is $10,000 per beneficiary per year.

EXAMPLE Walt and Skyler Blanco have two children, Jesse and Jane, and established 529 plans for both of them many years ago. Jesse is now in his second year of college at Albuquerque Community College and Jane is a junior at Albuquerque High School for Math and Science, a private high school. In 2022, the Blancos have $3,500 distributed from the 529 plan with Jesse as the named beneficiary to pay for his community college tuition, books, and course-related supplies. Jane's private school tuition is much higher and the Blancos distribute $12,000 from the 529 plan for which she is the beneficiary. $11,000 of the distribution is used to pay for tuition, $550 for books, and $450 for her private school uniforms. The Blancos may exclude $13,500 of the distributions. Jesse's $3,500 distribution meets the definition of qualified higher education expenses. Only $10,000 of Jane's distribution meets the definition of qualified higher education expenses. The remaining $1,000 of Jane's tuition is in excess of the annual limit and her books and uniform costs do not qualify. ♦

The definition of qualified higher education costs that are eligible for exclusion from income when distributed from a Section 529 plan was expanded to include distributions of up to $10,000 used to pay student loan principal or interest for the plan beneficiary, a sibling, or both. However, the $10,000 limit related to student loan principal or interest payments is a lifetime limit for any single beneficiary.

EXAMPLE Breonna graduated college in 2021 and has a remaining student loan debt balance in 2022 of $13,000. Breonna's brother Christian is a current college student and is the beneficiary of Section 529 qualified tuition plan. In 2022, a $16,000 distribution is made to Christian to pay for his qualified higher education expenses. In addition, the same plan makes a $10,000 distribution to Breonna to pay her student loans. Neither Breonna nor Christian will be required to include the distribution in income. Breonna will not be eligible for any additional exclusion on Section 529 distributions for loans in the future as she has met her lifetime limit; however, if Christian finishes college with student loan debt, his $10,000 lifetime limit remains available. ♦

Taxpayers may not exclude student loan interest under these provisions and also deduct the same interest as a for AGI student loan interest deduction (see Chapter 5). In an additional expansion of qualified higher education costs, 529 distributions used to pay for costs for apprenticeship programs which are registered and certified are now eligible to be excluded from income. The U.S. Department of Labor certifies such programs.

The earnings portion of 529 plan distributions that are not used for qualified tuition expenses are includable in the distributee's gross income under the annuity income rules and are subject to a 10-percent early withdrawal penalty.

Unlike Educational Savings Accounts, discussed later in this section, there is no income limit on the amount of contributions to a Section 529 plan. Like an Educational Savings Account, however, the contributions are not deductible. Any contributions are gifts, and thus subject to the gift tax rules. In addition, most programs impose some form of overall maximum contribution for each beneficiary based on estimated future higher education expenses.

EXAMPLE Bill has AGI of $275,000 and has two children. He chooses to contribute $9,000 (he is allowed to contribute any amount up to the limit imposed by his state's law) to a QTP for each of his children in 2022, even with his high AGI. The $18,000 is not deductible to Bill. Any earnings on the contribution accumulate tax free and are excluded from gross income if used for future qualified higher education expenses. ♦

A taxpayer may claim an American Opportunity credit or lifetime learning credit (discussed in detail in Chapter 7) for a tax year and exclude from gross income amounts distributed (both the principal and the earnings portions) from a qualified tuition program on behalf of the same student. This is true as long as the distribution is not used for the same expenses for which a credit was claimed. However, the amount of qualified higher education expenses for a tax year for purposes of calculating the exclusion from income must be reduced by scholarships, veterans' benefits, military reserve benefits, employer-provided educational assistance amounts, and the tuition amounts used to generate the American Opportunity and lifetime learning credits.

EXAMPLE In 2022, Sammy receives $15,000 from a qualified tuition program. He uses the funds to pay for his college tuition and other qualified higher education expenses. Sammy also claims an American Opportunity credit of $1,500 for the year, using the expenses paid from the Section 529 plan funds. For purposes of the Section 529 plan exclusion calculation, the $15,000 must be reduced to $13,500 ($15,000 − $1,500). ♦

The tax law provides that if the total distributions from a Section 529 plan and from an educational savings account exceed the total amount of qualified higher education expenses, the taxpayer will have to allocate the expenses among the distributions for purposes of determining how much of each distribution is excludable.

If Section 529 funds are used to pay for qualified higher education expenses that are then refunded because of classes being canceled or university housing closing, and if those funds are redeposited within 60 days of the refund, the tax and 10-percent penalty are waived.

2-14b Educational Savings Accounts

Taxpayers are allowed to set up educational savings accounts, also known as Coverdell Education Savings Accounts, to pay for qualified education expenses. The maximum amount a taxpayer can contribute annually to an educational savings account for a beneficiary is $2,000. Contributions are not deductible and are subject to income limits. Contributions cannot be made to an educational savings account after the date on which the designated beneficiary becomes 18 years old. In addition, contributions cannot be made to a beneficiary's educational savings account during any year in which contributions are made to a qualified state tuition program (such as a 529 saving plan) on behalf of the same beneficiary. The educational savings account exclusion for distributions of income is available in any tax year in which the beneficiary claims the American Opportunity credit or the lifetime learning credit (see Chapter 7), provided the distribution is not used for the same expenses for which the credit was claimed.

Contributions to educational savings accounts are phased out between AGIs of $95,000 and $110,000 for single taxpayers and $190,000 and $220,000 for married couples who file a joint return (these limits are not adjusted annually for inflation). Like regular and Roth IRAs, contributions applied to the current tax year must be made by April 15 (or the next business day, if April 15 falls on a weekend or holiday) of the following year.

EXAMPLE Joe, who is single, would like to contribute $2,000 to an educational savings account for his 12-year-old son. However, his AGI is $105,000, so his contribution is limited to $667, calculated as follows:

$$\frac{(\$110{,}000 \text{ upper limit} - \$105{,}000 \text{ AGI})}{\$15{,}000} \times \$2{,}000 = \$667 \text{ contribution}$$

$15,000 is the difference between the upper ($110,000) and lower ($95,000) phase-out limits. ♦

TAX BREAK

For parents with income above the allowable limit, a gift may be made to a child and the child may make the contribution to an educational savings account. There is no requirement that the contributor have earned income as there is for IRAs.

Amounts received from an educational savings account are tax-free if they are used for qualified education expenses. Qualified education expenses include tuition, fees, books, supplies, and related equipment for private, elementary, and secondary school expenses as well as for college. Room and board also qualify if the student's course load is at least 50 percent of the full-time course load. If the distributions during a tax year exceed qualified education expenses, part of the excess is treated as a return of capital (the contributions), and part is treated as a distribution of earnings. The distribution is presumed to be pro rata from each category. The exclusion for the distribution of earnings is calculated as follows:

$$\frac{\text{Qualified education expenses}}{\text{Total distribution}} \times \text{Earnings} = \text{Exclusion}$$

EXAMPLE Amy receives a $2,000 distribution from her educational savings account. She uses $1,800 to pay for qualified education expenses. Immediately prior to the distribution, Amy's account balance is $5,000, $3,000 of which are her contributions. Because 60 percent ($3,000/$5,000) of her account balance represents her contributions, $1,200 ($2,000 × 60%) of the distribution is a tax-free return of capital and $800 ($2,000 × 40%) is a distribution of earnings. The excludable amount of the earnings is calculated as follows:

$$\frac{\$1{,}800}{\$2{,}000} \times \$800 = \$720$$ is excludable (thus, the amount taxable is $80, or $800 − $720).

Amy's adjusted basis for her educational savings account is reduced to $1,800 ($3,000 − $1,200). ♦

Self-Study Problem 2.14 *See Appendix E for Solutions to Self-Study Problems*

a. Abby has a distribution of $10,000 from a qualified tuition program, of which $3,000 represents earnings. The funds are used to pay for her daughter's qualified higher education expenses. How much of the $10,000 distribution is taxable to the daughter?

b. During 2022, Henry (a single taxpayer) has a salary of $85,000 and interest income of $4,000. Henry has no other income or deductions. Calculate the maximum contribution Henry is allowed for an educational savings account.

Learning Objective 2.15

Describe the tax treatment of unemployment compensation.

2-15 UNEMPLOYMENT COMPENSATION

Unemployment compensation payments are generally fully taxable. Unemployment compensation is generally reported on a Form 1099-G.

EXAMPLE Genny was unemployed for several months during 2022 and received unemployment compensation of $4,000. The $4,000 is included in Genny's taxable income for 2022. ♦

Self-Study Problem 2.15 *See Appendix E for Solutions to Self-Study Problems*

Bear was unemployed during part of 2022 and received the following Form 1099-G:

☐ CORRECTED (if checked)

PAYER'S name, street address, city or town, state or province, country, ZIP or foreign postal code, and telephone no.		1 Unemployment compensation	OMB No. 1545-0120	
North Carolina Division of Employment Security PO Box 25900 Raleigh, NC 27611		$ 3,200.00	Form **1099-G** (Rev. January 2022) For calendar year 20 22	**Certain Government Payments**
		2 State or local income tax refunds, credits, or offsets $		
PAYER'S TIN 21-4321234	RECIPIENT'S TIN 239-03-0045	3 Box 2 amount is for tax year	**4 Federal income tax withheld** $ 230.00	**Copy B** **For Recipient**
RECIPIENT'S name Bear Shaw		5 RTAA payments $	6 Taxable grants $	This is important tax information and is being furnished to the IRS. If you are required to file a return, a negligence penalty or other sanction may be imposed on you if this income is taxable and the IRS determines that it has not been reported.
Street address (including apt. no.) 118 E. North Street		7 Agriculture payments $	8 If checked, box 2 is trade or business income ▶ ☐	
City or town, state or province, country, and ZIP or foreign postal code Raleigh, NC 27601		9 Market gain $		
Account number (see instructions)		10a State / 10b State identification no.	11 State income tax withheld $ $	

Form **1099-G** (Rev. 1-2022) (keep for your records) www.irs.gov/Form1099G Department of the Treasury - Internal Revenue Service

How much unemployment compensation is included in Bear's gross income?

2-16 SOCIAL SECURITY BENEFITS

2.16 Learning Objective

Apply the rules governing inclusion of Social Security benefits in gross income.

Some taxpayers may exclude all of their Social Security benefits from gross income. However, most middle-income and upper-income Social Security recipients may have to include up to 85 percent of their benefits in gross income. The formula to determine taxable Social Security income is based on *modified adjusted gross income* (MAGI). Generally, MAGI is the taxpayer's adjusted gross income (without Social Security benefits) plus any tax-free interest income. On rare occasions, taxpayers will also have to add back unusual items such as the foreign earned income exclusion, employer-provided adoption benefits, or interest on education loans. If MAGI plus 50 percent of Social Security benefits is less than the base amount shown below (base amounts are not adjusted for inflation), benefits are excluded from income.

Base Amounts	*Applies To*
$32,000	Married filing jointly
0	Married taxpayers who did not live apart for the entire year and still filed separate returns
25,000	All other taxpayers

The formula for calculating the taxable amount of Social Security is complex and time-consuming. Many taxpayers rely on tax-preparation software to perform the calculation. For preparation by hand, the Form 1040 Instructions include a full-page worksheet that takes taxpayers through the calculation one step at a time.

Originally, Social Security benefits were not taxed; however, starting in 1984, a portion of Social Security benefits became taxable using the now familiar $25,000 and $32,000 base amounts. At the time, the explanation used to support the change was that one-half of the tax was paid by employers and employees were not taxed on that benefit. The base amounts have not changed since 1984. Using the Consumer Price Index Inflation Calculator (**www.bls.gov/data/inflation_calculator.htm**), one would need more than $73,000 to equal the purchasing power of $25,000 in 1984. As a result, a much larger percentage of taxpayers are paying tax on their Social Security benefits.

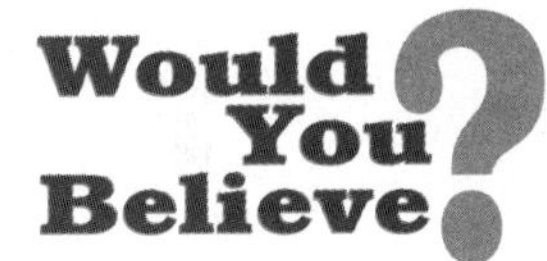

EXAMPLE For the 2022 tax year, Nancy, a single taxpayer, receives $7,000 in Social Security benefits. She has adjusted gross income of $20,000, not including any Social Security income, and receives $10,000 of tax-exempt municipal bond interest. Nancy must include $3,500 of her Social Security benefits in gross income as determined as follows:

SIMPLIFIED TAXABLE SOCIAL SECURITY WORKSHEET (FOR MOST PEOPLE)

1. Enter the total amount of Social Security income.	1. $ 7,000
2. Enter one-half of line 1.	2. 3,500
3. Enter the total of taxable income items on Form 1040 except Social Security income.	3. 20,000
4. Enter the amount of tax-exempt interest income.	4. 10,000
5. Add lines 2, 3, and 4.	5. 33,500
6. Enter all adjustments for AGI except for student loan interest deduction.	6. -0-
7. Subtract line 6 from line 5. If zero or less, stop here, none of the Social Security benefits are taxable.	7. 33,500

8. Enter $25,000 ($32,000 if married filing jointly; $0 if married filing separately and living with spouse at any time during the year).	8. 25,000
9. Subtract line 8 from line 7. If zero or less, enter –0–.	9. 8,500

Note: *If line 9 is zero or less, stop here;* ***none of your benefits are taxable.*** *Otherwise, go on to line 10.*

10. Enter $9,000 ($12,000 if married filing jointly; $0 if married filing separately and living with spouse at any time during the year).	10. 9,000
11. Subtract line 10 from line 9. If zero or less, enter –0–.	11. –0–
12. Enter the **smaller** of line 9 or line 10.	12. 8,500
13. Enter one-half of line 12.	13. 4,250
14. Enter the **smaller** of line 2 or line 13.	14. 3,500
15. Multiply line 11 by 85% (.85). If line 11 is zero, enter –0–.	15. –0–
16. Add lines 14 and 15.	16. 3,500
17. Multiply line 1 by 85% (.85).	17. 5,950
18. **Taxable benefits.** Enter the **smaller** of line 16 or line 17.	18. $ 3,500

♦

EXAMPLE Linda, a widow, is retired and receives Social Security benefits of $14,000 in 2022. She has MAGI of $47,000. Linda must include $11,900 of her Social Security benefits in gross income as determined as follows:

SIMPLIFIED TAXABLE SOCIAL SECURITY WORKSHEET (FOR MOST PEOPLE)

1. Enter the total amount of Social Security income.	1. $14,000
2. Enter one-half of line 1.	2. 7,000
3. Enter the total of taxable income items on Form 1040 except Social Security income.	3. 47,000
4. Enter the amount of tax-exempt interest income.	4. –0–
5. Add lines 2, 3, and 4.	5. 54,000
6. Enter all adjustments for AGI except for student loan interest deduction.	6. –0–
7. Subtract line 6 from line 5. If zero or less, stop here, none of the Social Security benefits are taxable.	7. 54,000
8. Enter $25,000 ($32,000 if married filing jointly; $0 if married filing separately and living with spouse at any time during the year).	8. 25,000
9. Subtract line 8 from line 7. If zero or less, enter –0–.	9. 29,000

Note: *If line 9 is zero or less, stop here;* ***none of your benefits are taxable.*** *Otherwise, go on to line 10.*

10. Enter $9,000 ($12,000 if married filing jointly; $0 if married filing separately and living with spouse at any time during the year).	10. 9,000

11. Subtract line 10 from line 9. If zero or less, enter -0-.	11. 20,000
12. Enter the **smaller** of line 9 or line 10.	12. 9,000
13. Enter one-half of line 12.	13. 4,500
14. Enter the **smaller** of line 2 or line 13.	14. 4,500
15. Multiply line 11 by 85% (.85). If line 11 is zero, enter -0-.	15. 17,000
16. Add lines 14 and 15.	16. 21,500
17. Multiply line 1 by 85% (.85).	17. 11,900
18. **Taxable benefits.** Enter the **smaller** of line 16 or line 17.	18. $11,900

♦

A summary of the tax treatment of Social Security benefits is presented in Table 2.4.

TABLE 2.4 SOCIAL SECURITY INCOME INCLUSION FORMULAS

Filing Status	MAGI + 50% SS	Amount of SS That Is Included in Taxable Income
Single, HOH, Surviving Spouse, MFS (Living apart)	Under $25,000	No SS benefits included in taxable income
	$25,000–$34,000	The lesser of: 50% of SS benefits, or 50% of (MAGI + 50%SS, over $25,000)
	Over $34,000	The lesser of: 85% of SS benefits, or (lesser of box above or $4,500) + 85% of (MAGI + 50%SS, over $34,000)
Married Filing Jointly	Under $32,000	No SS benefits included in taxable income
	$32,000–$44,000	The lesser of: 50% of SS benefits, or 50% of (MAGI + 50%SS, over $32,000)
	Over $44,000	The lesser of: 85% of SS benefits, or (lesser of box above or $6,000) + 85% of (MAGI + 50%SS, over $44,000)

Note: The Social Security income inclusion formulas in the table above are shown for information only. No problems in the textbook will require the use of these formulas.

ProConnect™ Tax TIP

Social Security benefits are entered under the same heading in Income as alimony discussed in LO 2.13.

Self-Study Problem 2.16

See Appendix E for Solutions to Self-Study Problems

For the 2022 tax year, Kim and Edward are married and file a joint return. They have Social Security benefits of $13,000 and their adjusted gross income is $20,000, not including any Social Security income. They also receive $30,000 in tax-free municipal bond interest. How much, if any, of the Social Security benefits should Kim and Edward include in gross income? Use the worksheet below to compute your answer.

Simplified Taxable Social Security Worksheet (for most people)

1. Enter the total amount of Social Security income.	1. $________
2. Enter one-half of line 1.	2. ________
3. Enter the total of taxable income items on Form 1040 except Social Security income.	3. ________
4. Enter the amount of tax-exempt interest income.	4. ________
5. Add lines 2, 3, and 4.	5. ________
6. Enter all adjustments for AGI except for student loan interest deduction.	6. ________
7. Subtract line 6 from line 5. If zero or less, stop here, none of the Social Security benefits are taxable.	7. ________
8. Enter $25,000 ($32,000 if married filing jointly; $0 if married filing separately and living with spouse at any time during the year).	8. ________
9. Subtract line 8 from line 7. If zero or less, enter –0–.	9. ________
Note: *If line 9 is zero or less, stop here;* ***none of your benefits are taxable.*** *Otherwise, go on to line 10.*	
10. Enter $9,000 ($12,000 if married filing jointly; $0 if married filing separately and living with spouse at any time during the year).	10. ________
11. Subtract line 10 from line 9. If zero or less, enter –0–.	11. ________
12. Enter the **smaller** of line 9 or line 10.	12. ________
13. Enter one-half of line 12.	13. ________
14. Enter the **smaller** of line 2 or line 13.	14. ________
15. Multiply line 11 by 85% (.85). If line 11 is zero, enter –0–.	15. ________
16. Add lines 14 and 15.	16. ________
17. Multiply line 1 by 85% (.85).	17. ________
18. **Taxable benefits.** Enter the **smaller** of line 16 or line 17.	18. $________

2-17 COMMUNITY PROPERTY

2.17 Learning Objective

Distinguish between the different rules for married taxpayers residing in community property states when filing separate returns.

When married couples file separate income tax returns, a special problem arises. Income derived from property held by a married couple, either jointly or separately, as well as wages and other income earned by a husband and wife, must be allocated between the spouses. State law becomes important in making this allocation.

The law in nine states is based on a community property system of marital law. In these states, the property rights of married couples differ from the property rights of married couples residing in the remaining common law states. The nine states that are community property states are:

Arizona	Louisiana	Texas
California	Nevada	Washington
Idaho	New Mexico	Wisconsin

Note: In Alaska, spouses may elect to treat income as community income.

Under the community property system, all property is deemed to be either separate property or community property. Separate property includes property acquired by a spouse before marriage or received after marriage as a gift or inheritance. All other property owned by a married couple is presumed to be community property. For federal income tax purposes, each spouse is automatically taxed on half of the income from community property.

The tax treatment of income from separate property depends on the taxpayer's state of residence. In Idaho, Louisiana, Texas, and Wisconsin, income from separate property produces community income. Thus, just as each spouse is taxed on half of the income from community property, each spouse is also taxed on half of the income from separate property. In the other five community property states, income on separate property is separate income and is reported in full on the tax return of the spouse who owns the property. Income such as nontaxable dividends or royalties from mineral interests assumes the classification of the asset from which the income is derived. Capital gains also retain their classification based on the classification of the property from which the gain arises.

EXAMPLE John and Marsha are married and live in Texas. John owns, as his separate property, stock in AT&T Corporation. During the year, John receives dividends of $4,000. Assuming John and Marsha file separate returns, each of them must report $2,000 of the dividends. On the other hand, if John and Marsha lived in California, John would report the entire $4,000 of the dividends on his tax return and Marsha would not include any of the dividend income on her tax return. ♦

In all of the community property states, income from salary and wages is generally treated as having been earned one-half by each spouse.

EXAMPLE Robert and Linda are married but file separate tax returns. Robert receives a salary of $30,000 and has interest income of $500 from a savings account which is in his name. The savings account was established with salary earned by Robert since his marriage. Linda collects $20,000 in dividends on stock she inherited from her father. The amount of income which Linda must report on her separate income tax return depends on the state in which Robert and Linda reside. Three different assumptions are presented below:

State of Residence

Linda's Income:	*Texas*	*California*	*Common Law States*
Salary	$15,000	$15,000	$ 0
Dividends	10,000	20,000	20,000
Interest	250	250	0
Total	$25,250	$35,250	$20,000

♦

2-17a Spouses Living Apart

To simplify problems that could arise when married spouses residing in a community property state do not live together, the tax law contains an exception to the above community property rules. Under this special provision, a spouse will be taxed only on his or her actual earnings from personal services. For this provision to apply, the following conditions must be satisfied:

1. The individuals must live apart for the entire year,
2. They must not file a joint return, and
3. No portion of the earned income may be transferred between the spouses.

EXAMPLE Bill and Betty, both residents of Nevada, are married but live apart for the entire year. Bill has a salary of $30,000 and Betty has a salary of $35,000. Normally, Bill and Betty would each report $32,500. However, if the required conditions are met, Bill and Betty would each report their own salary. If Bill and Betty had any unearned income, such as dividends or interest, the income would be reported under the general community property rules. The special provision applies only to earned income of the spouses. ♦

Another provision addresses the problem of spouses who fail to qualify for the above special exception because they do not live apart for the entire year. In certain cases, a spouse who fails to include in income his or her share of community income, as required by the community property laws, may be relieved of any liability related to this income. To be granted relief, the taxpayer must not know of or have reason to know of the omitted community property income.

Self-Study Problem 2.17

See Appendix E for Solutions to Self-Study Problems

Tom and Rachel are married and living together in California. Their income is as follows:

Tom's salary	$40,000
Rachel's salary	30,000
Dividends (Tom's property)	5,000
Dividends (Rachel's property)	3,000
Interest (community property)	4,000
Total	$82,000

a. If Rachel files a separate tax return, what should Rachel report as income?

b. If Tom and Rachel lived in Texas, what should Rachel report as income?

2-18 FORGIVENESS OF DEBT INCOME

2.18 Learning Objective

Describe the inclusion and exclusion of cancellation of debt income.

The cancellation of debt represents an economic benefit to the taxpayer that receives the debt relief. Unsurprisingly, the broad definition of gross income generally treats the amount forgiven as income to the taxpayer. This can also be referred to as forgiveness of debt income or discharge of indebtedness income.

EXAMPLE Howard borrowed funds from Usury National Bank so he could start a small business. Unfortunately, Howard's business failed and he was unable to pay back the entire loan balance. Howard and the bank agreed to settle Howard's $50,000 outstanding debt for only $40,000. Howard has $10,000 of cancellation of debt income. ♦

There are a number of provisions provided to exclude forgiveness of debt from gross income including:

- The taxpayer is bankrupt or insolvent at the time the debt is cancelled or reduced
- The debt is qualified real property business debt
- The debt is qualified principal residence debt
- The debt is certain types of student loan debt that is forgiven under certain conditions

If a taxpayer's debt has been discharged in a bankruptcy, the tax law recognizes that requiring a bankrupt individual to pay taxes on debt that was required to be forgiven because the taxpayer lacks the ability to repay the debt would not make economic sense. As a result, this cancellation of debt income is generally excluded from gross income.

EXAMPLE Sharon borrowed funds from Usury National Bank so she could start a small business. Unfortunately, Sharon's business failed and her entire debt was discharged in a bankruptcy proceeding. Sharon may exclude the debt discharged. ♦

Often times debt is associated with the acquisition of real property, for example, land, a building used in business, or a house; and that property serves as collateral on the debt. If that property is qualified business property or the taxpayer's principal residence, an exclusion of the cancellation of debt income may apply. In the case of business property, the debt generally must have been incurred with respect to the acquisition, construction, or a substantial improvement to real property used in a trade or business.

EXAMPLE Heidi's small business purchased a warehouse to store inventory. The acquisition was funded by a loan from a local bank. The loan is secured by the building. Heidi found herself unable to make the loan payments and the bank agreed to cancel $15,000 of the loan. Heidi will be able to exclude the cancellation of debt income under the qualified real property business debt provisions. ♦

Similarly, debt incurred by a taxpayer to purchase, build, or substantially improve the taxpayer's principal residence is afforded similar treatment when forgiven. To qualify, the debt must be secured by the principal residence. The provision to exclude qualified principal residence debt forgiven currently is scheduled to expire at the end of 2025.

EXAMPLE Tyra acquired a new principal residence for $250,000 using a $200,000 mortgage that was secured by the home. In 2022, when the balance of the loan was $190,000, Tyra lost her job and was struggling to continue to make mortgage payments. The bank agreed to lower Tyra's loan principal to $160,000. Tyra may exclude the $30,000 of cancellation of debt income. ♦

When cancellation of debt income is excluded under the qualified business property and principal resident provisions, the basis in the underlying property is adjusted to reflect that exclusion amount.

EXAMPLE Muffy purchased her principle residence for $160,000 in 2012. In 2022, Muffy was required to renegotiate the mortgage on her principle residence. Although Muffy was solvent at the time, she was unable to make mortgage payments due to losing her job. The mortgage balance was $100,000 and she was able to reduce the balance to $75,000, which in turn reduced her monthly mortgage payments. The $25,000 cancellation of mortgage debt will be excluded from Muffy's gross income. Accordingly, Muffy will need to reduce her basis in the home to $135,000 ($160,000 − $25,000 debt forgiven). ♦

The amount of excludable income under the qualified principal residence exception is limited to $750,000 ($375,000 for married taxpayers filing separately).

Because taxpayers that exclude cancellation of debt income under any of these provisions are often bankrupt, insolvent, or both, the tax rules require that the cancellation be attributed first to bankruptcy, if that applies and next to insolvency, if that applies.

In order to encourage students to pursue careers in certain occupations or locations that have unmet needs, the cancellation of certain student loans is also excluded from income. The student loan generally must be issued by a university or government agency.

EXAMPLE Yousef attended Grays Medical University to become a pediatrician. Due to the cost of medical education, Yousef incurred substantial student loan debt. When Yousef graduated, he entered Grays Native American Loan Repayment Program. This program will refinance Yousef's existing student loans and then cancel Yousef's debt if he agrees to serve as a pediatrician for 5 years at a Native American reservation hospital. ♦

More broadly, student loans discharged before 2026 for any reason are also excluded from income.

The rules related to the exclusion of cancellation of debt can be complex and this section provides only a basic overview. Taxpayers report exclusions from bankruptcy, insolvency, and qualified business or principal residence property on Form 982.

Self-Study Problem 2.18

See Appendix E for Solutions to Self-Study Problems

In 2022, Stuart loses his job when his employer closes. Because Stuart is struggling to pay his monthly expenses, he arranges a decrease in his mortgage from $160,000 to $120,000 with his mortgage lender. His basis in the home is $200,000 and the fair market value at the time of the mortgage reduction is $250,000. Stuart also has $10,000 of student loan debt forgiven in 2022 under a federal program to forgive students loans for lower-income individuals.

a. What amount of the cancellation of debt must Stuart include in his income in 2022?
b. What is Stuart's basis in his home after applying exclusion provisions (if any)?

KEY TERMS

gross income, 2-2
barter, 2-2
exclusions, 2-2
inclusions – gross income, 2-3
exclusions – gross income, 2-3
Form W-2, 2-4
employee, 2-6
independent contractor, 2-6
employee fringe benefits, 2-12
flexible spending accounts, 2-12
health care flexible spending accounts, 2-12
dependent care flexible spending accounts, 2-12
qualified transportation benefits, 2-13

de minimis transportation benefits, 2-13
dependent care assistance programs, 2-14
group term life insurance, 2-14
education assistance plans, 2-15
tuition reduction, 2-15
no-additional-cost services, 2-15
qualified employee discounts, 2-15
working condition fringe benefits, 2-16
de minimis fringe benefits, 2-16
athletic facilities, 2-17
retirement planning fringe benefit, 2-17
tangible personal property, 2-19
qualified plan award, 2-19
annuities, 2-20
the simplified method, 2-21
exclusion ratio, 2-22
the general rule, 2-22
accelerated death benefits, 2-24
viatical settlements, 2-24
interest income, 2-25
municipal bond interest, 2-25
Schedule B, 2-25
U.S. savings bonds, 2-25
U.S. Treasury Bills, 2-26
corporate bonds, 2-27
zero coupon bonds, 2-27
original issue discount (OID), 2-27
state and local bonds (municipals), 2-27
market discount and premium, 2-28
gift loans, 2-29
Form 1099-INT, 2-29
ordinary and qualified dividends, 2-33
nontaxable distributions, 2-33
capital gain distributions 2-33
Form 1099-DIV, 2-35
gift, 2-37
inheritance, 2-37
scholarship, 2-38
alimony, 2-38
property transfers, 2-39
child support, 2-39
qualified tuition programs (Section 529 tuition plan), 2-41
educational savings account (Coverdell Education Savings Accounts), 2-42
modified adjusted gross income (MAGI), 2-45
community property, 2-49
separate property, 2-49
cancellation of debt income, 2-51
qualified real property business debt, 2-51
qualified principal residence debt, 2-51

KEY POINTS

Learning Objectives	Key Points
LO 2.1: Apply the definition of gross income.	• Gross income means "all income from whatever source derived." • Gross income includes everything a taxpayer receives unless it is specifically excluded from gross income by the tax law.
LO 2.2: Describe salaries and wages income reporting and inclusion in gross income.	• The primary form of reporting wages to an employee is through Form W-2. • Employers should report the employee's taxable wages, salary, bonuses, awards, commissions, and almost every other type of taxable compensation in Box 1 of the Form W-2. • If a taxpayer receives more than one Form W-2 or is jointly filing with a spouse having their own Form W-2, the amounts in Box 1 are combined before entering the total on Line 1 of the Form 1040. • Other Form W-2 information such as federal and state income taxes paid will also be reported by the taxpayer on the Form 1040. • The classification of employees and independent contractors is a function of law and each is subject to income and employment taxes differently. • The classification of a worker as an employee or independent contractor depends on the degree of control and independence between the individual and the business.
LO 2.3: Explain the general tax treatment of health insurance.	• Taxpayers may exclude health insurance premiums paid by their employer. • Taxpayers are allowed an exclusion for payments received from accident and health plans. The taxpayer may exclude the total amount received for payment of medical care, including any amount paid for the medical care of the taxpayer, his or her spouse, or dependents.
LO 2.4: Determine when meals and lodging may be excluded from taxable income.	• Meals and lodging are excluded from gross income provided they are for the convenience of the employer and they are furnished on the business premises. Lodging must be a condition of employment to be excluded.

LO 2.5: Identify the common employee fringe benefit income exclusions.	• Certain fringe benefits provided to employees may be excluded from the employees' gross income. These include dependent care and health care flexible spending accounts, transportation (commuter) benefits, dependent care assistance programs, group term life insurance (up to $50,000), education assistance plans, and others.
LO 2.6: Determine when prizes and awards are included in income.	• Amounts received from prizes and awards are normally taxable income unless refused by the taxpayer. • Certain small prizes of tangible personal property (generally under $400) for length of service and safety achievement are excluded from gross income. If the award is a "qualified plan award," up to $1,600 of the value of the award may be excluded.
LO 2.7: Calculate the taxable and nontaxable portions of annuity payments.	• Under both the simplified method and the general method, annuity payments received by a taxpayer may have an element of taxable income and an element of tax-free return of the original purchase price. • Individual taxpayers generally must use the "simplified" method to calculate the taxable amount from a qualified annuity starting after November 18, 1996. • The part of the payment that is excluded from income is the ratio of the investment in the contract to the total expected return. • The total expected return is the annual payment multiplied by the life expectancy of the annuitant, based on mortality tables provided by the IRS.
LO 2.8: Describe the tax treatment of life insurance proceeds.	• Life insurance proceeds are generally excluded from gross income. If the proceeds are taken over several years instead of in a lump sum, any interest on the unpaid proceeds is generally taxable income. • Early payouts of life insurance are excluded from gross income for certain terminally or chronically ill taxpayers. • All or a portion of the proceeds from a life insurance policy transferred to another person for valuable consideration may be taxable to the recipient.
LO 2.9: Identify the tax treatment of interest income.	• Interest income is taxable except for certain state and municipal bond interest. • Interest income exceeding $1,500 per year must be reported in detail on Schedule B of Form 1040. • Series EE and Series I Savings Bond interest is taxable in the year the bonds are cashed unless a taxpayer elects to report the interest each year as it accrues. • Under certain circumstances, interest income from EE and I Savings Bonds can be excluded if used for higher education expenses. • Interest must be adjusted for purchases and sales between interest payments, and at times, for market discount and premium. • Interest from an obligation of a state, territory, or possession of the United States, or of a political subdivision of the foregoing, or of the District of Columbia, is excluded from gross income.
LO 2.10: Identify the tax treatment of dividend income.	• Ordinary dividends are also qualifying dividends if the stock is held for a certain length of time (usually 60 days) and is issued by a U.S. corporation. • If ordinary dividends are not qualifying dividends, they are taxed as ordinary income, which is generally a higher rate than the long-term capital gains rate. • Qualified dividends are taxed at rates ranging from 0 percent to 20 percent and possibly included in the 3.8 percent net investment income tax for high-income taxpayers. • Like interest income, ordinary dividend income exceeding $1,500 per year must be reported in detail on Schedule B of Form 1040. Ordinary dividends $1,500 or less and qualified dividends of any amount are reported on Lines 3a and 3b of Form 1040.
LO 2.11: Identify the general rules for the tax treatment of gifts and inheritances.	• The receipt of gifts and inheritances is usually excludable from gross income. Income received from the property after the transfer may be taxable to the recipient.

LO 2.12: Describe the elements of scholarship income that are excluded from tax.	• Scholarships granted to degree candidates are excluded from gross income if spent for tuition, fees, books, and course-required supplies and equipment. Amounts received for items such as room and board are taxable to the recipient.
LO 2.13: Describe the tax treatment of alimony and child support.	• Alimony paid in cash is taxable to the person who receives it and is deductible to the person who pays it, for divorce agreements dated prior to January 1, 2019. • Alimony is neither included in nor deducted from taxable income beginning with divorce or separation agreements after December 31, 2018. • Child support is not alimony and is not taxable when received, nor deductible when paid. • A spouse who transfers property in settlement of a marital obligation is not required to recognize any gain as a result of the property's appreciation. The receiving spouse assumes the tax basis of the property.
LO 2.14: Explain the tax implications of using educational savings vehicles.	• A Qualified Tuition Program (Section 529 plan) allows taxpayers (1) to buy in-kind tuition credits or certificates for qualified higher education expenses (a prepaid tuition plan) or (2) to contribute to an account established to meet qualified higher education expenses (a savings-type plan). Distributions from the account are not taxable if the proceeds are used for qualified higher education expenses. • Qualified higher education expenses include tuition, fees, books, supplies, and equipment required for the enrollment or attendance at an eligible educational institution. In addition, taxpayers are allowed reasonable room and board costs, subject to certain limitations. • The maximum exclusion for elementary or secondary education (K-12) for tuition only, is $10,000 per beneficiary per year. • Distributions from a Section 529 plan may be used for student loan payments up to a lifetime limit of $10,000 per beneficiary or beneficiary's siblings. • Taxpayers can annually contribute $2,000 to an educational savings account (Coverdell) for a beneficiary, subject to income and other limitations.
LO 2.15: Describe the tax treatment of unemployment compensation.	• Unemployment compensation is taxable.
LO 2.16: Apply the rules governing inclusion of Social Security benefits in gross income.	• Taxpayers with income under $25,000 ($32,000 for Married Filing Jointly) exclude all of their Social Security benefits from gross income. • Middle-income and upper-income Social Security recipients, however, may have to include up to 85 percent of their benefits in gross income. • Calculating the taxable amount of Social Security is complex and most easily performed using a worksheet, such as the one provided in this chapter, or by using a tax program such as ProConnect Tax.
LO 2.17: Distinguish between the different rules for married taxpayers residing in community property states when filing separate returns.	• Income derived from community property held by a married couple, either jointly or separately, as well as wages and other income earned by a married couple, must be allocated between the spouses, if filing separately. • Nine states use a community property system of marital law. These states are Arizona, California, Idaho, Louisiana, Nevada, New Mexico, Texas, Washington, and Wisconsin. In Alaska, spouses may elect to treat income as community property. • In general, in a community property state, income is split one-half (50 percent) to each spouse. There are exceptions for certain separate property (e.g., property owned prior to marriage, inherited property, etc.).
LO 2.18: Describe the inclusion and exclusion of cancellation of debt income.	• Generally, cancellation of debt results in taxable income. • Income from the cancellation of debt due to bankruptcy, insolvency, associated with qualified real business property or a qualified primary residence, and certain student loan debt can be excluded from gross income.

QUESTIONS and PROBLEMS

GROUP 1: MULTIPLE CHOICE QUESTIONS

LO 2.1

1. The definition of gross income in the tax law is:
   a. All items specifically listed as income in the tax law
   b. All cash payments received for goods provided and services performed
   c. All income from whatever source derived
   d. All income from whatever source derived unless the income is earned illegally

LO 2.1

2. Which of the following is excluded from gross income for income tax purposes in 2022?
   a. Commissions
   b. Severance pay
   c. Qualified dividends
   d. Unemployment compensation
   e. Life insurance proceeds

LO 2.1

3. In 2022, all of the following items are gross income to the taxpayer receiving them, *except*:
   a. Damages for personal injury
   b. Hobby income
   c. Embezzled funds
   d. Gains from illegal activities
   e. Gambling winnings

LO 2.1

4. In 2022, which of the following types of income is excluded from gross income?
   a. Unemployment compensation
   b. Income earned illegally
   c. Dividends from foreign corporations
   d. Corporate bond interest income
   e. Scholarship used for tuition

LO 2.1

5. Which of the following is included in gross income?
   a. Loans
   b. Scholarships for room and board
   c. Gifts
   d. Health insurance proceeds
   e. Child support payments received

LO 2.2

6. Annual wages subject to income tax are reported:
   a. On Form W-4
   b. On Form W-2 in Box 1
   c. On Form W-2 in Boxes 1, 3, and 5
   d. On Form 1099-W in Box 1

LO 2.2

7. The classification of a worker as an employee or an independent contractor is:
   a. Made by the employer
   b. Made by the employee
   c. Based on a negotiation between the employer and employee
   d. Based on a set of common law factors related to control and independence

LO 2.2

8. Which of the following is likely to indicate classification of a worker as an employee:
   a. The worker must provide their own tools and equipment.
   b. The worker can provide services at a location they choose.
   c. The worker receives benefits like health care.
   d. The worker makes their services available to the general public.

LO 2.2

9. State income tax withholding is reported on:
   a. Form W-2S
   b. Form W-4
   c. Each state has a unique reporting form
   d. Form W-2 on Box 17

LO 2.3

10. In 2022, Jonah's employer pays $8,700 for health insurance premiums for Jonah, Jonah's spouse, and Jonah's three dependent children. Jonah has $100 per month withheld from his pay toward the cost as well. Jonah's employer covers the entire cost ($1,400 for the year) of Jonah's dental plan for his household. How much gross income will Jonah report from his employer's payments for his health and dental plan premiums?
    a. $0
    b. $1,400
    c. $8,900
    d. $10,100

LO 2.3

11. Taylor's 2022 health insurance premiums of $7,800 are paid by her employer. During 2022, Taylor requires surgery on her vocal chords. The cost of the surgery is $10,000 and Taylor's insurance covers all but $500, which Taylor pays herself. How much is Taylor's gross income from these health-related transactions?
    a. $0
    b. $7,800
    c. $9,500
    d. $10,000
    e. $17,800

LO 2.4

12. George works at the Springfield Nuclear Plant as a nuclear technician. The plant is located 15 miles from the town of Springfield. George likes to eat his lunch at the plant's cafeteria because he is required to be available for nuclear emergencies during his shift. No other eating establishments are located near the plant. George estimates the value of the meals he was provided during the current year as $1,300. He estimates the cost for him to have prepared those lunches for himself as about $560. The cost of the meals to the power company was $470. How much income does George need to recognize from the meals?
    a. $1,300
    b. $560
    c. $470
    d. $830 ($1,300 − $470)
    e. None of the above

LO 2.4

13. In which of the following situations is the value of employer-provided meals included in gross income?
    a. An employee that is not required to eat at the company cafeteria but often does. The majority of other employees at this location are required to eat in the cafeteria for business reasons.
    b. An employee of a quick-service restaurant that eats a meal at the end of his work shift each day.
    c. An employee that eats two to three doughnuts on Doughnut Day (the third Friday of each month) while most employees eat one or none.
    d. An employee who occasionally receives a free meal when working overtime
    e. None of these meals are included in gross income.

LO 2.5

14. Which of the following is a fringe benefit excluded from income?
    a. A mechanic at Denise's employer, a car rental company, provides $1,000 of repair services to Denise's personal car for free
    b. Alfa-Bet, a high-tech corporation, pays for each employee's membership at the 24 Hour Biceps Gym closest to each Alfa-Bet office
    c. Quickchat Inc. gives each employee a $10 giftcard to the local coffee shop on National Coffee Day
    d. Hedaya, a doctoral student at Ivy University, receives a full tuition waiver while serving as research assistant

LO 2.5

15. Which of the following will result in the recognition of gross income?
    a. Gail's employer allows her to set aside $4,000 from her wages to cover the cost of daycare for Gail's 4-year-old daughter. Gail's daycare costs are $4,300 for the year.
    b. Hannah purchases a new sofa from her employer, Sofas-R-Us, for $1,200. The cost of the sofa to the furniture store is $1,100 and the sofa normally sells for $1,700.
    c. Jayden's employer purchases her commuting pass for the subway at a cost of $325 per month.
    d. Havana is a lawyer. The law firm she works for pays for her subscription to Lawyer's Weekly, a trade magazine for attorneys.
    e. None of the above will result in recognition of gross income.

LO 2.5

16. In 2022, the limit for contributions to a health care flexible spending account is:
    a. $500
    b. $1,200
    c. $2,850
    d. $5,000

LO 2.5

17. Veruca's employer offers both a dependent care flexible spending account (FSA) and a dependent care assistance program in which employees can receive occasional dependent care at no cost. In 2022, the maximum total amount Veruca can exclude from her gross income for both dependent care programs is:
    a. $0
    b. $2,850
    c. $5,000
    d. $10,000

LO 2.5

18. Which of the following transportation-related costs paid by an employer to or on behalf of an employee cannot be excluded from gross income?
    a. Providing bus passes to employees for a $20 discount.
    b. Paying for the parking of only senior executives at a cost of $250 per month.
    c. Paying the occasional ride-sharing fare for an employee that has worked overtime late into the evening.
    d. Paying $10 per month for bicycle storage for employees that bike to work.

LO 2.5

19. Air Suppliers Inc. provides group term insurance to all its employees for policies up to $250,000. Michelle, an Air Suppliers employee, has a $100,000 policy. The cost of the policy is $50 per month, all of which is paid by Air Suppliers. Which of the following best describes how much gross income Michelle will recognize for this employee benefit?
    a. Michelle will recognize no gross income.
    b. Michelle will recognize gross income for the value of the life insurance above $50,000.
    c. Michelle must recognize the annual cost of the policy ($600) as gross income.
    d. Michelle will recognize no gross income but if she dies, the beneficiary will pay taxes on the life insurance benefits paid.

LO 2.5

20. Which of the following fringe benefits can be offered to only executives and remain excluded from employee gross income?
   a. Parking
   b. Group term life insurance up to $50,000
   c. De minimis cafeteria provided meals
   d. Employee discounts

LO 2.6

21. Which of the following prizes or awards is *not* taxable?
   a. A crystal paperweight worth $125 given to an employee for achieving 10 years of service to the company
   b. Prizes from a television game show
   c. Awards for superior performance on the job
   d. A $100 gift card received as a prize in a raffle run by the local school parent-teacher organization
   e. All of the above are taxable

LO 2.6

22. Huihana receives four tickets to the local professional football game for achieving twenty years of employment with her employer. The tickets cost the employer $390 and have a market value of the same on the date awarded. Huihana is in the highest tax bracket for single taxpayers. How much gross income will Huihana recognize on the receipt of the tickets?
   a. $390
   b. $200
   c. $25
   d. $0
   e. $50 or $59.50 including the net investment income tax

LO 2.7

23. A 67-year-old taxpayer retires this year and receives the first payment on a qualified annuity that was purchased several years ago. The taxpayer's investment in the annuity is $94,500, and the annuity pays $1,000 per month for the remainder of the taxpayer's life. Based on IRS mortality tables, the taxpayer is expected to live another twenty years. If the taxpayer receives $4,000 in annuity payments in the current year, the nontaxable portion calculated using the simplified method is:
   a. $0
   b. $1,500
   c. $1,800
   d. $4,000
   e. None of the above

LO 2.7

24. Amara has an annuity and over time has recovered her entire investment but it continues to pay her $450 per month. Amara should recognize how much of each monthly payment as gross income?
   a. $0
   b. Some amount greater than $450
   c. Some amount between $0 and $450
   d. $450

LO 2.8

25. Which of the following might result in life insurance proceeds that are taxable to the recipient?
   a. A life insurance policy in which the insured is the son of the taxpayer and the beneficiary is the taxpayer
   b. A life insurance policy transferred by a partner to the partnership
   c. A life insurance policy transferred to a creditor in payment of a debt
   d. A life insurance policy purchased by a taxpayer insuring his or her spouse
   e. A life insurance policy purchased by a corporation insuring an officer

LO 2.8

26. Lupita dies in 2022 but has a $1 million life insurance policy that lists her spouse, M'Baku as the beneficiary. M'Baku elects to receive all $1 million in a lump sum and spends $200,000 immediately on a new yacht. M'Baku's gross income from the life insurance is:
    a. $0
    b. $200,000
    c. $800,000
    d. $1,000,000

LO 2.9

27. Rebecca, a single taxpayer, owns a Series I U.S. Savings Bond that increased in value by $46 during the year. She makes no special election. How much income must Rebecca recognize this year?
    a. $0
    b. $46
    c. $23
    d. $0 if in first 5 years or $46 thereafter

LO 2.9

28. Interest from which of the following types of bonds is included in federal taxable income?
    a. State of California bond
    b. City of New Orleans bond
    c. Bond of the Commonwealth of Puerto Rico
    d. U.S. Treasury Bond
    e. All of the above are excluded from income

LO 2.9

29. Which of the following best describes the treatment of U.S. obligation interest income?
    a. Excluded from federal and state gross income
    b. Excluded from federal gross income but included for most states
    c. Included in federal gross income but excluded for most states
    d. Included in gross income for federal and state purposes

LO 2.9

30. In 2022, Yui, a single mother, redeems Series EE bonds and uses the total proceeds ($6,700 par value and $1,300 interest) to pay for her daughter's college education. If Yui's 2022 AGI is $75,000, how much of the proceeds from the redemption of the EE bonds can she exclude?
    a. $0
    b. $1,300
    c. $6,700
    d. $8,000

LO 2.9

31. On September 22, 2022, Jerry purchases a corporate bond. The bond pays interest each sixth months on June 30 and December 31 of each year. On December 31, 2022, Jerry receives an interest payment of $400. The amount of interest Jerry will need to include in gross income is:
    a. None
    b. Exactly $400
    c. More than $400
    d. Less than $400

LO 2.9

32. A bond is issued in 2020 at its face value of $10,000 with an interest rate of 5 percent. In 2022, the bond is sold when prevailing interest rates have increased. When recognizing gross income from the interest on the bond, the buyer of the bond in 2022 will have to consider:
    a. market bond discount
    b. original issue discount
    c. market bond premium
    d. in-kind dividends

LO 2.9

33. Helen loans her son Ricky, $25,000 to help with the purchase of a car and other personal expenses. Due to her affection for her son, Helen charges Ricky zero interest. Which of these statements best describes the result of this below-market loan?
   a. Ricky will have interest income.
   b. Helen will have interest income and an offsetting gift to Ricky.
   c. Helen will have interest expense since she is out the interest she could have earned.
   d. Ricky will have interest income since he is better off by not having to pay interest.

LO 2.10

34. Nomi is in the highest individual tax bracket and receives $375 in qualified dividends from Omega Corp. Nomi's tax liability (not including any net investment income tax) with respect to these dividends is:
   a. $0
   b. $277.20
   c. $100.00
   d. $75.00
   e. $50.00

LO 2.10

35. The distinction between qualified dividends and ordinary dividends is:
   a. There is no distinction.
   b. Ordinary dividends are taxed at preferential rates.
   c. Qualified dividends are taxed at preferential rates and are a subset of ordinary dividends.
   d. Qualified dividends are excluded from gross income.

LO 2.11

36. Which of the following gifts would probably be taxable to the person receiving the gift?
   a. One thousand dollars given to a taxpayer by his or her father
   b. An acre of land given to a taxpayer by a friend
   c. A car given to a loyal employee by her supervisor when she retired to recognize her faithful service
   d. A Mercedes-Benz given to a taxpayer by his cousin
   e. An interest in a partnership given to a taxpayer by his or her uncle

LO 2.12

37. Kelly receives a $40,000 scholarship to Ivy University. She uses $35,000 on tuition and books and $5,000 for rent while at school. How much gross income will Kelly recognize, if any?
   a. $0
   b. $5,000
   c. $10,000
   d. $30,000
   e. $40,000

LO 2.13

38. Hillary gets divorced in 2020 and is required to pay her ex-spouse $200 per month until her son reaches 18 years of age in seven years and $120 per month thereafter. How much of her 2021 payments are deductible as alimony?
   a. $0
   b. $2,400
   c. $1,440
   d. $960

LO 2.13

39. Donald and Michelle are divorced in the current year. As part of the divorce settlement, Michelle transfers a plot of land in Long Island, NY to Donald. Michelle's basis in the property was $20,000 and the market value of the property was $250,000 when transferred. Donald holds the property through the end of the year in hopes of building a residence on it. How much income do Michelle and Donald recognize in the current year?
   a. $0 for Michelle and $20,000 for Donald
   b. $230,000 for Michelle and $20,000 for Donald
   c. $230,000 for Michelle and $0 for Donald
   d. $0 for both Michelle and Donald
   e. $0 for Michelle and $250,000 for Donald

LO 2.14

40. Gina receives a $2,900 distribution from her educational savings account. She uses $1,500 to pay for qualified higher education expenses and $1,400 on a vacation. Immediately prior to the distribution, Gina's account balance is $5,000, $3,000 of which is her contributions. What is Gina's taxable income (after any exclusion) from the distribution?
    a. $1,400
    b. $560
    c. $840
    d. $0
    e. Some other amount

LO 2.14

41. Which of the following is correct for Qualified Tuition Programs (Section 529 plans)?
    a. Contributions are deductible, and qualified educational expense distributions are tax-free.
    b. Contributions are not deductible, and qualified educational expense distributions are tax-free.
    c. Contributions are deductible, and qualified educational expense distributions are taxable.
    d. Contributions are not deductible, and qualified educational expense distributions are taxable.

LO 2.14

42. In 2022, Amy receives $8,000 (of which $3,000 is earnings) from a qualified tuition program. She uses the funds to pay for tuition and other qualified higher education expenses. What amount is taxable to Amy?
    a. $0
    b. $8,000
    c. $3,000
    d. $11,000

LO 2.14

43. For married taxpayers filing a joint return in 2022, at what AGI level does the phase-out limit for contributions to Section 529 plans start?
    a. $110,000
    b. $190,000
    c. $220,000
    d. There is no phase-out limit on Section 529 plan contributions

LO 2.14

44. Which of the following is true with respect to education incentives?
    a. The contributions to qualified tuition programs (Section 529 plans) are deductible.
    b. The contributions to educational savings accounts (Coverdell ESA) are deductible.
    c. Tuition paid by a taxpayer earning $300,000 of income is deductible.
    d. Married taxpayers have no income limit to contribute to a qualified tuition program (Section 529 plan).

LO 2.14

45. During 2022, Carl (a single taxpayer) has a salary of $91,500 and interest income of $11,000. Calculate the maximum contribution Carl is allowed for an educational savings account (Coverdell).
    a. $0
    b. $400
    c. $1,000
    d. $2,000
    e. Some other amount

LO 2.15

46. Alicia loses her job part way through 2022. Her employer pays her wages of $15,450 up through her date of termination. After that, she received $1,600 of unemployment compensation from the state until she gets a new job for which she is paid wages of $1,400 through year-end. Based on this information, Alicia's gross income for 2022 is:
    a. $15,450
    b. $16,850

c. $17,050
d. $18,450
e. $21,850

LO 2.16

47. For 2021, the maximum percentage of Social Security benefits that could be included in a taxpayer's gross income is:
a. 0%
b. 25%
c. 50%
d. 75%
e. 85%

LO 2.16

48. Generally, when calculating the taxable portion of Social Security benefits, modified adjusted gross income (MAGI) is adjusted gross income (without Social Security benefits):
a. Plus tax-exempt interest
b. Less personal and dependency exemptions
c. Less itemized deductions
d. Less tax-exempt interest plus any foreign income exclusion
e. Less tax-exempt interest income

LO 2.17

49. Dana and Larry are married and live in Texas. Dana earns a salary of $45,000 and Larry has $25,000 of rental income from his separate property. If Dana and Larry file separate tax returns, what amount of income must Larry report?
a. $0
b. $22,500
c. $25,000
d. $47,500
e. None of the above

LO 2.17

50. Which of the following conditions need *not* be satisfied in order for a married taxpayer, residing in a community property state, to be taxed only on his or her separate salary?
a. The husband and wife must live apart for the entire year.
b. A minor child must be living with the spouse.
c. The husband and wife must not file a joint income tax return.
d. The husband and wife must not transfer earned income between themselves.
e. All of the above must be satisfied.

LO 2.18

51. Jack borrows $13,000 from Sawyer Savings and Loan and uses the proceeds to acquire a used car. When the loan balance is $12,000, Jack loses his job and is unable to make payments for three months. When Jack gets a new job, the bank agrees to forgive the missed principal payments and reduces his loan to $11,500. Jack remains solvent even when unemployed. How much cancellation of debt income does Jack have?
a. $0
b. $500
c. $1,500
d. $2,000

LO 2.18

52. Kate acquires a principal residence in 2017 for $200,000 secured by a $180,000 mortgage. In 2022, Kate misses work for three months. Her employer stops paying her after ten days. In 2022 when the mortgage balance is $170,000, Kate and the bank revise her terms and lower the loan balance to $150,000. The market value of the home remains above $200,000. How much cancellation of debt income will Kate recognize?
a. $0
b. $20,000
c. $10,000
d. $150,000
e. $170,000

LO 2.18

53. Mike, a single taxpayer, has $10,000 of student loans forgiven in 2022 under a federal student loan forgiveness program. His total student loan balance was $34,000. His 2022 AGI is $55,000. How much cancellation of debt income will Mike need to recognize in 2022?
    a. $0
    b. $10,000
    c. $5,000
    d. $24,000

GROUP 2: PROBLEMS

LO 2.1

1. Indicate whether each of the items listed below would be included in or excluded from gross income for the 2022 tax year.
    a. Welfare payments
    b. Commissions
    c. Hobby income
    d. Scholarships for room and board
    e. $300 set of golf clubs, an employee award for length of service
    f. Severance pay
    g. Ordinary dividend of $50
    h. Accident insurance proceeds received for personal bodily injury
    i. Inheritances
    j. Gifts
    k. Tips and gratuities

LO 2.1

2. Jane is a roofing contractor. Jane's friend needed a new roof but did not have the cash to pay. Jane's friend instead paid with a used truck that Jane could use in her roofing business. The truck had originally cost the friend $17,500 but it was gently used and only worth $6,000. Jane did not actually need the truck and ended up selling it to a used car dealer for $5,200 a few months later. Explain what amount of gross income Jane must recognize as a result of the truck payment and why.

LO 2.1

3. Larry is a tax accountant and Sheila is a hairdresser. Larry prepares Sheila's tax return for free and Sheila agrees to style Larry's hair six times for free in return for the tax return. The value of the tax return is approximately $300 and the hair styling work is approximately $300.
    a. How much of the $300 is includable income to Larry? Why?
    b. How much of the $300 is includable income to Sheila? Why?

LO 2.1

4. Kerry and Jim have a successful marijuana farm in the woods around Humboldt County, California. Growing marijuana is illegal for federal purposes. Are Kerry and Jim required by law to report the income from their farm on their tax return? Why?

LO 2.2

5. Kristen, a single taxpayer, receives two 2022 Forms W-2 from the two employers she worked for during the year. One Form W-2 lists her wages in Boxes 1, 3, and 5 as $18,700. Her other employer's Form W-2 has $43,000 in Box 1 but $46,500 in both Box 3 and Box 5. Kristen participated in the second employer's 401(k) plan. She also received health care from her second employer. Lastly, her second employer provided $30,000 of group term life insurance to Kristen.
    a. What amount should Kristen report as taxable wages in 2022?
    b. What could explain the difference between Box 1 wages and Boxes 3 and 5 on her second employer's W-2?

LO 2.2

6. List four behavioral factors that could be used to classify a worker as either an employee or an independent contractor and provide a brief example.

LO 2.3

7. Skyler is covered by his company's health insurance plan. The health insurance costs his company $9,500 a year. During the year, Skyler is diagnosed with a serious illness and health insurance pays $100,000 for surgery and treatment. How much of the insurance and treatment payments are taxable to Skyler?

LO 2.3

8. Malin is a married taxpayer and has three dependent children. Malin's employer offers health insurance for employees and Malin takes advantage of the benefit for her entire family (her spouse's employer also offers health insurance but they opt out). During the year, Malin paid $1,200 toward her family's health insurance premiums through payroll deductions while the employer paid the remaining $9,200. Malin's family visited health care professionals numerous times during the year and made total co-payments toward medical services of $280. Malin's daughter had knee surgery due to a soccer injury and the insurance company paid the hospital $6,700 directly and reimbursed Malin $400 for her out-of-pocket health care expenses related to the surgery. Explain how much gross income should Malin recognize related to her health insurance and why?

LO 2.4

9. For each of the following, explain whether the value of the meals provided to the taxpayer are part of the taxpayer's gross income and why:
   a. Milton is a nurse whose employer provided meals for him on the employer's premises, since he is given only 30 minutes for lunch.
   b. Mary is a San Diego ambulance driver. The city provides Mary with meals while she is working so she will be available for emergencies.
   c. Indigo is the head of security at a casino. The casino operator frequently provides meals from the casino buffett to Indigo as a gesture of goodwill for the great job she is doing.
   d. Kerrie works at Sante Fe Memorial Hospital as an administrative assistant. Sante Fe operates a heavily subsidized on-site cafeteria because the majority of Sante Fe employees are required to eat lunch on the premises to be available for emergencies. Kerrie's job description has no such requirement and she is free to eat anywhere during a typical lunch hour. Kerrie likes the cafeteria and generally eats her meals there anyway. Kerrie estimates the value of her 2022 meals at the cafeteria as $2,750. Her records show she paid $400 for these meals.

LO 2.5

10. Linda and Richard are married and file a joint return for 2022. During the year, Linda, who works as an accountant for a national airline, used $2,100 worth of free passes for travel on the airline; Richard used the same amount. Linda and Richard also used $850 worth of employee vouchers for hotel rooms at the hotel chain that is also owned by the airline. Richard is employed at State University as an accounting clerk. Under a tuition reduction plan, Richard saved $4,000 in tuition fees during 2022. He is taking classes toward a master's degree in business at night while still working full-time. Richard also had $30 worth of personal typing done by his administrative assistant at the University. What is the amount of fringe benefits that should be included in Linda and Richard's gross income on their 2022 tax return?

LO 2.5

11. Ellen's tax client, Tom, is employed at a large company that offers health care flexible spending accounts to its employees. Tom must decide at the beginning of the year whether he wants to put as much as $2,850 of his salary into the health care flexible spending account. He expects that he will have to pay for at least $8,000 of medical expenses for his family during the year since his wife is seeing a psychiatrist every week and his daughter and son are both having their teeth straightened. Tom does not itemize deductions. Should Ellen recommend that Tom put the maximum amount in his health care flexible spending account, and if so, why?

LO 2.6

12. How much of each of the following is included in gross income?
    a. Cheline, an actress, received a $7,600 gift bag for attending the Academy Awards Ceremony during 2022.
    b. Jon received a gold watch worth $700 for twenty-five years of service to his accounting firm (not a qualified award).
    c. Kerry won $1,000,000 in her state lottery.
    d. Deborah is a professor who received $30,000 as an award for her scientific research from the university that employs her.

LO 2.6
LO 2.12

13. For each of the following independent cases, indicate the amount of gross income that must be included on the taxpayer's 2022 income tax return.
    a. Malchia won a $4,000 humanitarian award.
    b. Rob won a new automobile (with a sticker price of $15,700 and a market value of $14,500) for being the best junior tennis player in 2022.
    c. George received a $3,500 tuition and fees scholarship to attend Western University.

LO 2.7

14. Lola, age 67, began receiving a $1,000 monthly annuity in the current year upon the death of her husband. She received seven payments in the current year. Her husband contributed $48,300 to the qualified employee plan. Use the Simplified Method Worksheet below to calculate Lola's taxable amount from the annuity.

SIMPLIFIED METHOD WORKSHEET

1. Enter total amount received this year. 1. ________
2. Enter cost in the plan at the annuity starting date. 2. ________
3. Age at annuity starting date

	Enter
55 and under	360
56–60	310
61–65	260
66–70	210
71 and older	160

3. ________

4. Divide line 2 by line 3. 4. ________
5. Multiply line 4 by the number of monthly payments this year. If the annuity starting date was before 1987, also enter this amount on line 8, and skip lines 6 and 7. Otherwise, go to line 6. 5. ________
6. Enter the amount, if any, recovered tax free in prior years. 6. ________
7. Subtract line 6 from line 2. 7. ________
8. Enter the smaller of line 5 or 7. 8. ________
9. Taxable amount this year: Subtract line 8 from line 1. Do not enter less than zero. 9. ________

LO 2.8

15. Sharon transfers to Russ a life insurance policy with a cash surrender value of $30,000 and a face value of $100,000 in exchange for real estate. Russ continues to pay the premiums on the policy until Sharon dies 7 years later. At that time, Russ has paid $12,000 in premiums, and he collects the $100,000 face value. Explain how much of the proceeds is taxable to Russ and why?

LO 2.8

16. Greg died on July 1, 2021, and left Lea, his wife, a $45,000 life insurance policy which she elects to receive at $9,000 per year plus interest for five years. In the current year, Lea receives $9,500. How much should Lea include in her gross income?

LO 2.8

17. David is certified by his doctor as terminally ill with liver disease. His doctor certifies that he cannot reasonably be expected to live for more than a year. He sells his life insurance policy to Viatical Settlements, Inc., for $250,000. He has paid $20,000 so far for the policy. How much of the $250,000 must David include in his taxable income?

LO 2.8

18. Helen receives a $200,000 lump sum life insurance payment when her friend Alice dies. How much of the payment is taxable to Helen?

LO 2.9

19. Describe the methods that an individual taxpayer that holds Series I Bonds can use to recognize interest.

LO 2.9

20. Yorick purchases a $10,000 bond with a 5 percent interest rate from Hamlet on March 31, 2022. The bond pays interest semiannually on June 30 and December 31. Prevailing interest rates have risen since Hamlet first purchased the bond for $10,000 at issuance. Yorick pays $9,561 for the bond. Explain the items that are affecting Yorick's purchase price for the bond and what effect these items will have on Yorick's gross income?

LO 2.9

21. Vandell is a taxpayer in the 22-percent tax bracket. He invests in Otay Mesa Water District Bonds that pay 4.5 percent interest. What interest on a taxable bond would provide the same after-tax return to Vandell?

LO 2.9

22. Karen is a wealthy retired investment advisor who is in the 35-percent tax bracket. She has a choice between investing in a high-quality municipal bond paying 5 percent or a high-quality corporate bond paying 7 percent. What is the after-tax return of each bond and which one should Karen invest in? Explain your answer.

LO 2.10

23. How are qualified dividends taxed in 2022? Please give the rates of tax which apply to qualified dividends, and specify when each of these rates applies.

LO 2.9
LO 2.10

24. Sally and Charles Colonel received the following Form 1099-DIV in 2022:

☐ CORRECTED (if checked)

Dividends and Distributions — OMB No. 1545-0110 — Form **1099-DIV** (Rev. January 2022) — For calendar year 2022 — **Copy B For Recipient**

PAYER'S name, street address, city or town, state or province, country, ZIP or foreign postal code, and telephone no.	Kentucky East Corporation 500 Lancaster Avenue Richmond, KY 40475
PAYER'S TIN	45-6067473
RECIPIENT'S TIN	313-13-1313
RECIPIENT'S name	Sally Colonel
Street address (including apt. no.)	1045 Gibson Bay Drive
City or town, state or province, country, and ZIP or foreign postal code	Richmond, KY 40475
11 FATCA filing requirement	☐
Account number (see instructions)	
1a Total ordinary dividends	$ 700.00
1b Qualified dividends	$ 694.00
2a Total capital gain distr.	$ 180.00
2b Unrecap. Sec. 1250 gain	$
2c Section 1202 gain	$
2d Collectibles (28%) gain	$
2e Section 897 ordinary dividends	$
2f Section 897 capital gain	$
3 Nondividend distributions	$
4 Federal income tax withheld	$ 0.00
5 Section 199A dividends	$
6 Investment expenses	$
7 Foreign tax paid	$
8 Foreign country or U.S. possession	
9 Cash liquidation distributions	$
10 Noncash liquidation distributions	$
12 Exempt-interest dividends	$
13 Specified private activity bond interest dividends	$
14 State	
15 State identification no.	
16 State tax withheld	$ $

This is important tax information and is being furnished to the IRS. If you are required to file a return, a negligence penalty or other sanction may be imposed on you if this income is taxable and the IRS determines that it has not been reported.

Form **1099-DIV** (Rev. 1-2022) (keep for your records) www.irs.gov/Form1099DIV Department of the Treasury - Internal Revenue Service

The Colonels also received the following dividends and interest in 2022 (Forms 1099-DIV not shown):

	Sally	*Charles*	*Jointly*
Ordinary and qualifying dividends:			
Altus Inc.	$2,000		
Buller Corp.		$400	
Gene Corporation			$3,000
Interest:			
Porcine Bank			1,200
River Bank			700
City of Richmond, KY Bonds		400	

a. Assuming the Colonels file a joint tax return, complete Schedule B of Form 1040 (on Page 2-69) for them for the 2022 tax year.
b. What amounts are reported on Lines 2a and 2b of Form 1040?
c. What amounts are reported on Lines 3a and 3b of Form 1040?

LO 2.11

25. In June of 2022, Kevin inherits stock worth $125,000. During the year, he collects $5,600 in dividends from the stock. Explain how much of these amounts, if any, should Kevin include in his gross income for 2022 and why?

LO 2.11

26. Gwen is a tax accountant who works very hard for a large corporate client. The client is pleased and gives her a gift of $10,000 at year-end. How much of the gift is taxable to Gwen?

LO 2.11

27. Charlene receives a gift from her boyfriend of $10,000. He knows she is having financial problems and wants to help her. How much of the gift is taxable to Charlene?

LO 2.12

28. Robbie receives a scholarship of $20,000 to an elite private college. $12,000 of the scholarship is earmarked for tuition, and $8,000 covers his room and board. How much of the scholarship, if any, is taxable to Robbie?

LO 2.13

29. Answer the following questions:
    a. Under a 2017 divorce agreement, Joan is required to pay her ex-husband, Bill, $700 a month until their daughter is 18 years of age. At that time, the required payments are reduced to $450 per month.
        1. How much of each $700 payment may be deducted as alimony by Joan?
        2. How much of each $700 payment must be included in Bill's taxable income?
        3. How much would be deductible/included if the divorce agreement were dated 2022?
    b. Under the terms of a property settlement executed during 2022, Jane transferred property worth $450,000 to her ex-husband, Tom. The property has a tax basis to Jane of $425,000.
        1. How much taxable gain must be recognized by Jane at the time of the transfer?
        2. What is the amount of Tom's tax basis in the property he received from Jane?

SCHEDULE B (Form 1040)

Department of the Treasury
Internal Revenue Service

Interest and Ordinary Dividends

Go to *www.irs.gov/ScheduleB* for instructions and the latest information.
Attach to Form 1040 or 1040-SR.

OMB No. 1545-0074

2022

Attachment Sequence No. **08**

Name(s) shown on return | Your social security number

Part I Interest

(See instructions and the Instructions for Form 1040, line 2b.)

Note: If you received a Form 1099-INT, Form 1099-OID, or substitute statement from a brokerage firm, list the firm's name as the payer and enter the total interest shown on that form.

			Amount
1	List name of payer. If any interest is from a seller-financed mortgage and the buyer used the property as a personal residence, see the instructions and list this interest first. Also, show that buyer's social security number and address:	1	
2	Add the amounts on line 1	2	
3	Excludable interest on series EE and I U.S. savings bonds issued after 1989. Attach Form 8815	3	
4	Subtract line 3 from line 2. Enter the result here and on Form 1040 or 1040-SR, line 2b	4	

Note: If line 4 is over $1,500, you must complete Part III.

Part II Ordinary Dividends

(See instructions and the Instructions for Form 1040, line 3b.)

Note: If you received a Form 1099-DIV or substitute statement from a brokerage firm, list the firm's name as the payer and enter the ordinary dividends shown on that form.

			Amount
5	List name of payer:	5	
6	Add the amounts on line 5. Enter the total here and on Form 1040 or 1040-SR, line 3b	6	

Note: If line 6 is over $1,500, you must complete Part III.

Part III Foreign Accounts and Trusts

Caution: If required, failure to file FinCEN Form 114 may result in substantial penalties. Additionally, you may be required to file Form 8938, Statement of Specified Foreign Financial Assets. See instructions.

You must complete this part if you **(a)** had over $1,500 of taxable interest or ordinary dividends; **(b)** had a foreign account; or **(c)** received a distribution from, or were a grantor of, or a transferor to, a foreign trust.

		Yes	No
7a	At any time during 2022, did you have a financial interest in or signature authority over a financial account (such as a bank account, securities account, or brokerage account) located in a foreign country? See instructions		
	If "Yes," are you required to file FinCEN Form 114, Report of Foreign Bank and Financial Accounts (FBAR), to report that financial interest or signature authority? See FinCEN Form 114 and its instructions for filing requirements and exceptions to those requirements		
b	If you are required to file FinCEN Form 114, list the name(s) of the foreign country(-ies) where the financial account(s) are located:		
8	During 2022, did you receive a distribution from, or were you the grantor of, or transferor to, a foreign trust? If "Yes," you may have to file Form 3520. See instructions		

For Paperwork Reduction Act Notice, see your tax return instructions. Cat. No. 17146N **Schedule B (Form 1040) 2022**

LO 2.13

30. Arlen is required by his 2022 divorce agreement to pay alimony of $2,000 a month and child support of $2,000 a month to his ex-wife Jane. What is the tax treatment of these two payments for Arlen? What is the tax treatment of these two payments for Jane?

LO 2.13

31. As part of the property settlement related to their divorce, Cindy must give Allen the house that they have been living in, while she gets 100 percent of their savings accounts. The house in southern California was purchased 20 years ago for $90,000 and is now worth $700,000. How much gain must Cindy recognize on the transfer of the house to Allen? What is Allen's tax basis in the house for calculating tax on any future sale of the house?

LO 2.14

32. Jose paid the following amounts for his son to attend Big State University in 2022:

Tuition	$6,400
Room and board	4,000
Books	772
A car to use at school	1,932
Student football tickets	237
Spending money	4,775

How much of the above is a qualified higher education expense for purposes of his Section 529 plan?

LO 2.14

33. In 2022, Van receives $20,000 (of which $4,000 is earnings) from a Section 529 plan. He uses the funds to pay for his college tuition and other qualified higher education expenses. How much of the $20,000 is taxable to Van?

LO 2.15

34. Lydia, a married individual, was unemployed for a few months during 2021. During the year, she received $3,250 in unemployment compensation payments. How much of her unemployment compensation payments must be included in gross income?

LO 2.16

35. During the 2022 tax year, Brian, a single taxpayer, received $7,600 in Social Security benefits. His adjusted gross income for the year was $14,700 (not including the Social Security benefits) and he received $30,000 in tax-exempt interest income and has no for AGI deductions. Calculate the amount of the Social Security benefits that Brian must include in his gross income for 2022.

Simplified Taxable Social Security Worksheet (for most people)

1. Enter the total amount of Social Security income. 1. ________
2. Enter one-half of line 1. 2. ________
3. Enter the total of taxable income items on Form 1040 except Social Security income. 3. ________
4. Enter the amount of tax-exempt interest income. 4. ________
5. Add lines 2, 3, and 4. 5. ________
6. Enter all adjustments for AGI except for student loan interest deduction. 6. ________
7. Subtract line 6 from line 5. If zero or less, stop here, none of the Social Security benefits are taxable. 7. ________
8. Enter $25,000 ($32,000 if married filing jointly; $0 if married filing separately and living with spouse at any time during the year). 8. ________

9. Subtract line 8 from line 7. If zero or less, enter –0–. 9. ________

Note: *If line 9 is zero or less, stop here;* ***none of your benefits are taxable.*** *Otherwise, go on to line 10.*

10. Enter $9,000 ($12,000 if married filing jointly; $0 if married filing separately and living with spouse at any time during the year). 10. ________
11. Subtract line 10 from line 9. If zero or less, enter –0–. 11. ________
12. Enter the **smaller** of line 9 or line 10. 12. ________
13. Enter one-half of line 12. 13. ________
14. Enter the **smaller** of line 2 or line 13. 14. ________
15. Multiply line 11 by 85% (.85). If line 11 is zero, enter –0–. 15. ________
16. Add lines 14 and 15. 16. ________
17. Multiply line 1 by 85% (.85). 17. ________
18. **Taxable benefits**. Enter the **smaller** of line 16 or line 17. 18. ________

LO 2.16

36. Please answer the following questions regarding the taxability of Social Security:
    a. A 68-year-old taxpayer has $20,000 in Social Security income and $100,000 in tax-free municipal bond income. Does the municipal bond income affect the amount of Social Security the taxpayer must include in income?
    b. A 68-year-old taxpayer has $20,000 in Social Security income and no other taxable or tax-free income. How much of the Social Security income must the taxpayer include in taxable income?
    c. A 68-year-old taxpayer has $20,000 in Social Security income and has significant other taxable retirement income. What is the maximum percentage of Social Security that the taxpayer might be required to include in taxable income?

LO 2.17

37. In 2022, Kelly and Kerry live in California and are married and live together but plan to file separately. Their income for the year is as follows:

	Kelly	*Kerry*	*Joint*
Wages	$40,000	$30,000	
Investment income from Kelly's family inheritance			$8,000
Investment income from joint brokerage account			$1,600

    a. Compute the separate gross income for Kelly and Kerry.
    b. Assume they live in Texas instead of California. Compute the separate gross income for Kelly and Kerry.

LO 2.18

38. In 2021, Son loses his job and he is able to reduce his mortgage debt on his principle residence by $30,000 and remains solvent. Explain how much cancellation of debt income Son will recognize and what exception provision might apply, if any.

GROUP 3:
WRITING ASSIGNMENT

RESEARCH

Vanessa Lazo was an amazing high school student and so it was no great surprise when she was accepted into Prestige Private University (PPU). To entice Vanessa to attend PPU, the school offered her a reduced tuition of $13,000 per year (full-time tuition would typically be $43,000 per year). PPU also has a scholarship program thanks to a large donation from William Gatos. Vanessa was the Gatos Scholarship winner and will receive a scholarship for $20,000. Vanessa is required to use the scholarship first to pay her $13,000 tuition and the remainder is to cover room and board at PPU. Lastly, PPU also offered Vanessa a part-time job on the PPU campus as a student lab assistant in the Biology Department of PPU for which she is paid $1,500.

Required: Go to the IRS website (**www.irs.gov**) and locate Publication 970. Review the section on Scholarships. Write a letter to Vanessa Lazo stating how much of the PPU package is taxable.
(An example of a client letter is available at the website for this textbook, located at **www.cengage.com**.)

GROUP 4:
COMPREHENSIVE PROBLEMS

1. Donna and Chris Hoser have been married for three years. Donna works as nurse at Tarleton Memorial Hospital. Chris is a full-time student at Southwest Texas State University (STSU) and also works part-time during the summer at Tarleton Hospital. Chris' birthdate is January 12, 1996, and Donna's birthdate is November 4, 1998. Donna and Chris' earnings and income tax withholdings are reported on the following Forms W-2:

a Employee's social security number	465-74-3322
OMB No. 1545-0008	Safe, accurate, FAST! Use IRS e-file. Visit the IRS website at www.irs.gov/efile
b Employer identification number (EIN)	31-1238977
c Employer's name, address, and ZIP code	Tarleton Memorial Hospital Corp. 412 N. Belknap Street Stephenville, TX 76401
d Control number	
e Employee's first name and initial / Last name / Suff.	Donna Hoser 1313 W. Washington Street Stephenville, TX 76401
f Employee's address and ZIP code	
1 Wages, tips, other compensation	50,198.00
2 Federal income tax withheld	4,020.30
3 Social security wages	50,198.00
4 Social security tax withheld	3,112.28
5 Medicare wages and tips	50,198.00
6 Medicare tax withheld	727.87
7 Social security tips	
8 Allocated tips	
9	
10 Dependent care benefits	
11 Nonqualified plans	
12a See instructions for box 12	C 48.00
12b	DD 5,700.00
12c	
12d	
13 Statutory employee / Retirement plan / Third-party sick pay	☐ ☐ ☐
14 Other	FSA $2,850
15 State / Employer's state ID number	TX
16 State wages, tips, etc.	
17 State income tax	
18 Local wages, tips, etc.	
19 Local income tax	
20 Locality name	

Form **W-2** Wage and Tax Statement 2022

Department of the Treasury—Internal Revenue Service

Copy B—To Be Filed With Employee's FEDERAL Tax Return.
This information is being furnished to the Internal Revenue Service.

	a Employee's social security number 465-57-9935	OMB No. 1545-0008	Safe, accurate, FAST! Use IRS e-file	Visit the IRS website at www.irs.gov/efile
b Employer identification number (EIN) 31-1238977			1 Wages, tips, other compensation 3,200.00	2 Federal income tax withheld 150.00
c Employer's name, address, and ZIP code Tarleton Memorial Hospital Corp. 412 N. Belknap Street Stephenville, TX 76401			3 Social security wages 3,200.00	4 Social security tax withheld 198.40
			5 Medicare wages and tips 3,200.00	6 Medicare tax withheld 46.40
			7 Social security tips	8 Allocated tips
d Control number			9	10 Dependent care benefits
e Employee's first name and initial Last name Suff. Chris Hoser 1313 W. Washington Street Stephenville, TX 76401 f Employee's address and ZIP code			11 Nonqualified plans	12a See instructions for box 12
			13 Statutory employee ☐ Retirement plan ☐ Third-party sick pay ☐	12b
			14 Other	12c
				12d

15 State	Employer's state ID number	16 State wages, tips, etc.	17 State income tax	18 Local wages, tips, etc.	19 Local income tax	20 Locality name
TX						

Form **W-2** **Wage and Tax Statement** 2022 Department of the Treasury—Internal Revenue Service

Copy B—To Be Filed With Employee's FEDERAL Tax Return.
This information is being furnished to the Internal Revenue Service.

Donna and Chris received the following Forms 1099-INT and 1099-DIV:

☐ CORRECTED (if checked)

PAYER'S name, street address, city or town, state or province, country, ZIP or foreign postal code, and telephone no.		Payer's RTN (optional)	OMB No. 1545-0112 Form **1099-INT** (Rev. January 2022)	**Interest Income**
Lone Star State Bank 1000 N. Wolfe Nursery Road Stephenville, TX 76401		1 Interest income $ 623.63	For calendar year 20 22	
		2 Early withdrawal penalty $		**Copy B** **For Recipient**
PAYER'S TIN 33-1234556	RECIPIENT'S TIN 465-74-3322	3 Interest on U.S. Savings Bonds and Treasury obligations $		
RECIPIENT'S name Donna and Chris Hoser		**4 Federal income tax withheld** $	5 Investment expenses $	This is important tax information and is being furnished to the IRS. If you are required to file a return, a negligence penalty or other sanction may be imposed on you if this income is taxable and the IRS determines that it has not been reported.
Street address (including apt. no.) 1313 W. Washington Street		6 Foreign tax paid $	7 Foreign country or U.S. possession	
City or town, state or province, country, and ZIP or foreign postal code Stephenville, TX 76401		8 Tax-exempt interest $	9 Specified private activity bond interest $	
		10 Market discount $	11 Bond premium $	
	FATCA filing requirement ☐	12 Bond premium on Treasury obligations $	13 Bond premium on tax-exempt bond $	
Account number (see instructions)		14 Tax-exempt and tax credit bond CUSIP no.	15 State / 16 State identification no.	17 State tax withheld $ $

Form **1099-INT** (Rev. 1-2022) (keep for your records) www.irs.gov/Form1099INT Department of the Treasury - Internal Revenue Service

☐ CORRECTED (if checked)

PAYER'S name, street address, city or town, state or province, country, ZIP or foreign postal code, and telephone no.	1 Original issue discount for the year*	OMB No. 1545-0117	
Stephenville Indep. School District 2655 West Overhill Drive Stephenville, Texas 76401	$ * This may not be the correct figure to report on your income tax return. See instructions on the back.	Form **1099-OID** (Rev. October 2019)	**Original Issue Discount**
	2 Other periodic interest $	For calendar year 20 22	
PAYER'S TIN: 13-3229985 / RECIPIENT'S TIN: 465-74-3322	3 Early withdrawal penalty $	**4 Federal income tax withheld** $	**Copy B**
	5 Market discount $	6 Acquisition premium $	**For Recipient**
RECIPIENT'S name Donna Hoser Street address (including apt. no.) 1313 W. Washington Street	7 Description STEPHENVILLE TEX INDPT S CUSIP 859128HW3 0% DUE 02/15/23		This is important tax information and is being furnished to the IRS. If you are required to file a return, a negligence penalty or other sanction may be imposed on you if this income is taxable and the IRS determines that it has not been reported.
City or town, state or province, country, and ZIP or foreign postal code Stephenville, TX 76401	8 Original issue discount on U.S. Treasury obligations* $	9 Investment expenses $	
FATCA filing requirement ☐	10 Bond premium $	11 Tax-exempt OID $ 122.00	
Account number (see instructions)	12 State / 13 State identification no.	14 State tax withheld $ $	

Form **1099-OID** (Rev. 10-2019) (keep for your records) www.irs.gov/Form1099OID Department of the Treasury - Internal Revenue Service

☐ CORRECTED (if checked)

PAYER'S name, street address, city or town, state or province, country, ZIP or foreign postal code, and telephone no.	1a Total ordinary dividends	OMB No. 1545-0110	
Ozark Corporation 900 South Orange Avenue Springfield, MO 62126	$ 320.00	Form **1099-DIV**	**Dividends and Distributions**
	1b Qualified dividends $ 320.00	(Rev. January 2022) For calendar year 20 22	
	2a Total capital gain distr. $	2b Unrecap. Sec. 1250 gain $	**Copy B** **For Recipient**
PAYER'S TIN: 33-1122335 / RECIPIENT'S TIN: 465-57-9935	2c Section 1202 gain $	2d Collectibles (28%) gain $	
	2e Section 897 ordinary dividends $	2f Section 897 capital gain $	
RECIPIENT'S name Chris Hoser	3 Nondividend distributions $	**4 Federal income tax withheld** $	This is important tax information and is being furnished to the IRS. If you are required to file a return, a negligence penalty or other sanction may be imposed on you if this income is taxable and the IRS determines that it has not been reported.
Street address (including apt. no.) 1313 W. Washington Street	5 Section 199A dividends $	6 Investment expenses $	
City or town, state or province, country, and ZIP or foreign postal code Stephenville, TX 76401	7 Foreign tax paid $	8 Foreign country or U.S. possession	
	9 Cash liquidation distributions $	10 Noncash liquidation distributions $	
11 FATCA filing requirement ☐	12 Exempt-interest dividends $	13 Specified private activity bond interest dividends $	
Account number (see instructions)	14 State / 15 State identification no.	16 State tax withheld $ $	

Form **1099-DIV** (Rev. 1-2022) (keep for your records) www.irs.gov/Form1099DIV Department of the Treasury - Internal Revenue Service

Chris is an excellent student at STSU. He was given a $1,750 scholarship by the university to help pay educational expenses. The scholarship funds were used by Chris for tuition and books.

Chris entered the Compositors Expanse Residence (CER) sweepstakes and ended up winning $10,000. Chris took advantage of the no-purchase-required option and paid nothing to join the sweepstakes. He received a 1099-MISC (not shown) reporting the prize.

Donna is a valued employee at the hospital. Her supervisor gave her two tickets to a single game of the nearby professional football team that were worth $100 each. The hospital also sent Donna flowers valued at $40 when her mother passed away during 2022.

Chris has a 4-year-old son, Robert R. Hoser, from a prior marriage that ended in divorce in 2019. During 2022, he paid his ex-wife $300 per month in child support. Robert is claimed as a dependent by Chris's ex-wife.

During 2022, Chris' aunt died. The aunt, in her will, left Chris $15,000 in cash. Chris deposited this money in the Lone Star State Bank savings account.

Required: Complete the Hoser's federal tax return for 2022 on Form 1040, Schedule 1, and the Qualified Dividends and Capital Gain Tax Worksheet.

2A. Ray and Maria Gomez have been married for eight years. Ray is an oil rig maintenance supervisor for Palm Oil Corporation and Maria works as a cashier for Lowes Depot. Ray's birthdate is February 21, 1989, and Maria's is December 30, 1991. Ray and Maria have a 9-year-old son named Jaime Gomez, born 3/22/2013 (Social Security number 721-34-1134). Ray and Maria's earnings are reported on the following Forms W-2:

a Employee's social security number	469-21-5523
OMB No. 1545-0008	Safe, accurate, FAST! Use IRS e-file. Visit the IRS website at www.irs.gov/efile
b Employer identification number (EIN)	21-7654321
c Employer's name, address, and ZIP code	Palm Oil Corporation 11134 E. Pecan Blvd. McAllen, TX 78501
d Control number	
e Employee's first name and initial / Last name / Suff.	Ray Gomez 1610 Sonora Avenue McAllen, TX 78503
f Employee's address and ZIP code	
1 Wages, tips, other compensation	43,230.00
2 Federal income tax withheld	5,031.00
3 Social security wages	45,150.00
4 Social security tax withheld	2,799.30
5 Medicare wages and tips	45,150.00
6 Medicare tax withheld	654.68
7 Social security tips	
8 Allocated tips	
9	
10 Dependent care benefits	600.00
11 Nonqualified plans	
12a See instructions for box 12	D 1,920.00
12b	DD 8,800.00
12c	
12d	
13 Statutory employee / Retirement plan / Third-party sick pay	Retirement plan: X
14 Other	FSA Health 2,850.00
15 State / Employer's state ID number	TX
16 State wages, tips, etc.	
17 State income tax	
18 Local wages, tips, etc.	
19 Local income tax	
20 Locality name	

Form **W-2** Wage and Tax Statement **2022** Department of the Treasury—Internal Revenue Service

Copy B—To Be Filed With Employee's FEDERAL Tax Return.
This information is being furnished to the Internal Revenue Service.

a Employee's social security number	444-65-9912
OMB No. 1545-0008	Safe, accurate, FAST! Use IRS e-file. Visit the IRS website at www.irs.gov/efile
b Employer identification number (EIN)	23-4444321
c Employer's name, address, and ZIP code	Lowes Depot 1300 W. Houston Ave. McAllen, TX 78501
d Control number	
e Employee's first name and initial / Last name / Suff.	Maria Gomez 1610 Sonora Avenue McAllen, TX 78503
f Employee's address and ZIP code	
1 Wages, tips, other compensation	32,750.00
2 Federal income tax withheld	2,620.00
3 Social security wages	32,750.00
4 Social security tax withheld	2,030.50
5 Medicare wages and tips	32,750.00
6 Medicare tax withheld	474.88
7 Social security tips	
8 Allocated tips	
9	
10 Dependent care benefits	
11 Nonqualified plans	
12a See instructions for box 12	
12b	
12c	
12d	
13 Statutory employee / Retirement plan / Third-party sick pay	
14 Other	Educ Asst Plan $5,250.00
15 State / Employer's state ID number	TX
16 State wages, tips, etc.	
17 State income tax	
18 Local wages, tips, etc.	
19 Local income tax	
20 Locality name	

Form **W-2** Wage and Tax Statement **2022** Department of the Treasury—Internal Revenue Service

Copy B—To Be Filed With Employee's FEDERAL Tax Return.
This information is being furnished to the Internal Revenue Service.

Ray took advantage of his employer-provided dependent care assistance program on a small number of days when Jaime was sick and unable to go to school. The value of dependent care assistance was $600.

Once each week, Ray is required to work at the site of the oil drilling rig for a 24-hour period to provide on-call maintenance on the rig. On those days, Palm Oil requires Ray to stay in an apartment building that sits on the oil rig site. Because different maintenance workers stay each night, the building has a cook and dining room that prepares meals for the crew. All crew members must take their meals in the dining room when staying the night. The value of the lodging provided to Ray is $6,000 and the value of the meals provided to Ray is $750.

Maria frequently takes advantage of the 10-percent employee discount on merchandise from Lowes Depot. The discount is available to all employees of Lowes Depot and the company still makes a small profit on the items after the discount. Maria estimates her employee discounts in 2022 total $780.

Ray and Maria have investment income as reported on the attached Form 1099-INT and brokerage statement:

☐ CORRECTED (if checked)

PAYER'S name, street address, city or town, state or province, country, ZIP or foreign postal code, and telephone no.		Payer's RTN (optional)	OMB No. 1545-0112 Form **1099-INT** (Rev. January 2022) For calendar year 20 22	**Interest Income**
McAllen State Bank 3302 N. 10th Street McAllen, TX 78501		1 Interest income $ 723.61		
		2 Early withdrawal penalty $		**Copy B** **For Recipient**
PAYER'S TIN 34-7657651	RECIPIENT'S TIN 444-65-9912	3 Interest on U.S. Savings Bonds and Treasury obligations $		
RECIPIENT'S name Maria Gomez		**4 Federal income tax withheld** $	5 Investment expenses $	This is important tax information and is being furnished to the IRS. If you are required to file a return, a negligence penalty or other sanction may be imposed on you if this income is taxable and the IRS determines that it has not been reported.
Street address (including apt. no.) 1610 Sonora Avenue		6 Foreign tax paid $	7 Foreign country or U.S. possession	
City or town, state or province, country, and ZIP or foreign postal code McAllen, TX 78503		8 Tax-exempt interest $	9 Specified private activity bond interest $	
		10 Market discount $	11 Bond premium $	
	FATCA filing requirement ☐	12 Bond premium on Treasury obligations $	13 Bond premium on tax-exempt bond $	
Account number (see instructions)		14 Tax-exempt and tax credit bond CUSIP no.	15 State / 16 State identification no.	17 State tax withheld $ $

Form **1099-INT** (Rev. 1-2022) (keep for your records) www.irs.gov/Form1099INT Department of the Treasury - Internal Revenue Service

2022 Combined Forms 1099

This is important tax information and is being furnished to the IRS (except as indicated). If you are required to file a return, a negligence penalty or other sanction may be imposed on you if this income is taxable and the IRS determines that it has not been reported.

Copy B For Recipient
OMB No. 1545-0110

Friar Tuck Investments
38 Wall Street, 8th Floor
New York, NY 10005

Ray and Maria Gomez
1610 Sonora Ave.
McAllen, TX 78503

Account Number	Tax ID
4500881661	***-**-9912
Payer's Federal Tax ID	
33-1357246	
Financial Adviser/Phone	
Ray Greenleaf 888-555-1212	

Form 1099-INT **Interest Income**

Box 1 Interest income	Box 2 Early withdrawal penalty	Box 3 Interest on U.S. Savings Bonds and Treasury obligations
23.88		600.00
Box 4 Federal income tax withheld	Box 5 Investment expenses	Box 6 Foreign Tax Paid
Box 7 Foreign country or U.S. possession	Box 8 Tax-exempt interest	Box 9 Specified private activity bond interest
	400.00	
Box 10 Market Discount	Box 11 Bond Premium	
Box 12 Bond premium on Treasury obligations	Box 13 Bond premium on tax-exempt bond	

Form 1099-DIV **Dividend Income**

Box 1a Total ordinary dividends	Box 1b Qualified dividends	Box 2a Total capital gain distr.
1,000.00	1,000.00	60.00
Box 2b Unrecap Sec 1250 gain	Box 2c Section 1202 gain	Box 2d Collectibles (28%) gain
Box 2e Section 897 ordinary dividends	Box 2f Section 897 capital gain	Box 3 Nondividend distributions
Box 4 Federal income tax withheld	Box 5 Section 199A dividends	Box 6 Investment expenses
Box 7 Foreign taxes paid	Box 8 Foreign country or possession	Box 9 Cash liquidation distributions

Ray has an ex-wife named Judy Gomez. Pursuant to their January 27, 2016, divorce decree, Ray pays her $200 per month in alimony. All payments were made on time in 2022. Judy's Social Security number is 566-74-8765.

During 2022, Ray was in the hospital for a successful operation. His health insurance company reimbursed Ray $4,732 for all of his hospital and doctor bills.

In June of 2022, Maria's father died. Under a life insurance policy owned and paid for by her father, Maria was paid death benefits of $25,000. She used $7,800 to cover a portion of the funeral costs for her father.

Maria bought a Texas lottery ticket on impulse during 2022. Her ticket was lucky and she won $1,000. The winning amount was paid to Maria in November 2022 with no income tax withheld.

Maria is pursuing a Masters of Business Administration from McAllen State University. Lowes Depot operates an employee assistance plan that she takes full advantage of. She is also the beneficiary of the $1,000 Lowes Depot Adult Learner Scholarship. All of the scholarship is used to pay for tuition and books.

Ray and Maria are eligible for a $2,000 child tax credit in 2022.

Required: Complete the Gomez's federal tax return for 2022 on Form 1040, Schedule B, and Schedule 1. Form 8812 for the child tax credit does not need to be completed.

2B. Carl Conch and Mary Duval are married and file a joint return. Carl is retired US Army but likes to stay busy, and so he works as a part-time baker at the Key Lime Pie Company. Mary is unemployed since losing her job in 2021. Carl's birth date is June 14, 1957, and Mary's is October 2, 1967.

Carl and Mary help support an old Army friend of Carl's named Buster Crabbe. Buster is 72 years old and lives in an over-55 community in Key West near Carl and Mary's apartment. Buster has a small Social Security benefit of $6,000 per year, and so Carl and Mary provide for more than half of his support. Buster's birth date is June 12, 1950, and his Social Security number is 454-11-1719.

Carl's W-2, 1099-R (Army pension), and Social Security benefits statement are presented below:

a Employee's social security number: 835-21-5423 — OMB No. 1545-0008 — Safe, accurate, FAST! Use IRS e-file — Visit the IRS website at www.irs.gov/efile

b Employer identification number (EIN)	61-7651234
c Employer's name, address, and ZIP code	Key Lime Pie Company 223 Key Deer Blvd. Big Pine Key, FL 33043
d Control number	
e Employee's first name and initial / Last name / Suff.	Carl Conch 1234 Mallory Square, Apt #64 Key West, FL 33040
f Employee's address and ZIP code	
1 Wages, tips, other compensation	23,000.00
2 Federal income tax withheld	2,400.00
3 Social security wages	23,000.00
4 Social security tax withheld	1,426.00
5 Medicare wages and tips	23,000.00
6 Medicare tax withheld	333.50
7 Social security tips	
8 Allocated tips	
9	
10 Dependent care benefits	
11 Nonqualified plans	
12a See instructions for box 12	
12b	
12c	
12d	
13 Statutory employee / Retirement plan / Third-party sick pay	☐ / ☐ / ☐
14 Other	

15 State Employer's state ID number	16 State wages, tips, etc.	17 State income tax	18 Local wages, tips, etc.	19 Local income tax	20 Locality name
FL					

Form **W-2** Wage and Tax Statement **2022** — Department of the Treasury—Internal Revenue Service

Copy B—To Be Filed With Employee's FEDERAL Tax Return.
This information is being furnished to the Internal Revenue Service.

☐ CORRECTED (if checked)

Distributions From Pensions, Annuities, Retirement or Profit-Sharing Plans, IRAs, Insurance Contracts, etc. — OMB No. 1545-0119 — **2022** — Form **1099-R**

PAYER'S name, street address, city or town, state or province, country, ZIP or foreign postal code, and telephone no.	Defense Finance and Accounting Service U.S. Military Retired Pay 8899 E 56th Street Indianapolis IN 46249-1200
PAYER'S TIN	22-4564561
RECIPIENT'S TIN	835-21-5423
RECIPIENT'S name	Carl Conch
Street address (including apt. no.)	1234 Mallory Square, Apt 64
City or town, state or province, country, and ZIP or foreign postal code	Key West, FL 33040
1 Gross distribution	$ 13,400.00
2a Taxable amount	$ 13,400.00
2b Taxable amount not determined	☐
Total distribution	☐
3 Capital gain (included in box 2a)	$
4 Federal income tax withheld	$ 1,200.00
5 Employee contributions/Designated Roth contributions or insurance premiums	$
6 Net unrealized appreciation in employer's securities	$
7 Distribution code(s)	7
IRA/SEP/SIMPLE	☐
8 Other	$ %
9a Your percentage of total distribution	%
9b Total employee contributions	$ 0.00
10 Amount allocable to IRR within 5 years	$
11 1st year of desig. Roth contrib.	
12 FATCA filing requirement	☐
13 Date of payment	
14 State tax withheld	$ $
15 State/Payer's state no.	
16 State distribution	$ $
17 Local tax withheld	$ $
18 Name of locality	
19 Local distribution	$ $
Account number (see instructions)	

Copy B — **Report this income on your federal tax return. If this form shows federal income tax withheld in box 4, attach this copy to your return.**

This information is being furnished to the IRS.

Form **1099-R** www.irs.gov/Form1099R Department of the Treasury - Internal Revenue Service

FORM SSA-1099 – SOCIAL SECURITY BENEFIT STATEMENT		
2022	• Part of your social security benefits shown in box 5 may be taxable income • See reverse side for more information	
Box 1 Name Carl Conch		Box 2 Beneficiary's Social Security Number 835-21-5423
Box 3 Benefits Paid in 2022 $7,600.00	Box 4 Benefits Repaid to SSA in 2022	Box 5 Net Benefits for 2022 $7,600.00
Description of Amount in Box 3 Paid by direct deposit $7,600.00 Benefits for 2022: $7,600.00	Description of Amount in Box 4	
	Box 6 Voluntary Federal Income Tax Withheld $500.00	
	Box 7 Address 1234 Mallory Square, Apt #64 Key West, FL 33040	
	Box 8 Claim Number	
Form SSA-1099-SM (1-2022)	DO NOT RETURN THIS FORM TO SSA OR IRS	

Mary is divorced, and she pays her ex-husband (Tom Tortuga) child support. Pursuant to their January 12, 2019, divorce decree, Mary pays Tom $500 per month in child support. All payments were made on time in 2022.

In early 2022, when Mary was struggling financially due to the loss of her job, she was able to renegotiate her auto loan and had the balance reduced by $4,000. The Form 1099-C is presented below:

☐ CORRECTED (if checked)

CREDITOR'S name, street address, city or town, state or province, country, ZIP or foreign postal code, and telephone no.		1 Date of identifiable event	OMB No. 1545-1424	
Tesla Finance LLC 4500 Deer Creek Rd Palo Alto, CA 94304		3/15/2022 2 Amount of debt discharged $ 4,000.00 3 Interest, if included in box 2 $	Form **1099-C** (Rev. January 2022) For calendar year 20 22	**Cancellation of Debt**
CREDITOR'S TIN 46-3896777	DEBTOR'S TIN 633-65-7912	4 Debt description Auto loan 2019 Tesla Model S		**Copy B** **For Debtor**
DEBTOR'S name Mary Duval				This is important tax information and is being furnished to the IRS. If you are required to file a return, a negligence penalty or other sanction may be imposed on you if taxable income results from this transaction and the IRS determines that it has not been reported.
Street address (including apt. no.) 1234 Mallory Sq #64		5 If checked, the debtor was personally liable for repayment of the debt . . . . ☒		
City or town, state or province, country, and ZIP or foreign postal code Key West, FL 33040				
Account number (see instructions)		6 Identifiable event code F	7 Fair market value of property $	

Form **1099-C** (Rev. 1-2022) (keep for your records) www.irs.gov/Form1099C Department of the Treasury - Internal Revenue Service

Sadly, in June 2022, Mary's father passed away and left her $75,000.

Mary also received unemployment compensation as shown on the following Form 1099-G:

☐ CORRECTED (if checked)

PAYER'S name, street address, city or town, state or province, country, ZIP or foreign postal code, and telephone no.
Florida Dept. of Economic Opportunity
107 E. Jefferson Blvd.
Tallahassee, FL 32399

1 Unemployment compensation $ 2,300.88
2 State or local income tax refunds, credits, or offsets $
OMB No. 1545-0120
Form **1099-G** (Rev. January 2022)
For calendar year 20 22
Certain Government Payments

PAYER'S TIN 21-5556666
RECIPIENT'S TIN 633-65-7912
3 Box 2 amount is for tax year
4 Federal income tax withheld $ 200.00
Copy B For Recipient

RECIPIENT'S name
Mary Duval
5 RTAA payments $
6 Taxable grants $
7 Agriculture payments $
8 If checked, box 2 is trade or business income ▶ ☐

Street address (including apt. no.)
1234 Mallory Sq. Apt 64
9 Market gain $

City or town, state or province, country, and ZIP or foreign postal code
Key West, FL 33040
10a State
10b State identification no.
11 State income tax withheld $ $

Account number (see instructions)

This is important tax information and is being furnished to the IRS. If you are required to file a return, a negligence penalty or other sanction may be imposed on you if this income is taxable and the IRS determines that it has not been reported.

Form **1099-G** (Rev. 1-2022) (keep for your records) www.irs.gov/Form1099G Department of the Treasury - Internal Revenue Service

The Key Lime Pie Company provides all employees with a gym on the premises of the pie factory that Carl works at. Carl uses the gym at least three days a week. The value of a similar gym membership would be $1,200.

Required: Complete Carl and Mary's federal tax return for 2022 on Form 1040 and Schedule 1. If not using software, consider completing the Simplified Taxable Social Security Worksheet found in Chapter 2 to determine the taxable portion of Social Security benefits.

GROUP 5: CUMULATIVE SOFTWARE PROBLEM

1. The following additional information is available for the family of Albert and Allison Gaytor.

In 2022, Albert received a Form W-2 from his employer, Coconut Grove Fishing Charters, Inc. (hint: slightly modified from Chapter 1):

a Employee's social security number 255-51-1966
OMB No. 1545-0008
Safe, accurate, FAST! Use IRS e-file
Visit the IRS website at www.irs.gov/efile

b Employer identification number (EIN) 60-3456789
1 Wages, tips, other compensation 67,917.71
2 Federal income tax withheld 5,478.87

c Employer's name, address, and ZIP code
Coconut Grove Fishing Charters, Inc.
2432 Bay Blvd.
Coconut Grove, FL 33133
3 Social security wages 67,917.71
4 Social security tax withheld 4,120.90
5 Medicare wages and tips 67,917.71
6 Medicare tax withheld 984.81
7 Social security tips
8 Allocated tips

d Control number
9
10 Dependent care benefits

e Employee's first name and initial Last name Suff.
Albert T. Gaytor
12340 Cocoshell Road
Coral Gables, FL 33134
11 Nonqualified plans
12a See instructions for box 12: DD | 8,900.00
13 Statutory employee ☐ Retirement plan ☐ Third-party sick pay ☐
12b
14 Other: Parking $1,680.00
12c
12d

f Employee's address and ZIP code

15 State Employer's state ID number	16 State wages, tips, etc.	17 State income tax	18 Local wages, tips, etc.	19 Local income tax	20 Locality name
FL					

Form **W-2** Wage and Tax Statement **2022** Department of the Treasury—Internal Revenue Service

Copy B—To Be Filed With Employee's FEDERAL Tax Return.
This information is being furnished to the Internal Revenue Service.

In addition to the interest from Chapter 1, Albert and Allison also received four Forms 1099:

☐ CORRECTED (if checked)

PAYER'S name, street address, city or town, state or province, country, ZIP or foreign postal code, and telephone no.		Payer's RTN (optional)	OMB No. 1545-0112 Form **1099-INT** (Rev. January 2022) For calendar year 20 22	**Interest Income**
Department of Treasury Bureau of the Fiscal Service PO Box 7105 Minneapolis, MN 55480		1 Interest income $		
		2 Early withdrawal penalty $		**Copy B** **For Recipient**
PAYER'S TIN 53-0247776	RECIPIENT'S TIN 266-51-1966	3 Interest on U.S. Savings Bonds and Treasury obligations $ 826.33		
RECIPIENT'S name Albert T. Gaytor		**4 Federal income tax withheld** $	5 Investment expenses $	This is important tax information and is being furnished to the IRS. If you are required to file a return, a negligence penalty or other sanction may be imposed on you if this income is taxable and the IRS determines that it has not been reported.
Street address (including apt. no.) 12340 Cocoshell Road		6 Foreign tax paid $	7 Foreign country or U.S. possession	
		8 Tax-exempt interest $	9 Specified private activity bond interest $	
City or town, state or province, country, and ZIP or foreign postal code Coral Gables, FL 33134		10 Market discount $	11 Bond premium $	
	FATCA filing requirement ☐	12 Bond premium on Treasury obligations $	13 Bond premium on tax-exempt bond $	
Account number (see instructions)		14 Tax-exempt and tax credit bond CUSIP no.	15 State / 16 State identification no.	17 State tax withheld $ $

Form **1099-INT** (Rev. 1-2022) (keep for your records) www.irs.gov/Form1099INT Department of the Treasury - Internal Revenue Service

☐ CORRECTED (if checked)

PAYER'S name, street address, city or town, state or province, country, ZIP or foreign postal code, and telephone no.		1a Total ordinary dividends $ 1,200.00	OMB No. 1545-0110 Form **1099-DIV**	**Dividends and Distributions**
Everglades Boating Corp. 1500 S. Krome Avenue Homestead, FL 33034		1b Qualified dividends $ 1,100.00	(Rev. January 2022) For calendar year 20 22	
		2a Total capital gain distr. $	2b Unrecap. Sec. 1250 gain $	**Copy B** **For Recipient**
PAYER'S TIN 57-4443344	RECIPIENT'S TIN 266-34-1967	2c Section 1202 gain $	2d Collectibles (28%) gain $	
		2e Section 897 ordinary dividends $	2f Section 897 capital gain $	
RECIPIENT'S name Allison Gaytor		3 Nondividend distributions $	**4 Federal income tax withheld** $ 0.00	This is important tax information and is being furnished to the IRS. If you are required to file a return, a negligence penalty or other sanction may be imposed on you if this income is taxable and the IRS determines that it has not been reported.
Street address (including apt. no.) 12340 Cocoshell Rd.		5 Section 199A dividends $	6 Investment expenses $	
		7 Foreign tax paid $	8 Foreign country or U.S. possession	
City or town, state or province, country, and ZIP or foreign postal code Coral Gables, FL 33134		9 Cash liquidation distributions $	10 Noncash liquidation distributions $	
	11 FATCA filing requirement ☐	12 Exempt-interest dividends $	13 Specified private activity bond interest dividends $	
Account number (see instructions)		14 State / 15 State identification no.	16 State tax withheld $ $	

Form **1099-DIV** (Rev. 1-2022) (keep for your records) www.irs.gov/Form1099DIV Department of the Treasury - Internal Revenue Service

☐ CORRECTED (if checked)

Form 1099-DIV — Dividends and Distributions (OMB No. 1545-0110, Rev. January 2022, For calendar year 2022) — Copy B For Recipient

PAYER'S name, street address, city or town, state or province, country, ZIP or foreign postal code, and telephone no.	Grapefruit Mutual Fund 1500 S. Orange Blossom Trail Orlando, FL 32809
PAYER'S TIN	51-3332215
RECIPIENT'S TIN	266-34-1967
RECIPIENT'S name	Allison A. Gaytor
Street address (including apt. no.)	12340 Cocoshell Road
City or town, state or province, country, and ZIP or foreign postal code	Coral Gables, FL 33134
11 FATCA filing requirement	☐
Account number (see instructions)	
1a Total ordinary dividends	$ 400.00
1b Qualified dividends	$ 380.00
2a Total capital gain distr.	$ 150.00
2b Unrecap. Sec. 1250 gain	$
2c Section 1202 gain	$
2d Collectibles (28%) gain	$
2e Section 897 ordinary dividends	$
2f Section 897 capital gain	$
3 Nondividend distributions	$
4 Federal income tax withheld	$ 0.00
5 Section 199A dividends	$
6 Investment expenses	$
7 Foreign tax paid	$
8 Foreign country or U.S. possession	
9 Cash liquidation distributions	$
10 Noncash liquidation distributions	$
12 Exempt-interest dividends	$
13 Specified private activity bond interest dividends	$
14 State	
15 State identification no.	
16 State tax withheld	$ $

This is important tax information and is being furnished to the IRS. If you are required to file a return, a negligence penalty or other sanction may be imposed on you if this income is taxable and the IRS determines that it has not been reported.

Form 1099-DIV (Rev. 1-2022) (keep for your records) www.irs.gov/Form1099DIV Department of the Treasury - Internal Revenue Service

☐ CORRECTED (if checked)

Form 1099-INT — Interest Income (OMB No. 1545-0112, Rev. January 2022, For calendar year 2022) — Copy B For Recipient

PAYER'S name, street address, city or town, state or province, country, ZIP or foreign postal code, and telephone no.	Miami-Dade County Airport Department General Revenue Bonds 111 NW 1st Street, 25th Floor Miami, FL 33128
Payer's RTN (optional)	
PAYER'S TIN	24-6767888
RECIPIENT'S TIN	266-51-1966
RECIPIENT'S name	Albert Gaytor
Street address (including apt. no.)	12340 Cocoshell Road
City or town, state or province, country, and ZIP or foreign postal code	Coral Gables, FL 33134
FATCA filing requirement	☐
Account number (see instructions)	
1 Interest income	$
2 Early withdrawal penalty	$
3 Interest on U.S. Savings Bonds and Treasury obligations	$
4 Federal income tax withheld	$
5 Investment expenses	$
6 Foreign tax paid	$
7 Foreign country or U.S. possession	
8 Tax-exempt interest	$ 800.00
9 Specified private activity bond interest	$
10 Market discount	$
11 Bond premium	$
12 Bond premium on Treasury obligations	$
13 Bond premium on tax-exempt bond	$
14 Tax-exempt and tax credit bond CUSIP no.	
15 State	
16 State identification no.	
17 State tax withheld	$ $

This is important tax information and is being furnished to the IRS. If you are required to file a return, a negligence penalty or other sanction may be imposed on you if this income is taxable and the IRS determines that it has not been reported.

Form 1099-INT (Rev. 1-2022) (keep for your records) www.irs.gov/Form1099INT Department of the Treasury - Internal Revenue Service

The interest from US Treasury notes was from bonds purchased between interest payments. Included in the purchase price was $148.76 of accrued interest. There is no market discount or bond premium on the bonds.

Albert went to the casino on his birthday and won big, as reflected on the following Form W-2G:

☐ CORRECTED (if checked)

PAYER'S name, street address, city or town, province or state, country, and ZIP or foreign postal code		1 Reportable winnings	2 Date won	OMB No. 1545-0238 **Form W-2G** **Certain Gambling Winnings** (Rev. January 2021) For calendar year 20 ____
Mikkosukee Resort and Gaming 1321 Tamiami Hwy Miami, FL 33194		$ 5,600.00		
		3 Type of wager Slot machine	**4 Federal income tax withheld** $ 1,500.00	
		5 Transaction	6 Race	
PAYER'S federal identification number	PAYER'S telephone number	7 Winnings from identical wagers $	8 Cashier	
22-7778877	305-555-1212	9 Winner's taxpayer identification no. 266-51-1966	10 Window	This information is being furnished to the Internal Revenue Service.
WINNER'S name Albert T. Gaytor		11 First identification	12 Second identification	
Street address (including apt. no.) 12340 Cocoshell Road		13 State/Payer's state identification no.	14 State winnings $	**Copy B**
City or town, province or state, country, and ZIP or foreign postal code Coral Gables, FL 33134		15 State income tax withheld $	16 Local winnings $	**Report this income on your federal tax return. If this form shows federal income tax withheld in box 4, attach this copy to your return.**
		17 Local income tax withheld $	18 Name of locality	

Under penalties of perjury, I declare that, to the best of my knowledge and belief, the name, address, and taxpayer identification number that I have furnished correctly identify me as the recipient of this payment and any payments from identical wagers, and that no other person is entitled to any part of these payments.

Signature ▶ **Date ▶**

Form **W-2G** (Rev. 1-2021) www.irs.gov/FormW2G Department of the Treasury - Internal Revenue Service

Albert had no other gambling income or losses for the year.

In February, Allison received $50,000 in life insurance proceeds from the death of her friend, Sharon.

In July, Albert's uncle Ivan died and left him real estate (undeveloped land) worth $72,000.

Five years ago, Albert and Allison divorced. Albert married Iris, but the marriage did not work out, and they divorced a year later. Under the July 1, 2017 divorce decree, Albert pays Iris $12,000 per year in alimony. All payments were on time in 2022 and Iris' Social Security number is 667-34-9224. Three years ago, Albert and Allison were remarried.

Coconut Fishing Charters, Inc. pays Albert's captain's license fees and membership dues to the Charter Fisherman's Association. During 2022, Coconut Fishing paid $1,300 for such dues and fees for Albert.

Allison was laid off from her job on January 2, 2022. She received a Form 1099-G for unemployment benefits:

☐ CORRECTED (if checked)

PAYER'S name, street address, city or town, state or province, country, ZIP or foreign postal code, and telephone no.		1 Unemployment compensation	OMB No. 1545-0120	**Certain Government Payments**
Florida Dept. of Economic Opportunity 107 E. Jefferson Blvd. Tallahassee, FL 32399		$ 3,950.00	Form **1099-G** (Rev. January 2022)	
		2 State or local income tax refunds, credits, or offsets $	For calendar year 20 22	
PAYER'S TIN 21-5556666	RECIPIENT'S TIN 633-65-7912	3 Box 2 amount is for tax year	**4 Federal income tax withheld** $ 225.00	**Copy B For Recipient**
RECIPIENT'S name Allison Gaytor		5 RTAA payments $	6 Taxable grants $	This is important tax information and is being furnished to the IRS. If you are required to file a return, a negligence penalty or other sanction may be imposed on you if this income is taxable and the IRS determines that it has not been reported.
Street address (including apt. no.) 12340 Cocoshell Road		7 Agriculture payments $	8 If checked, box 2 is trade or business income ▶ ☐	
City or town, state or province, country, and ZIP or foreign postal code Coral Gables, FL 33134		9 Market gain $		
Account number (see instructions)		10a State / 10b State identification no.	11 State income tax withheld $ $	

Form **1099-G** (Rev. 1-2022) (keep for your records) www.irs.gov/Form1099G Department of the Treasury - Internal Revenue Service

Albert and his family are covered by an employee-sponsored health plan at his work. Coconut Fishing pays $742 per month in premiums for Albert and his family. During the year, Allison was in the hospital for appendix surgery. The bill for the surgery was $10,100 of which the health insurance reimbursed Albert the full $10,100.

Coconut Fishing also paid for Albert's parking at the marina for the six months he worked there. The monthly cost is $280.

Required: Combine this new information about the Gaytor family with the information from Chapter 1 and complete a revised 2022 tax return for Albert and Allison. Be sure to save your data input files since this case will be expanded with more tax information in later chapters.

CHAPTER 3

Business Income and Expenses

LEARNING OBJECTIVES

After completing this chapter, you should be able to:

LO 3.1 Complete a basic Schedule C (Profit or Loss from Business).

LO 3.2 Describe the tax treatment of inventories and cost of goods sold.

LO 3.3 Identify the requirements for deducting transportation expenses.

LO 3.4 Identify the requirements for deducting travel expenses.

LO 3.5 Determine the requirements for deducting meals.

LO 3.6 Identify the requirements for claiming business education expenses.

LO 3.7 Identify the tax treatment of dues and subscriptions.

LO 3.8 Determine which clothing and uniforms may be treated as tax deductions.

LO 3.9 Explain the special limits for business gift deductions.

LO 3.10 Explain the tax treatment of bad debt deductions.

LO 3.11 Ascertain when a home office deduction may be claimed and how the deduction is computed.

LO 3.12 Apply the factors used to determine whether an activity is a hobby, and understand the tax treatment of hobby losses.

OVERVIEW

This chapter covers Schedule C, "Profit or Loss from Business (Sole Proprietorship)," and many of the common business expenses allowed as deductions in arriving at net taxable business income. Schedule C is filed by self-employed taxpayers, such as accountants, doctors, lawyers, architects, consultants, small manufacturers, restaurateurs, store owners, gardeners, event planners, bookkeepers, and other small businesses. This form is one of the most commonly used tax forms and, for many taxpayers, the net income reported on Schedule C is the primary component of their adjusted gross income. With the qualified business income (QBI) deduction, the sole proprietorship, along with income from rental properties (see Chapter 4), partnerships (see Chapter 10), and S corporations (see Chapter 11), may enjoy a reduction in tax rate in an attempt to match the 21 percent corporate tax rate. The QBI deduction is covered in detail in Chapter 4.

The business expenses discussed in this chapter include travel, transportation, bad debts, inventory, home office, meals and entertainment, business education, dues, subscriptions, publications, special clothing, uniforms, and business gifts. While these expenses are often associated with Schedule C (sole proprietorship income), they may also be reported with rental and royalty income on Schedule E, or farm and ranch income on Schedule F. Employee business expenses are covered in Chapter 5.

Learning Objective 3.1

Complete a basic Schedule C (Profit or Loss from Business).

3-1 SCHEDULE C

A taxpayer who operates a trade or business or practices a profession as a sole proprietorship must file a Schedule C with the Form 1040, reporting their taxable income or loss from the activity. Schedule C is similar to the income statement in financial accounting. Taxable income from a business or profession is reported on either Schedule C or Schedule F (a specialized version of Schedule C for farmers and ranchers).

3-1a Trade or Business

The term *trade or business* is not formally defined, although the term is used often in the Internal Revenue Code (the Code). For example, Section 162 of the Code states that a taxpayer is allowed to deduct all the ordinary and necessary expenses in carrying on a trade or business. Generally, a "trade or business" for tax purposes is any activity engaged in for profit. Note that a taxpayer does not have to actually make a profit, but they should be seeking to make a profit through regular and continual effort. Intermittent activities (e.g., casual craft sales) or leisure pursuits (e.g., wine making) do not always rise to the level of a trade or business and may require reporting under the hobby loss rules discussed later in this chapter.

3-1b Tests for Deductibility

Expenses must meet several general tests to qualify as a tax deduction. Listed below are three common tests for deductibility. These tests give guidelines for deductibility, but often in practice it is a matter of judgment as to whether an expense is considered a deductible business expense. Taxpayers and IRS agents frequently disagree as to whether specific expenses pass the following tests, and many court cases have been devoted to resolving these disagreements. The tests below overlap and an expense may fail more than one test.

- **The Ordinary and Necessary Test:** Under the tax law, for trade or business expenses to be deductible they must be ordinary and necessary. Generally, this means that the expense is commonly found in the specific business, and is helpful and appropriate in running the business.

EXAMPLE Rob is a CPA who goes to a "tax boot camp" which offers intensive training on tax return preparation every year. Rob also hires a trainer at his local gym to work out with him to help him maintain the strength and endurance needed to handle the rigors of tax season. The cost of the "tax boot camp" would be deductible. The cost of the personal trainer is not a common or ordinary expense of CPA firms and is not necessary for preparing tax returns and therefore would not be deductible. ♦

- **The Business Purpose Test:** Expenses must have a legitimate business purpose to be considered deductible.

EXAMPLE Larry is an independent consultant who maintains an office in his home, although he always meets with clients at their place of business. He spent $75,000 upgrading his office to include a large attached glass sunroom and a display area for his orchid collection. This home office upgrade would likely be considered to serve no business purpose, so the expenses related to the improvements would not be allowed. ♦

- **The Reasonableness Test:** The tax law requires that deductions be reasonable to be deducted.

EXAMPLE Derek owns a small business and takes one of his clients, who is also a friend, to an expensive business dinner every week. They enjoy a variety of restaurants and fine wines, and always spend some time talking about their joint business interests. The yearly cost of the meetings and meals is $20,000, and Derek generates $15,000 of fees from his friend each year. This lavish and extravagant business entertainment would likely not be considered reasonable given the circumstances. If they had met for pizza and a business discussion every week, the expense would likely be considered reasonable and deductible. ♦

The IRS and courts have taken a fairly permissive perspective on the deduction of business expenses; however, the Code does restrict the deduction of certain expenses such as the following:

- Personal, living, and family expenses (although see itemized deductions in Chapter 5)
- Capital expenditures (see Chapter 8)
- Expenses related to tax-exempt income
- Expenditures related to the sale of illegal drugs
- Illegal bribes and kickbacks
- Fines, penalties, and other payments to governments related to the violation of law
- Lobbying and political expenditures
- Settlement or attorney fees related to sexual abuse or harassment if subject to a non-disclosure agreement

Taxes are specifically excepted from the restriction on fines and penalties as are payments made to bring the taxpayer into compliance with the law or as restitution.

EXAMPLE Maria owns and operates a small pizza shop in the city. The City Council is considering new zoning laws that would permit the creation of a large hotel and theme park next to Maria's restaurant which she expects would increase her business significantly. She pays $10,000 to have a study prepared to show the economic benefits of the new zoning to the City Council at a future meeting. Maria also has been a Republican since she was old enough to vote and makes a $1,000 contribution to the Republican National Committee. The $10,000 fee and her contribution to the RNC are lobbying and political expenditures and are not deductible. ♦

3-1c Schedule C

Schedule C is used by sole proprietors to report profit or loss from their businesses. The first section (lines A to J) of Schedule C requires disclosure of basic information such as the business name and location, the accounting method (cash, accrual, or other, as covered in Chapter 6), material participation in the business (for passive activity loss classification purposes, see Chapter 4), and whether the business was started or acquired during the year.

Schedule C requires the taxpayer to provide a principal business or professional activity code (see Figure 3.1). These codes are used to classify sole proprietorships by the type of business activity. For example, a full-service restaurant is code 722511, as shown in Figure 3.1.

FIGURE 3.1 **PRINCIPAL BUSINESS OR PROFESSIONAL ACTIVITY CODES EXCERPT**

Principal Business or Professional Activity Codes

These codes for the Principal Business or Professional Activity classify sole proprietorships by the type of activity they are engaged in to facilitate the administration of the Internal Revenue Code. These six-digit codes are based on the North American Industry Classification System (NAICS).

Select the category that best describes your primary business activity (for example, Real Estate). Then select the activity that best identifies the principal source of your sales or receipts (for example, real estate agent). Now find the six-digit code assigned to this activity (for example, 531210, the code for offices of real estate agents and brokers) and enter it on Schedule C, line B.

Note. If your principal source of income is from farming activities, you should file Schedule F.

Accommodation, Food Services, & Drinking Places

Accommodation

721310 Rooming & boarding houses, dormitories, & workers' camps
721210 RV (recreational vehicle) parks & recreational camps
721100 Traveler accommodation (including hotels, motels, & bed & breakfast inns)

Food Services & Drinking Places

722514 Cafeterias & buffets
722410 Drinking places (alcoholic beverages)
722511 Full-service restaurants
722513 Limited-service restaurants
722515 Snack & non-alcoholic beverage bars

115110 Support activities for crop production (including cotton ginning, soil preparation, planting, & cultivating)
115310 Support activities for forestry

Arts, Entertainment, & Recreation

Amusement, Gambling, & Recreation Industries

713100 Amusement parks & arcades
713200 Gambling industries
713900 Other amusement & recreation services (including golf courses, skiing facilities, marinas, fitness centers, bowling centers, skating rinks, miniature golf courses)

Museums, Historical Sites, & Similar Institutions

238990 All other specialty trade contractors

Educational Services

611000 Educational services (including schools, colleges, & universities)

Finance & Insurance

Credit Intermediation & Related Activities

522100 Depository credit intermediation (including commercial banking, savings institutions, & credit unions)
522200 Nondepository credit intermediation (including sales financing & consumer lending)
522300 Activities related to credit intermediation (including loan brokers)

624310 Vocational rehabilitation services

Information

511000 Publishing industries (except Internet)

Broadcasting (except Internet) & Telecommunications

515000 Broadcasting (except Internet)
517000 Telecommunications & Internet service providers

Data Processing Services

518210 Data processing, hosting, & related services
519100 Other information services (including news syndicates & libraries, Internet publishing & broadcasting)

Motion Picture & Sound Recording

2021 Schedule C instructions presented. 2022 not available as we went to print.

3-1d Schedule C Income (Part I)

Part I of Schedule C (Figure 3.2) contains the calculation of the taxpayer's gross income from the business or profession. The calculation starts with gross receipts or sales (line 1). Returns and allowances (line 2) and cost of goods sold (line 4) are subtracted to arrive at the gross profit from the activity. Other related income from the business (line 6) is added to the gross profit to produce the Schedule C gross income (line 7).

FIGURE 3.2 **SCHEDULE C INCOME (PART I)**

Part I Income

1	Gross receipts or sales. See instructions for line 1 and check the box if this income was reported to you on Form W-2 and the "Statutory employee" box on that form was checked ☐	1	
2	Returns and allowances	2	
3	Subtract line 2 from line 1	3	
4	Cost of goods sold (from line 42)	4	
5	**Gross profit.** Subtract line 4 from line 3	5	
6	Other income, including federal and state gasoline or fuel tax credit or refund (see instructions)	6	
7	**Gross income.** Add lines 5 and 6	7	

3-1e Schedule C Expenses (Part II)

The taxpayer reports the expenses from their business or profession in Part II of Schedule C (Figure 3.3). Expenses such as advertising, insurance, interest, rent, travel, wages, and utilities are reported on lines 8 through 27. Some expenses such as depreciation may require additional supporting information from another schedule. The expenses are totaled on line 28 and subtracted from gross income (line 7) to arrive at the tentative profit or loss from the activity (line 29). An expense for business use of a taxpayer's home (see LO 3.11) is computed on Form 8829 or using the simplified method. The deductible portion of home office expenses is

FIGURE 3.3 SCHEDULE C EXPENSES (PART II)

Part II **Expenses.** Enter expenses for business use of your home **only** on line 30.

Line	Description	Box	Amount	Line	Description	Box	Amount
8	Advertising	8		18	Office expense (see instructions) .	18	
9	Car and truck expenses (see instructions) . . .	9		19	Pension and profit-sharing plans .	19	
				20	Rent or lease (see instructions):		
10	Commissions and fees .	10		a	Vehicles, machinery, and equipment	20a	
11	Contract labor (see instructions)	11		b	Other business property . . .	20b	
12	Depletion	12		21	Repairs and maintenance . . .	21	
13	Depreciation and section 179 expense deduction (not included in Part III) (see instructions)	13		22	Supplies (not included in Part III) .	22	
				23	Taxes and licenses	23	
				24	Travel and meals:		
14	Employee benefit programs (other than on line 19) .	14		a	Travel	24a	
15	Insurance (other than health)	15		b	Deductible meals (see instructions)	24b	
16	Interest (see instructions):			25	Utilities	25	
a	Mortgage (paid to banks, etc.)	16a		26	Wages (less employment credits)	26	
b	Other	16b		27a	Other expenses (from line 48) . .	27a	
17	Legal and professional services	17		b	**Reserved for future use** . . .	27b	

28	**Total expenses** before expenses for business use of home. Add lines 8 through 27a	28	
29	Tentative profit or (loss). Subtract line 28 from line 7	29	
30	Expenses for business use of your home. Do not report these expenses elsewhere. Attach Form 8829 unless using the simplified method. See instructions. **Simplified method filers only:** Enter the total square footage of (a) your home: ______ and (b) the part of your home used for business: ______. Use the Simplified Method Worksheet in the instructions to figure the amount to enter on line 30	30	
31	**Net profit or (loss).** Subtract line 30 from line 29. • If a profit, enter on both **Schedule 1 (Form 1040), line 3,** and on **Schedule SE, line 2.** (If you checked the box on line 1, see instructions.) Estates and trusts, enter on **Form 1041, line 3.** • If a loss, you **must** go to line 32.	31	
32	If you have a loss, check the box that describes your investment in this activity. See instructions. • If you checked 32a, enter the loss on both **Schedule 1 (Form 1040), line 3,** and on **Schedule SE, line 2.** (If you checked the box on line 1, see the line 31 instructions.) Estates and trusts, enter on **Form 1041, line 3.** • If you checked 32b, you **must** attach **Form 6198.** Your loss may be limited.	32a ☐ All investment is at risk. 32b ☐ Some investment is not at risk.	

entered on line 30 and subtracted from tentative profit, resulting in the net profit or loss (line 31) from the activity. Common business expenses are covered in detail later in this chapter.

3-1f Schedule C Cost of Goods Sold (Part III)

The calculation of cost of goods sold is reported in Part III (Figure 3.4) of Schedule C. In Part III lines 33 and 34, taxpayers must answer questions about the methods used to calculate inventory. Cost of goods sold (line 42) is equal to the beginning inventory (line 35) plus purchases (line 36), labor (line 37), materials and supplies (line 38), and other costs (line 39) less ending inventory (line 41). Please see LO 3.2 for a more detailed discussion of inventories.

3-1g Schedule C Vehicle Information (Part IV)

If a taxpayer uses a car or truck in their sole proprietorship, then Part IV of Schedule C (Figure 3.5) must be completed to provide the IRS with supplemental vehicle information. In Part IV, a taxpayer should provide the date the vehicle was placed in service for business use (line 43), the business miles driven (line 44a), the commuting miles driven (line 44b), and other miles driven (line 44c). On lines 45 to 47 of Part IV, taxpayers must answer questions relevant to obtaining a deduction for business use of a vehicle.

According to the Small Business Administration, almost 50 percent of small businesses fail in the first five years and about two-thirds fail within ten years. To assist small business owners with winding up their tax affairs, the IRS provides a website devoted to this unenviable task. Go to **www.irs.gov/businesses/small-businesses-self-employed/closing-a-business** and select the type of entity (sole proprietor, corporation, etc.).

FIGURE 3.4 COST OF GOODS SOLD (PART III)

Part III **Cost of Goods Sold** (see instructions)

33	Method(s) used to value closing inventory: **a** ☐ Cost **b** ☐ Lower of cost or market **c** ☐ Other (attach explanation)		
34	Was there any change in determining quantities, costs, or valuations between opening and closing inventory? If "Yes," attach explanation . . . ☐ **Yes** ☐ **No**		
35	Inventory at beginning of year. If different from last year's closing inventory, attach explanation . . .	**35**	
36	Purchases less cost of items withdrawn for personal use . . .	**36**	
37	Cost of labor. Do not include any amounts paid to yourself . . .	**37**	
38	Materials and supplies . . .	**38**	
39	Other costs . . .	**39**	
40	Add lines 35 through 39 . . .	**40**	
41	Inventory at end of year . . .	**41**	
42	**Cost of goods sold.** Subtract line 41 from line 40. Enter the result here and on line 4 . . .	**42**	

FIGURE 3.5 VEHICLE INFORMATION (PART IV)

Part IV **Information on Your Vehicle.** Complete this part **only** if you are claiming car or truck expenses on line 9 and are not required to file Form 4562 for this business. See the instructions for line 13 to find out if you must file Form 4562.

43 When did you place your vehicle in service for business purposes? (month/day/year) ______/______/______

44 Of the total number of miles you drove your vehicle during 2022, enter the number of miles you used your vehicle for:

a Business ____________ **b** Commuting (see instructions) ____________ **c** Other ____________

45 Was your vehicle available for personal use during off-duty hours? . . . ☐ **Yes** ☐ **No**

46 Do you (or your spouse) have another vehicle available for personal use?. . . ☐ **Yes** ☐ **No**

47a Do you have evidence to support your deduction? . . . ☐ **Yes** ☐ **No**

b If "Yes," is the evidence written? . . . ☐ **Yes** ☐ **No**

3-1h Schedule C Other Expenses (Part V)

The expenses section of Schedule C (Part II), line 27a contains an entry for other miscellaneous expenses. These other expenses must be itemized in Part V of Schedule C and include deductible items which do not have specific lines already assigned in the expenses section (Part II). Expenses for business gifts, education, professional dues, and consulting fees are commonly listed.

3-1i Self-Employment Tax

Self-employed taxpayers, sole proprietors, and independent contractors with net earnings of $400 or more, many of whom report income on Schedule C, must pay self-employment tax calculated on Schedule SE with their Form 1040. For new business owners, the self-employment tax may come as a particularly unpleasant and costly surprise if they are not aware of its existence.

The self-employment tax is made up of two taxes, the Social Security tax, which is meant to fund old age and disability insurance payments, and the Medicare tax. For 2022, the Social Security tax rate of 12.4 percent applies to the first $147,000 of net self-employment income, while the Medicare tax rate of 2.9 percent applies to all net self-employment income, with no income ceiling. Half of the self-employment tax is allowed as a deduction on Line 15 of Schedule 1 of Form 1040 in arriving at adjusted gross income. Self-employment taxes are similar to FICA taxes, which are levied on employees partly through payroll withholding and partly through employer contributions. FICA taxes are not paid with Form 1040 as self-employment taxes are. Self-employed Social Security and Medicare taxes, including the 0.9 percent additional Medicare tax, are covered in detail in Chapter 6.

ProConnect™ Tax TIP

To report profits from a sole proprietorship in ProConnect Tax, under Income use Business Income (Schedule C) to enter information. Additional businesses can be added using the [+] tab at the top of the main window.

Self-Study Problem 3.1 *See Appendix E for Solutions to Self-Study Problems*

Teri Kataoka is self-employed as a professional golf instructor. She uses the cash method of accounting, and her Social Security number is 466-47-8833. Her principal business code is 812990. Teri's business is located at 4300 Diamond Head Rd, Honolulu, HI 96816. During 2022, Teri had the following income and expenses:

Fees from golf lessons	$40,125
Expenses:	
Car expenses (5,000 business miles)	3,025
Business liability insurance	475
Office expense	660
Rent on office space	2,700
City business license	250
Travel expense	3,000
Meals (deductible portion)	985
Utilities	515
Membership in professional golfers' association	500

Teri bought her car on January 1, 2022. In addition to the business miles listed above, she commuted 1,200 miles and she drove 4,500 miles for nonbusiness purposes.

Complete Schedule C on Pages 3-8 and 3-9 for Teri showing her net income from self-employment. Make realistic assumptions about any missing data.

3-2 INVENTORIES

3.2 Learning Objective

Describe the tax treatment of inventories and cost of goods sold.

Inventory is the stock of goods or materials that a business holds for the purpose of resale to generate a profit. The purchase or sale of merchandise is almost always an income-producing factor for manufacturers, retailers, and wholesalers, and cost of goods sold is often the largest expense for these types of businesses.

Self-Study Problem 3.1

SCHEDULE C (Form 1040)

Department of the Treasury Internal Revenue Service

Profit or Loss From Business

(Sole Proprietorship)

Go to *www.irs.gov/ScheduleC* for instructions and the latest information.

Attach to Form 1040, 1040-SR, 1040-NR, or 1041; partnerships must generally file Form 1065.

OMB No. 1545-0074

2022

Attachment Sequence No. **09**

Name of proprietor | **Social security number (SSN)**

A Principal business or profession, including product or service (see instructions) | **B Enter code from instructions**

C Business name. If no separate business name, leave blank. | **D Employer ID number (EIN)** (see instr.)

E Business address (including suite or room no.)

City, town or post office, state, and ZIP code

F Accounting method: **(1)** ☐ Cash **(2)** ☐ Accrual **(3)** ☐ Other (specify)

G Did you "materially participate" in the operation of this business during 2022? If "No," see instructions for limit on losses . ☐ **Yes** ☐ **No**

H If you started or acquired this business during 2022, check here . . . ☐

I Did you make any payments in 2022 that would require you to file Form(s) 1099? See instructions . . ☐ **Yes** ☐ **No**

J If "Yes," did you or will you file required Form(s) 1099? . . . ☐ **Yes** ☐ **No**

Part I Income

1	Gross receipts or sales. See instructions for line 1 and check the box if this income was reported to you on Form W-2 and the "Statutory employee" box on that form was checked . . . ☐	1	
2	Returns and allowances . . .	2	
3	Subtract line 2 from line 1 . . .	3	
4	Cost of goods sold (from line 42) . . .	4	
5	**Gross profit.** Subtract line 4 from line 3 . . .	5	
6	Other income, including federal and state gasoline or fuel tax credit or refund (see instructions) . . .	6	
7	**Gross income.** Add lines 5 and 6 . . .	7	

Part II Expenses. Enter expenses for business use of your home **only** on line 30.

8	Advertising . . .	8		18	Office expense (see instructions) .	18	
9	Car and truck expenses (see instructions) . . .	9		19	Pension and profit-sharing plans .	19	
				20	Rent or lease (see instructions):		
10	Commissions and fees .	10		a	Vehicles, machinery, and equipment	20a	
11	Contract labor (see instructions)	11		b	Other business property . . .	20b	
12	Depletion . . .	12		21	Repairs and maintenance . . .	21	
13	Depreciation and section 179 expense deduction (not included in Part III) (see instructions) . . .	13		22	Supplies (not included in Part III) .	22	
				23	Taxes and licenses . . .	23	
				24	Travel and meals:		
14	Employee benefit programs (other than on line 19) .	14		a	Travel . . .	24a	
15	Insurance (other than health)	15		b	Deductible meals (see instructions) . . .	24b	
16	Interest (see instructions):			25	Utilities . . .	25	
a	Mortgage (paid to banks, etc.)	16a		26	Wages (less employment credits)	26	
b	Other . . .	16b		27a	Other expenses (from line 48) . .	27a	
17	Legal and professional services	17		b	**Reserved for future use** . . .	27b	

28	**Total expenses** before expenses for business use of home. Add lines 8 through 27a . . .	28	
29	Tentative profit or (loss). Subtract line 28 from line 7 . . .	29	
30	Expenses for business use of your home. Do not report these expenses elsewhere. Attach Form 8829 unless using the simplified method. See instructions. **Simplified method filers only:** Enter the total square footage of (a) your home: ______ and (b) the part of your home used for business: ______ . Use the Simplified Method Worksheet in the instructions to figure the amount to enter on line 30 . . .	30	
31	**Net profit or (loss).** Subtract line 30 from line 29. • If a profit, enter on both **Schedule 1 (Form 1040), line 3,** and on **Schedule SE, line 2.** (If you checked the box on line 1, see instructions.) Estates and trusts, enter on **Form 1041, line 3.** • If a loss, you **must** go to line 32.	31	
32	If you have a loss, check the box that describes your investment in this activity. See instructions. • If you checked 32a, enter the loss on both **Schedule 1 (Form 1040), line 3,** and on **Schedule SE, line 2.** (If you checked the box on line 1, see the line 31 instructions.) Estates and trusts, enter on **Form 1041, line 3.** • If you checked 32b, you **must** attach **Form 6198.** Your loss may be limited.		**32a** ☐ All investment is at risk. **32b** ☐ Some investment is not at risk.

For Paperwork Reduction Act Notice, see the separate instructions. Cat. No. 11334P **Schedule C (Form 1040) 2022**

Schedule C (Form 1040) 2022 Page 2

Part III Cost of Goods Sold (see instructions)

33	Method(s) used to value closing inventory: a ☐ Cost b ☐ Lower of cost or market c ☐ Other (attach explanation)		
34	Was there any change in determining quantities, costs, or valuations between opening and closing inventory? If "Yes," attach explanation . . . ☐ Yes ☐ No		
35	Inventory at beginning of year. If different from last year's closing inventory, attach explanation	35	
36	Purchases less cost of items withdrawn for personal use	36	
37	Cost of labor. Do not include any amounts paid to yourself	37	
38	Materials and supplies	38	
39	Other costs	39	
40	Add lines 35 through 39	40	
41	Inventory at end of year	41	
42	**Cost of goods sold.** Subtract line 41 from line 40. Enter the result here and on line 4	42	

Part IV Information on Your Vehicle.

Complete this part **only** if you are claiming car or truck expenses on line 9 and are not required to file Form 4562 for this business. See the instructions for line 13 to find out if you must file Form 4562.

43 When did you place your vehicle in service for business purposes? (month/day/year) ____/____/____

44 Of the total number of miles you drove your vehicle during 2022, enter the number of miles you used your vehicle for:

a Business ____________ **b** Commuting (see instructions) ____________ **c** Other ____________

45 Was your vehicle available for personal use during off-duty hours? . . . ☐ Yes ☐ No

46 Do you (or your spouse) have another vehicle available for personal use?. . . ☐ Yes ☐ No

47a Do you have evidence to support your deduction? . . . ☐ Yes ☐ No

b If "Yes," is the evidence written? . . . ☐ Yes ☐ No

Part V Other Expenses.

List below business expenses not included on lines 8–26 or line 30.

48 Total other expenses. Enter here and on line 27a	48	

Schedule C (Form 1040) 2022

EXAMPLE Yashida operates a small business that sells crafts over the Internet. The crafts are manufactured in her small factory. The purchase and sale of merchandise is clearly an income-producing factor for this business. ♦

EXAMPLE Alan is a lawyer that specializes in consumer class-action lawsuits against large corporations. Because his primary product is legal services, inventory is not a significant income-producing factor for Alan's business. ♦

When a business supplies goods in conjunction with providing services to customers, it is not always clear whether providing goods is an income-producing factor that requires the business to keep inventories.

Accounting for inventory can be complex. One of the primary steps in inventory accounting is to measure ending inventory at the end of the accounting period (usually at year-end). To do so often requires a physical inventory, which is a process by which the actual count of goods is taken. An additional step is to assign an inventory flow method such as first-in, first-out (FIFO) or last-in, first-out (LIFO). Once ending inventory is established, cost of goods sold can be computed as follows:

Beginning inventory	$ 75,000
Add: purchases	250,000
Costs of goods available for sale	325,000
Less: ending inventory	(100,000)
Cost of goods sold	$ 225,000

Because of the time and effort associated with tracking inventory, the tax law permits small businesses to use the cash method for accounting for inventory. For purposes of this tax provision, a business with three-year average gross receipts of less than $27 million is considered a small business. Under the cash method, the taxpayer has three options:

1. treat inventory as non-incidental materials and supplies,
2. treat inventory the same as on the applicable financial statements of the business, or
3. for taxpayers without applicable financial statements, treat inventory as it conforms with the business books and records.

Non-incidental materials and supplies (NIMS) are deducted either in the year that the merchandise is sold or the year in which the inventory is paid for, whichever is later.

EXAMPLE Geoff purchases unique goods from a variety of manufacturers and then sells those items over the Internet. Geoff's business is small and he treats inventory as NIMS. He will include the cost of the goods in his cost of goods sold when the items are sold. ♦

The treatment of inventory as NIMS does not differ considerably from typical inventory accounting, which also generally would recover the cost of inventory when the inventory is sold.

The second option is to treat inventory the same as that of applicable financial statements (or AFS) of the business. AFS are generally financial statements that have been prepared in accordance with generally accepted accounting principles (GAAP). Since GAAP is going to require proper inventory accounting, this option provides no significant relief from inventory accounting.

The last option is to use the same accounting for inventory as is used on the books and records of the business. Under this option, if a business chooses to expense inventory when purchased, the business would be permitted to deduct the costs in the same year for tax purposes.

EXAMPLE Sue operates a garage that repairs European-made automobiles. As part of the service, the garage purchases and eventually sells a variety of car parts, including oil filters, brake pads, various belts, and motors (such as alternators). Sue expenses any part or supply as it is purchased, in spite of the item not yet being sold. For example, Sue may purchase five oil filters (when only one is needed for a current repair) with the expectation that the remaining four filters will be sold in the near future. Sue does not prepare applicable financial statements for her business. Sue will be able to conform her tax accounting for inventory with her books and records and thus will deduct inventory when purchased. ♦

However, the regulations surrounding this tax law appear to increase the likelihood that *any* use of typical inventory accounting may preclude deducting the cost of inventory at any time except when sold.

EXAMPLE Sasha is engaged in the retail business of selling beer, wine, and liquor. Sasha has average annual gross receipts for the prior three taxable years of less than $27 million and thus uses the cash method of accounting. Sasha treats all merchandise costs paid during the taxable year as expensed on the bookkeeping software. However, as part of its regular business practice, Sasha takes a physical count of inventory of merchandise on hand at year end. Sasha also makes representations to its creditor of the amount of inventory on hand. Because Sasha's books and records do not accurately reflect the inventory records used for non-tax purposes in its regular business activity, Sasha must use the physical inventory count to determine its ending inventory and thus will deduct only the cost of inventory sold based on that count. ♦

The above examples of the three options for cash-basis inventory accounting show that only a small business that pays very little attention to inventory, can use the cash-basis method of inventory. To the extent that the purchase or sale of merchandise is a significant income-producing activity, recommended business practices would not permit such transactions without some form of tracking and accounting controls. Tax law generally requires the capitalization of certain indirect costs into inventory under Section 263A, sometimes known as the Uniform Capitalization (UNICAP) rules. Businesses with gross receipts of no more than $27 million are not required to apply the UNICAP rules. The details of the UNICAP rules are beyond the scope of this textbook.

As a result of the current interpretation of inventory tax law, most businesses must calculate cost of goods sold by determining the value of the beginning and ending inventories of the business. This involves determining the cost of the items on hand. This process is not as easy as it seems, since the taxpayer will often have paid different prices during the year for the same item. There are two common methods of inventory valuation used by taxpayers: first in, first out (FIFO) and last in, first out (LIFO). The FIFO method is based on the assumption that the first merchandise acquired is the first to be sold. Accordingly, the inventory on hand consists of the most recently acquired goods. Alternatively, when the taxpayer uses the LIFO method, it is assumed that the most recently acquired goods are sold first and the inventory on hand consists of the earliest purchases. FIFO and LIFO are simply calculation assumptions; the goods that are actually on hand do not have to correspond to the assumptions of the method selected. In addition to the LIFO and FIFO methods which are commonly used by taxpayers in valuing beginning and ending inventories, taxpayers may specifically identify the goods that are sold and the goods that are in ending inventory. However, the process of specifically identifying items sold and on hand is not a practical alternative for most taxpayers.

EXAMPLE Paige made the following purchases of a particular inventory item during the current year:

March 1	50 units at $120 per unit	$ 6,000
August 1	40 units at $130 per unit	5,200
December 1	25 units at $140 per unit	3,500
Total		$14,700

If the ending inventory is 60 units, it is valued under the FIFO method as illustrated below:

25 units at $140 each	$3,500
35 units at $130 each	4,550
Ending inventory	$8,050

Assuming that Paige had no beginning inventory of the item, the same ending inventory (60 units) would be valued using the LIFO method as follows:

50 units at $120 each	$6,000
10 units at $130 each	1,300
Ending inventory	$7,300

The cost of goods sold for both the FIFO and LIFO methods are presented below:

	FIFO	*LIFO*
Beginning inventory	$ 0	$ 0
Add: purchases	14,700	14,700
Cost of goods available for sale	$14,700	$14,700
Less: ending inventory	(8,050)	(7,300)
Cost of goods sold	$ 6,650	$ 7,400

Notice that taxable income will be $750 more when the FIFO method is used instead of the LIFO method. During periods of rising inventory prices, taxpayers have lower taxable income and pay less tax if they use the LIFO inventory valuation method. ♦

A taxpayer may adopt the LIFO method by using it in a tax return and attaching Form 970 to make the election. Once the election is made, the method may be changed only with the consent of the IRS. Also, if the LIFO election is made for reporting taxable income, taxpayers must use the same method for preparing their financial statements. In other words, a taxpayer may not use LIFO for their tax return and use FIFO for financial statements presented to a bank. This rule is strictly enforced by the IRS.

Self-Study Problem 3.2 *See Appendix E for Solutions to Self-Study Problems*

Kelly owns a small retail store. During the year, Kelly purchases $178,750 worth of inventory. Her beginning inventory is $62,500 and her ending inventory is $68,400. Use Part III of Schedule C below to calculate Kelly's cost of goods sold for the year.

Part III **Cost of Goods Sold** (see instructions)

33 Method(s) used to value closing inventory: a ☐ Cost b ☐ Lower of cost or market c ☐ Other (attach explanation)

34 Was there any change in determining quantities, costs, or valuations between opening and closing inventory? If "Yes," attach explanation . . . ☐ Yes ☐ No

35	Inventory at beginning of year. If different from last year's closing inventory, attach explanation	35	
36	Purchases less cost of items withdrawn for personal use	36	
37	Cost of labor. Do not include any amounts paid to yourself	37	
38	Materials and supplies	38	
39	Other costs	39	
40	Add lines 35 through 39	40	
41	Inventory at end of year	41	
42	**Cost of goods sold.** Subtract line 41 from line 40. Enter the result here and on line 4	42	

3-3 TRANSPORTATION

3.3 Learning Objective

Identify the requirements for deducting transportation expenses.

Certain transportation expenses for business purposes are deductible by self-employed taxpayers and employers. Deductible expenses include travel by airplane, rail, and bus, and the cost of operating and maintaining an automobile. Meals and lodging are *not* included in the transportation expense deduction; those expenses may be deducted as travel expenses (see LO 3.4). Transportation expenses may be deducted even if the taxpayer is not away from his or her tax home.

Not since 2011 has the IRS increased the standard mileage rate in the middle of a tax year but due to the high cost of fuel, the 2022 rate increased from 58.5 cents per mile for the first half of the year to 62.5 cents per mile starting July 1, 2022. The medical mileage rate also increased from 18 cents per mile to 22 cents per mile; however, the charity mileage rate is fixed by law at 14 cents per mile and did not change.

Deductible transportation costs do not include the normal costs of commuting. Commuting includes the expenses of buses, subways, taxis, and operating a private car between home and the taxpayer's principal place of work, and is generally a nondeductible personal expense. The cost of transportation between the taxpayer's home and a work location is generally not deductible, except in the three sets of circumstances described below:

1. A taxpayer is allowed to deduct daily transportation expenses incurred in going between the taxpayer's residence and work locations outside the metropolitan area where the taxpayer lives and normally works.
2. If the taxpayer has a regular place of business, daily expenses for transportation between the taxpayer's home and temporary work locations are deductible.
3. A taxpayer may deduct daily expenses for transportation between the taxpayer's home and other regular or temporary work locations if the taxpayer's residence is the

taxpayer's principal place of business, based on the home office rules, which are discussed later in this chapter.

In all cases, the additional costs of hauling tools and instruments are deductible. For example, the cost of renting a trailer to haul tools to a job site is deductible.

If the taxpayer works at two or more jobs during the same day, he or she may deduct the cost of going from one job to the other or from one business location to another. The deductible expense is based on the cost of travel by the shortest, most normally traveled route, even if the taxpayer uses another route. If the taxpayer works at a second job on a day that he or she does not work at the first job, the commuting expenses to the second job are not deductible.

EXAMPLE Walter is a self-employed CPA working full time Monday through Friday. On Tuesday night he teaches an accounting class at a local university. Walter leaves the office at 5:30 p.m. on his class day and, after dinner at a local cafe, teaches his class from 7:00 p.m. to 10:00 p.m. The distance from Walter's home to his office is twelve miles, the distance from his office to the university is fifteen miles, and the distance from the university to his home is eighteen miles. If Walter teaches the class thirty-two times a year, his mileage deduction is based on 480 miles (32 × 15 miles). While he is traveling from home to the office (twelve miles) and from the university to home (eighteen miles), he is commuting and the mileage is not deductible. If Walter taught the class in the afternoon and returned to his regular job before going home, he could claim a deduction based on the round-trip mileage from his office to and from the university, thirty miles (2 × 15 miles). Alternatively, if he taught the course on a day (Saturday) when he did not work at his full-time job, Walter would not be entitled to any mileage deduction. ♦

Taxpayers may deduct the actual expenses of transportation, or they may be entitled to use a standard mileage rate to calculate their deduction for transportation costs. The standard mileage rate for 2022 is 58.5 cents per mile through June 30. Because of the increase in fuel prices, the rate was increased to 62.5 cents per mile on or after July 1. Most costs associated with the operation of an automobile, such as gasoline, oil, insurance, repairs, and maintenance, as well as depreciation, are built into the standard mileage rate. The deduction for parking and toll fees related to business transportation (not commuting) and the deduction for interest on car loans and state and local personal property taxes on the automobile are determined separately. Self-employed taxpayers deduct the business portion of the state and local personal property taxes and interest on automobile loans on Schedule C or F. To use the standard mileage method, the taxpayer must:

1. own or lease the automobile,
2. not operate a fleet of automobiles, using five or more at the same time,
3. not have claimed depreciation on the automobile using any method other than straight-line depreciation, and
4. not have claimed Section 179 (expense election) depreciation or bonus depreciation on the automobile (see Chapter 8 for a complete discussion of depreciation).

If the taxpayer is entitled to use either the actual cost or the standard mileage method, they may select the method that results in the largest tax deduction for the first year. If the taxpayer does not use the standard mileage method in the first year, the method is no longer available for any subsequent year. A change to the actual cost method can be made any year. If, after using the standard mileage method, the taxpayer uses actual costs to determine the automobile expense deduction, depreciation on the automobile must be calculated using straight-line depreciation (see Chapter 8). The standard mileage method may be used for a car for hire, such as a taxi, if the automobile meets the other requirements for use of this method.

Taxpayers who use the actual cost method to calculate their transportation deductions must keep adequate cost records. The deductible portion of the total automobile expenses is based on the ratio of the number of business miles driven during the year to the total miles driven during the tax year multiplied by the total automobile expenses for the year. The business-use percentage is applied to the total automobile expenses for the year, including depreciation, but excluding any expenses which are directly attributable to business use of the automobile, such as business parking fees and tolls. The deduction for interest and personal property taxes is also separately computed.

EXAMPLE T.J. is a self-employed salesman who drove his automobile 22,500 total miles ratably during the 2022 tax year. The business use of the automobile was 80 percent of the total miles driven. The actual cost of gasoline, oil, repairs, depreciation, and insurance for the year was $10,000. The automobile expense deduction is calculated as follows:

1. Standard mileage method:

Business mileage = 18,000 miles (22,500 miles × 80%)	
9,000 × 58.5 cents/mile	$ 5,265
9,000 × 62.5 cents/mile	5,625
Total	$10,890

2. Actual cost method:

80% × $10,000 (total actual cost)	$ 8,000

T.J. is permitted to deduct the larger amount. ♦

ProConnect™ Tax TIP

Vehicle expenses are reported on Form 2106 and are carried over to Schedule C or other forms. To enter deductions associated with a business vehicle, go to Vehicle/Employee Business Expense (2106) under the general Deductions item in the left margin. The deduction can be connected to the appropriate Schedule C or other business using a dropdown box.

Self-Study Problem 3.3

See Appendix E for Solutions to Self-Study Problems

Marc Lusebrink, sole proprietor of Oak Company, bought a used automobile and drove it 6,000 miles through June 30, 2022 and another 7,000 miles during the remainder of the year, all for business purposes. Total miles (including business miles) is 16,000. His total expenses for his automobile for the year are:

Gasoline	$2,061
Oil changes	92
Insurance	1,030
Tires	225
Repairs	620
Total	$4,028

The automobile cost $20,000 on January 1, and depreciation expense for the year, including business use, was $4,000. His business parking and toll fees for business amount to $327. Calculate Marc's transportation expense deduction for the year.

Learning Objective 3.4

Identify the requirements for deducting travel expenses.

3-4 TRAVEL EXPENSES

Travel expenses are defined as ordinary and necessary expenses incurred in traveling away from home in pursuit of the taxpayer's trade or business. These expenses are deductible as long as they can be substantiated and are not lavish or extravagant. Transportation expenses incurred while not away from home such as business gifts are not included as travel expenses, although these items may be separately deductible, subject to certain limitations. Expenses included as part of the travel deduction include the cost of such items as meals, lodging, taxis, tips, and laundry. Most travel expenses are fully deductible, but Congress decided that a portion of the cost of meals is a personal expense. Therefore, only 50 percent of the cost of meals is deductible. If an employer reimburses an employee for the cost of meals, then the 50 percent limitation applies to the employer so that the employer can deduct only 50 percent of the expense. Temporarily for 2022, the cost of business meals purchased at a restaurant is 100 percent deductible.

To deduct travel expenses, a taxpayer must be away from home "overnight." Overnight does not literally mean 24 hours; it is a period of time longer than an ordinary work day in which rest or relief from work is required. Also, the taxpayer must be away from his or her "tax home" to be on travel status. A tax home is the taxpayer's principal place of business or employment, and not necessarily the same location as their family residence. If the taxpayer has two or more places of business, the taxpayer's tax home is at the principal place of business. Factors that determine the principal place of business include total time spent in each location, the degree of business activity, and the relative amount of income from each location.

Expenses of a temporary assignment are deductible if it is not practical to return home at the end of each day's work or if the employer requires the employee's attendance at a business meeting, training activity, or other overnight business function. If the assignment is for a long period of time or indefinite (generally more than one year), the new location may be considered the taxpayer's new tax home and they may lose the travel deduction. If the travel costs are not deductible, an employee must include as income any reimbursements of non-deductible travel expenses.

Taxpayers who make a combined business and pleasure trip within the United States may deduct all of the costs incurred in traveling to and from the business destination (for example, airfare) provided the trip is primarily for business. Once at the destination, only the business portion of the travel costs for meals, lodging, local transportation, and incidental expenses may be deducted; any costs which are not associated with the taxpayer's business are not deductible. If a taxpayer makes a trip which is primarily for pleasure, the travel expenses to and from the destination are not deductible even though the taxpayer engages in some business activity while at the destination. Although the traveling expenses to and from the destination are not deductible, any expenses incurred while at the destination that are related to the taxpayer's business are deductible.

Special rules and limitations apply to combined business and pleasure travel outside the United States. Even though a trip is primarily for business, if the trip has any element of pleasure, the cost of traveling to and from the destination must be allocated between the business and personal portions of the trip. The travel expenses for transportation to and from the destination must be allocated based on the number of business days compared to the total number of days outside the United States. The rules for travel costs to and from the destination where the trip is primarily for pleasure are the same as the rules for travel within the United States; none of the travel costs are deductible. Once at the destination, the taxpayer's expenses directly related to the taxpayer's business are deductible. For a complete explanation of travel outside the United States, see IRS Publication 463.

No deduction for travel expenses is allowed unless the taxpayer keeps proper expense records. Taxpayers must substantiate the following:

1. The amount of each separate expenditure, such as airfare and lodging. Expenses such as meals and taxi fares may be accumulated and reported in reasonable categories. As an alternative to reporting actual expenses, a per diem method may be used in certain circumstances.

2. The dates of departure and return for each trip and the number of business days on the trip.
3. The destination or locality of the travel described by the name of the city or town.
4. The business reason for the travel or the business benefit expected to be gained from the travel.

EXAMPLE During 2022, Susan travels from Los Angeles to Hawaii for a three-day business trip and pays $450 for the airfare. While in Hawaii, Susan spends 3 days on business and an additional 2 days on vacation. The lodging and meal costs are $300 and $120, respectively, for the business portion of the trip. All meals were purchased at restaurants. The total cost of meals and lodging for the personal portion of the trip is $260. Susan may deduct $450 for the airfare, $300 for the business lodging, and $120 (100 percent of $120 in 2022) for the business meals. None of the $260 of personal expenses is deductible. ♦

3-4a **Per Diem Substantiation**

Instead of requiring actual expense records, employers who reimburse employees for travel expenses can choose a per diem method of substantiation. Per diem is a daily allowance used for business travel expenses while away from an employee's tax home. The primary advantage of using a per diem method to substantiate expenses is that it eliminates much of the record keeping usually associated with travel expenses. The IRS has approved two per diem methods to substantiate travel expenses: (1) the standard per diem method and (2) the high-low per diem method. Employers can use per diem for all travel expenses including lodging, meals, and incidentals or an employer can use per diem for only meals and incidentals. Self-employed taxpayers may only use per diem for meals and incidentals.

1. *The Standard Federal Rate Method*. Under this method, the employee is allowed a per diem amount for travel equal to the current federal per diem rate which varies based on the travel location. A complete list of the regular per diem rates in effect for each area of the United States is available at the U.S. General Services Administration website (**www.gsa.gov**). The GSA also offers a mobile app.
2. *The High-Low Method*. The high-low method provides a simplified way of computing the federal per diem rate for travel within the United States. This method avoids the need to keep a current list of the per diem rates for all localities in the United States. Under this method a small number of locations are designated as high-cost localities and all other locations are deemed to be low-cost areas. Starting in October 2022, the high-cost allowance is $297 per day and the low-cost amount is $202 per day. If an employer uses this method to reimburse an employee any time during a calendar year, this method must be used for all travel for that employee in the same calendar year.

Under either the standard method or the high-low method, the employee can use a current per diem amount for meals and incidental expenses (M&IE) only. Actual cost records are required for lodging expenses. The M&IE rate may be taken from the standard per diem rate tables or the high-low method may be used. For 2022, the M&IE allowance using the high-low method is $74 per day for high-cost localities and $64 per day for low-cost localities. Employees and self-employed taxpayers who do not incur meal expenses when traveling are allowed an incidental expense allowance of $5 per day.

Per diem rates are revised on October 1 every year with additional revisions made for specific locations throughout the year. For purposes of illustration and problems, the rates above are assumed to be chosen for the full year. Different rates than those shown above may apply.

Self-Study Problem 3.4 *See Appendix E for Solutions to Self-Study Problems*

Byron is a certified public accountant who is self-employed. He is required to make a 5-day business trip to Salt Lake City for an audit. Since he is going to be in Utah, Byron decides to stay for the weekend and go skiing. His expenses for the trip are as follows:

Airfare to Salt Lake City and return	$ 480
Hotel while on the audit (5 nights at $165 per night)	825
Deductible portion of meals while on the audit	168
Laundry in Salt Lake City	22
Taxi fares in Salt Lake City	72
Transportation from Salt Lake City to and from Park City ski resort	100
Lodging at Park City ski resort	380
Lift tickets	99
Ski rental	89
Meals at Park City	182
Total	$2,417

If Byron has proper records to substantiate the above expenses, how much may he deduct as travel expenses for the 7-day trip?

Learning Objective 3.5

Determine the requirements for deducting meals.

3-5 MEALS AND ENTERTAINMENT

There is no deduction for (1) an activity generally considered to be entertainment, amusement, or recreation, (2) membership dues for any club organized for business, pleasure, recreation, or other social purposes, or (3) a facility used in connection with any of the above items. Entertainment costs related to a recreation, social, or similar activities for the benefit of employees remain deductible.

EXAMPLE Dee Skotech operates a small business and hosted two parties at a local night club during 2022. The first was a party for all of her clients to celebrate a great year and to thank them for their loyalty. The second party was a holiday celebration for all the employees in Dee's company. The costs associated with the client party are nondeductible entertainment costs. The costs for the employee holiday party are 100 percent deductible. ♦

Because meals and entertainment are often closely aligned, taxpayers should be cautious in attempting to deduct meals associated with an entertainment event. Client meals in which business is conducted (and the taxpayer or taxpayer's employee is present) and which are not lavish or extravagant are typically 50 percent deductible. However, in 2022, business meals are 100 percent deductible if the meal is provided by a restaurant. Under IRS rules, a restaurant is a business that prepares and sells food or beverages to retail customers for immediate consumption. Note that the food and beverages do not need to be consumed at the restaurant for the 100-percent deduction to apply. Businesses that predominantly sell pre-packaged food or beverages such as grocery stores, liquor stores, and specialty food stores are not restaurants. Eating facilities located at an employer's business that provide meals that are excluded from the employees' gross income, or that are considered a de minimis fringe benefit are also not restaurants. An entertainment-related meal such as one associated with a cocktail party, theatre, golf outing, or other entertainment event is only deductible if the meal is purchased or invoiced separately.

EXAMPLE Beau Gee is a salesperson for Hamilton Company. Beau has a meeting with an important customer at a local diner. Business is conducted at the meal as

Beau and the customer discuss pricing, delivery dates, and other particulars, although no sale is actually closed. After the meal, Beau suggests they play a round of golf at the local golf course. After playing a round of golf, Beau and the customer stop in the golf club's restaurant and have a drink or two and some appetizers. Because business was conducted at the diner, which is a restaurant, the cost of the first meal is 100 percent deductible; however, the golf is entertainment and is not deductible. If the drinks and appetizers are separately purchased, the cost is 100 percent deductible. ♦

In addition to celebratory meals such as holiday parties and company picnics, other meals remain either 50 or 100-percent deductible:

Type of meal	*Deductible*
Meals for the convenience of the employer	50 percent (see Chapter 2) until after 2025 and thereafter, not deductible
Water, coffee, and other office snacks	50 percent deductible
Restaurant meals provided for in-office meetings with employees	100 percent deductible
Restaurant meals during business travel	100 percent deductible
Meals offered for free to the public (e.g., a free seminar)	100 percent deductible
Food and beverages from a grocery store or liquor store	50 percent deductible

Although entertainment-related club dues are nondeductible, dues paid to professional organizations, such as bar or medical organizations, are deductible. Dues paid to civic or public organizations, such as Chambers of Commerce, Kiwanis, and Rotary, are also allowed as legitimate business deductions. These clubs do public service work and are not organizations like country clubs which are entertainment or pleasure driven. Many business people belong to clubs such as Kiwanis or Rotary to network, meet potential clients, and increase their visibility in the community, but the club must do significant service work for the members' dues to qualify as deductions.

Self-Study Problem 3.5

See Appendix E for Solutions to Self-Study Problems

Milly operates a small business and incurs the following expenses:

Annual dues Tampa Bay Golf Club	$2,000
Restaurant meals with clients after golf	500
Meals with clients at the Club's dining room where business was conducted	600
Greens fees (personal and with clients)	700
Meals (personal)	250
Total	$4,050

Calculate the portion of the $4,050 that Milly can deduct.

3-6 EDUCATIONAL EXPENSES

3.6 Learning Objective

Identify the requirements for claiming business education expenses.

Please note: Educational incentives such as qualified tuition programs and educational savings accounts are discussed in Chapter 2. The deduction for education loan interest is discussed in Chapter 5. Education tax credits are discussed in Chapter 7.

Because there are numerous education incentives, the tax law in this area has become very complex. There may be more than one tax option for treating a particular education expense. This section deals primarily with the deduction of continuing education expenses incurred by self-employed taxpayers. The suspension of the deduction for miscellaneous expenses subject to 2 percent of AGI has effectively eliminated the deduction of unreimbursed educational costs for employees.

TAX BREAK

Taxpayers have been able to manage a handful of wins against the IRS when it comes to claiming a deduction for the cost of an MBA degree. In *Zuo v. Comm.* (2021), an entrepreneur was permitted an unreimbursed employee business deduction after demonstrating that the MBA did not prepare him for a new job since he was already an entrepreneur before starting the degree. This follows a series of cases such as *Blair v. Comm.* (1980), *Beatty v. Comm.* (1980), *Allemeier v. Comm.* (2005), *Singleton-Clarke v. Comm.* (2009), *Long v. Comm.* (2016) in which the court held that the MBA did not qualify an already experienced businessperson for a new job and permitted a deduction. In *Zhao Creigh v. Comm.*; however, the court held the opposite since the taxpayers' role prior to the MBA differed substantially from her role afterward. Note that the temporary repeal of unreimbursed employee business expenses limits this deduction to self-employed only through 2025.

There are two tests related to the deduction of educational expenses, at least one of which must be met to deduct the expenses. The tests are:

1. the educational expenses must be paid to meet *the requirements of the taxpayer's employer or the requirements of law or regulation* for keeping the taxpayer's salary, status, or job, or
2. the educational expenses must be paid to *maintain* or *improve existing skills* required in performing the duties of the taxpayer's present work.

Educational expenses meeting one of the above tests, which have a bona fide business purpose, may be deducted even if the education leads to a college degree.

Educational expenses are not deductible, even if one of the above tests is met, if (1) the education is required to meet the minimum requirements for the taxpayer's current job, or (2) the education is part of a program that will lead to a new trade or business even if the taxpayer does not intend to enter that new trade or business.

3-6a Education Required by Employer or Law

Taxpayers who are required to meet educational standards beyond minimum requirements may deduct the expenses of the education. However, the expenses must be paid for education to maintain the taxpayer's current job, not to meet the minimum requirements for that job. If the education qualifies the taxpayer for a new trade or business, the expenses are not deductible.

EXAMPLE Jenny is a high school teacher working under a temporary teaching certificate. The state in which she teaches requires a master's degree to receive a permanent certificate, and Jenny only has a bachelor's degree. Her expenses to obtain a master's degree are not deductible even though the degree is required by her school district, since she has not yet met the minimum educational requirements to be a permanent teacher.

However, Jenny may qualify for the lifetime learning credit discussed in Chapter 7. ♦

3-6b Maintaining or Improving Existing Skills

Expenses that are paid by a taxpayer for education to maintain or improve existing skills are deductible. Expenses deductible under this category include the costs of continuing education courses and academic work at a college or university. However, the education must not lead to qualification in a new trade or business. The deduction of a review course for the CPA exam and bar exam is consistently disallowed by the IRS.

EXAMPLE John is a certified public accountant (CPA) in practice with a CPA firm. He decides a law degree would be helpful to him in his present job since he does a lot of income tax planning for clients. He enrolls in a night program at a local law school. John's educational expenses are not deductible since the program leads to a new trade or business, the practice of law. Whether or not John plans to practice law is not relevant. However, John may qualify for the lifetime learning credit discussed in Chapter 7 ♦

EXAMPLE Kenzie recently completed her degree in accounting and went to work for a local CPA firm. She spends $1,000 for a CPA exam review course to help her pass the exam. The $1,000 is not deductible since passing the CPA exam leads to a new trade or business, that of being a licensed CPA as opposed to an accountant. Depending on whether Kenzie takes this course at a qualified institution of higher education, and other circumstances, she may qualify for the lifetime learning credit discussed in Chapter 7 ♦

3-6c Expenses of Travel for Educational Purposes

Travel expenses incurred while away from home for trips that are primarily to obtain qualifying education are also deductible. For example, a taxpayer may deduct travel expenses for attending a continuing education course in a distant city. Whether a trip is primarily personal or primarily educational depends on the relative amount of time devoted to each activity. If the trip qualifies as primarily for educational purposes, the cost of transportation to and from the destination is fully deductible. The lodging and meal expenses directly connected with the educational activity are also deductible. As is the case with travel expenses, the cost of meals is only 50 percent deductible, unless provided by a restaurant. Expenses for "travel as a form of education" are not deductible.

EXAMPLE Jay is a self-employed doctor who attended a continuing education seminar in New York. His expenses related to attendance at the program are as follows:

Lodging in New York	$ 350
Transportation	700
Restaurant meals	150
Fee for the course	250
Total	$1,450

Jay's educational expense deduction for the seminar would be $1,450 including lodging of $350, transportation of $700, meals of $150, and the course fee of $250. ♦

EXAMPLE Natalie is an instructor of Japanese at Big State University. She spends the summer traveling in Japan to improve her understanding of the Japanese language and culture. Although Natalie arranges her trip to improve her ability to teach the Japanese language, no education deduction is allowed for the travel expenses. ♦

Self-Study Problem 3.6 *See Appendix E for Solutions to Self-Study Problems*

Nadine is a self-employed attorney. Her expenses for continuing legal education are as follows:

Lodging in Tempe, Arizona	$1,200
Transportation	350
Snacks and drinks purchased at a convenience store	30
Meals purchased at restaurants	170
Books	175
Tuition	550
Weekend trip to the Grand Canyon	175
Total	$2,650

Calculate Nadine's educational expense deduction for the current year. Assume Nadine's household income is too high for her to qualify for the lifetime learning credit discussed in Chapter 7.

Learning Objective 3.7

Identify the tax treatment of dues and subscriptions.

3-7 DUES, SUBSCRIPTIONS, AND PUBLICATIONS

Doctors, lawyers, accountants, engineers, teachers, and other professionals who are self-employed or are employers may deduct certain dues and the costs of certain subscriptions and publications. Included in this category of deductions are items such as membership to the local bar for a lawyer, dues to the American Institute of Certified Public Accountants (AICPA) for an accountant, and the cost of subscriptions to any journal that is directly related to the taxpayer's profession. Due to the suspension of miscellaneous deductions subject to 2 percent of AGI through 2025, only self-employed taxpayers can deduct dues and subscriptions. Employees can no longer deduct these costs; however, if the dues or subscription costs are reimbursed by the employer, the employer can deduct those costs.

EXAMPLE Hal is a federal law enforcement officer who pays $200 per year for a subscription to the official agency work manual. The agency provides a manual in the office for its employees, but Hal spends a lot of time on the road away from the office. As an employee, Hal may not deduct the cost of the subscription. If Hal's employer reimbursed Hal for the manual, the employer could deduct the cost. If Hal were self-employed, the cost would be deductible. ♦

Self-Study Problem 3.7 *See Appendix E for Solutions to Self-Study Problems*

Indicate which of the following dues, subscriptions, and publications are deductible and which are not deductible.

1. Dues to the American Medical Association paid by a self-employed physician.
2. A subscription to a tax journal paid for by an accounting professor.
3. Dues to a health spa paid by a lawyer.
4. Union dues paid by a carpenter that works for a large construction company.
5. Subscription to *Motor Trend* magazine paid for by a registered nurse.

3-8 SPECIAL CLOTHING AND UNIFORMS

3.8 Learning Objective

Determine which clothing and uniforms may be treated as tax deductions.

Self-employed individuals and employers are allowed a deduction for the costs of special work clothing or uniforms. The deduction is not allowed for the general cost and upkeep of normal work clothes; the clothing must be specialized. To be deductible, the clothing or uniforms must (1) be required as a condition of employment, and (2) not be suitable for everyday use. Both conditions must be met for the deduction to be allowed. It is not enough that the taxpayer is required to wear special clothing if the clothing can be worn while the taxpayer is not on the job. The costs of protective clothing, such as safety shoes, hard hats, and rubber boots, required for the job are also deductible. If the clothing or uniforms qualify, the costs of purchase, alterations, laundry, and their maintenance are deductible. Any uniforms purchased by an employer for its employees are deductible by the employer.

The suspension of miscellaneous deductions subject to 2 percent of AGI has severely limited the deduction of uniforms and related costs by employees. In the past, uniforms worn by police officers, firefighters, nurses, and letter carriers would have qualified as an unreimbursed employee business expense. Because of the suspension of these miscellaneous deductions, taxpayers that serve in these roles as an employee are no longer permitted to deduct uniform costs. To the extent they serve as an independent contractor or are self-employed, qualifying uniform costs may be deducted. Similar to dues and subscriptions, if the employer reimburses the employee for qualifying uniform costs, the employer may deduct the costs. Self-employed taxpayers deduct special clothing and uniforms on Schedule C.

TAX BREAK

For the cost of uniforms to be deductible, it is not enough that the taxpayer does not use the apparel for normal everyday wear, the standard is much higher in demanding that the clothes may not be adaptable to general use as ordinary clothing outside of employment. A recent court case found that a nurse that purchased clothing for work in accordance with her employer's dress code was not adaptable as it "resembled scrubs." Although unreimbursed employee business expenses are not deductible through 2025, this interpretation could affect self-employed taxpayers in the medical field.

Self-Study Problem 3.8 *See Appendix E for Solutions to Self-Study Problems*

Steve has his own business as an installer for the light company, and he wears typical work clothes that cost $400 during the year. Also, Steve must wear safety shoes and an orange neon vest on the job that cost $650 this year, and he purchased pole-climbing equipment, spikes, and a safety belt that cost $275. What is Steve's deduction on Schedule C for these items?

3-9 BUSINESS GIFTS

3.9 Learning Objective

Explain the special limits for business gift deductions.

Within limits, taxpayers are allowed a deduction for business gifts. Salespersons and other taxpayers may deduct up to $25 per year per donee. For purposes of this limitation, a husband and wife count as one donee. Thus, the maximum that a taxpayer could deduct for gifts to a client or potential client and their spouse is a total of $25 per year, unless the spouse is also a client, in which case the spouse may receive a separate $25 gift. Incidental expenses such as gift wrapping and shipping may be excluded from the limitation and are fully deductible. Recall from Chapter 2 that transfers of value to employees are rarely going to be classified as a gift that can be excluded from gross income.

There is no limitation for small business gifts costing up to $4 each that have the taxpayer's name or company name imprinted on them, such as pencils and calendars, and no limitation on promotional materials, such as signs and display racks. Also, the cost of gifts of tangible personal property made to employees for length of service on the job and safety achievement may be deducted up to a limit of $400 per employee per year. If the gift is made in conjunction with a "qualified plan," the limit is raised to $1,600. Gifts made to a taxpayer's supervisor (or individuals at a higher employment level) are not deductible. Those gifts are considered nondeductible personal expenses.

EXAMPLE Marc is a salesperson who gives gifts to his clients. During the year, Marc gives Mr. Alford a gift costing $20 and Mrs. Alford (not a client) a gift costing $15. He also gives Ms. Bland a gift that cost $24 plus $2 for wrapping. Marc may deduct a total of $25 for the two gifts to Mr. and Mrs. Alford, and $26 for the gift to Ms. Bland. The $2 gift-wrapping charge is not included as part of the $25 limitation on the gift to Ms. Bland. ♦

3-9a Substantiation Requirement

To deduct meals and business gifts, taxpayers must be able to substantiate the deduction. The four items that must be substantiated to deduct meals expenses and gifts are the:

1. Amount of the expense,
2. Date and description,
3. Business purpose, and
4. Business relationship.

If any of the above information is not available, the IRS will disallow the deduction for meals expenses or gifts.

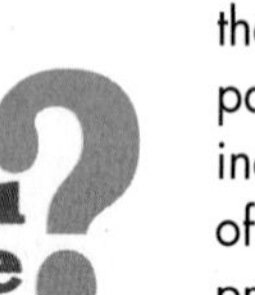

A taxpayer from Oklahoma recently discovered that lying to the IRS can have consequences. In spite of the taxpayer initially reporting that he had one bank account, owned only his home and his body shop business property, and three cars, the IRS revenue agent eventually determined that the taxpayer had five bank accounts, three unreported rental properties, and had made payments on car loans for fifteen vehicles during the audit period. Amazingly, his taxable income for the same periods was $0, $0, and $114. The court affirmed the IRS assessment of a 75-percent fraud penalty. See *Clark v. Comm'r*, T.C. Memo 2021–114 in which the court provides a detailed discussion of the audit process undertaken.

Self-Study Problem 3.9 *See Appendix E for Solutions to Self-Study Problems*

Carol makes the following business gifts during the tax year:

Donee	Amount
1. Mr. Jones (a client)	$ 20
2. Mr. Brown (a client)	32
3. Mrs. Green (a client) received a $15 gift while her husband, Mr. Green (a non-client) received an $18 gift	33
4. Ms. Gray (Carol's supervisor)	45
5. Mr. Edwards (a client) receiving a display rack with Carol's company name on it	75
6. Various customers (receiving ball point pens with the company name on them)	140

Calculate Carol's allowed deduction for each business gift and her total allowed deduction.

3-10 BAD DEBTS

3.10 Learning Objective

Explain the tax treatment of bad debt deductions.

When a taxpayer sells goods or services on credit and the accounts receivable subsequently become worthless (uncollectible), a bad debt deduction is allowed to the extent that income arising from the sales was previously included in income. Taxpayers must use the specific charge-off method and are allowed deductions for bad debts only after the debts are determined to be partially or completely worthless.

A taxpayer who uses the specific charge-off method must be able to satisfy the IRS requirement that the debt is worthless and demonstrate the amount of the worthlessness. For a totally worthless account, a deduction is allowed for the entire amount of the taxpayer's basis in the account in the year the debt becomes worthless. The taxpayer's basis in the debt is the amount of income recognized from the recording of the debt, or the amount paid for the debt if it was purchased.

EXAMPLE Todd owns a small retail store. During the current tax year, Todd has $8,500 worth of uncollectible accounts receivable. Assuming he reported $7,800 in sales income from the accounts, that amount is his basis in the accounts receivable. Therefore, Todd's deduction for bad debts is limited to $7,800 for the year. ♦

3-10a Business and Nonbusiness Bad Debts

Bad debts fall into two categories, business bad debts and nonbusiness bad debts. Debts that arise from the taxpayer's trade or business are classified as business bad debts, while all other debts are considered nonbusiness bad debts. The distinction between the two types of debts is important, since business bad debts are ordinary deductions and nonbusiness bad debts are short-term capital losses. Short-term and long-term capital gains may be offset by short-term capital losses. If there are net capital losses, only $3,000 of net capital losses may be deducted against ordinary income in any one tax year. Unused short-term capital losses are carried forward and may be deductible in future years, subject to the $3,000 annual limitation. The treatment of capital gains and losses is discussed in Chapter 4.

EXAMPLE Robert loaned his friend, Calvin, $5,000 to start a business. In the current year, Calvin went bankrupt and the debt became completely worthless. Since the debt is a nonbusiness debt, Robert may claim only a $3,000 short-term capital loss deduction this year (assuming no other capital transactions). The $2,000 unused deduction may be carried forward to the next year. This is not a business bad-debt deduction, because Robert is not in the business of loaning funds. ♦

ProConnect™ Tax TIP

Nonbusiness bad debts are treated as short-term capital losses. To report these items, use the Schedule D/4797/etc., item under Income. Drill down into the Schedule D entry form and select the Nonbusiness Bad Debt button after entering the other relevant information.

Self-Study Problem 3.10 *See Appendix E for Solutions to Self-Study Problems*

Indicate whether the debt in each of the following cases is a business or nonbusiness debt.

1. Accounts receivable of a doctor from patients
2. A father loans his son $2,000 to buy a car
3. A corporate president personally loans another corporation $100,000
4. Loans by a bank to its customers
5. A taxpayer loans her sister $15,000 to start a business

Sign Here — Under penalties of perjury, I declare that I have examined this return and accompanying schedules and statements, and to the best of my knowledge and belief, they are true, correct, and complete. Declaration of preparer (other than taxpayer) is based on all information of which preparer has any knowledge.

Joint return? See instructions. Keep a copy for your records.	Your signature	Date	Your occupation	If the IRS sent you an Identity Protection PIN, enter it here (see inst.) ▶
	Spouse's signature. If a joint return, **both** must sign.	Date	Spouse's occupation	If the IRS sent your spouse an Identity Protection PIN, enter it here (see inst.) ▶
	Phone no.	Email address		

Paid Preparer Use Only	Preparer's name	Preparer's signature	Date	PTIN	Check if: ☐ Self-employed
	Firm's name ▶			Phone no.	
	Firm's address ▶			Firm's EIN ▶	

Would You Sign This Tax Return?

Your clients, Tom (age 48) and Teri (age 45) Trendy, have a son, Tim (age 27). Tim lives in Hawaii, where he studies the effects of various sunscreens on his ability to surf. Last year, Tim was out of money and wanted to move back home and live with Tom and Teri. To prevent this, Tom lent Tim $20,000 with the understanding that he would stay in Hawaii and not come home. Tom had Tim sign a formal note, including a stated interest rate and due date. Tom has a substantial portfolio of stocks and bonds and has generated a significant amount of capital gains in the current year. He concluded that Tim is unlikely to repay the loan and the $20,000 note is worthless. Consequently, Tom wants to report Tim's bad debt on his and Teri's current tax return and net it against his other capital gains and losses. Tom is adamant about this. Would you sign the Paid Preparer's declaration (see example above) on this return? Why or why not?

Learning Objective 3.11

Ascertain when a home office deduction may be claimed and how the deduction is computed.

3-11 OFFICE IN THE HOME

Some taxpayers operate a trade or business in their homes and qualify for home office deductions. The tax law imposes strict limits on the availability of the deduction. In fact, the deduction for an office in the home is allowed by exception. The general rule for a home office deduction states that a taxpayer will not be allowed a deduction for the use of a dwelling unit used by the taxpayer as a residence. The law provides four exceptions to the general rule under which a deduction may be allowed.

Under the first exception, a deduction is allowed if the home office is used on a regular basis and exclusively as the self-employed taxpayer's principal place of business. To meet the exclusive use test, a specific area of the home must be used only for the trade or business. If the area is used for both business and personal purposes, no home office deduction is allowed.

A second exception states that a deduction is allowed if the home office is used exclusively and on a regular basis by patients, clients, or customers in meetings or dealings with the taxpayer in the normal course of a trade or business. This exception allows doctors and salespeople to deduct home office expenses even though they maintain another office away from their residence, and even though the office is not the self-employed taxpayer's principal place of business.

Under the third exception, the deduction of home office expenses is allowed if the home office is a separate structure not attached to the dwelling unit and is used exclusively and on a regular basis in the taxpayer's trade or business.

The fourth and final exception to the rule allows a deduction of a portion of the cost of a dwelling unit if it is used on a regular basis for the storage of business inventory or product samples held for use in the self-employed taxpayer's trade or business of selling products. Under this fourth exception, the taxpayer's home must be the taxpayer's sole place of business.

3-11a The Income Limitation

The home office deduction may not reduce the net income from the business below zero, except for mortgage interest and property taxes allocable to the office, which are generally tax deductible anyway. The other costs of operating a home, which are included in the home office allocation, include rent, home insurance, repairs, cleaning, utilities and other services, homeowners' association dues, and depreciation on the cost of the home. Depreciation expense is considered only after all other expenses have been allowed. These expenses are typically allocated to the home office on the basis of the square footage of the office to the total square footage of the home. Any unused deductions may be carried over to offset income in future years.

EXAMPLE Jane, an accounting professor, maintains an office in her apartment where she conducts a small tax practice. Jane properly allocates $1,500 in rent to the home office, and during the year she collects $1,400 in fees from various clients. Assuming Jane has no other expenses associated with her practice, only $1,400 of the rent may be claimed as a home office deduction, since she may not show a loss from the practice due to the gross income limitation. The unused portion is carried over to the next taxable year. ♦

EXAMPLE Assume the same facts as those in the previous example, except Jane owns her home. She has real estate taxes of $100, mortgage interest of $600, maintenance expenses of $200, and depreciation of $1,000 attributable to the home office. Her deduction for home office expenses is calculated as follows:

Gross income from tax practice	$1,400
Less: mortgage interest and real estate taxes	(700)
Balance	700
Less: maintenance expense	(200)
Balance	500
Depreciation (maximum allowed)	(500)
Net income from tax practice	$ 0

Note that the only way the home office can generate an overall business loss for Jane is if her home office mortgage interest and taxes exceed her gross business income. The unused portion of depreciation is carried over to the next taxable year. ♦

If a home office is used for both business and personal purposes, no deduction is allowed. For example, Professor Jane in the previous example would not be allowed a deduction for any expenses associated with the office in her home if the office was also used for personal activities, such as watching television or as a guest room.

3-11b The Home Office Allocation

The calculation of home office expenses involves the allocation of the total expenses of a self-employed taxpayer's dwelling between business and personal use. This allocation is usually made on the basis of the number of square feet of business space as a percentage of the total number of square feet in the residence, or on the basis of the number of rooms devoted to business use as a percentage of the total number of rooms in the dwelling.

EXAMPLE Lois operates a hair-styling salon in her rental home. The salon occupies 400 square feet of her residence, which has a total of 1,600 square feet. Her expenses for her residence are presented below and allocated as shown.

Expenses	***Total Amount***	***Business Percentage****	***Business Portion***
Rent	$10,000	25%	$2,500
Utilities	4,000	25%	1,000
Cleaning	2,000	25%	500

*400 sq. ft./1,600 sq. ft. ♦

Self-employed taxpayers filing Schedule C and claiming a deduction for home office expenses are required to file Form 8829, Expenses for Business Use of Your Home.

3-11c **Optional Safe Harbor Method**

In an effort to reduce the complexity of the home office deduction, the IRS has introduced a simplified method. Under the simplified method, the self-employed taxpayer may deduct home office expenses at the applicable rate ($5) multiplied by the number of square feet used in the home office, up to a maximum of 300 square feet, thus limiting the home office deduction under the safe harbor to $1,500. The deduction is still limited to the net profit from the business. Any deduction in excess of the income limit may not be carried forward. The same home office qualifications apply but no allocations are required. A taxpayer that uses the simplified method may deduct mortgage interest and property taxes as itemized deductions (see Chapter 5) without having to allocate a portion to the home office.

EXAMPLE Martha operates a business that generates $6,700 of income before the home office deduction. She has a qualifying home office of 350 square feet in her home. She properly allocates $1,200 of household expenses to her home office. Under the safe harbor method, Martha's home office deduction is $1,500 ($5 per square foot × maximum 300 square feet). Martha should elect the larger safe harbor home office deduction. ♦

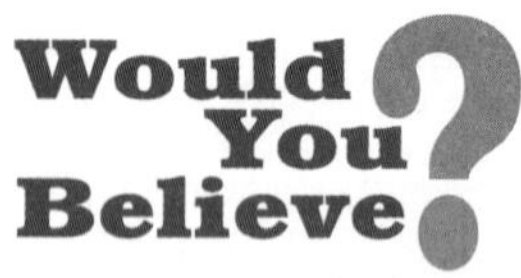

In 2013, when the safe harbor was introduced at $5 per square foot, the IRS notice stated "The Service and the Treasury Department may update this rate from time to time as warranted." At the start of 2013, the median cost of a home in the US was about $180,000. In the second quarter of 2022, the median price was $388,000, an increase of 115%. An increase might be warranted.

ProConnect™ Tax TIP

Similar to auto expenses, the home office deduction is not entered into Schedule C directly, but rather under Deductions and then Business Use of the Home. The interaction between the cap on taxes (see Chapter 5) and the allocation of property taxes can create complexity in this area for certain taxpayers.

TAX BREAK

The simplified method may hold advantages that extend beyond ease of use. One possible advantage is that no depreciation is deducted from the basis of a taxpayer's home and thus "depreciation recapture" (see LO 8.8) can be avoided and the exclusion of the gain on the sale of a principal residence (see LO 4.6) can still apply. A second advantage is that the property taxes and interest allocated to the small business can still be deducted on Schedule A as an itemized deduction (see Chapter 5).

3-11d Home Office Deduction for an Employee

Prior to 2018, under certain circumstances, an employee was eligible to take a home office deduction. One of the most important requirements was that the use of the home office was for the convenience of the employer. The deduction of unreimbursed employee business expenses is suspended through 2025.

Self-Study Problem 3.11 *See Appendix E for Solutions to Self-Study Problems*

Terry is a self-employed lawyer who maintains an office in her home. The office is used exclusively for client work, and clients regularly visit her home office. The mortgage interest and real estate taxes allocated to the business use of the home amount to $2,100, and maintenance, utilities, and cleaning service allocable to the business use of the home total $1,400. The depreciation allocated to business use is $4,000. If gross billings of Terry's practice are $3,900 for this year and Terry has no other expenses allocable to the business, calculate the net income or loss she may report from the practice.

3-12 HOBBY LOSSES

3.12 Learning Objective

Apply the factors used to determine whether an activity is a hobby, and understand the tax treatment of hobby losses.

If a taxpayer enters into an activity without a profit motive, the tax law limits the amount of tax deductions available. Under the hobby loss provisions, a taxpayer may not show a loss from an activity that is not engaged in for profit.

EXAMPLE The breeding of race horses is an activity which might not be considered a trade or business when carried on by a full-time dentist. The IRS might contend that the activity was for personal enjoyment and disallow any loss for tax purposes. ♦

Despite the limitation on losses, any profits from hobbies must be included in taxable income. Hobby income is reported on Line 8j, Other income on Schedule 1 of Form 1040.

3-12a Operational Rules

Individual taxpayers (or S corporations) can avoid the hobby loss rules if they can show that the activity was conducted with the intent to earn a profit. To determine whether the activity was engaged in for profit, the IRS will look at the following factors:

1. carrying on the activity in a businesslike manner,
2. the time and effort put into the activity indicate an intent to make it profitable,
3. dependence on the income for the taxpayer's livelihood,
4. whether the losses are due to circumstances beyond the taxpayer's control (or are normal in the startup phase of this type of business),
5. attempts to change methods of operation to improve profitability,
6. the taxpayer or advisors have the knowledge needed to carry on the activity as a successful business,
7. success in making a profit in similar activities in the past,
8. the activity makes a profit in some years, and
9. the activity is expected to make a future profit from the appreciation of the assets used in the activity.

The tax law provides a rebuttable presumption that if an activity shows a profit for three of the five previous years (two of the seven previous years for activities involving horses), the activity is engaged in for profit. For example, if an activity shows a profit for three of the previous five years, it is presumed to be a trade or business, and the IRS has the burden to prove that it is a hobby.

EXAMPLE Dean Copper is an auto mechanic but also likes to create sculptures from scrap iron materials. Dean's sculpting business turned a small profit in 2017, 2019, and 2021 but had modest losses in 2018 and 2020. Because Dean's sculpting activity has profits in three of the previous five years, the presumption is that the activity is not a hobby.

3-12b **Loss Limitations**

Historically, the deduction of hobby expenses have been limited. Hobby expenses were deductible to the extent of hobby income (unless otherwise deductible such as mortgage interest and property taxes) and claimed as a miscellaneous itemized deduction subject to 2 percent of AGI floor. Thus, hobby expenses were only available to deduct if the taxpayer itemized deductions.

The miscellaneous expense deduction for items subject to the 2 percent of AGI floor is suspended through 2025; thus, no miscellaneous hobby expenses are deductible. Hobby expenses associated with other allowable itemized deductions (e.g., taxes or interest) are deductible subject to the limitations on those items (see Chapter 5). The income, net of cost of goods sold, must still be reported as other income on Schedule 1, Line 8j.

EXAMPLE Fred, the president of a bank, decides that he wants to be a famous wine maker. He has the following expenses related to this activity:

Costs of the wine sold	$2,000
Personal property taxes on equipment	2,500
Advertising costs	4,600

During the year, Fred sells 200 cases of wine for $7,500. If the activity is not a hobby, then Fred may take a loss, against his other income, of $1,600 ($7,500 − $2,000 − $2,500 − $4,600). However, if the activity is deemed to be a hobby, Fred would potentially be allowed to deduct the property taxes of $2,500 as an itemized deduction. The cost of the wine sold can be netted against the revenue. The advertising expenses are not deductible. ♦

ProConnect™ Tax TIP

Hobby income can be entered under Income and then Alimony and Other Income. Be sure and net the cost of goods sold against gross income when reporting this amount. Hobby expenses are not deductible.

Self-Study Problem 3.12 *See Appendix E for Solutions to Self-Study Problems*

Kana is a CPA who loves chinchillas. She breeds chinchillas as pets (she currently owns thirteen of them) and every so often sells a baby chinchilla to a suitable family to keep as a pet. In the current year, she sells $250 worth of chinchillas and incurs the following expenses:

Chinchilla cages	$ 300
Advertising for chinchilla sales	$2,500

This activity is considered a hobby. Kana has adjusted gross income of $72,000. What is the amount of income and expense Kana recognizes (assume she itemizes deductions) associated with her chinchilla hobby?

KEY TERMS

Schedule C, 3-2
trade or business, 3-2
cost of goods sold, 3-5
self-employment tax, 3-7
inventory, 3-7
first in, first out (FIFO), 3-10
last in, first out (LIFO), 3-10
non-incidental materials and supplies (NIMS), 3-10
commuting, 3-13
standard mileage rate, 3-14
standard mileage method, 3-14
actual cost method, 3-14
tax home, 3-16
per diem substantiation, 3-17
standard federal rate method, 3-17
high-low method, 3-17
business gifts, 3-23
business and nonbusiness bad debts, 3-25
home office, 3-26
simplified method, 3-28
hobby losses, 3-29

KEY POINTS

Learning Objectives	Key Points
LO 3.1: Complete a basic Schedule C (Profit or Loss from Business).	• Taxpayers who operate a business or practice a profession as a sole proprietorship must file a Schedule C to report the net profit or loss from the sole proprietorship. • Deductions taken on Schedule C must be ordinary and necessary, reasonable, and have a business purpose. • Schedule C filers such as sole proprietors and independent contractors with net earnings of $400 or more must pay a self-employment tax calculated on Schedule SE with their Form 1040.
LO 3.2: Describe the tax treatment of inventories and cost of goods sold.	• Inventory is the stock of goods or materials that a business holds for the purpose of resale to generate a profit. • Cost of goods sold, which is the largest single deduction for many businesses, is calculated as follows: beginning inventory + purchases − ending inventory. • Small businesses are permitted to use the cash method to account for inventory but in many instances, typical inventory accounting is still used. • There are two common methods of inventory valuation used by taxpayers: first in, first out (FIFO) and last in, first out (LIFO).
LO 3.3: Identify the requirements for deducting transportation expenses.	• Deductible transportation expenses include travel by airplane, rail, bus, and automobile. Normal commuting costs to and from the taxpayer's place of regular employment are not deductible. • If the taxpayer works at two or more jobs during the same day, they may deduct the cost of going from one job to the other or from one business location to another. • The standard mileage rate for 2022 is 58.5 cents per mile through June 30 and 62.5 cents per mile thereafter.
LO 3.4: Identify the requirements for deducting travel expenses.	• Travel expenses are defined as ordinary and necessary expenses incurred in traveling away from home in pursuit of the taxpayer's trade or business. • Deductible travel expenses include the cost of such items as meals, lodging, taxis, tips, and laundry. • A taxpayer must be away from home "overnight" in order to deduct travel expenses. Overnight is a period of time longer than an ordinary work day in which rest or relief from work is required. Also, the taxpayer must be away from their "tax home" to be on travel status. • Taxpayers must substantiate the following: the amount of each separate expenditure, the dates of departure and return for each trip and the number of business days on the trip, the destination or locality of the travel, and the business reason for the travel. • As an alternative to reporting actual expenses, a per diem method may be used in certain circumstances.

LO 3.5: Determine the requirements for deducting meals.	• Business meals are generally subject to a 50-percent limitation; however, in 2022, business meals provided by restaurants are 100 percent deductible. • Generally, entertainment costs are not deductible. • Certain meals and entertainment costs are deductible in full when celebratory for all employees.
LO 3.6: Identify the requirements for claiming business education expenses.	• To be deductible as a business expense, education expenditures must be paid to meet the requirements of the taxpayer's employer or the requirements of law or regulation for keeping the taxpayer's salary, status, or job, or the expenses must be paid to maintain or improve existing skills required in performing the duties of the taxpayer's present work.
LO 3.7: Identify the tax treatment of dues and subscriptions.	• Self-employed professionals may deduct dues and the costs of subscriptions and publications. Employees may no longer deduct these costs due to the suspension of miscellaneous deductions subject to 2 percent of AGI through 2025.
LO 3.8: Determine which clothing and uniforms may be treated as tax deductions.	• Self-employed individuals and employers are allowed a deduction for the costs of special work clothing or uniforms. • In order to be deductible, clothing or uniforms must (1) be required as a condition of employment, and (2) not be suitable for everyday use.
LO 3.9: Explain the special limits for business gift deductions.	• Taxpayers are allowed a deduction for business gifts up to $25 per year per donee. For purposes of this limitation, a husband and wife count as one donee, unless the husband and wife are both clients. • To deduct meals and business gifts, taxpayers must be able to substantiate the deduction with the expense amounts, the dates and descriptions, the business purposes, and the business relationships.
LO 3.10: Explain the tax treatment of bad debt deductions.	• Bad debts are classified as either business bad debts or nonbusiness bad debts. Debts arising from a taxpayer's trade or business are classified as business bad debts, while all other debts are considered nonbusiness bad debts. • Business bad debts are treated as ordinary deductions and nonbusiness bad debts are treated as short-term capital losses, of which only $3,000 can be deducted against ordinary income each year.
LO 3.11: Ascertain when a home office deduction may be claimed and how the deduction is computed.	• A home office is generally not deductible, allowed only by exception. There are four exceptions to the general rule. • A home office deduction is allowed if the home office is used on a regular basis and exclusively as the self-employed taxpayer's principal place of business. • A home office deduction is allowed if the home office is used exclusively and on a regular basis by patients, clients, or customers in meetings or dealings with the self-employed taxpayer in the normal course of a trade or business. • The deduction of home office expenses is allowed if the home office is a separate structure not attached to the dwelling unit and is used exclusively and on a regular basis in the self-employed taxpayer's trade or business. • A home office deduction of a portion of the cost of a dwelling unit is allowed if it is used on a regular basis for the storage of business inventory or product samples and is the sole place of business. • The home office deduction is limited by the amount of net income from the associated trade or business. • A simplified home office deduction is also available at $5 per square foot up to an annual maximum of $1,500. • Employees may no longer deduct a home office, even when at the convenience of their employer, due to the suspension of the miscellaneous business expense deduction.

LO 3.12: Apply the factors used to determine whether an activity is a hobby, and understand the tax treatment of hobby losses.	• Under the hobby loss provisions, a taxpayer may not show a loss from an activity that is not engaged in for profit. • To determine whether the activity was engaged in for profit, the IRS will look at numerous factors including whether the activity is conducted like a business. • Hobby expenses are no longer deductible due to the TCJA suspension of miscellaneous itemized deductions subject to the 2 percent of AGI floor.

QUESTIONS and PROBLEMS

GROUP 1: MULTIPLE CHOICE QUESTIONS

LO 3.1

1. Which of the following is *not* a test for the deductibility of a business expense?
   a. Ordinary and necessary test
   b. Sales generation test
   c. Reasonableness test
   d. Business purpose test

LO 3.1

2. In the current year, Mary started a profitable housekeeping business as a sole proprietor. She has ten housekeepers working for her and spends her time selling their services and coordinating her employees' time. Mary made $50,000 in her first year of operations. In addition to filing a Schedule C to report her business earnings, Mary *must* also file
   a. Schedule A
   b. Schedule F
   c. Schedule B
   d. Schedule SE
   e. None of the above

LO 3.1
LO 3.3
LO 3.4
LO 3.5

3. Daniel just became a self-employed consultant. Prior to this year he was always an employee. He comes to discuss his new business with you. As his tax accountant, you should:
   a. Discuss setting up a good record-keeping system for his new business
   b. Discuss the substantiation requirements for meals
   c. Discuss the self-employment tax, as well as the income tax, on business earnings in order to help Daniel estimate what he might owe in taxes for the year
   d. Discuss the rules for deducting automobile expenses
   e. Discuss all of the above

LO 3.1

4. Which of the following expenses is generally deductible in the year incurred?
   a. Capital expenditures for land and buildings
   b. Illegal bribes or kickbacks
   c. Continuing legal training for a practicing professional attorney
   d. Political contributions

LO 3.1

5. Which of the following expenses is generally deductible in the year incurred?
   a. Payments to remediate the contaminated ground water surrounding an oil refinery
   b. Interest expense associated with debt incurred to purchase municipal bonds
   c. A speeding fine paid by an express delivery company for one of its drivers
   d. Rent for a retail store in which medical marijuana is sold

LO 3.2

6. A small business that qualifies for the cash method may use which method to account for inventory?
   a. Treat as non-incidental materials and supplies
   b. Treat the same as in the applicable financial statements

c. Treat the same as books and records if no applicable financial statements
d. Under the accrual method
e. All of these choices are suitable for accounting for inventory

LO 3.2

7. If a taxpayer has beginning inventory of $45,000, purchases of $175,000, and ending inventory of $25,000, what is the amount of the cost of goods sold for the current year?
a. $155,000
b. $180,000
c. $175,000
d. $195,000
e. None of the above

LO 3.3

8. Which of the following taxpayers may use the standard mileage method of calculating transportation costs?
a. A taxi driver who owns a fleet of six cars for hire
b. A taxpayer who used accelerated depreciation on his automobile
c. A business executive who claimed bonus depreciation in the first year she used the car
d. An attorney who uses his European sports car for calling on clients
e. None of the above

LO 3.3

9. Heather drives her minivan 450 miles through June 30 and another 475 miles for business purposes in the second half of 2022. She elects to use the standard mileage rate for her auto expense deduction. Her deduction will be
a. $506
b. $515
c. $519
d. $553
e. $560

LO 3.3

10. Which of the following is not considered commuting miles?
a. The miles from a taxpayer's home to their regular place of work
b. The miles to a taxpayer's home from a regular second job
c. The miles from a taxpayer's main job to a temporary work location
d. The miles from a temporary work location to a taxpayer's home (and the taxpayer has a main work location)

LO 3.4

11. In which of the following cases is the employer entitled to a travel expense deduction?
a. An employee, who worked in the Salt Lake City plant of a company, who is assigned to the Denver plant of the company for four years
b. An employee who travels between several business locations within the same city each day
c. A manager of a chain of department stores who works in the main store three weeks out of every month and visits distant branch locations on overnight trips during the remainder of the month
d. An employee who resigns from his current job and accepts a new job in a city 500 miles away from his current residence
e. A bank employee who travels to a branch office for a couple of hours of work and decides to stay overnight to attend a play

LO 3.4

12. Which of the following expenses incurred while the taxpayer is away from home "overnight" is *not* included as a travel expense?
a. Laundry expenses
b. Transportation expenses
c. Meal expenses
d. Business gifts
e. Lodging expenses

LO 3.4

13. Under the high-low method, the federal per diem amount is
    a. The same in every city in the U.S.
    b. Different for every city in the U.S.
    c. The same for most cities but higher in certain locations
    d. An average of the highest and lowest costs for that city
    e. The boundary for expenses incurred in a city (never higher than the high amount but never lower than the low amount)

LO 3.4

14. Joe is a self-employed information technology consultant from San Francisco. He takes a week-long trip to Chicago primarily for business. He takes two personal days to go to museums and see the sights of Chicago. How should he treat the expenses related to this trip?
    a. One hundred percent of the trip should be deducted as a business expense since the trip was primarily for business.
    b. Half of the trip should be deducted as a business expense since the IRS limits such business expenses to 50 percent of the actual cost.
    c. The cost of all of the airfare and the business days should be deducted, while the cost of the personal days are not deductible.
    d. None of the expenses are deductible since there was an element of personal enjoyment in the trip.

LO 3.5

15. Which of the following expenses is deductible as an entertainment expense?
    a. The depreciation on an airplane used to entertain customers
    b. The cost of a hunting camp used to entertain customers
    c. The dues of a racquet club used to keep in shape
    d. The cost of a paintball party for clients paid for by a computer salesman at a computer fair
    e. None of these are deductible

LO 3.5

16. Which of the following is *not* likely to be a deductible expense?
    a. The cost of tickets to a stage play for a client and the taxpayer.
    b. The cost for Rosa to take a potential customer to lunch to describe a new service Rosa's company is offering. Unfortunately, the customer explains that they are not interested in the service.
    c. The cost of a party for all of Dan's employees to celebrate a record-breaking profits year.
    d. The dues for Charles Coke to join the City Chamber of Commerce to generally improve the reputation of his business in the community.
    e. None of the above are deductible expenses.

LO 3.5

17. In 2022, Values R Us, a real estate appraising firm, incurs the following meals expenses:
    - $1,200 restaurant meals with business clients
    - $1,600 for an end of year celebratory company dinner for all employees
    - $400 for bagels once a month for all employees
    - $300 for pre-packaged snacks offered to potential clients at a business fair
    - $40 for non-restaurant travel snacks consumed by employees while on business travel
    - $800 of restaurant meals consumed by employees while on business travel

    What is Values R Us' deductible meals expense in 2022?
    a. $2,770
    b. $3,320
    c. $4,120
    d. $4,340

LO 3.6

18. Which of the following taxpayers may *not* deduct their educational expense?
    a. A CPA who attends a course to review for the real estate agents' exam
    b. An independent sales representative who attends a customer relations course at a local university
    c. A self-employed attorney who attends a course on computing legal damages
    d. An independent real estate broker who attends a college course on real estate law
    e. All of the above are deductible

LO 3.6

19. Which of the following is likely a deductible business educational expense?
    a. Leah is a self-employed tax preparer. The State Board of Taxation requires Leah to attend federal and state taxation training each year to maintain her tax preparation licence.
    b. Mike is an auto mechanic. He decides he wants to be a high school math teacher but the state Department of Education requires Mike to earn a bachelor's degree in education.
    c. John teaches European History at Ridgemont High School. In order to better understand the material he teaches, John takes a summer trip with *American Geographic* magazine to tour Western Europe.
    d. Becca is an auto mechanic. She sees that the local community college is offering courses in jet engine repair which would prepare her to work for one of the airlines. Becca would like to work for an airline because they let employees fly for free.

LO 3.7

20. Which of the following is *not* deductible by the self-employed taxpayer?
    a. A subscription to *The CPA Journal* by a CPA
    b. A subscription to *The Yale Medical Journal* by a doctor
    c. A subscription to *Financial Management* by a financial planner
    d. A subscription to *The Harvard Law Review* by a lawyer
    e. All of the above are deductible

LO 3.8

21. Which of the following self-employed taxpayers are most likely permitted to deduct the cost of their uniform?
    a. A lawyer who wears a business suit
    b. A furnace repairman who must wear overalls while on the job
    c. A nurse who can wear casual clothes while on duty
    d. A butcher who wears stainless steel safety gloves

LO 3.9

22. Which of the following business gifts are fully deductible?
    a. A gift to a client that cost $35
    b. A gift to an employee, for ten years of continued service, that cost $250
    c. A gift to a client and her nonclient spouse that cost $45
    d. A gift to an employee paid under a qualified plan, for not having an on-the-job injury for twenty-five years, that cost $1,650
    e. None of the above are fully deductible

LO 3.9

23. Which of the following statements about business gift deductions is *not* true?
    a. A taxpayer can provide two gifts to a client during the year and the maximum deduction is $50.
    b. Reasonable shipping costs do not count toward the $25 business gift limit.
    c. Employee gifts for a significant number of years of service can exceed $25 and remain deductible.
    d. A holiday gift from an employee to their supervisor is a non-deductible personal expense.

LO 3.10

24. Grady operates a lawn maintenance business using the accrual method. He estimates that 5 percent, or about $2,500 of his 2022 year-end customers' invoices will never be paid. During 2022, he wrote off $13,500 of his receivables as uncollectible. Grady's bad debt expense deduction is:
    a. $0
    b. $2,500
    c. $13,500
    d. $16,000

LO 3.10

25. Loren loaned a friend $9,000 as financing for a new business venture. In the current year, Loren's friend declares bankruptcy and the debt is considered totally worthless. What amount may Loren deduct on his individual income tax return for the current year as a result of the worthless debt, assuming he has no other capital gains or losses for the year?
    a. $9,000 ordinary loss
    b. $9,000 short-term capital loss
    c. $3,000 short-term capital loss
    d. $3,000 ordinary loss
    e. $6,000 short-term capital loss

LO 3.11

26. Kathy is a self-employed taxpayer working exclusively from her home office. Before the home office deduction, Kathy has $3,000 of net income. Her allocable home office expenses are $5,000 in total (includes $2,000 of allocated interest and property taxes). How are the home office expenses treated on her current year tax return?
    a. All home office expenses may be deducted, resulting in a business loss of $2,000.
    b. Only $3,000 of home office expenses may be deducted, resulting in net business income of zero. None of the extra $2,000 of home office expenses may be carried forward or deducted.
    c. Only $3,000 of home office expenses may be deducted, resulting in net business income of zero. The extra $2,000 of home office expenses may be carried forward and deducted in a future year against home office income.
    d. None of the home office expenses may be deducted since Kathy's income is too low.

LO 3.11

27. Which of the following taxpayers qualifies for a home office deduction?
    a. An attorney who is employed by a law firm and has a home office in which to read cases
    b. A doctor who has a regular office downtown and a library at home to store medical journals
    c. An accounting student who maintains a home office used exclusively for her business preparing tax returns
    d. A nurse who maintains a home office to pay bills and read nursing journals
    e. A corporate president who uses his home office to entertain friends and customers

LO 3.11

28. Carol maintains an office in her home where she conducts a dressmaking business. During the year she collects $4,000 from sales, pays $1,300 for various materials and supplies, and properly allocates $2,500 of rent expense and $500 of her utilities expense to the use of her home office. What amount of the rent and utilities expense may Carol deduct in the current year in computing her net income or loss from the dressmaking business?
    a. $0
    b. $500
    c. $2,500
    d. $2,700
    e. $3,000

LO 3.12

29. Which of the following factors is not considered by the IRS in determining whether an activity is a hobby?
    a. Whether the activity is conducted like a business
    b. The time and effort expended by the taxpayer
    c. Whether there have been changes in the methods of operation in an attempt to improve profitability
    d. Income and loss history of the activity
    e. All of the above are considered to determine if an activity is a hobby

LO 3.12

30. Stewie, a single taxpayer, operates an activity as a hobby. Brian operates a similar activity as a bona fide business. Stewie's gross income from his activity is $5,000 and his expenses are $6,000. Brian's gross income and expenses are coincidentally the same as Stewie. Neither Stewie nor Brian itemize, but both have other forms of taxable income. What is the impact on taxable income for Stewie and Brian from these activities?
    a. Stewie will report $0 income and Brian will report a $1,000 loss.
    b. Stewie will report $5,000 income and $0 deduction and Brian will report a $1,000 loss.
    c. Stewie and Brian will report $0 taxable income.
    d. Stewie and Brian will report a $1,000 loss.
    e. Stewie will report a $1,000 loss and Brian will report $5,000 income.

GROUP 2:
PROBLEMS

LO 3.1
LO 3.3
LO 3.5
LO 3.7

1. Scott Butterfield is self-employed as a CPA. He uses the cash method of accounting, and his Social Security number is 644-47-7833. His principal business code is 541211. Scott's CPA practice is located at 678 Third Street, Riverside, CA 92860. Scott's income statement for the year shows the following:

Income Statement

Scott Butterfield, CPA
Income Statement
12/31/2022

	Current Period 1/1/2022 to 12/31/2022	Prior Period 1/1/2021 to 12/31/2021
REVENUES		
Tax Services	$ 76,124	$ 75,067
Accounting Services	49,081	48,860
Other Consulting Services	10,095	10,115
TOTAL REVENUES	**135,300**	**134,042**
COST OF SERVICES		
Salaries	35,000	30,100
Payroll Taxes	3,098	2,387
Supplies	1,302	1,548
TOTAL COST OF SERVICES	39,400	34,035
GROSS PROFIT (LOSS)	95,900	100,007
OPERATING EXPENSES		
Advertising and Promotion	250	350
Business Licenses and Permits	300	250
Charitable Contributions	400	275
Continuing Education	500	300
Dues and Subscriptions	2,800	3,500
Insurance	900	875
Meals and Entertainment	4,400	5,500
Office Expense	200	150
Postage and Delivery	100	50
Printing and Reproduction	50	100
Office Rent	12,000	14,000
Travel	900	865
Utilities	3,000	2,978
TOTAL OPERATING EXPENSES	25,800	29,193
NET INCOME (LOSS)	**$ 70,100**	**$ 70,814**

Scott also mentioned the following:

- The expenses for dues and subscriptions were his country club membership dues for the year.
- $400 of the charitable contributions were made to a political action committee.
- Scott does not generate income from the sale of goods and therefore does not record supplies and wages as part of cost of goods sold.
- Scott placed a business auto in service on January 1, 2019 and drove it 4,000 miles for business (equally over the course of the year), 3,250 miles for commuting, and 4,500 miles for nonbusiness purposes. No business expenses for the car are included above. Scott wishes to use the standard mileage method. His wife has a car for personal use.

- Meals and Entertainment expense includes $2,500 related to golf greens fees for entertaining clients, $1,000 for business meals provided by restaurants, and $900 for the bagels and doughnuts once a month for all employees.

Complete Schedule C on Pages 3-41 and 3-42 for Scott showing Scott's net taxable profit from self-employment.

SCHEDULE C (Form 1040)

Department of the Treasury Internal Revenue Service

Profit or Loss From Business

(Sole Proprietorship)

Go to *www.irs.gov/ScheduleC* for instructions and the latest information.

Attach to Form 1040, 1040-SR, 1040-NR, or 1041; partnerships must generally file Form 1065.

OMB No. 1545-0074

2022

Attachment Sequence No. **09**

Name of proprietor | **Social security number (SSN)**

A Principal business or profession, including product or service (see instructions) | **B Enter code from instructions**

C Business name. If no separate business name, leave blank. | **D Employer ID number (EIN)** (see instr.)

E Business address (including suite or room no.)

City, town or post office, state, and ZIP code

F Accounting method: **(1)** ☐ Cash **(2)** ☐ Accrual **(3)** ☐ Other (specify)

G Did you "materially participate" in the operation of this business during 2022? If "No," see instructions for limit on losses . ☐ **Yes** ☐ **No**

H If you started or acquired this business during 2022, check here . . . . ☐

I Did you make any payments in 2022 that would require you to file Form(s) 1099? See instructions . . . . . ☐ **Yes** ☐ **No**

J If "Yes," did you or will you file required Form(s) 1099? . . . . ☐ **Yes** ☐ **No**

Part I Income

1	Gross receipts or sales. See instructions for line 1 and check the box if this income was reported to you on Form W-2 and the "Statutory employee" box on that form was checked . . . . . ☐	**1**	
2	Returns and allowances . . .	**2**	
3	Subtract line 2 from line 1 . . .	**3**	
4	Cost of goods sold (from line 42) . . .	**4**	
5	**Gross profit.** Subtract line 4 from line 3 . . .	**5**	
6	Other income, including federal and state gasoline or fuel tax credit or refund (see instructions) . . .	**6**	
7	**Gross income.** Add lines 5 and 6 . . .	**7**	

Part II Expenses. Enter expenses for business use of your home **only** on line 30.

8	Advertising . . .	**8**		**18**	Office expense (see instructions) .	**18**	
9	Car and truck expenses (see instructions) . . .	**9**		**19**	Pension and profit-sharing plans .	**19**	
				20	Rent or lease (see instructions):		
10	Commissions and fees .	**10**		**a**	Vehicles, machinery, and equipment	**20a**	
11	Contract labor (see instructions)	**11**		**b**	Other business property . . .	**20b**	
12	Depletion . . .	**12**		**21**	Repairs and maintenance . . .	**21**	
13	Depreciation and section 179 expense deduction (not included in Part III) (see instructions) . . .	**13**		**22**	Supplies (not included in Part III) .	**22**	
				23	Taxes and licenses . . .	**23**	
				24	Travel and meals:		
14	Employee benefit programs (other than on line 19) .	**14**		**a**	Travel . . .	**24a**	
15	Insurance (other than health)	**15**		**b**	Deductible meals (see instructions) . . .	**24b**	
16	Interest (see instructions):			**25**	Utilities . . .	**25**	
a	Mortgage (paid to banks, etc.)	**16a**		**26**	Wages (less employment credits)	**26**	
b	Other . . .	**16b**		**27a**	Other expenses (from line 48) . .	**27a**	
17	Legal and professional services	**17**		**b**	**Reserved for future use** . . .	**27b**	

28	**Total expenses** before expenses for business use of home. Add lines 8 through 27a . . .	**28**	
29	Tentative profit or (loss). Subtract line 28 from line 7 . . .	**29**	
30	Expenses for business use of your home. Do not report these expenses elsewhere. Attach Form 8829 unless using the simplified method. See instructions. **Simplified method filers only:** Enter the total square footage of (a) your home: ________ and (b) the part of your home used for business: ________ . Use the Simplified Method Worksheet in the instructions to figure the amount to enter on line 30 . . .	**30**	
31	**Net profit or (loss).** Subtract line 30 from line 29. • If a profit, enter on both **Schedule 1 (Form 1040), line 3,** and on **Schedule SE, line 2.** (If you checked the box on line 1, see instructions.) Estates and trusts, enter on **Form 1041, line 3.** • If a loss, you **must** go to line 32.	**31**	

32 If you have a loss, check the box that describes your investment in this activity. See instructions.

- If you checked 32a, enter the loss on both **Schedule 1 (Form 1040), line 3,** and on **Schedule SE, line 2.** (If you checked the box on line 1, see the line 31 instructions.) Estates and trusts, enter on **Form 1041, line 3.**
- If you checked 32b, you **must** attach **Form 6198.** Your loss may be limited.

32a ☐ All investment is at risk.
32b ☐ Some investment is not at risk.

For Paperwork Reduction Act Notice, see the separate instructions. Cat. No. 11334P **Schedule C (Form 1040) 2022**

Schedule C (Form 1040) 2022 Page **2**

Part III **Cost of Goods Sold** (see instructions)

33 Method(s) used to value closing inventory: a ☐ Cost b ☐ Lower of cost or market c ☐ Other (attach explanation)

34 Was there any change in determining quantities, costs, or valuations between opening and closing inventory? If "Yes," attach explanation . . . ☐ **Yes** ☐ **No**

35	Inventory at beginning of year. If different from last year's closing inventory, attach explanation	35	
36	Purchases less cost of items withdrawn for personal use	36	
37	Cost of labor. Do not include any amounts paid to yourself	37	
38	Materials and supplies	38	
39	Other costs	39	
40	Add lines 35 through 39	40	
41	Inventory at end of year	41	
42	**Cost of goods sold.** Subtract line 41 from line 40. Enter the result here and on line 4	42	

Part IV **Information on Your Vehicle.** Complete this part **only** if you are claiming car or truck expenses on line 9 and are not required to file Form 4562 for this business. See the instructions for line 13 to find out if you must file Form 4562.

43 When did you place your vehicle in service for business purposes? (month/day/year) ____ / ____ / ____

44 Of the total number of miles you drove your vehicle during 2022, enter the number of miles you used your vehicle for:

a Business ____________ **b** Commuting (see instructions) ____________ **c** Other ____________

45 Was your vehicle available for personal use during off-duty hours? . . . ☐ **Yes** ☐ **No**

46 Do you (or your spouse) have another vehicle available for personal use?. . . ☐ **Yes** ☐ **No**

47a Do you have evidence to support your deduction? . . . ☐ **Yes** ☐ **No**

b If "Yes," is the evidence written? . . . ☐ **Yes** ☐ **No**

Part V **Other Expenses.** List below business expenses not included on lines 8–26 or line 30.

48 **Total other expenses.** Enter here and on line 27a	48	

Schedule C (Form 1040) 2022

LO 3.1
LO 3.3
LO 3.4
LO 3.5
LO 3.9
LO 3.11

2. Margaret started her own business in the current year and will report a profit for her first year. Her results of operations are as follows:

Gross income	$45,000
Travel	1,000
Contribution to Presidential Election Campaign	100
Transportation 5,300 miles equally across the year, using standard mileage method	?
Entertainment in total	4,200
Nine gifts at $50 each	450
Rent and utilities for apartment in total (25 percent is used for a home office)	10,500

What is the net income Margaret should show on her Schedule C? Show the calculation of her gross income, expenses, and taxable business income.

LO 3.2

3. Lawrence owns a small candy store that sells one type of candy. His beginning inventory of candy was made up of 10,000 boxes costing $1.50 per box ($15,000), and he made the following purchases of candy during the year:

March 1	10,000 boxes at $1.55	$15,500
August 15	20,000 boxes at $1.65	33,000
November 20	10,000 boxes at $1.70	17,000

At the end of the year, Lawrence's inventory consisted of 16,000 boxes of candy.

a. Calculate Lawrence's ending inventory and cost of goods sold using the FIFO inventory valuation method.
b. Calculate Lawrence's ending inventory and cost of goods sold using the LIFO inventory valuation method.

LO 3.2

4. Kevin owns a retail store, and during the current year he purchased $580,000 worth of inventory. Kevin's beginning inventory was $60,000, and his ending inventory is $80,000. During the year, Kevin withdrew $1,000 in inventory for his personal use. Use Part III of Schedule C below to calculate Kevin's cost of goods sold for the year.

Part III **Cost of Goods Sold** (see instructions)

33	Method(s) used to value closing inventory: a ☐ Cost b ☐ Lower of cost or market c ☐ Other (attach explanation)		
34	Was there any change in determining quantities, costs, or valuations between opening and closing inventory? If "Yes," attach explanation . . . ☐ Yes ☐ No		
35	Inventory at beginning of year. If different from last year's closing inventory, attach explanation . . .	35	
36	Purchases less cost of items withdrawn for personal use . . .	36	
37	Cost of labor. Do not include any amounts paid to yourself . . .	37	
38	Materials and supplies . . .	38	
39	Other costs . . .	39	
40	Add lines 35 through 39 . . .	40	
41	Inventory at end of year . . .	41	
42	**Cost of goods sold.** Subtract line 41 from line 40. Enter the result here and on line 4 . . .	42	

LO 3.2

5. Frank owns an auto repair shop that serves a particular model of auto and he tends to purchase parts in bulk. Frank is eligible to treat inventory as non-incidental materials and could elect to do so. In December of 2021 he purchases twenty-four oil filters. He uses one filter to service an auto in January 2022, and then about two filters per month and ends 2022 with 14 filters. Frank's business has gross receipts of around $1.2 million per year. Frank expenses oil filters when he purchases them on his book and records (Frank does not have financial statements other than for taxes). Explain how Frank could treat his oil filter inventory.

LO 3.3

6. Teresa is a self-employed civil engineer who uses her automobile for business. Teresa drove her automobile a total of 12,000 miles during 2022, of which 5,600 were business miles before July 1 and 4,000 were business miles after June 30. The actual cost of gasoline, oil, depreciation, repairs, and insurance for the year was $6,400. Teresa is eligible to use the actual or standard method.
   a. How much is Teresa's transportation deduction based on the standard mileage method?
   b. How much is Teresa's transportation deduction based on the actual cost method?
   c. Which method should Teresa use to calculate her transportation deduction? Why?

LO 3.3

7. Art is a self-employed installer of home entertainment systems, and he drives his car frequently to installation locations. Art drove his car 15,000 miles for business purposes and 20,000 miles in total. His actual expenses, including depreciation, for operating the auto are $10,000 since he had to have the car repaired several times. Art has always used the actual cost method in the past. How much is Art's deductible auto expense for the year?

LO 3.3

8. Martha is a self-employed tax accountant who drives her car to visit clients on a regular basis. She drives her car 3,000 miles for business before July 1, 1,000 miles for business after June 30, and 10,000 miles for commuting and other personal use. Assuming Martha uses the standard mileage method, how much is her auto expense for the year? Where on her tax return should Martha claim this deduction?

LO 3.4

9. Joan is a self-employed attorney in New York City. Joan took a trip to San Diego, CA, primarily for business, to consult with a client and take a short vacation. On the trip, Joan incurred the following expenses:

Airfare to and from San Diego	$ 480
Hotel charges while on business	440
Restaurant meals while on business	260
Car rental while on business (she drove 240 miles)	110
Hotel charges while on vacation	460
Restaurant meals while on vacation	290
Car rental while on vacation	180
Total	$2,220

Calculate Joan's travel expense deduction for the trip, assuming the trip was made in 2022.

LO 3.4

10. Go to the U.S. General Services Administration (GSA) website (**www.gsa.gov**). For the month of September 2022, what is the per diem rate for each of the following towns:
   a. Flagstaff, AZ
   b. Palm Springs, CA
   c. Atlanta, GA

LO 3.4
LO 3.5
LO 3.6

11. Bob is a self-employed lawyer and is required to take a week of continuing legal education every year to maintain his license. This year he paid $1,400 in course fees for his continuing legal education in a different city. He also paid $500 for airfare

and a hotel room and paid $300 for meals, all of which were provided by the hotel's restaurant. Bob also purchased a $10 bag of snacks from a newsstand while waiting for his plane in the airport because he missed lunch. What is the total amount he can deduct on his Schedule C related to these expenses?

LO 3.5

12. Grace is a self-employed sales consultant who spends significant time entertaining potential customers. She keeps all the appropriate records to substantiate her entertainment. She has the following expenses in the current year:

Restaurant meals where business was conducted	$5,000
Greens fees (all business)	500
Tickets to baseball games (all business)	500
Country Club dues (all business use)	6,000

What are the tax-deductible meals and entertainment expenses Grace may claim in the current year? On which tax form should she claim the deduction?

LO 3.5

13. Marty is a sales consultant. Marty incurs the following expenses related to the entertainment of his clients in the current year:

Dues to a country club (The country club was used for business 25 days of the total 75 days that it was used.)	$4,500
Business meals at the country club restaurant not associated with golf or tennis	1,400
Dues to a tennis club (The club was used 75 percent for directly related business.)	1,000
Tennis fees (personal use)	300
Business meals at various restaurants	1,900

a. How much is Marty's deduction for meals and entertainment expenses for the current year?
b. For each item listed above that you believe is not allowed as a deduction, explain the reason it is not allowed.

LO 3.6

14. a. Loren is a secretary in a lawyer's office. Since he often deals with legal matters, Loren feels that a law degree will be beneficial to him. Explain whether Loren may deduct his educational expenses for law school?
b. Alicia is an employee in the sales department for an international firm. She wishes to learn Spanish to improve her ability to communicate with foreign clients. Explain whether Alicia may deduct her educational expenses for language school as a miscellaneous itemized deduction?
c. Joan is a practicing lawyer. She enrolls in a local medical school and works toward a medical degree in her spare time. Explain whether Joan may deduct her educational expenses for the medical classes?

LO 3.7

15. Carey opens a law office in Chicago on January 1, 2022. On January 1, 2022, Carey purchases an annual subscription to a law journal for $240 and a one-year legal reference service for $3,500. Carey also subscribes to *Chicago Magazine* for $60 so she can find great places to take clients to dinner and review the "Best 50 Lawyers in Chicago" list published each year. Calculate Carey's deduction for the above items for the 2022 tax year.

LO 3.8

16. Cooper and Brandy are married and file a joint income tax return with two separate Schedule Cs. Cooper is an independent security specialist who spent $400 on uniforms during the year. His laundry expenses for the uniforms were $160 for this year, plus $85 for altering them. Brandy works as a drill press operator and wears jeans and a work shirt on the job, which cost $175 this year. Her laundry costs were

$50 for the work clothes. Brandy is also required by state regulators to wear safety glasses and safety shoes when working, which cost a total of $125.

a. How much is Cooper's total deduction on his Schedule C for special clothing and uniforms?
b. How much is Brandy's total deduction on her Schedule C for special clothing and uniforms?

LO 3.9

17. Sam owns an insurance agency and makes the following business gifts during the year. Calculate Sam's deduction for business gifts.

Donee	*Amount*
Ms. Sears (a client)	$35, plus $4 shipping
Mr. Williams (a tennis partner, not a business prospect or client)	55
Mr. Sample (a client) received $22 and Mrs. Sample (nonclient spouse of Mr. Sample) received a gift valued at $20	42
Various customers (calendars costing $3 each with the company name on them)	300
Mr. Shiver (an employee gift, a watch, for 25 years of continuous service)	175

LO 3.10

18. Steinar loaned a friend $9,500 to buy some stock three years ago. In the current year the debt became worthless.
a. How much is Steinar's deduction for the bad debt for this year? (Assume he has no other capital gains or losses.)
b. What can Steinar do with the deduction not used this year?

LO 3.10

19. Sharon is an orthopedic surgeon. She performed a surgery two years ago and billed $10,000 to her patient. After two years of attempting to collect the money, it is clear that Sharon will not be able to collect anything. Sharon reports income on her tax return on the cash basis, so she only reports the income she actually receives in cash each year. Can she claim a bad debt deduction for the $10,000?

LO 3.10

20. Carrie loaned her friend $4,500 to buy a used car. She had her friend sign a note with repayment terms and set a reasonable interest rate on the note because the $4,500 was most of her savings. Her friend left town without a forwarding address and nobody Carrie knows has heard from the friend in the last year. How should Carrie treat the bad loan for tax purposes?

LO 3.11

21. Cindy operates a computerized engineering drawing business from her home. Cindy maintains a home office and properly allocates the following expenses to her office:

Depreciation	$1,500
Utilities	500
Real estate taxes	325
Mortgage interest (100 percent deductible)	500

a. Assume that Cindy earns income of $4,400 from her business for the year before deducting home office expenses. She has no other expenses associated with the business. Calculate Cindy's deduction for home office expenses.

b. Assume that Cindy earns income of $2,600 from her business during the year before deducting home office expenses. Calculate Cindy's deduction for home office expenses.

LO 3.11

22. Pete qualifies for a home office deduction. The amount of space devoted to business use is 300 square feet of the total 1,200 square feet in his apartment. Pete's total rent for the year is $9,600, and he pays utilities (other than telephone) of $2,500 for the year. Calculate Pete's deduction for home office expenses (rent and utilities, other than telephone) before the gross income limitation.

LO 3.11

23. Randi qualifies for a home deduction. The amount of space devoted to business use is 400 square feet of the total 2,000 square feet of her home. Randi's mortgage interest and property taxes in total are $1,600. Other deductions properly allocated to the home office total $300. In addition, Randi purchases and uses business supplies costing $200 during the year. Assume Randi earns income of $3,400 for the year before deducting any home office or supplies deduction. Calculate the largest deduction Randi can take for her home office (ignore self-employment taxes).

LO 3.11

24. Ann is a self-employed restaurant critic who does her work exclusively from a home office. Ann's income is $25,000 before the home office deduction this year. Her office takes up 200 square feet of her 1,000-square-foot apartment. The total expenses for her apartment are $6,000 for rent, $1,000 for utilities, $200 for renter's insurance, and $800 for pest control and other maintenance. What is Ann's home office deduction? Please show your calculations.

LO 3.12

25. Lew is a practicing CPA who decides to raise bonsai as a business. Lew engages in the activity and has the following revenue and expenses:

Sales	$ 5,000
Depreciation on greenhouse	10,000
Fertilizer, soil, pots	1,500

a. What are the factors that the IRS will consider when evaluating whether the activity is a business or a hobby?
b. If the activity is deemed to be a regular business, what is the amount of Lew's loss from the activity?
c. If the activity is deemed to be a hobby, what is the amount of Lew's expenses (if any) from the activity that may be deducted?

GROUP 3: WRITING ASSIGNMENT

ETHICS

1. Bobby Reynolds, a new client of yours, is a self-employed caterer in Santa Fe, New Mexico. Bobby drives his personal van when delivering catered meals to customers. You have asked him to provide the amount of business miles driven using his vehicle. You are planning on using the standard mileage method to calculate Bobby's deduction for transportation costs. Bobby has responded by saying, "Well, I don't really keep track of my miles. I guess I drove around 3,000 miles last year for the business." What would you say to Bobby?

RESEARCH

2. Your supervisor has asked you to research a potential tax deduction for a client, Randall Stevens. Randall is a self-employed loan agent that lives in Portland, Maine. His specialty is marine loans; in particular, loans for the renovation of classic boats. Over the years, Randall has developed a very unique expertise in valuation of classic boats and is considered a global expert in the field. In 2022, Randall is hoping to attend the North American Classic Marine Boat Show that takes place in Zihuatanejo, Mexico. Randall attends the show more or less every year in order to stay current on classic boat valuations. Interested parties from around the world attend the show in the quaint Mexican coastal town. Randall's costs to attend are $800 for show registration, $1,750 for airfare from Portland to Zihuatanejo, $2,400 for lodging. Meals are estimated at $600. Please prepare a letter for Randall that describes the issues he will face when attempting to deduct the cost of attending the show. Use IRS Publication 463 (available at **www.irs.gov**) to assist you.

   (An example of a client letter is available at the website for this textbook located at **www.cengage.com.**)

GROUP 4:
COMPREHENSIVE PROBLEMS

1. Gordon Temper is a single taxpayer (birthdate July 1, 1985 and Social Security number 242-11-6767) that operates a food truck that specializes in food from South Africa. His business is named "Mobile Peri Peri" and although the truck moves around quite a bit, he generally parks it in an office park where he maintains an office and a supply of inventory. The business address is 150 Erie Street, Laramie, WY 82070. The principal business code is 722300.

Gordon's food truck business is fairly new, so he also works part-time as a cook at a steak house restaurant in Laramie. His 2022 Form W-2 follows:

a Employee's social security number: 242-11-6767 — OMB No. 1545-0008	Safe, accurate, FAST! Use IRS e-file	Visit the IRS website at www.irs.gov/efile
b Employer identification number (EIN): 37-9019012	1 Wages, tips, other compensation: 21,000.00	2 Federal income tax withheld: 1,600.00
c Employer's name, address, and ZIP code: Tenderloin of Laramie, 2400 Grand Avenue, Laramie, WY 82070	3 Social security wages: 21,000.00	4 Social security tax withheld: 1,302.00
	5 Medicare wages and tips: 21,000.00	6 Medicare tax withheld: 304.50
	7 Social security tips	8 Allocated tips
d Control number	9	10 Dependent care benefits
e Employee's first name and initial / Last name / Suff.: Gordon Temper, 116 S 6th Street Unit 3D, Laramie, WY 82070	11 Nonqualified plans	12a See instructions for box 12
	13 Statutory employee ☐ Retirement plan ☐ Third-party sick pay ☐	12b
	14 Other	12c
f Employee's address and ZIP code		12d

15 State / Employer's state ID number	16 State wages, tips, etc.	17 State income tax	18 Local wages, tips, etc.	19 Local income tax	20 Locality name
WY					

Form **W-2** Wage and Tax Statement 2022 — Department of the Treasury—Internal Revenue Service

Copy B—To Be Filed With Employee's FEDERAL Tax Return.
This information is being furnished to the Internal Revenue Service.

Gordon provided the following financial information related to Mobile Peri Peri:

Revenues	$78,000
Beginning Inventory	5,600
Purchases	43,000
Ending inventory	7,800
Truck rental	24,000
Office rental	8,600
Advertising	500
Insurance	3,000
Food license	450
Uniforms	200
Dues	100
Travel	1,600
Office expense	400

Mobile Peri Peri uses the cash method of accounting and the cost method for inventory.

Gordon also provided a transportation log that shows that the truck drove 2,600 business miles between January 1 and June 30 and 3,000 miles from July 1 through the end of 2022. Gordon's log also listed total mileage of 680 miles for his drive in his personal car from the Mobile Peri Peri office to his second job at the steak house. He did not provide mileage from his apartment to or from either work location.

Dues are for a subscription to *Food Truck Monthly*, a trade magazine.

His travel expense of $1,600 is for a trip to Steamboat Springs, CO, for a one-day seminar on South African cuisine. He spent the day at the seminar and then went snow-skiing for two days before returning to Laramie. His airfare to Steamboat Springs was $400, his lodging was $300 per night for three nights, and his meals were all restaurant meals at a cost of $100 per day. The uniforms are white chef's coats and puffy chef's hats embroidered with the South African flag and the Mobile Peri Peri logo on front and back.

Gordon was divorced in 2017. His ex-spouse, Tanya Ramsey, pays him alimony of $300 per month. She also has custody of their five children. One of the Ramsey's children, Buffy, age 17, lived with Gordon for five months during 2022 and he estimates he provided more than one-half of her support. Buffy has a part-time job at Taco Shell fast-food restaurant and made $5,000 in 2022.

Gordon received a sizable property settlement as part of the divorce and has invested wisely. He received the following Forms 1099 for 2022:

☐ CORRECTED (if checked)

PAYER'S name, street address, city or town, state or province, country, ZIP or foreign postal code, and telephone no.	Investcorp Bond Fund PO Box 11234 Valley Forge, PA 19481
Payer's RTN (optional)	
OMB No. 1545-0112	Form **1099-INT** (Rev. January 2022) For calendar year 20 22
1 Interest income	$ 3,200.00
2 Early withdrawal penalty	$
PAYER'S TIN	43-98712361
RECIPIENT'S TIN	242-11-6767
3 Interest on U.S. Savings Bonds and Treasury obligations	$
RECIPIENT'S name	Gordon Temper
4 Federal income tax withheld	$
5 Investment expenses	$
6 Foreign tax paid	$
7 Foreign country or U.S. possession	
Street address (including apt. no.)	116 S. 6th St 3D
8 Tax-exempt interest	$
9 Specified private activity bond interest	$
City or town, state or province, country, and ZIP or foreign postal code	Laramie, WY 82070
10 Market discount	$
11 Bond premium	$
FATCA filing requirement	☐
12 Bond premium on Treasury obligations	$
13 Bond premium on tax-exempt bond	$
Account number (see instructions)	
14 Tax-exempt and tax credit bond CUSIP no.	
15 State	
16 State identification no.	
17 State tax withheld	$ $

Interest Income

Copy B

For Recipient

This is important tax information and is being furnished to the IRS. If you are required to file a return, a negligence penalty or other sanction may be imposed on you if this income is taxable and the IRS determines that it has not been reported.

Form **1099-INT** (Rev. 1-2022) (keep for your records) www.irs.gov/Form1099INT Department of the Treasury - Internal Revenue Service

☐ CORRECTED (if checked)

PAYER'S name, street address, city or town, state or province, country, ZIP or foreign postal code, and telephone no.	Investcorp Small Cap Equity Fund PO Box 11234 Valley Forge, PA 19481
1a Total ordinary dividends	$ 5,678.12
OMB No. 1545-0110	Form **1099-DIV** (Rev. January 2022) For calendar year 20 22
1b Qualified dividends	$ 5,478.12
2a Total capital gain distr.	$ 1,045.67
2b Unrecap. Sec. 1250 gain	$
PAYER'S TIN	42-1313445
RECIPIENT'S TIN	242-11-6767
2c Section 1202 gain	$
2d Collectibles (28%) gain	$
2e Section 897 ordinary dividends	$
2f Section 897 capital gain	$
RECIPIENT'S name	Gordon Temper
3 Nondividend distributions	$
4 Federal income tax withheld	$
5 Section 199A dividends	$
6 Investment expenses	$
Street address (including apt. no.)	116 S. 6th Street #3D
7 Foreign tax paid	$
8 Foreign country or U.S. possession	
City or town, state or province, country, and ZIP or foreign postal code	Laramie, WY 82070
9 Cash liquidation distributions	$
10 Noncash liquidation distributions	$
11 FATCA filing requirement	☐
12 Exempt-interest dividends	$
13 Specified private activity bond interest dividends	$
Account number (see instructions)	
14 State	
15 State identification no.	
16 State tax withheld	$ $

Dividends and Distributions

Copy B

For Recipient

This is important tax information and is being furnished to the IRS. If you are required to file a return, a negligence penalty or other sanction may be imposed on you if this income is taxable and the IRS determines that it has not been reported.

Form **1099-DIV** (Rev. 1-2022) (keep for your records) www.irs.gov/Form1099DIV Department of the Treasury - Internal Revenue Service

Required: Complete Gordon's federal income tax return for 2022 on Form 1040, Schedule 1, Schedule B, Schedule C, and the Qualified Dividends and Capital Gains Tax Worksheet.

2A. Russell (birthdate February 2, 1971) and Linda (birthdate August 30, 1976) Long have brought you the following information regarding their income and expenses for the current year. Russell owns and operates a landscaping business called Lawns and Landscapes Unlimited (EIN: 32-1456789). The business is operated out of their home, located at 1234 Cherry Lane, Nampa, ID 83687. The principal business code is 561730. Russell's bookkeeper provided the following income statement from the landscaping business:

Lawns and Landscapes
Income Statement
12/31/2022

	Current Period 1/1/2022 to 12/31/2022	Prior Period 1/1/2021 to 12/31/2021
REVENUES		
Lawn maintenance	$ 85,000	$ 71,998
Lawn and plant installation	35,000	48,576
Other	17,100	8,001
TOTAL REVENUES	**137,100**	**128,575**
COST OF SERVICES		
Salaries	85,000	78,445
Payroll Taxes	6,800	6,432
Equipment Rental	12,500	10,651
Maintenance (Equipment)	8,300	8,435
Special Clothing and Safety Shoes	660	200
Contract Labor	7,780	6,790
TOTAL COST OF SERVICES	121,040	110,953
GROSS PROFIT (LOSS)	16,060	17,622
OPERATING EXPENSES		
Advertising and Promotion	1,500	700
Donations	600	500
Insurance	4,000	870
Meals and Entertainment	2,300	2,100
Subscriptions	120	120
Business Gifts	790	600
Telephone	2,015	1,956
Training	1,975	-
Travel	865	750
Other	1,700	2,724
TOTAL OPERATING EXPENSES	15,865	10,320
NET INCOME (LOSS)	**$ 195**	**$ 7,302**

The bookkeeper provided the following additional information:

- Donations expense is a $600 donation to the Campaign to Re-Elect Senator Ami Dahla.
- Training includes $575 for an educational seminar on bug control. It also includes the cost for Russell to attend an online certificate program in landscaping in order to improve his skills and advertise his designation as a certified landscaper. The tuition, fees, and books cost $1,400.
- No business gift exceeded $22 in value.
- The subscription is for a trade magazine titled *Plants Unlimited.*
- Meals and entertainment expense is $1,500 of restaurant business meals and $800 for season tickets to Boise State University that Russell uses to entertain potential clients.

- Russell drove his pickup truck (purchased 3/14/2021) 200 business miles through June 30 and 800 business miles for the remainder of 2022. He also drove the truck 2,300 commuting miles and 3,000 other miles. The Longs have another car available for personal use. Truck business mileage is not reflected in the income statement.

The business uses the cash method of accounting and has no accounts receivable or inventory held for resale.

In addition to the above expenses, the Longs have set aside one room of their house as a home office. The room is 192 square feet and their house has a total of 1,600 square feet. They pay $13,200 per year rental on their house, and the utilities amount to $1,800 for the year.

The Longs inherited a large number of acres of farm land from Linda's father in 2021 and sold it immediately for its market value of $1,000,000. They invested the proceeds in the Potato Dividend High Yield Fund and received the following Form 1099-DIV.

☐ CORRECTED (if checked)

PAYER'S name, street address, city or town, state or province, country, ZIP or foreign postal code, and telephone no.
Potato Dividend High Yield Fund
1100 W. Front Street, 8th Fl.
Boise, ID 83702

1a Total ordinary dividends $ 26,000.00
1b Qualified dividends $ 26,000.00

OMB No. 1545-0110
Form 1099-DIV
(Rev. January 2022)
For calendar year 20 22

Dividends and Distributions

2a Total capital gain distr. $
2b Unrecap. Sec. 1250 gain $

Copy B For Recipient

PAYER'S TIN: 12-3144562
RECIPIENT'S TIN: 554-98-3946

2c Section 1202 gain $
2d Collectibles (28%) gain $
2e Section 897 ordinary dividends $
2f Section 897 capital gain $

RECIPIENT'S name
Linda Long

3 Nondividend distributions $
4 Federal income tax withheld $

Street address (including apt. no.)
1234 Cherry Lane

5 Section 199A dividends $
6 Investment expenses $
7 Foreign tax paid $
8 Foreign country or U.S. possession

City or town, state or province, country, and ZIP or foreign postal code
Nampa, ID 83687

9 Cash liquidation distributions $
10 Noncash liquidation distributions $

11 FATCA filing requirement ☐
12 Exempt-interest dividends $
13 Specified private activity bond interest dividends $

Account number (see instructions)

14 State
15 State identification no.
16 State tax withheld $ / $

This is important tax information and is being furnished to the IRS. If you are required to file a return, a negligence penalty or other sanction may be imposed on you if this income is taxable and the IRS determines that it has not been reported.

Form 1099-DIV (Rev. 1-2022) (keep for your records) www.irs.gov/Form1099DIV Department of the Treasury - Internal Revenue Service

Linda lost her job in late 2021 and collected unemployment as shown on the following Form 1099-G.

☐ CORRECTED (if checked)

PAYER'S name, street address, city or town, state or province, country, ZIP or foreign postal code, and telephone no.
Idaho Department of Labor
317 W. Main St.
Boise, Idaho 83735

1 Unemployment compensation $ 800.00
2 State or local income tax refunds, credits, or offsets $

OMB No. 1545-0120
Form 1099-G
(Rev. January 2022)
For calendar year 20 22

Certain Government Payments

PAYER'S TIN: 11-2456871
RECIPIENT'S TIN: 554-98-3946

3 Box 2 amount is for tax year
4 Federal income tax withheld $

Copy B For Recipient

RECIPIENT'S name
Linda Long

5 RTAA payments $
6 Taxable grants $
7 Agriculture payments $
8 If checked, box 2 is trade or business income ▶ ☐

Street address (including apt. no.)
1234 Cherry Lane

9 Market gain $

City or town, state or province, country, and ZIP or foreign postal code
Nampa, ID 83687

Account number (see instructions)

10a State
10b State identification no.
11 State income tax withheld $ / $

This is important tax information and is being furnished to the IRS. If you are required to file a return, a negligence penalty or other sanction may be imposed on you if this income is taxable and the IRS determines that it has not been reported.

Form 1099-G (Rev. 1-2022) (keep for your records) www.irs.gov/Form1099G Department of the Treasury - Internal Revenue Service

Russell was divorced on April 1, 2020 and pays his ex-spouse, Lois Long (SSN 313-29-3133) alimony of $200 per month in 2022.

Russell's Social Security number is 664-98-5678 and Linda's is 554-98-3946. They made an estimated tax payment to the IRS of $300 on December 31, 2022.

Required: Complete the Longs' federal tax return for 2022 on Form 1040, Schedule 1, Schedule B, Schedule C, Form 8829, and the Qualified Dividends and Capital Gain Tax Worksheet. Do not complete Form 4562 (depreciation).

2B. Christopher Crosphit (birthdate April 28, 1980, Social Security number 565-12-6789) and Traynor Crosphit (birthdate July 17, 1979) are married filing jointly in 2022. They have a dependent son, Arnold (Social Security number 276-23-3954). Arnold (birthdate July 1, 2004) is a high school student; he does not qualify for the child tax credit but does qualify for the $500 other dependent credit.

Chris owns and operates a health club called "Catawba Fitness." The business is located at 4321 New Cut Road, Spartanburg, SC 29303. The principal business code is 812190 and the EIN is 12-3456789. Chris had the following income and expenses from the health club:

Income	216,000
Expenses	
Business insurance	3,500
Office supplies	3,400
Payroll	99,000
Payroll taxes	9,000
Travel	2,500
Meals	2,100
Business gifts	800
Equipment maintenance	10,700
Cleaning service	8,800
Equipment rent	22,500
Utilities	14,000
Telephone	2,700
Rent	32,000
Advertising	4,000
Special workout clothes and boxing gloves	750
Subscription to Biceps Monthly magazine	100
Online educational seminar on gym safety	800
Other expenses	1,800

The business uses the cash method of accounting and has no accounts receivable or inventory held for resale.

Travel includes a trip to a weight-lifting seminar in Miami, FL. The one-day seminar cost $400. Chris took Traynor and Arnold with him. Airfare was $400 for each of them. The seminar started early in the morning, so they flew down the night before and then left the following morning since the seminar ended late in the day. Traynor and Arnold went to Miami Beach for the day. Lodging was $250 per night for two nights and meals were $100 for each of the three of them ($300 total). They also paid $100 for ground transportation from the airport to the hotel hosting the seminar.

Meals includes $1,000 for a staff party for all employees of Catawba Fitness, $800 in restaurant meals, and $300 in non-restaurant meals.

Chris purchased business gifts for 20 customers at a cost of $40 each.

The Crosphits live next door to the health club at 4323 New Cut Road. Chris does all the administrative work for the health club out of an office in their home. The room is 171 square feet and the house has a total of 1,800 square feet. The Crosphits pay $20,000 per year in rent and $4,000 in utilities. Chris would prefer to use the simplified method to deduct his home office if possible.

Traynor works as a sales representative for an online manufacturer and distributor of exercise bicycles. Her W-2 follows:

a Employee's social security number: 712-22-9881	OMB No. 1545-0008	Safe, accurate, FAST! Use IRS e-file	Visit the IRS website at www.irs.gov/efile
b Employer identification number (EIN): 47-3533716		1 Wages, tips, other compensation: 48,040.00	2 Federal income tax withheld: 2,200.00
c Employer's name, address, and ZIP code: Pack of Bikes, Inc., 120 East 25th Street, 10th Floor, New York, NY 10001		3 Social security wages: 48,040.00	4 Social security tax withheld: 2,978.48
		5 Medicare wages and tips: 48,040.00	6 Medicare tax withheld: 969.58
		7 Social security tips	8 Allocated tips
d Control number		9	10 Dependent care benefits
e Employee's first name and initial, Last name, Suff.: Traynor Crosphit, 4323 New Cut Road, Spartanburg, SC 29303		11 Nonqualified plans	12a See instructions for box 12: C 40.00
		13 Statutory employee ☐ Retirement plan ☐ Third-party sick pay ☐	12b: DD 6,500.00
		14 Other: FSA Health $2,850.00	12c
f Employee's address and ZIP code			12d

15 State	Employer's state ID number	16 State wages, tips, etc.	17 State income tax	18 Local wages, tips, etc.	19 Local income tax	20 Locality name
SC	10008723	48,040.00	600.00			

Form **W-2** Wage and Tax Statement **2022** Department of the Treasury—Internal Revenue Service

Copy B—To Be Filed With Employee's FEDERAL Tax Return.
This information is being furnished to the Internal Revenue Service.

Chris ran up credit card debt in 2022 and was able to negotiate a reduction of his balance. He received the following 1099-C:

☐ CORRECTED (if checked)

CREDITOR'S name, street address, city or town, state or province, country, ZIP or foreign postal code, and telephone no.		1 Date of identifiable event: 3/19/2022	OMB No. 1545-1424	
Explorer Card Services, 100 N Phillips Ave., Sioux Falls, SD 57104		2 Amount of debt discharged: $ 4,000.00	Form **1099-C** (Rev. January 2022)	**Cancellation of Debt**
		3 Interest, if included in box 2: $	For calendar year 20 22	
CREDITOR'S TIN: 31-4543431	DEBTOR'S TIN: 565-12-6789	4 Debt description: Credit card debt		**Copy B For Debtor**
DEBTOR'S name: Christopher Crosphit				This is important tax information and is being furnished to the IRS. If you are required to file a return, a negligence penalty or other sanction may be imposed on you if taxable income results from this transaction and the IRS determines that it has not been reported.
Street address (including apt. no.): 4323 New Cut Road		5 If checked, the debtor was personally liable for repayment of the debt ☒		
City or town, state or province, country, and ZIP or foreign postal code: Spartanburg, SC 29303				
Account number (see instructions)		6 Identifiable event code: F	7 Fair market value of property: $	

Form **1099-C** (Rev. 1-2022) (keep for your records) www.irs.gov/Form1099C Department of the Treasury - Internal Revenue Service

Chris also dabbles as a broker of antique and rare books. He acquires and scavenges for books and then sells them on the Internet. He generated $4,000 of sales in 2022 and the books he sold cost $3,500. He also incurred $7,600 in travel and other expenses related to this activity. Chris has never turned a profit in the book business, but he loves books and book selling and does not mind losing money doing it.

The Crosphits withdrew $2,000 from the health care flexible account with Traynor's employer to pay for Arnold's orthodontic work.

Chris made an estimated tax payment to the IRS of $500 on April 15, 2021.

Required: Complete the Crosphit's federal tax return for 2022 on Form 1040, Schedule 1, and Schedule C. Do not complete Form 4562 (depreciation).

GROUP 5:

CUMULATIVE SOFTWARE PROBLEM

1. The following additional information is available for the Albert and Allison Gaytor family from Chapters 1 and 2.

   On September 1, Allison opened a retail store that specializes in sports car accessories. The name of the store is "Toge Pass." The store is located at 617 Crandon Boulevard, Key Biscayne, FL 33149. The store uses the cash method of accounting for everything except inventory which is kept on an accrual basis. The store's EIN is 98-7321654. Allison purchased inventory in August and then started her business on September 1 with $40,100 of inventory. The Toge Pass accountant provided the following financial information:

Income Statement

Toge Pass Auto Parts
Calendar Year 2022

Financial Statements in U.S. Dollars

Revenue		
Gross Sales	64,600	
Less: Sales Returns and Allowances	400	
Net Sales		64,200
Cost of Goods Sold		
Beginning Inventory	40,100	
Add: Purchases	37,900	
Inventory Available	78,000	
Less: Ending Inventory	37,850	
Cost of Goods Sold		40,150
Gross Profit (Loss)		24,050
Expenses		
Advertising	3,000	
Dues and Subscriptions	-	
Gifts	180	
Insurance	900	
Interest	1,650	
Legal and Professional Fees	300	
Licenses and Fees	900	
Miscellaneous	100	
Office Expense	1,280	
Payroll Taxes	500	
Postage	-	
Rent	7,500	
Repairs and Maintenance	400	
Supplies	650	
Telephone	750	
Travel	950	
Uniforms	400	
Utilities	975	
Vehicle Expenses	-	
Wages	3,470	
Total Expenses		23,905
Net Operating Income		145
Other Income		
Gain (Loss) on Sale of Assets		
Interest Income		
Total Other Income		-
Net Income (Loss)		145

A review of the expense account detail reveals the following:

- The travel expense includes the costs Allison incurred to attend a seminar on sports car accessories. She spent $300 on airfare, $400 on lodging, $100 on a rental car, and $150 on restaurant meals. Allison has proper receipts for these amounts.
- The gift account details show that Allison gave a $30 gift to each of her six best suppliers.

- The supplies expense account detail reflects the purchase of 250 pens with the "Toge Pass" logo inscribed on each pen. Allison gave the pens away to suppliers, customers, and other business contacts before the end of the year.
- Uniforms expense reflects the cost to purchase polo shirts Allison provided for each employee (but not herself). The shirts have the Toge Pass logo printed on the front and back and are the required apparel while working but otherwise are just like any other polo shirts.
- The license and fee account includes a $600 fine Toge Pass paid to the state of Washington for environmental damage resulting from an oil spill.

Allison drove her 2014 Ford Explorer 1,686 miles (all after June 30, 2022) for business related to Toge Pass. The Explorer was driven a total of 11,450 miles for the year. Included in the total 11,450 miles is 5,000 miles spent commuting to the store. Allison has the required substantiation for business mileage. She uses the standard mileage method.

In July, Albert loaned a friend $7,000 so he could buy a car. Albert's friend lost his job in 2022 and stopped making payments on the loan. He plans to start making payments again, however, with additional interest as soon as he has new employment.

In late 2022, Albert started to mount and stuff some of his trophy fish to display in his "man cave" at the Gaytor's home. Some of his friends liked Albert's taxidermy work and asked him to prepare a couple of trophy fish for them as well. Although he doubts he will ever sell any more stuffed fish, he received $150 and had no expenses related to this activity in 2022.

Required: Combine this new information about the Gaytor family with the information from Chapters 1 and 2 and complete a revised 2022 tax return for Albert and Allison. Be sure to save your data input files since this case will be expanded with more tax information in later chapters.

CHAPTER 4

Additional Income and the Qualified Business Income Deduction

Andriy Blokhin/Shutterstock.com

LEARNING OBJECTIVES

After completing this chapter, you should be able to:

LO 4.1 Define the term "capital asset."

LO 4.2 Apply the holding period for long-term and short-term capital gains and losses.

LO 4.3 Calculate the gain or loss on the disposition of an asset.

LO 4.4 Compute the tax on capital gains.

LO 4.5 Describe the treatment of capital losses.

LO 4.6 Apply the exclusion of gain from personal residence sales.

LO 4.7 Apply the tax rules for rental property and vacation homes.

LO 4.8 Explain the treatment of passive income and losses.

LO 4.9 Describe the basic tax treatment of deductions for net operating losses.

LO 4.10 Calculate and report the self-employment tax (both Social Security and Medicare portions) for self-employed taxpayers.

LO 4.11 Compute the qualified business income (QBI) deduction.

OVERVIEW

Chapter 4 covers additional important elements of income and expense which enter into the calculation of adjusted gross income (AGI). The first part of this chapter includes capital gains and other items reported through Schedule D. The second part covers the tax rules for rental properties and other business activities including limitations on passive activities reported through Schedule E. This chapter concludes with the self-employment tax and the qualified business income deduction introduced in 2018. The business income and expenses included in this chapter are all part of the calculation of a taxpayer's AGI.

Learning Objective 4.1

Define the term "capital asset."

4-1 WHAT IS A CAPITAL ASSET?

When taxpayers dispose of property, they must calculate any gain or loss on the transaction and report the gain or loss on their tax returns. The gain or loss realized is equal to the difference between the amount realized on the sale or exchange of the property and the taxpayer's adjusted basis in the property. How gains and losses are reported is dependent on the nature of the property and the length of time the property has been owned. Gains and losses on the sale of capital assets are known as capital gains and losses and are classified as either short-term or long-term. For a gain or loss on the sale of a capital asset to be classified as a long-term capital gain or loss, the taxpayer must have held the asset for the required holding period.

The tax law defines a capital asset as any property, whether used in a trade or business or not, other than:

1. Stock in trade, inventory, or property held primarily for sale to customers in the ordinary course of a trade or business;
2. Depreciable property or real property used in a trade or business (Section 1231 assets);
3. A patent, invention, model or design (whether or not patented), a secret formula or process, a copyright, a literary, musical, or artistic composition, a letter or memorandum, or similar property, if the property is created by the taxpayer;
4. Accounts or notes receivable; and
5. Certain U.S. government publications.

The definition of a capital asset is a definition by exception. All property owned by a taxpayer, other than property specifically noted as an exception, is a capital asset. Depreciable property and real estate used in a trade or business are referred to as Section 1231 assets and will be discussed in Chapter 8 because special rules apply to such assets.

4-1a Virtual Currency

Virtual currency is a digital representation of value that functions as a medium of exchange, a unit of account, or a store of value. Cryptocurrency is a type of virtual currency that utilizes blockchain to validate and secure transactions that are digitally recorded on a distributed ledger.

Some virtual currencies, such as Bitcoin, have an equivalent value in real currency. For example, Bitcoin can be digitally traded between users and can be purchased for, or exchanged into, U.S. dollars, Euros, and other real currencies.

EXAMPLE Micah, a cash-basis single taxpayer, has a customer that paid him 2.25 units of Bitcoin for the services he provided as part of his business. Later in the year, Micah exchanged 2.00 units of his Bitcoin for an automobile when the value of the Bitcoin was $19,000 per unit. ♦

In general, virtual currency is treated the same as property. For most taxpayers, the rules will follow those laid out in this chapter.

EXAMPLE Continuing with the previous example, Micah will be required to recognize the fair market value of the Bitcoin ($18,000 per unit times 2.25 units or $40,500 total) received as gross income in payment for his services. His basis in the Bitcoin will be $18,000 per unit. When he exchanges 2.00 units of Bitcoin for an auto, the value has increased to $19,000 per unit. As a result, Micah will recognize a gain of $2,000 (amount realized of $38,000 less adjusted basis of $36,000). The character of the gain depends on the character of the virtual currency to Micah, which appears to be a capital asset. ♦

Self-Study Problem 4.1 *See Appendix E for Solutions to Self-Study Problems*

Determine whether each of the following properties is a capital asset.

Property

1. Shoes held by a shoe store
2. A taxpayer's personal residence
3. A painting held by the artist
4. Accounts receivable of a dentist
5. A copyright purchased from a company
6. A truck used in the taxpayer's business
7. IBM stock owned by an investor
8. AT&T bonds owned by an investor
9. Land held as an investment
10. A taxpayer's television
11. Automobiles for sale owned by a car dealer
12. A taxpayer's investment in virtual currency

4-2 HOLDING PERIOD

4.2 Learning Objective

Apply the holding period for long-term and short-term capital gains and losses.

Assets must be held for more than one year for the gain or loss to be considered long-term. A capital asset sold before it is owned for the required holding period results in a short-term capital gain or loss. A net short-term capital gain is treated as ordinary income for tax purposes. In calculating the holding period, the taxpayer excludes the date of acquisition and includes the date of disposition.

EXAMPLE Glen purchased stock as an investment on March 27, 2021. The first day the stock may be sold for long-term capital gain treatment is March 28, 2022. ♦

To satisfy the long-term holding period requirement, a capital asset acquired on the last day of a month must not be disposed of before the first day of the thirteenth month following the month of purchase.

EXAMPLE If Elwood purchases a painting on March 31, 2021, the first day the painting may be sold for long-term capital gain treatment is April 1, 2022. ♦

For inherited property, the holding period is deemed to be over one year, regardless of actual holding period. For property received as a gift, the holding period from the donor will "tack on" if the basis carries over; otherwise, the holding period starts at the date of the gift. See the basis rules in the next section for additional details.

Self-Study Problem 4.2 *See Appendix E for Solutions to Self-Study Problems*

Determine whether a gain or loss realized in each of the following situations would be long-term or short-term.

Date Acquired	***Date Sold***
1. October 16, 2021	May 30, 2022
2. May 2, 2021	October 12, 2022
3. July 18, 2021	July 18, 2022
4. August 31, 2020	March 1, 2022

Learning Objective 4.3

Calculate the gain or loss on the disposition of an asset.

4-3 CALCULATION OF GAIN OR LOSS

A taxpayer must calculate the amount realized and the adjusted basis of property sold or exchanged to arrive at the amount of the gain or loss realized on the disposition. The taxpayer's gain or loss is calculated using the following formula:

Amount realized − Adjusted basis = Gain or loss realized

4-3a Sale or Exchange

The realization of a gain or loss requires the "sale or exchange" of an asset. The term "sale or exchange" is not defined in the tax law, but a sale generally requires the receipt of money or the relief from liabilities in exchange for property. An exchange is the transfer of ownership of one property for another property.

EXAMPLE Maggie sells virtual currency for $8,500 that she purchased 2 years ago for $6,000. Maggie's adjusted basis in the virtual currency is its cost, $6,000; therefore, she realizes a long-term capital gain of $2,500 ($8,500 − $6,000) on the sale. ♦

EXAMPLE Art owns a home which has increased in value during the tax year. If Art does not sell the home, there is no realized gain during the tax year. ♦

4-3b Amount Realized

The amount realized from a sale or other disposition of property is equal to the sum of the money received, plus the fair market value of other property received, less the costs paid to transfer the property. If the taxpayer is relieved of a liability, the amount of the liability is added to the amount realized.

EXAMPLE During the tax year, Ted sells real estate held as an investment for $75,000 in cash, and the buyer assumes the mortgage on the property of $120,000. Ted pays real estate commissions and other transfer costs of $11,000. The amount realized on the sale is calculated as:

Cash received	$ 75,000
Liabilities transferred	120,000
Total sales price	195,000
Less: transfer costs	(11,000)
Amount realized	$ 184,000

♦

4-3c Adjusted Basis

The adjusted basis of property is equal to the original basis adjusted by adding capital (major) improvements and deducting depreciation allowed or allowable, as illustrated by the following formula:

Adjusted basis = Original basis + Capital improvements − Accumulated depreciation

The original basis of property is usually its cost. The cost is the amount paid in cash, debt obligations, other property, or services. The original basis also includes amounts you pay for the sales tax, freight, installation and testing, excise taxes, revenue stamps, recording fees, and real estate taxes if you assume the liability of the seller. If the acquired asset is real property, certain fees and other expenses are part of the cost basis in the property such as the settlement fees and closing costs you paid for buying the property but does not include fees and costs for getting a loan on the property.

The following are some of the settlement fees or closing costs included in the basis of real property:

- Charges for installing utility services
- Legal fees (including fees for the title search and preparation of the sales contract and deed)
- Recording fees
- Survey fees
- Transfer taxes
- Owner's title insurance
- Any amounts the seller owes that you agree to pay, such as back taxes or interest, recording or mortgage fees, charges for improvements or repairs, and sales commissions

The following are some of the settlement fees and closing costs that cannot be included in the basis of property:

- Amounts placed in escrow for the future payment of items such as taxes and insurance
- Casualty insurance premiums
- Rent for occupancy of the property before closing
- Charges for utilities or other services related to occupancy of the property before closing
- Charges connected with getting a loan, such as points (discount points, loan origination fees), mortgage insurance premiums, loan assumption fees, cost of a credit report, and fees for an appraisal required by a lender

Capital improvements are major expenditures for permanent improvements to or restoration of the taxpayer's property. These expenditures include amounts which result in an increase in the value of the taxpayer's property or substantially increase the useful life of the property, as well as amounts which are spent to adapt property to a new use. For example, architect fees paid to plan an addition to a building, as well as the cost of the addition, must be added to the original basis of the asset as capital improvements. Ordinary repairs and maintenance expenditures are not capital expenditures.

EXAMPLE Alan and his wife purchased a house on September 15, 2022. Their closing statement for the purchase is illustrated on Pages 4-6 and 4-7. Their original tax basis in the house is equal to the purchase price of $130,000 plus the incidental costs of the owner's title insurance (not lender's), government recording fees, and transfer taxes. Therefore, their original basis is $130,740 ($130,000 + $500 + $50 + $190). The loan origination fee represents "points" on the mortgage loan. If the house is their principal residence, the points are deductible as interest in the year of payment. The prorated interest and taxes affect their deductions for interest and taxes, as described in Chapter 5. The homeowners' insurance is a nondeductible personal expense, assuming the house is their personal residence. ♦

EXAMPLE Paul acquired a rental house four years ago for $91,000. Depreciation claimed on the house for the four years totals $14,000. Paul installed a new patio at a cost of $2,500. The adjusted basis of the house is $79,500, as calculated below:

Adjusted basis = original basis + capital improvements − accumulated depreciation

$79,500 = $91,000 + $2,500 − $14,000 ♦

If property is received from a decedent (as an inheritance), the original basis is generally equal to the fair market value at the decedent's date of death. For property acquired as a gift, the amount of the donee's basis depends on whether the property is

OMB Approval No. 2502-0265

A. Settlement Statement (HUD-1)

B. Type of Loan

1. [ ] FHA 2. [ ] RHS 3. [X] Conv. Unins. 4. [ ] VA 5. [ ] Conv. Ins.	6. File Number:	7. Loan Number:	8. Mortgage Insurance Case Number:

C. Note: This form is furnished to give you a statement of actual settlement costs. Amounts paid to and by the settlement agent are shown. Items marked "(p.o.c.)" were paid outside the closing; they are shown here for informational purposes and are not included in the totals.

D. Name & Address of Borrower:	E. Name & Address of Seller:	F. Name & Address of Lender:
Alan & Julie Young 66 W. 2nd Street, Apt. 3F Peru, IN 46970	Chris and Fiona Everett 89 Payson Street Denver, IN 46926	2nd Farmers Bank 120 N. Broadway Peru, IN 46970
G. Property Location: 68 W. Canal Street Peru, IN 46970	H. Settlement Agent: Place of Settlement:	I. Settlement Date:

J. Summary of Borrower's Transaction

100. Gross Amount Due from Borrower	
101. Contract sales price	$130,000.00
102. Personal property	
103. Settlement charges to borrower (line 1400)	$4,354.40
104.	
105.	
Adjustment for items paid by seller in advance	
106. City/town taxes to	
107. County taxes 10/1/2022 to 12/31/2022	$1,000.00
108. Assessments to	
109.	
110.	
111.	
112.	
120. Gross Amount Due from Borrower	$135,354.40
200. Amount Paid by or in Behalf of Borrower	
201. Deposit or earnest money	$1,000.00
202. Principal amount of new loan(s)	$104,000.00
203. Existing loan(s) taken subject to	
204.	
205.	
206.	
207.	
208.	
209.	
Adjustments for items unpaid by seller	
210. City/town taxes to	
211. County taxes to	
212. Assessments to	
213.	
214.	
215.	
216.	
217.	
218.	
219.	
220. Total Paid by/for Borrower	$105,000.00
300. Cash at Settlement from/to Borrower	
301. Gross amount due from borrower (line 120)	$135,354.40
302. Less amounts paid by/for borrower (line 220)	( )
303. Cash [X] **From** [ ] **To Borrower**	$30,354.40

K. Summary of Seller's Transaction

400. Gross Amount Due to Seller	
401. Contract sales price	$130,000.00
402. Personal property	
403.	
404.	
405.	
Adjustment for items paid by seller in advance	
406. City/town taxes to	
407. County taxes 10/1/2022 to 12/31/2022	$1,000.00
408. Assessments to	
409.	
410.	
411.	
412.	
420. Gross Amount Due to Seller	$131,000.00
500. Reductions In Amount Due to seller	
501. Excess deposit (see instructions)	
502. Settlement charges to seller (line 1400)	$8,240.00
503. Existing loan(s) taken subject to	
504. Payoff of first mortgage loan	
505. Payoff of second mortgage loan	
506.	
507.	
508.	
509.	
Adjustments for items unpaid by seller	
510. City/town taxes to	
511. County taxes to	
512. Assessments to	
513.	
514.	
515.	
516.	
517.	
518.	
519.	
520. Total Reduction Amount Due Seller	$8,240.00
600. Cash at Settlement to/from Seller	
601. Gross amount due to seller (line 420)	$131,000.00
602. Less reductions in amounts due seller (line 520)	($8,240.00)
603. Cash [X] **To** [ ] **From Seller**	$122,760.00

The Public Reporting Burden for this collection of information is estimated at 35 minutes per response for collecting, reviewing, and reporting the data. This agency may not collect this information, and you are not required to complete this form, unless it displays a currently valid OMB control number. No confidentiality is assured; this disclosure is mandatory. This is designed to provide the parties to a RESPA covered transaction with information during the settlement process.

L. Settlement Charges		
700. Total Real Estate Broker Fees $7,800	Paid From Borrower's Funds at Settlement	Paid From Seller's Funds at Settlement
Division of commission (line 700) as follows :		
701. $ 3,900.00 to ABC Realtor		
702. $ 3,900.00 to XYZ Realtor		
703. Commission paid at settlement		$7,800.00
704.		
800. Items Payable in Connection with Loan		
801. Our origination charge incl. origination points (1% or $1,040.00) $ 1,040.00 (from GFE #1)		
802. Your credit or charge (points) for the specific interest rate chosen $ (from GFE #2)		
803. Your adjusted origination charges (from GFE #A)	$1,040.00	
804. Appraisal fee to Appraisers R Us (from GFE #3)	$400.00	
805. Credit report to Equifacts (from GFE #3)	$50.00	
806. Tax service to (from GFE #3)		
807. Flood certification to (from GFE #3)		
808.		
809.		
810.		
811.		
900. Items Required by Lender to be Paid in Advance		
901. Daily interest charges from 9/15/22 to 10/31/22 @ $ 11.40 /day (from GFE #10)	$524.40	
902. Mortgage insurance premium for months to (from GFE #3)		
903. Homeowner's insurance for 1 years to ($600 P.O.C.) (from GFE #11)		
904.		
1000. Reserves Deposited with Lender		
1001. Initial deposit for your escrow account (from GFE #9)	$250.00	
1002. Homeowner's insurance 1 months @ $ 50.00 per month $ 50.00		
1003. Mortgage insurance months @ $ per month $		
1004. Property Taxes 2 months @ $ 100.00 per month $ 200.00		
1005. months @ $ per month $		
1006. months @ $ per month $		
1007. Aggregate Adjustment -$		
1100. Title Charges		
1101. Title services and lender's title insurance (from GFE #4)	$1,350.00	
1102. Settlement or closing fee $ 100.00		$250.00
1103. Owner's title insurance Title Company, Inc. (from GFE #5)	$500.00	
1104. Lender's title insurance $ 500.00		
1105. Lender's title policy limit $ 130,000.00		
1106. Owner's title policy limit $ 130,000.00		
1107. Agent's portion of the total title insurance premium to Title Company Inc $ 300.00		
1108. Underwriter's portion of the total title insurance premium to Underwriter $ 75.00		
1109.		
1110.		
1111.		
1200. Government Recording and Transfer Charges		
1201. Government recording charges (from GFE #7)	$50.00	
1202. Deed $ 25.00 Mortgage $ 25.00 Release $ 15.00		$15.00
1203. Transfer taxes (from GFE #8)	$190.00	
1204. City/County tax/stamps Deed $ 130.00 Mortgage $		
1205. State tax/stamps Deed $ 60.00 Mortgage $		
1206.		
1300. Additional Settlement Charges		
1301. Required services that you can shop for (from GFE #6)		
1302. Pest Inspection $ 75.00		$75.00
1303. Home warranty $ 100.00		$100.00
1304.		
1305.		
1400. Total Settlement Charges (enter on lines 103, Section J and 502, Section K)	$4,354.40	$8,240.00

sold for a gain or a loss by the donee. If a gain results from the disposition of the property, the donee's basis is equal to the donor's basis. If the disposition of the property results in a loss, the donee's basis is equal to the lesser of the donor's basis or the fair market value of the property on the date of the gift. When property acquired by gift is disposed of at an amount between the basis for gain and the basis for loss, no gain or loss is recognized. Note that the basis for gain and the basis for loss will be different only where the gifted property has a fair market value, on the date of the gift, that is less than the donor's adjusted basis in the property.

EXAMPLE Ron received AT&T stock upon the death of his grandfather. The stock cost his grandfather $6,000 forty years ago and was worth $97,000 on the date of his grandfather's death. Ron's basis in the stock is $97,000. ♦

EXAMPLE Jane received a gift of stock from her mother. The stock cost her mother $9,000 five years ago and was worth $6,500 on the date of the gift. If the stock is sold by Jane for $12,000, her gain would be $3,000 ($12,000 – $9,000). However, if the stock is sold for $5,000, the loss would be only $1,500 ($5,000 – $6,500). If the stock is sold for an amount between $6,500 and $9,000, no gain or loss is recognized on the sale. ♦

Self-Study Problem 4.3 *See Appendix E for Solutions to Self-Study Problems*

Supply the missing information in the following blanks:

	Original Cost	Accumulated Depreciation	Capital Improvements	Adjusted Basis
1.	$15,000	$5,000	$1,000	$______
2.	15,000	8,000	______	9,000
3.	30,000	______	2,000	17,000
4.	______	9,000	4,000	18,000

Learning Objective 4.4

Compute the tax on capital gains.

4-4 NET CAPITAL GAINS

In recent years, the tax rates on long-term and short-term capital gains have become complex. Short-term capital gains are taxed as ordinary income, while there are various different preferential long-term capital gains tax rates. The 2022 capital gains tax rates are as follows:

Type of Gains	*Tax Rate**
Short-Term Capital Gains	Taxed at ordinary income rates consistent with filing status
Typical Long-Term Capital Gains	Taxed at 0, 15, or 20 percent depending on level of other taxable income (see Chapter 2)
Long-Term Unrecaptured Section 1250 Gain (see Chapter 8)	Capped at 25 percent
Long-Term Collectibles Gains (Art, Gems, Coins, Stamps, etc.)	Capped at 28 percent

*The 3.8 percent Medicare tax on net investment income, including qualifying dividends, applies to high-income taxpayers with income over certain thresholds. Please see Chapter 6 for further details.

The application of the typical long-term capital gains rates of 0, 15, or 20 percent depends on the taxable income and filing status of the taxpayer. Formerly, the different rates applied to a taxpayer depending on which ordinary tax bracket the taxpayer was in (e.g., a taxpayer in the 12-percent tax bracket would pay tax on long-term gains at 0 percent since 15 percent is not preferential). The current long-term capital gains tax rates do not align perfectly with the existing ordinary income tax rates. For 2022, typical long-term capital gains (and dividends as discussed in Chapter 2) are taxed as follows:

Income level	*Long-term capital gains rate**
Married filing jointly	
$0–$83,350	0%
$83,351–$517,600	15%
>$517,600	20%
Single	
$0–$41,675	0%
$41,676–$459,750	15%
>$459,750	20%
Head of household	
$0–$55,800	0%
$55,801–$488,500	15%
>$488,500	20%
Married filing separately	
$0–$41,675	0%
$41,676–$258,600	15%
>$258,600	20%

*Special higher rates for "high-income" taxpayers are covered in Chapter 6.

The 2022 break points between the ordinary rates and the typical long-term capital gains rates differ by minor amounts. For example, a single taxpayer moves from an ordinary income tax rate of 12 percent to 22 percent at $41,775; whereas the same taxpayer moves from a 0 percent to 15 percent long-term capital gains tax rate at $41,675.

EXAMPLE Dee is a single taxpayer with wage income of $47,000 and long-term capital gains of $8,000 in 2022. Assume Dee has no other deductions or income except the standard deduction. Dee's taxable income is

Wage income	$47,000
Long-term capital gains	8,000
Standard deduction	(12,950)
Taxable income	$42,050

Dee's income now must be separated into the ordinary and long-term capital gain portions:

Taxable income	$42,050
Long-term capital gains	(8,000)
Ordinary income	$34,050

The 2022 tax on $34,050 of ordinary income is $3,884. Dee's taxable income without the long-term gain is below the 15-percent threshold of $41,675 for a single taxpayer in 2022, but her taxable income with the long-term gain is above the threshold; thus, a portion of the long-term gain will be taxed at 0 percent and a portion at 15 percent. Of her $8,000 long-term capital gain, $7,625 is below the threshold and taxed at 0 percent while $375 is above the threshold and is taxed at 15 percent for an additional capital gains tax of $56 to bring Dee's total tax liability to $3,940. The Qualified Dividends and Capital Gain Tax Worksheet introduced in Chapter 2 may be used to calculate the ordinary and long-term capital gains tax. ♦

4-4a Ordering Rules for Capital Gains

Since there are multiple kinds of capital gains on which to calculate tax, an ordering system is necessary to know which capital gains to tax at what rates. The various kinds of gains are included in taxable income in the following order:

1. Short-term capital gains
2. Unrecaptured Section 1250 gains on real estate
3. Gains on collectibles
4. Long-term capital gains

If taxpayers (or tax practitioners) have several different types of capital gains that interact with each other, the calculation may become very complex. A good tax preparation software will provide the calculation along with supporting worksheets for further review. The rules for the taxation of capital gains are exceptionally complex, and a complete discussion of them is beyond the scope of this textbook.

4-4b Calculation of a Net Capital Position

If a taxpayer has a "net long-term capital gain" (net long-term capital gain in excess of net short-term capital loss), the gain is subject to a preferential tax rate as discussed above. Thus, a taxpayer has to net all of the long-term and short-term capital transactions that take place during a year to calculate tax liability. In calculating a taxpayer's net capital gain or net capital loss, the following procedure is followed:

1. Capital gains and losses are classified into two groups, long-term and short-term.
2. Long-term capital gains are offset by long-term capital losses, resulting in either a net long-term capital gain or a net long-term capital loss.
3. Short-term capital gains are offset by short-term capital losses, resulting in a net short-term capital gain or a net short-term capital loss.
4. If Step 2 above results in a net long-term capital gain, it is offset by any net short-term capital loss (Step 3), resulting in either a net long-term capital gain (net long-term capital gain exceeds net short-term capital loss) or a net short-term capital loss (net short-term capital loss exceeds net long-term capital gain). If Step 2 above results in a net long-term capital loss, it is offset against any net short-term capital gain (Step 3), resulting in either a net long-term capital loss (net long-term capital loss exceeds net short-term capital gain) or ordinary income (net short-term capital gain exceeds net long-term capital loss).

EXAMPLE The net capital gain computation is illustrated in the following table:

Taxpayer	*Net LT Capital Gain or (Loss)*	*Net ST Capital Gain or (Loss)*	*Net Capital Position*	*Taxable LT Gain*	*Taxable ST Gain*
A.	$10,000	$ 0	$ 10,000	$10,000	$ 0
B.	10,000	(4,000)	6,000	6,000	0
C.	0	20,000	20,000	0	20,000
D.	0	(20,000)	(20,000)	0	0
E.	10,000	8,000	18,000	10,000	8,000
F.	(8,000)	12,000	4,000	0	4,000
G.	(8,000)	(6,000)	(14,000)	0	0

♦

Self-Study Problem 4.4 *See Appendix E for Solutions to Self-Study Problems*

In October 2022, Jack, a single taxpayer, sold IBM stock for $12,000, which he purchased four years ago for $4,000. He also sold GM stock for $14,000, which cost $17,500 three years ago, and he had a short-term capital loss of $1,800 on the sale of land. If Jack's other taxable income (salary) is $78,000, what is the amount of Jack's tax on these capital transactions?

4-5 NET CAPITAL LOSSES

4.5 Learning Objective

Describe the treatment of capital losses.

4-5a Calculation of Net Capital Losses

The computation of an individual taxpayer's net capital loss is accomplished in a manner similar to the computation of a net capital gain. A net capital loss is incurred when the total capital losses for the period exceed the total capital gains for the period.

EXAMPLE Connie has net long-term capital gains of $6,500 and a short-term capital loss of $8,000. The net short-term capital loss is $1,500 ($6,500 − $8,000). ♦

EXAMPLE Delvin has net long-term capital losses of $8,000 and a short-term capital gain of $4,500. The net long-term capital loss is $3,500 ($4,500 − $8,000). ♦

4-5b Treatment of Net Capital Losses

Individual taxpayers may deduct net capital losses against ordinary income in amounts up to $3,000 per year. Unused capital losses in a particular year may be carried forward indefinitely. Capital losses and capital loss carryovers first offset capital gains using the ordering rules discussed below. Any remaining net capital loss may be used to offset ordinary income, subject to the $3,000 annual limitation.

EXAMPLE Carter has a net long-term capital loss of $15,000 and other taxable income for the year of $25,000. He may deduct $3,000 of the loss against the $25,000 of other taxable income. The remaining capital loss of $12,000 ($15,000 − $3,000) is carried forward to future years. ♦

When unused capital losses are carried forward, they maintain their character as either long-term or short-term. If an individual taxpayer has both net long-term losses and net short-term losses in the same year, the net short-term losses are deducted first.

EXAMPLE Frances has a long-term capital loss of $7,000 and a $2,000 short-term capital loss in Year 1. For that year, Frances may deduct $3,000 in capital losses, the $2,000 short-term capital loss, and $1,000 of the long-term capital loss. Her carryforward would be a $6,000 long-term capital loss. If Frances has no capital gains or losses in Year 2, she would deduct $3,000 in long-term capital losses and carry forward $3,000 ($6,000 − $3,000) to Year 3. Assuming she has no other capital gains and losses, the deduction of losses by year can be summarized as follows:

	Year 1	*Year 2*	*Year 3*
Long-term capital loss	$7,000	$6,000	$3,000
Short-term capital loss	2,000	0	0
Deduction	3,000	3,000	3,000
Long-term capital loss used	1,000	3,000	3,000
Carryforward, long-term capital loss	6,000	3,000	0 ♦

TAX BREAK Taxpayers who have recognized a large capital loss during the year may wish to sell appreciated stock or other property to generate enough capital gains prior to year-end to use up all but $3,000 of the capital loss. This way, the capital loss in excess of $3,000 will be used in the current period rather than carried forward, and the capital gains will be fully sheltered from tax.

4-5c Ordering Rules for Capital Losses

When a taxpayer ends up with net capital losses, the losses offset capital gains using the following ordering rules:

- Net short-term capital losses first reduce 28-percent gains, then 25-percent gains, then regular long-term capital gains.
- Net long-term capital losses first reduce 28-percent gains, then 25-percent gains, then any short-term capital gains.

As with the ordering rules for capital gains, the ordering calculation may become quite complex when different classes of capital assets are present. A detailed discussion is beyond the scope of this textbook.

4-5d Personal Capital Losses

Losses from the sale of personal capital assets are not allowed for tax purposes. For instance, the sale of a personal automobile at a loss or the sale of a personal residence at a loss does not generate a tax-deductible capital loss for individual taxpayers.

EXAMPLE Rosa moved to a nursing home in 2022 and sold both her personal auto and her principal residence. She originally purchased her auto for $20,000 and sold it for $10,000. She originally purchased her residence for $125,000 and sold it for $100,000. The losses on these sales are not tax deductible to Rosa because the assets were personal-use assets. ♦

4-5e Reporting Capital Gains and Losses

Capital gains and losses are frequently reported in a two-step process. First, report each item on Form 8949 and then report aggregated data from Form 8949 onto Schedule D. If reporting each trade, the first step is to list each sale on Form 8949. Part I of Form 8949 is used to report the details of short-term capital gains and losses and Part II (the opposite side of the form) is used to report long-term capital gains and losses. Generally, each sale will be listed and the acquisition date, sale date, sale proceeds (amount realized) and cost basis (adjusted basis) will be reported along with the resulting capital gain or loss. Form 8949 also requires the taxpayer to indicate an explanation code (column f) and an exclusion or adjustment to the gain or loss amount (column g). Common codes are H for the exclusion of gain on the sale of a principal residence; Q for the exclusion of gain on the sale of small business stock (§1202 stock); W for a nondeductible wash sale; and L for a nondeductible loss such as a disallowed related party loss. The complete set of codes can be found in the Form 8949 instructions.

EXAMPLE Maria sells her primary residence for a gain of $270,000. She is eligible to exclude $250,000 of that gain. She will report the acquisition and sales dates, the proceeds from the sale and basis, as is typical. Because she is excluding a part of the gain, she will also enter code H in column f and $250,000 in column g to adjust the gain recognized to $20,000, the amount in excess of the exclusion. ♦

Form 8949 also requires that the taxpayer indicate whether the sales were reported on Form 1099-B and if so, whether the Form 1099-B reported the basis to the IRS. These are indicated with boxes in Part I (short-term) and Part II (long-term) as follows:

Box	*Part I (short-term)*	*Part II (long-term)*
Sales reported on Form 1099-B and basis provided to IRS	A	D
Sales reported on Form 1099-B and basis not reported to IRS	B	E
Sales not reported on Form 1099-B	C	F

If a taxpayer has capital transactions classified in more than one box, a separate Form 8949 should be completed.

EXAMPLE Greta traded a number of stocks in the current year. Her broker sent her a 1099-B with the following activity:

- Two short-term trades for which basis was provided to the IRS (A)
- One short-term trade for which no basis was provided to the IRS (B)
- Three long-term trades for which basis was reported to the IRS (D)

Greta also made one short-term trade that was not reported on a Form 1099-B (C).

Greta will need to complete three different Parts I of Form 8949 since she has three different types of short-term trades, all of which require a different box. She can use the reverse side of any of the Forms 8949 to report her one type of long-term trading activity. ♦

To save taxpayer's time and effort, under certain circumstances, the capital gains and losses can aggregated and reported directly on Schedule D. In order to aggregate either short-term or long-term trades into a single amount, all the trades must be of either Type A for short-term or Type D for long-term and require no adjustments, for example, a wash sale deferral. Figure 4-1 presents Line 1a on Part I of Schedule D where aggregated data can be reported.

FIGURE 4.1

SCHEDULE D (Form 1040)
Department of the Treasury Internal Revenue Service

Capital Gains and Losses

Attach to Form 1040, 1040-SR, or 1040-NR.
Go to *www.irs.gov/ScheduleD* for instructions and the latest information.
Use Form 8949 to list your transactions for lines 1b, 2, 3, 8b, 9, and 10.

OMB No. 1545-0074
2022
Attachment Sequence No. 12

Name(s) shown on return | Your social security number

Did you dispose of any investment(s) in a qualified opportunity fund during the tax year? ☐ Yes ☐ No
If "Yes," attach Form 8949 and see its instructions for additional requirements for reporting your gain or loss.

Part I **Short-Term Capital Gains and Losses—Generally Assets Held One Year or Less** (see instructions)

See instructions for how to figure the amounts to enter on the lines below. This form may be easier to complete if you round off cents to whole dollars.	(d) Proceeds (sales price)	(e) Cost (or other basis)	(g) Adjustments to gain or loss from Form(s) 8949, Part I, line 2, column (g)	(h) Gain or (loss) Subtract column (e) from column (d) and combine the result with column (g)
1a Totals for all short-term transactions reported on Form 1099-B for which basis was reported to the IRS and for which you have no adjustments (see instructions). However, if you choose to report all these transactions on Form 8949, leave this line blank and go to line 1b .				
1b Totals for all transactions reported on Form(s) 8949 with **Box A** checked				

EXAMPLE Gunter spent a fair amount of his time trading stocks in 2022. As a result, he has twenty-four short-term gain transactions for which the basis was reported to the IRS and two short-term transactions for which no basis was reported to the IRS. Gunter will report the two trades for which no basis was reported on Forms 8949 and select Box B and carry the totals to Line 2 of Part I of Schedule D. The aggregate data for the twenty-four trades can all be reported directly on Line 1a of Part I of Schedule D and no reporting on Form 8949 is required. ♦

ProConnect™ Tax TIP

When entering capital gains and losses in ProConnect, whether using the Quick Entry or Detail screen, if the box for Basis Reported to the IRS is left blank, ProConnect will automatically aggregate those items and report them directly on Schedule D and bypass Form 8949 as permitted. If aggregated data is entered with no date acquired or disposed, the classification of short-term or long-term can be selected by using the 1=short-term, 2=long-term [Override] box.

Self-Study Problem 4.5

See Appendix E for Solutions to Self-Study Problems

During 2022, Louis Winthorp, who is single, received the following Form 1099-B:

☐ CORRECTED (if checked)

PAYER'S name, street address, city or town, state or province, country, ZIP or foreign postal code, and telephone no. Duke Brothers Brokerage 135 S. Broad Street Philadelphia, PA 19103	Applicable checkbox on Form 8949 D	OMB No. 1545-0715 2022 Form 1099-B	Proceeds From Broker and Barter Exchange Transactions
	1a Description of property (Example: 100 sh. XYZ Co.) 100 shs. Second Maid Juice Corp.		
	1b Date acquired 06/12/2013	1c Date sold or disposed 08/15/2022	
PAYER'S TIN 34-9876543 / RECIPIENT'S TIN 123-44-3214	1d Proceeds $ 18,000.00	1e Cost or other basis $ 12,500.00	Copy B For Recipient
	1f Accrued market discount $	1g Wash sale loss disallowed $	
RECIPIENT'S name Louis Winthorpe	2 Short-term gain or loss ☐ Long-term gain or loss ☒ Ordinary ☐	3 If checked, proceeds from: Collectibles ☐ QOF ☐	This is important tax information and is being furnished to the IRS. If you are required to file a return, a negligence penalty or other sanction may be imposed on you if this income is taxable and the IRS determines that it has not been reported.
Street address (including apt. no.) 2014 Delancey Street	4 Federal income tax withheld $	5 If checked, noncovered security ☐	
City or town, state or province, country, and ZIP or foreign postal code Philadelphia, PA 19103	6 Reported to IRS: Gross proceeds ☐ Net proceeds ☒	7 If checked, loss is not allowed based on amount in 1d ☐	
Account number (see instructions)	8 Profit or (loss) realized in 2022 on closed contracts $	9 Unrealized profit or (loss) on open contracts—12/31/2021 $	
CUSIP number / FATCA filing requirement ☐	10 Unrealized profit or (loss) on open contracts—12/31/2022 $	11 Aggregate profit or (loss) on contracts $	
14 State name / 15 State identification no. / 16 State tax withheld $ $	12 If checked, basis reported to IRS ☒	13 Bartering $	

Form **1099-B** (Keep for your records) www.irs.gov/Form1099B Department of the Treasury - Internal Revenue Service

He also received the following 1099-B from a different broker:

2022 Combined Forms 1099

This is important tax information and is being furnished to the IRS (except as indicated). If you are required to file a return, a negligence penalty or other sanction may be imposed on you if this income is taxable and the IRS determines that it has not been reported.

Copy B For Recipient
OMB No. 1545-0110

Friar Tuck Investments
38 Wall Street, 8th Floor
New York, NY 10005

Louis Winthorpe
2014 Delancey Street
Philadelphia, PA 19103

Account Number: 5600911452 Tax ID: ***-**-3214
Payer's Federal Tax ID: 33-1357246
Financial Adviser/Phone: Marion Maide 888-555-1212

Form 1099-B **Proceeds from Broker and Barter Exchange Transactions**

Box 6: Gross Proceeds; Box 5: Not checked; Box 3: Basis reported to IRS; Box 2: Type of Gain or Loss: Short Term

Box 1 Security description (CUSIP)	Quantity sold	Box 1b Date acquired	Box 1c Date sold or disposed	Box 1d Proceeds	Box 1e Cost or other basis	Box 1g Wash sale loss disallowed	Gain/(Loss) amount
Sargent Corp	100	04/18/2022	12/07/2022	12,000	19,200	-	(7,200)

Box 6: Gross Proceeds; Box 5: Not checked; Box 3: Basis reported to IRS; Box 2: Type of Gain or Loss: Long Term

Box 1 Security description (CUSIP)	Quantity sold	Box 1b Date acquired	Box 1c Date sold or disposed	Box 1d Proceeds	Box 1e Cost or other basis	Box 1g Wash sale loss disallowed	Gain/(Loss) amount
Reynolds Corp	50	12/18/2013	10/02/2022	25,000	21,000	-	4,000

Louis' taxable income is $59,000 (including gains and losses from above). Calculate Louis' net capital gain or loss and tax liability using Schedule D of Form 1040, Parts I, II, and III; Form 8949, Parts I and II; and the Qualified Dividends and Capital Gain Tax Worksheet on Pages 4-17 to 4-21.

Self-Study Problem 4.5

SCHEDULE D (Form 1040)

Department of the Treasury
Internal Revenue Service

Capital Gains and Losses

Attach to Form 1040, 1040-SR, or 1040-NR.
Go to *www.irs.gov/ScheduleD* for instructions and the latest information.
Use Form 8949 to list your transactions for lines 1b, 2, 3, 8b, 9, and 10.

OMB No. 1545-0074
2022
Attachment Sequence No. **12**

Name(s) shown on return | **Your social security number**

Did you dispose of any investment(s) in a qualified opportunity fund during the tax year? ☐ **Yes** ☐ **No**
If "Yes," attach Form 8949 and see its instructions for additional requirements for reporting your gain or loss.

Part I **Short-Term Capital Gains and Losses—Generally Assets Held One Year or Less** (see instructions)

See instructions for how to figure the amounts to enter on the lines below. This form may be easier to complete if you round off cents to whole dollars.	**(d)** Proceeds (sales price)	**(e)** Cost (or other basis)	**(g)** Adjustments to gain or loss from Form(s) 8949, Part I, line 2, column (g)	**(h) Gain or (loss)** Subtract column (e) from column (d) and combine the result with column (g)
1a Totals for all short-term transactions reported on Form 1099-B for which basis was reported to the IRS and for which you have no adjustments (see instructions). However, if you choose to report all these transactions on Form 8949, leave this line blank and go to line 1b .				
1b Totals for all transactions reported on Form(s) 8949 with **Box A** checked				
2 Totals for all transactions reported on Form(s) 8949 with **Box B** checked				
3 Totals for all transactions reported on Form(s) 8949 with **Box C** checked				

4 Short-term gain from Form 6252 and short-term gain or (loss) from Forms 4684, 6781, and 8824 . .	**4**	
5 Net short-term gain or (loss) from partnerships, S corporations, estates, and trusts from Schedule(s) K-1	**5**	
6 Short-term capital loss carryover. Enter the amount, if any, from line 8 of your **Capital Loss Carryover Worksheet** in the instructions	**6**	( )
7 **Net short-term capital gain or (loss).** Combine lines 1a through 6 in column (h). If you have any long-term capital gains or losses, go to Part II below. Otherwise, go to Part III on the back	**7**	

Part II **Long-Term Capital Gains and Losses—Generally Assets Held More Than One Year** (see instructions)

See instructions for how to figure the amounts to enter on the lines below. This form may be easier to complete if you round off cents to whole dollars.	**(d)** Proceeds (sales price)	**(e)** Cost (or other basis)	**(g)** Adjustments to gain or loss from Form(s) 8949, Part II, line 2, column (g)	**(h) Gain or (loss)** Subtract column (e) from column (d) and combine the result with column (g)
8a Totals for all long-term transactions reported on Form 1099-B for which basis was reported to the IRS and for which you have no adjustments (see instructions). However, if you choose to report all these transactions on Form 8949, leave this line blank and go to line 8b .				
8b Totals for all transactions reported on Form(s) 8949 with **Box D** checked				
9 Totals for all transactions reported on Form(s) 8949 with **Box E** checked				
10 Totals for all transactions reported on Form(s) 8949 with **Box F** checked.				

11 Gain from Form 4797, Part I; long-term gain from Forms 2439 and 6252; and long-term gain or (loss) from Forms 4684, 6781, and 8824	**11**	
12 Net long-term gain or (loss) from partnerships, S corporations, estates, and trusts from Schedule(s) K-1	**12**	
13 Capital gain distributions. See the instructions	**13**	
14 Long-term capital loss carryover. Enter the amount, if any, from line 13 of your **Capital Loss Carryover Worksheet** in the instructions	**14**	( )
15 **Net long-term capital gain or (loss).** Combine lines 8a through 14 in column (h). Then, go to Part III on the back	**15**	

For Paperwork Reduction Act Notice, see your tax return instructions. Cat. No. 11338H **Schedule D (Form 1040) 2022**

Schedule D (Form 1040) 2022 Page **2**

Part III **Summary**

16 Combine lines 7 and 15 and enter the result **16**

- If line 16 is a **gain**, enter the amount from line 16 on Form 1040, 1040-SR, or 1040-NR, line 7. Then, go to line 17 below.
- If line 16 is a **loss**, skip lines 17 through 20 below. Then, go to line 21. Also be sure to complete line 22.
- If line 16 is **zero**, skip lines 17 through 21 below and enter -0- on Form 1040, 1040-SR, or 1040-NR, line 7. Then, go to line 22.

17 Are lines 15 and 16 **both** gains?
☐ **Yes.** Go to line 18.
☐ **No.** Skip lines 18 through 21, and go to line 22.

18 If you are required to complete the **28% Rate Gain Worksheet** (see instructions), enter the amount, if any, from line 7 of that worksheet **18**

19 If you are required to complete the **Unrecaptured Section 1250 Gain Worksheet** (see instructions), enter the amount, if any, from line 18 of that worksheet **19**

20 Are lines 18 and 19 both zero or blank and you are not filing Form 4952?
☐ **Yes.** Complete the **Qualified Dividends and Capital Gain Tax Worksheet** in the instructions for Form 1040, line 16. **Don't** complete lines 21 and 22 below.

☐ **No.** Complete the **Schedule D Tax Worksheet** in the instructions. **Don't** complete lines 21 and 22 below.

21 If line 16 is a loss, enter here and on Form 1040, 1040-SR, or 1040-NR, line 7, the **smaller** of:

- The loss on line 16; or
- ($3,000), or if married filing separately, ($1,500) } . . . . **21** ( )

Note: When figuring which amount is smaller, treat both amounts as positive numbers.

22 Do you have qualified dividends on Form 1040, 1040-SR, or 1040-NR, line 3a?

☐ **Yes.** Complete the **Qualified Dividends and Capital Gain Tax Worksheet** in the instructions for Form 1040, line 16.

☐ **No.** Complete the rest of Form 1040, 1040-SR, or 1040-NR.

Schedule D (Form 1040) 2022

Self-Study Problem 4.5

Form **8949**

Department of the Treasury
Internal Revenue Service

Sales and Other Dispositions of Capital Assets

Go to *www.irs.gov/Form8949* for instructions and the latest information.

File with your Schedule D to list your transactions for lines 1b, 2, 3, 8b, 9, and 10 of Schedule D.

OMB No. 1545-0074

2022

Attachment Sequence No. **12A**

Name(s) shown on return | **Social security number or taxpayer identification number**

Before you check Box A, B, or C below, see whether you received any Form(s) 1099-B or substitute statement(s) from your broker. A substitute statement will have the same information as Form 1099-B. Either will show whether your basis (usually your cost) was reported to the IRS by your broker and may even tell you which box to check.

Part I **Short-Term.** Transactions involving capital assets you held 1 year or less are generally short-term (see instructions). For long-term transactions, see page 2.

Note: You may aggregate all short-term transactions reported on Form(s) 1099-B showing basis was reported to the IRS and for which no adjustments or codes are required. Enter the totals directly on Schedule D, line 1a; you aren't required to report these transactions on Form 8949 (see instructions).

You *must* check Box A, B, *or* C below. Check only one box. If more than one box applies for your short-term transactions, complete a separate Form 8949, page 1, for each applicable box. If you have more short-term transactions than will fit on this page for one or more of the boxes, complete as many forms with the same box checked as you need.

☐ **(A)** Short-term transactions reported on Form(s) 1099-B showing basis was reported to the IRS (see **Note** above)
☐ **(B)** Short-term transactions reported on Form(s) 1099-B showing basis **wasn't** reported to the IRS
☐ **(C)** Short-term transactions not reported to you on Form 1099-B

1 (a) Description of property (Example: 100 sh. XYZ Co.)	(b) Date acquired (Mo., day, yr.)	(c) Date sold or disposed of (Mo., day, yr.)	(d) Proceeds (sales price) (see instructions)	(e) Cost or other basis See the **Note** below and see *Column (e)* in the separate instructions.	Adjustment, if any, to gain or loss. If you enter an amount in column (g), enter a code in column (f). See the separate instructions. (f) Code(s) from instructions	(g) Amount of adjustment	(h) Gain or (loss) Subtract column (e) from column (d) and combine the result with column (g).
2 Totals. Add the amounts in columns (d), (e), (g), and (h) (subtract negative amounts). Enter each total here and include on your Schedule D, **line 1b** (if **Box A** above is checked), **line 2** (if **Box B** above is checked), or **line 3** (if **Box C** above is checked) . .							

Note: If you checked Box A above but the basis reported to the IRS was incorrect, enter in column (e) the basis as reported to the IRS, and enter an adjustment in column (g) to correct the basis. See *Column (g)* in the separate instructions for how to figure the amount of the adjustment.

Form 8949 (2022) Attachment Sequence No. **12A** Page **2**

Name(s) shown on return. Name and SSN or taxpayer identification no. not required if shown on other side	**Social security number or taxpayer identification number**

Before you check Box D, E, or F below, see whether you received any Form(s) 1099-B or substitute statement(s) from your broker. A substitute statement will have the same information as Form 1099-B. Either will show whether your basis (usually your cost) was reported to the IRS by your broker and may even tell you which box to check.

Part II **Long-Term.** Transactions involving capital assets you held more than 1 year are generally long-term (see instructions). For short-term transactions, see page 1.

Note: You may aggregate all long-term transactions reported on Form(s) 1099-B showing basis was reported to the IRS and for which no adjustments or codes are required. Enter the totals directly on Schedule D, line 8a; you aren't required to report these transactions on Form 8949 (see instructions).

You *must* check Box D, E, *or* F below. Check only one box. If more than one box applies for your long-term transactions, complete a separate Form 8949, page 2, for each applicable box. If you have more long-term transactions than will fit on this page for one or more of the boxes, complete as many forms with the same box checked as you need.

☐ **(D)** Long-term transactions reported on Form(s) 1099-B showing basis was reported to the IRS (see **Note** above)
☐ **(E)** Long-term transactions reported on Form(s) 1099-B showing basis **wasn't** reported to the IRS
☐ **(F)** Long-term transactions not reported to you on Form 1099-B

1 (a) Description of property (Example: 100 sh. XYZ Co.)	(b) Date acquired (Mo., day, yr.)	(c) Date sold or disposed of (Mo., day, yr.)	(d) Proceeds (sales price) (see instructions)	(e) Cost or other basis See the **Note** below and see *Column (e)* in the separate instructions.	Adjustment, if any, to gain or loss If you enter an amount in column (g), enter a code in column (f). **See the separate instructions.** (f) Code(s) from instructions	(g) Amount of adjustment	(h) Gain or (loss) Subtract column (e) from column (d) and combine the result with column (g).
2 Totals. Add the amounts in columns (d), (e), (g), and (h) (subtract negative amounts). Enter each total here and include on your Schedule D, **line 8b** (if **Box D** above is checked), **line 9** (if **Box E** above is checked), or **line 10** (if **Box F** above is checked) . .							

Note: If you checked Box D above but the basis reported to the IRS was incorrect, enter in column (e) the basis as reported to the IRS, and enter an adjustment in column (g) to correct the basis. See *Column (g)* in the separate instructions for how to figure the amount of the adjustment.

Form **8949** (2022)

Self-Study Problem 4.5

Qualified Dividends and Capital Gain Tax Worksheet—Line 16

Keep for Your Records

Before you begin:
√ See the earlier instructions for line 16 to see if you can use this worksheet to figure your tax.
√ Before completing this worksheet, complete Form 1040 or 1040-SR through line 15.
√ If you don't have to file Schedule D and you received capital gain distributions, be sure you checked the box on Form 1040 or 1040-SR, line 7.

1. Enter the amount from Form 1040 or 1040-SR, line 15. However, if you are filing Form 2555 (relating to foreign earned income), enter the amount from line 3 of the Foreign Earned Income Tax Worksheet . . . . . . 1. ______
2. Enter the amount from Form 1040 or 1040-SR, line 3a* . . . . . . 2. ______
3. Are you filing Schedule D?*
   ☐ **Yes.** Enter the **smaller** of line 15 or 16 of Schedule D. If either line 15 or 16 is blank or a loss, enter -0-.
   ☐ **No.** Enter the amount from Form 1040 or 1040-SR, line 7. } 3. ______
4. Add lines 2 and 3 . . . . . . 4. ______
5. Subtract line 4 from line 1. If zero or less, enter -0- . . . . . . 5. ______
6. Enter:
   $41,675 if single or married filing separately,
   $83,350 if married filing jointly or qualifying widow(er),
   $55,800 if head of household. } . . . . . . 6. ______
7. Enter the smaller of line 1 or line 6 . . . . . . 7. ______
8. Enter the smaller of line 5 or line 7 . . . . . . 8. ______
9. Subtract line 8 from line 7. This amount is taxed at 0% . . . . . . 9. ______
10. Enter the smaller of line 1 or line 4 . . . . . . 10. ______
11. Enter the amount from line 9 . . . . . . 11. ______
12. Subtract line 11 from line 10 . . . . . . 12. ______
13. Enter:
    $459,750 if single,
    $258,600 if married filing separately,
    $517,200 if married filing jointly or qualifying widow(er),
    $488,500 if head of household. } . . . . . . 13. ______
14. Enter the smaller of line 1 or line 13 . . . . . . 14. ______
15. Add lines 5 and 9 . . . . . . 15. ______
16. Subtract line 15 from line 14. If zero or less, enter -0- . . . . . . 16. ______
17. Enter the smaller of line 12 or line 16 . . . . . . 17. ______
18. Multiply line 17 by 15% (0.15) . . . . . . 18. ______
19. Add lines 9 and 17 . . . . . . 19. ______
20. Subtract line 19 from line 10 . . . . . . 20. ______
21. Multiply line 20 by 20% (0.20) . . . . . . 21. ______
22. Figure the tax on the amount on line 5. If the amount on line 5 is less than $100,000, use the Tax Table to figure the tax. If the amount on line 5 is $100,000 or more, use the Tax Computation Worksheet . . . . . . 22. ______
23. Add lines 18, 21, and 22 . . . . . . 23. ______
24. Figure the tax on the amount on line 1. If the amount on line 1 is less than $100,000, use the Tax Table to figure the tax. If the amount on line 1 is $100,000 or more, use the Tax Computation Worksheet . . . . . . 24. ______
25. **Tax on all taxable income.** Enter the **smaller** of line 23 or 24. Also include this amount on the entry space on Form 1040 or 1040-SR, line 16. If you are filing Form 2555, don't enter this amount on the entry space on Form 1040 or 1040-SR, line 16. Instead, enter it on line 4 of the Foreign Earned Income Tax Worksheet . . . . . . 25. ______

* *If you are filing Form 2555, see the footnote in the Foreign Earned Income Tax Worksheet before completing this line.*

This worksheet adapted from the 2021 worksheet.

4-6 SALE OF A PERSONAL RESIDENCE

4.6 Learning Objective

Apply the exclusion of gain from personal residence sales.

4-6a Sales After May 6, 1997

For gains on the sale of a personal residence after May 6, 1997, a seller who has owned and used a home as a principal residence for at least two of the last five years before the sale can exclude from income up to $250,000 of gain ($500,000 for joint return filers). In general, this personal residence exclusion can be used only once every two years. A personal residence includes single-family homes, mobile homes, houseboats, condominiums, cooperative apartments, duplexes, or row houses.

EXAMPLE Joe, a single taxpayer, bought his home twenty-two years ago for $25,000. He has lived in the home continuously since he purchased it. In November 2022, he sells his home for $300,000. Therefore, his realized gain on the sale of his personal residence is $275,000 ($300,000 − $25,000). Joe's recognized taxable gain on this sale is $25,000, which is his total gain of $275,000 less the exclusion of $250,000. ♦

A seller otherwise qualified to exclude gain on a principal residence who fails to satisfy the two-year ownership and use requirements may calculate the amount of excluded gain by prorating the exclusion amount if the residence sale is due to an employment-related move, health, or unforeseen circumstances. Unforeseen circumstances include death, divorce or separation, a change in employment that leaves the taxpayer unable to pay the mortgage, multiple births from the same pregnancy, and becoming eligible for unemployment compensation. The $250,000 or $500,000 exclusion amount is prorated by multiplying the exclusion amount by the length of time the taxpayer owned and used the home divided by 2 years.

EXAMPLE John is a single taxpayer who owns and uses his principal residence for 1 year. He then sells the residence due to an employment-related move at a $100,000 gain. Because he may exclude up to one-half (1 year divided by 2 years) of the $250,000 exclusion amount, or $125,000, none of his gain is taxable. ♦

4-6b Married Taxpayers

Taxpayers who are married and file a joint return for the year of sale may exclude up to $500,000 of gain realized on the sale of a personal residence. The full $500,000 for a married couple can be excluded if:

1. Either spouse owned the home for at least two of the five years before the sale,
2. Both spouses used the home as a principal residence for at least two of the last five years, and
3. Neither spouse has used the exclusion during the prior two years.

EXAMPLE Don and Dolly have been married for twenty years. At the time they were married, they purchased a home for $200,000 and have lived in the home since their marriage. Don and Dolly sell their home for $800,000 and retire to Arizona. Their realized gain on the sale is $600,000 ($800,000 − $200,000), of which only $100,000 is taxable because of the $500,000 exclusion. ♦

The $500,000 exclusion for married taxpayers has been extended to spouses who sell the residence within two years of their spouse's death. If a portion of the sale of a residence is taxable, then it should be reported on Form 8949 using Code H and Schedule D. If no portion is taxable, then no reporting is generally required.

Beginning in 2009, Congress closed a loophole in the residence gain exclusion laws, which was used effectively by some owners of multiple rental properties. Under the residence gain exclusion laws in operation prior to 2009, taxpayers with multiple rental properties could move into a previously rented property every two years, reside in the property for the required two-year period, and then sell the property using the $250,000 or $500,000 gain exclusion. Over a period of 10 years, a married couple could theoretically exclude $2.5 million of taxable gain on five separate properties. Beginning in 2009, taxpayers who rent their residence prior to their two years of personal use are generally limited to an exclusion smaller than the full $250,000 or $500,000 amounts. For details, examples, and exceptions to the law, visit **www.irs.gov.**

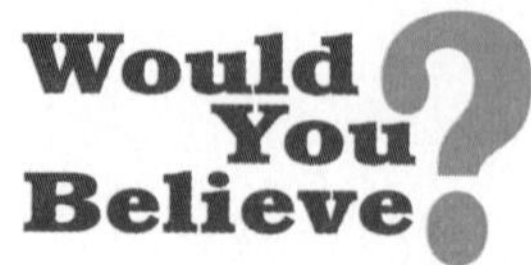

The exclusion of the gain on the sale of a principal residence in its current form was introduced in 1997. The $250,000 and $500,000 (MFJ) exclusions were certainly considered generous at the time. A married filing jointly taxpayer with a 15-percent capital gains rate can save up to $75,000 ($500,000 × 15%) in taxes with this provision. Amazingly, the 25-year-old provision is finally starting to show its age. The median value of a home in 2000 was just under $120,000. According to data provided by the S&P/Case-Shiller U.S. National Home Price Index, that value has tripled since 2000. Unsurprisingly, homes in cities such as San Francisco, Los Angeles, and Miami have increased more than $500,000 since 2000 but more modest cities such as Denver, Phoenix, and Boston have also seen values increase by more than the exclusion amount. For example, a home in Denver valued at $350,000 in 2000 is now estimated to be worth just over $976,000.

4-6c Sales Before May 7, 1997

Please note: The law below no longer applies to sales of principal residences. However, because many taxpayers still own residences with "rollover" basis determined under this law, it is important to understand how the law operated.

For sales of a personal residence before May 7, 1997, taxpayers did not have to recognize gain on the sale if they rolled the gain into a new house with a cost as high as the adjusted sales price of the old residence. The adjusted sales price was the amount realized on the sale less any qualified fixing-up expenses. Fixing-up expenses must have been incurred within 90 days prior to the date of sale and paid within thirty days after the date of sale. In addition, the purchase of the new residence had to be within two years of the date of sale of the old residence to qualify for nonrecognition of the gain. The adjusted basis of the new residence was reduced by any gain not recognized on the sale of the old residence.

EXAMPLE Mary sold her personal residence for $60,000 in 1994 and paid selling expenses of $3,600. Mary had fixing-up expenses of $1,400, and the basis of her old residence was $40,000. If Mary purchased a new residence within two years for $85,000, her recognized gain and the basis of the new residence was calculated as follows:

1. Sales price	$ 60,000
Less: selling expenses	(3,600)
Amount realized	56,400
Adjusted basis of the old residence	(40,000)
Gain realized on the sale	$ 16,400
2. Amount realized	$ 56,400
Less: fixing-up expenses	(1,400)
Adjusted sales price	55,000
Less: cost of the new residence	(85,000)
Gain recognized	$ 0
3. Gain realized	$ 16,400
Less: gain recognized	(0)
Gain not recognized (deferred)	$ 16,400
4. Cost of the new residence	$ 85,000
Less: gain deferred	(16,400)
Basis of the new residence	$ 68,600

♦

EXAMPLE Assume instead that Mary paid only $50,000 for a new residence. The gain and basis of the new residence are calculated as follows:

1. Adjusted sales price (from above)	$ 55,000
Less: cost of new residence	(50,000)
Gain recognized	$ 5,000
2. Gain realized (from above example)	$ 16,400
Less: gain recognized	(5,000)
Gain not recognized (deferred)	$ 11,400
3. Cost of the new residence	$ 50,000
Less: gain deferred	(11,400)
Basis of the new residence	$ 38,600

◆

The calculations on the previous page show that a taxpayer who sold one or more principal residences over a period of years and has a "rollover" basis under the old law may have a principal residence basis that is far lower than the cost of the taxpayer's residence. Because the current law does not require rollover treatment, taxpayers receive a fresh basis in a newly purchased residence which is equal to the purchase price.

Self-Study Problem 4.6

See Appendix E for Solutions to Self-Study Problems

Mike, a single taxpayer, purchased a house twenty years ago for $30,000. He sells the house in December 2022 for $350,000. He has always lived in the house.

a. How much taxable gain does Mike have from the sale of his personal residence?

b. Assume Mike married Mary three years ago and she has lived in the house since their marriage. If they sell the house in December 2022 for $350,000, what is their taxable gain on a joint tax return?

c. Assume Mike is not married and purchased the house only one year ago for $200,000, and he sells the house for $350,000 due to an employment-related move. What is Mike's taxable gain?

Sign Here

Under penalties of perjury, I declare that I have examined this return and accompanying schedules and statements, and to the best of my knowledge and belief, they are true, correct, and complete. Declaration of preparer (other than taxpayer) is based on all information of which preparer has any knowledge.

Joint return? See instructions. Keep a copy for your records.

Your signature	Date	Your occupation	If the IRS sent you an Identity Protection PIN, enter it here (see inst.) ▶
Spouse's signature. If a joint return, **both** must sign.	Date	Spouse's occupation	If the IRS sent your spouse an Identity Protection PIN, enter it here (see inst.) ▶
Phone no.	Email address		

Paid Preparer Use Only

Preparer's name	Preparer's signature	Date	PTIN	Check if: ☐ Self-employed
Firm's name ▶			Phone no.	
Firm's address ▶			Firm's EIN ▶	

Would You Sign This Tax Return?

Ivy Tower (age 45), a history professor at Coastal State University, recently purchased a house near the beach. In the current year, she accepted an offer from a buyer who wants to make the house into a bed and breakfast. Ivy sold her personal residence for a $100,000 gain. She owned the house eleven months as of the date of sale. After the sale closed, she discovered that the $100,000 is taxable as a short-term taxable gain (i.e., ordinary income) because she had not lived there the two years required for exclusion of gain on the sale of a residence. She is upset that she will have to pay substantial tax on the sale. Her best friend's husband is a physician who signed a letter that Ivy had to move due to the dampness and humidity at the beach. She is not a regular patient of the doctor, and Ivy has no history of respiratory problems. Ivy claims she meets the medical extraordinary circumstances exception and therefore refuses to report the gain on her Form 1040. If Ivy were your tax client, would you sign the Paid Preparer's declaration (see example above) on her return? Why or why not?

Learning Objective 4.7

Apply the tax rules for rental property and vacation homes.

4-7 RENTAL INCOME AND EXPENSES

The net income from rental property is taxable income to the taxpayer. In most cases, rental income is reported with the related expenses on Part I of Schedule E. If services are provided to the tenant beyond those customarily provided, such as cleaning and maid services, the income is reported on Schedule C and is subject to the self-employment tax. Expenditures deductible as rental expenses include real estate taxes, mortgage interest, insurance, commissions, repairs, and depreciation.

EXAMPLE June Sanchez owns a house that she rents to a tenant for $600 per month. The following are her expenses for the year:

Real estate taxes	$ 800
Mortgage interest	2,000
Insurance	200
Rent collection commissions	432
General repairs	350

June bought the property on July 1, 2006, and her original basis for depreciation of the house is $55,000. She uses straight-line depreciation with a 27.5 year life.

In 2022, June bought a new stove for the rental house that cost $500. The stove has a five-year life, and 20 percent of the stove's cost is depreciated this year. June's net rental income for the year is calculated as follows:

Rental income ($600 × 12)		$ 7,200
Less expenses:		
Real estate taxes	$ 800	
Mortgage interest	2,000	

Insurance	200	
Commissions	432	
General repairs	350	
Depreciation:		
House ($55,000/27.5)	2,000	
Stove ($500 × 20%)	100	
Total expenses		(5,882)
Net rental income		$ 1,318

Please note that depreciation is an advanced topic which will be covered in detail in Chapter 8. ♦

4-7a Vacation Homes

Many taxpayers own residences which they use personally as part-year residences and rent during the remainder of the year. Such part-year rental properties are often referred to as "vacation homes." The tax law limits the deduction of expenses associated with the rental of vacation homes.

EXAMPLE Jean owns a condo in Vail, Colorado. The condo is rented for three months during the year and is used by Jean for one month. If there were no vacation home limitations, Jean could deduct eleven months' worth of depreciation, maintenance, and other costs associated with the property. The resulting loss could then be deducted against Jean's other taxable income. ♦

To prevent taxpayers from claiming a deduction for expenses effectively personal in nature (associated with a personal residence), the tax law limits the deductions a taxpayer can claim for expenses associated with a vacation home. Deductions attributable to vacation homes used primarily as personal residences are limited to the income generated from the rental of the property. In general, only profit or breakeven (no loss) tax situations are allowed on the rental of vacation homes.

The expenses associated with the rental of a residence used for both personal and rental purposes are subject to three possible tax treatments. The tax treatment depends on the period of time the residence is used for personal versus rental purposes.

1. **Primarily Personal Use**
   If a residence is rented for fewer than fifteen days during the year, the rental period is disregarded and it is treated as a personal residence for tax purposes. The rental income is not taxable and the mortgage interest and real estate taxes may be allowed as itemized deductions. Other expenses, such as utilities and maintenance, are considered nondeductible personal expenses.

EXAMPLE Glenn owns a lake home. During the year he rented the home for $1,800 for two weeks, lived in the home for three months, and left the home vacant during the remainder of the year. The expenses for the lake home included $5,000 in mortgage interest, $700 in property taxes, $2,100 in utilities and maintenance, and $3,000 in depreciation. Since the lake home was rented for fewer than fifteen days, Glenn would not report the $1,800 of income and would deduct only the interest and property taxes as itemized deductions on Schedule A. The other expenses are nondeductible personal expenses. ♦

2. **Primarily Rental Use**
   If the residence is rented for fifteen days or more and is used for personal purposes for not more than *fourteen days or 10 percent of the days rented, whichever is greater,* the residence is treated as rental property. The expenses must then be allocated between the personal and rental days. If this is the case, the rental expenses may exceed the rental income, and the resulting loss would be deducted against other income, subject to the passive loss rules. (See LO 4.8 for further details.)

EXAMPLE Assume the same facts as in the preceding example except that the $1,800 rental fee is for twenty days and Glenn uses the lake home for only ten days during the year. Since the lake home is now rented for fifteen days or more and Glenn's use of the home is not more than fourteen days (or 10 percent of the days rented, if greater), the property is treated as primarily a rental property. Allocation of expenses associated with the home is based on the number of days of rental or personal use compared to the total number of days of use. Glenn's personal use percentage is 33.33 percent (10 days/30 days) and the rental portion is 66.67 percent (20 days/30 days). For tax purposes, the rental income or loss is calculated as follows:

	Rental (66.67%)	***Personal (33.33%)***
Income	$ 1,800	$ 0
Interest and taxes	(3,800)	(1,900)
Utilities and maintenance	(1,400)	(700)
Depreciation	(2,000)	(1,000)
Rental loss	$(5,400)	$ 0

The interest and taxes allocable to Glenn's personal use of the property may be deductible as itemized deductions on Schedule A (see Chapter 5). The personal portion of utilities, maintenance, and depreciation are nondeductible personal expenses. ♦

3. **Rental/Personal Use**

   If the residence is rented for fifteen days or more and is used for personal purposes for more than *fourteen days or 10 percent of the days rented, whichever is greater,* allocable rental expenses are allowed only to the extent of rental income. Allocable rental expenses are deducted in three separate steps: first, the interest and taxes are deducted; second, utilities and maintenance expenses are deducted; and third, depreciation expense is deducted. For utilities, maintenance, and depreciation expenses to be deductible, there must be positive income following the deduction of items in the preceding step(s). In addition, the expenses, other than interest and taxes, are only deductible to the extent of that positive income. Expenses are allocated between the rental and personal days before the limits are applied. The IRS requires that the allocation be on the basis of the total days of rental use or personal use divided by the total days of use.

EXAMPLE Assume Glenn rents the lake home for $2,500 for twenty days and uses it for personal purposes for sixty days. Assume Glenn has the same operating expenses as in the previous examples. Since the lake home is rented for fifteen days or more and Glenn uses the home for personal purposes for more than fourteen days (or 10 percent of the days rented, if greater), the property is subject to the vacation home limitations. Glenn's personal use percentage is 75 percent (60 days/80 days) and the rental portion is 25 percent (20 days/80 days). The IRS requires that the rental income or loss be calculated as follows:

Gross rental income	$ 2,500
Less: interest and taxes ($5,700 × 25%)	(1,425)
Balance	1,075
Less: utilities and maintenance ($2,100 × 25%)	(525)
Balance	550
Less: depreciation ($3,000 × 25%, limited to $550)	(550)
Net income	$ 0

The interest and taxes allocable to Glenn's personal use of the property may be deductible as itemized deductions on Schedule A (see Chapter 5). The personal portion of utilities, maintenance, and depreciation are nondeductible personal expenses. The depreciation that is limited by income can be carried forward to the next tax year. ♦

It should be noted that the U.S. Tax Court has allowed taxpayers to use 365 days for the allocation of interest and taxes. Under the Tax Court rules, the interest and taxes allocable to the rental use of the property in the above example would be 5.5 percent (20 days/365 days) instead of 25 percent (20 days/80 days). The allocation of utilities and maintenance would remain unchanged, while the full $750 of depreciation (25% of $3,000) would be allowed. The remaining interest and taxes (345 days/365 days) may be included in itemized deductions on Schedule A.

ProConnect™ Tax TIP

Rental activity is entered under Income and then Rental and Royalty Income (Schedule E). Key fields to consider are the Type of Property (dropdown), the number of days rented, the number of days of personal use (located below the expenses fields), and the number of days owned (if the Tax Court method is to be used).

4-7b **Other Rental Issues**

Many rental property owners collect deposits up front from tenants. If the deposit is a security deposit to be returned at the end of the lease (assuming no damage), that amount should generally not be included in the taxpayer's gross rental income. Any amount kept during or at the end of the lease is rental income at the time the deposit will no longer be returned. Collections of rent in advance are generally rental income at the time of collection, regardless of what time period the rent is intended to apply to.

EXAMPLE Sadie rents an apartment to Brendan for $2,000 per month for twelve months starting July 1, 2022. The terms of the lease require Brendan to provide Sadie with the first and last months' rent, and a security deposit of one month's rent at the start of the lease. Brandon pays Sadie $6,000 when he signs the lease. Sadie will include $4,000 of rental income in 2022 for the first and last month's rent that was collected; however, the deposit is not rental income. In 2023, at the end of the lease, Sadie determines that Brendan has caused $800 of damage to the unit and under the terms of the security deposit clause in the lease, she will keep $800 and return the remaining $1,200 deposit to him. Sadie will include the $800 of the security deposit in her 2023 rental income. ♦

Occasionally, a tenant will pay expenses on behalf of the rental property owner. Generally, these must be included in rental income.

EXAMPLE Hugo rents a condominium to Caroline. During the lease, the condo has a plumbing issue and because Hugo was out of town, Caroline contacted a plumber directly and had the $300 of repairs made. Caroline then deducted $300 from her next monthly rent payment. Hugo is required to include $300 in rental income, but, assuming the repairs are deductible, may deduct the repairs as a rental expense. ♦

Self-Study Problem 4.7 *See Appendix E for Solutions to Self-Study Problems*

Nancy Kapiolani lives in a duplex that she owns at 1218 Park Ave S., Tacoma, WA 98447. Nancy rents one-half of her duplex and lives in the other half. In 2022, her existing tenant's lease expires and the tenant moves out. The tenant paid $2,500 in rent during 2022. Nancy had collected first and last months' rent from the tenant in 2021. Due to the condition of the unit, Nancy keeps $200 of the security deposit to make repairs. Her new tenant moves in and pays $1,000 per month for a one-year lease starting July 1, 2022. The new tenant is also required to pay Nancy first and last months' rent plus a $500 security deposit. The unit is rented for 365 days during 2022.

Nancy's basis for depreciation on the rental portion is $120,000, and she uses straight-line depreciation with a 27.5 year useful life. Repairs to the rental half of the unit are $400 (including the $200 from the security deposit). On the whole duplex, real estate taxes are $2,200, interest on the mortgage is $3,400, utilities are $1,800, and insurance is $450. Use Part I of Schedule E on Page 4-31 to report Nancy's income from the rental of part of the duplex.

Learning Objective 4.8

Explain the treatment of passive income and losses.

4-8 PASSIVE LOSS LIMITATIONS

Because of past abuses primarily involving tax shelters and loss deductions from rental real estate, Congress enacted legislation limiting the deduction of certain "passive" losses from other taxable income. A passive activity is a trade or business in which the taxpayer does not materially participate and includes most rental real estate activity. Because the most common passive loss seen on tax returns is from ordinary real estate rental activities, many taxpayers with an investment in a real estate rental property are affected by these rules. In establishing the limitations, the tax law classifies individual income into three categories. These categories are (1) active income (e.g., wages, self-employment income, and salaries), (2) portfolio income (e.g., dividends and interest), and (3) passive income and losses (e.g., rental real estate income and loss, and income and loss passed through from limited partnerships and other ventures in which the taxpayer has minimal or no involvement).

Generally, passive losses cannot be used to offset either active or portfolio income. Also, any tax credits derived from passive activities can only offset income taxes attributable to passive income. Any unused passive losses and credits are carried over and may be used to offset future passive income or taxes attributable to such income, respectively. Generally, losses remaining when the taxpayer disposes of his or her entire interest in the passive activity may be used in full; however, the taxpayer can only use remaining credits to offset the income tax arising from any gain recognized on the disposition of the activity.

EXAMPLE Mike's income and loss items for 2022 are:

Salary	$40,000
Sales commissions	15,000
Dividends on Microsoft stock	2,000
Rental income from real estate	5,000
Loss from limited partnership	(9,000)
Interest on savings account	4,000

Mike's active income for the year is $55,000 ($40,000 + $15,000), his portfolio income is $6,000 ($2,000 + $4,000), and his passive loss is $4,000 ($5,000 − $9,000). Mike must report gross income of $61,000 ($55,000 + $6,000), since the passive loss cannot be used to offset his active or portfolio income. The net passive loss of $4,000 will be carried over to 2023. ♦

Self-Study Problem 4.7

SCHEDULE E (Form 1040)

Department of the Treasury Internal Revenue Service

Supplemental Income and Loss

(From rental real estate, royalties, partnerships, S corporations, estates, trusts, REMICs, etc.)

Attach to Form 1040, 1040-SR, 1040-NR, or 1041.

Go to *www.irs.gov/ScheduleE* for instructions and the latest information.

OMB No. 1545-0074

2022

Attachment Sequence No. 13

Name(s) shown on return | **Your social security number**

Part I Income or Loss From Rental Real Estate and Royalties

Note: If you are in the business of renting personal property, use **Schedule C**. See instructions. If you are an individual, report farm rental income or loss from **Form 4835** on page 2, line 40.

A Did you make any payments in 2022 that would require you to file Form(s) 1099? See instructions . . . . . ☐ **Yes** ☐ **No**

B If "Yes," did you or will you file required Form(s) 1099? . . . . . ☐ **Yes** ☐ **No**

1a	Physical address of each property (street, city, state, ZIP code)
A	
B	
C	

1b	Type of Property (from list below)	**2** For each rental real estate property listed above, report the number of fair rental and personal use days. Check the QJV box only if you meet the requirements to file as a qualified joint venture. See instructions.		**Fair Rental Days**	**Personal Use Days**	**QJV**
A			**A**			☐
B			**B**			☐
C			**C**			☐

Type of Property:

1 Single Family Residence
2 Multi-Family Residence
3 Vacation/Short-Term Rental
4 Commercial
5 Land
6 Royalties
7 Self-Rental
8 Other (describe) ________

			Properties:		
			A	**B**	**C**
Income:					
3	Rents received	**3**			
4	Royalties received	**4**			
Expenses:					
5	Advertising	**5**			
6	Auto and travel (see instructions)	**6**			
7	Cleaning and maintenance	**7**			
8	Commissions	**8**			
9	Insurance	**9**			
10	Legal and other professional fees	**10**			
11	Management fees	**11**			
12	Mortgage interest paid to banks, etc. (see instructions)	**12**			
13	Other interest	**13**			
14	Repairs	**14**			
15	Supplies	**15**			
16	Taxes	**16**			
17	Utilities	**17**			
18	Depreciation expense or depletion	**18**			
19	Other (list) ________	**19**			
20	Total expenses. Add lines 5 through 19	**20**			
21	Subtract line 20 from line 3 (rents) and/or 4 (royalties). If result is a (loss), see instructions to find out if you must file **Form 6198**	**21**			
22	Deductible rental real estate loss after limitation, if any, on **Form 8582** (see instructions)	**22**	( )	( )	( )

23a	Total of all amounts reported on line 3 for all rental properties	**23a**	
b	Total of all amounts reported on line 4 for all royalty properties	**23b**	
c	Total of all amounts reported on line 12 for all properties	**23c**	
d	Total of all amounts reported on line 18 for all properties	**23d**	
e	Total of all amounts reported on line 20 for all properties	**23e**	
24	**Income.** Add positive amounts shown on line 21. **Do not** include any losses	**24**	
25	**Losses.** Add royalty losses from line 21 and rental real estate losses from line 22. Enter total losses here	**25**	( )
26	**Total rental real estate and royalty income or (loss).** Combine lines 24 and 25. Enter the result here. If Parts II, III, IV, and line 40 on page 2 do not apply to you, also enter this amount on Schedule 1 (Form 1040), line 5. Otherwise, include this amount in the total on line 41 on page 2 .	**26**	

For Paperwork Reduction Act Notice, see the separate instructions. Cat. No. 11344L **Schedule E (Form 1040) 2022**

Under the passive loss rules, real estate rental activities are specifically defined as passive, even if the taxpayer actively manages the property and even if the activity is not conducted as a partnership. Individual taxpayers, however, may deduct up to $25,000 of rental property losses against other income, if they are actively involved in the management of the property and their income does not exceed certain limits. The $25,000 loss deduction is phased out when the taxpayer's modified adjusted gross income (adjusted gross income before passive losses and Individual Retirement Account deductions) exceeds $100,000. The $25,000 is reduced by 50 cents for each $1.00 the taxpayer's modified adjusted gross income exceeds that amount. Therefore, no deduction is allowed when the taxpayer's modified adjusted gross income reaches $150,000 (this threshold is not adjusted for inflation). Special limitations apply to taxpayers filing as Married, Filing Separately and claiming a deduction for real estate rental losses under this special rule.

EXAMPLE Mary has modified AGI before passive losses of $120,000. In addition, she has a rental house that she actively manages which shows a loss of $18,000 for the year. She may deduct only $15,000 ($25,000 − 50% of $20,000) of the loss because of the phase-out of the $25,000 allowance for passive rental losses where modified AGI is over $100,000. ♦

ProConnect™ Tax TIP

ProConnect Tax assumes that a rental property is actively managed and will apply the appropriate phase-out based on the modified AGI information entered elsewhere. There is a box to check on the General Information page of the rental property section to indicate otherwise.

4-8a Real Estate Rental as Trade or Business

Taxpayers heavily involved in real estate rental activities may qualify as having an active business rather than a passive activity. If so, the income and losses from qualified rental activities are not subject to passive loss limitations. For a real estate rental to be considered active, the taxpayer must materially participate in the activity. An individual will satisfy this requirement if both of the following are met:

1. More than 50 percent of the individual's personal service during the tax year is performed in real property trades or businesses, and
2. The individual performs more than 750 hours of service during the tax year in the real property trade or business in which he or she claims material participation.

EXAMPLE In 2022, Allan owns eighteen rental houses and spends 100 percent of his personal service time (1,800 hours in 2022) managing them. Allan spends his 1,800 hours of management time doing repairs, landscaping, collecting rents, cleaning and painting vacant houses, advertising for and interviewing new tenants, doing bookkeeping, and purchasing/installing new appliances, drapes, carpets, and toilets. He keeps a log to prove how many hours he works on his property. Since both the above tests are met, Allan's real estate rental activity is not a passive activity. If Allan has an overall loss of $40,000 on the real estate rentals, he can deduct the entire loss on his tax return as an active business, not a passive loss. ♦

TAX BREAK

Real estate professionals who report large losses tend to attract the attention of the IRS. The real estate professional exception to the passive loss rules considers a two-step hurdle for deducting losses: (1) the real estate professional exception is used to overcome the presumption that a rental real estate activity is a passive activity but that does not guarantee treatment as non-passive; (2) the taxpayer is still going to have to demonstrate material participation. When multiple properties are owned, electing to treat them as a single activity can be useful for meeting the material participations rules.

Income from passive activities can be used by taxpayers to absorb passive losses that would otherwise be disallowed. The passive loss limitations are very complex. Certain oil and gas investments are not subject to the passive loss limitations, and special rules apply to investments in qualified low-income housing.

ProConnect™ Tax TIP

Rental real estate is a common form of passive income and is input through the Rental and Royalty Income (Schedule E) window. Another source of passive income is from partnerships, LLCs or S corporations. As discussed in Chapters 10 and 11, these entities report income to individual owners through a Schedule K-1. K-1 income is input under Income in the left margin and the applicable Partnership K-1 or S Corporation K-1 input.

Self-Study Problem 4.8 *See Appendix E for Solutions to Self-Study Problems*

Sherry Lockey has a new limited partnership investment in a commercial rental project in which she has no personal involvement. During 2022, her share of the partnership loss equals $15,000. Sherry also has a new rental house that she actively manages, and this activity generated a $9,000 loss for 2022. Sherry had no passive loss carryover from prior years. If Sherry's modified adjusted gross income before passive losses is $138,000, calculate the deduction amounts for Sherry's 2022 tax return using page 1 of Form 8582 on Page 4-35.

Learning Objective 4.9

Describe the basic tax treatment of deductions for net operating losses.

4-9 NET OPERATING LOSSES

Most taxpayers are required to file an annual tax return. The pattern of a taxpayer's income, however, can lead to inequities among taxpayers with the same total amount of taxable income over a number of years. To alleviate this problem, Congress enacted the Net Operating Loss (NOL) provision.

The NOL provision is primarily designed to provide relief for trade or business losses. Generally, only losses from the operation of a trade or business and casualty and theft losses can generate a net operating loss. Thus, individual taxpayers with only wages, itemized deductions (except casualty losses), and personal exemptions (although currently suspended) cannot generate a net operating loss.

The tax law is designed to permit individuals to deduct business NOLs and prevent the deductions of nonbusiness NOLs. Thus, the NOL computation for individual taxpayers requires the categorization of items of income, deductions, gains, and losses as either business or nonbusiness related. The NOL is not simply the total taxable loss shown at the bottom of page 1 of Form 1040. In general, when calculating a current net operating loss, the following tax items should be considered:

- No personal or dependency exemptions (exemptions are suspended after 2017)
- No deduction for an NOL from a different year
- Capital losses in excess of capital gains are not allowed
- "Nonbusiness" capital losses (those arising outside of a trade or business, or employment) can only be used against "nonbusiness" capital gains. Excess capital losses cannot increase the NOL
- "Business" capital losses can only be used against "business" capital gains, except that they can be used to offset a net nonbusiness capital gain if one exists
- "Nonbusiness" deductions (e.g., charitable donations, deductible medical expenses, mortgage interest, alimony, etc.) can only be used against "nonbusiness" income (interest, dividends, etc.). However, if nonbusiness capital gains exceed nonbusiness capital losses (see above), "excess" nonbusiness deductions can be offset against these gains. (Note that casualty losses are treated as "business deductions" for NOL purposes.)

Self-Study Problem 4.8

Form **8582**

Department of the Treasury
Internal Revenue Service

Passive Activity Loss Limitations

See separate instructions.
Attach to Form 1040, 1040-SR, or 1041.
Go to *www.irs.gov/Form8582* for instructions and the latest information.

OMB No. 1545-1008
2022
Attachment Sequence No. **858**

Name(s) shown on return | **Identifying number**

Part I **2022 Passive Activity Loss**
Caution: Complete Parts IV and V before completing Part I.

Rental Real Estate Activities With Active Participation (For the definition of active participation, see ***Special Allowance for Rental Real Estate Activities*** in the instructions.)

1a	Activities with net income (enter the amount from Part IV, column (a))	1a			
b	Activities with net loss (enter the amount from Part IV, column (b))	1b	( )		
c	Prior years' unallowed losses (enter the amount from Part IV, column (c))	1c	( )		
d	Combine lines 1a, 1b, and 1c			1d	

All Other Passive Activities

2a	Activities with net income (enter the amount from Part V, column (a))	2a			
b	Activities with net loss (enter the amount from Part V, column (b))	2b	( )		
c	Prior years' unallowed losses (enter the amount from Part V, column (c))	2c	( )		
d	Combine lines 2a, 2b, and 2c			2d	
3	Combine lines 1d and 2d. If this line is zero or more, stop here and include this form with your return; all losses are allowed, including any prior year unallowed losses entered on line 1c or 2c. Report the losses on the forms and schedules normally used			3	

If line 3 is a loss and:
- Line 1d is a loss, go to Part II.
- Line 2d is a loss (and line 1d is zero or more), skip Part II and go to line 10.

Caution: If your filing status is married filing separately and you lived with your spouse at any time during the year, **do not** complete Part II. Instead, go to line 10.

Part II **Special Allowance for Rental Real Estate Activities With Active Participation**
Note: Enter all numbers in Part II as positive amounts. See instructions for an example.

4	Enter the **smaller** of the loss on line 1d or the loss on line 3			4	
5	Enter $150,000. If married filing separately, see instructions	5			
6	Enter modified adjusted gross income, but not less than zero. See instructions	6			
	Note: If line 6 is greater than or equal to line 5, skip lines 7 and 8 and enter -0- on line 9. Otherwise, go to line 7.				
7	Subtract line 6 from line 5	7			
8	Multiply line 7 by 50% (0.50). **Do not** enter more than $25,000. If married filing separately, see instructions			8	
9	Enter the **smaller** of line 4 or line 8			9	

Part III **Total Losses Allowed**

10	Add the income, if any, on lines 1a and 2a and enter the total	10	
11	**Total losses allowed from all passive activities for 2022.** Add lines 9 and 10. See instructions to find out how to report the losses on your tax return	11	

Part IV **Complete This Part Before Part I, Lines 1a, 1b, and 1c.** See instructions.

Name of activity	Current year		Prior years	Overall gain or loss	
	(a) Net income (line 1a)	**(b)** Net loss (line 1b)	**(c)** Unallowed loss (line 1c)	**(d)** Gain	**(e)** Loss
Total. Enter on Part I, lines 1a, 1b, and 1c					

For Paperwork Reduction Act Notice, see instructions. Cat. No. 63704F Form **8582** (2022)

EXAMPLE Yujian, a single taxpayer, has completed her 2022 Schedule C and her net loss is $70,000. She also has wages of $45,000 and interest income from her savings of $500. Her business sold property during the year and generated a $3,000 ordinary gain and a separate $5,000 long-term capital gain. Yujian also had several capital gains and losses from the sale of stock investments. Her net results are a $17,000 short-term capital gain and a $6,000 long-term capital loss from these stock sales. Yujian itemizes her deductions and her Schedule A reports the following:

Taxes paid	$ 8,500
Mortgage interest	6,000
Charitable gifts	500
Casualty loss (federal disaster area loss)	2,500
Total itemized deductions	$ 17,500

Yujian calculates her taxable income as follows:

Wages	$ 45,000
Interest income	500
Business loss	(70,000)
Capital gains[1]	16,000
Other gains	3,000
Total income (loss) and AGI	(5,500)
Itemized deductions	(17,500)
Taxable income (loss)	$(23,000)

To compute Yujian's NOL, we need to categorize business and nonbusiness items:

	Business	***Nonbusiness***
Wages	$ 45,000	
Interest income		$ 500
Business loss	(70,000)	
Capital gains	5,000	11,000
Other gains	3,000	
Itemized deductions	(2,500)	(15,000)
Total loss	$(19,500)	$ (3,500)

Using the above information, we can modify taxable income to compute the NOL.

Step 1: Excess nonbusiness capital losses cannot exceed nonbusiness capital gains.

Since the $6,000 nonbusiness capital losses do not exceed $17,000 of nonbusiness capital gains, no adjustment is required. In addition, we can use the $11,000 "excess" nonbusiness capital gain to absorb any nonbusiness deductions in the next step.

Step 2: Nonbusiness deductions cannot exceed nonbusiness income.

Nonbusiness deductions $15,000 − Nonbusiness income $500 = Net nonbusiness deductions $14,500

[1]$1,000 long-term capital loss ($5,000 long-term capital gain from business less $6,000 long-term capital loss from stocks) netted against $17,000 short-term capital gain from stocks.

However, as previously mentioned, net nonbusiness deductions can also offset any net nonbusiness capital gains. Thus $11,000 of the nonbusiness deductions can be used; however, the remaining $3,500 ($14,500 − $11,000) are not deductible and must be added back to the tentative NOL $(23,000) + $3,500 = $(19,500).

Step 3: The business capital (casualty) loss of $2,500 can only be offset by business capital gains of $5,000. There is no excess loss and thus no adjustment is needed.

This agrees to the business category total loss of $19,500 above which is consistent with the NOL representing only business losses.

Yujian may carryforward (or temporarily carryback) the NOL of $19,500 to offset future income. ♦

4-9a NOL Carryforward and Carryback

The rules related to NOLs have changed three times in recent years and with each change, NOLs are treated slightly differently. The three periods are: (1) the pre-2018 period, (2) the 2018–2020 period (due to COVID-19 provisions), and (3) the post-2020 period.

In the pre-2018 period, NOLs were eligible to be carried back two years and forward for 20 years. Any NOL carryforward or carryback could be used to offset 100 percent of the income generated in the carryback or forward period. NOLs generated in this period can continue to be utilized in the same manner.

EXAMPLE Henri generated a loss in 2017 of $45,000. His business income was $2,000 and $5,000 in 2015 and 2016, respectively. Henri will first carryback the NOL to offset the income generated in 2015 and 2016. The remaining NOL of $38,000 can be carried forward for twenty years and offset any income generated in those years. ♦

The TCJA of 2017 changed the treatment of NOLs to permit only the indefinite carryforward of NOLs generated after 2017. In addition, the use of an NOL generated after December 31, 2017, is limited to 80 percent of the current year's taxable income (without regard to the NOL deduction) when used.

EXAMPLE Zlatan generated an NOL in 2018 of $10,000. At that time, he is unable to carry the NOL back and must carry it forward only. In 2019, Zlatan generates $11,000 of business income. Zlatan may only offset up to 80 percent or $8,800 of the 2019 income ($11,000 × 80%). The remaining $1,200 NOL can be carried forward indefinitely. ♦

In the COVID-19 pandemic period (2018–2020), a number of retroactive provisions regarding NOLs were put into place to assist taxpayers with remaining financially viable during the economic downturn. NOLs generated in 2018, 2019, and 2020 were given a 5-year carryback period (but keep the indefinite carryforward) and the 80-percent income limitation was suspended on NOLs generated and used in those three years.

EXAMPLE Zlatan (from the previous example) may now carryback his 2018 $10,000 NOL up to five years (to 2013). If no income was available in the carryback years (or Zlatan elects out of the carryback), the NOL can be used to offset any income in the future year. Thus, Zlatan could carry the $10,000 NOL forward to 2019 and reduce 2019 income to $1,000 (no 80-percent limitation). ♦

Pre-COVID but post-2018 NOL rules are effective after 2020. NOLs generated in 2021 and after may only be carried forward and any post-2017 NOLs will again be limited to 80 percent.

EXAMPLE Lionel started his sole proprietorship in 2018 and generated an NOL of $5,000 in 2018 and another NOL of $8,000 in 2019. In 2020, Lionel made a very small business profit of $2,000. In 2021, he generated $11,000 of business income. Because he has no pre-2018 business income, Lionel is unable to carryback any of the 2018 NOL and instead carries it forward. He offsets the entire $2,000 of 2020 income (no 80-percent limitation) leaving $3,000 of 2018 NOL and $8,000 of 2019 NOL. In 2021, he is limited to using only $8,800 ($11,000 × 80%) of the NOLs. Lionel can carry the $2,200 [($3,000 + $8,000) − $8,800 limitation] forward indefinitely, subject to the 80-percent limitation of future income. ♦

4-9b **Overall Business Loss Limitation**

To reduce the potential for large business losses being claimed in a single year, starting in 2018, the tax law places an annual limitation on noncorporate business losses for taxpayers. After adjusting for inflation, the 2022 limits were set to be $540,000 for married filing jointly and $270,000 for all other returns. The business loss limitation is in place for 2021 through the end of 2028.

EXAMPLE Bettina is a single taxpayer with wages of $20,000 and a business with income of $5,000 in 2022. In addition, Bettina disposed of a passive loss activity for which she has accumulated suspended losses of $280,000 (including her share of the current year loss). Bettina's excess business loss is $275,000 ($280,000 − $5,000) less the single threshold for 2022 of $270,000 yielding an excess loss of $5,000. This amount will become part of Bettina's net operating loss and subject to the NOL limitation and carryforward rules. ♦

ProConnect™ Tax TIP

When a taxpayer creates a net operating loss (NOL), no specific entry is required by the preparer. Instead, supplemental schedules that track the NOL will be created automatically by the software.

Self-Study Problem 4.9 *See Appendix E for Solutions to Self-Study Problems*

Indicate whether the following statements are true or false as of December 31, 2022.

1. NOL deductions from 2022 are first carried back two years and then forward twenty years.
2. The itemized deduction for home mortgage interest can generate an NOL for an individual taxpayer.
3. An individual taxpayer's NOL is equal to the net taxable loss from page 1 of Form 1040.
4. Individual taxpayers' total business losses can be limited.
5. There is no limitation for using a 2022 NOL against the taxable income in 2023.

Sign Here

Under penalties of perjury, I declare that I have examined this return and accompanying schedules and statements, and to the best of my knowledge and belief, they are true, correct, and complete. Declaration of preparer (other than taxpayer) is based on all information of which preparer has any knowledge.

Your signature	Date	Your occupation	If the IRS sent you an Identity Protection PIN, enter it here (see inst.) ▶
Spouse's signature. If a joint return, **both** must sign.	Date	Spouse's occupation	If the IRS sent your spouse an Identity Protection PIN, enter it here (see inst.) ▶
Phone no.	Email address		

Joint return? See instructions. Keep a copy for your records.

Paid Preparer Use Only

Preparer's name	Preparer's signature	Date	PTIN	Check if: ☐ Self-employed
Firm's name ▶			Phone no.	
Firm's address ▶			Firm's EIN ▶	

Would You Sign This Tax Return?

Mark (age 44) and Mary (age 41) Mower are your tax clients. They have two children, Matthew (age 20) and Mindy (age 17), who live at home. Mindy is a senior in high school and Matthew commutes to a local college where he is studying soil management. Mark owns and operates a successful lawn maintenance and landscaping business. He has six employees and three pick-up trucks used for transportation to the job sites. The business has a credit card in its name for use by the employees and Mark, who fills the trucks with gas almost daily. Mark gave a business credit card to Mary, Matthew, and Mindy and told them to use it to buy gas for their automobiles used for shopping, going to school, and short trips. In the current year, his wife and children put \$5,210 of gasoline in their automobiles using the business credit card. Mark is adamant that the \$5,210 be deducted on his Schedule C. He feels the amount is small compared to the business gas purchases of approximately \$28,000. Mark says the amounts charged are spread throughout the credit card statements and would be very difficult for the IRS to detect in an audit. Would you sign the Paid Preparer's declaration (see example above) on this return? Why or why not?

Learning Objective 4.10

Calculate and report the self-employment tax (both Social Security and Medicare portions) for self-employed taxpayers.

4-10 SELF-EMPLOYMENT TAX

The Federal Insurance Contributions Act (FICA) imposes Social Security (Old Age, Survivors, and Disability Insurance (OASDI)) and Medicare taxes. As discussed in Chapter 9, employees and their employers are both required to pay FICA taxes. Employers withhold a specified percentage of each employee's wages up to a maximum base amount, match the amount withheld with an equal amount, and pay the total to the IRS.

Self-employed individuals pay self-employment taxes instead of FICA taxes. Since these individuals have no employers, the entire tax is paid by self-employed individuals. Like the FICA taxes to which employees and their employers are subject, the self-employment tax also consists of two parts, Social Security and Medicare. The maximum base amount of earnings subject to the Social Security portion of the self-employment tax is \$147,000 in 2022. All earnings are subject to the Medicare portion of the self-employment tax. The Social Security tax rate is 12.4 percent and the Medicare tax rate is 2.9 percent. The self-employment tax rates and the maximum base amounts for five years are illustrated in the following table:

Year	*Maximum \$ Base for 12.4%*	*Maximum \$ Base for 2.90%**
2018	128,400	Unlimited
2019	132,900	Unlimited
2020	137,700	Unlimited
2021	142,800	Unlimited
2022	147,000	Unlimited

*A 0.9 percent additional Medicare tax on self-employment income over \$250,000 for married filing jointly filing status, \$200,000 for single, head of household and surviving spouse, and \$125,000 for married filing separately. See Chapter 6 for more information.

If a self-employed individual also receives wages subject to FICA taxes during a tax year, the Social Security tax maximum base amount for self-employment taxes is reduced by the amount of wages. Therefore, the total amount of earnings subject to the Social Security tax portion of both FICA and self-employment tax for 2022 cannot exceed $147,000.

The self-employment tax is imposed on net earnings of $400 or more from self-employment. Net earnings from self-employment include gross income from a trade or business less trade or business deductions, the distributive share of partnership income from a trade or business, and net income earned as an independent contractor. Gains and losses from property transactions, except inventory transactions, and other unearned income are not considered self-employment income. In arriving at net earnings for purposes of computing the self-employment tax, self-employed taxpayers are allowed a deduction for AGI of one-half of the otherwise applicable self-employment tax. A shortcut to arriving at the self-employment income subject to self-employment tax is to multiply the net earnings from self-employment by 92.35 percent. This shortcut is used on Schedule SE as illustrated below.

EXAMPLE Norman is a self-employed accountant in 2022. From his practice, Norman earns $147,000, and has wages subject to FICA from a part-time job of $12,000. Norman's self-employment tax is calculated as follows:

Step 1:

Net earnings from self-employment, before the self-employment tax deduction	$147,000
	× 92.35%
Tentative net earnings from self-employment after deduction for self-employment tax	$135,755

Step 2:

	Social Security	***Medicare***
Maximum base for 2022	$147,000	Unlimited
Less: FICA wages	(12,000)	Not Applicable
Maximum self-employment tax base	$135,000	Unlimited
Lesser of net earnings from self-employment after deduction for self-employment tax or maximum base	$135,000	$135,755
Self-employment tax rate	12.4%	2.9%
Self-employment tax for 2022	$ 16,740	$ 3,937

Norman's total self-employment tax for 2022 is $20,677 ($16,740 + $3,937). On his 2022 income tax return, Norman will report net earnings from self-employment of $147,000, a deduction for adjusted gross income of $10,339 (50% × $20,677), and a self-employment tax liability of $20,677. ♦

The calculation of self-employment tax is reported on page 1 of Schedule SE, Part I, and must be included with a taxpayer's Form 1040.

4-10a COVID-Related Provisions for Self-Employed

During early 2020 and into 2021, many businesses were forced to close or reduce commercial activity due to the COVID-19 pandemic. To provide financial support for businesses, a series of temporary changes to payroll taxes were implemented. Although originally set to expire on December 31, 2020, most of these measures were extended until December 31, 2021, but are not expected to affect payroll taxes in 2022 and after (except where indicated). For employers, these provisions are covered in Chapter 9; however, many self-employed individuals may also find their business eligible for the benefits and thus, those provisions are covered here.

Self-Employment Tax Deferral

In 2020, a deferral was available for one-half of the Social Security portion (12.4 percent) of self-employment tax for net business profits from March 27 through December 31, 2020. Half of the payroll taxes deferred are due by the end of 2021 and the remaining half by the end of 2022.

EXAMPLE In 2020, Kathy determines that 77.5 percent of her $50,029 of net profits are allocable to the period March 27 through December 31, 2020. As a result she deferred one-half of the Social Security tax as follows:

$50,029 × 77.5% = $38,772
$38,772 × 0.9235 = $35,806
$35,806 × 6.2% = $2,220

Kathy was able to defer $2,220 of the Social Security tax in 2020. A payment of $1,110 is due by the end of 2021 and the remainder is due by the end of 2022. ♦

Self-Study Problem 4.10 ***See Appendix E for Solutions to Self-Study Problems***

1. Joanne Plummer is self-employed in 2022. Her Schedule C net income is $36,600 for the year, and Joanne also has a part-time job and earned $4,400 that was subject to FICA tax. Joanne received taxable dividends of $1,110 during the year, and she has a capital gain on the sale of stock of $9,100. Joanne did not elect to defer her payroll taxes in 2020. Calculate Joanne's self-employment tax using Schedule SE of Form 1040 on Page 4-43.

Self-Study Problem 4.10

SCHEDULE SE (Form 1040)
Department of the Treasury
Internal Revenue Service

Self-Employment Tax

Go to *www.irs.gov/ScheduleSE* for instructions and the latest information.
Attach to Form 1040, 1040-SR, or 1040-NR.

OMB No. 1545-0074
2022
Attachment Sequence No. 17

Name of person with self-employment income (as shown on Form 1040, 1040-SR, or 1040-NR) | Social security number of person with **self-employment** income

Part I Self-Employment Tax

Note: If your only income subject to self-employment tax is **church employee income**, see instructions for how to report your income and the definition of church employee income.

A If you are a minister, member of a religious order, or Christian Science practitioner **and** you filed Form 4361, but you had $400 or more of **other** net earnings from self-employment, check here and continue with Part I . . . ☐

Skip lines 1a and 1b if you use the farm optional method in Part II. See instructions.

1a	Net farm profit or (loss) from Schedule F, line 34, and farm partnerships, Schedule K-1 (Form 1065), box 14, code A			1a	
b	If you received social security retirement or disability benefits, enter the amount of Conservation Reserve Program payments included on Schedule F, line 4b, or listed on Schedule K-1 (Form 1065), box 20, code AH			1b	( )
	Skip line 2 if you use the nonfarm optional method in Part II. See instructions.				
2	Net profit or (loss) from Schedule C, line 31; and Schedule K-1 (Form 1065), box 14, code A (other than farming). See instructions for other income to report or if you are a minister or member of a religious order			2	
3	Combine lines 1a, 1b, and 2			3	
4a	If line 3 is more than zero, multiply line 3 by 92.35% (0.9235). Otherwise, enter amount from line 3			4a	
	Note: If line 4a is less than $400 due to Conservation Reserve Program payments on line 1b, see instructions.				
b	If you elect one or both of the optional methods, enter the total of lines 15 and 17 here			4b	
c	Combine lines 4a and 4b. If less than $400, **stop**; you don't owe self-employment tax. **Exception:** If less than $400 and you had **church employee income**, enter -0- and continue			4c	
5a	Enter your **church employee income** from Form W-2. See instructions for definition of church employee income	5a			
b	Multiply line 5a by 92.35% (0.9235). If less than $100, enter -0-			5b	
6	Add lines 4c and 5b			6	
7	Maximum amount of combined wages and self-employment earnings subject to social security tax or the 6.2% portion of the 7.65% railroad retirement (tier 1) tax for 2022			7	147,000
8a	Total social security wages and tips (total of boxes 3 and 7 on Form(s) W-2) and railroad retirement (tier 1) compensation. If $147,000 or more, skip lines 8b through 10, and go to line 11	8a			
b	Unreported tips subject to social security tax from Form 4137, line 10	8b			
c	Wages subject to social security tax from Form 8919, line 10	8c			
d	Add lines 8a, 8b, and 8c			8d	
9	Subtract line 8d from line 7. If zero or less, enter -0- here and on line 10 and go to line 11			9	
10	Multiply the **smaller** of line 6 or line 9 by 12.4% (0.124)			10	
11	Multiply line 6 by 2.9% (0.029)			11	
12	**Self-employment tax.** Add lines 10 and 11. Enter here and on **Schedule 2 (Form 1040), line 4**			12	
13	**Deduction for one-half of self-employment tax.** Multiply line 12 by 50% (0.50). Enter here and on **Schedule 1 (Form 1040), line 15**	13			

Part II Optional Methods To Figure Net Earnings (see instructions)

Farm Optional Method. You may use this method **only** if **(a)** your gross farm income[1] wasn't more than $9,060, **or (b)** your net farm profits[2] were less than $6,540.

14	Maximum income for optional methods	14	6,040
15	Enter the **smaller** of: two-thirds (2/3) of gross farm income[1] (not less than zero) **or** $6,040. Also, include this amount on line 4b above	15	

Nonfarm Optional Method. You may use this method **only** if **(a)** your net nonfarm profits[3] were less than $6,540 and also less than 72.189% of your gross nonfarm income,[4] **and (b)** you had net earnings from self-employment of at least $400 in 2 of the prior 3 years. **Caution:** You may use this method no more than five times.

16	Subtract line 15 from line 14	16	
17	Enter the **smaller** of: two-thirds (2/3) of gross nonfarm income[4] (not less than zero) **or** the amount on line 16. Also, include this amount on line 4b above	17	

[1] From Sch. F, line 9; and Sch. K-1 (Form 1065), box 14, code B.
[2] From Sch. F, line 34; and Sch. K-1 (Form 1065), box 14, code A—minus the amount you would have entered on line 1b had you not used the optional method.
[3] From Sch. C, line 31; and Sch. K-1 (Form 1065), box 14, code A.
[4] From Sch. C, line 7; and Sch. K-1 (Form 1065), box 14, code C.

For Paperwork Reduction Act Notice, see your tax return instructions. Cat. No. 11358Z **Schedule SE (Form 1040) 2022**

4-11 QUALIFIED BUSINESS INCOME (QBI) DEDUCTION

4.11 Learning Objective

Compute the qualified business income (QBI) deduction.

The Qualified Business Income (QBI) deduction was introduced in 2018 and applies to tax years through 2025. The QBI deduction is a deduction for individual taxpayers reporting business income from a passthrough entity such as a sole proprietorship, partnership, limited liability company, or S corporation. It is also referred to as the Section 199A deduction, the passthrough deduction, or the QBI deduction. The QBI deduction requires no additional outlay or investment of funds but is simply granted as a function of legislative grace. A discussion of the QBI deduction related specifically to partnerships and S corporations is covered in Chapters 10 and 11, respectively.

The QBI deduction is available to individual taxpayers as a "below the line" deduction (after adjusted gross income) and is also available to taxpayers who take the standard deduction. The deduction is generally 20 percent of a taxpayer's qualified business income (QBI) from a partnership (including LLC if so treated), S corporation, or sole proprietorship.

4-11a Definition of Qualified Business Income

Qualified business income for a tax year is the net amount of qualified items of income, gain, deduction, and loss relating to any qualified trade or business of the taxpayer in the United States (foreign income is not considered). QBI excludes the following:

- Short-term capital gain, short-term capital loss, long-term capital gain, or long-term capital loss
- Dividend income
- Interest income
- Commodity transaction income or foreign currency gain or loss
- Any item of income, gain, deduction, or loss relating to certain notional principal contracts
- Amounts received from an annuity that is not received in connection with the trade or business
- Any item of deduction or loss properly allocable to an amount described in any of the preceding items in this list (e.g., interest expense associated with investment income)

Reasonable employee compensation paid to the taxpayer by the qualified trade or business and guaranteed payments to a partner are not QBI and therefore the QBI deduction is not applicable to such income. For a sole proprietor, QBI is often the net profit reported on Line 31 less any for AGI deductions associated with the business such as one-half of self-employment taxes.

EXAMPLE Princess is a single taxpayer and operates a small business as a sole proprietor. In 2022, her business generates $80,000 of gross business income, $50,000 of business expenses, $3,000 of interest income, and a $2,000 capital gain. Her deduction for one-half of self-employment taxes is $4,500. Princess' QBI is $25,500 ($80,000 − $50,000 − $4,500). The interest and capital gains are excluded from QBI. ♦

With respect to the QBI deduction, the term "*qualified* trade or business" means any trade or business other than a specified service trade or business, or the trade or business of performing services as an employee. Unfortunately, "trade or business" is not defined in the tax law. The regulations interpret trade or business to be consistent with the same phrase in Internal Revenue Code Section 162 related to the deduction of trade or business expenses. This does not provide an exceptional level of guidance for many businesses but certainly hobby activities (Chapter 3) would not qualify. The tax law provides a safe-harbor under which income from rental real estate (even if treated as passive) can qualify as qualified business income. The requirements are:

1. 250 hours or more are spent by the taxpayer with respect to the rental activity
2. Contemporaneous records of the time spent are maintained
3. Separate books and records for the rental activity are maintained

Note that 250 hours per year amounts to an average of over 20 hours per month. Time spent related to the rental activity on advertising, negotiating with tenants, verifying applications, daily operation, repair and maintenance, purchase of materials, and supervision of employees all count toward the required 250 hours. Time spent purchasing or financing the acquisition of the property and time spent traveling to and from the property do not generally qualify.

4-11b QBI Deduction Taxable Income Limitation

The QBI deduction is subject to a number of limitations and exceptions. A limitation that applies to all taxpayers is that the QBI deduction cannot exceed 20 percent of the taxpayer's taxable income (excluding net long-term capital gains and qualified dividend income).

EXAMPLE Alice operates a small accounting business that generates $60,000 of qualified business income. She also operates a separate investment advising business that focuses on providing crypto-currency investment advice that lost $20,000. Both of Alice's businesses are sole proprietorships. Her pre-limitation QBI deduction is $8,000 [($60,000 − $20,000) × 20%]. Alice also earned $5,000 in net capital gains but had no other forms of income and elects the standard deduction. In 2022, Alice's taxable income subject to the 20-percent limit is $27,050 ($40,000 of business income less her standard deduction of $12,950; capital gains are excluded from this calculation). Her QBI deduction is limited to $5,410 ($27,050 × 20%). ♦

4-11c Wage Limitation

The two additional limitations on the QBI deduction are (1) the wage limitation and (2) the specified service business limitation. These limitations apply to taxpayers that have taxable income (*total* taxable income not just *business* income, and including long-term capital gains or qualified dividends) above the threshold amounts, which in 2022 are $340,100 for married filing jointly and $170,050 for all other taxpayers. These threshold amounts are indexed for inflation each year. The limitations are computed before considering the QBI deduction.

For taxpayers with income below the thresholds, the QBI deduction is as described above. For taxpayers with taxable income above the threshold amounts, the two limitations apply and subject to a complex phase-out.

The wage limitation is the greater of:

- 50 percent of the allocable share of W-2 wages with respect to the business (the "wage limit") or
- 25 percent of the allocable share of W-2 wages with respect to the business plus 2.5 percent of the unadjusted basis of all qualified business property (the "wage and capital limit")

W-2 wages are defined as wages paid to employees (not independent contractors) including deferrals into Section 401(k) plans and the like. The term allocable share pertains to the allocation of wages similar to that associated with the allocation of partnership income (see further discussion of allocation of wages in Chapter 10). Because the tax law was designed to encourage investment in employees and business capital investment, the wage and capital limit includes a percentage of the unadjusted basis (basis prior to any depreciation) of business property.

EXAMPLE Pat operates a sole proprietorship which generates $200,000 of qualified business income that includes the deduction for wages of $66,000 that Pat pays to employees. Pat's business has invested $20,000 in qualified business property. Pat has no other sources of income and files as a single taxpayer and elects the standard deduction. Pat's initial QBI deduction is $200,000 × 20% or $40,000 which is limited to 20 percent of Pat's taxable income [$187,050 ($200,000 – standard deduction of $12,950) × 20% = $37,410]. Furthermore, since Pat's income exceeds the $170,050 threshold, the wage limit applies. The wage limit is the greater of 50 percent of the wages ($66,000 × 50% = $33,000) or the wage and capital limit of 25 percent of the wages ($66,000 × 25% = $16,500) plus 2.5 percent of the unadjusted basis of qualified business property ($20,000 × 2.5% = $500) which totals $17,000. The greater of the two wage-limit amounts applies and thus, Pat's QBI deduction is limited to $33,000. Pat's final taxable income will be $154,050 ($200,000 – $33,000 – $12,950). Recall that the wage limit applies if the taxpayer's taxable income *before* the QBI deduction exceeds the threshold. ♦

Qualified business property for purposes of the wage and capital limit is defined as tangible property subject to depreciation (i.e., not inventory or land) for which the depreciable period has not ended before the close of the taxable year, held by the business at year end, and used at any point during the year in the production of QBI. If the "depreciation period" for a property ended in any prior tax year, that property is not included in the calculation of tangible property. The depreciable period is defined as starting when the property was placed in service and ending on the later of (1) 10 years or (2) the last day in the last year of the property's regular depreciation.

EXAMPLE Josh, a single taxpayer, operates a sole proprietorship. He qualifies for the QBI deduction and his taxable income subjects him to the wage and capital limitations. Josh has purchased and placed in service the following property (all of which is currently being used in 2022):

Year	5-year recovery period	39-year recovery period
2011	$20,000	$600,000
2012	0	0
2013	4,000	0
2014	0	0
2015	0	0
2016	0	0
2017	25,000	0
2018	0	0
2019	10,000	0
2020	2,000	0
2021	50,000	0
2022	13,000	0
Total	$124,000	$600,000

Qualified business property still within recovery period

In determining qualified business property for purposes of the QBI wage limit in 2022, Josh's property must still be within the depreciable period which ends on the later of the last full year of the recovery period or ten years. The 2011–2017 five-year property is fully depreciated BUT only the property placed in service before 2013 is no longer qualified; thus, Josh has $104,000 of qualified five-year property. In spite of being placed in service more than ten years ago, all of the building in the 39-year category is qualified as it is still being depreciated. Josh's total qualified property under the wage and capital limit for the QBI deduction is $704,000 ($104,000 + $600,000). ♦

Recall that the wage limitations apply only if the taxpayer's taxable income exceeds the threshold amount ($340,100 for married filing jointly and $170,050 for all others). As is typical in the tax law, a taxpayer's opportunity to use the QBI deduction does not cease entirely if the threshold is exceeded. Instead, the QBI deduction is subject to a phase-out up to an excess of $100,000 for married filing jointly taxpayers and $50,000 for all others. First, the QBI deduction is computed as if no wage limitation applies. The next step is to compute the QBI deduction including the wage limitation. The excess of the QBI deduction with no limitation over the QBI deduction with limitation is known as the "excess amount." The excess amount is subject to a pro rata phase-out based on the taxpayer's income over the threshold amount.

EXAMPLE Phil is a single taxpayer with a QBI eligible small business and his taxable income as measured for the QBI deduction is $182,650 and thus exceeds the $170,050 threshold. Phil's QBI is $150,000 and his business paid wages of $42,000 in 2022 and has qualified business property of $660,000.

Phil's QBI deduction with no limitation = $30,000 ($150,000 × 20%)
The wage limitation is $27,000, which is the greater of:

$21,000 ($42,000 wages × 50%) or

$27,000 [($42,000 × 25%) + ($660,000 × 2.5%)]

Phil's QBI deduction is limited to $27,000; however, Phil is not subject to the entire wage limitation as his income is not $50,000 or more over the threshold amount. Thus, the wage limitation is "phased-in."

Phil's taxable income for QBI deduction purposes	$182,650
Phil's threshold amount (single taxpayer)	170,050
Excess	$ 12,600
Excess divided by the phase-out range	$12,600/$50,000 = 25.2%

Thus Phil will lose 25.2 percent of his "excess amount" of $3,000 ($30,000 QBI deduction without limit less $27,000 QBI deduction with limit) or $756. Phil's QBI deduction is $29,244 ($30,000 − $756). ♦

To summarize thus far, the QBI deduction is 20 percent of qualified business income, which is the income of a business held in any form but the corporate form. QBI excludes forms of "portfolio" income such as interest, dividends, and gains. For taxpayers below the income thresholds ($340,100 for married filing joint returns, $170,050 for all other returns), there are no explicit limitations other than the taxable income limit. For those with taxable income above the thresholds, the QBI deduction is limited by the wage limitation and also by the specified service business limitation (which is covered in the following section).

4-11d **Specified Service Business Limitation**

For taxpayers with income in excess of the threshold, certain types of businesses are not eligible for the QBI deduction:

1. a taxpayer whose business is being an employee, and
2. a specified service trade or business.

A specified service trade or business is defined as any trade or business involving the performance of services in the fields of health, law, accounting, actuarial science, performing arts, consulting, athletics, financial services, brokerage services, or any trade or business where the principal asset of such trade or business is the reputation or skill of one or more of its owners or employees. Also, specified service businesses include those involved in investing and investment management, trading, or dealing in securities, partnership interests, or commodities.

To be clear, recall that a taxpayer in a specified service business is not necessarily prohibited from the QBI deduction but rather is not eligible for the QBI deduction if the taxpayer's taxable income exceeds the aforementioned thresholds. The same phase-out for the wage limitation also applies to a specified service business (i.e., the with and without comparison of the QBI deduction and pro-rata reduction of the excess amount). However, the phase-out applies in a two-step process that is almost certainly better left to tax software.

EXAMPLE Jenny and Jason file jointly in 2022. Jenny is a physician and works for her pass-through business that has QBI of $310,000 in 2022. The S corporation paid Jenny wages of $80,000 and her employee wages of $40,000 in 2022. Jenny and Jason's taxable income before any QBI deduction is $385,000. Jenny's S corporation has qualified business property of $300,000.

Jenny's QBI without any limits would be $62,000 ($310,000 × 20%). However, Jenny and Jason exceed the threshold income by $44,900 ($385,000 − $340,100). The excess income of $44,900 is 44.9 percent of the phase-out range of $100,000 for married filing jointly taxpayers and thus Jenny is eligible for only 55.1 percent of the benefits from the deduction. This eligible share is applied to each of the limits as follows:

QBI is $310,000 × 55.1% = $170,810
W-2 wages of $120,000 × 55.1% = $66,120
Qualified business property $300,000 × 55.1% = $165,300

Using this information, Jenny's tentative QBI deduction under the general rules is:

20% of QBI: $34,162 ($170,810 × 20%)
Or the greater of
Wages limit: $33,060 ($66,120 × 50%) or
Wages and capital limit: $20,663 [($66,120 × 25%) + $165,300 × 2.5%]

Under the first step, the QBI deduction would be $33,060. But now, the phase-out associated with income over the threshold must be applied based on these amounts. Jenny's QBI would be $34,162 with no limitation and $33,060 with limitation or an excess QBI deduction of $1,102. As previously calculated, Jenny and Jason's income exceeds the threshold by $44,900 or 44.9 percent of the phase-out range of $100,000. Thus, Jenny is going to lose $495 of the QBI deduction (44.9 percent of the excess QBI deduction of $1,102).

As a result of the above steps, Jenny's QBI deduction for 2022 is $33,667 ($34,162 − $495). ♦

If a taxpayer has net QBI from one or more businesses that is less than zero, no QBI deduction is permitted and the QBI loss is carried over to the following year.

EXAMPLE Alice operates a small business that generates $20,000 of qualified business income. She also operates a separate business that lost $60,000. Both of Alice's businesses are sole proprietorships. Alice's total net QBI is less than

$0 ($40,000 net loss). As a result, Alice is not permitted a QBI deduction in the current year and will carry the QBI loss forward to next year. ♦

The regulations that cover the QBI deduction are complex and the calculation of the QBI deduction can become unwieldy when a taxpayer subject to the limitations has multiple businesses eligible for the QBI deduction and some of these businesses operate at a loss and others generate income. These computations are beyond the scope of this textbook.

4-11e Reporting the QBI Deduction

Forms 8995 and 8995-A are used for reporting the QBI deduction. Form 8995 is for taxpayers whose taxable income before the QBI deduction does not exceed the phase-out thresholds ($340,100 for married filing joint returns, $170,050 for all other returns in 2022). Otherwise, taxpayers must use Form 8995-A. As the complexity of the QBI deduction increases, taxpayers may also need to use four accompanying schedules (A–D) that are part of Form 8995-A. These additional schedules are beyond the scope of this textbook.

Self-Study Problem 4.11

See Appendix E for Solutions to Self-Study Problems

Determine whether the following taxpayers are eligible for the QBI deduction and the deduction amount, if any.

a. Aretha is a married taxpayer filing jointly and a shareholder in Soul Corporation (not an S corporation). She owns 10 percent of the outstanding stock and the corporation generates $700,000 of taxable income from its business operations and distributes a $70,000 dividend to Aretha. Her total taxable income before the QBI deduction is $92,000.

b. Terri Jones is a single taxpayer and sole proprietor who operates a small chain of hair salons called The Bee Hive that specializes in obscure hair colors. Her business has no employees since all the stylists operate as independent contractors. The taxpayer identification number of the Bee Hive is 317-65-4321. Terri's business generated business income of $120,000 in 2022. Her taxable income before any QBI deduction is $133,000. Use Form 8995 on Page 4-51 to determine her QBI deduction.

c. Alice Delvecchio is married and files a joint return with her spouse, Chris Delvecchio. Alice operates a small family restaurant called D's Pizza as a sole proprietor (taxpayer identification number 565-22-4321). She pays wages of $36,000, has qualified property with a basis of $67,000, and the QBI from the restaurant is $100,000. Chris has wages of $250,000 and their joint taxable income before the QBI deduction is $366,000 and includes $12,000 of qualified dividends. Use Form 8995-A on Pages 4-52 and 4-53 to determine their QBI deduction amount.

ProConnect™ Tax TIP

All of the different entry points for information for a tax return are located on the left-hand margin of ProConnect Tax. At the top of that list are two tabs: All and In Use. The All tab shows all of the possible data entry points and aids in the prevention of overlooking a tax item while preparing the return. For reviewing a return, the In Use tab hides the areas not in use and can be very helpful.

Self-Study Problem 4.11b

Form **8995**

Department of the Treasury
Internal Revenue Service

Qualified Business Income Deduction Simplified Computation

▶ Attach to your tax return.

▶ Go to *www.irs.gov/Form8995* for instructions and the latest information.

OMB No. 1545-2294

2021*

Attachment Sequence No. 55

Name(s) shown on return	Your taxpayer identification number

Note. *You can claim the qualified business income deduction* **only** *if you have qualified business income from a qualified trade or business, real estate investment trust dividends, publicly traded partnership income, or a domestic production activities deduction passed through from an agricultural or horticultural cooperative. See instructions.*
Use this form if your taxable income, before your qualified business income deduction, is at or below $164,900 ($164,925 if married filing separately; $329,800 if married filing jointly), and you aren't a patron of an agricultural or horticultural cooperative.

1	(a) Trade, business, or aggregation name	(b) Taxpayer identification number	(c) Qualified business income or (loss)
i			
ii			
iii			
iv			
v			

2	Total qualified business income or (loss). Combine lines 1i through 1v, column (c)	2			
3	Qualified business net (loss) carryforward from the prior year	3	( )		
4	Total qualified business income. Combine lines 2 and 3. If zero or less, enter -0-	4			
5	Qualified business income component. Multiply line 4 by 20% (0.20)			5	
6	Qualified REIT dividends and publicly traded partnership (PTP) income or (loss) (see instructions)	6			
7	Qualified REIT dividends and qualified PTP (loss) carryforward from the prior year	7	( )		
8	Total qualified REIT dividends and PTP income. Combine lines 6 and 7. If zero or less, enter -0-	8			
9	REIT and PTP component. Multiply line 8 by 20% (0.20)			9	
10	Qualified business income deduction before the income limitation. Add lines 5 and 9			10	
11	Taxable income before qualified business income deduction (see instructions)	11			
12	Net capital gain (see instructions)	12			
13	Subtract line 12 from line 11. If zero or less, enter -0-	13			
14	Income limitation. Multiply line 13 by 20% (0.20)			14	
15	Qualified business income deduction. Enter the smaller of line 10 or line 14. Also enter this amount on the applicable line of your return (see instructions) ▶			15	
16	Total qualified business (loss) carryforward. Combine lines 2 and 3. If greater than zero, enter -0-			16	( )
17	Total qualified REIT dividends and PTP (loss) carryforward. Combine lines 6 and 7. If greater than zero, enter -0-			17	( )

For Privacy Act and Paperwork Reduction Act Notice, see instructions. Cat. No. 37806C Form **8995** (2021)

*Please go to **www.irs.gov** to download the latest Form 8995. The 2022 version of Form 8995 was not available as we went to print.

Self-Study Problem 4.11c

Form **8995-A** Department of the Treasury Internal Revenue Service

Qualified Business Income Deduction

▶ Attach to your tax return.
▶ Go to *www.irs.gov/Form8995A* for instructions and the latest information.

OMB No. 1545-2294
2021*
Attachment Sequence No. 55A

Name(s) shown on return | **Your taxpayer identification number**

Note: *You can claim the qualified business income deduction* **only** *if you have qualified business income from a qualified trade or business, real estate investment trust dividends, publicly traded partnership income, or a domestic production activities deduction passed through from an agricultural or horticultural cooperative. See instructions. Use this form if your taxable income, before your qualified business income deduction, is above $164,900 ($164,925 if married filing separately; $329,800 if married filing jointly), or you're a patron of an agricultural or horticultural cooperative.*

Part I Trade, Business, or Aggregation Information

Complete Schedules A, B, and/or C (Form 8995-A), as applicable, before starting Part I. Attach additional worksheets when needed. See instructions.

1	(a) Trade, business, or aggregation name	(b) Check if specified service	(c) Check if aggregation	(d) Taxpayer identification number	(e) Check if patron
A		☐	☐		☐
B		☐	☐		☐
C		☐	☐		☐

Part II Determine Your Adjusted Qualified Business Income

			A	B	C
2	Qualified business income from the trade, business, or aggregation. See instructions	2			
3	Multiply line 2 by 20% (0.20). If your taxable income is $164,900 or less ($164,925 if married filing separately; $329,800 if married filing jointly), skip lines 4 through 12 and enter the amount from line 3 on line 13	3			
4	Allocable share of W-2 wages from the trade, business, or aggregation	4			
5	Multiply line 4 by 50% (0.50)	5			
6	Multiply line 4 by 25% (0.25)	6			
7	Allocable share of the unadjusted basis immediately after acquisition (UBIA) of all qualified property	7			
8	Multiply line 7 by 2.5% (0.025)	8			
9	Add lines 6 and 8	9			
10	Enter the greater of line 5 or line 9	10			
11	W-2 wage and UBIA of qualified property limitation. Enter the smaller of line 3 or line 10	11			
12	Phased-in reduction. Enter the amount from line 26, if any. See instructions	12			
13	Qualified business income deduction before patron reduction. Enter the greater of line 11 or line 12	13			
14	Patron reduction. Enter the amount from Schedule D (Form 8995-A), line 6, if any. See instructions	14			
15	Qualified business income component. Subtract line 14 from line 13	15			
16	Total qualified business income component. Add all amounts reported on line 15 ▶	16			

For Privacy Act and Paperwork Reduction Act Notice, see separate instructions. Cat. No. 71661B Form **8995-A** (2021)

*Please go to **www.irs.gov** to download the latest Form 8995-A. The 2022 version of Form 8995-A was not available as we went to print. If using the prior year form included in the textbook, be sure and use updated income limits on Line 3 and Line 21 ($340,100 for married filing joint returns, $170,050 for all other returns).

Form 8995-A (2021) Page **2**

Part III Phased-in Reduction

Complete Part III only if your taxable income is more than $164,900 but not $214,900 ($164,925 and $214,925 if married filing separately; $329,800 and $429,800 if married filing jointly) and line 10 is less than line 3. Otherwise, skip Part III.

					A	B	C
17	Enter the amounts from line 3			17			
18	Enter the amounts from line 10			18			
19	Subtract line 18 from line 17			19			
20	Taxable income before qualified business income deduction	20					
21	Threshold. Enter $164,900 ($164,925 if married filing separately; $329,800 if married filing jointly)	21					
22	Subtract line 21 from line 20	22					
23	Phase-in range. Enter $50,000 ($100,000 if married filing jointly)	23					
24	Phase-in percentage. Divide line 22 by line 23	24	%				
25	Total phase-in reduction. Multiply line 19 by line 24			25			
26	Qualified business income after phase-in reduction. Subtract line 25 from line 17. Enter this amount here and on line 12, for the corresponding trade or business			26			

Part IV Determine Your Qualified Business Income Deduction

27	Total qualified business income component from all qualified trades, businesses, or aggregations. Enter the amount from line 16	27			
28	Qualified REIT dividends and publicly traded partnership (PTP) income or (loss). See instructions	28			
29	Qualified REIT dividends and PTP (loss) carryforward from prior years	29	( )		
30	Total qualified REIT dividends and PTP income. Combine lines 28 and 29. If less than zero, enter -0-	30			
31	REIT and PTP component. Multiply line 30 by 20% (0.20)	31			
32	Qualified business income deduction before the income limitation. Add lines 27 and 31 ▶			32	
33	Taxable income before qualified business income deduction	33			
34	Net capital gain. See instructions	34			
35	Subtract line 34 from line 33. If zero or less, enter -0-			35	
36	Income limitation. Multiply line 35 by 20% (0.20)			36	
37	Qualified business income deduction before the domestic production activities deduction (DPAD) under section 199A(g). Enter the smaller of line 32 or line 36 ▶			37	
38	DPAD under section 199A(g) allocated from an agricultural or horticultural cooperative. Don't enter more than line 33 minus line 37			38	
39	Total qualified business income deduction. Add lines 37 and 38 ▶			39	
40	Total qualified REIT dividends and PTP (loss) carryforward. Combine lines 28 and 29. If zero or greater, enter -0-			40	( )

Form **8995-A** (2021)

KEY TERMS

capital asset, 4-2
capital gain or loss, 4-2
Section 1231 assets, 4-2
virtual currency, 4-2
cryptocurrency, 4-2
bitcoin, 4-2
holding period, 4-3
"sale or exchange," 4-4
amount realized, 4-4
adjusted basis, 4-4
capital improvements, 4-5
net capital gains, 4-8
net capital losses, 4-11
capital loss carryovers, 4-11
personal residence exclusion, 4-23
vacation homes, 4-27
primarily personal use, 4-27
primarily rental use, 4-27
passive activity, 4-30
passive income and losses, 4-30
net operating loss (NOL), 4-34
business loss limitation, 4-39
self-employment tax, 4-40
qualified business income (QBI) deduction, 4-45
wage limitation, 4-46
wage and capital limit, 4-46
qualified business property, 4-47
specified service business limitation, 4-48

KEY POINTS

Learning Objectives	Key Points
LO 4.1: Define the term "capital asset."	• A capital asset is any property, whether or not used in a trade or business, except: (1) inventory, (2) depreciable property or real property used in a trade or business, (3) patents, inventions, models or designs, secret formulas or processes, copyrights, literary, musical, or artistic compositions, letters or memorandums, or similar property, if the property is created by the taxpayer, (4) accounts or notes receivable, and (5) certain U.S. government publications. • Virtual currency is a digital representation of value that functions as a medium of exchange, a unit of account, or a store of value. • Cryptocurrency is a type of virtual currency that utilizes blockchain to validate and secure transactions that are digitally recorded on a distributed ledger.
LO 4.2: Apply the holding period for long-term and short-term capital gains and losses.	• Assets must be held for more than one year for the gain or loss to be considered long-term. • A capital asset held one year or less results in a short-term capital gain or loss. • A net short-term capital gain is treated as ordinary income. • In calculating the holding period, the taxpayer excludes the date of acquisition and includes the date of disposition.
LO 4.3: Calculate the gain or loss on the disposition of an asset.	• The taxpayer's gain or loss is calculated using the following formula: amount realized − adjusted basis = gain or loss realized. • The amount realized from a sale or other disposition of property is equal to the sum of the money received, plus the fair market value of other property received, plus any liabilities relieved, less the costs paid to transfer the property. • The adjusted basis of property is equal to: the original basis + capital improvements − accumulated depreciation. • In most cases, the original basis is the cost of the property at the date of acquisition, plus any costs incidental to the purchase, such as title insurance, escrow fees, and inspection fees (but not fees or costs for getting a loan on the property). • Capital improvements are major expenditures for permanent improvements to or restoration of the taxpayer's property. • Basis of property received from inheritance is equal to the fair market value at the date of the decedent's death. • Basis of property acquired as a gift depends on whether the property is sold for a gain or loss by the donee.

LO 4.4: Compute the tax on capital gains.	• Short-term capital gains are taxed as ordinary income, while there are various different preferential long-term capital gains tax rates. • Net long-term capital gains may be subject to rates ranging from 0 percent to 28 percent (an additional 3.8 percent Medicare tax on net investment income applies to high-income individuals). • Special rates apply to long-term gains on collectibles (e.g., art, stamps, gems, coins, etc.) and depreciation recapture on the disposition of certain Section 1250 assets.
LO 4.5: Describe the treatment of capital losses.	• Individual taxpayers may deduct net capital losses against ordinary income in amounts up to $3,000 per year with any unused capital losses carried forward indefinitely. • When a taxpayer ends up with net capital losses, the losses offset capital gains as follows: (1) net short-term capital losses first reduce 28-percent gains, then 25-percent gains, then regular long-term capital gains, and (2) net long-term capital losses first reduce 28-percent gains, then 25-percent gains, then any short-term capital gains. • Personal capital losses are not deductible for tax purposes.
LO 4.6: Apply the exclusion of gain from personal residence sales.	• Taxpayers who have owned their personal residence and lived in it for at least two of the five years before the sale can exclude from income up to $250,000 of gain ($500,000 for joint return filers).
LO 4.7: Apply the tax rules for rental property and vacation homes.	• Rental income and related expenses are reported on Schedule E. • Rental expenses include real estate taxes, mortgage interest, insurance, commissions, repairs, and depreciation. • If a residence is rented for fewer than fifteen days during the year, the rental income is disregarded and the property is treated as a personal residence for tax purposes. • If the residence is rented for fifteen days or more and is used for personal purposes for not more than fourteen days or 10 percent of the days rented, whichever is greater, the residence is treated as a rental property. • If the residence is rented for fifteen days or more and is used for personal purposes for more than fourteen days or 10 percent of the days rented, whichever is greater, allocable rental expenses are allowed only to the extent of rental income.
LO 4.8: Explain the treatment of passive income and losses.	• The tax law defines three categories of income: (1) active income, (2) portfolio income, and (3) passive income and losses. • Normally, passive losses cannot be used to offset either active or portfolio income. Passive losses not used to offset passive income are carried forward indefinitely. • Generally, losses remaining when the taxpayer disposes of his or her entire interest in a passive activity may be used in full. • Under the passive loss rules, real estate rental activities are specifically defined as passive, even if the taxpayer actively manages the property. • Individual taxpayers may deduct up to $25,000 of rental property losses against other income, if they are actively involved in the management of the property and their modified adjusted gross income does not exceed certain limits. • Taxpayers heavily involved in real estate rental activities may qualify as running an active trade or business rather than a passive activity and may fully deduct all rental losses.
LO 4.9: Describe the basic tax treatment of deductions for net operating losses.	• Computation of an individual taxpayer NOL requires classification of income and deductions as business and nonbusiness. • An NOL generated after 2020 may be carried forward only and may only offset up to 80 percent of a future year's income. • An NOL generated between 2018 and 2020 may be carried back five years and carried forward indefinitely. The 80 percent income limit does not apply to these NOLs. • An NOL generated in 2017 or before may be carried back two years and forward twenty years. • Total business losses generated between 2021 and 2028 are limited.

LO 4.10: Calculate and report the self-employment tax (both Social Security and Medicare portions) for self-employed taxpayers.	• Self-employed individuals pay self-employment (SE) taxes instead of FICA taxes and, since these individuals have no employers, the entire tax is paid by the self-employed individuals. • For 2022, the Social Security (OASDI) tax rate is 12.4 percent, with a maximum base amount of earnings subject to the Social Security portion of $147,000. The Medicare tax rate is 2.9 percent with all earnings subject to the Medicare portion, without limitation. • If an individual, subject to SE taxes, also receives wages subject to FICA taxes during a tax year, the individual's maximum base amount for SE taxes is reduced by the amount of the wages when calculating the SE taxes. • Net earnings from self employment include gross income from a trade or business less trade or business deductions, the distributive share of partnership income from a trade or business, and net income earned as an independent contractor. • Self-employed taxpayers are allowed a deduction for AGI of one-half of the SE tax.
LO 4.11: Compute the qualified business income (QBI) deduction.	• Flow-through entities are eligible for a deduction of 20 percent of QBI, subject to limitations. • QBI is business income only and generally does not include interest, dividends, or capital gains. • Tax law provides a safe-harbor under which income from rental real estate can qualify as QBI if it meets the necessary requirements. • The QBI deduction may not exceed 20 percent of taxable income. • If taxable income exceeds $340,100 for married filing joint returns, $170,050 for all other returns, the QBI deduction is limited by the wage limitation, which is the greater of the wage limit (50 percent of wages) or the wage and capital limit [(25 percent of wages) plus (2.5 percent of qualified business property)]. • QBI from service-related business may also be subject to limitation if income thresholds are surpassed.

QUESTIONS and PROBLEMS

GROUP 1: MULTIPLE CHOICE QUESTIONS

LO 4.1

1. All of the following assets are capital assets, *except*:
   a. A personal automobile
   b. IBM stock
   c. A child's bicycle
   d. Personal furniture
   e. Used car inventory held by a car dealer

LO 4.1

2. Which of the following is a capital asset?
   a. Account receivable
   b. Copyright created by the taxpayer
   c. Copyright (held by the writer)
   d. Business inventory
   e. A taxpayer's residence

LO 4.2

3. Yasmeen purchases stock on January 30, 2021. If she wishes to achieve a long-term holding period, what is the first date that she can sell the stock as a long-term gain?
   a. January 20, 2022
   b. January 31, 2022
   c. February 1, 2022
   d. July 31, 2021
   e. July 30, 2021

LO 4.2

4. To calculate the number of days in the holding period, a taxpayer should:
   a. Include the date of acquisition
   b. Exclude the date of disposition
   c. Exclude the date of acquisition
   d. Include the date of acquisition and disposition

LO 4.3

5. Vijay sells land and receives $5,000 cash, a motorcycle worth $1,600, and two tickets to the Super Bowl with a total face value (cost) of $800 but worth $1,200. In addition, the buyer assumes the mortgage on the land of $12,000. What is Vijay's amount received in this transaction?
   a. $5,000
   b. $7,800
   c. $8,200
   d. $19,800
   e. $20,200

LO 4.3

6. Jaye purchased a building for $100,000. After deducting depreciation of $12,000 through the date of sale, Jaye sells the building for $120,000. What is Jaye's adjusted basis for computing realized gain or loss?
   a. $100,000
   b. $120,000
   c. $88,000
   d. $108,000

LO 4.3

7. Agnes passes away in 2022 and leaves her daughter, Sam, 100 shares of stock. Agnes purchased the stock for $1,000 over twenty-five years ago. It was worth $10,000 on the date of Agnes' death. Sam sells the stock a short time later for $10,500. What is the basis of the stock for computing Sam's realized gain or loss?
   a. $1,000
   b. $10,000
   c. $10,500
   d. Some other amount

LO 4.3

8. Grady gives a watch to his nephew, Fred. Grady's original basis in the watch is $100 and the value of the watch on the date of the gift is $1,000. Fred keeps the watch for a year or two and then sells it for $1,200. What is Fred's basis in the watch for computing his realized gain or loss?
   a. $0. It's a gift so Fred has no basis.
   b. $100. Grady's basis carries over to Fred.
   c. $1,000. Fred takes basis as the market value on the date of the gift.
   d. $1,200. Fred's basis should result in no gain or loss on a gift property.

LO 4.3

9. Bob sells a stock investment for $35,000 cash, and the purchaser assumes Bob's $32,500 debt on the investment. The basis of Bob's stock investment is $55,000. What is the gain or loss realized on the sale?
   a. $10,000 loss
   b. $10,000 gain
   c. $12,500 gain
   d. $22,500 loss
   e. $22,500 gain

LO 4.4

10. In 2022, what is the top tax rate for individual long-term capital gains and the top tax rate for long-term capital gains of collectible items assuming that the net investment income tax does not apply.
   a. 10; 20
   b. 20; 28
   c. 15; 25
   d. 25; 28

LO 4.4

11. In November 2022, Ben and Betty (married, filing jointly) have a long-term capital gain of $54,000 on the sale of stock. They have no other capital gains and losses for the year. Their ordinary income for the year after the standard deduction is $72,500, making their total taxable income for the year $126,500 ($72,500 + $54,000). In 2022, married taxpayers pay 0 percent on long-term gains up to $83,350. What will be their 2022 total tax liability assuming a tax of $8,292 on the $72,500 of ordinary income?
    a. $8,100
    b. $15,160
    c. $14,765
    d. $0

LO 4.4

12. Harold, a single taxpayer, has $30,000 of ordinary income after the standard deduction, and $10,000 in long-term capital gains, for total taxable income of $40,000. For 2022, single taxpayers pay 0 percent on long-term gains up to $41,675. Assuming a tax of $3,398 on the $30,000 of ordinary income, what is Harold's total income tax?
    a. $3,404
    b. $3,398
    c. $1,500
    d. $4,094
    e. $4,898

LO 4.4
LO 4.5

13. In 2022, Tim, a single taxpayer, has ordinary income of $30,000. In addition, he has $2,000 in short-term capital gains, long-term capital losses of $10,000, and long-term capital gains of $4,000. What is Tim's AGI for 2022?
    a. $26,000
    b. $27,000
    c. $30,000
    d. $32,000

LO 4.5

14. Angela sold her personal auto in 2022 for $8,000. She purchased the car for $26,000 in 2015. She has long-term capital gains of $4,000 from the sale of stock in 2022. What is Angela's net recognized capital gain or loss in 2022?
    a. Gain of $4,000
    b. Gain of $1,000
    c. Loss of $14,000
    d. Loss of $3,000

LO 4.5

15. If an individual taxpayer generates a net capital loss in excess of $3,000 in 2022:
    a. The loss can be carried back for 3 years and forward for 5 years
    b. The loss can be carried back for 2 years and forward for 20 years
    c. The loss can be carried forward indefinitely
    d. The loss can be carried forward indefinitely but only offset 80 percent of a future year's capital gains

LO 4.5

16. Serena, a married filing jointly taxpayer, has the following capital gains and losses in 2022:
    - $4,000 short-term capital gain
    - $2,000 short-term capital loss
    - $2,000 long-term capital gains
    - $8,000 long-term capital loss

    What is the amount and nature of Serena's net capital loss carryforward into 2023?
    a. $1,000 long-term loss carryforward
    b. $3,000 long-term loss carryforward
    c. $4,000 long-term loss carryforward
    d. $6,000 long-term loss carryforward

LO 4.6

17. Oscar, a single taxpayer, sells his residence of the last 10 years in January of 2022 for $190,000. Oscar's basis in the residence is $45,000, and his selling expenses are $11,000. If Oscar does not buy a new residence, what is the taxable gain on the sale of his residence?
    a. $145,000
    b. $134,000
    c. $45,000
    d. $9,000
    e. $0

LO 4.6

18. Jim, a single taxpayer, bought his home 25 years ago for $25,000. He has lived in the home continuously since he purchased it. In 2022, he sells his home for $300,000. What is Jim's taxable gain on the sale?
    a. $0
    b. $25,000
    c. $125,000
    d. $275,000

LO 4.6

19. Susan, a single taxpayer, bought her home 25 years ago for $30,000. She has lived in the home continuously since she purchased it. In 2022, she sells her home for $200,000. What is Susan's taxable gain on the sale?
    a. $0
    b. $20,000
    c. $250,000
    d. $170,000

LO 4.6

20. Kevin purchased a house 20 years ago for $100,000 and he has always lived in the house. Three years ago Kevin married Karen, and she has lived in the house since their marriage. If they sell Kevin's house in December 2022 for $425,000, what is their taxable gain on a joint tax return?
    a. $0
    b. $75,000
    c. $125,000
    d. $250,000

LO 4.6

21. Gene, a single taxpayer, purchased a house eighteen months ago for $350,000. If Gene sells his house due to unforeseen circumstances for $550,000 after living in it for a full eighteen months, what is his taxable gain?
    a. $0
    b. $12,500
    c. $50,000
    d. $200,000

LO 4.7

22. Which of the following is *true* about the rental of real estate?
    a. Depreciation and maintenance expenses for an apartment complex are deductible.
    b. The expenses deductions for a home rented for 100 days and used for personal use for seventeen days will be limited to the gross rental income.
    c. If a home is rented for less than fifteen days a year, the rent is not taxable.
    d. Repairs on rental property are deductible by the taxpayer.
    e. All of the above.

LO 4.7

23. Jonathan rents his home for twelve days during the 2022 World Cup of US Soccer. Due to the popularity of the event, he earns $4,000 in rent. He spends $150 on a cleaning service immediately after the rental. He does not rent the home otherwise during the year. What is Jonathan's rental income and deductions from this short-term rental?
    a. $0 income and $0 deduction
    b. $4,000 income and $150 deduction
    c. $4,000 income and $0 deduction
    d. $4,000 income and $5 (12/365 × $150)

LO 4.7

24. Juanita rents a vacation condo for 120 days and uses the condo for herself for twenty days. What allocation percentage will Juanita apply to the condo's operating expenses (for example, insurance, utilities, etc.) to compute the rental portion under the IRS allocation method?
    a. 32.8 percent (120/365)
    b. 5.4 percent (20/365)
    c. 85.7 percent (120/140)
    d. 38.4 percent (140/365)

LO 4.7

25. John owns a second home in Palm Springs, CA. During the year, he rented the house for $5,000 for fifty-six days and used the house for fourteen days during the summer. The house remained vacant during the remainder of the year. The expenses for the home included $5,000 in mortgage interest, $850 in property taxes, $900 for utilities and maintenance, and $3,500 of depreciation. What is John's deductible rental loss, before considering the passive loss limitations?
    a. $0
    b. $200
    c. $875
    d. $2,500
    e. $3,200

LO 4.8

26. Helen, a single taxpayer, has modified adjusted gross income (before passive losses) of $126,000. During the tax year, Helen's rental house generated a loss of $15,000. Assuming Helen is actively involved in the management of the property, what is the amount of Helen's passive loss deduction from the rental house?
    a. $0
    b. $3,000
    c. $10,000
    d. $12,000
    e. $13,000

LO 4.8

27. Which of the following is *not* classified as portfolio income for tax purposes?
    a. Interest income on savings accounts
    b. Dividends paid from a credit union
    c. Net rental income from real estate partnership
    d. Dividend income from stock
    e. All of the above are classified as portfolio income

LO 4.8

28. Which of the following types of income is passive income?
    a. Net rental income from real estate limited partnership investments
    b. Dividends from domestic corporations
    c. Wages
    d. Interest income from certificates of deposit
    e. None of the above

LO 4.8

29. Which of the following is classified as active income?
    a. Self-employment income from a small business
    b. Interest income
    c. Limited partnership income
    d. Bonus paid by an employer to an employee
    e. a. and d.

LO 4.8

30. Nancy has active modified adjusted gross income before passive losses of $75,000. She has a loss of $5,000 on a rental property she actively manages. How much of the loss is she allowed to take against the $75,000 of other income?
    a. None
    b. $2,500
    c. $5,000
    d. $25,000

LO 4.8

31. Ned has active modified adjusted gross income before passive losses of $250,000. He has a loss of $15,000 on rental property he actively manages. How much of the loss is he allowed to take against the $250,000 of other income?
    a. $15,000
    b. $10,000
    c. $5,000
    d. None

LO 4.8

32. Norm is a real estate professional with a real estate trade or business as defined in the tax law. He has $80,000 of business income and $40,000 of losses from actively managed real estate rentals. How much of the $40,000 in losses is he allowed to claim on his tax return?
    a. $40,000
    b. $25,000
    c. $20,000
    d. None

LO 4.9

33. Bonita earns $31,000 from her job, and she has $1,000 of interest income. She has itemized deductions of $35,000. There are no casualty or theft losses in the itemized deductions. What is Bonita's net operating loss for the current year?
    a. $0
    b. $1,000
    c. $3,000
    d. $4,000
    e. Some other amount

LO 4.9

34. Jim has a net operating loss in 2022. If he does not make any special elections, what is the first year to which Jim carries the net operating loss?
    a. 2017
    b. 2018
    c. 2019
    d. 2021
    e. 2023

LO 4.10

35. For 2022, Roberta is a self-employed truck driver with earnings of $45,000 from her business. During the year, Roberta received $2,500 in interest income and dividends of $500. She also sold investment property and recognized a $1,500 gain. What is the amount of Roberta's self-employment tax (Social Security and Medicare taxes) liability for 2022?
    a. $7,304
    b. $6,641
    c. $6,358
    d. $6,885
    e. $7,455

LO 4.10

36. Which of the following is not subject to self-employment tax?
    a. Gain on the sale of real estate held for investment
    b. Net earnings of a self-employed lawyer
    c. Distributive share of earnings of a partnership
    d. Net earnings of the owner of a shoe store
    e. Net earnings of the owner of a dry cleaner

LO 4.10

37. Katrina has wages of $150,000 in 2022. She also operates a small business that generated net profits of $10,000. What is Katrina's total self-employment tax?
    a. $0
    b. $267.82
    c. $290.00
    d. $1,530.00

LO 4.11

38. The qualified business income deduction is unavailable to which of the following businesses:
    a. A sole proprietor dental practice that generates about $70,000 in income each year
    b. An incorporated small tools manufacturer
    c. A partnership operated by a husband and wife that sells wood carvings over the Internet
    d. An S corporation that owns and operates a restaurant. The S corporation has six different owners.
    e. The QBI deduction is available to all of the above.

LO 4.11

39. Qualified business income does not include which of the following:
    a. Income from sales of goods
    b. Deductions related to cost of goods sold
    c. Deductions for business expenses such as rent
    d. Interest income from an investment in bonds

LO 4.11

40. In 2022, Tracy generates a $10,000 loss from an otherwise qualified business activity. Fortunately, she also works as an employee and has taxable wages of $40,000. Tracy's 2022 QBI deduction is
    a. $0
    b. $2,000
    c. $8,000
    d. $6,000

GROUP 2: PROBLEMS

LO 4.1 LO 4.2 LO 4.3

1. Martin sells a stock investment for $26,000 on August 2, 2022. Martin's adjusted basis in the stock is $15,000.
    a. If Martin acquired the stock on November 15, 2020, calculate the amount and the nature of the gain or loss.
    b. If Martin had acquired the stock on September 10, 2021, calculate the amount and nature of the gain or loss.

LO 4.1 LO 4.2 LO 4.3 LO 4.5

2. During 2022, Tom sold GM stock for $10,000. The stock was purchased four years ago for $13,000. Tom also sold Ford Motor Company bonds for $35,000. The bonds were purchased two months ago for $30,000. Home Depot stock, purchased two years ago for $1,000, was sold by Tom for $2,500. Calculate Tom's net gain or loss, and indicate the nature of the gain or loss.

LO 4.1
LO 4.2
LO 4.3
LO 4.5

3. Charu Khanna received a Form 1099-B showing the following stock transactions and basis during 2022:

2022 Combined Forms 1099

This is important tax information and is being furnished to the IRS (except as indicated). If you are required to file a return, a negligence penalty or other sanction may be imposed on you if this income is taxable and the IRS determines that it has not been reported.

Copy B For Recipient
OMB No. 1545-0110

Friar Tuck Investments
38 Wall Street, 8th Floor
New York, NY 10005

Chari Khanna
206 Commonwealth Ave, Apt 3B.
Boston, MA 02116

Account Number	Tax ID
5612311789	***-**-4023
Payer's Federal Tax ID	
33-1357246	
Financial Adviser/Phone	
John Little 888-555-1212	

Form 1099-B — Proceeds from Broker and Barter Exchange Transactions

Box 6: Gross Proceeds Box 1 Security description (CUSIP)	Quantity sold	Box 5: Not checked Box 1b Date acquired	Box 1c Date sold or disposed	Box 3: Basis reported to IRS Box 1d Proceeds	Box 1e Cost or other basis	Box 2: Type of Gain or Loss: Short Term Box 1g Wash sale loss disallowed	Gain/(Loss) amount
Gold Corp	500	02/12/2022	09/05/2022	50,000	61,500	-	(11,500)
Orange Corp	100	11/15/2021	07/12/2022	21,000	19,200		1,800

Box 6: Gross Proceeds Box 1 Security description (CUSIP)	Quantity sold	Box 5: Not checked Box 1b Date acquired	Box 1c Date sold or disposed	Box 3: Basis reported to IRS Box 1d Proceeds	Box 1e Cost or other basis	Box 2: Type of Gain or Loss: Long Term Box 1g Wash sale loss disallowed	Gain/(Loss) amount
Green Corp	4,000	06/04/2011	08/05/2022	11,500	3,200	-	8,300
Blue Corp	50	02/04/2012	10/01/2022	16,000	21,700		(5,700)

None of the stock is qualified small business stock. The stock basis was reported to the IRS. Calculate Charu's net capital gain or loss using Schedule D only on Pages 4-65 through 4-66.

LO 4.3

4. Jocasta owns an apartment complex that she purchased six years ago for $700,000. Jocasta has made $65,000 of capital improvements on the complex, and her depreciation claimed on the building to date is $125,000. Calculate Jocasta's adjusted basis in the building.

LO 4.3

5. Chrissy receives 200 shares of Chevron stock as a gift from her father. The father purchased the stock for $8,000 10 years ago and it is worth $10,000 at the date of the gift.
   a. If Chrissy sells the stock for $11,200, calculate the amount of the realized gain or loss on the sale.
   b. If Chrissy sells the stock for $7,500, calculate the amount of the realized gain or loss on the sale.

LO 4.3

6. John receives 200 shares of Chevron stock as a gift from his mother. The mother purchased the stock for $10,000 eight years ago and it is now worth $8,000 at the date of the gift.
   a. If John sells the stock for $11,200, calculate the amount of the realized gain or loss on the sale.
   b. If John sells the stock for $7,500, calculate the amount of the realized gain or loss.
   c. If John sells the stock for $9,000, calculate the amount of the realized gain or loss.

LO 4.4
LO 4.5

7. In 2022, Michael has net short-term capital losses of $1,700, a net long-term capital loss of $17,000, and other ordinary taxable income of $45,000.
   a. Calculate the amount of Michael's deduction for capital losses for 2022.
   b. Calculate the amount and nature of his capital loss carryforward.
   c. For how long may Michael carry forward the unused loss?

LO 4.6 8. Larry Gaines, a single taxpayer, age 42, sells his personal residence on November 12, 2022, for $168,000. He lived in the house for seven years. The expenses of the sale are $10,080, and he has made capital improvements of $8,800. Larry's cost basis in his residence is $87,500. On November 30, 2021, Larry purchases and occupies a new residence at a cost of $155,000. Calculate Larry's realized gain, recognized gain, and the adjusted basis of his new residence.

LO 4.6 9. On July 1, 2022, Ted, age 73 and single, sells his personal residence of the last thirty years for $365,000. Ted's basis in his residence is $50,000. The expenses associated with the sale of his home total $21,000. On December 15, 2022, Ted purchases and occupies a new residence at a cost of $225,000. Calculate Ted's realized gain, recognized gain, and the adjusted basis of his new residence.

LO 4.6 10. Kendra and Lloyd get married on July 1, 2022 and will file jointly in 2022. Both of them owned a home prior to marriage, but they agree that they wish to no live together in one of the homes. Kendra's home was purchased on September 1, 2021 for $270,000 and is now worth $290,000. Lloyd's home was purchased in 2018 for $170,000 and is now worth $215,000. Both believe that the housing market in their area will remain strong (and maybe prices will increase). They also plan to start having children in two or three years and expect to have to move into a larger home than either of their existing homes now. Describe the possible alternatives available to Kendra and Lloyd with respect to excluding the gain on the sale of the homes.

LO 4.7 11. Dick owns a house that he rents to college students. Dick receives $800 per month rent and incurs the following expenses during the year:

Real estate taxes	$1,250
Mortgage interest	1,500
Insurance	425
Repairs	562
Association dues	1,500

Dick purchased the house in 1988 for $48,000. The house is fully depreciated. Calculate Dick's net rental income for the year, assuming the house was rented for a full twelve months.

LO 4.7 12. Sherry rents her vacation home for six months and lives in it for six months during the year. Her gross rental income during the year is $6,000. Total real estate taxes for the home are $2,200, and interest on the home mortgage is $4,000. Annual utilities and maintenance expenses total $2,000, and depreciation expense is $4,500. Calculate Sherry's deductible depreciation, the net income or loss from the vacation home, and the loss carryforward, if any.

LO 4.7 13. On May 1, 2022, Ella leases her condo to Fitz for a 12-month lease period starting May 1 for $1,000 per month. Ella requires that Fitz pay first month's rent, last month's rent and a $1,000 security deposit (total $3,000) prior to turning over the keys to Fitz. The security deposit is refundable as long as Fitz abides by the terms of the lease agreement. Compute the amount of gross rental income Ella will recognize in 2022.

LO 4.8 14. Walter, a single taxpayer, purchased a limited partnership interest in a tax shelter in 1995. He also acquired a rental house in 2022, which he actively manages. During 2022, Walter's share of the partnership's losses was $30,000, and his rental house generated $20,000 in losses. Walter's modified adjusted gross income before passive losses is $120,000.

a. Calculate the amount of Walter's allowable loss for rental house activities for 2022.
b. Calculate the amount of Walter's allowable loss for the partnership activities for 2022.
c. What may be done with the unused losses, if anything?

SCHEDULE D
(Form 1040)

Department of the Treasury
Internal Revenue Service

Capital Gains and Losses

Attach to Form 1040, 1040-SR, or 1040-NR.
Go to *www.irs.gov/ScheduleD* for instructions and the latest information.
Use Form 8949 to list your transactions for lines 1b, 2, 3, 8b, 9, and 10.

OMB No. 1545-0074
2022
Attachment Sequence No. **12**

Name(s) shown on return | **Your social security number**

Did you dispose of any investment(s) in a qualified opportunity fund during the tax year? ☐ **Yes** ☐ **No**
If "Yes," attach Form 8949 and see its instructions for additional requirements for reporting your gain or loss.

Part I Short-Term Capital Gains and Losses—Generally Assets Held One Year or Less (see instructions)

See instructions for how to figure the amounts to enter on the lines below. This form may be easier to complete if you round off cents to whole dollars.	**(d)** Proceeds (sales price)	**(e)** Cost (or other basis)	**(g)** Adjustments to gain or loss from Form(s) 8949, Part I, line 2, column (g)	**(h) Gain or (loss)** Subtract column (e) from column (d) and combine the result with column (g)
1a Totals for all short-term transactions reported on Form 1099-B for which basis was reported to the IRS and for which you have no adjustments (see instructions). However, if you choose to report all these transactions on Form 8949, leave this line blank and go to line 1b .				
1b Totals for all transactions reported on Form(s) 8949 with **Box A** checked				
2 Totals for all transactions reported on Form(s) 8949 with **Box B** checked				
3 Totals for all transactions reported on Form(s) 8949 with **Box C** checked				

4 Short-term gain from Form 6252 and short-term gain or (loss) from Forms 4684, 6781, and 8824 . .	**4**	
5 Net short-term gain or (loss) from partnerships, S corporations, estates, and trusts from Schedule(s) K-1	**5**	
6 Short-term capital loss carryover. Enter the amount, if any, from line 8 of your **Capital Loss Carryover Worksheet** in the instructions	**6**	( )
7 **Net short-term capital gain or (loss).** Combine lines 1a through 6 in column (h). If you have any long-term capital gains or losses, go to Part II below. Otherwise, go to Part III on the back	**7**	

Part II Long-Term Capital Gains and Losses—Generally Assets Held More Than One Year (see instructions)

See instructions for how to figure the amounts to enter on the lines below. This form may be easier to complete if you round off cents to whole dollars.	**(d)** Proceeds (sales price)	**(e)** Cost (or other basis)	**(g)** Adjustments to gain or loss from Form(s) 8949, Part II, line 2, column (g)	**(h) Gain or (loss)** Subtract column (e) from column (d) and combine the result with column (g)
8a Totals for all long-term transactions reported on Form 1099-B for which basis was reported to the IRS and for which you have no adjustments (see instructions). However, if you choose to report all these transactions on Form 8949, leave this line blank and go to line 8b .				
8b Totals for all transactions reported on Form(s) 8949 with **Box D** checked				
9 Totals for all transactions reported on Form(s) 8949 with **Box E** checked				
10 Totals for all transactions reported on Form(s) 8949 with **Box F** checked.				

11 Gain from Form 4797, Part I; long-term gain from Forms 2439 and 6252; and long-term gain or (loss) from Forms 4684, 6781, and 8824	**11**	
12 Net long-term gain or (loss) from partnerships, S corporations, estates, and trusts from Schedule(s) K-1	**12**	
13 Capital gain distributions. See the instructions	**13**	
14 Long-term capital loss carryover. Enter the amount, if any, from line 13 of your **Capital Loss Carryover Worksheet** in the instructions	**14**	( )
15 **Net long-term capital gain or (loss).** Combine lines 8a through 14 in column (h). Then, go to Part III on the back	**15**	

For Paperwork Reduction Act Notice, see your tax return instructions. Cat. No. 11338H **Schedule D (Form 1040) 2022**

Schedule D (Form 1040) 2022 Page **2**

Part III **Summary**

16 Combine lines 7 and 15 and enter the result **16**

- If line 16 is a **gain**, enter the amount from line 16 on Form 1040, 1040-SR, or 1040-NR, line 7. Then, go to line 17 below.
- If line 16 is a **loss**, skip lines 17 through 20 below. Then, go to line 21. Also be sure to complete line 22.
- If line 16 is **zero**, skip lines 17 through 21 below and enter -0- on Form 1040, 1040-SR, or 1040-NR, line 7. Then, go to line 22.

17 Are lines 15 and 16 **both** gains?
☐ **Yes.** Go to line 18.
☐ **No.** Skip lines 18 through 21, and go to line 22.

18 If you are required to complete the **28% Rate Gain Worksheet** (see instructions), enter the amount, if any, from line 7 of that worksheet **18**

19 If you are required to complete the **Unrecaptured Section 1250 Gain Worksheet** (see instructions), enter the amount, if any, from line 18 of that worksheet **19**

20 Are lines 18 and 19 both zero or blank and you are not filing Form 4952?
☐ **Yes.** Complete the **Qualified Dividends and Capital Gain Tax Worksheet** in the instructions for Form 1040, line 16. **Don't** complete lines 21 and 22 below.

☐ **No.** Complete the **Schedule D Tax Worksheet** in the instructions. **Don't** complete lines 21 and 22 below.

21 If line 16 is a loss, enter here and on Form 1040, 1040-SR, or 1040-NR, line 7, the **smaller** of:

- The loss on line 16; or
- ($3,000), or if married filing separately, ($1,500) } . . . . **21** (   )

Note: When figuring which amount is smaller, treat both amounts as positive numbers.

22 Do you have qualified dividends on Form 1040, 1040-SR, or 1040-NR, line 3a?

☐ **Yes.** Complete the **Qualified Dividends and Capital Gain Tax Worksheet** in the instructions for Form 1040, line 16.

☐ **No.** Complete the rest of Form 1040, 1040-SR, or 1040-NR.

Schedule D (Form 1040) 2022

LO 4.8

15. Clifford Johnson has a limited partnership investment and a rental condominium. Clifford actively manages the rental condominium. During 2022, his share of the loss from the limited partnership was $11,000, and his loss from the rental condo was $18,000. Assuming Clifford's modified adjusted gross income is $132,000 for 2022, and he has no prior year unallowed losses from either activity, complete page 1 of Form 8582 on Page 4-69.

LO 4.9

16. Tyler, a single taxpayer, generates business income of $3,000 in 2019. In 2020, he generates an NOL of $5,000. In 2021, he generates business income of $1,000. In 2022, his business generates income of $1,100. What is Tyler's NOL carryforward into 2023, if any?

LO 4.9

17. Julie, a single taxpayer, has completed her 2022 Schedule C and her net loss is $40,000. Her only other income is wages of $30,000. Julie takes the standard deduction of $12,950 in 2022.
    a. Calculate Julie's taxable income or loss.
    b. Calculate the business and nonbusiness portions of her taxable income or loss.
    c. Determine Julie's 2022 NOL.

LO 4.10

18. Tommy Staples is a self-employed surfboard maker in 2022. His Schedule C net income is $128,000 for the year. He also has a part-time job and earns $29,000 in wages subject to FICA taxes. Calculate James' self-employment tax for 2022 using Schedule SE on Page 4-71.

LO 4.11

19. Sanjay is a single taxpayer that operates a curry cart on the streets of Baltimore. The business is operated as a sole proprietorship with no employees (Sanjay does everything). Sanjay's Schedule C reports income of $87,000. His taxable income is $80,000 and includes no capital gains. Compute Sanjay's QBI deduction.

LO 4.11

20. Rob Wriggle operates a small plumbing supplies business as a sole proprietor. In 2022, the plumbing business has gross business income of $421,000 and business expenses of $267,000, including wages paid of $58,000. The business sold some land that had been held for investment generating a long-term capital gain of $15,000. The business has $300,000 of qualified business property in 2022. Rob's wife, Marie, has wage income of $250,000. They jointly sold stocks in 2022 and generated a long-term capital gain of $13,000. Rob and Marie have no dependents and in 2022, they take the standard deduction of $25,900.
    a. What is Rob and Marie's taxable income before the QBI deduction?
    b. What is Rob and Marie's QBI?
    c. What is Rob and Marie's QBI deduction?
    d. Complete Form 8995-A on Pages 4-73 and 4-74 to report Rob's QBI deduction.

GROUP 3:
WRITING ASSIGNMENT

RESEARCH

You recently received the following e-mail from a client and friend:

Hey Great Student,

I cannot believe it is almost year-end! Only a few days before it's 2023.

As you recall, I was lucky enough to win big at the casino back on New Year's Day earlier this year (thanks for celebrating with me). I took the $3,000 I won and bought 100 shares of stock in that cool new smartphone app company, TriviaAddiction. I just love playing that game. Anyway, the stock has done well, and I am thinking of selling before year end now that the price has reached $240 per share. Since you are my tax adviser, I thought I'd ask a couple of questions:

1. Is there any reason to wait and sell later?
2. If I don't sell, the price might go down (TriviaMaster seems to be replacing TriviaAddiction as the "hot" new game). I'm thinking the price might be as low as $220 by early next year.

My taxable income this year and next year is expected to be $40,000 (not including the stock sale). I think that puts me in the 12-percent tax bracket? Any suggestions on what I should do?

Thanks!

Sue

Prepare an e-mail to your friend Sue addressing her questions. Be certain to include estimates of the different after-tax outcomes she is suggesting. Sue is a single taxpayer and not a tax expert and so your language should reflect her limited understanding of tax law and avoid technical jargon. Although Sue is your friend, she is also a client and your e-mail should maintain a professional style.

Form **8582**

Department of the Treasury
Internal Revenue Service

Passive Activity Loss Limitations

See separate instructions.
Attach to Form 1040, 1040-SR, or 1041.
Go to *www.irs.gov/Form8582* for instructions and the latest information.

OMB No. 1545-1008
2022
Attachment Sequence No. **858**

Name(s) shown on return | **Identifying number**

Part I **2022 Passive Activity Loss**
Caution: Complete Parts IV and V before completing Part I.

Rental Real Estate Activities With Active Participation (For the definition of active participation, see ***Special Allowance for Rental Real Estate Activities*** in the instructions.)

1a	Activities with net income (enter the amount from Part IV, column (a))	**1a**			
b	Activities with net loss (enter the amount from Part IV, column (b))	**1b**	( )		
c	Prior years' unallowed losses (enter the amount from Part IV, column (c))	**1c**	( )		
d	Combine lines 1a, 1b, and 1c			**1d**	

All Other Passive Activities

2a	Activities with net income (enter the amount from Part V, column (a))	**2a**			
b	Activities with net loss (enter the amount from Part V, column (b))	**2b**	( )		
c	Prior years' unallowed losses (enter the amount from Part V, column (c))	**2c**	( )		
d	Combine lines 2a, 2b, and 2c			**2d**	
3	Combine lines 1d and 2d. If this line is zero or more, stop here and include this form with your return; all losses are allowed, including any prior year unallowed losses entered on line 1c or 2c. Report the losses on the forms and schedules normally used			**3**	

If line 3 is a loss and:
- Line 1d is a loss, go to Part II.
- Line 2d is a loss (and line 1d is zero or more), skip Part II and go to line 10.

Caution: If your filing status is married filing separately and you lived with your spouse at any time during the year, **do not** complete Part II. Instead, go to line 10.

Part II **Special Allowance for Rental Real Estate Activities With Active Participation**
Note: Enter all numbers in Part II as positive amounts. See instructions for an example.

4	Enter the **smaller** of the loss on line 1d or the loss on line 3			**4**	
5	Enter $150,000. If married filing separately, see instructions	**5**			
6	Enter modified adjusted gross income, but not less than zero. See instructions	**6**			
	Note: If line 6 is greater than or equal to line 5, skip lines 7 and 8 and enter -0- on line 9. Otherwise, go to line 7.				
7	Subtract line 6 from line 5	**7**			
8	Multiply line 7 by 50% (0.50). **Do not** enter more than $25,000. If married filing separately, see instructions			**8**	
9	Enter the **smaller** of line 4 or line 8			**9**	

Part III **Total Losses Allowed**

10	Add the income, if any, on lines 1a and 2a and enter the total	**10**	
11	**Total losses allowed from all passive activities for 2022.** Add lines 9 and 10. See instructions to find out how to report the losses on your tax return	**11**	

Part IV **Complete This Part Before Part I, Lines 1a, 1b, and 1c.** See instructions.

Name of activity	Current year		Prior years	Overall gain or loss	
	(a) Net income (line 1a)	**(b)** Net loss (line 1b)	**(c)** Unallowed loss (line 1c)	**(d)** Gain	**(e)** Loss
Total. Enter on Part I, lines 1a, 1b, and 1c					

SCHEDULE SE (Form 1040) Department of the Treasury Internal Revenue Service	**Self-Employment Tax** Go to *www.irs.gov/ScheduleSE* for instructions and the latest information. Attach to Form 1040, 1040-SR, or 1040-NR.	OMB No. 1545-0074 **2022** Attachment Sequence No. **17**

Name of person with self-employment income (as shown on Form 1040, 1040-SR, or 1040-NR)	Social security number of person with **self-employment** income

Part I Self-Employment Tax

Note: If your only income subject to self-employment tax is **church employee income**, see instructions for how to report your income and the definition of church employee income.

A If you are a minister, member of a religious order, or Christian Science practitioner **and** you filed Form 4361, but you had $400 or more of **other** net earnings from self-employment, check here and continue with Part I . . . . ☐

Skip lines 1a and 1b if you use the farm optional method in Part II. See instructions.

1a	Net farm profit or (loss) from Schedule F, line 34, and farm partnerships, Schedule K-1 (Form 1065), box 14, code A			**1a**	
b	If you received social security retirement or disability benefits, enter the amount of Conservation Reserve Program payments included on Schedule F, line 4b, or listed on Schedule K-1 (Form 1065), box 20, code AH			**1b**	( )
	Skip line 2 if you use the nonfarm optional method in Part II. See instructions.				
2	Net profit or (loss) from Schedule C, line 31; and Schedule K-1 (Form 1065), box 14, code A (other than farming). See instructions for other income to report or if you are a minister or member of a religious order			**2**	
3	Combine lines 1a, 1b, and 2			**3**	
4a	If line 3 is more than zero, multiply line 3 by 92.35% (0.9235). Otherwise, enter amount from line 3 . **Note:** If line 4a is less than $400 due to Conservation Reserve Program payments on line 1b, see instructions.			**4a**	
b	If you elect one or both of the optional methods, enter the total of lines 15 and 17 here			**4b**	
c	Combine lines 4a and 4b. If less than $400, **stop**; you don't owe self-employment tax. **Exception:** If less than $400 and you had **church employee income**, enter -0- and continue			**4c**	
5a	Enter your **church employee income** from Form W-2. See instructions for definition of church employee income	**5a**			
b	Multiply line 5a by 92.35% (0.9235). If less than $100, enter -0-			**5b**	
6	Add lines 4c and 5b			**6**	
7	Maximum amount of combined wages and self-employment earnings subject to social security tax or the 6.2% portion of the 7.65% railroad retirement (tier 1) tax for 2022			**7**	147,000
8a	Total social security wages and tips (total of boxes 3 and 7 on Form(s) W-2) and railroad retirement (tier 1) compensation. If $147,000 or more, skip lines 8b through 10, and go to line 11	**8a**			
b	Unreported tips subject to social security tax from Form 4137, line 10 . . .	**8b**			
c	Wages subject to social security tax from Form 8919, line 10	**8c**			
d	Add lines 8a, 8b, and 8c			**8d**	
9	Subtract line 8d from line 7. If zero or less, enter -0- here and on line 10 and go to line 11			**9**	
10	Multiply the **smaller** of line 6 or line 9 by 12.4% (0.124)			**10**	
11	Multiply line 6 by 2.9% (0.029)			**11**	
12	**Self-employment tax.** Add lines 10 and 11. Enter here and on **Schedule 2 (Form 1040), line 4** . .			**12**	
13	**Deduction for one-half of self-employment tax.** Multiply line 12 by 50% (0.50). Enter here and on **Schedule 1 (Form 1040), line 15**	**13**			

Part II Optional Methods To Figure Net Earnings (see instructions)

Farm Optional Method. You may use this method **only** if **(a)** your gross farm income[1] wasn't more than $9,060, **or (b)** your net farm profits[2] were less than $6,540.

14	Maximum income for optional methods	**14**	6,040
15	Enter the **smaller** of: two-thirds (2/3) of gross farm income[1] (not less than zero) **or** $6,040. Also, include this amount on line 4b above	**15**	

Nonfarm Optional Method. You may use this method **only** if **(a)** your net nonfarm profits[3] were less than $6,540 and also less than 72.189% of your gross nonfarm income,[4] **and (b)** you had net earnings from self-employment of at least $400 in 2 of the prior 3 years. **Caution:** You may use this method no more than five times.

16	Subtract line 15 from line 14	**16**	
17	Enter the **smaller** of: two-thirds (2/3) of gross nonfarm income[4] (not less than zero) **or** the amount on line 16. Also, include this amount on line 4b above	**17**	

[1] From Sch. F, line 9; and Sch. K-1 (Form 1065), box 14, code B.

[2] From Sch. F, line 34; and Sch. K-1 (Form 1065), box 14, code A—minus the amount you would have entered on line 1b had you not used the optional method.

[3] From Sch. C, line 31; and Sch. K-1 (Form 1065), box 14, code A.

[4] From Sch. C, line 7; and Sch. K-1 (Form 1065), box 14, code C.

For Paperwork Reduction Act Notice, see your tax return instructions. Cat. No. 11358Z **Schedule SE (Form 1040) 2022**

Form **8995-A** Department of the Treasury Internal Revenue Service

Qualified Business Income Deduction

▶ Attach to your tax return.

▶ Go to *www.irs.gov/Form8995A* for instructions and the latest information.

OMB No. 1545-2294 2021* Attachment Sequence No. **55A**

Name(s) shown on return | **Your taxpayer identification number**

Note: *You can claim the qualified business income deduction* **only** *if you have qualified business income from a qualified trade or business, real estate investment trust dividends, publicly traded partnership income, or a domestic production activities deduction passed through from an agricultural or horticultural cooperative. See instructions. Use this form if your taxable income, before your qualified business income deduction, is above $164,900 ($164,925 if married filing separately; $329,800 if married filing jointly), or you're a patron of an agricultural or horticultural cooperative.*

Part I Trade, Business, or Aggregation Information

Complete Schedules A, B, and/or C (Form 8995-A), as applicable, before starting Part I. Attach additional worksheets when needed. See instructions.

1	(a) Trade, business, or aggregation name	(b) Check if specified service	(c) Check if aggregation	(d) Taxpayer identification number	(e) Check if patron
A		☐	☐		☐
B		☐	☐		☐
C		☐	☐		☐

Part II Determine Your Adjusted Qualified Business Income

			A	B	C
2	Qualified business income from the trade, business, or aggregation. See instructions	2			
3	Multiply line 2 by 20% (0.20). If your taxable income is $164,900 or less ($164,925 if married filing separately; $329,800 if married filing jointly), skip lines 4 through 12 and enter the amount from line 3 on line 13	3			
4	Allocable share of W-2 wages from the trade, business, or aggregation	4			
5	Multiply line 4 by 50% (0.50)	5			
6	Multiply line 4 by 25% (0.25)	6			
7	Allocable share of the unadjusted basis immediately after acquisition (UBIA) of all qualified property	7			
8	Multiply line 7 by 2.5% (0.025)	8			
9	Add lines 6 and 8	9			
10	Enter the greater of line 5 or line 9	10			
11	W-2 wage and UBIA of qualified property limitation. Enter the smaller of line 3 or line 10	11			
12	Phased-in reduction. Enter the amount from line 26, if any. See instructions	12			
13	Qualified business income deduction before patron reduction. Enter the greater of line 11 or line 12	13			
14	Patron reduction. Enter the amount from Schedule D (Form 8995-A), line 6, if any. See instructions	14			
15	Qualified business income component. Subtract line 14 from line 13	15			
16	Total qualified business income component. Add all amounts reported on line 15 ▶	16			

For Privacy Act and Paperwork Reduction Act Notice, see separate instructions. Cat. No. 71661B Form **8995-A** (2021)

*Please go to **www.irs.gov** to download the latest Form 8995-A. The 2022 version of Form 8995-A was not available as we went to print. If using the prior year form included in the textbook, be sure and use updated income limits on Line 3 and Line 21 ($340,100 for married filing joint returns, $170,050 for all other returns).

Form 8995-A (2021) Page **2**

Part III Phased-in Reduction

Complete Part III only if your taxable income is more than $164,900 but not $214,900 ($164,925 and $214,925 if married filing separately; $329,800 and $429,800 if married filing jointly) and line 10 is less than line 3. Otherwise, skip Part III.

				A	B	C
17	Enter the amounts from line 3		17			
18	Enter the amounts from line 10		18			
19	Subtract line 18 from line 17		19			
20	Taxable income before qualified business income deduction	20				
21	Threshold. Enter $164,900 ($164,925 if married filing separately; $329,800 if married filing jointly)	21				
22	Subtract line 21 from line 20	22				
23	Phase-in range. Enter $50,000 ($100,000 if married filing jointly)	23				
24	Phase-in percentage. Divide line 22 by line 23	24 %				
25	Total phase-in reduction. Multiply line 19 by line 24		25			
26	Qualified business income after phase-in reduction. Subtract line 25 from line 17. Enter this amount here and on line 12, for the corresponding trade or business		26			

Part IV Determine Your Qualified Business Income Deduction

27	Total qualified business income component from all qualified trades, businesses, or aggregations. Enter the amount from line 16	27			
28	Qualified REIT dividends and publicly traded partnership (PTP) income or (loss). See instructions	28			
29	Qualified REIT dividends and PTP (loss) carryforward from prior years	29	( )		
30	Total qualified REIT dividends and PTP income. Combine lines 28 and 29. If less than zero, enter -0-	30			
31	REIT and PTP component. Multiply line 30 by 20% (0.20)	31			
32	Qualified business income deduction before the income limitation. Add lines 27 and 31 ▶			32	
33	Taxable income before qualified business income deduction	33			
34	Net capital gain. See instructions	34			
35	Subtract line 34 from line 33. If zero or less, enter -0-			35	
36	Income limitation. Multiply line 35 by 20% (0.20)			36	
37	Qualified business income deduction before the domestic production activities deduction (DPAD) under section 199A(g). Enter the smaller of line 32 or line 36 ▶			37	
38	DPAD under section 199A(g) allocated from an agricultural or horticultural cooperative. Don't enter more than line 33 minus line 37			38	
39	Total qualified business income deduction. Add lines 37 and 38 ▶			39	
40	Total qualified REIT dividends and PTP (loss) carryforward. Combine lines 28 and 29. If zero or greater, enter -0-			40	( )

Form **8995-A** (2021)

GROUP 4:
COMPREHENSIVE PROBLEMS

1. Theodore E. Lariat is a single taxpayer born on September 22, 1974. He was appointed the new coach of the Nashville Country Stars soccer team in January 2022. His address, Social Security number and wages are reported on his Form W-2:

a Employee's social security number	775-89-9532
OMB No. 1545-0008	Safe, accurate, FAST! Use IRS e-file. Visit the IRS website at www.irs.gov/efile
b Employer identification number (EIN)	36-1389676
c Employer's name, address, and ZIP code	Nashville Country Stars Soccer Club 501 Interstate Blvd S 10th Floor Nashville, TN 37210
d Control number	
e Employee's first name and initial / Last name / Suff.	Theodore Lariat 140 Whitsett Road Nashville, TN 37210
f Employee's address and ZIP code	
1 Wages, tips, other compensation	124,800.00
2 Federal income tax withheld	20,000.00
3 Social security wages	130,000.00
4 Social security tax withheld	8,060.00
5 Medicare wages and tips	130,000.00
6 Medicare tax withheld	1,885.00
7 Social security tips	
8 Allocated tips	
9	
10 Dependent care benefits	
11 Nonqualified plans	
12a See instructions for box 12	DD 5,700.00
12b	D 5,200.00
12c	
12d	
13 Statutory employee / Retirement plan / Third-party sick pay	☐ / ☒ / ☐
14 Other	
15 State / Employer's state ID number	TN
16 State wages, tips, etc.	
17 State income tax	
18 Local wages, tips, etc.	
19 Local income tax	
20 Locality name	

Form **W-2** Wage and Tax Statement 2022 Department of the Treasury—Internal Revenue Service

Copy B—To Be Filed With Employee's FEDERAL Tax Return.
This information is being furnished to the Internal Revenue Service.

Theodore was previously the coach at a different soccer club in a different state. He sold his previous home for $528,000. His basis in the home was $400,000. Theodore purchased his previous home on January 5, 2021, and sold it on January 6, 2022. Obviously, he would not have sold the home if it were not for the new job. He is currently renting the home he lives in.

Theodore was welcomed back to the Nashville area as he was formerly a star player on the Country Stars team. During his playing time he had purchased a modest home in Nashville but did not sell it, instead choosing to rent the home over the years. His rental home is located at 2300 Bransford Ave., Nashville, TN 37204 and was rented all year to his tenant. The tenant occupied the home on January 1, 2022, and pays rent of $1,500 per month for each month of 2022 (the lease is a two-year lease); however, Theodore required first and last months' rent and a security deposit of $500 and all were paid on January 1, 2022. Theodore's rental expenses for the year are:

Mortgage interest	$16,000
Real estate taxes	10,000
Insurance	3,000
Depreciation (fully depreciated)	0
Repairs	1,000
Lawn and other maintenance	3,000

Now that Theodore is back in Nashville, he actively manages the rental home. He probably spends about ten hours per month on the rental.

Theodore received the following 1099-B from his broker:

2022 Combined Forms 1099

This is important tax information and is being furnished to the IRS (except as indicated). If you are required to file a return, a negligence penalty or other sanction may be imposed on you if this income is taxable and the IRS determines that it has not been reported.

Copy B For Recipient
OMB No. 1545-0110

Clay Investments
40 Wall Street, 24th Floor
New York, NY 10005

Theodore Lariat
140 Whitsett Road
Nashville, TN 37210

Account Number	Tax ID
	***-**-9532
Payer's Federal Tax ID	
32-9863145	
Financial Adviser/Phone	
Stephen Mason 888-555-1212	

Form 1099-B **Proceeds from Broker and Barter Exchange Transactions**

Box 6: Gross Proceeds	Box 5: Not checked		Box 3: Basis reported to IRS		Box 2: Type of Gain or Loss: Short Term		
Box 1 Security description (CUSIP)	Quantity sold	Box 1b Date acquired	Box 1c Date sold or disposed	Box 1d Proceeds	Box 1e Cost or other basis	Box 1g Wash sale loss disallowed	Gain/(Loss) amount
Jars Corp	100	04/27/2022	12/15/2022	3,400	3,000	-	400
Hands Inc	50	10/01/2021	04/28/2022	5,600	5,800		(200)
Box 6: Gross Proceeds	**Box 5: Not checked**		**Box 3: Basis reported to IRS**		**Box 2: Type of Gain or Loss: Long Term**		
Box 1 Security description (CUSIP)	Quantity sold	Box 1b Date acquired	Box 1c Date sold or disposed	Box 1d Proceeds	Box 1e Cost or other basis	Box 1g Wash sale loss disallowed	Gain/(Loss) amount
Mizer Corp	130	01/17/2011	08/21/2022	11,500	11,000	-	500
Moses Inc	50	03/25/2018	06/01/2022	1,000	5,200		(4,200)

Form 1099-INT **Interest Income**

Box 1 Interest income	Box 2 Early withdrawal penalty	Box 3 Interest on U.S. Savings Bonds and Treasury obligations
138.29		
Box 4 Federal income tax withheld	Box 5 Investment expenses	Box 6 Foreign Tax Paid
Box 7 Foreign country or U.S. possession	Box 8 Tax-exempt interest	Box 9 Specified private activity bond interest
Box 10 Market Discount	Box 11 Bond Premium	
Box 12 Bond premium on Treasury obligations	Box 13 Bond premium on tax-exempt bond	

Required: Complete Theodore's federal tax return for 2022. Determine if Form 8949 and Schedule D are required. If so, use those forms and Form 1040, Schedule E (page 1 only), and Form 8582 (page 1 only) to complete this tax return. Do not complete Form 4562 for reporting depreciation.

2A. Skylar and Walter Black have been married for 25 years. They live at 883 Scrub Brush Street, Unit 52B, Las Vegas, NV 89125. Skylar is self-employed and Walt is a high school teacher. Skylar's Social Security number is 222-43-7690 and Walt's is 700-01-0002. Walter's birthdate is January 21, 1967, and Skylar's is February 14, 1980. The Blacks provide all the support for Skylar's mother, Rebecca Backin (Social Security number 411-66-2121), who lives in a nursing home in Reno, NV, and has no income.

Walter's father, Alton Black (Social Security number 343-22-8899), lives with the Blacks in Las Vegas. Although Alton received Social Security benefits of $7,600 in 2022, the Blacks provide more than half of Alton's support. If Rebecca or Alton qualify as dependents, Skylar and Walt can claim a $500 other dependent credit for each.

Walt's earnings from teaching are:

a Employee's social security number: 700-01-0002

OMB No. 1545-0008 Safe, accurate, FAST! Use IRS e-file. Visit the IRS website at www.irs.gov/efile

b Employer identification number (EIN): 31-1239876

c Employer's name, address, and ZIP code:
Las Vegas School District
2234 Vegas Valley Drive
Las Vegas, NV 89169

d Control number

e Employee's first name and initial / Last name / Suff.
Walter Black
883 Scrub Brush Street, 52B
Las Vegas, NV 89125

f Employee's address and ZIP code

1 Wages, tips, other compensation	55,000.00	2 Federal income tax withheld	3,800.00
3 Social security wages	55,000.00	4 Social security tax withheld	3,410.00
5 Medicare wages and tips	55,000.00	6 Medicare tax withheld	797.50
7 Social security tips		8 Allocated tips	
9		10 Dependent care benefits	
11 Nonqualified plans		12a See instructions for box 12	Code DD 7,900.00
13 Statutory employee ☐ Retirement plan ☒ Third-party sick pay ☐		12b	
14 Other	Educ Assist Plan $5,250	12c	
		12d	

15 State / Employer's state ID number	16 State wages, tips, etc.	17 State income tax	18 Local wages, tips, etc.	19 Local income tax	20 Locality name
NV					

Form **W-2** Wage and Tax Statement 2022

Department of the Treasury—Internal Revenue Service

Copy B—To Be Filed With Employee's FEDERAL Tax Return.
This information is being furnished to the Internal Revenue Service.

The Blacks moved from Maine to Nevada. As a result, they sold their house in Maine on January 4, 2022. They originally paid $80,000 for the home on July 3, 1996, but managed to sell it for $598,000. They spent $14,000 on improvements over the years.

The Blacks own a ski condo located at 123 Buncombe Lane, Brian Head, UT 84719. The condo was rented for 189 days during 2022 and used by the Blacks for 21 days. The rental activity does not rise to the level to qualify for the QBI deduction. Pertinent information about the condo rental is as follows:

Rental income	$25,000
Mortgage interest reported on Form 1098	12,000
Homeowners' association dues	4,200
Utilities	4,400
Maintenance	4,600
Depreciation (assume fully depreciated)	0

The above amounts do not reflect any allocation between rental and personal use of the condo. The Blacks are active managers of the condo.

Skylar runs a small car wash in Las Vegas as a sole proprietor. The business name is A1A Car Wash and is located at 4900 Cutler Ave NE, Las Vegas, NV 89146. The employer identification number is 19-3451234. She uses the cash method of accounting and does not track inventory of the sundries she sells (air fresheners, etc.). She therefore does not have beginning or ending inventories and recognizes the cost as supplies expense. The business code for a car wash is 811192. Her financial results for 2022 were as follows:

Revenues:	
Car Wash	$ 32,000
Sundries	3,000
Total	$ 35,000
Expenses:	
Payroll	$ 22,000
Utilities	2,000
Depreciation	0
Taxes	1,000
Licenses	300
Sundries cost	600
Insurance	900
Advertising	500
Total	$ 27,300
Net profit	$ 7,700

The business office at the car wash is not conducive to any type of work. It is basically a glorified broom closet. As a result, Skylar has a home office in their primary residence (which they rent). The office is 200 square feet in their 2,000 square foot home. They pay rent of $16,000 per year and their 2022 utilities are $1,200.

In 2018, Walter loaned his friend, Hank Shorter $5,000. In 2022, Hank declared bankruptcy and Walter is certain he will never get paid.

Walt is attending the Las Vegas Polytechnical University, pursuing a master's degree in chemistry. His employer has an education assistance program that paid Walt $5,250 in 2022. His total 2022 tuition was $10,000. The remaining tuition was paid for through the Los Gatos Hermanos Foundation scholarship for adult learners.

Walter has been experimenting with a new candy formula in his garage chemistry lab. He has been working on a new blueberry flavor that tastes more like real blueberries. For the past few years, he has spent between $1,000 and $2,000 per year on this venture but has never made any money. In 2022, a bakery in town bought some of Walter's formula for $700 to try a new blueberry muffin formula but did not purchase any additional formula after the first attempt. Walter spent $1,000 on lab supplies during 2022. Walter does not realistically expect to ever turn a profit, he just does not care for the existing artificial blueberry flavors.

Required: Complete the Black's federal tax return for 2022. Use Form 1040, Schedule 1, Schedule 2, Schedule C, Schedule D, Form 8949, Schedule E (page 1 only), Schedule SE, Form 8995, and Form 8829 to complete their tax return.

2B. Ryan and Blake Lively are married filing jointly taxpayers. Ryan's birthdate is August 10, 1982 and Social Security number is 434-14-4448. Blake's birthdate is March 19, 1983 and their Social Security number is 763-16-1562. They live at 22 Thornton Road, Nashua, NH 03063. Both are self-employed.

The Livelys received the following statement from their brokerage account:

2022 Combined Forms 1099

This is important tax information and is being furnished to the IRS (except as indicated). If you are required to file a return, a negligence penalty or other sanction may be imposed on you if this income is taxable and the IRS determines that it has not been reported.

Copy B For Recipient
OMB No. 1545-0110

Pooled Investments
40 Wall Street, 24th Floor
New York, NY 10005

Ryan and Blake Lively
22 Thornton Road
Nashua, NH 03063

Account Number	Tax ID
2345660009	***-**-4448
Payer's Federal Tax ID	
32-9863145	
Financial Adviser/Phone	
Monty Cook 888-555-1212	

Form 1099-B — **Proceeds from Broker and Barter Exchange Transactions**

Box 6: Gross Proceeds | **Box 5: Not checked** | **Box 3: Basis reported to IRS** | **Box 2: Type of Gain or Loss: Long Term**

Box 1 Security description (CUSIP)	Quantity sold	Box 1b Date acquired	Box 1c Date sold or disposed	Box 1d Proceeds	Box 1e Cost or other basis	Box 1g Wash sale loss disallowed	Gain/(Loss) amount
Green Lantern Inc	1,000	04/21/2017	03/22/2022	35,000	3,000	-	32,000

Form 1099-INT — **Interest Income**

58Box 1 Interest income	Box 2 Early withdrawal penalty	Box 3 Interest on U.S. Savings Bonds and Treasury obligations
57.89		600.00
Box 4 Federal income tax withheld	Box 5 Investment expenses	Box 6 Foreign Tax Paid
Box 7 Foreign country or U.S. possession	Box 8 Tax-exempt interest	Box 9 Specified private activity bond interest
Box 10 Market Discount	Box 11 Bond Premium	
Box 12 Bond premium on Treasury obligations	Box 13 Bond premium on tax-exempt bond	

Form 1099-DIV — **Dividend Income**

Box 1a Total ordinary dividends	Box 1b Qualified dividends	Box 2a Total capital gain distr.
2,500.00	2,500.00	
Box 2b Unrecap Sec 1250 gain	Box 2c Section 1202 gain	Box 2d Collectibles (28%) gain
Box 2e Section 897 ordinary dividends	Box 2f Section 897 capital gain	Box 3 Nondividend distributions
Box 4 Federal income tax withheld	Box 5 Section 199A dividends	Box 6 Investment expenses
Box 7 Foreign taxes paid	Box 8 Foreign country or possession	Box 9 Cash liquidation distributions

The U.S. Treasury interest is associated with bonds that also have market discount. The accrued market discount in 2022 was $45.02. The Livelys elect to recognize market discount in the year earned.

Blake started a new life coach business in 2022 as a sole proprietor. The business office is located at 4 Townsend W, Suite 8, Nashua, NH 03063. The business code is 812990. The financial results are:

Client revenue	$ 5,000
Office rent expense	12,000
Supplies	1,000
Utilities	300
Telephone	360

During 2022, Ryan invested in Vaporcoin, a virtual currency. He purchased 40 units of Vaporcoin for $3,000 on February 2, 2022. On May 15, 2022, he exchanged the Vaporcoin into dollars when the value was $3,500. He did not receive a 1099-B from the Vaporcoin account.

Ryan also operates a small business teaching fitness classes in a park near their house. The business code is 812190. Ryan has a loyal clientele, and the books and records show the following:

Exercise class receipts	$4,000
Exercise clothes	1,000
Various exercise supplies	1,700

The exercise clothes that Blake purchased are not dissimilar to any other type of workout clothing.

Neither business has employees, an EIN or inventory. Both businesses are accounted for using the cash basis of accounting.

Ryan and Blake own a rental property located at 52 Charlotte Ave, Nashua, NH 03064. The condo was rented all year but is in need of an update. The condo's finances are as follows:

Rent	$ 8,000
Interest	10,000
Property taxes	3,000
Utilities	1,400
Maintenance	100

Ryan and Blake made a $400 estimated payment on September 15, 2022.

Required: Complete the Livelys' federal tax return for 2022. Use Form 1040, Schedule 1, Schedule 2, Schedule B, Schedule C (two of them), Schedule D, Form 8949, Schedule E, Schedule SE, Form 8995, Form 8582 (page 1 only) to complete this tax return. Also, to compute the Livelys' net operating loss carryforward, prepare only Schedule A of Form 1045.

GROUP 5:
CUMULATIVE SOFTWARE PROBLEM

1. The following additional information is available for the Albert and Allison Gaytor family.

   The Gaytors own a rental beach house in Hawaii. The beach house was rented for the full year during 2022 and was not used by the Gaytors during the year. The Gaytors were active participants in the management of the rental house but the activity is not eligible for a QBI deduction. Pertinent information about the rental house is as follows:

   Address: 1237 Pineapple St., Lihue, HI 96766

Gross rental income	$20,000
Mortgage interest	8,000
Real estate taxes	2,200
Utilities	1,500
Cleaning	2,500
Repairs	600

   The house is fully depreciated so there is no depreciation expense.

Albert and Allison received the following combined statements 1099-DIV and 1099-B from their investment manager:

IMPORTANT TAX DOCUMENT
2022 Form 1099-DIV
Dividends and Distributions

RECIPIENT'S TIN: 266-51-1966

Albert T. Gaytor
Allison A Gaytor
JT TEN WROS
12340 Cocoshell Rd
Coral Gables, FL 33134

Fortress Securities
PO Box 1300
Gaithersburg, MD 20877
Copy B for Recipient

Fund Name	*Total Ordinary Dividends*	*Qualified Dividends*	*Capital Gain Distrib*	*Unrecap 1250 Gain*	*Nondividend Distrib*	*Fed Tax Withheld*	*Exempt-Interest Dividends*	*State Tax Withheld*
Peach Fund	0.00	0.00	480.00			0.00		

2022 Form 1099-B

Proceeds from Broker and Barter Exchange Transactions

Descript.	*Date Acq*	*Date Sold*	*Proceeds*	*Cost*	*Proceeds Reported to IRS*	*Basis Reported to IRS*
100 shs. Orange Co	02/11/2022	04/16/2022	$3,000	$2,300	Net	Yes
100 shs. Banana Co.	07/17/2021	07/31/2022	2,200	4,200	Net	Yes
100 shs Grape Corp	12/18/2021	09/01/2022	9,000	10,400	Net	Yes
5 $1,000 Par Value Bonds due 4/2021	12/30/2012	01/02/2022	5,100	5,415	Net	Yes
5,011.23 shs. Peach Mutual Fund	05/30/2013	08/22/2022	59,800	56,000	Net	Yes

On January 12, 2022, Albert and Allison sold their personal residence for $716,500 and purchased a new house for $725,000. The house they sold was their personal residence before and after the divorce (they have lived in it together for three years since remarrying). The sold house cost $120,200 back in January of 2009 and the Gaytors added on a new bedroom and bathroom a few years ago for a cost of $20,100. They also built a pool for a cost of $61,400. They moved into their new house on January 19, 2022.

Required: Combine this new information about the Gaytor family with the information from Chapters 1–3 and complete a revised 2022 tax return for Albert and Allison. Be sure to save your data input files since this case will be expanded with more tax information in later chapters.

CHAPTER 5

Deductions For and From AGI

Andrei Dodonov/Dreamstime.com

LEARNING OBJECTIVES

After completing this chapter, you should be able to:

LO 5.1 Explain how Health Savings Accounts (HSAs) can be used for tax-advantaged medical care.

LO 5.2 Describe the self-employed health insurance deduction.

LO 5.3 Explain the treatment of Individual Retirement Accounts (IRAs), including Roth IRAs.

LO 5.4 Explain the general contribution rules for small business and self-employed retirement plans.

LO 5.5 Describe other adjustments for adjusted gross income.

LO 5.6 Calculate the itemized deduction for medical expenses.

LO 5.7 Calculate the itemized deduction for taxes.

LO 5.8 Apply the rules for an individual taxpayer's interest deduction.

LO 5.9 Determine the charitable contributions deduction.

LO 5.10 Describe other itemized deductions.

OVERVIEW

Deductions related to a business (for example, Schedule C in Chapter 3) or the production of income or investment (for example, Schedules D and E in Chapter 4) represent deductions that are for AGI (above-the-line). The business deductions are generally reported on the separate schedules. However, the tax law permits additional for AGI deductions that may be associated with business activity or, in some instances unrelated to business activity, such as the student loan interest deduction, as simply a matter of legislative grace for individual taxpayers. These additional deductions are reported on Part II of Schedule 1 of Form 1040. Included among the more common for AGI deductions is:

- Individual retirement account (IRA) contributions,
- One-half of self-employment taxes,
- Student loan interest, and
- Self-employed health care and qualified retirement plan contributions.

Deductions that occur after AGI (from AGI deductions, or below-the-line) include the standard deduction discussed in Chapter 1, the qualified business income deduction discussed in Chapter 4, and Schedule A itemized deductions, introduced here in Chapter 5. Itemized deductions fall into six categories: medical and dental expenses, state and local taxes, interest expenses, charitable contributions, casualty and theft losses, and miscellaneous deductions.

Recall from Chapter 1, that when calculating taxable income, individuals determine their standard deduction and their allowable itemized deductions and use the larger of the two. For example, if a taxpayer's standard deduction is $12,950 and her itemized deductions are $18,100, she would use her itemized deductions in calculating taxable income. On the other hand, if her itemized deductions were $9,500, she would use the larger standard deduction of $12,950 in computing taxable income.

A number of limitations are placed on itemized deductions. One example is the $10,000 limit on state and local taxes. For federal budget reasons, many of these limitations only suspend, rather than repeal the deduction. The suspensions are largely scheduled to end after 2025. As a result, brief explanations of the pre-limitation deductions are provided.

Learning Objective 5.1

Explain how Health Savings Accounts (HSAs) can be used for tax-advantaged medical care.

5-1 HEALTH SAVINGS ACCOUNTS

There are four types of tax-favored medical spending plans available to taxpayers:

1. Health care flexible spending arrangements or FSAs (covered in Chapter 2) in which employees can set aside money to cover medical expenses and exclude the funds from gross income.
2. Health Reimbursement Arrangements (HRAs) in which the employer funds an account that may be used by employees for medical expenses (these do not generally affect an individual taxpayer's taxable income and thus are not covered in detail in this textbook).
3. Medical Savings Accounts (MSAs or Archer MSAs) which permit (limited) deductions for amounts contributed to an account established to cover medical expenses for small business and self-employed individuals. Effective January 1, 2008, no new MSA accounts may be established, and thus, these are not covered in detail in this textbook. Note that an Archer MSA can be rolled over into an HSA.
4. Health Savings Accounts (HSAs) are a type of savings account which may be established for the purpose of paying unreimbursed medical expenses by taxpayers who carry qualifying high-deductible medical insurance.

Contributions to HSAs are a deduction for AGI and are limited to certain dollar amounts depending on age and whether the high-deductible insurance covers an individual or a family. Earnings and unused contributions accumulated in an HSA are not taxed, and distributions to cover medical expenses are not taxed or penalized.

Health insurance with a high deductible is less expensive than standard health insurance since the issuing insurance company does not have to pay any of the taxpayer's medical expenses until a certain threshold (the deductible plus any other required out-of-pocket medical costs) is reached. The funds contributed to the HSA may then be used by the taxpayer to pay medical expenses not covered by health insurance. This popular combination of tax benefits and less expensive insurance is designed to encourage taxpayers to carry health insurance.

5-1a Deductions for Contributions to HSAs

The following table shows the contribution limits for HSA deductions for 2022. The table also shows the additional "catch-up" contributions allowed for individuals beginning at age 55 and ending at age 65, the age for Medicare eligibility. Individuals are not allowed to make contributions to HSAs once they attain the age of 65 and qualify for Medicare coverage. Finally, the table shows the lower and upper deductible and out-of-pocket medical expense limits (excluding the actual cost of insurance) required for insurance to qualify as a high-deductible health plan.

2022 Limits for HSAs

	Family	*Self-Only*
Contribution limit	$ 7,300	$ 3,650
Additional catch-up contribution for taxpayer age 55 or older	1,000 per qualifying spouse	1,000
Minimum health insurance deductible	2,800	1,400
Maximum health insurance out-of-pocket	14,100	7,050

Although the out-of-pocket limits under the Affordable Care Act (ACA) are slightly higher than those listed above, the IRS limits determine tax compliance for HSAs. Contributions to HSAs must generally be made by April 15 of the year following the year for which the contribution is made. IRS Form 8889 is used to provide information to the IRS regarding HSA deductions claimed on Line 13 of Schedule 1 of Form 1040 and to compute the deduction amount.

EXAMPLE Gary is 35 years old and carries self-only coverage in a qualifying high-deductible health insurance plan during 2022. Gary may contribute up to $3,650 to his HSA account and deduct this amount for AGI. Gary may use some or all of the contributions to pay medical expenses he has incurred. Any amount he leaves in the HSA account will accumulate earnings tax free and carry forward to be available for payment of qualifying medical expenses in the future. ♦

5-1b Distributions

Distributions from HSAs are excluded from income when used to pay for qualified medical expenses. Distributions which are not used to pay for qualified medical expenses are subject to both income tax and a 20-percent penalty. Once a taxpayer is 65 years old, distributions may be taken for nonmedical expenses and will be subject to income tax, but not the 20-percent penalty. Distributions from an HSA are reported on Form 1099-SA. The amount of the distribution is reported in Box 1 and codes indicating the proper treatment are provided in Box 3. A normal distribution is coded 1.

ProConnect™ Tax TIP

To report HSA information and complete a Form 8889, the input area can be found in the left-hand margin under Deductions/Adjustments to Income. The input area is conveniently called Health Savings Account (Form 8889).

EXAMPLE Debbie is 66 years old and has $30,000 in her HSA. She can withdraw the $30,000 to purchase a new car, but will have to pay income tax on the distribution. If she takes the distribution to pay medical expenses, no income tax will be due. If Debbie was under age 65 and took a distribution from her HSA to buy a car, she would owe both income tax and a 20-percent penalty on the distribution. ♦

5-1c Guidance

The rules governing HSAs are more detailed and lengthy than the summaries above. IRS Publication 969 is a good source of information on a range of additional issues related to HSAs and their operation.

Self-Study Problem 5.1 ***See Appendix E for Solutions to Self-Study Problems***

a. Determine the deductible HSA amount for each of the following taxpayers for 2022:
   1. Amy is 40 years old, has a qualifying high-deductible health plan, carries family coverage, and contributes the maximum amount to her family HSA.
   2. Cary is 60 years old, has self-only health insurance with no deductible, and contributes $1,200 to an HSA.
   3. Annabelle is 52 years old and contributes $2,000 to her HSA. She has qualifying self-only coverage in a high-deductible health plan.
   4. Lucille is 70 years old and is covered by Medicare. She contributes $3,050 to her HSA.

b. Alex Morton is a single taxpayer, age 34. She is part of a qualifying high-deductible health plan. In 2022, Alex made contributions of $3,000 to her HSA. Alex's employer reported making $240 of contributions to her HSA in Box 12 of her Form W-2 (code W). Alex spent $2,000 on qualified medical expenses. Alex received the following Form 1099-SA from her HSA administrator:

☐ CORRECTED (if checked)

TRUSTEE'S/PAYER'S name, street address, city or town, state or province, country, ZIP or foreign postal code, and telephone number Heritage Health Partners PO Box 12345 Dallas, TX 75621		OMB No. 1545-1517 Form **1099-SA** (Rev. November 2019) For calendar year 2022	**Distributions From an HSA, Archer MSA, or Medicare Advantage MSA**
PAYER'S TIN 13-0080072	RECIPIENT'S TIN 213-21-3121	1 Gross distribution $ 1,924.78	2 Earnings on excess cont. $
RECIPIENT'S name Alex Morton		3 Distribution code 1	4 FMV on date of death $
Street address (including apt. no.) 1921 S. Orange Avenue City or town, state or province, country, and ZIP or foreign postal code Orlando, FL 32806		5 HSA ☒ Archer MSA ☐ MA MSA ☐	
Account number (see instructions)			

Copy B For Recipient

This information is being furnished to the IRS.

Form **1099-SA** (Rev. 11-2019) (keep for your records) www.irs.gov/Form1099SA Department of the Treasury - Internal Revenue Service

Prepare Form 8889 on Page 5-5 to determine Alex's HSA deduction and taxable HSA distribution.

Self-Study Problem 5.1

Form **8889** — Department of the Treasury, Internal Revenue Service

Health Savings Accounts (HSAs)

Attach to Form 1040, 1040-SR, or 1040-NR.
Go to *www.irs.gov/Form8889* for instructions and the latest information.

OMB No. 1545-0074 — 2022 — Attachment Sequence No. 52

Name(s) shown on Form 1040, 1040-SR, or 1040-NR | Social security number of HSA beneficiary. If both spouses have HSAs, see instructions.

Before you begin: Complete Form 8853, Archer MSAs and Long-Term Care Insurance Contracts, if required.

Part I **HSA Contributions and Deduction.** See the instructions before completing this part. If you are filing jointly and both you and your spouse each have separate HSAs, complete a separate Part I for each spouse.

1	Check the box to indicate your coverage under a high-deductible health plan (HDHP) during 2022. See instructions . . . ☐ Self-only ☐ Family		
2	HSA contributions you made for 2022 (or those made on your behalf), including those made in 2023 by the unextended due date of your tax return that were for 2022. **Do not** include employer contributions, contributions through a cafeteria plan, or rollovers. See instructions . . .	2	
3	If you were under age 55 at the end of 2022 and, on the first day of **every** month during 2022, you were, or were considered, an eligible individual with the **same** coverage, enter $3,650 ($7,300 for family coverage). **All others**, see the instructions for the amount to enter . . .	3	
4	Enter the amount you and your employer contributed to your Archer MSAs for 2022 from Form 8853, lines 1 and 2. If you or your spouse had family coverage under an HDHP at any time during 2022, also include any amount contributed to your spouse's Archer MSAs . . .	4	
5	Subtract line 4 from line 3. If zero or less, enter -0- . . .	5	
6	Enter the amount from line 5. But if you and your spouse each have separate HSAs and had family coverage under an HDHP at any time during 2022, see the instructions for the amount to enter . .	6	
7	If you were age 55 or older at the end of 2022, married, and you or your spouse had family coverage under an HDHP at any time during 2022, enter your additional contribution amount. See instructions .	7	
8	Add lines 6 and 7 . . .	8	
9	Employer contributions made to your HSAs for 2022 . . . 9		
10	Qualified HSA funding distributions . . . 10		
11	Add lines 9 and 10 . . .	11	
12	Subtract line 11 from line 8. If zero or less, enter -0- . . .	12	
13	**HSA deduction.** Enter the **smaller** of line 2 or line 12 here and on Schedule 1 (Form 1040), Part II, line 13	13	
	Caution: If line 2 is more than line 13, you may have to pay an additional tax. See instructions.		

Part II **HSA Distributions.** If you are filing jointly and both you and your spouse each have separate HSAs, complete a separate Part II for each spouse.

14a	Total distributions you received in 2022 from all HSAs (see instructions) . . .	14a	
b	Distributions included on line 14a that you rolled over to another HSA. Also include any excess contributions (and the earnings on those excess contributions) included on line 14a that were withdrawn by the due date of your return. See instructions . . .	14b	
c	Subtract line 14b from line 14a . . .	14c	
15	Qualified medical expenses paid using HSA distributions (see instructions) . . .	15	
16	**Taxable HSA distributions.** Subtract line 15 from line 14c. If zero or less, enter -0-. Also, include this amount in the total on Schedule 1 (Form 1040), Part I, line 8f . . .	16	
17a	If any of the distributions included on line 16 meet any of the **Exceptions to the Additional 20% Tax** (see instructions), check here . . . ☐		
b	**Additional 20% tax** (see instructions). Enter 20% (0.20) of the distributions included on line 16 that are subject to the additional 20% tax. Also, include this amount in the total on Schedule 2 (Form 1040), Part II, line 17c . . .	17b	

Part III **Income and Additional Tax for Failure To Maintain HDHP Coverage.** See the instructions before completing this part. If you are filing jointly and both you and your spouse each have separate HSAs, complete a separate Part III for each spouse.

18	Last-month rule . . .	18	
19	Qualified HSA funding distribution . . .	19	
20	**Total income.** Add lines 18 and 19. Include this amount on Schedule 1 (Form 1040), Part I, line 8f .	20	
21	**Additional tax.** Multiply line 20 by 10% (0.10). Include this amount in the total on Schedule 2 (Form 1040), Part II, line 17d . . .	21	

For Paperwork Reduction Act Notice, see your tax return instructions. Cat. No. 37621P Form **8889** (2022)

5-2 SELF-EMPLOYED HEALTH INSURANCE DEDUCTION

5.2 Learning Objective

Describe the self-employed health insurance deduction.

Self-employed taxpayers are allowed an above-the-line deduction for the cost of providing health insurance for themselves and their families. This deduction is meant to give self-employed taxpayers the same tax treatment available to employees who are offered health insurance as a tax-free benefit of employment. Deductible insurance includes the following:

- Medical and dental insurance paid to cover the self-employed taxpayer, spouse, and dependents;
- Medical and dental insurance paid for children under the age of 27 who are not dependents;
- Medicare premiums;
- Long-term care insurance paid for the taxpayer and the family of the taxpayer within certain dollar limitations shown below.

EXAMPLE Joe has a barbershop and earns $60,000 in 2022, which he reports on Schedule C. Joe pays $10,000 in health and dental insurance costs for himself, his unemployed wife, and his 10-year-old daughter. The full $10,000 is a deduction for Joe's AGI. ♦

5-2a Special Rules

The following special rules limit the treatment of health insurance as a deduction for AGI:

- Other Health Care Plan Available: The self-employed health insurance deduction is not allowed for any months in which the taxpayer is eligible to participate in a subsidized health care plan offered by an employer of either the taxpayer or the spouse of the taxpayer.
- Definition of Self-Employment: Taxpayers with income reportable on Schedule C are generally considered self-employed. However, taxpayers with earnings from certain partnerships, S corporations, limited liability corporations (LLCs), and farm businesses may also be considered self-employed and may be allowed the above-the-line deduction for self-employed health insurance. Taxpayers with income from these sources sometimes present more complex health insurance deduction issues which should be researched as they appear.
- Deductible Portion: Self-employed taxpayers that receive advance premium tax credits under the ACA may deduct only the portion paid out of pocket, not the portion covered by the premium tax credit.
- Earned Income Limitation: The deduction for self-employed health insurance is only allowed to the extent of the taxpayer's net self-employed earned income. For example, a taxpayer with a Schedule C business loss would not be allowed to claim a self-employed health insurance deduction even though they paid for health insurance. The deduction would instead be allowed as an itemized medical deduction subject to the limits discussed in LO 5.6.
- Long-Term Care Premium Limitation: The individual limitations on the deduction of long-term care premiums are as follows:

Attained Age Before the Close of the Taxable Year	*2022 Limitation on Premiums*
40 or less	$ 450
More than 40 but not more than 50	850
More than 50 but not more than 60	1,690
More than 60 but not more than 70	4,510
More than 70	5,640

ProConnect™ Tax TIP

To enter self-employed health insurance and many of the other for-AGI deductions, go to Deductions/Adjustments to Income. There is a long input page, and a number of subheadings are available in the left-hand margin.

EXAMPLE Candace is a 55-year-old massage therapist who earns $40,000 of net self-employment income in 2022. She pays $6,000 for medical insurance and $1,690 for long-term care insurance. Candace can take $7,690 ($6,000 + $1,690) as a deduction for AGI. ♦

Self-Study Problem 5.2 *See Appendix E for Solutions to Self-Study Problems*

During the 2022 tax year, Gwen supports her family as a physical therapist. She reports $90,000 of earned income on her Schedule C and paid the following insurance premiums:

- Family health insurance: $15,000
- Family dental insurance: $2,000
- Health insurance for her 24-year-old son who is not a dependent: $3,000
- Long-term care insurance for her 49-year-old husband: $900

What is Gwen's self-employed health insurance deduction for 2022?

Learning Objective 5.3

Explain the treatment of Individual Retirement Accounts (IRAs), including Roth IRAs.

5-3 INDIVIDUAL RETIREMENT ACCOUNTS

The two principal types of individual retirement accounts (IRAs) are the *traditional IRA* and the *Roth IRA*. Generally, annual contributions to a traditional IRA are deductible, and retirement distributions are taxable. Annual contributions to a Roth IRA are not deductible, but retirement distributions are nontaxable. Earnings in both types of IRAs are not taxable in the current year.

EXAMPLE Gene has $30,000 in his IRA in 2022. The earnings for the year on this IRA are $1,600. These earnings are not taxed to Gene in the current year. ♦

5-3a IRA Annual Contributions and Deductions

There are annual contribution limits for both traditional and Roth IRAs. In 2022, the maximum annual contribution that may be made to both types of IRAs combined in total is equal to the lesser of (1) 100 percent of the taxpayer's compensation or self-employment income (earned income) or (2) $6,000 (or $12,000 if an additional $6,000 is contributed to a spouse's IRA, and the spouse has no earned income). It is possible for a taxpayer to contribute $4,000 to a traditional IRA and up to $2,000 to a Roth IRA. The maximum contribution to a spouse's IRA may not exceed $6,000. In 2022, an additional $1,000 annual "catch-up" contribution is allowed for taxpayers and spouses age 50 and over, increasing the maximum contribution to $7,000.

EXAMPLE Quincy, age 31, works for Big Corporation and has a salary of $40,000 for 2022. Quincy is eligible to contribute the maximum $6,000 to his traditional or Roth IRA for 2022. If Quincy has a spouse who does not work, he could also contribute $6,000 into her IRA or Roth IRA. If Quincy is 55 years old instead of 31 years old, he could contribute $7,000 to his traditional or Roth IRA, and $6,000 or $7,000 for his spouse, depending on whether she is old enough to qualify for the $1,000 "catch-up" contribution. ♦

The annual deduction maximums on the previous page may be reduced for traditional IRAs if the taxpayer is an active participant in another qualified retirement plan. The annual contribution allowed for a Roth IRA is reduced for all taxpayers over certain income levels, but is not affected by whether the taxpayer or spouse is an active participant in another retirement plan. In each case, the maximum annual contribution is phased out proportionately between certain adjusted gross income ranges, as shown in Table 5.1 below.

TABLE 5.1 PHASE OUT $ LIMITS FOR CONTRIBUTIONS TO IRAs

		Traditional IRA		
	Roth IRA	***No Active Participant***	***One Active Participant***	***Both Active Participants***
Single or Head of Household	129,000–144,000	No phase-out	68,000–78,000	N/A
Married Filing Jointly	204,000–214,000	No phase-out	Active spouse 109,000–129,000 Nonactive spouse 204,000–214,000	109,000–129,000
Married Filing Separately	0–10,000	0–10,000	0–10,000	0–10,000

When one spouse is an active participant in a retirement plan and the other is not, two separate income limitations apply but both measure the joint income of the married couple.

A nondeductible traditional IRA contribution may be made by taxpayers with income over the phase-out ranges shown above. Although the taxpayer cannot deduct the contribution, all income earned in the IRA account is sheltered from tax until the earnings are withdrawn. When there have been nondeductible IRA contributions, the taxable portion of the withdrawn IRA money is calculated similar to the treatment of annuities discussed in Chapter 2. Many high-income taxpayers make nondeductible traditional IRA contributions each year because of the deferral of tax on the earnings of the IRA.

EXAMPLE Ed, age 31, is single and is covered by a retirement plan. If his modified adjusted gross income is $69,000, Ed's maximum deductible traditional IRA contribution is $5,400. With income of $69,000, his $6,000 contribution is proportionately phased out by dividing the amount remaining in his phase-out range, $78,000 − $69,000, or $9,000, by the $10,000 phase-out range (the difference between the bottom and top of the $68,000 and $78,000 phase-out range) and multiplying this by the $6,000 maximum IRA deduction as follows:

$$\frac{(\$78{,}000 - \$69{,}000)}{\$10{,}000} \times \$6{,}000 = \$5{,}400 \text{ allowed IRA deduction}$$

Ed may choose to contribute the $6,000 maximum to a traditional IRA, but the remaining $600 will not be deductible. Alternatively, he may contribute the remaining $600 to a Roth IRA since his income is below the phase-out range for Roth IRA contributions. He could also choose to ignore the allowed traditional IRA contribution and contribute the full nondeductible $6,000 to a Roth IRA. In any event, he cannot contribute more than $6,000 in total to IRAs, and his maximum allowed tax deduction for a traditional IRA contribution will be $5,400. ♦

EXAMPLE Ann, who is 36 and single, would like to contribute $6,000 to her Roth IRA. However, her AGI is $136,000, so her contribution is limited to $3,200 calculated as follows:

$$\frac{(\$144{,}000 - \$136{,}000)}{\$15{,}000} \times \$6{,}000 = \$3{,}200 \text{ allowed Roth IRA}$$

The $15,000 denominator in the calculation above is the amount of the phase-out range between $129,000 and $144,000. If she were 50 or older and wanted to contribute $7,000, her contribution would be limited to $3,733. ♦

EXAMPLE Paul and Lucy are married and are both 36 years old. Lucy is covered by a retirement plan and earns $70,000. Paul is not covered by a retirement plan and earns $66,000. Lucy cannot make a deductible contribution to a traditional IRA since the income on their joint tax return is greater than the $129,000 maximum phase-out range for married couples. Paul, however, can make a fully deductible IRA contribution of $6,000 since Paul and Lucy's AGI is below the $204,000–$214,000 phase-out range used when one spouse is an active participant in a plan and the other is not. Lucy could still choose to make a $6,000 contribution to a Roth IRA since their joint income is below the Roth IRA phase-out range for married couples. Paul would have a choice between making a $6,000 deductible contribution to a traditional IRA or a contribution of $6,000 to a Roth IRA or some combination thereof, not greater than $6,000. ♦

Contributions made above the maximum permitted for that year are subject to a 6-percent excise tax for each year the excess amount has not been withdrawn.

An IRA contribution may be made at any time before the original due date of the tax return for the year in which the deduction is to be claimed. This means, for example, that an individual can contribute to an IRA as late as the filing deadline of April 18, 2023, and still deduct the amount on the 2022 tax return.

5-3b **Roth IRA Conversions**

Taxpayers may benefit from a rule allowing conversions of traditional IRAs into Roth IRAs. Although the income generated by the conversion is subject to current income tax, taxpayers with certain factors in their favor such as number of years to retirement, a low current tax bracket, or a high expected tax bracket in retirement may wish to convert. Also, taxpayers with negative taxable income due to large personal deductions may wish to convert enough of their regular IRAs to Roth IRAs to bring taxable income to zero. This way the conversion can be done with no tax cost since deductions which would otherwise be lost are used to offset the taxable IRA income.

5-3c **Traditional IRA Distributions**

Money removed from a traditional IRA is taxable as ordinary income and may be subject to a 10-percent penalty for early withdrawal.

EXAMPLE Tomas is 48 years old and decides he must have a red sports car. He withdraws $35,000 from his traditional IRA to purchase the car. Tomas does not qualify for any of the penalty-free withdrawals listed below. The $35,000 is taxable to Tomas as ordinary income and he is subject to a $3,500 (10% × $35,000) penalty for removing the funds before age 59½. ♦

To avoid the 10-percent penalty, distributions from an IRA generally cannot begin before age 59½. However, penalty-free withdrawals from IRAs may be made by taxpayers under age 59½ who are:

1. Disabled
2. Using a special level payment option
3. Using the withdrawals for unreimbursed medical expenses in excess of 7.5 percent of their AGI
4. The recipients of at least twelve weeks of unemployment compensation and to the extent they are paying medical insurance premiums for their dependents
5. Paying the costs of higher education, including tuition, fees, books, and room and board for the taxpayers or their spouses, children, or grandchildren
6. Withdrawing up to $10,000 for first-time home-buying expenses
7. Beneficiaries due to the death of the IRA owner
8. Withdrawing funds due to an IRS levy
9. A qualified reservist
10. Withdrawing up to $5,000 within a year of a qualified birth or adoption

Due to COVID-related financial distress, the CARES Act extends the 10-percent penalty waiver to distributions of up to $100,000 made on or after March 27, 2020, and before December 31, 2020, to a taxpayer (or spouse or dependent) diagnosed with COVID-19 (using a CDC-approved test) or to a taxpayer that experiences adverse financial consequences as a result of quarantine, business closure, layoff, or reduced hours due to the virus. As with other exempted withdrawals, this exception does not apply to the normal income tax on the income; however, two special rules do apply. The first is that the taxpayer may include the income ratably over a three-year period starting in 2020. The second exception is that amounts recontributed to the qualified retirement plan within three years can be treated as a rollover and thus the original distribution would not be subject to tax.

EXAMPLE Juanita's spouse is stricken with COVID-19, and she and her spouse are unable to work for three months in 2020. To cover expenses, Juanita takes a $30,000 COVID-related distribution from her IRA. The income is recognized ratably over 2020, 2021, and 2022. In 2022, Juanita contributes $30,000 to her IRA and may amend her 2020 and 2021 tax returns to exclude the income from the distribution. She is not required to report any distribution income on her 2022 tax return. ♦

Traditional IRAs have required minimum distributions (RMDs) to prevent taxpayers from keeping funds in a traditional IRA indefinitely. RMDs must begin in the year a taxpayer turns age 72; however, the first distribution can be deferred until April 1 of the following year.

EXAMPLE Wade turns 72 in February 2022. He is required to take an RMD for 2022 but may defer that initial distribution until April 1, 2023. He will also be required to take a 2023 RMD by December 31, 2023. ♦

Once the first year of RMDs begin, all future RMDs must be paid by December 31. Plan sponsors or financial institutions generally take on the burden of calculating RMDs for taxpayers.

A taxpayer who has reached age 70½, may make a qualified charitable distribution of up to $100,000 and the amount of the distribution will not be included in taxable income; thus, avoiding tax on the income altogether. The qualified charitable distribution is also counted toward the taxpayer's RMD.

For any year that a taxpayer fails to take an RMD, a 50-percent tax applies on the difference between the required distribution and the actual distribution.

EXAMPLE Dalton, age 73, takes a distribution of $40,000 in the current year. His RMD amount was $60,000 and thus his distributions were $20,000 below the RMD. Dalton will owe a 50-percent excise tax of $10,000 ($20,000 × 50%). ♦

5-3d **Roth IRA Distributions**

Unlike a traditional IRA, distributions from a Roth IRA are not generally subject to tax and a Roth IRA does not have RMDs. If the funds have been in the Roth IRA for a five-year holding period, distributions will be tax-free if any of the following requirements are satisfied:

1. The distribution is made on or after the date on which the participant attains age 59½.
2. The distribution is made to a beneficiary (or the participant's estate) on or after the participant's death.
3. The participant becomes disabled.
4. The distribution is used to pay for qualified first-time home-buyer's expenses.

EXAMPLE Bob establishes a Roth IRA at age 50 and contributes to the Roth each year for ten years. The account is now worth $61,000, consisting of $35,000 of nondeductible contributions and $26,000 in earnings that have not been taxed. Bob may withdraw the $61,000 tax-free from the Roth IRA because he is over age 59½ and has met the five-year holding period requirement. ♦

The distributions may be taxable if the taxpayer receives distributions from a Roth IRA and does not satisfy the above requirements. The part of the distributions that represents a return of capital is tax-free, and the part that represents a payout of earnings is taxable. Under the ordering rules for Roth IRA distributions, distributions are treated as first made from contributions (return of capital) and then from earnings.

EXAMPLE Assume the same facts in the previous example, except that Bob is only age 56 and receives distributions of $10,000. Assume his adjusted basis for the Roth IRA is $35,000 (contributions made of $5,000 × 7 years). The distribution is tax-free and his adjusted basis is reduced to $25,000 ($35,000 − $10,000). ♦

5-3e **Prohibited Transactions**

IRA owners and family members of the owner are not generally permitted to engage in certain transactions with the IRA account itself. Most IRAs are held by large financial institutions and invest overwhelmingly in publicly-traded investments and the risk of a prohibited transaction is extremely low. Self-directed IRAs that are controlled directly by the IRA owner and invest in non-publicly-traded assets are far more likely to be at risk for a prohibited transaction. The following are likely to be prohibited transactions:

- Borrowing money from the IRA
- Selling property to the IRA
- Using the funds in the IRA as security for a loan
- Buying property for personal use (present or future) with IRA funds

If an IRA engages in a prohibited transaction, it ceases to be an IRA at that time and is treated as having distributed all of the assets of the IRA to the beneficiary at fair market value on the first day of the year, triggering tax on any amounts in excess of basis.

EXAMPLE Cliven's self-directed IRA invests in a small corporation over which Cliven or a member of his family has significant influence (for example, greater-than-50-percent ownership). This is a prohibited transaction. All of Cliven's contributions to the IRA were deductible and he therefore has no basis. The IRA is deemed to have made a taxable distribution of the market value of the IRA to Cliven. ♦

EXAMPLE Ammon's self-directed IRA has a 98-percent ownership of an LLC. The LLC pays Ammon a salary as compensation. The investment is a prohibited transaction due to the salary payment. ♦

If an IRA invests in collectibles such as artworks, antiques, metals, gems, and coins, the amount invested is considered to have been distributed to the owner as of the date of the investment.

A gift of a contribution to a Roth IRA for a child or grandchild with a summer job can grow into a very large gift over time. The amount that may be contributed to a child's Roth IRA is the lesser of $6,000 or the child's earnings. A child with $6,000 in a Roth IRA at age 16 will have well over $100,000 at age 65 if the Roth IRA investment earns 7 percent annually.

Self-Study Problem 5.3 *See Appendix E for Solutions to Self-Study Problems*

a. During 2022, George (a 24-year-old single taxpayer) has a salary of $52,000, dividend income of $14,000, and interest income of $4,000. In addition, he has rental income of $1,000. George is covered by a qualified retirement plan. Calculate the maximum regular IRA deduction that George is allowed.

b. During 2022, Irene (a single taxpayer, under age 50) has a salary of $121,000 and dividend income of $10,000. Calculate Irene's maximum contribution to a Roth IRA.

c. Wanda, a single taxpayer age 63, takes a $10,000 distribution from her traditional IRA to purchase furniture for her home. Over the years she has contributed $36,000 to the IRA which had a $50,000 balance at the time of the distribution. Determine how much of Wanda's distribution is taxable.

d. Same as part c., except the distribution is from a Roth IRA.

5-4 SMALL BUSINESS AND SELF-EMPLOYED RETIREMENT PLANS

5.4 Learning Objective

Explain the general contribution rules for small business and self-employed retirement plans.

The tax law provides employees, employers, and the self-employed with an incentive to plan for retirement through qualified retirement plans. Under the tax law, favorable tax treatment is granted to contributions, by or for employees, to qualified retirement plans. Employers may claim a deduction in the current year for contributions to qualified retirement plans on the employees' behalf, while the employees do not include the employer contributions in income until the contributed amounts are distributed (generally during their retirement years). Tax on earnings on the amounts contributed to the plan is also deferred. This deferral of income taxation is a significant benefit to most taxpayers.

EXAMPLE In the current year, Polly's employer makes a $2,000 contribution to a qualified plan for Polly's retirement. The $2,000 is deductible to the employer in the current year and is not taxable to Polly until she withdraws the money from the plan. Any earnings on the money contributed to the plan are also taxable only upon withdrawal from the plan. ♦

The tax code provides for a number of different types of plans for taxpayers to save for retirement. Most retirement plans have a number of requirements in order to be classified as "qualified," thereby extending the tax benefits described previously:

- Funding requirements: Most plans require that the benefit be extended to all employees and not favor only the highly-compensated (nondiscriminatory).

- Fiduciary responsibility: Most plans require a separate account to hold the retirement assets, typically handled by a bank or financial institution.
- Early withdrawals: Most plans penalize or prohibit early distributions from the plan with limited hardship exceptions.
- Vesting requirement: Some plans require immediate "vesting" of contributions (i.e., the contributions are immediately set aside for an employee and will not be returned to the employer even if the employee leaves the company).

The retirement plan area has become one of the most complex areas of the tax law. Many tax accountants refer taxpayers to a specialist for help in choosing a plan and for guidance with the ongoing employee coverage, tax reporting, and contribution requirements. The coverage in this textbook is meant to give a simple overview of several common options available to taxpayers for tax-deferred retirement plans, which remain some of the best completely legal tax shelters available. Retirement plans for small businesses are covered here while large retirement plans, which are generally operated by larger employers, are covered in Chapter 9.

5-4a Self-Employed and Small Business Retirement Plan Options

Although available to small businesses, complex retirement plans such as defined-benefit plans or employee stock ownership plans are generally used by only large companies due to their complexity and cost to operate (see Chapter 9). However, over time, the tax law has created a number of retirement plans directed at the small business owner or even a self-employed sole proprietor.

5-4b IRA-Based Plans

IRA-based plans include the Payroll Deduction IRA, the Simplified Employee Pension (SEP or SEP IRA), and the SIMPLE IRA. All are quite easy to establish and require no annual reporting by the employer.

A Payroll Deduction IRA is probably the easiest type of plan to offer. Contributions are withheld from an employee's pay and directed into a traditional IRA account. No plan setup is necessary other than having the employee direct the payroll withholding to the IRA custodian. Contribution limits are the same as the traditional IRA limits ($6,000 or $7,000, if a catch-up contribution). There are no requirements for minimum employee coverage and employees can elect how much they want directed to the IRA at any time.

A SEP is an IRA-based retirement plan available to any employer (including a self-employed individual). These plans are simple to establish; the IRS even provides a one-page Form 5305-SEP that can be used to set up the plan. SEPs have flexible funding requirements in case funding the plan with consistent contribution amounts might be an issue for the underlying business. The amount of contributions can change from year-to-year and can be zero. Employees that meet the SEP requirements for minimum age (21) and years of service (employed by the employer for at least three of the last five years), and make at least $650 in annual compensation, *must* be offered an opportunity to participate in the SEP.

SEP contributions and deductions are limited under different rules for employees versus a self-employed business owner. The maximum contribution made for an employee and the related deduction cannot exceed the lesser of 25 percent of the employee's compensation or $61,000 in 2022. For the self-employed business owner, the contribution maximum is the same 25 percent as for employees; however, the deduction limit considers the net self-employment income after consideration of the deduction for the contribution to the SEP. As a result, the deduction available for the self-employed will be slightly lower than that of an employee and is derived by taking the plan contribution rate and dividing by one plus the contribution rate; thus, effectively lowering the maximum contribution rate to 20 percent (0.25 ÷ 1.25).

EXAMPLE Dan is a self-employed doctor. His net earned income (Schedule C net income less one-half of self-employment tax) from his practice is $125,000. Under the terms of his SEP plan, Dan contributes 20 percent of compensation (up to the maximum allowable) to the plan for his employees. Dan's maximum deduction is calculated as follows: Dan's self-employed rate is 0.20 ÷ 1.20 = 0.1666 or 16.667 percent. His maximum deduction is $20,834, which is the lesser of 16.667% × $125,000 ($20,834) or $61,000. ♦

A SIMPLE IRA is available to any employer with 100 or fewer employees (including a self-employed individual). SIMPLE IRAs are also easy to establish (Form 5304-SIMPLE or 5305-SIMPLE) and administer. Both the employee and the employer are eligible to contribute with an annual limit of $14,000 ($17,000 for taxpayers age 50 or older) in 2022. The SIMPLE IRA must be offered to employees with compensation of at least $5,000 in any prior two years and are expected to have compensation of $5,000 in the current year. Unlike a SEP, a SIMPLE IRA requires certain contributions *must* be made by the employer. Employees decide how much they would like to contribute and the employer must match employees for the first 3 percent of compensation (with some flexibility) or 2 percent of each eligible employee's compensation regardless of the employee's contributions.

5-4c **401(k)-Based Plans**

One of the more popular qualified retirement plans is the Section 401(k) plan, which permits an employee to choose to receive a direct payment of compensation in cash or to defer the amount through an employer contribution on behalf of the employee to plan. Such a plan may be structured as a salary reduction agreement. The agreement may allow the employee to reduce their compensation or forgo an increase in compensation, with the amount contributed to the qualified retirement plan, thereby deferring tax on the compensation. Employees choose the percentage of their pay which will be withheld and contributed to the plan. Some employers match employee contributions up to a certain percentage in order to encourage participation.

EXAMPLE In 2022, Margo elects to defer 5 percent of her next year's salary into her company's 401k plan. Margo's 2022 salary is $50,000 and thus $2,500 ($50,000 × 5%) will be contributed to the 401k plan. Her taxable wages for 2022 will be $47,500. ♦

Any matching amount contributed to the plan by the employer on behalf of the employee is also excluded from the employee's gross income. The contributions and the earnings on the amounts invested in the plan are taxable when withdrawn.

EXAMPLE In the previous example, Margo's employer matches contributions up to 4 percent and thus contributes an additional $2,000 ($50,000 × 4 percent) to Margo's 401k plan. The $2,000 is also excluded from Margo's taxable wages. ♦

Employment taxes (covered in Chapter 9) apply to the employee's contribution but do not apply to the employer's match.

In all 401(k) plans, contributions are limited in two ways: (1) for 2022, an employee may elect to make an annual contribution up to $20,500 ($26,500 for taxpayers age 50 or older) to a Section 401(k) plan, and (2) the amount of total contributions (employee plus employer) made to the Section 401(k) plan are also subject to the limitations applicable to all qualified plans (25 percent of compensation, subject to a limit of $61,000, not including catch-up contributions if over age 50). The annual maximum ($20,500, or $26,500 if age 50 or over, in 2022) is reduced dollar for dollar by amounts contributed as a result of the employee's participation in other salary reduction plans of any employer. Contributions in excess of the maximum allowed may be subject to a 10-percent excise tax imposed on the employer.

EXAMPLE Carol, age 48, participates in a Section 401(k) plan. Carol's salary is $30,000 per year and she chooses to contribute 15 percent to the 401(k) plan. The maximum amount she may contribute on a tax-deferred basis to the Section 401(k) plan under a salary reduction agreement is $4,500 (15% × $30,000, not to exceed $20,500, in 2022). ♦

Finally, Section 401(k) plans must meet certain requirements in addition to the general qualification requirements for all qualified plans. Generally, any employee who is at least 21 years old with at least 1,000 hours of work performed in a previous year, must be permitted to participate. An employee with over 500 hours in each of three consecutive years must also be permitted to participate. The amount deferred must be 100-percent vested and may be distributed only upon retirement, death, disability, or other separation from service, attainment of age 59½, or hardship.

A traditional 401(k) plan can be used by any type of company but is generally thought to be more appropriate for business with at least twenty employees due to the cost to establish and administer the plan. An annual reporting of the plan assets is required (Form 5500) and special annual IRS testing is required to ensure that the plan does not favor highly-compensated employees. One of the newest types of traditional 401k plans is the automatic enrollment 401k. As the name describes, in this type of plan employees are automatically enrolled in the plan unless they opt out. Not only do auto-enroll plans nudge employees into saving for retirement, the typically higher participation rates decrease the chances of the plan favoring highly-compensated employees. To provide incentive to employers to create auto-enroll plans, there is an annual $500 Small Employer Automatic Enrollment credit which can be claimed for up to three years for certain qualified employers.

For small businesses with employees, a safe harbor 401(k) plan operates like other 401(k) plans with one important distinction: it must provide for employer contributions that are fully vested when made. These contributions may be employer-matching contributions, limited to employees who defer, or employer contributions made on behalf of all eligible employees, regardless of whether they make elective deferrals. The safe harbor 401(k) plan is not subject to the complex annual nondiscrimination tests that apply to traditional 401(k) plans.

Employers can also set up Roth 401(k)s for their employees. The amounts allowed to be set aside are the same as for regular 401(k)s, but the dollars paid in do not reduce the employees' taxable income, which is similar to the tax treatment of Roth IRAs. Withdrawals, including earnings, are generally tax-free based on rules similar to those for Roth IRA withdrawals. Roth 401(k)s are popular because they allow a significantly higher Roth contribution than a Roth IRA and because there is no AGI limitation, they may be used by high-income taxpayers.

A self-employed 401(k) or solo 401(k) is designed for self-employed individuals with no employees (spouse is permitted). Setup and maintenance of the plan are relatively inexpensive and easy.

Self-Study Problem 5.4 *See Appendix E for Solutions to Self-Study Problems*

a. Lewis, a self-employed individual, has net earned income of $50,000 in 2022. If Lewis has no employees, calculate the maximum contribution to a SEP plan that he may deduct from his adjusted gross income.

b. During 2022, Linda, age 32, has a salary of $40,000. She participates in a Section 401(k) plan and chooses to defer 25 percent of her compensation.

   i. What is the maximum amount Linda can contribute to the Section 401(k) plan on a tax-deferred basis?

   ii. If Linda's salary was $125,000, instead of $40,000, what is the maximum amount that she could contribute to the Section 401(k) plan on a tax-deferred basis?

c. Laura contributed $78,000 (including employer match) of pre-tax salary to her 401(k) plan over the years. In 2022, at age 62, she retires and takes a distribution of $25,000 when the 401(k) has an account balance of $164,000. Compute the taxable portion of Laura's distribution.

5-5 OTHER FOR AGI DEDUCTIONS

5.5 Learning Objective

Describe other adjustments for adjusted gross income.

There are a number of other deductions for AGI available under the tax law. Because of the limited nature of these deductions, a less detailed description is provided. The deduction for one-half of self-employment tax, which affects almost all self-employed taxpayers, is described in Chapter 4.

5-5a Educator Expenses

Eligible educators may deduct up to $300 for the unreimbursed cost of classroom materials such as books, supplies, computer equipment, supplementary materials, and personal protective equipment and supplies used for the prevention of the spread of COVID-19 as a deduction in arriving at AGI. An eligible educator is a K-12 teacher, instructor, counselor, principal or aide who works at least 900 hours a school year in a school that provides elementary or secondary education. If a married couple filing jointly are both eligible educators, the total deduction is up to $600 but not more than $300 for either spouse.

EXAMPLE Glen and Iris Holland are a married couple that files jointly, and both are high school teachers. In 2022, Glen and Iris spent $320 and $120 on various school supplies, respectively. The Hollands are eligible for a $420 ($300 + $120) educator expense for AGI deduction. ♦

5-5b Unreimbursed Business Expenses for Performing Artists and Others

As discussed later in this chapter, employees that incur business expenses are no longer permitted to deduct those costs as an itemized deduction subject to a 2 percent of AGI floor. Certain employee taxpayers, however, are eligible to take a for AGI deduction for unreimbursed employee costs and thus, are not required to itemize to deduct these costs.

There are three different types of taxpayers eligible for this deduction (and the rules are different for each one):

1. Performing artists who worked for two or more employers during the year
2. National Guard or Reserve member
3. Fee-basis government officials

Performing artists may deduct employee business expenses as a for AGI deduction if they meet the following qualifications:

1. The taxpayer was paid for providing performing arts as an employee for at least two employers.
2. The taxpayer received at least $200 each from any two of these employers.
3. The related performing-arts business expenses are more than 10 percent of gross income from the performance of those services, and
4. AGI is not more than $16,000 before deducting these business expenses.

Members of a reserve component of the Armed Forces of the United States that travel more than 100 miles away from home in connection with services in the reserves can deduct travel expenses. The travel expense deduction is limited to the regular federal per diem rate (for lodging, meals, and incidental expenses) and the standard mileage rate (for car expenses) plus any parking fees, ferry fees, and tolls. Per diems are discussed in Chapter 3.

Certain fee-basis officials can claim their employee business expenses. Fee-basis officials are persons who are employed by a state or local government and who are paid in whole or in part on a fee basis.

EXAMPLE Sally is a building inspector for the city of Hickory, Indiana. Sally is compensated solely from fees paid directly to her by clients and is not considered an employee of Hickory. Sally's travel and other business expenses can be deducted as a for AGI deduction. ♦

Unreimbursed business expenses that are deductible are claimed on Form 2106.

5-5c Moving Expenses

In the past, the tax law provided a deduction for moving expenses to help relieve taxpayers of a portion of the financial burden of moving from one job location to another. The deduction for moving expenses is currently suspended (through 2025) for all taxpayers except members of the Armed Forces of the United States on active duty whose move is pursuant to a military order and incident to a permanent change of station.

Reimbursements to an employee from an employer for qualified moving costs are no longer excluded from the employee's income.

Under the former law, taxpayers (except for those in the Armed Forces) had to meet three tests in order to deduct moving costs:

1. The taxpayer must change job sites.
2. The taxpayer must move so that the distance from the taxpayer's former residence to the new job location must be at least 50 miles more than the distance from the former residence to the former job location.
3. The taxpayer must remain at the new job location for a certain period of time, generally, thirty-nine weeks. Taxpayers who were self-employed had to work at least seventy-eight weeks at the new location.

Taxpayers in the Armed Forces are not required to meet the time or distance tests.

For the members of the military that qualify, moving expenses are reported on Form 3903.

Self-Study Problem 5.5 *See Appendix E for Solutions to Self-Study Problems*

For each of the following situations, determine the amount of the for AGI deduction for each taxpayer:

a. Professor Hill teaches at Bunker Hall Community College. In 2022, he spent $307 on supplies for his classroom and was not reimbursed.
b. Jackie Rights played the lead role in two different plays in 2022 in the local community theatre. Two different production companies sponsored the plays and so she was an employee of both in 2022 and was paid the same by both employers: $4,000 per play. Jackie spent $1,100 in business expenses such as new business cards, personal management fees, and new head-shots for her portfolio. Her 2022 AGI was $15,200 (she also generated income as a shared-ride vehicle driver).
c. Lieutenant Dan of the U.S. Army was stationed in Fort Bragg, NC. In 2022, his permanent post was moved from Bragg to Fort Jackson. The unreimbursed moving costs for he and his wife are $4,500.

5-6 MEDICAL EXPENSES

5.6 Learning Objective

Calculate the itemized deduction for medical expenses.

Medical expenses are the first itemized deduction listed on Schedule A. Taxpayers are allowed a deduction for the medical expenses paid for themselves, their spouse, and dependents. Unreimbursed medical expenses can only be deducted to the extent that they exceed 7.5 percent of the taxpayer's AGI. The formula for calculating a taxpayer's medical expense deduction is as follows:

Prescription medicines and drugs, insulin, doctors, dentists, hospitals, medical insurance premiums	$ xxx
Other medical and dental expenses, such as lodging, transportation, eyeglasses, contact lenses, etc.	xxx
Less: insurance reimbursements	(xxx)
Subtotal	xxx
Less: 7.5 percent of adjusted gross income	(xxx)
Excess expenses qualifying for the medical deduction	$ xxx

5-6a What Qualifies as a Medical Expense?

Expenses that are deductible as medical expenses include the cost of items for the diagnosis, cure, mitigation, treatment, and prevention of disease. Also included are expenditures incurred that affect any structure or function of the body. Therefore, amounts for all of the following categories of expenditures qualify as medical expenses:

- Prescription medicines and drugs and insulin
- Fees for doctors, dentists, nurses, and other medical professionals
- Hospital fees
- Hearing aids, dentures, prescription eyeglasses, and contact lenses
- Medical transportation and lodging
- Medical aids, such as crutches, wheelchairs, and guide dogs

- Birth control prescriptions
- Acupuncture
- Psychiatric care
- Medical insurance premiums, including Medicare premiums
- Certain capital expenditures deemed medically necessary by a doctor
- Nursing home care for the chronically ill (e.g., Alzheimer's disease care)

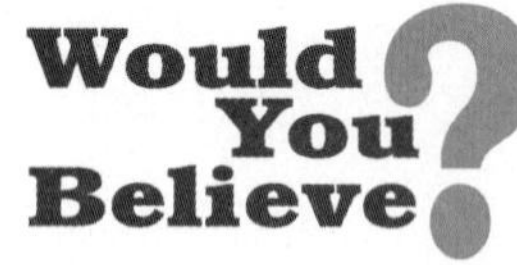

The IRS has allowed a deduction for the following unusual medical expenses:
- Long-distance phone calls made to a psychological counselor
- Hair transplants for premature baldness
- A wig prescribed by a psychiatrist for a taxpayer upset by hair loss
- A mobile phone for a taxpayer who may need instantaneous medical help
- Treatments provided by a Native American medicine man

Certain medical expenses are not deductible. For example, the cost of travel for the general improvement of the taxpayer's health is not deductible. The expense of a swimming pool is not deductible unless the pool is designed specially for the hydrotherapeutic treatment of the taxpayer's illness. No deduction is allowed for the cost of weight-loss programs (unless prescribed by a doctor; diet foods do not qualify) or marriage counseling. Medical expenses for unnecessary cosmetic surgery or similar procedures are not deductible. Cosmetic surgery is considered unnecessary unless it corrects (1) a congenital abnormality, (2) a personal injury resulting from an accident or trauma, or (3) a disfiguring disease. In general, unnecessary cosmetic surgery is any procedure which is directed at improving the patient's appearance and does not meaningfully promote the proper function of the body or prevent or treat illness or disease.

Taxpayers that do not spend medical expenses greater than 7.5 percent of AGI can still enjoy the tax benefit associated with the deduction by using the medical flexible spending account discussed in Chapter 2. By excluding up to $2,850 from gross income, the after-tax savings is basically identical to taking the medical expense deduction for the same amount.

5-6b **Medical Insurance**

Medical insurance includes standard health policies, whether the benefits are paid to the taxpayer or to the provider of the services directly. In addition, the premiums paid for membership in health maintenance plans are deductible as medical insurance, as are supplemental payments for optional Medicare coverage. Insurance policies that pay a specific amount each day or week the taxpayer is hospitalized are not considered medical insurance and the premiums are not deductible. Premiums paid for qualified long-term care insurance policies are also deductible medical expenses up to specified limits which change each year and are based on the age of the taxpayer.

Self-employed taxpayers are allowed, subject to certain limitations, a deduction for adjusted gross income for the medical insurance premiums paid for themselves and their families. Long-term care insurance premiums, up to a specified amount based on the taxpayer's age, are considered health insurance for this purpose. These deductions are covered earlier in this chapter. If a deduction is taken for these items in arriving at AGI, then these same expenses are excluded from the medical expense deduction on Schedule A. However, if the self-employed insurance deduction is limited by net self-employment income, the excess medical insurance expenses can be included on Schedule A.

5-6c Medicines and Drugs

Prescription medicines and drugs and insulin are the only drugs deductible as medical expenses. No deduction is allowed for drugs purchased illegally from abroad, including Canada and Mexico. Nonprescription medicines such as over-the-counter antacids, allergy medications, and pain relievers, even if recommended by a physician, are not deductible as a medical expense.

5-6d Capital Expenditures

Payments for capital improvements purchased and installed in the taxpayer's home for medical reasons may also be deductible. Examples include support railings, lowering kitchen cabinets, and medically necessary swimming pools. Unlike other capital expenditures, allowable amounts are deducted fully in the year the item is purchased. If the expenditure is for an improvement that increases the value of the taxpayer's property, the deduction is limited to the amount by which the expenditure exceeds the increase in the value of the property. If the value of the property does not increase as a result of the expenditure, the entire cost is deductible. The cost of upkeep and operation of an item, the cost of which qualified as a medical expense, is also deductible, provided the medical reason for the improvement or special equipment still exists. To take advantage of this deduction, the taxpayer must show the improvement is used primarily for and directly related to medical care. A doctor's recommendation is an important factor in supporting the deduction.

EXAMPLE A taxpayer has a heart condition and installs an elevator in his home at a cost of $6,000. The value of the home is increased by $4,000 as a result of the improvement. The taxpayer is allowed a deduction of $2,000 ($6,000 − $4,000), the excess of the cost of the equipment over the increase in the value of the taxpayer's home. ♦

5-6e Transportation

Transportation expenses primarily and necessary for medical care are deductible, including amounts paid for taxis, trains, buses, airplanes, and ambulances. Taxpayers may also claim a deduction for the use of their personal automobile for medical transportation. However, only out-of-pocket expenses such as the cost of gas and oil are deductible. Maintenance, insurance, general repair, and depreciation expenses are not deductible. If the taxpayer does not wish to deduct actual costs of transportation by personal automobile, the standard mileage rate for medical care purposes is 18 cents per mile through June 30th and 22 cents per mile thereafter in 2022. In addition to the deduction for actual automobile costs or the standard mileage amount, parking and toll fees for medical transportation are deductible medical expenses. If the transportation expenses are for the medical care of a dependent child, the amounts are deductible by the parent.

5-6f Lodging for Medical Care

Taxpayers may deduct the cost of lodging up to $50 per night, per person, on a trip primarily for and essential to medical care provided by a physician or a licensed hospital. The deduction is allowed for the patient and an individual accompanying the patient, such as the parent of a child. However, no deduction is allowed if the trip involves a significant element of recreation or vacation. No deduction is allowed for meal costs.

TAX BREAK

The cost of buying, training, and maintaining a service animal to assist a visually impaired person, a hearing disabled person, or a person with other physical disabilities, qualifies as a medical expense.

ProConnect™ Tax TIP

Itemized deductions are located under Deductions/Itemized Deductions (Schedule A). Subheadings for each of the itemized deductions will be found in the left-hand margin.

Self-Study Problem 5.6 *See Appendix E for Solutions to Self-Study Problems*

During the 2022 tax year, Frank (age 65) and Betty (age 63) paid the following medical expenses:

Medical insurance	$ 425
Prescription medicines and drugs	364
Hospital bills	2,424
Health club dues	725
Prescription eyeglasses for Frank's dependent mother	75
Doctor bills for Betty's sister, who is claimed as a dependent by Frank and Betty	220

In addition, during 2022, they drove 700 miles (all after June 30) for medical transportation in their personal automobile. Their insurance company reimbursed Frank and Betty $1,400 during the year for the medical expenses. If their adjusted gross income for the year is $25,000, calculate their medical expense deduction. Use the Medical and Dental Expenses section of Schedule A of Form 1040 on Page 5-23.

Learning Objective 5.7

Calculate the itemized deduction for taxes.

5-7 TAXES

Taxpayers are allowed to deduct certain state, local, and foreign taxes paid during the year. The purpose of the deduction for taxes is to relieve the burden of multiple taxation of the same income. However, the tax law distinguishes between a "tax" and a "fee." A tax is imposed by a government to raise revenue for general public purposes, and a fee is a charge with a direct benefit to the person paying the fee. Taxes are generally deductible; fees are not deductible. For example, postage, fishing licenses, and dog tags are considered fees that are not deductible as taxes.

Prior to the enactment of the TCJA, tax law provided for an itemized deduction for the following taxes:

- State, local, and foreign income taxes
- Sales taxes (in lieu of state and local income taxes)
- State, local, and foreign real property taxes
- State, local, and foreign personal property taxes

After the TCJA, these taxes largely remain deductible; however, foreign property taxes are only deductible if incurred in carrying on a business or for the production of income (e.g., rental activity). In addition, the aggregate amount of the deduction for state and local real property taxes, state and local personal property taxes, state and local, and foreign, income taxes, and general sales taxes (if elected) for any tax year is limited to $10,000 ($5,000 for married filing separately). But, the $10,000 aggregate limitation rule does not apply to (i) foreign income taxes; (ii) state and local, and foreign real property taxes; and (iii) state and local personal property taxes, if these taxes are paid or accrued in carrying on a business or for the production of income. In other words, taxes deductible on an individual's Schedule C, Schedule E, or Schedule F remain fully deductible and are not subject to the limitation. Note that state and local *income* taxes are not included in the business-related exclusion from the limitation as these taxes have always been deductible as an itemized deduction on an individual's Schedule A. These provisions (the loss of the foreign property tax deduction and $10,000 deduction limitation) apply through 2025.

Self-Study Problems 5.6, 5.7, 5.8, 5.9, and 5.10

SCHEDULE A (Form 1040)
Department of the Treasury
Internal Revenue Service

Itemized Deductions

Go to *www.irs.gov/ScheduleA* for instructions and the latest information.
Attach to Form 1040 or 1040-SR.
Caution: If you are claiming a net qualified disaster loss on Form 4684, see the instructions for line 16.

OMB No. 1545-0074
2022
Attachment Sequence No. **07**

Name(s) shown on Form 1040 or 1040-SR | **Your social security number**

Section	Line	Description	Box	Amount	Box	Amount
Medical and Dental Expenses		**Caution:** Do not include expenses reimbursed or paid by others.				
	1	Medical and dental expenses (see instructions)	1			
	2	Enter amount from Form 1040 or 1040-SR, line 11 [2]				
	3	Multiply line 2 by 7.5% (0.075)	3			
	4	Subtract line 3 from line 1. If line 3 is more than line 1, enter -0-			4	
Taxes You Paid	5	State and local taxes.				
	a	State and local income taxes or general sales taxes. You may include either income taxes or general sales taxes on line 5a, but not both. If you elect to include general sales taxes instead of income taxes, check this box ☐	5a			
	b	State and local real estate taxes (see instructions)	5b			
	c	State and local personal property taxes	5c			
	d	Add lines 5a through 5c	5d			
	e	Enter the smaller of line 5d or $10,000 ($5,000 if married filing separately)	5e			
	6	Other taxes. List type and amount:	6			
	7	Add lines 5e and 6			7	
Interest You Paid Caution: Your mortgage interest deduction may be limited. See instructions.	8	Home mortgage interest and points. If you didn't use all of your home mortgage loan(s) to buy, build, or improve your home, see instructions and check this box ☐				
	a	Home mortgage interest and points reported to you on Form 1098. See instructions if limited	8a			
	b	Home mortgage interest not reported to you on Form 1098. See instructions if limited. If paid to the person from whom you bought the home, see instructions and show that person's name, identifying no., and address	8b			
	c	Points not reported to you on Form 1098. See instructions for special rules	8c			
	d	Reserved for future use	8d			
	e	Add lines 8a through 8c	8e			
	9	Investment interest. Attach Form 4952 if required. See instructions	9			
	10	Add lines 8e and 9			10	
Gifts to Charity Caution: If you made a gift and got a benefit for it, see instructions.	11	Gifts by cash or check. If you made any gift of $250 or more, see instructions	11			
	12	Other than by cash or check. If you made any gift of $250 or more, see instructions. You **must** attach Form 8283 if over $500	12			
	13	Carryover from prior year	13			
	14	Add lines 11 through 13			14	
Casualty and Theft Losses	15	Casualty and theft loss(es) from a federally declared disaster (other than net qualified disaster losses). Attach Form 4684 and enter the amount from line 18 of that form. See instructions			15	
Other Itemized Deductions	16	Other—from list in instructions. List type and amount:			16	
Total Itemized Deductions	17	Add the amounts in the far right column for lines 4 through 16. Also, enter this amount on Form 1040 or 1040-SR, line 12			17	
	18	If you elect to itemize deductions even though they are less than your standard deduction, check this box ☐				

For Paperwork Reduction Act Notice, see the Instructions for Form 1040. Cat. No. 17145C **Schedule A (Form 1040) 2022**

EXAMPLE Britney and Brad are married taxpayers filing jointly. In 2022, Britney has $7,800 in state income taxes withheld by her employer from her wages. Brad operates a sole proprietorship that owns a building and pays property taxes of $2,300. Brad also pays estimated state income tax payments on his business of $4,000. Lastly, in 2022 Brad and Britney pay property taxes on their home of $1,600. The $2,300 of property taxes associated with the business building are deductible on Schedule C as a business deduction. The $13,400 of itemized deduction for taxes includes Britney's state income taxes ($7,800), Brad's estimated tax payments ($4,000), and the property taxes on their home ($1,600). However, the itemized deduction for taxes is limited to $10,000 in 2022. ♦

The following taxes are not deductible:

- Federal income taxes
- Employee portion of Social Security taxes
- Estate, inheritance, and gift taxes (except in unusual situations not discussed here)
- Excise taxes and gasoline taxes (except when business-related)
- Foreign income taxes if the taxpayer elects a foreign tax credit

5-7a **Income Taxes and Sales Taxes**

Taxpayers may elect to deduct either state and local sales and use taxes or state and local income taxes as itemized deductions. The election to deduct state and local sales tax instead of income tax primarily benefits taxpayers in states with no income taxes or low income tax rates.

For taxpayers electing to deduct state and local income taxes paid during 2022, the amount of the deduction is the total amount of state and local taxes withheld from wages plus any amounts actually paid during the year, even if the tax payments are for a prior year's tax liability. If the taxpayer receives a refund of taxes deducted in a previous year, the refund must generally be included in gross income (e.g., Line 1 on Schedule 1 of the Form 1040) in the year the refund is received. Taxes which did not provide any tax benefit (reduction in taxes) in the year paid are not required to be included in income in the year received as a refund. For example, a taxpayer claiming the standard deduction in the year taxes are paid does not receive a tax benefit for the payment and is not required to include in income a tax refund received the following year.

EXAMPLE For 2022, Mary's total itemized deductions are $4,500, including state income tax withheld of $1,800. As a result, Mary uses the standard deduction of $12,950. When Mary prepares her 2022 state income taxes, she realizes that she overpaid state income tax through withholding by $200 and receives a refund in 2023. In early 2024, she receives a Form 1099-G reporting her $200 state income tax refund. Because Mary did not benefit from the state tax deduction since she used the standard deduction, she is not required to include the $200 refund in income. ♦

EXAMPLE Damone paid state income and property taxes of $10,250 in 2022. Damone claimed total itemized deductions of $13,200, including the $10,000 limit on state and local taxes. In 2023, Damone received a state income tax refund of $1,000. If Damone had deducted the actual amount of state taxes in 2022, he would have deducted on $9,250 ($10,250 paid in 2022 less $1,000 refund). His adjusted total itemized deductions would have been $12,450. As a result, Damone would have elected the standard deduction of $12,950 in 2022. The difference between his 2022-claimed itemized deductions ($13,200) and his properly adjusted standard deduction ($12,950) is $250. Thus, he received a $250 benefit from the overpayment of taxes, and Damone must include $250 in his 2023 income. ♦

For taxpayers electing to deduct sales taxes in 2022, the deduction is calculated by using either (a) actual sales taxes paid or (b) estimated sales taxes from IRS tables. Actual sales and use tax expenses are based on a "general sales tax," which is a tax imposed at one rate with respect to the retail sale of a broad range of classes of items. To the extent a higher sales tax rate than the general rate applies to motor vehicles, that excess amount is specifically excluded from the deduction amount.

The actual sales taxes paid method requires a taxpayer to maintain extensive records to substantiate the sales and use taxes paid during the year. To ease the burden on taxpayers, the tax law also permits taxpayers to use estimated state sales tax tables to calculate the deduction. Taxpayers using the estimation tables may add the sales taxes paid on items that include motor vehicles (car, truck, van, motor home, recreational vehicle), aircraft, boats, a home or a substantial addition or renovation to a home. The estimated state sales tax tables are based on the taxpayer's adjusted gross income modified by adding back certain tax-exempt sources of income such as tax-exempt interest, workers compensation, and the nontaxable parts of Social Security or qualified retirement plan distributions. The estimated sales tax also differs by the number of dependents a taxpayer has. The following is a portion of the sales tax estimation table:

2021 Optional State Sales Tax Tables

Income		Family Size						Family Size						Family Size					
At least	But less than	1	2	3	4	5	Over 5	1	2	3	4	5	Over 5	1	2	3	4	5	Over 5
		Alabama			**1**		**4.0000%**	**Arizona**			**2**		**5.6000%**	**Arkansas**			**2**		**6.5000%**
$0	$20,000	252	294	323	345	363	389	246	280	302	319	332	352	283	318	341	358	372	391
$20,000	$30,000	360	421	461	493	519	555	363	413	445	470	491	519	433	488	523	549	571	600
$30,000	$40,000	415	485	531	567	597	639	423	481	519	548	572	605	513	578	620	651	677	712
$40,000	$50,000	461	538	590	630	663	710	475	540	582	615	641	678	582	656	704	739	768	808
$50,000	$60,000	502	586	642	685	721	772	520	591	638	674	703	744	645	726	779	819	851	895
$60,000	$70,000	538	628	688	735	773	827	561	638	688	727	758	802	701	790	848	891	926	975
$70,000	$80,000	571	666	730	780	821	878	599	681	734	775	809	856	754	849	911	958	996	1048
$80,000	$90,000	601	702	769	821	864	925	634	720	777	820	856	906	802	905	971	1020	1061	1116
$90,000	$100,000	630	735	805	860	905	968	666	757	817	863	900	952	849	957	1027	1079	1122	1181
$100,000	$120,000	667	778	853	911	958	1025	709	806	870	919	959	1014	910	1027	1102	1158	1204	1267
$120,000	$140,000	716	835	915	976	1028	1099	765	870	939	991	1034	1094	991	1118	1199	1261	1311	1380
$140,000	$160,000	760	887	971	1037	1091	1167	817	929	1002	1058	1104	1168	1066	1203	1291	1358	1412	1486
$160,000	$180,000	801	934	1023	1092	1149	1229	865	983	1061	1120	1169	1236	1136	1282	1376	1447	1505	1584
$180,000	$200,000	839	978	1072	1144	1204	1288	910	1034	1116	1178	1229	1300	1202	1357	1456	1532	1593	1677
$200,000	$225,000	878	1024	1122	1198	1260	1348	956	1087	1173	1238	1292	1367	1271	1435	1541	1620	1685	1774
$225,000	$250,000	920	1073	1176	1255	1320	1412	1006	1143	1234	1303	1359	1438	1346	1519	1631	1716	1784	1879
$250,000	$275,000	960	1119	1226	1308	1376	1472	1052	1196	1291	1363	1423	1505	1416	1599	1717	1806	1878	1977
$275,000	$300,000	997	1162	1273	1359	1430	1529	1097	1247	1346	1421	1483	1568	1484	1675	1799	1892	1968	2072
$300,000	or more	1213	1414	1549	1653	1739	1859	1358	1544	1666	1759	1835	1941	1887	2132	2290	2409	2506	2640
Income		**California**			**3**		**7.2500%**	**Colorado**			**2**		**2.9000%**	**Connecticut**			**4**		**6.3500%**
$0	$20,000	314	356	384	405	422	446	127	138	144	150	154	159	218	237	248	257	264	273
$20,000	$30,000	458	520	560	591	616	651	191	208	218	226	232	241	337	366	384	397	408	423
$30,000	$40,000	532	603	650	686	715	755	225	245	257	266	273	283	401	435	457	473	486	503
$40,000	$50,000	595	674	726	766	799	844	254	276	290	301	309	320	457	496	521	539	553	573
$50,000	$60,000	650	737	794	837	873	922	280	305	320	331	341	353	508	551	578	598	614	636
$60,000	$70,000	700	793	855	901	940	993	304	330	347	359	369	383	554	601	631	653	670	694
$70,000	$80,000	745	845	910	960	1001	1057	325	354	372	385	396	410	597	648	680	703	722	747
$80,000	$90,000	787	892	961	1014	1057	1117	346	376	395	409	420	435	637	691	725	750	771	798
$90,000	$100,000	827	937	1009	1064	1110	1172	364	396	416	431	443	459	675	733	769	795	817	845
$100,000	$120,000	879	996	1073	1131	1179	1246	390	424	445	461	474	491	726	788	827	855	878	909
$120,000	$140,000	946	1072	1155	1218	1270	1341	422	459	483	500	514	532	793	861	903	934	959	993
$140,000	$160,000	1008	1143	1231	1298	1353	1429	453	493	517	536	551	571	856	929	974	1008	1035	1072

*The 2022 version of the Optional State Sales Tax Tables was not available as we went to print. Please check the IRS website (**www.irs.gov**) for updates to the instructions for Form 1040 Schedule A.

Because a number of states permit localities to also charge a general sale tax, a local sales tax table for some of the states is provided to assist with that calculation. Because the estimation method is fairly complex, the IRS provides a worksheet to assist with the deduction calculation and most tax preparation software will compute the amounts as well.

ProConnect™ Tax TIP

When it comes to entering state tax deduction information, much of the work will be done elsewhere. For example, income taxes withheld are generally input as part of the W-2 input. Estimated payments are input under the primary heading Payments, Penalties, and Extensions. Lastly, ProConnect Tax has the state sales tax calculator built in and does not require the manual completion of the state and local sales tax worksheet.

State and Local General Sales Tax Deduction Worksheet—Line 5a*

Keep for Your Records 

Instead of using this worksheet, you can find your deduction by using the Sales Tax Deduction Calculator at IRS.gov/SalesTax.

Before you begin: See the instructions for line 1 of the worksheet if you:

√ Lived in more than one state during 2022, or

√ Had any **nontaxable** income in 2022.

1. Enter your **state** general sales taxes from the 2022 Optional State Sales Tax Table . . . . **1.** $________

Next. If, for all of 2022, you lived only in Connecticut, the District of Columbia, Indiana, Kentucky, Maine, Maryland, Massachusetts, Michigan, New Jersey, or Rhode Island, skip lines 2 through 5, enter -0- on line 6, and go to line 7. Otherwise, go to line 2.

2. Did you live in Alaska, Arizona, Arkansas, Colorado, Georgia, Illinois, Louisiana, Mississippi, Missouri, New York, North Carolina, South Carolina, Tennessee, Utah, or Virginia in 2022?

☐ **No.** Enter -0-.

☐ **Yes.** Enter your base **local** general sales taxes from the 2022 Optional Local Sales Tax Tables. . . . . **2.** $________

3. Did your locality impose a **local** general sales tax in 2022? Residents of California and Nevada, see the instructions for line 3 of the worksheet.

☐ **No.** Skip lines 3 through 5, enter -0- on line 6, and go to line 7.

☐ **Yes.** Enter your **local** general sales tax rate, but omit the percentage sign. For example, if your local general sales tax rate was 2.5%, enter 2.5. If your local general sales tax rate changed or you lived in more than one locality in the same state during 2022, see the instructions for line 3 of the worksheet . . . . **3.** ____.____

4. Did you enter -0- on line 2?

☐ **No.** Skip lines 4 and 5 and go to line 6.

☐ **Yes.** Enter your **state** general sales tax rate (shown in the table heading for your state), but omit the percentage sign. For example, if your state general sales tax rate is 6%, enter 6.0 . . . . **4.** ____.____

5. Divide line 3 by line 4. Enter the result as a decimal (rounded to at least three places) . . . . **5.** ____.____

6. Did you enter -0- on line 2?

☐ **No.** Multiply line 2 by line 3.

☐ **Yes.** Multiply line 1 by line 5. If you lived in more than one locality in the same state during 2022, see the instructions for line 6 of the worksheet. . . . . **6.** $________

7. Enter your state and local general sales taxes paid on specified items, if any. See the instructions for line 7 of the worksheet . . . . **7.** $________

8. **Deduction for general sales taxes.** Add lines 1, 6, and 7. Enter the result here and the total from all your state and local general sales tax deduction worksheets, if you completed more than one, on Schedule A, line 5a. Be sure to check the **box** on that line . . . . **8.** $________

*Download the latest version of this worksheet from the Schedule A instructions available at www.irs.gov. The 2022 worksheet was not available as we went to print. This worksheet is adapted from the 2021 version.

The IRS also provides an online sales tax deduction calculator at **www.irs.gov**.

EXAMPLE Jason and Tina Sterling are married filing jointly taxpayers and residents of Brentwood, Tennessee (Davidson County, zip code 37027). They have no dependents and their AGI for 2022 is $85,000. Brentwood has a 9.25 percent sales tax that includes 7 percent for the state portion and 2.25 percent for the local portion. The Sterlings paid no sales tax on specified items during the year.

The state sales tax table for Tennessee provides a general sales tax amount for income between $80,000 and $90,000 for married filing jointly as $1,116. Tennessee permits a local general sales tax, and thus the Sterlings use the Local Sales Tax Table for income between $80,000 and $90,000 with two family members to derive a local sales tax estimate of $186. Using the sales tax deduction worksheet, the local amount of $186 is multiplied by 2.25 to yield a total local sales tax amount of $419. Thus the total sales tax deduction is $1,535. ♦

This example uses 2021 state and local general sales tax estimates as the 2022 amounts were not available as we went to print.

When a married couple files separately, if one spouse uses the optional sales tax tables, the other spouse must use the optional sales tax tables as well.

5-7b **Property Taxes**

Taxes that are levied on state and local real property for the general public welfare are deductible. However, special assessments charged to provide local benefit to property owners are not deductible; these amounts increase the basis of the taxpayer's property. Also, service fees, such as garbage fees and homeowner association fees, are not deductible as property taxes.

If real estate is sold during the year, the taxes must be allocated between the buyer and the seller, and the division must be made according to the number of days in the year that each taxpayer held the property. The seller is generally responsible for the property taxes up to, but not including, the date the house was sold.

EXAMPLE Sally sells her home to Patty on March 3, 2022. The taxes for 2022 are paid by Patty and they total $1,825, or $5.00 per day ($1,825/365 days). The purchaser is treated as the owner on the day of sale. Sally is entitled to deduct sixty-one days of real property taxes or $305 (61 days × $5.00 per day). Patty deducts $1,520 (304 days × $5.00 per day). ♦

Generally, the escrow company or closing agent handling the sale of the property will make the allocation of taxes between the buyer and the seller and the result will be reflected in the settlement charges on the transfer of the title. These amounts are itemized on closing statements for the sale, which are provided to the buyer and the seller (see Chapter 4 for an example).

EXAMPLE William purchased a residence from John in 2022. William's closing statement shows that he receives a credit for $299.80 in taxes that he will pay later in the year on behalf of the seller. Assuming that William pays $525.00 in total taxes on the property later in 2022, his property tax deduction for 2022 would be $225.20 ($525.00 − $299.80). John, the seller, would be allowed a deduction for $299.80 plus any other taxes he paid during the year prior to selling the property. ♦

5-7c Personal Property Taxes

To be deductible as an itemized deduction, personal property taxes must be levied based on the value of the property. Taxes of a fixed amount, or those calculated on a basis other than value, are not deductible. For example, automobile fees that are calculated on the basis of the automobile's weight are not deductible.

EXAMPLE Rich lives in a state that charges $20 per year plus 2 percent of the value of the automobile for vehicle registration. If Rich pays $160 [$20 + (2% × $7,000)] for his automobile registration, he may deduct only $140, the amount that is based on the value of the automobile. ♦

Self-Study Problem 5.7 *See Appendix E for Solutions to Self-Study Problems*

Sharon is single, lives in Idaho, and has adjusted gross income of $130,000 for 2022. Sharon deducts state income tax rather than state sales tax. The tax withheld from her salary for state income taxes in 2022 is $6,600, and in May of 2022 she received a $225 refund on her state income tax return for the prior year. Sharon paid real estate taxes on her house of $3,300 for the year and an automobile registration fee of $140, of which $20 is based on the weight of the automobile and the balance on the value of the property. Use the Taxes You Paid section of Schedule A on Page 5-23 to report Sharon's deduction for state and local taxes.

5-8 INTEREST

5.8 Learning Objective

Apply the rules for an individual taxpayer's interest deduction.

Taxpayers are allowed a deduction for certain interest paid or accrued during the tax year. Interest is defined as an amount paid for the use of borrowed funds. The type and amount of the deduction depend on the purpose for which the money is borrowed. Interest on loans for business, rent, and royalty activities is deducted for adjusted gross income. Certain interest on personal loans is deductible as an itemized deduction. The following types of personal interest are deductible:

- Qualified residence interest (mortgage interest)
- Mortgage interest prepayment penalties
- Investment interest
- Certain interest associated with a passive activity

Interest on other loans for personal purposes which do not fall into one of the above categories is generally referred to as consumer interest and is not deductible. Consumer interest includes interest on any loan, the proceeds of which are used for personal purposes, such as credit card interest, finance charges, and automobile loan interest. Interest on loans used to acquire assets generating tax-exempt income is also not deductible.

The following items are not considered "interest" and, therefore, are not deductible as an itemized deduction for interest:

- Service charges
- Credit investigation fees
- Loan fees other than "points" discussed later under Prepaid Interest
- Interest paid to carry single premium life insurance
- Premium on convertible bonds

Many lenders require that home mortgage borrowers purchase private mortgage insurance (PMI) to protect the lender. The deduction for PMI expired at the end of 2021. This provision has been permitted to expire in previous years only to be extended with late legislation. The deduction for PMI phased out for taxpayers with AGI between $100,000 and $109,000.

EXAMPLE Fred and Betty Pebblestone, married filing jointly taxpayers, acquired their principal residence in 2014. The Pebblestone's AGI has never exceeded $100,000. At the time of the mortgage, the lender required that the Pebblestones acquire private mortgage insurance. In 2022, the Pebblestones paid PMI premiums of $1,700. Because the provision to deduct PMI expired in 2021, the Pebblestones will be unable to include the PMI premiums as an itemized deduction for interest. ♦

As we go to print, it is unknown whether Congress will extend the PMI deduction after 2021.

5-8a Taxpayer's Obligation

To deduct interest on a debt, the taxpayer must be legally liable for the debt. No deduction is allowed for payments made for another's obligation, where the taxpayer is not liable for payment. Also, both the lender and the borrower must intend for the loan to be repaid.

EXAMPLE Bill makes a payment on his son's home mortgage since his son is unable to make the current payment. The interest included in the mortgage payment is not deductible by Bill since the mortgage is not his obligation. Bill's son cannot deduct the interest since he did not make the payment. ♦

EXAMPLE Mary loans her daughter $50,000 to start a business. The daughter is 19 years old and unsophisticated in business. No note is signed and no repayment date is mentioned. Mary would be surprised if the daughter's business venture is a success. In all likelihood, a true debtor-creditor relationship is not created. ♦

A taxpayer who assumes the benefits and burdens of ownership, and is considered to essentially be an owner under state law, may be allowed to deduct mortgage interest on a residence even if not directly liable on the mortgage. This situation is not typical and the deduction is allowed only on a case-by-case basis.

5-8b Prepaid Interest

Cash-basis taxpayers are required to use the accrual basis for deducting prepaid interest. Prepaid interest must be capitalized and the deduction spread over the life of the loan. This requirement does not apply to points paid on a mortgage loan for purchasing or improving a taxpayer's principal residence, provided points are customarily charged and they do not exceed the normal rate. Such points paid on a mortgage for the purchase or improvement of a personal residence may be deducted in the year they are paid. Points paid to refinance a home mortgage are not deductible when paid, but must be capitalized and the deduction spread over the life of the loan. Points charged for specific loan services, such as the lender's appraisal fee and other settlement fees, are not deductible.

EXAMPLE On November 1, 2022, Allen, a cash-basis taxpayer, obtains a six-month loan of $500,000 on a new apartment building. On November 1, Allen prepays $36,000 interest on the loan. He must capitalize the prepaid interest and deduct it over the 6-month loan period. Therefore, his interest deduction for 2022 is $12,000 ($36,000/6 months × 2 months). ♦

5-8c Qualified Residence, Home Equity, and Consumer Interest

No deduction is available for consumer (personal) interest, such as interest on credit cards and loans for personal automobiles. Qualified residence interest, however, is a type of personal interest specifically allowed as a deduction. The term "qualified residence interest" is the interest paid on "qualified residence acquisition debt." The term "qualified residence acquisition debt" is defined as debt secured by the taxpayer's principal or second residence in acquiring, constructing, or substantially improving that residence. Qualified residence acquisition debt can include the original mortgage, home equity debt, or refinanced debt. Refinanced debt is treated as acquisition debt only to the extent it does not exceed the principal amount of acquisition debt immediately before the refinancing.

For mortgage debt incurred on or before December 15, 2017, interest is deductible on the first $1 million ($500,000 for married filing separately) of debt. After December 15, 2017, interest related to the first $750,000 of mortgage debt is deductible.

After 2025, the qualified mortgage debt limit returns to $1 million, regardless of the date of the mortgage. Refinancing of pre-TCJA qualified mortgage debt retains the $1 million limit as long as the refinanced debt does not exceed the debt balance at the time of the refinancing.

In order to take a home mortgage interest deduction, debt must be secured by a qualified home (primary residence or second home). A "home" includes a house, condominium, cooperative, and mobile home. A home also includes house trailer, recreational vehicle, boat, or similar property that has sleeping, cooking, and toilet facilities.

EXAMPLE Klaus and Len file jointly in 2022. They purchased their primary residence in New Jersey in January 2016 using a thirty-year mortgage of $1,000,000. In 2022, Klaus and Len decide to refinance the full amount of their $950,000 mortgage balance. Because the refinanced amount is the same or less than the mortgage balance at the time of the refinancing, the interest on the entire $950,000 balance will remain deductible. ♦

EXAMPLE Meredith and Scott file jointly in 2022. They purchase their primary residence in Palo Alto, CA, in January 2022 using a thirty-year mortgage of $1,000,000. In 2022, Meredith and Scott pay interest of $38,000 and make no payments toward loan principle and thus the average loan balance is $1,000,000. Because Meredith and Scott's 2022 mortgage exceeds $750,000, the interest deduction will be limited to $28,500 ($38,000 × $750,000/$1,000,000). ♦

The previously permitted deduction of interest on up to $100,000 of home equity debt has been suspended through 2025 (unless the home equity debt is qualified acquisition debt). Interest on home equity loans incurred prior to 2018 is also not deductible.

EXAMPLE Michael and Jeanette Stern file jointly in 2022. In 2006, the Sterns purchased a home using a mortgage of $400,000. In 2016, when the mortgage balance was $50,000, the Sterns used a $300,000 home equity loan to build a substantial addition to their home. The home equity loan is treated as acquisition financing and thus is treated as qualified mortgage debt and the interest remains deductible. The Sterns could also have used the home equity to refinance the original mortgage debt and retained the deduction of interest. ♦

EXAMPLE Barb is a single taxpayer. In 2022, she uses a home equity loan of $46,000 to pay for a new car and part of her nephew's college tuition. Barb may not deduct any of the interest on the home equity loan. ♦

In certain circumstances, when the debt balance exceeds the purchase price or the fair market value of the home, the amount of deductible interest can be further limited. If loan proceeds are used in part for a qualified residence and part for other purposes, the amount of debt attributable to the residence will need to be determined using tracing rules. See IRS Publication 936 for more information.

If the sum of mortgage interest and other itemized deductions is less than the standard deduction, no tax benefit is received from the mortgage interest payments. In this case, a taxpayer may wish to pay the mortgage off as quickly as possible if the taxpayer believes its investments will generate an after-tax rate of return greater than the interest rate on the home mortgage.

5-8d **Education Loan Interest**

Taxpayers are allowed a deduction for adjusted gross income (above-the-line) for certain interest paid on qualified education loans. The deduction is limited to $2,500 for 2022, and is phased out for single taxpayers with modified AGI of $70,000 to $85,000 and for married taxpayers with modified AGI of $145,000 to $175,000. Qualified higher education expenses include tuition, room and board, and related expenses.

EXAMPLE Sam graduated from college in 2020, taking a job with a salary of $55,000 per year. During 2022, he pays $2,500 interest on qualified education loans. Because his income is below the $70,000 phase-out amount for individual taxpayers, he can deduct the full $2,500 of the interest in arriving at adjusted gross income on his 2022 tax return. If he had paid more than $2,500 in interest, the excess would be considered nondeductible consumer interest. ♦

If the interest is paid through the use of funds from a Section 529 program or through an employer's education assistance program, the interest may not also be deducted as an itemized deduction.

5-8e **Investment Interest**

To prevent abuses by taxpayers, the Internal Revenue Code includes a provision limiting the deduction of investment interest expense. This provision limits the amount of deductible interest on loans to finance investments. The investment interest deduction is limited to the taxpayer's net investment income. Net investment income is income such as dividends and interest, less investment expenses other than interest. Special rules apply to dividends and capital gains included as investment income due to their preferential tax rates. The general rule is that they may only be included as investment income if the taxpayer chooses to calculate tax on them at ordinary income rates. Any disallowed interest expense is carried over and may be deducted in succeeding years, but only to the extent that the taxpayer's net investment income exceeds investment interest expense for the year. The investment interest deduction is reported on Form 4952.

EXAMPLE Karen borrows $150,000 at 12 percent interest on January 1, 2022. The proceeds are used to purchase $100,000 worth of land and a $50,000 Certificate of Deposit (CD). During 2022, the CD pays interest of $1,700. Karen incurs expenses (for example, property taxes) attributable to the investment property of $500. Of the $18,000 (12% × $150,000) interest expense incurred in 2022, $1,200 is deductible due to being limited by the total net investment income in 2022. The deduction is computed as follows:

Investment income	$1,700
Less: investment expenses	(500)
Net investment income	$1,200
Interest deductible in 2022	$1,200

The unused deduction of $16,800 ($18,000 − $1,200) is carried forward and may be used as an interest deduction in future years, subject to the net investment income limitation. ♦

Self-Study Problem 5.8 *See Appendix E for Solutions to Self-Study Problems*

Dorothie paid the following amounts during the current year:

Interest on her home mortgage (pre-12/16/17)	$9,250
Service charges on her checking account	48
Credit card interest	168
Auto loan interest	675
Interest from a home equity line of credit (HELOC)	2,300
Interest from a loan used to purchase stock	1,600
Credit investigation fee for loan	75

Dorothie's residence has a fair market value of $250,000. The mortgage is secured by the home at the time of purchase and has a balance of $180,000. Dorothie used the same home to secure her HELOC with a balance of $50,000. Dorothie used the proceeds of her HELOC to pay for college and to buy a new car. Dorothie has $1,000 of net investment income. Compute Dorothie's interest deduction in the following scenarios:

a. Use the Interest You Paid section of Schedule A on Page 5-23 to calculate Dorothie's interest deduction for 2022.

b. Same as part a, and Dorothie used the HELOC proceeds to add a new bedroom to her home.

c. Same as part a, but Dorothie's home is valued at $1.2 million and her mortgage balance is $900,000.

5-9 CHARITABLE CONTRIBUTIONS

5.9 Learning Objective

Determine the charitable contributions deduction.

To encourage individuals to be socially responsible, the Internal Revenue Code allows a deduction for charitable contributions. To be deductible, the donation must be made in cash or property; the value of free use of the taxpayer's property by the charitable organization does not qualify.

EXAMPLE Lucille allows the Red Cross to use her building rent-free for 8 months. The building normally rents for $600 per month. There is no deduction allowed for the free use of the building. ♦

In addition, out-of-pocket expenses related to qualified charitable activities are deductible as charitable contributions.

EXAMPLE Jerry drives his car 200 miles during 2022 to take a church group to a meeting out of town. Jerry is permitted a charitable deduction of $28 (200 miles × 14 cents per mile).

To be deductible, donations must be made to a qualified recipient as listed in the tax law, including:

1. the United States, a state, or political subdivision thereof, if the donation is made for exclusively public purposes (such as a contribution to pay down the federal debt);
2. domestic organizations operated exclusively for charitable, religious, educational, scientific, or literary purposes, or for the prevention of cruelty to children or animals;
3. church, synagogue, or other religious organizations;
4. war veterans' organizations;
5. civil defense organizations;

6. fraternal societies operating under the lodge system, but only if the contribution is used for one or more of the charitable purposes listed in (2) above; and
7. certain nonprofit cemetery companies.

The following contributions are not deductible:

1. Gifts to nonqualified recipients, for example, needy individuals, social clubs, labor unions, international organizations, and political parties;
2. Contributions of time, service, the use of property, or blood;
3. Contributions where benefit is received from the contribution, for example, tuition at a parochial school; and
4. Wagering losses, such as church bingo and raffle tickets.

If a taxpayer has doubt as to the deductibility of a payment to a specific organization, they should review the IRS's online search tool called "Tax Exempt Organization Search."

If cash is donated, the deduction is equal to the amount of the cash. For donated property other than cash, the general rule is that the deduction is equal to the fair market value of the property at the time of the donation. The fair market value is the price at which the property would be sold between a willing buyer and seller. There is an exception to this general rule for property that would have resulted in ordinary income or short-term capital gain had it been sold on the date of the contribution. In that situation, the deduction for the contribution is equal to the property's fair market value less the amount of the ordinary income or short-term capital gain that would have resulted from sale of the property. If the sale of the property would have produced a long-term capital gain, the deduction is generally equal to the fair market value of the property. However, the fair market value is reduced by the amount of the potential long-term capital gain, if the donation is made to certain private nonoperating foundations or the donation is a contribution of tangible personal property to an organization that uses the property for a purpose unrelated to the organization's primary purpose.

EXAMPLE Jeano donates a painting acquired five years ago at a cost of $4,000 to a museum for exhibition. The painting's fair market value is $12,000. If Jeano had sold the painting, the difference between the sales price ($12,000) and its cost ($4,000) would have been a long-term capital gain. The deduction is $12,000, and it is not reduced by the amount of the appreciation, since the painting was put to a use related to the museum's primary purpose. If the painting had been donated to a hospital, the deduction would be $4,000, which is $12,000 less $8,000 ($12,000 − $4,000), the amount of the long-term capital gain that would have resulted if the painting had been sold. ♦

5-9a Percentage Limitations

Different limits apply to different types of charitable contributions and depend on to whom the contribution is made. The rules for charitable contributions classify organizations as either: (1) a "50-percent organization" or (2) any other charitable organization (a non-50-percent organization). Public charities, churches, most educational institutions, hospitals, the United States or any state or local government, all private operating foundations, and private nonoperating foundations if they distribute their contributions to public charities within a specified time period, are all 50-percent charities. Any other qualified organization is a non-50-percent organization.

There are currently four different limitations, all of which represent a percentage of the taxpayer's AGI:

1. 60-percent limitation
2. 50-percent limitation
3. 30-percent limitation
4. 20-percent limitation

Given the complexity of the charitable contribution limits, the IRS provides a worksheet in Publication 526 which has been adapted and presented on Page 5-35.

Step 1. Enter charitable contributions made during the year.

1 Enter contributions of capital gain property to non-50 percent qualified organizations

2 Enter other contributions to qualified organizations that are non-50 percent organizations. Do not include any contributions entered on the previous line

3 Enter contributions of capital gain property to 50% limit organizations deducted at fair market value. Do not include any contributions entered on a previous line

4 Enter noncash contributions to 50% limit organizations other than capital gain property deducted at fair market value. Be sure to include contributions of capital gain property to 50% limit organizations if electing to deduct at basis. Do not include any contributions entered on a previous line

5 Enter cash contributions to 50% limit organizations. Do not include any contributions entered on a previous line

Step 2. Figure the deduction for the year (if any result is zero or less, enter -0-)

6 Enter adjusted gross income (AGI)

Cash contributions subject to the limit based on 60% of AGI (If line 5 is zero, enter -0- on lines 7 through 9)

7 Multiply line 6 by 0.6

8 Deductible amount. Enter the smaller of line 5 or line 7

9 Carryover. Subtract line 8 from line 5

Noncash contributions subject to the limit based on 50% of AGI (If line 4 is zero, enter -0- on lines 10 through 13)

10 Multiply line 6 by 0.5

11 Subtract line 8 from line 10

12 Deductible amount. Enter the smaller of line 4 or line 11

13 Carryover. Subtract line 12 from line 4

Contributions (other than capital gain property) subject to limit based on 30% of AGI (If line 2 is zero, enter -0- on lines 14

14 Multiply line 6 by 0.5

15 Add lines 3, 4, and 5

16 Subtract line 15 from line 14

17 Multiply line 6 by 0.3

18 Enter line 2

19 Deductible amount. Enter the smallest of line 16, 17, or 18

20 Carryover. Subtract line 19 from line 18

Contributions of capital gain property subject to limit based on 30% of AGI (If line 3 is zero, enter -0- on lines 21 through 26.)

21 Multiply line 6 by 0.5

22 Add lines 4 and 5

23 Subtract line 22 from line 21

24 Multiply line 6 by 0.3

25 Deductible amount. Enter the smallest of line 3, 23, or 24

26 Carryover. Subtract line 25 from line 3

Contributions subject to the limit based on 20% of AGI (If line 1 is zero, enter -0- on lines 27 through 36)

27 Multiply line 6 by 0.5

28 Add lines 8, 12, 19, and 25

29 Subtract line 28 from line 27

30 Multiply line 6 by 0.3

31 Subtract line 19 from line 30

32 Subtract line 25 from line 30

33 Multiply line 6 by 0.2

34 Enter line 1

35 Deductible amount. Enter the smallest of line 29, 31, 32, 33, or 34

36 Carryover. Subtract line 35 from line 34

37 Deduction for the year. Add lines 8, 12, 19, 25, and 35

60-Percent Limitation

For tax years from 2022 to 2025, the limit for cash contributions to 50-percent organizations is 60 percent of AGI.

EXAMPLE In 2022, Doug, a single taxpayer, donates $25,000 in cash to a public charity (a 50-percent organization). Doug's 2022 AGI is $30,000. Doug may deduct only $18,000 ($30,000 × 60%) of the donation. The remaining contribution of $7,000 may be carried forward for up to 5 years. ♦

50-percent Limitation

For noncash contributions to a 50-percent organization, the limit is 50 percent of AGI less any deductions that were subject to the 60-percent limit.

EXAMPLE In 2022, Jill, a single taxpayer with AGI of $30,000, makes the following donations:

Amount	***Organization***
$10,000 cash	50-percent organization
$7,000 non-cash (not capital gain property)	50-percent organization

- The $10,000 is below the 60-percent limit of $18,000 ($30,000 × 60%) and thus, is deductible.
- The non-cash donation is subject to a limit of 50-percent of AGI decreased by any deductions taken at the 60-percent level. The $7,000 donation is limited to $5,000 [($30,000 × 50%) − $10,000 previous deduction].
- The excess contribution of $2,000 may be carried forward for up to 5 years. ♦

30-percent Limitation

The 30-percent limit applies to cash donations made to a non-50-percent organization. The 30-percent limit also applies to capital gain property donated to a 50-percent organization for which the taxpayer is taking a deduction for the fair market value of the property. The 50-percent limit also applies in that the total deduction cannot exceed 50 percent of AGI less any previously deducted donations.

EXAMPLE In 2022, Nicole, a single taxpayer with AGI of $36,000, makes the following donations:

Amount	***Organization***
$10,000 cash	50-percent organization
$7,000 non-cash (not capital gain property)	50-percent organization
$4,000 cash	Non-50-percent organization

- The $10,000 is below the 60-percent limit of $21,600 ($36,000 × 60%) and thus, is deductible.
- The non-cash donation is subject to a limit of 50 percent of AGI decreased by any deductions taken at the 60-percent level. The $7,000 donation is less than $8,000 ($36,000 × 50% less the previous deduction of $10,000) and can be deducted.

- The cash donation of $4,000 to a non-50-percent organization is subject to the 30 percent of AGI limit ($10,800) but also may not exceed $1,000 [50% of AGI ($18,000) less any deductible contributions previously made to a 50-percent organization ($17,000)].
- Nicole may carryforward the excess $3,000 donation for up to 5 years. ♦

If a taxpayer donates both types of 30-percent limitation property (capital gains property to a 50-percent organization and cash to a non-50-percent organization), one deduction does not reduce the 30-percent limitation of the other; however, neither may exceed 50 percent of AGI less deductible contributions previously made to a 50-percent organization.

EXAMPLE In 2022, Darby, a single taxpayer with AGI of $46,000, makes the following donations:

Amount	*Organization*
$10,000 cash	50-percent organization
$7,000 non-cash (not capital gain property)	50-percent organization
$5,000 capital gain property (basis $2,000)	50-percent organization
$4,000 cash	Non-50-percent organization

- The $10,000 cash donation is below the 60-percent limit of $27,600 ($46,000 × 60%) and thus, is deductible.
- The non-cash donation of $7,000 is subject to a limit of 50 percent of AGI decreased by any deductions taken at the 60-percent level. The $7,000 donation is less than $13,000 ($46,000 × 50% less the previous deduction of $10,000) and can be deducted.
- The $5,000 capital gain property donation is less than the 30-percent of AGI limit ($13,800) and also less than $6,000, which is the 50-percent limitation of $23,000 less $17,000 ($10,000 + $7,000) of other donations subject to the 50-percent limitation.
- The $4,000 cash donation to a non-50-percent organization is less than the 30-percent limitation ($13,800) but is not less than the 50-percent limitation of $23,000 less all other donations subject to the 50-percent limitation of $22,000 ($10,000 + $7,000 + $5,000) leaving only $1,000 available against which to deduct the $4,000.
- The remaining $3,000 is carried forward for up to 5 years.

As a result, Darby's total deduction is $23,000 ($10,000 + $7,000 + $1,000 + $5,000) or 50 percent of AGI, with an excess of $3,000 remaining that can be carried forward for up to 5 years. ♦

A taxpayer that donates capital gains property to a 50-percent organization can elect to deduct their basis in the property rather than fair market value. If this election is made, the 50-percent limit would apply instead of the 20-percent limit.

EXAMPLE If in the previous example, Darby instead elects to deduct his $2,000 basis in the capital gain property, rather than the $5,000 market value.

- The $10,000 cash donation is below the 60-percent limit of $27,600 ($46,000 × 60%) and thus, is deductible.
- The non-cash donation of $7,000 plus the capital gain property basis of $2,000 are subject to a limit of 50 percent of AGI decreased by any deductions taken at the 60-percent level. The $9,000 donation is less than

$13,000 ($46,000 × 50% less the previous deduction of $10,000) and can be deducted.

- The $4,000 donation to a non-50-percent organization Is subject to the 30-percent limit ($13,800) or 50 percent of AGI ($23,000) less all donations to 50-percent organizations, which is now only $19,000 ($10,000 + $7,000 + $2,000) leaving $4,000 against which to deduct the $4,000. No amount is carried forward. ♦

20-percent Limitation

The final limit of 20 percent of AGI applies to non-cash contributions of capital gain property to other non-50-percent charitable organizations. The deductible amount of 20-percent contributions is subject to the same cascading effect of previous limits as shown with the 50 and 30-percent limits.

In practice, there are additional contribution limitations such as donations for the use of an organization (as opposed to directly to the organization), qualified conservation contributions, and qualified disaster relief donations. These more complex limitations are outside the scope of this textbook.

In general, any contributions not allowed due to the adjusted gross income limitations may be carried forward for up to 5 years. The contributions may be deducted in the carryover years subject to the same percentage of income limitations which were applicable to the contributions in the year they originated. Contribution carryovers are allowed only after taking into account the current year contributions in the same category.

In summary, if a taxpayer's total contributions total 20 percent or less of their AGI, then none of these limits apply.

No charitable contribution deduction is permitted for a payment to a college or university in exchange for the right to purchase tickets or seating at an athletic event. Pre-2018 law permitted an 80-percent deduction for such contributions.

EXAMPLE In 2022, Marco donates $5,000 to Big State University in exchange for the right to purchase 2022 season tickets to Big State football games. Marco may not deduct any of the $5,000 payment. ♦

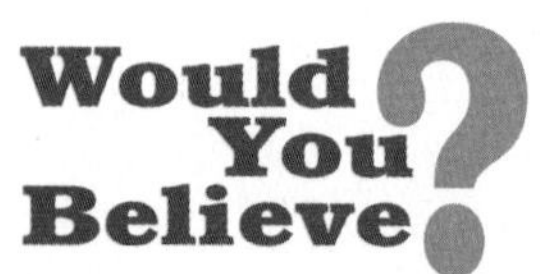

A tax lawyer pleaded guilty to tax evasion in Federal District Court for substantially overstating his charitable contributions. He told an IRS agent that he put $500 in cash into the church collection basket each week. His pastor, however, said that the church never received more than $500 in currency at all of its weekly church services combined.

5-9b **Substantiation Rules**

Taxpayers should keep records, receipts, cancelled checks, and other proof of charitable contributions. For gifts of property, such as clothes and household goods given to the Salvation Army, totaling over $500, the taxpayer must attach a Form 8283 to their return giving the name and address of the donee, the date of the contribution, a description of the property, the approximate date of acquisition of the property, and certain other required information. For large gifts of property worth $5,000 or more, the donor must also obtain and submit an appraisal.

No charitable deduction is allowed for contributions of $250 or more unless the taxpayer substantiates the contributions with written acknowledgments from the recipient charitable organizations. The acknowledgments must contain this information:

- The amount of cash and a description (but not the value) of property other than cash contributed.
- Whether the charitable organization provided any goods or services in consideration, in whole or in part, for any property contributed. (If a payment is partly a gift and

partly in consideration for goods or services provided to the donor, it is a "quid pro quo contribution" and special rules apply.)

- A description and good-faith estimate of the value of any goods or services provided by the donor, or, if the goods and services consist solely of intangible religious benefits, a statement to that effect. Intangible religious benefits are any benefits provided by organizations formed exclusively for religious purposes and not generally sold in a commercial setting. For example, attendance at church is considered an intangible religious benefit while attendance at a private religious school is not. Therefore, a donation made at a church service is generally considered a charitable contribution while tuition paid to a private religious school is not considered a charitable contribution.

Taxpayers donating amounts of cash smaller than the $250 limit are required to keep a bank record (cancelled check) or a written communication from the charity. Taxpayers who itemize deductions should use checks or a credit card instead of cash for church and similar cash donations.

Gifts of clothing and household items (including furnishings, electronics, appliances, and linens) must be in "good" condition or better to qualify for a deduction. Also, charitable deductions may be denied for contributions of items with minimal value, such as used socks and undergarments. The rules for noncash contributions were enacted because some taxpayers significantly overstated the value of noncash contributions deducted.

No particular form is prescribed for the written acknowledgment, nor does the donor's tax identification number have to be contained on the acknowledgment. It may be a receipt, letter, postcard, or computer form. The acknowledgment must be obtained on or before the date on which the tax return for the tax year of the contribution is filed, or by the due date (plus extensions) if it is earlier than the actual filing date.

Taxpayers donating used vehicles to charity cannot claim a deduction greater than the amount for which the charity actually sells the vehicle. The charity is required to provide the resale information on Form 1098-C to taxpayers donating vehicles. The same rule also applies to boats and planes donated to charity. Taxpayers must attach Form 1098-C to their tax return to substantiate the deduction. Taxpayers may claim an estimated value for the automobile if the charity does not sell it but rather uses it or gives it to a needy individual. The charity must certify that an exception applies if no resale amount is provided on Form 1098-C.

For quid pro quo contributions (donations involving the receipt of goods or services by the donee), written statements (disclosures) are required from the charitable organization to donors making contributions of more than $75. The disclosures need not be individual letters to donors; they simply need to provide the donors with good-faith estimates of the value of the goods or services and inform the donors that only the amounts of the contributions in excess of the value of the goods or services are deductible for federal income tax purposes.

A charitable organization knowingly providing false written acknowledgments is subject to penalty (generally $1,000) for aiding and abetting in the understatement of tax liability. A penalty of $10 per contribution per event, capped at $5,000, may be imposed on charities failing to make the required disclosures for quid pro quo contributions.

TAX BREAK

A cash-basis taxpayer may charge year-end expenses on a credit card and still deduct the expenses even when payment on the credit card is not made until the next year. Instead of paying medical bills, charitable contributions, or even property taxes by check at year-end, the taxpayer may prefer to charge the expense. Note however, that the credit card may not be one issued by the company supplying the deductible goods or services, but must be a card issued by a third party.

Self-Study Problem 5.9 *See Appendix E for Solutions to Self-Study Problems*

In 2022, Jon makes the following donations:

a. $8,000 cash to his church
b. $500 check to the Guayaquil Soup Kitchen, a charity based in Ecuador
c. 100 shares of stock with a fair market value of $11,000 and a cost basis of $2,000 to a local university
d. $1,500 to Rhode Island State University (his alma mater) for the right to purchase season tickets to the Fightin' Nutmeggers basketball games
e. $3,200 cash to the Stonecutters, a fraternal benefit society (a non-50-percent charitable organization)
f. Clothing and household items valued at $1,000 donated to a public charity.
g. 10 shares of stock with a value of $1,500 (basis of $100) donated to a non-50-percent organization

Jon's 2022 AGI is $45,000. Use the worksheet on Page 5-35 to determine the charitable contribution deduction and then report that amount in the Gifts to Charity section of Schedule A on Page 5-23. You are not required to complete Form 8283.

Learning Objective 5.10

Describe other itemized deductions.

5-10 OTHER ITEMIZED DEDUCTIONS

The final portion of this chapter discusses casualty and theft losses, other miscellaneous deductions, and the phase-out of itemized deductions for high-income taxpayers (the "Pease" phase-out).

5-10a Casualty and Theft Losses

Taxpayers are allowed deductions for certain casualty and theft losses. The deductions may be itemized deductions or, if related to a business, deductions for adjusted gross income. A casualty is a complete or partial destruction of property resulting from an identifiable event of a sudden, unexpected, or unusual nature. Examples of casualties include property damage from storms, floods, shipwrecks, fires, automobile accidents, and vandalism. For damage from weather conditions to be deductible, the condition must be unusual for the particular region. To qualify as a casualty, an automobile accident must not be caused by the taxpayer's willful act or willful negligence.

EXAMPLE A taxpayer has an automobile that he decides is a lemon, and he wants to get rid of it. He drives the automobile to the top of a cliff and pushes it off. There is no casualty loss deduction since the act is willful. ♦

Many events do not qualify as casualties. For example, progressive deterioration from rust or corrosion and disease or insect damage are usually not "sudden" enough to qualify as casualties. The IRS has held that termite damage is not deductible as a casualty; however, several courts have in the past allowed the deduction. Indirect losses, such as losses in property value due to damage to neighboring property, also are not deductible.

If the taxpayer can establish that theft occurred, certain theft losses are deductible. It is important to show that the item was not simply misplaced. Theft losses are deductible in the year the theft is discovered, not in the year the theft took place. This is important in cases of embezzlement, where the theft has gone on for many years and the statute of limitations has run out on earlier years, otherwise preventing the taxpayer from amending returns for those years.

As a general rule, casualty losses are deductible in the year of occurrence, but there is an exception for federally declared disaster area losses. Taxpayers may elect to treat the losses in a disaster area as a deduction in the year prior to the year the casualty occurred. If a return has already been filed for the prior year, an amended return may be filed and a refund claimed for the prior year's taxes paid. This provision is designed to provide taxpayers with cash on a more timely basis when they have suffered severe casualties.

EXAMPLE In May of 2022, Amy's house is damaged by flooding. Shortly thereafter, the president of the United States declared the region a disaster area. The damage to the house is $6,000 and the loss may be deducted in 2021 or 2022, even if the 2021 return has already been filed. If Amy elects to take the deduction in 2021, she may immediately file an amended tax return for that year and collect a refund of previously paid taxes. ♦

5-10b **Measuring the Loss**

The amount of the casualty or theft loss is measured by one of the following two rules:

Rule A—The deduction is based on the decrease in fair market value of the property, not to exceed the adjusted basis of the property.

Rule B—The deduction is based on the adjusted basis of the property.

Rule A applies to the partial destruction of business or investment property and the partial or complete destruction of personal property, while Rule B applies to the complete destruction of business and investment property. The cost of repairs is usually used for the measurement of loss from automobile damage. Repair costs may also be used to measure losses involving other types of property, but it is not a controlling factor. Indirect costs, such as cleanup costs, are part of the loss, provided the payments do not restore the property to better than its previous condition.

EXAMPLE A taxpayer purchased his house fifteen years ago for $25,000. Today it is worth $160,000, and heavy rains cause the house to slide into a canyon and be completely destroyed. The taxpayer's casualty loss deduction under Rule A is the decrease in fair market value ($160,000 − $0) not to exceed the taxpayer's basis ($25,000). Thus, the deduction is limited to $25,000. ♦

5-10c **Deduction Limitations**

Personal casualty losses are only deductible if associated with a federally declared disaster. The restriction to a federally declared disaster applies to tax years 2018 to 2025. Such losses are subject to a $100 floor per casualty and must exceed 10 percent of AGI to be deducted. If a taxpayer has a net casualty gain, the declared disaster restriction does not apply to the extent of the gain. If related to business property, there is no federally declared disaster restriction, no adjusted gross income limitation or dollar reduction applicable to casualty and theft losses; such losses are deductions for adjusted gross income.

EXAMPLE In 2022, Wanda incurs a loss due to a complete destruction of her personal-use car due to a casualty event not attributable to a federally declared disaster. Her adjusted basis in the car was $19,000 and the fair market value at the time of the loss was $8,000. Wanda's AGI is $55,000. Wanda was not insured for this type of loss and received no reimbursement. Wanda will not be able to deduct any of her loss as it was not attributable to a federally declared disaster.

If instead Wanda's loss was attributable to a federally declared disaster, she can deduct $8,000 less the $100 floor and also less 10 percent of her AGI:

$2,400 = $8,000 − $100 − $5,500 ♦

EXAMPLE Cosmo incurs two personal losses during 2022. His car was stolen and destroyed by the thieves. His basis in the car was $22,000 and the fair market value at the time of the theft was $16,000. Cosmo also lost a family heirloom watch with a basis of $4,000 in a different theft. Neither of these losses is attributable to a federally declared disaster. Cosmo's insurance covered the auto and reimbursed him $22,000 but the loss of the watch was not covered. Cosmo's casualty gain on the auto is $6,000 ($22,000 − $16,000) and his loss on the watch is $3,900 ($4,000 − $100 floor). Because Cosmo experienced a net casualty gain of $2,100, he may offset the casualty loss against the gain despite the loss not being attributable to a federally declared disaster. ♦

Certain disasters can be deemed "qualified" federal disasters and were eligible for additional relief. For example, certain areas affected by Hurricanes Harvey, Irma, and Maria as well as the California wildfires, were declared qualified federal disaster areas. The rules for qualified federal disasters require the taxpayer to use a $500 floor (instead of $100) but do not subject the casualty loss to the 10 percent AGI limitation. In addition, taxpayers that do not itemize were permitted to add the qualified federal disaster area loss to the standard deduction. At the time we go to print, no events in 2022 have been declared a qualified federal disaster.

A casualty or theft loss is reported on Form 4684 and then the deductible amount is generally taken as an itemized deduction on Schedule A.

ProConnect™ Tax TIP

Entering the loss from a casualty is input on the left navigation menu. Select Income and then Schedule D/4797/etc. Scroll down to Casualties and Thefts (4868).

5-10d **Miscellaneous Expenses**

Miscellaneous itemized deductions are categorized into two types: (1) those subject to the 2 percent of AGI floor and (2) those not subject to the 2 percent of AGI floor.

Miscellaneous itemized deductions subject to the 2 percent of AGI rule have been suspended through 2025. The most common deductions subject to the 2 percent of AGI rule are:

- Unreimbursed employee business expenses and employee expenses reimbursed under a nonaccountable plan
- Investment expenses
- Other miscellaneous expenses including the all-important tax preparation fees

The most common unreimbursed employee expenses are included in the following list:

- Business bad debt of an employee
- Business liability insurance premiums
- Damages paid to a former employer for breach of an employment contract
- Depreciation on a computer your employer requires you to use in your work
- Dues to a chamber of commerce if membership helps you do your job
- Dues to professional societies
- Educator expenses
- Home office or part of your home used regularly and exclusively in your work
- Job search expenses in your present occupation
- Laboratory breakage fees
- Legal fees related to your job
- Licenses and regulatory fees
- Malpractice insurance premiums
- Medical examinations required by an employer
- Occupational taxes
- Passport for a business trip
- Repayment of an income aid payment received under an employer's plan
- Research expenses of a college professor
- Rural mail carriers' vehicle expenses
- Subscriptions to professional journals and trade magazines related to your work
- Tools and supplies used in your work
- Travel, transportation, meals, entertainment, gifts, and local lodging related to your work
- Union dues and expenses
- Work clothes and uniforms, if required and not suitable for everyday use
- Work-related education

The repeal of miscellaneous deductions subject to the 2 percent floor could result in an employee being subject to additional tax liability when receiving reimbursement from an employer without an accountable plan. Since changing from an employee to an independent contractor is generally not possible without a significant change in the relationship between the individual and the business (this is a matter of law, not a choice by either the employee or employer), taxpayers that are employees in this situation may want to inquire if an accountable plan can be implemented by their employer going forward.

Miscellaneous itemized deductions not subject to the 2 percent floor were not affected by the TCJA. This category of expenses includes the following items:

- Amortizable premium on taxable bonds
- Casualty and theft losses from income-producing property
- Federal estate tax on income in respect of a decedent
- Gambling losses up to the amount of gambling winnings
- Impairment-related work expenses of persons with disabilities
- Loss from other activities from Schedule K-1 (Form 1065-B), Box 2
- Losses from Ponzi-type investment schemes
- Repayments of more than $3,000 under a claim of right
- Unrecovered investment in an annuity

Gambling losses are not subject to the 2-percent limitation and are not directly limited, but gambling losses are only deductible for taxpayers that itemize deductions. Gambling winnings must be reported as other income on Schedule 1 and losses may be deducted on Schedule A only to the extent of winnings.

5-10e Phase-out of Itemized Deductions

Prior to 2018, certain high-income taxpayers were subject to limits on the amount of itemized deductions. Certain AGI limits for different filing status triggered a reduction in itemized deductions by the lesser of 3 percent of the excess of the taxpayer's AGI over the threshold amount or 80 percent of itemized deductions excluding the deductions for medical expenses, investment interest expense, casualty and theft losses, and gambling losses to the extent of gambling income. The so-called "Pease phase-out" is suspended through 2025.

Self-Study Problem 5.10 ***See Appendix E for Solutions to Self-Study Problems***

During 2022, Robert (a single taxpayer) is an employee and has AGI of $35,000. He lives in Tulsa, OK 74119.

a. Robert's community was struck by a flood. During the flood, his car was destroyed. The flood was declared a federal disaster (FEMA Code DR-4657-OK). The market value of the car on the date of destruction was $14,000. Robert purchased the car in July 2019 at a cost of $18,500. Robert's car was only partially covered for this type of loss and his insurance paid him $5,000. Calculate Robert's casualty or theft loss on Form 4684 on Page 5-45 and carry any deductible amount to the Casualty and Theft Losses section of the Schedule A on Page 5-23.

b. Robert also incurs the following expenses:

Safe-deposit box rental (for investments)	$ 25
Tax return preparation fees	450
Professional dues	175
Trade journals	125
Bank trust fees	1,055
Qualifying job hunting expenses	1,400
Total	$3,230

Robert also had a big day at the casinos and won $1,400. Over the year, he had substantiation for $1,700 in gambling losses. Assuming Robert is not self-employed, calculate any miscellaneous deductions and enter them in the Other Itemized Deductions section of Schedule A on Page 5-23.

Self-Study Problem 5.10

Form **4684** Department of the Treasury Internal Revenue Service	**Casualties and Thefts** Go to *www.irs.gov/Form4684* for instructions and the latest information. Attach to your tax return. Use a separate Form 4684 for each casualty or theft.	OMB No. 1545-0177 **2022** Attachment Sequence No. **26**
Name(s) shown on tax return		**Identifying number**

SECTION A—Personal Use Property (Use this section to report casualties and thefts of property **not** used in a trade or business or for income-producing purposes. For tax years 2018 through 2025, if you are an individual, casualty or theft losses of personal-use property are deductible only if the loss is attributable to a federally declared disaster. You must use a separate Form 4684 (through line 12) for each casualty or theft event involving personal-use property. **If reporting a qualified disaster loss, see the instructions for special rules that apply before completing this section.**)

If the casualty or theft loss is attributable to a federally declared disaster, check here ☐ and enter the DR-_______ or EM-_______ declaration number assigned by FEMA. (See instructions.)

1 Description of properties (show type, location (city, state, and ZIP code), and date acquired for each property). Use a separate line for each property lost or damaged from the same casualty or theft. If you checked the box and entered the FEMA disaster declaration number above, enter the ZIP code for the property most affected on the line for Property **A**.

	Type of Property	City and State	ZIP Code	Date Acquired
Property **A**				
Property **B**				
Property **C**				
Property **D**				

		Properties			
		A	**B**	**C**	**D**
2 Cost or other basis of each property	2				
3 Insurance or other reimbursement (whether or not you filed a claim) (see instructions). **Note:** If line 2 is **more** than line 3, skip line 4.	3				
4 Gain from casualty or theft. If line 3 is **more** than line 2, enter the difference here and skip lines 5 through 9 for that column. See instructions if line 3 includes insurance or other reimbursement you did not claim, or you received payment for your loss in a later tax year	4				
5 Fair market value **before** casualty or theft	5				
6 Fair market value **after** casualty or theft	6				
7 Subtract line 6 from line 5	7				
8 Enter the **smaller** of line 2 or line 7	8				
9 Subtract line 3 from line 8. If zero or less, enter -0-	9				

10 Casualty or theft loss. Add the amounts on line 9 in columns A through D	10	
11 Enter $100 ($500 if qualified disaster loss rules apply; see instructions)	11	
12 Subtract line 11 from line 10. If zero or less, enter -0-	12	
Caution: Use only one Form 4684 for lines 13 through 18.		
13 Add the amounts on line 4 of all Forms 4684	13	
14 Add the amounts on line 12 of all Forms 4684. If you have losses not attributable to a federally declared disaster, see the instructions	14	
Caution: See instructions before completing line 15.		
15 • If line 13 is **more** than line 14, enter the difference here and on Schedule D. **Do not** complete the rest of this section. • If line 13 is **equal** to line 14, enter -0- here. **Do not** complete the rest of this section. • If line 13 is **less** than line 14, and you have no qualified disaster losses subject to the $500 reduction on line 11 on any Form(s) 4684, enter -0- here and go to line 16. If you have qualified disaster losses subject to the $500 reduction, subtract line 13 from line 14 and enter the smaller of this difference or the amount on line 12 of the Form(s) 4684 reporting those losses. Enter that result here and on Schedule A (Form 1040), line 16; or Schedule A (Form 1040-NR), line 7. If you claim the standard deduction, also include on Schedule A (Form 1040), line 16, the amount of your standard deduction (see the Instructions for Form 1040). Do not complete the rest of this section if all of your casualty or theft losses are subject to the $500 reduction.	15	
16 Add lines 13 and 15. Subtract the result from line 14	16	
17 Enter 10% of your adjusted gross income from Form 1040, 1040-SR, or 1040-NR, line 11. Estates and trusts, see instructions	17	
18 Subtract line 17 from line 16. If zero or less, enter -0-. Also, enter the result on Schedule A (Form 1040), line 15; or Schedule A (Form 1040-NR), line 6. Estates and trusts, enter the result on the "Other deductions" line of your tax return	18	

For Paperwork Reduction Act Notice, see instructions. Cat. No. 12997O Form **4684** (2022)

KEY TERMS

Health Savings Accounts (HSAs), 5-2
traditional IRA, 5-8
Roth IRA, 5-8
annual contribution limits, 5-8
"catch-up" contribution, 5-8
nondeductible traditional IRA, 5-9
excise tax, 5-10
Roth IRA conversions, 5-10
early withdrawal, 5-10
distributions, 5-11
required minimum distributions (RMDs), 5-11
qualified charitable distribution, 5-11
qualified retirement plans, 5-13
nondiscriminatory, 5-13
Payroll Deduction IRA, 5-14
SEP IRA, 5-14
SIMPLE IRA, 5-15
Section 401(k) plan, 5-15
automatic enrollment 401(k), 5-16
Small Employer Automatic Enrollment credit, 5-16
safe harbor 401(k), 5-16
Roth 401(k), 5-16
self-employed or solo 401(k), 5-16
tax, 5-22
fee, 5-22
estimated sales taxes from IRS tables, 5-26
consumer interest, 5-29
prepaid interest, 5-30
qualified residence interest (mortgage interest), 5-30
qualified residence acquisition debt, 5-31
home equity debt, 5-31
investment interest, 5-32
charitable contributions, 5-33
qualified recipient, 5-33
nonqualified recipients, 5-34
Tax Exempt Organization Search, 5-34
50-percent organization, 5-34
60-percent limitation, 5-36
50-percent limitation, 5-36
30-percent limitation, 5-36
20-percent limitation, 5-38
substantiation rules, 5-38
quid pro quo contributions, 5-39
casualty, 5-40
"qualified" federal disasters, 5-42

KEY POINTS

Learning Objectives	Key Points
LO 5.1: Explain how Health Savings Accounts (HSAs) can be used for tax-advantaged medical care.	• Health Savings Accounts (HSAs) are used for the purpose of paying unreimbursed medical expenses. • HSAs have an annual age-based contribution dollar limitation for deductions for individuals ($3,650) and families ($7,300). There is an additional $1,000 "catch-up" contribution allowed for individuals beginning at age 55 and ending at age 65, the age for Medicare eligibility. • Distributions from HSAs are tax-exempt when used to pay for qualified medical expenses. Distributions which are not used to pay for qualified medical expenses may be subject to income tax and a 20-percent penalty. • Once a taxpayer is 65 years old, distributions may be taken for nonmedical expenses and will be subject to income tax, but not the 20-percent penalty.
LO 5.2: Describe the self-employed health insurance deduction.	• Deductible health insurance includes: (1) medical and dental insurance paid to cover the self-employed taxpayer, spouse, and dependents; (2) medical and dental insurance paid for children under the age of 27 who are not dependents; (3) Medicare premiums; and (4) long-term care insurance paid for the taxpayer and the family of the taxpayer. • Taxpayers with income reportable on Schedule C are generally considered self-employed. • Taxpayers with earnings from certain partnerships, S corporations, LLCs, and farm businesses may also be considered self-employed and may be allowed the deduction for self-employed health insurance. • The deduction for self-employed health insurance is only allowed to the extent of the taxpayer's net self-employed income.

LO 5.3: Explain the treatment of Individual Retirement Accounts (IRAs), including Roth IRAs.	• Generally, annual contributions to a traditional IRA are deductible and retirement distributions are taxable; whereas, annual contributions to a Roth IRA are not deductible and retirement distributions are nontaxable. • Earnings in both types of IRAs are not taxable in the current year. • In 2022, the maximum annual contribution that may be made to either type of IRA is equal to the lesser of (1) 100 percent of the taxpayer's compensation or self-employment income (earned income) or (2) $6,000 (plus an additional $6,000 which may be contributed on behalf of a spouse with no earned income). An additional catch-up $1,000 annual contribution is allowed for taxpayers age 50 and over. • The tax deduction for contributions to traditional IRAs is limited for taxpayers who are active participants in qualified retirement plans and have income over certain limits. Contributions to Roth IRAs are limited for taxpayers with income over certain limits; however, they are not affected by taxpayer participation in other retirement plans. • Taxpayers may benefit from a rule allowing conversions of traditional IRAs into Roth IRAs. • Generally, money distributed from a traditional IRA is taxable as ordinary income and may be subject to a 10-percent penalty for early withdrawal (before age 59½). Some types of early withdrawals may be made without penalty. • A taxpayer can make tax-free withdrawals from a Roth IRA after a five-year holding period if the distribution is made on or after the date on which the participant attains age 59½. Other tax-free withdrawals may also apply.
LO 5.4: Explain the general contribution rules for small business and self-employed retirement plans.	• Employers may claim a deduction in the current year for contributions to qualified retirement plans on employees' behalf. The employees do not include the employer contributions in income until the contributed amounts are distributed. • For 2022, the maximum employee contribution to a SEP is the lesser of 25 percent of compensation or $61,000. • For 2022, contributions to retirement plans by self-employed taxpayers are generally limited to the lesser of 20 percent of their net earned income before the contribution deduction or $61,000. • For 2022, an employee may elect to make an annual contribution up to $20,500 to a Section 401(k) plan. In addition, any matching amount contributed to the plan by the employer on behalf of the employee is excluded from the employee's gross income.
LO 5.5: Describe other adjustments for adjusted gross income.	• Eligible educators may deduct up to $300 for the unreimbursed cost of classroom materials as a for AGI deduction. • Certain performing artists, reservists, and fee-basis government officials can deduct unreimbursed employee expenses as a for AGI deduction. • Starting in 2018, moving expenses are only deductible for members of the Armed Forces pursuant to a military order and permanent change of station.
LO 5.6: Calculate the itemized deduction for medical expenses.	• Taxpayers are allowed an itemized deduction on Schedule A for medical expenses paid for themselves, their spouse, and their dependents. • Qualified medical expenses are deductible only to the extent they exceed 7.5 percent of a taxpayer's adjusted gross income. • Qualified medical expenses include such items as prescription medicines and drugs, insulin, fees for doctors, dentists, nurses, and other medical professionals, hospital fees, hearing aids, dentures, prescription eyeglasses, contact lenses, medical transportation and lodging, crutches, wheelchairs, guide dogs, birth control prescriptions, acupuncture, psychiatric care, medical and Medicare insurance premiums, and various other listed medical expenses.

LO 5.7: Calculate the itemized deduction for taxes.	• The following taxes are deductible on Schedule A: state and local income taxes or state and local sales taxes, real property taxes (state and local), and personal property taxes (state and local). • The itemized deduction for taxes is limited to $10,000. • Nondeductible taxes include the following: federal income taxes, employee portion of Social Security taxes, estate, inheritance, and gift taxes (except in unusual situations), gasoline taxes, excise taxes, and foreign taxes if the taxpayer elects a foreign tax credit. • If real estate is sold during the year, the taxes must be allocated between the buyer and seller based on the number of days in the year that each taxpayer held the property to determine each party's deductible amount. • To be deductible, personal property taxes must be levied based on the value of the property. Personal property taxes of a fixed amount, or those calculated on a basis other than value, are not deductible.
LO 5.8: Apply the rules for an individual taxpayer's interest deduction.	• Deductible personal interest includes qualified residence interest (mortgage interest), mortgage interest prepayment penalties, investment interest, and certain interest associated with a passive activity. • Nondeductible consumer interest includes interest on any loan, the proceeds of which are used for personal purposes, such as credit card interest, finance charges, and automobile loan interest. • "Qualified residence interest" is the sum of the interest paid on "qualified residence acquisition debt." • Taxpayers are allowed a deduction for AGI for certain interest paid on qualified education loans. • Deductible investment interest is limited to the taxpayer's net investment income, which is investment income such as dividends and interest, less investment expenses other than interest.
LO 5.9: Determine the charitable contributions deduction.	• To be deductible, the donation must be made in cash or property. • For donated property other than cash, the general rule is that the deduction is equal to the fair market value of the property at the time of the donation. • Donations are limited to 60, 50, 30, or 20 percent of AGI in certain cases. • Excess contributions due to the limitations may be carried forward up to 5 years.
LO 5.10: Describe other itemized deductions.	• A loss from a personal casualty such as property damage from storms, floods, shipwrecks, fires, automobile accidents, and vandalism is only deductible if associated with a federally declared disaster. • For the partial destruction of business or investment property and the partial or complete destruction of personal property, the deduction is based on the decrease in fair market value of the property, not to exceed the adjusted basis of the property. • For the complete destruction of business and investment property, the deduction is based on the adjusted basis of the property. • The amount of each personal casualty loss attributable to a federally declared disaster, is reduced by $100 and only the excess over 10 percent of the taxpayer's AGI is deductible. • The deduction for miscellaneous expenses subject to the 2 percent of AGI limit is suspended until 2025. • Miscellaneous expenses not subject to the 2 percent of AGI limit such as gambling losses to the extent of gambling winnings, handicapped "impairment-related work expenses," certain estate taxes, amortizable bond premiums, and unrecovered annuity costs at death remain deductible. • The phase-out of itemized deductions for high-income taxpayers has been suspended.

QUESTIONS and PROBLEMS

GROUP 1:
MULTIPLE CHOICE QUESTIONS

LO 5.1

1. Which of the following is a *false* statement about Health Savings Accounts (HSAs)?
   a. Taxpayers who contribute to an HSA must carry qualifying high-deductible health insurance.
   b. HSAs are available to any taxpayer using a health plan purchased through the state or federal exchange under the Affordable Care Act.
   c. Distributions from HSAs are not taxable when used to pay qualifying medical expenses.
   d. Taxpayers must contribute to the HSA by April 15 of the year following the tax year for which they want the deduction.
   e. Distributions from HSAs which are not used to pay qualifying medical expenses are generally subject to a 20-percent penalty as well as income taxes.

LO 5.1

2. Charlene has single coverage in a qualifying high-deductible health insurance plan. She is 47 years old and wishes to contribute the maximum amount to her HSA. How much is she allowed to contribute and deduct in 2022?
   a. $1,000
   b. $1,300
   c. $3,600
   d. $3,650
   e. $7,300

LO 5.2

3. Kidd is a self-employed single taxpayer in 2022 that files Schedule C for his sole proprietorship. He pays for his own health insurance and the premiums are less than his net profits. Kidd will deduct his self-employed health insurance on which form?
   a. Schedule C
   b. Form 1040 as a from AGI deduction
   c. Form 1040 as a for AGI deduction
   d. Self-employed health care insurance is not deductible

LO 5.2

4. Which type of insurance is *not* deductible as self-employed health insurance?
   a. Medical insurance
   b. Disability insurance
   c. Dental insurance
   d. Long-term care insurance
   e. Spousal medical insurance

LO 5.2

5. Which of the following is *true* about the self-employed health insurance deduction?
   a. The deduction cannot be claimed when a subsidized employer health insurance plan is also available.
   b. The deduction can be claimed if the taxpayer has an overall business loss from self-employment.
   c. Long-term care premiums may not be deducted within specified dollar limitations based on age.
   d. The self-employed health insurance deduction is a from AGI deduction.
   e. Dental insurance is not included as deductible self-employed health insurance.

LO 5.3

6. Lyndon, age 24, has a nonworking spouse and earns wages of $36,000 for 2022. He also received rental income of $5,000 and dividend income of $900 for the year. Assuming Lyndon's employer does not offer a retirement plan, what is the maximum

amount Lyndon can deduct for contributions to his and his wife's individual retirement accounts for the 2022 tax year?

a. $11,000
b. $5,500
c. $6,000
d. $12,000
e. None of the above

LO 5.3

7. Martha and Rob, a married couple, under 50 years of age, have adjusted gross income on their 2022 joint income tax return of $45,000, before considering any IRA deduction. Martha and Rob have no earned income. What is the amount of Martha's maximum deductible IRA contribution?
   a. $2,700
   b. $3,500
   c. $6,000
   d. $12,000
   e. $0

LO 5.3

8. Donna, age 42 and a single taxpayer, has a salary of $112,000 and interest income of $20,000. What is the maximum amount Donna can contribute to a Roth IRA for 2022?
   a. $4,800
   b. $5,400
   c. $5,800
   d. $6,000
   e. Some other amount

LO 5.3

9. Mary has a Roth IRA held more than five years to which she has contributed $30,000. The IRA has a current value of $62,000. Mary is 55 years old and she takes a distribution of $40,000. How much of the distribution will be taxable to Mary?
   a. $0
   b. $8,000
   c. $10,000
   d. $40,000
   e. Some other amount

LO 5.3

10. Marge has a Roth IRA held more than five years to which she has contributed $38,000. The IRA has a current value of $62,000. Marge is 65 years old and she takes a distribution of $40,000. How much of the distribution will be taxable to Marge?
    a. $0
    b. $8,000
    c. $30,000
    d. $40,000
    e. Some other amount

LO 5.3

11. Mindy has a Roth IRA held longer than five years to which she has contributed $30,000. The IRA has a current value of $62,000. Mindy is 55 years old and she takes a distribution of $40,000 after retiring on disability. How much of the distribution will be taxable to Mindy?
    a. $0
    b. $8,000
    c. $30,000
    d. $40,000
    e. Some other amount

LO 5.3

12. What is the deadline for making a contribution to a traditional IRA or a Roth IRA for 2022?
    a. April 18, 2023
    b. July 15, 2022
    c. December 31, 2022
    d. October 15, 2023

LO 5.3

13. Which of the following would *not* be considered a prohibited transaction between an IRA and its owner?
    a. The owner taking a loan from the IRA
    b. The owner selling property to the IRA
    c. Investing in foreign stocks
    d. Buying property for personal use with IRA funds

LO 5.4

14. Which of the following statements with respect to a qualified retirement plan is accurate?
    a. Self-employed individuals are not eligible to be members of a SEP.
    b. Contributions to SIMPLE IRAs are limited to 15 percent of the taxpayer's net earned income or $100,000, whichever is greater.
    c. Employer matching of employee contributions to a 401(k) plan is not taxable in the year contributed.
    d. Taxpayers must begin receiving distributions from a qualified plan by the age of 65.
    e. None of these statements are accurate.

LO 5.4

15. What is the maximum tax-deferred contribution that can be made to a Section 401(k) plan by an employee under age 50 in 2022?
    a. $19,000
    b. $20,000
    c. $19,500
    d. $20,500
    e. $61,000

LO 5.4

16. Paul, age 37, participates in a Section 401(k) plan which allows employees to contribute up to 15 percent of their salary. His annual salary is $125,000 in 2022. What is the maximum he can contribute, on a tax-deferred basis under a salary reduction agreement, to this plan?
    a. $24,000
    b. $20,500
    c. $18,500
    d. $18,750
    e. None of the above

LO 5.5
LO 5.10

17. Eliza is a kindergarten teacher for Alexander Hamilton Elementary School. Eliza decorates her classroom with new artwork, posters, bulletin boards, etc. In 2022, she spends $470 on materials and supplies for her classroom. The school reimburses her $100 (the annual reimbursement limit). Eliza can deduct ____________ for AGI and ____________ from AGI.
    a. $0 for and $0 from AGI
    b. $370 for and $0 from AGI
    c. $250 for and $0 from AGI
    d. $300 for and $0 from AGI
    e. $0 for and $370 from AGI

LO 5.5

18. Jessica is a U.S. Army Reservist and in 2022 traveled 130 miles each way to serve duty at a local military installation. She was required to report four times in 2022, two times before June 30 and two times after. Her normal route from home to the base included a $1.75 toll each way. Jessica's for AGI deduction for these costs is:
    a. $0
    b. $622.40
    c. $596.40
    d. $643.00
    e. $643.20

LO 5.6

19. The cost of which of the following expenses is *not* deductible as a medical expense on Schedule A, before the 7.5 percent of adjusted gross income limitation?
    a. A psychiatrist
    b. Botox treatment to reduce wrinkles around eyes
    c. Acupuncture
    d. Expense to hire and train a guide dog for a visually-impaired taxpayer

LO 5.6

20. The cost of which of the following is deductible as a medical expense?
    a. Travel to a warm climate
    b. Birth control pills
    c. A disability insurance policy that pays $200 for each day the taxpayer is in the hospital
    d. Liposuction to reduce waist size

LO 5.6

21. Which of the following is not considered a deductible medical expense?
    a. Once daily multivitamin
    b. Prescription eyeglasses
    c. Acupuncture
    d. Filling a tooth cavity

LO 5.7

22. Which of the following taxes may be deducted as an itemized deduction?
    a. State gasoline taxes
    b. Local property taxes
    c. Federal income taxes
    d. Social Security taxes
    e. Medicare taxes

LO 5.7

23. In April 2022, Fred paid $40 of state income tax that was due when he filed his 2021 income tax return. During 2022, Fred's employer withheld $1,200 of state income tax from his pay. In April 2023, Fred determined that his 2022 state tax liability was $1,100 and received his state income tax refund of $100 in May 2023. Assuming Fred itemizes, how much state income tax deduction should he report on his 2022 federal income tax return?
    a. $1,200
    b. $1,240
    c. $1,100
    d. $1,140
    e. $1,000

LO 5.7

24. Antonio is a small business owner and files jointly with his spouse. In 2022, he generates $100,000 of net profits from his business. His spouse, Maria, has $4,000 of state income tax withheld from her wages in 2022. They also pay $4,500 in property taxes on their home. Antonio determines that their state income taxes associated with his business are about $5,600 and makes estimated state income tax payments of that amount in 2022. How much should Antonio and Maria deduct for state taxes?
    a. Itemized deductions of $9,500 and deduct $5,600 for taxes on Antonio's Schedule C for his business
    b. Itemized deductions of $10,000 and deduct $5,100 for taxes on Antonio's Schedule C for his business
    c. Itemized deductions of $10,000
    d. Itemized deductions of $4,000 and deduct $5,600 for taxes on Antonio's Schedule C for his business

LO 5.7

25. The itemized deduction for state and local taxes in 2022 is
    a. Total taxes less 10 percent of AGI
    b. Limited to no more than $10,000
    c. Unlimited
    d. Only deductible if the taxes are business related
    e. Deductible if your home value is less than $750,000

LO 5.8

26. Which of the following is deductible as interest on Schedule A?
   a. Fees for having the home's value assessed by the bank for purposes of getting a mortgage
   b. Purchase mortgage insurance paid in 2022
   c. Interest on a credit card balance from the purchase of home furnishings.
   d. Interest on loans to finance tax-exempt bonds
   e. None of the above are deductible as interest

LO 5.8

27. Carrie, a single taxpayer, finished her undergraduate degree using money from a student loan. She earned $56,000 her first year and paid $2,600 in interest in 2022. She can take a deduction for student loan interest in the amount of:
   a. $2,600
   b. $2,500
   c. $1,500
   d. $0
   e. None of the above

LO 5.8

28. Which of the following interest expense amounts is *not* deductible in the current year?
   a. Education loan interest of $2,000, assuming the taxpayer has income of $30,000.
   b. Home equity loan interest of $6,000, on a loan of $90,000, the proceeds of which were used to add a new bedroom and bathroom to an existing primary residence.
   c. Investment interest expense of $1,200, assuming the taxpayer has no investment income.
   d. Qualified residence interest of $70,000 on a $730,000 loan used to purchase a luxury apartment in downtown San Diego.

LO 5.9

29. Which of the following donations are *not* deductible as a charitable contribution?
   a. A donation of clothing to Goodwill Industries
   b. A cash contribution to a church
   c. A contribution of stock to a public university
   d. A contribution of a taxpayer's time picking up trash on the beach
   e. A painting contributed to a museum

LO 5.9

30. Stanley donates a hotel to a university for use as a conference center. The building was purchased three years ago for $1,200,000 and has a fair market value of $1,500,000 on the date the contribution is made. If Stanley had sold the building, the $300,000 difference between the sales price and cost would have been a long-term capital gain. What is the amount of Stanley's deduction for this contribution, before considering any limitation based on adjusted gross income?
   a. $1,800,000
   b. $1,500,000
   c. $1,900,000
   d. $1,200,000
   e. $0

LO 5.9

31. Rico a single taxpayer, makes $5,000 of cash donations in 2022. His standard deduction exceeds his itemized deductions including the contribution. What amount will Rico deduct for charitable contributions? His AGI in 2022 is $48,000.
   a. $300
   b. $5,000
   c. $4,800
   d. $0
   e. $48,000

LO 5.9

32. Which of the following gifts is a deductible contribution?
   a. A gift of $100 to a homeless person
   b. A $500 gift to the Democratic National Committee
   c. $1,000 spent on church bingo games
   d. A $200 contribution to your child's public elementary school

LO 5.10

33. Which of the following would typically be deductible as a casualty loss in 2022?
   a. Long-term damage to a home from termites
   b. An automobile accident during the daily commute
   c. A theft of a big screen television
   d. Dropping your smartphone in the pool
   e. None of the above

LO 5.10

34. Which of the following is *not* a possible limitation on the deduction of a personal casualty loss?
   a. The lesser of the fair market value of the property or the adjusted basis at the time of the loss
   b. A $100 floor for each casualty event
   c. A 10 percent of AGI floor for all casualty losses during the year
   d. A personal casualty not associated with a federally declared disaster
   e. All of the above are possible limitations on a personal casualty loss

LO 5.10

35. Which of the following is deductible as a miscellaneous itemized deduction in 2022?
   a. Tax preparation fees
   b. Gambling losses in excess of gambling winnings
   c. Losses from Ponzi-type schemes
   d. Job-hunting expenses subject to the 2 percent of AGI floor
   e. None of the above are deductible as a miscellaneous itemized deduction.

LO 5.10

36. Which of the following items is deductible as a miscellaneous deduction on Schedule A?
   a. Investment expenses
   b. Gambling losses to the extent of gambling winnings
   c. Unreimbursed business expenses
   d. Subscriptions to professional publications
   e. Charitable contributions

GROUP 2: PROBLEMS

LO 5.1

1. Evan participates in an HSA carrying family coverage for himself, his spouse, and two children. In 2022, Evan has $200 per month deducted from his paycheck and contributed to the HSA. In addition, Evan makes a one-time contribution of $2,000 on April 15, 2023 when he files his tax return. Evan also receives a 2022 Form 1099-SA that reports distributions to Evan of $3,200 which Evan used for medical expenses. Compute the effect of the HSA transactions on Evan's adjusted gross income.

LO 5.2

2. Serena is a 48-year-old single taxpayer. She operates a small business on the side as a sole proprietor. Her 2022 Schedule C reports net profits of $15,000. Her employer does not offer health insurance. Serena pays health insurance premiums of $7,800 in 2022. Serena also pays long-term care insurance premiums of $1,200 in 2022. Calculate Serena's self-employed health care deduction.

LO 5.3

3. Karen, 28 years old and a single taxpayer, has a salary of $38,000 and rental income of $33,000 for the 2022 calendar tax year. Karen is covered by a pension through her employer.
   a. What is the maximum amount that Karen may deduct for contributions to her IRA for 2022?
   b. If Karen is a calendar year taxpayer and files her tax return on August 15, what is the last date on which she can make her contribution to the IRA and deduct it for 2022?

LO 5.3

4. Phil and Linda are 25-year-old newlyweds and file a joint tax return. Linda is covered by a retirement plan at work, but Phil is not.
   a. Assuming Phil's wages were $27,000 and Linda's wages were $18,500 for 2022 and they had no other income, what is the maximum amount of Phil and Linda's deductions for contributions to a traditional IRA for 2022?
   b. Assuming Phil's wages were $60,000 and Linda's wages were $71,000 for 2022 and they had no other income, what is the maximum amount of Phil and Linda's deductions for contributions to a traditional IRA for 2022?

LO 5.3

5. What is the maximum amount a 45-year-old taxpayer and 45-year-old spouse can put into a Traditional or Roth IRA for 2022 (assuming they have sufficient earned income, but do not have an income limitation and are not covered by another pension plan)?

LO 5.3

6. What is the maximum amount a 55-year-old taxpayer and 52-year-old spouse can put into a Traditional or Roth IRA for 2022, assuming they earn $70,000 in total and are not participants in pension plans?

LO 5.3

7. Barry is a single, 40-year-old software engineer earning $140,000 a year and is not covered by a pension plan at work. How much can he put into a Roth IRA in 2022?

LO 5.3

8. Bob is a single, 40-year-old doctor earning $190,000 a year and is not covered by a pension plan at work. What is the maximum deductible contribution into a Traditional IRA in 2022?

LO 5.3

9. Dori is 58 years old and retired in 2022. She receives a pension of $25,000 a year and no other income. She wishes to put the maximum allowed into an IRA. How much can she contribute to her IRA?

LO 5.4

10. During 2022, Jerry is a self-employed therapist, and his net earned income is $160,000 from his practice. Jerry's SEP Plan, a defined contribution plan, states that he will contribute the maximum amount allowable. Calculate Jerry's contribution.

LO 5.4

11. Tony is a 45-year-old psychiatrist who has net earned income of $320,000 in 2022. What is the maximum amount he can contribute to his SEP for the year?

LO 5.4

12. Mario, a self-employed plumber, makes a maximum contribution to a SEP for his employee, Peach. Peach's compensation is $50,000 for the year. How much is he allowed to contribute to the plan for Peach?

LO 5.4

13. During 2022, Jill, age 39, participated in a Section 401(k) plan which provides for maximum employee contributions of 12 percent. Jill's salary was $80,000 for the year. Jill elects to make the maximum contribution. What is Jill's maximum tax-deferred contribution to the plan for the year?

LO 5.4

14. Determine the outcome of each of the following contributions or distributions from a small-business qualified retirement plan:
    a. As an employee of Wumbo Company, Margo is enrolled in the SEP and in 2022, Wumbo provides a contribution of 5 percent of Margo's salary or $2,500. Describe the taxation of the contribution to Margo and Wumbo.
    b. Patrick works at the Krab Shack as a manager. In 2022, the Krab Shack operates a SIMPLE IRA plan and Patrick contributes $10,000 (10 percent of his $100,000 salary). Krab Shack matches the first 3 percent of the employee's annual wages. Describe the tax treatment of Patrick's contribution and the Krab Shack's match to the SIMPLE IRA. Explain whether Patrick has exceeded the maximum contribution allowed to the SIMPLE IRA versus a traditional or Roth IRA in 2022 assuming he is age 45 versus age 55.

c. As an employee of Undersea Labs, in 2022 Sandy, age 35, elects to defer $6,000 of her salary into the company's Roth 401(k) plan. Sandy's salary is $160,000 in 2022. Explain how the Roth 401(k) contribution limitations apply to Sandy.

LO 5.6

15. Linda installed a special pool for the hydrotherapeutic treatment of severe arthritis, as prescribed by her doctor. The cost of installing the pool was $20,000, and her insurance company paid $5,000 toward its cost. The pool increased the value of Linda's house by $7,000, and it has a useful life of ten years. Determine the amount of the deduction Linda is entitled to and explain why.

LO 5.6

16. In 2022, Margaret and John Murphy (both over age 65) are married taxpayers who file a joint tax return with AGI of $27,507. During the year they incurred the following expenses:

Medical insurance premiums	$1,200
Premiums on an insurance policy that pays $100 per day for each day Margaret is hospitalized	400
Medical care lodging (two people, one night)	160
Hospital bills	2,500
Herbal supplements	75
Dentist bills	250
Prescription drugs and medicines	360
Cosmetic surgery	400

In addition, they drove 122 miles (all before June 30) for medical transportation, and their insurance company reimbursed them $500 for the above expenses. On the following segment of Schedule A of Form 1040, calculate the Murphy's medical expense deduction.

Medical and Dental Expenses	**Caution:** Do not include expenses reimbursed or paid by others.				
	1 Medical and dental expenses (see instructions)	1			
	2 Enter amount from Form 1040 or 1040-SR, line 11 [2]				
	3 Multiply line 2 by 7.5% (0.075)	3			
	4 Subtract line 3 from line 1. If line 3 is more than line 1, enter -0-			4	

LO 5.6

17. Janet needs an elevator seat attached to her stairs since she has a medical condition that makes her unable to climb the stairs in her house. The $10,000 spent on the elevator seat does not increase the value of her house according to a local appraiser. How much of the capital asset is deductible in Janet's tax return as a medical expense?

LO 5.7

18. Lyndon's employer withheld $8,700 in state income taxes from Lyndon's wages in 2022. Lyndon obtained a refund of $1,700 this year for overpayment of state income taxes for 2021. State income taxes were an itemized deduction on his 2021 return. His 2022 liability for state income tax is $8,500. Indicate the amount of Lyndon's deduction for state income taxes on his federal tax return assuming he elects to deduct state income taxes for 2022.

LO 5.7

19. Mike sells his home to Jane on April 2, 2022. Jane pays the property taxes covering the full calendar year in October, which amount to $2,500. How much may Mike and Jane each deduct for property taxes in 2022?

LO 5.7 20. Laura is a single taxpayer living in New Jersey with adjusted gross income for the 2022 tax year of $86,000. Laura's employer withheld $8,400 in state income tax from her salary. In May of 2022, she received a $400 state income tax refund from her prior year's tax return. The real estate taxes on her home are $2,100 for 2022, and her personal property taxes, based on the value of the property, amount to $130. Also, she paid $80 for state gasoline taxes for the year. Complete the taxes section of Schedule A below to report Laura's 2022 deduction for taxes assuming she chooses to deduct state and local income taxes.

Taxes You Paid	5 State and local taxes.			
	a State and local income taxes or general sales taxes. You may include either income taxes or general sales taxes on line 5a, but not both. If you elect to include general sales taxes instead of income taxes, check this box . . . . ☐	5a		
	b State and local real estate taxes (see instructions)	5b		
	c State and local personal property taxes	5c		
	d Add lines 5a through 5c	5d		
	e Enter the smaller of line 5d or $10,000 ($5,000 if married filing separately)	5e		
	6 Other taxes. List type and amount: --	6		
	7 Add lines 5e and 6		7	

LO 5.7 21. Mary paid $2,000 of state income taxes in 2022. She paid $1,500 of state sales tax on the purchase of goods and she also purchased a car in 2022 and paid sales tax of $3,000. How should Mary treat the taxes paid on her 2022 tax return?

LO 5.8 22. Mary's mother defaults on a home loan and Mary pays $600 in loan payments, including $175 in interest. Mary is not legally obligated on the loan and has no ownership interest in her mother's home.

a. What amount, if any, may Mary claim as an itemized deduction for the current tax year?

b. Why?

LO 5.8 23. Matthew borrows $250,000 to invest in bonds. During the current year, his interest on the loan is $30,000. Matthew's taxable interest income from the bonds is $10,000. This is Matthew's only investment income and he has no other investment expenses other than the interest on the loan.

a. Calculate Matthew's itemized deduction for investment interest expense for this year.

b. Is Matthew entitled to a deduction in future years? Explain your rationale.

LO 5.8 24. Ken paid the following amounts for interest during 2022:

Qualified interest on home mortgage	$7,300
Auto loan interest	800
"Points" on the mortgage for acquisition of his personal residence	1,100
Home equity loan interest (proceeds used to pay for an addition to his home)	1,300
Mastercard interest	300

The amount of debt secured by Ken's home is less than $700,000. Calculate Ken's itemized deduction for interest on the following portion of Schedule A.

Interest You Paid				
Caution: Your mortgage interest deduction may be limited. See instructions.	**8** Home mortgage interest and points. If you didn't use all of your home mortgage loan(s) to buy, build, or improve your home, see instructions and check this box . . . . ☐			
	a Home mortgage interest and points reported to you on Form 1098. See instructions if limited	8a		
	b Home mortgage interest not reported to you on Form 1098. See instructions if limited. If paid to the person from whom you bought the home, see instructions and show that person's name, identifying no., and address	8b		
	c Points not reported to you on Form 1098. See instructions for special rules	8c		
	d Reserved for future use	8d		
	e Add lines 8a through 8c	8e		
	9 Investment interest. Attach Form 4952 if required. See instructions .	9		
	10 Add lines 8e and 9			10

LO 5.8

25. Janet and James purchased their personal residence fifteen years ago for $300,000. For the current year, they have an $80,000 first mortgage on their home, on which they paid $6,000 in interest. They also have a home equity loan to pay for the children's college tuition secured by their home with a balance throughout the year of $150,000. They paid interest on the home equity loan of $9,000 for the year.
    a. Calculate the qualified residence acquisition debt interest for the current year.
    b. Calculate the qualified home equity debt interest for the current year.

LO 5.8

26. Helen paid the following amounts of interest during the 2022 tax year:

Mortgage interest on Dallas residence (loan balance $50,000)	$1,600
Automobile loan interest (personal use only)	440
Mortgage interest on Vail residence (loan balance $50,000)	3,100
Student loan interest	775

Calculate the amount of Helen's itemized deduction for interest (after limitations, if any) for 2022.

LO 5.8

27. At the end of 2022, Mark owes $250,000 on the mortgage related to the 2016 purchase of his residence. When his daughter went to college in the fall of 2022, he borrowed $20,000 through a home equity loan on his house to help pay for her education. The interest expense on the main mortgage is $15,000, and the interest expense on the home equity loan is $1,500. How much of the interest is deductible as an itemized deduction and why?

LO 5.9

28. Barbara donates a painting that she purchased three years ago for $8,000, to a university for display in the president's office. The fair market value of the painting on the date of the gift is $14,000. If Barbara had sold the painting, the difference between the sales price and her cost would have been a long-term capital gain.
    a. How much is Barbara's charitable contribution deduction for this donation (before any AGI-based limitations)?
    b. Explain why.

LO 5.9

29. Jerry made the following contributions during 2022:

His synagogue (by check)	$4,500
The Republican Party (by check)	400
The American Red Cross (by check)	1,000
His fraternal organization for tickets to a holiday party	100
A baseball autographed by hall-of-fame baseball pitcher Sandy Koufax (basis $0) donated to a public charity	6,000

In addition, Jerry donated used furniture to the Salvation Army that he purchased years ago for $10,000 with a fair market value of $2,000. Assuming Jerry has adjusted gross income of $25,000, has the necessary written acknowledgments, and itemizes deductions, complete the charitable deduction limitations worksheet on Page 5-61 and then complete the Gifts to Charity section of Schedule A below.

Gifts to Charity **Caution:** If you made a gift and got a benefit for it, see instructions.	11 Gifts by cash or check. If you made any gift of $250 or more, see instructions	11		
	12 Other than by cash or check. If you made any gift of $250 or more, see instructions. You **must** attach Form 8283 if over $500. . . .	12		
	13 Carryover from prior year	13		
	14 Add lines 11 through 13		14	

LO 5.9

30. Richard donates publicly traded Gold Company stock with a basis of $1,000 and a fair market value of $15,000 to the college he attended, which is considered a public charity. Richard has owned the shares for 10 years. How is this contribution treated on Richard's tax return?

LO 5.9

31. Kathy, a single taxpayer, donates cash of $600 and also provides some gently-used clothing worth $150 to a local church. Kathy does not itemize deductions. What is the nature of any deduction for these items for Kathy in 2022?

LO 5.10

32. On January 3, 2022, Carey discovers his diamond bracelet has been stolen. The bracelet had a fair market value and adjusted basis of $7,500. Assuming Carey had no insurance coverage on the bracelet and his adjusted gross income for 2022 is $45,000, calculate the amount of his theft loss deduction.

LO 5.10

33. Kerry's car is totaled in tornado that is declared a federal disaster. The car originally cost $18,000, but is worth $7,500 at the time of the accident. Kerry's insurance company gives her a check for $5,000. Kerry has $30,000 of adjusted gross income. How much can Kerry claim as a casualty loss on her tax return? Please explain.

LO 5.10

34. During the 2022 tax year, Irma incurred the following expenses:

Union dues	$244
Tax return preparation fee	150
Brokerage fees for the purchase of stocks	35
Uniform expenses not reimbursed by her employer	315

If Irma's adjusted gross income is $23,000, calculate her miscellaneous deductions.

Step 1. Enter charitable contributions made during the year.

1 Enter contributions of capital gain property to non-50 percent qualified organizations

2 Enter other contributions to qualified organizations that are non-50 percent organizations. Do not include any contributions entered on the previous line

3 Enter contributions of capital gain property to 50% limit organizations deducted at fair market value. Do not include any contributions entered on a previous line

4 Enter noncash contributions to 50% limit organizations other than capital gain property deducted at fair market value. Be sure to include contributions of capital gain property to 50% limit organizations if electing to deduct at basis. Do not include any contributions entered on a previous line

5 Enter cash contributions to 50% limit organizations. Do not include any contributions entered on a previous line

Step 2. Figure the deduction for the year (if any result is zero or less, enter -0-)

6 Enter adjusted gross income (AGI)

Cash contributions subject to the limit based on 60% of AGI (If line 5 is zero, enter -0- on lines 7 through 9)

7 Multiply line 6 by 0.6

8 Deductible amount. Enter the smaller of line 5 or line 7

9 Carryover. Subtract line 8 from line 5

Noncash contributions subject to the limit based on 50% of AGI (If line 4 is zero, enter -0- on lines 10 through 13)

10 Multiply line 6 by 0.5

11 Subtract line 8 from line 10

12 Deductible amount. Enter the smaller of line 4 or line 11

13 Carryover. Subtract line 12 from line 4

Contributions (other than capital gain property) subject to limit based on 30% of AGI (If line 2 is zero, enter -0- on lines 14

14 Multiply line 6 by 0.5

15 Add lines 3, 4, and 5

16 Subtract line 15 from line 14

17 Multiply line 6 by 0.3

18 Enter line 2

19 Deductible amount. Enter the smallest of line 16, 17, or 18

20 Carryover. Subtract line 19 from line 18

Contributions of capital gain property subject to limit based on 30% of AGI (If line 3 is zero, enter -0- on lines 21 through 26.)

21 Multiply line 6 by 0.5

22 Add lines 4 and 5

23 Subtract line 22 from line 21

24 Multiply line 6 by 0.3

25 Deductible amount. Enter the smallest of line 3, 23, or 24

26 Carryover. Subtract line 25 from line 3

Contributions subject to the limit based on 20% of AGI (If line 1 is zero, enter -0- on lines 27 through 36)

27 Multiply line 6 by 0.5

28 Add lines 8, 12, 19, and 25

29 Subtract line 28 from line 27

30 Multiply line 6 by 0.3

31 Subtract line 19 from line 30

32 Subtract line 25 from line 30

33 Multiply line 6 by 0.2

34 Enter line 1

35 Deductible amount. Enter the smallest of line 29, 31, 32, 33, or 34

36 Carryover. Subtract line 35 from line 34

37 Deduction for the year. Add lines 8, 12, 19, 25, and 35

GROUP 3:
WRITING ASSIGNMENT

ETHICS

1. While preparing Massie Miller's 2022 Schedule A, you review the following list of possible charitable deductions provided by Massie:

Cash contribution to a family whose house burned down	$1,000
Time while working as a volunteer at Food Bank (five hours @ $50/hour)	250
Cash contribution to United Methodist Church (receipt provided)	800
Cash contribution to Salvation Army *(note from Massie: "I can't remember exactly the amount that I gave and I can't find the receipt. I think it was around $500.")*	500
Total	$2,550

What would you say to Massie regarding her listed deductions? How much of the deduction is allowed for charitable contributions?

RESEARCH

2. In 2022, Gale and Cathy Alexander hosted an exchange student, Axel Muller, for 9 months. Axel was part of International Student Exchange Programs (a qualified organization). Axel attended tenth grade at the local high school. Gale and Cathy did not claim Axel as a dependent but paid the following items for Axel's well-being:

Food and clothing	$1,500
Medical care	200
Fair market value of lodging	2,700
Entertainment	100
Total	$4,500

Gale and Cathy have asked for your help in determining if any of the $4,500 can be deducted as a charitable contribution.

Required: Go to the IRS website **(www.irs.gov)** and locate Publication 526. Write a letter to Gale and Cathy answering their question. If they can claim a deduction, be sure to include in your letter the amount that can be deducted and any substantiation requirements. (An example of a client letter is available at the website for this textbook located at **www.cengage.com.**)

GROUP 4:
COMPREHENSIVE PROBLEMS

1. Anthony Stork (birthdate August 2, 1978) is a single taxpayer. Anthony's earnings and withholdings as the manager of a local casino for 2022 are reported on his Form W-2:

a Employee's social security number 555-94-6767	OMB No. 1545-0008	Safe, accurate, FAST! Use IRS e-file. Visit the IRS website at www.irs.gov/efile
b Employer identification number (EIN) 34-4453987	1 Wages, tips, other compensation 77,000.00	2 Federal income tax withheld 3,400.00
c Employer's name, address, and ZIP code Stork Industries, Inc. 722 Centinela Ave. Inglewood, CA 90302	3 Social security wages 77,000.00	4 Social security tax withheld 4,774.00
	5 Medicare wages and tips 77,000.00	6 Medicare tax withheld 1,116.50
	7 Social security tips	8 Allocated tips
d Control number	9	10 Dependent care benefits
e Employee's first name and initial / Last name / Suff. Anthony Stork 800 N. Sierra Street Reno, NV 89503	11 Nonqualified plans	12a See instructions for box 12 W 1,000.00
	13 Statutory employee ☐ Retirement plan ☒ Third-party sick pay ☐	12b D 3,000.00
	14 Other	12c
f Employee's address and ZIP code		12d

15 State Employer's state ID number	16 State wages, tips, etc.	17 State income tax	18 Local wages, tips, etc.	19 Local income tax	20 Locality name
NV					

Form **W-2** Wage and Tax Statement 2022 Department of the Treasury—Internal Revenue Service

Copy B—To Be Filed With Employee's FEDERAL Tax Return.
This information is being furnished to the Internal Revenue Service.

Anthony pays his ex-spouse, Salty Pans, $3,900 per month in accordance with their February 12, 2020 divorce decree. When their 12-year-old child (in the ex-wife's custody) reaches the age of 18, the payments are reduced to $2,800 per month. His ex-wife's Social Security number is 554-44-5555.

In 2022, Anthony purchased a new car and so he kept track of his sales tax receipts during the year. His actual sales tax paid was $3,450 for the car and $925 for all other purchases.

Anthony participates in a high-deductible health plan and is eligible to contribute to a health savings account. His HSA earned $75 in 2022.

During the year, Anthony paid the following amounts (all of which can be substantiated):

Credit card interest	$1,760
Auto loan interest	2,300
Auto insurance	900
Property taxes on personal residence	3,400
Contributions to HSA	2,650
Income tax preparation fee	900
Charitable contributions (all cash):	
Boy Scouts of America	1,200
St. Matthews Church	3,100
Nevada Democratic Party	250
Fund-raising dinner for the Reno Auto Museum (value of dinner is $45)	100

In 2022, Anthony inherited over $500,000 from his father, Howard, who died in 2022. Although Anthony invested a large portion, he also contributed $50,000 cash to the newly named Stork School of Engineering at Reno State University.

Anthony also received the following Form 1098:

☐ CORRECTED (if checked)

RECIPIENT'S/LENDER'S name, street address, city or town, state or province, country, ZIP or foreign postal code, and telephone no. Reno Savings & Loan 49 Commerce Street Reno, NV 89501	*Caution: The amount shown may not be fully deductible by you. Limits based on the loan amount and the cost and value of the secured property may apply. Also, you may only deduct interest to the extent it was incurred by you, actually paid by you, and not reimbursed by another person.	OMB No. 1545-1380 Form **1098** (Rev. January 2022) For calendar year 20 22	**Mortgage Interest Statement**
	1 Mortgage interest received from payer(s)/borrower(s)* $ 9,870.78		**Copy B For Payer/ Borrower**
RECIPIENT'S/LENDER'S TIN 33-1234569 / PAYER'S/BORROWER'S TIN 555-94-6767	2 Outstanding mortgage principal $ 345,002.60	3 Mortgage origination date 03/05/2009	The information in boxes 1 through 9 and 11 is important tax information and is being furnished to the IRS. If you are required to file a return, a negligence penalty or other sanction may be imposed on you if the IRS determines that an underpayment of tax results because you overstated a deduction for this mortgage interest or for these points, reported in boxes 1 and 6; or because you didn't report the refund of interest (box 4); or because you claimed a nondeductible item.
PAYER'S/BORROWER'S name Anthony Stork	4 Refund of overpaid interest $	5 Mortgage insurance premiums $	
	6 Points paid on purchase of principal residence $		
Street address (including apt. no.) 800 N. Sierra Street	7 ☒ If address of property securing mortgage is the same as PAYER'S/BORROWER'S address, the box is checked, or the address or description is entered in box 8.		
City or town, state or province, country, and ZIP or foreign postal code Reno, NV 89503	8 Address or description of property securing mortgage		
9 Number of properties securing the mortgage 1 / 10 Other			11 Mortgage acquisition date
Account number (see instructions)			

Form **1098** (Rev. 1-2022) (Keep for your records) www.irs.gov/Form1098 Department of the Treasury - Internal Revenue Service

Required: Complete Anthony's federal tax return for 2022. Use Form 1040, Schedule 1, Schedule A, and Form 8889 to complete this tax return. Make realistic assumptions about any missing data.

2A. Bea Krump (birthdate 3/27/1987) moved from Texas to Florida in January 2022 after divorcing her spouse in 2021. She and her daughter, Dee Krump (birthdate 5/30/2012, Social Security number 121-44-6666) live at 654 Ocean Way, Gulfport, FL 33707. Bea provides all of Dee's support. Bea can claim a child tax credit for Dee. Bea's Social Security number is 466-78-6700 and she is single.

Bea owns and operates a shrimping business called Bea Krump's Shrimp. She uses a rented boat to shrimp and has a home office located in their home. The principal business code is 114110. Bea's bookkeeper provided the following income statement from the shrimping business:

Revenues	$43,000
Shrimp boat rental	16,000
Payroll	6,000
Payroll taxes	480
Bait and tackle	3,300
Boat fuel	2,400
Shrimping permit	800
Miscellaneous supplies	900
Health insurance premiums (for Bea and Dee)	3,700
Insurance	800

Bea sells her entire catch at the end of each day and thus has no inventory. She uses the cash method of accounting and has no depreciation. Bea uses her home office exclusively for conducting business. The office is 160 square feet in her 2,000 square foot home. Other than the interest and taxes reported below, her only other cost is utilities of $1,200. Assume no depreciation. Bea's health insurance is a high-deductible plan.

Because the shrimping business is seasonal, Bea also works at a local restaurant as a server. Her 2022 W-2 is below:

a Employee's social security number 466-78-6700	OMB No. 1545-0008 Safe, accurate, FAST! Use IRS e-file. Visit the IRS website at www.irs.gov/efile
b Employer identification number (EIN) 34-9172555	1 Wages, tips, other compensation 39,132.89
	2 Federal income tax withheld 2,400.00
c Employer's name, address, and ZIP code Bubble Gum Shrimp Diner 7821 Gulf Blvd. St Pete Beach, FL 33706	3 Social security wages 39,132.89
	4 Social security tax withheld 2,426.24
	5 Medicare wages and tips 39,132.89
	6 Medicare tax withheld 567.43
	7 Social security tips
	8 Allocated tips
d Control number	9
	10 Dependent care benefits
e Employee's first name and initial / Last name / Suff. Bea Krump 654 Ocean Way Gulfport, FL 33707	11 Nonqualified plans
	12a See instructions for box 12
	13 Statutory employee / Retirement plan / Third-party sick pay
	12b
	14 Other
	12c
	12d
f Employee's address and ZIP code	

15 State	Employer's state ID number	16 State wages, tips, etc.	17 State income tax	18 Local wages, tips, etc.	19 Local income tax	20 Locality name
FL						

Form **W-2** **Wage and Tax Statement** 2022 Department of the Treasury—Internal Revenue Service

Copy B—To Be Filed With Employee's FEDERAL Tax Return.
This information is being furnished to the Internal Revenue Service.

Bea received the following 1099-INT:

☐ CORRECTED (if checked)

PAYER'S name, street address, city or town, state or province, country, ZIP or foreign postal code, and telephone no. St. Pete Bank of Florida 958 Pasadena Ave S. South Pasadena, FL 33707	Payer's RTN (optional)	OMB No. 1545-0112 Form **1099-INT** (Rev. January 2022) For calendar year 20 22
	1 Interest income $ 89.38	**Interest Income**
	2 Early withdrawal penalty $	**Copy B** **For Recipient**
PAYER'S TIN 13-2278912 / RECIPIENT'S TIN 466-78-6700	3 Interest on U.S. Savings Bonds and Treasury obligations $	
RECIPIENT'S name Bea Krump	4 Federal income tax withheld $	5 Investment expenses $
Street address (including apt. no.) 654 Ocean Way	6 Foreign tax paid $	7 Foreign country or U.S. possession
City or town, state or province, country, and ZIP or foreign postal code Gulfport, FL 33707	8 Tax-exempt interest $ 340.00	9 Specified private activity bond interest $
	10 Market discount $	11 Bond premium $
FATCA filing requirement ☐	12 Bond premium on Treasury obligations $	13 Bond premium on tax-exempt bond $
Account number (see instructions)	14 Tax-exempt and tax credit bond CUSIP no.	15 State / 16 State identification no. / 17 State tax withheld $ $

This is important tax information and is being furnished to the IRS. If you are required to file a return, a negligence penalty or other sanction may be imposed on you if this income is taxable and the IRS determines that it has not been reported.

Form **1099-INT** (Rev. 1-2022) (keep for your records) www.irs.gov/Form1099INT Department of the Treasury - Internal Revenue Service

Bea also receives $600 per month in alimony from her ex-spouse in accordance with their 2021 divorce decree.

In order to move herself and Dee, Bea spent $800 moving her household goods (trailer rental), $200 on meals and $300 on lodging while traveling between Texas and Florida. The drive was 1,005 miles.

After moving to Gulfport, Bea sent Dee to a local private school for the remainder of 5th grade. Bea used $4,000 from Dee's Section 529 plan to pay for private school tuition as reported on the Form 1099-Q on Page 5-66. Dee had always attended public schools in Texas.

☐ CORRECTED (if checked)

PAYER'S/TRUSTEE'S name, street address, city or town, state or province, country, ZIP or foreign postal code, and telephone no.		1 Gross distribution	OMB No. 1545-1760	Payments From Qualified Education Programs (Under Sections 529 and 530)
Texas College Savings Plan PO Box 13400 Austin, TX 78711		$ 4,000.00	Form **1099-Q** (Rev. November 2019)	
		2 Earnings $ 254.00	For calendar year 20 22	
PAYER'S/TRUSTEE'S TIN 22-1456712	RECIPIENT'S TIN 121-44-6666	3 Basis $ 3,746.00	4 Trustee-to-trustee transfer ☐	**Copy B For Recipient**
RECIPIENT'S name Dee Krump		5 Distribution is from: • Qualified tuition program— Private ☐ or State ☒ • Coverdell ESA ☐	6 If this box is checked, the recipient is not the designated beneficiary ☐	This is important tax information and is being furnished to the IRS. If you are required to file a return, a negligence penalty or other sanction may be imposed on you if this income is taxable and the IRS determines that it has not been reported.
Street address (including apt. no.) 654 Ocean Way		If the fair market value (FMV) is shown below, see **Pub. 970**, Tax Benefits for Education, for how to figure earnings.		
City or town, state or province, country, and ZIP or foreign postal code Gulfport, FL 33707		Dist Code = 1		
Account number (see instructions)				

Form **1099-Q** (Rev. 11-2019) (keep for your records) www.irs.gov/Form1099Q Department of the Treasury - Internal Revenue Service

During 2022, Bea paid the following amounts (all of which can be substantiated):

Home mortgage interest (1098 not shown)	$8,820
Auto loan interest	2,300
Property taxes on personal residence	5,040
Out-of-pocket doctor bills	2,788
Income tax preparation fee	600
Job-hunting expenses	925
Contribution to HSA	3,300
Cash donations to church	$4,000

Bea paid for the out-of-pocket doctor bills with a distribution from her HSA account. See Form 1099-SA below:

☐ CORRECTED (if checked)

TRUSTEE'S/PAYER'S name, street address, city or town, state or province, country, ZIP or foreign postal code, and telephone number			OMB No. 1545-1517	Distributions From an HSA, Archer MSA, or Medicare Advantage MSA
Tampa Health Savings Admin Inc. 720 N Franklin Street Tampa, FL 33602			Form **1099-SA** (Rev. November 2019) For calendar year 2022	
PAYER'S TIN 57-8712353	RECIPIENT'S TIN 466-78-6700	1 Gross distribution $ 2,788.00	2 Earnings on excess cont. $	**Copy B For Recipient**
RECIPIENT'S name Bea Krump		3 Distribution code 1	4 FMV on date of death $	
Street address (including apt. no.) 654 Ocean Way		5 HSA ☒ Archer MSA ☐ MA MSA ☐		This information is being furnished to the IRS.
City or town, state or province, country, and ZIP or foreign postal code Gulfport, FL 33707				
Account number (see instructions)				

Form **1099-SA** (Rev. 11-2019) (keep for your records) www.irs.gov/Form1099SA Department of the Treasury - Internal Revenue Service

After the divorce, Bea had to purchase a car for herself and all the furnishings for her home. She kept her receipts and had total sales taxes of $3,881, which exceeds the sales tax estimate from the IRS tables.

Required: Complete Bea's federal tax return for 2022. Use Form 1040, Schedule 1, Schedule 2, Schedule A, Schedule C, Schedule SE, Form 8829, Form 8889 and Form 8995 to complete this tax return. Make realistic assumptions about any missing data.

2B. John Fuji (birthdate June 6, 1983) received the following Form W-2 from his employer related to his job as a manager at a Washington apple-processing plant:

a Employee's social security number 571-78-5974	OMB No. 1545-0008	Safe, accurate, FAST! Use IRS e-file	Visit the IRS website at www.irs.gov/efile
b Employer identification number (EIN) 34-7654321		1 Wages, tips, other compensation 80,125.00	2 Federal income tax withheld 10,100.00
c Employer's name, address, and ZIP code Granny Smith Apple Co. 200 Ahtanum Road Yakima, WA 98903		3 Social security wages 80,125.00	4 Social security tax withheld 4,967.75
		5 Medicare wages and tips 80,125.00	6 Medicare tax withheld 1,161.81
		7 Social security tips	8 Allocated tips
d Control number		9	10 Dependent care benefits
e Employee's first name and initial / Last name / Suff. John Fuji 468 Bonnie Doon Avenue Yakima, WA 98902		11 Nonqualified plans	12a See instructions for box 12
		13 Statutory employee ☐ Retirement plan ☒ Third-party sick pay ☐	12b
		14 Other	12c
f Employee's address and ZIP code			12d

15 State	Employer's state ID number	16 State wages, tips, etc.	17 State income tax	18 Local wages, tips, etc.	19 Local income tax	20 Locality name
WA						

Form **W-2** **Wage and Tax Statement** 2022 Department of the Treasury—Internal Revenue Service

Copy B—To Be Filed With Employee's FEDERAL Tax Return.
This information is being furnished to the Internal Revenue Service.

John has income reported to him on a 1099-DIV from his investment in mutual funds:

☐ CORRECTED (if checked)

PAYER'S name, street address, city or town, state or province, country, ZIP or foreign postal code, and telephone no. Honeycrisp Equity Fund 900 Western Ave, 12th Fl Seattle, WA 98104		1a Total ordinary dividends $ 4,000.00	OMB No. 1545-0110 Form **1099-DIV** (Rev. January 2022)	**Dividends and Distributions**
		1b Qualified dividends $ 4,000.00	For calendar year 20 22	
		2a Total capital gain distr. $ 1,200.00	2b Unrecap. Sec. 1250 gain $	**Copy B For Recipient**
PAYER'S TIN 33-9871012	RECIPIENT'S TIN 571-78-5974	2c Section 1202 gain $	2d Collectibles (28%) gain $	
		2e Section 897 ordinary dividends $	2f Section 897 capital gain $	
RECIPIENT'S name John Fuji		3 Nondividend distributions $	4 Federal income tax withheld $ 0.00	This is important tax information and is being furnished to the IRS. If you are required to file a return, a negligence penalty or other sanction may be imposed on you if this income is taxable and the IRS determines that it has not been reported.
Street address (including apt. no.) 468 Bonnie Doon Avenue		5 Section 199A dividends $	6 Investment expenses $	
		7 Foreign tax paid $	8 Foreign country or U.S. possession	
City or town, state or province, country, and ZIP or foreign postal code Yakima, WA 98902		9 Cash liquidation distributions $	10 Noncash liquidation distributions $	
	11 FATCA filing requirement ☐	12 Exempt-interest dividends $	13 Specified private activity bond interest dividends $	
Account number (see instructions)		14 State / 15 State identification no.	16 State tax withheld $ $	

Form **1099-DIV** (Rev. 1-2022) (keep for your records) www.irs.gov/Form1099DIV Department of the Treasury - Internal Revenue Service

Also, in accordance with the January 2016 divorce decree John receives $500 per month alimony from his ex-wife (Dora Fuji, Social Security number 573-79-6075) in 2022.

On December 30, 2022, John sold his primary residence after living there since October 2012. The proceeds from the sale were $560,677 and his basis was $292,000. The closing statement for the sale indicated that John owed property taxes of $323 at the time of closing and the seller reduced his net proceeds by that amount. Those property taxes are not reflected on John's 1098.

☐ CORRECTED (if checked)

RECIPIENT'S/LENDER'S name, street address, city or town, state or province, country, ZIP or foreign postal code, and telephone no.
Braeburn National Bank
1600 W. Nob Hill Blvd.
Yakima, WA 98902

*Caution: The amount shown may not be fully deductible by you. Limits based on the loan amount and the cost and value of the secured property may apply. Also, you may only deduct interest to the extent it was incurred by you, actually paid by you, and not reimbursed by another person.

OMB No. 1545-1380
Form **1098**
(Rev. January 2022)
For calendar year 20 22

Mortgage Interest Statement

1 Mortgage interest received from payer(s)/borrower(s)* $ 9,835.12

Copy B For Payer/ Borrower

RECIPIENT'S/LENDER'S TIN 54-9019016

PAYER'S/BORROWER'S TIN 571-78-5974

2 Outstanding mortgage principal $ 302,458.90

3 Mortgage origination date 10/01/2012

4 Refund of overpaid interest $

5 Mortgage insurance premiums $

PAYER'S/BORROWER'S name John Fuji

6 Points paid on purchase of principal residence $

Street address (including apt. no.) 468 Bonnie Doon Avenue

7 ☒ If address of property securing mortgage is the same as PAYER'S/BORROWER'S address, the box is checked, or the address or description is entered in box 8.

City or town, state or province, country, and ZIP or foreign postal code Yakima, WA 98902

8 Address or description of property securing mortgage

9 Number of properties securing the mortgage 1

10 Other Prop Tax $3,480.00

The information in boxes 1 through 9 and 11 is important tax information and is being furnished to the IRS. If you are required to file a return, a negligence penalty or other sanction may be imposed on you if the IRS determines that an underpayment of tax results because you overstated a deduction for this mortgage interest or for these points, reported in boxes 1 and 6; or because you didn't report the refund of interest (box 4); or because you claimed a nondeductible item.

Account number (see instructions)

11 Mortgage acquisition date

Form **1098** (Rev. 1-2022) (Keep for your records) www.irs.gov/Form1098 Department of the Treasury - Internal Revenue Service

John tried his hand at day trading for one week in February 2022. He received a substitute Form 1099-B from his broker. Because the IRS was provided the acquisition date and basis for all trades and none required any adjustments or codes, these can be entered as a summary entry into Schedule D and no Form 8949 needs to be prepared.

Little John Brokerage Statement
100 Nottingham Street
Sherwood Forest, MA 01233
Substitute Form 1099-B
Tax Year 2022

John Fuji
468 Bonnie Doon Ave.
Yakima, WA 98902
XXX-XX-5974

1a		1b	1c	1d	1e	Net Gain	2
Descrip	**Shares**	**Date Acq**	**Date Sold**	**Proceeds**	**Cost Basis**	**or Loss**	**ST/LT**
Moderni Pharm	44	2/3/2022	2/3/2022	910.00	888.00	22.00	ST
Moderni Pharm	37	2/3/2022	2/3/2022	740.00	738.00	2.00	ST
Moderni Pharm	31	2/3/2022	2/3/2022	623.00	473.00	150.00	ST
Moderni Pharm	28	2/3/2022	2/3/2022	569.00	593.00	(24.00)	ST
Moderni Pharm	34	2/3/2022	2/3/2022	683.00	443.00	240.00	ST
Moderni Pharm	21	2/4/2022	2/4/2022	422.00	172.00	250.00	ST
Moderni Pharm	40	2/4/2022	2/4/2022	786.00	667.00	119.00	ST
Moderni Pharm	32	2/4/2022	2/4/2022	646.00	464.00	182.00	ST
Moderni Pharm	35	2/4/2022	2/4/2022	692.00	495.00	197.00	ST
Moderni Pharm	30	2/4/2022	2/4/2022	595.00	478.00	117.00	ST
Moderni Pharm	42	2/5/2022	2/5/2022	847.00	579.00	268.00	ST
Moderni Pharm	28	2/5/2022	2/5/2022	565.00	433.00	132.00	ST
Moderni Pharm	33	2/5/2022	2/5/2022	664.00	421.00	243.00	ST
Moderni Pharm	21	2/5/2022	2/5/2022	422.00	277.00	145.00	ST
Moderni Pharm	32	2/5/2022	2/5/2022	630.00	478.00	152.00	ST
Moderni Pharm	39	2/6/2022	2/6/2022	780.00	509.00	271.00	ST
Moderni Pharm	40	2/6/2022	2/6/2022	796.00	711.00	85.00	ST
Moderni Pharm	38	2/6/2022	2/6/2022	754.00	484.00	270.00	ST
Moderni Pharm	34	2/6/2022	2/6/2022	674.00	424.00	250.00	ST
				12,798.00	9,727.00	3,071.00	

During 2022, John paid the following amounts (all of which can be substantiated):

Auto loan interest	1,575
Credit card interest	655
State sales tax (actual exceeds estimated)	2,022
Doctor bills	4,000
Other deductible medical expenses	1,800
Income tax preparation fee	500
Job-hunting expenses	925
Cash charitable donation to the Jonagold Research Center	2,500
Federal estimated tax payment 12/30/2022	5,000

John's employer offers a retirement plan, but John does not participate. Instead, he made a $6,000 contribution to a Roth IRA.

John owns a condo in Seattle that he lived in years ago and now rents. His rental condo is located at 1012 E Terrace Street Unit 1204, Seattle, WA 98122 and was rented all year to his tenant. The tenant occupied the home on January 1, 2022 and pays rent of $2,000 per month for each month of 2022 (a 12-month lease). John demanded first and last month rent and a security deposit of $500 and all were paid January 1, 2022. Upon the tenant's departure on December 31, John noted damages and is going to retain $200 of the security deposit. John's rental expenses for the year are:

Mortgage interest	$9,500
Real estate taxes	7,000
Insurance	2,000
Depreciation (fully depreciated)	0
Repairs	1,000
Homeowner's association fees	5,600

John actively manages the rental home. He probably spends about seven hours per month on the rental.

Required: Complete John's federal tax return for 2021. Use Form 1040, Schedule 1, Schedule A, and Schedule D as needed to complete this tax return. Make realistic assumptions about any missing data.

GROUP 5:
CUMULATIVE SOFTWARE PROBLEM

1. The following information is available for the Albert and Allison Gaytor family in addition to that provided in Chapters 1–4.
   Albert and Allison received the following form:

☐ CORRECTED (if checked)

RECIPIENT'S/LENDER'S name, street address, city or town, state or province, country, ZIP or foreign postal code, and telephone no.		*Caution: The amount shown may not be fully deductible by you. Limits based on the loan amount and the cost and value of the secured property may apply. Also, you may only deduct interest to the extent it was incurred by you, actually paid by you, and not reimbursed by another person.	OMB No. 1545-1380 Form **1098** (Rev. January 2022) For calendar year 20 22	**Mortgage Interest Statement**
Vizcaya National Bank 9871 Coral Way Miami, FL 33134		1 Mortgage interest received from payer(s)/borrower(s)* $ 11,489.32		**Copy B** **For Payer/ Borrower** The information in boxes 1 through 9 and 11 is important tax information and is being furnished to the IRS. If you are required to file a return, a negligence penalty or other sanction may be imposed on you if the IRS determines that an underpayment of tax results because you overstated a deduction for this mortgage interest or for these points, reported in boxes 1 and 6; or because you didn't report the refund of interest (box 4); or because you claimed a nondeductible item.
RECIPIENT'S/LENDER'S TIN 60-7654321	PAYER'S/BORROWER'S TIN 266-51-1966	2 Outstanding mortgage principal $ 318,055.12	3 Mortgage origination date 03/01/2007	
PAYER'S/BORROWER'S name Albert and Allison Gaytor		4 Refund of overpaid interest $	5 Mortgage insurance premiums $	
		6 Points paid on purchase of principal residence $		
Street address (including apt. no.) 12340 Cocoshell Road		7 ☒ If address of property securing mortgage is the same as PAYER'S/BORROWER'S address, the box is checked, or the address or description is entered in box 8.		
City or town, state or province, country, and ZIP or foreign postal code Coral Gables, FL 33134		8 Address or description of property securing mortgage		
9 Number of properties securing the mortgage 1	10 Other			
Account number (see instructions)				11 Mortgage acquisition date

Form **1098** (Rev. 1-2022) (Keep for your records) www.irs.gov/Form1098 Department of the Treasury - Internal Revenue Service

Albert and Allison paid the following in 2022 (all by check or can otherwise be substantiated):

Contributions to St. Anne's Catholic Church	$ 600
Tuition to St. Anne's Catholic School for Crocker (spring 2022)	6,000
Clothes to Salvation Army (10 bags in good condition)	250
Contributions to Marcus Rubius Congressional campaign	250
Psychotherapy for Allison	2,300
Prescription eyeglasses for Crocker	400
Prescription medication and drugs	1,900
Credit card interest	1,345
Interest on Albert's college loans	3,125
Actual state sales tax (including sales tax on new auto of $2,000)	3,750
Investment interest expense on stock margin account	350
Auto loan interest reported on Form 1098 (not shown here; auto was paid for by a home equity loan on residence)	860
Auto insurance	1,600
Cosmetic surgery for Albert	4,500
Dave Deduction, CPA, for preparation of last year's tax return	765
Safe-deposit box for storage of stocks and tax data	100
Contribution to an educational savings account for Crocker	1,000
Home property taxes	4,500
Unreimbursed business expense (seminar on dealing with hijacking at sea)	700

In August 2022, Crocker was on an out-of-town field trip with the university band and his appendix burst. He required immediate surgery which was considered "out of network" for the Gaytor's health plan, resulting in hospital and doctor's fees of $3,200 not covered by insurance. In addition, Allison drove 300 miles round trip to be with Crocker after the surgery and drove him home after he recovered. She spent two nights in a hotel at a cost of $170 per night.

In June, Albert purchased a new professional digital SLR camera for $7,950. While the Gaytors were on vacation in August, someone broke into their residence and stole the camera. Albert's homeowners' insurance did not reimburse him for any part of the loss since he declined the special premium add-on for high value items required by his policy.

For the 2022 tax year, on April 15, 2023, Albert contributes $6,000 to his traditional IRA and Allison contributes $6,000 to her traditional IRA. Albert is not covered by a qualified retirement plan at work.

Albert managed to gather his gambling loss documentation and can substantiate gambling losses of $5,781 in 2022 (refer back to Chapter 2 for gambling winnings).

Required: Combine this new information about the Gaytor family with the information from Chapters 1–4 and complete a revised 2022 tax return for Albert and Allison. Be sure to save your data input files since this case will be expanded with more tax information in later chapters.

CHAPTER 6

Accounting Periods and Other Taxes

valentinrussanov/Getty Images

LEARNING OBJECTIVES

After completing this chapter, you should be able to:

- **LO 6.1** Determine the different accounting periods allowed for tax purposes.
- **LO 6.2** Determine the different accounting methods allowed for tax purposes.
- **LO 6.3** Determine whether parties are considered related for tax purposes, and classify the tax treatment of certain related-party transactions.
- **LO 6.4** Apply the rules for computing tax on the unearned income of minor children and certain students (the "kiddie tax").
- **LO 6.5** Calculate a basic alternative minimum tax.
- **LO 6.6** Apply the special tax and reporting requirements for household employees (the "nanny tax").
- **LO 6.7** Compute the special taxes for high-income taxpayers.
- **LO 6.8** Describe the basic rules surrounding special taxpayer situations such as divorce, deceased taxpayers, nonresident taxpayers, and farmers.

OVERVIEW

Taxpayers operating a business, whether professional, rental, manufacturing, or another activity, should have an understanding of the accounting periods (calendar, fiscal, or short-period tax years) and accounting methods (cash, accrual, or hybrid methods) allowed. Transactions involving related parties often have different rules for inclusion or exclusion of income and deductions. This chapter begins by addressing how and when individual, partnership, and corporate taxpayers should report taxable income.

In addition to the typical income tax, a number of other taxes are also reported through the individual income tax return. On the 2022 Form 1040, Schedule 2 is the primary reporting mechanism for additional taxes. This chapter covers the computation of taxes such as the "kiddie tax," the "nanny tax," the alternative minimum tax, the net investment income tax, and the additional Medicare tax.

Learning Objective 6.1

Determine the different accounting periods allowed for tax purposes.

6-1 ACCOUNTING PERIODS

6-1a Individual Tax Years

Almost all individuals file tax returns using a calendar-year accounting period. Individuals reporting for tax purposes on a fiscal year other than a calendar year are extremely rare since the tax system is set up to accommodate calendar-year taxpayers. However, there are no restrictions on an individual taking a tax year other than a calendar year. The choice to file on a fiscal-year basis must be made with an initial tax return, and books and records must be kept on that basis. An individual may also request IRS approval to change to a fiscal year if certain conditions are met.

6-1b Partnership and Corporation Tax Years

Many individual tax returns include the pass-through of income from partnerships, limited liability companies, S corporations, and personal service corporations. The income or loss from partnerships and S corporations is passed through on Schedule K-1 to the owners and taxed on the owners' personal tax returns. Partnerships and S corporations are not generally taxable entities, only reporting entities. Similarly, wages are passed through to doctors, lawyers, accountants, actuaries, and other professionals from personal service corporations owned by them. Many individuals carry on businesses in partnerships which comprise a large part of the income shown on their tax returns. Other individuals make investments, including the operation of real estate rental activities, in these pass-through entities. Because the pass-through of income and loss from partnerships and S corporations plays a large role in the taxation of many individuals, it is important to understand the rules governing the allowed accounting periods for these entities.

Partnerships and corporations had a great deal of freedom in selecting a tax year in the past. However, Congress decided that this freedom often resulted in an inappropriate deferral of taxable income. For example, if an individual taxpayer has a calendar tax year and receives income from a partnership with a tax year ending September 30, the taxpayer is able to defer three months of partnership income for an indefinite period of time. Therefore, the tax law was changed to include provisions that specify the required tax year for many partnerships and certain corporations, reducing the opportunities for deferring income.

Corporations have much more flexibility and can generally choose any fiscal year-end for tax purposes. The primary restriction on choosing a fiscal year-end for a corporation is that its books and records must also be maintained on the same fiscal year-end. Fiscal year-ends must always occur on the last day of a month unless the taxpayer adopts a 52–53-week year, which permits the year-end to always fall on the same day of the week. That day of the week must be the one closest to the last day of the month.

Most partnerships, S corporations, and personal service corporations owned by individual taxpayers now conform to the same calendar-year reporting used by almost all individuals. These entities are allowed a September, October, or November year-end if the owners make an annual cash deposit on behalf of the entity or perform other required calculations to assure the IRS that they are not using the fiscal year to defer the payment of federal taxes. The details of the complex requirements which must be met by entities filing non-calendar tax years are beyond the scope of this textbook.

6-1c Short-Period Taxable Income

If taxpayers have a short year other than their first or last year of operations, they are required to annualize their taxable income to calculate the tax for the short period. The tax liability is calculated for the annualized period and allocated back to the short period. With the flat 21 percent corporate tax rate, the annualization method is somewhat simplified.

EXAMPLE Omoto Corporation obtains permission from the IRS to change from a calendar year to a fiscal year ending August 31. For the short period, January 1 through August 31, 2022, the corporation's taxable income was $40,000. Omoto Corporation's tax for the short period is calculated as follows:

Step 1: Annualize the income	$40,000 × 12/8 = $60,000
Step 2: Tax on annualized income	21% × $60,000 = $12,600
Step 3: Short period tax	$12,600 × 8/12 = $ 8,400

With a flat tax rate, this short-period taxable income calculation is equivalent to $40,000 × 21 percent. ♦

Self-Study Problem 6.1

See Appendix E for Solutions to Self-Study Problems

For the following taxpayers, determine the choice of year-end and place an X in the correct column(s).

Taxpayer	Calendar year-end	Fiscal year-end	Fiscal year-end but some restrictions
1. Individual with no separate books and records	______	______	______
2. Partnership for which all the partners are calendar year-end individuals	______	______	______
3. A corporation that keeps in book and records on a fiscal year ending June 30	______	______	______
4. An S corporation for which all shareholders are calendar year-end individuals	______	______	______

6-2 ACCOUNTING METHODS

6.2 Learning Objective

Determine the different accounting methods allowed for tax purposes.

The tax law requires taxpayers to report taxable income using the method of accounting regularly used by the taxpayer in keeping their books, provided the method clearly reflects the taxpayer's income. The cash receipts and disbursements method, the accrual method, and the hybrid method are accounting methods specifically recognized in the tax law.

The cash receipts and disbursements method of accounting (commonly referred to as the cash method or cash basis) is used by most individuals for their overall method of accounting. Generally, wages, interest and dividend income, capital gains, and personal deductions are accounted for on the cash basis for individuals. Individuals may choose to account for a particular business, such as a sole proprietorship reported on Schedule C, using the accrual or hybrid method of accounting. If a taxpayer has two businesses, a different method of accounting may be used for each. The choice of a tax accounting method is a general rule which will be overridden by tax laws for some items of income and expense. For example, individuals reporting on a cash basis may deduct IRAs or pension contributions which are paid in cash in the year following the deduction, the income from savings bonds may be included in taxable income even though it is not received in cash, and prepaid interest may not be allowed as a deduction in the year paid.

The cash method generally results in the recognition of income when it is actually or constructively received; deductions are recognized in the year of payment. Taxpayers on the accrual basis generally recognize income when it is earned, regardless of when it is received, and generally recognize deductions when they are incurred, regardless of when they are paid. Cash-basis taxpayers may not use the cash method for all expenses. Tax rules require cash-basis taxpayers to always use the accrual basis for prepayments of interest. Other business expenses such as rent must also follow the accrual method if the prepayment extends substantially (generally twelve months) beyond the end of the tax year. Conversely, accrual-basis taxpayers who receive certain types of prepaid income, such as rent in advance, must generally recognize the income on the cash basis.

EXAMPLE On December 1, 2022, Carol entered into a lease on a building for use in her business for $2,000 per month. Under the lease terms, Carol pays eighteen months' rent ($36,000) in advance on December 1. Carol may deduct only one month's rent ($2,000) for the calendar year ended December 31, 2022, because the prepayment extends substantially beyond the end of the tax year, even though she is a cash-basis taxpayer. The remainder of the prepaid rent is deducted at $2,000 per month in 2023 and 2024. The taxpayer receiving the rent must report all $36,000 as income even if they are an accrual-basis taxpayer. ♦

EXAMPLE If in the previous example, the lease was for only 12 months, then as a cash-basis taxpayer, Carol could deduct the entire $36,000 in 2022 at the time of payment. ♦

The accrual method of accounting requires that income be recognized when (1) all events have occurred which fix the right to receive the income, and (2) the amount of income can be estimated with reasonable accuracy. An expense is deductible in the year in which all events have occurred that determine a liability exists and the amount can be estimated with reasonable accuracy. Also, "economic performance" must occur before an accrual-basis deduction can be claimed. Economic performance means that all activities related to the incurrence of the liability have been performed. For example, economic performance occurs for the purchase of services when the taxpayer uses the services.

A hybrid method of accounting involves the use of both the cash and accrual methods of accounting. The tax law permits the use of a hybrid method, provided the taxpayer's income is clearly reflected by the method. An example of a hybrid method is the use of the accrual method for cost of products sold by the business and the use of the cash method for income and other expenses.

Taxpayers make an election to use an accounting method when they file an initial tax return and use that method. To change methods, taxpayers must obtain permission from the IRS.

TAX BREAK

The cash method allows a certain amount of flexibility in tax planning. Payment of business expenses may be accelerated before year-end to generate additional deductions, if desired. In addition, billings for services may be postponed at year-end so payment will not be received and included in income until the following year. Some itemized deductions such as property taxes, state income taxes, and charitable contributions may also be paid before year-end for an immediate deduction.

6-2a Restrictions on the Use of the Cash Method

The tax law contains certain restrictions on the use of the cash method of accounting. Regular corporations, partnerships that have a regular corporation as a partner, and tax-exempt trusts with unrelated business income are generally prohibited from using the cash method. However, this requirement does not apply to farming businesses, qualified personal service corporations, and entities with average annual gross receipts of $27 million or less in 2022.

EXAMPLE Orange Associates is a manufacturer of light bulbs with average gross receipts of $28 million. Orange would not be allowed to use the cash method of accounting for tax purposes. ♦

Self-Study Problem 6.2 ***See Appendix E for Solutions to Self-Study Problems***

a. Melaleuca, Inc., is an accrual-basis taxpayer with the following transactions during the calendar tax year:

Accrual business income (except rent and interest)	$63,000
Accrual business expenses (except rent)	42,000
Three months' rent received on a leased building on November 1 of this year	9,000
Prepaid interest for one year received on a note on July 1 of the current year	12,000
Six months' rent paid on December 1 for business property	7,200

Calculate Melaleuca, Inc.'s, net income for this year.

b. Determine whether or not each of the following entities may use the cash method for tax purposes during 2022.

1. A corporation engaged in orange farming.
2. A dentist with a personal service corporation.
3. A corporate car dealer with sales of $28 million per year.
4. A corporation engaged in certified public accounting.

6-3 RELATED PARTIES (SECTION 267)

6.3 Learning Objective

Determine whether parties are considered related for tax purposes, and classify the tax treatment of certain related-party transactions.

When taxpayers who are related to each other engage in transactions, there is potential for abuse of the tax system. To prevent this abuse, the tax law contains provisions that govern related-party transactions. Under these rules, related parties who undertake certain types of transactions may find the timing of income or deduction recognition differs from typical rules.

There are two types of transactions between related parties restricted by Section 267 of the tax law. These transactions are:

1. Sales of property at a loss
2. Unpaid expenses and interest

6-3a Losses

Under the tax law "losses from sale or exchange of property . . . directly or indirectly" are disallowed between related parties. When the property is later sold to an unrelated party, any disallowed loss may be used to offset gain on that transaction.

EXAMPLE Mary sells IBM stock with a basis of $10,000 to her son, Steve, for $8,000, resulting in a disallowed loss of $2,000. Three years later, Steve sells the stock to an unrelated party for $13,000. Steve has a gain on the sale of $5,000 ($13,000 − $8,000). However, only $3,000 ($5,000 − $2,000) of the gain is taxable to Steve since the previously disallowed loss can reduce his gain. ♦

EXAMPLE Assume the same facts as in the example above, except the IBM stock is sold for $9,500 (instead of $13,000). None of the gain of $1,500 ($9,500 − $8,000) would be taxable, because the disallowed loss would absorb it. $500 of Mary's disallowed loss is not available to her son. ♦

EXAMPLE Assume the same facts as in the example above, except Steve sells the IBM stock three years later for $7,000 (instead of $9,500). Steve now has a $1,000 realized loss, which can be deducted subject to any capital loss limitations. Because there is no gain on this transaction, the tax benefit of Mary's $2,000 disallowed loss is not available to her son. ♦

6-3b Unpaid Expenses and Interest

Under Section 267, related taxpayers are prevented from engaging in tax avoidance schemes in which one taxpayer uses the cash method of accounting and the other taxpayer uses the accrual method.

EXAMPLE Ficus Corporation, an accrual-basis taxpayer, is owned by Bill, an individual who uses the cash method of accounting for tax purposes. On December 31, Ficus Corporation accrues interest expense of $10,000 on a loan from Bill, but the interest is not paid to him. Ficus Corporation may not deduct the $10,000 until the tax year in which it is actually paid to Bill. This rule also applies to other expenses such as salaries and bonuses. ♦

6-3c Relationships

Section 267 has a complex set of rules to define who is a related party for disallowance purposes. The common related parties under Section 267 include the following:

1. Family members. A taxpayer's family includes brothers and sisters (whole or half), a spouse, ancestors (parents, grandparents, etc.), and lineal descendants (children, grandchildren, etc.).
2. A corporation or an individual who directly or indirectly owns more than 50 percent of the corporation.
3. Two corporations that are members of the same controlled group.
4. Trusts, corporations, and certain charitable organizations. They are subject to a complex set of relationship rules.

EXAMPLE Kalmia Corporation is owned 70 percent by Jim and 30 percent by Kathy. Jim and Kathy are unrelated to each other. Since Jim owns over 50 percent of the corporation, he is deemed to be a related party to the corporation.

As a result, if Jim sells property to the corporation at a loss, the loss will be disallowed. Since Kathy is not related to the corporation, the rules of Section 267 do not apply to Kathy. ♦

Related-party rules also consider constructive ownership in determining whether parties are related to each other. Under these rules, taxpayers are deemed to own stock owned by certain relatives and related entities. The common constructive ownership rules are as follows:

1. A taxpayer is deemed to own all the stock owned by their spouse, brothers and sisters (whole or half), ancestors, and lineal descendants.
2. A taxpayer is deemed to own their proportionate share of stock owned by any partnership, corporation, trust, or estate in which they are a partner, shareholder, or beneficiary.
3. A taxpayer is deemed to own any stock owned directly or indirectly by a partner.

EXAMPLE ABC Corporation is owned 40 percent by Andy, 30 percent by Betty, and 30 percent by Chee. Betty and Chee are married to each other. For purposes of related-party rules, Andy is not a related party to the corporation since he does not own more than 50 percent of the corporation. Betty is a related party because she is a 60-percent shareholder (30 percent directly and 30 percent from her husband, Chee). Using the same rule, Chee is also a related party since he also owns 60 percent (30 percent directly and 30 percent from his wife, Betty). ♦

EXAMPLE Robert owns 40 percent of R Corporation and 40 percent of T Corporation. T Corporation owns 60 percent of R Corporation. Robert is deemed to own 64 percent of R Corporation; therefore, he is a related party to R Corp.The 64 percent is calculated as 40 percent direct ownership and 24 percent (40% × 60%) constructive ownership. ♦

There are other sets of related-party and constructive ownership rules in the tax law, which differ from the related-party rules discussed in this section and should not be confused with the Section 267 related-party provisions.

Self-Study Problem 6.3

See Appendix E for Solutions to Self-Study Problems

EFG Corporation is owned 40 percent by Ed, 20 percent by Frank, 20 percent by Gene, and 20 percent by X Corporation. X Corporation is owned 80 percent by Ed and 20 percent by an unrelated party. Frank and Gene are brothers. Answer each of the following questions about EFG under the constructive ownership rules of Section 267.

1. What is Ed's percentage ownership?
2. What is Frank's percentage ownership?
3. What is Gene's percentage ownership?
4. If EFG sells property to Ed for a $15,000 loss, what amount of that loss can be recognized for tax purposes?

Learning Objective 6.4

Apply the rules for computing tax on the unearned income of minor children and certain students (the "kiddie tax").

6-4 UNEARNED INCOME OF MINOR CHILDREN AND CERTAIN STUDENTS

A child generally computes their income tax liability the same as any other taxpayer except that the decreased standard deduction is claimed if the child is a dependent. However, many parents have found it beneficial from a tax-planning standpoint to give income-earning assets, such as stocks, bonds, bank certificates of deposit, and mutual funds, to their minor children. Since minor children are generally in a lower income tax bracket, the unearned income from assets such as interest, dividends, and capital gains on stock sales would have been taxed at a lower rate than the parents' rate. However, one of the provisions of the tax law is that certain unearned income can be taxed at their parent's rate, if higher. This is commonly referred to as the "kiddie tax."

A child is subject to the kiddie tax if:

- the child is required to file a tax return
- the child's unearned income is more than $2,300 (in 2022)
- either parent is alive
- the child
  - Is under 18, or
  - Is age 18 and does not provide more than one-half of their own support, or
  - Is age 19–24, a full-time student, and does not provide more than one-half of their own support

Although there is no statutory definition for a parent, the term is generally considered to mean a parent or step-parent of the child. For purposes of determining the child's (or young adult's) income subject to the parental tax rate, net unearned income is never considered to include wages or salary of a minor child and is computed as follows:

Unearned income	$xxxx.xx
Less the greater of:	
1. $1,150 (child's standard deduction), or	
2. The allowable itemized deductions directly connected with the production of the unearned income	(xxx.xx)
	xxxx.xx
Less the 2022 statutory standard deduction	(1,150)
Net unearned income	$xxxx.xx

If the net unearned income is zero or less, the child's tax is calculated using the child's tax rate. However, if the net earned income amount is positive, the child's tax is calculated by applying the parents' tax rate, if higher, to that amount.

EXAMPLE Don and Melanie are a high-income married couple in the 37-percent tax bracket. Their 11-year-old son, Boris, generates $5,000 of interest income from investments. The tax on Boris' income will be computed at his parents' tax rate as follows:

Unearned income	$5,000
Standard deduction	(1,150)
Statutory standard deduction for 2022	(1,150)
Net unearned income	2,700
Taxed at parent's rate	37%
Tax	999
Statutory standard deduction	1,150
Taxed at child's rate	10%
Tax	115
Total tax	$1,114

♦

The more precise method of describing the computation of the kiddie tax is to compute the parent's tax without the child's unearned income and the recompute the parent's tax with the child's unearned income. If more than one child is subject to the kiddie tax, then a complex allocation of the tax to each child is required. The kiddie tax is reported on Form 8615.

The taxation of a child's unearned income is made even more complex in situations where the child's earned income is unusually high (over approximately $70,000) or where the unearned income is subject to preferential rates such as qualified dividends or long-term capital gains. These situations are beyond the scope of this textbook.

ProConnect™ Tax TIP

Although the computation of the kiddie tax is complex, having ProConnect Tax compute the kiddie tax requires no extra input on the part of the preparer. If the taxpayer is noted as being claimed as a dependent, fits the age requirements, and unearned income that exceeds the threshold is input (for example, Forms 1099-INT or 1099-DIV), the software will automatically generate and populate the Form 8615 and calculate the kiddie tax.

6-4a Election to Include a Child's Unearned Income on Parents' Return

If certain conditions are met, parents may elect to include a child's gross income on the parents' tax return. The election eliminates the child's return filing requirements and saves the parents from the trouble of filing the special calculation on Form 8615 for the "kiddie tax." To qualify for this election, the following conditions must be met:

1. The child's gross income is from interest and dividends only.
2. The gross income is more than $1,150 and less than $11,500 (or ten times the lower amount).
3. No estimated tax has been paid in the name of the child and the child is not subject to backup withholding.

EXAMPLE Sam Jackson is 12 years old and has $2,300 of interest from a savings account established for him by his grandparents. This is Sam's only income for the year. Instead of completing Form 8615 and paying the kiddie tax on his $2,300 in income, Sam's parents, Michael and Janet, may elect to include the $2,300 on their tax return, thereby eliminating Sam's filing requirement. ♦

The election to include the income of a minor child on the parents' return is made on Form 8814, as illustrated on Page 6-13.

Self-Study Problem 6.4 *See Appendix E for Solutions to Self-Study Problems*

Bill and Janet are a married couple filing jointly in 2022. They have one 12-year-old child, Robert, whose only income in 2022 is $3,000 of interest income. Bill and Janet's AGI in 2022 is $71,500, taxed at ordinary rates. Their only other deduction is the $25,900 standard deduction. Bill and Janet are eligible for a $2,000 child tax credit

a. Complete Form 8615 (Page 6-11) assuming Bill and Janet do not make the election to include Robert's income on their tax return.

b. Complete Form 8814 (Page 6-13) assuming Bill and Janet make the election to include Robert's income on their tax return.

Form **8615**

Department of the Treasury
Internal Revenue Service

Tax for Certain Children Who Have Unearned Income

Attach only to the child's Form 1040 or 1040-NR.
Go to *www.irs.gov/Form8615* for instructions and the latest information.

OMB No. 1545-0074
2022
Attachment Sequence No. **33**

Child's name shown on return | **Child's social security number**

A Parent's name (first, initial, and last). **Caution:** See instructions before completing. | **B Parent's social security number**

C Parent's filing status (check one):
☐ Single ☐ Married filing jointly ☐ Married filing separately ☐ Head of household ☐ Qualifying widow(er)

Part I Child's Net Unearned Income

1	Enter the child's unearned income. See instructions	1	
2	If the child **did not** itemize deductions on **Schedule A** (Form 1040) or **Schedule A** (Form 1040-NR), enter $2,300. Otherwise, see instructions	2	
3	Subtract line 2 from line 1. If zero or less, **stop**; do not complete the rest of this form but **do** attach it to the child's return	3	
4	Enter the child's **taxable income** from Form 1040 or 1040-NR, line 15. If the child files Form 2555, see the instructions	4	
5	Enter the **smaller** of line 3 or line 4. If zero, **stop**; do not complete the rest of this form but **do** attach it to the child's return	5	

Part II Tentative Tax Based on the Tax Rate of the Parent

6	Enter the parent's **taxable income** from Form 1040 or 1040-NR, line 15. If zero or less, enter -0-. If the parent files Form 2555, see the instructions	6	
7	Enter the total, if any, from Forms 8615, line 5, of **all other** children of the parent named above. **Do not** include the amount from line 5 above	7	
8	Add lines 5, 6, and 7. See instructions	8	
9	Enter the tax on the amount on line 8 based on the **parent's** filing status above. See instructions. If the Qualified Dividends and Capital Gain Tax Worksheet, Schedule D Tax Worksheet, or Schedule J (Form 1040) is used to figure the tax, check here ☐	9	
10	Enter the parent's tax from Form 1040 or 1040-NR, line 16, minus any alternative minimum tax. **Do not** include any tax from **Form 4972** or **Form 8814**, or any tax from the recapture of an education credit. If the parent files Form 2555, see the instructions. If the Qualified Dividends and Capital Gain Tax Worksheet, Schedule D Tax Worksheet, or Schedule J (Form 1040) was used to figure the tax, check here ☐	10	
11	Subtract line 10 from line 9 and enter the result. If line 7 is blank, also enter this amount on line 13 and go to **Part III**	11	
12a	Add lines 5 and 7 — 12a		
b	Divide line 5 by line 12a. Enter the result as a decimal (rounded to at least three places)	12b	× .
13	Multiply line 11 by line 12b	13	

Part III Child's Tax—If lines 4 and 5 above are the same, enter -0- on line 15 and go to line 16.

14	Subtract line 5 from line 4 — 14		
15	Enter the tax on the amount on line 14 based on the **child's** filing status. See instructions. If the Qualified Dividends and Capital Gain Tax Worksheet, Schedule D Tax Worksheet, or Schedule J (Form 1040) is used to figure the tax, check here ☐	15	
16	Add lines 13 and 15	16	
17	Enter the tax on the amount on line 4 based on the **child's** filing status. See instructions. If the Qualified Dividends and Capital Gain Tax Worksheet, Schedule D Tax Worksheet, or Schedule J (Form 1040) is used to figure the tax, check here ☐	17	
18	Enter the **larger** of line 16 or line 17 here and on the **child's** Form 1040 or 1040-NR, line 16. If the child files Form 2555, see the instructions	18	

For Paperwork Reduction Act Notice, see your tax return instructions. Cat. No. 64113U Form **8615** (2022)

Form **8814**

Department of the Treasury
Internal Revenue Service

Parents' Election To Report Child's Interest and Dividends

Go to *www.irs.gov/Form8814* for the latest information.
Attach to parents' Form 1040, 1040-SR, or 1040-NR.

OMB No. 1545-0074
2022
Attachment Sequence No. **40**

Name(s) shown on your return | **Your social security number**

Caution: The federal income tax on your child's income, including qualified dividends and capital gain distributions, may be less if you file a separate tax return for the child instead of making this election. This is because you cannot take certain tax benefits that your child could take on his or her own return. For details, see *Tax benefits you cannot take* in the instructions.

A Child's name (first, initial, and last) | **B Child's social security number**

C If more than one Form 8814 is attached, check here . . . ☐

Part I Child's Interest and Dividends To Report on Your Return

1a	Enter your child's **taxable** interest. If this amount is different from the amounts shown on the child's Forms 1099-INT and 1099-OID, see the instructions		1a
b	Enter your child's **tax-exempt** interest. **Do not** include this amount on line 1a	1b	
2a	Enter your child's ordinary dividends, including any Alaska Permanent Fund dividends. If your child received any ordinary dividends as a nominee, see the instructions		2a
b	Enter your child's qualified dividends included on line 2a. See the instructions	2b	
3	Enter your child's capital gain distributions. If your child received any capital gain distributions as a nominee, see the instructions		3
4	Add lines 1a, 2a, and 3. If the total is $2,300 or less, skip lines 5 through 12 and go to line 13. If the total is $11,500 or more, **do not** file this form. Your child **must** file his or her own return to report the income		4
5	Base amount. Enter 2,300		5
6	Subtract line 5 from line 4		6
	If both lines 2b and 3 are zero or blank, skip lines 7 through 10, enter -0- on line 11, and go to line 12. Otherwise, go to line 7.		
7	Divide line 2b by line 4. Enter the result as a decimal (rounded to at least three places)	7 .	
8	Divide line 3 by line 4. Enter the result as a decimal (rounded to at least three places)	8 .	
9	Multiply line 6 by line 7. Enter the result here. See the instructions for where to report this amount on your return	9	
10	Multiply line 6 by line 8. Enter the result here. See the instructions for where to report this amount on your return	10	
11	Add lines 9 and 10		11
12	Subtract line 11 from line 6. Include this amount in the total on Schedule 1 (Form 1040), line 8z. In the space next to that line, enter "Form 8814" and show the amount. If you checked the box on line C above, see the instructions. Go to line 13 below		12

Part II Tax on the First $2,300 of Child's Interest and Dividends

13	Amount not taxed. Enter 1,150	13
14	Subtract line 13 from line 4. If the result is zero or less, enter -0-	14
15	**Tax.** Is the amount on line 14 less than $1,150? ☐ **No.** Enter $115 here and see the **Note** below. ☐ **Yes.** Multiply line 14 by 10% (0.10). Enter the result here and see the **Note** below.	15

Note: If you checked the box on line C above, see the instructions. Otherwise, include the amount from line 15 in the tax you enter on Form 1040,1040-SR, or 1040-NR, line 16. Be sure to check box 1 on Form 1040, 1040-SR, or 1040-NR, line 16.

For Paperwork Reduction Act Notice, see your tax return instructions. Cat. No. 10750J Form **8814** (2022)

6-5 THE INDIVIDUAL ALTERNATIVE MINIMUM TAX (AMT)

6.5 Learning Objective

Calculate a basic alternative minimum tax.

A small number of individual taxpayers are subject to two parallel tax calculations, the regular tax and the alternative minimum tax (AMT). The AMT was designed in the 1960s to ensure that wealthy taxpayers could not take advantage of special tax write-offs (tax preferences and other adjustments) to avoid paying tax. In general, taxpayers must pay the alternative minimum tax if their AMT tax liability is larger than their regular tax liability.

The AMT is calculated on Form 6251, using the following formula simplified for purposes of this textbook:

Regular taxable income (before standard deduction)
± Plus or minus AMT preferences and adjustments
= Equals alternative minimum taxable income (AMTI)
− Less AMT exemption (phased out to zero as AMTI increases)
= Equals amount subject to AMT
× Multiplied by the AMT tax rate(s)
= Equals tentative minimum tax
− Less regular tax
= Equals amount of AMT due with tax return, if a positive amount

6-5a Common AMT Adjustments and Preferences

The terms "AMT adjustments" and "AMT preferences" are often used interchangeably, though they have slightly different meanings. In general, adjustments are *timing* differences that arise because of differences in the regular and AMT tax calculations (e.g., depreciation timing differences), while preferences are special provisions for the regular tax that are not allowed for the AMT (e.g., state income taxes). Both terms refer to items which adjust regular taxable income to arrive at income which is subject to alternative minimum tax. There are more than twenty different types of adjustments and preferences used in the calculation of AMT on Form 6251. Some of the common adjustments and preferences are as follows:

- The standard deduction allowed for regular tax is not allowed for AMT.
- The deductions for property tax, state income tax, and other taxes allowed as itemized deductions for regular tax are not allowed for AMT.
- Depreciation is generally calculated over a longer life for AMT, sometimes using a different method.
- Net operating losses are calculated differently for AMT and often result in an adjustment when they are present.
- State income tax refunds are not considered income for AMT since the state income tax deduction is not allowed for AMT.
- Interest from specified private activity bonds is not taxed for regular tax purposes, but is taxable for AMT.
- Other less commonly seen AMT differences include such items as the calculations related to incentive stock options, oil and gas depletion, research and development expenses, gains on asset sales such as rental real estate, passive losses, and the gain exclusion for small business stock and other items.

The expansion of the AMT exemption and income thresholds in 2017 had a profound effect on the number of taxpayers subject to AMT. In 2017, under the old AMT rules, more than 5 million taxpayers reported over $36 billion in AMT. Based on preliminary data from the IRS, in 2020 less than 150,000 taxpayers reported AMT totaling only about $3 billion. The expanded amounts are currently scheduled to expire at the end of 2025.

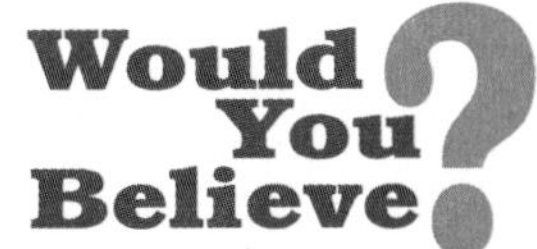

The actual details of the calculation of several of the AMT tax preferences and adjustments are complex and infrequently seen in practice. For further information, please consult the IRS website, a tax service, or an advanced tax textbook.

6-5b AMT Exemption

To reduce the chances of subjecting a greater number of taxpayers to the AMT, an exemption amount is permitted as a deduction against AMT income. The 2022 AMT exemptions and thresholds are:

	Married filing jointly	*Single and H of H*	*Married filing separately*
Exemption amount	$ 118,100	$ 75,900	$ 59,050
Threshold	1,079,800	539,900	539,900

The exemption amount is phased out (reduced) 25 cents for each dollar by which the taxpayer's alternative minimum taxable income exceeds the threshold amounts.

EXAMPLE Abby, a single taxpayer, has AMTI of $126,000 in 2022. Her AMT exemption is $75,900 as she has not reached the threshold for phase-out. ♦

EXAMPLE Damon and Tiffany are married and file jointly. They have AMTI of $1,234,000 in 2022. Their AMT exemption is $79,550 [$118,100 – (($1,234,000 – $1,079,800) × 25%)]. ♦

The exemption amounts and phase-out thresholds are both indexed for inflation, but the amounts are scheduled to be reduced significantly after 2025.

6-5c Alternative Minimum Tax Rates

For 2022, the alternative minimum tax rates for calculating the tentative minimum tax are 26 percent of the first $206,100 ($103,050 for married taxpayers filing separately), plus 28 percent on amounts above $206,100 (amounts above $103,050 for married filing separately). These rates are applied to the taxpayer's alternative minimum tax base from the formula above. The alternative minimum tax rate for capital gains and dividends is limited to the rate paid for regular tax purposes (e.g., capital gain or qualified dividends taxed at 15 percent for regular tax purposes will also be taxed at a 15 percent alternative minimum tax rate).

EXAMPLE Teddy has alternative minimum taxable income after the exemption deduction of $270,000, none of which is from capital gains. His tentative minimum tax is $71,478, which is calculated as (26% × $206,100) + (28% × [$270,000 – $206,100]). ♦

The large AMT exemption amount and exemption phase-out threshold in conjunction with the limitation on the itemized deduction for state and local taxes and the suspension of miscellaneous itemized deduction subject to the 2 percent floor, results in few taxpayers being subject to the AMT.

EXAMPLE Gram and Sally are married taxpayers who file a joint tax return in 2022. Their taxable income and regular tax liability can be calculated as follows:

Adjusted gross income	$200,000
Itemized deductions:	
State income tax	10,000
Home mortgage interest	20,000
Contributions	1,906
Total itemized deductions	(31,906)
Taxable income	$168,094
Tax from rate schedule	$ 28,215

Gram and Sally have $30,000 of private activity bond interest which is taxable for AMT but not for regular tax. The AMT is calculated as follows (same format as shown on Form 6251 presented on Page 6-19):

Taxable income	$168,094
Interest on private activity bonds	30,000
Add back:	
Taxes	10,000
Alternative minimum taxable income	208,094
AMT exemption	(118,100)
AMT Base	$ 89,994
Tentative minimum tax	$ 23,398
AMT	$ 0

Because the regular tax of $28,215 exceeds the tentative minimum tax of $23,398 in 2022, no AMT is due. ♦

Self-Study Problem 6.5

See Appendix E for Solutions to Self-Study Problems

Harold Brown, a single taxpayer, has adjusted gross income of $600,000. He has a deduction for home mortgage interest of $23,000, cash contributions of $11,000, state income taxes of $10,000, and private activity bond interest income of $100,000. Assuming Harold's regular tax liability is $168,675, use Form 6251 on Page 6-19 to calculate the amount of Harold's net alternative minimum tax.

Self-Study Problem 6.5

Form **6251**

Department of the Treasury
Internal Revenue Service

Alternative Minimum Tax—Individuals

Go to *www.irs.gov/Form6251* for instructions and the latest information.
Attach to Form 1040, 1040-SR, or 1040-NR.

OMB No. 1545-0074
2022
Attachment Sequence No. **32**

Name(s) shown on Form 1040, 1040-SR, or 1040-NR | **Your social security number**

Part I **Alternative Minimum Taxable Income** (See instructions for how to complete each line.)

1	Enter the amount from Form 1040 or 1040-SR, line 15, if more than zero. If Form 1040 or 1040-SR, line 15, is zero, subtract line 14 of Form 1040 or 1040-SR from line 11 of Form 1040 or 1040-SR and enter the result here. (If less than zero, enter as a negative amount.)	1	
2a	If filing Schedule A (Form 1040), enter the taxes from Schedule A, line 7; otherwise, enter the amount from Form 1040 or 1040-SR, line 12	2a	
b	Tax refund from Schedule 1 (Form 1040), line 1 or line 8z	2b	( )
c	Investment interest expense (difference between regular tax and AMT)	2c	
d	Depletion (difference between regular tax and AMT)	2d	
e	Net operating loss deduction from Schedule 1 (Form 1040), line 8a. Enter as a positive amount	2e	
f	Alternative tax net operating loss deduction	2f	( )
g	Interest from specified private activity bonds exempt from the regular tax	2g	
h	Qualified small business stock, see instructions	2h	
i	Exercise of incentive stock options (excess of AMT income over regular tax income)	2i	
j	Estates and trusts (amount from Schedule K-1 (Form 1041), box 12, code A)	2j	
k	Disposition of property (difference between AMT and regular tax gain or loss)	2k	
l	Depreciation on assets placed in service after 1986 (difference between regular tax and AMT)	2l	
m	Passive activities (difference between AMT and regular tax income or loss)	2m	
n	Loss limitations (difference between AMT and regular tax income or loss)	2n	
o	Circulation costs (difference between regular tax and AMT)	2o	
p	Long-term contracts (difference between AMT and regular tax income)	2p	
q	Mining costs (difference between regular tax and AMT)	2q	
r	Research and experimental costs (difference between regular tax and AMT)	2r	
s	Income from certain installment sales before January 1, 1987	2s	( )
t	Intangible drilling costs preference	2t	
3	Other adjustments, including income-based related adjustments	3	
4	**Alternative minimum taxable income.** Combine lines 1 through 3. (If married filing separately and line 4 is more than $776,100, see instructions.)	4	

Part II **Alternative Minimum Tax (AMT)**

5 Exemption.

IF your filing status is...	**AND line 4 is not over...**	**THEN enter on line 5...**
Single or head of household	$ 539,900	$ 75,900
Married filing jointly or qualifying widow(er)	1,079,800	118,100
Married filing separately	539,900	59,050

If line 4 is **over** the amount shown above for your filing status, see instructions. — **5**

6	Subtract line 5 from line 4. If more than zero, go to line 7. If zero or less, enter -0- here and on lines 7, 9, and 11, and go to line 10	6	
7	• If you are filing Form 2555, see instructions for the amount to enter. • If you reported capital gain distributions directly on Form 1040 or 1040-SR, line 7; you reported qualified dividends on Form 1040 or 1040-SR, line 3a; **or** you had a gain on both lines 15 and 16 of Schedule D (Form 1040) (as refigured for the AMT, if necessary), complete Part III on the back and enter the amount from line 40 here. • **All others:** If line 6 is $206,100 or less ($103,050 or less if married filing separately), multiply line 6 by 26% (0.26). Otherwise, multiply line 6 by 28% (0.28) and subtract $4,122 ($2,061 if married filing separately) from the result.	7	
8	Alternative minimum tax foreign tax credit (see instructions)	8	
9	Tentative minimum tax. Subtract line 8 from line 7	9	
10	Add Form 1040 or 1040-SR, line 16 (minus any tax from Form 4972), and Schedule 2 (Form 1040), line 2. Subtract from the result Schedule 3 (Form 1040), line 1 and any negative amount reported on Form 8978, line 14 (treated as a positive number). If zero or less, enter -0-. If you used Schedule J to figure your tax on Form 1040 or 1040-SR, line 16, refigure that tax without using Schedule J before completing this line. See instructions	10	
11	**AMT.** Subtract line 10 from line 9. If zero or less, enter -0-. Enter here and on Schedule 2 (Form 1040), line 1	11	

Sign Here	Under penalties of perjury, I declare that I have examined this return and accompanying schedules and statements, and to the best of my knowledge and belief, they are true, correct, and complete. Declaration of preparer (other than taxpayer) is based on all information of which preparer has any knowledge.			
	Your signature	Date	Your occupation	If the IRS sent you an Identity Protection PIN, enter it here (see inst.) ▶
Joint return? See instructions. Keep a copy for your records.	Spouse's signature. If a joint return, **both** must sign.	Date	Spouse's occupation	If the IRS sent your spouse an Identity Protection PIN, enter it here (see inst.) ▶
	Phone no.	Email address		

Paid Preparer Use Only	Preparer's name	Preparer's signature	Date	PTIN	Check if: ☐ Self-employed
	Firm's name ▶			Phone no.	
	Firm's address ▶			Firm's EIN ▶	

Your client, William Warrant, was hired for a management position at an Internet company planning to start a website called "indulgedanimals.com" for dogs, cats, and other pets. When he was hired, William was given an incentive stock option (ISO) worth $500,000, which he exercised during the year. Exercise of the ISO creates a tax preference item for alternative minimum tax (AMT) and causes him to have to pay substantial additional tax when combined with his other tax items for the year. He is livid about the extra tax and refuses to file the AMT Form 6251 with his tax return because the AMT tax is "unfair" and "un-American" according to him. Would you sign this tax return?

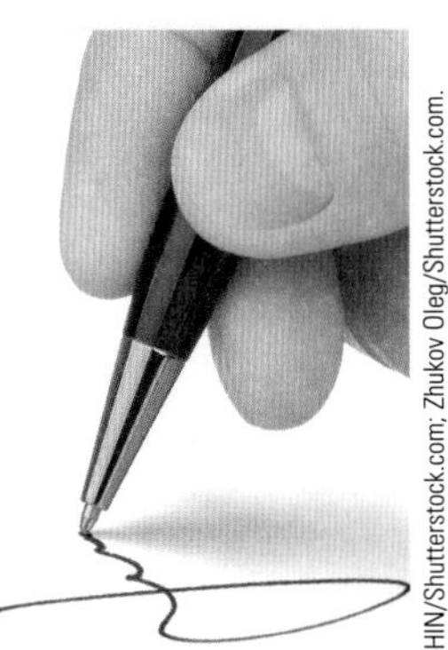

ILYA AKINSHIN/Shutterstock.com; Zhukov Oleg/Shutterstock.com.

Would You Sign This Tax Return?

6-6 THE NANNY TAX

6.6 Learning Objective

Apply the special tax and reporting requirements for household employees (the "nanny tax").

Over the years, the taxation and reporting of household employees' wages has caused many problems for taxpayers and the IRS. The threshold for filing was low ($50 per quarter of wages), and the tax forms to be completed were complex. As a result, many taxpayers ignored the reporting of household workers' wages and taxes. Congress addressed this problem by enacting what are commonly referred to as the "nanny tax" provisions. These provisions simplified the reporting process for employers of domestic household workers.

Household employers are not required to pay FICA taxes on cash payments of less than $2,400 paid to any household employee in a calendar year. If the cash payment to any household employee is $2,400 or more in a calendar year, all the cash payments (including the first $2,400) are subject to FICA taxes (see LO 9.2). The $2,400 threshold is adjusted for inflation each year. Household employers must also withhold income taxes if requested by the employee and are required to pay FUTA (Federal Unemployment Tax Act) tax (see LO 9.6) if more than $1,000 in cash wages are paid to household employees during any calendar quarter. The federal unemployment tax rate is 6 percent of an employee's wages up to $7,000.

A taxpayer is a household employer if they hire workers to perform household services in or around the taxpayer's home that are subject to the "will and control" of the taxpayer. Examples of household workers include:

- Babysitters
- Caretakers
- Cooks
- Drivers
- Gardeners
- Housekeepers
- Maids

If the household worker has an employee-employer relationship with the taxpayer, it does not matter if the worker is called something else, such as "independent contractor." Also, it does not matter if the worker is full-time or part-time. The household employer is responsible for the proper reporting, withholding, and payment of any taxes due.

The following workers are not subject to FICA taxes on wages paid for *work in the home*:

- The taxpayer's spouse
- The taxpayer's father or mother

- The taxpayer's children under 21 years of age
- Anyone who is under age 18 during the year, unless providing household services is their principal occupation (being a student is considered an occupation for purposes of this requirement)

EXAMPLE Allison is a 17-year-old high school student. During the year, she earns $2,400 by babysitting for a neighbor with four children. Any amount she earns is exempt from FICA requirements. However, if Allison is not a student and works full-time as a nanny, she will be subject to the general FICA withholding requirements under the nanny tax rules. ♦

Under the nanny tax provisions, household employers only have to report FICA, federal income tax withholding, and FUTA tax once a year. The taxpayer completes Schedule H and files it with his or her individual Form 1040. Taxpayers who have nonhousehold worker(s) in addition to household worker(s) can elect to report any FICA taxes and withholding on Forms 941 and 940 with their regular employees. Also, at the close of a tax year, taxpayers must file Form W-2 (Copy A) and Form W-3 with the Social Security Administration for each household employee who earned $2,400 or more in cash wages subject to FICA tax or had federal income taxes withheld from wages. For complete details on reporting the wages of household employees, see IRS Publication 926.

ProConnect™ Tax TIP

Taxes for household employees are input in ProConnect Tax under Taxes. There is a separate subheading for Household Employment Taxes (Schedule H).

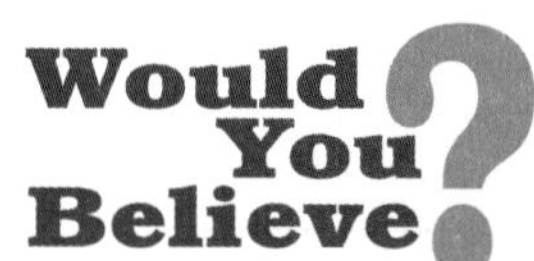

In 1993, shortly after he was elected, President Bill Clinton nominated Zoë Baird as U.S. Attorney General. Her nomination was derailed in what would become known as "Nannygate" when it was discovered that Baird had hired household employees and not paid taxes. During that time, the level of scrutiny on this type of arrangement increased significantly and some Americans were being asked if they had a "Zoë Baird problem." Based on a 2006 study, some of the fear of Nannygate has subsided as filing rates for Schedule H have dropped on average across the United States. Interestingly, the filing rate for Schedule H was more than three times greater if you lived in or around Washington, DC.

Self-Study Problem 6.6 *See Appendix E for Solutions to Self-Study Problems*

Susan Green lives in Virginia and hires Helen in February 2022 to clean her house for $80 per week. Susan does not withhold income taxes from Helen's wages. Helen's quarterly wages are as follows:

1st quarter	$ 480	($80 × 6 weeks)
2nd quarter	1,040	($80 × 13 weeks)
3rd quarter	1,040	($80 × 13 weeks)
4th quarter	1,040	($80 × 13 weeks)
Total	$3,600	

Assume Susan pays her state unemployment of $194 to the state of Virginia during the year. Complete her 2022 Schedule H (Form 1040) on Pages 6-23 and 6-24, using the above information.

Self-Study Problem 6.6

SCHEDULE H (Form 1040)
Department of the Treasury Internal Revenue Service

Household Employment Taxes

(For Social Security, Medicare, Withheld Income, and Federal Unemployment (FUTA) Taxes)
Attach to Form 1040, 1040-SR, 1040-NR, 1040-SS, or 1041.
Go to *www.irs.gov/ScheduleH* for instructions and the latest information.

OMB No. 1545-0074
2022
Attachment Sequence No. **44**

Name of employer | **Social security number**
Employer identification number

Calendar year taxpayers having no household employees in 2022 don't have to complete this form for 2022.

A Did you pay **any one** household employee cash wages of $2,400 or more in 2022? (If any household employee was your spouse, your child under age 21, your parent, or anyone under age 18, see the line A instructions before you answer this question.)
- ☐ **Yes.** Skip lines B and C and go to line 1a.
- ☐ **No.** Go to line B.

B Did you withhold federal income tax during 2022 for any household employee?
- ☐ **Yes.** Skip line C and go to line 7.
- ☐ **No.** Go to line C.

C Did you pay **total** cash wages of $1,000 or more in **any** calendar **quarter** of 2021 or 2022 to **all** household employees? (**Don't** count cash wages paid in 2021 or 2022 to your spouse, your child under age 21, or your parent.)
- ☐ **No. Stop.** Don't file this schedule.
- ☐ **Yes.** Skip lines 1a–9 and go to line 10.

Part I Social Security, Medicare, and Federal Income Taxes

1a	Total cash wages subject to social security tax	1a	
b	Qualified sick and family leave wages paid in 2022 for leave taken after March 31, 2020, and before April 1, 2021, included on line 1a	1b	
2a	Social security tax. Multiply line 1a by 12.4% (0.124)	2a	
b	Employer share of social security tax on qualified sick and family leave wages paid in 2022 for leave taken after March 31, 2020, and before April 1, 2021. Multiply line 1b by 6.2% (0.062)	2b	
c	Total social security tax. Subtract line 2b from line 2a	2c	
3	Total cash wages subject to Medicare tax	3	
4	Medicare tax. Multiply line 3 by 2.9% (0.029)	4	
5	Total cash wages subject to Additional Medicare Tax withholding	5	
6	Additional Medicare Tax withholding. Multiply line 5 by 0.9% (0.009)	6	
7	Federal income tax withheld, if any	7	
8a	Total social security, Medicare, and federal income taxes. Add lines 2c, 4, 6, and 7	8a	
b	Nonrefundable portion of credit for qualified sick and family leave wages for leave taken before April 1, 2021	8b	
c	Nonrefundable portion of credit for qualified sick and family leave wages for leave taken after March 31, 2021, and before October 1, 2021	8c	
d	Total social security, Medicare, and federal income taxes after nonrefundable credits. Add lines 8b and 8c and then subtract that total from line 8a	8d	
e	Refundable portion of credit for qualified sick and family leave wages for leave taken before April 1, 2021	8e	
f	Refundable portion of credit for qualified sick and family leave wages for leave taken after March 31, 2021, and before October 1, 2021	8f	
g	Qualified sick leave wages for leave taken before April 1, 2021	8g	
h	Qualified health plan expenses allocable to qualified sick leave wages reported on line 8g	8h	
i	Qualified family leave wages for leave taken before April 1, 2021	8i	
j	Qualified health plan expenses allocable to qualified family leave wages reported on line 8i	8j	
k	Qualified sick leave wages for leave taken after March 31, 2021, and before October 1, 2021	8k	
l	Qualified health plan expenses allocable to qualified sick leave wages reported on line 8k	8l	
m	Qualified family leave wages for leave taken after March 31, 2021, and before October 1, 2021	8m	
n	Qualified health plan expenses allocable to qualified family leave wages reported on line 8m	8n	

9 Did you pay **total** cash wages of $1,000 or more in **any** calendar **quarter** of 2021 or 2022 to **all** household employees? (**Don't** count cash wages paid in 2021 or 2022 to your spouse, your child under age 21, or your parent.)
- ☐ **No. Stop.** Include the amount from line 8d above on Schedule 2 (Form 1040), line 9. Include the amounts, if any, from line 8e on Schedule 3 (Form 1040), line 13b, and line 8f on Schedule 3 (Form 1040), line 13h. If you're not required to file Form 1040, see the line 9 instructions.
- ☐ **Yes.** Go to line 10.

Schedule H (Form 1040) 2022 Page **2**

Part II **Federal Unemployment (FUTA) Tax**

			Yes	No
10	Did you pay unemployment contributions to only one state? If you paid contributions to a credit reduction state, see instructions and check "**No**"	10		
11	Did you pay all state unemployment contributions for 2022 by April 18, 2023? Fiscal year filers, see instructions	11		
12	Were all wages that are taxable for FUTA tax also taxable for your state's unemployment tax?	12		

Next: If you checked the "**Yes**" box on **all** the lines above, complete Section A.
If you checked the "**No**" box on **any** of the lines above, skip Section A and complete Section B.

Section A

13 Name of the state where you paid unemployment contributions ______

14 Contributions paid to your state unemployment fund . . . 14

15 Total cash wages subject to FUTA tax . . . 15

16 **FUTA tax.** Multiply line 15 by 0.6% (0.006). Enter the result here, skip Section B, and go to line 25 . 16

Section B

17 Complete all columns below that apply (if you need more space, see instructions):

(a) Name of state	(b) Taxable wages (as defined in state act)	(c) State experience rate period From	(c) State experience rate period To	(d) State experience rate	(e) Multiply col. (b) by 0.054	(f) Multiply col. (b) by col. (d)	(g) Subtract col. (f) from col. (e). If zero or less, enter -0-.	(h) Contributions paid to state unemployment fund

18 Totals . . . 18

19 Add columns (g) and (h) of line 18 . . . 19

20 Total cash wages subject to FUTA tax (see the line 15 instructions) . . . 20

21 Multiply line 20 by 6.0% (0.06) . . . 21

22 Multiply line 20 by 5.4% (0.054) . . . 22

23 Enter the **smaller** of line 19 or line 22.
(If you paid state unemployment contributions late or you're in a credit reduction state, see instructions and check here) . . . ☐ 23

24 **FUTA tax.** Subtract line 23 from line 21. Enter the result here and go to line 25 . . . 24

Part III **Total Household Employment Taxes**

25 Enter the amount from line 8d. If you checked the "**Yes**" box on line C of page 1, enter -0- . . . 25

26 Add line 16 (or line 24) and line 25 . . . 26

27 Are you required to file Form 1040?

☐ **Yes. Stop.** Include the amount from line 26 above on Schedule 2 (Form 1040), line 9. Include the amounts, if any, from line 8e on Schedule 3 (Form 1040), line 13b, and line 8f on Schedule 3 (Form 1040), line 13h. **Don't** complete Part IV below.

☐ **No.** You may have to complete Part IV. See instructions for details.

Part IV **Address and Signature** — Complete this part **only** if required. See the line 27 instructions.

Address (number and street) or P.O. box if mail isn't delivered to street address | Apt., room, or suite no.

City, town or post office, state, and ZIP code

Under penalties of perjury, I declare that I have examined this schedule, including accompanying statements, and to the best of my knowledge and belief, it is true, correct, and complete. No part of any payment made to a state unemployment fund claimed as a credit was, or is to be, deducted from the payments to employees. Declaration of preparer (other than taxpayer) is based on all information of which preparer has any knowledge.

Employer's signature | Date

Paid Preparer Use Only	Print/Type preparer's name	Preparer's signature	Date	Check ☐ if self-employed	PTIN
	Firm's name			Firm's EIN	
	Firm's address			Phone no.	

Schedule H (Form 1040) 2022

6-7 SPECIAL TAXES FOR HIGH-INCOME TAXPAYERS

6.7 Learning Objective

Compute the special taxes for high-income taxpayers.

There are two separate Medicare taxes for certain high-income taxpayers to help cover the cost of the Affordable Care Act (ACA). The first is the 3.8 percent net investment income tax. The second is a 0.9 percent additional Medicare tax on wages and self-employment income.

6-7a The 3.8 Percent Medicare Tax on Net Investment Income

The ACA imposes a 3.8 percent Medicare tax on the net investment income of individuals with modified AGI over $250,000 for joint filers ($125,000 if married filing separate), and $200,000 for single filers (note that these amounts are not adjusted for inflation). Modified AGI is adjusted gross income increased by certain foreign earned income amounts not covered in this textbook. Investment income subject to the additional 3.8 percent tax includes the following:

- Interest and dividends (excluding tax-exempt interest)
- Royalties
- Annuities
- Net rental income, with some exceptions
- Passive activities
- Most gains on the sale of capital and other assets

Income not subject to the 3.8 percent tax includes the following:

- Tax-exempt interest
- Excluded gain on the sale of a principal residence
- Distributions from retirement plans and individual retirement accounts
- Wages and self-employment income (earned income); however, this income may be subject to a 0.9 percent Medicare tax

Deductions allowed in arriving at net investment income subject to tax include:

- State income taxes reasonably allocated to the investment income
- Investment interest expense

The $3,000 net deduction allowed for capital losses in excess of capital gains for regular tax purposes and net operating losses is not allowed to reduce net investment income. Additional rules govern which income and deductions are included in calculating net investment income. The net investment income tax is reported on Form 8960 shown on Page 6-29.

EXAMPLE Consider each of the following single taxpayers:

Taxpayer	*A*	*B*	*C*
Investment Income	$ 50,000	$ 80,000	$ 80,000
Modified AGI	190,000	220,000	340,000

The 3.8 percent net investment income tax would be calculated in each case as follows:

Taxpayer	*A*	*B*	*C*
Modified AGI	$190,000	$220,000	$340,000
Threshold	200,000	200,000	200,000
Excess over Threshold	n/a	20,000	140,000
Investment Income	50,000	80,000	80,000
Lesser of Excess or Investment Income	n/a	20,000	80,000
Tax Rate	3.8%	3.8%	3.8%
Net Investment Income Tax	$ 0	$ 760	$ 3,040

♦

6-7b The 0.9 Percent Additional Medicare Tax on Earned Income

In addition to the 3.8 percent Medicare tax on net investment income, the ACA imposed a 0.9 percent Medicare tax on high-income taxpayers' earned income such as salaries, wages, and self-employment income. The 0.9 percent tax applies to high-income taxpayers defined as taxpayers with earned income from wages, compensation, and self-employment income over the following thresholds (which are not adjusted for inflation each year):

a. $250,000 for joint filers
b. $125,000 if married filing separately
c. $200,000 for single filers (including head of household and qualifying widow(er)s)

The ordinary Medicare tax is 2.9 percent of earned income with no upper limitation. Employees split the cost of this tax with employers, with the employee paying 1.45 percent through withholding, and the employer paying 1.45 percent directly. Self-employed individuals pay the full 2.9 percent as calculated on Schedule SE with their Form 1040 income tax return. There is no employer match for the 0.9 percent tax. The 0.9 percent Medicare tax is reported on Form 8959 (see Page 6-31).

6-7c Employees

The 0.9 percent Medicare tax must be withheld from each employee with a salary in excess of $200,000, whether single or married. Married couples must combine their earned income and compare the total with the $250,000 threshold for married taxpayers to determine if they owe the 0.9 percent Medicare tax. Depending on the income of each spouse, the couple may owe more 0.9 percent Medicare tax when computing the 0.9 percent Medicare tax on their Form 1040 to make up for amounts not fully withheld, or they may treat the excess amount withheld as an additional tax payment. The withholding is reported on each individual's Form W-2 along with other Medicare withholding.

EXAMPLE Will and Karen are married. Will earns $225,000 in 2022 and Karen does not work. They have no other income in 2022. Will's employer must withhold $225 [0.9% × ($225,000 − $200,000)], from his wages. Because Will and Karen do not have earned income in their joint return in excess of the $250,000 threshold for joint filers, the $225 withholding will be treated as an additional payment when they file their Form 1040 income tax return for 2022. ♦

EXAMPLE Fran and Steve are married and each has wages of $150,000. Because they each earn less than $200,000, their employers are not required to withhold the 0.9 percent Medicare tax. However, when they file their 2022 Form 1040, they will be required to pay $450 (0.9% × $50,000) with their tax return since their $300,000 in joint earnings exceeds the $250,000 threshold for married taxpayers filing jointly. ♦

EXAMPLE Johnny is single and changes jobs during 2022. His wages are $175,000 from each job for a total of $350,000 of wage income. Johnny's employers are not required to withhold any 0.9 percent Medicare tax from his wages since he does not reach the $200,000 threshold in either job. Johnny must pay $1,350 (0.9% × $150,000, the excess of $350,000 over the $200,000 single threshold amount) with his tax return for 2022. ♦

6-7d Self-Employed Taxpayers

Self-employed taxpayers generally report earnings on Schedule C, Schedule F, and Schedule E in the case of earned royalty income and partnership income passed through on Schedule K-1. The 0.9 percent Medicare tax for self-employed taxpayers must be paid with Form 1040. The following additional rules apply to high-income, self-employed taxpayers:

a. The 0.9 percent Medicare tax is not allowed as part of the computation of the deductible self-employment tax adjustment for AGI shown on the front page of Form 1040.
b. A loss from self-employment may offset gains from another self-employment enterprise by the same individual. In the case of married individuals, a loss incurred by one spouse may offset the income earned by the other self-employed spouse for purposes of the 0.9 percent Medicare tax. This is not true for the 2.9 percent Medicare tax on self-employment income because the 2.9 percent Medicare tax of each spouse is required to be computed separately.
c. Losses from self-employment are not allowed to offset salary or wages for purposes of the 0.9 percent Medicare tax.

EXAMPLE In 2022, Barry is single and earns $500,000 from his construction business, and has a loss of $100,000 from his commercial nursery business. Both businesses are reported on Schedule C in his income tax return. His net self-employment earnings of $400,000 exceed the single individual threshold by $200,000. He must pay $1,800 with his 2022 Form 1040 (0.9% × $200,000) to cover his 0.9 percent Medicare tax. None of the $1,800 is allowed as part of the computation of the self-employment tax adjustment included with his deductions for AGI. ♦

Self-Study Problem 6.7

See Appendix E for Solutions to Self-Study Problems

A. Ronald Trunk is single and independently wealthy. His wages come from his job as a vice-president at a local bank (founded by his great-grandfather) and all of his interest, dividends, and capital gains are from his large investment portfolio of publicly-traded stocks and bonds. He also operates a small business in which he actively participates.

His 2022 Form 1040 is almost complete and reports the following amounts:

Line 1: $200,000
Line 2a: $48,000
Line 2b: $53,000
Line 3a: $33,000
Line 3b: $45,000
Line 7: $23,000
Line 8 and Schedule 1, Line 3: $12,000
Line 11: $333,000

He has no investment expenses associated with this income, no foreign earnings exclusion, and lives where there is no state income tax. Complete Form 8960 on Page 6-29 to calculate Ronald's 2022 net investment income tax.

B. Meng and Eang Ung are married. Meng is self-employed and generates self-employment income of $130,000. Eang is a physician at a local hospital and earns Social Security (Box 5) wages of $265,000. Her Medicare withholding (Box 6) is $4,427.50. Eang and Meng have no other earned or unearned income. Complete Form 8959 on Page 6-31 to determine how much 0.9 percent additional Medicare tax on earned income Meng and Eang must pay with their joint tax return in 2022 and what 0.9 percent additional Medicare tax withholding will they report?

TAX BREAK

The IRS recommends considering the following when getting married:

- Social Security numbers on the tax return need to match the Social Security Administration's (SSA) records. Be sure and report any name changes to the SSA.
- Taxpayers may want to consider changing their withholding, especially if both spouses work.
- Marriage is likely to trigger a "change in circumstance" if a taxpayer is receiving advance payments on the premium tax credit. The appropriate health insurance marketplace should be notified.
- Change of address with the U.S. Postal Service (online) and with the IRS (Form 8822).
- Change in filing status to married filing jointly or separately should be considered.

Self-Study Problem 6.7A

Form **8960** | **Net Investment Income Tax—Individuals, Estates, and Trusts** | OMB No. 1545-2227

Department of the Treasury Internal Revenue Service

Attach to your tax return.

Go to *www.irs.gov/Form8960* for instructions and the latest information.

2022 Attachment Sequence No. **72**

Name(s) shown on your tax return | **Your social security number or EIN**

Part I Investment Income ☐ Section 6013(g) election (see instructions) ☐ Section 6013(h) election (see instructions) ☐ Regulations section 1.1411-10(g) election (see instructions)

1	Taxable interest (see instructions)			1	
2	Ordinary dividends (see instructions)			2	
3	Annuities (see instructions)			3	
4a	Rental real estate, royalties, partnerships, S corporations, trusts, etc. (see instructions)	4a			
b	Adjustment for net income or loss derived in the ordinary course of a non-section 1411 trade or business (see instructions)	4b			
c	Combine lines 4a and 4b			4c	
5a	Net gain or loss from disposition of property (see instructions)	5a			
b	Net gain or loss from disposition of property that is not subject to net investment income tax (see instructions)	5b			
c	Adjustment from disposition of partnership interest or S corporation stock (see instructions)	5c			
d	Combine lines 5a through 5c			5d	
6	Adjustments to investment income for certain CFCs and PFICs (see instructions)			6	
7	Other modifications to investment income (see instructions)			7	
8	Total investment income. Combine lines 1, 2, 3, 4c, 5d, 6, and 7			8	
Part II	**Investment Expenses Allocable to Investment Income and Modifications**				
9a	Investment interest expenses (see instructions)	9a			
b	State, local, and foreign income tax (see instructions)	9b			
c	Miscellaneous investment expenses (see instructions)	9c			
d	Add lines 9a, 9b, and 9c			9d	
10	Additional modifications (see instructions)			10	
11	Total deductions and modifications. Add lines 9d and 10			11	
Part III	**Tax Computation**				
12	Net investment income. Subtract Part II, line 11, from Part I, line 8. Individuals, complete lines 13–17. Estates and trusts, complete lines 18a–21. If zero or less, enter -0-			12	
	Individuals:				
13	Modified adjusted gross income (see instructions)	13			
14	Threshold based on filing status (see instructions)	14			
15	Subtract line 14 from line 13. If zero or less, enter -0-	15			
16	Enter the smaller of line 12 or line 15			16	
17	Net investment income tax for individuals. Multiply line 16 by 3.8% (0.038). **Enter here and include on your tax return** (see instructions)			17	
	Estates and Trusts:				
18a	Net investment income (line 12 above)	18a			
b	Deductions for distributions of net investment income and deductions under section 642(c) (see instructions)	18b			
c	Undistributed net investment income. Subtract line 18b from line 18a (see instructions). If zero or less, enter -0-	18c			
19a	Adjusted gross income (see instructions)	19a			
b	Highest tax bracket for estates and trusts for the year (see instructions)	19b			
c	Subtract line 19b from line 19a. If zero or less, enter -0-	19c			
20	Enter the smaller of line 18c or line 19c			20	
21	Net investment income tax for estates and trusts. Multiply line 20 by 3.8% (0.038). **Enter here and include on your tax return** (see instructions)			21	

For Paperwork Reduction Act Notice, see your tax return instructions. Cat. No. 59474M Form **8960** (2022)

Self-Study Problem 6.7B

Form **8959**
Department of the Treasury
Internal Revenue Service

Additional Medicare Tax

If any line does not apply to you, leave it blank. See separate instructions.
Attach to Form 1040, 1040-SR, 1040-NR, 1040-PR, or 1040-SS.
Go to *www.irs.gov/Form8959* for instructions and the latest information.

OMB No. 1545-0074
2022
Attachment Sequence No. **71**

Name(s) shown on return | **Your social security number**

Part I Additional Medicare Tax on Medicare Wages

1	Medicare wages and tips from Form W-2, box 5. If you have more than one Form W-2, enter the total of the amounts from box 5	1			
2	Unreported tips from Form 4137, line 6	2			
3	Wages from Form 8919, line 6	3			
4	Add lines 1 through 3	4			
5	Enter the following amount for your filing status: Married filing jointly $250,000; Married filing separately $125,000; Single, Head of household, or Qualifying widow(er) $200,000	5			
6	Subtract line 5 from line 4. If zero or less, enter -0-			6	
7	Additional Medicare Tax on Medicare wages. Multiply line 6 by 0.9% (0.009). Enter here and go to Part II			7	

Part II Additional Medicare Tax on Self-Employment Income

8	Self-employment income from Schedule SE (Form 1040), Part I, line 6. If you had a loss, enter -0- (Form 1040-PR or 1040-SS filers, see instructions.)	8			
9	Enter the following amount for your filing status: Married filing jointly $250,000; Married filing separately $125,000; Single, Head of household, or Qualifying widow(er) $200,000	9			
10	Enter the amount from line 4	10			
11	Subtract line 10 from line 9. If zero or less, enter -0-	11			
12	Subtract line 11 from line 8. If zero or less, enter -0-			12	
13	Additional Medicare Tax on self-employment income. Multiply line 12 by 0.9% (0.009). Enter here and go to Part III			13	

Part III Additional Medicare Tax on Railroad Retirement Tax Act (RRTA) Compensation

14	Railroad retirement (RRTA) compensation and tips from Form(s) W-2, box 14 (see instructions)	14			
15	Enter the following amount for your filing status: Married filing jointly $250,000; Married filing separately $125,000; Single, Head of household, or Qualifying widow(er) $200,000	15			
16	Subtract line 15 from line 14. If zero or less, enter -0-			16	
17	Additional Medicare Tax on railroad retirement (RRTA) compensation. Multiply line 16 by 0.9% (0.009). Enter here and go to Part IV			17	

Part IV Total Additional Medicare Tax

18	Add lines 7, 13, and 17. Also include this amount on Schedule 2 (Form 1040), line 11 (Form 1040-PR or 1040-SS filers, see instructions), and go to Part V	18	

Part V Withholding Reconciliation

19	Medicare tax withheld from Form W-2, box 6. If you have more than one Form W-2, enter the total of the amounts from box 6	19			
20	Enter the amount from line 1	20			
21	Multiply line 20 by 1.45% (0.0145). This is your regular Medicare tax withholding on Medicare wages	21			
22	Subtract line 21 from line 19. If zero or less, enter -0-. This is your Additional Medicare Tax withholding on Medicare wages			22	
23	Additional Medicare Tax withholding on railroad retirement (RRTA) compensation from Form W-2, box 14 (see instructions)			23	
24	**Total Additional Medicare Tax withholding.** Add lines 22 and 23. Also include this amount with federal income tax withholding on Form 1040, 1040-SR, or 1040-NR, line 25c (Form 1040-PR or 1040-SS filers, see instructions)			24	

6-8 SPECIAL TAXPAYER SITUATIONS

6.8 Learning Objective

Describe the basic rules surrounding special taxpayer situations such as divorce, deceased taxpayers, nonresident taxpayers, and farmers.

The section of the textbook is designed to provide modest exposure to some of the unique situations that tax preparers may encounter. The tax law in these areas tends to be complex and could provide enough content to fill its own textbook. Each of the areas selected were compiled from a review of various state requirements for federal income tax preparation in states which have such requirements (Oregon, California, and Maryland) and from the IRS' annual filing season program.

6-8a Tax Return Errors

From time to time, a taxpayer or an employer will make a mistake in preparing an income tax return or an information reporting return such as Form W-2. Understanding that mistakes are occasionally made by taxpayers and tax preparers, the IRS has created procedures to address such situations.

W-2 or 1099-R Wrong or Not Received

If a taxpayer does not receive Forms W-2 or 1099-R (the deadline to send these forms is generally January 31 of the following year), the first and obvious step is to contact the employer or payer and request the missing form. If the forms cannot be obtained, the next step is to call the IRS and provide identification information and if requested, the dates of employment. The IRS recommends contacting them at or around the end of February. The IRS will also send a Form 4852 to the taxpayer if needed. If the missing form is not received by the filing deadline, the taxpayer uses Form 4852 as a substitute Form W-2 or 1099-R based on the year-to-date information known (from paystubs or pension statements). Filing a Form 4852 may cause delays in processing a refund payment.

If a taxpayer receives incorrect Forms W-2 or 1099-R, the first step is to contact the payer to get a corrected form. An employer should provide a Form W-2c (a corrected Form W-2). This form reports the original information and the corrected information on the face of the form (see excerpt in Figure 6.1). A pension recipient will receive a corrected 1099-R, which is the typical Form 1099-R with the Corrected box marked.

For a missing or corrected form, if the taxpayer has already filed a tax return using incorrect data, the taxpayer has a responsibility to file an amended tax return (Form 1040-X) as discussed in the next section. Taxpayers wishing to avoid amending a tax return may want to wait as long as possible to file the original return to increase the chance of receiving the corrected information before the deadline and thus avoid the need to amend.

Amended Tax Returns

When a taxpayer files an incorrect tax return, the taxpayer is responsible for amending that return and filing a corrected version on Form 1040-X (which, since 2019 can be electronically filed if amending Forms 1040 or 1040-SR). Corrections to Form 1040-NR must be paper filed. In general, Form 1040-X requires the taxpayer to report the original amount of income, deductions, credits, or payments and the corrected amount of the same items. See Form 1040-X on Page 6-35

However, there are a large number of reasons to file a Form 1040-X besides an incorrect amount (for minor math errors, conventional wisdom is to not file an amended return and let the IRS send a correction notice to the taxpayer first).

Additional common reasons to amend include:

- Change in filing status
- Change from resident taxpayer to nonresident
- Incorrect or missing dependent
- Claim a refund due to a casualty loss or net operating loss in a subsequent year being carried back

FIGURE 6.1

44444 | For Official Use Only ► OMB No. 1545-0008 | Safe, accurate, FAST! Use IRS e-file | Visit the IRS website at **www.irs.gov.**

a Employer's name, address, and ZIP code

b Employer's Federal EIN

c Tax year/Form corrected / **W-2**

d Employee's correct SSN

e Corrected SSN and/or name (Check this box and complete boxes f and/or g if incorrect on form previously filed.) ☐

Complete boxes f and/or g only if incorrect on form **previously filed** ►

f Employee's **previously reported** SSN

g Employee's **previously reported** name

h Employee's first name and initial | Last name | Suff.

i Employee's address and ZIP code

Note. Only complete money fields that are being corrected (exception: for corrections involving MQGE, see the General Instructions for Forms W-2 and W-3, under Specific Instructions for Form W-2c, boxes 5 and 6).

Previously reported	Correct information	Previously reported	Correct information
1 Wages, tips, other compensation	1 Wages, tips, other compensation	2 Federal income tax withheld	2 Federal income tax withheld
3 Social security wages	3 Social security wages	4 Social security tax withheld	4 Social security tax withheld
5 Medicare wages and tips	5 Medicare wages and tips	6 Medicare tax withheld	6 Medicare tax withheld
7 Social security tips	7 Social security tips	8 Allocated tips	8 Allocated tips
9	9	10 Dependent care benefits	10 Dependent care benefits
11 Nonqualified plans	11 Nonqualified plans	12a See instructions for box 12 Code	12a See instructions for box 12 Code
13 Statutory employee ☐ Retirement plan ☐ Third-party sick pay ☐	13 Statutory employee ☐ Retirement plan ☐ Third-party sick pay ☐	12b Code	12b Code
14 Other (see instructions)	14 Other (see instructions)	12c Code	12c Code
		12d Code	12d Code

EXAMPLE Martha paper-filed her original tax return and made a mathematical error when computing her tax liability. She ended up paying too much tax as a result. Martha should consider waiting until the IRS has processed her tax return and send her a correction notice rather than file an amended return. ♦

EXAMPLE Lew filed his tax return and omitted self-employment income. This error is not likely to be identified by the IRS while processing Lew's return and he should file an amended return. ♦

When preparing a Form 1040-X, the taxpayer should generally prepare amended versions of forms that are affected.

EXAMPLE Hayder accidentally failed to report any deductible charitable contributions on his Schedule A. When preparing the Form 1040-X, Hayder should also prepare a revised Schedule A to attached to his Form 1040-X. ♦

In some instances, the instructions for Form 1040-X permit the amended return to omit certain items.

Form **1040-X** (Rev. July 2021)

Department of the Treasury—Internal Revenue Service

Amended U.S. Individual Income Tax Return

▶ Use this revision to amend 2019 or later tax returns.
▶ Go to *www.irs.gov/Form1040X* for instructions and the latest information.

OMB No. 1545-0074

This return is for calendar year (enter year) **or fiscal year** (enter month and year ended)

Your first name and middle initial	Last name		Your social security number
If joint return, spouse's first name and middle initial	Last name		Spouse's social security number
Current home address (number and street). If you have a P.O. box, see instructions.		Apt. no.	Your phone number
City, town or post office, state, and ZIP code. If you have a foreign address, also complete spaces below. See instructions.			
Foreign country name	Foreign province/state/county		Foreign postal code

Amended return filing status. You **must** check one box even if you are not changing your filing status. **Caution:** In general, you can't change your filing status from married filing jointly to married filing separately after the return due date.

☐ Single ☐ Married filing jointly ☐ Married filing separately (MFS) ☐ Head of household (HOH) ☐ Qualifying widow(er) (QW)

If you checked the MFS box, enter the name of your spouse. If you checked the HOH or QW box, enter the child's name if the qualifying person is a child but not your dependent ▶

Enter on lines 1 through 23, columns A through C, the amounts for the return year entered above. Use Part III on page 2 to explain any changes.		A. Original amount reported or as previously adjusted (see instructions)	B. Net change—amount of increase or (decrease)—explain in Part III	C. Correct amount
Income and Deductions				
1 Adjusted gross income. If a net operating loss (NOL) carryback is included, check here . . . ▶ ☐	1			
2 Itemized deductions or standard deduction . . .	2			
3 Subtract line 2 from line 1 . . .	3			
4a Reserved for future use . . .	4a			
b Qualified business income deduction . . .	4b			
5 Taxable income. Subtract line 4b from line 3. If the result is zero or less, enter -0- . . .	5			
Tax Liability				
6 Tax. Enter method(s) used to figure tax (see instructions):	6			
7 Nonrefundable credits. If a general business credit carryback is included, check here . . . ▶ ☐	7			
8 Subtract line 7 from line 6. If the result is zero or less, enter -0- . . .	8			
9 Reserved for future use . . .	9			
10 Other taxes . . .	10			
11 Total tax. Add lines 8 and 10 . . .	11			
Payments				
12 Federal income tax withheld and excess social security and tier 1 RRTA tax withheld. (**If changing,** see instructions.) . . .	12			
13 Estimated tax payments, including amount applied from prior year's return	13			
14 Earned income credit (EIC) . . .	14			
15 Refundable credits from: ☐ Schedule 8812 Form(s) ☐ 2439 ☐ 4136 ☐ 8863 ☐ 8885 ☐ 8962 or ☐ other (specify):	15			
16 Total amount paid with request for extension of time to file, tax paid with original return, and additional tax paid after return was filed . . .			16	
17 Total payments. Add lines 12 through 15, column C, and line 16 . . .			17	
Refund or Amount You Owe				
18 Overpayment, if any, as shown on original return or as previously adjusted by the IRS . . .			18	
19 Subtract line 18 from line 17. (If less than zero, see instructions.) . . .			19	
20 **Amount you owe.** If line 11, column C, is more than line 19, enter the difference . . .			20	
21 If line 11, column C, is less than line 19, enter the difference. This is the amount **overpaid** on this return			21	
22 Amount of line 21 you want **refunded to you** . . .			22	
23 Amount of line 21 you want **applied to your (enter year):** **estimated tax**	23			

Complete and sign this form on page 2.

For Paperwork Reduction Act Notice, see separate instructions. Cat. No. 11360L Form **1040-X** (Rev. 7-2021)

Form 1040-X (Rev. 7-2021) Page **2**

Part I Dependents

Complete this part to change any information relating to your dependents. This would include a change in the number of dependents. Enter the information for the return year entered at the top of page 1.		**A. Original number of dependents** reported or as previously adjusted	**B. Net change — amount of increase or (decrease)**	**C. Correct number**
24 Reserved for future use	**24**			
25 Your dependent children who lived with you	**25**			
26 Your dependent children who didn't live with you due to divorce or separation	**26**			
27 Other dependents	**27**			
28 Reserved for future use	**28**			
29 Reserved for future use	**29**			

30 List **ALL** dependents (children and others) claimed on this amended return.

Dependents (see instructions):

If more than four dependents, see instructions and check here ▶ ☐

(a) First name	Last name	(b) Social security number	(c) Relationship to you	(d) ✓ if qualifies for (see instructions): Child tax credit	Credit for other dependents
				☐	☐
				☐	☐
				☐	☐
				☐	☐

Part II Presidential Election Campaign Fund (for the return year entered at the top of page 1)

Checking below won't increase your tax or reduce your refund.

☐ Check here if you didn't previously want $3 to go to the fund, but now do.

☐ Check here if this is a joint return and your spouse did not previously want $3 to go to the fund, but now does.

Part III Explanation of Changes. In the space provided below, tell us why you are filing Form 1040-X.

▶ Attach any supporting documents and new or changed forms and schedules.

Sign Here

Remember to keep a copy of this form for your records.

Under penalties of perjury, I declare that I have filed an original return, and that I have examined this amended return, including accompanying schedules and statements, and to the best of my knowledge and belief, this amended return is true, correct, and complete. Declaration of preparer (other than taxpayer) is based on all information about which the preparer has any knowledge.

▶ Your signature | Date | Your occupation

▶ Spouse's signature. If a joint return, **both** must sign. | Date | Spouse's occupation

Paid Preparer Use Only

Print/Type preparer's name	Preparer's signature	Date	Check ☐ if self-employed	PTIN
Firm's name ▶			Firm's EIN ▶	
Firm's address ▶			Phone no.	

For forms and publications, visit *www.irs.gov/Forms.* Form **1040-X** (Rev. 7-2021)

EXAMPLE Louisa accidentally filed a Form 1040 as a resident taxpayer, not realizing she is a nonresident for the current tax year and should have filed Form 1040-NR. The Form 1040-X instructions instruct Louisa to provide her identifying information at the top of page 1 of Form 1040-X but not complete any of the income, deductions, credits or tax information nor any of Parts I or II. Instead, Louisa is instructed to complete a new Form 1040-NR and submit the entire return with her Form 1040-X on which she provides the reason for the amendment in Part III. ♦

With the advent of electronic filing of amended returns, tax preparers should pay careful attention to the Form 1040-X instructions as they provide detailed instructions for a number of special situations and are subject to change.

6-8b Divorce and Separation

Recent data shows that somewhere between 750,000 and 1 million people get divorced in the United States each year and that about one-third of all Americans over the age of 20 have been divorced once. The tax consequences of divorce extend beyond filing status (Chapter 1) and alimony, child support, and property divisions (Chapter 2). This section considers some of the more common tax-related outcomes of divorce.

Divorce is a determination made at the state level. The authority to marry and divorce is vested in states and thus not all states follow the same rules or even use the same language when discussing the dissolution of a marriage. The tax rules that define "married status" for purposes of determination of filing status indicate that a taxpayer is unmarried if the taxpayer is single (never married) or has obtained a final decree of divorce or separate maintenance by the last day of the tax year and under state law the taxpayer is divorced or legally separated.

In most states, a divorce is considered final when a judge approves or signs the divorce decree or divorce settlement agreement. Unlike a divorce, a separation may have a number of different stages. For example, a trial separation generally does not require any court filings or approval by the state and simply entails the two spouses living apart. In most states, a legal separation is awarded through a court process and approved by a judge. Some states also offer a marriage annulment. An annulment is the state's recognition that a marriage was never legal (and often require amending prior year returns). If the separation, divorce, or annulment are recognized by the state, the tax rules will generally follow and treat these taxpayers as unmarried (the abandoned spouse exception is covered in Chapter 1).

As discussed in Chapter 2, the division of property between ex-spouses is not generally a taxable event. Technically, the transfers that are incident to a divorce are treated as a non-taxable gift if made within one year of the divorce. Special rules apply to property divisions of qualified retirement plan assets such as pensions, 401(k), and other similar plans. Typically, distributions from qualified plans are subject to income tax and, if the taxpayer is under age 59 and one-half, a 10-percent penalty is assessed. A distribution pursuant to a qualified domestic relations order (QDRO); however, is not generally subject to the tax or penalty. A QDRO is issued by the court and recognizes that some form of retirement assets should also be divided between ex-spouses. The tax treatment that would have applied to the original owner of the retirement assets will apply to the new owner when distributions are made.

EXAMPLE As part of Brad and Angelina' divorce, the court issues a QDRO providing that one-half of Angelina's 401(k) balance of $40,000. be transferred to Brad. Angelina and Angelina's employer had made only pre-tax contributions to the 401(k) and thus Angelina had no basis in the plan assets. Brad will receive a distribution of $20,000 and if he places the transferred funds in a retirement account such as a rollover IRA, he will not be taxed on the transfer. When Brad turns 65 and starts taking distributions from the IRA, he will be taxed just as Angelina would have. ♦

Division of the assets in a health savings account work in the same fashion.

Tax Liability Issues with a Current or Former Spouse

When a married couple files a joint tax return, they are both liable for the entire tax liability. There are three different ways a spouse can request relief from joint liability:

1. Innocent Spouse Relief
2. Separation of Liability Relief
3. Equitable Relief

As soon as a spouse determines they might be liable for a tax liability that should be attributed to only their spouse or former spouse, a Form 8857 should be filed to claim one of the above three forms of relief.

Innocent spouse relief provides relief from tax liability to a spouse or ex-spouse that was not aware of the liability when they signed the tax return. To qualify for innocent spouse relief, a taxpayer must must the requirements presented in Figure 6.2 (from IRS Publication 971)

FIGURE 6.2 **INNOCENT SPOUSE RELIEF DECISION TREE**

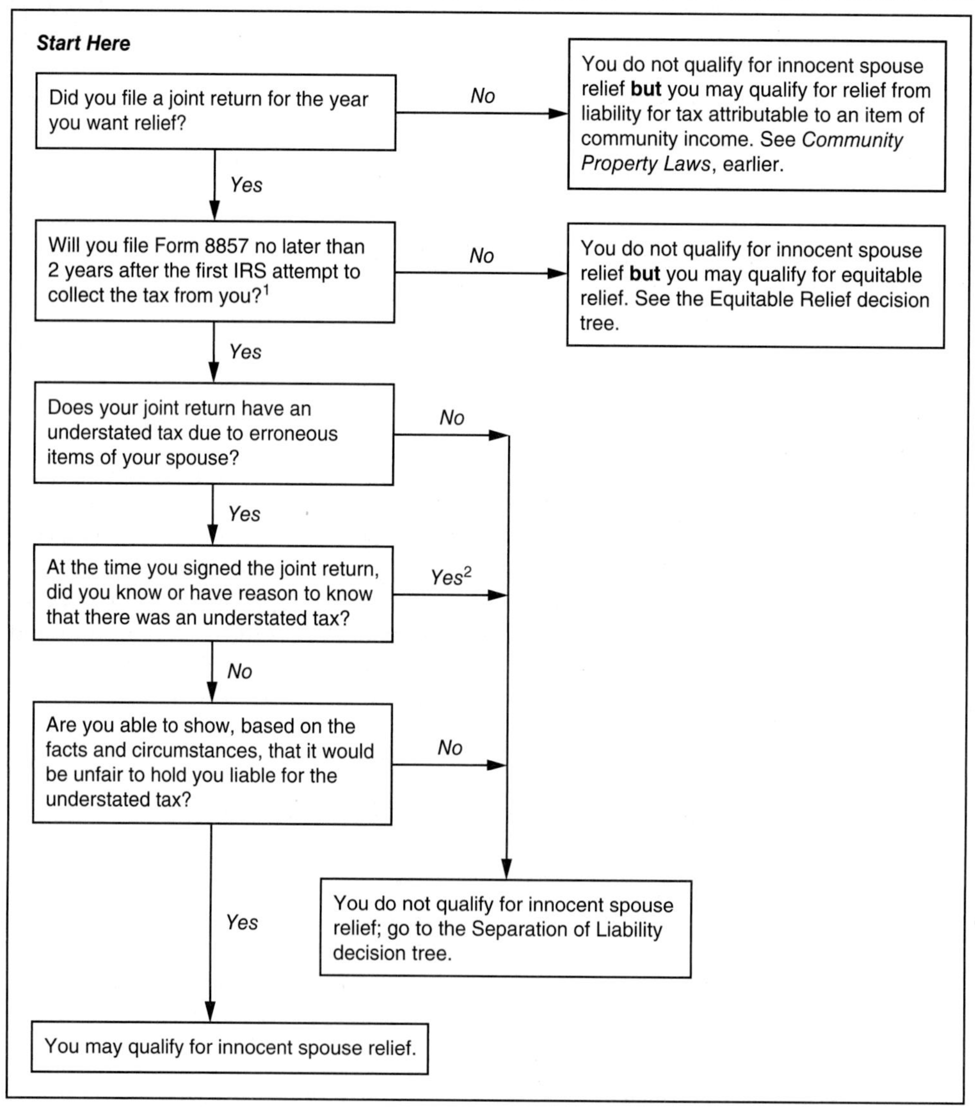

Source: IRS Publication 971

[1] Collection activities that may start the 2-year period are described earlier under *How To Request Relief.*

[2] You may qualify for partial relief if, at the time you filed your return, you knew or had reason to know of only a portion of an erroneous item.

Separation of liability relief pertains to situations in which the ex-spouse wishes to allocate the joint liability on a previously filed return to reflect each spouse's share of liability. Separation of liability relief is available only to taxpayers that have a final divorce decree or a legal separation and do not live in the same household for a 12-month period.

EXAMPLE Bill and Karen filed a joint return in 2021. Karen reported wages of $50,000 and Bill reported self-employment income of $10,000. Subsequent to Bill and Karen's divorce, it was discovered that Bill should have reported an additional $20,000 of self-employment income. If Karen can demonstrate she qualifies for separation of liability relief, Bill will be separately liable for the tax, penalties, and interest on his understatement of income. ♦

Separation of liability relief requires that the spouse requesting relief have had no actual knowledge of the erroneous information at the time of the filing. There are exceptions to this requirement if the spouse was a victim of domestic violence or spousal abuse. Figure 6.3 shows the requirements for separation of liability relief.

Equitable relief is available only of the taxpayer does not qualify for innocent spouse or separation of liability relief. Of the three types of relief, only equitable relief will provide relief from an unpaid tax.

EXAMPLE Brad and Jennifer's joint return shows that tax owed is $5,000 of which only $2,000 was paid with the return. Jennifer might be able to claim equitable relief from the remaining $3,000 tax to be paid. ♦

The requirements for equitable relief are shown in Figure 6.4.

All three claims for relief require that the taxpayer and spouse or former spouse did not transfer assets to one another as a part of a fraudulent scheme for the main purpose of avoiding tax or the payment of tax.

Innocent spouse relief should not be confused with injured spouse relief. Injured spouse relief is when a joint return is filed and the refund is used to pay one spouse's past-due federal tax, state income tax, state unemployment compensation debts, child support, spousal support, or federal nontax debt, such as a student loan, the other spouse may be considered an injured spouse. An injured spouse can get back his or her share of the joint overpayment using Form 8379. To be an injured spouse, the taxpayer must not be legally obligated to pay the past-due amount, and meet *any* of the following conditions: (1) the taxpayer claiming to be an injured spouse made and reported tax payments (such as federal income tax withholding or estimated tax payments), (2) the taxpayer had earned income (such as wages, salaries, or self-employment income) and claimed the earned income credit or the additional child tax credit, or (3) the taxpayer claimed a refundable tax credit, such as the health coverage tax credit or the refundable credit for prior year minimum tax.

Dependents of Divorced Spouses

In most instances, the dependent child of a divorced couple will be claimed by the custodial parent (due to the domicile test – see Chapter 1). A child of divorced or separated parents can be a dependent of the noncustodial parent if all the following requirements are met:

- The parents are divorced, legally separated under a maintenance or written agreement or have lived apart for the last six months of the year
- The child received over half of the support from the parents
- The child is in the custody of one or both the parents for more than one-half of the year
- The custodial parent signs a written declaration (Form 8332) that they will not claim the child that year

FIGURE 6.3 SEPARATION OF LIABILITY RELIEF DECISION TREE

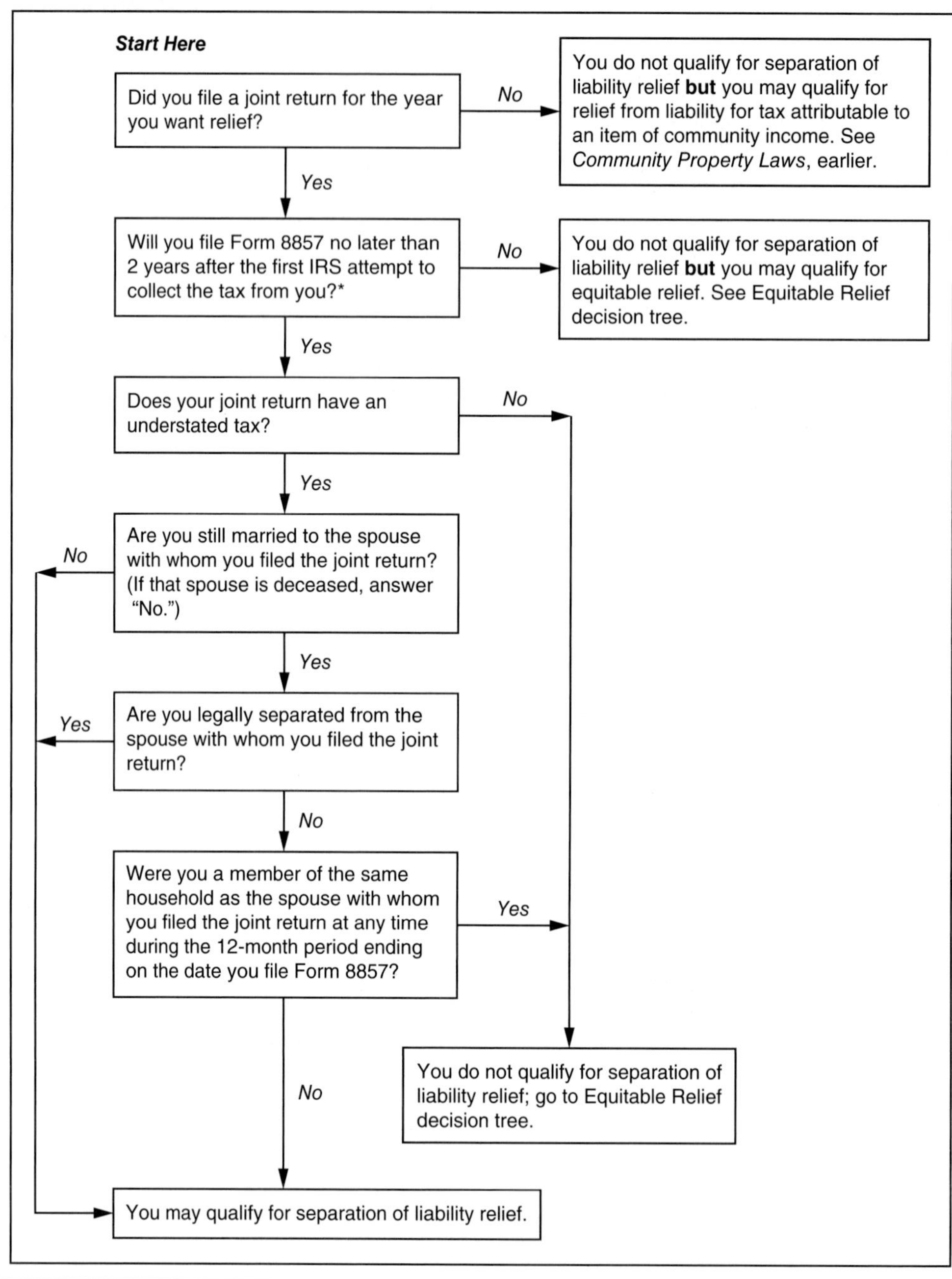

Source: IRS Publication 971

*Collection activities that may start the 2-year period are described earlier under *How To Request Relief.*

In certain instances, a child can be claimed by both divorced parents.

EXAMPLE Brad and Gwyneth, married couple, lived together with their son, Davos through the end of July 2022 at which time they legally separated. Davos moved with Gwyneth after the separation. If both parents wish to claim Davos, the IRS will grant the dependency to Gwyneth because Davos lived with her for more of the year. ♦

FIGURE 6.4 **EQUITABLE RELIEF DECISION TREE**

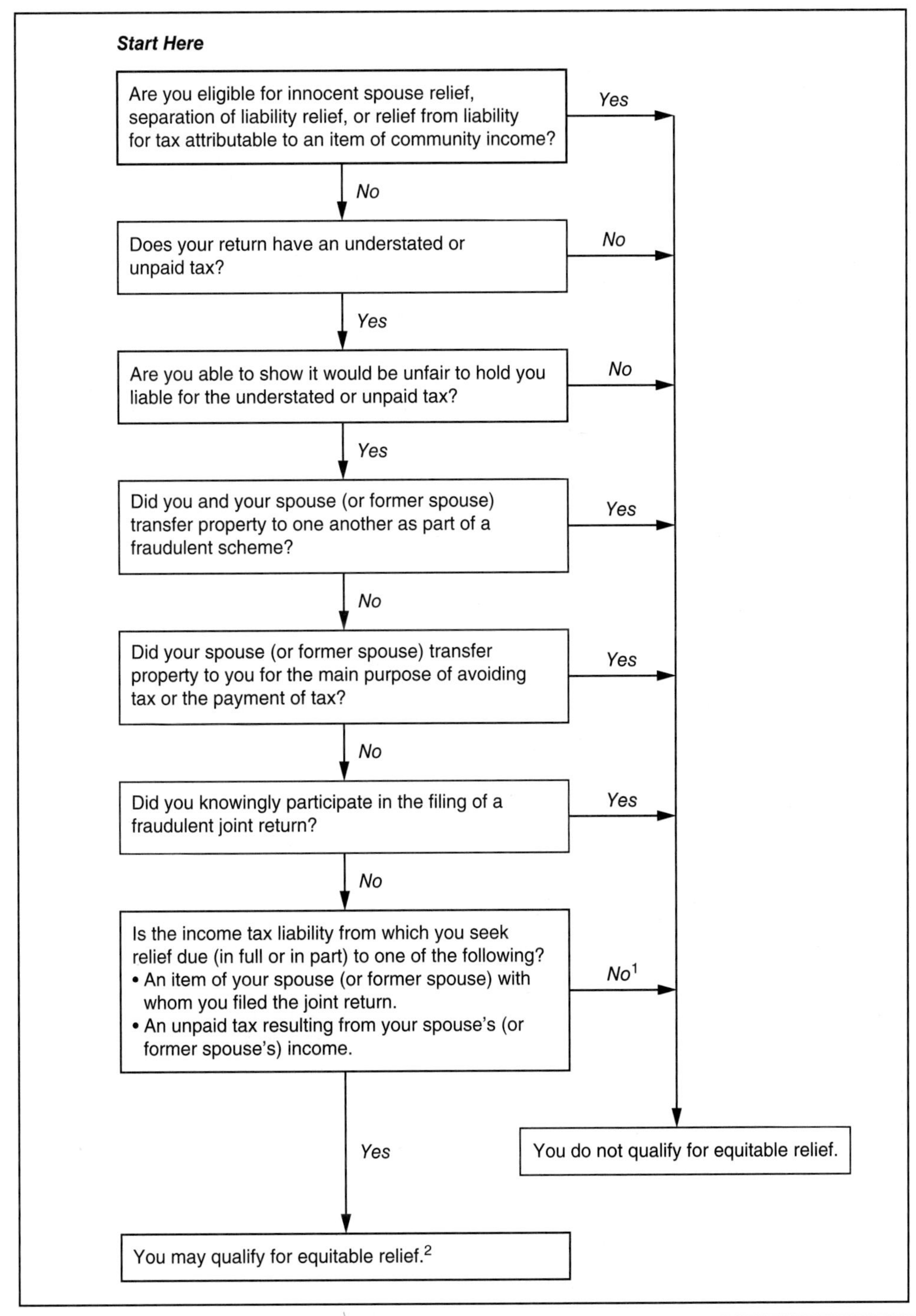

Source: IRS Publication 971

[1] You may qualify for equitable relief if you meet any of the exceptions to condition (7) discussed earlier under *Conditions for Getting Equitable Relief.*

[2] You must file Form 8857 by the filing deadlines explained earlier in *Exception for equitable relief* under *How To Request Relief.*

Nondeductible Divorce Expenses

Legal fees and court costs associated with a divorce are nondeductible. Fees paid to accountants for determining the correct tax, appraisers, actuaries and other experts are also nondeductible.

6-8c Death of the Taxpayer

In 1789, Benjamin Franklin is purported to have said, "nothing is certain but death and taxes." This section discusses that death and taxes do intersect, as even death does not preclude the payment of taxes.

When a taxpayer dies, a final income tax return will generally need to be prepared by a personal representative of the decedent. If the taxpayer was married, the personal representative can be, but is not required to be, the surviving spouse. As discussed in Chapter 1, if a spouse dies, the surviving spouse can file married filing jointly for the year of death (and may be eligible for surviving spouse for two years thereafter). A taxpayer's death can introduce many different tax consequences such as estate and gift taxes, and under certain circumstances, an income tax requirement for the decedent's estate.

EXAMPLE Paloma died in 2022. Among her assets is a closely-held corporation for which she was both the sole shareholder and an employee. Under the provisions of Paloma's will, her corporation became the property of a trust owned by her estate. The trust was designed to operate the business until such time as the business could be sold. Paloma will likely have a final personal income tax return and an estate tax return to report the transfer of her assets. Her trust, through its ownership of a business, will also need to file an income tax return. ♦

Estate and gift taxes and the income taxation of estates and trusts are beyond the scope of this textbook.

The final individual income tax return is due at the normal income tax filing deadline of April 15 (or later of a weekend or holiday) and if not filing jointly, should state "deceased" on the top of the return. The determination of what income to include on the decedent's final return is based on the accounting method (cash or accrual) the taxpayer was using. If the cash method, only income constructively received at the time of the decedent's death is included and generally only items paid by the decedent's death can be deducted.

EXAMPLE Drake, a single taxpayer, died in August of 2022. In March and June, Drake received dividends from his stock investment in Big Corp. The dividends paid by Big Corp. in September and December were paid to Drake's estate and thus are not reported on Drake's final income tax return. ♦

If the final return includes the standard deduction, the full amount of the standard deduction is permitted. Income that the decedent would have included, if not for death, is classified as income in respect of a decedent or IRD. IRD must be reported by the party that received the income after death.

EXAMPLE Continuing from the previous example, Drake's estate, as the recipient of the last two dividends payments, will include that income on the estate income tax return for 2022. ♦

For married couples, IRD is often received by the surviving spouse making reporting a simple matter.

EXAMPLE Joan and Edgar and married. After Joan passes away in 2022, Edgar will file jointly for the tax year. Joan's will transferred ownership of all of the investment to Edgar at death. The income that Joan would have earned in 2022 but for her death is now Edgar's income and he may report that on the joint return. ♦

Because certain income will be allocated to the decedent's final tax return and IRD may be allocated to another income tax return, deductions may also need to be allocated between the two income tax returns. Deductions in respect of a decedent are reported on the return of the party that captured the income.

EXAMPLE Gretchen died in 2022. Gretchen was operating a business on the cash basis, and the income of her business after death became the IRD of her estate. The business deductions that were incurred but not paid until after her death are deducted on her estate income tax. ♦

IRD can be included in the estate of the decedent (as part of estate tax) on which estate taxes are paid and the same IRD can also reported on the estate's income tax return. In this situation, the estate's income tax return may deduct the estate taxes paid that are associated with the IRD.

If the estate of the decedent is terminated and the estate's final return results in unused NOL carryforwards or excess deductions (other than the charitable contributions deduction), the beneficiaries of the estate may claim the deductions on the beneficiary's tax return.

EXAMPLE Amanda died in 2021. In 2022, her estate is winding up and reports an unused NOL of $10,000. All of Amanda's estate is being transferred to her daughter, Sarah. Sarah may use the estate's NOL on her own income tax return as permitted. ♦

The final tax liability is forgiven in its entirety for an armed forces member killed in combat, by military action, or by terrorist action, or that of an astronaut killed in the line of duty.

If the personal representative filing the final income tax return is not a spouse or court appointed representative, Form 1310 must be filed in order to receive a refund.

The estate, trust, and gift tax consequences of the death of a taxpayer are complex. This section of the textbook provides an overview to enable awareness of the issues but does not contemplate a complete discussion of all the possible tax consequences associated with the death of a taxpayer.

6-8e **Nonresident and International Issue**

Taxpayers that are U.S. citizens, green card holders, or meet the requirements of the substantial presence test are treated as tax residents for income tax purposes. Any other individual that earns U.S. sourced income is treated as a nonresident for tax purposes.

EXAMPLE Luka, a Croatian citizen, is in the U.S. for 190 days of 2022 working for his employer's office located in Dallas, TX. Luka is not considered a resident for U.S. tax purposes, but his income will be sourced from the U.S. and thus subject to US income taxation. ♦

Nonresidents have a very different income tax regime in the U.S. and file a different tax form (Form 1040-NR). A nonresident that is married to a U.S. resident; however, can make an election to file a married filing jointly return. The election applies for the entire year in which it is made.

EXAMPLE Bao and Hien are married, and both are nonresident aliens at the beginning of the year. In June, Bao became a resident alien and remained a resident for the rest of the year. Bao and Hien both elect to be treated as resident aliens. Bao and Hien must file a joint return for the year they make the choice, but they can file either joint or separate returns for later years. ♦

The substantial presence test and the many additional differences between a nonresident and resident tax return are outside the scope of this textbook. Additional details can be found in the instructions to Form 1040-NR, IRS Publication 519, and IRS Publication 901.

Form 843

Most nonresidents are not subject to Social Security or Medicare taxes, but many employers will mistakenly withhold these not realizing the exclusion. If a nonresident taxpayer has Social Security or Medicare taxes withheld in error, the taxpayer should contact the employer who withheld the taxes for a refund. If unable to get a full refund of the amount from the employer, the nonresident taxpayer should file a claim for refund with the IRS on Form 843 and attached the following items as appropriate:

- A copy of your Form W-2 to prove the amount of social security and Medicare taxes withheld.
- A copy of your visa.
- Form I-94 (or other documentation showing your dates of arrival or departure).
- A statement from the employer indicating the amount of the reimbursement the employer provided and the amount of the credit or refund the employer claimed or was authorized to claim. If this statement cannot be obtained from the employer, this information must be provided on Form 843 explaining why no statement from the employer is attached or include Form 8316.

Form 843 and attachments are filed at the Department of the Treasury Internal Revenue Service Center Ogden, UT 84201-0038 regardless of where the original tax return was filed.

Reporting Foreign Financial Accounts (FBAR, FinCEN, and Form 8938)

A U.S. person is subject to two separate reporting responsibilities with respect to a financial interest or signatory authority of a foreign financial account:

1. Reporting foreign financial accounts in the U.S. Treasury's Financial Crimes Enforcement Network (FinCEN)
2. Reporting specified foreign financial assets on Form 8938

If an individual has an interest in or authority over foreign financial accounts for which the aggregate value of all accounts exceeds $10,000 at any time during the year, the individual is required to complete Report 114 in FinCEN's Bank Secrecy Act E-Filing System (**https://bsaefiling.fincen.treas.gov/main.html**), commonly known as FBAR.

EXAMPLE Paula is a U.S. citizen. In 2022, Paula's father, who is a citizen and resident of Spain dies, and she inherits his bank account in a Spanish bank that holds the equivalent of US$12,000. Paula has an FBAR filing requirement in 2022. ♦

EXAMPLE Heather is a citizen of Nigeria but has been in the US for three years and files as a US tax resident starting in 2022. She maintains a joint personal bank account in Nigeria with her parents. If her Nigerian bank account has a value of over US$10,000 at any time during the year, Heather has a FBAR filing requirement. ♦

EXAMPLE Gabe, a US citizen, has signatory authority over three bank accounts in three different countries outside the Unites States. The bank accounts hold the equivalent of US$3,000, US$4,000 and US$8,000 during 2022. Gabe is required to report all three accounts because the aggregate value exceeds US$10,000. ♦

Form 8938 is used to report specified foreign assets if the value of those assets exceeds a specified reporting threshold. Table 6.1 presents common filing thresholds for individual taxpayers.

TABLE 6.1 FORM 8938 FILING THRESHOLDS

Filing Status	Timing	Living in US	Living outside US
Married filing jointly	End of year	$100,000	$400,000
	During year	150,000	600,000
All Others	End of year	50,000	200,000
	During year	75,000	300,000

EXAMPLE Joe is a single, U.S. citizen that lives in the U.S. in 2022. He owns specified foreign assets valued at $60,000. Joe is required to file Form 8938 since his assets exceed the $50,000 threshold for an unmarried individual living in the U.S. ♦

Filing FBAR does not relieve an individual from the requirements to file Form 8938 and vice versa.

EXAMPLE In the previous example, Joe files Form 8938 with the IRS. Joe is also required to file FBAR since he has more than $10,000 in foreign financial assets. ♦

6-8f Farmers

According to the U.S. Department of Agriculture, in 2020 there were over 1.7 million family-owned farms. The business of farming is the cultivation, operation, or management of a farm for profit, either as owner or tenant. A farm includes livestock, dairy, poultry, fish, fruit, and truck farms. It also includes plantations, ranches, ranges, and orchards and groves.

Farmers that operate their farms individually or with their spouse (as a qualified joint venture – see Chapter 10) report farming income and expenses on Schedule F of Form 1040. The tax law includes a number of special provisions that apply to farmers, making this area of taxation a specialty area that should not be taken on by a tax preparer without considerable additional training. Table 6.2 provides a selection of special tax provisions for farmers.

TABLE 6.2 SPECIAL TAX PROVISIONS FOR FARMERS

Provisions	Overview
Farm-price inventory method	Value at market price less cost to sell
Unit-livestock-price inventory method	Use a standard price for livestock based on age and type
Crop method of accounting	For crops not planted and harvested in the same year
Agricultural program payments	Government payments typically income
Commodity Credit Corporation loans	Treat loan as sale if production used as collateral
Conservation Reserve Program	Payments generally income
Crop Insurance and Disaster Payments	Generally income but can be deferred
Feed Assistance	Income in year received
Qualified farm debt	Exclude from cancellation of debt income
Income averaging	Use average tax rate from prior three years
Prepaid farm supplies	Cash-basis deduction can be limited
Prepaid livestock feed	Cash-basis deduction can be limited
Breeding fees	May need to be capitalized
Forestation and reforestation costs	Election to deduct
Soil and water conservation expenses	May be immediately deductible but limited
Livestock sales	Can be treated as Sec 1231
Farm and nonfarm optional methods of self-employment tax	Can reduce self-employment tax for low-income farmers
Fuel excise tax credit/refund	Credit or refund of excise taxes for fuel used for farming purposes
Estimated taxes	Payment timing can be later if qualify

Source: Adapted from IRS Publication 225

Self-Study Problem 6.8

See Appendix E for Solutions to Self-Study Problems

Determine whether each statement is true or false.

1. If a taxpayer does not receive a Form W-2, the first step is to contact the IRS.
2. An amended income tax return is filed on Form 1040-C.
3. A married couple in a trial separation should file as unmarried.
4. A division of the assets of a qualified retirement plan incident to divorce is handled by a QDRO.
5. If Mary believes that she should be relieved of the income tax liability that is unpaid at the time of filing, she should file for injured spouse relief
6. Most individuals are not required to file an income tax return in the year of death
7. Chamu's employer withheld Social Security and Medicare taxes from her wages even though Chamu is a nonresident and is not liable for employment taxes. Chamu should file a Form 1040-X
8. A taxpayer that properly files Form 8938 to report foreign assets is not required to also file FBAR since the Form 8938 thresholds to file are higher.
9. Individual farmers file Schedule F to report farm income

KEY TERMS

accounting periods, 6-2
fiscal year-end, 6-2
short-period taxable income, 6-2
annualized period, 6-2
accounting methods, 6-3
cash method, 6-4
accrual method, 6-4
economic performance, 6-4
hybrid method, 6-4
Section 267, 6-5
related parties, 6-6
constructive ownership, 6-7
"kiddie tax," 6-8
alternative minimum tax (AMT), 6-15
AMT adjustments, 6-15
AMT preferences, 6-15
AMT exemption, 6-16
alternative minimum tax rates, 6-16
nanny tax, 6-21
household workers, 6-21
net investment income tax, 6-25
0.9 percent additional Medicare tax, 6-26
Form W-2C, 6-33
Form 1040-X, 6-33
Married status, 6-37
annulment, 6-37
qualified domestic relations order (QDRO), 6-37
innocent spouse relief, 6-38
separation of liability relief, 6-39
equitable relief, 6-39
income in respect of a decedent (IRD), 6-42
tax residents, 6-43
nonresident, 6-43
Form 1040-NR, 6-43
Form 843, 6-43
FinCEN, 6-44
FBAR, 6-44

KEY POINTS

Learning Objectives	Key Points
LO 6.1: Determine the different accounting periods allowed for tax purposes.	• Almost all individuals file tax returns using a calendar-year accounting period. • Partnerships and corporations had a great deal of freedom in selecting a tax year in the past. However, Congress set limits on this freedom when it resulted in an inappropriate deferral of taxable income. • A personal service corporation is a corporation whose shareholder-employees provide personal services (e.g., medical, legal, accounting, actuarial, or consulting services) for the corporation's patients or clients. Personal service corporations generally must adopt a calendar year-end. • If taxpayers have a short year other than their first or last year of operations, they are required to annualize their taxable income to calculate the tax for the short period.
LO 6.2: Determine the different accounting methods allowed for tax purposes.	• The tax law requires taxpayers to report taxable income using the method of accounting regularly used by the taxpayer in keeping their books, provided the method clearly reflects the taxpayer's income. • The cash receipts and disbursements (cash) method, the accrual method, and the hybrid method are accounting methods specifically recognized in the tax law.
LO 6.3: Determine whether parties are considered related for tax purposes, and classify the tax treatment of certain related-party transactions.	• The two types of disallowed related-party transactions are (1) sales of property at a loss and (2) unpaid expenses and interest. • Any loss or deduction arising from transactions between related parties are disallowed by Section 267. • The common related parties under Section 267 include brothers and sisters (whole or half), a spouse, ancestors (parents, grandparents, etc.), lineal descendants (children, grandchildren, etc.), and a corporation or an individual shareholder who directly or constructively owns more than 50 percent of the corporation. • Related-party rules also consider constructive ownership in determining whether parties are related to each other (e.g., taxpayers are deemed to own stock owned by certain relatives and related entities).
LO 6.4: Apply the rules for computing tax on the unearned income of minor children and certain students (the "kiddie tax").	• The tax law contains provisions that limit the benefit of shifting income to certain dependent children. • The net unearned income of dependent children ("kiddie tax") may be taxed at the parent's rate, if higher. • The kiddie tax applies to dependent children who are required to file a tax return, are ages 18 or younger, or are students ages 19 through 24, who have at least one living parent, and who have "net unearned income" of more than \$2,300 for 2022. • If certain conditions are met, parents may elect to include a child's gross income on the parents' tax return. The election eliminates the child's return filing requirements, including the special calculation on Form 8615 for the kiddie tax.

LO 6.5: Calculate a basic alternative minimum tax.	• The AMT was designed to ensure that wealthy taxpayers could not take advantage of special tax write-offs (tax preferences and other adjustments) to avoid paying tax. In general, taxpayers must pay the AMT if their AMT liability is greater than their regular tax liability. • Adjustments are timing differences that arise because of differences in the regular and AMT calculations (e.g., depreciation timing differences), while preferences are special provisions for the regular tax that are not allowed for the AMT (e.g., state income taxes). • For 2022, the AMT exemption allowance is $118,100 for married taxpayers filing joint returns, $75,900 for single and head of household taxpayers, and $59,050 for married taxpayers filing separate returns. The AMT exemption allowance amount is phased out for high-income taxpayers. • For 2022, the alternative minimum tax rates for calculating the tentative minimum tax are 26 percent of the first $206,100 ($103,050 for married taxpayers filing separately), plus 28 percent on amounts above $208,100 applied to the taxpayer's alternative minimum tax base. • The increases in the AMT exemptions and thresholds coupled with the limitations or suspension of certain itemized deductions are expected to reduce the number of taxpayers subject to the AMT.
LO 6.6: Apply the special tax and reporting requirements for household employees (the "nanny tax").	• The "nanny tax" provisions provide a simplified reporting process for employers of household workers. • Household employers are not required to pay FICA taxes on cash payments of less than $2,400 paid to any household employee in a calendar year. • If the cash payment to any household employee is $2,400 or more in a calendar year, all the cash payments (including the first $2,400) are subject to Social Security and Medicare taxes. • If more than $1,000 in cash wages are paid to household employees during any calendar quarter, employers are required to pay FUTA taxes. • A taxpayer is a household employer if they hire workers to perform household services in or around the taxpayer's home that are subject to the "will and control" of the taxpayer (e.g., babysitters, caretakers, cooks, drivers, gardeners, housekeepers, and maids). • Certain workers are not subject to Social Security and Medicare taxes on wages paid for work in the home. These workers include the taxpayer's spouse, the taxpayer's father or mother, the taxpayer's children under 21 years of age, and anyone who is under age 18 during the year, unless providing household services is their principal occupation. • Under the nanny tax provisions, a household employer must report Social Security and Medicare taxes, federal income tax withholding, and FUTA tax once a year by filing Schedule H with his or her individual Form 1040. • At the close of the tax year, household employers must also file Form W-2 (copy A) and Form W-3 for each household employee whose income is reflected on Schedule H or had federal income tax withheld from wages.
LO 6.7 Compute the special taxes for high-income taxpayers.	• The Affordable Care Act (ACA) added a 3.8 percent Medicare tax on net investment income and a 0.9 percent additional Medicare tax on earned income for certain high-income taxpayers. • The 3.8 percent net investment income tax applies to the net investment income of individuals with modified AGI over $250,000 for joint filers ($125,000 if married filing separate), and $200,000 for single filers. • The 0.9 percent Medicare tax is imposed on earned income from salaries, wages, and self-employment income of joint filers with earned income over $250,000 ($125,000 if married filing separate) and single taxpayers with earned income over $200,000. • Employers are required to withhold the 0.9 percent Medicare tax when a taxpayer's salary exceeds $200,000. • Self-employed taxpayers must pay the tax with their individual income tax returns.

LO 6.8 Describe the basic rules surrounding special taxpayer situations such as divorce, deceased taxpayers, nonresident taxpayers, and farmers.	• Taxpayers should contact payer first if Forms W-2 and 1099-R are missing or incorrect. • Amended tax returns are filed on Form 1040-X. • Divorce and legal separation are determined under state law. • Spouses and ex-spouses can seek relief from tax under innocent spouse, separation of liability, or equitable relief using Form 8857. • Deceased taxpayers may need to file a final tax return. • Income in respect of a decedent (IRD) is income that would have been reported by the taxpayer if not for death. • A nonresident married to a resident can file a joint resident return. • Tax residents with foreign financial accounts may need to report them in two ways: FBAR or Form 8938. • Individual farmers report income on Schedule F and are subject to many special tax provisions.

QUESTIONS and PROBLEMS

GROUP 1: MULTIPLE CHOICE QUESTIONS

LO 6.1

1. E Corporation is a subchapter S corporation owned by three individuals with calendar year-ends. The corporation sells a sports drink as its principal product and has similar sales each month. What options does E Corporation have in choosing a tax year?
   a. E Corporation may choose any month end as its tax year.
   b. Because the owners of E Corporation have tax years ending in December, E Corporation must also choose a December year-end.
   c. E Corporation may choose an October, November, or December tax year-end.
   d. E Corporation may choose a tax year ending in September, October, or November, but only if the corporation also makes an annual cash deposit and adjusts the amount every year depending on the income deferred.

LO 6.1

2. Income and loss from which of the following entities is passed through and taxed on the individual's personal tax returns?
   a. S corporation
   b. Partnership
   c. Sole proprietor
   d. All of the above

LO 6.1

3. Which of the following entities is likely to have the greatest flexibility in choosing a year-end other than a calendar year-end?
   a. Sole proprietor
   b. General partnership
   c. Corporation
   d. S corporation

LO 6.2

4. Which of the following is an acceptable method of accounting under the tax law?
   a. The accrual method
   b. The hybrid method
   c. The cash method
   d. All of the above are acceptable
   e. None of the above

LO 6.2

5. Which of the following entities is required to report on the accrual basis?
   a. An accounting firm operating as a Personal Service Corporation.
   b. A manufacturing business with $30 million of gross receipts operating as a regular C corporation.
   c. A corporation engaged in tropical fruit farming in Southern California.
   d. A partnership with gross receipts of $13 million and all of the partners are individuals with a December year-end.

LO 6.2

6. A cash-basis taxpayer will recognize gross income when:
   a. earned
   b. actually or constructively received
   c. when reasonably estimable
   d. when shipped for goods and when provided for services

LO 6.2

7. In addition to the liability existing in an estimable amount, an accrual-based taxpayer cannot deduct an expense without this also occurring.
   a. The expense is paid
   b. An invoice has been received for the expense
   c. Economic performance has occurred
   d. The expense has been paid in cash

LO 6.3

8. Pekoe sold stock to his sister Rose for $12,000, its fair market value. Pekoe bought the stock 5 years ago for $16,000. Also, Pekoe sold Earl (an unrelated party) stock for $6,500 that he bought 3 years ago for $8,500. What is Pekoe's recognized gain or loss?
   a. $6,500 loss
   b. $6,000 loss
   c. $3,000 loss
   d. $2,000 loss
   e. $1,000 gain

LO 6.3

9. B Corporation, a calendar year-end, accrual-basis taxpayer, is owned 75 percent by Bonnie, a cash-basis taxpayer. On December 31, 2022, the corporation accrues interest of $4,000 on a loan from Bonnie and also accrues a $15,000 bonus to Bonnie. The bonus is paid to Bonnie on February 1, 2023; the interest is not paid until 2024. How much can B Corporation deduct on its 2022 tax return for these two expenses?
   a. $0
   b. $4,000
   c. $15,000
   d. $19,000
   e. $12,000

LO 6.3

10. B Corporation, a calendar year-end, accrual-basis taxpayer, is owned 75 percent by Bonnie, a cash-basis taxpayer. On December 31, 2022, the corporation accrues interest of $4,000 on a loan from Bonnie and also accrues a $15,000 bonus to Bonnie. The bonus is paid to Bonnie on February 1, 2023; the interest is not paid until 2024. How much can B Corporation deduct on its 2023 tax return for these two expenses?
    a. $0
    b. $4,000
    c. $15,000
    d. $19,000
    e. $12,000

LO 6.3

11. BJT Corporation is owned 40 percent by Bill, 30 percent by Jack, and 30 percent by the Trumpet Partnership. Bill and Jack are father and son. Jack has a 10 percent interest in Trumpet Partnership. What is Jack's total direct and constructive ownership of BJT Corporation under Section 267?
    a. 30 percent
    b. 70 percent
    c. 100 percent
    d. 73 percent
    e. 33 percent

LO 6.4

12. Which of the following is required for a taxpayer to be subject to the tax on unearned income of minors (kiddie tax) in 2022?
    a. Must have no earned income
    b. 21 years of age or younger
    c. Both parents must be living
    d. Net unearned income must exceed $2,300
    e. All of the above are required

LO 6.4

13. Which of the following is an option for a minor with unearned income of $3,500?
    a. Pay tax at trust and estate rates
    b. Pay tax at the parent's rate
    c. Pay $0 tax since the income is unearned
    d. Pay at the minor's individual tax rate

LO 6.5

14. An individual taxpayer will be liable for alternative minimum tax when:
    a. The regular tax liability exceeds the tentative minimum tax
    b. The tentative minimum tax exceeds the regular tax liability
    c. The taxpayer's income is below the filing threshold
    d. The standard deduction or any credit is claimed

LO 6.5

15. Which of the following is an adjustment for AMT purposes?
    a. Itemized deduction for home mortgage interest
    b. Itemized deduction for charitable contributions
    c. State income tax refunds
    d. Itemized deduction for medical expenses in excess of 7.5 percent of AGI

LO 6.5

16. The alternative minimum tax exemption:
    a. Is a direct reduction of the tentative minimum tax
    b. Is a reduction of alternative minimum taxable income for certain taxpayers
    c. Permits certain taxpayers to elect to treat AMT as a reduction of tax
    d. Is subject to carryback and carryforward provisions
    e. Increases the effects of tax preference items

LO 6.5

17. Alternative minimum tax rates in individuals:
    a. Are the same as regular tax rates but on adjusted minimum taxable income
    b. Higher than the highest marginal tax rate for individuals depending on filing status
    c. Are 26 percent and 28 percent
    d. Are 21 percent

LO 6.6

18. Bob employs a maid to clean his house. He pays her $1,040 during the current year. What is the proper tax treatment of the Social Security and Medicare tax for the maid?
    a. Bob is not required to pay or withhold Social Security and Medicare taxes on the $1,040.
    b. The $1,040 is subject to the Medicare tax, but not the Social Security tax.
    c. $500 is subject to the Social Security and Medicare tax.
    d. Bob is required to withhold Social Security and Medicare taxes on the entire $1,040.

LO 6.6

19. Which of the following employees would *not* be exempt from Social Security and Medicare taxes on wages paid for household work?
    a. The taxpayer's 16-year-old daughter
    b. The taxpayer's wife
    c. The taxpayer's 20-year-old sister
    d. The 14-year-old babysitter from down the street

LO 6.6

20. Individual taxpayers may pay withholding taxes due with their individual income tax returns using Schedule H for each of the following workers *except*:
    a. A nanny hired to watch their children
    b. A maid hired to clean house and cook every day
    c. An attorney with her own business, hired to handle a legal dispute with the taxpayers' neighbor
    d. An unlicensed caregiver for a disabled spouse

LO 6.7

21. The 3.8 percent Medicare tax on net investment income applies to:
    a. Tax-exempt interest income
    b. Interest and dividends
    c. IRA distributions
    d. Wages

LO 6.7

22. Skylar is single and earns $410,000 in salary during 2022. What is the amount of 0.9 percent Medicare tax for high-income taxpayers that his employer must withhold from his wages?
    a. $1,890
    b. $1,800
    c. $1,440
    d. $900

LO 6.7

23. Christine and Doug are married. In 2022, Christine earns a salary of $250,000 and Doug earns a salary of $50,000. They have no other income and work for the same employers for all of 2022. How much 0.9 percent Medicare tax for high-income taxpayers will Christine and Doug have to pay with their 2022 income tax return?
    a. $450
    b. $900
    c. $2,700
    d. None

LO 6.8

24. If a taxpayer did not receive a copy of their Form W-2:
    a. They should request a copy from the Social Security Administration.
    b. They should file a tax return and *not* include the income.
    c. They should attach a Form 4852 reporting the missing Form W-2 if a copy cannot be obtained.
    d. They should file a Form 1040-X which is the form used for missing information returns

LO 6.8

25. If a taxpayer discovers a math error on their tax return in which two lines were added incorrectly:
    a. Conventional wisdom is that they simply wait for the IRS to send them a notice addressing the mistake
    b. They should immediately file a Form 1040-X
    c. They should prepare a new tax return and submit that electronically
    d. Prepare the page of the tax return that was wrong and resubmit only that page

LO 6.8

26. Ben and Jennifer get divorced in 2022. Which of the following statements is *true* regarding the tax consequences of the divorce?
   a. Ben will be able to deduct any alimony paid to Jennifer in future years.
   b. Any property divided between the two will be subject to gain or loss recognition.
   c. If a QDRO is issued regarding Ben's qualified retirement plan assets, Jennifer will "step into Ben's shoes" for the plan assets that are transferred to her and will not be taxed on the distribution if rolled over into a new qualified plan.
   d. They will file as married filing separately until one of them remarries.

LO 6.8

27. Which of the following is *not* a form of relief from tax liability available to a spouse or ex-spouse?
   a. Protective custody relief
   b. Innocent spouse relief
   c. Separation of liability relief
   d. Equitable relief

LO 6.8

28. Helen was a retired 77-year-old teacher who died in 2022. In 2022, Helen's pension paid her $45,000 up to her date of death and $13,000 afterward. Which of the following statements best describes Helen's tax situation for 2022?
   a. Her tax liability is reduced to zero due to her death
   b. All of her income will be income in respect of a decedent and will be taxed to her estate
   c. All of her income will be reported on a Form 1040-X which is the form for deceased taxpayers.
   d. She will be required to file a final tax return for 2022 that includes her income and deductions up through the date of her death.

LO 6.8

29. If an estate is being terminated but has an NOL carryforward on the final income tax return, which of the following best describes the tax options for the NOL?
   a. It expires unused.
   b. It can be included on the return of the estate beneficiaries.
   c. It can be deducted on the estate's final return and create a refund.
   d. It can be used to lower any estate taxes.

LO 6.8

30. Rhianna is a tax resident of the U.S. and has a bank account in in Switzerland with a balance equivalent to about US$14,000. Which of the following best describes Rhianna's foreign bank account reporting requirements?
   a. Rhianna should file FBAR only using the electronic filing system.
   b. Rhianna should complete Form 8938 only and file with her tax return.
   c. Rhianna should file both FBAR and Form 8938 and submit both with her tax return.
   d. Rhianna does not need to report a foreign bank account.

GROUP 2: PROBLEMS

LO 6.1

1. Explain why the tax law prefers flowthrough entities like partnerships and S corporations to have a year-end that matches the year-end of its owners.

LO 6.2

2. Yolanda is a cash-basis taxpayer with the following transactions during the year:

Cash received from sales of products	$70,000
Cash paid for expenses (except rent and interest)	40,000
Rent prepaid on a leased building for 18 months beginning December 1	45,000
Prepaid interest on a bank loan, paid on December 31 for the next 3 months	5,000

Calculate Yolanda's income from her business for this calendar year.

LO 6.2

3. Geraldine is an accrual-basis taxpayer who has the following transactions during the current calendar tax year:

Accrued business income (except rent)	$220,000
Accrued business expenses (except rent)	170,000
Rental income on a building lease for the next 6 months, received on December 1	21,000
Prepaid rent expense for six months, paid on December 1	9,000

Calculate Geraldine's net income from her business for the current year.

LO 6.2

4. Amy is a calendar-year taxpayer reporting on the cash basis. Please indicate how she should treat the following items for 2022:
   a. She makes a deductible contribution to an IRA on April 15, 2023 .
   b. She has made an election to accrue the increase in value of savings bonds even though the increase is not received in cash.
   c. She prepays half a year of interest in advance on her mortgage on the last day of 2022.
   d. She pays all of her outstanding invoices for standard business expenses in the last week of December.
   e. She sends out a big bill to a customer on January 1, 2023, even though she did all of the work in December of 2022.

LO 6.3

5. JBC Corporation is owned 20 percent by John, 30 percent by Brian, 30 percent by Charlie, and 20 percent by Z Corporation. Z Corporation is owned 80 percent by John and 20 percent by an unrelated party. Brian and Charlie are brothers. Answer each of the following questions about JBC under the constructive ownership rules of Section 267:
   a. What is John's percentage ownership?
   b. What is Brian's percentage ownership?
   c. What is Charlie's percentage ownership?
   d. If Brian sells property to JBC for a $6,000 loss, what amount of that loss can be recognized for tax purposes (before any annual limitations)?

LO 6.3

6. You have a problem and need a full-text copy of the Related Party Code Section 267. Go to the Office of the Law Revision Counsel of the United States House of Representatives website (**uscode.house.gov**) and enter Title 26 (the Internal Revenue Code) and Section 267 in the Jump To boxes. Print out a copy of Section 267(a).

LO 6.4

7. Explain the purpose of the provision in the tax law that taxes unearned income of certain minor children at their parents' tax rates.

LO 6.4

8. Brian and Kim have a 12-year-old child, Stan. For 2022, Brian and Kim have taxable income of $52,000, and Stan has interest income of $4,500. No election is made to include Stan's income on Brian and Kim's return.
   a. For purposes of the tax on a child's unearned income, calculate Stan's taxable income.
   b. Calculate Stan's net unearned income.
   c. Calculate Stan's tax for 2022.
   d. If there was no kiddie tax and Stan were taxed at his own rate, what would the tax on Stan's income be?

LO 6.4

9. Explain the two different ways that the tax on unearned income of minor children, or "kiddie tax," can be reported.

LO 6.4

10. Does the tax on unearned income of minor children, or "kiddie tax," apply to wages earned by minors in summer and other jobs?

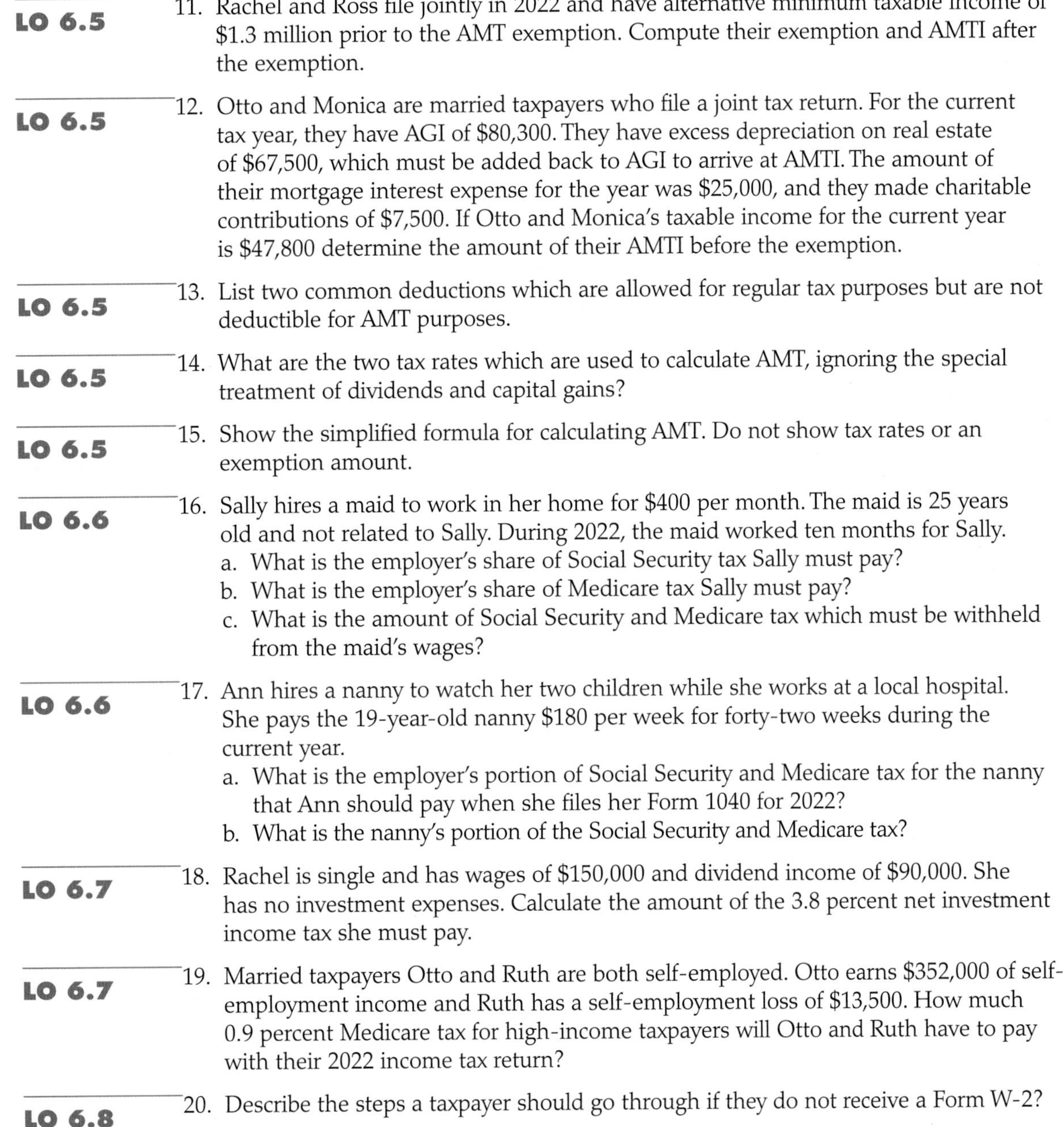

LO 6.5

11. Rachel and Ross file jointly in 2022 and have alternative minimum taxable income of $1.3 million prior to the AMT exemption. Compute their exemption and AMTI after the exemption.

LO 6.5

12. Otto and Monica are married taxpayers who file a joint tax return. For the current tax year, they have AGI of $80,300. They have excess depreciation on real estate of $67,500, which must be added back to AGI to arrive at AMTI. The amount of their mortgage interest expense for the year was $25,000, and they made charitable contributions of $7,500. If Otto and Monica's taxable income for the current year is $47,800 determine the amount of their AMTI before the exemption.

LO 6.5

13. List two common deductions which are allowed for regular tax purposes but are not deductible for AMT purposes.

LO 6.5

14. What are the two tax rates which are used to calculate AMT, ignoring the special treatment of dividends and capital gains?

LO 6.5

15. Show the simplified formula for calculating AMT. Do not show tax rates or an exemption amount.

LO 6.6

16. Sally hires a maid to work in her home for $400 per month. The maid is 25 years old and not related to Sally. During 2022, the maid worked ten months for Sally.
    a. What is the employer's share of Social Security tax Sally must pay?
    b. What is the employer's share of Medicare tax Sally must pay?
    c. What is the amount of Social Security and Medicare tax which must be withheld from the maid's wages?

LO 6.6

17. Ann hires a nanny to watch her two children while she works at a local hospital. She pays the 19-year-old nanny $180 per week for forty-two weeks during the current year.
    a. What is the employer's portion of Social Security and Medicare tax for the nanny that Ann should pay when she files her Form 1040 for 2022?
    b. What is the nanny's portion of the Social Security and Medicare tax?

LO 6.7

18. Rachel is single and has wages of $150,000 and dividend income of $90,000. She has no investment expenses. Calculate the amount of the 3.8 percent net investment income tax she must pay.

LO 6.7

19. Married taxpayers Otto and Ruth are both self-employed. Otto earns $352,000 of self-employment income and Ruth has a self-employment loss of $13,500. How much 0.9 percent Medicare tax for high-income taxpayers will Otto and Ruth have to pay with their 2022 income tax return?

LO 6.8

20. Describe the steps a taxpayer should go through if they do not receive a Form W-2?

LO 6.8

21. Define income in respect of a decedent and provide an example of IRD.

GROUP 3: WRITING ASSIGNMENT

ETHICS

Charlie's Green Lawn Care is a cash-basis taxpayer. Charlie Adame, the sole proprietor, is considering delaying some of his December 2022 customer billings for lawn care into the next year. In addition, he is thinking about paying some of the bills in late December 2022, which he would ordinarily pay in January 2023. This way, Charlie claims, he will have "less income and more expenses, thereby paying less tax!" Is Charlie's way of thinking acceptable?

GROUP 4:
COMPREHENSIVE PROBLEMS

1A. Richard McCarthy (born 2/14/1968; Social Security number 100-10-9090) and Christine McCarthy (born 6/1/1970; Social Security number 101-21-3434) have a 19-year-old son Jack, (born 10/2/2003; Social Security number 555-55-1212), who is a full-time student at the University of Key West. The McCarthys also have a 12-year-old daughter Justine, (born 12/09/2010; Social Security number 444-23-1212), who lives with them. The McCarthys can claim a $2,000 child tax credit for Justine and a $500 other dependent credit for Jack. Richard is the CEO at a paper company. His 2022 Form W-2:

a Employee's social security number: 100-10-9090	OMB No. 1545-0008	Safe, accurate, FAST! Use IRS e-file. Visit the IRS website at www.irs.gov/efile
b Employer identification number (EIN): 32-5656567	1 Wages, tips, other compensation: 231,500.00	2 Federal income tax withheld: 55,820.00
c Employer's name, address, and ZIP code: Mufflin-Dunder Paper, 302 Lackawanna Avenue, Scranton, PA 18503	3 Social security wages: 147,000.00	4 Social security tax withheld: 9,114.00
	5 Medicare wages and tips: 237,500.00	6 Medicare tax withheld: 3,781.25
	7 Social security tips	8 Allocated tips
d Control number	9	10 Dependent care benefits
e Employee's first name and initial, Last name, Suff.: Richard McCarthy, 32 Sleepy Hollow Road, Clarks Summit, PA 18411	11 Nonqualified plans	12a See instructions for box 12: D 6,000.00
	13 Statutory employee ☐ Retirement plan ☒ Third-party sick pay ☐	12b DD 11,412.90
	14 Other	12c
f Employee's address and ZIP code		12d

15 State	Employer's state ID number	16 State wages, tips, etc.	17 State income tax	18 Local wages, tips, etc.	19 Local income tax	20 Locality name
PA	1PA300906	231,500.00	13,900.00			

Form **W-2** Wage and Tax Statement 2022 Department of the Treasury—Internal Revenue Service

Copy B—To Be Filed With Employee's FEDERAL Tax Return.
This information is being furnished to the Internal Revenue Service.

Christine is an optometrist and operates her own practice ("The Eyes of March") in town as a sole proprietor. The shop address is 1030 Morgan Highway, Clarks Summit, PA 18411 and the business code is 621320. Christine keeps her books on the cash basis and her bookkeeper provided the following information:

Gross sales		$292,000
Returns		8,300
Inventory:		
Beginning inventory	$ 25,000	
Purchases	122,000	
Ending inventory	28,000	
Rent		42,000
Insurance		11,500
Professional fees		3,200
Payroll		35,000
Payroll taxes		2,800
Utilities		4,000
Office expenses		2,000
Depreciation		5,000

Christine paid her rent in 2022 month-to-month, but paid $24,000 in December 2022 for a 12-month lease on her office for all of 2023. One of Christine's customers is a large state prison that purchases special eye glasses for the the inmates that meet prison safety standards. Because the order is large, Christine was paid a $20,000 advance payment in December 2022 for glasses she delivered in January 2023. The rent and advance payment are included in her financial figures on the previous page.

The McCarthys have a nanny/housekeeper whom they paid $13,000 during 2022. They did not withhold income or FICA taxes. The McCarthys paid Pennsylvania state unemployment tax of $380 in 2022.

Christine received a 2022 Form 1099-INT from the National Bank of Scranton that listed interest income of $23,500. Note that McCarthys reasonably allocate $751 to state income tax expense for purposes of the net investment income tax. Christine's uncle that lives in Scotland dies in 2022 and left her a checking account at the Royal Bank of Glasgow with a balance of £18,000 or about US$20,000. The account did not earn any interest. Christine reported the account on the FinCEN website.

The McCarthys received a Form 1099-G from Pennsylvania that reported a $477 state income tax refund from 2021. The McCarthys filed a Schedule A in 2021 and had $14,223 of state income tax expense that was limited to a $10,000 deduction.

The McCarthys paid the following in 2022:

Home mortgage interest reported on Form 1098 on mortgage of less than $750,000	$15,600
Property taxes	5,600
Estimated state income tax payments	2,425
Estimated Federal income tax payments	4,700
Charitable contributions (all cash)	7,600
Student loan interest	2,700

Required: Complete the McCarthys' federal tax return for 2022. Use Form 1040, Schedule 1, Schedule 2, Schedule A, Schedule B, Schedule C, Schedule H, Schedule SE, Form 8995, Form 8959, and Form 8960 to complete this tax return. Make realistic assumptions about any missing data and ignore any alternative minimum tax. Do not complete Form 4952, which is used for depreciation.

1B. Complete Problem 1A above before completing Problem 1B. Richard and Christine McCarthy have a 19-year-old son Jack, (born 10/2/2003; Social Security number 555-55-1212), who is a full-time student at the University of Key West. Years ago, the McCarthys shifted a significant amount of investments into Jack's name. In 2022, Jack received Forms 1099-INT and 1099-DIV that reported the following:

Tandy Corporation Bonds interest	$14,500

In addition, Jack works part-time as a waiter in an upscale seafood restaurant in Miami, FL. His 2022 Form W-2 reported:

Wages	$12,900
Federal withholding	1,100

In spite of his fairly large income, the McCarthys provide more than 50 percent of his support and claim Jack as a dependent in 2022. Jack's mailing address is 100 Duval Street, Apt. #B12, Key West, FL 33040. Use the parent's information from Problem 1A, Form 1040, Schedule B, and Form 8615, to compute Jack's 2022 income tax.

2A. Warner Robins (born July 4, 1987) and Augustine Robins (born Nov 11, 1987) have been married for nine years, have no dependents, and file jointly. Warner is the president of Jaystar Corporation located in Macon, Georgia. The Jaystar stock is owned 40 percent by Warner, 40 percent by Augustine, and 20 percent by Warner's father. Warner and Augustine received the following tax documents:

a Employee's social security number: 798-09-8526	OMB No. 1545-0008	Safe, accurate, FAST! Use IRS e-file. Visit the IRS website at www.irs.gov/efile
b Employer identification number (EIN): 43-4321567	1 Wages, tips, other compensation: 133,600.00	2 Federal income tax withheld: 6,200.00
c Employer's name, address, and ZIP code: Jaystar Corp. 1776 Eisenhower Pkwy. Macon, GA 31206	3 Social security wages: 133,600.00	4 Social security tax withheld: 8,238.20
	5 Medicare wages and tips: 133,600.00	6 Medicare tax withheld: 1,937.20
	7 Social security tips	8 Allocated tips
d Control number	9	10 Dependent care benefits
e Employee's first name and initial / Last name / Suff.: Warner Robins 638 Russell Parkway Macon, GA 31207	11 Nonqualified plans	12a See instructions for box 12
	13 Statutory employee ☐ Retirement plan ☐ Third-party sick pay ☐	12b
	14 Other	12c
f Employee's address and ZIP code		12d

15 State	Employer's state ID number	16 State wages, tips, etc.	17 State income tax	18 Local wages, tips, etc.	19 Local income tax	20 Locality name
GA	5643E25	133,600.00	3,600.00			

Form **W-2** **Wage and Tax Statement** 2022 Department of the Treasury—Internal Revenue Service

Copy B—To Be Filed With Employee's FEDERAL Tax Return.
This information is being furnished to the Internal Revenue Service.

☐ CORRECTED (if checked)

PAYER'S name, street address, city or town, state or province, country, ZIP or foreign postal code, and telephone no.: Georgia National Bank 520 Walnut Street Macon, GA 31201	Payer's RTN (optional)	OMB No. 1545-0112 Form **1099-INT** (Rev. January 2022) For calendar year 20 22	**Interest Income**
	1 Interest income: $ 540.00		
	2 Early withdrawal penalty: $ 250.00		**Copy B**
PAYER'S TIN: 23-8787878 / RECIPIENT'S TIN: 445-81-1423	3 Interest on U.S. Savings Bonds and Treasury obligations: $		**For Recipient**
RECIPIENT'S name: Augustine and Warner Robins	4 Federal income tax withheld: $	5 Investment expenses: $	This is important tax information and is being furnished to the IRS. If you are required to file a return, a negligence penalty or other sanction may be imposed on you if this income is taxable and the IRS determines that it has not been reported.
Street address (including apt. no.): 638 Russell Parkway	6 Foreign tax paid: $	7 Foreign country or U.S. possession	
City or town, state or province, country, and ZIP or foreign postal code: Macon, GA 31207	8 Tax-exempt interest: $	9 Specified private activity bond interest: $	
	10 Market discount: $	11 Bond premium: $	
FATCA filing requirement ☐	12 Bond premium on Treasury obligations: $	13 Bond premium on tax-exempt bond: $	
Account number (see instructions)	14 Tax-exempt and tax credit bond CUSIP no.	15 State / 16 State identification no.	17 State tax withheld: $ $

Form **1099-INT** (Rev. 1-2022) (keep for your records) www.irs.gov/Form1099INT Department of the Treasury - Internal Revenue Service

☐ CORRECTED (if checked)

RECIPIENT'S/LENDER'S name, street address, city or town, state or province, country, ZIP or foreign postal code, and telephone no.		*Caution: The amount shown may not be fully deductible by you. Limits based on the loan amount and the cost and value of the secured property may apply. Also, you may only deduct interest to the extent it was incurred by you, actually paid by you, and not reimbursed by another person.	OMB No. 1545-1380 Form **1098** (Rev. January 2022) For calendar year 20 22	**Mortgage Interest Statement**
Georgia National Bank 520 Walnut Street Macon, GA 31201		1 Mortgage interest received from payer(s)/borrower(s)* $ 27,400.00		**Copy B For Payer/ Borrower**
RECIPIENT'S/LENDER'S TIN 23-8787878	PAYER'S/BORROWER'S TIN 798-09-8526	2 Outstanding mortgage principal $ 790,000.00	3 Mortgage origination date 10/13/2014	The information in boxes 1 through 9 and 11 is important tax information and is being furnished to the IRS. If you are required to file a return, a negligence penalty or other sanction may be imposed on you if the IRS determines that an underpayment of tax results because you overstated a deduction for this mortgage interest or for these points, reported in boxes 1 and 6; or because you didn't report the refund of interest (box 4); or because you claimed a nondeductible item.
		4 Refund of overpaid interest $	5 Mortgage insurance premiums $	
PAYER'S/BORROWER'S name Warner and Augustine Robins		6 Points paid on purchase of principal residence $		
Street address (including apt. no.) 638 Russell Parkway		7 ☒ If address of property securing mortgage is the same as PAYER'S/BORROWER'S address, the box is checked, or the address or description is entered in box 8.		
City or town, state or province, country, and ZIP or foreign postal code Macon, GA 31207		8 Address or description of property securing mortgage		
9 Number of properties securing the mortgage 1	10 Other Prop tax $6,650.00			11 Mortgage acquisition date
Account number (see instructions)				

Form **1098** (Rev. 1-2022) (Keep for your records) www.irs.gov/Form1098 Department of the Treasury - Internal Revenue Service

☐ CORRECTED (if checked)

PAYER'S name, street address, city or town, state or province, country, ZIP or foreign postal code, and telephone no.		1 Unemployment compensation	OMB No. 1545-0120 Form **1099-G** (Rev. January 2022) For calendar year 20 22	**Certain Government Payments**
State of Georgia Treasurer 200 Piedmont Ave SE, Ste 1204 Atlanta, GA 30334		$ 2 State or local income tax refunds, credits, or offsets $ 710.00		
PAYER'S TIN 21-4315123	RECIPIENT'S TIN 798-09-8526	3 Box 2 amount is for tax year	**4 Federal income tax withheld** $	**Copy B For Recipient**
RECIPIENT'S name Warner and Augustine Robins		5 RTAA payments $	6 Taxable grants $	This is important tax information and is being furnished to the IRS. If you are required to file a return, a negligence penalty or other sanction may be imposed on you if this income is taxable and the IRS determines that it has not been reported.
Street address (including apt. no.) 638 Russell Parkway		7 Agriculture payments $	8 If checked, box 2 is trade or business income ▶ ☐	
City or town, state or province, country, and ZIP or foreign postal code Macon, GA 31207		9 Market gain $		
Account number (see instructions)		10a State | 10b State identification no.	11 State income tax withheld $ $	

Form **1099-G** (Rev. 1-2022) (keep for your records) www.irs.gov/Form1099G Department of the Treasury - Internal Revenue Service

Macon Museum of Arts
3231 Vineville Ave.
Macon, GA 31204

November 23, 2022

Mr. and Mrs. Warner and Augustine Robins
638 Russell Parkway
Macon, GA 31207

Dear Mr. and Mrs. Robins:

Thank you for your contribution of the original album cover art for the Almond Sisters Band to the Macon Museum of Arts.

This gift supports the Macon Museum's efforts to bring original and locally-sourced art work to Macon. This continuing support will guarantee our ability to display Almond Sister art work for many years to come.

We have attached a copy of the appraiser's market valuation. Her analysis estimates the value of the painting at $54,000.

Please keep this written acknowledgement of your donation for your tax records. As a token of our appreciation for your support, we have mailed you the Macon Museum tote bag. We estimate the value of the tote bag to be $25. We are required to inform you that your federal income tax deduction for your contribution is the amount of your contribution less the value of the tote bag. Thank you for your continuing support for our important work in this field!

Please retain this letter as proof of your charitable contribution.

Sincerely,

Jack T. Mann

Jack T. Mann
Art Development Officer

Employer Identification Number **22-1234567**
Macon Museum of Arts is a registered 501(c)(3) corporation

The Robins paid the following amounts (all can be substantiated):

General state sales tax	2,120
Auto loan interest	4,800
Medical insurance	11,400
Income tax preparation fee	750
Charitable contributions in cash:	
Church	2,700
Central Georgia Technical University	5,000
Safe-deposit box	200

The Robins had total itemized deductions of $33,567 in 2021 which included a $9,600 state tax deduction.

The tax basis for the donated album cover art is $25,000 and has been owned by Warner and Augustine for five years.

Jaystar does not cover health insurance for its employees. In addition to Warner and Augustine's health insurance premiums shown above, Augustine required surgery which cost $6,500 for which only $3,200 was covered by insurance. In September 2022, Warner had to drive Augustine 130 miles each way to a surgical center.

On January 1, 2022, Warner sold land to Jaystar Corporation for $75,000. He acquired the land 5 years ago for $160,000. No Form 1099-B was filed for this transaction.

Augustine decided to become a management consultant in late 2022 and provided consulting services to her only client, Jaystar, in 2022 and billed them $7,500 on December 27, 2022. Jaystar is an accrual-based corporation and accrued the consulting expense of $7,500. Jaystar paid Augustine in January 2023 and expects to issue her a 1099-NEC in 2023. This was Augustine's only consulting work in 2022, and she is a cash-based business. She incurred no business-related expenses in 2022.

Jaystar Corporation does not have a qualified pension plan or Section 401(k) plan for its employees. Therefore, Warner deposited $12,000 ($6,000 each) into traditional IRA accounts for Augustine and himself (neither are covered by a qualified plan at work).

Required: Complete the Robins' federal tax return for 2022. Use Form 1040, Schedule 1, Schedule A, Schedule D, and Form 8949 to complete this tax return. Make realistic assumptions about any missing data and ignore any alternative minimum tax. Do not complete Form 8283, which is used when large noncash donations are made to charity.

2B. Complete Problem 2A above before starting Problem 2B. The Robins received their income tax refund for 2022 in May 2023. On July 14, 2023, the Robins' primary home in Macon (Bibb County, GA) was hit by the remnants of Hurricane Gator (DR-4690-GA) and suffered damage that decreased the fair market value of their home from $900,000 to $880,000. They originally paid $800,000 for the home. Because Macon is not normally hit by hurricanes, the Robins' had only limited insurance and received $3,000 to cover the cost of repairs. Because this was declared a federal disaster, the Robins wish to amend their 2022 return and obtain an immediate refund. In accordance with IRS guidance, the Form 4684 should state "Section 165(i) Election" at the top of the form and the explanation for the amendment on Form 1040-X should include (1) the name or a description of the disaster and date or dates of the disaster which gave rise to the loss, and (2) the address, including the city, town, county, parish, State, and zip code, where the damaged or destroyed property was located at the time of the disaster.

Required: Complete the Robins' 2022 amended federal tax return. Use Form 1040-X, Form 1040, Schedule A, and Form 4684 to complete this tax return. Make realistic assumptions about any missing data. Note: Because the ProConnect software requires an *actual* federal declared disaster, this problem cannot be completed in the software and must be completed manually.

GROUP 5:
CUMULATIVE SOFTWARE PROBLEM

1. The following information is available for the Albert and Allison Gaytor family in addition to that provided in Chapters 1–5.

Allison discovered a bookkeeping error in her business records. The revenues from Toge Pass should have been $80,000 (not the $64,600 originally recorded).

Albert owned 1,000 shares of Behemoth Airline stock with a basis of $25 per share. The stock was purchased six years ago on June 10. Albert sells 500 shares of Behemoth stock to his uncle Seth and 500 of the shares to his sister Sara for $5 per share on December 31, 2022. These sales were not reported on Form 1099-B.

Required: Combine this new information about the Gaytor family with the information from Chapters 1–5 and complete a revised 2022 tax return for Albert and Allison. Be sure to save your data input files since this case will be expanded with more tax information in the next chapter.

CHAPTER 7

Tax Credits

Thomas Imo/Alamy Stock Photo

LEARNING OBJECTIVES

After completing this chapter, you should be able to:

LO 7.1 Calculate the child tax credit.

LO 7.2 Determine the earned income credit (EIC).

LO 7.3 Compute the child and dependent care credit for an individual taxpayer.

LO 7.4 Calculate the premium tax credit available under the Affordable Care Act.

LO 7.5 Apply the special rules applicable to the American Opportunity tax credit (AOTC) and lifetime learning credit.

LO 7.6 Compute the foreign income exclusion and tax credit.

LO 7.7 Determine the proper use and calculation of the adoption credit.

LO 7.8 Recognize other basic individual credits.

LO 7.9 Calculate the low-income Retirement Plan Contribution Credit.

OVERVIEW

This chapter covers the most common tax credits. Credits differ from deductions. A credit is a direct reduction in tax liability while a deduction decreases taxable income. Credits are used because they target tax relief to certain groups of taxpayers. Because of the progressive rate structure of the income tax, a deduction provides greater benefit to higher-income taxpayers, while a tax credit provides equal benefit, regardless of the taxpayer's income level.

A deduction reduces taxable income by the amount of the deduction and thus results in a tax savings equal to the deduction multiplied by the tax rate. A credit is a dollar-for-dollar reduction of the taxpayer's tax liability. If a taxpayer has a choice between a credit or a deduction of equal amounts, generally the credit will result in greater tax savings.

Many credits exist in the tax law that are not covered here, such as the credit for research and development, the Work Opportunity Tax Credit, and the credit for the elderly and disabled.

EXAMPLE Gordon is a single taxpayer. His 2022 taxable income is $60,000 placing him in the 22-percent tax bracket for ordinary income. His income tax liability is $8,823. Not included in the $60,000 of taxable income is a choice between a $1,000 deduction or a $1,000 credit.

	Deduction	***Credit***
Taxable income	$60,000	$60,000
Deduction	(1,000)	n/a
Revised taxable income	59,000	60,000
Tax on revised income	8,603	8,823
Tax credit	n/a	(1,000)
Tax after credits	8,603	7,823
Original tax	8,823	8,823
Tax savings	$ 220	$ 1,000

Gordon saves $1,000 (a dollar-for-dollar reduction in tax liability) with the credit. He saves $220 ($1,000 × 22% tax rate) for the deduction. ♦

Most tax credits are limited to the amount of total tax liability that a taxpayer has and thus are "nonrefundable." Certain credits allow taxpayers to claim the credit even when the amount of the credit exceeds their tax liability—these are known as refundable credits since they result in a "refund" of taxes that were never actually paid by the taxpayer.

EXAMPLE Sandy is a taxpayer who files as head of household, with taxable income of $16,125 and a tax liability of $1,642 before any tax credits. Sandy has total tax payments (including withholding) of $2,200. Sandy is eligible for a tax credit of $2,000. Sandy's refund is calculated as follows if the credit is refundable versus nonrefundable:

	Nonrefundable	***Refundable***
Total tax before credits	$1,642	$1,642
Tax credit	(1,642)	(2,000)
Tax after credits	0	(358)
Tax payments	(2,200)	(2,200)
Total refund	$(2,200)	$(2,558)

The refundable credit increases Sandy's refund to an amount in excess of her taxes paid. ♦

Learning Objective 7.1

Calculate the child tax credit.

7-1 CHILD TAX CREDIT

The child tax credit permits individual taxpayers to take a tax credit based on the number of their qualifying dependent children. The child tax credit is amidst a temporary expansion. The TCJA made three significant, but temporary, changes to the child tax credit that apply in 2022: (1) increased the credit per child to $2,000, (2) increased the threshold for which the phase-out starts, and (3) increased the refundable amount of the credit for taxpayers whose credit is limited by their pre-credit tax liability. In addition, the TCJA added a new qualifying dependent credit of $500 for certain dependents. All of these provisions are scheduled to expire after 2025.

7-1a Child Tax Credit

To qualify for the child tax credit, the child must be under age 17, a U.S. citizen or U.S. resident alien, claimed as a dependent on the taxpayer's return, and meet the definition of "qualifying child" as discussed in Chapter 1. Thus, the child must meet the six tests outlined in LO 1.6: (1) relationship test, (2) domicile test, (3) age test (except in the case of the child tax credit, the child must be under age 17), (4) joint return test, (5) citizenship test, and (6) self-support test. All qualifying children must have a Social Security number at the time of filing.

The maximum credit is $2,000 per qualifying child; however, the available credit begins phasing out when AGI reaches $400,000 for joint filers and $200,000 for all other taxpayers. The credit is phased out by $50 for each $1,000 (or part thereof) of AGI above the threshold amounts. Since the maximum credit available depends on the number of qualifying children, the income level at which the credit is fully phased out also depends on the number of children qualifying for the credit. The phase-out thresholds for the child tax credit are currently not adjusted for cost-of-living increases.

EXAMPLE Donna and Chris Howser are married and file a joint tax return. They have two children, ages 5 and 7, that are qualifying children under the dependency rules. All members of the family are U.S. citizens with Social Security numbers. In 2022, their AGI was $120,006. In 2022, both children qualify for the child tax credit of $2,000; thus, the maximum credit is $4,000. Because the phase-out for married filing jointly taxpayers in 2022 starts at $400,000, the Howsers are eligible for the maximum credit of $4,000. ♦

EXAMPLE Fiona and Kris Everest are married and file a joint return. They have one child, age 13. Each member of the Everest family has a Social Security number and their 2022 AGI is $409,100. The maximum child tax credit in 2022 is $2,000 per child; however, the Everest's AGI exceeds the $400,000 threshold. The phase-out amount is $500.

$409,100 − $400,000 = $9,100

$9,100/$1,000 = 9.1 rounded to 10

10 × $50 = $500

The Everest's child tax credit is limited to $1,500 ($2,000 − $500). ♦

The nonrefundable portion of the child tax credit is limited to the amount of tax liability before taking the child tax credit. Because taxpayers may be eligible for other tax credits that also reduce tax liability, the tax law prescribes a "pecking order" to prevent taxpayers from claiming more than one nonrefundable tax credit and creating a refundable credit. The child tax credit comes after the foreign tax credit, the credit for child and dependent care expenses, education credits, and the saver's credit.

EXAMPLE In 2022, Eugene has a tax liability of $2,200 before any tax credits. Eugene has determined he is eligible for an education credit of $400 and a child tax credit of $2,000. Because his two nonrefundable credits exceed his tax liability, Eugene will take a $400 education credit, and his nonrefundable child tax credit will be limited to $1,800 ($2,200 − $400). ♦

The refundable portion of the child tax credit is the amount of child tax credit that was limited by the taxpayer's tax liability.

EXAMPLE Eugene, in the previous example, was eligible for a total child tax credit of $2,000; however, he could only take a credit of $1,800 due to the tax liability limitation. The $200 unclaimed child tax credit *may* be refundable. ♦

If the taxpayer has fewer than three children that are eligible for the child tax credit, the refundable portion of the child tax credit is subject to two additional limitations. The first limitation is that the additional child tax credit cannot exceed $1,500 per child. The second limitation is that the refundable child tax credit cannot exceed 15 percent of the taxpayer's earned income over $2,500. The lower of these two amounts will apply.

EXAMPLE In 2022, Mike and Laura, married filing jointly taxpayers, have two qualifying children, AGI of $72,000 (all earned income) and tax liability before any credits of $1,043. As a result, their child tax credit of $4,000 is limited to $1,043. However, Mike and Laura can claim the refundable portion of child tax credit of $3,000; the lesser of the unclaimed child tax credit $2,957 ($4,000 – $1,043) or 15 percent of earned income over $2,500 [($72,000 – $2,500) × 15% = $10,425], limited to $3,000 ($1,500 per qualifying child). ♦

For taxpayers with three or more qualifying children, the child tax credit amount in excess of tax liability is subject to limitations. The same overall $1,500 limit per child applies. The refundable child tax credit is also limited by the greater of (1) 15 percent of earned income over $2,500 or (2) the amount of Social Security and Medicare taxes paid, up to the unclaimed child tax credit. For purposes of the refundable child tax credit, Social Security and Medicare taxes are the amounts withheld for the employee and 50 percent of self-employment taxes.

EXAMPLE Molly and Sam are married, file a joint tax return, have five qualifying children, and earned income of $6,000 in 2022. The children are qualifying children for purposes of the child tax credit, but do not qualify under the earned income tax credit. Molly and Sam had $459 of Social Security and Medicare taxes withheld by their employers. Their pre-credit tax liability is $0. Because their pre-credit tax liability is $0, Molly and Sam are not eligible for the $10,000 ($2,000 × 5 children) child tax credit. The refundable portion of the child tax credit is $525, which starts at $10,000 but is first limited to $7,500 ($1,500 × 5) and then further limited to the greater of $459 or $525 [($6,000 – $2,500) × 15%]. ♦

For 2022, the child tax credit is claimed on Schedule 8812 (see Page 7-7). Most taxpayers will complete Part I and those with a limited credit will also complete Part II-A of Schedule 8812. The other portion of the form is for taxpayers with three of more children eligible for the child tax credit.

For dependents that do not qualify for the child tax credit, a $500 "other dependent credit" also exists. For example, a dependent parent or dependent child age 17 or older can still qualify as eligible dependents for the other dependent credit. The qualifying relative test for purposes of the other dependent credit requires the individual must be a U.S. citizen, a U.S. national, or a U.S. resident in order to be eligible for the credit. A Social Security number is not required for the other dependent credit and the credit is nonrefundable. The other dependent credit is also reported on Schedule 8812 in 2022.

EXAMPLE Alex is a single taxpayer with a 15-year-old child. Alex also takes care of her elderly mother, who qualifies as a dependent. Alex is eligible for a possible $2,000 child tax credit and a $500 other dependent credit for her mother. ♦

EXAMPLE Marty is a single taxpayer with a dependent 21-year-old child who is a full-time student. Marty also takes care of his elderly mother who qualifies as a dependent. Marty is eligible for a $1,000 other dependent tax credit for his child and his mother. ♦

A taxpayer who erroneously claims the child tax credit due to reckless or intentional disregard of rules or regulations is ineligible to claim the credit for a period of two tax years. If the IRS determines the claim for the credit was fraudulent, the ineligibility window is extended to ten years.

If the IRS rejects a child tax credit for any reason other than a math or clerical error, the taxpayer must complete a Form 8862 in a year after a rejection. Form 8862 is also used for claiming an earned income credit or American Opportunities credit after rejection. Tax preparers that prepare returns on which the child tax credit is claimed are required to complete Form 8867, a due diligence checklist that was also discussed in Chapter 1 when the filing status is head of household.

The IRS will not issue refunds for any tax returns that claim a child tax credit (or earned income credit) until February 15 of the year following the tax year. This tax provision is intended to provide the IRS with additional time to review refund claims that stem from refundable credit claims.

ProConnect™ Tax TIP

The child tax credit is handled by ProConnect Tax in an almost seamless fashion. By entering the dependent's birthdate and status (e.g., full-time student) the software will automatically compute the child tax credit, other dependent credit, and additional child tax credit. A number of dropdown boxes are available under the Dependent entry screen that permit overrides and other options for these credits. For this reason, child tax credits or related information will not be found under the Credits input.

Self-Study Problem 7.1 *See Appendix E for Solutions to Self-Study Problems*

a. Jose and Jane are married and file a joint tax return claiming their three children, ages 4, 5, and 18, as dependents. Their AGI for 2022 is $125,400 and their pre-credit tax liability is $14,000. They are not claiming any other tax credits in 2022. Determine Jose and Jane's child tax credit for 2022.

b. Herb and Carol are married and file a joint tax return claiming their three children, ages 4, 5, and 18, as dependents. Their AGI for 2022 is $405,600 and their pre-credit tax liability is about $84,000. What is Herb and Carol's child tax credit for 2022?

c. Marie and Pierre Curry are married and file a joint tax return claiming their three children, ages 4, 5, and 16, as dependents. Their AGI for 2022 is $26,400 (all wage income) and their pre-credit tax liability is $50. Marie and Pierre's employers withheld $2,020 in Social Security and Medicare taxes in 2022. They are not claiming any other tax credits. Complete Schedule 8812 on Pages 7-7 and 7-8 to determine Marie and Pierre's child tax credit and additional refundable child tax credit, if any, for 2022.

Learning Objective 7.2

Determine the earned income credit (EIC).

7-2 EARNED INCOME CREDIT

The earned income credit (EIC or sometimes referred to as EITC) is available to qualifying individuals with earned income and AGI below certain levels. The earned income credit is meant to assist the working poor by reducing their tax burden and to supplement wage income through a refundable credit when earnings are less than the taxpayer's maximum income for their filing status. Qualifying taxpayers can receive a refundable EIC even in situations when they have no filing requirement, owe no tax, and had no income tax withheld. Similar to the additional child tax credit, the refundable EIC can in effect produce a "negative" income tax.

Proper calculation of the EIC requires a taxpayer to answer three important questions:

(1) Does the taxpayer qualify for the EIC?
(2) Does the taxpayer have a qualifying child?
(3) What is the amount of the EIC?

7-2a Does the Taxpayer Qualify?

There are seven rules that all taxpayers must meet in order to claim the EIC and the taxpayer must meet *all seven* rules. Failure to meet just one precludes the taxpayer from claiming the EIC. The seven rules fall into the following categories:

1. AGI limit–AGI limits are indexed for inflation and can change each year. In addition, the AGI limits vary based on filing status and number of qualifying children. The EIC phases out for taxpayers with income over the limits. For 2022, the limits are:

	Other Than Joint Filers		*Joint Filers*	
Qualifying Children	Phase-out Begins	Phase-out Ends	Phase-out Begins	Phase-out Ends
None	$9,160	$16,480	$15,290	$22,610
1	20,130	43,492	26,260	49,622
2	20,130	49,399	26,260	55,529
3 or more	20,130	53,057	26,260	59,187

   The limits for taxpayers with no qualifying children had been adjusted upward for only 2021 but have returned to pre-2021 levels adjusted for inflation. The phase-out percentages vary; however, only the IRS EIC Tables (Appendix B) may be used to calculate the EIC amount.

2. Social Security numbers—The taxpayer (and spouse, if filing jointly) plus any qualifying children, must all have valid Social Security numbers. If a taxpayer's child(ren) does not have a Social Security number, the taxpayer may still claim the EIC for no children if qualified otherwise.
3. Married filing separate not allowed unless one spouse lives with a qualifying child for at least one-half of the year and has not lived in the same abode as the other spouse for the last six months of the year or has a separation decree.
4. U.S. citizenship or resident alien status is required for the entire tax year.
5. Foreign income exclusion not allowed—tax law provides for certain taxpayers to exclude income earned overseas (reported on Form 2555 or Form 2555-EZ). The foreign income exclusion is beyond the scope of this textbook.
6. Investment income limit—generating a certain amount of "disqualified" income ($10,300 in 2022) precludes claiming the EIC. Disqualified income includes most typical forms of investment income such as interest, dividends, net income from rents and royalties and most forms of capital gains.
7. Earned income requirement—Since the design of the EIC is to assist the working poor, an obvious requirement is that the taxpayer (or spouse, if filing jointly) have earned

Self-Study Problem 7.1c

SCHEDULE 8812 (Form 1040)

Department of the Treasury
Internal Revenue Service

Credits for Qualifying Children and Other Dependents

Attach to Form 1040, 1040-SR, or 1040-NR.

Go to *www.irs.gov/Schedule8812* for instructions and the latest information.

OMB No. 1545-0074

2022

Attachment Sequence No. **47**

Name(s) shown on return | **Your social security number**

Part I — Child Tax Credit and Credit for Other Dependents

1	Enter the amount from line 11 of your Form 1040, 1040-SR, or 1040-NR			1	
2a	Enter income from Puerto Rico that you excluded	2a			
b	Enter the amounts from lines 45 and 50 of your Form 2555	2b			
c	Enter the amount from line 15 of your Form 4563	2c			
d	Add lines 2a through 2c			2d	
3	Add lines 1 and 2d			3	
4	Number of qualifying children under age 17 with the required social security number	4			
5	Multiply line 4 by $2,000			5	
6	Number of other dependents, including any qualifying children who are not under age 17 or who do not have the required social security number	6			
	Caution: Do not include yourself, your spouse, or anyone who is not a U.S. citizen, U.S. national, or U.S. resident alien. Also, do not include anyone you included on line 4.				
7	Multiply line 6 by $500			7	
8	Add lines 5 and 7			8	
9	Enter the amount shown below for your filing status. • Married filing jointly—$400,000 • All other filing statuses—$200,000			9	
10	Subtract line 9 from line 3. • If zero or less, enter -0-. • If more than zero and not a multiple of $1,000, enter the next multiple of $1,000. For example, if the result is $425, enter $1,000; if the result is $1,025, enter $2,000, etc.			10	
11	Multiply line 10 by 5% (0.05)			11	
12	Is the amount on line 8 more than the amount on line 11?			12	
	☐ **No. STOP.** You cannot take the child tax credit, credit for other dependents, or additional child tax credit. Skip Parts II-A and II-B. Enter -0- on lines 14 and 27.				
	☐ **Yes.** Subtract line 11 from line 8. Enter the result.				
13	Enter the amount from the **Credit Limit Worksheet A**			13	
14	Enter the smaller of line 12 or 13. **This is your child tax credit and credit for other dependents** **Enter this amount on Form 1040, 1040-SR, or 1040-NR, line 19.**			14	

If the amount on line 12 is more than the amount on line 14, you may be able to take the **additional child tax credit** on Form 1040, 1040-SR, or 1040-NR, line 28. Complete your Form 1040, 1040-SR, or 1040-NR through line 27 (also complete Schedule 3, line 11) before completing Part II-A.

For Paperwork Reduction Act Notice, see your tax return instructions. Cat. No. 59761M **Schedule 8812 (Form 1040) 2022**

Schedule 8812 (Form 1040) 2022 Page **2**

Part II-A Additional Child Tax Credit for All Filers

Caution: If you file Form 2555, you cannot claim the additional child tax credit.

15	Check this box if you **do not** want to claim the additional child tax credit. Skip Parts II-A and II-B. Enter -0- on line 27 . . . . . . ☐		
16a	Subtract line 14 from line 12. If zero, **stop here**; you cannot take the additional child tax credit. Skip Parts II-A and II-B. Enter -0- on line 27 . . .	16a	
b	Number of qualifying children under 17 with the required social security number: ________ x $1,500. Enter the result. If zero, **stop here**; you cannot claim the additional child tax credit. Skip Parts II-A and II-B. Enter -0- on line 27 . . .	16b	
	TIP: The number of children you use for this line is the same as the number of children you used for line 4.		
17	Enter the **smaller** of line 16a or line 16b . . .	17	
18a	Earned income (see instructions) . . . 18a		
b	Nontaxable combat pay (see instructions) . . . 18b		
19	Is the amount on line 18a more than $2,500? ☐ **No.** Leave line 19 blank and enter -0- on line 20. ☐ **Yes.** Subtract $2,500 from the amount on line 18a. Enter the result . . . 19		
20	Multiply the amount on line 19 by 15% (0.15) and enter the result . . .	20	
	Next. On line 16b, is the amount $4,500 or more? ☐ **No.** If you are a bona fide resident of Puerto Rico, go to line 21. Otherwise, skip Part II-B and enter the **smaller** of line 17 or line 20 on line 27. ☐ **Yes.** If line 20 is equal to or more than line 17, skip Part II-B and enter the amount from line 17 on line 27. Otherwise, go to line 21.		

Part II-B Certain Filers Who Have Three or More Qualifying Children and Bona Fide Residents of Puerto Rico

21	Withheld social security, Medicare, and Additional Medicare taxes from Form(s) W-2, boxes 4 and 6. If married filing jointly, include your spouse's amounts with yours. If your employer withheld or you paid Additional Medicare Tax or tier 1 RRTA taxes, see instructions . . . 21		
22	Enter the total of the amounts from Schedule 1 (Form 1040), line 15; Schedule 2 (Form 1040), line 5; Schedule 2 (Form 1040), line 6; and Schedule 2 (Form 1040), line 13 . 22		
23	Add lines 21 and 22 . . . 23		
24	**1040 and 1040-SR filers:** Enter the total of the amounts from Form 1040 or 1040-SR, line 27, and Schedule 3 (Form 1040), line 11. **1040-NR filers:** Enter the amount from Schedule 3 (Form 1040), line 11. 24		
25	Subtract line 24 from line 23. If zero or less, enter -0- . . .	25	
26	Enter the **larger** of line 20 or line 25 . . .	26	
	Next, enter the **smaller** of line 17 or line 26 on line 27.		

Part II-C Additional Child Tax Credit

27	**This is your additional child tax credit. Enter this amount on Form 1040, 1040-SR, or 1040-NR, line 28** . .	27	

Schedule 8812 (Form 1040) 2022

income. For self-employed taxpayers, earned income includes income reported on Schedule SE. The earned income limits for 2022 are:

	Other Than Joint Filers		*Joint Filers*	
Qualifying Children	Minimum Earned Income	Maximum Earned Income	Minimum Earned Income	Maximum Earned Income
None	$1	$16,480	$1	$22,610
1	1	43,492	1	49,622
2	1	49,399	1	55,529
3 or more	1	53,057	1	59,187

EXAMPLE Doug is married but files separately in 2022. Doug has no qualifying children. Doug is not qualified for the EIC in 2022 because he does not meet the specific qualifications for separated spouses. ♦

EXAMPLE In 2022, Jane has income of $7,000, is single, has a valid Social Security number, and is not a qualifying child of another taxpayer. Her income includes $4,500 of interest on a corporate bond. Jane is eligible for the EIC because her investment income does not exceed $10,300. ♦

EXAMPLE In 2022, Eddie and Lindsey had a new baby. Their earned income and AGI in 2022 was $12,500, they filed jointly, lived in the United States, and had no investment income. Eddie and Lindsey have Social Security numbers but have not had the time to get a Social Security number for the baby yet. Eddie and Lindsey may claim an EIC in 2022 but only with no qualifying child since the baby does not have a valid Social Security number. They should consider applying for a Social Security number by the filing deadline. ♦

EXAMPLE In 2022, Jerry earns wages of $22,000 from his job and has no adjustments or other forms of income. He has no qualifying children and no investment income. Even if Jerry meets all the other requirements (Social Security number, U.S. residence, etc.), he will not be eligible for the EIC as his AGI exceeds the threshold amount for an unmarried taxpayer with no qualifying children ($16,480 in 2022). ♦

7-2b **Does the Taxpayer Have a Qualifying Child?**

Determining whether the taxpayer has a qualifying child is important because the eligibility rules differ based on whether a qualifying child is claimed or not. Because the rules defining a qualifying child for the EIC are similar to the rules for claiming a dependent, a review of the rules in Chapter 1 is suggested.

7-2c **Taxpayer with No Qualifying Child**

If the taxpayer does not have a qualifying child, the previous seven rules *must* be met along with four additional rules:

1. Taxpayer's age—in 2022, the taxpayer or the spouse (but not both) must be at least 25 years of age by the end of the tax year but less than 65 years of age.
2. Dependency status—the taxpayer (or spouse, if filing jointly) must not be eligible to be claimed as a dependent on another taxpayer's return, whether they are claimed or not.
3. Cannot be a qualifying child—the taxpayer claiming the EIC may not be the qualifying child of another taxpayer. Note the qualifying child definition discussed in Chapter 1 applies here with two notable exceptions: (1) the child need not meet the support test, and (2) the child must live in a U.S. home for more than one-half of the year (a slight extension of the domicile test).

4. U.S. home—the taxpayer must have lived in the United States for more than one-half of the tax year.

EXAMPLE Marco and Llewelyn are married and file jointly with no qualifying children in 2022 and meet the general rules to claim the EIC. Marco turned 66 on December 14, 2022, and Llewelyn turned 65 on April 3, 2022. Marco and Llewelyn do not qualify to claim the 2022 EIC. ♦

EXAMPLE Monica is a 23-year-old single taxpayer with no qualifying children in 2022. She is a full-time student at State College and generates enough income to live on from her nontaxable scholarships and a job on campus; however, she lets her father claim her as a dependent as the scholarship money is not included in her support test. Even if Monica meets the seven general rules, because she is claimed as a dependent by another taxpayer, she is not eligible to claim the EIC. ♦

7-2d Taxpayer with a Qualifying Child

To claim an EIC with a qualifying child, three additional rules must be considered:

1. Qualifying child tests—the child must meet the qualifying child tests. These are the same tests as discussed in Chapter 1 with two notable exceptions: (1) the child need not meet the support test, and (2) the child must live in a U.S. home for more than one-half of the year (a slight extension of the domicile test).
2. Qualifying child cannot be claimed by more than one person–only one taxpayer may claim a qualifying child for the EIC. If the child meets the definition of a qualifying child for more than one taxpayer, tiebreaker rules similar to those discussed in Chapter 1 must be applied.
3. Taxpayer cannot be a qualifying child of another taxpayer–see rule 3 under taxpayer with no qualifying child at Section 7-2c.

With so many qualification rules, it is no wonder that taxpayers and tax preparers have been known to make numerous errors when determining the EIC. Numerous checklists and aids have been prepared to assist taxpayers with preparing the EIC calculation. IRS Publication 596 contains an EIC Eligibility Checklist as shown on Page 7-11.

In addition to checklists, the IRS has implemented some additional procedural steps to ensure the EIC is not being abused by taxpayers. Similar to the child tax credit rules, taxpayers claiming an earned income credit must have a Social Security number for the taxpayer, spouse (if married), and each qualifying child by the due date (including extensions) of the return.

If the IRS rejects an earned income credit for any reason other than a math or clerical error, the taxpayer must complete a Form 8862 in order to claim the earned income credit in a future year.

In addition, a taxpayer who erroneously claims the earned income credit due to reckless or intentional disregard of rules or regulations is ineligible to claim the credit for a period of two tax years. If the IRS determines the claim for the credit was fraudulent, the ineligibility window is extended to ten years.

The IRS will not issue refunds for any tax returns that claim an earned income credit until February 15th of the following year to provide the IRS with additional time to review refund claims that stem from refundable earned income credit claims.

To assist tax preparers with the accurate completion of the EIC (and the child tax credit and American Opportunities tax credit), Form 8867 (see also Chapter 1) must be prepared and filed with the tax return and a copy retained by the tax preparer. If a taxpayer is claiming more than one of the credits covered by Form 8867, only one form is required to be filed. Failure to file Form 8867 could result in a $560 penalty.

7-2e What Is the Amount of the EIC?

Taxpayers are required to have some earned income to qualify for the EIC; however, too much earned income renders the taxpayer ineligible for the EIC. As stated previously, the

EIC amount must be derived from the EIC Tables in Appendix B and should not be calculated using the statutory credit percentages to avoid rounding issues. To find the correct amount of EIC in the EIC Tables, the taxpayer must compare the EIC Table amount based on the taxpayer's earned income with the EIC Table amount associated with the taxpayer's AGI. The taxpayer is required to claim the smaller of the two EIC amounts.

Part of the complexity of the EIC is that a number of the thresholds, amounts, and limits change each year. As a result, new EIC tables must be used each year. The EIC is reported on Line 27 of Form 1040. Similar to the child tax credit, a specific form to support the EIC computation is not always required to be prepared and filed. Instead, a series of supporting worksheets found within the instructions to the Form 1040 are available to assist with preparation. Worksheet A is used for taxpayers with wage income only and Worksheet B is used by taxpayers with self-employment income. For taxpayers claiming a qualifying child for the EIC, Schedule EIC must also be filed.

EIC Eligibility Checklist

1. Is your AGI less than: ☐ Yes ☐ No
   - $16,480 ($22,610 for married filing jointly) if you do not have a qualifying child,
   - $43,492 ($49,622 for married filing jointly) if you have one qualifying child,
   - $49,399 ($55,529 for married filing jointly) if you have two qualifying children, or
   - $53,057 ($59,187 for married filing jointly) if you have more than two qualifying children?
2. Do you and your spouse each have a valid SSN (by the due date of your return including extensions)? ☐ Yes ☐ No
3. Is your filing status married filing jointly, head of household, qualifying widow(er), or single? ☐ Yes ☐ No
4. Answer "**Yes**" if you are not filing Form 2555 or Form 2555-EZ. Otherwise, answer "**No**." ☐ Yes ☐ No
5. Is your investment income $10,300 or less? ☐ Yes ☐ No
6. Is your total earned income at least $1 but less than: ☐ Yes ☐ No
   - $16,480 ($22,610 for married filing jointly) if you do not have a qualifying child,
   - $43,492 ($49,622 for married filing jointly) if you have one qualifying child,
   - $49,399 ($55,529 for married filing jointly) if you have two qualifying children, or
   - $53,057 ($59,187 for married filing jointly) if you have more than two qualifying children?
7. Answer "**Yes**" if (a) you are not a qualifying child of another taxpayer or (b) you are filing a joint return. Otherwise, answer "NO." ☐ Yes ☐ No
8. Does your child meet the relationship, age, residency, and joint return tests for a qualifying child and have a Social Security number received by the due date of the tax return (including extensions)? ☐ Yes ☐ No
9. Is your child a qualifying child only for you? Answer "**Yes**" if (a) your qualifying child does not meet the tests to be a qualifying child of any other person or (b) your qualifying child meets the tests to be a qualifying child of another person but you are the person entitled to treat the child as a qualifying child under the tiebreaker rules. Answer "**No**" if the other person is the one entitled to treat the child as a qualifying child under the tiebreaker rules. ☐ Yes ☐ No
10. Were you (or your spouse if filing a joint return) at least age 25 but under age 65 at the end of 2022? ☐ Yes ☐ No
11. Answer "**Yes**" if (a) you cannot be claimed as a dependent on anyone else's return or (b) you are filing a joint return. Otherwise, answer "**No**." ☐ Yes ☐ No
12. Was your main home (and your spouse's if filing a joint return) in the United States for more than half the year? ☐ Yes ☐ No

PERSONS WITH A QUALIFYING CHILD: If you answered "**Yes**" to questions 1 through 9, you can claim the EIC. Remember to fill out Schedule EIC and attach it to your Form 1040. If you answered "**Yes**" to questions 1 through 7 and "**No**" to question 8, answer questions 10 through 12 to see if you can claim the EIC without a qualifying child.

PERSONS WITHOUT A QUALIFYING CHILD: If you answered "**Yes**" to questions 1 through 7, and 10 through 12, you can claim the EIC.

If you answered "No" to any questions that applies to you: You cannot claim the EIC.

EXAMPLE Ying and Michael are married filing jointly taxpayers with earned income and AGI of $23,200 in 2022. They have two children ages 3 and 5. All members of the family have Social Security numbers, are U.S. citizens, and lived together in the United States all year. Ying had $820 of tax withheld from her wages during the year. Michael did not work. Ying and Michael can claim the EIC as they meet all the tests for taxpayers with a qualifying child. Based on earned income of $23,200, filing jointly with two qualifying children, their EIC per the 2022 table (Appendix B) is $6,164. ♦

Self-Study Problem 7.2

See Appendix E for Solutions to Self-Study Problems

Dennis and Lynne have a 5-year-old child. Dennis has a salary of $16,200. Lynne is self-employed with a loss of $400 from her business. Dennis and Lynne receive $100 of taxable interest income during the year. Their earned income for the year is $15,800 and their adjusted gross income is $15,900 ($16,200 − $400 + $100).

Use the worksheet below and calculate their earned income credit from the EIC table in Appendix B.

Worksheet A—2022 EIC—Line 27a* *Keep for Your Records*

Before you begin: √ Be sure you are using the correct worksheet. Use this worksheet only if you answered "No" to Step 5, question 2. Otherwise, use Worksheet B.

Part 1

All Filers Using Worksheet A

1. Enter your earned income from Step 5. **1** ______

2. Look up the amount on line 1 above in the EIC Table (right after Worksheet B) to find the credit. Be sure you use the correct column for your filing status and the number of qualifying children you have who have a valid SSN as defined earlier. Enter the credit here. **2** ______

   If line 2 is zero, STOP You can't take the credit. Enter "No" on the dotted line next to Form 1040 or 1040-SR, line 27.

3. Enter the amount from Form 1040 or 1040-SR, line 11. **3** ______

4. Are the amounts on lines 3 and 1 the same?

   ☐ **Yes.** Skip line 5; enter the amount from line 2 on line 6.

   ☐ **No.** Go to line 5.

Part 2

Filers Who Answered "No" on Line 4

5. If you have:
   - No qualifying children who have a valid SSN, is the amount on line 3 less than $9,200 ($15,300 if married filing jointly)?
   - 1 or more qualifying children who have a valid SSN, is the amount on line 3 less than $20,150 ($26,300 if married filing jointly)?

   ☐ **Yes.** Leave line 5 blank; enter the amount from line 2 on line 6.

   ☐ **No.** Look up the amount on line 3 in the EIC Table to find the credit. Be sure you use the correct column for your filing status and the number of qualifying children you have who have a valid SSN. Enter the credit here. Look at the amounts on lines 5 and 2. Then, enter the **smaller** amount on line 6. **5** ______

Part 3

Your Earned Income Credit

6. **This is your earned income credit.** **6** ______

   Enter this amount on Form 1040 or 1040-SR, line 27.

Reminder—

√ If you have a qualifying child, complete and attach Schedule EIC.

1040 or 1040-SR | EIC | 1040 or 1040-SR

CAUTION *If your EIC for a year after 1996 was reduced or disallowed, see Form 8862, who must file, earlier, to find out if you must file Form 8862 to take the credit for 2022.*

*Download the latest version of this worksheet from the Form 1040 Instructions available at www.irs.gov. The 2022 worksheet was not available as we went to print. This worksheet is adapted from the 2021 version.

ProConnect™ Tax TIP

ProConnect Tax determines whether the earned income credit applies based on the information that the preparer inputs (most importantly, income and dependent information). However, if the earned income credit is not computing and the preparer believes the taxpayer is eligible, the earned income credit worksheets can be produced by ProConnect Tax to allow for review of the calculation. To produce the EIC worksheets, click on the Credits section and on the EIC, Residential Energy, Other Credits screen, expand the Earned Income Credit section and scroll down to the bottom to select the box Force Earned Income Credit Worksheets.

7-3 CHILD AND DEPENDENT CARE CREDIT

7.3 Learning Objective

Compute the child and dependent care credit for an individual taxpayer.

Congress enacted tax laws to provide benefits to taxpayers with dependents who must be provided with care and supervision while the taxpayers work. Taxpayers are allowed a credit for expenses for the care of their children and certain other dependents. Form 2441 is used to calculate and report the credit for child and dependent care expenses. To be eligible for the child and dependent care credit, the dependent must either be under the age of 13 or be a dependent or spouse of any age who is incapable of self-care. If a child's parents are divorced, the child need not be the dependent of the taxpayer claiming the credit, but the child must live with that parent more than he or she lives with the other parent. For example, a divorced mother with custody of a child may be entitled to the credit even though the child is a dependent of the father.

7-3a Qualified Expenses

The expenses that qualify for the credit include amounts paid to enable both the taxpayer and his or her spouse to be employed. Qualified expenses include amounts paid for in-home care, such as a nanny, as well as out-of-home care, such as a day care center. Overnight camps do not qualify for the credit, nor do activities providing standard education such as kindergarten. Day camps such as soccer camps, music camps, math camps, and dinosaur camps do qualify for the credit since they are not considered standard education. Payments to relatives are eligible for the credit, unless the payments are to a dependent of the taxpayer or to the taxpayer's child who is under the age of 19 at the end of the tax year. To claim the credit, the taxpayer must include on his or her tax return, the name, address, and taxpayer identification number of the person or organization providing the care. Qualified expenses do not include amounts provided under an employer dependent care assistance program as discussed in Chapter 2.

7-3b Allowable Credit

For taxpayers with AGI of less than $15,000, the child and dependent care credit is equal to 35 percent of the qualified expenses. For taxpayers with AGI of $15,000 or more, the applicable percentage of qualified expenses is reduced by 1 percent for each $2,000 (or part thereof) of AGI above $15,000 but not below 20 percent. In determining the credit, the maximum amount of qualified expenses to which the applicable percentage is applied is $3,000 for one dependent and $6,000 for two or more dependents.

TAX BREAK

The cost of summer camp for dependents often meets the definition of qualified expenses for the child and dependent care credit, even when the camp is centered around sports or fun activities. Overnight camps and summer school; however, do not qualify. See IRS Publication 503 for more details.

EXAMPLE Heather and Kamal are married filing jointly. They have one child and pay $4,000 for child care expenses during the year. Kamal earns $16,000 and Heather earns $8,500 during the year, resulting in adjusted gross income of $24,500. The 2022 child care credit is calculated as follows:

Qualified expenses	$3,000
Credit percentage from Form 2441	× 30%
Credit allowed	$ 900

♦

EXAMPLE Janie and Bongsik are married filing jointly. They have two children and pay $17,000 for child care expenses during the year. Janie earns $86,000 and Bongsik earns $38,500 during the year, resulting in adjusted gross income of $124,500. The 2022 child care credit is calculated as follows:

Qualified expenses	$17,000
Maximum for more than one dependent	6,000
Credit percentage from Form 2441	× 20%
Credit allowed	$ 1,200

♦

Married taxpayers must generally file a joint return to claim the child and dependent care credit unless legally separated. If the taxpayer is married but files separately, has lived apart from their spouse for the last six months of the tax year, and provided one-half the cost for a principal abode for a qualifying individual, the credit can be claimed. When filing jointly, the qualifying dependent care expenses are limited to the lesser of either spouse's earned income.

EXAMPLE Jeff and Janie file jointly in 2022. Janie makes $22,000 and Jeff earns $1,500, and they spend $1,900 on child care. The maximum qualifying expenses are $1,500, the lower of earned income from the lowest earning spouse or the qualifying expenses. ♦

A special rule applies when a taxpayer or spouse is a full-time student or disabled. Full-time students or disabled taxpayers with little or no income are deemed to have earned income of $250 per month for one dependent and $500 per month for two or more dependents for purposes of calculating this limitation.

EXAMPLE Lin and Leon file jointly in 2022. Lin earns $36,000 and Leon is a full-time student for nine months of the year and has no income. The maximum amount of the qualifying expenses for the care of one dependent is $2,250 ($250 per month × 9 months). ♦

The child and dependent care expense credit is nonrefundable.

Self-Study Problem 7.3 *See Appendix E for Solutions to Self-Study Problems*

Julie Brown (Social Security number 456-23-6543) has been widowed for five years and has one dependent child, Chuck Brown (Social Security number 123-33-4444). Julie's adjusted gross income and her earned income are $90,000. Julie's employer withheld $5,000 in the dependent care flexible spending account (see Chapter 2) that was used toward Chuck's child care. This amount was excluded from her wage income. Assume her taxable income is $44,450, and her regular tax is $5,044 (line 10 on Form 2441). Julie paid child care expenses of $8,500 (including $5,000 from the flexible spending account) to Ivy Childcare (1 Sunflower Street, Terre Haute, IN 47803, EIN 56-7654321) and expenses for the care of her disabled dependent mother, Devona Neuporte (Social Security number 214-55-6666), of $3,400 paid to De Anza Adult Care (13 Fort Harrison Rd., Dewey, IN 47805, EIN 43-1234567). Calculate Julie's child and dependent care credit for 2022 using Form 2441 on Pages 7-17 and 7-18. Make realistic assumptions about any missing data.

ProConnect™ Tax TIP

The child and dependent care credit is a function of two entry points in ProConnect Tax. The first is the input in Dependents as discussed in Chapter 1 and in the other credits mentioned earlier in this chapter. The second important input occurs under Credits/Ind Qualifying for Dependent Care Credit. This screen and the Persons and Expenses Qualifying for the Dependent Care Credit are where you identify the dependent for which the expenses were incurred. The provider of the care is entered in the Provider of Dependent Care screen.

7-4 THE AFFORDABLE CARE ACT

7.4 Learning Objective

Calculate the premium tax credit available under the Affordable Care Act.

The Affordable Care Act (also called the "ACA" or "Obamacare") contains a number of different provisions that affect a taxpayer's income tax liability and reporting. The net investment income tax of 3.8 percent and 0.9 percent Medicare tax (both discussed in Chapter 6) are additional taxes for certain high-income taxpayers.

Changes to the tax law now leave only one significant tax provision that relates to individuals from the ACA: health insurance premium tax credits. The individual shared responsibility was repealed starting in 2019.

7-4a Premium Tax Credit

Under the ACA, eligible taxpayers may receive a tax credit intended to lower the cost of health care. To be eligible, a taxpayer must meet all of the following requirements:

- Health insurance is purchased through one of the state exchanges or the federal exchange
- The taxpayer is not eligible for coverage through an employer or government plan
- The taxpayer does not file Married Filing Separately except under very limited conditions
- The taxpayer cannot be claimed as a dependent by another

Calculating the premium tax credit is similar to the EIC in that specific tables are required to compute the allowable credit. The credit is intended to take the form of the lesser of (1) actual health care premiums paid or (2) benchmark plan premiums, less the amount the taxpayer is expected to contribute to health care. To calculate the premium tax credit, the following steps are required:

Step 1. Calculate modified AGI for all members of the household. This is AGI for all individuals claimed as a dependent (dependent's income is includable if they are required to file a tax return) adjusted for a number of items including tax-exempt interest and nontaxable Social Security benefits.

Step 2. Compare the household income to the previous year's federal poverty line (FPL). Under the ACA, the FPL is set in the *previous* year during open enrollment (around October). The FPL is defined in three ways: (a) the forty-eight contiguous states and the District of Columbia, (b) Alaska, or (c) Hawaii. The FPL selected is based on the household's state of residence (see FPL amounts below).

Persons in Family/Household	*2022 FPL for 48 States and DC*
1	$12,880
2	17,420
3	21,960
4	26,500
5	31,040
6	35,580
7	40,120
8	44,660
Each additional person	+ 4,540

The household income is then expressed as a percentage of the FPL.

Step 3. The amount of income deemed appropriately spent on health care premiums is then identified on the 2022 Applicable Figure Table shown on Page 7-19. The applicable figure is designed to represent the maximum percentage of income a household will spend on health care premiums.

EXAMPLE Ed and Milly are married with two children under the age of 21. Household income is $53,000. Ed and Milly's household income is at 200 percent of the FPL ($53,000 ÷ $26,500 = 2.0 or 200%). For household income of 200 percent of the FPL, the applicable figure is 0.0200; thus the intended or deemed to be paid for annual health care premiums is $53,000 × 2.00% or $1,060. ♦

Step 4. The amount of the credit is based on comparing the cost of premiums for a designated benchmark plan in the taxpayer's state with the deemed premium cost calculated above. For example, if the deemed annual premium to be paid by the taxpayer is $1,060 and the annual cost of a benchmark plan for that household is $8,000 then the premium tax credit is $6,940 ($8,000 − $1,060). For households that did not have coverage for the entire year, the credit is prorated based on the number of months coverage was maintained.

Step 5. Lastly, the amount calculated in steps 1–4 is compared to the actual premiums paid and the lesser of the two is the premium tax credit (i.e., the credit cannot exceed the actual premiums paid).

EXAMPLE Thus, to continue with the example above, if Ed and Milly paid annual health care premiums of $6,500, their premium tax credit calculated of $6,940 is limited to $6,500. ♦

Self-Study Problem 7.3

Form **2441** | **Child and Dependent Care Expenses** | OMB No. 1545-0074
Department of the Treasury Internal Revenue Service
Attach to Form 1040, 1040-SR, or 1040-NR.
Go to *www.irs.gov/Form2441* for instructions and the latest information.
2022 Attachment Sequence No. **21**

Name(s) shown on return | **Your social security number**

A You can't claim a credit for child and dependent care expenses if your filing status is married filing separately unless you meet the requirements listed in the instructions under *Married Persons Filing Separately*. If you meet these requirements, check this box . . ☐

B If you or your spouse was a student or was disabled during 2022 and you're entering deemed income of $250 or $500 a month on Form 2441 based on the income rules listed in the instructions under *If You or Your Spouse Was a Student or Disabled*, check this box . ☐

Part I **Persons or Organizations Who Provided the Care—**You **must** complete this part.
If you have more than three care providers, see the instructions and check this box . . . . ☐

1 (a) Care provider's name	(b) Address (number, street, apt. no., city, state, and ZIP code)	(c) Identifying number (SSN or EIN)	(d) Was the care provider your household employee in 2022? For example, this generally includes nannies but not daycare centers. (see instructions)	(e) Amount paid (see instructions)
			☐ Yes ☐ No	
			☐ Yes ☐ No	
			☐ Yes ☐ No	

Did you receive **dependent care benefits?**
- **No** — Complete only Part II below.
- **Yes** — Complete Part III on page 2 next.

Caution: If the care provider is your household employee, you may owe employment taxes. For details, see the Instructions for Schedule H (Form 1040). If you incurred care expenses in 2022 but didn't pay them until 2023, or if you prepaid in 2022 for care to be provided in 2023, don't include these expenses in column (d) of line 2 for 2022. See the instructions.

Part II **Credit for Child and Dependent Care Expenses**

2 Information about your **qualifying person(s)**. If you have more than three qualifying persons, see the instructions and check this box ☐

(a) Qualifying person's name — First	Last	(b) Qualifying person's social security number	(c) Check here if the qualifying person was over age 12 and was disabled. (see instructions)	(d) Qualified expenses you incurred and paid in 2022 for the person listed in column (a)
			☐	
			☐	
			☐	

3 Add the amounts in column (d) of line 2. **Don't** enter more than $3,000 if you had one qualifying person or $6,000 if you had two or more persons. If you completed Part III, enter the amount from line 31 . . . **3**

4 Enter your **earned income**. See instructions **4**

5 If married filing jointly, enter your spouse's earned income (if you or your spouse was a student or was disabled, see the instructions); **all others**, enter the amount from line 4 . . . . **5**

6 Enter the **smallest** of line 3, 4, or 5 . . . . **6**

7 Enter the amount from Form 1040, 1040-SR, or 1040-NR, line 11 . . . **7**

8 Enter on line 8 the decimal amount shown below that applies to the amount on line 7.

If line 7 is: Over — But not over	Decimal amount is	If line 7 is: Over — But not over	Decimal amount is	If line 7 is: Over — But not over	Decimal amount is
$0—15,000	.35	$25,000—27,000	.29	$37,000—39,000	.23
15,000—17,000	.34	27,000—29,000	.28	39,000—41,000	.22
17,000—19,000	.33	29,000—31,000	.27	41,000—43,000	.21
19,000—21,000	.32	31,000—33,000	.26	43,000—No limit	.20
21,000—23,000	.31	33,000—35,000	.25		
23,000—25,000	.30	35,000—37,000	.24		

8 X.

9a Multiply line 6 by the decimal amount on line 8 . . . . **9a**

b If you paid 2021 expenses in 2022, complete Worksheet A in the instructions. Enter the amount from line 13 of the worksheet here. Otherwise, enter -0- on line 9b and go to line 9c **9b**

c Add lines 9a and 9b and enter the result **9c**

10 Tax liability limit. Enter the amount from the Credit Limit Worksheet in the instructions **10**

11 **Credit for child and dependent care expenses.** Enter the **smaller** of line 9c or line 10 here and on Schedule 3 (Form 1040), line 2 . . . . **11**

Form 2441 (2022) Page **2**

Part III **Dependent Care Benefits**

12	Enter the total amount of **dependent care benefits** you received in 2022. Amounts you received as an employee should be shown in box 10 of your Form(s) W-2. **Don't** include amounts reported as wages in box 1 of Form(s) W-2. If you were self-employed or a partner, include amounts you received under a dependent care assistance program from your sole proprietorship or partnership			12	
13	Enter the amount, if any, you carried over from 2020 and/or 2021 and used in 2022. See instructions			13	
14	If you forfeited or carried over to 2023 any of the amounts reported on line 12 or 13, enter the amount. See instructions			14	( )
15	Combine lines 12 through 14. See instructions			15	
16	Enter the total amount of **qualified expenses** incurred in 2022 for the care of the **qualifying person(s)**	16			
17	Enter the **smaller** of line 15 or 16	17			
18	Enter your **earned income**. See instructions	18			
19	Enter the amount shown below that applies to you. • If married filing jointly, enter your spouse's earned income (if you or your spouse was a student or was disabled, see the instructions for line 5). • If married filing separately, see instructions. • All others, enter the amount from line 18.	19			
20	Enter the **smallest** of line 17, 18, or 19	20			
21	Enter $5,000 ($2,500 if married filing separately **and** you were required to enter your spouse's earned income on line 19). If you entered an amount on line 13, add it to the $5,000 or $2,500 amount you enter on line 21. However, don't enter more than the maximum amount allowed under your dependent care plan. If your dependent care plan uses a non-calendar plan year, see instructions	21			
22	Is any amount on line 12 or 13 from your sole proprietorship or partnership? ☐ **No.** Enter -0-. ☐ **Yes.** Enter the amount here			22	
23	Subtract line 22 from line 15	23			
24	**Deductible benefits.** Enter the **smallest** of line 20, 21, or 22. Also, include this amount on the appropriate line(s) of your return. See instructions			24	
25	**Excluded benefits.** If you checked "No" on line 22, enter the smaller of line 20 or 21. Otherwise, subtract line 24 from the smaller of line 20 or line 21. If zero or less, enter -0-			25	
26	**Taxable benefits.** Subtract line 25 from line 23. If zero or less, enter -0-. Also, enter this amount on Form 1040, 1040-SR, or 1040-NR, line 1e			26	

To claim the child and dependent care credit, complete lines 27 through 31 below.

27	Enter $3,000 ($6,000 if two or more qualifying persons)	27	
28	Add lines 24 and 25	28	
29	Subtract line 28 from line 27. If zero or less, **stop**. You can't take the credit. **Exception.** If you paid 2021 expenses in 2022, see the instructions for line 9b	29	
30	Complete line 2 on page 1 of this form. **Don't** include in column (d) any benefits shown on line 28 above. Then, add the amounts in column (d) and enter the total here	30	
31	Enter the **smaller** of line 29 or 30. Also, enter this amount on line 3 on page 1 of this form and complete lines 4 through 11	31	

Form **2441** (2022)

2022 Applicable Figure Table

TIP *If the amount on line 5 is 150 or less, your applicable figure is 0.0000. If the amount on line 5 is 400 or more, your applicable figure is 0.0850.*

IF Form 8962, line 5, is . . .	**ENTER** on Form 8962, line 7 . . .	**IF** Form 8962, line 5, is . . .	**ENTER** on Form 8962, line 7 . . .	**IF** Form 8962, line 5, is . . .	**ENTER** on Form 8962, line 7 . . .	**IF** Form 8962, line 5, is . . .	**ENTER** on Form 8962, line 7 . . .	**IF** Form 8962, line 5, is . . .	**ENTER** on Form 8962, line 7 . . .
less than 150	0.0000	200	0.0200	251	0.0404	302	0.0605	353	0.0733
150	0.0000	201	0.0204	252	0.0408	303	0.0608	354	0.0735
151	0.0004	202	0.0208	253	0.0412	304	0.0610	355	0.0738
152	0.0008	203	0.0212	254	0.0416	305	0.0613	356	0.0740
153	0.0012	204	0.0216	255	0.0420	306	0.0615	357	0.0743
154	0.0016	205	0.0220	256	0.0424	307	0.0618	358	0.0745
155	0.0020	206	0.0224	257	0.0428	308	0.0620	359	0.0748
156	0.0024	207	0.0228	258	0.0432	309	0.0623	360	0.0750
157	0.0028	208	0.0232	259	0.0436	310	0.0625	361	0.0753
158	0.0032	209	0.0236	260	0.0440	311	0.0628	362	0.0755
159	0.0036	210	0.0240	261	0.0444	312	0.0630	363	0.0758
160	0.0040	211	0.0244	262	0.0448	313	0.0633	364	0.0760
161	0.0044	212	0.0248	263	0.0452	314	0.0635	365	0.0763
162	0.0048	213	0.0252	264	0.0456	315	0.0638	366	0.0765
163	0.0052	214	0.0256	265	0.0460	316	0.0640	367	0.0768
164	0.0056	215	0.0260	266	0.0464	317	0.0643	368	0.0770
165	0.0060	216	0.0264	267	0.0468	318	0.0645	369	0.0773
166	0.0064	217	0.0268	268	0.0472	319	0.0648	370	0.0775
167	0.0068	218	0.0272	269	0.0476	320	0.0650	371	0.0778
168	0.0072	219	0.0276	270	0.0480	321	0.0653	372	0.0780
169	0.0076	220	0.0280	271	0.0484	322	0.0655	373	0.0783
170	0.0080	221	0.0284	272	0.0488	323	0.0658	374	0.0785
171	0.0084	222	0.0288	273	0.0492	324	0.0660	375	0.0788
172	0.0088	223	0.0292	274	0.0496	325	0.0663	376	0.0790
173	0.0092	224	0.0296	275	0.0500	326	0.0665	377	0.0793
174	0.0096	225	0.0300	276	0.0504	327	0.0668	378	0.0795
175	0.0100	226	0.0304	277	0.0508	328	0.0670	379	0.0798
176	0.0104	227	0.0308	278	0.0512	329	0.0673	380	0.0800
177	0.0108	228	0.0312	279	0.0516	330	0.0675	381	0.0803
178	0.0112	229	0.0316	280	0.0520	331	0.0678	382	0.0805
179	0.0116	230	0.0320	281	0.0524	332	0.0680	383	0.0808
180	0.0120	231	0.0324	282	0.0528	333	0.0683	384	0.0810
181	0.0124	232	0.0328	283	0.0532	334	0.0685	385	0.0813
182	0.0128	233	0.0332	284	0.0536	335	0.0688	386	0.0815
183	0.0132	234	0.0336	285	0.0540	336	0.0690	387	0.0818
184	0.0136	235	0.0340	286	0.0544	337	0.0693	388	0.0820
185	0.0140	236	0.0344	287	0.0548	338	0.0695	389	0.0823
186	0.0144	237	0.0348	288	0.0552	339	0.0698	390	0.0825
187	0.0148	238	0.0352	289	0.0556	340	0.0700	391	0.0828
188	0.0152	239	0.0356	290	0.0560	341	0.0703	392	0.0830
189	0.0156	240	0.0360	291	0.0564	342	0.0705	393	0.0833
190	0.0160	241	0.0364	292	0.0568	343	0.0708	394	0.0835
191	0.0164	242	0.0368	293	0.0572	344	0.0710	395	0.0838
192	0.0168	243	0.0372	294	0.0576	345	0.0713	396	0.0840
193	0.0172	244	0.0376	295	0.0580	346	0.0715	397	0.0843
194	0.0176	245	0.0380	296	0.0584	347	0.0718	398	0.0845
195	0.0180	246	0.0384	297	0.0588	348	0.0720	399	0.0848
196	0.0184	247	0.0388	298	0.0592	349	0.0723	400 or more	0.0850
197	0.0188	248	0.0392	299	0.0596	350	0.0725		
198	0.0192	249	0.0396	300	0.0600	351	0.0728		
199	0.0196	250	0.0400	301	0.0603	352	0.0730		

The premium tax credit can be obtained at two different times: (1) in advance (i.e., as a direct reduction in the monthly health care premiums) or (2) at the end of the year when the tax return is filed. If the taxpayer elects to have the credit paid in advance, the exchange will automatically adjust the premiums to reflect an estimated credit based on estimated household income. Since the actual premium tax credit is not known until household income can be computed after the end of the tax year, Form 8962, shown on Page 7-23, provides a reconciliation of the estimated credit and the actual credit. If the actual credit is greater than the estimated credit, the difference between the two amounts is a refundable credit on the taxpayer's tax return. If the estimated credit taken throughout the year is greater than the actual credit, the difference is treated as additional tax due on the taxpayer's tax return. However, as long as the household income is below 400 percent of the FPL, the repayment amount of the credit is limited:

	Single	*Taxpayers Other Than Single*
Less than 200%	$ 325	$ 650
At least 200% but less than 300%	825	1,650
At least 300% but less than 400%	1,400	2,800
At least 400%	No limit	No limit

Form 1095-A reports the taxpayer's actual premiums paid, the cost of the benchmark plan, and any advance credits received during the year from the exchange on which they purchased the insurance.

Self-Study Problem 7.4

See Appendix E for Solutions to Self-Study Problems

Marco and Tracy Brigantine live in California, are married filing jointly, under age 65, and have three children ages 14, 16, and 26. However, the oldest child is not claimed as a dependent and does not live at home. Tracy's adjusted gross income is $46,490 and Marco's is $49,560 and both are self-employed. They also have $2,000 in interest income from tax-exempt bonds. The Brigantines are enrolled in health insurance for all of 2022 through their state exchange and elected to have the credit paid in advance. Using the Brigantine's 2022 Form 1095-A on Page 7-21, complete the Form 8962 on Page 7-23 to determine the following:

1. The actual premium tax credit (Line 24).
2. The net premium tax credit to be claimed on the return, if any (Line 26) or the excess advance payment, if any (Line 27).
3. The repayment amount required, if any (line 29).

Self-Study Problem 7.4

Form **1095-A** Department of the Treasury Internal Revenue Service

Health Insurance Marketplace Statement

Do not attach to your tax return. Keep for your records.
Go to *www.irs.gov/Form1095A* for instructions and the latest information.

☐ VOID ☐ CORRECTED

OMB No. 1545-2232

2022

Part I Recipient Information

1 Marketplace identifier	2 Marketplace-assigned policy number	3 Policy issuer's name	
12-3456999	34589A	Covered California	
4 Recipient's name		5 Recipient's SSN	6 Recipient's date of birth
Tracy Brigantine		123-44-5555	07/01/1970
7 Recipient's spouse's name		8 Recipient's spouse's SSN	9 Recipient's spouse's date of birth
Marco Brigantine		124-55-6666	09/22/1974
10 Policy start date	11 Policy termination date	12 Street address (including apartment no.)	
01/01/2022	12/31/2022	3167 Kendra Lane	
13 City or town	14 State or province	15 Country and ZIP or foreign postal code	
Poway	CA	92064	

Part II Covered Individuals

	A. Covered individual name	B. Covered individual SSN	C. Covered individual date of birth	D. Coverage start date	E. Coverage termination date
16	Tracy Brigantine	123-44-5555	07/01/1970	01/01/2022	12/31/2022
17	Marco Brigantine	124-55-6666	09/22/1974	01/01/2022	12/31/2022
18	Alex Brigantine	503-11-2222	04/28/2008	01/01/2022	12/31/2022
19	Bryan Brigantine	867-53-0922	01/28/2006	01/01/2022	12/31/2022
20					

Part III Coverage Information

Month	A. Monthly enrollment premiums	B. Monthly second lowest cost silver plan (SLCSP) premium	C. Monthly advance payment of premium tax credit
21 January	965.00	832.00	490.00
22 February	965.00	832.00	490.00
23 March	965.00	832.00	490.00
24 April	965.00	832.00	490.00
25 May	965.00	832.00	490.00
26 June	965.00	832.00	490.00
27 July	965.00	832.00	490.00
28 August	965.00	832.00	490.00
29 September	965.00	832.00	490.00
30 October	965.00	832.00	490.00
31 November	965.00	832.00	490.00
32 December	965.00	832.00	490.00
33 Annual Totals	11,580.00	9,984.00	5,880.00

For Privacy Act and Paperwork Reduction Act Notice, see separate instructions. Cat. No. 60703Q Form **1095-A** (2022)

Self-Study Problem 7.4

Form **8962**

Department of the Treasury
Internal Revenue Service

Premium Tax Credit (PTC)

Attach to Form 1040, 1040-SR, or 1040-NR.
Go to *www.irs.gov/Form8962* for instructions and the latest information.

OMB No. 1545-0074
2022
Attachment Sequence No. 73

Name shown on your return | Your social security number

A. You cannot take the PTC if your filing status is married filing separately unless you qualify for an exception. See instructions. If you qualify, check the box ☐

Part I Annual and Monthly Contribution Amount

1	Tax family size. Enter your tax family size. See instructions	1	
2a	Modified AGI. Enter your modified AGI. See instructions	2a	
b	Enter the total of your dependents' modified AGI. See instructions	2b	
3	Household income. Add the amounts on lines 2a and 2b. See instructions	3	
4	Federal poverty line. Enter the federal poverty line amount from Table 1-1, 1-2, or 1-3. See instructions. Check the appropriate box for the federal poverty table used. a ☐ Alaska b ☐ Hawaii c ☐ Other 48 states and DC	4	
5	Household income as a percentage of federal poverty line (see instructions)	5	%
6	Reserved for future use		
7	Applicable figure. Using your line 5 percentage, locate your "applicable figure" on the table in the instructions	7	
8a	Annual contribution amount. Multiply line 3 by line 7. Round to nearest whole dollar amount **8a** ; **b** Monthly contribution amount. Divide line 8a by 12. Round to nearest whole dollar amount	8b	

Part II Premium Tax Credit Claim and Reconciliation of Advance Payment of Premium Tax Credit

9 Are you allocating policy amounts with another taxpayer or do you want to use the alternative calculation for year of marriage? See instructions.
☐ **Yes.** Skip to Part IV, Allocation of Policy Amounts, or Part V, Alternative Calculation for Year of Marriage. ☐ **No.** Continue to line 10.

10 See the instructions to determine if you can use line 11 or must complete lines 12 through 23.
☐ **Yes.** Continue to line 11. Compute your annual PTC. Then skip lines 12–23 and continue to line 24.
☐ **No.** Continue to lines 12–23. Compute your monthly PTC and continue to line 24.

Annual Calculation	(a) Annual enrollment premiums (Form(s) 1095-A, line 33A)	(b) Annual applicable SLCSP premium (Form(s) 1095-A, line 33B)	(c) Annual contribution amount (line 8a)	(d) Annual maximum premium assistance (subtract (c) from (b); if zero or less, enter -0-)	(e) Annual premium tax credit allowed (smaller of (a) or (d))	(f) Annual advance payment of PTC (Form(s) 1095-A, line 33C)
11 Annual Totals						

Monthly Calculation	(a) Monthly enrollment premiums (Form(s) 1095-A, lines 21–32, column A)	(b) Monthly applicable SLCSP premium (Form(s) 1095-A, lines 21–32, column B)	(c) Monthly contribution amount (amount from line 8b or alternative marriage monthly calculation)	(d) Monthly maximum premium assistance (subtract (c) from (b); if zero or less, enter -0-)	(e) Monthly premium tax credit allowed (smaller of (a) or (d))	(f) Monthly advance payment of PTC (Form(s) 1095-A, lines 21–32, column C)
12 January						
13 February						
14 March						
15 April						
16 May						
17 June						
18 July						
19 August						
20 September						
21 October						
22 November						
23 December						

24	Total premium tax credit. Enter the amount from line 11(e) or add lines 12(e) through 23(e) and enter the total here	24	
25	Advance payment of PTC. Enter the amount from line 11(f) or add lines 12(f) through 23(f) and enter the total here	25	
26	Net premium tax credit. If line 24 is greater than line 25, subtract line 25 from line 24. Enter the difference here and on Schedule 3 (Form 1040), line 9. If line 24 equals line 25, enter -0-. Stop here. If line 25 is greater than line 24, leave this line blank and continue to line 27	26	

Part III Repayment of Excess Advance Payment of the Premium Tax Credit

27	Excess advance payment of PTC. If line 25 is greater than line 24, subtract line 24 from line 25. Enter the difference here	27	
28	Repayment limitation (see instructions)	28	
29	Excess advance premium tax credit repayment. Enter the smaller of line 27 or line 28 here and on Schedule 2 (Form 1040), line 2	29	

7-5 EDUCATION TAX CREDITS

7.5 Learning Objective

Apply the special rules applicable to the American Opportunity tax credit and lifetime learning credit.

The tax law contains a number of provisions that are intended to reduce the cost of education for taxpayers. Educational credits represent the last of these provisions covered in this textbook:

Educational Tax Benefit	*Learning Objective*
Exclusion from gross income for scholarships	2.12
Employer-provided education assistance plans	2.5
Tuition reduction for school employees	2.5
Deduction of business educational expenses	3.6
Student loan interest deduction	5.8
Qualified tuition programs (529 plans)	2.14
Coverdell educational savings accounts	2.14
American Opportunity tax credit	7.5
Lifetime learning credit	7.5

7-5a American Opportunity Tax Credit

The American Opportunity tax credit (AOTC) is an education credit available to help qualifying low-income and middle-income individuals defray the cost of higher education.

The AOTC is a credit for students in their first four years of postsecondary education. The AOTC may be claimed for the expenses of students pursuing bachelor's or associate's degrees or vocational training. To be eligible, the student must meet all of the following:

- Pursuing a degree or recognized credential,
- Enrolled at least half-time for one semester, quarter, trimester, etc. starting during the tax year,
- Received a Form 1098-T from the eligible education institution,
- Not have completed the first four years of higher education at the start of the tax year,
- The AOTC has not been claimed for more than four years, and
- Has not been convicted of a felony drug conviction.

Meeting either of the following criteria precludes claiming the AOTC:

- Married filing separate status, or
- Taxpayer is listed as a dependent on another's return.

EXAMPLE Alice is a single parent filing as head of household. Alice has been taking nursing classes at night to help her improve her job performance at the hospital. Alice has a 19-year-old daughter, Melanie, who is a second-year full-time student at Wake Tech Community College pursing her associate degree in accounting. She might go on to pursue a four-year degree at some later date. Alice claims Melanie as a dependent but Melanie files her own tax return to report the income she earns from her part-time job. Alice claimed the AOTC for Melanie last year. As Melanie is enrolled in school at least half-time, is pursuing a degree, and has not claimed the AOTC for more than four years, she is an eligible student for the AOTC. Although Alice's school expense does not qualify for the AOTC, since she is not pursuing a degree or certification, she may qualify for the lifetime learning credit (LLC) discussed below. ♦

Like many other education tax benefits, the AOTC depends on an accurate computation of "qualified higher education expenses." The table below shows how qualified educational expenses can differ across some of the common education benefits.

Qualifying expenses for the AOTC can be paid on behalf of the taxpayer, his or her spouse, or dependents. As noted previously, expenses paid for room and board, nonacademic fees or for expenses that are not related to the student's course of instruction, do not qualify. Also, expenses for courses that involve sports, games, and hobbies do not qualify for the credit unless the course is part of a degree program. Expenses paid from a gift or inheritance (which is tax-free) do qualify for credits.

EXAMPLE Trinity's grandmother paid Trinity's $4,000 tuition directly to the university. Assuming Trinity meets the qualifying requirements for the AOTC otherwise, Trinity's parents may include the $4,000 as a qualifying expense when calculating the AOTC. ♦

Qualified Educational Expenses

Cost	*Scholarship*	*AOTC*	*Lifetime Learning Credit*	*Student Loan Interest*	*Coverdell*	*QTP (529 Plan)*	*Employer Provided Education Assistance Plan*	*Business Deduction for Work-related Education*
Tuition and enrollment fees	X	X	X	X	X	X	X	X
Course-related Books	X	X	X[a]	X	X	X	X	X
Course-related supplies and equipment	X	X	X[a]	X	X	X	X	X
Room and board				X	X	X		
Transportation				X				X
Certain K-12 education costs					X	X		
Student loan payments						X	X	
Other necessary expenses including special needs services				X	X	X		X

[a] Only if required to be paid to educational institution

Qualifying expenses must be reduced by any tax-free scholarships, grants or other education assistance. Taxpayers claiming the AOTC must have received a Form 1098-T (shown below) and must report the employer identification number of the educational institution on Form 8863.

☐ CORRECTED

FILER'S name, street address, city or town, state or province, country, ZIP or foreign postal code, and telephone number	1 Payments received for qualified tuition and related expenses	OMB No. 1545-1574	
Wake Tech 1909 Fayetteville Blvd. Raleigh, NC 27603	$ 4,000.00 2	2022 Form **1098-T**	**Tuition Statement**
FILER'S employer identification no. 45-3213211 / STUDENT'S TIN 455-22-1234	3		**Copy B For Student**
STUDENT'S name Melanie	4 Adjustments made for a prior year $	5 Scholarships or grants $ 1,000.00	This is important tax information and is being furnished to the IRS. This form must be used to complete Form 8863 to claim education credits. Give it to the tax preparer or use it to prepare the tax return.
Street address (including apt. no.) City or town, state or province, country, and ZIP or foreign postal code	6 Adjustments to scholarships or grants for a prior year $	7 Checked if the amount in box 1 includes amounts for an academic period beginning January–March 2023 ☐	
Service Provider/Acct. No. (see instr.) / 8 Checked if at least half-time student ☒	9 Checked if a graduate student ☐	10 Ins. contract reimb./refund $	

Form **1098-T** (keep for your records) www.irs.gov/Form1098T Department of the Treasury - Internal Revenue Service

EXAMPLE Alice's daughter Melanie is an eligible student for the AOTC. Melanie received a 2022 Form 1098-T from Wake Tech as shown above. Additionally, Alice paid $400 for course-related books and materials related to Melanie's school in 2022. Qualified education expenses for the AOTC are $3,400 ($4,000 of tuition and fees less $1,000 of tax-free scholarships plus $400 for books). ♦

The AOTC is calculated as 100 percent of the first $2,000 of qualified expenses paid, and 25 percent of the next $2,000, for a maximum annual credit of $2,500 per student. The AOTC is phased out ratably for joint return filers with income between $160,000 and $180,000 and for single, head of household, or qualifying widow(er) filers with income between $80,000 and $90,000 (these amounts are not adjusted for inflation). The AOTC is 40 percent refundable, so up to $1,000 (40 percent of $2,500) may be refunded to the taxpayer if the credit exceeds the taxpayer's tax liability.

Many college students earn income and provide some of their own support. As a result, many parents of college-age students start to consider the consequences of claiming a child as a dependent versus allowing the child to claim themselves as a dependent on the student's own tax return (of course, the support test and others discussed in Chapter 1 generally dictate whether a full-time college student can be claimed by their parents). In order to prevent abuse of the AOTC by students attempting to maximize the credit by filing their own tax return, there are special rules related to the refundable portion of the AOTC. If a student under the age of 24, with at least one parent still living, is filing his or her own tax return (is not a joint return), and any of the following apply, they may not claim the *refundable* portion of the AOTC:

- Under age 18 at end of 2022, or
- At age 18 and earned income is less than one-half of support, or
- Over age 18 and a full-time student and earned income is less than one-half of support

EXAMPLE Vance Wilder is a single, 20-year-old full-time student at Harrison College. Vance earned $11,000 from his part-time accounting job and in 2022, provided over one-half of his own support. As a result, his parents no longer claim him as a dependent. Although Vance has a living parent and is not filing a joint return, because he is over age 18 and a full-time student whose earned income is over one-half of his support, he is eligible for the refundable portion of the AOTC. ♦

EXAMPLE Jenny graduates from high school in June 2022. In the fall, she enrolls for twelve units at Gwinett University. Gwinett University considers students who take twelve or more units to be full-time students. Jenny's father pays her tuition and fees of $2,300. The American Opportunity tax credit for Jenny is $2,075 [(100% × $2,000) + (25% × $300)]. ♦

EXAMPLE Jason, a single father, has AGI of $85,000 in 2022 and pays $5,000 in qualified tuition for his son, who just started at Alamance University. Without any limitations, Jason would be entitled to a maximum American Opportunity tax credit of $2,500. However, after applying the AGI limitations, Jason's American Opportunity tax credit is reduced by $1,250 ($2,500 × ($90,000 − $85,000)/$10,000), resulting in a credit of $1,250. ♦

Qualifying expenses must be paid during the tax year for education during an academic year beginning within that tax year. If tuition expenses are paid during the tax year for an academic period beginning during the first three months of the following tax year, the expenses may be claimed during the payment year.

Similar to the child tax credit rules, a taxpayer identification number (Social Security number or individual tax identification number) is required for each AOTC qualifying student by the due date of the return (including extensions).

If the IRS rejects an AOTC for any reason other than a math or clerical error, the taxpayer must complete Form 8862 used for claiming certain credits in a year after a rejection.

In addition, a taxpayer who erroneously claims the AOTC due to reckless or intentional disregard of rules or regulations is ineligible to claim the credit for a period of two tax years. If the IRS determines the claim for the credit was fraudulent, the ineligibility window is extended to ten years.

Unlike the child tax credit and EIC, no time restriction was placed on the IRS issuing refunds for any tax returns that claim an AOTC.

Form 8867, a due diligence checklist for tax preparers is required for returns claiming the AOTC. Failure to file Form 8867 could result in a $560 penalty.

7-5b **Lifetime Learning Credit**

Taxpayers can elect a nonrefundable tax credit of 20 percent of qualified expenses of up to $10,000, for a maximum credit of $2,000. The lifetime learning credit is available for qualified expenses paid for education of the taxpayer, his or her spouse, and dependents. The credit is available for undergraduate, graduate, or professional courses at eligible educational institutions. The student can be enrolled in just one course and still get the credit. There is no limit on the number of years a taxpayer can claim the credit. The credit is not subject to felony drug offense restrictions. The purpose of this credit is to encourage taxpayers to take courses at eligible institutions to acquire or improve job skills.

EXAMPLE In September 2022, Scott pays $1,200 to take a course to improve his job skills to qualify for a new position at work. His lifetime learning credit for 2022 is $240 (20% × $1,200). ♦

The lifetime learning credit is phased out at the same income levels as the American Opportunity tax credit. Joint return filers with AGI between $160,000 and $180,000 and single, head of household, or qualifying widow(er) filers with income between $80,000 and $90,000, must phase the credit out evenly over the phase-out range.

EXAMPLE During 2022, Jason, a single father with AGI of $85,000, paid $2,500 of tuition for a master's degree program in fine arts which he has been attending with the hope of eventually becoming a writer. Without any limitations, Jason would be entitled to a maximum lifetime learning credit of $500 (20% × $2,500). However, due to the income phase-out ranges for the lifetime learning credit, his credit is $250 [$500 × (90,000 − $85,000)/$10,000]. ♦

7-5c **Using Both Credits**

Taxpayers cannot take both the American Opportunity tax credit and the lifetime learning credit for the same student in the same tax year. An American Opportunity tax credit can be claimed for one or more students, and the lifetime learning credit can be claimed for other students in the same tax year. Also, the choice in one year does not bind the taxpayer for future years. For example, a taxpayer can claim the American Opportunity tax credit for a student in one tax year and take the lifetime learning credit for the same student the following year. Taxpayers should claim the credit or combination of credits that provides the best tax benefit. Both the AOTC and the lifetime learning credit are claimed using Form 8863 (see Pages 7-31 and 7-32).

ProConnect™ Tax TIP

Education credits are input under Credits/Education Tuition (1098-T). The typical starting point would be to enter the information obtained from the student's 1098-T.

Self-Study Problem 7.5

See Appendix E for Solutions to Self-Study Problems

a. Judy Estudiante graduates from high school in June 2022. In the fall, she enrolls for twelve units in Southwest University and receives the following Form 1098-T.

☐ CORRECTED

FILER'S name, street address, city or town, state or province, country, ZIP or foreign postal code, and telephone number		1 Payments received for qualified tuition and related expenses	OMB No. 1545-1574	
Southwest University 1234 Cleveland Avenue El Paso, TX 79925		$ 3,950.00 2	2022 Form **1098-T**	**Tuition Statement**
FILER'S employer identification no. 12-7652311	STUDENT'S TIN 434-11-7812	3		**Copy B For Student**
STUDENT'S name Judy Estudiante		4 Adjustments made for a prior year $	5 Scholarships or grants $	This is important tax information and is being furnished to the IRS. This form must be used to complete Form 8863 to claim education credits. Give it to the tax preparer or use it to prepare the tax return.
Street address (including apt. no.) 12 Fannin Street		6 Adjustments to scholarships or grants for a prior year $	7 Checked if the amount in box 1 includes amounts for an academic period beginning January–March 2023 ☐	
City or town, state or province, country, and ZIP or foreign postal code Van Horn, TX 79855				
Service Provider/Acct. No. (see instr.)	8 Checked if at least half-time student ☒	9 Checked if a graduate student ☐	10 Ins. contract reimb./refund $	

Form **1098-T** (keep for your records) www.irs.gov/Form1098T Department of the Treasury - Internal Revenue Service

Judy spends $275.00 on textbooks during the fall semester. Judy's parents, Santiago and Sophia Estudiante, pay her tuition and fees, have AGI of $170,000, have pre-credit tax liability of over $20,000, are claiming no other tax credits, and claim Judy as a dependent. Judy has never been arrested or convicted of any crimes. Complete Form 8863 on Pages 7-31 and 7-32 to determine what is the refundable and nonrefundable American Opportunity tax credit Judy's parents can claim for Judy if they file a joint return.

b. In September 2022, Gene pays $5,200 to take a course to improve his job skills at work. Gene's AGI is $35,000 for 2022. What is Gene's lifetime learning credit for 2022?

Self-Study Problem 7.5a

Form **8863**

Department of the Treasury
Internal Revenue Service

Education Credits
(American Opportunity and Lifetime Learning Credits)

Attach to Form 1040 or 1040-SR.
Go to *www.irs.gov/Form8863* for instructions and the latest information.

OMB No. 1545-0074
2022
Attachment Sequence No. **50**

Name(s) shown on return | **Your social security number**

CAUTION *Complete a separate Part III on page 2 for each student for whom you're claiming either credit before you complete Parts I and II.*

Part I Refundable American Opportunity Credit

1	After completing Part III for each student, enter the total of all amounts from all Parts III, line 30		1
2	Enter: $180,000 if married filing jointly; $90,000 if single, head of household, or qualifying widow(er)	2	
3	Enter the amount from Form 1040 or 1040-SR, line 11. If you're filing Form 2555 or 4563, or you're excluding income from Puerto Rico, see Pub. 970 for the amount to enter	3	
4	Subtract line 3 from line 2. If zero or less, **stop**; you can't take any education credit	4	
5	Enter: $20,000 if married filing jointly; $10,000 if single, head of household, or qualifying widow(er)	5	
6	If line 4 is: • Equal to or more than line 5, enter 1.000 on line 6 • Less than line 5, divide line 4 by line 5. Enter the result as a decimal (rounded to at least three places)		6 .
7	Multiply line 1 by line 6. **Caution:** If you were under age 24 at the end of the year **and** meet the conditions described in the instructions, you **can't** take the refundable American opportunity credit; skip line 8, enter the amount from line 7 on line 9, and check this box ☐		7
8	**Refundable American opportunity credit.** Multiply line 7 by 40% (0.40). Enter the amount here and on Form 1040 or 1040-SR, line 29. Then go to line 9 below.		8

Part II Nonrefundable Education Credits

9	Subtract line 8 from line 7. Enter here and on line 2 of the Credit Limit Worksheet (see instructions)		9
10	After completing Part III for each student, enter the total of all amounts from all Parts III, line 31. If zero, skip lines 11 through 17, enter -0- on line 18, and go to line 19		10
11	Enter the smaller of line 10 or $10,000		11
12	Multiply line 11 by 20% (0.20)		12
13	Enter: $180,000 if married filing jointly; $90,000 if single, head of household, or qualifying widow(er)	13	
14	Enter the amount from Form 1040 or 1040-SR, line 11. If you're filing Form 2555 or 4563, or you're excluding income from Puerto Rico, see Pub. 970 for the amount to enter	14	
15	Subtract line 14 from line 13. If zero or less, skip lines 16 and 17, enter -0- on line 18, and go to line 19	15	
16	Enter: $20,000 if married filing jointly; $10,000 if single, head of household, or qualifying widow(er)	16	
17	If line 15 is: • Equal to or more than line 16, enter 1.000 on line 17 and go to line 18 • Less than line 16, divide line 15 by line 16. Enter the result as a decimal (rounded to at least three places)		17 .
18	Multiply line 12 by line 17. Enter here and on line 1 of the Credit Limit Worksheet (see instructions)		18
19	**Nonrefundable education credits.** Enter the amount from line 7 of the Credit Limit Worksheet (see instructions) here and on Schedule 3 (Form 1040), line 3		19

For Paperwork Reduction Act Notice, see your tax return instructions. Cat. No. 25379M Form **8863** (2022)

Self-Study Problem 7.5a

Form 8863 (2022) Page **2**

Name(s) shown on return	**Your social security number**

CAUTION ***Complete Part III for each student for whom you're claiming either the American opportunity credit or lifetime learning credit. Use additional copies of page 2 as needed for each student.***

Part III **Student and Educational Institution Information.** See instructions.

20 Student name (as shown on page 1 of your tax return)	**21** Student social security number (as shown on page 1 of your tax return)

22 Educational institution information (see instructions)

a. Name of first educational institution	**b.** Name of second educational institution (if any)
(1) Address. Number and street (or P.O. box). City, town or post office, state, and ZIP code. If a foreign address, see instructions.	**(1)** Address. Number and street (or P.O. box). City, town or post office, state, and ZIP code. If a foreign address, see instructions.
(2) Did the student receive Form 1098-T from this institution for 2022? ☐ Yes ☐ No	**(2)** Did the student receive Form 1098-T from this institution for 2022? ☐ Yes ☐ No
(3) Did the student receive Form 1098-T from this institution for 2021 with box 7 checked? ☐ Yes ☐ No	**(3)** Did the student receive Form 1098-T from this institution for 2021 with box 7 checked? ☐ Yes ☐ No
(4) Enter the institution's employer identification number (EIN) if you're claiming the American opportunity credit or if you checked "Yes" in **(2)** or **(3).** You can get the EIN from Form 1098-T or from the institution. __ __ - __ __ __ __ __ __ __	**(4)** Enter the institution's employer identification number (EIN) if you're claiming the American opportunity credit or if you checked "Yes" in **(2)** or **(3).** You can get the EIN from Form 1098-T or from the institution. __ __ - __ __ __ __ __ __ __

23	Has the American opportunity credit been claimed for this student for any 4 tax years before 2022?	☐ Yes — **Stop!** Go to line 31 for this student.	☐ No — Go to line 24.
24	Was the student enrolled at least half-time for at least one academic period that began or is treated as having begun in 2022 at an eligible educational institution in a program leading towards a postsecondary degree, certificate, or other recognized postsecondary educational credential? See instructions.	☐ Yes — Go to line 25.	☐ No — **Stop!** Go to line 31 for this student.
25	Did the student complete the first 4 years of postsecondary education before 2022? See instructions.	☐ Yes — **Stop!** Go to line 31 for this student.	☐ No — Go to line 26.
26	Was the student convicted, before the end of 2022, of a felony for possession or distribution of a controlled substance?	☐ Yes — **Stop!** Go to line 31 for this student.	☐ No — Complete lines 27 through 30 for this student.

CAUTION *You* ***can't*** *take the American opportunity credit and the lifetime learning credit for the* ***same student*** *in the same year. If you complete lines 27 through 30 for this student, don't complete line 31.*

American Opportunity Credit

27	Adjusted qualified education expenses (see instructions). **Don't enter more than $4,000**	**27**	
28	Subtract $2,000 from line 27. If zero or less, enter -0-	**28**	
29	Multiply line 28 by 25% (0.25)	**29**	
30	If line 28 is zero, enter the amount from line 27. Otherwise, add $2,000 to the amount on line 29 and enter the result. Skip line 31. Include the total of all amounts from all Parts III, line 30, on Part I, line 1 .	**30**	

Lifetime Learning Credit

31	Adjusted qualified education expenses (see instructions). Include the total of all amounts from all Parts III, line 31, on Part II, line 10	**31**	

Form **8863** (2022)

7-6 FOREIGN EXCLUSION AND TAX CREDIT

7.6 Learning Objective

Compute the foreign income exclusion and tax credit.

Some of the most sweeping changes to the tax law under the TCJA are related to the taxation of international income but virtually all of these changes were directed at U.S. corporations; with little applying specifically to individuals. However, there are two main provisions related to U.S. taxation of international income that apply to individuals: (1) the foreign income exclusion and (2) the foreign tax credit.

7-6a Foreign Income Exclusion

Certain taxpayers working and living outside the U.S. are eligible to exclude a certain portion of their foreign income from taxable income under the foreign income exclusion. In addition, certain foreign housing can also be excluded or deducted. To qualify, the taxpayer must have a bona fide tax home outside the U.S. for a certain number of days. The exclusion limit in 2022 is $112,000.

EXAMPLE John Adams, a single U.S. citizen, is an employee of a large multinational corporation and works at the company's Mexican subsidiary. He has established a bona fide tax home in Mexico. During the year, John spent 355 days in Mexico and 10 days vacationing in Hawaii. His employer paid him wages of $115,000 in 2022. John excludes $112,000 of his wages from U.S. taxable income. John will not be eligible to claim a foreign tax credit (see below) on the wages excluded. ♦

The foreign income exclusion is claimed on Form 2555. Use of the foreign income exclusion precludes the use of certain credits or deductions (for example, the EITC). In addition, a number of provisions that require the computation of modified taxable income require the foreign income exclusion to be added back (for example, the limits for a deduction for contributions to an IRA).

Employees and self-employed taxpayers that qualify for the foreign income exclusion are also eligible for a housing exclusion or deduction. The foreign housing exclusion is an additional exclusion designed to represent the incremental cost of housing in a foreign country above a base amount. The details are beyond the scope of this textbook.

7-6b Foreign Tax Credit

An individual will typically incur foreign taxes under two possible scenarios: (1) they have engaged in work outside the United States as either an employee or as a self-employed individual (expat) or (2) as a result of foreign investments either directly or through an investment portfolio such as a mutual fund or exchange-traded fund. Although the tax treatment of expats is beyond the scope of this textbook, aside from the benefit available for many expats under the foreign income exclusions described above, an expat may use a foreign tax credit for foreign taxes paid to reduce their U.S. income tax liability. The same is true of an investor whose income is subject to foreign taxes. In both cases, the amount of the credit is limited to the U.S. tax that applies to that income.

EXAMPLE Tom Jefferson, a single U.S. citizen, works for his employer in France and he is not eligible to use the foreign income exclusion. In 2022, Tom paid income taxes in France of $3,500 on his income of $50,000. This was his only income during the year (U.S. or otherwise). Tom claims the standard deduction. Tom's foreign-sourced income is $37,050 ($50,000 less standard deduction of $12,950). His U.S. income for purposes of the foreign tax credit limitation is also $37,050. Tom calculates his U.S. income tax liability before any credits as $4,244. His foreign tax credit limit in this case is:

$$\frac{\text{Net foreign income } \$37{,}050}{\text{Total taxable income } \$37{,}050} \times \text{U.S. tax liability } \$4{,}244 = \$4{,}244$$

Tom's actual foreign taxes paid are $3,500; thus, his foreign tax credit is not limited and he is eligible for a $3,500 foreign tax credit. ♦

EXAMPLE Alexander Hamilton held shares in the Federalist International Stock Fund, a mutual fund with extensive foreign holdings. Alexander's earnings of $2,300 from the fund and foreign taxes paid of $632 were reported to him on a Form 1099-DIV. This was Alexander's only portfolio income during the year. Alexander's taxable income was $75,950 and his tax liability before the credit was $12,332 including Alexander's U.S. tax liability associated with dividend income of $345. Alexander's limitation is calculated as

$$\frac{\text{Net foreign income } \$2{,}300}{\text{Total taxable income } \$75{,}950} \times \text{U.S. tax liability } \$12{,}332 = \$373$$

As a result, Alexander's foreign tax credit is limited to $373. The unused credit of $259 ($632 foreign taxes paid less $373 limitation) can be carried back 1 year or forward for up to ten years. ♦

A number of simplifications were used in the above examples and the actual computation of the limit can be considerably more complex. Different rules apply to income earned in a U.S. possession. The foreign tax credit is typically claimed on Form 1116 and the rules are explained in the instructions to Form 1116.

A simplified foreign tax credit that does not require the completion of Form 1116 is available if you meet all of the following requirements:

1. All of the foreign-sourced gross income was "passive category income" (which includes most interest and dividends).
2. All the income and any foreign taxes paid on it were reported on a qualified payee statement such as a Form 1099-DIV, Form 1099-INT, Schedule K-1, or similar substitute statements.
3. Total creditable foreign taxes aren't more than $300 ($600, if married filing a joint return).

If the Form 1116 is not used, the foreign tax credit is entered directly on Schedule 3 of Form 1040, Line 1. The foreign tax credit is nonrefundable, and thus, limited to the pre-credit tax amount. Use of the simplified method precludes a carryback of any limited foreign tax credit but the unused credit can be carried forward up to ten years.

As a reminder, this is just an overview of these areas which are, in most instances, extremely complex. Useful publications are IRS Publication 54, Form 1116 and instructions, and Form 2555 and instructions.

ProConnect™ Tax TIP

One of the most common ways to pay foreign taxes is through an investment in a mutual fund that happens to hold some international investments and pays foreign taxes at the fund level. The foreign tax payments are generally reported on the taxpayer's Form 1099-DIV and are entered into ProConnect Tax as part of recording the dividend income.

Self-Study Problem 7.6 *See Appendix E for Solutions to Self-Study Problems*

Benny Franklin receives a Form 1099-DIV from his investment manager that lists foreign taxes paid of $432 and Benny's foreign investment earnings of $1,500. Benny had no other investment earnings and his total taxable income for the year is $58,000. Benny's tax liability before any foreign taxes is $8,383. Calculate the amount of the foreign tax credit.

7-7 ADOPTION EXPENSES

7.7 Learning Objective

Determine the proper use and calculation of the adoption credit.

Taxpayers are allowed two tax breaks for adoption expenses. A tax credit is allowed for qualified adoption expenses paid by taxpayers, and an exclusion from W-2 income is allowed for qualified adoption expenses paid by taxpayers' employers.

7-7a Adoption Credit

Individuals are allowed a nonrefundable income tax credit for qualified adoption expenses. Form 8839 is used to calculate and report the adoption credit. The total expense that can be taken as a credit for all tax years with respect to an adoption of a child is $14,890 for 2022. The credit is the total amount for each adoption and is not an annual amount (i.e., there is only one $14,890 credit per adopted child). The amount of the credit allowable for any tax year is reduced for taxpayers with AGI over $223,410 and is fully phased out when AGI reaches $263,410. The amount of the credit is reduced (but not below zero) by a factor equal to the excess of the taxpayer's AGI over $223,410 divided by $40,000. In some cases, beyond the scope of this textbook, AGI must be modified prior to calculating the adoption credit phase-out. For additional information on calculating modified adjusted gross income (MAGI) with respect to the adoption credit, see the IRS website at **www.irs.gov.**

EXAMPLE Ben and Beverly pay $5,000 of qualified adoption expenses in 2022 to adopt a qualified child. Their AGI is $227,410 for 2022, which reduces the adoption credit for 2022 by $500 [$5,000 × ($227,410 − $223,410) / $40,000)]. Thus, Ben and Beverly's allowable adoption credit for 2022 is $4,500 ($5,000 − $500). ♦

The credit is not refundable; however, the unused portion may be carried forward for five years. To claim the credit, married individuals must file jointly, and the taxpayer must include (if known) the name, age, and taxpayer identification number (TIN) of the child on the return.

7-7b Domestic Multiyear Adoptions

In the case of the adoption of an eligible child who is a U.S. citizen or resident of the United States at the time the adoption commenced, the credit for qualified adoption expenses is allowed for the tax year that follows the year during which the expenses are paid or incurred, unless the expenses are paid or incurred in the tax year the adoption becomes final. If the expenses are paid or incurred during the tax year in which the adoption becomes final, the credit is allowed for that year. The full $14,890 credit is allowed in special-needs adoptions regardless of the amount of qualified adoption expenses paid.

EXAMPLE In connection with the adoption of an eligible child who is a U.S. citizen and is not a child with special needs, a taxpayer pays $7,000 of qualified adoption expenses in 2021 and $8,600 of qualified adoption expenses in 2022. The adoption is not finalized until 2023. The $7,000 of expenses paid or incurred in 2021 would be allowed in 2022, and $7,890 of the $8,600 paid or incurred in 2022 would be allowed in 2023. On the other hand, if the adoption were finalized in 2022, then $14,890 of qualified expenses would be allowed in 2022 (the maximum credit permitted as of 2022). ♦

7-7c Foreign Multiyear Adoptions

In the case of the adoption of a child who is *not* a U.S. citizen or resident of the United States, the credit for qualified adoption expenses is not available unless the adoption becomes final. Qualified adoption expenses paid or incurred before the tax year in which the adoption becomes final are taken into account for the credit as if the expenses were paid or incurred in the tax year in which the adoption becomes final. Therefore, the credit for qualified adoption expenses paid or incurred in the tax year in which the adoption becomes final, or in any earlier tax year, is allowed only in the tax year the adoption becomes final.

EXAMPLE In 2020 and 2021, a taxpayer pays $3,000 and $6,000, respectively, of qualified adoption expenses in connection with the adoption of an eligible child who is not a U.S. citizen or resident of the United States. In 2022, the year the adoption becomes final, the taxpayer pays an additional $3,000 of qualified expenses. The taxpayer may claim a credit of $12,000 on their income tax return for 2022 (the year the adoption becomes final). If a foreign adoption does not become final, no credit is allowed. ♦

7-7d Employer-Provided Adoption Assistance

An employee may exclude from W-2 earnings amounts paid or expenses incurred by his or her employer for qualified adoption expenses connected with the adoption of a child by the employee, if the amounts are furnished under an adoption assistance program. The total amount excludable per child is the same as the adoption credit amount ($14,890). The phase-out is calculated in the same manner as the phase-out for the adoption credit. An individual may claim both a credit and an exclusion in connection with the adoption of an eligible child, but may not claim both a credit and an exclusion for the same expense.

Self-Study Problem 7.7

See Appendix E for Solutions to Self-Study Problems

James and Michael Bass finalized the adoption of their daughter Allison in October 2022, one month after her birth. Allison is a U.S. citizen and is not a child with special needs. Her Social Security number is 466-47-3311. In 2022, James and Michael paid $17,000 in qualified adoption expenses. In addition, Michael's employer paid $4,000 directly to an adoption agency as an employer-provided adoption benefit. The Bass' AGI for 2022 is $231,410 (assume adjusted gross income and modified adjusted gross income are the same for purposes of this problem). The Bass' tax liability is $28,300 and they are not using tax credits except the adoption credit. Use Form 8839 on Pages 7-37 and 7-38 to calculate the Bass' adoption credit and the amount of any employee adoption exclusion.

Self-Study Problem 7.7

Form **8839** | **Qualified Adoption Expenses** | OMB No. 1545-0074
Department of the Treasury Internal Revenue Service
Attach to Form 1040, 1040-SR, or 1040-NR.
Go to *www.irs.gov/Form8839* for instructions and the latest information.
2022 Attachment Sequence No. **38**

Name(s) shown on return | **Your social security number**

Part I Information About Your Eligible Child or Children—You **must** complete this part. See instructions for details, including what to do if you need more space.

1	(a) Child's name First	Last	(b) Child's year of birth	Check if child was— (c) born **before 2005** and disabled	(d) a child with special needs	(e) a foreign child	(f) Child's identifying number	(g) Check if adoption became final in 2022 or earlier
Child 1				☐	☐	☐		☐
Child 2				☐	☐	☐		☐
Child 3				☐	☐	☐		☐

Caution: If the child was a foreign child, see **Special rules** in the instructions for line 1, column (e), before you complete Part II or Part III. If you received **employer-provided adoption benefits**, complete Part III on the back next.

Part II Adoption Credit

			Child 1	Child 2	Child 3		
2	Maximum adoption credit per child. Enter $14,890 (see instructions)	2					
3	Did you file Form 8839 for a prior year for the same child? ☐ **No.** Enter -0-. ☐ **Yes.** See instructions for the amount to enter.	3					
4	Subtract line 3 from line 2	4					
5	**Qualified adoption expenses** (see instructions)	5					
	Caution: Your qualified adoption expenses may not be equal to the adoption expenses you paid in 2022.						
6	Enter the **smaller** of line 4 or line 5	6					
7	Enter modified adjusted gross income (see instructions)			7			
8	Is line 7 more than $223,410? ☐ **No.** Skip lines 8 and 9, and enter -0- on line 10. ☐ **Yes.** Subtract $223,410 from line 7			8			
9	Divide line 8 by $40,000. Enter the result as a decimal (rounded to at least three places). Do not enter more than 1.000					9	× .
10	Multiply each amount on line 6 by line 9	10					
11	Subtract line 10 from line 6	11					
12	Add the amounts on line 11					12	
13	Credit carryforward, if any, from prior years. See your Adoption Credit Carryforward Worksheet in the 2021 Form 8839 instructions					13	
14	Add lines 12 and 13					14	
15	Enter the amount from line 5 of the Credit Limit Worksheet in the instructions					15	
16	**Adoption Credit.** Enter the smaller of line 14 or line 15 here and on Schedule 3 (Form 1040), line 6c. If line 15 is smaller than line 14, you may have a credit carryforward (see instructions)					16	

For Paperwork Reduction Act Notice, see your tax return instructions. Cat. No. 22843L Form **8839** (2022)

Form 8839 (2022) Page **2**

Part III Employer-Provided Adoption Benefits

			Child 1	Child 2	Child 3		
17	Maximum exclusion per child. Enter $14,890 (see instructions)	17					
18	Did you receive employer-provided adoption benefits for a prior year for the same child? ☐ **No.** Enter -0-. ☐ **Yes.** See instructions for the amount to enter.	18					
19	Subtract line 18 from line 17	19					
20	Employer-provided adoption benefits you received in 2022. This amount should be shown in box 12 of your 2022 Form(s) W-2 with code **T**	20					
21	Add the amounts on line 20					21	
22	Enter the **smaller** of line 19 or line 20. But if the child was a child with special needs and the adoption became final in 2022, enter the amount from line 19 .	22					
23	Enter modified adjusted gross income (from the worksheet in the instructions)	23					
24	Is line 23 more than $223,410? ☐ **No.** Skip lines 24 and 25, and enter -0- on line 26. ☐ **Yes.** Subtract $223,410 from line 23	24					
25	Divide line 24 by $40,000. Enter the result as a decimal (rounded to at least three places). Do not enter more than 1.000	25	× .				
26	Multiply each amount on line 22 by line 25	26					
27	**Excluded benefits.** Subtract line 26 from line 22 . .	27					
28	Add the amounts on line 27					28	
29	**Taxable benefits.** Is line 28 more than line 21? ☐ **No.** Subtract line 28 from line 21. Also, include this amount, if more than zero, on line 1f of Form 1040, 1040-SR, or 1040-NR. ☐ **Yes.** Subtract line 21 from line 28. Enter the result as a negative number. Also, enter the result on line 1f of Form 1040, 1040-SR, or 1040-NR.					29	

You may be able to claim the adoption credit in Part II on the front of this form if any of the following apply.

- You paid adoption expenses in 2021, those expenses were not fully reimbursed by your employer or otherwise, and the adoption was not final by the end of 2021.
- The total adoption expenses you paid in 2022 were not fully reimbursed by your employer or otherwise, and the adoption became final in 2022 or earlier.
- You adopted a child with special needs and the adoption became final in 2022.

Form **8839** (2022)

7-8 OTHER CREDITS

7.8 Learning Objective

Recognize other basic individual credits.

In addition to the credits discussed previously in this chapter, there are many other credits that are directed at individuals, businesses in general, and specific types of businesses, especially those involved in renewable energy or energy efficiency products. This list of credits is immense, and many are temporary. Table 7.1 provides a partial list of individual credits that are available and the target taxpayer-type who might benefit from such credits.

TABLE 7.1 SELECTED INDIVIDUAL TAX CREDITS

Credit	Target	Comments
Elderly or disabled credit	Taxpayers 65 or over or disabled	$563 to $1,125 depending on filing status. Phases out starting at AGI $7,500 ($10,000 MFJ)
Mortgage interest credit	Individuals with mortgage credit certificate	Credit for certain interest paid up to $2,000 each year
First-time homebuyer credit	Homebuyers before 2011	Credit is in repayment phase

For businesses, there are many unique credits that fit within what is known as the general business credit. Each of the credits are calculated separately but are aggregated into the general business credit on Form 3800 and generally subject to a limitation of 25 percent of the tax liability in excess of $25,000 (the actual limitation is much more nuanced and outside the scope of this textbook). Credits in the general business credit are not refundable. The number of separate credits within the general business credit is immense and constantly subject to change. Part III of Form 3800 lists most of the available credits in any given tax year. Table 7.2 lists a small selection of the over two dozen credits available inside the general business credit in 2022.

TABLE 7.2 SELECTED BUSINESS CREDITS

Credit	Comments
Research and experimentation credit	Credit is a given percentage of incremental additional research and experimentation costs
Work opportunity credit	Credit is a percentage of certain wages paid to workers from targeted hard-to-employ groups
Rehabilitation credit	Credit is a percentage of the costs paid to rehabilitate certain historical buildings
Low-income housing credit	Credit for a certain amount of the cost of low-income housing constructed, rehabilitated or acquired
New markets credit	Credit for a certain percentage of business investment in low-income communities

7-8a Energy Credits

Over the past decade, the tax law has included a number of personal tax credits associated with energy-efficient products. These credits have been slowly expiring. By design, many tax credits are temporary additions to the tax law and are designed to create short-term or limited changes in taxpayer behavior as mentioned in Chapter 1. The status of many of these credits is presented in Table 7.3.

TABLE 7.3 INDIVIDUAL ENERGY CREDITS

Credit	Code Section	Status
Clean vehicle credit	30D	Extended through 12/31/2032
Energy efficient home improvement credit (formerly nonbusiness energy property credit)	25C	Extended through 12/31/2031
Residential clean energy credit (formerly residential energy efficient property (REEP) credit)	25D	Extended through 12/31/2034
Qualified fuel cell motor vehicle credit	30B	Expired at end of 2021

Because credits are often retroactively extended, be sure and check **www.irs.gov** for any changes that may have occurred after we went to print.

Three of the remaining credits are discussed here.

7-8b Clean Vehicle Credit

The former electric vehicle credit underwent substantial changes starting in 2022. The clean vehicle credit has two parts: (1) a $3,750 credit if the critical minerals in the battery are domestically sourced and (2) a $3,750 credit of the battery components are domestically produced. The credit is not available for taxpayers with AGI above $300,000 for married filing jointly, $225,000 for head of household, and $150,000 for all others. The credit is not available for vehicles that have a manufacturer's suggested retail price (MSRP) of over $55,000 or $80,000 if a van, SUV, or pickup truck. For vehicles sold after 2022, the previous production limitations (200,000 units) on a particular model have been repealed.

A new used clean vehicle credit of 30 percent of the price up to $4,000 has been added after 2022 and before 2033. The sales price cannot exceed $25,000. The AGI limits of the used clean vehicle credit are $150,000 for married filing jointly, $112,500 for head of household, and $75,000 for all others. The used clean vehicle credit may not be claimed more than once every three years.

EXAMPLE Greta, a single taxpayer, purchases a new plug-in electric vehicle that qualifies for the clean energy vehicle credit. Her AGI is $80,000. She will claim a $7,500 credit. ♦

7-8c Energy Efficient Home Improvement Credit

Taxpayers may claim a credit of 30 percent of the amount paid for the installation of qualified energy efficiency improvements (building envelope components) or 100 percent of qualified residential energy property expenditures (furnaces and certain fans, central air conditioners, water heaters, and certain heat pumps on or in connection with the taxpayer's principal residence), subject to limitations depending on the type of property installed. The lifetime credits previously in place have been replaced with annual limits such as $600 on exterior windows and skylights, $250 for any exterior door with an aggregate limit of $500 for all exterior doors. Electric or gas heat pumps and water heaters have a $600 per item limit and a $2,000 aggregate limit per year. The energy efficient home improvement credit and the residential clean energy credit are both reported on Form 5695.

7-8d Residential Clean Energy Credit

Taxpayers may claim a credit of 30 percent of the amount paid for qualified solar electric property (property which uses solar power to generate electricity in a home), qualified solar water-heating property, qualified fuel cell property, qualified small wind energy property, and qualified geothermal heat pump property through 2032. Starting in 2023, the credit can be applied to battery storage technology.

The residential clean energy credit may be claimed for both principal residences and vacation homes. No credit is allowed for installations used to heat swimming pools or hot tubs.

EXAMPLE In 2022, Mary buys $30,000 of solar electric property for her second (vacation) home. The equipment is not used to heat her swimming pool or hot tub. She may claim a credit of $9,000 ($30,000 × 30%) for 2022. ♦

Self-Study Problem 7.8 *See Appendix E for Solutions to Self-Study Problems*

Calculate the energy credit allowed for the following purchases:

a. Geoffrey purchases a Nissan Leaf in May of 2022. His 2022 AGI is $100,000.
b. Betty purchases a solar system to heat her hot tub for $2,000 and a second, certified, energy-efficient solar system to heat her home for $10,000 in 2022.

7-9 LOW-INCOME RETIREMENT PLAN CONTRIBUTION CREDIT

7.9 Learning Objective

Calculate the low-income Retirement Plan Contribution Credit.

Certain low-income taxpayers may claim a nonrefundable "Low-Income Retirement Plan Contribution Credit," also called the "Saver's Credit," to encourage them to participate in tax-saving retirement plans, including IRAs. The credit rate is 50 percent, 20 percent, or 10 percent depending on the taxpayer's filing status and adjusted gross income. The credit is a direct deduction from income taxes otherwise payable, and the cash saved may be used to make part of the contribution to the plan. Taxpayers receive up to a 50-percent credit for contribution amounts up to $2,000 ($4,000 married filing jointly) or a maximum credit of $1,000 ($2,000 for married filing jointly). The credit phases out for adjusted gross income over certain income limits, as shown below.

Filing Status/Adjusted Gross Income for 2022—Saver's Credit

		Filing Status		
If AGI is		*Up to $4,000*	*Up to $2,000*	
Over	*But not over*	*Married Filing Jointly*	*Head of Household*	*All Others*
$ 0	$20,500	50%	50%	50%
20,500	22,000	50	50	20
22,000	30,750	50	50	10
30,750	33,000	50	20	10
33,000	34,000	50	10	10
34,000	41,000	50	10	0
41,000	44,000	20	10	0
44,000	51,000	10	10	0
51,000	68,000	10	0	0
68,000	---	0	0	0

EXAMPLE In 2022, Teddy and Abby file a joint tax return with AGI of $29,000. Teddy contributes $1,500 to a Section 401(k) plan at work. Teddy and Abby are entitled to a $750 (50% × $1,500) Retirement Plan Contribution Credit. The credit is in addition to any deduction or exclusion allowed for the contribution. ♦

The Saver's Credit is claimed on Form 8880. Because the Saver's Credit is nonrefundable, the amount of the credit is limited to the income tax liability after reflecting any foreign tax credit, child and dependent care expense credit, educations credits, or credit for the elderly and disabled.

EXAMPLE In 2022, Whitney and Melissa file a joint tax return that reflects AGI of $37,100, income tax liability before any credits of $1,123, and a lifetime learning credit of $240. If Whitney and Melissa contribute $2,100 to an IRA, their Saver's Credit is $883 calculated as the credit amount of $1,050 ($2,100 × 50%) limited to tax liability before the credit of $883 ($1,123 − $240). ♦

Self-Study Problem 7.9

See Appendix E for Solutions to Self-Study Problems

Steve and Robin Harrington are married filing jointly taxpayers, both 61 years of age and semi-retired. Robin earns wages of $32,000 as a part-time school librarian, and Steve sharpens knives as a hobby, and their 2022 AGI is $39,500. Their tax liability before any credit is $1,363. The Harringtons are not eligible for any other tax credits. Neither Harrington is active in any other income deferral plans. Because the Harringtons have limited financial needs, they also made an IRA contribution of $12,000 ($6,000 each) trying to get ready for retirement. Use the Form 8880 on Page 7-43 to determine the Harrington's Saver's Credit.

Self-Study Problem 7.9

Form **8880**

Department of the Treasury
Internal Revenue Service

Credit for Qualified Retirement Savings Contributions

Attach to Form 1040, 1040-SR, or 1040-NR.
Go to *www.irs.gov/Form8880* for the latest information.

OMB No. 1545-0074
2022
Attachment Sequence No. **54**

Name(s) shown on return | **Your social security number**

*You **cannot** take this credit if **either** of the following applies.*

- *The amount on Form 1040, 1040-SR, or 1040-NR, line 11, is more than $34,000 ($51,000 if head of household; $68,000 if married filing jointly).*
- *The person(s) who made the qualified contribution or elective deferral **(a)** was born after January 1, 2005; **(b)** is claimed as a dependent on someone else's 2022 tax return; or **(c)** was a **student** (see instructions).*

			(a) You	(b) Your spouse
1	Traditional and Roth IRA contributions, and ABLE account contributions by the designated beneficiary for 2022. **Do not** include rollover contributions	1		
2	Elective deferrals to a 401(k) or other qualified employer plan, voluntary employee contributions, and 501(c)(18)(D) plan contributions for 2022 (see instructions) . .	2		
3	Add lines 1 and 2	3		
4	Certain distributions received **after** 2019 and **before** the due date (including extensions) of your 2022 tax return (see instructions). If married filing jointly, include **both** spouses' amounts in **both** columns. See instructions for an exception . . .	4		
5	Subtract line 4 from line 3. If zero or less, enter -0-	5		
6	In each column, enter the **smaller** of line 5 or $2,000	6		

7 Add the amounts on line 6. If zero, **stop**; you can't take this credit . . . . . | 7 |

8 Enter the amount from Form 1040, 1040-SR, or 1040-NR, line 11* . . . . | 8 |

9 Enter the applicable decimal amount from the table below. | 9 | x 0.

If line 8 is—		And your filing status is—		
Over—	But not over—	Married filing jointly	Head of household	Single, Married filing separately, or Qualifying widow(er)
		Enter on line 9—		
---	$20,500	0.5	0.5	0.5
$20,500	$22,000	0.5	0.5	0.2
$22,000	$30,750	0.5	0.5	0.1
$30,750	$33,000	0.5	0.2	0.1
$33,000	$34,000	0.5	0.1	0.1
$34,000	$41,000	0.5	0.1	0.0
$41,000	$44,000	0.2	0.1	0.0
$44,000	$51,000	0.1	0.1	0.0
$51,000	$68,000	0.1	0.0	0.0
$68,000	---	0.0	0.0	0.0

Note: If line 9 is zero, **stop**; you can't take this credit.

10	Multiply line 7 by line 9	10	
11	Limitation based on tax liability. Enter the amount from the Credit Limit Worksheet in the instructions	11	
12	**Credit for qualified retirement savings contributions.** Enter the **smaller** of line 10 or line 11 here and on Schedule 3 (Form 1040), line 4	12	

* See Pub. 590-A for the amount to enter if you claim any exclusion or deduction for foreign earned income, foreign housing, or income from Puerto Rico or for bona fide residents of American Samoa.

For Paperwork Reduction Act Notice, see your tax return instructions. Cat. No. 33394D Form **8880** (2022)

KEY TERMS

nonrefundable, 7-2
refundable, 7-2
child tax credit, 7-2
qualifying dependent credit, 7-2
qualifying child, 7-2
nonrefundable child tax credit, 7-3
additional child tax credit, 7-4
refundable child tax credit, 7-4
earned income credit (EIC), 7-6
"negative" income tax, 7-6
child and dependent care credit, 7-13
Affordable Care Act (ACA), 7-15
premium tax credit, 7-15
federal poverty line (FPL), 7-16
applicable figure, 7-16
Form 1095-A, 7-20
American Opportunity tax credit, 7-25
qualified higher education expenses, 7-25
lifetime learning credit, 7-28
foreign income exclusion, 7-33
foreign tax credit, 7-33
adoption credit, 7-35
energy credit, 7-39
low-income Retirement Plan Contribution Credit, 7-41
Saver's Credit, 7-41

KEY POINTS

Learning Objectives	Key Points
LO 7.1: Calculate the child tax credit.	• Credits are a direct reduction in tax liability instead of a deduction from income. • The child tax credit is $2,000 per qualifying child. • All qualifying children must have a Social Security number at the time of filing. • The child tax credit begins phasing out when AGI reaches $400,000 for joint filers and $200,000 for all others. • A portion of the child tax credit in 2022 is refundable. • The child tax credit also includes an "other dependent credit" of $500 for taxpayers with dependents that do not qualify for the child tax credit.
LO 7.2: Determine the earned income credit (EIC).	• The earned income credit (EIC) is available to qualifying individuals with earned income and AGI below certain levels and is meant to assist the working poor. • The EIC formula for calculating the credit is based on the AGI of the taxpayer and the number of qualifying children of the taxpayer. • To compute the credit, the taxpayer must fill out a worksheet calculating the credit from the tables based on earned income from wages, salaries, and self-employment income. • To be eligible for the credit with no qualifying children, a worker must be over 25 years old and under 65 years old and not be claimed as a dependent by another taxpayer.
LO 7.3: Compute the child and dependent care credit for an individual taxpayer.	• To be eligible for the child and dependent care credit, the dependent must either be under the age of 13 or be a dependent or spouse of any age who is incapable of self-care. • If a child's parents are divorced, the child need not be the dependent of the taxpayer claiming the credit, but the child must live with that parent more than they live with the other parent. • The expenses that qualify for the credit include amounts paid to enable both the taxpayer and their spouse to be employed. • For taxpayers with AGI of less than $15,000, the child and dependent care credit is equal to 35 percent of the qualified expenses. For taxpayers with AGI of $15,000 or more, the credit gradually decreases from 35 percent to 20 percent. • Full-time students and disabled taxpayers with little or no income are deemed to have earned income of $250 per month for one dependent and $500 per month for two or more dependents for purposes of calculating this limitation.

	• In determining the credit, the maximum amount of qualified expenses to which the applicable percentage is applied is $3,000 for one dependent and $6,000 for two or more dependents. • Qualified dependent care expenses are limited to the lesser of either spouse's earned income.
LO 7.4: Calculate the premium tax credit available under the Affordable Care Act.	• Certain lower income taxpayers may be eligible for a premium tax credit to offset some or all of the cost of health care purchased through an exchange. • The premium tax credit can be received in advance or at the time the tax return is filed. • The advanced premium tax credit and the actual premium tax credit are reconciled at the time the tax return is prepared. Repayments may be limited.
LO 7.5: Apply the special rules applicable to the American Opportunity tax credit and lifetime learning credit.	• The partially refundable American Opportunity tax credit is 100 percent of the first $2,000 of tuition, fees, books, and course materials paid and 25 percent of the next $2,000, for a total maximum annual credit of $2,500 per student. • The American Opportunity tax credit is available for the first four years of post-secondary education. • Taxpayers can elect a nonrefundable lifetime learning credit of 20 percent of the first $10,000 in qualified expenses for education. • The American Opportunity tax credit and the lifetime learning credit are phased out for joint filers with income between $160,000 and $180,000 and for single and head of household filers with income between $80,000 and $90,000. • Taxpayers cannot take both the American Opportunity tax credit and the lifetime learning credit for the same student in the same tax year.
LO 7.6: Compute the foreign income exclusion and tax credit.	• The foreign income exclusion amount for 2022 is $112,000. • U.S. taxpayers are allowed to claim a foreign tax credit on income earned in a foreign country and subject to income taxes in that country. • Generally, the foreign tax credit is equal to the amount of the taxes paid to foreign governments; however, there is an "overall" limitation on the amount of the credit, which is calculated as the ratio of net foreign income to U.S. taxable income multiplied by the U.S. tax liability. • Unused foreign tax credits may be carried back 1 year and forward 10 years to reduce any tax liability in those years.
LO 7.7: Determine the proper use and calculation of the adoption credit.	• Individuals are allowed an income tax credit for qualified adoption expenses. The maximum total expense that can be taken as a credit for all tax years with respect to an adoption of a child is $14,890 for 2022. • The maximum exclusion from income for benefits under an employer's adoption assistance program is $14,890. • These amounts are phased out if modified AGI is between $223,410 and $263,410.
LO 7.8: Recognize other basic individual credits.	• A tax credit of up to $7,500 for the purchase of new clean vehicle is available, subject to AGI limits and car price limits. • Taxpayers may claim a 30-percent credit of the amount paid for qualified property such as solar electric property and solar water-heating property.
LO 7.9: Calculate the low-income Retirement Plan Contribution Credit.	• Certain low-income taxpayers may claim a nonrefundable low-income Retirement Plan Contribution. Credit, also called the "Saver's Credit," to encourage them to participate in tax-saving retirement plans.

QUESTIONS and PROBLEMS

GROUP 1: MULTIPLE CHOICE QUESTIONS

LO 7.1

1. Which of the following will qualify for the child tax credit of $2,000 in 2022?
   a. A dependent child age 17
   b. A dependent child age 21 and a full-time student
   c. A dependent child age 13
   d. A dependent parent age 67 that lives with the taxpayer

LO 7.1

2. Which of the following best describes the child tax credit?
   a. A $2,000 credit available to taxpayers with AGI under certain limits and children under age 17.
   b. A $500 credit for a dependent that lives with the taxpayer.
   c. A credit for a percentage of the expenses paid for child or dependent care.
   d. A nonrefundable credit based on a percentage of income.

LO 7.1

3. Russ and Linda are married and file a joint tax return claiming their three children, ages 4, 7, and 18, as dependents. Their adjusted gross income for 2022 is $421,400. What is Russ and Linda's total child and other dependent tax credit for 2022?
   a. $2,000
   b. $3,400
   c. $4,900
   d. $6,000
   e. $9,600

LO 7.1

4. Jennifer is divorced and files a head of household tax return claiming her children, ages 4, 7, and 11, as dependents. Her adjusted gross income for 2022 is $81,200. What is Jennifer's total child tax credit for 2022?
   a. $500
   b. $4,500
   c. $6,000
   d. $9,000
   e. $9,600

LO 7.2

5. Which of the following is *not* a requirement to claim the earned income credit?
   a. The taxpayer (and spouse if filing jointly) have a valid Social Security number.
   b. The taxpayer's investment income is less than $4,400.
   c. You cannot claim the foreign income exclusion by filing Form 2555.
   d. You have at least $1 of earned income.

LO 7.2

6. Which of the following taxpayers would most likely be eligible to claim an earned income credit with a qualifying child?
   a. Marco is a single parent and files head of household. Marco's child, Rebecca, obtained her Social Security number after the extended filing deadline for the tax year.
   b. Bart, a single parent filing head of household, has two daughters ages 21 and 25. The 25-year-old is not supported by Bart. The 21-year-old is a full-time student that does not provide more than half of her own support and lived with Bart and his ex-spouse (and the daughter's mother) until August 2022. After the divorce, Bart and the daughter moved to a new home together.
   c. Julia and Todd take care of Julia's elderly mother and provide all of her support.
   d. Howard and Anne (married filing jointly) have two dependent children under the age of 13. Howard's 2022 earned income is $80,000. Anne does not work.

LO 7.2

7. Assuming they all meet the income requirements, which of the following taxpayers qualify for the earned income credit in 2022?
   a. A married taxpayer that lives with their spouse and who files a separate tax return and has a dependent child
   b. A single taxpayer who waited on tables for three months of the tax year and is claimed as a dependent by her mother
   c. A single taxpayer who is self-employed and has a dependent child
   d. a and c above
   e. None of the above qualify for the earned income credit

LO 7.3

8. Which of the following payments does *not* qualify as a child care expense for purposes of the child and dependent care credit?
   a. Payments to a day care center
   b. Payments to the taxpayer's sister (21 years old) for daytime babysitting
   c. Payments to a housekeeper who also babysits the child
   d. Payments to the taxpayer's dependent brother (16 years old) for daytime babysitting
   e. All of the above qualify for the child and dependent care credit

LO 7.3

9. Mabel and Marty are married filing jointly and incurred $8,900 of child care expenses in 2022 for their 6-year-old son. Mabel has earned income of $35,000. Marty is a student and attended classes for eight months in 2022. What is the amount of qualified expenses for which Mable and Marty will determine the allowable child and dependent care credit?
   a. $0
   b. $2,000
   c. $3,000
   d. $4,000
   e. $8,900

LO 7.4

10. Which of the following is *not* a requirement to receive the premium tax credit for health care in 2022?
    a. Health care through the employer is not available
    b. Health insurance is purchased through the state or federal exchange
    c. Income must be below 200 percent of the federal poverty line
    d. The taxpayer cannot be claimed as a dependent

LO 7.4

11. For purposes of determining income eligibility for the premium tax credit, household AGI is
    a. AGI for the taxpayer and spouse
    b. AGI for the taxpayer, spouse, and any other household members required to file a tax return
    c. AGI for the taxpayer, spouse, and any other household members required to file a tax return plus any tax-exempt income
    d. AGI for the taxpayer, spouse, and any other household members required to file a tax return plus any tax-exempt income and nontaxable Social Security benefits

LO 7.5

12. The American Opportunity tax credit is 100 percent of the first ____ of tuition and fees paid and 25 percent of the next ____.
    a. $600; $1,200
    b. $1,100; $550
    c. $2,000; $2,000
    d. $1,100; $5,500
    e. None of the above

LO 7.5

13. Jane graduates from high school in June 2022. In the fall, she enrolls for twelve units at Big State University. Big State University considers students who take twelve or more units to be full-time. Jane's father pays her tuition and fees of $2,500 for the fall semester and in December 2022 prepays $2,500 for the spring semester. In 2022, the American Opportunity tax credit for Jane's tuition and fees before any AGI limitation is:
    a. $5,000
    b. $2,500
    c. $2,200
    d. $2,000
    e. Some other amount

LO 7.5

14. Which of the following costs is *not* a qualified education expense for the American Opportunity tax credit?
    a. Tuition
    b. Student loan payments
    c. Course-related books
    d. Lab supplies required by the course

LO 7.5

15. In September 2022, Sam pays $1,100 to take a course to improve his job skills to qualify for a new position at work. Assuming there is no phase-out of the credit, his lifetime learning credit for 2022 is:
    a. $220
    b. $1,100
    c. $275
    d. $1,000
    e. None of the above

LO 7.5

16. In November 2022, Simon pays $1,000 to take a course to improve his job skills to qualify for a new position at work. Simon's employer reimbursed him for the cost of the course. For 2022, Simon's lifetime learning credit is:
    a. $200
    b. $500
    c. $1,000
    d. $2,500
    e. None of the above

LO 7.5

17. John, a single father, has AGI of $83,000 in 2022. During the year, he pays $4,000 in qualified tuition for his dependent son, who just started attending Small University. What is John's American Opportunity tax credit for 2022?
    a. $0
    b. $1,750
    c. $2,250
    d. $2,500
    e. $4,000

LO 7.5

18. Joan, a single mother, has AGI of $92,000 in 2022. In September 2022, she pays $5,000 in qualified tuition for her dependent son who just started at Big University. What is Joan's American Opportunity credit for 2022?
    a. $0
    b. $1,250
    c. $2,125
    d. $2,500
    e. Some other amount

LO 7.5

19. Becky, a college freshman, works part-time and pays $1,650 of her college tuition expenses. Although Becky files her own tax return, her parents claim her as a dependent on their tax return. Becky's parents file jointly and have AGI of $50,000. What is the amount of American Opportunity tax credit her parents can claim on their tax return for the tuition Becky paid?
    a. $0
    b. $413
    c. $1,600
    d. $1,650
    e. Some other amount

LO 7.6

20. Lucas, a single U.S. citizen, works in Denmark for MNC Corp during all of 2022. His MNC salary is $187,000. Lucas may exclude from his gross income wages of:
    a. $0
    b. $108,700
    c. $112,000
    d. $187,000

LO 7.6

21. Taxpayer L has income of $55,000 from Norway, which imposes a 40 percent income tax, and income of $45,000 from France, which imposes a 30 percent income tax. L has additional taxable income from U.S. sources of $200,000 and U.S. tax liability before credits of $105,000. What is the amount of the foreign tax credit?
    a. $16,500
    b. $35,000
    c. $35,500
    d. $100,000
    e. $45,000

LO 7.7

22. John and Joan pay $16,500 of qualified adoption expenses in 2022 to finalize the adoption of a qualified child. Their AGI is $199,000 for 2022. What is their adoption credit for 2022?
    a. $0
    b. $16,500
    c. $14,440
    d. $14,890

LO 7.7

23. In connection with the adoption of an eligible child who is a U.S. citizen and who is not a child with special needs, Sean pays $4,000 of qualified adoption expenses in 2021 and $3,000 of qualified adoption expenses in 2022. The adoption is finalized in 2022. There is no phase-out of the adoption credit. What are the adoption credits for both 2021 and 2022, respectively?
    a. $0; $7,000
    b. $4,000; $1,000
    c. $4,000; $3,000
    d. $7,000; $0

LO 7.7

24. If a taxpayer does not have enough tax liability to use all the available adoption credit, the unused portion may be carried forward for how many years?
    a. Two
    b. Three
    c. Five
    d. There is no carryforward

LO 7.8

25. Barbara purchased a new Honda Clarity electric vehicle in 2022 for $36,000. Her federal tax credit will be:
   a. $0
   b. $2,500
   c. $5,000
   d. $7,500
   e. $10,000

LO 7.9

26. Virginia and Richard are married taxpayers with adjusted gross income of $43,000 in 2022. If Virginia is able to make a $1,500 contribution to her IRA and Richard makes a $1,500 contribution to his IRA, what is the Saver's Credit Virginia and Richard will be eligible for?
   a. $0
   b. $600
   c. $1,500
   d. $3,000
   e. $4,000

GROUP 2: PROBLEMS

LO 7.1

1. Calculate the total 2022 child and other dependent credit for the following taxpayers. Please show your work.
   a. Jeremy is a single (head of household) father with $80,100 of AGI and has a dependent 8-year-old son.
   b. Jerry and Ann have $100,000 of AGI, file jointly, and claim two dependent preschool (under the age of 6) children.
   c. James and Apple have AGI of $430,300, file jointly, and claim three dependent children (ages 7, 10, and 19).

LO 7.2

2. How does the earned income credit (EIC) produce a "negative" income tax?

LO 7.2

3. List the seven rules that all taxpayers must meet in order to claim the EIC.

LO 7.2

4. List the four rules that apply to taxpayers without a qualifying child in order to claim the EIC.

LO 7.2

5. List the three rules that apply to taxpayers with a qualifying child in order to claim the EIC.

LO 7.2

6. Diane is a single taxpayer who qualifies for the earned income credit. Diane has two qualifying children who are 3 and 5 years old. During 2022, Diane's wages are $19,800 and she receives dividend income of $1,200. Calculate Diane's earned income credit using the EIC table in Appendix B.

LO 7.2

7. Margaret and David Simmons are married and file a joint income tax return. They have two dependent children, Margo, 5 years old (Social Security number 316-31-4890), and Daniel, who was born during the year (Social Security number 316-31-7894). Margaret's wages are $3,000, and David has wages of $14,000. In addition, they receive interest income of $200 during the year. Margaret and David do not have any other items of income and do not have any deductions for adjusted gross income. Assuming the Simmons file Form 1040 for 2022, complete Schedule EIC and the Earned Income Credit Worksheet A, on Pages 7-55 and 7-56. (The EIC table is in Appendix B.)

LO 7.2

8. What is the maximum investment income a taxpayer is allowed to have and still be allowed to claim the earned income credit? Please speculate as to why there is an investment income limit in the tax law.

LO 7.3

9. Calculate the amount of the child and dependent care credit allowed before any tax liability limitations or other credits for 2022 in each of the following cases, assuming the taxpayers had no income other than the stated amounts.
   a. William and Carla file a joint tax return. Carla earned $27,500 during the year, while William attended law school full-time for nine months and earned no income. They paid $3,500 for the care of their 3-year-old child, Carl.
   b. Raymond and Michele file a joint tax return. Raymond earned $83,000 during the year, while Michele earned $139,000 for the year from a part-time job. They paid $17,000 for the care of their two children under age 13.

LO 7.2
LO 7.3

10. Clarita is an unmarried taxpayer with two dependent children, ages 10 and 12. Clarita pays $3,000 in qualified child care expenses during the year. If her adjusted gross income (all from wages) for the year is $21,400 and she takes the standard deduction, calculate Clarita's earned income credit and child and dependent care credit for 2022.

LO 7.2
LO 7.3

11. Redo Problem 10 above except assume that Clarita's earned income is $70,000. Determine the net effect of the additional income on her total credits.

LO 7.3

12. Mary and John are married and have AGI of $100,000 and two young children. John doesn't work, and they pay $6,000 a year to day care providers so he can shop, clean, and read a little bit in peace. How much child and dependent care credit can Mary and John claim? Why?

LO 7.3

13. Martha has a 3-year-old child and pays $10,000 a year in day care costs. Her salary is $45,000. How much is her 2022 child and dependent care credit?

LO 7.3

14. Marty and Jean are married and have 4-year-old twins. Jean is going to school full-time for nine months of the year, and Marty earns $45,000. The twins are in day care so Jean can go to school while Marty is at work. The cost of day care is $10,000. What is their 2022 child and dependent care credit? Please explain your calculation.

LO 7.4

15. Susan and Stan Collins live in Iowa, are married and have two children ages 6 and 10. In 2022, Susan's income is $43,120 and Stan's is $12,000 and both are self-employed. They also have $500 in interest income from tax-exempt bonds. The Collins enrolled in health insurance for all of 2022 through their state exchange but did not elect to have the credit paid in advance. The 2022 Form 1095-A that the Collins received from the exchange lists the following information:

Annual premiums	$9,800
Annual premium for the designated benchmark plan in the state	$10,800

Compute the Collins' premium tax credit for 2022.

LO 7.4

16. Using the information in the previous question, assume that the Collins' Form 1095-A also indicated that the total advance payment of the premium tax credit was $11,200. Calculate the excess advance premium tax credit and the repayment amount for 2022.

LO 7.5

17. What is the reason there are education tax credits in the tax law?

LO 7.5

18. Please explain the difference between the types of education covered by the American Opportunity tax credit and the lifetime learning credit.

LO 7.5

19. Janie graduates from high school in 2022 and enrolls in college in the fall. Her parents pay $4,000 for her tuition and fees.
    a. Assuming Janie's parents have AGI of $172,000, what is the American Opportunity tax credit they can claim for Janie?
    b. Assuming Janie's parents have AGI of $75,000, what is the American Opportunity tax credit they can claim for Janie?

LO 7.5

20. Jasper is single and is a computer software consultant with a college degree. He feels that one of the reasons for his success is that he continually updates his knowledge by taking classes at the local college in various areas related to software design and information technology. This year he spent $2,000 on course tuition and fees.
    a. Assuming Jasper has AGI of $86,000, how much lifetime learning credit can Jasper claim on his tax return? Would the answer be different if Jasper were married and supporting a wife who was not working?

LO 7.6

21. Martha and Lew are married taxpayers with $400 of foreign tax withholding from dividends in a mutual fund. They have enough foreign income from the mutual fund to claim the full $400 as a foreign tax credit. Their tax bracket is 24 percent and they itemize deductions. Should they claim the foreign tax credit or a deduction for foreign taxes on their Schedule A? Why?

LO 7.7

22. Carl and Jenny adopt a Korean orphan. The adoption takes 2 years and two trips to Korea and is finalized in 2022. They pay $8,000 in 2021 and $7,500 in 2022 for qualified adoption expenses. In 2022, Carl and Jenny have AGI of $150,000.
    a. What is the adoption credit Carl and Jenny can claim in 2022?
    b. How much credit could they claim if the adoption falls through and is never finalized?
    c. How much credit could they claim if their AGI was $229,410?

LO 7.8

23. Mike bought a solar electric pump to heat his pool at a cost of $2,500 in 2022. What is Mike's credit?

LO 7.8

24. In 2022, Jeff spends $6,000 on solar panels to heat water for his main home. What is Jeff's credit for his 2022 purchases?

LO 7.9

25. George and Amal file a joint return in 2022 and have AGI of $38,200. They each make a $1,600 contribution to their respective IRAs. Assuming that they are not eligible for any other credits, what is the amount of their Saver's Credit?

GROUP 2:
PROBLEM 7

SCHEDULE EIC (Form 1040)	**Earned Income Credit** Qualifying Child Information	OMB No. 1545-0074
Department of the Treasury Internal Revenue Service	**Complete and attach to Form 1040 or 1040-SR only if you have a qualifying child. Go to *www.irs.gov/ScheduleEIC* for the latest information.**	**2022** Attachment Sequence No. **43**

Name(s) shown on return | **Your social security number**

If you are separated from your spouse, filing a separate return, and meet the requirements to claim the EIC (see instructions), check here ☐

Before you begin:
- See the instructions for Form 1040, line 27, to make sure that **(a)** you can take the EIC, and **(b)** you have a qualifying child.
- Be sure the child's name on line 1 and social security number (SSN) on line 2 agree with the child's social security card. Otherwise, at the time we process your return, we may reduce your EIC. If the name or SSN on the child's social security card is not correct, call the Social Security Administration at 800-772-1213.
- If you have a child who meets the conditions to be your qualifying child for purposes of claiming the EIC, but that child doesn't have an SSN as defined in the instructions for Form 1040, line 27, see the instructions.

- *You can't claim the EIC for a child who didn't live with you for more than half of the year.*
- *If your child doesn't have an SSN as defined in the instructions for Form 1040, line 27, see the instructions.*
- *If you take the EIC even though you are not eligible, you may not be allowed to take the credit for up to 10 years. See the instructions for details.*
- *It will take us longer to process your return and issue your refund if you do not fill in all lines that apply for each qualifying child.*

Qualifying Child Information	Child 1	Child 2	Child 3
1 Child's name If you have more than three qualifying children, you have to list only three to get the maximum credit.	First name Last name	First name Last name	First name Last name
2 Child's SSN The child must have an SSN as defined in the instructions for Form 1040, line 27, unless the child was born and died in 2022 or you are claiming the self-only EIC; see instructions. If your child was born and died in 2022 and did not have an SSN, enter "Died" on this line and attach a copy of the child's birth certificate, death certificate, or hospital medical records showing a live birth.			
3 Child's year of birth	Year ___ ___ ___ ___ *If born after 2003 **and** the child is younger than you (or your spouse, if filing jointly), skip lines 4a and 4b; go to line 5.*	Year ___ ___ ___ ___ *If born after 2003 **and** the child is younger than you (or your spouse, if filing jointly), skip lines 4a and 4b; go to line 5.*	Year ___ ___ ___ ___ *If born after 2003 **and** the child is younger than you (or your spouse, if filing jointly), skip lines 4a and 4b; go to line 5.*
4a Was the child under age 24 at the end of 2022, a student, and younger than you (or your spouse, if filing jointly)?	☐ **Yes.** *Go to line 5.* ☐ **No.** *Go to line 4b.*	☐ **Yes.** *Go to line 5.* ☐ **No.** *Go to line 4b.*	☐ **Yes.** *Go to line 5.* ☐ **No.** *Go to line 4b.*
b Was the child permanently and totally disabled during any part of 2022?	☐ **Yes.** *Go to line 5.* ☐ **No.** The child is not a qualifying child.	☐ **Yes.** *Go to line 5.* ☐ **No.** The child is not a qualifying child.	☐ **Yes.** *Go to line 5.* ☐ **No.** The child is not a qualifying child.
5 Child's relationship to you (for example, son, daughter, grandchild, niece, nephew, eligible foster child, etc.)			
6 Number of months child lived with you in the United States during 2022 • If the child lived with you for more than half of 2022 but less than 7 months, enter "7." • If the child was born or died in 2022 and your home was the child's home for more than half the time he or she was alive during 2022, enter "12."	______ months *Do not enter more than 12 months.*	______ months *Do not enter more than 12 months.*	______ months *Do not enter more than 12 months.*

For Paperwork Reduction Act Notice, see your tax return instructions. Cat. No. 13339M **Schedule EIC (Form 1040) 2022**

GROUP 2:
PROBLEM 7

Worksheet A—2022 EIC—Line 27*

Keep for Your Records 

Before you begin: √ Be sure you are using the correct worksheet. Use this worksheet only if you answered "No" to Step 5, question 2. Otherwise, use Worksheet B.

Part 1

All Filers Using Worksheet A

1. Enter your earned income from Step 5. **1** ______

2. Look up the amount on line 1 above in the EIC Table (right after Worksheet B) to find the credit. Be sure you use the correct column for your filing status and the number of children you have. Enter the credit here. **2** ______

   If line 2 is zero, STOP You can't take the credit.
   Enter "No" on the dotted line next to Form 1040 or 1040-SR, line 27.

3. Enter the amount from Form 1040 or 1040-SR, line 11. **3** ______

4. Are the amounts on lines 3 and 1 the same?

   ☐ **Yes.** Skip line 5; enter the amount from line 2 on line 6.

   ☐ **No.** Go to line 5.

Part 2

Filers Who Answered "No" on Line 4

5. If you have:
   - No qualifying children, is the amount on line 3 less than $9,200 ($15,300 if married filing jointly)?
   - 1 or more qualifying children, is the amount on line 3 less than $20,150 ($26,300 if married filing jointly)?

   ☐ **Yes.** Leave line 5 blank; enter the amount from line 2 on line 6.

   ☐ **No.** Look up the amount on line 3 in the EIC Table to find the credit. Be sure you use the correct column for your filing status and the number of children you have. Enter the credit here. **5** ______
   Look at the amounts on lines 5 and 2.
   Then, enter the **smaller** amount on line 6.

Part 3

Your Earned Income Credit

6. **This is your earned income credit.** **6** ______

   Enter this amount on Form 1040 or 1040-SR, line 27.

Reminder—

√ If you have a qualifying child, complete and attach Schedule EIC.

1040 or 1040-SR | EIC | 1040 or 1040-SR

CAUTION *If your EIC for a year after 1996 was reduced or disallowed, see* Form 8862, who must file, *earlier, to find out if you must file Form 8862 to take the credit for 2022.*

*Download the latest version of this worksheet from the Form 1040 Instructions available at www.irs.gov. The 2022 worksheet was not available as we went to print. This worksheet is adapted from the 2021 version.

GROUP 3: WRITING ASSIGNMENT

RESEARCH

Your supervisor has asked you to research the following situation concerning Scott and Heather Moore. Scott and Heather are married and file a joint return. Scott works full-time as a wildlife biologist, and Heather is a full-time student enrolled at Online University. Scott's earned income for the year is $36,000. Heather does not have a job and concentrates solely on her schoolwork. The university she is enrolled in offers courses only through the Internet. Scott and Heather have one child, Elizabeth (age 8), and pay $3,000 for child care expenses during the year.

Required: Go to the IRS website **(www.irs.gov)**. Locate and review Publication 503. Write a file memorandum stating the amount of child and dependent care credit that Scott and Heather Moore can claim. (An example of a file memorandum is available at the website for this textbook located at **www.cengage.com.)**

GROUP 4: COMPREHENSIVE PROBLEMS

1. David and Darlene Jasper have one child, Sam, who is 6 years old (birthdate July 1, 2016). The Jaspers reside at 4639 Honeysuckle Lane, Apt. 1201, Los Angeles, CA 90248. David's Social Security number is 577-11-3311, Darlene's is 477-98-4731, and Sam's is 589-22-1142. David's birthdate is May 29, 1989 and Darlene's birthday is January 31, 1991. David and Darlene's earnings and withholdings for 2022 are:

David:	Earnings from Apple Company (office manager)	$27,100
	Federal income tax withheld	800
	State income tax withheld	1,050
Darlene:	Earnings from Rose Company (perfume tester)	$26,500
	Federal income tax withheld	1,050
	State income tax withheld	1,000

Their other income includes interest from Pine Tree Savings and Loan of $1,000. David made a $500 contribution to his IRA (he does not have an retirement plan at work).

David and Darlene received the following letter from Sam's daycare provider:

KIDDIECARE INC.
10250 Santa Monica Blvd.
Los Angeles, CA 90067
EIN: 13-3345678

January 14, 2023

David and Darlene Jasper
4639 Honeysuckle Lane Unit 1201
Los Angeles, CA 90248

Dear David and Darlene,

Thank you for your patronage of our day care center with your child, Sam Jasper, in 2022. This statement serves as a record of the cost of daycare services we provided during calendar year 2022:

Child	Amount	Dates of Service
Sam Jasper	$3,680.00	1/1/2022 – 8/25/2022

Sincerely,

/s/ Marcia Clarke

Marcia Clarke
Director, KiddieCare Inc.

Required: Complete the Jaspers' federal tax return for 2022. Use Form 1040, Schedule 1, Schedule 3, Schedule A, Form 2441, Schedule 8812, and Form 8880, as needed. Make realistic assumptions about any missing data.

2A. Steve Jackson (birthdate December 13, 1969) is a single taxpayer living at 3215 Pacific Dr., Apt. B, Pacific Beach, CA 92109. His Social Security number is 465-88-9415. In 2022, Steve's earnings and income tax withholding as laundry attendant of a local hotel are:

Earnings from the Ocean View Hotel	$22,600
Federal income tax withheld	220
State income tax withheld	100

Steve has a daughter, Janet, from a previous marriage. Janet is 11 years old (Social Security number 654-12-6543). Steve provides all Janet's support. Also living with Steve is his younger brother, Reggie (Social Security number 667-21-8998). Reggie, age 47, is unable to care for himself due to a disability. On a reasonably regular basis, Steve has a caregiver come to the house to help with Reggie. He uses a company called HomeAid, 456 La Jolla Dr., San Diego, CA 92182 (EIN 17-9876543). Steve made payments of $1,000 to HomeAid in 2022. Janet receives free after-school care provided by the local school district.

Required: Complete Steve's federal tax return for 2022. Use Form 1040, Schedule 3, Form 2441, Form 8812, EITC Worksheet A, and Schedule EIC.

2B. David Fleming is a single taxpayer living at 169 Trendie Street, Apartment 6B, La Jolla, CA 92037. His Social Security number is 865-68-9635 and his birthdate is September 18, 1977.

David was employed as a cook for a local pizza restaurant. David's W-2 showed the following:

a Employee's social security number	865-68-9635
OMB No. 1545-0008	Safe, accurate, FAST! Use IRS e-file. Visit the IRS website at www.irs.gov/efile
b Employer identification number (EIN)	23-4567321
c Employer's name, address, and ZIP code	California Pizza Cafe 231 Foodie Street La Jolla, CA 92037
d Control number	
e Employee's first name and initial / Last name / Suff.	David Fleming 169 Trendie Street, Apt 6B La Jolla, CA 92037
f Employee's address and ZIP code	
1 Wages, tips, other compensation	24,000.00
2 Federal income tax withheld	1,290.00
3 Social security wages	24,000.00
4 Social security tax withheld	1,488.00
5 Medicare wages and tips	24,000.00
6 Medicare tax withheld	348.00
7 Social security tips	
8 Allocated tips	
9	
10 Dependent care benefits	
11 Nonqualified plans	
12a See instructions for box 12	
12b	
12c	
12d	
13 Statutory employee / Retirement plan / Third-party sick pay	☐ ☐ ☐
14 Other	

15 State	Employer's state ID number	16 State wages, tips, etc.	17 State income tax	18 Local wages, tips, etc.	19 Local income tax	20 Locality name
CA	D4567221	24,000.00	400.00			

Form **W-2** Wage and Tax Statement 2022

Department of the Treasury—Internal Revenue Service

Copy B—To Be Filed With Employee's FEDERAL Tax Return.
This information is being furnished to the Internal Revenue Service.

David's only other source of income during the year was a prize he won appearing on a game show. The game show sent David home with a Form 1099-MISC:

☐ CORRECTED (if checked)

PAYER'S name, street address, city or town, state or province, country, ZIP or foreign postal code, and telephone no.	Price is Accurate Studios Studio 44 Studio City, CA 91604
PAYER'S TIN	21-8675309
RECIPIENT'S TIN	865-68-9635
RECIPIENT'S name	David Fleming
Street address (including apt. no.)	169 Trendie St, Apt 6B
City or town, state or province, country, and ZIP or foreign postal code	La Jolla, CA 92037
13 FATCA filing requirement	☐
Account number (see instructions)	
1 Rents	$
2 Royalties	$
3 Other income	$ 10,000.00
4 Federal income tax withheld	$ 2,400.00
5 Fishing boat proceeds	$
6 Medical and health care payments	$
7 Payer made direct sales totaling $5,000 or more of consumer products to recipient for resale	☐
8 Substitute payments in lieu of dividends or interest	$
9 Crop insurance proceeds	$
10 Gross proceeds paid to an attorney	$
11 Fish purchased for resale	$
12 Section 409A deferrals	$
14 Excess golden parachute payments	$
15 Nonqualified deferred compensation	$
16 State tax withheld	$ 200.00 $
17 State/Payer's state no.	
18 State income	$ $

OMB No. 1545-0115
Form **1099-MISC** (Rev. January 2022)
For calendar year 20 22

Miscellaneous Information

Copy B For Recipient

This is important tax information and is being furnished to the IRS. If you are required to file a return, a negligence penalty or other sanction may be imposed on you if this income is taxable and the IRS determines that it has not been reported.

Form **1099-MISC** (Rev. 1-2022) (keep for your records) www.irs.gov/Form1099MISC Department of the Treasury - Internal Revenue Service

David attended community college full-time in 2022 as a second-year student. He intends to transfer to a four-year university to complete his degree. David received the following Form 1098-T.

☐ CORRECTED

FILER'S name, street address, city or town, state or province, country, ZIP or foreign postal code, and telephone number Windandsea Community College 1300 Genesee Street San Diego, CA 92037	1 Payments received for qualified tuition and related expenses $ 1,800.00 2	OMB No. 1545-1574 2022 Form 1098-T	Tuition Statement
FILER'S employer identification no. 12-7652444 — STUDENT'S TIN 865-68-9635	3		Copy B For Student
STUDENT'S name David Fleming	4 Adjustments made for a prior year $	5 Scholarships or grants $	This is important tax information and is being furnished to the IRS. This form must be used to complete Form 8863 to claim education credits. Give it to the tax preparer or use it to prepare the tax return.
Street address (including apt. no.) 169 Trendie Street, Apt. 6B City or town, state or province, country, and ZIP or foreign postal code La Jolla, CA 92037	6 Adjustments to scholarships or grants for a prior year $	7 Checked if the amount in box 1 includes amounts for an academic period beginning January–March 2023 ☐	
Service Provider/Acct. No. (see instr.) — 8 Checked if at least half-time student ☒	9 Checked if a graduate student ☐	10 Ins. contract reimb./refund $	

Form **1098-T** (keep for your records) www.irs.gov/Form1098T Department of the Treasury - Internal Revenue Service

David's textbooks cost $340. David wishes to claim whatever educational credits he is eligible for. He has not claimed any educational credits in the past and has not been convicted of a felony drug conviction. Unfortunately, David's employer did not provide health care to its employees but David signed up for coverage through his state's health care exchange. The exchange sent him a Form 1095-A as shown on Page 7-61.

Required: Complete David's federal tax return for 2022. Use Form 1040, Schedule 1, Schedule 3, Form 8863, and Form 8962. Make realistic assumptions about any missing data.

Form **1095-A**

Department of the Treasury
Internal Revenue Service

Health Insurance Marketplace Statement

Do not attach to your tax return. Keep for your records.
Go to *www.irs.gov/Form1095A* for instructions and the latest information.

☐ VOID
☐ CORRECTED

OMB No. 1545-2232

2022

Part I Recipient Information

1 Marketplace identifier	2 Marketplace-assigned policy number	3 Policy issuer's name	
31-9876543	B1234TH	Covered California	
4 Recipient's name		5 Recipient's SSN	6 Recipient's date of birth
David Fleming		865-68-9635	09/18/1977
7 Recipient's spouse's name		8 Recipient's spouse's SSN	9 Recipient's spouse's date of birth
10 Policy start date	11 Policy termination date	12 Street address (including apartment no.)	
Jan 1, 2022	Dec 31, 2022	169 Trendie St., Apt. 6B	
13 City or town	14 State or province	15 Country and ZIP or foreign postal code	
La Jolla	CA	92037	

Part II Covered Individuals

	A. Covered individual name	B. Covered individual SSN	C. Covered individual date of birth	D. Coverage start date	E. Coverage termination date
16	David Fleming	865-68-9635	09/18/1977	01/01/2022	12/31/2022
17					
18					
19					
20					

Part III Coverage Information

Month	A. Monthly enrollment premiums	B. Monthly second lowest cost silver plan (SLCSP) premium	C. Monthly advance payment of premium tax credit
21 January	316.00	350.00	152.00
22 February	316.00	350.00	152.00
23 March	316.00	350.00	152.00
24 April	316.00	350.00	152.00
25 May	316.00	350.00	152.00
26 June	316.00	350.00	152.00
27 July	316.00	350.00	152.00
28 August	316.00	350.00	152.00
29 September	316.00	350.00	152.00
30 October	316.00	350.00	152.00
31 November	316.00	350.00	152.00
32 December	316.00	350.00	152.00
33 Annual Totals	3,792.00	4,200.00	1,824.00

For Privacy Act and Paperwork Reduction Act Notice, see separate instructions. Cat. No. 60703Q Form **1095-A** (2022)

GROUP 5:
CUMULATIVE SOFTWARE PROBLEM

1. The following information is available for the Albert and Allison Gaytor family in addition to that provided in Chapters 1–6.

The Gaytors paid tuition and fees for both Crocker and Cayman to attend college. Recall that Crocker is a freshman at Brickell State and Cayman is a part-time student in community college. Crocker received a $1,300 scholarship from Brickell State. Crocker's Form 1098-T is shown below. The Gaytors paid tuition and fees of $1,400 for Cayman in 2022.

☐ CORRECTED

FILER'S name, street address, city or town, state or province, country, ZIP or foreign postal code, and telephone number		1 Payments received for qualified tuition and related expenses	OMB No. 1545-1574	
Brickell State University 605 Crandon Blvd. Key Biscayne, FL 33149		$ 4,950.00 2	2022 Form 1098-T	Tuition Statement
FILER'S employer identification no. 44-3421456	STUDENT'S TIN 261-55-1212	3		Copy B For Student
STUDENT'S name Crocker Gaytor		4 Adjustments made for a prior year $	5 Scholarships or grants $ 1,300.00	This is important tax information and is being furnished to the IRS. This form must be used to complete Form 8863 to claim education credits. Give it to the tax preparer or use it to prepare the tax return.
Street address (including apt. no.) 12340 Cocoshell Rd City or town, state or province, country, and ZIP or foreign postal code Coral Gables, FL 33134		6 Adjustments to scholarships or grants for a prior year $	7 Checked if the amount in box 1 includes amounts for an academic period beginning January–March 2023 ☐	
Service Provider/Acct. No. (see instr.)	8 Checked if at least half-time student ☒	9 Checked if a graduate student ☐	10 Ins. contract reimb./refund $	

Form **1098-T** (keep for your records) www.irs.gov/Form1098T Department of the Treasury - Internal Revenue Service

In December 2021, Albert's 82 year-old aunt, Virginia Everglades (Social Security number 699-19-9000), was unable to support herself and moved in with the Gaytors. She lived with them for all of 2022. The Gaytors provided more than one-half of Aunt Virginia's support. Virginia's only source of income is a small annuity that paid her $3,100 in 2022. While Albert and Allison were working, the Gaytors hired a nanny service from time to time to take care of Aunt Virginia. The Gaytors paid $3,400 to Nannys R Us in 2022. Nannys R Us (EIN 34-1234123) is located at 80 SW 22nd Avenue, Miami, FL 33133.

Required: Combine this new information about the Gaytor family with the information from Chapters 1–6 and complete a revised 2022 tax return for Albert and Allison. Be sure to save your data input files since this case will be expanded and completed with more tax information in Chapter 8.

CHAPTER 8

Depreciation and Sale of Business Property

photosvit/Getty Images

LEARNING OBJECTIVES

After completing this chapter, you should be able to:

LO 8.1 Explain the concept of capitalization and depreciation.
LO 8.2 Calculate depreciation expense using the MACRS tables.
LO 8.3 Identify when a Section 179 election to expense the cost of property may be used.
LO 8.4 Apply the limitations placed on depreciation of "listed property."
LO 8.5 Apply the limitations on depreciation of "luxury automobiles."
LO 8.6 Calculate the amortization of goodwill and certain other intangibles.
LO 8.7 Classify gains and losses from Section 1231 assets.
LO 8.8 Apply the depreciation recapture rules.
LO 8.9 Apply the general treatment of casualty gains and losses for business purposes.
LO 8.10 Compute the gain on installment sales.
LO 8.11 Calculate recognized and deferred gains on like-kind exchanges.
LO 8.12 Calculate recognized and deferred gains on involuntary conversions.

OVERVIEW

The decisions to capitalize an expenditure has significant effects on taxable income. The immediate deduction of a cost versus the slower recovery of a cost over time through depreciation can create a considerable difference in the cash flows of a business. Tax depreciation is largely computed under the Modified Accelerated Cost Recovery System (MACRS) under U.S. tax law. Because the financial impact of depreciation can be significant, lawmakers have frequently created a number of temporary provisions such as bonus depreciation and permanent but limited provisions such as the Section 179 election to expense to accelerate the recovery of costs for property that must be capitalized.

As discussed in Chapter 4, realized gains and losses are generally recognized for tax purposes unless there is a tax provision that specifically allows for a different treatment. This chapter focuses on business-related gains and losses. Transactions covered in this chapter include:

- Section 1231 (business) gains and losses
- Depreciation recapture on business assets
- Installment sales
- Like-kind exchanges
- Involuntary conversions

Unlike capital gains and losses which are generally reported on Schedule D, many business asset sale transactions are reported on Form 4797, and installment sales are reported on Form 6252.

Learning Objective 8.1

Explain the concept of capitalization and depreciation.

8-1 CAPITALIZATION AND DEPRECIATION

In accounting, capitalization is the process of recording an expenditure for an item that is likely to provide benefits over a long period of time (or at least beyond the end of the year) as an asset on the balance sheet as opposed to an expense on the income statement. In Chapter 4 of Statement of Concepts 8, the Financial Accounting Standards Board defines an asset as "a present right of an entity to an economic benefit." The tax law does not provide as elegant a definition, but rather provides that "no deduction shall be allowed for any amount paid out for new buildings or for permanent improvements or betterments made to increase the value of any property or estate." With so little guidance provided in the statutory law, unsurprisingly, a bevy of administrative and judicial law has been constructed to assist taxpayers with the decision as to whether to deduct or capitalize and depreciate. Many times, the choice to capitalize or deduct is obvious.

EXAMPLE Caroline purchases an office building and the land on which it sits for $400,000. The cost of the building and land both must be capitalized. ♦

Other times, especially when related to an improvement or repair to property, the choice is less obvious:

EXAMPLE Tonya owns a building with 22 apartments. The ice maker in the refrigerator of one of the apartments breaks and Tanya has a repairman install a new icemaker for $250. This expenditure could require capitalization or could be deducted as routine maintenance and repairs. ♦

8-1a Capitalization

Generally, an expenditure for property will require capitalization if the expenditure is any of the following:

1. A betterment
2. An adaption to a new or better use
3. A restoration

A betterment is an amount paid to fix a material condition or defect that existed prior to acquisition or that arose while the property was created. Expenditures for material additions including enlargement, extension, or the addition of a major component are generally treated as a betterment. Expenditures that are expected to increase the productivity, efficiency, strength, quality, or output of the property are considered a betterment.

EXAMPLE Troy is adding a new extension to his existing factory building. By enlarging the building, he has an expenditure that qualifies as a betterment and should be capitalized. ♦

EXAMPLE Petro Inc. acquires land that had a leaking underground storage tank. Petro incurs costs to remove the tank and clean up the land. These costs are a betterment as they correct a material defect in the property when acquired. ♦

EXAMPLE Amon-Ra is renovating the lobby of his office building. The footprint of the building will not be enlarged, and the work does not affect the structure of the building. The work is largely decorative and aesthetic in nature. The existing lobby was fully functional prior to the remodel. This expenditure does not qualify as a betterment. ♦

An adaptation is an expenditure that allows the property to be used in a new or different use.

EXAMPLE Carpets R Us owns a building in Georgia that is used as a factory to manufacture carpets. When Carpets decides to move its manufacturing facility overseas, the company incurs the cost to convert the factory building into a retail showroom by making modifications to the structure and systems (for example, HVAC and plumbing) of the building. These expenditures represent an adaptation and should be capitalized. ♦

A restoration is the replacement of a major component, a substantial structural part, or combination of parts that make up a substantial component of the property. A restoration also includes amounts paid to return property to its normal operating condition if the property has deteriorated and is no longer functional for its intended use. Amounts paid to rebuild property to return it to a like-new condition after the end of its useful life are also considered a restoration. Lastly, expenditures to replace property for which a gain or loss and associated basis adjustment have been taken are considered restorations.

EXAMPLE Rexford Soccer Club has a set of bleacher seats that face the northern goal of the soccer field. Because the bleachers have not been maintained, they have fallen into a state of disrepair and cannot be used to seat spectators. Rexford incurs the costs to replace the seats, floors and railings of the bleachers so that spectators may sit in that section again. Because the bleachers were returned to their normal operating condition, the expenditures are a restoration and should be capitalized. ♦

EXAMPLE Fiona owns a building that was partially damaged by a hurricane. She recognizes a casualty loss of $10,000 on the building and thus reduces the building's basis by $10,000. When later Fiona elects to make repairs to the damaged building, the amounts paid to restore the property are considered a restoration and should be capitalized. ♦

If the expenditure does not meet any of the above, the cost can generally be deducted as repairs or maintenance. Costs associated with inventory may require an additional analysis that is outside the scope of this textbook.

Although the guidance on the capitalize versus deduct decision is somewhat voluminous, the decision is not always clear and thus the IRS has created a number of safe harbor provisions that allow taxpayers to treat an item as a deductible repair or maintenance cost if the safe harbor is met.

De Minimis Safe Harbor Election

A taxpayer is permitted to deduct an item of tangible property to the extent that item is deducted on the taxpayer's books and records up to a specific dollar limit. The dollar limit is $5,000 per invoice or item if the taxpayer has applicable financial statements (AFS). For a taxpayer without AFS, the limit is $2,500. AFS are financial statements filed with the

Securities and Exchange Commission, audited financial statements with an accompanying CPA report including those prepared for a creditor, reporting to shareholders, or provided to the state or federal government or agency thereof. Taxpayers with AFS must have a written accounting policy that supports the expensing of de minimis items up to the dollar limit. No written policy is required for taxpayers without AFS, but the books and records of the taxpayer must demonstrate that the policy is being consistently followed.

EXAMPLE Dalvin operates a small business that does not prepare applicable financial statements. Dalvin's accounting policy is to expense any item under $2,000, regardless of the item's useful life. Dalvin may deduct the cost of the same items on his tax return. ♦

Safe Harbor for Routine Maintenance

For non-building property, there is an additional safe harbor associated with restoration costs. Under this safe harbor, costs incurred to restore property can be deducted if the restoration is an activity that would be reasonably expected to be performed at least twice during the useful life of the property.

EXAMPLE Najee takes his business auto in to the auto shop for repairs. The auto undergoes an oil and filter change, a transmission fluid replacement, a brake pad replacement, and also has a leaky radiator replaced. The recovery period of the auto is five years. Typically, Najee's business autos have the oil and filter changed twice a year and the transmission fluid and brake pads changed every two years. The radiator is not normally replaced during the life of the auto. Najee can elect to deduct the costs of the oil and filter, transmission fluid and brake pads under the safe harbor as all of these activities would be expected to be performed at least twice during the 5-year recovery period. The radiator repair does not qualify for the safe harbor and must be capitalized. ♦

Building property has a slightly different safe harbor. The cost to perform restoration activities can be deducted if the activity is expected to be performed more than once during a 10-year period starting when the property was placed in service.

EXAMPLE Cooper Corporation owns a large office building in downtown Metropolis. During 2022, Cooper completed three projects on the building: (1) installed new fiber-optic wiring throughout the building to provide faster connectivity, (2) replaced the plumbing fixtures in a number of the building's restrooms, and (3) replaced the security cameras located on the exterior of the building. The new fiber optic wiring is not a restoration and should be classified as a betterment and thus is not eligible for the safe harbor and should be capitalized. The plumbing fixtures are not routinely replaced by Cooper every 10 years. These fixtures are more than 15 years old. As a result, the cost of the plumbing work does not meet the safe harbor and must be capitalized. The security cameras placed on the exterior of the building are subject to the weather and Cooper expects to replace them about every 4 years. Since the cameras are expected to be restored more than once in a 10-year period, the cost to replace them meets the safe harbor and can be deducted. ♦

These safe harbors cannot be applied to inventory costs or betterments.

Small Business Safe Harbor

Lastly, there is a safe harbor for small businesses with annual gross receipts of $10 million or less and ownership or lease of buildings with an adjusted basis of $1 million or less.

This safe harbor permits the deduction of costs for work performed on owned or leased buildings if the total amount paid during the year does not exceed the lesser of:

1. 2 percent of the unadjusted basis of building property or
2. $10,000

EXAMPLE Ja'Marr qualifies as a small business for safe harbor election. His total unadjusted basis of buildings is $400,000 and he spends $5,000 on new exterior siding for the building. Since the cost is below $8,000 (lesser of $10,000 or $400,000 × 2%), Ja'Marr may deduct the $5,000. ♦

8-1b Depreciation

Since many long-lived assets are used in business production over a number of years, accrual-based income is not properly measured if the entire cost of these assets is deducted in the year the assets are purchased. Depreciation is the accounting process of allocating and deducting the cost of an asset over a period of years. The term *depreciation* does not necessarily mean physical deterioration or loss of value of the asset. In fact, in some cases the value of the asset may increase while it is being depreciated. In Accounting Standards Codification 360-10-35-4, depreciation is defined as follows:

> A system of accounting which aims to distribute the cost or other basic value of tangible capital assets, less salvage (if any), over the estimated useful life of the unit (which may be a group of assets) in a systematic and rational manner. It is a process of allocation, not of valuation.

EXAMPLE Arike operates a small business with two assets: an auto and a building. Although the value of the auto decreases over time and the value of the building increases over time, both will be depreciated for accounting and tax purposes. ♦

Certain assets, such as land, cannot be depreciated for tax purposes. These assets remain on the taxpayer's records at original cost.

Self-Study Problem 8.1

See Appendix E for Solutions to Self-Study Problems

Determine whether each of the following expenditures should be capitalized or deducted or both for tax purposes.

a. Taxpayer pays $12,000 to acquire new tangible personal property (a machine)
b. Taxpayer pays $9,000 to acquire a machine that is not in working condition and spends an additional $3,000 getting the machine ready for use. The taxpayer does not have applicable financial statements or any policies on expensing repairs.
c. Taxpayer incurs cost of $3,000 to perform maintenance on a building system. This maintenance was designed to improve the efficiency of the system.
d. Taxpayer with applicable financial statements and a written policy that calls for expensing all costs under $3,000, purchases ten computers at a cost of $2,000 each.
e. Taxpayer adds a new wing to his factory to warehouse additional supplies at a cost of $16,000.

Learning Objective 8.2

Calculate depreciation expense using the MACRS tables.

8-2 MODIFIED ACCELERATED COST RECOVERY SYSTEM (MACRS) AND BONUS DEPRECIATION

For tax years after 1980, modifications in the tax law were made to encourage capital investment. As a major part of this tax law change, the Accelerated Cost Recovery System (ACRS) was enacted and later modified in 1986 to become the current tax depreciation system referred to as the Modified Accelerated Cost Recovery System (MACRS). The current MACRS allows taxpayers who invest in capital assets to write off an asset's cost over a period designated in the tax law and to use an accelerated method for depreciation of assets other than real estate. The minimum number of years over which the cost of an asset may be deducted (the recovery period) depends on the type of the property and the year in which the property was acquired. The recovery periods are based on asset depreciation ranges (ADRs) as published by the IRS. A schedule of the recovery periods for assets acquired after 1986 is presented in Table 8.1. The recovery period classification for assets acquired after 1980, but before 1987, differs from the recovery period classification presented in Table 8.1.

TABLE 8.1 RECOVERY PERIODS FOR ASSETS PLACED IN SERVICE AFTER 1986

Recovery Period	Recovery Method	Assets
3-year	200% declining balance	ADR midpoint life of four years or less, excluding cars and light trucks.
5-year	200% declining balance	ADR midpoint life of more than four years but less than ten years, cars and light trucks, office machinery, certain energy property, R&D property, computers, and certain equipment.
7-year	200% declining balance	ADR midpoint life of ten years or more but less than sixteen years and property without an ADR life (e.g., most business furniture and certain equipment).
10-year	200% declining balance	ADR midpoint life of sixteen years or more but less than 20 years, including trees and vines.
15-year	150% declining balance	ADR midpoint life of twenty years or more but less than 25 years, including treatment plants and land improvements (sidewalks, roads, fences, and landscaping).
20-year	150% declining balance	ADR midpoint life of 25 years or more, other than real property with an ADR life of 27.5 years or longer and municipal sewers.
27.5-year	Straight-line	Residential rental real estate, elevators, and escalators.
39-year	Straight-line	Other real property purchased generally on or after May 13,1993 (previously 31.5-year straight-line).

Under MACRS, taxpayers calculate the depreciation of an asset using a table which contains a percentage rate for each year of the property's recovery period. The yearly rate is applied to the cost of the asset. The cost of the property to which the rate is applied is not reduced for prior years' depreciation. For personal property (all property except real estate) the percentages in Table 8.2 apply.

EXAMPLE Assume a taxpayer acquires an asset (five-year class property) in 2022 with a cost basis of $15,000 and uses accelerated depreciation under MACRS. The depreciation expense deduction for each year of the asset's life is calculated (using the percentages in Table 8.2) as follows:

Year	Percent		Cost		Deduction
2022	20.00	×	$15,000	=	$ 3,000
2023	32.00	×	15,000	=	4,800
2024	19.20	×	15,000	=	2,880
2025	11.52	×	15,000	=	1,728
2026	11.52	×	15,000	=	1,728
2027	5.76	×	15,000	=	864
Total	100.00%				$15,000

♦

In the above example, note that even though the asset is a 5-year class property, the cost is written off over a period of 6 tax years. This is due to the convention under MACRS which provides for 6 months of depreciation during the year the asset is first placed in service and 6 months of depreciation during the year the asset is fully depreciated, sold, or disposed. This convention is referred to as the *half-year convention* since only one-half of the year of depreciation is allowed in both the year of acquisition and the year of disposition, regardless of the actual acquisition and disposition dates. The half-year convention is built into the rates in Table 8.2.

TABLE 8.2 ACCELERATED DEPRECIATION FOR PERSONAL PROPERTY ASSUMING HALF-YEAR CONVENTION (FOR PROPERTY PLACED IN SERVICE AFTER DECEMBER 31, 1986)

Recovery Year	3-Year (200% DB)	5-Year (200% DB)	7-Year (200% DB)	10-Year (200% DB)	15-Year (150% DB)	20-Year (150% DB)
1	33.33	20.00	14.29	10.00	5.00	3.750
2	44.45	32.00	24.49	18.00	9.50	7.219
3	14.81*	19.20	17.49	14.40	8.55	6.677
4	7.41	11.52*	12.49	11.52	7.70	6.177
5		11.52	8.93*	9.22	6.93	5.713
6		5.76	8.92	7.37	6.23	5.285
7			8.93	6.55*	5.90*	4.888
8			4.46	6.55	5.90	4.522
9				6.56	5.91	4.462*
10				6.55	5.90	4.461
11				3.28	5.91	4.462
12					5.90	4.461
13					5.91	4.462
14					5.90	4.461
15					5.91	4.462
16					2.95	4.461
17						4.462
18						4.461
19						4.462
20						4.461
21						2.231

*Switch to straight-line depreciation.

For property (other than real estate), a taxpayer may elect to use straight-line depreciation instead of the accelerated depreciation rates under MACRS. The taxpayer must use the straight-line MACRS tables for assets for which a straight-line election has been made. The annual percentage rates to be applied to the cost of an asset for which a straight-line election under MACRS has been made are presented in Table 8.3.

TABLE 8.3 STRAIGHT-LINE DEPRECIATION FOR PERSONAL PROPERTY, ASSUMING HALF-YEAR CONVENTION* (FOR PROPERTY PLACED IN SERVICE AFTER DECEMBER 31, 1986)

Recovery Period	% First Recovery Year	Other Recovery Years: Years	Other Recovery Years: %	Last Recovery Year	Last Recovery Years %
3-year	16.67	2–3	33.33	4	16.67
5-year	10.00	2–5	20.00	6	10.00
7-year	7.14	2–7	14.29	8	7.14
10-year	5.00	2–10	10.00	11	5.00
15-year	3.33	2–15	6.67	16	3.33
20-year	2.50	2–20	5.00	21	2.50

*The official table contains a separate row for each year. For ease of presentation, certain years are grouped together in this table. In some instances, this will cause a difference of 0.01 percent for the last digit when compared with the official table.

EXAMPLE On April 1, 2022, Lori purchased and placed in service a specialized computer for use in her business. The computer cost $18,000 and Lori elects to use straight-line depreciation over 5 years instead of accelerated depreciation under MACRS. The annual deduction for depreciation over the life of the computer is calculated below (the percentages are taken from Table 8.3).

Year	*Percent*		*Cost*		*Deduction*
2022	10.00	×	$18,000	=	$ 1,800
2023	20.00	×	18,000	=	3,600
2024	20.00	×	18,000	=	3,600
2025	20.00	×	18,000	=	3,600
2026	20.00	×	18,000	=	3,600
2027	10.00	×	18,000	=	1,800
Total	100.00%				$18,000

Note that Lori receives a deduction based on 6 months in the year of purchase (half-year convention), even though the asset was put into service on April 1. If the asset had been placed into service on September 1, Lori still would have received a deduction for six months of depreciation. ♦

Under MACRS, the same method of depreciation (accelerated or straight-line) must be used for all property in a given class placed in service during that year.

8-2a Mid-Quarter Convention

When a taxpayer acquires a significant amount of assets during the last quarter of the tax year, the half-year convention, referred to in the above examples, is replaced by the *mid-quarter convention*. The mid-quarter convention must be applied if more than 40 percent of the total cost of a taxpayer's property acquired during the year, other than real property, is placed in service during the last three months of the tax year. The mid-quarter convention treats all property placed in service during any quarter of the tax year as being placed in service on the midpoint of the quarter. The mid-quarter convention, if applied in the year the asset is acquired, also applies upon the disposition of the asset. Assets placed in service and disposed of during the same tax year are not considered in determining

TABLE 8.4 ACCELERATED DEPRECIATION FOR PERSONAL PROPERTY ASSUMING MID-QUARTER CONVENTION* (FOR PROPERTY PLACED IN SERVICE AFTER DECEMBER 31, 1986)

Recovery Year	3-Year (200% DB)	5-Year (200% DB)	7-Year (200% DB)
First Quarter			
1	58.33	35.00	25.00
2	27.78	26.00	21.43
3	12.35	15.60	15.31
4	1.54	11.01	10.93
5		11.01	8.75
Second Quarter			
1	41.67	25.00	17.85
2	38.89	30.00	23.47
3	14.14	18.00	16.76
4	5.30	11.37	11.97
5		11.37	8.87
Third Quarter			
1	25.00	15.00	10.71
2	50.00	34.00	25.51
3	16.67	20.40	18.22
4	8.33	12.24	13.02
5		11.30	9.30
Fourth Quarter			
1	8.33	5.00	3.57
2	61.11	38.00	27.55
3	20.37	22.80	19.68
4	10.19	13.68	14.06
5		10.94	10.04

*For ease of presentation, only 3-year, 5-year, and 7-year property and only depreciation rates for the first 5 years are provided. The official table also includes 10- ,15- , and 20-year property. See IRS Publication 946 for the complete table.

whether the taxpayer meets the 40-percent test. An excerpt from the mid-quarter tables can be found in Table 8.4. Complete mid-quarter tables may be found in IRS Publication 946.

EXAMPLE Jane, a calendar-year taxpayer, purchases the following property during 2022 for use in her business:

Placed in Service	*Property*	*Original Cost*	*Recovery Period*
March 2	Office furniture	$ 3,000	7 years
July 31	Apartment building	200,000	27.5 years
November 1	Automobile	18,000	5 years

Jane does not elect Section 179 and elects out of bonus depreciation. The cost of the automobile acquired during the last three months of the year represents 86 percent of the total cost of assets, other than real property, acquired during the tax year. Since more than 40 percent of Jane's purchases, other than real property, were made during the last three months of the tax year, the mid-quarter convention would apply. Depreciation for 2022 on the furniture is $750 ($3,000 × 25%) and on the auto is $900 ($18,000 × 5%). ♦

8-2b Bonus Depreciation

Because the cost recovery of long-lived assets occurs over many years, one way to lower the after-tax cost of capitalized expenditures is through accelerated depreciation. At times, the tax law has provided for "bonus depreciation," which is the immediate deduction of all or some of the cost of otherwise slowly depreciated property. The TCJA increased the bonus depreciation percentage to 100 percent for qualified property acquired and placed in service after September 27, 2017, and through December 31, 2022 (certain long-lived assets have an additional year), but the 100-percent bonus depreciation phases out starting in 2023 as follows:

Year	*Bonus Percentage*
2023	80
2024	60
2025	40
2026	20
2027	0

The bonus depreciation rules allow taxpayers purchasing property with a MACRS recovery period of 20 years or less (see Table 8.1), computer software, and qualified improvement property to directly write off up to 100 percent of the cost of the assets in the year placed in service. Bonus depreciation is presumed to apply unless the taxpayer elects out of the provision. The taxable income limits and thresholds associated with Section 179 (see LO 8.3) do not apply to bonus depreciation.

Both new and used property are generally eligible for bonus depreciation.

EXAMPLE Mary places a new 5-year MACRS-class machine costing $20,000 into service on March 1, 2022. She does not elect out of bonus depreciation on the machine. The bonus depreciation on the machine for 2022 is $20,000. The basis is reduced to $0 and no additional MACRS depreciation on the machine is deducted. ♦

Between bonus depreciation and the expanded immediate expensing under Section 179, small businesses are not likely to capitalize the cost of any non-real property unless they have a net operating loss or anticipate using larger depreciation deductions during higher tax bracket years in the future.

In previous years, certain categories of real property qualified for bonus depreciation. For example, qualified leasehold improvements were eligible for bonus depreciation if placed in service before 2016. Currently, qualified improvement property (QIP) has a 15-year life and is eligible for bonus depreciation. QIP is defined as an internal improvement to nonresidential property, excluding escalators, elevators, internal structural framework, and enlargements to the building.

EXAMPLE In 2022, Bordeaux decided to upgrade the office building that it owns. The lobby area was completely redesigned to reflect the current standards for security and aesthetics. Also, additional space was added to the rear of the building to provide for storage for some high-value goods that need additional security not available in the existing building. The redesign of the lobby (unless changes were made to the structure of the building) is likely to qualify for bonus depreciation, whereas the expansion for additional space will not. ♦

Bonus depreciation starts to decrease in years after 2022. In 2023, the percentage eligible for immediate write-off is reduced to 80 percent and decreases by 20 percent every year until 2027.

8-2c Real Estate

For real estate acquired after 1986, MACRS requires the property to be depreciated using the straight-line method. The straight-line MACRS realty tables for residential realty (e.g., an apartment building) provide for depreciation over 27.5 years. Nonresidential realty (e.g., an office building) is depreciated over 39 years (31.5 years for realty acquired generally before May 13, 1993). The annual depreciation percentages for real estate under MACRS are shown in Table 8.5.

TABLE 8.5 STRAIGHT-LINE DEPRECIATION FOR REAL PROPERTY ASSUMING MID-MONTH CONVENTION* 27.5-YEAR RESIDENTIAL REAL PROPERTY

The applicable annual percentage is (use the column for the month in the first year the property is placed in service):

Recovery Year(s)	1	2	3	4	5	6	7	8	9	10	11	12
1	3.485	3.182	2.879	2.576	2.273	1.970	1.667	1.364	1.061	0.758	0.455	0.152
2–18	3.636	3.636	3.636	3.636	3.636	3.636	3.636	3.636	3.636	3.636	3.636	3.636
19–27	3.637	3.637	3.637	3.637	3.637	3.637	3.637	3.637	3.637	3.637	3.637	3.637
28	1.970	2.273	2.576	2.879	3.182	3.485	3.636	3.636	3.636	3.636	3.636	3.636
29	0.000	0.000	0.000	0.000	0.000	0.000	0.152	0.455	0.758	1.061	1.364	1.667

39-Year Nonresidential Real Property

The applicable annual percentage is (use the column for the month in the first year the property is placed in service):

Recovery Year(s)	1	2	3	4	5	6	7	8	9	10	11	12
1	2.461	2.247	2.033	1.819	1.605	1.391	1.177	0.963	0.749	0.535	0.321	0.107
2–39	2.564	2.564	2.564	2.564	2.564	2.564	2.564	2.564	2.564	2.564	2.564	2.564
40	0.107	0.321	0.535	0.749	0.963	1.177	1.391	1.605	1.819	2.033	2.247	2.461

*The official tables contain a separate row for each year. For ease of presentation, certain years are grouped together in these two tables. In some instances, this will produce a difference of 0.001 percent when compared with the official tables.

EXAMPLE Carlos purchases a rental house on September 3, 2022, for $90,000 (the land is accounted for separately). The house is already rented to a tenant. The annual depreciation expense deduction under MACRS for each of the first 4 years is illustrated below (the percentages are taken from Table 8.5, 27.5-Year Residential Real Property).

Year	*Percent*		*Cost*		*Deduction*
2022	1.061	×	$90,000	=	$ 955
2023	3.636	×	90,000	=	3,272
2024	3.636	×	90,000	=	3,272
2025	3.636	×	90,000	=	3,272

Note that the percentages are taken from Table 8.5 under column 9, because the month of acquisition (September) is the ninth month of the year. ♦

Most real property (except QIP) is not eligible for bonus depreciation or Section 179 immediate expensing (see LO 8.3).

8-2d Mid-Month Convention

For the depreciation of real property under MACRS, a *mid-month convention* replaces the half-year convention. Real estate is treated as placed in service in the middle of the month the property is placed in service. Likewise, a disposition during a month is treated as occurring on the midpoint of such month. For example, under the mid-month convention, an asset purchased and placed in service on April 2 is treated as being placed in service on April 15. The mid-month convention is built into the first year's rates in Table 8.5.

8-2e Reporting Depreciation Expense

Depreciation expense is reported on Form 4562, Depreciation and Amortization. Individual taxpayers who have no current year asset additions and who are not reporting depreciation on listed property (see LO 8.4) are not required to file Form 4562 with their federal tax return.

ProConnect™ Tax TIP

ProConnect Tax includes a powerful depreciation calculator included as part of the software. There are two ways to report depreciation. The first method is to enter the property details into the software. Property can be entered through either a quick entry or detailed input screen, both of which are located under Deductions. The first subheading in the left-hand margin is Depreciation. The property is linked to a business (for example, Schedule C or Schedule E). Based on the type and cost of property placed in service, the software will automatically apply bonus depreciation ("SDA") unless overridden in the detail screen. Section 179 immediate expensing can be input directly. The second method is to compute depreciation outside the ProConnect Tax software and input the deduction as an override. The screens for direct input are located under the normal depreciation screens in the left-hand margin.

Self-Study Problem 8.2 *See Appendix E for Solutions to Self-Study Problems*

During 2022, Mary Moser purchases the following items for use in her business:

Manufacturing equipment (7-year property, placed in service August 1)	$ 11,000
Office furniture (7-year property, placed in service December 15)	6,000
Office building, land is accounted for separately (placed in service April 30)	180,000

Assume that Mary uses the accelerated depreciation method under MACRS.

a. Use page 1 of Form 4562 on Page 8-15 to report Mary's depreciation deduction for 2022 including bonus depreciation.

b. Calculate Mary's depreciation on each property (but do not complete Form 4562) assuming she elects out of bonus depreciation.

c. Calculate Mary's depreciation deduction on the assets for 2023 (Year 2). Compute amounts assuming bonus depreciation was taken in 2022.

8-3 ELECTION TO EXPENSE (SECTION 179)

8.3 Learning Objective

Identify when a Section 179 election to expense the cost of property may be used.

As part of the landmark Tax Reform Act of 1986, Internal Revenue Code Section 179 was implemented to decrease the cost of investments in business property by permitting small businesses to expense the costs of certain property that would otherwise be capitalized and depreciated over time.

Under Section 179, taxpayers may elect to expense the acquisition cost of certain property, subject to certain limitations. This cost would otherwise have been deducted over a period of time using the regular cost recovery depreciation rules. Similar to bonus depreciation, the Section 179 deduction applies to both new and used property. Property that qualifies for Section 179 includes personal property (property other than real estate), QIP, and improvements to nonresidential real property that are placed in service after the nonresidential real property was first placed in service, such as roofs; heating, ventilation, and air-conditioning property; fire protection and alarm systems; and security systems.

Section 179 places three limitations on the expensing election: (1) a maximum on the annual amount expensed, (2) a phase-out of the annual amount limit, and (3) the taxable income limit.

Originally, the maximum annual expensing amount was a modest $10,000. Over the years the amount was adjusted for inflation and also increased with economic stimulus in mind. As a result of the financial crisis, the annual maximum was increased to $250,000 in 2008 and then increased again to $500,000 in 2010. Although subject to repeated expiration and extension, the limit had remained at $500,000 until 2015 when it was made permanent and subject to inflation adjustment each year. The maximum annual amount that can be expensed under Section 179 is $1,080,000 in 2022.

The annual maximum expense amount is reduced dollar-for-dollar by the amount of Section 179 property acquired during the year in excess of a threshold amount. Similar to the annual limit, the Section 179 phase-out threshold amount has fluctuated over time. In 2022, the threshold is $2,700,000. As a result, a taxpayer that acquires $3,780,000 or more of Section 179 property during 2022 may not immediately expense in 2022 under Section 179.

Lastly, the amount of acquired qualified property that may be expensed annually is limited to the taxpayer's taxable income, before considering any amount expensed under the Section 179 election, from any trade or business of the taxpayer. Any amount which is limited due to the taxable income limitation may be carried over to succeeding tax years.

EXAMPLE During 2022, Bob buys used equipment that cost $1,520,000 for his factory. Bob's business generates taxable income of well over $3,000,000 and he elects out of bonus depreciation. Bob's Section 179 property placed in service is below $2,700,000 and thus is not subject to phase-out. With $3 million in taxable income, Bob's Section 179 deduction is not subject to the income limitation. Bob may immediately expense $1,080,000 of his equipment. The remaining $440,000 of equipment cost will be depreciated over the recovery period under MACRS. ♦

EXAMPLE During 2022, Shuri places in service used manufacturing equipment for use in her business. The machinery cost $2,000,000. Shuri has taxable income (after considering any MACRS depreciation) from her business of $200,000. Under the annual maximum limitation, Shuri can immediately expense up to $1,080,000 and would depreciate the remaining $20,000 under MACRS. However, the maximum amount allowed under the taxable income limitation is only $200,000. The remaining $880,000 ($1,080,000 annual maximum less $200,000 permitted under the income limit) is carried forward to succeeding tax years. ♦

EXAMPLE During 2022, Portia purchased $2,760,000 of new equipment for use in her business. Portia's taxable income before considering immediate expensing is over $4 million. Because the amount of Section 179 property placed in service during the year exceeds the phase-out threshold of $2,700,000, Portia's annual Section 179 expensing limit of $1,080,000 is reduced by the $60,000 phase-out ($2,760,000 − $2,700,000), resulting in a maximum allowable expensing amount of only $1,020,000 ($1,080,000 − $60,000). ♦

A taxpayer who has made the Section 179 election to expense must reduce the basis of the asset by the amount expensed before calculating regular MACRS depreciation on the remaining cost of the asset. Even if the taxpayer is not able to deduct the full amount expensed in the current year due to the *taxable income limitation,* the basis must be reduced by the full amount of the Section 179 expense election.

When calculating depreciation on an asset, if an election to expense only part of the asset has been made, the amount of the Section 179 election to expense must be decided first. When a taxpayer decides to take only a portion of the cost of the asset as a Section 179 deduction, the rest of the cost of the asset must be depreciated. The depreciation must be deducted from taxable income to determine the income limitation for the Section 179 deduction.

EXAMPLE On August 1, 2022, Joan purchases a machine for use in her business. It is her only purchase of business property in 2022. The machine cost $1,100,000 and qualifies as 5-year MACRS property. Her business income before any cost recovery is $1,020,000. Joan elects to immediately expense $1,080,000. She elects out of bonus depreciation, thus $20,000 of remaining basis ($2,000,000 − $1,080,000) is subject to MACRS depreciation of $4,000 ($20,000 × 0.20 depreciation factor). As a result of deducting MACRS depreciation of $4,000, Joan's taxable income before Section 179 is reduced to $1,016,000. Joan may only immediately expense $1,016,000 due to the income limit. The excess $64,000 ($1,080,000 − $1,016,000) of Section 179 deduction will be carried forward to 2023. ♦

Self-Study Problem 8.2

Form **4562** Department of the Treasury Internal Revenue Service

Depreciation and Amortization

(Including Information on Listed Property)
Attach to your tax return.
Go to *www.irs.gov/Form4562* for instructions and the latest information.

OMB No. 1545-0172 **2022** Attachment Sequence No. **179**

Name(s) shown on return	Business or activity to which this form relates	**Identifying number**

Part I Election To Expense Certain Property Under Section 179
Note: If you have any listed property, complete Part V before you complete Part I.

1	Maximum amount (see instructions)	1	
2	Total cost of section 179 property placed in service (see instructions)	2	
3	Threshold cost of section 179 property before reduction in limitation (see instructions)	3	
4	Reduction in limitation. Subtract line 3 from line 2. If zero or less, enter -0-	4	
5	Dollar limitation for tax year. Subtract line 4 from line 1. If zero or less, enter -0-. If married filing separately, see instructions	5	

6	(a) Description of property	(b) Cost (business use only)	(c) Elected cost

7	Listed property. Enter the amount from line 29	7	
8	Total elected cost of section 179 property. Add amounts in column (c), lines 6 and 7	8	
9	Tentative deduction. Enter the **smaller** of line 5 or line 8	9	
10	Carryover of disallowed deduction from line 13 of your 2021 Form 4562	10	
11	Business income limitation. Enter the smaller of business income (not less than zero) or line 5. See instructions	11	
12	Section 179 expense deduction. Add lines 9 and 10, but don't enter more than line 11	12	
13	Carryover of disallowed deduction to 2023. Add lines 9 and 10, less line 12	13	

Note: Don't use Part II or Part III below for listed property. Instead, use Part V.

Part II Special Depreciation Allowance and Other Depreciation (Don't include listed property. See instructions.**)**

14	Special depreciation allowance for qualified property (other than listed property) placed in service during the tax year. See instructions	14	
15	Property subject to section 168(f)(1) election	15	
16	Other depreciation (including ACRS)	16	

Part III MACRS Depreciation (Don't include listed property. See instructions.**)**

Section A

17	MACRS deductions for assets placed in service in tax years beginning before 2022	17	
18	If you are electing to group any assets placed in service during the tax year into one or more general asset accounts, check here ☐		

Section B—Assets Placed in Service During 2022 Tax Year Using the General Depreciation System

(a) Classification of property	(b) Month and year placed in service	(c) Basis for depreciation (business/investment use only—see instructions)	(d) Recovery period	(e) Convention	(f) Method	(g) Depreciation deduction
19a 3-year property						
b 5-year property						
c 7-year property						
d 10-year property						
e 15-year property						
f 20-year property						
g 25-year property			25 yrs.		S/L	
h Residential rental			27.5 yrs.	MM	S/L	
property			27.5 yrs.	MM	S/L	
i Nonresidential real			39 yrs.	MM	S/L	
property				MM	S/L	

Section C—Assets Placed in Service During 2022 Tax Year Using the Alternative Depreciation System

20a Class life					S/L	
b 12-year			12 yrs.		S/L	
c 30-year			30 yrs.	MM	S/L	
d 40-year			40 yrs.	MM	S/L	

Part IV Summary (See instructions.)

21	Listed property. Enter amount from line 28	21	
22	**Total.** Add amounts from line 12, lines 14 through 17, lines 19 and 20 in column (g), and line 21. Enter here and on the appropriate lines of your return. Partnerships and S corporations—see instructions	22	
23	For assets shown above and placed in service during the current year, enter the portion of the basis attributable to section 263A costs	23	

For Paperwork Reduction Act Notice, see separate instructions. Cat. No. 12906N Form **4562** (2022)

Form 4562 (2022) Page **2**

Part V **Listed Property** (Include automobiles, certain other vehicles, certain aircraft, and property used for entertainment, recreation, or amusement.)

Note: For any vehicle for which you are using the standard mileage rate or deducting lease expense, complete **only** 24a, 24b, columns (a) through (c) of Section A, all of Section B, and Section C if applicable.

Section A—Depreciation and Other Information (Caution: See the instructions for limits for passenger automobiles.**)**

24a Do you have evidence to support the business/investment use claimed? ☐ **Yes** ☐ **No** **24b** If "Yes," is the evidence written? ☐ **Yes** ☐ **No**

(a) Type of property (list vehicles first)	(b) Date placed in service	(c) Business/ investment use percentage	(d) Cost or other basis	(e) Basis for depreciation (business/investment use only)	(f) Recovery period	(g) Method/ Convention	(h) Depreciation deduction	(i) Elected section 179 cost
25 Special depreciation allowance for qualified listed property placed in service during the tax year and used more than 50% in a qualified business use. See instructions .						**25**		
26 Property used more than 50% in a qualified business use:								
		%						
		%						
		%						
27 Property used 50% or less in a qualified business use:								
		%				S/L –		
		%				S/L –		
		%				S/L –		
28 Add amounts in column (h), lines 25 through 27. Enter here and on line 21, page 1 .						**28**		
29 Add amounts in column (i), line 26. Enter here and on line 7, page 1							**29**	

Section B—Information on Use of Vehicles

Complete this section for vehicles used by a sole proprietor, partner, or other "more than 5% owner," or related person. If you provided vehicles to your employees, first answer the questions in Section C to see if you meet an exception to completing this section for those vehicles.

	(a) Vehicle 1		(b) Vehicle 2		(c) Vehicle 3		(d) Vehicle 4		(e) Vehicle 5		(f) Vehicle 6	
30 Total business/investment miles driven during the year (**don't** include commuting miles) .												
31 Total commuting miles driven during the year												
32 Total other personal (noncommuting) miles driven												
33 Total miles driven during the year. Add lines 30 through 32												
	Yes	**No**	**Yes**	**No**	**Yes**	**No**	**Yes**	**No**	**Yes**	**No**	**Yes**	**No**
34 Was the vehicle available for personal use during off-duty hours?												
35 Was the vehicle used primarily by a more than 5% owner or related person? . .												
36 Is another vehicle available for personal use?												

Section C—Questions for Employers Who Provide Vehicles for Use by Their Employees

Answer these questions to determine if you meet an exception to completing Section B for vehicles used by employees who **aren't** more than 5% owners or related persons. See instructions.

	Yes	**No**
37 Do you maintain a written policy statement that prohibits all personal use of vehicles, including commuting, by your employees?		
38 Do you maintain a written policy statement that prohibits personal use of vehicles, except commuting, by your employees? See the instructions for vehicles used by corporate officers, directors, or 1% or more owners . .		
39 Do you treat all use of vehicles by employees as personal use?		
40 Do you provide more than five vehicles to your employees, obtain information from your employees about the use of the vehicles, and retain the information received?		
41 Do you meet the requirements concerning qualified automobile demonstration use? See instructions		
Note: If your answer to 37, 38, 39, 40, or 41 is "Yes," don't complete Section B for the covered vehicles.		

Part VI **Amortization**

(a) Description of costs	(b) Date amortization begins	(c) Amortizable amount	(d) Code section	(e) Amortization period or percentage	(f) Amortization for this year
42 Amortization of costs that begins during your 2022 tax year (see instructions):					
43 Amortization of costs that began before your 2022 tax year				**43**	
44 **Total.** Add amounts in column (f). See the instructions for where to report				**44**	

Form **4562** (2022)

The effects of bonus depreciation, Section 179 and MACRS depreciation can combine to create substantially accelerated cost recovery. If a taxpayer elects Section 179 immediate expensing and uses bonus depreciation, the cost basis of the property is first reduced by the Section 179 deduction, then by bonus depreciation and lastly, by typical MACRS depreciation. With 100-percent bonus depreciation, the need to deduct Section 179 and then bonus depreciation is an unlikely occurrence since the entire cost of many types of property can be recovered under bonus depreciation without annual or income limits.

Self-Study Problem 8.3 *See Appendix E for Solutions to Self-Study Problems*

On June 15, 2022, Chang purchases $2,837,000 of equipment (7-year property) for use in her business. It is her only purchase of business property in 2022. Chang has taxable income from her business of $2.5 million before any cost recovery.

a. Assuming Chang does not elect Section 179 and elects out of bonus depreciation, what is her total 2022 cost recovery?
b. Assuming Chang elects the maximum Section 179 deduction allowable and elects out of bonus depreciation, what is her total 2022 cost recovery?
c. Assuming Chang does not elect Section 179 deduction allowable and does not elect out of bonus depreciation, what is her total 2022 cost recovery?

8-4 LISTED PROPERTY

8.4 Learning Objective

Apply the limitations placed on depreciation of "listed property."

Congress felt some taxpayers were using the favorable tax incentives of the accelerated cost recovery system and the limited expensing election to claim depreciation deductions on assets used for personal purposes. To curtail this perceived abuse of the tax system, Congress enacted special rules which apply to the depreciation of "listed property." Listed property includes those types of assets which lend themselves to personal use, including the following:

1. Passenger automobiles, defined to include any four-wheeled vehicle manufactured primarily for use on public streets, roads, and highways, rated at 6,000 pounds or less unloaded gross vehicle weight. Specifically excluded from the definition of passenger automobiles are vehicles used directly in the trade or business of transporting persons or property, ambulances and hearses used in a trade or business, and certain trucks and vans not likely to be used more than a de minimis amount for personal purposes, including vehicles which display the company name or advertising.
2. Other property used as a means of transportation (trucks, buses, boats, airplanes, and motorcycles), except vehicles which are not likely to be used for personal purposes, such as marked police cars, school buses, and tractors, or vehicles used for transporting persons or cargo for compensation.
3. Property generally used for entertainment, recreation, or amusement (video recording equipment, communication equipment, etc.).

If listed property is used 50 percent or less in a qualified business use, any depreciation deduction must be calculated using the straight-line method of depreciation over an alternate recovery period, and the special election to expense under Section 179 and bonus depreciation are not allowed.

Qualified business use does not include investment use or the use of property owned by an employee in performing services as an employee, unless the use meets the convenience-of-employer and condition-of-employment tests. In addition, the excess depreciation allowed by reason of the property meeting the more-than-50-percent-use test must be included in income if property which meets the test in one year subsequently fails to meet the more-than-50-percent-use test in a succeeding year.

EXAMPLE Oscar has an automobile he uses 45 percent of the time for personal use and 55 percent of the time in his accounting business. Since Oscar's business-use percentage of 55 percent exceeds 50 percent, Oscar is not required to use the straight-line method in calculating depreciation. The accelerated depreciation method and the election to expense may be used by Oscar. ♦

Self-Study Problem 8.4 *See Appendix E for Solutions to Self-Study Problems*

For each of the following independent situations, indicate if the taxpayer is required to depreciate the property using the straight-line method over the alternate recovery period:

1. Alvarez uses an automobile 20 percent for his business and 80 percent for personal reasons.
2. Laura has a truck she uses in her business 55 percent of the time, 15 percent for her real estate investment, and 30 percent for personal use.

Learning Objective 8.5

Apply the limitations on depreciation of "luxury automobiles."

8-5 LIMITATION ON DEPRECIATION OF LUXURY AUTOMOBILES

In addition to the limitations on the depreciation of passenger automobiles imposed by the listed property rules discussed in the preceding section, the depreciation of passenger automobiles is subject to an additional limitation, commonly referred to as the "luxury automobile" limitation. Regardless of the method of depreciation used by the taxpayer, accelerated or straight-line, the election to expense, or bonus depreciation, the amount of depreciation expense that may be claimed on a passenger automobile is subject to an annual dollar limitation. The annual dollar limitations that apply to passenger automobiles acquired in 2022 are listed below. Any automobile which would have actual MACRS depreciation exceeding the limits is considered a "luxury automobile" by the IRS for purposes of the depreciation limitation rules.

Annual Automobile Depreciation Limitations

Year of Use	*2022 Limits*
Year 1	$19,200*
Year 2	18,000
Year 3	10,800
Year 4 (and subsequent years until fully depreciated)	6,460

*Additional bonus depreciation of $8,000 is included in this amount. If bonus is elected out of, the limit is $11,200.

Separate higher depreciation limits apply for certain trucks and vans and also for electric automobiles.

Some sport utility vehicles fall outside of the definition of passenger automobiles and can be depreciated or expensed under Section 179 or the bonus depreciation rules without regard to the automobile depreciation limits. To qualify for the exception, the sport utility vehicle must have a gross vehicle weight rating above 6,000 pounds. Vehicles that meet the large sport utility vehicle exception are limited to $27,000 (2022 limit) in Section 179 expensing but may depreciate using the 5-year MACRS percentages without the typical auto depreciation limitations.

The annual limitations must be reduced to reflect the actual business-use percentage where business use is less than 100 percent.

EXAMPLE Sally purchased a new car for $65,000 in September 2022 which she uses 75 percent for business. Sally elects out of bonus depreciation. Depreciation on the automobile is calculated as follows:

Total cost		$65,000
		× 0.75
Limited to business use		$48,750
MACRS depreciation (half-year convention)	$48,750 × 20% =	$ 9,750
Compared to:		
Maximum luxury automobile depreciation allowed**	$11,200 × 75% =	$ 8,400

Because the luxury automobile limitation is less than the actual depreciation calculated, Sally's depreciation deduction is limited to $8,400. ♦

**$19,200 limit less $8,000 bonus depreciation Sally elected out of.

EXAMPLE In September 2022, Joan purchased a passenger automobile which cost $65,000. The automobile is used 100 percent for business purposes and Joan elects out of bonus depreciation. A comparison of MACRS, with and without the limitation, is as follows:

	Five-Year MACRS	***Annual Limit***
Year 1	$13,000	$11,200
Year 2	20,800	18,000
Year 3	12,480	10,800
Year 4	7,488	6,460
Year 5	7,488	6,460
Year 6	3,744	6,460
Year 7		5,620

Note that, although the automobile is a 5-year property, it will take 7 years to recover the entire cost of the asset because of the annual dollar limits, assuming no election to expense under Section 179 or bonus depreciation. ♦

TAX BREAK

Taxpayers hoping to get around the luxury auto depreciation limits by leasing an auto should be aware that there is a rule designed to put them in the same economic position as if they had purchased the auto. The IRS issued tables for computation of an "income inclusion" which must be used to reduce the lease expense deduction for leased autos.

Bonus depreciation on autos is subject to annual depreciation limits also. For years after the first year, the unrecovered basis of the auto is subject to MACRS depreciation but remains limited by the auto limits.

EXAMPLE Sally purchased a new automobile for $66,000 in September 2022 which she uses 100 percent for business during the life of the auto. Assuming half-year convention, bonus depreciation and no Section 179 depreciation, Sally's 2022 cost recovery is computed as follows:

Cost basis	$66,000
Depreciation limit for autos, Year 1	19,200
Basis unrecovered at end of 2022	$46,800

In 2023, MACRS depreciation is $14,976 (unrecovered basis of $46,800 × 32%, which is the depreciation factor for the second year of 5-year property). The second-year limit of $18,000 exceeds the deduction and thus does not apply. ♦

Self-Study Problem 8.5

See Appendix E for Solutions to Self-Study Problems

On June 17, 2022, Travis purchased a passenger automobile at a cost of $58,000. The automobile is used 90 percent for qualified business use and 10 percent for personal purposes. Calculate the depreciation expense (without bonus depreciation) for the automobile for 2022, 2023, and 2024, assuming half-year convention and no Section 179 immediate expensing.

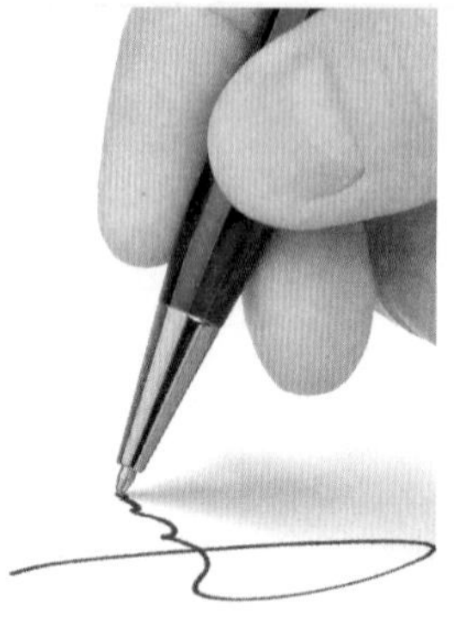

Sign Here — Under penalties of perjury, I declare that I have examined this return and accompanying schedules and statements, and to the best of my knowledge and belief, they are true, correct, and complete. Declaration of preparer (other than taxpayer) is based on all information of which preparer has any knowledge.

Joint return? See instructions. Keep a copy for your records.	Your signature	Date	Your occupation	If the IRS sent you an Identity Protection PIN, enter it here (see inst.) ▶
	Spouse's signature. If a joint return, **both** must sign.	Date	Spouse's occupation	If the IRS sent your spouse an Identity Protection PIN, enter it here (see inst.) ▶
	Phone no.	Email address		

Paid Preparer Use Only				
Preparer's name	Preparer's signature	Date	PTIN	Check if: ☐ Self-employed
Firm's name ▶				Phone no.
Firm's address ▶				Firm's EIN ▶

Would You Sign This Tax Return?

Duncan Devious (age 52) is a self-employed attorney. Duncan loves to be noticed in public and, therefore, he drives a 7,000-pound, military-type, SUV, the only vehicle he owns. When you are preparing his tax return, you notice that he claims 90 percent of his total auto expenses as a business deduction on his Schedule C and 10 percent as personal use, with total miles driven in 2022 as 10,000. You note from his home and office addresses on his tax return that he lives approximately 15 miles from his office. The total of the expenses (i.e., gas, oil, maintenance, depreciation) he claims is $31,200. He does not have a mileage log to substantiate the business use of the SUV. Would you sign the Paid Preparer's declaration (see example above) on this return? Why or why not?

8-6 INTANGIBLES

8.6 Learning Objective

Calculate the amortization of goodwill and certain other intangibles.

The current tax guidance provides for two main categories of intangibles: (1) Section 197 intangibles and (2) non-Section 197 intangibles. Section 197 intangibles are those acquired by a taxpayer as part of the acquisition of a trade or business. Section 197 intangibles are amortized over a 15-year period, beginning with the month of acquisition. Amortization is a cost recovery method similar to depreciation in that it spreads the cost recovery over a fixed period of years. It differs from depreciation in that it is applied to intangible assets rather than tangible personal or real property and does not include the half-year or mid-quarter conventions. The 15-year life applies regardless of the actual useful life of the intangible asset. No other amortization or depreciation method may be claimed on Section 197 assets. When acquired as part of a trade or business, the following are defined as qualified Section 197 intangibles:

- Goodwill
- Going-concern value
- Workforce in place
- Information bases, including business books and records and operating systems
- Know-how
- Customer-based intangibles
- License, permit, or right granted by a governmental unit
- Covenant not to compete
- Franchise, trademark, or trade name

EXAMPLE In March 2022, Mary purchases a business from Bill for $250,000. Section 197 goodwill of $36,000 is included in the $250,000 purchase price. Mary amortizes the goodwill over a 15-year period at the rate of $200 per month, starting with the month of purchase. ♦

8-6a Exclusions

Many intangible assets are specifically excluded from the definition of Section 197 intangibles. Examples of these Section 197 exclusions include items which are not generally amortizable:

- Interests in a corporation, partnership, trust, or estate
- Interests in land

Section 197 exclusions that are generally amortizable:

- Computer software readily available for purchase by the general public
- Interests in films, sound recordings, video recordings, and similar property
- Self-created intangible assets

Non-Section 197 intangibles that are separately acquired are generally amortized over their remaining useful life using the straight-line method. For example, a patent could be acquired as part of the purchase of a business (Section 197 intangible) or a patent could be acquired separately (non-Section 197 intangible). A franchise, trademark, or tradename is treated as a Section 197 intangible whether acquired as part of a business or not.

EXAMPLE Sam purchases computer software sold to the general public for $20,000. The $20,000 is not a Section 197 intangible and therefore the amount would be amortized under regular amortization rules (typically 3 years). ♦

Amortization expense is reported on the bottom of page 2 in Part VI of Form 4562.

ProConnect™ Tax TIP

Amortization is entered into the software in the Depreciation section. Select Non-recovery/Straight-line as the depreciation method. The recovery period (e.g., 15 years for Section 197 intangibles) must be input. An amortization code is available in the detailed input screen.

Self-Study Problem 8.6 *See Appendix E for Solutions to Self-Study Problems*

Determine whether the following items are generally amortizable over 15 years, amortized over their useful life, or not amortized.

1. Patent acquired as part of a business
2. Separately acquired film rights
3. Computer software sold at an office supply store
4. Goodwill
5. Franchise
6. Land
7. Trademark
8. Interest in a corporation

Learning Objective 8.7

Classify gains and losses from Section 1231 assets.

8-7 SECTION 1231 GAINS AND LOSSES

The first part of this chapter has dealt with the acquisition and cost recovery of business property. The remaining sections deal with the sale, exchange, or disposal of business property. The tax rules on capital gains and losses covered in Chapter 4 continue to apply here, but the tax law has been crafted in a way to provide capital treatment for certain business gains and losses and ordinary treatment for others. Unlike much of the tax law covered elsewhere in this textbook, these tax concepts often refer to the Internal Revenue Code section number as the identifying name. For example, Section 1231 is used to describe property used in a trade or business and held for more than one year. Depreciation recapture is commonly referred to as Section 1245 or Section 1250 recapture.

Section 1231 assets are not capital assets (see Chapter 4), but they are given special tax treatment. Gains on Section 1231 assets may be treated as long-term capital gains, while losses in some cases may be deducted as ordinary losses. Section 1231 assets include:

1. Depreciable or real property used in a trade or business;
2. Timber, coal, or domestic iron ore;
3. Livestock (not including poultry) held for draft, breeding, dairy, or sporting purposes; and
4. Unharvested crops on land used in a trade or business.

Any property held one year or less, inventory and property held for sale to customers, and copyrights, paintings, government publications, etc., are not Section 1231 property.

The calculation of net Section 1231 gains and losses is summarized as follows:

Combine *all* Section 1231 gains and losses to compute *net* Section 1231 gains or losses. If the gains exceed the losses, the excess is a long-term capital gain. When the losses exceed the gains, all gains are treated as ordinary income, and all losses are fully deductible as ordinary losses.

EXAMPLE Frank Harper had the following business gains and (losses) on the sale of business property during the current year:

Sale of land held for four years	$ 9,500
Sale of truck held for three years	(2,100)
Sale of inventory	6,000

Frank's Section 1231 gains and losses would be calculated as follows:

Gain on land	$ 9,500
Loss on truck	(2,100)
Net Section 1231 gain	$ 7,400

The $7,400 net Section 1231 gain would be treated as a long-term capital gain and would be reported on Form 4797 and transferred to Line 11 of Schedule D of Form 1040. Inventory is not Section 1231 property and thus, results in ordinary income ♦

8-7a Section 1231 Lookback

The result of Section 1231 generally favor taxpayers—long-term capital gain treatment for gain, which often enjoy preferential rates and ordinary character for losses, which are much less likely to be subject to limitation than capital losses. To prevent taxpayers from abusing the preferred treatment under Section 1231, the tax law includes a lookback provision that requires a taxpayer that has net Section 1231 gains for the current year to recharacterize the current year gain to the extent of Section 1231 losses in the prior 5 years.

EXAMPLE Eddie Mahoney operates a small business that started in 2019. His 1231 gains and losses through 2022 are as follows:

Year	***Net Section 1231 Gain/(Loss)***
2019	0
2020	(4,000)
2021	(2,000)
2022	7,000

In 2022, Eddie will lookback over the prior five years and recharacterize $6,000 of the $7,000 Section 1231 gains as ordinary gains under the lookback rule. The remaining $1,000 gain will remain a Section 1231 gain. If Eddie generates a $5,000 Section 1231 gain in 2023, the gain will remain Section 1231 since no unrecharacterized Section 1231 losses exist due to the previous recharacterization in 2022. ♦

EXAMPLE Roger Nelson generated the following Section 1231 gains and losses:

Year	***Net Section 1231 Gain/(Loss)***
2019	0
2020	4,000
2021	2,000
2022	(7,000)

In 2022, Roger will not be required to recharacterize his loss. Only Section 1231 *gains* are subject to the lookback rule. Should Roger generate Section 1231 gains through 2027, his 2022 loss would be subject to recharacterization. ♦

Self-Study Problem 8.7 *See Appendix E for Solutions to Self-Study Problems*

Serena had the following sales of business property during the 2022 tax year:

1. Sold land acquired on December 3, 2010, at a cost of $24,000, for $37,000 on January 5, 2022. The cost of selling the land was $500, and there was no depreciation allowable or capital improvements made to the asset over the life of the asset.
2. Sold a business computer with an adjusted basis of $20,700 that was acquired on April 5, 2020. The original cost was $53,906, and accumulated depreciation was $33,206. The computer was sold on May 2, 2022, for $14,000, resulting in a $6,700 loss.
3. Sold equipment on July 22, 2022 for gross proceeds of $16,000. The equipment was acquired on October 21, 2021 at a cost of $28,177 and accumulated depreciation was $7,477 at the time of the sale. Serena used an equipment broker on this sale and paid a sales commission of $1,600.

Calculate Serena's net gain or loss and determine the character as either capital or ordinary (ignore any depreciation recapture).

Learning Objective 8.8

Apply the depreciation recapture rules.

8-8 DEPRECIATION RECAPTURE

Since long-term capital gains traditionally have been taxed at a lower tax rate than ordinary income, taxpayers have attempted to maximize the amount of income treated as capital gain. Congress enacted depreciation recapture provisions to prevent taxpayers from converting ordinary income into capital gains by claiming maximum depreciation deductions over the life of the asset and then selling the asset and receiving capital gain treatment on the resulting gain at the time of the sale. There are three major depreciation recapture provisions: (1) Section 1245, which generally applies to personal property, (2) Section 1250, which applies to real estate, and (3) "unrecaptured depreciation" previously taken on real estate. The depreciation recapture provisions are extremely complex. Only a brief overview of the general provisions contained in the tax law is presented here.

8-8a Section 1245 Recapture

Under the provisions of Section 1245, any gain recognized on the disposition of a Section 1245 asset will be classified as ordinary income up to an amount equal to the depreciation claimed. Any gain in excess of depreciation taken is classified as a Section 1231 gain. Section 1245 property is:

- Depreciable tangible personal property such as furniture, machines, computers, and automobiles
- Amortizable intangible personal property such as patents, copyrights, leaseholds, and professional sports contracts

- Other tangible property (except buildings) used as an integral part of manufacturing, production or extraction
- Single purpose agricultural or horticultural structures

Section 1245 recapture potential is defined as the total depreciation claimed on Section 1245 property. The amount of ordinary income recognized upon the sale of an asset under Section 1245 is equal to the lesser of (1) total depreciation claimed on the asset, or (2) the amount of the realized gain on the sale. Any gain recognized in excess of the amount of ordinary income is a Section 1231 gain.

EXAMPLE On March 1 of the current year, Melvin sells Section 1245 property, which was purchased 4 years ago for $6,000. Melvin had claimed depreciation on the property of $2,500, and sold the property for $5,000. The recapture under Section 1245 is calculated below:

Amount realized	$5,000
Adjusted basis ($6,000 – $2,500)	3,500
Realized gain	$1,500
Total depreciation taken	$2,500

The amount of Section 1245 recapture (the gain characterized as ordinary) is $1,500, which is the lesser of the realized gain ($1,500) or the total depreciation taken ($2,500). ♦

EXAMPLE Assume the same facts as in the previous example, except that the property is sold for $7,800. The recapture under Section 1245 is calculated below:

Amount realized	$7,800
Adjusted basis ($6,000 – $2,500)	3,500
Realized gain	$4,300
Total depreciation taken	$2,500

The amount of Section 1245 recapture (the gain characterized as ordinary) is $2,500, which is the lesser of the realized gain ($4,300) or the total depreciation taken ($2,500). The residual gain of $1,800 ($4,300 – $2,500) is a Section 1231 gain. ♦

EXAMPLE Assume the same facts as in the previous example, except that the property is sold for $2,800. Because the property is sold at a loss of $700 ($2,800 – $3,500), Section 1245 recapture does not apply and the loss is treated as a Section 1231 loss. ♦

8-8b **Section 1250 Recapture**

Section 1250 applies to the gain on the sale of depreciable real property, other than real property included in the definition of Section 1245 property. The amount of Section 1250 recapture potential is equal to the excess of depreciation expense claimed over the life of the asset under an *accelerated* method of depreciation over the amount of depreciation that would have been allowed if the straight-line method of depreciation had been used. If property is depreciated using the straight-line method, there is no Section 1250 recapture potential. Since the use of the straight-line method is required for real property acquired after 1986, there will be no Section 1250 recapture on the disposition of such property. In practice, Section 1250 recapture is rarely seen.

8-8c "Unrecaptured Depreciation" on Real Estate—25 Percent Rate

For non-corporate taxpayers, a special 25-percent tax rate applies to real property gains attributable to depreciation previously taken and not already recaptured under the Section 1245 or Section 1250 rules discussed above. Any remaining gain attributable to "unrecaptured depreciation"previously taken, including straight-line depreciation, is taxed at 25 percent rather than the long-term capital gain rate of 15 percent. When the taxpayer's ordinary tax rate is below 25 percent, the depreciation recapture will be taxed at the lower ordinary tax rate to the extent of the remaining amount in the less than 25 percent bracket and then at 25 percent. The application of the 25 percent rate for "unrecaptured depreciation" is frequently seen in practice because it applies to every rental property which is depreciated and then sold at a gain. If the 3.8 percent net investment income tax discussed in Chapter 6 applies, the 25 percent rate will be increased to 28.8 percent and the 15 percent rate will be increased to 18.8 percent.

EXAMPLE Lew, an individual taxpayer, acquired an apartment building in 2012 for $300,000, and he sells it in October 2022 for $500,000. The accumulated straight-line depreciation on the building at the time of the sale is $45,000. Lew is in the 35-percent tax bracket for ordinary income. Lew's gain on the sale of the property is $245,000 ($500,000 less adjusted basis of $255,000). Note that $45,000 of the gain is attributable to unrecaptured depreciation and is taxed at 25 percent, while the remaining $200,000 gain is taxed at the 15-percent long-term capital gains rate. Lew may also be subject to the 3.8 percent net investment income tax which is discussed in Chapter 6. ♦

The reporting of unrecaptured depreciation on 1250 property gains subject to the 25-percent rate is considerably complex. The amounts from the Form 4797 are reported on Schedule D and the use of the Unrecaptured Section 1250 Gain Worksheet from the Schedule D instructions is also suggested. Amounts from this worksheet are transferred to the Schedule D Tax worksheet (also part of the Schedule D instructions) which is similar to the Qualified Dividends and Capital Gain Tax Worksheet used in earlier chapters of this textbook.

8-8d Section 291 Recapture for Corporations

The tax rules associated with unrecaptured Section 1250 gains are different between corporate taxpayers and individual taxpayers. Under Section 291, corporations are required to recharacterize 20 percent of unrecaptured depreciation as ordinary and the remaining gain is treated as Section 1231 gain. Losses are not subject to Section 291 recapture.

EXAMPLE Lewis Corporation acquired an apartment building in 2012 for $300,000, and sells the building in October 2022 for $500,000. The accumulated straight-line depreciation on the building at the time of the sale is $45,000. Lewis Corporation's gain on the sale of the property is $245,000 ($500,000 less adjusted basis of $255,000). Twenty percent of the amount of unrecaptured depreciation ($9,000 = $45,000 × 20%) of the gain will be characterized as ordinary and the remaining $236,000 will remain Section 1231 gain. ♦

Self-Study Problem 8.8 *See Appendix E for Solutions to Self-Study Problems*

The following information is from Self-Study Problem 8.7:

Serena, an individual taxpayer, had the following sales of business property during the 2022 tax year:

1. Sold land acquired on December 3, 2010, at a cost of $24,000, for $37,000 on January 5, 2022. The cost of selling the land was $500, and there was no depreciation allowable or capital improvements made to the asset over the life of the asset.
2. Sold a business computer with an adjusted basis of $20,700 that was acquired on April 5, 2020. The original cost was $53,906, and accumulated depreciation was $33,206. The computer was sold on May 2, 2022, for $14,000, resulting in a $6,700 loss.
3. Sold equipment on July 22, 2022, for gross proceeds of $16,000. The equipment was acquired on October 21, 2021, at a cost of $28,177 and accumulated depreciation was $7,477 at the time of the sale. Serena used an equipment broker on this sale and paid a sales commission of $1,600.

Add this new information:

4. Sold a building on October 7, 2022, for $340,000, net of sales commissions of $15,000. Serena acquired the building on December 3, 2010, at a cost of $320,000. Accumulated depreciation has been computed using the straight-line method since acquisition and totaled $126,050 at the time of the sale.
5. Sold furniture on October 7, 2022, for $7,600. The furniture was acquired on December 3, 2010, for $15,000 and accumulated depreciation was $15,000 at the time of the sale.

Serena's employer identification number is 74-8976432. Use Form 4797 on Pages 8-29 and 8-30 to report the above gains and losses (hint: do **not** ignore depreciation recapture and complete Part III first).

ProConnect™ Tax TIP

The sale of business property is entered on the Sale of Asset 4797/6252 screens under deductions.

8-9 BUSINESS CASUALTY GAINS AND LOSSES

8.9 Learning Objective

Apply the general treatment of casualty gains and losses for business purposes.

The treatment of casualty gains and losses differs depending on whether the property involved is held for personal use or held for business or investment purposes. Therefore, a taxpayer's business and investment casualty gains and losses are computed separately from personal casualty gains and losses. Deductions for personal casualty losses are restricted to those associated with a federally-declared disaster area. Since the casualty loss is an itemized deduction, the rules for personal casualties are discussed in Chapter 5.

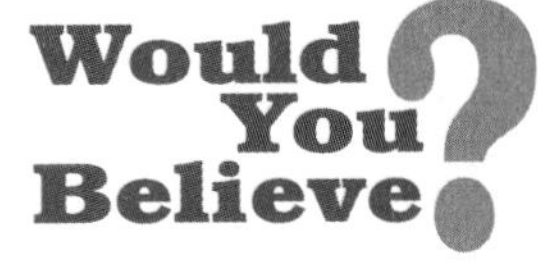

The Ninth Circuit Court decided that a man's payment to a woman to keep her from revealing their extramarital affair was not a deductible casualty loss.

The amount of a business casualty or loss depends on whether the property was completely or partially destroyed. If business property is completely destroyed, the loss is the adjusted basis of the property less any insurance reimbursement. If business property is partially destroyed, the loss is insurance proceeds less the lesser of the adjusted basis at the time of the casualty or the decrease in the property's fair market value associated with the casualty.

EXAMPLE Joan's business suffered two casualties in the current year. Theft 1: One of Joan's employees stole a business vehicle and ended up abandoning the vehicle. The car was vandalized and damaged. The adjusted basis of the car was $14,000 at the time of the theft and the car was repairable but decreased in value $7,000 because of the damage. Theft 2: A car owned by Joan's business was stolen. The thief was involved in a traffic accident and the car was totally destroyed. The basis of the car was $7,600 at the time of the theft and had a fair market value of $5,000 before the crash. Joan's insurance company reimbursed her $6,000 for the first theft and $4,000 for the second. Theft 1 is a partial destruction and the lesser of the decrease in market value or the adjusted basis is used to compute the loss. Theft 2 is a complete destruction and so the adjusted basis is used to compute the loss.

	Theft 1 Partial Destruction	*Theft 2 Complete Destruction*
Insurance proceeds	$ 6,000	$ 4,000
Adjusted basis	14,000	**7,600**
Decrease in FMV	**7,000**	n/a
Loss	$(1,000)	$(3,600)

◆

Business and investment property must be identified as a capital asset, trade or business property subject to an allowance for depreciation, or ordinary income property. The following rules apply to the treatment of business or investment property:

1. Property held for 1 year or less—gains from trade or business property (including property used in the production of rental or royalty income) and gains from investment property are netted against losses from trade or business property, and the resulting net gain or loss is treated as ordinary income or loss. Losses from investment property are considered separately.
2. Property held over 1 year—gains and losses from trade or business property and investment property are netted.
   a. Net gain—if the result is a net gain, the net gain is included in the calculation of the net Section 1231 gain or loss (the gains and losses are treated as Section 1231 gains and losses).
   b. Net loss—if the result is a net loss, the gains and losses from business and investment property are excluded from Section 1231 treatment.

The tax treatment of the gains and losses depends on whether the property was used in the taxpayer's trade or business or held for investment. Gains and losses from business-use assets are treated as ordinary income and ordinary losses, respectively.

If the taxpayer recognizes a gain as a result of a casualty, and the property involved is depreciable property, the depreciation recapture provisions may cause all or a part of the gain to be treated as ordinary income. A casualty involving business property is included in the definition of an involuntary conversion, so that gain realized may be eligible for deferral under the special involuntary conversion provisions discussed in LO 8.12 of this chapter.

Self-Study Problem 8.8

Form **4797**

Department of the Treasury
Internal Revenue Service

Sales of Business Property
(Also Involuntary Conversions and Recapture Amounts Under Sections 179 and 280F(b)(2))
Attach to your tax return.
Go to *www.irs.gov/Form4797* for instructions and the latest information.

OMB No. 1545-0184
2022
Attachment Sequence No. **27**

Name(s) shown on return | **Identifying number**

1a	Enter the gross proceeds from sales or exchanges reported to you for 2022 on Form(s) 1099-B or 1099-S (or substitute statement) that you are including on line 2, 10, or 20. See instructions	1a	
b	Enter the total amount of gain that you are including on lines 2, 10, and 24 due to the partial dispositions of MACRS assets	1b	
c	Enter the total amount of loss that you are including on lines 2 and 10 due to the partial dispositions of MACRS assets	1c	

Part I **Sales or Exchanges of Property Used in a Trade or Business and Involuntary Conversions From Other Than Casualty or Theft—Most Property Held More Than 1 Year** (see instructions)

2	(a) Description of property	(b) Date acquired (mo., day, yr.)	(c) Date sold (mo., day, yr.)	(d) Gross sales price	(e) Depreciation allowed or allowable since acquisition	(f) Cost or other basis, plus improvements and expense of sale	(g) Gain or (loss) Subtract (f) from the sum of (d) and (e)

3	Gain, if any, from Form 4684, line 39	3	
4	Section 1231 gain from installment sales from Form 6252, line 26 or 37	4	
5	Section 1231 gain or (loss) from like-kind exchanges from Form 8824	5	
6	Gain, if any, from line 32, from other than casualty or theft	6	
7	Combine lines 2 through 6. Enter the gain or (loss) here and on the appropriate line as follows	7	
	Partnerships and S corporations. Report the gain or (loss) following the instructions for Form 1065, Schedule K, line 10, or Form 1120-S, Schedule K, line 9. Skip lines 8, 9, 11, and 12 below. **Individuals, partners, S corporation shareholders, and all others.** If line 7 is zero or a loss, enter the amount from line 7 on line 11 below and skip lines 8 and 9. If line 7 is a gain and you didn't have any prior year section 1231 losses, or they were recaptured in an earlier year, enter the gain from line 7 as a long-term capital gain on the Schedule D filed with your return and skip lines 8, 9, 11, and 12 below.		
8	Nonrecaptured net section 1231 losses from prior years. See instructions	8	
9	Subtract line 8 from line 7. If zero or less, enter -0-. If line 9 is zero, enter the gain from line 7 on line 12 below. If line 9 is more than zero, enter the amount from line 8 on line 12 below and enter the gain from line 9 as a long-term capital gain on the Schedule D filed with your return. See instructions	9	

Part II **Ordinary Gains and Losses** (see instructions)

10 Ordinary gains and losses not included on lines 11 through 16 (include property held 1 year or less):

11	Loss, if any, from line 7	11	( )
12	Gain, if any, from line 7 or amount from line 8, if applicable	12	
13	Gain, if any, from line 31	13	
14	Net gain or (loss) from Form 4684, lines 31 and 38a	14	
15	Ordinary gain from installment sales from Form 6252, line 25 or 36	15	
16	Ordinary gain or (loss) from like-kind exchanges from Form 8824	16	
17	Combine lines 10 through 16.	17	
18	For all except individual returns, enter the amount from line 17 on the appropriate line of your return and skip lines a and b below. For individual returns, complete lines a and b below.		
a	If the loss on line 11 includes a loss from Form 4684, line 35, column (b)(ii), enter that part of the loss here. Enter the loss from income-producing property on Schedule A (Form 1040), line 16. (Do not include any loss on property used as an employee.) Identify as from "Form 4797, line 18a." See instructions	18a	
b	Redetermine the gain or (loss) on line 17 excluding the loss, if any, on line 18a. Enter here and on Schedule 1 (Form 1040), Part I, line 4	18b	

For Paperwork Reduction Act Notice, see separate instructions. Cat. No. 13086I Form **4797** (2022)

Form 4797 (2022) Page **2**

Part III Gain From Disposition of Property Under Sections 1245, 1250, 1252, 1254, and 1255 (see instructions)

19 (a) Description of section 1245, 1250, 1252, 1254, or 1255 property:	(b) Date acquired (mo., day, yr.)	(c) Date sold (mo., day, yr.)
A		
B		
C		
D		

These columns relate to the properties on lines 19A through 19D.		Property A	Property B	Property C	Property D
20 Gross sales price (**Note:** *See line 1a before completing.*)	20				
21 Cost or other basis plus expense of sale	21				
22 Depreciation (or depletion) allowed or allowable	22				
23 Adjusted basis. Subtract line 22 from line 21	23				
24 Total gain. Subtract line 23 from line 20	24				
25 **If section 1245 property:**					
a Depreciation allowed or allowable from line 22	25a				
b Enter the **smaller** of line 24 or 25a	25b				
26 **If section 1250 property:** If straight line depreciation was used, enter -0- on line 26g, except for a corporation subject to section 291.					
a Additional depreciation after 1975. See instructions	26a				
b Applicable percentage multiplied by the **smaller** of line 24 or line 26a. See instructions	26b				
c Subtract line 26a from line 24. If residential rental property **or** line 24 isn't more than line 26a, skip lines 26d and 26e	26c				
d Additional depreciation after 1969 and before 1976	26d				
e Enter the **smaller** of line 26c or 26d	26e				
f Section 291 amount (corporations only)	26f				
g Add lines 26b, 26e, and 26f	26g				
27 **If section 1252 property:** Skip this section if you didn't dispose of farmland or if this form is being completed for a partnership.					
a Soil, water, and land clearing expenses	27a				
b Line 27a multiplied by applicable percentage. See instructions	27b				
c Enter the **smaller** of line 24 or 27b	27c				
28 **If section 1254 property:**					
a Intangible drilling and development costs, expenditures for development of mines and other natural deposits, mining exploration costs, and depletion. See instructions	28a				
b Enter the **smaller** of line 24 or 28a	28b				
29 **If section 1255 property:**					
a Applicable percentage of payments excluded from income under section 126. See instructions	29a				
b Enter the **smaller** of line 24 or 29a. See instructions	29b				

Summary of Part III Gains. Complete property columns A through D through line 29b before going to line 30.

30 Total gains for all properties. Add property columns A through D, line 24	30	
31 Add property columns A through D, lines 25b, 26g, 27c, 28b, and 29b. Enter here and on line 13	31	
32 Subtract line 31 from line 30. Enter the portion from casualty or theft on Form 4684, line 33. Enter the portion from other than casualty or theft on Form 4797, line 6	32	

Part IV Recapture Amounts Under Sections 179 and 280F(b)(2) When Business Use Drops to 50% or Less (see instructions)

		(a) Section 179	(b) Section 280F(b)(2)
33 Section 179 expense deduction or depreciation allowable in prior years	33		
34 Recomputed depreciation. See instructions	34		
35 Recapture amount. Subtract line 34 from line 33. See the instructions for where to report	35		

Form **4797** (2022)

The interaction of Section 1231 and casualty gains and losses from business or investment property is complex. Taxpayers should follow the instructions included with Form 4684 and Form 4797. See the IRS website (**www.irs.gov**) for samples of these forms and instructions.

EXAMPLE Two pieces of manufacturing equipment used by Robert in his business are completely destroyed by fire. One of the pieces of equipment had an adjusted basis of $5,000 ($11,000 original basis less $6,000 accumulated depreciation) and a fair market value of $3,000 on the date of the fire. The other piece of equipment had an adjusted basis of $7,000 ($18,000 original basis less $11,000 of accumulated depreciation) and a fair market value of $10,000. Robert receives $3,000 from his insurance company to compensate him for the loss of the first piece of equipment, and he receives $8,000 for the second piece of equipment. As a result of the casualty, Robert's casualty gain or loss is calculated as follows:

	Item 1	*Item 2*
Insurance proceeds	$ 3,000	$ 8,000
Adjusted basis of property	(5,000)	(7,000)
(Loss) gain	$(2,000)	$ 1,000

The netting of the business casualty gains and losses results in a net loss of $1,000; thus, the gains and losses are excluded from Section 1231 treatment. Since the loss on Item 1 represents a loss arising from an asset used in the taxpayer's business (not an asset held for investment), the loss is considered an ordinary loss. The $1,000 gain from Item 2 is treated as ordinary income under Section 1245 recapture. ♦

Self-Study Problem 8.9 *See Appendix E for Solutions to Self-Study Problems*

Jonathan has the following separate casualties during the year:

	Decrease in Fair Market Value	*Adjusted Basis*	*Insurance Reimbursement*	*Holding Period*
Business furniture	$ 4,000	$ 5,000	$ 0	3 years
Business machinery	15,000	14,000	10,000	3 years

The furniture was completely destroyed while the machinery was partially destroyed. Jonathan also sold business land for a Section 1231 gain of $10,000. Calculate the amount and nature of Jonathan's gains and losses as a result of these casualties.

8-10 INSTALLMENT SALES

8.10 Learning Objective

Compute the gain on installment sales.

Some taxpayers sell property and do not receive payment immediately. Instead, they take a note from the purchaser and receive payments over an extended period of time. It might be a financial hardship to require those taxpayers to pay tax on all of the gain on the sale of the property in the year of sale when they may not have received enough cash to cover the taxes. To provide equity in such situations, Congress passed the installment sale provision. The installment sale provision allows taxpayers to spread the gain (but not a loss) over the tax years in which payments are received. On an installment sale, the taxable gain reported each year is determined as follows:

$$\text{Taxable gain} = \frac{\text{Total gain realized on the sale}}{\text{Contract price}} \times \text{Cash collections during the year}$$

Taxpayers who receive payments over a period of time automatically report gain on the installment method, unless they elect to report all the gain in the year of the sale. An election to report all the gain in the year of sale is made by including all the gain in income for the year of the sale. Taxpayers use Form 6252, Installment Sale Income, to report the installment sale gain on their income tax returns.

EXAMPLE Howard Scripp sells land with an adjusted basis of $20,000 for $50,000. He receives $10,000 in the year of sale, and the balance is payable at $8,000 per year for 5 years, plus a reasonable amount of interest. If Howard elects not to report under the installment method, the gain in the year of sale would be calculated in the following manner:

Cash	$ 10,000
Note at fair market value	40,000
Amount realized	50,000
Less: the land's basis	(20,000)
Taxable gain	$ 30,000

♦

EXAMPLE If, instead, Howard reports the gain on the installment method, the amount of the taxable gain in the year of sale is $6,000, which is calculated below.

$$\text{Taxable gain} = \frac{\text{Total gain}}{\text{Contract price}} \times \text{Cash collections}$$

$$\text{Taxable gain} = \frac{\$30{,}000}{\$50{,}000} \times \$10{,}000 = \$6{,}000$$

If $8,000 is collected in the first year after the year of sale, the gain in that year would be $4,800, as illustrated below.

$$\text{Taxable gain} = \frac{\$30{,}000}{\$50{,}000} \times \$8{,}000 = \$4{,}800$$

Of course, any interest income received on the note is also included in income as portfolio income. ♦

Complex installment sale rules apply to taxpayers who regularly sell real or personal property and to taxpayers who sell certain business or rental real property. For example, any recapture under Section 1245 or Section 1250 must be reported in full in the year of sale, regardless of the taxpayer's use of the installment method. Any remaining gain may be reported under the installment method. In addition, certain limitations apply where there is an installment sale between related parties.

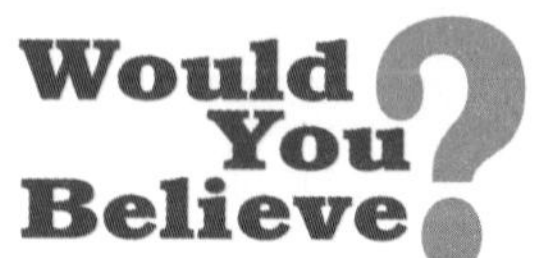

The installment method requires that payments be received in a tax year after the year of sale. In a recent decision (*Merchia v. United States IRS*, 565 F. Supp. 3d 26), the court held that the promissory note used to establish the future payment did not provide for any dates for future payments, and therefore, was considered a demand note under applicable state law. Since demand notes are not eligible for installment sale treatment, the entire gain was recognized in the year of sale.

8-10a The Contract Price

The contract price used in calculating the taxable gain is the amount the seller will ultimately collect from the purchaser (other than interest). This amount is usually the sale price of the property. However, the purchaser will occasionally assume the seller's liability on the property, in which case the contract price is computed by subtracting from the selling price any mortgage or notes assumed by the buyer. If the mortgage or notes assumed by the buyer exceed the adjusted basis of the property, the excess is treated as a cash payment received in the year of sale and must be included in the contract price.

EXAMPLE Roger receives the following for an installment sale of real estate:

Cash	$ 3,000
Roger's mortgage assumed by the purchaser	9,000
Note payable to Roger from the purchaser	39,000
Selling price	$ 51,000

Roger's total gain is computed as follows:

Selling price	$ 51,000
Less: selling expenses	(1,500)
Amount realized	49,500
Less: Roger's basis in the property	(30,000)
Total gain	$ 19,500

The contract price is $42,000 ($51,000 − $9,000), and assuming the $3,000 is the only cash received in the year of sale, the taxable gain in the year of sale is $1,393 as shown below:

$$\text{Taxable gain} = \frac{\$19{,}500}{\$42{,}000} \times \$3{,}000 = \$1{,}393$$ ♦

Self-Study Problem 8.10 ***See Appendix E for Solutions to Self-Study Problems***

Brian acquired a rental house on January 1, 2006, for a cost of $80,000. Straight-line depreciation on the property of $26,000 has been claimed by Brian. On January 15, 2022, he sells the property for $120,000, receiving $8,000 cash, the buyer's assumption of the remaining $12,000 mortgage on the house, and a note from the buyer for $100,000 at 10 percent interest. The note is payable at $10,000 per year for 10 years, with the first payment to be received 1 year after the date of sale. Use Form 6252 on Page 8-35 to calculate his taxable gain under the installment method for the year of sale of the rental house.

Taxpayers may wish to elect out of the installment treatment for a sale which could qualify, and instead recognize all of the gain in the year of sale when they have low income and expect that the gain would be taxed at a higher rate if deferred to later years.

TAX BREAK

Learning Objective 8.11

Calculate recognized and deferred gains on like-kind exchanges.

8-11 LIKE-KIND EXCHANGES

Although a taxpayer realizes a gain or loss on the sale or exchange of property, the recognition of the gain or loss may be deferred for tax purposes. One example of such a situation arises when a taxpayer exchanges real property for other real property of a like kind. Under certain circumstances, the transaction may be nontaxable. To qualify as a nontaxable exchange, the property exchanged must be real property, held for productive use in a trade or business, or held for investment. Exchanges of personal or intangible property used in a business or for investment such as machines, cars, trucks, patents, furniture, etc., do not qualify as like-kind. Property held for personal purposes, such as a taxpayer's residence, also does not qualify for a like-kind exchange.

When the exchange involves only qualified like-kind property, no gain or loss is recognized. However, some exchanges include cash or other property in addition to the like-kind property. Even when the exchange is not solely for like-kind assets, the nontaxable treatment usually is not completely lost. Gain is recognized in an amount equal to the lesser of (1) the gain realized or (2) the "boot" received. Boot is money or the fair market value of other property received in addition to the like-kind property. Relief from a liability is the same as receiving cash and is treated as boot.

The basis of other property received as boot in an exchange is its fair market value on the date of the exchange. The basis of the like-kind property received is:

The basis of the like-kind property given up
+ Any boot paid
− Any boot received
+ Any gain recognized
Basis of property received

The holding period for property acquired in a like-kind exchange includes the holding period of the property exchanged. For example, if long-term capital gain property is exchanged today, the new property may be sold immediately, and the gain recognized would be long-term capital gain.

Taxpayers must file Form 8824, Like-Kind Exchanges, to report the exchange of property. This form must be completed even if no gain is recognized.

EXAMPLE Janis and Kevin exchange real estate held as an investment. Janis gives up property with an adjusted basis of $350,000 and a fair market value of $560,000. The property is subject to a mortgage of $105,000 which is assumed by Kevin. In return for this property, Janis receives from Kevin land with a fair market value of $420,000 and cash of $35,000. Kevin's adjusted basis in the property he exchanges is $280,000.

1. Janis recognizes a gain of $140,000, equal to the lesser of the gain realized or the boot received as calculated below.

Calculation of gain realized:	
Fair market value of property received	$ 420,000
Cash received	35,000
Liability assumed by Kevin	105,000
Total amount realized	$ 560,000
Less: the adjusted basis of the property given up	(350,000)
Gain realized	$ 210,000
Calculation of boot received:	
Cash received	$ 35,000
Liability assumed by Kevin	105,000
Total boot received	$ 140,000
Gain recognized: Lesser of gain realized or boot received	$ 140,000

Self-Study Problem 8.10

Form **6252** | **Installment Sale Income** | OMB No. 1545-0228
Department of the Treasury Internal Revenue Service

Attach to your tax return.
Use a separate form for each sale or other disposition of property on the installment method.
Go to *www.irs.gov/Form6252* for the latest information.

2022 Attachment Sequence No. **67**

Name(s) shown on return | **Identifying number**

1 Description of property

2a Date acquired (mm/dd/yyyy) **b** Date sold (mm/dd/yyyy)

3 Was the property sold to a related party? See instructions. If "Yes," complete Part III for the year of sale and 2 years after the year of the sale unless you received the final payment during the tax year. If "No," skip line 4 . ☐ **Yes** ☐ **No**

4 Did you sell the property to an intermediary? If "Yes," provide the name and address of the intermediary on line 27 ☐ **Yes** ☐ **No**

Part I Gross Profit and Contract Price. Complete this part for all years of the installment agreement.

5	Selling price including mortgages and other debts. **Don't** include interest, whether stated or unstated		5
6	Mortgages, debts, and other liabilities the buyer assumed or took the property subject to (see instructions)	6	
7	Subtract line 6 from line 5	7	
8	Cost or other basis of property sold	8	
9	Depreciation allowed or allowable	9	
10	Adjusted basis. Subtract line 9 from line 8	10	
11	Commissions and other expenses of sale	11	
12	Income recapture from Form 4797, Part III (see instructions)	12	
13	Add lines 10, 11, and 12		13
14	Subtract line 13 from line 5. If zero or less, **don't** complete the rest of this form. See instructions		14
15	If the property described on line 1 above was your main home, enter the amount of your excluded gain. See instructions. Otherwise, enter -0-		15
16	**Gross profit.** Subtract line 15 from line 14		16
17	Subtract line 13 from line 6. If zero or less, enter -0-		17
18	**Contract price.** Add line 7 and line 17		18

Part II Installment Sale Income. Complete this part for all years of the installment agreement.

19	Gross profit percentage (expressed as a decimal amount). Divide line 16 by line 18. (For years after the year of sale, see instructions.)		19
20	If this is the year of sale, enter the amount from line 17. Otherwise, enter -0-		20
21	Payments received during year (see instructions). **Don't** include interest, whether stated or unstated		21
22	Add lines 20 and 21		22
23	Payments received in prior years (see instructions). **Don't** include interest, whether stated or unstated	23	
24	**Installment sale income.** Multiply line 22 by line 19		24
25	Enter the part of line 24 that is ordinary income under the recapture rules. See instructions		25
26	Subtract line 25 from line 24. Enter here and on Schedule D or Form 4797. See instructions		26

Part III Related Party Installment Sale Income. Don't complete if you received the final payment this tax year.

27 Name, address, and taxpayer identifying number of related party

28 Did the related party resell or dispose of the property ("second disposition") during this tax year? ☐ **Yes** ☐ **No**

29 **If the answer to question 28 is "Yes," complete lines 30 through 37 below unless one of the following conditions is met. Check the box that applies.**

a ☐ The second disposition was more than 2 years after the first disposition (other than dispositions of marketable securities). If this box is checked, enter the date of disposition (mm/dd/yyyy)

b ☐ The first disposition was a sale or exchange of stock to the issuing corporation.

c ☐ The second disposition was an involuntary conversion and the threat of conversion occurred after the first disposition.

d ☐ The second disposition occurred after the death of the original seller or buyer.

e ☐ It can be established to the satisfaction of the IRS that tax avoidance wasn't a principal purpose for either of the dispositions. If this box is checked, attach an explanation. See instructions.

30	Selling price of property sold by related party (see instructions)	30
31	Enter contract price from line 18 for year of first sale	31
32	Enter the **smaller** of line 30 or line 31	32
33	Total payments received by the end of your 2022 tax year (see instructions)	33
34	Subtract line 33 from line 32. If zero or less, enter -0-	34
35	Multiply line 34 by the gross profit percentage on line 19 for year of first sale	35
36	Enter the part of line 35 that is ordinary income under the recapture rules. See instructions	36
37	Subtract line 36 from line 35. Enter here and on Schedule D or Form 4797. See instructions	37

For Paperwork Reduction Act Notice, see page 4. Cat. No. 13601R Form **6252** (2022)

2. The basis of Janis's property is calculated below.

Basis of the property given up	$ 350,000
+ Boot paid	0
− Boot received	(140,000)
+ Gain recognized	140,000
Basis of the like-kind property received	$ 350,000

3. Kevin's recognized gain is equal to the lesser of the gain realized or the boot received. Since he received no boot, the recognized gain is zero.

Calculation of gain realized:	
Fair market value of the property received	$ 560,000
Less: boot paid ($105,000 + $35,000)	(140,000)
Less: adjusted basis of property given up	(280,000)
Gain realized	$ 140,000
Boot received	$ 0

4. The basis of Kevin's new property is calculated below.

Basis of the property given up	$ 280,000
+ Boot paid	140,000
− Boot received	0
+ Gain recognized	0
Basis of the property received	$ 420,000

♦

8-11a Like-Kind Property

The term "like-kind property" does not include inventory, stocks, bonds, or other securities or any personal property such as equipment, cars, trucks, machines, and furniture. Real property is more or less considered to be like-kind with any other real property so long as the original property and the new property are both used in a trade or business or held for investment.

Although the repeal of like-kind treatment for personal property does not permit the deferral of gains on that type of property, this may result in some favorable outcomes as well. The deferral on a like-kind exchange is not elective, it is required. One of the most common forms of exchange for a small business is the trade-in of a business auto. Because the market value of a used auto is almost always below its adjusted basis, the losses were not deductible under the previous like-kind exchange rules. Now that personal property is not eligible for like-kind treatment, these losses may be deductible.

Self-Study Problem 8.11 *See Appendix E for Solutions to Self-Study Problems*

Daniel James exchanges land used in his business for a new parcel of land. Daniel's basis in the land acquired on February 14, 2015, is $18,000, and the land is subject to a mortgage of $8,000, which is assumed by the other party to the exchange. Daniel receives new land worth $22,000. The exchange agreement and delivery of the title to the land both took place on May 12, 2022. Use Part I and Part III only of Form 8824 on Pages 8-39 and 8-40 to calculate Daniel's recognized gain on the exchange and his basis in the new land.

Learning Objective 8.12

Calculate recognized and deferred gains on involuntary conversions.

8-12 INVOLUNTARY CONVERSIONS

Occasionally, taxpayers are forced to dispose of property as a result of circumstances beyond their control. At the election of the taxpayer, and provided certain conditions are met, the gain on an involuntary conversion of property may be deferred. The provisions require that the property must be replaced and the basis of the replacement property reduced by the amount of the gain deferred. An involuntary conversion is defined as the destruction of the taxpayer's property in whole or in part, or loss of the property by theft, seizure, requisition, or condemnation. Also, property sold pursuant to reclamation laws, and livestock destroyed by disease or drought, are subject to the involuntary conversion rules. To qualify for nonrecognition of gain, the taxpayer must obtain qualified replacement property. The replacement property must be "similar or related in service or use." This definition is narrower than the like-kind rule; the property must be very similar to the property converted. Generally, a taxpayer has 2 years after the close of the tax year in which a gain was realized to obtain replacement property.

A realized gain on the involuntary conversion of property occurs when the taxpayer receives insurance proceeds or other payments in excess of his or her adjusted basis in the converted property. Taxpayers need not recognize any gain if they completely reinvest the proceeds or payments in qualified replacement property within the required time period. If they do not reinvest the total amount of the payments received, they must recognize a gain equal to the amount of the payment not reinvested (but limited to the gain realized). The basis of the replacement property is equal to the cost of the replacement property reduced by any gain not recognized on the transaction. The holding period of the replacement property includes the period the original property was held.

EXAMPLE Tammy's office building, which has an adjusted basis of $600,000, is destroyed by fire in 2022. In the same year, Tammy receives $700,000 of insurance proceeds for the loss. She has until December 31, 2024, (2 years after the end of the taxable year in which the gain is realized), to acquire a replacement building. In 2023, Tammy replaces the building with a new building that cost $680,000. Her realized gain on the involuntary conversion is $100,000 ($700,000 − $600,000), and the gain recognized is $20,000, which is the $700,000 of cash received less the amount reinvested ($680,000). The basis of the new building is $600,000 ($680,000 − $80,000), the cost of the new building less the portion of the gain not recognized. ♦

The involuntary conversion provision applies only to gains, not to losses. The provision must be elected by the taxpayer. In contrast, the like-kind exchange provision discussed previously applies to both gains and losses and is not elective.

Self-Study Problem 8.12 *See Appendix E for Solutions to Self-Study Problems*

Sam's store is destroyed in 2022 as a result of a flood. The store has an adjusted basis of $70,000, and Sam receives insurance proceeds of $150,000 on the loss. Sam invests $135,000 in a replacement store in 2023. Calculate Sam's recognized gain, assuming an election under the involuntary conversion provision is made. Calculate Sam's basis in the replacement store.

Self-Study Problem 8.11

Form **8824**

Department of the Treasury
Internal Revenue Service

Like-Kind Exchanges

(and section 1043 conflict-of-interest sales)

Attach to your tax return.

Go to *www.irs.gov/Form8824* for instructions and the latest information.

OMB No. 1545-1190

2022

Attachment Sequence No. **109**

Name(s) shown on tax return | **Identifying number**

Part I **Information on the Like-Kind Exchange**

Note: Only real property should be described on lines 1 and 2. If the property described on line 1 or line 2 is real property located outside the United States, indicate the country.

1 Description of like-kind property given up:

2 Description of like-kind property received:

3	Date like-kind property given up was originally acquired (month, day, year)	3	MM/DD/YYYY
4	Date you actually transferred your property to the other party (month, day, year)	4	MM/DD/YYYY
5	Date like-kind property you received was identified by written notice to another party (month, day, year). See instructions for 45-day written identification requirement	5	MM/DD/YYYY
6	Date you actually received the like-kind property from other party (month, day, year). See instructions	6	MM/DD/YYYY

7 Was the exchange of the property given up or received made with a related party, either directly or indirectly (such as through an intermediary)? See instructions. If "Yes," complete Part II. If "No," go to Part III ☐ **Yes** ☐ **No**

Note: Do not file this form if a related party sold property into the exchange, directly or indirectly (such as through an intermediary); that property became your replacement property; and none of the exceptions on line 11 applies to the exchange. Instead, report the disposition of the property as if the exchange had been a sale. If one of the exceptions on line 11 applies to the exchange, complete Part II.

Part II **Related Party Exchange Information**

8 Name of related party	Relationship to you	Related party's identifying number

Address (no., street, and apt., room, or suite no.; city or town; state; and ZIP code)

9 During this tax year (and before the date that is 2 years after the last transfer of property that was part of the exchange), did the related party sell or dispose of any part of the like-kind property received from you (or an intermediary) in the exchange? ☐ **Yes** ☐ **No**

10 During this tax year (and before the date that is 2 years after the last transfer of property that was part of the exchange), did you sell or dispose of any part of the like-kind property you received? ☐ **Yes** ☐ **No**

*If both lines 9 and 10 are "No" and this is the year of the exchange, go to Part III. If both lines 9 and 10 are "No" and this is **not** the year of the exchange, stop here. If either line 9 or line 10 is "Yes," complete Part III and report on this year's tax return the deferred gain or (loss) from line 24 **unless** one of the exceptions on line 11 applies.*

11 If one of the exceptions below applies to the disposition, check the applicable box.

a ☐ The disposition was after the death of either of the related parties.

b ☐ The disposition was an involuntary conversion, and the threat of conversion occurred after the exchange.

c ☐ You can establish to the satisfaction of the IRS that neither the exchange nor the disposition had tax avoidance as one of its principal purposes. If this box is checked, attach an explanation. See instructions.

Form 8824 (2022) Page **2**

Name(s) shown on tax return. Do not enter name and social security number if shown on other side. | **Your social security number**

Part III Realized Gain or (Loss), Recognized Gain, and Basis of Like-Kind Property Received

Caution: If you transferred **and** received (**a**) more than one group of like-kind properties, or (**b**) cash or other (not like-kind) property, see ***Reporting of multi-asset exchanges*** in the instructions.

Note: Complete lines 12 through 14 **only** if you gave up property that was not like-kind. Otherwise, go to line 15.

12	Fair market value (FMV) of other property given up. See instructions	12	
13	Adjusted basis of other property given up	13	
14	Gain or (loss) recognized on other property given up. Subtract line 13 from line 12. Report the gain or (loss) in the same manner as if the exchange had been a sale	14	
	Caution: If the property given up was used previously or partly as a home, see ***Property used as home*** in the instructions.		
15	Cash received, FMV of other property received, plus net liabilities assumed by other party, reduced (but not below zero) by any exchange expenses you incurred. See instructions	15	
16	FMV of like-kind property you received	16	
17	Add lines 15 and 16	17	
18	Adjusted basis of like-kind property you gave up, net amounts paid to other party, plus any exchange expenses **not** used on line 15. See instructions	18	
19	**Realized gain or (loss).** Subtract line 18 from line 17	19	
20	Enter the smaller of line 15 or line 19, but not less than zero	20	
21	Ordinary income under recapture rules. Enter here and on Form 4797, line 16. See instructions	21	
22	Subtract line 21 from line 20. If zero or less, enter -0-. If more than zero, enter here and on Schedule D or Form 4797, unless the installment method applies. See instructions	22	
23	**Recognized gain.** Add lines 21 and 22	23	
24	Deferred gain or (loss). Subtract line 23 from line 19. If a related party exchange, see instructions	24	
25	**Basis of like-kind property received.** Subtract line 15 from the sum of lines 18 and 23. See instructions	25	

Part IV Deferral of Gain From Section 1043 Conflict-of-Interest Sales

Note: This part is to be used **only** by officers or employees of the executive branch of the federal government or judicial officers of the federal government (including certain spouses, minor or dependent children, and trustees as described in section 1043) for reporting nonrecognition of gain under section 1043 on the sale of property to comply with the conflict-of-interest requirements. This part can be used **only** if the cost of the replacement property is more than the basis of the divested property.

26 Enter the number from the upper right corner of your certificate of divestiture. (**Do not** attach a copy of your certificate. Keep the certificate with your records.) ______ -

27 Description of divested property ______

28 Description of replacement property ______

29	Date divested property was sold (month, day, year)	29	MM/DD/YYYY
30	Sales price of divested property. See instructions	30	
31	Basis of divested property	31	
32	**Realized gain.** Subtract line 31 from line 30	32	
33	Cost of replacement property purchased within 60 days after date of sale	33	
34	Subtract line 33 from line 30. If zero or less, enter -0-	34	
35	Ordinary income under recapture rules. Enter here and on Form 4797, line 10. See instructions	35	
36	Subtract line 35 from line 34. If zero or less, enter -0-. If more than zero, enter here and on Schedule D or Form 4797. See instructions	36	
37	**Deferred gain.** Subtract the sum of lines 35 and 36 from line 32	37	
38	**Basis of replacement property.** Subtract line 37 from line 33	38	

Form **8824** (2022)

KEY TERMS

capitalization, 8-2
betterment, 8-2
adaptation, 8-2
restoration, 8-2
depreciation, 8-5
Modified Accelerated Cost Recovery System (MACRS), 8-6
recovery period, 8-6
asset depreciation ranges (ADRs), 8-6
half-year convention, 8-7
straight-line depreciation, 8-7
mid-quarter convention, 8-8
bonus depreciation, 8-10
qualified improvement property (QIP), 8-10
mid-month convention, 8-12
Section 179, 8-13
election to expense, 8-13
listed property, 8-17
intangibles, 8-21
Section 197 intangibles, 8-21
amortization, 8-21
Section 1231 assets, 8-22
Section 1231 lookback, 8-23
depreciation recapture, 8-24
Section 1245 recapture, 8-24
Section 1250 recapture, 8-25
unrecaptured depreciation, 8-26
Section 291 recapture, 8-26
installment sales, 8-31
like-kind exchange, 8-34
boot, 8-34
like-kind property, 8-37
involuntary conversion, 8-38
qualified replacement property, 8-38

KEY POINTS

Learning Objectives	Key Points
LO 8.1: Explain the concept of capitalization and depreciation.	• Capitalization is the process of recording an expenditure for an item that is likely to provide benefits over a long period of time as an asset on the balance sheet rather than as an expense on the income statement. • Depreciation is the accounting process of allocating and deducting the cost of an asset over a period of years and does not necessarily mean physical deterioration or loss of value of the asset. • Land is not depreciated.
LO 8.2: Calculate depreciation expense using the MACRS tables.	• The Modified Accelerated Cost Recovery System (MACRS) allows taxpayers who invest in capital assets to write off an asset's cost over a period designated in the tax law and to use an accelerated method of depreciation for assets other than real estate. • The minimum number of years over which the cost of an asset may be deducted (the recovery period) depends on the type of property and the year in which the property was acquired. • Under MACRS, taxpayers calculate the depreciation of an asset using a table, which contains a percentage rate for each year of the property's recovery period and includes the half-year convention for personal property and mid-month convention for real property. • The mid-quarter convention must be applied if more than 40 percent of the total cost of a taxpayer's tangible property acquired during the year, other than real property, is placed in service during the last quarter of the tax year. • The bonus depreciation rules allow taxpayers purchasing new or used property with a MACRS recovery period of 20 years or less (see Table 8.1), computer software, and certain leasehold improvements to directly write off 100 percent of the cost of the assets in the year placed in service. Bonus depreciation is presumed to apply unless the taxpayer elects out of the provision. • There are no taxable income limits or thresholds associated with bonus depreciation. • For post-1986 acquired real estate, MACRS uses the straight-line method over 27.5 years for residential realty and 39 years for nonresidential realty (31.5 years for realty acquired generally before May 13, 1993).

LO 8.3: Identify when a Section 179 election to expense the cost of property may be used.	• Qualified Section 179 property is personal property (property other than real estate or assets used in residential real estate rental activities) placed in service during the year and used in a trade or business. • The maximum cost that may be expensed in the year of acquisition under Section 179 is $1,080,000 for 2022. The property may be new or used. • The $1,080,000 maximum is reduced dollar for dollar by the cost of qualifying property placed in service during the year in excess of $2,700,000. • The amount that may be expensed is limited to the taxpayer's taxable income, before considering any amount expensed under this election, from any trade or business of the taxpayer. Any excess amount resulting from the taxable income limitation may be carried forward to succeeding tax years. • Section 179 expensed amounts reduce the basis of the asset before calculating any regular MACRS depreciation on the remaining cost of the asset even when the taxpayer is unable to deduct the full amount expensed due to the taxable income limitation.
LO 8.4: Apply the limitations placed on depreciation of "listed property."	• Special rules apply to the depreciation of listed property. • Listed property includes those types of assets which lend themselves to personal use. • Listed property includes automobiles, certain other vehicles, and property used for entertainment, recreation, or amusement. • If listed property is used 50 percent or less in a qualified business use, any depreciation deduction must be calculated using the straight-line method of depreciation over an alternate recovery period, and the special election to expense under Section 179 and bonus depreciation are not allowed.
LO 8.5: Apply the limitations on depreciation of "luxury automobiles."	• The depreciation of passenger automobiles is subject to an annual dollar limitation, commonly referred to as the luxury automobile limitation. • For automobiles acquired in 2022, the maximum depreciation is $19,200 (including $8,000 bonus) (Year 1), $18,000 (Year 2), $10,800 (Year 3), and $6,460 (Year 4 and subsequent years, until fully depreciated).
LO 8.6: Calculate the amortization of goodwill and certain other intangibles.	• Section 197 intangibles are amortized over a 15-year period, beginning with the month of acquisition. • Qualified Section 197 intangibles include goodwill, going-concern value, workforce in place, information bases, know-how, customer-based intangibles, licenses, permits, rights granted by a governmental unit, covenants not to compete, franchises, trademarks, and trade names. • Examples of Section 197 exclusions are interests in a corporation, partnership, trust, or estate; interests in land; computer software readily available for purchase by the general public; interests in films, sound recordings, and video recordings; and self-created intangible assets.
LO 8.7: Classify gains and losses from Section 1231 assets.	• Section 1231 assets include (1) depreciable or real property used in a trade or business, (2) timber, coal, or domestic iron ore, (3) livestock (not including poultry) held for draft, breeding, dairy, or sporting purposes, and (4) unharvested crops on land used in a trade or business. • If net Section 1231 gains exceed the losses, the excess is a long-term capital gain. When the net Section 1231 losses exceed the gains, all gains are treated as ordinary income, and all losses are fully deductible as ordinary losses.

LO 8.8: Apply the depreciation recapture rules.	• Depreciation recapture provisions are meant to prevent taxpayers from converting ordinary income into capital gain by claiming maximum depreciation deductions over the life of the asset and then selling the asset and receiving capital gain treatment on the resulting gain at sale. • The tax law includes a lookback provision that requires a taxpayer that has net Section 1231 gains for the current year to recharacterize the current year gain to the extent of Section 1231 losses in the past 5 years. • Under Section 1245, any gain recognized on the disposition of a Section 1245 asset (generally personal property) will be classified as ordinary income up to an amount equal to the accumulated depreciation. Any gain in excess of depreciation taken is classified as a Section 1231 gain. • Section 1250 real property recapture is the excess of depreciation expense claimed, using an accelerated method of depreciation, over what would have been allowed if the straight-line method were used. • Since the straight-line method is required for real property acquired after 1986, there will be no Section 1250 recapture on the disposition of real property. • A special 25 or 28.8 percent tax rate applies to real property gains attributable to depreciation previously taken and not already recaptured under Section 1245 or Section 1250.
LO 8.9: Apply the general treatment of casualty gains and losses for business purposes.	• The amount of a partial casualty loss from business property is insurance proceeds less the decrease in the value of the property or the adjusted basis, whichever is smaller. • The amount of a casualty loss from a complete destruction of business property is the insurance proceeds less the adjusted basis of the property. • Gains and losses from business-use assets are generally treated as ordinary income and ordinary losses, respectively.
LO 8.10: Compute the gain on installment sales.	• On an installment sale, the taxable gain reported each year is determined as follows: taxable gain equals total gain realized on the sale, divided by the contract price, and multiplied by the payment received during the year.
LO 8.11: Calculate recognized and deferred gains on like-kind exchanges.	• To qualify as a nontaxable like-kind exchange, the property exchanged must be real property, held for use in a trade or business or held for investment, and exchanged for property of a like kind. • Personal property no longer qualifies for like-kind exchange treatment. • Like-kind gain is recognized in an amount equal to the lesser of (1) the gain realized or (2) the "boot" received. Boot is money or the fair market value of other property received in addition to the like-kind property. Relief from a liability is the same as receiving cash and is treated as boot. • If a transaction qualifies as a like-kind exchange, the like-kind exchange provisions must be followed.
LO 8.12: Calculate recognized and deferred gains on involuntary conversions.	• A realized gain on the involuntary conversion of property occurs when the taxpayer receives proceeds in excess of his or her adjusted basis. • Involuntary conversion gain is not recognized if the proceeds or payments are reinvested in qualified replacement property within the required time period and the taxpayer makes the proper election.

QUESTIONS and PROBLEMS

GROUP 1: MULTIPLE CHOICE QUESTIONS

LO 8.1

1. When a taxpayer capitalizes an expenditure:
   a. The taxpayer pays for it with debt or a liability
   b. The amount is expensed immediately in accordance with ordinary and necessary deduction rules
   c. The amount is generally placed on the balance sheet awaiting time or some future event for recognition as an expense
   d. the cost can be recovered only when the item is sold

LO 8.1

2. Which if the following is not generally required to be capitalized?
   a. An adaption to a better use
   b. A betterment by expanding the size of a building
   c. A routinely performed item of maintenance
   d. A restoration of a deteriorated property

LO 8.1

3. Micah's business has four different building projects underway. Select the project that is likely to be immediately deductible.
   a. Micah is installing a new roof on a warehouse. The roof has started to leak due to its age.
   b. Micah is repainting the first-floor restrooms in his showroom. The colors did not match the furniture in the lobby.
   c. Micah is expanding the size of his inventory warehouse. The project will double the size.
   d. Micah is redesigning a machine on the factory floor that is intended to increase the speed of the machine's operation.

LO 8.1

4. Proudfoot, Inc. would like to deduct expenditures for tangible personal property under $4,000 as maintenance and repairs costs. To implement this policy, which of the following is *not* required?
   a. A written policy describing a matching treatment for the company's financial statements.
   b. Proudfoot's financial statements are audited and have an accompanying opinion.
   c. Proudfoot must be a small business with gross income below $10 million.
   d. Proudfoot must also deduct expenses under $4,000 in its financial books and records.

LO 8.2

5. Alice purchases a rental house on June 22, 2022, for a cost of $174,000. Of this amount, $100,000 is considered to be allocable to the cost of the home, with the remaining $74,000 allocable to the cost of the land. What is Alice's maximum depreciation deduction for 2022 using MACRS?
   a. $1,970
   b. $1,667
   c. $1,177
   d. $1,061
   e. $3,485

LO 8.2

6. An asset (not an automobile) put in service in June 2022 has a depreciable basis of $25,000 and a recovery period of 5 years. Assuming half-year convention, no bonus depreciation, and no election to expense is made, what is the maximum amount of cost that can be deducted in 2022?
   a. $2,500
   b. $5,000
   c. $6,000
   d. $30,000
   e. None of the above

LO 8.2

7. An asset (not an automobile) put in service in June 2022 has a depreciable basis of $24,000 and a recovery period of 5 years. Assuming bonus depreciation is used, half-year convention and no election to expense is made, what is the maximum amount of cost that can be deducted in 2022?
   a. $4,800
   b. $12,000
   c. $24,000
   d. $2,000
   e. $5,600

LO 8.2

8. James purchased office equipment for his business. The equipment has a depreciable basis of $16,000 and was put in service on June 1, 2022. James decides to elect straight-line depreciation under MACRS for the asset over the minimum number of years (seven years), and does not use bonus depreciation or make the election to expense. What is the amount of his depreciation deduction for the equipment for the 2022 tax year?
   a. $16,000
   b. $14,000
   c. $2,000
   d. $7,321
   e. None of the above

LO 8.2

9. Which of the following statements with respect to the depreciation of property under MACRS is *incorrect*?
   a. Under the half-year convention, one-half year of depreciation is allowed in the year the property is placed in service.
   b. If a taxpayer elects to use the straight-line method of depreciation for property in the 5-year class, all other five-year class property acquired during the year must also be depreciated using the straight-line method.
   c. In some cases, when a taxpayer places a significant amount of property in service during the last quarter of the year, real property must be depreciated using a mid-quarter convention.
   d. Real property acquired after 1986 must be depreciated using the straight-line method.
   e. The cost of property to which the MACRS rate is applied is not reduced for estimated salvage value.

LO 8.2

10. Which of the following is *true* about the MACRS depreciation system:
   a. A salvage value must be determined before depreciation percentages are applied to depreciable real estate.
   b. Residential rental buildings are depreciated over 39 years straight-line.
   c. Commercial real estate buildings are depreciated over 27.5 years straight-line.
   d. No matter when during the month depreciable real estate is purchased, it is considered to have been placed in service at mid-month for MACRS depreciation purposes.

LO 8.3

11. On July 20, 2022, Kelli purchases office equipment at a cost of $24,000. Kelli elects out of bonus depreciation but makes the election to expense for 2022. She is self-employed as an attorney, and in 2022, her business has a net income of $6,000 before considering this election to expense. Kelli has no other income or expenses for the year. What is the maximum amount that Kelli may deduct for 2022 under the election to expense, assuming she elects to expense the entire $24,000 purchase?
    a. $24,000
    b. $12,000
    c. $6,000
    d. $3,000
    e. $1,000

LO 8.3

12. Which of the following is *not* considered a limit on the immediate expensing election of Section 179?
    a. Fifty percent of qualified improvement property
    b. Total Section 179-eligible property acquired in excess of $3,780,000
    c. The taxable income of the taxpayer considering all income and deductions except for Section 179 immediate expensing
    d. An annual limit of $1,080,000
    e. None of the above

LO 8.4

13. Which of the following is a *true* statement about depreciation on listed property?
    a. All listed property is not depreciable, and any costs are recovered when the property is sold.
    b. Cellphones and computers generally both meet the definition of listed property.
    c. Listed property includes school buses and tractors.
    d. If listed property is used less than 50 percent for business purposes, depreciation must be straight-line.

LO 8.5

14. In 2022, Ben purchases and places in service a new auto for his business. The auto costs $57,000 and will be used 60 percent for business. Assuming the half-year convention applies and Ben elects out of bonus depreciation and Section 179, what will be the depreciation on the auto in 2022?
    a. $11,200
    b. $6,840
    c. $6,720
    d. $6,120
    e. None of the above

LO 8.5

15. In 2022, Ben purchases and places in service a new auto for his business. The auto costs $57,000 and will be used 100 percent for business. Assuming the half-year convention applies and Ben does not elect out of bonus depreciation, what will be the depreciation on the auto in 2022?
    a. $57,000
    b. $18,200
    c. $19,200
    d. $11,200
    e. None of the above

LO 8.5

16. Tupper Corp. purchases a new auto in 2022 for $62,000. The auto is used 100 percent for business and the half-year convention applies. Tupper uses bonus depreciation when available. What is the *2023* depreciation for this auto?
    a. $12,400
    b. $13,696
    c. $18,000
    d. $19,200
    e. $19,840

LO 8.6

17. The amortization period for Section 197 intangibles is:
    a. 5 years
    b. 7 years
    c. 10 years
    d. 15 years
    e. 40 years

LO 8.6

18. Which of the following intangibles is defined as a Section 197 intangible asset?
    a. An interest in land
    b. A partnership interest
    c. An interest in a corporation
    d. A covenant not to compete acquired as part of a business
    e. A separately acquired sound recording

LO 8.7

19. Which of the following is Section 1231 property?
    a. Land held for investment purposes
    b. A machine used in a business
    c. Accounts receivable
    d. Inventory
    e. Paintings owned by the artist

LO 8.7

20. Which of the following taxpayers would be subject to the Section 1231 lookback rule?
    a. Gun-Joh sold depreciable business property held for more than one year at a gain this year and has Section 1231 losses in the prior year.
    b. Tawny sold business property held for less than one year at a gain.
    c. Hubie sold depreciable business property held for more than one year at a loss this year and has Section 1231 gains in the prior year.
    d. Li sold inventory at a loss in the prior year due to obsolescence but returned to profitable inventory sales in the current year.

LO 8.7
LO 8.8

21. In 2022, Mary sells for $24,000 a machine used in her business. The machine was purchased on May 1, 2019, at a cost of $21,000. Mary has deducted depreciation on the machine of $5,000. Mary has no previous Section 1231 gains or losses. What is the amount and nature of Mary's gain as a result of the sale of the machine?
    a. $8,000 Section 1231 gain
    b. $8,000 ordinary income under Section 1245
    c. $5,000 ordinary income and $3,000 Section 1231 gain
    d. $5,000 Section 1231 gain and $3,000 ordinary income under Section 1245
    e. None of the above

LO 8.7
LO 8.8

22. During 2022, Paul, an individual taxpayer, sells residential rental property for $180,000, which he acquired in 2001 for $160,000. Paul has claimed straight-line depreciation on the building of $50,000. What is the amount and nature of Paul's gain on the sale of the rental property?
    a. $70,000 ordinary income
    b. $10,000 ordinary income and $60,000 ordinary gain
    c. $70,000 Section 1231 gain
    d. $20,000 Section 1231 gain, $50,000 "unrecaptured depreciation"
    e. None of the above

LO 8.8

23. Jeanie acquires an apartment building in 2011 for $280,000 and sells it for $480,000 in 2022. At the time of sale there is $60,000 of accumulated straight-line depreciation on the apartment building. Assuming Jeanie is in the highest tax bracket for ordinary income and the Medicare tax on net investment income applies, how much of her gain is taxed at 28.8 percent?
    a. None
    b. $60,000
    c. $200,000
    d. $280,000
    e. $260,000

LO 8.8

24. During 2022, Peters Corporation sells rental real property for $180,000, which was acquired in 2001 for $160,000. Peters has claimed straight-line depreciation on the building of $50,000. What is the amount and nature of Peter's gain on the sale of the real property?
    a. $70,000 ordinary income
    b. $10,000 ordinary income and $60,000 Section 1231 gain
    c. $70,000 Section 1231 gain
    d. $20,000 Section 1231 gain, $50,000 "unrecaptured depreciation"

LO 8.9

25. Virginia has business property that is stolen and partially destroyed by the time it was recovered. She receives an insurance reimbursement of $5,000 on property that had a $14,000 basis and a decrease in market value of $10,000 due to damage caused by the theft. What is the amount of Virginia's casualty loss?
    a. $14,000
    b. $5,000
    c. $10,000
    d. $4,000
    e. None of the above

LO 8.9

26. Prashant has business property that is stolen and totally destroyed by the time it was recovered. He receives an insurance reimbursement of $5,000 on property that had a $14,000 basis and a market value of $20,000 before destruction. What is the amount of Prashant's casualty loss?
    a. $14,000
    b. $9,000
    c. $15,000
    d. $20,000
    e. None of the above

LO 8.10

27. Pat sells land for $20,000 cash and a $80,000 four-year note with a reasonable interest rate. If her basis in the property is $30,000 and she receives the $20,000 down payment and the first $20,000 payment on the note in the year of sale, how much is Pat's taxable gain in the year of sale using the installment sales method?
    a. $0
    b. $40,000
    c. $20,000
    d. $28,000
    e. $70,000

LO 8.11

28. Fred and Sarajane exchanged land in a qualifying like-kind exchange. Fred gives up land with an adjusted basis of $11,000 (fair market value of $16,000) in exchange for Sarajane's land with a fair market value of $12,000 plus $4,000 cash. How much gain should Fred recognize on the exchange?
    a. $5,000
    b. $4,000
    c. $1,000
    d. $0
    e. None of the above

LO 8.11

29. What is Sarajane's basis in the land received in the exchange described in Question 28, assuming her basis in the land given up was $12,000?
    a. $0
    b. $12,000
    c. $14,000
    d. $16,000
    e. None of the above

LO 8.12

30. Oscar owns a building that is destroyed in a hurricane. His adjusted basis in the building before the hurricane is $130,000. His insurance company pays him $140,000 and he immediately invests in a new building at a cost of $142,000. What is the amount of recognized gain or loss on the destruction of Oscar's building?
    a. $0
    b. $10,000 gain
    c. $8,000 gain
    d. $12,000 gain
    e. $2,000 loss

LO 8.12

31. Using the information from Question 30, what is Oscar's basis on his new building?
    a. $130,000
    b. $132,000
    c. $140,000
    d. $142,000

GROUP 2: PROBLEMS

LO 8.1

1. Define each of the following as it relates to the tax rules for capitalization of expenditures:
    a. Betterment
    b. Adaptation
    c. Restoration

LO 8.1

2. Describe the requirements to apply a de minimis safe harbor to tangible property expenditures for a business taxpayer.

LO 8.2

3. Is land allowed to be depreciated? Why or why not?

LO 8.2

4. Is it possible to depreciate a residential rental building when it is actually increasing in value? Why?

LO 8.2
LO 8.3

5. Mike purchases a new heavy-duty truck (five-year class recovery property) for his delivery service on March 30, 2022. No other assets were purchased during the year. The truck is not considered a passenger automobile for purposes of the listed property and luxury automobile limitations. The truck has a depreciable basis of $50,000 and an estimated useful life of 5 years. Assume half-year convention for tax.
    a. Calculate the amount of depreciation for 2022 using the straight-line depreciation election, using MACRS tables over the minimum number of years with no bonus depreciation or election to expense.
    b. Calculate the amount of depreciation for 2022, including bonus depreciation but no election to expense, that Mike could deduct using the MACRS tables.
    c. Calculate the amount of depreciation for 2022 including the election to expense but no bonus depreciation that Mike could deduct. Assume no income limit on the expense election.

LO 8.2

6. On June 8, 2022, Holly purchased a residential apartment building. The cost basis assigned to the building is $650,000. Holly also owns another residential apartment building that she purchased on October 15, 2022, with a cost basis of $400,000.
    a. Calculate Holly's total depreciation deduction for the apartments for 2022 using MACRS.
    b. Calculate Holly's total depreciation deduction for the apartments for 2023 using MACRS.

LO 8.2

7. Give the MACRS depreciation life of the following assets:
   a. An automobile
   b. Business furniture
   c. A computer
   d. Residential real estate
   e. Commercial real estate
   f. Land

LO 8.2

8. Explain the use of the mid-quarter convention for MACRS depreciation:

LO 8.2

9. Calculate the following:
   a. The first year of depreciation on a office building that cost $250,000 purchased June 2, 2022.
   b. The second year (2023) of depreciation on a computer that cost $5,000 purchased in May 2022, using the half-year convention and accelerated depreciation considering any bonus depreciation taken.
   c. The first year of depreciation on a computer costing $2,800 purchased in May 2022, using the half-year convention and straight-line depreciation with no bonus depreciation.
   d. The third year of depreciation on business furniture costing $10,000 purchased in March 2020, using the half-year convention and accelerated depreciation but no bonus depreciation.

LO 8.2
LO 8.3
LO 8.4
LO 8.5

10. During 2022, William purchases the following capital assets for use in his catering business:

New passenger automobile (September 30)	$66,000
Baking equipment (June 30)	10,000

Assume that William decides to use the election to expense on the baking equipment (and has adequate taxable income to cover the deduction) but not on the automobile, and he also uses the MACRS accelerated method to calculate depreciation but elects out of bonus depreciation. Calculate William's maximum depreciation deduction for 2022, assuming he uses the automobile 100 percent in his business.

LO 8.2
LO 8.4

11. On February 2, 2022, Alexandra purchases a personal computer. The computer cost $2,400. Alexandra uses the computer 75 percent of the time in her accounting business, and the remaining 25 percent of the time for various personal uses. Calculate Alexandra's maximum depreciation deduction for 2022 for the computer, assuming half-year convention and she does not use bonus depreciation or make the election to expense.

LO 8.2
LO 8.4
LO 8.5

12. On September 14, 2022, Jay purchased a passenger automobile that is used 75 percent in his business. The automobile has a basis for depreciation purposes of $48,000, and Jay uses the accelerated method under MACRS. Jay does not elect to expense. Calculate Jay's depreciation deduction for 2022 assuming bonus depreciation.

LO 8.2
LO 8.4
LO 8.5

13. During 2022, Pepe Guardio purchases the following property for use in his calendar year-end manufacturing business:

Item	*Date Acquired*	*Cost*
Manufacturing equipment (7 year)	June 2	$ 60,000
Office furniture	September 15	10,000
Office computer	November 18	1,600
Passenger automobile (used 90 percent for business)	May 31	55,000
Warehouse	May 9	
Building		180,000
Land		135,000

Pepe uses the accelerated depreciation method under MACRS, if available, and does not make the election to expense and elects out of bonus depreciation. Use Form 4562 on Pages 8-53 and 8-54 to report Pepe's depreciation expense for 2022.

LO 8.2
LO 8.4
LO 8.5

14. Go to the IRS website (**www.irs.gov**) and assuming bonus depreciation is used, redo Problem 13, using the most recent interactive Form 4562, Depreciation and Amortization. Print out the *completed Form 4562*.

LO 8.2
LO 8.3

15. Tom has a successful business with $100,000 of taxable income before the election to expense in 2022. He purchases one new asset in 2022, a new machine which is seven-year MACRS property and costs $25,000. If you are Tom's tax advisor, how would you advise Tom to treat the purchase for tax purposes in 2022? Why?

LO 8.6

16. Derek purchases a small business from Art on August 30, 2022. He paid the following amounts for the business:

Fixed assets	$170,000
Goodwill	50,000
Covenant not to compete	20,000
Total	$240,000

   a. How much of the $240,000 purchase price is for Section 197 intangible assets?
   b. What amount can Derek deduct on his 2022 tax return as Section 197 intangible amortization?

LO 8.6

17. Annie develops a successful tax practice. She sells the practice to her friend Carol for $54,000 and moves to Florida to retire. The tax practice has no assets except intangible benefits such as the goodwill and going-concern value Annie has developed over the years. How should Carol treat the $54,000 cost of the tax practice she has purchased?

LO 8.7
LO 8.8

18. Nadia Shalom has the following transactions during the year:
   - Sale of office equipment on March 15 that cost $21,500 when purchased on July 1, 2020. Nadia has claimed $21,500 in depreciation and sells the asset for $13,500 with no selling costs.
   - Sale of land on April 19 for $121,000. The land cost $128,000 when purchased on February 1, 2011. Nadia's selling costs are $4,700.
   - Sale of an office building on April 19 for $250,000. The building cost $230,000 when purchased on February 1, 2011, and Nadia has claimed $62,500 in depreciation. Nadia pays a sales commission of $12,500.
   - Assume there were no capital improvements on either business asset sold. Nadia's Social Security number is 924-56-5783.

   Complete Form 4797 on Pages 8-55 and 8-56 to report the above gains or losses.

LO 8.8
LO 8.10

19. Steve Drake sells a rental house on January 1, 2022, and receives $100,000 cash and a note for $50,000 at 7-percent interest. The purchaser also assumes the mortgage on the property of $30,000. Steve's original cost for the house was $175,000 on January 1, 2014, and accumulated depreciation was $30,000 on the date of sale. He collects only the $100,000 down payment in the year of sale.
   a. If Steve elects to recognize the total gain on the property in the year of sale, calculate the taxable gain.
   b. Assuming Steve uses the installment sale method, complete Form 6252 on Page 8-57 for the year of the sale.
   c. Assuming Steve collects $5,000 (not including interest) of the note principal in the year following the year of sale, calculate the amount of income recognized in that year under the installment sale method.

LO 8.7
LO 8.8

20. William sold Section 1245 property for $26,000 in 2022. The property cost $40,000 when it was purchased five years ago. The depreciation claimed on the property was $22,000.
    a. Calculate the adjusted basis of the property.
    b. Calculate the realized gain on the sale.
    c. Calculate the amount of ordinary income under Section 1245.
    d. Calculate the Section 1231 gain.

LO 8.9

21. An office machine with a market value of $10,000 used by Josie in her accounting business was completely destroyed by fire. The adjusted basis of the machine was $8,000 (original basis of $14,000 less accumulated depreciation of $6,000). The machine was not insured. Calculate the amount and nature of Josie's gain or loss as a result of this casualty.

LO 8.11

22. Carey exchanges land for other land in a qualifying like-kind exchange. Carey's basis in the land given up is $115,000, and the property has a fair market value of $150,000. In exchange for her property, Carey receives land with a fair market value of $100,000 and cash of $10,000. In addition, the other party to the exchange assumes a mortgage loan on Carey's property of $40,000.
    a. Calculate Carey's recognized gain, if any, on the exchange.
    b. Calculate Carey's basis in the property received.

LO 8.12

23. Teresa's manufacturing plant is destroyed by fire. The plant has an adjusted basis of $270,000, and Teresa receives insurance proceeds of $410,000 for the loss. Teresa reinvests $420,000 in a replacement plant within 2 years of receiving the insurance proceeds.
    a. Calculate Teresa's recognized gain if she elects to utilize the involuntary conversion provision.
    b. Calculate Teresa's basis in the new plant.

GROUP 2:
PROBLEM 13

Form **4562**
Department of the Treasury
Internal Revenue Service

Depreciation and Amortization
(Including Information on Listed Property)
Attach to your tax return.
Go to *www.irs.gov/Form4562* for instructions and the latest information.

OMB No. 1545-0172
2022
Attachment Sequence No. **179**

Name(s) shown on return	Business or activity to which this form relates	**Identifying number**

Part I **Election To Expense Certain Property Under Section 179**
Note: If you have any listed property, complete Part V before you complete Part I.

1	Maximum amount (see instructions)	1	
2	Total cost of section 179 property placed in service (see instructions)	2	
3	Threshold cost of section 179 property before reduction in limitation (see instructions)	3	
4	Reduction in limitation. Subtract line 3 from line 2. If zero or less, enter -0-	4	
5	Dollar limitation for tax year. Subtract line 4 from line 1. If zero or less, enter -0-. If married filing separately, see instructions	5	

6	(a) Description of property	(b) Cost (business use only)	(c) Elected cost

7	Listed property. Enter the amount from line 29	7	
8	Total elected cost of section 179 property. Add amounts in column (c), lines 6 and 7	8	
9	Tentative deduction. Enter the **smaller** of line 5 or line 8	9	
10	Carryover of disallowed deduction from line 13 of your 2021 Form 4562	10	
11	Business income limitation. Enter the smaller of business income (not less than zero) or line 5. See instructions	11	
12	Section 179 expense deduction. Add lines 9 and 10, but don't enter more than line 11	12	
13	Carryover of disallowed deduction to 2023. Add lines 9 and 10, less line 12	13	

Note: Don't use Part II or Part III below for listed property. Instead, use Part V.

Part II **Special Depreciation Allowance and Other Depreciation (Don't** include listed property. See instructions.**)**

14	Special depreciation allowance for qualified property (other than listed property) placed in service during the tax year. See instructions	14	
15	Property subject to section 168(f)(1) election	15	
16	Other depreciation (including ACRS)	16	

Part III **MACRS Depreciation (Don't** include listed property. See instructions.**)**

Section A

17	MACRS deductions for assets placed in service in tax years beginning before 2022	17	
18	If you are electing to group any assets placed in service during the tax year into one or more general asset accounts, check here ☐		

Section B—Assets Placed in Service During 2022 Tax Year Using the General Depreciation System

(a) Classification of property	(b) Month and year placed in service	(c) Basis for depreciation (business/investment use only—see instructions)	(d) Recovery period	(e) Convention	(f) Method	(g) Depreciation deduction
19a 3-year property						
b 5-year property						
c 7-year property						
d 10-year property						
e 15-year property						
f 20-year property						
g 25-year property			25 yrs.		S/L	
h Residential rental property			27.5 yrs.	MM	S/L	
			27.5 yrs.	MM	S/L	
i Nonresidential real property			39 yrs.	MM	S/L	
				MM	S/L	

Section C—Assets Placed in Service During 2022 Tax Year Using the Alternative Depreciation System

(a) Classification of property	(b)	(c)	(d)	(e)	(f)	(g)
20a Class life					S/L	
b 12-year			12 yrs.		S/L	
c 30-year			30 yrs.	MM	S/L	
d 40-year			40 yrs.	MM	S/L	

Part IV **Summary** (See instructions.)

21	Listed property. Enter amount from line 28	21	
22	**Total.** Add amounts from line 12, lines 14 through 17, lines 19 and 20 in column (g), and line 21. Enter here and on the appropriate lines of your return. Partnerships and S corporations—see instructions	22	
23	For assets shown above and placed in service during the current year, enter the portion of the basis attributable to section 263A costs	23	

Form 4562 (2022) Page **2**

Part V **Listed Property** (Include automobiles, certain other vehicles, certain aircraft, and property used for entertainment, recreation, or amusement.)

Note: For any vehicle for which you are using the standard mileage rate or deducting lease expense, complete **only** 24a, 24b, columns (a) through (c) of Section A, all of Section B, and Section C if applicable.

Section A—Depreciation and Other Information (Caution: See the instructions for limits for passenger automobiles.**)**

24a Do you have evidence to support the business/investment use claimed? ☐ **Yes** ☐ **No** | **24b** If "Yes," is the evidence written? ☐ **Yes** ☐ **No**

(a) Type of property (list vehicles first)	(b) Date placed in service	(c) Business/ investment use percentage	(d) Cost or other basis	(e) Basis for depreciation (business/investment use only)	(f) Recovery period	(g) Method/ Convention	(h) Depreciation deduction	(i) Elected section 179 cost
25 Special depreciation allowance for qualified listed property placed in service during the tax year and used more than 50% in a qualified business use. See instructions .						**25**		
26 Property used more than 50% in a qualified business use:								
		%						
		%						
		%						
27 Property used 50% or less in a qualified business use:								
		%				S/L –		
		%				S/L –		
		%				S/L –		
28 Add amounts in column (h), lines 25 through 27. Enter here and on line 21, page 1 .						**28**		
29 Add amounts in column (i), line 26. Enter here and on line 7, page 1							**29**	

Section B—Information on Use of Vehicles

Complete this section for vehicles used by a sole proprietor, partner, or other "more than 5% owner," or related person. If you provided vehicles to your employees, first answer the questions in Section C to see if you meet an exception to completing this section for those vehicles.

	(a) Vehicle 1		(b) Vehicle 2		(c) Vehicle 3		(d) Vehicle 4		(e) Vehicle 5		(f) Vehicle 6	
30 Total business/investment miles driven during the year (**don't** include commuting miles) .												
31 Total commuting miles driven during the year												
32 Total other personal (noncommuting) miles driven												
33 Total miles driven during the year. Add lines 30 through 32												
	Yes	**No**	**Yes**	**No**	**Yes**	**No**	**Yes**	**No**	**Yes**	**No**	**Yes**	**No**
34 Was the vehicle available for personal use during off-duty hours?												
35 Was the vehicle used primarily by a more than 5% owner or related person? . .												
36 Is another vehicle available for personal use?												

Section C—Questions for Employers Who Provide Vehicles for Use by Their Employees

Answer these questions to determine if you meet an exception to completing Section B for vehicles used by employees who **aren't** more than 5% owners or related persons. See instructions.

	Yes	**No**
37 Do you maintain a written policy statement that prohibits all personal use of vehicles, including commuting, by your employees?		
38 Do you maintain a written policy statement that prohibits personal use of vehicles, except commuting, by your employees? See the instructions for vehicles used by corporate officers, directors, or 1% or more owners . .		
39 Do you treat all use of vehicles by employees as personal use?		
40 Do you provide more than five vehicles to your employees, obtain information from your employees about the use of the vehicles, and retain the information received?		
41 Do you meet the requirements concerning qualified automobile demonstration use? See instructions		
Note: If your answer to 37, 38, 39, 40, or 41 is "Yes," don't complete Section B for the covered vehicles.		

Part VI **Amortization**

(a) Description of costs	(b) Date amortization begins	(c) Amortizable amount	(d) Code section	(e) Amortization period or percentage	(f) Amortization for this year
42 Amortization of costs that begins during your 2022 tax year (see instructions):					
43 Amortization of costs that began before your 2022 tax year				**43**	
44 **Total.** Add amounts in column (f). See the instructions for where to report				**44**	

Form **4562** (2022)

GROUP 2:

PROBLEM 18

Form **4797**

Department of the Treasury
Internal Revenue Service

Sales of Business Property

(Also Involuntary Conversions and Recapture Amounts Under Sections 179 and 280F(b)(2))

Attach to your tax return.

Go to *www.irs.gov/Form4797* for instructions and the latest information.

OMB No. 1545-0184

2022

Attachment Sequence No. **27**

Name(s) shown on return | **Identifying number**

1a	Enter the gross proceeds from sales or exchanges reported to you for 2022 on Form(s) 1099-B or 1099-S (or substitute statement) that you are including on line 2, 10, or 20. See instructions	1a	
b	Enter the total amount of gain that you are including on lines 2, 10, and 24 due to the partial dispositions of MACRS assets	1b	
c	Enter the total amount of loss that you are including on lines 2 and 10 due to the partial dispositions of MACRS assets	1c	

Part I **Sales or Exchanges of Property Used in a Trade or Business and Involuntary Conversions From Other Than Casualty or Theft—Most Property Held More Than 1 Year** (see instructions)

2 (a) Description of property	(b) Date acquired (mo., day, yr.)	(c) Date sold (mo., day, yr.)	(d) Gross sales price	(e) Depreciation allowed or allowable since acquisition	(f) Cost or other basis, plus improvements and expense of sale	(g) Gain or (loss) Subtract (f) from the sum of (d) and (e)

3	Gain, if any, from Form 4684, line 39	3	
4	Section 1231 gain from installment sales from Form 6252, line 26 or 37	4	
5	Section 1231 gain or (loss) from like-kind exchanges from Form 8824	5	
6	Gain, if any, from line 32, from other than casualty or theft	6	
7	Combine lines 2 through 6. Enter the gain or (loss) here and on the appropriate line as follows	7	
	Partnerships and S corporations. Report the gain or (loss) following the instructions for Form 1065, Schedule K, line 10, or Form 1120-S, Schedule K, line 9. Skip lines 8, 9, 11, and 12 below.		
	Individuals, partners, S corporation shareholders, and all others. If line 7 is zero or a loss, enter the amount from line 7 on line 11 below and skip lines 8 and 9. If line 7 is a gain and you didn't have any prior year section 1231 losses, or they were recaptured in an earlier year, enter the gain from line 7 as a long-term capital gain on the Schedule D filed with your return and skip lines 8, 9, 11, and 12 below.		
8	Nonrecaptured net section 1231 losses from prior years. See instructions	8	
9	Subtract line 8 from line 7. If zero or less, enter -0-. If line 9 is zero, enter the gain from line 7 on line 12 below. If line 9 is more than zero, enter the amount from line 8 on line 12 below and enter the gain from line 9 as a long-term capital gain on the Schedule D filed with your return. See instructions	9	

Part II **Ordinary Gains and Losses** (see instructions)

10 Ordinary gains and losses not included on lines 11 through 16 (include property held 1 year or less):

11	Loss, if any, from line 7	11	( )
12	Gain, if any, from line 7 or amount from line 8, if applicable	12	
13	Gain, if any, from line 31	13	
14	Net gain or (loss) from Form 4684, lines 31 and 38a	14	
15	Ordinary gain from installment sales from Form 6252, line 25 or 36	15	
16	Ordinary gain or (loss) from like-kind exchanges from Form 8824	16	
17	Combine lines 10 through 16	17	
18	For all except individual returns, enter the amount from line 17 on the appropriate line of your return and skip lines a and b below. For individual returns, complete lines a and b below.		
a	If the loss on line 11 includes a loss from Form 4684, line 35, column (b)(ii), enter that part of the loss here. Enter the loss from income-producing property on Schedule A (Form 1040), line 16. (Do not include any loss on property used as an employee.) Identify as from "Form 4797, line 18a." See instructions	18a	
b	Redetermine the gain or (loss) on line 17 excluding the loss, if any, on line 18a. Enter here and on Schedule 1 (Form 1040), Part I, line 4	18b	

For Paperwork Reduction Act Notice, see separate instructions. Cat. No. 13086I Form **4797** (2022)

Form 4797 (2022) Page 2

Part III Gain From Disposition of Property Under Sections 1245, 1250, 1252, 1254, and 1255 (see instructions)

19 (a) Description of section 1245, 1250, 1252, 1254, or 1255 property:	(b) Date acquired (mo., day, yr.)	(c) Date sold (mo., day, yr.)
A		
B		
C		
D		

These columns relate to the properties on lines 19A through 19D.		Property A	Property B	Property C	Property D
20 Gross sales price (**Note:** *See line 1a before completing.*)	20				
21 Cost or other basis plus expense of sale	21				
22 Depreciation (or depletion) allowed or allowable	22				
23 Adjusted basis. Subtract line 22 from line 21	23				
24 Total gain. Subtract line 23 from line 20	24				
25 **If section 1245 property:**					
a Depreciation allowed or allowable from line 22	25a				
b Enter the **smaller** of line 24 or 25a	25b				
26 **If section 1250 property:** If straight line depreciation was used, enter -0- on line 26g, except for a corporation subject to section 291.					
a Additional depreciation after 1975. See instructions	26a				
b Applicable percentage multiplied by the **smaller** of line 24 or line 26a. See instructions	26b				
c Subtract line 26a from line 24. If residential rental property **or** line 24 isn't more than line 26a, skip lines 26d and 26e	26c				
d Additional depreciation after 1969 and before 1976	26d				
e Enter the **smaller** of line 26c or 26d	26e				
f Section 291 amount (corporations only)	26f				
g Add lines 26b, 26e, and 26f	26g				
27 **If section 1252 property:** Skip this section if you didn't dispose of farmland or if this form is being completed for a partnership.					
a Soil, water, and land clearing expenses	27a				
b Line 27a multiplied by applicable percentage. See instructions	27b				
c Enter the **smaller** of line 24 or 27b	27c				
28 **If section 1254 property:**					
a Intangible drilling and development costs, expenditures for development of mines and other natural deposits, mining exploration costs, and depletion. See instructions	28a				
b Enter the **smaller** of line 24 or 28a	28b				
29 **If section 1255 property:**					
a Applicable percentage of payments excluded from income under section 126. See instructions	29a				
b Enter the **smaller** of line 24 or 29a. See instructions	29b				

Summary of Part III Gains. Complete property columns A through D through line 29b before going to line 30.

30 Total gains for all properties. Add property columns A through D, line 24	30	
31 Add property columns A through D, lines 25b, 26g, 27c, 28b, and 29b. Enter here and on line 13	31	
32 Subtract line 31 from line 30. Enter the portion from casualty or theft on Form 4684, line 33. Enter the portion from other than casualty or theft on Form 4797, line 6	32	

Part IV Recapture Amounts Under Sections 179 and 280F(b)(2) When Business Use Drops to 50% or Less (see instructions)

		(a) Section 179	(b) Section 280F(b)(2)
33 Section 179 expense deduction or depreciation allowable in prior years	33		
34 Recomputed depreciation. See instructions	34		
35 Recapture amount. Subtract line 34 from line 33. See the instructions for where to report	35		

Form **4797** (2022)

GROUP 2:

PROBLEM 19

Form **6252** Department of the Treasury Internal Revenue Service

Installment Sale Income

Attach to your tax return.

Use a separate form for each sale or other disposition of property on the installment method.

Go to *www.irs.gov/Form6252* for the latest information.

OMB No. 1545-0228 2022 Attachment Sequence No. 67

Name(s) shown on return | **Identifying number**

1 Description of property

2a Date acquired (mm/dd/yyyy) **b** Date sold (mm/dd/yyyy)

3 Was the property sold to a related party? See instructions. If "Yes," complete Part III for the year of sale and 2 years after the year of the sale unless you received the final payment during the tax year. If "No," skip line 4 . ☐ **Yes** ☐ **No**

4 Did you sell the property to an intermediary? If "Yes," provide the name and address of the intermediary on line 27 ☐ **Yes** ☐ **No**

Part I Gross Profit and Contract Price. Complete this part for all years of the installment agreement.

5	Selling price including mortgages and other debts. **Don't** include interest, whether stated or unstated		5
6	Mortgages, debts, and other liabilities the buyer assumed or took the property subject to (see instructions)	6	
7	Subtract line 6 from line 5	7	
8	Cost or other basis of property sold	8	
9	Depreciation allowed or allowable	9	
10	Adjusted basis. Subtract line 9 from line 8	10	
11	Commissions and other expenses of sale	11	
12	Income recapture from Form 4797, Part III (see instructions)	12	
13	Add lines 10, 11, and 12		13
14	Subtract line 13 from line 5. If zero or less, **don't** complete the rest of this form. See instructions		14
15	If the property described on line 1 above was your main home, enter the amount of your excluded gain. See instructions. Otherwise, enter -0-		15
16	**Gross profit.** Subtract line 15 from line 14		16
17	Subtract line 13 from line 6. If zero or less, enter -0-		17
18	**Contract price.** Add line 7 and line 17		18

Part II Installment Sale Income. Complete this part for all years of the installment agreement.

19	Gross profit percentage (expressed as a decimal amount). Divide line 16 by line 18. (For years after the year of sale, see instructions.)		19
20	If this is the year of sale, enter the amount from line 17. Otherwise, enter -0-		20
21	Payments received during year (see instructions). **Don't** include interest, whether stated or unstated		21
22	Add lines 20 and 21		22
23	Payments received in prior years (see instructions). **Don't** include interest, whether stated or unstated	23	
24	**Installment sale income.** Multiply line 22 by line 19		24
25	Enter the part of line 24 that is ordinary income under the recapture rules. See instructions		25
26	Subtract line 25 from line 24. Enter here and on Schedule D or Form 4797. See instructions		26

Part III Related Party Installment Sale Income. Don't complete if you received the final payment this tax year.

27 Name, address, and taxpayer identifying number of related party

28 Did the related party resell or dispose of the property ("second disposition") during this tax year? ☐ **Yes** ☐ **No**

29 **If the answer to question 28 is "Yes," complete lines 30 through 37 below unless one of the following conditions is met. Check the box that applies.**

a ☐ The second disposition was more than 2 years after the first disposition (other than dispositions of marketable securities). If this box is checked, enter the date of disposition (mm/dd/yyyy)

b ☐ The first disposition was a sale or exchange of stock to the issuing corporation.

c ☐ The second disposition was an involuntary conversion and the threat of conversion occurred after the first disposition.

d ☐ The second disposition occurred after the death of the original seller or buyer.

e ☐ It can be established to the satisfaction of the IRS that tax avoidance wasn't a principal purpose for either of the dispositions. If this box is checked, attach an explanation. See instructions.

30	Selling price of property sold by related party (see instructions)	30
31	Enter contract price from line 18 for year of first sale	31
32	Enter the **smaller** of line 30 or line 31	32
33	Total payments received by the end of your 2022 tax year (see instructions)	33
34	Subtract line 33 from line 32. If zero or less, enter -0-	34
35	Multiply line 34 by the gross profit percentage on line 19 for year of first sale	35
36	Enter the part of line 35 that is ordinary income under the recapture rules. See instructions	36
37	Subtract line 36 from line 35. Enter here and on Schedule D or Form 4797. See instructions	37

For Paperwork Reduction Act Notice, see page 4. Cat. No. 13601R Form **6252** (2022)

GROUP 3:
WRITING ASSIGNMENT

RESEARCH

1. Your supervisor has asked you to research the following situation concerning Owen and Lisa Cordoncillo. Owen and Lisa are brother and sister. In May 2022, Owen and Lisa exchange land they both held separately for investment. Lisa gives up a two-acre property in Texas with an adjusted basis of $2,000 and a fair market value of $6,000. In return for this property, Lisa receives from Owen a one-acre property in Arkansas with a fair market value of $5,500 and cash of $500. Owen's adjusted basis in the land he exchanges is $2,500. In March 2023, Owen sells the Texas land to a third party for $5,800.

   Required: Go to the IRS website (**www.irs.gov**). Locate and review Publication 544, Chapter 1, Nontaxable Exchanges. Write a file memorandum stating the amount of Owen and Lisa's gain recognition for 2022. Also determine the effect, if any, of the subsequent sale in 2023. (An example of a file memorandum is available at the website for this textbook located at **www.cengage.com.**)

GROUP 4:
COMPREHENSIVE PROBLEMS

1. Trish Himple owns a retail family clothing store. Her store is located at 4321 Heather Drive, Henderson, NV 89002. Her employer identification number is 95-1234321 and her Social Security number is 123-45-6789. Trish keeps her books on the cash basis. The income and expenses for the year are:

Gross sales		$350,000
Returns and allowances		15,000
Expenses:		
Beginning inventory (at cost)	$ 85,000	
Add: purchases	100,000	
Cost of goods available for sale	185,000	
Less: ending inventory (at cost)	72,000	
Cost of goods sold		$113,000
Rent		29,000
Insurance		3,000
Legal and accounting fees		5,000
Payroll		60,000
Payroll taxes		5,000
Utilities		2,200
Office supplies		800
Advertising		6,000

Trish's bookkeeper has provided the following *book-basis* fixed asset rollforward:

Himple Retail
Fixed Asset Rollforward
12/31/2022
(book basis)

ASSET	IN SERVICE	DEPR METHOD	LIFE	COST BASIS	2020 DEPR	2021 DEPR	2022 DEPR	ACCUM DEPR	NET BOOK VALUE
CASH REGISTER	8/15/2020	SL	5	10,000.00	833.33	2,000.00	2,000.00	4,833.33	5,166.67
2020 TOTAL ADDITIONS				10,000.00	833.33	2,000.00	2,000.00	4,833.33	5,166.67
RETAIL FIXTURES	6/21/2021	SL	7	5,500.00		458.33	785.71	1,244.04	4,255.96
FURNITURE	6/12/2021	SL	7	4,100.00		341.67	585.71	927.38	3,172.62
2021 TOTAL ADDITIONS				9,600.00	-	800.00	1,371.42	2,171.42	7,428.58
TOTAL				19,600.00	833.33	2,800.00	3,371.42	7,004.75	12,595.25
DELIVERY TRUCK	10/1/2022	SL	5	38,000.00			1,900.00	1,900.00	36,100.00
DESK AND CABINETRY	6/1/2022	SL	7	12,000.00			1,000.00	1,000.00	11,000.00
COMPUTER	6/1/2022	SL	5	3,000.00			350.00	350.00	2,650.00
2022 TOTAL ADDITIONS				53,000.00	-	-	3,250.00	3,250.00	49,750.00
TOTAL				72,600.00	833.33	2,800.00	6,621.42	10,254.75	62,345.25

The truck is not considered a passenger automobile for purposes of the luxury automobile limitations.

Trish also has a qualified home office of 250 sq. ft. Her home is 2,000 sq. ft. Her 2017 purchase price and basis in the home, not including land, is $100,000 (the home's market value is $150,000). She incurred the following costs in 2022 related to the entire home:

Utilities	$3,000
Cleaning	1,000
Insurance	1,100
Property taxes	2,000

Required: For tax purposes, Trish elected out of bonus depreciation in all years except 2022. She did not elect immediate expensing in any year. The tax lives of the assets are the same as the book lives shown in the fixed asset schedule above. Complete Trish's Schedule C, Form 8829, and Form 4562. Make realistic assumptions about any missing data.

2. Tsate Kongia (birthdate 02/14/1956) is an unmarried high school principal. Tsate received the following tax documents:

a Employee's social security number 467-98-9784
OMB No. 1545-0008
Safe, accurate, FAST! Use IRS e-file
Visit the IRS website at www.irs.gov/efile

b Employer identification number (EIN) 56-1357924
c Employer's name, address, and ZIP code
Shawnee Mission School District
8200 W. 71st Street
Shawnee Mission, KS 66204

1 Wages, tips, other compensation 57,500.00
2 Federal income tax withheld 6,300.00
3 Social security wages 60,500.00
4 Social security tax withheld 3,751.00
5 Medicare wages and tips 60,500.00
6 Medicare tax withheld 877.25
7 Social security tips
8 Allocated tips

d Control number
9
10 Dependent care benefits

e Employee's first name and initial Last name Suff.
Tsate Kongai
212 Quivera Road
Overland Park, KS 66210
f Employee's address and ZIP code

11 Nonqualified plans
12a See instructions for box 12 Code D 3,000.00
13 Statutory employee ☐ Retirement plan ☒ Third-party sick pay ☐
12b
14 Other
12c
12d

15 State Employer's state ID number	16 State wages, tips, etc.	17 State income tax	18 Local wages, tips, etc.	19 Local income tax	20 Locality name
KS 34511DF	57,500.00	1,200.00			

Form **W-2** Wage and Tax Statement **2022**
Department of the Treasury—Internal Revenue Service

Copy B—To Be Filed With Employee's FEDERAL Tax Return.
This information is being furnished to the Internal Revenue Service.

☐ CORRECTED (if checked)

PAYER'S name, street address, city or town, state or province, country, ZIP or foreign postal code, and telephone no. Olanthe National Bank 1240 E. Santa Fe Street Olanthe, KS 66061	Payer's RTN (optional)	OMB No. 1545-0112 Form **1099-INT** (Rev. January 2022)	**Interest Income**
	1 Interest income $ 219.78	For calendar year 20 22	
	2 Early withdrawal penalty $		**Copy B** **For Recipient**
PAYER'S TIN 44-1352469 / RECIPIENT'S TIN 467-98-9784	3 Interest on U.S. Savings Bonds and Treasury obligations $		
RECIPIENT'S name Tsate Kongai	**4 Federal income tax withheld** $	5 Investment expenses $	This is important tax information and is being furnished to the IRS. If you are required to file a return, a negligence penalty or other sanction may be imposed on you if this income is taxable and the IRS determines that it has not been reported.
Street address (including apt. no.) 212 Quivera Road	6 Foreign tax paid $	7 Foreign country or U.S. possession	
City or town, state or province, country, and ZIP or foreign postal code Overland Park, KS 66210	8 Tax-exempt interest $	9 Specified private activity bond interest $	
	10 Market discount $	11 Bond premium $	
FATCA filing requirement ☐	12 Bond premium on Treasury obligations $	13 Bond premium on tax-exempt bond $	
Account number (see instructions)	14 Tax-exempt and tax credit bond CUSIP no.	15 State / 16 State identification no.	17 State tax withheld $ $

Form **1099-INT** (Rev. 1-2022) (keep for your records) www.irs.gov/Form1099INT Department of the Treasury - Internal Revenue Service

☐ CORRECTED (if checked)

PAYER'S name, street address, city or town, state or province, country, ZIP or foreign postal code, and telephone no. Johnson Corporation 100 E. 49th Street New York, NY 10017	1a Total ordinary dividends $ 4,100.00	OMB No. 1545-0110 Form **1099-DIV** (Rev. January 2022)	**Dividends and Distributions**
	1b Qualified dividends $ 4,000.00	For calendar year 20 22	
	2a Total capital gain distr. $	2b Unrecap. Sec. 1250 gain $	**Copy B** **For Recipient**
PAYER'S TIN 17-2468135 / RECIPIENT'S TIN 467-98-9784	2c Section 1202 gain $	2d Collectibles (28%) gain $	
	2e Section 897 ordinary dividends $	2f Section 897 capital gain $	
RECIPIENT'S name Tsate Kongai	3 Nondividend distributions $	**4 Federal income tax withheld** $ 0.00	This is important tax information and is being furnished to the IRS. If you are required to file a return, a negligence penalty or other sanction may be imposed on you if this income is taxable and the IRS determines that it has not been reported.
Street address (including apt. no.) 212 Quivera Rd	5 Section 199A dividends $	6 Investment expenses $	
City or town, state or province, country, and ZIP or foreign postal code Overland Park, KS 66210	7 Foreign tax paid $	8 Foreign country or U.S. possession	
	9 Cash liquidation distributions $	10 Noncash liquidation distributions $	
11 FATCA filing requirement ☐	12 Exempt-interest dividends $	13 Specified private activity bond interest dividends $	
Account number (see instructions)	14 State / 15 State identification no.	16 State tax withheld $ $	

Form **1099-DIV** (Rev. 1-2022) (keep for your records) www.irs.gov/Form1099DIV Department of the Treasury - Internal Revenue Service

During the year, Tsate paid the following amounts (all of which can be substantiated):

Home mortgage interest reported on Form 1098 (not shown)	$9,600
KS state income tax payment for 2021	600
MasterCard interest	550
Life insurance (whole life policy)	750
Property taxes on personal residence	1,500
Blue Cross medical insurance premiums	300
Other medical expenses	800
Income tax preparation fee	300
Charitable contributions (in cash)	750

Tsate's sole stock transaction was reported on a Form 1099-B:

☐ CORRECTED (if checked)

PAYER'S name, street address, city or town, state or province, country, ZIP or foreign postal code, and telephone no.		Applicable checkbox on Form 8949	OMB No. 1545-0715	Proceeds From Broker and Barter Exchange Transactions
Little John Trading 123 Wall Street New York, NY 10014		A	2022 Form 1099-B	
		1a Description of property (Example: 100 sh. XYZ Co.) 100 shs Johnson Corp		
		1b Date acquired 12/31/2021	1c Date sold or disposed 11/05/2022	
PAYER'S TIN 11-0010011	RECIPIENT'S TIN 467-98-9784	1d Proceeds $ 14,000.00	1e Cost or other basis $ 35,000.00	Copy B For Recipient
		1f Accrued market discount $	1g Wash sale loss disallowed $	
RECIPIENT'S name Tsate Kongai		2 Short-term gain or loss ☐ Long-term gain or loss ☐ Ordinary ☐	3 If checked, proceeds from: Collectibles ☐ QOF ☐	This is important tax information and is being furnished to the IRS. If you are required to file a return, a negligence penalty or other sanction may be imposed on you if this income is taxable and the IRS determines that it has not been reported.
Street address (including apt. no.) 212 Quivera Road		4 Federal income tax withheld $	5 If checked, noncovered security ☐	
City or town, state or province, country, and ZIP or foreign postal code Overland Park, KS 66210		6 Reported to IRS: Gross proceeds ☐ Net proceeds ☒	7 If checked, loss is not allowed based on amount in 1d ☐	
Account number (see instructions)		8 Profit or (loss) realized in 2022 on closed contracts $	9 Unrealized profit or (loss) on open contracts—12/31/2021 $	
CUSIP number	FATCA filing requirement ☐	10 Unrealized profit or (loss) on open contracts—12/31/2022 $	11 Aggregate profit or (loss) on contracts $	
14 State name	15 State identification no. / 16 State tax withheld $ $	12 If checked, basis reported to IRS ☐	13 Bartering $	

Form **1099-B** (Keep for your records) www.irs.gov/Form1099B Department of the Treasury - Internal Revenue Service

On January 28, 2022, Tsate sold land for $170,000 (basis to Tsate of $130,000). The land was purchased 6 years ago as an investment. Tsate received $50,000 as a down payment and the buyer's 10-year note for $120,000. The note is payable at the rate of $12,000 per year plus 2.708 percent interest. On December 31, 2022, Tsate received a payment of $15,250 that included $3,250 of interest.

Tsate also helps support his father, Jay Hawke, who lives in a nearby senior facility. Jay's Social Security number is 433-33-2121. Tsate provides over one-half of Jay's support but Jay also has a pension that paid him income of $14,000 in 2022. Jay's Social Security benefits were $3,200 in 2022.

Required: Complete Tsate's federal tax return for 2022. Use Form 1040-SR, Schedule A, Schedule B, Schedule D, the Qualified Dividends and Capital Gain Tax Worksheet, and Form 6252, as needed, to complete this tax return. Make realistic assumptions about any missing data.

GROUP 5:
CUMULATIVE SOFTWARE PROBLEM

1. The following information is available for the Albert and Allison Gaytor family in addition to that provided in Chapters 1–7.

   On September 14, 2022, Allison purchased the building where her store is located. She paid $375,000 for the building (which includes $100,000 for the land it is located on). Allison's store is the only business in the building. The depreciation on the store needs to be reflected on Schedule C of the business.

Required: Combine this new information about the Gaytor family with the information from Chapters 1 to 7 and complete a revised 2022 tax return for Albert and Allison. This completes the Group 5 multichapter case.

CHAPTER 9

Employment Taxes, Estimated Payments, and Retirement Plans

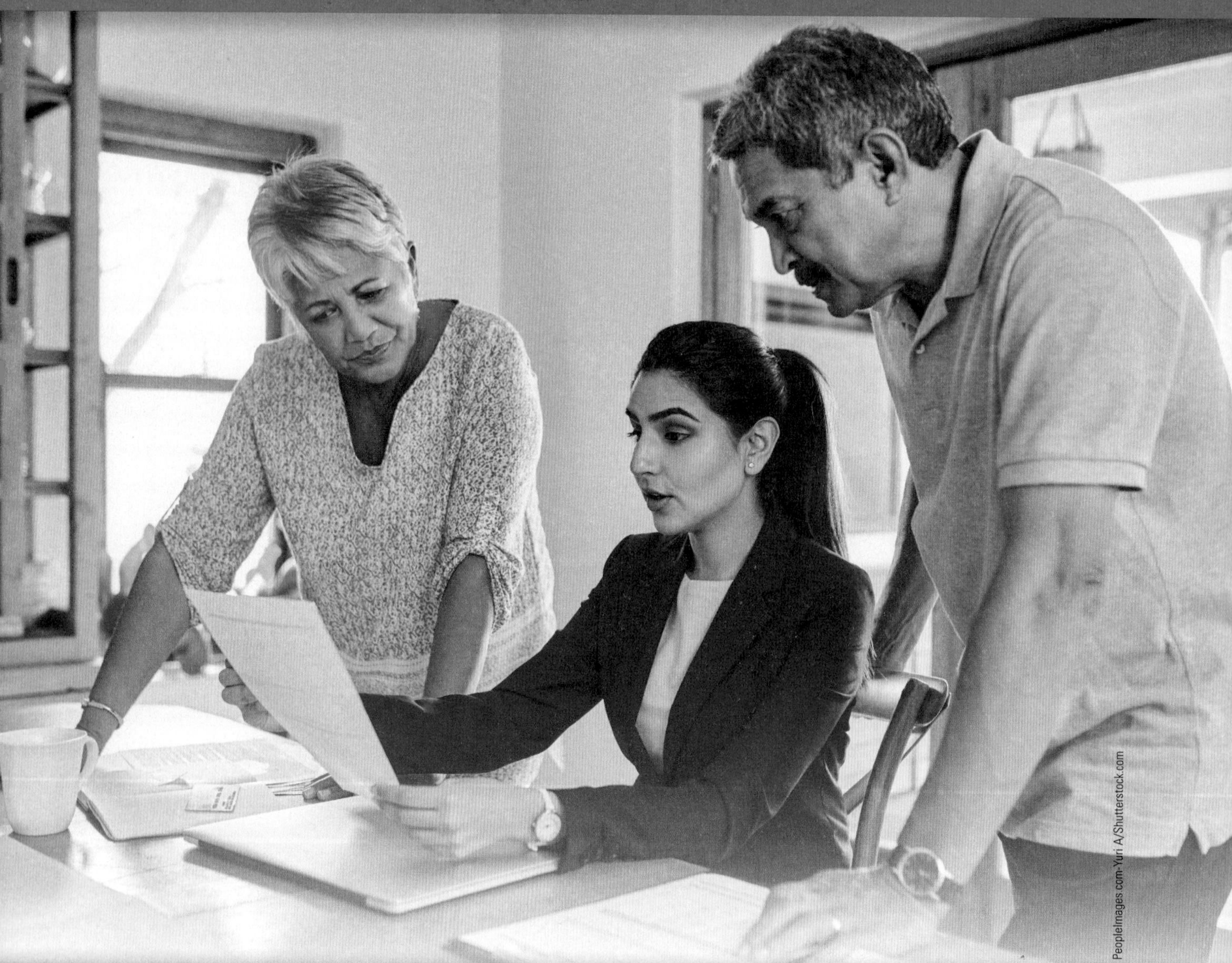

PeopleImages.com-Yuri A/Shutterstock.com

LEARNING OBJECTIVES

After completing this chapter, you should be able to:

LO 9.1 Compute the income tax withholding from employee wages.

LO 9.2 Compute the FICA tax.

LO 9.3 Determine taxpayers' quarterly estimated payments.

LO 9.4 Apply the federal deposit system to payroll withholding.

LO 9.5 Prepare employer payroll reporting.

LO 9.6 Compute the amount of FUTA tax for an employer.

LO 9.7 Describe the general rules for qualified retirement plans.

LO 9.8 Explain the pension plan rollover rules.

OVERVIEW

This chapter focuses on the payment and reporting of income and other taxes by employers, employees, and self-employed taxpayers. Payroll and other tax topics covered include withholding methods for employees, estimated payments, the FICA tax (Social Security and Medicare taxes), the federal tax deposit system, and employer reporting requirements. In addition, other payroll-related topics such as retirement plans and pensions are covered.

Much of the collection, payment, and reporting of employment taxes is handled by the employer, not the employee. In most instances, taxpayers are able to rely on the information provided by their employer such as Form W-2. However, understanding how employment taxes are computed remains an important issue for tax advisers and taxpayers.

Learning Objective 9.1

Compute the income tax withholding from employee wages.

9-1 WITHHOLDING METHODS

Employers are required to withhold income and employment taxes from amounts paid to employees for wages, including salaries, fees, bonuses, commissions, vacation and retirement pay. Employees complete Form W-4 to provide the information necessary for the employer to withhold income taxes at the prescribed amount. Although most taxpayers' income tax withholding should be adequate to result in an income tax refund at filing time, calculating withholding is more of an art than a science and is subject to the accurate estimation of income and deductions that are ultimately reported for the tax year.

The Form W-4 was redesigned in 2020. In previous years, withholding allowances were tied to the amount of the personal exemptions expected to be claimed by a taxpayer. Since exemptions are suspended from 2018–2025, the latest version of Form W-4 has been adapted and no longer requires an employee to report the number of withholding allowances that they expect to claim. Employees who submitted a Form W-4 in any year before 2020 are not required to submit a new Form W-4. Employers will continue to compute withholding based on the information from the employee's old Form W-4. The withholding tables published by the IRS allow employers to determine withholding based on old and new Forms W-4 under both the percentage and wage bracket methods. All new employees and any existing employees that wish to adjust withholding must use the new Form W-4.

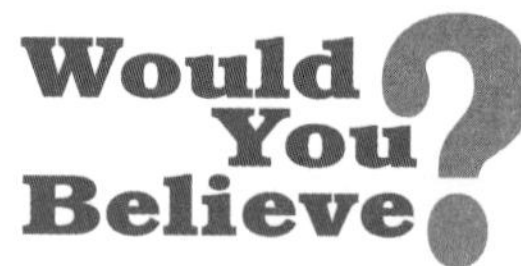

Predicting the outcomes from the scheduled 2025 sunset of the tax provisions associated with the Tax Cuts and Jobs Act of 2017 is a fool's errand at this point. However, should the suspended provisions around exemptions be reinstated, there is some chance that employers would need to consider three different types of Forms W-4.

9-1a The Form W-4 After 2019

The new Form W-4 (see Pages 9-5 to 9-8) is divided into five steps. Steps 1 and 5 are completed by all taxpayers. Step 1 asks for personal information such as name, address, and filing status. Step 5 is the taxpayer's signature. By design, Steps 1 and 5 are all that most taxpayers would need to complete, and withholding will be based on that taxpayer's wages and filing status only.

For taxpayers with more complex income tax situations—such as those with a working spouse, dependents, or having additional forms of income such as self-employment, investment income—or for taxpayers that itemize, two options for computing additional withholding are provided. The first option is for the taxpayer to use the IRS online withholding estimator (**www.irs.gov/individuals/tax-withholding-estimator**). The online estimator uses information from recent paystubs of the taxpayer and spouse, details from other sources of income, and a previous tax return to estimate any additional withholding needs. Using the online estimator can be a complex process that contemplates a wide variety of taxpayer situations and is similar to approximating a taxpayer's current year tax liability. As a result, the estimator requires the greatest amount of preparation and likely provides the most accurate result.

The second option is to use Steps 2–4 on Form W-4:

- Step 2 is for taxpayers with a working spouse or multiple jobs.
- Step 3 is for taxpayers with dependents.
- Step 4 is for taxpayers that have other forms of income or itemized or other deductions.

Under Step 2, if the taxpayer and the spouse have similar income, the taxpayer can simply check the box on line (c) (the spouse should do the same on their Form W-4) and withholding will be adjusted to reflect a two-income household by halving the standard deduction and tax brackets. Alternatively, the Form W-4 instructions include a multiple jobs worksheet that uses a series of tables to estimate the required additional withholding in situations where the taxpayer has multiple jobs or the spouse's wages differ from the taxpayer.

EXAMPLE Dot and Peg expect to file a joint tax return in 2022. Dot and Peg expect to be paid wages of $37,000 and $62,000, respectively. Dot is paid monthly, and Peg is paid every two weeks (26 times a year). Because Dot and Peg's wages are not similar in amount, they should use the Step 2(b) Multiple Jobs Worksheet included on page 3 of Form W-4 (see Page 9-7). Using the Married Filing Jointly table from page 4 of the Form W-4 (see Page 9-8), Line 1 of the Multiple Jobs Worksheet is $3,360 where the higher paying job of $62,000 and the lower paying job of $37,000 intersect in the table. Because Peg has the higher-paying job, 26 is entered on Line 3 to match the number of payroll periods during the year, and Line 4 of the Multiple Jobs Worksheet is $129.23 ($3,360 ÷ 26). Peg will carry that amount forward to Line 4(c) of page 1 of the Form W-4 as additional withholding for each pay period. ♦

Under Step 3, taxpayers report the impact of the child tax credit or the other dependent credit on tax liability. This amount will be used by the employer to compute withholding.

EXAMPLE Shirin and Hamed are married filing jointly and have two dependent children ages 13 and 17. Hamed expects his 2022 wages to be $78,000, and Shirin works part-time and expects to earn $45,000. Both are paid monthly. As the higher-paid spouse, Hamed completes a Form W-4 that reflects the additional withholding and dependents. Shirin would not need to reflect this information on her W-4. Using the Multiple Jobs Worksheet, Hamed reports $439.17 ($5,270 ÷ 12) on Line 4(c) of Form W-4. Hamed also reports $2,500 (one child under 17 at $2,000 and one other dependent at $500) on Line 3. ♦

Step 4 is associated with the complexities of other sources of income (e.g., interest, dividends, retirement) or other deductions such as itemized deductions, deductible IRA contributions, the qualified business income deduction, and student loan interest. Line 4(a) of Form W-4 is where the expected amount of any additional income is reported and Line 4(b) is where any additional deductions are reported. Step 4(b) refers the taxpayer to a simple deduction worksheet included with Form W-4 that ensures the taxpayer compares the total itemized deductions with the standard deduction to capture only the excess amount as an adjustment. A taxpayer that has a two-income household, non-wage income, dependents, and itemizes deductions is effectively estimating their current year taxes in preparing the W-4. Generally, only more sophisticated taxpayers would be required to estimate withholding using this degree of complexity.

EXAMPLE Fei and Zhi Han are married filing jointly and have three dependent children aged 13, 14, and 18. Zhi's older adult mother is also a dependent. Wage estimates for 2022 are $26,000 and $94,000 for Fei and Zhi, respectively. Both are paid semimonthly (24 times a year). They have an investment portfolio expected to pay $1,200 in interest and $2,300 in qualified dividends. They are not certain if they will have capital gains in 2022, since it depends on the stock market. The Hans own a home and estimate 2022 itemized deductions at $27,000. The Hans expect to make a $6,000 deductible IRA contribution and pay $3,200 in student loan interest. Zhi, as the higher-income spouse, will have a fairly complex Form W-4. Zhi should use the multiple jobs worksheet and will report $198.33 ($4,760 ÷ 24) on Line 4 of the worksheet. In Step 3, Zhi will report two qualifying children under 17 and two other dependents for a total of $5,000 ($2,000 × 2 plus $500 × 2). In Step 4, Zhi will include $3,500 of investment income on Line 4(a) of Form W-4. Zhi will complete the Deductions Worksheet and report $1,100 ($27,000 – $25,900) on Line 3 and $8,500 ($6,000 IRA deduction and the limit of $2,500 of deductible student loan interest) on Line 4, giving a total of $9,600 in Line 5 of the Deductions Worksheet. As a result, the first page of Zhi's W-4 will report $5,000 on Line 3, $3,500 on Line 4(a), $9,600 on Line 4(b) and $198.33 on Line 4(c). Note that the possible taxation of qualified dividends at a lower 15-percent rate, and the possibility that the student loan interest or the IRA contribution may not be deductible due to income limitations, would need to be considered by Zhi if she wanted to estimate withholding accurately. In this example, Zhi may want to consider using the IRS online withholding estimator. Zhi's completed Form W-4 is presented on Pages 9-5 to 9-8. ♦

The process is considerably more complex if for some reason a Form W-4 is completed during the middle of a year, since the withholding amounts are often associated with annual figures.

The amounts reported on Form W-4 will be used by the employer to make adjustments to the employee's tax withholding based on tables provided by the IRS. A taxpayer that is exempt from withholding should complete Steps 1 [do not check the box in 1(c)] and 5 and write "Exempt" in the space underneath Line 4(c). Employees are eligible to claim exempt if they had no federal tax liability in the prior year *and* expect to have no tax liability in 2022. If the employee completes any part of Form W-4 other than Steps 1(a) and 1(b) and Step 5, the Form W-4 for which exempt is claimed is considered invalid. A Form W-4 claiming exemption from withholding is effective only for that calendar year.

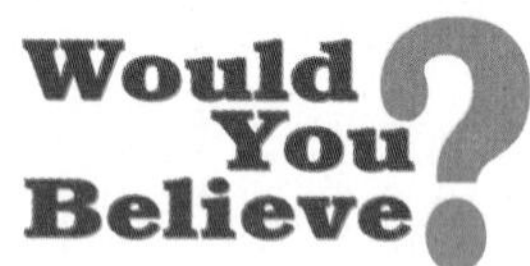

The 2022 version of Form W-4 is published in five different languages other than English: Korean, Spanish, Vietnamese, Russian, and traditional and simplified Chinese. Withholding knows no limits, language or otherwise!

An employer should withhold based on a valid Form W-4 authorized by the employee. If a valid Form W-4 has not been submitted, the employer should withhold based on a single taxpayer with no adjustments. There is no expectation that the employer confirm the information reported by the employee on a Form W-4; however, a Form W-4 is considered invalid if the employee clearly indicates information on Form W-4 is false by an oral or written statement.

Form **W-4**

Department of the Treasury
Internal Revenue Service

Employee's Withholding Certificate

▶ Complete Form W-4 so that your employer can withhold the correct federal income tax from your pay.
▶ Give Form W-4 to your employer.
▶ Your withholding is subject to review by the IRS.

OMB No. 1545-0074

2022

Step 1: Enter Personal Information

(a) First name and middle initial	Last name	(b) Social security number
Zhi	Han	
Address		▶ **Does your name match the name on your social security card?** If not, to ensure you get credit for your earnings, contact SSA at 800-772-1213 or go to *www.ssa.gov*.
City or town, state, and ZIP code		

(c) ☐ **Single** or **Married filing separately**
☑ **Married filing jointly** or **Qualifying widow(er)**
☐ **Head of household** (Check only if you're unmarried and pay more than half the costs of keeping up a home for yourself and a qualifying individual.)

Complete Steps 2–4 ONLY if they apply to you; otherwise, skip to Step 5. See page 2 for more information on each step, who can claim exemption from withholding, when to use the estimator at *www.irs.gov/W4App*, and privacy.

Step 2: Multiple Jobs or Spouse Works

Complete this step if you (1) hold more than one job at a time, or (2) are married filing jointly and your spouse also works. The correct amount of withholding depends on income earned from all of these jobs.

Do **only one** of the following.

(a) Use the estimator at *www.irs.gov/W4App* for most accurate withholding for this step (and Steps 3–4); **or**

(b) Use the Multiple Jobs Worksheet on page 3 and enter the result in Step 4(c) below for roughly accurate withholding; **or**

(c) If there are only two jobs total, you may check this box. Do the same on Form W-4 for the other job. This option is accurate for jobs with similar pay; otherwise, more tax than necessary may be withheld . . ▶ ☐

TIP: To be accurate, submit a 2022 Form W-4 for all other jobs. If you (or your spouse) have self-employment income, including as an independent contractor, use the estimator.

Complete Steps 3–4(b) on Form W-4 for only ONE of these jobs. Leave those steps blank for the other jobs. (Your withholding will be most accurate if you complete Steps 3–4(b) on the Form W-4 for the highest paying job.)

Step 3: Claim Dependents

If your total income will be $200,000 or less ($400,000 or less if married filing jointly):

Multiply the number of qualifying children under age 17 by $2,000 ▶	$ 4,000		
Multiply the number of other dependents by $500 . . . . ▶	$ 1,000		
Add the amounts above and enter the total here		3	$ 5,000

Step 4 (optional): Other Adjustments

(a) Other income (not from jobs). If you want tax withheld for other income you expect this year that won't have withholding, enter the amount of other income here. This may include interest, dividends, and retirement income	4(a)	$ 3,500
(b) Deductions. If you expect to claim deductions other than the standard deduction and want to reduce your withholding, use the Deductions Worksheet on page 3 and enter the result here	4(b)	$ 9,600
(c) Extra withholding. Enter any additional tax you want withheld each **pay period** . .	4(c)	$ 198.33

Step 5: Sign Here

Under penalties of perjury, I declare that this certificate, to the best of my knowledge and belief, is true, correct, and complete.

▶ **Employee's signature** (This form is not valid unless you sign it.) ▶ **Date**

Employers Only

Employer's name and address	First date of employment	Employer identification number (EIN)

For Privacy Act and Paperwork Reduction Act Notice, see page 3. Cat. No. 10220Q Form **W-4** (2022)

General Instructions

Section references are to the Internal Revenue Code.

Future Developments

For the latest information about developments related to Form W-4, such as legislation enacted after it was published, go to *www.irs.gov/FormW4*.

Purpose of Form

Complete Form W-4 so that your employer can withhold the correct federal income tax from your pay. If too little is withheld, you will generally owe tax when you file your tax return and may owe a penalty. If too much is withheld, you will generally be due a refund. Complete a new Form W-4 when changes to your personal or financial situation would change the entries on the form. For more information on withholding and when you must furnish a new Form W-4, see Pub. 505, Tax Withholding and Estimated Tax.

Exemption from withholding. You may claim exemption from withholding for 2022 if you meet both of the following conditions: you had no federal income tax liability in 2021 **and** you expect to have no federal income tax liability in 2022. You had no federal income tax liability in 2021 if (1) your total tax on line 24 on your 2021 Form 1040 or 1040-SR is zero (or less than the sum of lines 27a, 28, 29, and 30), or (2) you were not required to file a return because your income was below the filing threshold for your correct filing status. If you claim exemption, you will have no income tax withheld from your paycheck and may owe taxes and penalties when you file your 2022 tax return. To claim exemption from withholding, certify that you meet both of the conditions above by writing "Exempt" on Form W-4 in the space below Step 4(c). Then, complete Steps 1(a), 1(b), and 5. Do not complete any other steps. You will need to submit a new Form W-4 by February 15, 2023.

Your privacy. If you prefer to limit information provided in Steps 2 through 4, use the online estimator, which will also increase accuracy.

As an alternative to the estimator: if you have concerns with Step 2(c), you may choose Step 2(b); if you have concerns with Step 4(a), you may enter an additional amount you want withheld per pay period in Step 4(c). If this is the only job in your household, you may instead check the box in Step 2(c), which will increase your withholding and significantly reduce your paycheck (often by thousands of dollars over the year).

When to use the estimator. Consider using the estimator at *www.irs.gov/W4App* if you:

1. Expect to work only part of the year;

2. Have dividend or capital gain income, or are subject to additional taxes, such as Additional Medicare Tax;

3. Have self-employment income (see below); or

4. Prefer the most accurate withholding for multiple job situations.

Self-employment. Generally, you will owe both income and self-employment taxes on any self-employment income you receive separate from the wages you receive as an employee. If you want to pay these taxes through withholding from your wages, use the estimator at *www.irs.gov/W4App* to figure the amount to have withheld.

Nonresident alien. If you're a nonresident alien, see Notice 1392, Supplemental Form W-4 Instructions for Nonresident Aliens, before completing this form.

Specific Instructions

Step 1(c). Check your anticipated filing status. This will determine the standard deduction and tax rates used to compute your withholding.

Step 2. Use this step if you (1) have more than one job at the same time, or (2) are married filing jointly and you and your spouse both work.

Option **(a)** most accurately calculates the additional tax you need to have withheld, while option **(b)** does so with a little less accuracy.

If you (and your spouse) have a total of only two jobs, you may instead check the box in option **(c)**. The box must also be checked on the Form W-4 for the other job. If the box is checked, the standard deduction and tax brackets will be cut in half for each job to calculate withholding. This option is roughly accurate for jobs with similar pay; otherwise, more tax than necessary may be withheld, and this extra amount will be larger the greater the difference in pay is between the two jobs.

Multiple jobs. *Complete Steps 3 through 4(b) on only one Form W-4. Withholding will be most accurate if you do this on the Form W-4 for the highest paying job.*

Step 3. This step provides instructions for determining the amount of the child tax credit and the credit for other dependents that you may be able to claim when you file your tax return. To qualify for the child tax credit, the child must be under age 17 as of December 31, must be your dependent who generally lives with you for more than half the year, and must have the required social security number. You may be able to claim a credit for other dependents for whom a child tax credit can't be claimed, such as an older child or a qualifying relative. For additional eligibility requirements for these credits, see Pub. 501, Dependents, Standard Deduction, and Filing Information. You can also include **other tax credits** for which you are eligible in this step, such as the foreign tax credit and the education tax credits. To do so, add an estimate of the amount for the year to your credits for dependents and enter the total amount in Step 3. Including these credits will increase your paycheck and reduce the amount of any refund you may receive when you file your tax return.

Step 4 (optional).

Step 4(a). Enter in this step the total of your other estimated income for the year, if any. You shouldn't include income from any jobs or self-employment. If you complete Step 4(a), you likely won't have to make estimated tax payments for that income. If you prefer to pay estimated tax rather than having tax on other income withheld from your paycheck, see Form 1040-ES, Estimated Tax for Individuals.

Step 4(b). Enter in this step the amount from the Deductions Worksheet, line 5, if you expect to claim deductions other than the basic standard deduction on your 2022 tax return and want to reduce your withholding to account for these deductions. This includes both itemized deductions and other deductions such as for student loan interest and IRAs.

Step 4(c). Enter in this step any additional tax you want withheld from your pay **each pay period**, including any amounts from the Multiple Jobs Worksheet, line 4. Entering an amount here will reduce your paycheck and will either increase your refund or reduce any amount of tax that you owe.

Form W-4 (2022) Page **3**

Step 2(b)—Multiple Jobs Worksheet *(Keep for your records.)* 

If you choose the option in Step 2(b) on Form W-4, complete this worksheet (which calculates the total extra tax for all jobs) on **only ONE** Form W-4. Withholding will be most accurate if you complete the worksheet and enter the result on the Form W-4 for the highest paying job.

Note: If more than one job has annual wages of more than $120,000 or there are more than three jobs, see Pub. 505 for additional tables; or, you can use the online withholding estimator at *www.irs.gov/W4App*.

1	**Two jobs.** If you have two jobs or you're married filing jointly and you and your spouse each have one job, find the amount from the appropriate table on page 4. Using the "Higher Paying Job" row and the "Lower Paying Job" column, find the value at the intersection of the two household salaries and enter that value on line 1. Then, **skip** to line 3	1	$ 4,760
2	**Three jobs.** If you and/or your spouse have three jobs at the same time, complete lines 2a, 2b, and 2c below. Otherwise, skip to line 3.		
	a Find the amount from the appropriate table on page 4 using the annual wages from the highest paying job in the "Higher Paying Job" row and the annual wages for your next highest paying job in the "Lower Paying Job" column. Find the value at the intersection of the two household salaries and enter that value on line 2a	2a	$
	b Add the annual wages of the two highest paying jobs from line 2a together and use the total as the wages in the "Higher Paying Job" row and use the annual wages for your third job in the "Lower Paying Job" column to find the amount from the appropriate table on page 4 and enter this amount on line 2b	2b	$
	c Add the amounts from lines 2a and 2b and enter the result on line 2c	2c	$
3	Enter the number of pay periods per year for the highest paying job. For example, if that job pays weekly, enter 52; if it pays every other week, enter 26; if it pays monthly, enter 12, etc.	3	24
4	**Divide** the annual amount on line 1 or line 2c by the number of pay periods on line 3. Enter this amount here and in **Step 4(c)** of Form W-4 for the highest paying job (along with any other additional amount you want withheld)	4	$ 198.33

Step 4(b)—Deductions Worksheet *(Keep for your records.)*

1	Enter an estimate of your 2022 itemized deductions (from Schedule A (Form 1040)). Such deductions may include qualifying home mortgage interest, charitable contributions, state and local taxes (up to $10,000), and medical expenses in excess of 7.5% of your income	1	$ 27,000
2	Enter: { • $25,900 if you're married filing jointly or qualifying widow(er) • $19,400 if you're head of household • $12,950 if you're single or married filing separately }	2	$ 25,900
3	If line 1 is greater than line 2, subtract line 2 from line 1 and enter the result here. If line 2 is greater than line 1, enter "-0-"	3	$ 1,100
4	Enter an estimate of your student loan interest, deductible IRA contributions, and certain other adjustments (from Part II of Schedule 1 (Form 1040)). See Pub. 505 for more information	4	$ 8,500
5	**Add** lines 3 and 4. Enter the result here and in **Step 4(b)** of Form W-4	5	$ 9,600

Privacy Act and Paperwork Reduction Act Notice. We ask for the information on this form to carry out the Internal Revenue laws of the United States. Internal Revenue Code sections 3402(f)(2) and 6109 and their regulations require you to provide this information; your employer uses it to determine your federal income tax withholding. Failure to provide a properly completed form will result in your being treated as a single person with no other entries on the form; providing fraudulent information may subject you to penalties. Routine uses of this information include giving it to the Department of Justice for civil and criminal litigation; to cities, states, the District of Columbia, and U.S. commonwealths and possessions for use in administering their tax laws; and to the Department of Health and Human Services for use in the National Directory of New Hires. We may also disclose this information to other countries under a tax treaty, to federal and state agencies to enforce federal nontax criminal laws, or to federal law enforcement and intelligence agencies to combat terrorism.

You are not required to provide the information requested on a form that is subject to the Paperwork Reduction Act unless the form displays a valid OMB control number. Books or records relating to a form or its instructions must be retained as long as their contents may become material in the administration of any Internal Revenue law. Generally, tax returns and return information are confidential, as required by Code section 6103.

The average time and expenses required to complete and file this form will vary depending on individual circumstances. For estimated averages, see the instructions for your income tax return.

If you have suggestions for making this form simpler, we would be happy to hear from you. See the instructions for your income tax return.

Form W-4 (2022) Page 4

Married Filing Jointly or Qualifying Widow(er)

Higher Paying Job Annual Taxable Wage & Salary	Lower Paying Job Annual Taxable Wage & Salary											
	$0 - 9,999	$10,000 - 19,999	$20,000 - 29,999	$30,000 - 39,999	$40,000 - 49,999	$50,000 - 59,999	$60,000 - 69,999	$70,000 - 79,999	$80,000 - 89,999	$90,000 - 99,999	$100,000 - 109,999	$110,000 - 120,000
$0 - 9,999	$0	$110	$850	$860	$1,020	$1,020	$1,020	$1,020	$1,020	$1,020	$1,770	$1,870
$10,000 - 19,999	110	1,110	1,860	2,060	2,220	2,220	2,220	2,220	2,220	2,970	3,970	4,070
$20,000 - 29,999	850	1,860	2,800	3,000	3,160	3,160	3,160	3,160	3,910	4,910	5,910	6,010
$30,000 - 39,999	860	2,060	3,000	3,200	3,360	3,360	3,360	4,110	5,110	6,110	7,110	7,210
$40,000 - 49,999	1,020	2,220	3,160	3,360	3,520	3,520	4,270	5,270	6,270	7,270	8,270	8,370
$50,000 - 59,999	1,020	2,220	3,160	3,360	3,520	4,270	5,270	6,270	7,270	8,270	9,270	9,370
$60,000 - 69,999	1,020	2,220	3,160	3,360	4,270	5,270	6,270	7,270	8,270	9,270	10,270	10,370
$70,000 - 79,999	1,020	2,220	3,160	4,110	5,270	6,270	7,270	8,270	9,270	10,270	11,270	11,370
$80,000 - 99,999	1,020	2,820	4,760	5,960	7,120	8,120	9,120	10,120	11,120	12,120	13,150	13,450
$100,000 - 149,999	1,870	4,070	6,010	7,210	8,370	9,370	10,510	11,710	12,910	14,110	15,310	15,600
$150,000 - 239,999	2,040	4,440	6,580	7,980	9,340	10,540	11,740	12,940	14,140	15,340	16,540	16,830
$240,000 - 259,999	2,040	4,440	6,580	7,980	9,340	10,540	11,740	12,940	14,140	15,340	16,540	17,590
$260,000 - 279,999	2,040	4,440	6,580	7,980	9,340	10,540	11,740	12,940	14,140	16,100	18,100	19,190
$280,000 - 299,999	2,040	4,440	6,580	7,980	9,340	10,540	11,740	13,700	15,700	17,700	19,700	20,790
$300,000 - 319,999	2,040	4,440	6,580	7,980	9,340	11,300	13,300	15,300	17,300	19,300	21,300	22,390
$320,000 - 364,999	2,100	5,300	8,240	10,440	12,600	14,600	16,600	18,600	20,600	22,600	24,870	26,260
$365,000 - 524,999	2,970	6,470	9,710	12,210	14,670	16,970	19,270	21,570	23,870	26,170	28,470	29,870
$525,000 and over	3,140	6,840	10,280	12,980	15,640	18,140	20,640	23,140	25,640	28,140	30,640	32,240

Single or Married Filing Separately

Higher Paying Job Annual Taxable Wage & Salary	Lower Paying Job Annual Taxable Wage & Salary											
	$0 - 9,999	$10,000 - 19,999	$20,000 - 29,999	$30,000 - 39,999	$40,000 - 49,999	$50,000 - 59,999	$60,000 - 69,999	$70,000 - 79,999	$80,000 - 89,999	$90,000 - 99,999	$100,000 - 109,999	$110,000 - 120,000
$0 - 9,999	$400	$930	$1,020	$1,020	$1,250	$1,870	$1,870	$1,870	$1,870	$1,970	$2,040	$2,040
$10,000 - 19,999	930	1,570	1,660	1,890	2,890	3,510	3,510	3,510	3,610	3,810	3,880	3,880
$20,000 - 29,999	1,020	1,660	1,990	2,990	3,990	4,610	4,610	4,710	4,910	5,110	5,180	5,180
$30,000 - 39,999	1,020	1,890	2,990	3,990	4,990	5,610	5,710	5,910	6,110	6,310	6,380	6,380
$40,000 - 59,999	1,870	3,510	4,610	5,610	6,680	7,500	7,700	7,900	8,100	8,300	8,370	8,370
$60,000 - 79,999	1,870	3,510	4,680	5,880	7,080	7,900	8,100	8,300	8,500	8,700	8,970	9,770
$80,000 - 99,999	1,940	3,780	5,080	6,280	7,480	8,300	8,500	8,700	9,100	10,100	10,970	11,770
$100,000 - 124,999	2,040	3,880	5,180	6,380	7,580	8,400	9,140	10,140	11,140	12,140	13,040	14,140
$125,000 - 149,999	2,040	3,880	5,180	6,520	8,520	10,140	11,140	12,140	13,320	14,620	15,790	16,890
$150,000 - 174,999	2,040	4,420	6,520	8,520	10,520	12,170	13,470	14,770	16,070	17,370	18,540	19,640
$175,000 - 199,999	2,720	5,360	7,460	9,630	11,930	13,860	15,160	16,460	17,760	19,060	20,230	21,330
$200,000 - 249,999	2,970	5,920	8,310	10,610	12,910	14,840	16,140	17,440	18,740	20,040	21,210	22,310
$250,000 - 399,999	2,970	5,920	8,310	10,610	12,910	14,840	16,140	17,440	18,740	20,040	21,210	22,310
$400,000 - 449,999	2,970	5,920	8,310	10,610	12,910	14,840	16,140	17,440	18,740	20,040	21,210	22,470
$450,000 and over	3,140	6,290	8,880	11,380	13,880	16,010	17,510	19,010	20,510	22,010	23,380	24,680

Head of Household

Higher Paying Job Annual Taxable Wage & Salary	Lower Paying Job Annual Taxable Wage & Salary											
	$0 - 9,999	$10,000 - 19,999	$20,000 - 29,999	$30,000 - 39,999	$40,000 - 49,999	$50,000 - 59,999	$60,000 - 69,999	$70,000 - 79,999	$80,000 - 89,999	$90,000 - 99,999	$100,000 - 109,999	$110,000 - 120,000
$0 - 9,999	$0	$760	$910	$1,020	$1,020	$1,020	$1,190	$1,870	$1,870	$1,870	$2,040	$2,040
$10,000 - 19,999	760	1,820	2,110	2,220	2,220	2,390	3,390	4,070	4,070	4,240	4,440	4,440
$20,000 - 29,999	910	2,110	2,400	2,510	2,680	3,680	4,680	5,360	5,530	5,730	5,930	5,930
$30,000 - 39,999	1,020	2,220	2,510	2,790	3,790	4,790	5,790	6,640	6,840	7,040	7,240	7,240
$40,000 - 59,999	1,020	2,240	3,530	4,640	5,640	6,780	7,980	8,860	9,060	9,260	9,460	9,460
$60,000 - 79,999	1,870	4,070	5,360	6,610	7,810	9,010	10,210	11,090	11,290	11,490	11,690	12,170
$80,000 - 99,999	1,870	4,210	5,700	7,010	8,210	9,410	10,610	11,490	11,690	12,380	13,370	14,170
$100,000 - 124,999	2,040	4,440	5,930	7,240	8,440	9,640	10,860	12,540	13,540	14,540	15,540	16,480
$125,000 - 149,999	2,040	4,440	5,930	7,240	8,860	10,860	12,860	14,540	15,540	16,830	18,130	19,230
$150,000 - 174,999	2,040	4,460	6,750	8,860	10,860	12,860	15,000	16,980	18,280	19,580	20,880	21,980
$175,000 - 199,999	2,720	5,920	8,210	10,320	12,600	14,900	17,200	19,180	20,480	21,780	23,080	24,180
$200,000 - 449,999	2,970	6,470	9,060	11,480	13,780	16,080	18,380	20,360	21,660	22,960	24,250	25,360
$450,000 and over	3,140	6,840	9,630	12,250	14,750	17,250	19,750	21,930	23,430	24,930	26,420	27,730

An employee who submits a false Form W-4 may be subject to a $500 penalty. Willfully filing a fraudulent Form W-4 or failing to supply information that would increase the amount withheld can result in a fine of up to $1,000 or imprisonment for up to 1 year, or both. Employers must submit copies of Forms W-4 to the IRS only when directed to do so by written notice. Where there is significant underwithholding for a particular employee, the IRS may require the employer to withhold income tax at a higher rate and will notify the employer in writing (known as a "lock-in" letter). Employees are given the right to contest the IRS determination.

EXAMPLE Brianne is the payroll manager at her company and receives a Form W-4 from her employee, Mike. On his Form W-4, Mike indicated that he is a married employee with five children under age 17. Brianne also noted that Mike did not list a spouse or his children on his application or retirement plan paperwork and earlier mentioned that he was single. Based on both written and oral statements made by Mike, Brianne should ask Mike to prepare a corrected W-4. If he is unwilling to do so, she should withhold as if Mike is a single taxpayer. ♦

EXAMPLE George works in the payroll department and receives a Form W-4 from a new employee, Beatrice. Beatrice indicates married status and claims $4,000 on Step 3 for dependents on her Form W-4. George notes that her married status is consistent with her other paperwork and Beatrice has provided no oral or written statements that would indicate she is not married and has two children. George is not required to verify the existence of Beatrice's spouse and children. ♦

Although employers are not required to submit Forms W-4 to the Internal Revenue Service, that does not mean that new hires are not reported. In large part designed to assist with the enforcement of child support payments, the Personal Responsibility and Work Opportunity Reconciliation Act of 1996 (PRWORA) was passed requiring states to maintain a database of all new hires. Although many states use a specific form for reporting new hires, states will often also accept a completed Form W-4.

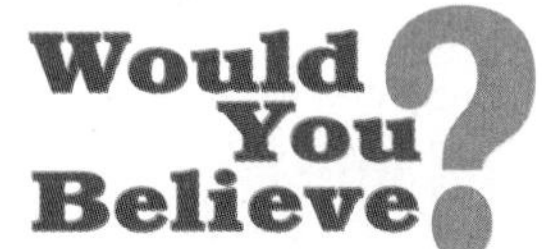

9-1b The Form W-4 Before 2020

As discussed previously, the former version of Form W-4 focused on the concept of "allowances" to determine the amount of income tax withholding. Employees would complete the Personal Allowances Worksheet and carry that information forward to the face of the Form W-4. The number of allowances was adjusted for two-wage earners, additional deductions, and credits. Employees who submitted a Form W-4 in any year before 2020 are not required to submit a new Form W-4. Employers will continue to compute withholding based on the information from the employee's old Form W-4. All new employees and any existing employees that wish to adjust withholding must use the new Form W-4.

EXAMPLE Using the information from the example of Fei and Zhi Han on Pages 9-3 and 9-4, a completed 2019 Form W-4 is presented on Pages 9-10 to 9-13. Note that this example presumes that Zhi completed this form in 2019 and that the employer would continue to use this information for withholding in 2022. ♦

Form W-4 (2019)

Future developments. For the latest information about any future developments related to Form W-4, such as legislation enacted after it was published, go to *www.irs.gov/FormW4*.

Purpose. Complete Form W-4 so that your employer can withhold the correct federal income tax from your pay. Consider completing a new Form W-4 each year and when your personal or financial situation changes.

Exemption from withholding. You may claim exemption from withholding for 2019 if **both** of the following apply.

• For 2018 you had a right to a refund of **all** federal income tax withheld because you had **no** tax liability, **and**

• For 2019 you expect a refund of **all** federal income tax withheld because you expect to have **no** tax liability.

If you're exempt, complete **only** lines 1, 2, 3, 4, and 7 and sign the form to validate it. Your exemption for 2019 expires February 17, 2020. See Pub. 505, Tax Withholding and Estimated Tax, to learn more about whether you qualify for exemption from withholding.

General Instructions

If you aren't exempt, follow the rest of these instructions to determine the number of withholding allowances you should claim for withholding for 2019 and any additional amount of tax to have withheld. For regular wages, withholding must be based on allowances you claimed and may not be a flat amount or percentage of wages.

You can also use the calculator at ***www.irs.gov/W4App*** to determine your tax withholding more accurately. Consider using this calculator if you have a more complicated tax situation, such as if you have a working spouse, more than one job, or a large amount of nonwage income not subject to withholding outside of your job. After your Form W-4 takes effect, you can also use this calculator to see how the amount of tax you're having withheld compares to your projected total tax for 2019. If you use the calculator, you don't need to complete any of the worksheets for Form W-4.

Note that if you have too much tax withheld, you will receive a refund when you file your tax return. If you have too little tax withheld, you will owe tax when you file your tax return, and you might owe a penalty.

Filers with multiple jobs or working spouses. If you have more than one job at a time, or if you're married filing jointly and your spouse is also working, read all of the instructions including the instructions for the Two-Earners/Multiple Jobs Worksheet before beginning.

Nonwage income. If you have a large amount of nonwage income not subject to withholding, such as interest or dividends, consider making estimated tax payments using Form 1040-ES, Estimated Tax for Individuals. Otherwise, you might owe additional tax. Or, you can use the Deductions, Adjustments, and Additional Income Worksheet on page 3 or the calculator at *www.irs.gov/W4App* to make sure you have enough tax withheld from your paycheck. If you have pension or annuity income, see Pub. 505 or use the calculator at *www.irs.gov/W4App* to find out if you should adjust your withholding on Form W-4 or W-4P.

Nonresident alien. If you're a nonresident alien, see Notice 1392, Supplemental Form W-4 Instructions for Nonresident Aliens, before completing this form.

Specific Instructions

Personal Allowances Worksheet

Complete this worksheet on page 3 first to determine the number of withholding allowances to claim.

Line C. *Head of household please note:* Generally, you may claim head of household filing status on your tax return only if you're unmarried and pay more than 50% of the costs of keeping up a home for yourself and a qualifying individual. See Pub. 501 for more information about filing status.

Line E. Child tax credit. When you file your tax return, you may be eligible to claim a child tax credit for each of your eligible children. To qualify, the child must be under age 17 as of December 31, must be your dependent who lives with you for more than half the year, and must have a valid social security number. To learn more about this credit, see Pub. 972, Child Tax Credit. To reduce the tax withheld from your pay by taking this credit into account, follow the instructions on line E of the worksheet. On the worksheet you will be asked about your total income. For this purpose, total income includes all of your wages and other income, including income earned by a spouse if you are filing a joint return.

Line F. Credit for other dependents. When you file your tax return, you may be eligible to claim a credit for other dependents for whom a child tax credit can't be claimed, such as a qualifying child who doesn't meet the age or social security number requirement for the child tax credit, or a qualifying relative. To learn more about this credit, see Pub. 972. To reduce the tax withheld from your pay by taking this credit into account, follow the instructions on line F of the worksheet. On the worksheet, you will be asked about your total income. For this purpose, total

---

Separate here and give Form W-4 to your employer. Keep the worksheet(s) for your records.

Form **W-4** | Department of the Treasury, Internal Revenue Service

Employee's Withholding Allowance Certificate

► **Whether you're entitled to claim a certain number of allowances or exemption from withholding is subject to review by the IRS. Your employer may be required to send a copy of this form to the IRS.**

OMB No. 1545-0074 | **2019**

1 Your first name and middle initial Zhi	Last name Han	**2 Your social security number**
Home address (number and street or rural route)	3 ☐ Single ☑ Married ☐ Married, but withhold at higher Single rate. **Note:** If married filing separately, check "Married, but withhold at higher Single rate."	
City or town, state, and ZIP code	**4 If your last name differs from that shown on your social security card, check here. You must call 800-772-1213 for a replacement card.** ► ☐	

5 Total number of allowances you're claiming (from the applicable worksheet on the following pages) **5** 5

6 Additional amount, if any, you want withheld from each paycheck . . . . **6** $

7 I claim exemption from withholding for 2019, and I certify that I meet **both** of the following conditions for exemption.

• Last year I had a right to a refund of **all** federal income tax withheld because I had **no** tax liability, **and**

• This year I expect a refund of **all** federal income tax withheld because I expect to have **no** tax liability.

If you meet both conditions, write "Exempt" here . . . . ► **7**

Under penalties of perjury, I declare that I have examined this certificate and, to the best of my knowledge and belief, it is true, correct, and complete.

Employee's signature
(This form is not valid unless you sign it.) ► **Date ►**

8 Employer's name and address (**Employer:** Complete boxes 8 and 10 if sending to IRS and complete boxes 8, 9, and 10 if sending to State Directory of New Hires.)	9 First date of employment	10 Employer identification number (EIN)

For Privacy Act and Paperwork Reduction Act Notice, see page 4. Cat. No. 10220Q Form **W-4** (2019)

income includes all of your wages and other income, including income earned by a spouse if you are filing a joint return.

Line G. Other credits. You may be able to reduce the tax withheld from your paycheck if you expect to claim other tax credits, such as tax credits for education (see Pub. 970). If you do so, your paycheck will be larger, but the amount of any refund that you receive when you file your tax return will be smaller. Follow the instructions for Worksheet 1-6 in Pub. 505 if you want to reduce your withholding to take these credits into account. Enter "-0-" on lines E and F if you use Worksheet 1-6.

Deductions, Adjustments, and Additional Income Worksheet

Complete this worksheet to determine if you're able to reduce the tax withheld from your paycheck to account for your itemized deductions and other adjustments to income, such as IRA contributions. If you do so, your refund at the end of the year will be smaller, but your paycheck will be larger. You're not required to complete this worksheet or reduce your withholding if you don't wish to do so.

You can also use this worksheet to figure out how much to increase the tax withheld from your paycheck if you have a large amount of nonwage income not subject to withholding, such as interest or dividends.

Another option is to take these items into account and make your withholding more accurate by using the calculator at *www.irs.gov/W4App*. If you use the calculator, you don't need to complete any of the worksheets for Form W-4.

Two-Earners/Multiple Jobs Worksheet

Complete this worksheet if you have more than one job at a time or are married filing jointly and have a working spouse. If you don't complete this worksheet, you might have too little tax withheld. If so, you will owe tax when you file your tax return and might be subject to a penalty.

Figure the total number of allowances you're entitled to claim and any additional amount of tax to withhold on all jobs using worksheets from only one Form W-4. Claim all allowances on the W-4 that you or your spouse file for the highest paying job in your family and claim zero allowances on Forms W-4 filed for all other jobs. For example, if you earn $60,000 per year and your spouse earns $20,000, you should complete the worksheets to determine what to enter on lines 5 and 6 of your Form W-4, and your spouse should enter zero ("-0-") on lines 5 and 6 of his or her Form W-4. See Pub. 505 for details.

Another option is to use the calculator at *www.irs.gov/W4App* to make your withholding more accurate.

Tip: If you have a working spouse and your incomes are similar, you can check the "Married, but withhold at higher Single rate" box instead of using this worksheet. If you choose this option, then each spouse should fill out the Personal Allowances Worksheet and check the "Married, but withhold at higher Single rate" box on Form W-4, but only one spouse should claim any allowances for credits or fill out the Deductions, Adjustments, and Additional Income Worksheet.

Instructions for Employer

Employees, do not complete box 8, 9, or 10. Your employer will complete these boxes if necessary.

New hire reporting. Employers are required by law to report new employees to a designated State Directory of New Hires. Employers may use Form W-4, boxes 8, 9, and 10 to comply with the new hire reporting requirement for a newly hired employee. A newly hired employee is an employee who hasn't previously been employed by the employer, or who was previously employed by the employer but has been separated from such prior employment for at least 60 consecutive days. Employers should contact the appropriate State Directory of New Hires to find out how to submit a copy of the completed Form W-4. For information and links to each designated State Directory of New Hires (including for U.S. territories), go to ***www.acf.hhs.gov/css/employers.***

If an employer is sending a copy of Form W-4 to a designated State Directory of New Hires to comply with the new hire reporting requirement for a newly hired employee, complete boxes 8, 9, and 10 as follows.

Box 8. Enter the employer's name and address. If the employer is sending a copy of this form to a State Directory of New Hires, enter the address where child support agencies should send income withholding orders.

Box 9. If the employer is sending a copy of this form to a State Directory of New Hires, enter the employee's first date of employment, which is the date services for payment were first performed by the employee. If the employer rehired the employee after the employee had been separated from the employer's service for at least 60 days, enter the rehire date.

Box 10. Enter the employer's employer identification number (EIN).

Form W-4 (2019) Page 3

Personal Allowances Worksheet (Keep for your records.)

A	Enter "1" for yourself	A	1
B	Enter "1" if you will file as married filing jointly	B	1
C	Enter "1" if you will file as head of household	C	
D	Enter "1" if: • You're single, or married filing separately, and have only one job; or • You're married filing jointly, have only one job, and your spouse doesn't work; or • Your wages from a second job or your spouse's wages (or the total of both) are $1,500 or less.	D	
E	**Child tax credit.** See Pub. 972, Child Tax Credit, for more information. • If your total income will be less than $71,201 ($103,351 if married filing jointly), enter "4" for each eligible child. • If your total income will be from $71,201 to $179,050 ($103,351 to $345,850 if married filing jointly), enter "2" for each eligible child. • If your total income will be from $179,051 to $200,000 ($345,851 to $400,000 if married filing jointly), enter "1" for each eligible child. • If your total income will be higher than $200,000 ($400,000 if married filing jointly), enter "-0-"	E	4
F	**Credit for other dependents.** See Pub. 972, Child Tax Credit, for more information. • If your total income will be less than $71,201 ($103,351 if married filing jointly), enter "1" for each eligible dependent. • If your total income will be from $71,201 to $179,050 ($103,351 to $345,850 if married filing jointly), enter "1" for every two dependents (for example, "-0-" for one dependent, "1" if you have two or three dependents, and "2" if you have four dependents). • If your total income will be higher than $179,050 ($345,850 if married filing jointly), enter "-0-"	F	1
G	**Other credits.** If you have other credits, see Worksheet 1-6 of Pub. 505 and enter the amount from that worksheet here. If you use Worksheet 1-6, enter "-0-" on lines E and F	G	
H	Add lines A through G and enter the total here ▶	H	7

For accuracy, **complete all worksheets that apply.**

- If you plan to **itemize** or **claim adjustments to income** and want to reduce your withholding, or if you have a large amount of nonwage income not subject to withholding and want to increase your withholding, see the **Deductions, Adjustments, and Additional Income Worksheet** below.
- If you **have more than one job at a time** or are **married filing jointly and you and your spouse both work,** and the combined earnings from all jobs exceed $53,000 ($24,450 if married filing jointly), see the **Two-Earners/Multiple Jobs Worksheet** on page 4 to avoid having too little tax withheld.
- If **neither** of the above situations applies, **stop here** and enter the number from line H on line 5 of Form W-4 above.

Deductions, Adjustments, and Additional Income Worksheet

Note: Use this worksheet *only* if you plan to itemize deductions, claim certain adjustments to income, or have a large amount of nonwage income not subject to withholding.

1	Enter an estimate of your 2019 itemized deductions. These include qualifying home mortgage interest, charitable contributions, state and local taxes (up to $10,000), and medical expenses in excess of 10% of your income. See Pub. 505 for details	1	$ 27,000
2	Enter: $24,400 if you're married filing jointly or qualifying widow(er); $18,350 if you're head of household; $12,200 if you're single or married filing separately	2	$ 24,400
3	**Subtract** line 2 from line 1. If zero or less, enter "-0-"	3	$ 2,600
4	Enter an estimate of your 2019 adjustments to income, qualified business income deduction, and any additional standard deduction for age or blindness (see Pub. 505 for information about these items)	4	$ 8,500 (a)
5	**Add** lines 3 and 4 and enter the total	5	$ 11,100
6	Enter an estimate of your 2019 nonwage income not subject to withholding (such as dividends or interest)	6	$ 3,500
7	**Subtract** line 6 from line 5. If zero, enter "-0-". If less than zero, enter the amount in parentheses	7	$ 7,600
8	**Divide** the amount on line 7 by $4,200 and enter the result here. If a negative amount, enter in parentheses. Drop any fraction	8	1
9	Enter the number from the **Personal Allowances Worksheet,** line H, above	9	7
10	**Add** lines 8 and 9 and enter the total here. If zero or less, enter "-0-". If you plan to use the **Two-Earners/Multiple Jobs Worksheet,** also enter this total on line 1 of that worksheet on page 4. Otherwise, **stop here** and enter this total on Form W-4, line 5, page 1	10	8

(a) The maximum IRA deduction was $6,000 and the maximum student loan interest deduction was $2,500 in 2019.

Form W-4 (2019) Page **4**

Two-Earners/Multiple Jobs Worksheet

Note: Use this worksheet *only* if the instructions under line H from the **Personal Allowances Worksheet** direct you here.

1 Enter the number from the **Personal Allowances Worksheet,** line H, page 3 (or, if you used the **Deductions, Adjustments, and Additional Income Worksheet** on page 3, the number from line 10 of that worksheet) . . . **1** 8

2 Find the number in **Table 1** below that applies to the **LOWEST** paying job and enter it here. **However,** if you're married filing jointly and wages from the highest paying job are $75,000 or less and the combined wages for you and your spouse are $107,000 or less, don't enter more than "3" . . . **2** 3

3 If line 1 is **more than or equal to** line 2, subtract line 2 from line 1. Enter the result here (if zero, enter "-0-") and on Form W-4, line 5, page 1. **Do not** use the rest of this worksheet . . . **3** 5

Note: If line 1 is **less than** line 2, enter "-0-" on Form W-4, line 5, page 1. Complete lines 4 through 9 below to figure the additional withholding amount necessary to avoid a year-end tax bill.

4 Enter the number from line 2 of this worksheet . . . **4** ______

5 Enter the number from line 1 of this worksheet . . . **5** ______

6 **Subtract** line 5 from line 4 . . . **6** ______

7 Find the amount in **Table 2** below that applies to the **HIGHEST** paying job and enter it here . . . **7** $ ______

8 **Multiply** line 7 by line 6 and enter the result here. This is the additional annual withholding needed . . . **8** $ ______

9 **Divide** line 8 by the number of pay periods remaining in 2019. For example, divide by 18 if you're paid every 2 weeks and you complete this form on a date in late April when there are 18 pay periods remaining in 2019. Enter the result here and on Form W-4, line 6, page 1. This is the additional amount to be withheld from each paycheck . . . **9** $ ______

Table 1

Married Filing Jointly		All Others	
If wages from **LOWEST** paying job are—	Enter on line 2 above	If wages from **LOWEST** paying job are—	Enter on line 2 above
$0 - $5,000	0	$0 - $7,000	0
5,001 - 9,500	1	7,001 - 13,000	1
9,501 - 19,500	2	13,001 - 27,500	2
19,501 - 35,000	3	27,501 - 32,000	3
35,001 - 40,000	4	32,001 - 40,000	4
40,001 - 46,000	5	40,001 - 60,000	5
46,001 - 55,000	6	60,001 - 75,000	6
55,001 - 60,000	7	75,001 - 85,000	7
60,001 - 70,000	8	85,001 - 95,000	8
70,001 - 75,000	9	95,001 - 100,000	9
75,001 - 85,000	10	100,001 - 110,000	10
85,001 - 95,000	11	110,001 - 115,000	11
95,001 - 125,000	12	115,001 - 125,000	12
125,001 - 155,000	13	125,001 - 135,000	13
155,001 - 165,000	14	135,001 - 145,000	14
165,001 - 175,000	15	145,001 - 160,000	15
175,001 - 180,000	16	160,001 - 180,000	16
180,001 - 195,000	17	180,001 and over	17
195,001 - 205,000	18		
205,001 and over	19		

Table 2

Married Filing Jointly		All Others	
If wages from **HIGHEST** paying job are—	Enter on line 7 above	If wages from **HIGHEST** paying job are—	Enter on line 7 above
$0 - $24,900	$420	$0 - $7,200	$420
24,901 - 84,450	500	7,201 - 36,975	500
84,451 - 173,900	910	36,976 - 81,700	910
173,901 - 326,950	1,000	81,701 - 158,225	1,000
326,951 - 413,700	1,330	158,226 - 201,600	1,330
413,701 - 617,850	1,450	201,601 - 507,800	1,450
617,851 and over	1,540	507,801 and over	1,540

Privacy Act and Paperwork Reduction Act Notice. We ask for the information on this form to carry out the Internal Revenue laws of the United States. Internal Revenue Code sections 3402(f)(2) and 6109 and their regulations require you to provide this information; your employer uses it to determine your federal income tax withholding. Failure to provide a properly completed form will result in your being treated as a single person who claims no withholding allowances; providing fraudulent information may subject you to penalties. Routine uses of this information include giving it to the Department of Justice for civil and criminal litigation; to cities, states, the District of Columbia, and U.S. commonwealths and possessions for use in administering their tax laws; and to the Department of Health and Human Services for use in the National Directory of New Hires. We may also disclose this information to other countries under a tax treaty, to federal and state agencies to enforce federal nontax criminal laws, or to federal law enforcement and intelligence agencies to combat terrorism.

You aren't required to provide the information requested on a form that's subject to the Paperwork Reduction Act unless the form displays a valid OMB control number. Books or records relating to a form or its instructions must be retained as long as their contents may become material in the administration of any Internal Revenue law. Generally, tax returns and return information are confidential, as required by Code section 6103.

The average time and expenses required to complete and file this form will vary depending on individual circumstances. For estimated averages, see the instructions for your income tax return.

If you have suggestions for making this form simpler, we would be happy to hear from you. See the instructions for your income tax return.

9-1c Computing Income Tax Withholding

The amount of income tax to be withheld by the employer is based on gross taxable wages before deducting FICA taxes, pension payments, union dues, insurance, and other deductions. An employer may elect to use any of several methods to determine the amount of the income tax withholding for each individual employee. Most commonly, withholding amounts are determined by use of the percentage method or by use of wage bracket tables.

The withholding tables published by the IRS allow employers to determine withholding based on old and new Forms W-4 under both the percentage and wage bracket methods.

To compute the withholding amount under the percentage method using a post-2019 ("new") Form W-4, the employer should use information from Form W-4 to prepare the adjusted wage amount, the tentative withholding amount, the adjustment for tax credits, and the final withholding. The steps can be summarized as:

1. Adjust the employee's wages for other forms of income [Line 4(a) from the employee's Form W-4] and excess deductions [Line 4(b) from the employee's Form W-4].
2. Determine the tentative withholding amount using the current year percentage method tables (reproduced here in Appendix C).
3. Account for tax credits.
4. Add any additional withholding requested to determine the final withholding amount.

Publication 15-T, Federal Income Tax Withholding Methods includes Worksheet 4 for employers to follow in computing withholding under the percentage method for an employee using a post-2019 ("new") Form W-4.

EXAMPLE Using the information presented in the Fei and Zhi Han example from Pages 9-3 and 9-4 and the new Form W-4 on Pages 9-5 to 9-8, Worksheet 4 is presented on Page 9-15 for one of Zhi's pay periods in 2022. The amount of withholding under the percentage method is $282.90. ♦

Under the wage bracket method of determining withholding, wage bracket tables are provided for weekly, biweekly, semimonthly, monthly, and daily payroll periods for both married, single, and head of household taxpayers. For a post-2019 Form W-4, the amount of withholding is obtained from the wage bracket method table for the appropriate payroll period and marital status and is based on the adjusted wage amount. The adjusted wage amount can be calculated using Worksheet 2 from Publication 15-T. The wage bracket method semimonthly tables for single and married taxpayers are reproduced in Appendix C. When using the new wage bracket method tables, care should be taken to select the proper tentative withholding amount from the table. There are two tentative withholding amount columns to choose from. The first column is for standard withholding and the second column is for when the taxpayer has checked the box on 2(c) of Form W-4, indicating that the taxpayer's spouse has wages similar to the taxpayer.

EXAMPLE Using the information presented in the Fei and Zhi Han example from Pages 9-3 and 9-4 and the new Form W-4 on Pages 9-5 to 9-8, Worksheet 2 is presented on Page 9-16 for one of Zhi's pay periods in 2022. The amount of withholding under the wage bracket method is $282.00. ♦

4. Percentage Method Tables for Manual Payroll Systems With Forms W-4 From 2020 or Later

If you compute payroll manually, your employee has submitted a Form W-4 for 2020 or later, and you prefer to use the Percentage Method or you can't use the Wage Bracket Method tables because the employee's annual wages exceed the amount from the last bracket of the table (based on marital status and pay period), use the worksheet below and the Percentage Method tables that follow to figure federal income tax withholding. This method works for any amount of wages.

Worksheet 4. Employer's Withholding Worksheet for Percentage Method Tables for Manual Payroll Systems With Forms W-4 From 2020 or Later

Keep for Your Records 

Table 6	Monthly	Semimonthly	Biweekly	Weekly	Daily
	12	24	26	52	260

Step 1. Adjust the employee's wage amount

1a	Enter the employee's total taxable wages this payroll period	1a	$ 3,916.67 *
1b	Enter the number of pay periods you have per year (see Table 6)	1b	24
1c	Enter the amount from Step 4(a) of the employee's Form W-4	1c	$ 3,500
1d	Divide line 1c by the number on line 1b	1d	$ 145.83
1e	Add lines 1a and 1d	1e	$ 4,062.50
1f	Enter the amount from Step 4(b) of the employee's Form W-4	1f	$ 9,600
1g	Divide line 1f by the number on line 1b	1g	$ 400
1h	Subtract line 1g from line 1e. If zero or less, enter -0-. This is the **Adjusted Wage Amount**	1h	$ 3,662.50

Step 2. Figure the Tentative Withholding Amount

based on your pay frequency, the employee's Adjusted Wage Amount, filing status (Step 1(c) of Form W-4), and whether the box in Step 2 of Form W-4 is checked.

2a	Find the row in the STANDARD Withholding Rate Schedules (if the box in Step 2 of Form W-4 is NOT checked) or the Form W-4, Step 2, Checkbox, Withholding Rate Schedules (if it HAS been checked) of the Percentage Method tables in this section in which the amount on line 1h is at least the amount in column A but less than the amount in column B, and then enter here the amount from column A of that row	2a	$ 1,935 **
2b	Enter the amount from column C of that row	2b	$ 85.60
2c	Enter the percentage from column D of that row	2c	12%
2d	Subtract line 2a from line 1h	2d	$ 1,727.50
2e	Multiply the amount on line 2d by the percentage on line 2c	2e	$ 207.30
2f	Add lines 2b and 2e. This is the **Tentative Withholding Amount**	2f	$ 292.90

Step 3. Account for tax credits

3a	Enter the amount from Step 3 of the employee's Form W-4	3a	$ 5,000
3b	Divide the amount on line 3a by the number of pay periods on line 1b	3b	$ 208.33
3c	Subtract line 3b from line 2f. If zero or less, enter -0-	3c	$ 84.57

Step 4. Figure the final amount to withhold

4a	Enter the additional amount to withhold from Step 4(c) of the employee's Form W-4	4a	$ 198.33
4b	Add lines 3c and 4a. **This is the amount to withhold from the employee's wages this pay period**	4b	$ 282.90

* Zhi's salary of $94,000 ÷ 24 semimonthly pay periods.

** Standard Withholding Rate Schedules of the Percentage Method tables are found in Appendix C.

2. Wage Bracket Method Tables for Manual Payroll Systems With Forms W-4 From 2020 or Later

If you compute payroll manually, your employee has submitted a Form W-4 for 2020 or later, and you prefer to use the Wage Bracket method, use the worksheet below and the Wage Bracket Method tables that follow to figure federal income tax withholding.

These Wage Bracket Method tables cover a limited amount of annual wages (generally, less than $100,000). If you can't use the Wage Bracket Method tables because taxable wages exceed the amount from the last bracket of the table (based on filing status and pay period), use the Percentage Method tables in section 4.

Worksheet 2. Employer's Withholding Worksheet for Wage Bracket Method Tables for Manual Payroll Systems With Forms W-4 From 2020 or Later

Keep for Your Records 

Table 5	Monthly	Semimonthly	Biweekly	Weekly	Daily
	12	24	26	52	260

Step 1. Adjust the employee's wage amount

1a	Enter the employee's total taxable wages this payroll period	1a	$ 3,916.67
1b	Enter the number of pay periods you have per year (see Table 5)	1b	24
1c	Enter the amount from Step 4(a) of the employee's Form W-4	1c	$ 3,500.00
1d	Divide the amount on line 1c by the number of pay periods on line 1b	1d	$ 145.83
1e	Add lines 1a and 1d	1e	$ 4,062.50
1f	Enter the amount from Step 4(b) of the employee's Form W-4	1f	$ 9,600.00
1g	Divide the amount on line 1f by the number of pay periods on line 1b	1g	$ 400.00
1h	Subtract line 1g from line 1e. If zero or less, enter -0-. This is the **Adjusted Wage Amount**	1h	$ 3,662.50

Step 2. Figure the Tentative Withholding Amount

2a	Use the amount on line 1h to look up the tentative amount to withhold in the appropriate Wage Bracket Method table in this section for your pay frequency, given the employee's filing status and whether the employee has checked the box in Step 2 of Form W-4. This is the **Tentative Withholding Amount**	2a	$ 292.00 **

Step 3. Account for tax credits

3a	Enter the amount from Step 3 of the employee's Form W-4	3a	$ 5,000.00
3b	Divide the amount on line 3a by the number of pay periods on line 1b	3b	$ 208.33
3c	Subtract line 3b from line 2a. If zero or less, enter -0-	3c	$ 83.67

Step 4. Figure the final amount to withhold

4a	Enter the additional amount to withhold from Step 4(c) of the employee's Form W-4	4a	$ 198.33
4b	Add lines 3c and 4a. **This is the amount to withhold from the employee's wages this pay period**	4b	$ 282.00

** Standard withholding from the Wage Bracket Method tables are found in Appendix C.

To compute the withholding amount under the percentage method using an old (before 2020) Form W-4, the employer should:

1. Multiply the number of allowances claimed by the employee (from Form W-4) by the allowance amount;
2. Subtract that amount from the employee's gross taxable wages for the pay period; and
3. Apply the result in Step 2 to the applicable withholding table in Appendix C for the appropriate marital status.

Publication 15-T provides Worksheet 5 to assist employers in calculating withholding under the percentage method for an old Form W-4. Note that although exemptions were repealed by the TCJA, allowance amounts are based on an exemption amount of $4,400 (in 2022).

EXAMPLE Using the information presented in the Fei and Zhi Han example from Pages 9-3 and 9-4 and the old Form W-4 on Pages 9-10 to 9-13, Worksheet 5 is presented below for one of Zhi's pay periods in 2022. The amount of withholding under the percentage method is $280.44. ♦

5. Percentage Method Tables for Manual Payroll Systems With Forms W-4 From 2019 or Earlier

If you compute payroll manually and your employee **has not** submitted a Form W-4 for 2020 or later, and you prefer to use the Percentage Method or you can't use the Wage Bracket Method tables because the employee's annual wages exceed the amount from the last bracket of the table (based on marital status and pay period) or the employee claimed more than 10 allowances, use the worksheet below and the Percentage Method tables that follow to figure federal income tax withholding. This method works for any number of withholding allowances claimed and any amount of wages.

Periodic payments of pensions or annuities with a 2021 or earlier Form W-4P. In lieu of Worksheet 1B and the Percentage Method tables in section 1, you may use Worksheet 5 and the Percentage Method tables in this section to figure federal income tax withholding on periodic payments of pensions or annuities with a 2021 or earlier Form W-4P. As an alternative, if you prefer to use the Wage Bracket Method of withholding, you may use Worksheet 3 and the Wage Bracket Method tables in section 3 to figure federal income tax withholding on periodic payments of pensions or annuities with a 2021 or earlier Form W-4P.

Worksheet 5. Employer's Withholding Worksheet for Percentage Method Tables for Manual Payroll Systems With Forms W-4 From 2019 or Earlier

Keep for Your Records 

Table 7	Annually	Semiannually	Quarterly	Monthly	Semimonthly	Biweekly	Weekly	Daily
	$4,300	$2,150	$1,075	$358	$179	$165	$83	$17

Step 1. Adjust the employee's wage amount

1a	Enter the employee's total taxable wages this payroll period	1a $ 3,916.67
1b	Enter the number of allowances claimed on the employee's most recent Form W-4	1b 5
1c	Multiply line 1b by the amount in Table 7 for your pay frequency	1c $ 895.00
1d	Subtract line 1c from line 1a. If zero or less, enter -0-. This is the **Adjusted Wage Amount**	1d $ 3,021.67

Step 2. Figure the Tentative Withholding Amount

based on your pay frequency, the employee's Adjusted Wage Amount, and marital status (line 3 of Form W-4).

2a	Find the row in the Percentage Method table in this section in which the amount on line 1d is at least the amount in column A but less than the amount in column B, and then enter here the amount from column A of that row	2a $ 1,398.00
2b	Enter the amount from column C of that row	2b $ 85.60
2c	Enter the percentage from column D of that row	2c 12%
2d	Subtract line 2a from line 1d	2d $ 1,623.67
2e	Multiply the amount on line 2d by the percentage on line 2c	2e $ 194.84
2f	Add lines 2b and 2e. This is the **Tentative Withholding Amount**	2f $ 280.44

Step 3. Figure the final amount to withhold

3a	Enter the additional amount to withhold from line 6 of the employee's Form W-4	3a $ 0.00
3b	Add lines 2f and 3a. **This is the amount to withhold from the employee's wages this pay period**	3b $ 280.44

The wage bracket method for an employee using an old (pre-2020) Form W-4 follows the same steps as a new (post-2019) Form W-4; however the tentative withholding is determined using Worksheet 3 and the associated wage bracket tables.

EXAMPLE Using the information presented in the Fei and Zhi Han example from Pages 9-3 and 9-4 *except that annual wages for Zhi are $74,000* and the old Form W-4 on Pages 9-10 to 9-13, Worksheet 3 is presented below for one of Zhi's pay periods in 2022. The amount of withholding under the wage bracket method is $178.00. ♦

3. Wage Bracket Method Tables for Manual Payroll Systems With Forms W-4 From 2019 or Earlier

If you compute payroll manually and your employee **has not** submitted a Form W-4 for 2020 or later, use the worksheet below and the Wage Bracket Method tables that follow to figure federal income tax withholding.

These Wage Bracket Method tables cover a limited amount of annual wages (generally, less than $100,000) and up to 10 allowances. If you can't use the Wage Bracket Method tables because taxable wages exceed the amount from the last bracket of the table (based on marital status and pay period) or the employee claimed more than 10 allowances, use the Percentage Method tables in section 5.

Periodic payments of pensions or annuities with a 2021 or earlier Form W-4P. In lieu of Worksheet 1B and the Percentage Method tables in section 1, you may use Worksheet 3 and the Wage Bracket Method tables in this section to figure federal income tax withholding on periodic payments of pensions or annuities with a 2021 or earlier Form W-4P. As an alternative, if you prefer to use the Percentage Method of withholding, you may use Worksheet 5 and the Percentage Method tables in section 5 to figure federal income tax withholding on periodic payments of pensions or annuities with a 2021 or earlier Form W-4P.

Worksheet 3. Employer's Withholding Worksheet for Wage Bracket Method Tables for Manual Payroll Systems With Forms W-4 From 2019 or Earlier *Keep for Your Records* 

Step 1.	**Figure the tentative withholding amount**			
	1a Enter the employee's total taxable wages this payroll period	1a	$	3,083.33
	1b Use the amount on line 1a to look up the tentative amount to withhold in the appropriate Wage Bracket Method table in this section for your pay frequency, given the employee's marital status (line 3 of Form W-4) and number of allowances claimed. This is the **Tentative Withholding Amount**	1b	$	178.00
Step 2.	**Figure the final amount to withhold**			
	2a Enter the additional amount to withhold from line 6 of the employee's Form W-4	2a	$	0.00
	2b Add lines 1b and 2a. **This is the amount to withhold from the employee's wages this pay period**	2b	$	178.00

The income tax withholding tables are constructed so that taxpayers that have completed their Form W-4 properly will receive an income tax refund during tax filing season. Many taxpayers are satisfied with the resulting refund even though a tax refund represents an interest-free loan to the government. The overpayment of taxes serves as a "forced" savings account which provides the opportunity to purchase a big ticket item in late spring when the refund is received. Taxpayers should also be aware that interest is not charged symmetrically: underpayments of tax may result in penalties and interest (see LO 9.3), while overpayments are not usually credited with interest.

9-1d Pension and Deferred Income

Income tax withholding is also required on pension and other deferred income payments based on Form W-4P, Withholding Certificate for Pension or Annuity Payments, as completed and signed by the taxpayer. Financial institutions and corporations must withhold on the taxable part of pension, profit sharing, stock bonus, and individual retirement account payments. The rates used for withholding vary depending on the nature of the payment, as described below:

1. Periodic payments (such as annuities): Rates are based on the taxpayer's Form W-4P or if no W-4P is filed, tax will be withheld as if the taxpayer was single with no adjustments for other income or deductions.
2. Nonperiodic payments: Withholding is deducted at a flat 10 percent rate, except for certain distributions from qualified retirement plans, which have a required 20 percent withholding tax rate. See LO 9.8 for a discussion of withholding on rollover distributions.

EXAMPLE Adam is a retired college professor and receives a pension of $775 per month. The payor should withhold on the pension, based on Adam's signed W-4P, in the same manner as if it were Adam's salary. ♦

9-1e Tip Reporting

Tips are a significant part of the compensation received by employees in many types of jobs such as the following:

- Barber
- Hairdresser
- Parking attendant
- Porter
- Food and beverage servers
- Busser and others who share restaurant tip pools
- Delivery driver
- Airport skycap
- Bartenders
- Hotel housekeepers
- Manicurists
- Taxi, Uber and Lyft drivers

Tips are generally not paid directly by the employer to the employee and as a result, create a unique challenge for tax reporting for both the employee and employer. Additionally, tips are often paid in cash, and capturing tips as income is difficult for the IRS.

To reduce the underreporting of tip income, the IRS requires employees to report tip income to their employers on Form 4070.

Form **4070** (Rev. August 2005) Department of the Treasury Internal Revenue Service	**Employee's Report of Tips to Employer**	OMB No. 1545-0074
Employee's name and address		**Social security number**
Employer's name and address (include establishment name, if different)		**1** Cash tips received
		2 Credit and debit card tips received
		3 Tips paid out
Month or shorter period in which tips were received from , , to ,		**4** Net tips (lines **1 + 2 - 3**)
Signature		Date

For Paperwork Reduction Act Notice, see the instructions on the back of this form. Cat. No. 41320P Form **4070** (Rev. 8-2005)

The employer uses the information from Form 4070 to properly withhold employment and income taxes on tip income. To provide some assurance that accurate tip income is being reported by employees in large food or beverage establishments, the employer must compare employee-reported tips to 8 percent of the employer's sales. If the reported tips are less than 8 percent of sales, the employer must allocate the difference to each employee and report this amount on each employee's Form W-2 in Box 8 (Allocated Tips). The allocation of tip income can be accomplished in one of three ways. The employer may allocate the amount based on (1) gross receipts per employee, (2) hours worked by each employee (available only to employers having fewer than the equivalent of twenty-five full-time employees), or (3) a good faith agreement as explained on Form 8027, Employer's Annual Information Return of Tip Income and Allocated Tips. For a detailed explanation of the allocation process, see the instructions for Form 8027. With the diversity of businesses and tipping customs, the IRS also permits employers to enter into the Tip Rate Determination/Education Program, in which the employer and the IRS work out a tip rate and reporting system. For more information on tip reporting in general, see the IRS website (**www.irs.gov**) or a tax research service.

TAX BREAK

The IRS has created two programs to help employers in businesses in which employees are compensated with tips: Tip Rate Determination Agreement (TRDA) and Tip Reporting Alternative Commitment (TRAC). These two programs are designed to help employers and employees more accurately report tip income and simplify the process for reporting tips by employees and employers.

9-1f **Backup Withholding**

In some situations, individuals may be subject to backup withholding on payments such as interest and dividends. The purpose of backup withholding is to ensure that income tax is paid on income reported on many of the different versions of Forms 1099. If backup withholding applies, the payor (e.g., bank or insurance company) must withhold 24 percent of the amount paid to the taxpayer. Payors are required to use backup withholding in the following cases:

1. The taxpayer does not give the payor his or her taxpayer identification number (e.g., Social Security number),
2. The taxpayer fails to certify that he or she is not subject to backup withholding,
3. The IRS informs the payor that the taxpayer gave an incorrect identification number, or
4. The IRS informs the payor to start withholding because the taxpayer has not reported the income on his or her tax return.

EXAMPLE Kamili earned $2,000 in interest income from Cactus Savings Bank. Kamili failed to certify that she was not subject to backup withholding. As a result, the bank must withhold taxes of $480 (24 percent of $2,000) from the interest payments to Kamili. ♦

Taxpayers who give false information to avoid backup withholding are subject to a $500 civil penalty and criminal penalties, including fines and/or imprisonment.

Self-Study Problem 9.1 *See Appendix E for Solutions to Self-Study Problems*

1. John and Lillian Miles intend to file jointly in 2022. The Miles' address is 456 Peachtree Court, Atlanta, GA 30310. John expects to earn wages of $40,000 in 2022 and Lillian's wages are expected to be very similar at $40,400. They have two dependent children aged 13 and 17. Lillian also has a small business that she expects to generate qualified business income of $6,500 in 2022. She would prefer to increase her withholding rather than make estimated tax payments. They expect to make a $4,000 deductible IRA contribution in 2022 and use the standard deduction. Assuming she is the higher income earner and is paid monthly, prepare a Form W-4 for Lillian Miles including worksheets for steps 2(b) and 4(b), if needed.
2. Assuming that Lillian is paid semimonthly ($1,683.33 per half-month) and using the Form W-4 prepared in part 1, compute Lillian's withholding using (a.) the percentage method and (b.) the wage bracket method. Use the worksheets in Appendix C.

9-2 THE FICA TAX

9.2 Learning Objective

Compute the FICA tax.

Note: Most of the employment tax provisions related to the COVID pandemic expired at the end of 2021.

9-2a FICA Taxes

The Federal Insurance Contributions Act (FICA) imposes Social Security and Medicare taxes. It was passed by Congress in 1935 to provide benefits for qualified retired and disabled workers. If a worker should die, it would also provide the family of the worker with benefits. The Medicare program for older adults is also funded by FICA taxes.

FICA taxes have two parts, Social Security (Old Age, Survivors, and Disability Insurance [OASDI]) and Medicare. Employees and their employers are both required to pay FICA taxes. Employers withhold a specified percentage of each employee's wages up to a maximum base amount, match the amount withheld with an equal amount, and pay the total to the IRS.

The Social Security (OASDI) tax rate is 6.2 percent and the Medicare tax rate is 1.45 percent each for employees and employers in 2022. The maximum wage subject to the Social Security portion of the FICA tax is $147,000 in 2022, and all wages are subject to the Medicare portion of the FICA tax. The maximum wages to which the rates apply have increased over the years as presented in the following table.

Year	*Maximum $ Base for 6.2% (employee and employer)*	*Maximum $ Base for 1.45% (employee and employer)**
2018	128,400	Unlimited
2019	132,900	Unlimited
2020	137,700	Unlimited
2021	142,800	Unlimited
2022	147,000	Unlimited

*Employees pay a 0.9 percent Medicare tax on wages over $200,000 if single and head of household ($250,000 if married filing jointly). See Chapter 6 for more information.

TAX BREAK

Taxpayers age 18 and older may request an online statement of Social Security benefits including estimates of projected retirement, survivors', and disability benefits. The statement also shows the taxpayer's Social Security earnings history, giving the taxpayer an opportunity to correct any errors or omissions. The personalized online statement is available at **www.ssa.gov/myaccount**. In some cases, the Social Security Administration will provide a paper version of this statement by mail.

EXAMPLE Katherine earns wages of $21,500 in 2022. The FICA tax on her wages is calculated as follows:

Katherine:	Soc. Sec. − 6.2% × $21,500	$1,333.00
	Medicare − 1.45% × $21,500	311.75
	Total employee FICA tax	$1,644.75
Katherine's employer:	Soc. Sec. − 6.2% × $21,500	$1,333.00
	Medicare − 1.45% × $21,500	311.75
	Total employer FICA tax	$1,644.75
Total FICA tax		$3,289.50

♦

EXAMPLE Nora is an employee of Serissa Company. Her salary for 2022 is $150,000. Nora's portion of the FICA tax is calculated as follows:

Soc. Sec. − 6.2% × $147,000	$9,114.00
Medicare − 1.45% × $150,000	2,175.00
Total employee FICA tax	$11,289.00

The total combined FICA tax (employee's and employer's share) is $22,578.00. ♦

EXAMPLE Haley, a single taxpayer, is an employee of Dunphee Company. Her wages in 2022 are $212,000. Haley's Social Security portion of the FICA tax is $147,000 (2022 FICA cap) × 6.2% or $9,114.00. The "regular" Medicare portion withheld will be $3,074.00 ($212,000 × 1.45%); however, Dunphee will also withhold the 0.9 percent additional Medicare tax as described in Chapter 6 on wages over $200,000 or $108.00 ($12,000 × 0.9%). Total withholding will be $12,296.00. Dunphee will pay a matching portion of Social Security ($9,114.00) and regular Medicare ($3,074.00) but is not required to pay the additional 0.9 percent Medicare tax on wages above $200,000. ♦

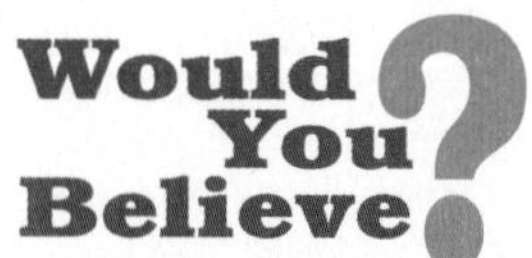

FICA taxes are paid one-half by employees through withholding and one-half by employers. Since the employer portion of the tax increases the cost of employees, many economists believe that even the employer's share of FICA tax is passed on to employees in the form of lower compensation. Thus, employees, like self-employed individuals, effectively bear both halves of FICA taxes.

9-2b Overpayment of Social Security Taxes

Taxpayers who work for more than one employer during the same tax year may pay more than the maximum amount of Social Security taxes. This occurs when the taxpayer's total wages are more than the maximum base amount for the year. When this happens, the taxpayer should compute the excess taxes paid, and report the excess on Line 11 of Schedule 3 of Form 1040 as an additional payment against their tax liability. This way, the taxpayer is refunded the excess Social Security tax. Note that the employer is not entitled to a similar refund for the overpaid matching Social Security tax.

EXAMPLE Jerry worked for two employers during 2022. The first employer withheld and paid Social Security taxes on $80,000 of salary paid to Jerry, and the second employer withheld and paid Social Security taxes on $71,000 of salary paid to Jerry. The amount of Jerry's excess Social Security taxes paid for 2022 is computed as follows: 6.2% (Social Security rate) × [$80,000 + $71,000 − $147,000 (maximum for Social Security portion of FICA tax)] = $248.00. Jerry receives credit against his 2022 income tax liability equal to the excess Social Security taxes of $248. No excess Medicare tax has been paid, as there is no upper limit on Medicare wages. ♦

9-2c FICA Taxes (Temporary COVID-19 Provisions)

During early 2020 and into 2021, many businesses were forced to close or reduce commercial activity due to the COVID-19 pandemic. To provide financial support for businesses, a series of temporary changes to payroll taxes were implemented. Special provisions for the employee retention credit, sick pay, and family leave pay credits related to COVID have all expired and would not be expected to affect payroll taxes in 2022.

Self-Study Problem 9.2 ***See Appendix E for Solutions to Self-Study Problems***

Hills Scientific Corp. (EIN 33-4434432) has 6 employees, including founder Juliette Hills. Payroll records indicate the wages paid to the employees during the first and second quarters of 2022:

Employee	*Title*	*Total Q1 Wages*	*Total Q2 Wages*	*Q2 Income Tax Withheld*
Juliette	CEO	$ 91,000	$ 60,000	$18,000
Yan	Head Scientist	40,000	40,000	10,000
Sai	Laboratory Manager	20,000	20,000	4,400
Yvette	Sr. Lab Analyst	15,000	15,000	3,150
Juan	Jr. Lab Analyst	9,000	9,000	1,350
Joe	Maintenance & Custodial	6,000	6,000	730
Total		$ 181,000	$ 150,000	$37,630

Compute Hills' portion of second quarter employment taxes:

a) Employee's portion Social Security tax
b) Employer's portion Social Security tax
c) Employee's portion Medicare tax
d) Employer's portion Medicare tax

Learning Objective 9.3

Determine taxpayers' quarterly estimated payments.

9-3 ESTIMATED PAYMENTS

Self-employed taxpayers are not subject to withholding; however, they must make quarterly estimated tax payments. Taxpayers with large amounts of interest, dividends, and other income not subject to withholding are also generally required to make estimated payments. Payments are made in four installments due April 15, June 15, and September 15 of the tax year, and January 15 of the following year (or the first business day after if the dates fall on a weekend or holiday), based on the taxpayer's estimate of the amount of the tax liability for the year. A taxpayer with self-employment income must begin making the payments when he or she first meets the filing requirements.

TAX BREAK

Never write out a check to the "IRS." The IRS issues this warning every year, because "IRS" may be easily changed to "MRS" plus an individual's name if the check falls into the wrong hands. Checks must be made payable to the U.S. Treasury, as a reminder that the IRS is merely the collector of revenue for the federal government. Alternatively, individual taxpayers can draft their bank account using Direct Pay or, for a fee, pay using a debit or credit card. Information regarding payment methods is available on the IRS website.

Any individual taxpayer who has estimated tax for the year of $1,000 or more, after subtracting withholding, and whose withholding does not equal or exceed the "required annual payment," must make quarterly estimated payments. The required annual payment is the smallest of the following amounts:

1. 90 percent of the tax shown on the current year's return,
2. 100 percent of the tax shown on the preceding year's return (such return must cover a full 12 months), or
3. 90 percent of the current-year tax determined by placing taxable income, alternative minimum taxable income, and adjusted self-employment income on an annualized basis for each quarter.

A special rule applies to individuals with adjusted gross income in excess of $150,000 for the previous year. These high-income taxpayers must pay 110 percent of the amount of tax shown on the prior year tax return for the current year estimated payments, instead of 100 percent, to meet the requirements in the second option.

Estimated payments need not be paid if the estimated tax, after subtracting withholding, can reasonably be expected to be less than $1,000. Therefore, employees who also have self-employment income may avoid making estimated payments by filing a new Form W-4 and increasing the amount of their withholding on their regular salary.

Estimating the required annual payment from the current-year tax is more of an art than a science, since it requires estimation of income, deductions, and credits. In addition, when computing the required annual payment, the amount of tax measured is the total of income tax plus any self-employment tax, net investment income tax, and additional Medicare tax (see Chapters 4 and 6 for additional discussion). For the prior year tax, these amounts can generally be found on Form 1040. For most taxpayers in 2021, the prior year tax is Line 24 from the Form 1040; however, this amount can be reduced by any earned income credit and the refundable portions of the child tax credit, American Opportunities credit, premium tax credit, and the child and dependent care credit, along with some other less common adjustments. To assist taxpayers with estimating the current-year tax, Form 1040-ES, Estimated Tax for Individuals includes a worksheet to assist in the calculation.

EXAMPLE Colin, a single taxpayer with no dependents, operates a small business as a sole proprietor. He expects to report a profit of $78,000 on his 2022 Schedule C, he has no other sources of income or deductions, and expects to take the standard deduction in 2022. Colin's prior year AGI was below

$150,000 and his Form 1040 Line 24 reported $14,000 of tax. He did not claim any refundable credits in 2021 or 2022. The worksheet below presents Colin's estimate of his 2022 tax, annual required payment, and first quarter estimated payment.

2022 Estimated Tax Worksheet *Keep for Your Records*

1	Adjusted gross income you expect in 2022 (see instructions)			1	72,489 (a)
2a	Deductions • If you plan to itemize deductions, enter the estimated total of your itemized deductions. • If you don't plan to itemize deductions, enter your standard deduction.			2a	12,950
b	If you can take the qualified business income deduction, enter the estimated amount of the deduction			2b	11,908 (b)
c	Add lines 2a and 2b ▶			2c	24,858
3	Subtract line 2c from line 1			3	47,631
4	**Tax.** Figure your tax on the amount on line 3 by using the **2022 Tax Rate Schedules.** **Caution:** *If you will have qualified dividends or a net capital gain, or expect to exclude or deduct foreign earned income or housing, see Worksheets 2-5 and 2-6 in Pub. 505 to figure the tax*			4	6,096 (c)
5	Alternative minimum tax from **Form 6251**			5	
6	Add lines 4 and 5. Add to this amount any other taxes you expect to include in the total on Form 1040 or 1040-SR, line 16			6	6,096
7	Credits (see instructions). **Do not** include any income tax withholding on this line			7	
8	Subtract line 7 from line 6. If zero or less, enter -0-			8	6,096
9	Self-employment tax (see instructions)			9	11,021
10	Other taxes (see instructions)			10	
11a	Add lines 8 through 10			11a	17,117
b	Earned income credit, refundable child tax credit* or additional child tax credit, fuel tax credit, net premium tax credit, refundable American opportunity credit, section 1341 credit, and refundable credit from Form 8885*			11b	
c	**Total 2022 estimated tax.** Subtract line 11b from line 11a. If zero or less, enter -0- ▶			11c	17,117
12a	Multiply line 11c by 90% (66⅔% for farmers and fishermen)	12a	15,405		
b	Required annual payment based on prior year's tax (see instructions)	12b	14,000		
c	**Required annual payment to avoid a penalty.** Enter the **smaller** of line 12a or 12b ▶			12c	14,000
	Caution: *Generally, if you do not prepay (through income tax withholding and estimated tax payments) at least the amount on line 12c, you may owe a penalty for not paying enough estimated tax. To avoid a penalty, make sure your estimate on line 11c is as accurate as possible. Even if you pay the required annual payment, you may still owe tax when you file your return. If you prefer, you can pay the amount shown on line 11c. For details, see chapter 2 of Pub. 505.*				
13	Income tax withheld and estimated to be withheld during 2022 (including income tax withholding on pensions, annuities, certain deferred income, etc.)			13	0
14a	Subtract line 13 from line 12c Is the result zero or less? ☐ **Yes.** Stop here. You are not required to make estimated tax payments. ☑ **No.** Go to line 14b.	14a	14,000		
b	Subtract line 13 from line 11c Is the result less than $1,000? ☐ **Yes.** Stop here. You are not required to make estimated tax payments. ☑ **No.** Go to line 15 to figure your required payment.	14b	17,117		
15	If the first payment you are required to make is due April 18, 2022, enter ¼ of line 14a (minus any 2021 overpayment that you are applying to this installment) here, and on your estimated tax payment voucher(s) if you are paying by check or money order			15	3,500

*If applicable.

(a) $78,000 − $5,511 (one-half self-employment tax)

(b) The QBI deduction before overall limitation is $78,000 − $5,511 (1/2 self-employment tax) × 20% = $14,498. The overall net income limitation is $11,908 [($78,000 − $5,511 − $12,950 standard deduction) × 20%]. Thus the QBI deduction is limited to $11,908.

(c) $4,807.50 + [($47,631 − $41,775) × 22%]. Note that Tax Tables are generally not available at the time of estimate and thus the tax rate schedules are used even when taxable income is less than $100,000. ♦

The IRS imposes a nondeductible penalty on the amounts of any underpayments of estimated tax. The penalty applies when any installment is less than the required annual payment divided by the number of installments that should have been made, which is usually four. Form 2210, Underpayment of Estimated Tax by Individuals, Estates, and Trusts, is used for the calculation of the penalty associated with the underpayment of estimated tax.

Good tax planning dictates that a taxpayer postpone payment of taxes as long as no penalty is imposed. Unpaid taxes are equivalent to an interest-free loan from the government. Therefore, taxpayers should base their estimated payments on the method which results in the lowest amount of required quarterly or annual payment. For example, a taxpayer who expects his tax liability to increase might base his or her estimated payments this year on the amount of the tax liability from the prior year. A taxpayer that overpays their tax liability has the option to receive the excess back as a refund or may apply the overpayment to the following year.

Individual taxpayers can pay estimated payments online through a number of different methods. Individual taxpayers with an IRS account can login and make payments through their account (**www.irs.gov/payments/your-online-account**). The IRS website (**www.irs.gov/payments**) provides a number of methods for payment, including Direct Pay (direct debit to your bank account), pay by debit card, credit card, digital wallet (for a fee), and via Electronic Federal Tax Payment System (EFTPS). Taxpayers may also pay estimated taxes using the IRS2Go app for mobile phones. Taxpayers paying online should take care to select the proper type of return (for example, Form 1040) and the proper tax year to increase the probability that the payment is credited to the proper tax type and period. Of course, taxpayers can pay by mail using a check. If paying by check, taxpayers should be certain to include the proper quarterly voucher from Form 1040-ES.

Self-Study Problem 9.3

See Appendix E for Solutions to Self-Study Problems

a. Ray Adams, a single taxpayer with no dependents, estimates his 2022 Schedule C net profits as $102,000, one-half of self-employment tax as $7,206, and his QBI deduction as $16,369. In 2021, Ray's AGI was below $150,000 and Line 24 of his 2021 Form 1040 was $21,000. He had no refundable credits last year. Ray's Social Security number is 321-45-9876 and he lives at 1905 Hardin Valley Road, Knoxville, TN 37932. Assuming no other sources of income, deductions, or refundable credits in 2022, calculate Ray's estimated income and required annual payment using the 2022 Estimated Tax Worksheet.

2022 Estimated Tax Worksheet

Keep for Your Records

1	Adjusted gross income you expect in 2022 (see instructions)	1	
2a	Deductions • If you plan to itemize deductions, enter the estimated total of your itemized deductions. • If you don't plan to itemize deductions, enter your standard deduction.	2a	
b	If you can take the qualified business income deduction, enter the estimated amount of the deduction	2b	
c	Add lines 2a and 2b ▶	2c	
3	Subtract line 2c from line 1	3	
4	**Tax.** Figure your tax on the amount on line 3 by using the **2022 Tax Rate Schedules.** **Caution:** *If you will have qualified dividends or a net capital gain, or expect to exclude or deduct foreign earned income or housing, see Worksheets 2-5 and 2-6 in Pub. 505 to figure the tax.*	4	
5	Alternative minimum tax from **Form 6251**	5	
6	Add lines 4 and 5. Add to this amount any other taxes you expect to include in the total on Form 1040 or 1040-SR, line 16	6	
7	Credits (see instructions). **Do not** include any income tax withholding on this line	7	
8	Subtract line 7 from line 6. If zero or less, enter -0-	8	
9	Self-employment tax (see instructions)	9	
10	Other taxes (see instructions)	10	
11a	Add lines 8 through 10	11a	
b	Earned income credit, refundable child tax credit* or additional child tax credit, fuel tax credit, net premium tax credit, refundable American opportunity credit, section 1341 credit, and refundable credit from Form 8885*	11b	
c	**Total 2022 estimated tax.** Subtract line 11b from line 11a. If zero or less, enter -0- ▶	11c	
12a	Multiply line 11c by 90% (66⅔% for farmers and fishermen) — 12a		
b	Required annual payment based on prior year's tax (see instructions) — 12b		
c	**Required annual payment to avoid a penalty.** Enter the **smaller** of line 12a or 12b ▶ **Caution:** *Generally, if you do not prepay (through income tax withholding and estimated tax payments) at least the amount on line 12c, you may owe a penalty for not paying enough estimated tax. To avoid a penalty, make sure your estimate on line 11c is as accurate as possible. Even if you pay the required annual payment, you may still owe tax when you file your return. If you prefer, you can pay the amount shown on line 11c. For details, see chapter 2 of Pub. 505.*	12c	
13	Income tax withheld and estimated to be withheld during 2022 (including income tax withholding on pensions, annuities, certain deferred income, etc.)	13	
14a	Subtract line 13 from line 12c — 14a Is the result zero or less? ☐ **Yes.** Stop here. You are not required to make estimated tax payments. ☐ **No.** Go to line 14b.		
b	Subtract line 13 from line 11c — 14b Is the result less than $1,000? ☐ **Yes.** Stop here. You are not required to make estimated tax payments. ☐ **No.** Go to line 15 to figure your required payment.		
15	If the first payment you are required to make is due April 18, 2022, enter ¼ of line 14a (minus any 2021 overpayment that you are applying to this installment) here, and on your estimated tax payment voucher(s) if you are paying by check or money order	15	

* If applicable.

Self-Study Problem 9.3, continued *See Appendix E for Solutions to Self-Study Problems*

b. Continuing from part a, assume that Ray had an overpayment of $475 in 2021 that he wishes to apply to his 2022 estimated taxes. Complete the 2022 first quarter voucher for Ray.

Form **1040-ES** Department of the Treasury Internal Revenue Service | **2022 Estimated Tax** | **Payment Voucher 1** | OMB No. 1545-0074

File only if you are making a payment of estimated tax by check or money order. Mail this voucher with your check or money order payable to **"United States Treasury."** Write your social security number and "2022 Form 1040-ES" on your check or money order. Do not send cash. Enclose, but do not staple or attach, your payment with this voucher.

Calendar year—Due April 18, 2022

Amount of estimated tax you are paying by check or money order.

Pay online at ***www.irs.gov/etpay***

Simple. Fast. Secure.

Print or type

Your first name and middle initial	Your last name	Your social security number
If joint payment, complete for spouse		
Spouse's first name and middle initial	Spouse's last name	Spouse's social security number
Address (number, street, and apt. no.)		
City, town, or post office. If you have a foreign address, also complete spaces below.	State	ZIP code
Foreign country name	Foreign province/county	Foreign postal code

For Privacy Act and Paperwork Reduction Act Notice, see instructions. **Form 1040-ES (2022)**

c. Continuing from parts a and b, assume that Ray's 2021 AGI was $155,000 and his current year tax remains the amount calculated in part a. Calculate Ray's 1st quarter estimated payment for 2022.

Learning Objective 9.4

Apply the federal deposit system to payroll withholding.

9-4 FEDERAL TAX DEPOSIT SYSTEM

Employers must make periodic deposits of the taxes that are withheld from employees' wages. The frequency of the deposits depends on the total income tax withheld and the total FICA taxes for all employees. Employers are either monthly depositors or semiweekly depositors. Prior to the beginning of each calendar year, taxpayers are required to determine which of the two deposit schedules they are required to use. Virtually all of the temporary changes made to payroll tax deposit rules as a result of the COVID-19 pandemic have expired.

9-4a Tax Deposits

Monthly or semiweekly deposit status is determined by using a lookback period, consisting of the four quarters beginning July 1 of the second preceding year and ending June 30 of the prior year. If the total income tax withheld from wages and FICA taxes attributable to wages for the four quarters in the lookback period is $50,000 or less, employers are monthly depositors for the current year. Monthly depositors must make deposits of employment taxes and taxes withheld by the fifteenth day of the month following the month of withholding. New employers are automatically monthly depositors.

If the total income tax withheld from wages and FICA attributable to wages for the four quarters in the lookback period is more than $50,000, the employer is a semiweekly depositor for the current year. Taxes on payments made on Wednesday, Thursday, or Friday must be deposited by the following Wednesday; taxes on payments made on the other days of the week must be deposited by the following Friday. If a deposit is scheduled for a day that is not a banking day, the deposit is considered to be made timely if it is made by the close of the next banking day. If income tax withholding and FICA taxes of $100,000 or more are accumulated at any time during the year, the depositor is required to make a deposit on the next business day. For new employers, required deposits during the lookback period are deemed to be zero and thus the employer will default to a monthly depositor.

EXAMPLE Tom runs a small business with ten employees. During the lookback period for the current year, the total withholding and FICA taxes amounted to $40,000. Since this is less than $50,000, Tom is a monthly depositor. His payroll tax deposits must be made by the fifteenth day of the month following the month of withholding. ♦

Tax payments (monthly, semiweekly, or daily for large depositors) must be made by Electronic Federal Tax Payment System (EFTPS), or by another electronic transfer method. Generally, employers must file Form 941, Employer's Quarterly Federal Tax Return, which reports the federal income taxes withheld from wages and the total FICA taxes attributable to wages paid during each quarter. Form 941 must be accompanied by any payroll taxes not yet deposited for the quarter. A specific deposit rule allows small employers who accumulate less than $2,500 tax liability during a quarter to skip monthly payments and pay the entire amount of their payroll taxes with their quarterly Form 941. Form 941 must be filed by the last day of the month following the end of the quarter. For example, the first quarter Form 941, covering the months of January through March, must be filed by April 30. The Form 941 e-file program allows taxpayers to electronically file Form 941 or Form 944.

Nearly a million very small employers with employment tax liability of $1,000 or less per year are allowed to file employment tax returns just once a year, instead of quarterly; for example, by January 31 of 2022 for 2021 employment taxes. Qualifying small employers receive written notification from the IRS that they should file using a Form 944 instead of the standard Form 941 used by most employers. The Form 944 is due annually, at the end of the month following the taxpayer's year end.

IRS Publications 15 (Circular E) and 15-T cover the rules regarding the calculation and deposit of payroll taxes in detail and are indispensable resources for those working in this complex area.

TAX BREAK

Many small businesses elect to outsource payroll processing to a third party. The IRS provides guidance to taxpayers on the differences among the four types of third-party arrangements for payroll outsourcing: (1) a payroll service provider, (2) a Reporting Agent, (3) a §3504 Agent, or (4) a Certified Professional Employer Organization. Taxpayers should take heed as to which arrangement they are engaged in since the permissible actions of the third-party and where ultimate liability resides may differ. See **www.irs.gov/businesses/small-businesses-self-employed/third-party-arrangement-chart**.

9-4b **Employer Payroll Tax Deferral (COVID-19 Provision)**

Under temporary provisions brought about by the COVID-19 pandemic, employers were eligible to defer the payment of the employer's portion of the Social Security portion of payroll tax for the period March 27 through December 31, 2020. Self-employed individuals can defer one-half of the 12.4 percent self-employment tax. One-half of the payment of these taxes can be deferred until December 31, 2021, and the other half can be deferred until December 31, 2022. The deferral applies to wages of any employee, not just those receiving benefits under some other COVID-19-related provisions. The IRS will be reminding employers during 2022 of any deferrals from 2020. The 2022 payments for the deferred employer's portion are not reported on Form 941.

Self-employed individuals were permitted to use any reasonable method to allocate 50 percent of the Social Security portion of self-employment tax attributable to net earnings from self-employment earned during March 27, 2020, through December 31, 2020. Just like the deferral for an employer's share of Social Security taxes, one-half of the self-employment tax must also be repaid by December 31, 2021, and the remainder by December 31, 2022.

EXAMPLE In 2020, Eddie deferred $2,130 of the Social Security portion of his self-employment taxes. Eddie will need to pay $1,065 (50% × $2,130) of the deferral by December 31, 2021, and the remaining $1,065 by December 31, 2022. ♦

Self-Study Problem 9.4 *See Appendix E for Solutions to Self-Study Problems*

1. Using the information from Self-Study Problem 9.2, complete Part I of Form 941 for the Hills Scientific Corp's second quarter on Pages 9-31 to 9-32. Assume that the company made deposits of $60,000 for the second quarter.

Self-Study Problem 9.4

950122

Form **941 for 2022: Employer's QUARTERLY Federal Tax Return**
(Rev. June 2022) Department of the Treasury — Internal Revenue Service
OMB No. 1545-0029

Employer identification number (EIN) ☐☐ – ☐☐☐☐☐☐☐

Name *(not your trade name)*

Trade name *(if any)*

Address
Number Street Suite or room number
City State ZIP code
Foreign country name Foreign province/county Foreign postal code

Report for this Quarter of 2022
(Check one.)

☐ **1:** January, February, March
☐ **2:** April, May, June
☐ **3:** July, August, September
☐ **4:** October, November, December

Go to *www.irs.gov/Form941* for instructions and the latest information.

Read the separate instructions before you complete Form 941. Type or print within the boxes.

Part 1: Answer these questions for this quarter.

1	**Number of employees who received wages, tips, or other compensation for the pay period including:** ***June 12*** **(Quarter 2),** ***Sept. 12*** **(Quarter 3), or** ***Dec. 12*** **(Quarter 4)**	1
2	**Wages, tips, and other compensation**	2 .
3	**Federal income tax withheld from wages, tips, and other compensation**	3 .
4	**If no wages, tips, and other compensation are subject to social security or Medicare tax**	☐ **Check and go to line 6.**

		Column 1		Column 2
5a	**Taxable social security wages***	.	× 0.124 =	.
5a	**(i) Qualified sick leave wages***	.	× 0.062 =	.
5a	**(ii) Qualified family leave wages***	.	× 0.062 =	.
5b	**Taxable social security tips**	.	× 0.124 =	.
5c	**Taxable Medicare wages & tips**	.	× 0.029 =	.
5d	**Taxable wages & tips subject to Additional Medicare Tax withholding**	.	× 0.009 =	.

**Include taxable qualified sick and family leave wages paid in this quarter of 2022 for leave taken after March 31, 2021, and before October 1, 2021, on line 5a. Use lines 5a(i) and 5a(ii) only for taxable qualified sick and family leave wages paid in this quarter of 2022 for leave taken after March 31, 2020, and before April 1, 2021.*

5e	**Total social security and Medicare taxes.** Add Column 2 from lines 5a, 5a(i), 5a(ii), 5b, 5c, and 5d	5e .
5f	**Section 3121(q) Notice and Demand—Tax due on unreported tips** (see instructions)	5f .
6	**Total taxes before adjustments.** Add lines 3, 5e, and 5f	6 .
7	**Current quarter's adjustment for fractions of cents**	7 .
8	**Current quarter's adjustment for sick pay**	8 .
9	**Current quarter's adjustments for tips and group-term life insurance**	9 .
10	**Total taxes after adjustments.** Combine lines 6 through 9	10 .
11a	**Qualified small business payroll tax credit for increasing research activities.** Attach Form 8974	11a .
11b	**Nonrefundable portion of credit for qualified sick and family leave wages for leave taken before April 1, 2021**	11b .
11c	**Reserved for future use**	11c .

► **You MUST complete all three pages of Form 941 and SIGN it.** Next ►

For Privacy Act and Paperwork Reduction Act Notice, see the back of the Payment Voucher. Cat. No. 17001Z Form **941** (Rev. 6-2022)

951222

Name *(not your trade name)*	Employer identification number (EIN) –

Part 1: Answer these questions for this quarter. *(continued)*

11d	**Nonrefundable portion of credit for qualified sick and family leave wages for leave taken after March 31, 2021, and before October 1, 2021**	11d	.
11e	**Reserved for future use**	11e	.
11f	**Reserved for future use**		
11g	**Total nonrefundable credits.** Add lines 11a, 11b, and 11d	11g	.
12	**Total taxes after adjustments and nonrefundable credits.** Subtract line 11g from line 10	12	.
13a	**Total deposits for this quarter, including overpayment applied from a prior quarter and overpayments applied from Form 941-X, 941-X (PR), 944-X, or 944-X (SP) filed in the current quarter**	13a	.
13b	**Reserved for future use**	13b	.
13c	**Refundable portion of credit for qualified sick and family leave wages for leave taken before April 1, 2021**	13c	.
13d	**Reserved for future use**	13d	.
13e	**Refundable portion of credit for qualified sick and family leave wages for leave taken after March 31, 2021, and before October 1, 2021**	13e	.
13f	**Reserved for future use**	13f	.
13g	**Total deposits and refundable credits.** Add lines 13a, 13c, and 13e	13g	.
13h	**Reserved for future use**	13h	.
13i	**Reserved for future use**	13i	.
14	**Balance due.** If line 12 is more than line 13g, enter the difference and see instructions	14	.
15	**Overpayment.** If line 13g is more than line 12, enter the difference [.] Check one: ☐ Apply to next return. ☐ Send a refund.		

Part 2: Tell us about your deposit schedule and tax liability for this quarter.

If you're unsure about whether you're a monthly schedule depositor or a semiweekly schedule depositor, see section 11 of Pub. 15.

16 Check one: ☐ **Line 12 on this return is less than $2,500 or line 12 on the return for the prior quarter was less than $2,500, and you didn't incur a $100,000 next-day deposit obligation during the current quarter.** If line 12 for the prior quarter was less than $2,500 but line 12 on this return is $100,000 or more, you must provide a record of your federal tax liability. If you're a monthly schedule depositor, complete the deposit schedule below; if you're a semiweekly schedule depositor, attach Schedule B (Form 941). Go to Part 3.

☐ **You were a monthly schedule depositor for the entire quarter.** Enter your tax liability for each month and total liability for the quarter, then go to Part 3.

Tax liability:	**Month 1**	.
	Month 2	.
	Month 3	.
Total liability for quarter		. **Total must equal line 12.**

☐ **You were a semiweekly schedule depositor for any part of this quarter.** Complete Schedule B (Form 941), Report of Tax Liability for Semiweekly Schedule Depositors, and attach it to Form 941. Go to Part 3.

► **You MUST complete all three pages of Form 941 and SIGN it.** Next ►

950922

Name *(not your trade name)* | **Employer identification number (EIN)** –

Part 3: Tell us about your business. If a question does NOT apply to your business, leave it blank.

17 If your business has closed or you stopped paying wages . . . . ☐ Check here, and

enter the final date you paid wages [/ /]; also attach a statement to your return. See instructions.

18 If you're a seasonal employer and you don't have to file a return for every quarter of the year . . . ☐ Check here.

19	Qualified health plan expenses allocable to qualified sick leave wages for leave taken before April 1, 2021	19	.
20	Qualified health plan expenses allocable to qualified family leave wages for leave taken before April 1, 2021	20	.
21	Reserved for future use	21	.
22	Reserved for future use	22	.
23	Qualified sick leave wages for leave taken after March 31, 2021, and before October 1, 2021	23	.
24	Qualified health plan expenses allocable to qualified sick leave wages reported on line 23	24	.
25	Amounts under certain collectively bargained agreements allocable to qualified sick leave wages reported on line 23	25	.
26	Qualified family leave wages for leave taken after March 31, 2021, and before October 1, 2021	26	.
27	Qualified health plan expenses allocable to qualified family leave wages reported on line 26	27	.
28	Amounts under certain collectively bargained agreements allocable to qualified family leave wages reported on line 26	28	.

Part 4: May we speak with your third-party designee?

Do you want to allow an employee, a paid tax preparer, or another person to discuss this return with the IRS? See the instructions for details.

☐ Yes. Designee's name and phone number [ ] [ ]

Select a 5-digit personal identification number (PIN) to use when talking to the IRS. ☐☐☐☐☐

☐ No.

Part 5: Sign here. You MUST complete all three pages of Form 941 and SIGN it.

Under penalties of perjury, I declare that I have examined this return, including accompanying schedules and statements, and to the best of my knowledge and belief, it is true, correct, and complete. Declaration of preparer (other than taxpayer) is based on all information of which preparer has any knowledge.

✗ **Sign your name here** [ ]

Print your name here [ ]

Print your title here [ ]

Date [/ /]

Best daytime phone [ ]

Paid Preparer Use Only

Check if you're self-employed . . . ☐

Preparer's name		PTIN	
Preparer's signature		Date	/ /
Firm's name (or yours if self-employed)		EIN	
Address		Phone	
City	State	ZIP code	

9-5 EMPLOYER REPORTING REQUIREMENTS

9.5 Learning Objective

Prepare employer payroll reporting.

On or before January 31 of the year following the calendar year of payment, an employer must furnish to each employee two copies of the employee's Wage and Tax Statement, Form W-2, for the previous calendar year. If employment is terminated before the end of the year and the employee requests a Form W-2, the employer must furnish the Form W-2 within 30 days after the last wage payment is made or after the employee request, whichever is later. Otherwise, the general rule requiring the W-2 to be furnished to the employee by January 31 applies. The original copy (Copy A) of all Forms W-2 and Form W-3 (Transmittal of Wage and Tax Statements) must be filed by the employer with the Social Security Administration by January 31 of the year following the calendar year of payment. Copy B of Form W-2 is filed with the employee's federal tax return. Employers retain Copy D of Form W-2 for their records. Extra copies of Form W-2 are prepared and provided to the employee to use when filing state and local tax returns. Starting in 2023, employers that need to file ten or more Forms W-2 must file them electronically.

Form W-2 is used to report wages, tips, and other compensation paid to an employee. Form W-2 also provides the employee with additional supplemental information. Among the items which must be reported on the employee's Form W-2 are the cost of employer-sponsored health care coverage, employer contributions to a health savings account (HSA), excess group-term life insurance premiums, Roth contributions to an employer plan, and certain reimbursements of travel and other ordinary and necessary expenses. Employers are permitted, but not required, to truncate all but the last four digits of the taxpayer's Social Security number on Form W-2, except for Copy A, which must include all digits. The details of the amounts included on Form W-2 are covered in Chapter 2.

Form W-3 is used to report the totals from all Forms W-2 for a particular employer.

EXAMPLE Nathan Orkney has two employees that work for his small business. The first employee reports Box 1 wages of $23,000 and the second employee reports Box 1 wages of $20,000. Nathan's Form W-3 will report $43,000 of Box 1 wages along with Copy A of Forms W-2 for both employees. ♦

A Form W-3 must be filed even when only one Form W-2 is being reported, including for household employees.

9-5a Business Expense Reimbursements

Special rules apply to the reimbursement of travel and other ordinary and necessary employee business expenses. If an employee is reimbursed for travel and other ordinary and necessary business expenses, income and employment tax withholding may be required. If a reimbursement payment is considered to have been made under an accountable plan, the amount is excluded from the employee's gross income and consequently is not required to be included on Form W-2, and no withholding is required. Alternatively, reimbursements of travel and other employee business expenses made under a nonaccountable plan must be included as wages on Form W-2, and the amounts are subject to withholding. Payments are considered made under a nonaccountable plan in the following circumstances: (1) the employee receives a reimbursement for expenses under an arrangement which does not require the employee to account adequately to the employer, or the employee receives advances under an arrangement which does not require the employee to return amounts in excess of substantiated expenses; or (2) the employee receives amounts under an arrangement that requires the employee to substantiate reimbursed expenses, but the amounts are not substantiated within a reasonable period of time, or the employee receives amounts under a plan which requires excess reimbursements to be returned to the employer, but the employee does not return such excess amounts within a reasonable period of time. In the first case, the entire amount paid under the expense account plan is considered wages subject to withholding, whereas under the circumstances described in the second situation, only the amounts in excess of the substantiated expenses are subject to withholding.

TAX BREAK

The Social Security Administration permits employers to prepare and file up to 50 Forms W-2 using their online business services. Employers should go to **www.ssa.gov** to register for the service.

9-5b Form W-2G

Gambling winnings are reported by gambling establishments on Form W-2G. Amounts that must be reported include certain winnings from horse and dog racing, jai alai, lotteries, state-conducted lotteries, sweepstakes, wagering pools, bingo, keno, and slot machines. In certain cases, withholding of income taxes is required. Forms W-2G must be transmitted to the taxpayer no later than January 31 of the year following the calendar year of payment, and to the IRS along with Form 1096 by March 1 following the calendar year of payment. Requirements to file Form W-2G can differ between the type of wagering or gaming. The due date is March 31 if transmitting electronically to the IRS. More information can be found in the instructions for Form W-2G.

9-5c Information Returns

Taxpayers engaged in a trade or business are required to file Form 1099 for each recipient of certain payments made in the course of their trade or business. Where applicable, federal income tax withheld with respect to the payment is also reported on Form 1099. The common types of payments and the related Form 1099 are summarized in Table 9.1.

TABLE 9.1 1099 FORMS

Form	Used For
1099-B	Payments of proceeds from brokers
1099-DIV	Dividend payments
1099-G	Certain government payments (state income tax refund)
1099-INT	Interest payments
1099-K	Merchant card and third-party network transactions
1099-MISC	Miscellaneous payments
1099-NEC	Payments to non-employees
1099-R	Payments of pension, annuity, profit sharing, retirement plan, IRA, insurance contracts, etc.
1099-S	Payments from real estate transactions

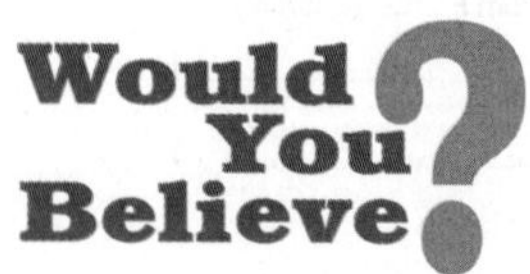

In 2021, during the COVID pandemic, the IRS inadvertently destroyed 30 million 2020 informational returns because the agency was unable to keep up with paper processing and to make space. Amazingly, the IRS reported that they successfully processed 3.2 billion informational returns filed for that year.

Forms 1099 must be mailed to the recipients by January 31 of the year following the calendar year of payment. However, payors are allowed until February 15 of the year following the calendar year of payment to provide Forms 1099-B, 1099-S, and certain 1099-MISC forms. A separate Form 1096 must be used to transmit each type of 1099 to the appropriate IRS Campus Processing Site. Different Forms 1099 have different due dates. The IRS publishes a guide titled *General Instructions for Certain Information Returns* each year which has a convenient table of due dates.

For most small businesses, the most commonly used information reporting form is the 1099-MISC. This is used to report payments that total $600 or more to virtually all non-corporate vendors. Taxpayers should use Form 1099-NEC to report nonemployee compensation of $600 or more. Nonemployee compensation is generally when an individual who does not qualify as an employee is paid for services provided.

9-5d Form 1099-K Reporting Merchant Card and Third-Party Payments

Banks and online payment networks ("payment settlement entities"), such as PayPal, Venmo, VISA, and MasterCard, are required to use Form 1099-K to report credit card sales and other reportable sales transactions to the IRS and to the businesses making reportable sales. The reporting requirement is triggered for an entity when the total dollar amount of specific transactions for a particular merchant exceeds $600.

If a taxpayer receives a Form 1099, the income reported on that form should generally be included on their tax return. The IRS is going to match the identification number on the Form 1099 to the taxpayer's tax return and likely will notice if that income is missing. A Form 1099 is not usually required to be attached to the taxpayer's return; however, if tax was withheld on the payment reported, the Form 1099 should be attached as necessary if paper filing.

9-5e Form W-9 Request for Taxpayer Identification Number

In order to assist in the preparation of information returns, one of the key forms that is often requested of non-employee vendors and others is the Form W-9, Request for Taxpayer Identification Number and Certification.

Form **W-9**
(Rev. October 2018)
Department of the Treasury
Internal Revenue Service

Request for Taxpayer Identification Number and Certification

▶ **Go to *www.irs.gov/FormW9* for instructions and the latest information.**

Give Form to the requester. Do not send to the IRS.

Print or type.
See Specific Instructions on page 3.

1 Name (as shown on your income tax return). Name is required on this line; do not leave this line blank.

2 Business name/disregarded entity name, if different from above

3 Check appropriate box for federal tax classification of the person whose name is entered on line 1. Check only **one** of the following seven boxes.

☐ Individual/sole proprietor or single-member LLC ☐ C Corporation ☐ S Corporation ☐ Partnership ☐ Trust/estate

☐ Limited liability company. Enter the tax classification (C=C corporation, S=S corporation, P=Partnership) ▶ ________

Note: Check the appropriate box in the line above for the tax classification of the single-member owner. Do not check LLC if the LLC is classified as a single-member LLC that is disregarded from the owner unless the owner of the LLC is another LLC that is **not** disregarded from the owner for U.S. federal tax purposes. Otherwise, a single-member LLC that is disregarded from the owner should check the appropriate box for the tax classification of its owner.

☐ Other (see instructions) ▶

4 Exemptions (codes apply only to certain entities, not individuals; see instructions on page 3):

Exempt payee code (if any) ________

Exemption from FATCA reporting code (if any) ________

(Applies to accounts maintained outside the U.S.)

5 Address (number, street, and apt. or suite no.) See instructions.

Requester's name and address (optional)

6 City, state, and ZIP code

7 List account number(s) here (optional)

Part I Taxpayer Identification Number (TIN)

Enter your TIN in the appropriate box. The TIN provided must match the name given on line 1 to avoid backup withholding. For individuals, this is generally your social security number (SSN). However, for a resident alien, sole proprietor, or disregarded entity, see the instructions for Part I, later. For other entities, it is your employer identification number (EIN). If you do not have a number, see *How to get a TIN,* later.

Note: If the account is in more than one name, see the instructions for line 1. Also see *What Name and Number To Give the Requester* for guidelines on whose number to enter.

Social security number

☐☐☐ - ☐☐ - ☐☐☐☐

or

Employer identification number

☐☐ - ☐☐☐☐☐☐☐

Part II Certification

The Form W-9 is used to capture two characteristics of payees: (1) the tax identification number and (2) the type of taxpayer (individual, corporation, etc.). This information is used to prepare the proper type of information reporting.

EXAMPLE Paola operates a small business and expects to make payments of $3,200 to a new vendor during the current year. Paola will request that the vendor provide a completed Form W-9 as part of the typical vendor set-up process, prior to making any payments to the vendor. The information from the Form W-9 will also be used to determine whether Paola will need to issue any information reporting for this vendor after the end of the year. ♦

Self-Study Problem 9.5

See Appendix E for Solutions to Self-Study Problems

David Flock (PO Box 12344, Melbourne, FL 32901; E.I.N. 95-1234567; telephone 800-555-1212) paid two employees for working for his small business in 2022. David does not offer a retirement plan for his employees. David's payroll records show the following:

Employee	Social Security Number	Hours Worked	Gross Wages	Federal Income Tax Withheld	State Income Tax Withheld	Social Security Withheld	Medicare Withheld	Net Pay
China Jones	398-22-4212	973.50	$17,523.12	$610.00	$0.00	$1,086.43	$254.09	$15,572.60
Lilly Smith	466-19-9001	875.00	14,000.00	235.00	0.00	868.00	203.00	12,694.00
Total			$31,523.12	$845.00	$0.00	$1,954.43	$457.09	$28,266.60

a. China's home address is 2702 Carlson Circle, Apt 2K, Melbourne FL 32901. Complete Copy B of the Form W-2 for China Jones.

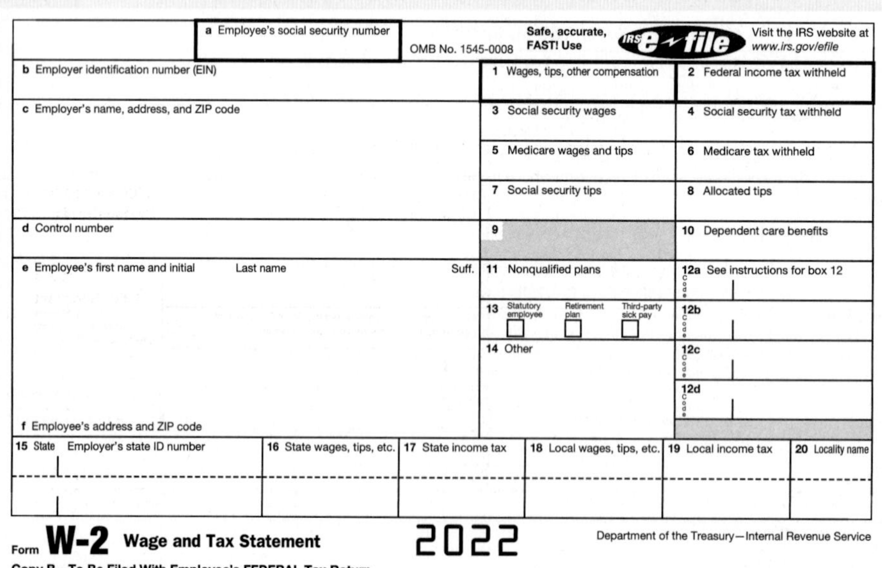

a Employee's social security number | OMB No. 1545-0008 | Safe, accurate, FAST! Use IRS e-file | Visit the IRS website at www.irs.gov/efile

b Employer identification number (EIN)

1 Wages, tips, other compensation | 2 Federal income tax withheld

c Employer's name, address, and ZIP code

3 Social security wages | 4 Social security tax withheld

5 Medicare wages and tips | 6 Medicare tax withheld

7 Social security tips | 8 Allocated tips

d Control number

9 | 10 Dependent care benefits

e Employee's first name and initial | Last name | Suff.

11 Nonqualified plans | 12a See instructions for box 12

13 Statutory employee | Retirement plan | Third-party sick pay | 12b

14 Other | 12c

12d

f Employee's address and ZIP code

15 State | Employer's state ID number | 16 State wages, tips, etc. | 17 State income tax | 18 Local wages, tips, etc. | 19 Local income tax | 20 Locality name

Form **W-2** Wage and Tax Statement 2022

Department of the Treasury—Internal Revenue Service

Copy B—To Be Filed With Employee's FEDERAL Tax Return.
This information is being furnished to the Internal Revenue Service.

Self-Study Problem 9.5, continued

See Appendix E for Solutions to Self-Study Problems

b. Assume David files a Form 941 to report his taxes. Complete David's Form W-3 for 2022.

33333 | a Control number | For Official Use Only ▶ OMB No. 1545-0008

b Kind of Payer (Check one): 941 ☐, Military ☐, 943 ☐, 944 ☐, CT-1 ☐, Hshld. emp. ☐, Medicare govt. emp. ☐

Kind of Employer (Check one): None apply ☐, 501c non-govt. ☐, State/local non-501c ☐, State/local 501c ☐, Federal govt. ☐

Third-party sick pay (Check if applicable) ☐

c Total number of Forms W-2	d Establishment number
1 Wages, tips, other compensation	2 Federal income tax withheld
e Employer identification number (EIN)	
3 Social security wages	4 Social security tax withheld
f Employer's name	
5 Medicare wages and tips	6 Medicare tax withheld
7 Social security tips	8 Allocated tips
9	10 Dependent care benefits
11 Nonqualified plans	12a Deferred compensation
g Employer's address and ZIP code	
h Other EIN used this year	
13 For third-party sick pay use only	12b
15 State Employer's state ID number	
14 Income tax withheld by payer of third-party sick pay	
16 State wages, tips, etc.	17 State income tax
18 Local wages, tips, etc.	19 Local income tax
Employer's contact person	Employer's telephone number
For Official Use Only	
Employer's fax number	Employer's email address

Under penalties of perjury, I declare that I have examined this return and accompanying documents, and, to the best of my knowledge and belief, they are true, correct, and complete.

Signature ▶ Title ▶ Date ▶

Form **W-3** **Transmittal of Wage and Tax Statements** 2022 Department of the Treasury Internal Revenue Service

c. David also occasionally pays Cielle Harris as a properly classified independent contractor to work for his business. In 2022, David paid Cielle $878.78 for services rendered. No taxes were withheld on payments to Cielle. Cielle lives at 224 Deland Avenue, Indialantic, FL 32903. Her Social Security number is 566-29-9819. Prepare Copy B of Cielle's Form 1099-NEC.

☐ CORRECTED (if checked)

PAYER'S name, street address, city or town, state or province, country, ZIP or foreign postal code, and telephone no.	OMB No. 1545-0116 Form **1099-NEC** (Rev. January 2022) For calendar year 20___ — **Nonemployee Compensation**
PAYER'S TIN	RECIPIENT'S TIN
1 Nonemployee compensation $	**Copy B For Recipient** This is important tax information and is being furnished to the IRS. If you are required to file a return, a negligence penalty or other sanction may be imposed on you if this income is taxable and the IRS determines that it has not been reported.
RECIPIENT'S name	
2 Payer made direct sales totaling $5,000 or more of consumer products to recipient for resale ☐	
Street address (including apt. no.)	3
City or town, state or province, country, and ZIP or foreign postal code	4 Federal income tax withheld $
Account number (see instructions)	
5 State tax withheld $ $	6 State/Payer's state no.
7 State income $ $	

Form **1099-NEC** (Rev. 1-2022) (keep for your records) www.irs.gov/Form1099NEC Department of the Treasury - Internal Revenue Service

Learning Objective 9.6

Compute the amount of FUTA tax for an employer.

9-6 THE FUTA TAX

Please note: Employers in jurisdictions that have not repaid money borrowed from the federal government for unemployment benefits will have a higher FUTA tax than the 0.6 percent illustrated below. At the time we go to print, 10 states are expected to be subject to a FUTA credit reduction in 2022 (official determinations are issued on or around November 10 each year). For purposes of the problems and examples in this textbook, assume that the employer does not reside in one of the jurisdictions where a higher FUTA tax applies.

The Federal Unemployment Tax Act (FUTA) instituted a tax that is not withheld from employees' wages, but instead is paid in full by employers. The federal unemployment tax rate is 6 percent of an employee's wages up to $7,000. A credit is allowed for state unemployment taxes of 5.4 percent. Therefore, the effective federal unemployment tax rate is only 0.6 percent if the state also assesses an unemployment tax.

EXAMPLE Karen has two employees in 2022: John, who earned $12,500 this year, and Sue, who earned $15,000. The FUTA tax is calculated as follows:

John's wages, $12,500 (maximum $7,000)	$ 7,000
Sue's wages, $15,000 (maximum $7,000)	7,000
Total FUTA wages	14,000
FUTA tax at 0.6%	$ 84

♦

TAX BREAK

One common income-shifting technique is to employ your children as part of your business. This creates an income tax deduction (at a presumably higher rate) and shifts the income to a (presumably) lower-taxed child. If the parent(s) operate(s) a sole proprietorship or a partnership in which both partners are parents of the child, wages paid to the child also escape FICA taxes before age 18 and escape FUTA taxes on the child's wages before age 21.

Employers report their FUTA liability for the year on Form 940, Employer's Annual Federal Unemployment (FUTA) Tax Return. Like federal income tax withholding and FICA taxes, federal unemployment taxes must be deposited by electronic funds transfer (EFTPS). A deposit is required when the FUTA taxes for the quarter, plus any amount not yet deposited for the prior quarter(s), exceed $500. If required, the deposit must be made by the last day of the month after the end of each quarter.

EXAMPLE Ti Corporation's federal unemployment tax liability, after reduction by the credit for state unemployment taxes, is $255 for the first quarter of 2022, $200 for the second quarter, $75 for the third quarter, and $25 for the fourth quarter. Ti Corporation must deposit $530, the sum of the first, second, and third quarters' liability, by October 31, 2022. The remaining $25 may be either deposited or paid with Form 940. ♦

Because states administer federal-state unemployment programs, most of the unemployment tax is paid to the state. Employers must pay all state unemployment taxes for the year by the due date of the federal Form 940 to get full credit for the state taxes against FUTA.

Self-Study Problem 9.6

See Appendix E for Solutions to Self-Study Problems

Your client has provided the following annual payroll summary for 2022:

Anatolian Corporation
400 8th Street N
La Crosse, WI 54601
EIN: 94-0001112
December 31, 2022

			Gross Wages ($)		
Employee	*Q1*	*Q2*	*Q3*	*Q4*	*YTD*
Nancy Wheeling	13,000	13,000	13,000	13,000	52,000
Dustin Hendrickson	6,000	7,500	8,200	7,700	29,400
John Myers	-	3,100	3,600	-	6,700
Ellie Veen	28,000	25,000	25,000	25,000	103,000
Mike Weeder	8,000	8,000	8,000	8,000	32,000
James Hopps	3,500	3,000	450	-	6,950
William Byars	-	6,700	5,890	-	12,590
Luke Éclair	-	-	3,300	3,400	6,700
Steve Harrison	5,700	5,700	5,700	5,700	22,800
Maxwell Maryfield	4,600	5,000	-	-	9,600
William Hargreaves	5,000	5,000	5,000	5,000	20,000
Joyce Byright	4,000	4,200	4,400	3,700	16,300
	77,800	86,200	82,540	71,500	318,040

Anatolian pays Wisconsin state unemployment tax and makes the *required* deposits of both federal and state unemployment taxes on a timely basis. There was no overpayment in 2021. Use this information to complete Parts 1–5 of Form 940 on Pages 9-43 and 9-44.

Due to the significant increase in unemployment claims during the COVID-19 pandemic, the U.S. Department of Labor expects the following states and territories to be subject to a FUTA credit reduction in 2022: CA, CO, CT, IL, MA, MN, NJ, NY, PA, and the U.S. Virgin Islands.

Learning Objective 9.7

Describe the general rules for qualified retirement plans.

9-7 QUALIFIED RETIREMENT PLANS

The discussion of qualified retirement plans in this chapter is focused on larger employers (see Chapter 5 for small business retirement plans). Qualified retirement plans generally offer potential tax savings in two primary ways:

1. Contributions to qualified plans are generally not subject to current income taxation.
2. The income generated by the funds in the plan are not subject to current taxation.

EXAMPLE In 2022, Gail contributes $2,400 from her $100,000 salary to her employer's qualified profit-sharing plan. Gail's employer contributes $3,600. Gail's wages subject to income tax in 2022 are reduced to $97,600 and the employer contribution of $3,600 is not subject to income taxation currently. ♦

EXAMPLE Bonnie and her employer have made substantial before-tax contributions to her qualified retirement plan for the past 30 years. In 2022, her retirement account, which is invested in a variety of mutual funds, generated interest income of $4,500, dividend income of $6,000 and capital gains of $14,000. If Bonnie's plan remains qualified and she does not withdraw any distributions from the plan, the earnings in her account are not subject to current income taxation in 2022. ♦

However, as was true with traditional Individual Retirement Accounts (as discussed in Chapter 5), because the initial contributions were not subject to income taxation, all of the distributions from the plan are generally subject to income tax.

EXAMPLE Continuing the previous example, Bonnie reaches age 60 and retires in 2023 and takes a distribution of $30,000 from her retirement account. Although the distribution may be in part her previous contributions or the employer's contributions or the earnings of her account, all of the $30,000 distribution is taxable. ♦

From an income tax planning perspective, the two primary benefits of qualified plans mentioned above create the possibility of three income tax benefits:

1. The deferral of paying income taxes on wages until a later year (taking advantage of the time value of money)
2. The deferral of paying income taxes on the retirement accounts earnings until a later year (also time value of money)
3. The possibility that income, and thus the marginal tax rate on that income, may be lower in a future period when the taxpayer is retired.

Tax planning is discussed further in Chapter 12.

9-7a Qualified Plans

For a retirement plan to be a qualified plan for income tax purposes, it must meet the following general requirements:

1. A plan must be created by an employer for the *exclusive benefit* of employees or their beneficiaries.
2. The contributions and benefits under a plan must *not discriminate in* favor of highly compensated employees.
3. A plan must meet certain *participation and coverage requirements*. The plan must provide that all employees who are at least 21 years old and who have completed at least one year of service with the employer are eligible to participate. If the plan provides for 100 percent vesting of accrued benefits upon commencement of participation in the plan, the one year of service requirement may be replaced with a requirement that the employee has completed at least two years of service.

Self-Study Problem 9.6

Form **940 for 2022: Employer's Annual Federal Unemployment (FUTA) Tax Return** 850113

Department of the Treasury — Internal Revenue Service OMB No. 1545-0028

Employer identification number (EIN) ☐☐ – ☐☐☐☐☐☐☐

Name *(not your trade name)*

Trade name *(if any)*

Address

Number Street Suite or room number

City State ZIP code

Foreign country name Foreign province/county Foreign postal code

Type of Return
(Check all that apply.)

☐ **a.** Amended

☐ **b.** Successor employer

☐ **c.** No payments to employees in 2022

☐ **d.** Final: Business closed or stopped paying wages

Go to *www.irs.gov/Form940* for instructions and the latest information.

Read the separate instructions before you complete this form. Please type or print within the boxes.

Part 1: Tell us about your return. If any line does NOT apply, leave it blank. See instructions before completing Part 1.

1a	**If you had to pay state unemployment tax in one state only, enter the state abbreviation** .	1a	☐☐
1b	**If you had to pay state unemployment tax in more than one state, you are a multi-state employer**	1b	☐ Check here. Complete Schedule A (Form 940).
2	**If you paid wages in a state that is subject to CREDIT REDUCTION**	2	☐ Check here. Complete Schedule A (Form 940).

Part 2: Determine your FUTA tax before adjustments. If any line does NOT apply, leave it blank.

3	**Total payments to all employees**	3	.
4	**Payments exempt from FUTA tax** . . . . 4 [.]		
	Check all that apply: 4a ☐ Fringe benefits; 4b ☐ Group-term life insurance; 4c ☐ Retirement/Pension; 4d ☐ Dependent care; 4e ☐ Other		
5	**Total of payments made to each employee in excess of $7,000** . . . 5 [.]		
6	**Subtotal** (line 4 + line 5 = line 6)	6	.
7	**Total taxable FUTA wages** (line 3 – line 6 = line 7). See instructions	7	.
8	**FUTA tax before adjustments** (line 7 x 0.006 = line 8)	8	.

Part 3: Determine your adjustments. If any line does NOT apply, leave it blank.

9	**If ALL of the taxable FUTA wages you paid were excluded from state unemployment tax, multiply line 7 by 0.054** (line 7 × 0.054 = line 9). Go to line 12	9	.
10	**If SOME of the taxable FUTA wages you paid were excluded from state unemployment tax, OR you paid ANY state unemployment tax late** (after the due date for filing Form 940), complete the worksheet in the instructions. Enter the amount from line 7 of the worksheet	10	.
11	**If credit reduction applies,** enter the total from Schedule A (Form 940)	11	.

Part 4: Determine your FUTA tax and balance due or overpayment. If any line does NOT apply, leave it blank.

12	**Total FUTA tax after adjustments** (lines 8 + 9 + 10 + 11 = line 12)	12	.
13	**FUTA tax deposited for the year, including any overpayment applied from a prior year**	13	.
14	**Balance due.** If line 12 is more than line 13, enter the excess on line 14. • If line 14 is more than $500, you must deposit your tax. • If line 14 is $500 or less, you may pay with this return. See instructions	14	.
15	**Overpayment.** If line 13 is more than line 12, enter the excess on line 15 and check a box below	15	.

You **MUST** complete both pages of this form and **SIGN** it. Check one: ☐ Apply to next return. ☐ Send a refund.

For Privacy Act and Paperwork Reduction Act Notice, see the back of the Payment Voucher. Cat. No. 11234O Form **940** (2022)

850212

Name *(not your trade name)* | Employer identification number (EIN) –

Part 5: Report your FUTA tax liability by quarter only if line 12 is more than $500. If not, go to Part 6.

16 Report the amount of your FUTA tax liability for each quarter; do NOT enter the amount you deposited. If you had no liability for a quarter, leave the line blank.

16a **1st quarter** (January 1 – March 31) . . . . 16a .

16b **2nd quarter** (April 1 – June 30) . . . . 16b .

16c **3rd quarter** (July 1 – September 30) . . . . 16c .

16d **4th quarter** (October 1 – December 31) . . . . 16d .

17 **Total tax liability for the year** (lines 16a + 16b + 16c + 16d = line 17) **17** . **Total must equal line 12.**

Part 6: May we speak with your third-party designee?

Do you want to allow an employee, a paid tax preparer, or another person to discuss this return with the IRS? See the instructions for details.

☐ **Yes.** Designee's name and phone number

Select a 5-digit personal identification number (PIN) to use when talking to the IRS.

☐ **No.**

Part 7: Sign here. You MUST complete both pages of this form and SIGN it.

Under penalties of perjury, I declare that I have examined this return, including accompanying schedules and statements, and to the best of my knowledge and belief, it is true, correct, and complete, and that no part of any payment made to a state unemployment fund claimed as a credit was, or is to be, deducted from the payments made to employees. Declaration of preparer (other than taxpayer) is based on all information of which preparer has any knowledge.

Sign your name here

Print your name here

Print your title here

Date / /

Best daytime phone

Paid Preparer Use Only

Check if you are self-employed ☐

Preparer's name | PTIN

Preparer's signature | Date / /

Firm's name (or yours if self-employed) | EIN

Address | Phone

City | State | ZIP code

4. *Minimum vesting* requirements must be met with respect to both employee and employer contributions.
5. *Uniform minimum distribution* rules must be met.

9-7b **Types of Qualified Plans**

The tax law provides for several types of qualified plans: pension plans, profit-sharing plans, stock bonus plans, and Employee Stock Ownership Plans (ESOPs). The pension plan can take one of two forms: the defined contribution plan or the defined benefit plan. Under a defined contribution plan, the amount of contribution for the employee is determined by reference to a formula based on the employee's current compensation. The employee's retirement benefits will be dependent upon the accumulated contributions and earnings in the account at the time of retirement. Under a defined benefit plan, the future retirement benefits of the employee are specified, and a formula is used to determine the contributions necessary to provide for the defined benefit. Defined benefit plans are being used more sparingly by employers over the last three decades. Profit-sharing plans are structured to allow the employee to share in company profits through employer contributions from such profits. Under a stock bonus plan, employer contributions on behalf of the employee consist of stock of the employer company.

EXAMPLE Heather is an employee who earned $30,000 during the current year. Her employer contributed $1,200 (4 percent of Heather's salary) to a qualified retirement plan. This plan is a defined contribution plan. ♦

EXAMPLE Alan works for an employer whose qualified retirement plan states that Alan will receive a retirement benefit at age 65 equal to 40 percent of his final year's salary. The employer must make adequate contributions to the plan to enable the stated retirement benefit to be paid (a sufficient amount of money must be in the plan upon Alan's retirement to pay for Alan's defined retirement benefit). This plan is a defined benefit plan. ♦

9-7c **Limitations on Contributions to and Benefits from Qualified Plans**

Employee and employer contributions to qualified plans are subject to certain dollar or percentage limitations. Under a defined contribution plan (including profit sharing plans), the annual addition to an employee's account is generally not allowed to exceed the lesser of $61,000 (in 2022) or 100 percent of the employee's compensation. Under a defined benefit plan, the annual benefit payable to an employee upon retirement is limited to the lesser of $245,000 (for 2022) or 100 percent of the employee's average compensation for the highest three consecutive years of employment. If an employee is the beneficiary of contributions to both a defined benefit and defined contribution plan, the limit is 25 percent of an employee's compensation or the required funding for the defined benefit plan, whichever is greater. The operational rules for qualified pension plans and the other types of qualified plans are complex.

Self-Study Problem 9.7 ***See Appendix E for Solutions to Self-Study Problems***

Jeannie is employed by a business that operates a qualified profit-sharing plan.

a. In 2022, when her compensation is $50,000, what is the maximum contribution the business can make for her?

b. If Jeannie's salary was $270,000, what is the maximum contribution?

Learning Objective 9.8

Explain the pension plan rollover rules.

9-8 ROLLOVERS

In many situations, taxpayers need to transfer assets from one retirement plan to another plan of the same or different type. For example, the taxpayer may change jobs, take early retirement, or simply seek a better retirement fund manager. There are two ways this transfer can be accomplished: (1) direct transfer, also known as a trustee-to-trustee transfer, and (2) rollover of the distribution, in whole or in part, to an IRA or other qualified plan. There are potentially different tax treatments for the two types of transfers.

9-8a Direct Transfers

In direct transfers, the taxpayer instructs the trustee of the retirement plan to transfer assets to the trustee of another plan. There are no current-year tax consequences for this transaction. Also, there is no limit to the dollar amount of the transfer or the number of times a taxpayer can do this in a single tax year.

EXAMPLE Juan has $90,000 in a Section 401(k) plan with his employer. He also has two IRAs, one with ABC Bank ($20,000) and one with XYZ Mutual Fund ($30,000). In March of 20XX, Juan instructs ABC Bank to make a direct transfer to XYZ Mutual Fund of all of his funds ($20,000). In August of 20XX, Juan quits his job and instructs the trustee of the Section 401(k) plan to transfer his $90,000 directly to XYZ Mutual Fund. On December 31, 20XX, Juan has $140,000 in his XYZ Mutual Fund IRA. Since the two transactions were direct transfers, there are no tax consequences to Juan in the current year. ♦

9-8b Distribution Rollovers

In a distribution rollover, the taxpayer receives a distribution of funds from a retirement plan and then transfers part or all of the funds to the new retirement plan trustee. The taxpayer has a maximum of sixty days in which to transfer funds to the new plan and avoid taxes and penalties. The sixty-day rollover period may be waived in cases of casualty, disaster, and other events beyond the reasonable control of the taxpayer such as death, disability, incarceration, and postal error. The sixty-day time limit is extended to 120 days for first-time home buyers.

The major drawback to distribution rollovers is that the trustee must withhold 20 percent of the amount distributed for federal income taxes, giving the taxpayer only 80 percent of the amount in his or her plan. However, the taxpayer must contribute 100 percent of the amount in the old plan to the new trustee within the required sixty-day period to avoid tax on the distribution. Amounts that are not placed in a new plan within the required period are taxable as ordinary income in the current year. Also, if the taxpayer is under 59½ years old, the portion of the retirement plan distribution not transferred will be subject to a 10 percent penalty tax.

The exception to mandatory withholding is a distribution from an IRA; such distributions are not subject to the 20 percent withholding tax. Also, taxpayers are allowed only one distribution rollover each year for transfers from one IRA to another IRA. There are many other complex rules concerning retirement plan rollovers.

EXAMPLE Bea is 50 years old, has worked for Gold Company for twenty-five years, and has $200,000 in her retirement plan. This year, Gold Company is purchased by Green Company. As a result of the takeover, Bea was laid off. Bea requests a distribution of her $200,000 from Gold Company's retirement plan. The trustee of Gold's retirement plan must withhold $40,000 (20 percent of $200,000) from the distribution. Bea only receives $160,000 from her retirement plan distribution. If Bea wants to roll her funds into an IRA and avoid taxes, she must contribute $200,000, even though she only received $160,000. If Bea has no other resources and cannot make up the $40,000, the amount not contributed to the IRA will be taxable income to her and subject to a 10 percent penalty. If Bea makes the total rollover contribution of $200,000 within the 60-day timeframe, then the distribution will be nontaxable. The $40,000 will be reported as taxes withheld on her tax return. ♦

If an individual misses the 60-day window to complete a rollover, generally the only way to avoid paying tax on the distribution is to request a private letter ruling from the IRS. The current cost for such a request is $10,000. Luckily, the IRS offers an automatic waiver in a number of circumstances including: (1) a misplaced check that was never cashed, (2) a distribution was mistakenly placed in an account that was thought to be an eligible retirement account, (3) the taxpayer's home was severely damaged, (4) a family member dies, (5) the taxpayer or a family member was seriously ill, (6) the taxpayer was incarcerated, (7) the post office made an error, and others.

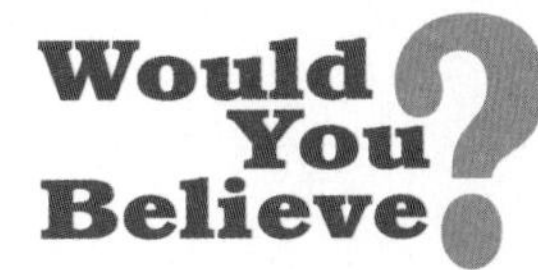

Self-Study Problem 9.8 *See Appendix E for Solutions to Self-Study Problems*

Carol, age 40, has an IRA with Blue Mutual Fund. Her balance in the fund is $150,000. She has heard good things about the management of Red Mutual Fund, so she opens a Red Fund IRA. Carol requests her balance from the Blue Fund be distributed to her on July 1, 20XX. She opted to have no withholding on the distribution.

a. How much will Carol receive from the Blue Fund IRA?

b. If the funds were distributed from a qualified retirement plan (not an IRA), how much would Carol receive?

c. When is the last day Carol can roll over the amount received into the Red Fund IRA and avoid taxation in the current year?

d. Assuming the funds were distributed from a qualified retirement plan, not from an IRA, how much will Carol have to contribute to the Red Fund IRA to avoid taxable income and any penalties?

KEY TERMS

Form W-4, 9-2
IRS online withholding estimator, 9-2
exempt, 9-4
"lock-in" letter, 9-9
percentage method, 9-14
IRS Publication 15-T, 9-14
wage bracket method, 9-14
Form W-4P, 9-19
backup withholding, 9-20
FICA, 9-21
Social Security, 9-21
Medicare, 9-21
OASDI, 9-21
estimated payments, 9-24
required annual payment, 9-24
monthly or semiweekly depositors, 9-28
lookback period, 9-28
Employee payroll tax deferral, 9-29
EFTPS, 9-29
Form 941, 9-29
Form W-2, 9-35
Form W-3, 9-35
Form W-2G, 9-36
Form 1099, 9-36
Form W-9, 9-37
FUTA, 9-40
Form 940, 9-40
qualified plan, 9-42
pension plans, 9-45
profit-sharing plans, 9-45
stock bonus plans, 9-45
Employee Stock Ownership Plans (ESOPs), 9-45
defined contribution plan, 9-45
defined benefit plan, 9-45
trustee-to-trustee transfer, 9-46
rollover, 9-46

KEY POINTS

Learning Objectives	Key Points
LO 9.1: Compute the income tax withholding from employee wages.	• Employers are required to withhold taxes from amounts paid to employees for wages, including salaries, fees, bonuses, commissions, vacation and retirement pay. • Form W-4, showing the filing status and possible adjustments to withholding, is furnished to the employer by the employee. • The percentage method and the wage bracket method of withholding are prescribed for the pre-2020 Form W-4 and post-2019 Form W-4. • Tip income must be reported using one of several methods.
LO 9.2: Compute the FICA tax.	• For 2022, the Social Security (OASDI) tax rate is 6.2 percent and the Medicare tax rate is 1.45 percent for employers and employees. The maximum wage subject to the Social Security portion of the FICA tax is $147,000 for 2022, and all wages are subject to the Medicare portion of the FICA tax. • Taxpayers working for more than one employer during the same tax year may pay more than the maximum amount of Social Security taxes. If this happens, the taxpayer should compute the excess taxes paid, and report the excess as a payment against his or her income tax liability on Line 11 of Schedule 3.
LO 9.3: Determine taxpayers' quarterly estimated payments.	• Self-employed taxpayers are not subject to withholding; however, they must make quarterly estimated tax payments. • Estimated payments are made in four installments on April 15, June 15, and September 15 of the tax year, and January 15 of the following year. • Any individual taxpayer who has estimated tax for the year of $1,000 or more, after subtracting withholding, and whose withholding does not equal or exceed the "required annual payment," must make quarterly estimated payments. • The required annual payment is the smallest of three amounts: (1) 90 percent of the tax shown on the current year's return, (2) 100 percent (or 110 percent at higher income levels) of the tax shown on the preceding year's return, or (3) 90 percent of the current-year tax determined each quarter on an annualized basis.
LO 9.4: Apply the federal deposit system to payroll withholding.	• Employers must make periodic deposits of the taxes that are withheld from employees' wages. Deposits must be made electronically. • Employers are either monthly or semiweekly depositors, depending on the total amount of income taxes withheld from wages and FICA taxes attributable to wages. However, if withholding and FICA taxes of $100,000 or more are accumulated at any time during the year, the depositor is subject to a special one-day deposit rule. • Due to the COVID-19 pandemic, a 2020 payroll tax deferral was implemented for the employer's share of Social Security tax, of which one-half can be deferred until December 31, 2021 and the remaining half can be deferred until December 31, 2022.
LO 9.5: Prepare employer payroll reporting.	• On or before January 31 of the year following the calendar year of payment, an employer must furnish to each employee two copies of the employee's Wage and Tax Statement, Form W-2, for the previous calendar year. • The original copy (Copy A) of all Forms W-2 and Form W-3 (Transmittal of Wage and Tax Statements) must be filed with the Social Security Administration by January 31 of the year following the calendar year of payment. • Forms 1099 must be mailed to the recipients by January 31 of the year following the calendar year of payment.

LO 9.6: Compute the amount of FUTA tax for an employer.	• The FUTA (Federal Unemployment Tax Act) tax is not withheld from employees' wages, but instead is paid in full by employers. • The federal unemployment tax rate is 6.0 percent of an employee's wages up to $7,000. A credit of up to 5.4 percent is allowed if state unemployment taxes are paid, resulting in a net effective federal unemployment tax rate of 0.6 percent.
LO 9.7: Describe the general rules for qualified retirement plans.	• In order to be qualified, retirement plans must meet certain requirements related to non-discrimination of lower compensated employees, participation eligibility, vesting requirements, and distribution rules.
LO 9.8: Explain the pension plan rollover rules.	• There are two ways to transfer assets from one retirement plan to another of the same or different type: (1) a direct transfer, also known as a trustee-to-trustee transfer, and (2) a rollover of an actual cash distribution, in whole or in part, to an IRA or other qualified plan. • There are no current-year tax consequences for a direct trustee-to-trustee transfer. • Distribution rollovers are subject to a 60-day time limit for completion and may also be subject to income tax withholding and tax penalties.

QUESTIONS and PROBLEMS

GROUP 1: MULTIPLE CHOICE QUESTIONS

LO 9.1

1. Which form is used by an employee to report the information necessary for income tax withholding to an employer?
   a. W-2
   b. W-3
   c. W-4
   d. 1099-NEC

LO 9.1

2. Abbe, age 56, started a new job in 2021. At Abbe's previous employer, she had filed a Form W-4 with 5 allowances. Abbe's new employer will:
   a. use a copy of Abbe's previous Form W-4 to calculate income tax withholding.
   b. permit Abbe to file a new W-4 using either the old allowances method or the new method.
   c. require Abbe to complete a new 2021 version of Form W-4.
   d. require Abbe to withhold as a single taxpayer with no dependents.
   e. require Abbe to use the IRS on-line withholding estimator.

LO 9.1

3. One of the primary differences between an "old" pre-2020 Form W-4 and a "new" post-2019 Form W-4 is:
   a. The new form does not require any additional work if the taxpayer has two jobs.
   b. The new form does not account for the possibility of child tax credits in determining the proper withholding.
   c. The new form does not rely on the number of allowances to determine withholding.
   d. The new form requires the taxpayer to sign the Form W-4.

LO 9.1

4. Flo is a server at a diner in Phoenix and earns a significant portion of her pay through tips from customers. Some of these tips are paid via credit card and others are paid in cash. Flo's employer will:

a. withhold employment taxes but no income taxes on the tips.
b. withhold both employment and income taxes on the cash tips but only employment taxes on the tips paid by credit card.
c. withhold both employment and income taxes on all tips.
d. not withhold any taxes on cash tips but will withhold both employment and income taxes on credit card tips.

LO 9.1

5. Gloria and Al intend to file jointly in 2022. Gloria's wages are expected to be $40,000 and Al's are expected to be about $39,500. When Gloria is completing a new 2022 Form W-4, the most convenient but reliable way to handle her working spouse is:
   a. Ignore the fact that her spouse has a job.
   b. Check box 2c. in Step 2 Multiple Jobs or Spouse Works on the new form.
   c. Complete the Multiple Jobs worksheet and use the Higher Paying Job column for her salary in determining the additional withholding required.
   d. Select the Head of household filing status in Step 1 of Form W-4.

LO 9.2

6. Which of the following is *not* true about FICA taxes?
   a. The FICA tax has two parts, Social Security (Old Age, Survivors, and Disability Insurance) and Medicare.
   b. In 2022, the maximum wage base for Social Security tax withholding is $147,000.
   c. In 2022, there is no maximum wage base for Medicare tax withholding.
   d. When employees work for more than one employer and exceed the maximum wage base for Social Security tax withholding in total, the additional Social Security tax is used to offset any Medicare taxes withheld otherwise.

LO 9.2

7. FICA taxes are generally paid as follows:
   a. One-half is withheld from the employee and the other half is paid by the employer.
   b. The entire amount of Social Security is paid by the employee and the employer pays the Medicare portion.
   c. The entire amount of Medicare is paid by the employee and the employer pays the Social Security portion.
   d. Both portions are paid by the employer and thus never withheld from an employee's pay.

LO 9.2

8. The rate for the Social Security portion of FICA taxes for a non-self-employed individual is:
   a. 12.4 percent for the employer.
   b. 15.3 percent for the employee.
   c. 7.65 percent total for the employee and employer.
   d. 6.2 percent each for the employee and employer up to the FICA cap amount.

LO 9.2

9. Carlotta is an employee and generates wages of $150,000 in 2022. Which of the following best describes the rate of tax associated with the Medicare portion of FICA taxes?
   a. 7.65 percent payable by Carlotta's employer.
   b. 1.45 percent payable by Carlotta and 6.2 percent payable by the employer.
   c. 1.45 percent each payable by Carlotta and the employer.
   d. 2.9 percent but only up to the current year FICA cap.

LO 9.2

10. Xinyi worked for two different employers in 2022 and her total wages were $80,000 for one and $87,000 for the other (total $167,000). Which of the following best describes Xinyi's 2022 FICA taxes?
    a. Xinyi and the employer will each pay half of Social Security and Medicare taxes on her total wages and both will claim an income tax credit for the portion of each tax in excess of the 2022 FICA cap.
    b. Xinyi and the employer will each pay half of Social Security and Medicare taxes on her total wages and only the employer will claim an income tax credit for the portion of each tax in excess of the 2022 FICA cap.

c. Xinyi and the employer will each pay half of Social Security and Medicare taxes on her total wages and only Xinyi will claim an income tax credit for the portion of each tax in excess of the 2022 FICA cap.
d. Xinyi and the employer will each pay half of Social Security and Medicare taxes on her total wages and only Xinyi will claim an income tax credit for the portion of only Social Security tax in excess of the 2022 FICA cap.

LO 9.2

11. For most taxpayers in 2022, which of the following temporary *COVID-related tax provisions* remains in place?
    a. The employee retention credit
    b. The sick pay credit
    c. The family leave credit
    d. All of these provisions remain in force in 2022
    e. None of these provisions remain in force in 2022.

LO 9.3

12. Typically, estimated payments for individual taxpayers are due on the following dates:
    a. Twice a year on April 15 and September 15
    b. Four installments on April 15, June 15, September 15, and January 15 of the next year
    c. Four times a year on April 15, July 15, September 15, and December 15
    d. Twice a year on June 15 and December 15

LO 9.3

13. Amy's prior year adjusted gross income was $70,000. In order to avoid penalty, what is the required annual payment Amy must make in the current year?
    a. 110% of the current year tax liability.
    b. Any amount that reduces the amount Amy owes for the current year to no less than $5,000.
    c. The lesser of 90 percent of the current year tax liability or 100 percent of the prior year tax liability.
    d. An amount that permits her to pay no more than $5,000 with her tax return when she files it on April 15th of the next year.

LO 9.3

14. When does the required annual payment for estimated income taxes increase to 110% of the prior year tax liability?
    a. When the current year taxable income exceeds $100,000.
    b. When prior year adjusted gross income is $150,000 or more.
    c. When prior year taxable income exceeds $125,000.
    d. When current year tax liability exceeds $20,000.

LO 9.4

15. Employers generally must file a quarterly tax return showing the amount of wages paid and the amount of income tax and FICA tax withholding due. This tax return is filed on:
    a. Form 944 or Form 945
    b. Schedule H
    c. Schedule SE
    d. Form 941

LO 9.4

16. Yamin operates a small business with a few part-time employees. Her annual employment tax withholding in 2022 is $467.80. Yamin should file which employment tax reporting form?
    a. Form 944
    b. Form 940
    c. Form 941
    d. Form 9000
    e. Form 409

LO 9.4

17. Under the special COVID tax provisions in 2020, Basalt Corporation elected to defer a portion of their payroll taxes. Which of the following best describes when Basalt must pay the deferred payroll taxes?
    a. The deferred payroll taxes must be repaid by December 31, 2022.
    b. The deferred payroll taxes must have been repaid by December 31, 2021.

c. The deferred payroll taxes were to be included in the normal payroll tax payments for 2021 and were due June 30, 2022.
d. The deferred payroll taxes were forgiven in 2021 and thus are not required to be paid.

LO 9.5

18. Which of the following forms is used to report wages, tips and other compensation paid to employees?
    a. Form W-4
    b. Form W-2G
    c. Form W-2
    d. Form 1099-R
    e. Form 1099-MISC

LO 9.5

19. Alexandra's nanny comes to work in Alexandra's home each weekday, and Alexandra pays the nanny $27,000 in 2022. Alexandra correctly withholds Social Security and Medicare tax but is not required to withhold income tax. At the end of 2022, Alexandra is required to prepare:
    a. Only a Form W-2 for the nanny.
    b. Only a Form W-3 for the nanny.
    c. A Form W-2 and a Form W-3 for the nanny.
    d. Nothing. Forms W-2 and W-3 are not required for household employees.

LO 9.5

20. Which of the following forms is used to report non-employee compensation?
    a. Form W-2G
    b. Form 1099-MISC
    c. Form 1099-G
    d. Form 1099-NEC
    e. Form 1099-Comp

LO 9.5

21. Griffin Inc. reimburses employees for travel and business expenses using an accountable plan. As a result:
    a. Griffin must include all reimbursements as compensation and withhold appropriately.
    b. Griffin must include travel and entertainment reimbursements as compensation and withhold only FICA taxes on the amount.
    c. Griffin must include all reimbursements as compensation but is only required to withhold income taxes in the amount.
    d. Griffin should not include reimbursements in compensation and no withholding is required.

LO 9.5

22. Which form is most likely to be issued to an individual that wins $10,000 on the slot machines at a casino?
    a. 1099-G
    b. W-2
    c. 1099-INT
    d. 1099-NEC
    e. W-2G

LO 9.5

23. Thibodeau Corporation pays Loretta $3,300 for providing services to Thibodeau during 2022. The nature and scope of the relationship between Thibodeau and Loretta is one of employer-employee. Which of the following best describes the income and employment tax requirements for Thibodeau?
    a. Withhold income and employment taxes and issue a timely Form W-2 to Loretta.
    b. Withhold income taxes but no employment taxes and issue a Form 1099-MISC to Loretta.
    c. Withhold no taxes and issue a Form 1099-NEC to Loretta.
    d. Withhold employment taxes but not income taxes and issue a 1099-K to Loretta.

LO 9.6

24. The FUTA tax is:
    a. An unemployment tax with a rate of 2.9 percent on wages up to $147,000 per employee.
    b. A disability tax with a rate of 2.9 percent on wages up to $7,000 per employee.
    c. An unemployment tax with a rate as low as 0.6 percent on wages up to $7,000 per employee.
    d. A disability tax with a rate of 0.6 percent on wages up to $100,000 per employee.

LO 9.6

25. Wei has four employees: Anna, Kenny, Stan, and Seth, who were paid $12,000, $5,000, $8,000, and $3,000, respectively. Assuming a full state credit, Wei's FUTA taxable wages for the year are:
    a. $28,000
    b. $21,000
    c. $22,000
    d. $186

LO 9.7

26. Which of the following best describes the typical treatment of contributions in an amount below the annual maximum to a qualified retirement plan?
    a. Employee contributions are currently taxable, but employer contributions are not currently taxable.
    b. Employee contributions are not currently taxable, but employer contributions are currently taxable.
    c. Employee and employer contributions are not currently taxable.
    d. Employee and employer contributions are both currently taxable.

LO 9.7

27. Greta and Greta's employer have both been making contributions to a qualified retirement plan for the last twenty-five years. Greta is looking forward to her retirement in a few more years and is extremely pleased to see a balance in her retirement account of $480,000 at the start of 2022. During 2022, the account earned interest, dividends, and capital gains and is now worth $500,000. Greta takes no distributions from the plan in 2022. What is the treatment of the $20,000 increase in Greta's retirement account?
    a. The interest, dividends, and realized capital gains (but not losses) are taxable in 2022.
    b. None of the increase is taxable in 2022.
    c. The interest and dividends are taxable in 2022 but the capital gains, both realized and unrealized, are not taxable in 2022.
    d. Only the unrealized capital gains and losses are taxable (if a net increase) in 2022. The other forms of income are not taxable in 2022.

LO 9.7

28. Gail's employer contributes $2,000 (5 percent of her $40,000 salary) to a qualified retirement plan for Gail. This pension plan is what kind of plan?
    a. Defined benefit plan
    b. Defined contribution plan
    c. Employee Stock Ownership Plan
    d. Profit-sharing plan
    e. None of the above

LO 9.8

29. When taxpayers receive distributions from qualified retirement plans, how much time is allowed to roll over the amount received into a new plan to avoid paying taxes on the distribution in the current year, assuming there are no unusual events?
    a. 180 days
    b. 90 days
    c. 60 days
    d. 1 year
    e. There is no time limit

LO 9.8

30. Tom quits his job with $150,000 in his employer's qualified retirement plan. Since he is broke, Tom instructs the plan trustee to pay him the balance in his retirement account. How much will Tom receive when he gets his check from the retirement plan?
    a. $120,000
    b. $100,000
    c. $96,000
    d. $24,000
    e. Some other amount

LO 9.8

31. Betty owns three separate IRA accounts with different banks. She wishes to consolidate her three IRAs into one IRA in 2022. How many distribution rollovers may Betty make in 2022?
    a. One
    b. Two
    c. Four
    d. Ten
    e. There is no limit

LO 9.8

32. Bonnie is getting close to retirement and realizes she has three different IRA accounts at three different financial institutions. To simplify her life, Bonnie wishes to consolidate her three IRAs into a single account in 2022 using trustee-to-trustee direct rollovers. How many rollovers of this type can Bonnie make in 2022?
    a. One
    b. Two
    c. Four
    d. Ten
    e. There is no limit

GROUP 2: PROBLEMS

LO 9.1

1. Phan Mai is single with two dependent children under age 17. Phan estimates her wages for the year will be $42,000 and her itemized deductions will be $14,000. In the previous year, Phan had a small tax liability. Assuming Phan files as head of household, use page 1 of Form W-4 on Page 9-57 determine what Phan should report on lines 3, 4(a), 4(b), and 4(c).

LO 9.1

2. Ralph and Kathy Gump are married with one 20-year-old dependent child. Ralph expects to earn $89,000 (paid monthly) and estimates their itemized deductions to be $30,000 for the year. Kathy expects to earn wages of $56,000. The Gumps expect to have for AGI deductions of $4,000. Use Form W-4 and worksheet on 9-61 to 9-64 to determine what Ralph should report on lines 3, 4(a), 4(b), and 4(c) of Form W-4.

LO 9.1

3. Sophie is a single taxpayer. For the first payroll period in July 2022, she is paid wages of $1,100 semimonthly. Sophie claims one allowance on her pre-2020 Form W-4. Utilize the Withholding Tables in Appendix C.
    a. Use the percentage method to calculate the amount of Sophie's withholding for a semimonthly pay period.
    b. Use the wage bracket method to determine the amount of Sophie's withholding for the same period.
    c. Use the percentage method assuming Sophie completed a post-2019 Form W-4 and checked only the single box in Step 1(c).
    d. Use the wage bracket method using the same assumptions in part c of this question.

LO 9.1

4. Beckett Rice submitted a new Form W-4 for 2022 as presented below. If Beckett is paid gross wages of $3,000 for the semimonthly period, determine Beckett's income tax withholding using the percentage method and the wage bracket method worksheets and tables from Appendix C.

Form **W-4** Department of the Treasury Internal Revenue Service	**Employee's Withholding Certificate** ▶ Complete Form W-4 so that your employer can withhold the correct federal income tax from your pay. ▶ Give Form W-4 to your employer. ▶ Your withholding is subject to review by the IRS.	OMB No. 1545-0074 **2022**

Step 1: Enter Personal Information	(a) First name and middle initial: Beckett	Last name: Rice	(b) Social security number: 344-56-7890
	Address: 6010 Middle Fiskville Road		▶ **Does your name match the name on your social security card?** If not, to ensure you get credit for your earnings, contact SSA at 800-772-1213 or go to *www.ssa.gov*.
	City or town, state, and ZIP code: Austin, TX 78752		
	(c) ☐ **Single** or **Married filing separately** ☑ **Married filing jointly** or **Qualifying widow(er)**		

Step 2: Multiple Jobs or Spouse Works

Complete this step if you (1) hold more than one job at a time, or (2) are married filing jointly and your spouse also works. The correct amount of withholding depends on income earned from all of these jobs.

Do **only one** of the following.

(a) Use the estimator at *www.irs.gov/W4App* for most accurate withholding for this step (and Steps 3–4); **or**

(b) Use the Multiple Jobs Worksheet on page 3 and enter the result in Step 4(c) below for roughly accurate withholding; **or**

(c) If there are only two jobs total, you may check this box. Do the same on Form W-4 for the other job. This option is accurate for jobs with similar pay; otherwise, more tax than necessary may be withheld . . ▶ ☑

Step 3: Claim Dependents	If your total income will be $200,000 or less ($400,000 or less if married filing jointly): Multiply the number of qualifying children under age 17 by $2,000 ▶ $ 4,000 Multiply the number of other dependents by $500 . . . . ▶ $ Add the amounts above and enter the total here	3	$ 4,000
Step 4 (optional): Other Adjustments	**(a) Other income (not from jobs).** If you want tax withheld for other income you expect this year that won't have withholding, enter the amount of other income here. This may include interest, dividends, and retirement income	4(a)	$ 5,600
	(b) Deductions. If you expect to claim deductions other than the standard deduction and want to reduce your withholding, use the Deductions Worksheet on page 3 and enter the result here	4(b)	$ 3,000
	(c) Extra withholding. Enter any additional tax you want withheld each **pay period** . .	4(c)	$ 0

LO 9.1

5. Cassie works at Capital Bank and is in charge of issuing Forms 1099 to bank customers. Please describe for Cassie the four possible situations that require the bank to implement backup withholding on a customer.

LO 9.2

6. Lamden Company paid its employee, Trudy, wages of $63,000 in 2022. Calculate each of the following: Social Security withheld from Trudy's wages, Medicare withheld from Trudy's wages, Social Security paid by Lamden, and Medicare paid by Lamden.

LO 9.2 7. Lamden Company paid its employee, Chuck, wages of $163,000 in 2022. Calculate each of the following: Social Security withheld from Chuck's wages, Medicare withheld from Chuck's wages, Social Security paid by Lamden, and Medicare paid by Lamden.

LO 9.2 8. Lamden Company paid its employee, William, wages of $263,000 in 2022. Calculate each of the following: Social Security withheld from William's wages, Medicare withheld from William's wages, Social Security paid by Lamden, and Medicare paid by Lamden.

LO 9.2 9. Thuy worked as the assistant manager at Burger Crown through August 2022 and received wages of $81,000. Thuy then worked at Up and Down Burger starting in September of 2022 and received wages of $76,000. Calculate the amount of Thuy's overpayment of Social Security taxes that she should report on her 2022 Form 1040.

LO 9.3 10. Sherina Smith (Social Security number 785-23-9873) lives at 536 West Lapham Street, Milwaukee, WI 53204, and is self-employed for 2022. She estimates her 2022 Schedule C net profit will be $50,000, one-half of self-employment tax will be $3,532, and her qualified business income deduction will be $5,414 in 2022. Sherina has no other forms of income or deductions. She has a dependent child aged 15 and files as head of household. Sherina expects to claim the child tax credit in 2022 but no other credits. Calculate her annual required payment based on 2022 estimates using the 2022 Estimated Tax Worksheet. Complete the worksheet through line 12a only. This question requires the use of the tax rate schedules in Appendix A.

2022 Estimated Tax Worksheet

Keep for Your Records

1	Adjusted gross income you expect in 2022 (see instructions)	1	
2a	Deductions • If you plan to itemize deductions, enter the estimated total of your itemized deductions. • If you don't plan to itemize deductions, enter your standard deduction.	2a	
b	If you can take the qualified business income deduction, enter the estimated amount of the deduction	2b	
c	Add lines 2a and 2b ▶	2c	
3	Subtract line 2c from line 1	3	
4	**Tax.** Figure your tax on the amount on line 3 by using the **2022 Tax Rate Schedules.** **Caution:** *If you will have qualified dividends or a net capital gain, or expect to exclude or deduct foreign earned income or housing, see Worksheets 2-5 and 2-6 in Pub. 505 to figure the tax*	4	
5	Alternative minimum tax from **Form 6251**	5	
6	Add lines 4 and 5. Add to this amount any other taxes you expect to include in the total on Form 1040 or 1040-SR, line 16	6	
7	Credits (see instructions). **Do not** include any income tax withholding on this line	7	
8	Subtract line 7 from line 6. If zero or less, enter -0-	8	
9	Self-employment tax (see instructions)	9	
10	Other taxes (see instructions)	10	
11a	Add lines 8 through 10	11a	
b	Earned income credit, refundable child tax credit* or additional child tax credit, fuel tax credit, net premium tax credit, refundable American opportunity credit, section 1341 credit, and refundable credit from Form 8885*	11b	
c	**Total 2022 estimated tax.** Subtract line 11b from line 11a. If zero or less, enter -0- ▶	11c	
12a	Multiply line 11c by 90% (66⅔% for farmers and fishermen) | 12a |		

Form **W-4**

Department of the Treasury
Internal Revenue Service

Employee's Withholding Certificate

▶ Complete Form W-4 so that your employer can withhold the correct federal income tax from your pay.
▶ Give Form W-4 to your employer.
▶ Your withholding is subject to review by the IRS.

OMB No. 1545-0074

2022

Step 1: Enter Personal Information

(a) First name and middle initial	Last name	(b) Social security number
Address		▶ **Does your name match the name on your social security card?** If not, to ensure you get credit for your earnings, contact SSA at 800-772-1213 or go to *www.ssa.gov*.
City or town, state, and ZIP code		

(c) ☐ **Single** or **Married filing separately**
☐ **Married filing jointly** or **Qualifying widow(er)**
☐ **Head of household** (Check only if you're unmarried and pay more than half the costs of keeping up a home for yourself and a qualifying individual.)

Complete Steps 2–4 ONLY if they apply to you; otherwise, skip to Step 5. See page 2 for more information on each step, who can claim exemption from withholding, when to use the estimator at *www.irs.gov/W4App*, and privacy.

Step 2: Multiple Jobs or Spouse Works

Complete this step if you (1) hold more than one job at a time, or (2) are married filing jointly and your spouse also works. The correct amount of withholding depends on income earned from all of these jobs.

Do **only one** of the following.

(a) Use the estimator at *www.irs.gov/W4App* for most accurate withholding for this step (and Steps 3–4); **or**

(b) Use the Multiple Jobs Worksheet on page 3 and enter the result in Step 4(c) below for roughly accurate withholding; **or**

(c) If there are only two jobs total, you may check this box. Do the same on Form W-4 for the other job. This option is accurate for jobs with similar pay; otherwise, more tax than necessary may be withheld . . ▶ ☐

TIP: To be accurate, submit a 2022 Form W-4 for all other jobs. If you (or your spouse) have self-employment income, including as an independent contractor, use the estimator.

Complete Steps 3–4(b) on Form W-4 for only ONE of these jobs. Leave those steps blank for the other jobs. (Your withholding will be most accurate if you complete Steps 3–4(b) on the Form W-4 for the highest paying job.)

Step 3: Claim Dependents

If your total income will be $200,000 or less ($400,000 or less if married filing jointly):

Multiply the number of qualifying children under age 17 by $2,000 ▶ $ ________

Multiply the number of other dependents by $500 . . . . ▶ $ ________

Add the amounts above and enter the total here . . . . **3** $

Step 4 (optional): Other Adjustments

(a) Other income (not from jobs). If you want tax withheld for other income you expect this year that won't have withholding, enter the amount of other income here. This may include interest, dividends, and retirement income . . . . **4(a)** $

(b) Deductions. If you expect to claim deductions other than the standard deduction and want to reduce your withholding, use the Deductions Worksheet on page 3 and enter the result here . . . . **4(b)** $

(c) Extra withholding. Enter any additional tax you want withheld each **pay period** . . **4(c)** $

Step 5: Sign Here

Under penalties of perjury, I declare that this certificate, to the best of my knowledge and belief, is true, correct, and complete.

▶ **Employee's signature** (This form is not valid unless you sign it.) ▶ **Date**

Employers Only	Employer's name and address	First date of employment	Employer identification number (EIN)

For Privacy Act and Paperwork Reduction Act Notice, see page 3. Cat. No. 10220Q Form **W-4** (2022)

Form W-4 (2022) Page **2**

General Instructions

Section references are to the Internal Revenue Code.

Future Developments

For the latest information about developments related to Form W-4, such as legislation enacted after it was published, go to *www.irs.gov/FormW4*.

Purpose of Form

Complete Form W-4 so that your employer can withhold the correct federal income tax from your pay. If too little is withheld, you will generally owe tax when you file your tax return and may owe a penalty. If too much is withheld, you will generally be due a refund. Complete a new Form W-4 when changes to your personal or financial situation would change the entries on the form. For more information on withholding and when you must furnish a new Form W-4, see Pub. 505, Tax Withholding and Estimated Tax.

Exemption from withholding. You may claim exemption from withholding for 2022 if you meet both of the following conditions: you had no federal income tax liability in 2021 **and** you expect to have no federal income tax liability in 2022. You had no federal income tax liability in 2021 if (1) your total tax on line 24 on your 2021 Form 1040 or 1040-SR is zero (or less than the sum of lines 27a, 28, 29, and 30), or (2) you were not required to file a return because your income was below the filing threshold for your correct filing status. If you claim exemption, you will have no income tax withheld from your paycheck and may owe taxes and penalties when you file your 2022 tax return. To claim exemption from withholding, certify that you meet both of the conditions above by writing "Exempt" on Form W-4 in the space below Step 4(c). Then, complete Steps 1(a), 1(b), and 5. Do not complete any other steps. You will need to submit a new Form W-4 by February 15, 2023.

Your privacy. If you prefer to limit information provided in Steps 2 through 4, use the online estimator, which will also increase accuracy.

As an alternative to the estimator: if you have concerns with Step 2(c), you may choose Step 2(b); if you have concerns with Step 4(a), you may enter an additional amount you want withheld per pay period in Step 4(c). If this is the only job in your household, you may instead check the box in Step 2(c), which will increase your withholding and significantly reduce your paycheck (often by thousands of dollars over the year).

When to use the estimator. Consider using the estimator at *www.irs.gov/W4App* if you:

1. Expect to work only part of the year;
2. Have dividend or capital gain income, or are subject to additional taxes, such as Additional Medicare Tax;
3. Have self-employment income (see below); or
4. Prefer the most accurate withholding for multiple job situations.

Self-employment. Generally, you will owe both income and self-employment taxes on any self-employment income you receive separate from the wages you receive as an employee. If you want to pay these taxes through withholding from your wages, use the estimator at *www.irs.gov/W4App* to figure the amount to have withheld.

Nonresident alien. If you're a nonresident alien, see Notice 1392, Supplemental Form W-4 Instructions for Nonresident Aliens, before completing this form.

Specific Instructions

Step 1(c). Check your anticipated filing status. This will determine the standard deduction and tax rates used to compute your withholding.

Step 2. Use this step if you (1) have more than one job at the same time, or (2) are married filing jointly and you and your spouse both work.

Option **(a)** most accurately calculates the additional tax you need to have withheld, while option **(b)** does so with a little less accuracy.

If you (and your spouse) have a total of only two jobs, you may instead check the box in option **(c)**. The box must also be checked on the Form W-4 for the other job. If the box is checked, the standard deduction and tax brackets will be cut in half for each job to calculate withholding. This option is roughly accurate for jobs with similar pay; otherwise, more tax than necessary may be withheld, and this extra amount will be larger the greater the difference in pay is between the two jobs.

Multiple jobs. *Complete Steps 3 through 4(b) on only one Form W-4. Withholding will be most accurate if you do this on the Form W-4 for the highest paying job.*

Step 3. This step provides instructions for determining the amount of the child tax credit and the credit for other dependents that you may be able to claim when you file your tax return. To qualify for the child tax credit, the child must be under age 17 as of December 31, must be your dependent who generally lives with you for more than half the year, and must have the required social security number. You may be able to claim a credit for other dependents for whom a child tax credit can't be claimed, such as an older child or a qualifying relative. For additional eligibility requirements for these credits, see Pub. 501, Dependents, Standard Deduction, and Filing Information. You can also include **other tax credits** for which you are eligible in this step, such as the foreign tax credit and the education tax credits. To do so, add an estimate of the amount for the year to your credits for dependents and enter the total amount in Step 3. Including these credits will increase your paycheck and reduce the amount of any refund you may receive when you file your tax return.

Step 4 (optional).

Step 4(a). Enter in this step the total of your other estimated income for the year, if any. You shouldn't include income from any jobs or self-employment. If you complete Step 4(a), you likely won't have to make estimated tax payments for that income. If you prefer to pay estimated tax rather than having tax on other income withheld from your paycheck, see Form 1040-ES, Estimated Tax for Individuals.

Step 4(b). Enter in this step the amount from the Deductions Worksheet, line 5, if you expect to claim deductions other than the basic standard deduction on your 2022 tax return and want to reduce your withholding to account for these deductions. This includes both itemized deductions and other deductions such as for student loan interest and IRAs.

Step 4(c). Enter in this step any additional tax you want withheld from your pay **each pay period**, including any amounts from the Multiple Jobs Worksheet, line 4. Entering an amount here will reduce your paycheck and will either increase your refund or reduce any amount of tax that you owe.

Step 2(b)—Multiple Jobs Worksheet *(Keep for your records.)*

If you choose the option in Step 2(b) on Form W-4, complete this worksheet (which calculates the total extra tax for all jobs) on **only ONE** Form W-4. Withholding will be most accurate if you complete the worksheet and enter the result on the Form W-4 for the highest paying job.

Note: If more than one job has annual wages of more than $120,000 or there are more than three jobs, see Pub. 505 for additional tables; or, you can use the online withholding estimator at *www.irs.gov/W4App*.

1 **Two jobs.** If you have two jobs or you're married filing jointly and you and your spouse each have one job, find the amount from the appropriate table on page 4. Using the "Higher Paying Job" row and the "Lower Paying Job" column, find the value at the intersection of the two household salaries and enter that value on line 1. Then, **skip** to line 3 . . . . 1 $ ________

2 **Three jobs.** If you and/or your spouse have three jobs at the same time, complete lines 2a, 2b, and 2c below. Otherwise, skip to line 3.

a Find the amount from the appropriate table on page 4 using the annual wages from the highest paying job in the "Higher Paying Job" row and the annual wages for your next highest paying job in the "Lower Paying Job" column. Find the value at the intersection of the two household salaries and enter that value on line 2a . . . . 2a $ ________

b Add the annual wages of the two highest paying jobs from line 2a together and use the total as the wages in the "Higher Paying Job" row and use the annual wages for your third job in the "Lower Paying Job" column to find the amount from the appropriate table on page 4 and enter this amount on line 2b . . . . 2b $ ________

c Add the amounts from lines 2a and 2b and enter the result on line 2c . . . . 2c $ ________

3 Enter the number of pay periods per year for the highest paying job. For example, if that job pays weekly, enter 52; if it pays every other week, enter 26; if it pays monthly, enter 12, etc. . . . . . . 3 ________

4 **Divide** the annual amount on line 1 or line 2c by the number of pay periods on line 3. Enter this amount here and in **Step 4(c)** of Form W-4 for the highest paying job (along with any other additional amount you want withheld) . . . . 4 $ ________

Step 4(b)—Deductions Worksheet *(Keep for your records.)*

1 Enter an estimate of your 2022 itemized deductions (from Schedule A (Form 1040)). Such deductions may include qualifying home mortgage interest, charitable contributions, state and local taxes (up to $10,000), and medical expenses in excess of 7.5% of your income . . . . 1 $ ________

2 Enter:
- $25,900 if you're married filing jointly or qualifying widow(er)
- $19,400 if you're head of household
- $12,950 if you're single or married filing separately

. . . . 2 $ ________

3 If line 1 is greater than line 2, subtract line 2 from line 1 and enter the result here. If line 2 is greater than line 1, enter "-0-" . . . . 3 $ ________

4 Enter an estimate of your student loan interest, deductible IRA contributions, and certain other adjustments (from Part II of Schedule 1 (Form 1040)). See Pub. 505 for more information . . . . 4 $ ________

5 **Add** lines 3 and 4. Enter the result here and in **Step 4(b)** of Form W-4 . . . . 5 $ ________

Form W-4 (2022) Page **4**

Married Filing Jointly or Qualifying Widow(er)

Higher Paying Job Annual Taxable Wage & Salary	Lower Paying Job Annual Taxable Wage & Salary											
	$0 - 9,999	$10,000 - 19,999	$20,000 - 29,999	$30,000 - 39,999	$40,000 - 49,999	$50,000 - 59,999	$60,000 - 69,999	$70,000 - 79,999	$80,000 - 89,999	$90,000 - 99,999	$100,000 - 109,999	$110,000 - 120,000
$0 - 9,999	$0	$110	$850	$860	$1,020	$1,020	$1,020	$1,020	$1,020	$1,020	$1,770	$1,870
$10,000 - 19,999	110	1,110	1,860	2,060	2,220	2,220	2,220	2,220	2,220	2,970	3,970	4,070
$20,000 - 29,999	850	1,860	2,800	3,000	3,160	3,160	3,160	3,160	3,910	4,910	5,910	6,010
$30,000 - 39,999	860	2,060	3,000	3,200	3,360	3,360	3,360	4,110	5,110	6,110	7,110	7,210
$40,000 - 49,999	1,020	2,220	3,160	3,360	3,520	3,520	4,270	5,270	6,270	7,270	8,270	8,370
$50,000 - 59,999	1,020	2,220	3,160	3,360	3,520	4,270	5,270	6,270	7,270	8,270	9,270	9,370
$60,000 - 69,999	1,020	2,220	3,160	3,360	4,270	5,270	6,270	7,270	8,270	9,270	10,270	10,370
$70,000 - 79,999	1,020	2,220	3,160	4,110	5,270	6,270	7,270	8,270	9,270	10,270	11,270	11,370
$80,000 - 99,999	1,020	2,820	4,760	5,960	7,120	8,120	9,120	10,120	11,120	12,120	13,150	13,450
$100,000 - 149,999	1,870	4,070	6,010	7,210	8,370	9,370	10,510	11,710	12,910	14,110	15,310	15,600
$150,000 - 239,999	2,040	4,440	6,580	7,980	9,340	10,540	11,740	12,940	14,140	15,340	16,540	16,830
$240,000 - 259,999	2,040	4,440	6,580	7,980	9,340	10,540	11,740	12,940	14,140	15,340	16,540	17,590
$260,000 - 279,999	2,040	4,440	6,580	7,980	9,340	10,540	11,740	12,940	14,140	16,100	18,100	19,190
$280,000 - 299,999	2,040	4,440	6,580	7,980	9,340	10,540	11,740	13,700	15,700	17,700	19,700	20,790
$300,000 - 319,999	2,040	4,440	6,580	7,980	9,340	11,300	13,300	15,300	17,300	19,300	21,300	22,390
$320,000 - 364,999	2,100	5,300	8,240	10,440	12,600	14,600	16,600	18,600	20,600	22,600	24,870	26,260
$365,000 - 524,999	2,970	6,470	9,710	12,210	14,670	16,970	19,270	21,570	23,870	26,170	28,470	29,870
$525,000 and over	3,140	6,840	10,280	12,980	15,640	18,140	20,640	23,140	25,640	28,140	30,640	32,240

Single or Married Filing Separately

Higher Paying Job Annual Taxable Wage & Salary	Lower Paying Job Annual Taxable Wage & Salary											
	$0 - 9,999	$10,000 - 19,999	$20,000 - 29,999	$30,000 - 39,999	$40,000 - 49,999	$50,000 - 59,999	$60,000 - 69,999	$70,000 - 79,999	$80,000 - 89,999	$90,000 - 99,999	$100,000 - 109,999	$110,000 - 120,000
$0 - 9,999	$400	$930	$1,020	$1,020	$1,250	$1,870	$1,870	$1,870	$1,870	$1,970	$2,040	$2,040
$10,000 - 19,999	930	1,570	1,660	1,890	2,890	3,510	3,510	3,510	3,610	3,810	3,880	3,880
$20,000 - 29,999	1,020	1,660	1,990	2,990	3,990	4,610	4,610	4,710	4,910	5,110	5,180	5,180
$30,000 - 39,999	1,020	1,890	2,990	3,990	4,990	5,610	5,710	5,910	6,110	6,310	6,380	6,380
$40,000 - 59,999	1,870	3,510	4,610	5,610	6,680	7,500	7,700	7,900	8,100	8,300	8,370	8,370
$60,000 - 79,999	1,870	3,510	4,680	5,880	7,080	7,900	8,100	8,300	8,500	8,700	8,970	9,770
$80,000 - 99,999	1,940	3,780	5,080	6,280	7,480	8,300	8,500	8,700	9,100	10,100	10,970	11,770
$100,000 - 124,999	2,040	3,880	5,180	6,380	7,580	8,400	9,140	10,140	11,140	12,140	13,040	14,140
$125,000 - 149,999	2,040	3,880	5,180	6,520	8,520	10,140	11,140	12,140	13,320	14,620	15,790	16,890
$150,000 - 174,999	2,040	4,420	6,520	8,520	10,520	12,170	13,470	14,770	16,070	17,370	18,540	19,640
$175,000 - 199,999	2,720	5,360	7,460	9,630	11,930	13,860	15,160	16,460	17,760	19,060	20,230	21,330
$200,000 - 249,999	2,970	5,920	8,310	10,610	12,910	14,840	16,140	17,440	18,740	20,040	21,210	22,310
$250,000 - 399,999	2,970	5,920	8,310	10,610	12,910	14,840	16,140	17,440	18,740	20,040	21,210	22,310
$400,000 - 449,999	2,970	5,920	8,310	10,610	12,910	14,840	16,140	17,440	18,740	20,040	21,210	22,470
$450,000 and over	3,140	6,290	8,880	11,380	13,880	16,010	17,510	19,010	20,510	22,010	23,380	24,680

Head of Household

Higher Paying Job Annual Taxable Wage & Salary	Lower Paying Job Annual Taxable Wage & Salary											
	$0 - 9,999	$10,000 - 19,999	$20,000 - 29,999	$30,000 - 39,999	$40,000 - 49,999	$50,000 - 59,999	$60,000 - 69,999	$70,000 - 79,999	$80,000 - 89,999	$90,000 - 99,999	$100,000 - 109,999	$110,000 - 120,000
$0 - 9,999	$0	$760	$910	$1,020	$1,020	$1,020	$1,190	$1,870	$1,870	$1,870	$2,040	$2,040
$10,000 - 19,999	760	1,820	2,110	2,220	2,220	2,390	3,390	4,070	4,070	4,240	4,440	4,440
$20,000 - 29,999	910	2,110	2,400	2,510	2,680	3,680	4,680	5,360	5,530	5,730	5,930	5,930
$30,000 - 39,999	1,020	2,220	2,510	2,790	3,790	4,790	5,790	6,640	6,840	7,040	7,240	7,240
$40,000 - 59,999	1,020	2,240	3,530	4,640	5,640	6,780	7,980	8,860	9,060	9,260	9,460	9,460
$60,000 - 79,999	1,870	4,070	5,360	6,610	7,810	9,010	10,210	11,090	11,290	11,490	11,690	12,170
$80,000 - 99,999	1,870	4,210	5,700	7,010	8,210	9,410	10,610	11,490	11,690	12,380	13,370	14,170
$100,000 - 124,999	2,040	4,440	5,930	7,240	8,440	9,640	10,860	12,540	13,540	14,540	15,540	16,480
$125,000 - 149,999	2,040	4,440	5,930	7,240	8,860	10,860	12,860	14,540	15,540	16,830	18,130	19,230
$150,000 - 174,999	2,040	4,460	6,750	8,860	10,860	12,860	15,000	16,980	18,280	19,580	20,880	21,980
$175,000 - 199,999	2,720	5,920	8,210	10,320	12,600	14,900	17,200	19,180	20,480	21,780	23,080	24,180
$200,000 - 449,999	2,970	6,470	9,060	11,480	13,780	16,080	18,380	20,360	21,660	22,960	24,250	25,360
$450,000 and over	3,140	6,840	9,630	12,250	14,750	17,250	19,750	21,930	23,430	24,930	26,420	27,730

LO 9.3

11. Kana is a single wage earner with no dependents and taxable income of $168,700 in 2022. Her 2021 taxable income was $155,000 and tax liability was $30,500. Calculate Kana's 2022 income tax liability and Kana's 2022 minimum required annual payment necessary to avoid penalty. (Note: this question requires the use of the tax rate schedules in Appendix A):

LO 9.4

12. Drew Fogelman operates a small business and his payroll records for the second quarter of 2022 reflect the following:

Employee	*Matt D.*	*Jack F.*	*Avery F.*	*Tiffany Y.*
Gross wages	$3,000.00	$1,400.00	$1,800.00	$4,200.00
Federal income tax withheld	45.00	18.00	25.00	191.00
FICA taxes	459.00	214.20	275.40	642.60

Drew's employee identification number is 34-4321321 and his business is located at 732 Nob Hill Blvd. in Yakima, WA 98902. Drew is eligible to pay his withholding at the time he files his quarterly Form 941. Complete pages 1 and 2 of Form 941 located on Pages 9-63 and 9-64 for Drew for the second quarter of 2022.

LO 9.4

13. Each of the three companies below have provided the amount of income taxes withheld plus the FICA taxes attributable to wages paid from their payroll records. Use this information to determine (1) what deposit schedule should each company be on and (2) what form should each company file (i.e., 941 or 944).

a. Pequeño Negocio Inc. has about four employees at any time during the year. The payroll records from 2020 and 2021 report the following:

Q1 2020	*Q2 2020*	*Q3 2020*	*Q4 2020*
$12,091	$10,138	$10,539	$12,064

Q1 2021	*Q2 2021*	*Q3 2021*	*Q4 2021*
$10,849	$12,213	$11,385	$12,782

b. Meniscus Corporation payroll records from 2020 and 2021 report the following:

Q1 2020	*Q2 2020*	*Q3 2020*	*Q4 2020*
$11,119	$12,023	$11,443	$11,194

Q1 2021	*Q2 2021*	*Q3 2021*	*Q4 2021*
$11,853	$13,868	$14,171	$16,782

c. Xochitl operates a small business and takes on part-time employees at certain times of the year. Her payroll records from 2020 and 2021 report the following:

Q1 2020	*Q2 2020*	*Q3 2020*	*Q4 2020*
$0	$0	$260	$312

Q1 2021	*Q2 2021*	*Q3 2021*	*Q4 2021*
$10	$0	$167	$328

LO 9.4

14. Consider each of the following employment tax deposit scenarios:
    a. Based on activity in the lookback period, Hugo Corp is on a semiweekly deposit schedule for income and employment taxes in 2022. In the weekly payroll period ending Sunday, March 13, 2022, Hugo paid executive bonuses that triggered income tax withheld and FICA taxes of $134,649 for that pay period. On what date is Hugo's next required deposit?
    b. Springs Corp. is a semiweekly depositor and processes a payroll on Thursday, September 22, 2022. The resulting tax deposit of income tax withholding and FICA taxes of $7,800 is due on what date?
    c. Rosarita Company is a semiweekly depositor and processes a payroll on Monday, April 11, 2022. The resulting tax deposit of income tax withholding and FICA taxes of $7,800 is due on what date?
    d. Encinitas Inc. is a new company and did not have any employees during the previous quarters. The first payroll is processed on August 9, 2022. The resulting tax deposit of income tax withholding and FICA taxes of $6,700 is due on what date?

LO 9.5

15. For each of the following payments, indicate the form that should be used to report the payment:
    a. Interest of $400 paid by a bank
    b. Payment of $400 in dividends by a corporation to a shareholder
    c. Periodic payments from a retirement plan
    d. Salary as president of the company
    e. Las Vegas keno winnings of $25,000
    f. Payments made to a non-employee

950122

Form **941 for 2022: Employer's QUARTERLY Federal Tax Return**
(Rev. June 2022) Department of the Treasury — Internal Revenue Service
OMB No. 1545-0029

Employer identification number (EIN) ☐☐ – ☐☐☐☐☐☐☐

Name *(not your trade name)*

Trade name *(if any)*

Address
Number Street Suite or room number
City State ZIP code
Foreign country name Foreign province/county Foreign postal code

Report for this Quarter of 2022
(Check one.)

- ☐ **1:** January, February, March
- ☐ **2:** April, May, June
- ☐ **3:** July, August, September
- ☐ **4:** October, November, December

Go to *www.irs.gov/Form941* for instructions and the latest information.

Read the separate instructions before you complete Form 941. Type or print within the boxes.

Part 1: Answer these questions for this quarter.

1	**Number of employees who received wages, tips, or other compensation for the pay period including:** ***June 12*** **(Quarter 2),** ***Sept. 12*** **(Quarter 3), or** ***Dec. 12*** **(Quarter 4)**			1	
2	**Wages, tips, and other compensation**			2	.
3	**Federal income tax withheld from wages, tips, and other compensation**			3	.
4	**If no wages, tips, and other compensation are subject to social security or Medicare tax**			☐	**Check and go to line 6.**

		Column 1		Column 2
5a	**Taxable social security wages***	.	× 0.124 =	.
5a	(i) **Qualified sick leave wages***	.	× 0.062 =	.
5a	(ii) **Qualified family leave wages***	.	× 0.062 =	.
5b	**Taxable social security tips**	.	× 0.124 =	.
5c	**Taxable Medicare wages & tips**	.	× 0.029 =	.
5d	**Taxable wages & tips subject to Additional Medicare Tax withholding**	.	× 0.009 =	.

Include taxable qualified sick and family leave wages paid in this quarter of 2022 for leave taken after March 31, 2021, and before October 1, 2021, on line 5a. Use lines 5a(i) and 5a(ii)* ***only* *for taxable qualified sick and family leave wages paid in this quarter of 2022 for leave taken after March 31, 2020, and before April 1, 2021.*

5e	**Total social security and Medicare taxes.** Add Column 2 from lines 5a, 5a(i), 5a(ii), 5b, 5c, and 5d	5e	.
5f	**Section 3121(q) Notice and Demand—Tax due on unreported tips** (see instructions)	5f	.
6	**Total taxes before adjustments.** Add lines 3, 5e, and 5f	6	.
7	**Current quarter's adjustment for fractions of cents**	7	.
8	**Current quarter's adjustment for sick pay**	8	.
9	**Current quarter's adjustments for tips and group-term life insurance**	9	.
10	**Total taxes after adjustments.** Combine lines 6 through 9	10	.
11a	**Qualified small business payroll tax credit for increasing research activities.** Attach Form 8974	11a	.
11b	**Nonrefundable portion of credit for qualified sick and family leave wages for leave taken before April 1, 2021**	11b	.
11c	**Reserved for future use**	11c	.

Next ▶

▶ **You MUST complete all three pages of Form 941 and SIGN it.**

951222

Name *(not your trade name)* | Employer identification number (EIN) –

Part 1: Answer these questions for this quarter. *(continued)*

11d	**Nonrefundable portion of credit for qualified sick and family leave wages for leave taken after March 31, 2021, and before October 1, 2021**	11d	.
11e	**Reserved for future use**	11e	.
11f	**Reserved for future use**		
11g	**Total nonrefundable credits.** Add lines 11a, 11b, and 11d	11g	.
12	**Total taxes after adjustments and nonrefundable credits.** Subtract line 11g from line 10	12	.
13a	**Total deposits for this quarter, including overpayment applied from a prior quarter and overpayments applied from Form 941-X, 941-X (PR), 944-X, or 944-X (SP) filed in the current quarter**	13a	.
13b	**Reserved for future use**	13b	.
13c	**Refundable portion of credit for qualified sick and family leave wages for leave taken before April 1, 2021**	13c	.
13d	**Reserved for future use**	13d	.
13e	**Refundable portion of credit for qualified sick and family leave wages for leave taken after March 31, 2021, and before October 1, 2021**	13e	.
13f	**Reserved for future use**	13f	.
13g	**Total deposits and refundable credits.** Add lines 13a, 13c, and 13e	13g	.
13h	**Reserved for future use**	13h	.
13i	**Reserved for future use**	13i	.
14	**Balance due.** If line 12 is more than line 13g, enter the difference and see instructions	14	.

15 **Overpayment.** If line 13g is more than line 12, enter the difference [.] Check one: ☐ Apply to next return. ☐ Send a refund.

Part 2: Tell us about your deposit schedule and tax liability for this quarter.

If you're unsure about whether you're a monthly schedule depositor or a semiweekly schedule depositor, see section 11 of Pub. 15.

16 Check one:

☐ **Line 12 on this return is less than $2,500 or line 12 on the return for the prior quarter was less than $2,500, and you didn't incur a $100,000 next-day deposit obligation during the current quarter.** If line 12 for the prior quarter was less than $2,500 but line 12 on this return is $100,000 or more, you must provide a record of your federal tax liability. If you're a monthly schedule depositor, complete the deposit schedule below; if you're a semiweekly schedule depositor, attach Schedule B (Form 941). Go to Part 3.

☐ **You were a monthly schedule depositor for the entire quarter.** Enter your tax liability for each month and total liability for the quarter, then go to Part 3.

Tax liability:	
Month 1	.
Month 2	.
Month 3	.
Total liability for quarter	.

Total must equal line 12.

☐ **You were a semiweekly schedule depositor for any part of this quarter.** Complete Schedule B (Form 941), Report of Tax Liability for Semiweekly Schedule Depositors, and attach it to Form 941. Go to Part 3.

► **You MUST complete all three pages of Form 941 and SIGN it.**

Next ■►

Form **941** (Rev. 6-2022)

LO 9.5

16. Philcon Corporation created the following 2022 employee payroll report for one of its employees.

Philcon Corporation **Employee Payroll Report**
2022

EIN: 12-3456789
PO Box 4563
Anchorage, AK 99508

Emp ID	Name	Wage Type	Date	Period Gross Pay	YTD Gross Pay	401k Contrib	Taxable Wages	YTD Tax Wages	FIT w/h	SS Tax w/h	Med Tax w/h	Net Pay
A1246G	Louise Alianait	Monthly	1/31/2022	12,175.00	12,175.00	487.00	11,688.00	11,688.00	2,032.48	754.85	176.54	8,724.13
A1246G	Louise Alianait	Monthly	2/28/2022	12,175.00	24,350.00	487.00	11,688.00	23,376.00	2,032.48	754.85	176.54	8,724.13
A1246G	Louise Alianait	Bonus	3/15/2022	6,400.00	30,750.00	-	6,400.00	29,776.00	1,408.00	396.80	92.80	4,502.40
A1246G	Louise Alianait	Monthly	3/31/2022	12,175.00	42,925.00	487.00	11,688.00	41,464.00	2,032.48	754.85	176.54	8,724.13
A1246G	Louise Alianait	Monthly	4/30/2022	12,175.00	55,100.00	487.00	11,688.00	53,152.00	2,032.48	754.85	176.54	8,724.13
A1246G	Louise Alianait	Monthly	5/31/2022	12,175.00	67,275.00	487.00	11,688.00	64,840.00	2,032.48	754.85	176.54	8,724.13
A1246G	Louise Alianait	Monthly	6/30/2022	12,175.00	79,450.00	487.00	11,688.00	76,528.00	2,032.48	754.85	176.54	8,724.13
A1246G	Louise Alianait	Monthly	7/31/2022	12,175.00	91,625.00	487.00	11,688.00	88,216.00	2,032.48	754.85	176.54	8,724.13
A1246G	Louise Alianait	Monthly	8/31/2022	12,175.00	103,800.00	487.00	11,688.00	99,904.00	2,032.48	754.85	176.54	8,724.13
A1246G	Louise Alianait	Monthly	9/30/2022	12,175.00	115,975.00	487.00	11,688.00	111,592.00	2,032.48	754.85	176.54	8,724.13
A1246G	Louise Alianait	Monthly	10/31/2022	12,175.00	128,150.00	487.00	11,688.00	123,280.00	2,032.48	754.85	176.54	8,724.13
A1246G	Louise Alianait	Monthly	11/30/2022	12,175.00	140,325.00	487.00	11,688.00	134,968.00	2,032.48	754.85	176.54	8,724.13
A1246G	Louise Alianait	Monthly	12/31/2022	12,175.00	152,500.00	487.00	11,688.00	146,656.00	2,032.48	413.85	176.54	9,065.13
A1246G	Louise Alianait	YTD Total		152,500.00		5,844.00	146,656.00		25,797.76	9,114.00	2,211.28	109,532.99

Employee Mailing Address:
Louise Alianait
5471 East Tudor Road
Anchorage, AK 99508
SSN: 545-64-7745

a. Complete the following Form W-2 for Louise Alianait from Philcon Corporation.

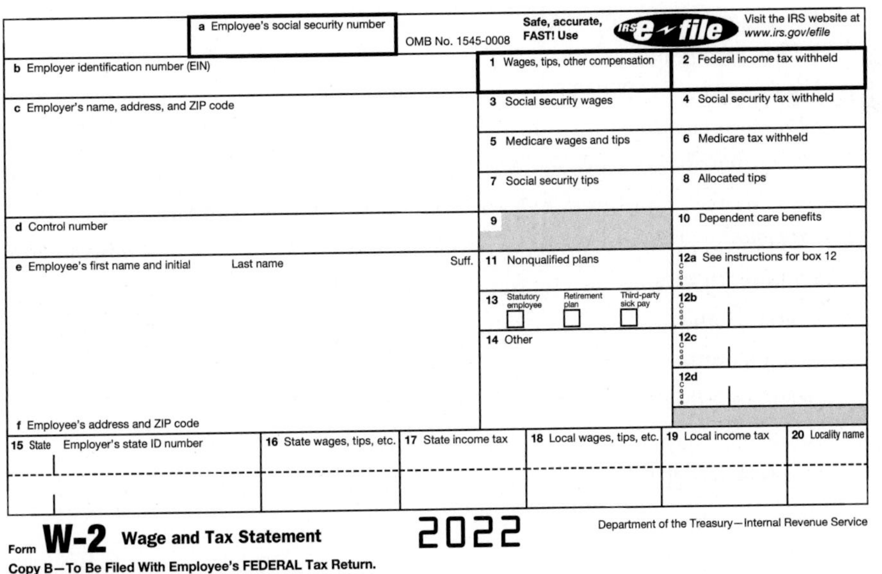
a Employee's social security number
OMB No. 1545-0008 Safe, accurate, FAST! Use IRS e-file Visit the IRS website at www.irs.gov/efile

b Employer identification number (EIN)
1 Wages, tips, other compensation
2 Federal income tax withheld
c Employer's name, address, and ZIP code
3 Social security wages
4 Social security tax withheld
5 Medicare wages and tips
6 Medicare tax withheld
7 Social security tips
8 Allocated tips
d Control number
9
10 Dependent care benefits
e Employee's first name and initial Last name Suff.
11 Nonqualified plans
12a See instructions for box 12
13 Statutory employee Retirement plan Third-party sick pay
12b
14 Other
12c
12d
f Employee's address and ZIP code
15 State Employer's state ID number
16 State wages, tips, etc.
17 State income tax
18 Local wages, tips, etc.
19 Local income tax
20 Locality name

Form **W-2** Wage and Tax Statement 2022
Department of the Treasury—Internal Revenue Service
Copy B—To Be Filed With Employee's FEDERAL Tax Return.
This information is being furnished to the Internal Revenue Service.

b. Philcon Corporation also paid $1,200 to Ralph Imiq for presenting a management seminar. Ralph is not a Philcon employee and lives at 1455 Raspberry Road, Anchorage, AK 99508, and his Social Security number is 475-45-3226. Complete the Form 1099-NEC located on the next page for the payment to Ralph from Philcon Corporation.

☐ CORRECTED (if checked)

PAYER'S name, street address, city or town, state or province, country, ZIP or foreign postal code, and telephone no.			OMB No. 1545-0116 Form **1099-NEC** (Rev. January 2022) For calendar year 20____	**Nonemployee Compensation**
PAYER'S TIN	RECIPIENT'S TIN	1 Nonemployee compensation $		**Copy B** **For Recipient** This is important tax information and is being furnished to the IRS. If you are required to file a return, a negligence penalty or other sanction may be imposed on you if this income is taxable and the IRS determines that it has not been reported.
RECIPIENT'S name Street address (including apt. no.) City or town, state or province, country, and ZIP or foreign postal code		2 Payer made direct sales totaling $5,000 or more of consumer products to recipient for resale ☐ 3 **4 Federal income tax withheld** $		
Account number (see instructions)		5 State tax withheld $ $	6 State/Payer's state no.	7 State income $ $

Form **1099-NEC** (Rev. 1-2022) (keep for your records) www.irs.gov/Form1099NEC Department of the Treasury - Internal Revenue Service

LO 9.6 17. Rebecca is an employer with three employees, Theodore, Roy, and Nathan. Theodore's 2022 wages are $46,200, Roy's wages are $14,600, and Nathan's wages are $4,500. The state unemployment tax rate is 5.4 percent. Calculate the following amounts for Rebecca:

a. FUTA tax before the state tax credit
b. State unemployment tax
c. FUTA tax after the state tax credit

LO 9.6 18. Your client has provided the following annual payroll summary for 2022:

Premium Court Corporation
1 First Street, NE
Washington, DC 20543
EIN: 44-1112223
December 31, 2022

			Gross Wages ($)		
Employee	*Q1*	*Q2*	*Q3*	*Q4*	*YTD*
Sammy Lightning	-	6,700	-	-	6,700
Clark Thomas	6,000	6,000	6,000	6,000	24,000
Rob Johnson	7,800	6,700	-	-	14,500
Stephanie Briar	20,000	20,000	20,000	20,000	80,000
Sonya Citimayor	8,000	8,000	8,000	8,000	32,000
Breck Cavendish	2,400	2,400	1,200	-	6,000
Ellen Caging	-	6,700	-	-	6,700
Neal Orbach	-	2,100	2,200	2,200	6,500
Amy Barry	5,700	5,700	5,700	5,700	22,800
	49,900	64,300	43,100	41,900	199,200

Premium Court pays District of Columbia (DC) unemployment tax and makes the required deposits of both federal and state unemployment taxes on a timely basis.

DC applies a rate of 0.7 percent to the first $9,000 of wages per employee and thus Premium Court paid state unemployment taxes of $496.30 to DC in 2022. DC is not subject to a credit reduction and there was no overpayment of FUTA in 2021. Use this information to complete Parts 1-5 (as necessary) of Form 940 on Pages 9-69 and 9-70.

LO 9.7

19. In 2022, Kwon Ah Bo is an employee at Sungsam Industries. Kwon is paid wages of $50,000 and is also a participant in the Sungsam 401(k) plan. Kwon contributes 6 percent of her salary to the 401(k) and Sungsam matches the first 3 percent of employee contributions.
    a. Describe how Kwon will be taxed on her 6 percent contribution to the 401(k) plan in 2022.
    b. Describe how Kwon will be taxed on the 3 percent match provided by Kwon's employer and contributed to the 401k plan.
    c. Compute the amount of wages subject to (i) income tax and (ii) FICA taxes
    d. Describe how Kwon will be taxed on withdrawals from the 401(k) assuming she reaches the age of 59 and one-half.

LO 9.7

20. Determine the 2022 maximum contributions to a qualified plan for each of the following taxpayers (assume no restrictions for highly-compensated employees):
    a. Vlad Zilinksy is paid wages of $150,000 and may contribute 20 percent of his wages and his employer matches the first 5 percent of employee contributions to the company profit sharing plan.
    b. Elina Kurlyenko is paid wages of $300,000 and may contribute toward a defined contributions plan through her employer.
    c. Oksana Biel is permitted to contribute up to 10 percent of her $30,000 wage to a qualified defined contribution plan.

LO 9.8

21. Telly, age 38, has a $140,000 IRA with Blue Mutual Fund. He has read good things about the management of Green Mutual Fund, so he opens a Green Fund IRA. Telly asked for a distribution rollover and received his balance from the Blue Fund on May 1, 2022. Telly opted to have no withholding on the distribution.
    a. What amount will Telly receive from the Blue Fund IRA?
    b. What amount must Telly contribute to the Green Fund IRA to avoid having taxable income and penalties for early withdrawal?
    c. When is the last day Telly can roll over the amount received into the Green Fund IRA and avoid taxation in the current year, assuming no unusual circumstances?
    d. What amount would Telly receive if the distribution were from his employer's qualified retirement plan?

LO 9.8

22. Allen (age 32) takes a distribution of $20,000 from his traditional IRA account which he plans to deposit into an IRA with a different bank. During the 60-day rollover period, he gambles and loses the entire IRA balance. What income and/or penalties must he show on his tax return related to the failed rollover?

Form **940 for 2022: Employer's Annual Federal Unemployment (FUTA) Tax Return** 850113

Department of the Treasury — Internal Revenue Service OMB No. 1545-0028

Employer identification number (EIN) ☐☐ – ☐☐☐☐☐☐☐

Name *(not your trade name)*

Trade name *(if any)*

Address

Number Street Suite or room number

City State ZIP code

Foreign country name Foreign province/county Foreign postal code

Type of Return
(Check all that apply.)

☐ **a.** Amended

☐ **b.** Successor employer

☐ **c.** No payments to employees in 2022

☐ **d.** Final: Business closed or stopped paying wages

Go to *www.irs.gov/Form940* for instructions and the latest information.

Read the separate instructions before you complete this form. Please type or print within the boxes.

Part 1: Tell us about your return. If any line does NOT apply, leave it blank. See instructions before completing Part 1.

1a	If you had to pay state unemployment tax in one state only, enter the state abbreviation .	1a	☐☐
1b	If you had to pay state unemployment tax in more than one state, you are a multi-state employer	1b	☐ Check here. Complete Schedule A (Form 940).
2	If you paid wages in a state that is subject to CREDIT REDUCTION	2	☐ Check here. Complete Schedule A (Form 940).

Part 2: Determine your FUTA tax before adjustments. If any line does NOT apply, leave it blank.

3 **Total payments to all employees** . . . . 3 ______ .

4 **Payments exempt from FUTA tax** . . . . 4 ______ .

Check all that apply: **4a** ☐ Fringe benefits **4c** ☐ Retirement/Pension **4e** ☐ Other
4b ☐ Group-term life insurance **4d** ☐ Dependent care

5 **Total of payments made to each employee in excess of $7,000** . . . . 5 ______ .

6 **Subtotal** (line 4 + line 5 = line 6) . . . . 6 ______ .

7 **Total taxable FUTA wages** (line 3 – line 6 = line 7). See instructions. . . . . 7 ______ .

8 **FUTA tax before adjustments** (line 7 x 0.006 = line 8) . . . . 8 ______ .

Part 3: Determine your adjustments. If any line does NOT apply, leave it blank.

9 **If ALL of the taxable FUTA wages you paid were excluded from state unemployment tax, multiply line 7 by 0.054** (line 7 × 0.054 = line 9). Go to line 12 . . . . 9 ______ .

10 **If SOME of the taxable FUTA wages you paid were excluded from state unemployment tax, OR you paid ANY state unemployment tax late** (after the due date for filing Form 940), complete the worksheet in the instructions. Enter the amount from line 7 of the worksheet . . 10 ______ .

11 **If credit reduction applies,** enter the total from Schedule A (Form 940) . . . . . 11 ______ .

Part 4: Determine your FUTA tax and balance due or overpayment. If any line does NOT apply, leave it blank.

12 **Total FUTA tax after adjustments** (lines 8 + 9 + 10 + 11 = line 12) . . . . . 12 ______ .

13 **FUTA tax deposited for the year, including any overpayment applied from a prior year** . 13 ______ .

14 **Balance due.** If line 12 is more than line 13, enter the excess on line 14.
- If line 14 is more than $500, you must deposit your tax.
- If line 14 is $500 or less, you may pay with this return. See instructions . . . . 14 ______ .

15 **Overpayment.** If line 13 is more than line 12, enter the excess on line 15 and check a box below 15 ______ .

You **MUST** complete both pages of this form and **SIGN** it. Check one: ☐ Apply to next return. ☐ Send a refund.

For Privacy Act and Paperwork Reduction Act Notice, see the back of the Payment Voucher. Cat. No. 11234O Form **940** (2022)

850212

Name *(not your trade name)*	Employer identification number (EIN) –

Part 5: Report your FUTA tax liability by quarter only if line 12 is more than $500. If not, go to Part 6.

16 **Report the amount of your FUTA tax liability for each quarter; do NOT enter the amount you deposited. If you had no liability for a quarter, leave the line blank.**

16a **1st quarter** (January 1 – March 31) . . . . **16a** [.]

16b **2nd quarter** (April 1 – June 30) . . . . **16b** [.]

16c **3rd quarter** (July 1 – September 30) . . . . **16c** [.]

16d **4th quarter** (October 1 – December 31) . . . . **16d** [.]

17 **Total tax liability for the year** (lines 16a + 16b + 16c + 16d = line 17) **17** [.] **Total must equal line 12.**

Part 6: May we speak with your third-party designee?

Do you want to allow an employee, a paid tax preparer, or another person to discuss this return with the IRS? See the instructions for details.

☐ **Yes.** Designee's name and phone number

Select a 5-digit personal identification number (PIN) to use when talking to the IRS.

☐ **No.**

Part 7: Sign here. You MUST complete both pages of this form and SIGN it.

Under penalties of perjury, I declare that I have examined this return, including accompanying schedules and statements, and to the best of my knowledge and belief, it is true, correct, and complete, and that no part of any payment made to a state unemployment fund claimed as a credit was, or is to be, deducted from the payments made to employees. Declaration of preparer (other than taxpayer) is based on all information of which preparer has any knowledge.

Sign your name here

Print your name here

Print your title here

Date / /

Best daytime phone

Paid Preparer Use Only

Check if you are self-employed ☐

Preparer's name

PTIN

Preparer's signature

Date / /

Firm's name (or yours if self-employed)

EIN

Address

Phone

City

State

ZIP code

GROUP 3:
WRITING ASSIGNMENT

ETHICS

Eric, your friend, received his Form W-2 from his employer (below) and has asked for your help. Eric's 2022 salary was $160,000 and he does not understand why the amounts in Boxes 1, 3, and 5 are not $160,000? His final paycheck for the year included the following information:

- Eric contributed 5 percent of his salary to the company 401(k) plan on a pre-tax basis.
- Eric is married with two children. He had $5,000 deducted from his wages for a Dependent Care Flexible Spending Account.
- Eric is enrolled in the company-sponsored life insurance program. He has a policy that provides a benefit of $150,000.
- Eric contributed the 2022 maximum amount to the Health Care Flexible Spending Account.

Using the information and Eric's Form W-2, prepare an email to Eric reconciling his salary of $160,000 to the amounts in Boxes 1, 3, and 5.

a Employee's social security number	791-51-4335
OMB No. 1545-0008	Safe, accurate, FAST! Use IRS e-file. Visit the IRS website at www.irs.gov/efile
b Employer identification number (EIN)	12-9456789
c Employer's name, address, and ZIP code	Ivy Technologies, Inc. 436 E. 35 Avenue Gary, IN 46409
d Control number	
e Employee's first name and initial / Last name / Suff.	Eric Hayes 555 E. 81st Street Merrillville, IN 46410
f Employee's address and ZIP code	
1 Wages, tips, other compensation	144,254.00
2 Federal income tax withheld	18,934.68
3 Social security wages	147,000.00
4 Social security tax withheld	9,114.00
5 Medicare wages and tips	152,254.00
6 Medicare tax withheld	2,207.68
7 Social security tips	
8 Allocated tips	
9	
10 Dependent care benefits	5,000.00
11 Nonqualified plans	
12a See instructions for box 12	D 8,000.00
12b	C 104.00
12c	DD 12,432.12
12d	
13 Statutory employee / Retirement plan / Third-party sick pay	Retirement plan: X
14 Other	

15 State	Employer's state ID number	16 State wages, tips, etc.	17 State income tax	18 Local wages, tips, etc.	19 Local income tax	20 Locality name
IN	00122231001	144,254.00	5,454.00	144,254.00	1,602.00	LAKE

Form **W-2** Wage and Tax Statement **2022**

Department of the Treasury—Internal Revenue Service

Copy B—To Be Filed With Employee's FEDERAL Tax Return.
This information is being furnished to the Internal Revenue Service.

GROUP 4:
PROBLEM

Ben Kenofee is a new company accountant for Richmond Industries, a small specialty manufacturing business located in The Woodlands, Texas. Ben is a new employee starting January 1, 2022 and expecting to earn wages of $55,000 and will be paid semimonthly. Ben's information is as follows:

- Name and address: Ben Kenofee, 2000 Berrywood Bend Drive, Apartment 3K, Tomball, TX 77375
- Social Security number: 613-27-7730
- Current year filing status: Married filing jointly

- Dependents: One child age 11.
- Spouse: Tala Kenofee, is self-employed and expects to earn $32,000 in 2022.
- Tala expects to pay *total* self-employment taxes of $4,521 and her self-employment income is eligible for a 2022 qualified business income deduction of $5,948 and will not be limited by taxable income or other limits.
- Ben and Tala expect to take the standard deduction and do not have any for AGI deductions in 2022.
- Both Ben and Tala are under age 65 and are not blind. They do not expect to claim any credits other than the child tax credit.
- Ben and Tala have a modest investment portfolio and expect to earn interest of $1,200 in 2022.

As the accountant for the company, Ben has access to the Richmond Industries Q4 payroll ledger for 2022 (but some of the information is missing and will need to be calculated):

Richmond Industries
4000 Research Forest Drive, The Woodlands, TX 77381
EIN: 56-8188324
Payroll Report
10-1-2022 to 12-31-2022

	Current Quarter				YTD			
Employee	Gross wages	FIT W/H	SS W/H	Medicare W/H	Gross wages	FIT W/H	SS W/H	Medicare W/H
Hannah Richmond 312-49-0025	40,000.00	8,800.00	1,674.00	580.00	160,000.00	35,200.00	9,114.00	2,320.00
Daniel Glover 429-97-7757	7,000.00	700.00	434.00	101.50	28,000.00	2,800.00	1,736.00	406.00
Jeff Proust 192-45-5518	5,800.00	696.00	359.60	84.10	6,430.00	734.00	398.66	93.24
Jane Thor 577-14-6389	-	-	-	-	14,300.00	2,150.00	886.60	207.35
Wilma Wildman 745-45-4641	1,200.00	232.00	74.40	17.40	15,600.00	3,016.00	967.20	226.20
Ben Kenofee 613-27-7730	13,750.00	?	852.50	199.38	55,000.00	?	3,410.00	797.50
Totals	67,750.00	?	3,394.50	982.38	279,330.00	?	16,512.46	4,050.29

Note that Ben's information on income tax withholding should be compiled using the answers from part b. Assume that Richmond pays the exact amount of their tax deposits each quarter and thus does not have overpayments or underpayments from the previous quarter. Richmond does not offer healthcare or a qualified retirement plan to its employees.

Requirements:

a. Prepare Ben's Form W-4 for 2022. Tala will be making estimated payments to cover her share of income taxes, but Ben will reflect the effects of her self-employment income on his W-4 like a second job to reduce the chances that he will be underwithheld. Ignore the for AGI deduction of one-half of Tala's self-employment taxes for purposes of this part.
b. Ben receives his first semimonthly paycheck for gross wages of $2,291.66 on January 15, 2022. Using the W-4 prepared in part a. and the percentage method for withholding, calculate Ben's income tax withholding on his first paycheck. Use Worksheet 4 from Appendix C to assist you.

c. Prepare the 2022 Estimated Tax Worksheet of Form 1040-ES to determine Tala's required annual required payment to avoid penalty and first quarter payment amount. Consider the following when completing this part:
   - Line 1: Total AGI will include her expected AGI plus Ben's wages
   - Lines 7 and 11b: Do not reflect any child tax credits
   - Line 12b: Prior year tax liability was $10,000.
   - Assume that withholding for Ben's wages is equal to the withholding calculated in part b above, multiplied by 24 pay periods.
   - There were no prior year overpayments applied to this year's first quarter payment.

d. Prepare Part 1 of Form 941 for Richmond Industries for the fourth quarter of 2022. Assume Richmond is a monthly depositor and has made payments of $11,738.16 for the fourth quarter thus far.

e. Prepare parts 1–4 (as needed) of Form 940 for Richmond Industries. Assume Richmond pays state unemployment to only Texas which taxes the first $9,000 of wages at a rate of 1.3%. Texas is not a credit reduction state in 2022.

f. Using the information from the Richmond payroll records and your results from part b., prepare Ben's Form W-2 for 2022 and the Richmond Industries' Form W-3.

g. Assume that Ben's actual 2022 wages are $55,000 and Tala's Schedule C net profits, self-employment tax, and qualified business income deduction are as assumed above. Assume Tala made four equal estimated payments based on the Estimated Tax Worksheet in part c. Compute the Kenofee's tax liability (use tax rate schedules instead of tax tables) and determine the amount of refund or overpayment.

CHAPTER 10

Partnership Taxation

Rowan Jordan/Getty Images

LEARNING OBJECTIVES

After completing this chapter, you should be able to:

- **LO 10.1** Define a partnership for tax purposes.
- **LO 10.2** Describe the basic tax rules for partnership formation and operation.
- **LO 10.3** Summarize the rules for partnership income reporting.
- **LO 10.4** Describe the tax treatment of partnership distributions.
- **LO 10.5** Determine partnership tax years.
- **LO 10.6** Describe the tax treatment of transactions between partners and their partnerships.
- **LO 10.7** Apply the qualified business income deduction to partners.
- **LO 10.8** Apply the at-risk rule to partnerships.
- **LO 10.9** Describe the tax treatment of limited liability companies (LLCs).

OVERVIEW

The partnership form allows taxpayers considerable flexibility in terms of contributions, income and loss allocations, and distributions. One of the primary benefits of the partnership is that partnership income is only taxed at the partner level. Corporate taxpayers (other than S corporations) pay tax at the corporate level and often again at the shareholder level (see Chapter 11), which results in corporate double taxation. Since a partnership's income passes through to the partners, there is no federal income tax at the entity level, only at the partner level. Currently, the tax law permits an additional qualified business income deduction for pass-through entities like partnerships.

One of the disadvantages of partnerships compared to corporations is the lack of limited liability for partners; whereas, corporate shareholders enjoy protection from liability to third parties (e.g., creditors of the corporation). The advent of the limited liability company (LLC) and the limited liability partnership (LLP) has provided partners this important liability protection. Because LLCs and LLPs are taxed like partnerships, they are included in this chapter on partnership taxation.

This chapter will provide an understanding of the tax treatment of partnerships and the tax forms (Form 1065 and Schedule K-1) related to reporting partnership income or loss.

Learning Objective 10.1

Define a partnership for tax purposes.

10-1 NATURE OF PARTNERSHIP TAXATION

Partnership federal income tax returns are information returns only. Returns show the amount of income by type and the allocation of the income to the partners. Partnership income and other items are passed through to the partners, and each partner is taxed on the individual's distributive share of partnership income. Partnership income is taxable to the partner even if they do not actually receive the income in cash.

EXAMPLE Mona is a 50-percent partner in the MAT Partnership. In 2022, MAT generates $10,000 in ordinary income but does not distribute any cash or property to the partners. Mona is allocated $5,000 ($10,000 × 50 percent) of ordinary income and will report this income on her individual income tax return. ♦

EXAMPLE Mona also owns 50 percent of the stock in AFM Corporation. AFM earns $10,000 of ordinary income in 2022 but does not distribute any cash or property to the shareholders. Corporate income is not allocated like partnership income and Mona will not report any of AFM's income on her individual income tax return. Corporations are discussed in Chapter 11. ♦

Even though the partnership tax return is only informational, partnerships do have to make various elections and select accounting methods and periods. For example, partnerships must select depreciation and inventory methods. In addition, partnerships are legal entities under civil law, and in most states have rights under the Uniform Partnership Act.

10-1a What Is a Partnership?

The tax law defines a partnership as a syndicate, group, pool, joint venture, or other unincorporated organization through or by means of which any business, financial operation, or venture is carried on, and which is not classified as a corporation, trust, or estate. Entities generally treated as partnerships for tax law purposes include limited partnerships, LLCs, and LLPs. The mere co-ownership of property does not constitute a partnership; the partners must engage in some type of business or financial activity.

EXAMPLE Avery and Roberta buy a rental house which they hold jointly. The house is rented and they share the income and expenses for the year. Avery and Roberta have not formed a partnership. However, if they had bought and operated a store together, a partnership would have been formed. Although the ownership of real estate may not rise to the level of a business requiring a partnership return, co-owners of real estate frequently do choose to operate in a partnership, limited partnership, LLP, or LLC form. ♦

Ordinary partnerships, or general partnerships as they are often called, may be formed by a simple verbal agreement or "handshake" between partners. In contrast, the formation of corporations, limited partnerships, limited liability companies, and limited liability partnerships must be documented in writing and the entity must be legally registered in the state in which it is formed. Even though general partnerships may be formed by verbal agreement between partners, partners usually document their agreement in writing with the help of attorneys in the event disagreements arise during the course of operations.

General partners usually take on the risk of legal liability for certain actions of the partnership or debts of the partnership, as specified under state law. To limit some of the liability exposure of operating a joint business, many partnerships are created formally as limited partnerships, LLCs, or LLPs. LLPs are used for licensed professionals such as attorneys and accountants.

Limited partnerships are a type of partnership that has one or more general partners and one or more limited partners. General partners participate in management and have unlimited liability for partnership obligations. Limited partners may not participate in management and have no liability for partnership obligations beyond their capital contributions. Many partnerships are formed as limited partnerships because the limited liability helps to attract passive investors. LLCs and LLPs are legal entities which combine the limited liability of corporations with the tax treatment of partnerships. LLCs and LLPs are discussed later in this chapter.

EXAMPLE The IAW Partnership is a limited partnership with three partners: Monica, who is the general partner, and Polly and Viktor, who are both limited partners. All three invested $5,000 in the partnership. Unfortunately, the partnership fails and has existing debts of $20,000. As limited partners, Polly and Viktor will lose their $5,000 investment but will not be personally responsible for the debts of the partnership while Monica, as the general partner, is personally liable for partnership debts. ♦

TAX BREAK

For federal tax purposes, an unincorporated business operated by spouses is considered a partnership. As a result, a business co-run by spouses is generally required to comply with filing and record-keeping requirements for partnerships and partners. Married co-owners wishing to avoid the burden of partnership documentation can form a qualified joint venture. The election to do so is made by simply reporting each spouse's share of income, losses, gains, and deductions on a Schedule C (along with other related forms) in respect of each spouse's interest in the joint venture.

Self-Study Problem 10.1

See Appendix E for Solutions to Self-Study Problems

The YKK partnership was formed by two unrelated individual taxpayers, Luis and Bheem, both 50-percent general partners. Each contributed $5,000 to form the partnership at the start of the current year. Determine whether the following statements are true or false:

1. If YKK owns a vacation home that Luis and Bheem use personally but do not rent, a partnership for tax purposes has been established.
2. If instead, YKK operates a small business, a partnership for tax purposes has been established.
3. Luis and Bheem are required to create a written partnership agreement for YKK to be taxed as a partnership.
4. In the current year, YKK generated $14,000 of taxable income and made a cash distribution of $1,000 each to the partners (not in excess of their basis). Luis will report $6,000 of partnership income on his individual income tax return.
5. At year-end, the partnership failed and the liabilities of the partnership exceed the assets. Bheem will be liable only for the $5,000 investment he made.

Learning Objective 10.2

Describe the basic tax rules for partnership formation and operation.

10-2 PARTNERSHIP FORMATION

Generally, there is no gain or loss recognized by a partnership or any of its partners when property is contributed to a partnership in exchange for an interest in the partnership. This rule applies to the formation of a partnership as well as any subsequent contributions to the partnership. However, there are exceptions to the nonrecognition rule. Income may be recognized when a partnership interest is received in exchange for services performed by the partner for the partnership or when a partner transfers to a partnership, property subject to a liability exceeding that partner's basis in the property transferred. In this situation, gain is recognized to the extent that the portion of the liability allocable to the other partners exceeds the basis of the property contributed. If a partner receives money or other property from the partnership, in addition to an interest in the partnership, the transaction may be considered in part a sale or exchange, and a gain or loss may be recognized.

EXAMPLE Dunn and Church form the Dunn & Church Partnership. Dunn contributes a building with a fair market value of $90,000 and an adjusted basis of $55,000 for a 50-percent interest in the partnership. Dunn does not recognize a gain on the transfer of the building to the partnership. Church performs services for the partnership for his 50-percent interest which is worth $90,000. Church must report $90,000 in ordinary income for the receipt of an interest in the partnership in exchange for services provided to the partnership. ♦

EXAMPLE Ann and Keith form the A&K Partnership. Ann contributes a building with a fair market value of $200,000 and an adjusted basis of $45,000 for a 50-percent interest in the partnership. The building is subject to a liability of $130,000. Keith contributes cash of $70,000 for a 50-percent interest in the partnership. Ann must recognize a gain on the transfer of the building to the partnership equal to $20,000, the amount by which the liability allocable to Keith, $65,000 (50% × $130,000), exceeds the basis of the building, $45,000. Keith does not recognize a gain on the contribution of cash to the partnership. ♦

A partner's initial basis in a partnership interest (often called outside basis) is equal to the basis of the property transferred plus cash contributed to the partnership. If gain is recognized on the transfer, the partner's basis in the partnership interest is increased by the gain recognized. The basis is reduced by any liabilities of the contributing partner assumed by the other partners through the partnership. For example, if a one-third partner is relieved of a $90,000 liability by the partnership, they would reduce by $60,000 (⅔ of $90,000) their partnership interest basis. After the initial basis in the partnership interest is established, the basis is adjusted for future earnings, losses, contributions to the partnership, and distributions from the partnership.

EXAMPLE Prentice contributes cash of $50,000 and property with a fair market value of $110,000 (adjusted basis of $30,000) to the P&H Partnership. Prentice's basis in the partnership interest is $80,000 ($50,000 + $30,000). ♦

EXAMPLE Assume that Prentice, in the example above, also received a partnership interest worth $15,000 for services provided to the partnership. She must recognize $15,000 as ordinary income, and her basis in the partnership interest is $95,000 ($80,000 + $15,000). ♦

EXAMPLE Darnell contributes property with a fair market value of $110,000 and an adjusted basis of $30,000, subject to a liability of $20,000, to a partnership in exchange for a 25-percent interest in the partnership. Darnell's basis in his partnership interest is $15,000 [$30,000 – ($20,000 × 75%)]. ♦

The partner's outside basis changes due to partnership activities. A partner's basis in their partnership interest is increased by the partner's share of (1) additional contributions to the partnership, (2) net ordinary taxable income of the partnership, and (3) capital gains and other income (including tax-exempt income such as municipal bond income) of the partnership. Alternatively, a partner's basis is reduced (but not below zero) by the partner's share of (1) distributions of partnership property, (2) losses from operations of the partnership, and (3) capital losses and other deductions (including disallowed tax deductions such as entertainment expenses) of the partnership. In addition, changes in the partner's share of partnership liabilities affects the basis of a partner's partnership interest.

EXAMPLE Reid has a 50-percent interest in the Reid Partnership. Her basis in her partnership interest at the beginning of the tax year is $12,000. For the current tax year, the partnership reports ordinary income of $15,000, a capital gain of $3,000, and charitable contributions of $700. The basis of Reid's partnership interest, after considering the above items, would be $20,650 ($12,000 beginning basis + $7,500 share of partnership ordinary income + $1,500 share of partnership capital gain – $350 share of partnership charitable contributions). ♦

The partnership's basis in property contributed by a partner is equal to the partner's adjusted basis in the property at the time of the contribution plus any gain recognized by the partner. The transfer of liabilities to the partnership by the partner does not impact the basis of the property to the partnership. The partnership's holding period for the property contributed to the partnership includes the partner's holding period. For example, long-term capital gain property may be transferred to a partnership by a partner and sold immediately, and any gain would be long-term, assuming the property is a capital asset to the partnership.

EXAMPLE Clark contributes property to the Rose Partnership in exchange for a partnership interest. The property contributed has an adjusted basis to Clark of $45,000 and a fair market value of $75,000 on the date of the contribution. The partnership's basis in the property is $45,000. ♦

Self-Study Problem 10.2

See Appendix E for Solutions to Self-Study Problems

John and Linda form the J&L Partnership. John contributes cash of $36,000 for a 40-percent interest in the partnership. Linda contributes equipment worth $54,000 with an adjusted basis of $17,500 for a 60-percent partnership interest.

1. What is John's recognized gain or loss on the contribution?
2. What is John's basis in his partnership interest?
3. What is Linda's recognized gain or loss on the contribution?
4. What is Linda's basis in her partnership interest?
5. What is J&L Partnership's basis in the equipment received from Linda?

Learning Objective 10.3

Summarize the rules for partnership income reporting.

10-3 PARTNERSHIP INCOME REPORTING

A partnership is required to report its income and other items on Form 1065, U.S. Return of Partnership Income, even though the partnership entity does not pay federal income tax. The tax return is due on the fifteenth day of the third month following the close of the partnership's tax year. When reporting partnership taxable income, certain transactions must be separated rather than being reported as part of ordinary income. The primary items that must be reported separately are net rental income, interest income, dividend income, capital gains and losses, Section 1231 gains and losses, Section 179 deductions, charitable deductions, tax-exempt income, non-deductible expenses, and most credits. These items are listed as separate income or expenses, since they are often subject to special calculations or limitations on the tax returns of the partners.

After the special items are separated, the partnership reports the remainder of its ordinary income or loss. The ordinary income or loss of a partnership is calculated in the same manner as that of an individual, except the partnership is not allowed to deduct the standard deduction, foreign taxes paid, charitable contributions, net operating losses, or personal itemized deductions. The ordinary business income of the partnership is reported in detail on page one of the Form 1065, Lines 1 through 22. The total from Line 22 is carried to the first line of Schedule K of Form 1065 and all other separately stated items for the total partnership are reported there as well. Schedule K-1 of Form 1065 presents the allocation of ordinary income or loss, special income and deductions, and gains and losses to each partner. The total of all Schedules K-1 should generally agree to the amounts reported on Schedule K for any particular line.

EXAMPLE WDL Partnership reports ordinary business income of $1,000. Mikey and Missy are both 50-percent partners in WDL and each receive a Schedule K-1 that reports $500 of ordinary business income on Line 1. The ordinary business income reported on Line 22 of the first page and Line 1 of Schedule K of the Form 1065 is $1,000. ♦

The Schedule K-1 is also used to report other important information such as self-employment income and qualified business income deduction information, including wages paid and the basis of qualified property. Different codes are used to identify the specific type of additional information. These codes can be found in the instructions to Schedule K-1. The partners report the amounts from their Schedules K-1 on their own individual tax returns.

A partner's deductible loss from a partnership is limited to the basis of the partner's partnership interest at the end of the year in which the loss was incurred. The partner's basis is not affected by the qualified business income deduction. The partner's partnership basis cannot be reduced below zero. Any unused losses may be carried forward and reported in a future year when there is partnership basis available to be reduced by the loss.

10-3a Guaranteed Payments

Payments made to a partner for services rendered or for the use of the partner's capital that are made without regard to the income of the partnership are termed guaranteed payments. Such payments are treated by the partnership in the same manner as payments made to a person who is not a partner. The payments are ordinary income to the partner and deductible by the partnership. Guaranteed payments are uniquely treated as both a deduction for ordinary business income and also separately reported on Line 4 of Schedule K-1.

EXAMPLE Alexander and Bryant operate the A&B Partnership. Alexander, a 50-percent partner, receives guaranteed payments of $15,000 for the year. If A&B has net ordinary income (after guaranteed payments) of $53,000, Alexander's total income from A&B is $41,500 ($15,000 + 50% of $53,000). Alexander's Schedule K-1 would report $26,500 on Line 1 (ordinary business income) and $15,000 on Line 4 (guaranteed payments). ♦

A partnership may show a loss after deducting guaranteed payments. In that case, the partner reports the guaranteed payments as income and reports their share of the partnership loss.

10-3b **Self-Employment Income for Partners**

A general partner is subject to self-employment tax on their distributive share of ordinary business income plus any guaranteed payments made to that partner. The treatment as self-employment income is not related to how much time the partner spent on partnership activities. A limited partner treats guaranteed payments as self-employment income but excludes the distributive share of ordinary income. Separately stated items are generally not self-employment income for either type of partner.

EXAMPLE Yorich is a general partner in the Shakespeare Partnership. His distributive share of ordinary income for the current year is $4,000 and he receives guaranteed payments of $12,000. He is also allocated $1,000 of net rental real estate income and $2,400 of long-term capital gains. Yorich's self-employment income is $16,000 ($4,000 ordinary income and $12,000 guaranteed payments). If Yorich were a limited partner, his self-employment income would be only $12,000 from the guaranteed payments. ♦

Self-employment income is reported on Line 14a of Schedule K-1 as an informational item.

In 2021, the IRS introduced a new Schedule K-2 and Schedule K-3 to provide a specific format to report international information related to pass-through entities. In some instances, a partnership or S corporation with no foreign partners, no assets generating foreign source income, and no foreign taxes paid may still need to report information on Schedules K-2 and K-3. For example, if the partner or shareholder claims the foreign tax credit, the partner generally needs certain information from the partnership on Schedule K-3, Parts II and III, to complete Form 1116.

Self-Study Problem 10.3

See Appendix E for Solutions to Self-Study Problems

Wita Caddoan and Sapat Illiniwek (SSN 444-14-1414) are equal general partners in the newly formed Cahokia Partnership. Cahokia is located at 40 Rainy Street, Collinsville, IL 62234. Cahokia's employee identification number is 44-4444444. During 2022, the partnership began operations and had the following income and expenses:

Gross income from operations	$255,600
Deductions:	
Salaries to employees (includes a $20,000 guaranteed payment to Sapat)	$168,000
Rent	12,000
Payroll taxes	6,100
Depreciation	9,250
Charitable contributions (to 50-percent organizations)	1,500
Cash withdrawals ($25,000 for each partner)	50,000

The partnership's balance sheet is as follows:

Cahokia Partnership Balance Sheet as of December 31, 2022

Assets:		
Cash		$ 27,000
Accounts receivable		10,000
Land		115,000
Building	$115,000	
Less: accumulated depreciation	(9,250)	105,750
Total Assets		$257,750
Liabilities and Partners' Capital:		
Accounts payable		$ 29,750
Mortgage payable		187,750
Partners' capital (includes $31,500 originally contributed, $15,750 by each partner)		40,250
Total Liabilities and Partners' Capital		$257,750

Cahokia is small advertising agency that is classified as business code 541800 and has no inventory. In spite of its small size, Cahokia uses the accrual method. Complete page 1 of Form 1065 on Page 10-9, and Schedules K, L, M-1, and M-2 on Pages 10-12 to 10-13 for Cahokia. Also, complete Schedule K-1 on Page 10-15 for Sapat. Form 4562 for depreciation, Schedule B-1 related to ownership, and Schedules K-2 and K-3 are not required.

Self-Study Problem 10.3

Form **1065** | **U.S. Return of Partnership Income** | OMB No. 1545-0123

Department of the Treasury Internal Revenue Service

For calendar year 2022, or tax year beginning ____________, 2022, ending ____________, 20___.

Go to www.irs.gov/Form1065 for instructions and the latest information.

2022

	Type or Print	
A Principal business activity	Name of partnership	D Employer identification number
B Principal product or service	Number, street, and room or suite no. If a P.O. box, see instructions.	E Date business started
C Business code number	City or town, state or province, country, and ZIP or foreign postal code	F Total assets (see instructions) $

G Check applicable boxes: (1) ☐ Initial return (2) ☐ Final return (3) ☐ Name change (4) ☐ Address change (5) ☐ Amended return

H Check accounting method: (1) ☐ Cash (2) ☐ Accrual (3) ☐ Other (specify):

I Number of Schedules K-1. Attach one for each person who was a partner at any time during the tax year:

J Check if Schedules C and M-3 are attached . . . ☐

K Check if partnership: (1) ☐ Aggregated activities for section 465 at-risk purposes (2) ☐ Grouped activities for section 469 passive activity purposes

Caution: Include **only** trade or business income and expenses on lines 1a through 22 below. See instructions for more information.

Income	1a	Gross receipts or sales	1a			
	b	Returns and allowances	1b			
	c	Balance. Subtract line 1b from line 1a			1c	
	2	Cost of goods sold (attach Form 1125-A)			2	
	3	Gross profit. Subtract line 2 from line 1c			3	
	4	Ordinary income (loss) from other partnerships, estates, and trusts (attach statement)			4	
	5	Net farm profit (loss) (attach Schedule F (Form 1040))			5	
	6	Net gain (loss) from Form 4797, Part II, line 17 (attach Form 4797)			6	
	7	Other income (loss) (attach statement)			7	
	8	**Total income (loss).** Combine lines 3 through 7			8	
Deductions (see instructions for limitations)	9	Salaries and wages (other than to partners) (less employment credits)			9	
	10	Guaranteed payments to partners			10	
	11	Repairs and maintenance			11	
	12	Bad debts			12	
	13	Rent			13	
	14	Taxes and licenses			14	
	15	Interest (see instructions)			15	
	16a	Depreciation (if required, attach Form 4562)	16a			
	b	Less depreciation reported on Form 1125-A and elsewhere on return	16b		16c	
	17	Depletion **(Do not deduct oil and gas depletion.)**			17	
	18	Retirement plans, etc.			18	
	19	Employee benefit programs			19	
	20	Other deductions (attach statement)			20	
	21	**Total deductions.** Add the amounts shown in the far right column for lines 9 through 20			21	
	22	**Ordinary business income (loss).** Subtract line 21 from line 8			22	
Tax and Payment	23	Interest due under the look-back method—completed long-term contracts (attach Form 8697)			23	
	24	Interest due under the look-back method—income forecast method (attach Form 8866)			24	
	25	BBA AAR imputed underpayment (see instructions)			25	
	26	Other taxes (see instructions)			26	
	27	**Total balance due.** Add lines 23 through 26			27	
	28	Payment (see instructions)			28	
	29	**Amount owed.** If line 28 is smaller than line 27, enter amount owed			29	
	30	**Overpayment.** If line 28 is larger than line 27, enter overpayment			30	

Sign Here

Under penalties of perjury, I declare that I have examined this return, including accompanying schedules and statements, and to the best of my knowledge and belief, it is true, correct, and complete. Declaration of preparer (other than partner or limited liability company member) is based on all information of which preparer has any knowledge.

Signature of partner or limited liability company member | Date

May the IRS discuss this return with the preparer shown below? See instructions. ☐ Yes ☐ No

Paid Preparer Use Only	Print/Type preparer's name	Preparer's signature	Date	Check ☐ if self-employed	PTIN
	Firm's name			Firm's EIN	
	Firm's address			Phone no.	

For Paperwork Reduction Act Notice, see separate instructions. Cat. No. 11390Z Form **1065** (2022)

Form 1065 (2022) Page **2**

Schedule B — Other Information

		Yes	No
1	What type of entity is filing this return? Check the applicable box: **a** ☐ Domestic general partnership **b** ☐ Domestic limited partnership **c** ☐ Domestic limited liability company **d** ☐ Domestic limited liability partnership **e** ☐ Foreign partnership **f** ☐ Other:		
2	At the end of the tax year:		
a	Did any foreign or domestic corporation, partnership (including any entity treated as a partnership), trust, or tax-exempt organization, or any foreign government own, directly or indirectly, an interest of 50% or more in the profit, loss, or capital of the partnership? For rules of constructive ownership, see instructions. If "Yes," attach Schedule B-1, Information on Partners Owning 50% or More of the Partnership		
b	Did any individual or estate own, directly or indirectly, an interest of 50% or more in the profit, loss, or capital of the partnership? For rules of constructive ownership, see instructions. If "Yes," attach Schedule B-1, Information on Partners Owning 50% or More of the Partnership		
3	At the end of the tax year, did the partnership:		
a	Own directly 20% or more, or own, directly or indirectly, 50% or more of the total voting power of all classes of stock entitled to vote of any foreign or domestic corporation? For rules of constructive ownership, see instructions. If "Yes," complete (i) through (iv) below		

(i) Name of Corporation	(ii) Employer Identification Number (if any)	(iii) Country of Incorporation	(iv) Percentage Owned in Voting Stock

b	Own directly an interest of 20% or more, or own, directly or indirectly, an interest of 50% or more in the profit, loss, or capital in any foreign or domestic partnership (including an entity treated as a partnership) or in the beneficial interest of a trust? For rules of constructive ownership, see instructions. If "Yes," complete (i) through (v) below		

(i) Name of Entity	(ii) Employer Identification Number (if any)	(iii) Type of Entity	(iv) Country of Organization	(v) Maximum Percentage Owned in Profit, Loss, or Capital

		Yes	No
4	Does the partnership satisfy **all four** of the following conditions?		
a	The partnership's total receipts for the tax year were less than $250,000.		
b	The partnership's total assets at the end of the tax year were less than $1 million.		
c	Schedules K-1 are filed with the return and furnished to the partners on or before the due date (including extensions) for the partnership return.		
d	The partnership is not filing and is not required to file Schedule M-3 If "Yes," the partnership is not required to complete Schedules L, M-1, and M-2; item F on page 1 of Form 1065; or item L on Schedule K-1.		
5	Is this partnership a publicly traded partnership, as defined in section 469(k)(2)?		
6	During the tax year, did the partnership have any debt that was canceled, was forgiven, or had the terms modified so as to reduce the principal amount of the debt?		
7	Has this partnership filed, or is it required to file, Form 8918, Material Advisor Disclosure Statement, to provide information on any reportable transaction?		
8	At any time during calendar year 2022, did the partnership have an interest in or a signature or other authority over a financial account in a foreign country (such as a bank account, securities account, or other financial account)? See instructions for exceptions and filing requirements for FinCEN Form 114, Report of Foreign Bank and Financial Accounts (FBAR). If "Yes," enter the name of the foreign country		
9	At any time during the tax year, did the partnership receive a distribution from, or was it the grantor of, or transferor to, a foreign trust? If "Yes," the partnership may have to file Form 3520, Annual Return To Report Transactions With Foreign Trusts and Receipt of Certain Foreign Gifts. See instructions		
10a	Is the partnership making, or had it previously made (and not revoked), a section 754 election? See instructions for details regarding a section 754 election.		
b	Did the partnership make for this tax year an optional basis adjustment under section 743(b) or 734(b)? If "Yes," attach a statement showing the computation and allocation of the basis adjustment. See instructions		
c	Is the partnership required to adjust the basis of partnership assets under section 743(b) or 734(b) because of a substantial built-in loss (as defined under section 743(d)) or substantial basis reduction (as defined under section 734(d))? If "Yes," attach a statement showing the computation and allocation of the basis adjustment. See instructions		

Form **1065** (2022)

Form 1065 (2022) Page 3

Schedule B **Other Information** *(continued)*

		Yes	No
11	Check this box if, during the current or prior tax year, the partnership distributed any property received in a like-kind exchange or contributed such property to another entity (other than disregarded entities wholly owned by the partnership throughout the tax year) . . . ☐		
12	At any time during the tax year, did the partnership distribute to any partner a tenancy-in-common or other undivided interest in partnership property? . . .		
13	If the partnership is required to file Form 8858, Information Return of U.S. Persons With Respect to Foreign Disregarded Entities (FDEs) and Foreign Branches (FBs), enter the number of Forms 8858 attached. See instructions . . . ______		
14	Does the partnership have any foreign partners? If "Yes," enter the number of Forms 8805, Foreign Partner's Information Statement of Section 1446 Withholding Tax, filed for this partnership . . . ______		
15	Enter the number of Forms 8865, Return of U.S. Persons With Respect to Certain Foreign Partnerships, attached to this return . . . ______		
16a	Did you make any payments in 2022 that would require you to file Form(s) 1099? See instructions . . .		
b	If "Yes," did you or will you file required Form(s) 1099? . . .		
17	Enter the number of Forms 5471, Information Return of U.S. Persons With Respect to Certain Foreign Corporations, attached to this return . . . ______		
18	Enter the number of partners that are foreign governments under section 892 . . . ______		
19	During the partnership's tax year, did the partnership make any payments that would require it to file Forms 1042 and 1042-S under chapter 3 (sections 1441 through 1464) or chapter 4 (sections 1471 through 1474)? . . .		
20	Was the partnership a specified domestic entity required to file Form 8938 for the tax year? See the Instructions for Form 8938 . . .		
21	Is the partnership a section 721(c) partnership, as defined in Regulations section 1.721(c)-1(b)(14)? . . .		
22	During the tax year, did the partnership pay or accrue any interest or royalty for which one or more partners are not allowed a deduction under section 267A? See instructions . . . If "Yes," enter the total amount of the disallowed deductions . . . $______		
23	Did the partnership have an election under section 163(j) for any real property trade or business or any farming business in effect during the tax year? See instructions . . .		
24	Does the partnership satisfy one or more of the following? See instructions . . . **a** The partnership owns a pass-through entity with current, or prior year carryover, excess business interest expense. **b** The partnership's aggregate average annual gross receipts (determined under section 448(c)) for the 3 tax years preceding the current tax year are more than $27 million and the partnership has business interest. **c** The partnership is a tax shelter (see instructions) and the partnership has business interest expense. If "Yes" to any, complete and attach Form 8990.		
25	Is the partnership attaching Form 8996 to certify as a Qualified Opportunity Fund? . . . If "Yes," enter the amount from Form 8996, line 15 . . . $______		
26	Enter the number of foreign partners subject to section 864(c)(8) as a result of transferring all or a portion of an interest in the partnership or of receiving a distribution from the partnership . . . ______ Complete Schedule K-3 (Form 1065), Part XIII, for each foreign partner subject to section 864(c)(8) on a transfer or distribution.		
27	At any time during the tax year, were there any transfers between the partnership and its partners subject to the disclosure requirements of Regulations section 1.707-8? . . .		
28	Since December 22, 2017, did a foreign corporation directly or indirectly acquire substantially all of the properties constituting a trade or business of your partnership, and was the ownership percentage (by vote or value) for purposes of section 7874 greater than 50% (for example, the partners held more than 50% of the stock of the foreign corporation)? If "Yes," list the ownership percentage by vote and by value. See instructions. Percentage: By vote: ______ By value: ______		
29	How many Schedules K-1 and Schedules K-3 were not furnished or will not be furnished timely? ______		
30	Is the partnership electing out of the centralized partnership audit regime under section 6221(b)? See instructions. If "Yes," the partnership must complete Schedule B-2 (Form 1065). Enter the total from Schedule B-2, Part III, line 3 . . . ______ If "No," complete Designation of Partnership Representative below.		

Designation of Partnership Representative (see instructions)
Enter below the information for the partnership representative (PR) for the tax year covered by this return.

Name of PR

U.S. address of PR		U.S. phone number of PR	

If the PR is an entity, name of the designated individual for the PR

U.S. address of designated individual		U.S. phone number of designated individual	

Form **1065** (2022)

Form 1065 (2022) Page 4

Schedule K — Partners' Distributive Share Items

				Total amount
Income (Loss)	1	Ordinary business income (loss) (page 1, line 22)	1	
	2	Net rental real estate income (loss) (attach Form 8825)	2	
	3a	Other gross rental income (loss) — 3a		
	b	Expenses from other rental activities (attach statement) — 3b		
	c	Other net rental income (loss). Subtract line 3b from line 3a	3c	
	4	Guaranteed payments: a Services 4a ___ b Capital 4b ___		
		c Total. Add lines 4a and 4b	4c	
	5	Interest income	5	
	6	Dividends and dividend equivalents: a Ordinary dividends	6a	
		b Qualified dividends 6b ___ c Dividend equivalents 6c ___		
	7	Royalties	7	
	8	Net short-term capital gain (loss) (attach Schedule D (Form 1065))	8	
	9a	Net long-term capital gain (loss) (attach Schedule D (Form 1065))	9a	
	b	Collectibles (28%) gain (loss) — 9b		
	c	Unrecaptured section 1250 gain (attach statement) — 9c		
	10	Net section 1231 gain (loss) (attach Form 4797)	10	
	11	Other income (loss) (see instructions) Type:	11	
Deductions	12	Section 179 deduction (attach Form 4562)	12	
	13a	Contributions	13a	
	b	Investment interest expense	13b	
	c	Section 59(e)(2) expenditures: (1) Type: ___ (2) Amount:	13c(2)	
	d	Other deductions (see instructions) Type:	13d	
Self-Employment	14a	Net earnings (loss) from self-employment	14a	
	b	Gross farming or fishing income	14b	
	c	Gross nonfarm income	14c	
Credits	15a	Low-income housing credit (section 42(j)(5))	15a	
	b	Low-income housing credit (other)	15b	
	c	Qualified rehabilitation expenditures (rental real estate) (attach Form 3468, if applicable)	15c	
	d	Other rental real estate credits (see instructions) Type:	15d	
	e	Other rental credits (see instructions) Type:	15e	
	f	Other credits (see instructions) Type:	15f	
International	16	Attach Schedule K-2 (Form 1065), Partners' Distributive Share Items—International, and check this box to indicate that you are reporting items of international tax relevance ☐		
Alternative Minimum Tax (AMT) Items	17a	Post-1986 depreciation adjustment	17a	
	b	Adjusted gain or loss	17b	
	c	Depletion (other than oil and gas)	17c	
	d	Oil, gas, and geothermal properties—gross income	17d	
	e	Oil, gas, and geothermal properties—deductions	17e	
	f	Other AMT items (attach statement)	17f	
Other Information	18a	Tax-exempt interest income	18a	
	b	Other tax-exempt income	18b	
	c	Nondeductible expenses	18c	
	19a	Distributions of cash and marketable securities	19a	
	b	Distributions of other property	19b	
	20a	Investment income	20a	
	b	Investment expenses	20b	
	c	Other items and amounts (attach statement)		
	21	Total foreign taxes paid or accrued	21	

Form **1065** (2022)

Form 1065 (2022) Page **5**

Analysis of Net Income (Loss) per Return

1	Net income (loss). Combine Schedule K, lines 1 through 11. From the result, subtract the sum of Schedule K, lines 12 through 13d, and 21					**1**	
2	Analysis by partner type:	**(i)** Corporate	**(ii)** Individual (active)	**(iii)** Individual (passive)	**(iv)** Partnership	**(v)** Exempt Organization	**(vi)** Nominee/Other
a	General partners						
b	Limited partners						

Schedule L **Balance Sheets per Books**

		Beginning of tax year		End of tax year	
	Assets	**(a)**	**(b)**	**(c)**	**(d)**
1	Cash				
2a	Trade notes and accounts receivable				
b	Less allowance for bad debts				
3	Inventories				
4	U.S. Government obligations				
5	Tax-exempt securities				
6	Other current assets (attach statement)				
7a	Loans to partners (or persons related to partners)				
b	Mortgage and real estate loans				
8	Other investments (attach statement)				
9a	Buildings and other depreciable assets				
b	Less accumulated depreciation				
10a	Depletable assets				
b	Less accumulated depletion				
11	Land (net of any amortization)				
12a	Intangible assets (amortizable only)				
b	Less accumulated amortization				
13	Other assets (attach statement)				
14	Total assets				
	Liabilities and Capital				
15	Accounts payable				
16	Mortgages, notes, bonds payable in less than 1 year				
17	Other current liabilities (attach statement)				
18	All nonrecourse loans				
19a	Loans from partners (or persons related to partners)				
b	Mortgages, notes, bonds payable in 1 year or more				
20	Other liabilities (attach statement)				
21	Partners' capital accounts				
22	Total liabilities and capital				

Schedule M-1 **Reconciliation of Income (Loss) per Books With Analysis of Net Income (Loss) per Return**

Note: The partnership may be required to file Schedule M-3. See instructions.

1	Net income (loss) per books		**6**	Income recorded on books this year not included on Schedule K, lines 1 through 11 (itemize):	
2	Income included on Schedule K, lines 1, 2, 3c, 5, 6a, 7, 8, 9a, 10, and 11, not recorded on books this year (itemize):		**a**	Tax-exempt interest $	
3	Guaranteed payments (other than health insurance)		**7**	Deductions included on Schedule K, lines 1 through 13d, and 21, not charged against book income this year (itemize):	
4	Expenses recorded on books this year not included on Schedule K, lines 1 through 13d, and 21 (itemize):		**a**	Depreciation $	
a	Depreciation $		**8**	Add lines 6 and 7	
b	Travel and entertainment $		**9**	Income (loss) (Analysis of Net Income (Loss), line 1). Subtract line 8 from line 5	
5	Add lines 1 through 4				

Schedule M-2 **Analysis of Partners' Capital Accounts**

1	Balance at beginning of year		**6**	Distributions: **a** Cash	
2	Capital contributed: **a** Cash			**b** Property	
	b Property		**7**	Other decreases (itemize):	
3	Net income (loss) (see instructions)				
4	Other increases (itemize):		**8**	Add lines 6 and 7	
5	Add lines 1 through 4		**9**	Balance at end of year. Subtract line 8 from line 5	

Form **1065** (2022)

Self-Study Problem 10.3

651121

☐ Final K-1 ☐ Amended K-1 OMB No. 1545-0123

Schedule K-1 (Form 1065) 2022
Department of the Treasury
Internal Revenue Service

For calendar year 2022, or tax year
beginning / / 2022 ending / /

Partner's Share of Income, Deductions, Credits, etc. See separate instructions.

Part I Information About the Partnership

A Partnership's employer identification number

B Partnership's name, address, city, state, and ZIP code

C IRS center where partnership filed return:

D ☐ Check if this is a publicly traded partnership (PTP)

Part II Information About the Partner

E Partner's SSN or TIN (Do not use TIN of a disregarded entity. See instructions.)

F Name, address, city, state, and ZIP code for partner entered in E. See instructions.

G ☐ General partner or LLC member-manager ☐ Limited partner or other LLC member

H1 ☐ Domestic partner ☐ Foreign partner

H2 ☐ If the partner is a disregarded entity (DE), enter the partner's:
TIN ________ Name ________

I1 What type of entity is this partner? ________

I2 If this partner is a retirement plan (IRA/SEP/Keogh/etc.), check here ☐

J Partner's share of profit, loss, and capital (see instructions):

	Beginning	Ending
Profit	%	%
Loss	%	%
Capital	%	%

Check if decrease is due to sale or exchange of partnership interest ☐

K Partner's share of liabilities:

	Beginning	Ending
Nonrecourse	$	$
Qualified nonrecourse financing	$	$
Recourse	$	$

Check this box if item K includes liability amounts from lower-tier partnerships ☐

L **Partner's Capital Account Analysis**

Beginning capital account $ ________
Capital contributed during the year $ ________
Current year net income (loss) $ ________
Other increase (decrease) (attach explanation) $ ________
Withdrawals and distributions $ (________)
Ending capital account $ ________

M Did the partner contribute property with a built-in gain (loss)?
☐ Yes ☐ No If "Yes," attach statement. See instructions.

N **Partner's Share of Net Unrecognized Section 704(c) Gain or (Loss)**
Beginning $ ________
Ending $ ________

Part III Partner's Share of Current Year Income, Deductions, Credits, and Other Items

1 Ordinary business income (loss)
2 Net rental real estate income (loss)
3 Other net rental income (loss)
4a Guaranteed payments for services
4b Guaranteed payments for capital
4c Total guaranteed payments
5 Interest income
6a Ordinary dividends
6b Qualified dividends
6c Dividend equivalents
7 Royalties
8 Net short-term capital gain (loss)
9a Net long-term capital gain (loss)
9b Collectibles (28%) gain (loss)
9c Unrecaptured section 1250 gain
10 Net section 1231 gain (loss)
11 Other income (loss)
12 Section 179 deduction
13 Other deductions
14 Self-employment earnings (loss)
15 Credits
16 Schedule K-3 is attached if checked ☐
17 Alternative minimum tax (AMT) items
18 Tax-exempt income and nondeductible expenses
19 Distributions
20 Other information
21 Foreign taxes paid or accrued
22 ☐ More than one activity for at-risk purposes*
23 ☐ More than one activity for passive activity purposes*

*See attached statement for additional information.

For IRS Use Only

For Paperwork Reduction Act Notice, see the Instructions for Form 1065. www.irs.gov/Form1065 Cat. No. 11394R Schedule K-1 (Form 1065) 2022

10-4 CURRENT DISTRIBUTIONS

10.4 Learning Objective

Describe the tax treatment of partnership distributions.

A partnership may make distributions of money or other property to the partners. A current distribution is defined as one which does not result in the complete termination of the partner's interest in the partnership.

In a current distribution, no gain is recognized by the partner receiving the distribution unless the partner's basis in the partnership has reached zero. In such a case, gain is recognized only to the extent that a distribution of money exceeds the partner's basis in their partnership interest.

The distribution of money or other property reduces the partner's basis in their partnership interest, but not below zero.

EXAMPLE Calvin is a partner in K&G Interests, and his basis in his partnership interest is $75,000. In the current tax year, Calvin receives a $45,000 cash distribution from the partnership. He does not recognize a gain or loss on the distribution, but his basis in his partnership interest is reduced to $30,000 ($75,000 − $45,000). If the distribution of cash were $80,000 instead of $45,000, Calvin would have a taxable gain of $5,000 ($80,000 − $75,000), and his basis in the partnership interest would be reduced to zero ($75,000 − $80,000 + $5,000). ♦

The basis of property received by a partner in a current distribution will generally be the same as the basis of the property to the partnership immediately prior to the distribution. An overall limitation is imposed, which states that the basis of the assets distributed cannot exceed the partner's basis in the partnership interest, reduced by any money distributed. In some cases, this overall limitation may require that the partner's basis in the partnership interest be allocated among the assets received in the distribution.

When determining the amount of a deductible loss, the partner's outside basis in the partnership is adjusted in a specific order. Outside basis is first increased by any partner contributions to the partnership and then the distributive share of income and income items (including tax-exempt items). Distributions are considered prior to deducting any losses. Any allocated losses in excess of outside basis are suspended and carried forward.

EXAMPLE Babek has a $5,000 outside basis in his partnership interest. The partnership allocates an ordinary business loss of $10,000 and tax-exempt income of $500 to Babek during the year. To determine the amount of deductible loss, Babek may first increase his outside basis to $5,500 by adding the $500 tax-exempt income. His deductible loss is limited to $5,500 and his basis is reduced to $0. The excess $4,500 loss is suspended and may be carried forward. ♦

EXAMPLE In the following year, Babek is allocated income of $6,000 and also receives a $6,000 cash distribution from the partnership. Although the income increases Babek's outside basis to $6,000, he must decrease his basis by the $6,000 cash distribution prior to attempting to deduct the loss suspended in the prior year and thus, may not deduct the loss. ♦

Self-Study Problem 10.4 *See Appendix E for Solutions to Self-Study Problems*

Jiang and Jackson are equal partners in J&J Partnership. Both partners start Year 1 with an outside basis of $10,000. Using the following information below, determine (1) the recognized income or loss for each partner and (2) the end-of-year outside basis for each partner:

1. J&J generates $6,000 of ordinary business income, allocates total municipal bond interest of $300 and allocates non-deductible fines of $100.
2. J&J generates a $20,000 loss that includes a deduction for a guaranteed payment of $2,000 to Jiang. Both Jiang and Jackson receive a cash distribution from the partnership of $7,100 each.
3. J&J generates ordinary business income of $4,000 and long-term capital gains of $1,000. Jiang receives a guaranteed payment of $2,000.

Learning Objective 10.5

Determine partnership tax years.

10-5 TAX YEARS

The tax law requires that each partner include in gross income for a particular tax year the individual's distributive share of income, including guaranteed payments, from a partnership whose tax year ends with or within that partner's tax year. For example, a calendar-year individual partner should report their income from a partnership with a tax year ending June 30, 2022, on his or her 2022 tax return. Since a partner reports only income reported by a partnership whose year ends with or within their tax year, it is possible to delay the reporting of partnership income and guaranteed payments for almost an entire year. This would happen, for example, if the partnership's year-end is January 31, and the partner's tax year is a calendar year. To prevent this deferral of income, rigid rules have been established regarding partnership tax years. Under these rules, unless a partnership can establish a business purpose for a fiscal year-end or meet certain tests, it must adopt the same taxable year as that of the majority partners. If such partners do not have the same tax year, then the partnership is required to adopt the tax year of all its principal partners. If neither of these rules can be met, the partnership must adopt a tax year based on the least aggregate deferral method (see IRS Publication 538 for more information).

Once established, a partnership will not close its tax year early unless the partnership is terminated. The tax year does not generally close upon the entry of a new partner, or the liquidation, sale, or exchange of an existing partnership interest. A partnership is terminated, and will close its tax year, if business activity by the partnership ceases.

Self-Study Problem 10.5 *See Appendix E for Solutions to Self-Study Problems*

R&S Associates is a partnership with a tax year that ends on August 31, 2022. During the partnership's tax year, Robert, a partner, received $1,000 per month as a guaranteed payment, and his share of partnership income after guaranteed payments was $21,000. For September through December of 2022, Robert's guaranteed payment was increased to $1,500 per month. Calculate the amount of income from the partnership that Robert should report for his 2022 calendar tax year.

10-6 TRANSACTIONS BETWEEN PARTNERS AND THE PARTNERSHIP

10.6 Learning Objective

Describe the tax treatment of transactions between partners and their partnerships.

When engaging in a transaction with a partnership, a partner is generally regarded as an outside party, and the transaction is reported as it would be if the two parties were unrelated. However, it is recognized that occasionally transactions may lack substance because one party to the transaction exercises significant influence over the other party. Therefore, losses are disallowed for (1) transactions between a partnership and a partner who has a direct or indirect capital or profit interest in the partnership of more than 50 percent, and (2) transactions between two partnerships owned more than 50 percent by the same partners. When a loss is disallowed, the purchaser may reduce a future gain on the disposition of the property by the amount of the disallowed loss.

EXAMPLE Kyle owns 55 percent of Willow Interests, a partnership. During the current year, Kyle sells property to the partnership for $60,000. Kyle's adjusted basis in the property is $75,000. The $15,000 loss is disallowed, since Kyle is a more than 50-percent partner. If later the partnership sells the property for $80,000, realizing a $20,000 gain ($80,000 − $60,000), only $5,000 of the gain is recognized, since the partnership can use Kyle's disallowed loss to offset $15,000 of the gain. ♦

In a transaction between a partner and a partnership, a gain will be taxed as ordinary income if the partner has more than a 50-percent interest in the partnership and the property sold or transferred is not a capital asset to the transferee. The interest may be owned directly or indirectly. For example, a taxpayer indirectly owns the interests owned by their spouse, brothers, sisters, ancestors, and lineal descendants.

EXAMPLE Amy is a 50-percent partner in the A&B Partnership, and her brother, Ben, is the other 50-percent partner. Amy sells for $65,000 a building (with a basis of $50,000) to the partnership for use in its business. The property qualifies as a long-term capital asset to Amy. The gain of $15,000 ($65,000 − $50,000), however, is ordinary income, since Amy is considered a 100-percent partner (50 percent directly and 50 percent indirectly) and the building is a Section 1231 asset to the partnership. ♦

Self-Study Problem 10.6 *See Appendix E for Solutions to Self-Study Problems*

Maxwell is a 50-percent partner in M&P Associates. Pam, Maxwell's daughter, owns the other 50-percent interest in the partnership. During the current tax year, Maxwell sells ordinary income property to M&P Associates for $70,000. The property's basis to Maxwell is $75,000. Also, Pam sells her personal Mercedes-Benz, with a basis of $25,000, for $40,000 to M&P Associates for use in the partnership's business.

1. What is the amount of Maxwell's recognized gain or loss on his transaction, and what is the nature of the gain or loss?
2. What is the amount and nature of Pam's gain or loss on her transaction with the partnership?

Learning Objective 10.7

Apply the qualified business income deduction to partners.

10-7 QUALIFIED BUSINESS INCOME DEDUCTION FOR PARTNERS

The qualified business income deduction is available to individual owners of pass-through businesses such as partnerships and LLCs. The deduction in general is covered in Chapter 4. This section covers some of the items applicable specifically to partnerships.

Qualified business income (QBI) generally includes all items of ordinary business income; however, the tax law specifically excludes certain items including guaranteed payments to partners and payments made to partners by the partnership in situations in which the partner is not acting in their capacity as a partner.

EXAMPLE Rigby is a 30-percent partner in Regular Partnership. In 2022, Regular has $50,000 of ordinary business income and no other separately stated items. In 2022, Rigby receives guaranteed payments of $10,000. Rigby also enters into a loan between himself and Regular and receives interest income from the partnership of $1,000. Regular makes a cash distribution to Rigby of $5,000 and Rigby maintains a positive basis at year-end. The loan is treated as a transaction in which Rigby is not acting in his capacity as a partner and thus the guaranteed payment and the interest are both excluded from Rigby's QBI. Rigby's QBI is $15,000 ($50,000 × 30%). ♦

Although guaranteed payments and payments to partners not acting as partners are not included in QBI, they are deductible by the partnership in computing ordinary business income (to the extent the items would be deductible otherwise).

TAX BREAK

Partners may want to reconsider a characterization away from guaranteed payments as part of a revision to the partnership agreement. Guaranteed payments and the allocation of business income to an individual partner are both generally subject to self-employment taxes; however, guaranteed payments are a deduction from ordinary business income while cash distributions from basis are not. In addition, guaranteed payments are not part of QBI. By treating former guaranteed payments instead as cash distributions, the partnership (and thus the partner) will have greater QBI eligible for the 20-percent QBI deduction. Of course, the "guarantee" of guaranteed payments will also be eliminated by the recharacterization.

For high-income taxpayers, the QBI deduction is limited by W-2 wages or a combination of W-2 wages and qualified property. A partner must be allocated their share of these items in order to properly apply the limitations when applicable.

EXAMPLE Mordecai is a 50-percent partner in Park Partnership. In 2022, Mordecai's taxable income is high enough to subject his QBI deduction to the wage limitation. Park pays W-2 wages of $70,000 and has qualified property of $300,000 in 2022. If these items are allocated in accordance with the partnership interest, Mordecai will be allocated $35,000 of W-2 wages ($70,000 × 50%) and $150,000 of qualified property ($300,000 × 50%) to compute his wage limitation. ♦

QBI deduction information is reported to partners on Schedule K-1. Informational items are frequently reported on Line 20 Other Information of Schedule K-1; however, due to the relative complexity of QBI deduction information, the IRS includes Statement A as part of the instructions for Form 1065 and encourages taxpayers to use this statement to report QBI deduction information. The regulations issued by the IRS indicate that failure to report QBI information to partners on the Schedule K-1 or attached Statement A is equivalent to reporting zero for each item.

Statement A—QBI Pass-Through Entity Reporting

Partnership's name:		Partnership's EIN:	
Partner's name:	Partner's identifying number:		
	Trade or Business 1	Trade or Business 2	Trade or Business 3
Partner's share of:	☐ PTP ☐ Aggregated ☐ SSTB	☐ PTP ☐ Aggregated ☐ SSTB	☐ PTP ☐ Aggregated ☐ SSTB
QBI or qualified PTP items subject to partner-specific determinations:			
Ordinary business income (loss)			
Rental income (loss)			
Royalty income (loss)			
Section 1231 gain (loss)			
Other income (loss)			
Section 179 deduction			
Other deductions			
W-2 wages			
UBIA of qualified property			
Section 199A dividends			

ProConnect™ Tax TIP

ProConnect automatically creates Statement A to Schedule K-1 to report qualified business income deduction information. To the extent more than one business is contained within the partnership or there is a need to report the unadjusted basis of qualified property or override wage information, the amounts can be input under Schedule K, Other Schedule K Items, QBI Reporting: Additional Trades or Businesses.

Self-Study Problem 10.7

See Appendix E for Solutions to Self-Study Problems

a. Dr. Marla Cratchitt is a single taxpayer and works as a cardiologist. Marla is an investor in Salem Healthcare LLC, a business that manufactures stents for a variety of cardiovascular issues. Marla's member's interest in Salem is 20 percent and the LLC agreement calls for guaranteed payments to Marla of $75,000 per year. In 2022, Marla's ordinary business income allocation from Salem is $200,000. Salem also allocated $5,000 of long-term capital gains to Marla. Salem paid wages to employees of $230,000 and has qualified property of $1,200,000. Marla has taxable income of $776,000 for purposes of the QBI limit. Compute Marla's QBI deduction.

b. Assume that same facts as above except that Salem is a service business. Compute Marla's QBI deduction.

Learning Objective 10.8

Apply the at-risk rule to partnerships.

10-8 THE AT-RISK RULE

The at-risk rule is designed to prevent taxpayers from deducting losses from activities in excess of their investment in those activities. Although the at-risk rule applies to most taxpayers, it is discussed here because the rule is a common problem related to investments in partnerships. In general, the at-risk rule limits the losses from a taxpayer's business activities to "amounts at risk" (AAR) in the activity.

To understand the at-risk rule, it is necessary to understand two related terms, "nonrecourse liabilities" and "encumbered property." A nonrecourse liability is a debt for which the borrower is not personally liable. If the debt is not paid, the lender generally can only repossess the property pledged as collateral on the loan. Encumbered property (also referred to as "collateral") is property pledged for the liability. The property is said to be encumbered in the amount of the liability. Taxpayers are at risk in amounts equal to their cash and property contributions to the activities, borrowed amounts to the extent of the property pledged, liabilities for which the taxpayers are personally liable, and retained profits of the activity. For contributions of unencumbered property, the amount considered at risk is the adjusted basis of the property contributed to the activity. For encumbered property, the amount at risk is also the adjusted basis of the property to the taxpayer if they are personally liable for repayment of the debt. If there is no personal liability for the debt, the amount at risk is the difference between the adjusted basis of the property and the amount of the nonrecourse debt on the property.

EXAMPLE A taxpayer contributes property with an adjusted basis of $100,000, subject to a recourse liability of $25,000 and a nonrecourse liability of $40,000. The taxpayer's AAR is the basis of the property less the amount of the nonrecourse liability, or $60,000 ($100,000 – $40,000). ♦

Under the at-risk rule, taxpayers are allowed a deduction for losses allocable to a business activity to the extent of (1) income received or accrued from the activity without regard to the amount at risk, or (2) the taxpayer's amount at risk at the end of the tax year. Any losses not allowed in the current year may be treated as deductions in succeeding years, with no limit on the number of years the losses may be carried forward. Remember that passive loss rules (discussed in Chapter 4) and the basis limitation (discussed earlier in this chapter) may also limit the taxpayer's ability to deduct certain losses.

EXAMPLE A taxpayer contributes $100,000 to an activity. Her amount at risk is $100,000. In the current year, the activity incurs losses of $250,000. For the current year, the taxpayer is allowed a loss of $100,000, the amount at risk. ♦

While real estate acquired before 1987 is not subject to the at-risk rules, the at-risk rules do apply to real estate acquired after 1986. For real estate acquired after 1986, "qualified nonrecourse financing" on real estate is considered to be an amount at risk. Qualified nonrecourse financing is debt that is secured by the real estate and loaned or guaranteed by a governmental agency or borrowed from any person who actively and regularly engages in the lending of money, such as a bank, savings and loan, or insurance company. A taxpayer is not considered at risk for financing obtained from sellers or promoters, including loans from parties related to the sellers or promoters.

EXAMPLE In the current tax year, Donna buys a real estate investment with a $20,000 cash down payment and $80,000 borrowed from a savings and loan company secured by a mortgage on the property. Donna has $100,000 at risk in this investment. If the mortgage were obtained from the seller, her amount at risk would be limited to her down payment of $20,000. ♦

Self-Study Problem 10.8 *See Appendix E for Solutions to Self-Study Problems*

During the current tax year, Joe is a partner in a plumbing business. His amount at risk at the beginning of the year is $45,000. During the year, Joe's share of loss is $60,000.

1. What is the amount of the loss that Joe may deduct for the current tax year?
2. If Joe has a profit of $31,000 in the following tax year, how much is taxable?

10-9 LIMITED LIABILITY COMPANIES

10.9 Learning Objective

Describe the tax treatment of limited liability companies (LLCs).

A limited liability company (LLC) is a hybrid form of business organization having some attributes of a partnership and other attributes of a corporation. Each owner, referred to as a member of an LLC, has limited liability, which may be similar to a stockholder in a corporation. However, an LLC is generally treated as a partnership for tax purposes. Because of this tax treatment, members of LLCs can have the tax advantages of a partnership and still have limited liability similar to a corporation. The benefits of LLCs have made them very popular as an entity choice for small businesses. LLCs are recognized legal entities in all 50 states and the District of Columbia. Many states prohibit certain licensed professionals such as attorneys, architects, and accountants from operating as an LLC but allow the formation of limited liability partnerships (LLPs) if these businesses wish to operate in a partnership form with legal liability protection similar to LLCs.

For the most part, LLCs follow partnership taxation rules. For example, taxable income and losses pass through to members; thereby, the LLC either avoids the corporate tax or allows its members to use the losses. An LLC may elect to be taxed like a corporation rather than a partnership, but very few do. Like partnerships, LLCs' items of income and expense retain their tax attributes (e.g., capital gains and charitable contributions). However, LLCs are not required to have a general partner; unlike a limited partnership, in which there has to be at least one general partner who does not have limited liability. Although not entirely settled tax law, the IRS has issued guidance indicating that LLC members actively engaged in the LLC's trade or business will be treated the same as general partners for self-employment tax purposes. Also, LLC members can participate in the management of the business. Because of the limited liability associated with LLCs, the debt of the LLC is generally treated as non-recourse. Lastly, LLCs may have a single member, whereas a partnership must have at least two partners. A single-member LLC is treated as a disregarded entity for tax purposes (i.e., the taxable income of the single-member LLC is reported directly on the tax return of its member, not on a separate Form 1065).

Self-Study Problem 10.9 *See Appendix E for Solutions to Self-Study Problems*

Determine whether the following statements are true or false.

1. A limited liability company is generally treated like a corporation for federal income tax purposes.
2. A general partner is required for a limited liability company.
3. Tax attributes of an LLC transaction pass through to the owners of the LLC.
4. Owners of an LLC can participate in the management of the LLC business.
5. Debt of an LLC is generally treated as recourse debt and thus included in a member's basis computations.

KEY TERMS

partnership, 10-2
general (ordinary) partnerships, 10-2
general partners, 10-3
limited partnerships, 10-3
limited partners, 10-3
initial basis, 10-4
outside basis, 10-4
basis, 10-4
Form 1065, 10-6
Schedule K-1, 10-6
guaranteed payments, 10-6
self-employment income, 10-7
current distribution, 10-17
qualified business income deduction, 10-20
qualified business income, 10-20
at-risk rule, 10-22
nonrecourse liabilities, 10-22
encumbered property ("collateral"), 10-22
qualified nonrecourse financing, 10-23
limited liability companies ("LLCs"), 10-23
limited liability partnerships ("LLPs"), 10-23

KEY POINTS

Learning Objectives	Key Points
LO 10.1: Define a partnership for tax purposes.	• A partnership is a syndicate, group, pool, joint venture, or other unincorporated organization through or by means of which any business, financial operation, or venture is carried on, and which is not classified as a corporation, trust, or estate. • Partnership federal tax returns are information returns only, which show the amount of income by type and the allocation of the income to the partners. • Partnership income is allocated and generally taxable to the partner even if that individual does not actually receive the income in cash. • Co-ownership of property does not constitute a partnership (e.g., owning investment property); the partners must engage in some type of business or financial activity. • Limited partnerships, limited liability partnerships (LLPs), and limited liability companies (LLCs) are generally treated as partnerships for tax law purposes.

LO 10.2: Describe the basic tax rules for partnership formation and operation.	• Generally, there is no gain or loss recognized by a partnership or any of its partners when property is contributed to a partnership in exchange for an interest in the partnership. • When a partner receives a partnership interest in exchange for providing services to the partnership, income is recognized by the partner. • When a partner transfers property to a partnership in exchange for a partnership interest and that property is subject to a liability exceeding the partner's basis, income may be recognized by the partner. • A partner's basis is increased by the partner's contributions to the partnership, net ordinary taxable income and capital gains of the partnership, and increases in the partner's share of partnership liabilities. • A partner's basis is decreased by distributions by the partnership, losses of the partnership, and decreases in the partner's share of partnership liabilities.
LO 10.3: Summarize the rules for partnership income reporting.	• A partnership is required to report its income and other items on Form 1065, U.S. Return of Partnership Income, even though the partnership entity does not pay federal income tax. • When reporting partnership taxable income, certain transactions must be separated rather than being reported as part of ordinary income. Separately reported items include net rental income, interest income, dividend income, capital gains and losses, Section 1231 gains and losses, Section 179 deductions, charitable deductions, tax-exempt income, non-deductible expenses, and most credits. • Schedule K-1 of Form 1065 presents the allocation of ordinary income or loss, special income and deductions, and gains and losses to each partner. The partners report the K-1 amounts on their own individual tax returns. • Payments made to a partner for services rendered or for the use of the partner's capital that are made without regard to the income of the partnership are termed *guaranteed payments*. • Guaranteed payments are ordinary income to the partner and deductible by the partnership. • A partnership may show a loss after deducting guaranteed payments, in which case, the partner reports the guaranteed payments as income and reports their share of the partnership loss. • Both general and limited partners are subject to self-employment tax on guaranteed payments received. Only general partners are subject to self-employment tax on their distributive share of ordinary business income. Separately stated items are not subject to self-employment tax.
LO 10.4: Describe the tax treatment of partnership distributions.	• A current distribution (of money or other property) does not result in the complete termination of the partner's interest in the partnership. • No gain is recognized by the partner receiving a current distribution unless the partner's basis in the partnership has reached zero. In such a case, gain is recognized only to the extent that a distribution of money exceeds the partner's basis in their partnership interest.
LO 10.5: Determine partnership tax years.	• Each partner includes in gross income for a particular tax year their individual distributive share of income, including guaranteed payments, from a partnership whose tax year ends with or within that tax year. • Unless a partnership can establish a business purpose for a fiscal year-end or meet certain tests, it must adopt the same taxable year as that of the majority partners. • If the majority partners do not have the same tax year, then the partnership is required to adopt the tax year of all its principal partners; otherwise, the partnership must adopt a tax year based on the least aggregate deferral method. • The tax year does not generally close upon the entry of a new partner, or upon the liquidation, sale, or exchange of an existing partnership interest. • A partnership will not close its tax year early unless the partnership is terminated, which occurs when business activity by the partnership ceases.

LO 10.6: Describe the tax treatment of transactions between partners and their partnerships.	• Generally, in a transaction with a partnership, a partner is regarded as an outside party, and the transaction is reported as it would be if the two parties were unrelated. • Losses, however, are disallowed for (1) transactions between a partnership and a partner who has a direct or indirect capital or profit interest in the partnership of more than 50 percent, and (2) transactions between two partnerships owned more than 50 percent by the same partners. • When a loss is disallowed, the purchaser may reduce a future gain on the disposition of the property by the amount of the disallowed loss. • A gain in a transaction between a partner and a partnership will be taxed as ordinary income if the partner has more than a 50-percent interest in the partnership and the property sold or transferred is not a capital asset to the transferee.
LO 10.7: Apply the qualified business income deduction to partners.	• Qualified business income does not include guaranteed payments or payments made to partners by the partnership in situations in which the partner is not acting in their capacity as a partner. • Partners are allocated their share of W-2 wages paid and qualified property of the partnership when computing the QBI deduction.
LO 10.8: Apply the at-risk rule to partnerships.	• In general, the at-risk rule limits the losses from a taxpayer's business activities to "amounts at risk" in the activity. • Taxpayers are at risk in amounts equal to their cash and property contributions to the activities, borrowed amounts to the extent of the property pledged, liabilities for which the taxpayers are personally liable, and retained profits of the activity. • Under the at-risk rule, taxpayers are allowed a deduction for losses allocable to a business activity to the extent of (1) income received or accrued from the activity without regard to the amount at risk, or (2) the taxpayer's amount at risk at the end of the tax year. • Any losses not allowed in the current year may be treated as deductions in succeeding years, with no limit on the number of years the losses may be carried forward.
LO 10.9: Describe the tax treatment of limited liability companies (LLCs).	• A limited liability company (LLC) is a hybrid form of business organization having some attributes of a partnership and other attributes of a corporation. • Each member of an LLC has limited liability similar to that of a stockholder in a corporation and at the same time has the tax advantages of a partnership (e.g., no tax at the entity level, loss pass-through, etc.). • Licensed professionals, such as attorneys, architects, and accountants, most often use a limited liability partnership (LLP) organizational structure, which is similar in many respects to an LLC. • An LLC can have a single member and in such cases, the LLC is treated as a disregarded entity for tax purposes.

QUESTIONS and PROBLEMS

GROUP 1: MULTIPLE CHOICE QUESTIONS

LO 10.1

1. Which of the following may *not* be treated as a partnership for tax purposes?
   a. Arnold and Willis operate a restaurant.
   b. Thelma and Louise establish an LLP to operate an accounting practice.
   c. Lucy and Desi purchase real estate together as a business.
   d. Jennifer and Ben form a corporation to purchase and operate a hardware store.
   e. All of the above are partnerships.

LO 10.1

2. Which of the following is a partnership for tax purposes?
   a. Monica and Chandler form a corporation to acquire a trucking business.
   b. Jimmy and Stephen both purchase a small stock interest in a manufacturing corporation as an investment.
   c. Emeril and Rachel purchase a food truck and sell prepared food dishes at various spots around the city.
   d. Melissa purchases a shoe store and hires her sister, Whitney, to manage the store.
   e. None of the above.

LO 10.1

3. In the current year, Hoffa Partnership allocates ordinary business income of $4,000 to Jimmy, a 40-percent partner. In addition, the partnership makes a cash distribution to Jimmy of $1,000, which is less than his basis in his partnership interest. What is the amount of partnership income Jimmy will need to recognize in the current year?
   a. $0
   b. $3,000
   c. $4,000
   d. $5,000

LO 10.1

4. Jekyll is a limited partner in the JH Partnership. His investment in JH is $10,000. If JH fails and if forced to wind up operations, Jekyll's liability is:
   a. unlimited
   b. limited to his investment in the partnership
   c. limited to his investment in the partnership plus his allocated share of the partnership liabilities
   d. zero, he has no liability

LO 10.1

5. Theodore has an investment in YYZ Corporation and a different investment in CXB Partnership. He has a 50-percent ownership stake in each. YYZ generates $100,000 of taxable income after paying corporate tax and makes no distribution to Theodore. CXB generates $50,000 of income and makes a $10,000 cash distribution (not in excess of Theodore's basis). Assuming he does not sell either investment, what is Theodore's taxable income from these investments in total?
   a. $0
   b. $10,000
   c. $25,000
   d. $35,000
   e. $85,000

LO 10.2

6. A partner's interest in a partnership is increased by:
   a. Capital losses of the partnership
   b. Tax-exempt interest earned by the partnership
   c. Losses of the partnership
   d. Distributions by the partnership
   e. None of the above

LO 10.2

7. A partner's interest in a partnership is decreased by:
   a. Increases in the partner's share of the partnership liabilities
   b. Debt relief that a partner experiences when contributing to the partnership property subject to a liability
   c. The partner's share of tax-exempt income earned by the partnership
   d. Contributions of cash from the partner to the partnership
   e. None of the above

LO 10.2

8. Abigail contributes land with an adjusted basis of $50,000 and a fair market value of $60,000 to Blair and Partners, a partnership. Abigail receives a 50-percent interest in Blair. What is Blair's basis in the land?
   a. $25,000
   b. $30,000
   c. $50,000
   d. $58,000
   e. $60,000

LO 10.2

9. Abigail contributes land with an adjusted basis of $50,000 and a fair market value of $60,000 to Blair and Partners, a partnership. Abigail receives a 50-percent interest in Blair. What is Abigail's basis in her partnership interest?
   a. $25,000
   b. $30,000
   c. $50,000
   d. $56,000
   e. $60,000

LO 10.2

10. Abigail contributes land with an adjusted basis of $50,000 and a fair market value of $60,000 to Blair and Partners, a partnership. Abigail receives a 50-percent interest in Blair. What is Abigail's recognized gain or loss on the contribution?
    a. $0
    b. $10,000 loss
    c. $10,000 gain
    d. $5,000 loss
    e. $5,000 gain

LO 10.2

11. Abigail contributes land with an adjusted basis of $50,000 and a fair market value of $60,000 to Blair and Partners, a partnership. Abigail receives a 50-percent interest in Blair. What is Blair's recognized gain or loss on the contribution?
    a. $0
    b. $10,000 loss
    c. $10,000 gain
    d. $5,000 loss
    e. $5,000 gain

LO 10.2

12. Blake and Ryan form the Poole Partnership. Blake contributes cash of $15,000. Ryan contributes land with an adjusted basis of $1,000 and a fair market value of $21,000. The land is subject to a $6,000 mortgage that Poole assumes. Blake and Ryan both receive a 50-percent interest in Poole. What is Ryan's recognized gain or loss on the contribution?
    a. $2,000
    b. $3,000
    c. $5,000
    d. $20,000
    e. None of the above

LO 10.3

13. Which of the following items do *not* have to be reported separately on a partnership return?
    a. Tax-exempt income
    b. Dividend income
    c. Typical MACRS depreciation expense
    d. Capital gains and losses
    e. Charitable contributions

LO 10.3

14. Which of the following items is generally reported as a separately stated item on a partnership return?
    a. Ordinary income from the operations of the partnership business
    b. Bonus depreciation
    c. Interest expense on business debts
    d. Net rental income
    e. Factory rent expense

LO 10.3
LO 10.7

15. When calculating ordinary income, partnerships are *not* allowed which of the following deductions?
    a. Miscellaneous expenses
    b. Qualified business income deduction
    c. Depreciation
    d. Cost of goods sold
    e. Employee wages

LO 10.3

16. Which of the following forms is used to report each partner's share of distributable income including separately stated items?
    a. Form 1065
    b. Schedule K
    c. Schedule K-1
    d. Schedule P

LO 10.3

17. TYVM Partnership allocates ordinary business income, long-term capital gains, and guaranteed payments of $13,000, $1,000, and $7,000, respectively, to Ariana Extensa, a general partner. Based on this information, what is Ariana's self-employment income?
    a. $0
    b. $7,000
    c. $8,000
    d. $20,000
    e. $21,000

LO 10.3

18. Which of the following items is generally reported as a separately stated item on a partnership return?
    a. Gross ordinary income from the operations of the partnership business
    b. Typical MACRS depreciation
    c. Employee salaries expense
    d. Insurance expense
    e. Guaranteed payments to a partner

LO 10.4

19. Feela is a one-third owner of Alchemy LLC, which is taxed as a partnership. Her basis prior to Alchemy paying Feela an $11,000 cash distribution is $6,000. How much income does Feela recognize from the distribution and what is her basis in her interest in Alchemy after the distribution?
    a. $11,000 income and $6,000 basis
    b. $6,000 income and $5,000 basis
    c. $5,000 income and $0 basis
    d. $0 income and negative $5,000 basis
    e. None of these choices

LO 10.4

20. Khushboo's basis in her 25-percent interest in the Rishi Partnership is $40,000 at the start of the current year. During the current year, Rishi reports ordinary business income of $80,000. Rishi also makes a $10,000 guaranteed payment and $16,000 cash distribution, both to Khushboo. What will Khushboo's basis be at the end of the current year and how much income will Khushboo recognize from these transactions?
    a. Basis of $44,000 and income of $30,000
    b. Basis of $34,000 and income of $80,000
    c. Basis of $34,000 and income of $20,000
    d. Basis of $60,000 and income of $20,000
    e. Basis of $50,000 and income of $16,000

LO 10.4

21. Laura is a non-passive general partner in the Douglass Partnership. At the start of 2022, her outside basis in Douglass is $10,000. During 2022, Douglass allocates loss of $8,000 to Laura and makes a $4,000 cash distribution to Laura. What is Laura's deductible loss for 2022 and what is her basis at year-end?
    a. $0 deductible loss and $0 basis.
    b. $8,000 deductible and $0 basis.
    c. $6,000 deductible and $4,000 basis.
    d. $6,000 deductible and $0 basis.
    e. $8,000 deductible and $2,000 basis.

LO 10.5

22. Which of the following circumstances will *not* cause a partnership to close its tax year early?
    a. The partnership terminates by agreement of the partners.
    b. The business activity of the partnership permanently ceases.
    c. All the partners decide to retire, permanently close their stores and stop conducting business.
    d. A new partner enters the partnership.

LO 10.5

23. Joe, Ben, and Melissa are partners in Collins Partnership. All three use a calendar year-end for their individual taxes. Collins Partnership's year-end is likely to be:
    a. October 31 since that is only three months prior to calendar year-end
    b. The end of any month during the year
    c. January 31 but only if Collins Partnership's accounting year-end is January 31
    d. December 31
    e. None of the above

LO 10.6

24. Kendra is an attorney and owns 60 percent of a law partnership. Kendra sells land to the partnership for $50,000 in the current tax year. She bought the land for $100,000 eight years ago when real estate prices were at their peak. How much gain or loss must Kendra recognize on the land sale to the partnership?
    a. No gain or loss
    b. $30,000 loss
    c. $50,000 loss
    d. $50,000 short-term capital loss, limited to $3,000 allowed per year

LO 10.6

25. A loss from the sale or exchange of property will be disallowed in which of the following situations?
    a. A transaction between a partnership and a partner who owns 40 percent of the partnership capital
    b. A transaction between a partnership and a partner who has a 40 percent profit interest in the partnership
    c. A transaction between two partnerships owned 80 percent by the same partners
    d. A transaction between two partners with investments in the same partnership
    e. None of the above

LO 10.7

26. In 2022, Gloria, a single taxpayer, receives a Schedule K-1 from a partnership in which she is invested. The K-1 reports ordinary business income of $30,000, dividend income of $500, tax-exempt interest of $300, and a guaranteed payment to Gloria of $10,000. Gloria's taxable income before the QBI deduction is $87,000. What is Gloria's QBI deduction?
    a. $6,160
    b. $6,000
    c. $4,000
    d. $17,400
    e. $8,000

LO 10.7

27. Jay is a 30-percent partner in the Closet Partnership. In 2022, Closet paid W-2 wages of $24,000 and held qualified property of $600,000. In 2022, Jay's QBI deduction is subject to the wage limitation due to his income. If Closet allocates wages and qualified property in the same manner as income (based on percentage ownership), what is Jay's wage and qualified property limit on the QBI deduction?
    a. $12,000
    b. $3,600
    c. $6,300
    d. $4,500

LO 10.7

28. A partnership should disclose qualified business income information on what supplemental form?
    a. Schedule K-2
    b. Statement A to the Schedule K-1
    c. Form 8995
    d. Schedule QBI

LO 10.8

29. Mike, an individual taxpayer, purchases a rental property for $200,000 using cash of $100,000 and borrowing the remaining $100,000 from a lending institution. The loan is considered to be qualified nonrecourse financing. What is Mike's at-risk amount?
    a. $300,000
    b. $200,000
    c. $100,000
    d. $0

LO 10.8

30. Gloria is a 30-percent general partner in the VH Partnership. During the year, VH borrows $40,000 from a bank to fund operations and is able to pay back $10,000 before year-end. VH also borrows $100,000 from Gloria's wealthy retired uncle on a non-recourse basis using land held by the partnership as the collateral. How much does Gloria's at-risk amount increase or decrease as a result of these transactions?
    a. $9,000 increase
    b. $30,000 decrease
    c. $12,000 increase
    d. $42,000 increase
    e. $42,000 decrease

LO 10.9

31. Which of the following properly describes a difference between a partnership and an LLC?
    a. Partnerships pass income and losses through to the partners while LLCs generally pay an entity level tax and owners pay tax on distributions.
    b. General partners are often personally responsible for the debts of the partnership while LLC members are not liable for LLC debt.
    c. Partnerships may have only one partner but LLCs must have more than one member.
    d. The tax attributes of income in a partnership are retained when included in the partner's income but LLC income is treated as capital income in all cases.

LO 10.9

32. Which of the following generate self-employment income for partners/members?
    a. Partnership income allocated to a limited partner
    b. Long-term capital gains allocated to an LLC member
    c. Income allocated to an LLC member that is actively engaged in the business
    d. Tax-exempt income allocated to both general partners and members

GROUP 2: PROBLEMS

LO 10.1

1. Debbie and Alan open a web-based bookstore together. They have been friends for so long that they start their business on a handshake after discussing how they will share both work and profits or losses from the business. Explain whether Debbie and Alan formed a partnership given that they have signed no written partnership agreement?

LO 10.1

2. Describe how the allocation of a partner's share of income and the distribution of cash to partners differ in triggering the recognition of income by the partner.

LO 10.1

3. Explain the difference in the treatment of liabilities between a general partner and a limited partner.

LO 10.2

4. Nan contributes property with an adjusted basis of $50,000 to a partnership. The property has a fair market value of $60,000 on the date of the contribution. What is the partnership's basis in the property contributed by Nan?

LO 10.2
LO 10.4

5. Elaine's original basis in the Hornbeam Partnership was $40,000. Her share of the taxable income from the partnership since she purchased the interest has been $70,000, and Elaine has received $80,000 in cash distributions from the partnership. Elaine did not recognize any gains as a result of the distributions. In the current year, Hornbeam also allocated $1,000 of tax-exempt interest to Elaine. Calculate Elaine's current basis in her partnership interest.

LO 10.2

6. Juanita contributes property with a fair market value of $30,000 and an adjusted basis of $16,000 to a partnership in exchange for an 10-percent partnership interest.
    a. Calculate the amount of gain recognized by Juanita as a result of the transfer of the property to the partnership.
    b. Calculate Juanita's basis in his partnership interest immediately following the contribution to the partnership.

LO 10.2

7. Mitchell, Max, and Romeo form a partnership to operate a grocery store. For each of the following contributions by the partners, indicate (1) the amount of income or gain recognized, if any, by the partner, and (2) the partner's basis in the partnership interest immediately after the contribution including the allocation of liabilities.
    a. Mitchell contributes property with a basis of $45,000 and subject to a $75,000 liability to the partnership for a one-third partnership interest worth $105,000. The partnership assumes the liability.
    b. Max contributes property with a basis of $25,000 and a fair market value of $105,000 to the partnership for a one-third partnership interest.
    c. Romeo performs services valued at $105,000 for the partnership for a one-third interest in the partnership.

LO 10.2

8. Kele and Nova wish to form the Sioux Partnership. Kele contributes property with an adjusted basis of $70,000, a fair market value of $200,000 that is subject to an $80,000 liability in exchange for 40 percent of Sioux. Nova receives a 60-percent interest in Sioux in exchange for providing services worth $10,000 and $170,000 cash.
    a. What amount of gain or loss must Kele recognize as a result of transferring property to the partnership?

b. What is Kele's basis in the partnership interest immediately after the formation of the partnership including allocation of partnership liabilities?
c. What is the partnership's basis in the property contributed by Kele?
d. What is Nova's basis in the partnership interest immediately after the formation of the partnership including allocation of partnership liabilities?
e. How much income does Nova recognize on the exchange?

LO 10.2
LO 10.4

9. Meredith has a 40-percent interest in the assets and income of the Gantt Partnership, and the basis in her partnership interest is $60,000 at the beginning of 2022. During 2022, the partnership's net loss is $45,000 and Meredith's share of the loss is $18,000. Also, Meredith receives a cash distribution from the partnership of $8,000 on June 30, 2022.
   a. Indicate the amount of income or loss from the partnership that should be reported by Meredith on her 2022 individual income tax return assuming she actively participates in the operations of the partnership.
   b. Calculate Meredith's basis in her partnership interest at the end of 2022.

LO 10.3

10. List five items of income or deductions that are required to be separately stated on Schedule K-1.

LO 10.3

11. K&T Company is a partnership with two equal partners, Kai and Taonga. The partnership has income of $60,000 for the year *before guaranteed payments*. Guaranteed payments of $25,000 are paid to Kai during the year. Calculate the amount of income that should be reported by Kai and Taonga from the partnership for the year.

LO 10.3

12. Georgina receives a Schedule K-1 for her general partner interest in the CCI Partnership that reports the following:
   - Ordinary business income $4,000
   - Net rental real estate income $2,000
   - Short-term capital gains $500
   - Section 1231 loss of $600
   - Guaranteed payments of $1,000
   - Cash distribution of $3,000

   Using the information from her Schedule K-1, compute Georgina's self-employment income:

LO 10.4

13. Elijah and Rona are both 50-percent partners in the Thakkar Partnership. At the start of the current year, Elijah's outside basis in Thakkar is $3,000 and Rona's outside basis in Thakkar is $7,000. During the current year, the distributive share of income for both Elijah and Rona is $500. There are no separately stated items in the current year except for a cash distribution of $5,000 each to Elijah and Rona. Provide an explanation of the computation of Elijah and Rona's income and ending outside basis for the current year.

LO 10.4

14. Walter receives cash of $18,000 and land with a fair market value of $75,000 (adjusted basis of $50,000) in a current distribution. His basis in his partnership interest is $16,000 before the distribution.
   a. What amount of gain must Walter recognize as a result of the current distribution?
   b. What amount of gain must the partnership recognize as a result of the distribution?
   c. What is Walter's basis in his partnership interest immediately after the distribution?

LO 10.5

15. Describe the rules for selecting a partnership year-end.

LO 10.5

16. Kiwi Interests is a partnership with a tax year that ends on September 30, 2022. During that year, Kereru, a partner, received $2,000 per month as a guaranteed payment, and his share of partnership income after guaranteed payments was $14,000. For October through December of 2022, Kereru received guaranteed payments of $3,000 per month. Calculate the amount of income from the partnership that Kereru should report for the tax year ending December 31, 2022.

LO 10.6

17. Louise owns 45 percent of a partnership, and her brother owns the remaining 55 percent interest. During the current tax year, Louise sold a building to the partnership for $160,000 to be used for the partnership's office. She had held the building for three years, and it had an adjusted basis of $120,000 at the time of the sale. What is the amount and nature of Louise's gain on this transaction?

LO 10.6

18. Rhianna owns a two-thirds interest in the ANTI Partnership and a 75-percent interest in the LOUD Partnership. In the current year, ANTI sells property to LOUD at a loss of $10,000. Later in the same year, LOUD sells the same property to an unrelated party for a $2,000 gain. What is the amount of gain or loss recognized by ANTI and LOUD on the sale of this property?

LO 10.7

19. Describe the consequences of not reporting qualified business income information to a partner on the partners' Schedule K-1.

LO 10.7

20. Janie owns a 30-percent interest in Chang Partnership. Chang has W-2 wages of $20,000 and qualified property of $900,000 in 2022.
    a. When computing the W-2 wages limitation, what is the amount of wages that will be allocated to Janie?
    b. What is the amount of qualified property that will be allocated to Janie?

LO 10.8

21. Van makes an investment in a partnership in the current year. Van's capital contributions to the partnership consist of $30,000 cash and a building with an adjusted basis of $70,000, subject to a nonrecourse liability (seller financing) of $20,000.
    a. Calculate the amount that Van has at risk in the partnership immediately after making the capital contributions.
    b. If Van's share of the loss from the partnership is $100,000 in the current year, and assuming that Van has sufficient amounts of passive income, how much of the loss may he deduct in the current year?
    c. What may be done with the nondeductible part of the loss in Part b?

LO 10.8

22. Octavio starts the year with outside basis of $23,000 and an amount at-risk of $23,000 in his 40-percent general partnership interest in Brown Partnership. In the current year, the partnership distributes $5,000 to Octavio. His share of allocated ordinary income is $3,000. The partnership also takes on nonrecourse debt of $20,000 (none of which is qualified nonrecourse financing). Compute Octavio's ending outside basis and amount at-risk.

LO 10.8
LO 10.9

23. Van makes an investment in an LLC in the current year. Van's capital contributions to the LLC consist of $30,000 cash and a building with an adjusted basis of $70,000, subject to a nonrecourse liability (seller financing) of $20,000. Calculate the amount that Van has at risk in the LLC immediately after making the capital contributions.

LO 10.9

24. Describe ways in which LLCs might differ from partnerships.

GROUP 3: COMPREHENSIVE PROBLEM

Emily Jackson (Social Security number 765-12-4326) and James Stewart (Social Security number 466-74-9932) are partners in a partnership that owns and operates a barber shop. The partnership's first year of operation is 2022. Emily and James divide income and expenses equally. The partnership name is J&S Barbers, it is located at 1023 Lexington Avenue, New York, NY 10128, and its Federal ID number is 95-6767676. The 2022 financial statements for the partnership are presented below.

J&S Barbers Income Statement for the Year Ending December 31, 2022

Gross income from operations	$349,000
Interest income	1,000
Deductions:	
Salaries to employees (includes guaranteed payments of $10,000 to Emily)	100,000
Payroll taxes	11,000
Supplies	7,900
Rent	90,000
Depreciation	32,100
Short-term capital loss	2,000
Non-deductible entertainment	3,000
Charitable contributions	1,000
Net income	$103,000
Partners' withdrawals (each partner)	$ 50,000

J&S Barbers Balance Sheet as of December 31, 2022

Assets:		
Cash		$92,000
Leasehold improvements	$ 3,100	
Equipment	32,000	
Accumulated depreciation	(32,100)	3,000
		$95,000
Liabilities and Capital:		
Recourse long-term debt		$52,000
Partners' capital ($20,000 contributed by each partner)		43,000
		$95,000

Emily lives at 456 E. 70th Street, New York, NY 10006, and James lives at 436 E. 63rd Street, New York, NY 10012.

Required: Complete J&S Barbers' Form 1065 and Emily and James' Schedules K-1. Do not fill in Schedule D for the capital loss, Form 4562 for depreciation, or Schedule B-1 related to ownership of the partnership. Make realistic assumptions about any missing data.

CHAPTER 11

The Corporate Income Tax

franckreporter/Getty Images

LEARNING OBJECTIVES

After completing this chapter, you should be able to:

- **LO 11.1** Employ the corporate tax rates to calculate corporate tax liability.
- **LO 11.2** Compute basic gains and losses for corporations.
- **LO 11.3** Apply special corporate deductions to corporate taxable income.
- **LO 11.4** Identify the components of Schedule M-1 and how they are reported to the IRS.
- **LO 11.5** Describe the corporate tax return filing and estimated tax payment requirements.
- **LO 11.6** Explain how an S corporation operates and is taxed.
- **LO 11.7** Describe the basic tax rules for the formation of a corporation.
- **LO 11.8** Describe the rules for the accumulated earnings tax and the personal holding company tax.

OVERVIEW

There are many forms of organization which may be used by taxpayers to operate a business. These include the sole proprietorship (Form 1040, Schedule C, covered in Chapter 3); the partnership, LLC, and LLP (Form 1065 covered in Chapter 10); and the regular C corporation and S corporation (covered in this chapter). Regular C corporations are taxed as separate legal taxpaying entities, and S corporations are taxed as flow-through entities similar to partnerships.

This chapter covers corporate tax rates, capital gains and losses, special deductions, the Schedule M-1, filing requirements, corporate formations, and corporate earnings accumulations. Additionally, basic coverage of the S corporation election and operating requirements are presented in this chapter.

This chapter provides a summary of corporate taxation and the tax forms (Form 1120, Form 1120S, and related schedules) associated with reporting C or S corporation income or loss.

Learning Objective 11.1

Employ the corporate tax rates to calculate corporate tax liability.

11-1 CORPORATE TAX RATES

Starting in 2018, corporations are subject to a flat income tax rate of 21 percent.

EXAMPLE Jasmine Corporation has taxable income of $175,000 for 2021. The corporation's tax liability for the year is calculated as follows:

Taxable income	$ 175,000
Corporate tax rate	21%
Tax liability	$ 36,750

♦

Unlike the individual alternative minimum tax (AMT), which remains in force, the corporate AMT was repealed for tax years after 2017 by the TCJA. Under the prior corporate AMT regime, a corporation subject to AMT may have had unused AMT credits that can be carried over indefinitely to offset regular tax. Under the CARES Act, any remaining AMT credit carryover could have been used as a refundable credit in 2019. Alternatively, an election could have been made by December 31, 2020, to take the entire credit amount in 2018. The likelihood of corporations having any remaining AMT credit carryforwards into 2022 is very low.

In 2022, a new version of a corporate alternative minimum tax was enacted in the Inflation Reduction Act of 2022. Described as a corporate minimum tax, the tax is 15 percent of adjusted financial statement income. The tax applies to corporations with average annual financial statement income of over $1 billion over a three-year period. An early analysis by the Joint Committee on Taxation estimates only 150 corporations will be subject to the tax.

Personal service corporations are taxed at the same 21 percent tax rate on all taxable income. A personal service corporation is substantially employee-owned and engages in one of the following activities:

- Health
- Law
- Engineering
- Architecture
- Accounting
- Actuarial science
- Performing arts
- Consulting

EXAMPLE Elm & Ash, Inc., is a professional service corporation of CPAs. For the current tax year, the corporation has taxable income of $175,000. Elm & Ash will have a 21 percent tax rate like any other corporation and thus a tax liability of $36,750 (21% × $175,000). ♦

Self-Study Problem 11.1 *See Appendix E for Solutions to Self-Study Problems*

Maple Corporation has taxable income of $335,000 for the current tax year. Calculate the corporation's tax liability, before tax credits.

Learning Objective 11.2

Compute basic gains and losses for corporations.

11-2 CORPORATE GAINS AND LOSSES

If a corporation generates a net capital gain, the net gain is included in ordinary income and the tax is computed at the regular rate except under very rare circumstances. The tax law provides for a maximum rate of 21 percent on corporate capital gains. Thus, Congress intends the ordinary income and capital gains rates to be the same for corporations, so there is no tax rate benefit to having long-term capital gains in a corporation. Net short-term capital gains of a corporation are also taxed as ordinary income.

11-2a **Capital Losses**

Corporations are not allowed to deduct capital losses against ordinary income. Capital losses may be used only to offset capital gains. If capital losses cannot be used in the year they occur, they may be carried back three years and forward five years to offset capital gains in those years. When a long-term capital loss is carried to another year, it is treated as a short-term capital loss, and may be offset against either long-term or short-term capital gains.

EXAMPLE In 2022, Eucalyptus Corporation incurs a long-term capital loss of $8,000, none of which may be deducted in that year. The loss is carried back to tax years 2019, 2020, and 2021, in that order. If the loss is not entirely used to offset capital gains in those years, it may be carried forward to 2023, 2024, 2025, 2026, and 2027, in that order. When the long-term loss is carried to another year, it is considered to be short term and may offset against either long-term or short-term capital gains. ♦

11-2b **Net Operating Losses**

As discussed in Chapter 4, corporations—similar to individuals—may also carryforward net operating losses (NOLs) to offset future taxable income. The TCJA made significant changes to the carryback and carryforward of NOLs after 2017, but most of these changes were temporarily suspended by the CARES Act in 2020 due to the COVID-19 pandemic. As a result, careful attention needs to be paid to when an NOL was created so that it can be tracked appropriately and afforded the proper treatment. An NOL created before 2018 had a two-year carryback and then a twenty-year carryforward (a taxpayer could elect out of the carryback) and the NOL could be used to offset 100 percent of the future year's taxable income.

EXAMPLE In 2017, Dez Corporation had a net operating loss of $10,000. Dez elected to forego any carryback and instead carried the NOL forward to 2018. In 2018, Dez generated taxable income of $12,000 eligible to be offset by 100 percent of the 2017 NOL. Dez's 2018 taxable income was $2,000, after the carryforward of the 2017 NOL. ♦

Under the TCJA, the use of an NOL generated after December 31, 2017, may only be carried forward (indefinitely) and was limited to 80 percent of the current year's taxable income (without regard to the NOL deduction) when used.

EXAMPLE Before the advent of the CARES Act, Fez Corporation had a net operating loss of $10,000 in 2018. Fez may only carry the NOL forward. In 2019, Fez generated taxable income of $12,000. Fez may only offset $9,600 ($12,000 × 80%) of its 2019 income which resulted in taxable income of $2,400. Fez may carryforward the remaining $400 2018 NOL to 2020. ♦

The CARES Act of 2020 suspended both the TCJA's 80-percent income limit rules and the carryforward only rule. Under the temporary rules, the 80-percent income limitation rule does not apply to a NOL created in 2018, 2019, or 2020, and those same NOLs may be carried back five years (unless carryback is waived). The carryforward remains indefinite. The TCJA rules are reinstated for years after 2020, thus an NOL carried forward into 2021 will be subject to the 80-percent limitation.

EXAMPLE Sez Corporation started in 2019 and generated taxable income in both 2019 and 2020; however, Sez generated a $10,000 loss in 2021. This NOL may not be carried back to any previous year and can be used to offset up to 80 percent of a future year's income with no expiration on any remaining NOL. ♦

The following table describes the treatment of NOLs since 2017:

NOL Year Generated	*Carryback*	*Carryforward*	*Limitation on use against future income*
Pre-2018	2 years	20 years	None
2018-2020	5 years	Indefinite	80% starting 2021
After 2020	None	Indefinite	80%

Self-Study Problem 11.2 ***See Appendix E for Solutions to Self-Study Problems***

a. During the current tax year, Taxus Corporation has ordinary income of $110,000, a long-term capital loss of $20,000, and a short-term capital loss of $5,000. Calculate Taxus Corporation's tax liability.

b. Maxus Corporation started business in 2020 and generated taxable income/(loss) of ($40,000), $45,000, and ($20,000) in 2020, 2021, and 2022, respectively. What is the NOL carryforward to 2023, if any?

11.3 Learning Objective

Apply special corporate deductions to corporate taxable income.

11-3 SPECIAL DEDUCTIONS AND LIMITATIONS

Corporations are allowed certain "special deductions," including the dividends received deduction and the deduction for organizational expenditures and start-up costs. In addition, the deduction for charitable contributions by a corporation is limited.

11-3a Dividends Received Deduction

When a corporation owns stock in another corporation, income earned by the first corporation could be taxed at least three times in the absence of a special provision. The income would be taxed to the first corporation when earned by the first corporation. Then it would be taxed to the corporation owning the stock in the first corporation when the income is distributed as dividend income. Finally, the income would be taxed to the shareholders of the second corporation when that corporation in turn distributes the earnings to its stockholders as dividends. To mitigate this potential for triple taxation of corporate earnings, corporations are allowed a deduction for all or a portion of dividends received from domestic corporations. Corporations are entitled to a dividends received deduction based on their percentage of ownership in the corporation paying the dividend. The deduction percentages are described as follows:

Percent Ownership	*Dividends Received Percentage*
Less than 20 percent	50%
20 percent or more, but less than 80 percent	65%
80 percent or more	100%

The dividends received deduction is limited to the applicable deduction percentage times the corporation's taxable income calculated before the dividends received deduction, the net operating loss deduction, and capital loss carrybacks. This taxable income limitation, however, does not apply if the receiving corporation has a net operating loss after reducing taxable income by the dividends received deduction. In other words, there is no taxable income limit if the dividends received deduction creates or increases a net operating loss.

EXAMPLE During the current year, Hackberry Corporation has the following income and expenses:

Gross income from operations excluding dividends	$240,000
Expenses from operations	200,000
Dividend received from a 30-percent-owned domestic corporation	100,000

The dividends received deduction is equal to the lesser of $65,000 (65% × $100,000) or 65 percent of taxable income before the dividends received deduction. Since taxable income (for computing this limitation) is $140,000 ($240,000 − $200,000 + $100,000) and 65 percent of $140,000 is $91,000, the full $65,000 is allowed as a deduction. ♦

EXAMPLE Assume the same facts as in the previous example, except Hackberry Corporation's gross income from operations is $190,000 (instead of $240,000). The dividends received deduction is equal to the lesser of $65,000 or 65 percent of $90,000 ($190,000 − $200,000 + $100,000), $58,500. Therefore, the dividends received deduction is limited to $58,500. Note that deducting the potential $65,000 dividends received deduction from taxable income does not generate a net operating loss. Accordingly, the taxable income limit is not avoided. ♦

11-3b Organizational Expenditures and Start-Up Costs

New businesses may incur organizational expenditures or start-up costs, or both, prior to starting a business. Organizational expenditures are incurred by partnerships, LLCs, and corporations in the process of forming an entity in which to operate a business. Start-up costs may be incurred by any business, including sole proprietorships reported on Schedule C, as well as the entities listed above.

In a scheme titled Private Tax Excepted Self Supporting Ministry (PTESSM), a taxpayer learned the consequences of attempting to deduct personal expenses by shifting them to a corporate entity. The taxpayer used a corporate credit card to pay for airfare, payments to video rental stores, grocery stores, fast-food restaurants, and other personal expenses. The IRS recharacterized these payments from business deductions to constructive dividends, which are not deductible. See *Combs v. Comm'r*, T.C. Memo 2019–96, and for information regarding the adviser of PTESSM see *United States v. Holcomb*, S.D. Cal. June 16, 2016.

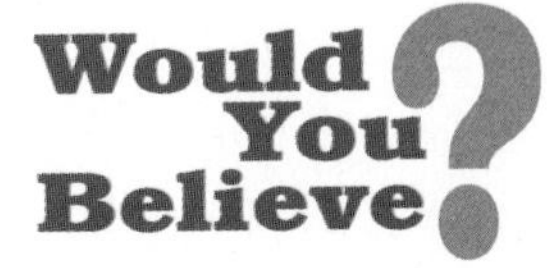

Corporations amortize qualifying *organizational* costs over 180 months, and there is no upper limit to the amount of qualifying costs that can be amortized. Corporations can elect to deduct up to $5,000 of organizational costs in the year they begin business. The $5,000 amount is reduced by each dollar of organizational expenses exceeding $50,000. Costs not expensed as part of the first-year election to expense are amortized ratably over the 180-month period beginning with the month the corporation begins business. Generally, organizational expenditures that qualify for amortization include legal and accounting services incident to organization, expenses of temporary directors and organizational meetings, and fees paid to the state for incorporation. Expenses such as the cost of transferring assets to the corporation and expenses connected with selling the corporation's stock are not organizational expenditures and, therefore, are not subject to amortization.

EXAMPLE In 2022, Coco Bola Corporation, an accrual-basis, calendar-year taxpayer, incurred $500 in fees to the state for incorporation, legal and accounting fees incident to the incorporation of $1,000, and temporary directors' expenses of $300. Assuming the corporation does not make an election to expense in the first year, the total $1,800 ($500 + $1,000 + $300) may be amortized over 15 years at a rate of $10 per month ($1,800/180 months). If the corporation began operations on June 1, 2022, $70 ($10 per month × 7 months) may be deducted for organizational expenditures for 2022. Alternatively, the corporation could elect to deduct the full $1,800 of organization costs in the first year of business. ♦

The *start-up costs* of a new business are given the same tax treatment as organizational costs, as illustrated in the previous paragraph and example. Start-up costs include both investigatory expenses and preopening costs. Investigatory expenses are expenses to investigate the potential success of a new business before the decision is made to actually pursue the business. Preopening costs are incurred after the taxpayer decides to start a new business but prior to the date the business actually begins. These expenses may include the training of new employees, advertising, and fees paid to consultants and professionals for advisory services.

For an existing business, exploratory (or expansion) costs are not treated the same as start-up costs.

EXAMPLE Donuts R Us Corp. owns a chain of donut shops in the northeast United States. DRU is considering opening new stores in southern California, and DRU's VP of Business Development visits a number of possible locations, meets with lawyers to discuss California regulation of food service and zoning rules, and engages a consulting firm to prepare a market study of the donut market in southern California. Because DRU is already in the donut business, the expenses incurred are considered ordinary and necessary expansion costs and are deductible. ♦

If a taxpayer attempts to expand into a new area of business, the costs are treated as start-up costs, and the resulting deduction is dependent on the type of taxpayer and whether the business is ever started.

EXAMPLE Donuts R Us Corp. owns a chain of donut shops in the northeast United States. DRU's CEO loves to surf, and so she is considering expanding DRU's operations into the surf shop business in southern California. The DRU VP of Business Development visits a number of locations, meets with lawyers to discuss California regulation of surf shops and zoning rules, and engages a consulting firm to prepare a market study of the surf apparel and surfboard market in Southern California. Because DRU is not in the surf shop business, these expenses are considered pre-operating start-up expenses. If DRU opens a California surf shop business, the expenses incurred are start-up costs and will be expensed or amortized as described previously. If DRU does not end up in the surfshop business, these costs are capitalized until such time as the "failure" occurs and are then deducted as a loss. Note that if DRU is not a corporation, the start-up costs associated with a failed venture are not deductible at all. ♦

11-3c Charitable Contributions

Corporations are allowed a deduction for contributions to qualified charitable organizations. Generally, a deduction is allowed in the year in which a payment is made. If, however, the directors of a corporation which maintains its books on the accrual basis make a pledge before year-end, and the payment is made on or before the fifteenth day of the third month after the close of the tax year, the deduction may be claimed in the year of the pledge.

Typically, a corporation's charitable contributions deduction is limited to 10 percent of taxable income, computed before the deduction for charitable contributions, net operating loss carrybacks, capital loss carrybacks, and the dividends received deduction. Any excess contributions may be carried forward to the five succeeding tax years, but carryforward amounts are subject to the 10 percent annual limitation in the carryover years, with the current year's contributions deducted first.

EXAMPLE Zircote Corporation had net operating income of $40,000 for the 2022 tax year and made a cash charitable contribution (not disaster relief) of $16,000 (not included in the operating income amount). Also not included in the operating income were dividends received of $10,000. The corporation's charitable contribution deduction is limited to 10 percent of $50,000 ($40,000 + $10,000), or $5,000. Note that the dividends received deduction is not used in calculating taxable income for purposes of determining the limitation on the charitable contribution deduction. The $11,000 ($16,000 − $5,000) of the charitable contribution that is disallowed in the current year is carried forward for up to five years. ♦

Self-Study Problem 11.3 ***See Appendix E for Solutions to Self-Study Problems***

a. During 2022, Fraxinia Corporation has the following income and expenses:

Gross income from operations, excluding dividends	$ 90,000
Expenses from operations	100,000
Dividends received from a 25-percent-owned domestic corporation	70,000

Calculate the amount of Fraxinia Corporation's dividends received deduction.

b. Boyce Inc., a calendar-year corporation, incurred organizational costs of $13,000 and start-up costs of $52,000 in 2022. Boyce started business on August 3, 2022. What is the maximum deduction for organizational and start-up costs for Boyce in 2022, and what is Boyce's 2023 deduction for the same costs?

c. Gant Corporation has income in 2022 of $65,000 after a dividends received deduction of $5,000 and a charitable contribution of $25,000. What is the deductible amount of the charitable contribution in 2022?

Learning Objective 11.4

Identify the components of Schedule M-1 and how they are reported to the IRS.

11-4 SCHEDULE M-1

A corporation is required to report its income and other items on Form 1120, U.S. Corporation Income Tax Return. Because of various provisions in the tax law, a corporation's taxable income seldom is the same as its accounting income (commonly referred to as "book income"). The purpose of Schedule M-1 of the Form 1120 corporate tax return is to reconcile a corporation's book income to its taxable income, computed before the net operating loss and special deductions such as the dividends received deduction. On the left side of Schedule M-1 are adjustments that must be added to book income, and on the right side of the schedule are adjustments that must be subtracted from book income to arrive at the amount of taxable income. The amounts that must be added to book income include the amount of federal income tax expense, net capital losses deducted for book purposes, income recorded on the tax return but not on the books, and expenses recorded on the books but not deducted on the tax return. Alternatively, the amounts that must be deducted from book income are income recorded on the books but not included on the tax return, and deductions on the return not deducted on the books.

EXAMPLE For the current tax year, Wisteria Corporation, an accrual-basis taxpayer, has net income reported on its books of $44,975. Included in this figure are the following items:

Net capital loss	$ 5,000
Interest income on tax-exempt bonds	9,000
Federal income tax expense	11,025
Depreciation deducted on the tax return, not deducted on the books	3,500
Interest deducted on the books, not deductible for tax purposes	4,000

Wisteria Corporation's Schedule M-1, Form 1120, is illustrated below.

Schedule M-1 **Reconciliation of Income (Loss) per Books With Income per Return**
Note: The corporation may be required to file Schedule M-3. See instructions.

1	Net income (loss) per books	44,975	7	Income recorded on books this year not included on this return (itemize): Tax-exempt interest $ 9,000	9,000
2	Federal income tax per books	11,025			
3	Excess of capital losses over capital gains				
4	Income subject to tax not recorded on books this year (itemize):		8	Deductions on this return not charged against book income this year (itemize):	
5	Expenses recorded on books this year not deducted on this return (itemize):		a	Depreciation $ 3,500	
a	Depreciation $		b	Charitable contributions $	3,500
b	Charitable contributions $				
c	Travel and entertainment $				
	Interest	4,000	9	Add lines 7 and 8	12,500
6	Add lines 1 through 5	65,000	10	Income (page 1, line 28)—line 6 less line 9	52,500

♦

Self-Study Problem 11.4 *See Appendix E for Solutions to Self-Study Problems*

Redwood Corporation has net income reported on its books of $115,600. For the current year, the corporation had federal income tax expense of $29,400, a net capital loss of $9,100, and tax-exempt interest income of $4,700. The company deducted depreciation of $17,000 on its tax return and $13,000 on its books. Using Schedule M-1 below, calculate Redwood Corporation's taxable income, before any net operating loss or special deductions, for the current year.

Schedule M-1 **Reconciliation of Income (Loss) per Books With Income per Return**
Note: The corporation may be required to file Schedule M-3. See instructions.

1	Net income (loss) per books		7	Income recorded on books this year not included on this return (itemize): Tax-exempt interest $	
2	Federal income tax per books				
3	Excess of capital losses over capital gains				
4	Income subject to tax not recorded on books this year (itemize):		8	Deductions on this return not charged against book income this year (itemize):	
5	Expenses recorded on books this year not deducted on this return (itemize):		a	Depreciation . . $	
a	Depreciation . . . . $		b	Charitable contributions $	
b	Charitable contributions . $				
c	Travel and entertainment . $		9	Add lines 7 and 8	
6	Add lines 1 through 5		10	Income (page 1, line 28)—line 6 less line 9	

11-5 FILING REQUIREMENTS AND ESTIMATED TAX

11.5 Learning Objective

Describe the corporate tax return filing and estimated tax payment requirements.

For all tax year-ends except for June 30, the due date for filing a corporate tax return is the fifteenth day of the fourth month after year-end. For June 30 year-end corporations, the filing due date is September 15 (fifteenth day of the third month). An extension provides an additional six months; thus, a calendar year-end corporation has an initial filing deadline of April 15 and an extended deadline of October 15 (six-month extension). However, corporations with tax years ending on June 30 will have an extended filing deadline of April 15 (seven-month extension). When the due date falls on a weekend or holiday, the due date is the next business day. To avoid penalties, a corporation must pay any unpaid tax liability by the original due date of the return.

Corporations must make estimated tax payments in a manner similar to those made by self-employed individual taxpayers. The payments are made in four installments due on the fifteenth day of the fourth, sixth, ninth, and twelfth months of the corporation's tax year.

EXAMPLE Grew Inc., is a calendar year-end corporation. Estimated payments are due April 15, June 15, September 15, and December 15. If Grew had a September 30 year-end, estimated payments would be due on January 15, March 15, June 15, and September 15. ♦

The penalty for failing to make adequate estimated payments applies when a corporation with an expected tax liability (after credits) of $500 or more fails to pay by the due date either (1) the current year tax liability or (2) an amount equal to the prior year tax liability. For large corporations (those with annual income of $1 million or more in any of the previous three years), use of prior year liability is limited to only the first quarter's estimated payment.

EXAMPLE Vector Corporation, a calendar year-end corporation that is not a large corporation, had tax liability of $14,000 last year and current year tax liability of $15,000. Vector can avoid penalties by making estimated payments of $14,000. If Vector was a large corporation, estimated payments of $15,000 are required to avoid penalties. ♦

Penalties for underpayment of estimated taxes by a corporation can also be avoided by use of the annualized income method. The annualized income method permits the corporation to estimate income for the first three quarters of the year and to determine required estimated payments. The annualized income method allows the corporation to estimate current year liability rather than wait for the end of the tax year to determine current year tax liability. Note that unlike individuals, a corporation's final quarter's payment is due the fifteenth day of the twelfth month, which is prior to the tax year-end. Under the annualized income method, each payment is designed to be 25 percent of the total tax liability based on estimates of annualized income.

EXAMPLE Minyon Corporation is a calendar year-end large corporation for purposes of estimated payments. Prior year tax liability was $250,000. Minyon estimates each quarter's *year-to-date income* as follows:

Q1	$ 300,000
Q2	700,000
Q3	950,000
Q4	1,300,000

The step-by-step process to compute the estimated tax payment for the first quarter payment is:

1. Annualize the first quarter's estimated income: $300,000 × 4 = $1,200,000
2. Compute the estimate of tax liability for the year: $1,200,000 × 21% = $252,000
3. Compute the first quarter's estimated payment requirement: $252,000 × 25% = $63,000

The first quarter's estimated payment can be based on either prior year $62,500 ($250,000 × 25%) or the annualized income method. Most corporations will choose to pay the lower amount and conserve cash.

The step-by-step process to compute the estimated tax payment for the second quarter payment is:

1. Annualize the *first* quarter's estimated income: $300,000 × 4 = $1,200,000 (note that the second quarter payment is due June 15 and thus, the second quarter's estimate of income is not yet known).
2. Compute the estimate of tax liability for the year: $1,200,000 × 21% = $252,000.
3. Compute the second quarter's estimated payment requirement: $252,000 × 50% = $126,000 less the previous payment of $62,500 results in a required second quarter estimated payment of $63,500.

Prior year tax liability is not permitted to be used to determine estimated tax payments after the first quarter for a large corporation such as Minyon.

The step-by-step process to compute the estimated tax payment for the third quarter payment is:

1. Annualize the *second* quarter's estimated income: $700,000 × 2 = $1,400,000 (note that the third quarter payment is due September 15 and thus the third quarter's estimate of income is not yet known).
2. Compute the estimate of tax liability for the year: $1,400,000 × 21% = $294,000.
3. Compute the third quarter's estimate payment requirement: $294,000 × 75% = $220,500 less previous payments of $126,000 results in a required estimated payment of $94,500.

The step-by-step process to compute the estimated tax payment for the fourth quarter payment is:

1. Annualize the *third* quarter's estimated income: $950,000 × 12/9 = $1,266,667 (note that the fourth quarter payment is due December 15 and thus the fourth quarter's estimate of income is not yet known).
2. Compute the estimate of tax liability for the year: $1,266,667 × 21% = $266,000.
3. Compute the fourth quarter's estimate payment requirement: $266,000 × 100% = $266,000 less previous payments of $220,500 results in a required estimated payment of $45,500. ♦

If estimates of annualized income have been prepared in accordance with regulations, the annualized estimates serve to replace the actual tax liability for the year. To the extent the actual tax liability exceeds the estimates, any payment is due at the original due date of the return. Overpayments can either be refunded or applied to the subsequent tax year.

EXAMPLE Minyon Corporation, from the previous example, has actual tax liability of $273,000 ($1,300,000 × 21%). The additional tax due of $7,000 ($273,000 − $266,000) must be paid by April 15 of the following year, the unextended due date of the corporate tax return. ♦

TAX BREAK

Small corporations (both S and C) with less than $250,000 in gross receipts and less than $250,000 in assets do not have to complete Schedule L (Balance Sheet) or Schedules M-1. A small C corporation does not have to complete Schedule M-2, while a C corporation does. The rule allows small businesses to keep records based on their checkbook or cash receipts and disbursements journal. This makes the reporting requirements for a small corporation similar to the reporting requirements for a Schedule C sole proprietorship.

Self-Study Problem 11.5

See Appendix E for Solutions to Self-Study Problems

1. Alberta Corp. is a calendar year-end corporation. In the previous three years, Alberta has reported taxable income of $680,000, $1,100,000 and $925,000. This year Alberta had the following year-to-date estimates of income for each quarter:

   Q1 $225,000
   Q2 $475,000
   Q3 $660,000
   Q4 $920,000

Self-Study Problem 11.5, continued

See Appendix E for Solutions to Self-Study Problems

Alberta's prior year tax liability was $194,250, and they applied an overpayment of $4,500 from the prior year to this year.

Using this information, calculate the required estimated payment for each quarter.

2. Aspen Corporation was formed and began operations on January 1, 2022. Aspen is located at 470 Rio Grande Place, Aspen, CO 81611 and the EIN is 92-2222222.

Aspen Corporation
Income Statement
for the Year Ended December 31, 2022

Gross income from operations		$ 285,000
Qualified dividends received from a 10 percent-owned domestic corporation		10,000
Total gross income		295,000
Cost of goods sold		(80,000)
Total income		215,000
Other expenses:		
Compensation of officers	$90,000	
Salaries and wages	82,000	
Repairs	8,000	
Depreciation expense for book and tax purposes	5,000	
Payroll taxes	11,000	
Total other expenses		(196,000)
Net income (before federal income tax expense)		$ 19,000

Aspen Corporation
Balance Sheet
as of December 31, 2022

Assets:		
Cash	$ 35,000	
Accounts receivable	10,000	
Land	18,000	
Building	125,000	
Less: accumulated depreciation	(5,000)	
Total assets		$ 183,000
Liabilities and owners' equity:		
Accounts payable	$ 26,940	
Common stock	140,000	
Retained earnings	16,060	
Total liabilities and owners' equity		$ 183,000

Aspen Corporation made estimated tax payments of $3,000.

Based on the above information, complete Form 1120 on Pages 11-13 to 11-18. Assume the corporation's book federal income tax expense is equal to its 2022 federal income tax liability and that any tax overpayment is to be applied to the next year's estimated tax. Schedule UTP, Form 4562, Form 1125-A, and Form 1125-E are not required. Make reasonable assumptions for any missing data.

Self-Study Problem 11.5

Form **1120** Department of the Treasury Internal Revenue Service

U.S. Corporation Income Tax Return

For calendar year 2022 or tax year beginning ________, 2022, ending ________, 20 ____

Go to *www.irs.gov/Form1120* for instructions and the latest information.

OMB No. 1545-0123 **2022**

A Check if:	TYPE OR PRINT		
1a Consolidated return (attach Form 851) ☐		Name	B Employer identification number
b Life/nonlife consolidated return . . ☐		Number, street, and room or suite no. If a P.O. box, see instructions.	C Date incorporated
2 Personal holding co. (attach Sch. PH) . ☐		City or town, state or province, country, and ZIP or foreign postal code	D Total assets (see instructions) $
3 Personal service corp. (see instructions) . ☐			
4 Schedule M-3 attached ☐		E Check if: (1) ☐ Initial return (2) ☐ Final return (3) ☐ Name change (4) ☐ Address change	

Income	1a	Gross receipts or sales	1a	
	b	Returns and allowances	1b	
	c	Balance. Subtract line 1b from line 1a		1c
	2	Cost of goods sold (attach Form 1125-A)		2
	3	Gross profit. Subtract line 2 from line 1c		3
	4	Dividends and inclusions (Schedule C, line 23)		4
	5	Interest		5
	6	Gross rents		6
	7	Gross royalties		7
	8	Capital gain net income (attach Schedule D (Form 1120))		8
	9	Net gain or (loss) from Form 4797, Part II, line 17 (attach Form 4797)		9
	10	Other income (see instructions—attach statement)		10
	11	**Total income.** Add lines 3 through 10		11
Deductions (See instructions for limitations on deductions.)	12	Compensation of officers (see instructions—attach Form 1125-E)		12
	13	Salaries and wages (less employment credits)		13
	14	Repairs and maintenance		14
	15	Bad debts		15
	16	Rents		16
	17	Taxes and licenses		17
	18	Interest (see instructions)		18
	19	Charitable contributions		19
	20	Depreciation from Form 4562 not claimed on Form 1125-A or elsewhere on return (attach Form 4562)		20
	21	Depletion		21
	22	Advertising		22
	23	Pension, profit-sharing, etc., plans		23
	24	Employee benefit programs		24
	25	Reserved for future use		25
	26	Other deductions (attach statement)		26
	27	**Total deductions.** Add lines 12 through 26		27
	28	Taxable income before net operating loss deduction and special deductions. Subtract line 27 from line 11.		28
	29a	Net operating loss deduction (see instructions)	29a	
	b	Special deductions (Schedule C, line 24)	29b	
	c	Add lines 29a and 29b		29c
Tax, Refundable Credits, and Payments	30	**Taxable income.** Subtract line 29c from line 28. See instructions		30
	31	Total tax (Schedule J, Part I, line 11)		31
	32	Reserved for future use		32
	33	Total payments and credits (Schedule J, Part III, line 23)		33
	34	Estimated tax penalty. See instructions. Check if Form 2220 is attached ☐		34
	35	**Amount owed.** If line 33 is smaller than the total of lines 31 and 34, enter amount owed		35
	36	**Overpayment.** If line 33 is larger than the total of lines 31 and 34, enter amount overpaid		36
	37	Enter amount from line 36 you want: **Credited to 2023 estimated tax**	Refunded	37

Sign Here

Under penalties of perjury, I declare that I have examined this return, including accompanying schedules and statements, and to the best of my knowledge and belief, it is true, correct, and complete. Declaration of preparer (other than taxpayer) is based on all information of which preparer has any knowledge.

Signature of officer | Date | Title

May the IRS discuss this return with the preparer shown below? See instructions. ☐ Yes ☐ No

Paid Preparer Use Only

Print/Type preparer's name	Preparer's signature	Date	Check ☐ if self-employed	PTIN
Firm's name			Firm's EIN	
Firm's address			Phone no.	

For Paperwork Reduction Act Notice, see separate instructions. Cat. No. 11450Q Form **1120** (2022)

Form 1120 (2022) Page 2

Schedule C **Dividends, Inclusions, and Special Deductions** (see instructions)	**(a)** Dividends and inclusions	**(b)** %	**(c)** Special deductions **(a)** × **(b)**
1 Dividends from less-than-20%-owned domestic corporations (other than debt-financed stock)		50	
2 Dividends from 20%-or-more-owned domestic corporations (other than debt-financed stock)		65	
3 Dividends on certain debt-financed stock of domestic and foreign corporations		See instructions	
4 Dividends on certain preferred stock of less-than-20%-owned public utilities		23.3	
5 Dividends on certain preferred stock of 20%-or-more-owned public utilities		26.7	
6 Dividends from less-than-20%-owned foreign corporations and certain FSCs		50	
7 Dividends from 20%-or-more-owned foreign corporations and certain FSCs		65	
8 Dividends from wholly owned foreign subsidiaries		100	
9 **Subtotal.** Add lines 1 through 8. See instructions for limitations		See instructions	
10 Dividends from domestic corporations received by a small business investment company operating under the Small Business Investment Act of 1958		100	
11 Dividends from affiliated group members		100	
12 Dividends from certain FSCs		100	
13 Foreign-source portion of dividends received from a specified 10%-owned foreign corporation (excluding hybrid dividends) (see instructions)		100	
14 Dividends from foreign corporations not included on line 3, 6, 7, 8, 11, 12, or 13 (including any hybrid dividends)			
15 Reserved for future use			
16a Subpart F inclusions derived from the sale by a controlled foreign corporation (CFC) of the stock of a lower-tier foreign corporation treated as a dividend (attach Form(s) 5471) (see instructions)		100	
b Subpart F inclusions derived from hybrid dividends of tiered corporations (attach Form(s) 5471) (see instructions)			
c Other inclusions from CFCs under subpart F not included on line 16a, 16b, or 17 (attach Form(s) 5471) (see instructions)			
17 Global Intangible Low-Taxed Income (GILTI) (attach Form(s) 5471 and Form 8992)			
18 Gross-up for foreign taxes deemed paid			
19 IC-DISC and former DISC dividends not included on line 1, 2, or 3			
20 Other dividends			
21 Deduction for dividends paid on certain preferred stock of public utilities			
22 Section 250 deduction (attach Form 8993)			
23 **Total dividends and inclusions.** Add column (a), lines 9 through 20. Enter here and on page 1, line 4			
24 **Total special deductions.** Add column (c), lines 9 through 22. Enter here and on page 1, line 29b			

Form **1120** (2022)

Form 1120 (2022) Page 3

Schedule J Tax Computation and Payment (see instructions)

Part I—Tax Computation

1	Check if the corporation is a member of a controlled group (attach Schedule O (Form 1120)). See instructions ☐				
2	Income tax. See instructions			2	
3	Base erosion minimum tax amount (attach Form 8991)			3	
4	Add lines 2 and 3			4	
5a	Foreign tax credit (attach Form 1118)	5a			
b	Credit from Form 8834 (see instructions)	5b			
c	General business credit (attach Form 3800)	5c			
d	Credit for prior year minimum tax (attach Form 8827)	5d			
e	Bond credits from Form 8912	5e			
6	**Total credits.** Add lines 5a through 5e			6	
7	Subtract line 6 from line 4			7	
8	Personal holding company tax (attach Schedule PH (Form 1120))			8	
9a	Recapture of investment credit (attach Form 4255)	9a			
b	Recapture of low-income housing credit (attach Form 8611)	9b			
c	Interest due under the look-back method—completed long-term contracts (attach Form 8697)	9c			
d	Interest due under the look-back method—income forecast method (attach Form 8866)	9d			
e	Alternative tax on qualifying shipping activities (attach Form 8902)	9e			
f	Interest/tax due under section 453A(c) and/or section 453(l)	9f			
g	Other (see instructions—attach statement)	9g			
10	**Total.** Add lines 9a through 9g			10	
11	**Total tax.** Add lines 7, 8, and 10. Enter here and on page 1, line 31			11	

Part II—Reserved For Future Use

12	Reserved for future use	12	

Part III—Payments and Refundable Credits

13	2021 overpayment credited to 2022			13	
14	2022 estimated tax payments			14	
15	2022 refund applied for on Form 4466			15	( )
16	Combine lines 13, 14, and 15			16	
17	Tax deposited with Form 7004			17	
18	Withholding (see instructions)			18	
19	**Total payments.** Add lines 16, 17, and 18			19	
20	Refundable credits from:				
a	Form 2439	20a			
b	Form 4136	20b			
c	Reserved for future use	20c			
d	Other (attach statement—see instructions)	20d			
21	**Total credits.** Add lines 20a through 20d			21	
22	Reserved for future use			22	
23	**Total payments and credits.** Add lines 19 and 21. Enter here and on page 1, line 33			23	

Form **1120** (2022)

Form 1120 (2022) Page **4**

Schedule K **Other Information** (see instructions)

		Yes	No
1	Check accounting method: **a** ☐ Cash **b** ☐ Accrual **c** ☐ Other (specify)		
2	See the instructions and enter the:		
a	Business activity code no.		
b	Business activity		
c	Product or service		
3	Is the corporation a subsidiary in an affiliated group or a parent–subsidiary controlled group? . . . . If "Yes," enter name and EIN of the parent corporation		
4	At the end of the tax year:		
a	Did any foreign or domestic corporation, partnership (including any entity treated as a partnership), trust, or tax-exempt organization own directly 20% or more, or own, directly or indirectly, 50% or more of the total voting power of all classes of the corporation's stock entitled to vote? If "Yes," complete Part I of Schedule G (Form 1120) (attach Schedule G)		
b	Did any individual or estate own directly 20% or more, or own, directly or indirectly, 50% or more of the total voting power of all classes of the corporation's stock entitled to vote? If "Yes," complete Part II of Schedule G (Form 1120) (attach Schedule G) .		
5	At the end of the tax year, did the corporation:		
a	Own directly 20% or more, or own, directly or indirectly, 50% or more of the total voting power of all classes of stock entitled to vote of any foreign or domestic corporation not included on **Form 851,** Affiliations Schedule? For rules of constructive ownership, see instructions. If "Yes," complete (i) through (iv) below.		

(i) Name of Corporation	**(ii)** Employer Identification Number (if any)	**(iii)** Country of Incorporation	**(iv)** Percentage Owned in Voting Stock

		Yes	No
b	Own directly an interest of 20% or more, or own, directly or indirectly, an interest of 50% or more in any foreign or domestic partnership (including an entity treated as a partnership) or in the beneficial interest of a trust? For rules of constructive ownership, see instructions. If "Yes," complete (i) through (iv) below.		

(i) Name of Entity	**(ii)** Employer Identification Number (if any)	**(iii)** Country of Organization	**(iv)** Maximum Percentage Owned in Profit, Loss, or Capital

		Yes	No
6	During this tax year, did the corporation pay dividends (other than stock dividends and distributions in exchange for stock) in excess of the corporation's current and accumulated earnings and profits? See sections 301 and 316 . . . . If "Yes," file **Form 5452,** Corporate Report of Nondividend Distributions. See the instructions for Form 5452. If this is a consolidated return, answer here for the parent corporation and on Form 851 for each subsidiary.		
7	At any time during the tax year, did one foreign person own, directly or indirectly, at least 25% of the total voting power of all classes of the corporation's stock entitled to vote or at least 25% of the total value of all classes of the corporation's stock? . For rules of attribution, see section 318. If "Yes," enter: **(a)** Percentage owned ________ and **(b)** Owner's country ________ **(c)** The corporation may have to file **Form 5472,** Information Return of a 25% Foreign-Owned U.S. Corporation or a Foreign Corporation Engaged in a U.S. Trade or Business. Enter the number of Forms 5472 attached ________		
8	Check this box if the corporation issued publicly offered debt instruments with original issue discount . . . . ☐ If checked, the corporation may have to file **Form 8281,** Information Return for Publicly Offered Original Issue Discount Instruments.		
9	Enter the amount of tax-exempt interest received or accrued during the tax year $ ________		
10	Enter the number of shareholders at the end of the tax year (if 100 or fewer) ________		
11	If the corporation has an NOL for the tax year and is electing to forego the carryback period, check here (see instructions) ☐ If the corporation is filing a consolidated return, the statement required by Regulations section 1.1502-21(b)(3) must be attached or the election will not be valid.		
12	Enter the available NOL carryover from prior tax years (do not reduce it by any deduction reported on page 1, line 29a.) . . . . $		

Form **1120** (2022)

Form 1120 (2022) Page **5**

Schedule K **Other Information** *(continued from page 4)*

		Yes	No
13	Are the corporation's total receipts (page 1, line 1a, plus lines 4 through 10) for the tax year **and** its total assets at the end of the tax year less than $250,000?		
	If "Yes," the corporation is not required to complete Schedules L, M-1, and M-2. Instead, enter the total amount of cash distributions and the book value of property distributions (other than cash) made during the tax year $ ________		
14	Is the corporation required to file Schedule UTP (Form 1120), Uncertain Tax Position Statement? See instructions		
	If "Yes," complete and attach Schedule UTP.		
15a	Did the corporation make any payments in 2022 that would require it to file Form(s) 1099?		
b	If "Yes," did or will the corporation file required Form(s) 1099?		
16	During this tax year, did the corporation have an 80%-or-more change in ownership, including a change due to redemption of its own stock?		
17	During or subsequent to this tax year, but before the filing of this return, did the corporation dispose of more than 65% (by value) of its assets in a taxable, non-taxable, or tax deferred transaction?		
18	Did the corporation receive assets in a section 351 transfer in which any of the transferred assets had a fair market basis or fair market value of more than $1 million?		
19	During the corporation's tax year, did the corporation make any payments that would require it to file Forms 1042 and 1042-S under chapter 3 (sections 1441 through 1464) or chapter 4 (sections 1471 through 1474) of the Code?		
20	Is the corporation operating on a cooperative basis?		
21	During the tax year, did the corporation pay or accrue any interest or royalty for which the deduction is not allowed under section 267A? See instructions		
	If "Yes," enter the total amount of the disallowed deductions $ ________		
22	Does the corporation have gross receipts of at least $500 million in any of the 3 preceding tax years? (See sections 59A(e)(2) and (3))		
	If "Yes," complete and attach Form 8991.		
23	Did the corporation have an election under section 163(j) for any real property trade or business or any farming business in effect during the tax year? See instructions		
24	Does the corporation satisfy one or more of the following? See instructions		
a	The corporation owns a pass-through entity with current, or prior year carryover, excess business interest expense.		
b	The corporation's aggregate average annual gross receipts (determined under section 448(c)) for the 3 tax years preceding the current tax year are more than $27 million and the corporation has business interest expense.		
c	The corporation is a tax shelter and the corporation has business interest expense.		
	If "Yes," complete and attach Form 8990.		
25	Is the corporation attaching Form 8996 to certify as a Qualified Opportunity Fund?		
	If "Yes," enter amount from Form 8996, line 15 $		
26	Since December 22, 2017, did a foreign corporation directly or indirectly acquire substantially all of the properties held directly or indirectly by the corporation, and was the ownership percentage (by vote or value) for purposes of section 7874 greater than 50% (for example, the shareholders held more than 50% of the stock of the foreign corporation)? If "Yes," list the ownership percentage by vote and by value. See instructions		
	Percentage: By Vote ________ By Value ________		

Form **1120** (2022)

Form 1120 (2022) Page **6**

Schedule L **Balance Sheets per Books**

	Assets	Beginning of tax year (a)	(b)	End of tax year (c)	(d)
1	Cash				
2a	Trade notes and accounts receivable				
b	Less allowance for bad debts	( )		( )	
3	Inventories				
4	U.S. government obligations				
5	Tax-exempt securities (see instructions)				
6	Other current assets (attach statement)				
7	Loans to shareholders				
8	Mortgage and real estate loans				
9	Other investments (attach statement)				
10a	Buildings and other depreciable assets				
b	Less accumulated depreciation	( )		( )	
11a	Depletable assets				
b	Less accumulated depletion	( )		( )	
12	Land (net of any amortization)				
13a	Intangible assets (amortizable only)				
b	Less accumulated amortization	( )		( )	
14	Other assets (attach statement)				
15	Total assets				
	Liabilities and Shareholders' Equity				
16	Accounts payable				
17	Mortgages, notes, bonds payable in less than 1 year				
18	Other current liabilities (attach statement)				
19	Loans from shareholders				
20	Mortgages, notes, bonds payable in 1 year or more				
21	Other liabilities (attach statement)				
22	Capital stock: **a** Preferred stock				
	b Common stock				
23	Additional paid-in capital				
24	Retained earnings—Appropriated (attach statement)				
25	Retained earnings—Unappropriated				
26	Adjustments to shareholders' equity (attach statement)				
27	Less cost of treasury stock		( )		( )
28	Total liabilities and shareholders' equity				

Schedule M-1 **Reconciliation of Income (Loss) per Books With Income per Return**

Note: The corporation may be required to file Schedule M-3. See instructions.

1	Net income (loss) per books		7	Income recorded on books this year not included on this return (itemize): Tax-exempt interest $	
2	Federal income tax per books				
3	Excess of capital losses over capital gains				
4	Income subject to tax not recorded on books this year (itemize):		8	Deductions on this return not charged against book income this year (itemize):	
5	Expenses recorded on books this year not deducted on this return (itemize):		a	Depreciation $	
a	Depreciation $		b	Charitable contributions $	
b	Charitable contributions $				
c	Travel and entertainment $				
			9	Add lines 7 and 8	
6	Add lines 1 through 5		10	Income (page 1, line 28)—line 6 less line 9	

Schedule M-2 **Analysis of Unappropriated Retained Earnings per Books (Schedule L, Line 25)**

1	Balance at beginning of year		5	Distributions: **a** Cash	
2	Net income (loss) per books			**b** Stock	
3	Other increases (itemize):			**c** Property	
			6	Other decreases (itemize):	
			7	Add lines 5 and 6	
4	Add lines 1, 2, and 3		8	Balance at end of year (line 4 less line 7)	

Form **1120** (2022)

11-6 S CORPORATIONS

11.6 Learning Objective

Explain how an S corporation operates and is taxed.

Qualified corporations may elect to be taxed under Subchapter S of the Internal Revenue Code in a manner similar to partnerships. An S corporation does not generally pay tax and each shareholder reports it's share of corporate income on their individual tax return. The S corporation election is designed to relieve corporations of certain corporate tax disadvantages, such as the double taxation of income.

To elect S corporation status, a corporation must have the following characteristics:

1. The corporation must be a domestic corporation;
2. The corporation must have 100 or fewer shareholders who are either individuals, estates, certain trusts, certain financial institutions, or certain exempt organizations;
3. The corporation must have only one class of stock; and
4. All shareholders must be U.S. citizens or resident aliens.

The S corporation election must be made during the prior year or the first two months and 15 days of the current tax year to obtain the status for the current year. Relief provisions may apply for elections that are filed late.

EXAMPLE Laurel Corporation is a calendar-year corporation that makes an S corporation election on November 2, 2022. The corporation does not qualify for any of the relief provisions for late S corporation elections for the 2022 tax year. The corporation is not an S corporation until the 2023 tax year; it is a regular C corporation for 2022. ♦

After electing S corporation status, the corporation retains the status until the election is voluntarily revoked or statutorily terminated. If the corporation ceases to qualify as an S corporation (e.g., it has 102 shareholders during the year), the election is statutorily terminated. Also, the election is terminated when a corporation receives 25 percent or more of its gross income from passive investments for three consecutive tax years and the corporation has accumulated earnings and profits at the end of each of those years. If a corporation experiences an involuntary termination of S corporation status, the election is terminated on the day the status changes. For example, the loss of S corporation status on June 1 causes the corporation to be a regular C corporation from that day on.

Upon consent of shareholders owning a majority of the voting stock, an S corporation election can be voluntarily revoked. If the consent to revoke the election is made during the first two months and fifteen days of the tax year, the S corporation status will be considered voluntarily terminated effective at the beginning of that year. Shareholders may specify a date on or after the date of the revocation as the effective date for the voluntary termination of the S corporation election. If a prospective revocation date is not specified, and the consent to revoke the election is made after two months and fifteen days of the tax year, the earliest that the S corporation status can be terminated is the first day of the following tax year.

EXAMPLE On January 20, 2022, Juniper Corporation, a calendar-year corporation, files a consent to revoke its S corporation election. No date is specified in the consent as the effective date of the revocation. The corporation is no longer an S corporation effective January 1, 2022. If the election were made after March 15, the corporation would not become a regular C corporation until the 2023 tax year. ♦

11-6a Reporting Income

An S corporation is required to report its income and other items on Form 1120S, U.S. Income Tax Return for an S Corporation, even though the corporate entity does not pay federal income tax. The tax return is due on the fifteenth day of the third month following the close of the corporation's tax year. S corporations may request a six-month extension for filing its tax return. Each shareholder of an S corporation reports their share of corporate income based on their stock ownership during the year. The taxable income of an S corporation is computed in the same manner as a partnership.

Each shareholder of an S corporation takes into account separately their share of items of income, deductions, and credits on a per share per day basis. Schedule K-1 of Form 1120S is used to report the allocation of ordinary income or loss, plus all separately stated items of income or loss, to each of the shareholders. Each shareholder's share of these items is included in the shareholder's computation of taxable income for the tax year during which the corporation's year ends. In the case of the death of a shareholder, the shareholder's portion of S corporation items will be taken into account on the shareholder's final tax return.

EXAMPLE Freda is the sole shareholder of the Freda Corporation, which has an S corporation election in effect. During calendar year 2022, the corporation has ordinary taxable income of \$100,000. Freda must report \$100,000 on her individual income tax return for 2022 as income from the Freda Corporation. ♦

11-6b S Corporation Losses

Losses from an S corporation also pass through to the shareholders. However, the amount of loss from an S corporation that a shareholder may report is limited to their adjusted basis in the corporation's stock plus the amount of any loans from the shareholder to the corporation. Any loss in excess of the shareholder's basis in the stock of the corporation plus loans is disallowed and becomes a carryforward loss. If a shareholder was not a shareholder for the entire tax year, losses must be allocated to the shareholder on a daily basis (the seller gets credit for the date of sale). This prevents a shareholder from selling losses late in the year to another taxpayer by selling the stock of an S corporation.

EXAMPLE Lawson and Mary are equal shareholders in L&M Corporation, an S corporation. On December 1, 2022, Mary sells her interest to Connley for \$15,000. Lawson's basis in his L&M Corporation stock is \$10,000. For the 2022 tax year, the corporation has a loss of \$24,000. Lawson can deduct only \$10,000 of his half of the loss (\$12,000), since that is the amount of his stock basis. Even though she is not a shareholder at year-end, Mary may deduct \$11,014 of the loss, which is 335/365 of \$12,000, assuming her basis was at least that amount. Connley may deduct \$986, 30/365 of \$12,000. In leap years, the amounts would be \$11,016 (336/366 × \$12,000) and \$984 (30/366 × \$12,000) for Mary and Connley, respectively. ♦

11-6c Pass-Through Items

Certain items pass through from an S corporation to the shareholders and retain their tax attributes on the shareholders' tax returns. The following are examples of pass-through items that are separately stated on the shareholders' Schedule K-1:

- Capital gains and losses
- Section 1231 gains and losses
- Dividend income
- Charitable contributions
- Tax-exempt interest
- Most credits

Unlike partnerships, S corporations do not have guaranteed payments to owners. If an S corporation shareholder provides services to the S corporation, a reasonable wage must be paid and reported on a Form W-2, like any other employee. The S corporation deducts reasonable wages from taxable income.

11-6d **Qualified Business Income Deduction**

Similar to partnerships, S corporations are flow-through entities that may generate qualified business income (QBI) and thus individual shareholders may be eligible for the QBI deduction. The same wage and service business limits apply as with other flow-through entities.

S corporations have a unique interaction between wages and qualified business income. The wages paid to an S corporation shareholder are not considered part of qualified business income; however, the wages count toward the wage limit, to the extent one applies to the taxpayer:

EXAMPLE Hogarth is a single taxpayer and the sole shareholder of Giant Corporation, which is an S corporation for tax purposes. Giant pays reasonable wages to Hogarth, the only employee, of $80,000 and allocates $100,000 of income. Hogarth's taxable income is above the threshold for a single taxpayer and he is required to apply the wage limitation to his QBI deduction. Hogarth can include $40,000 ($80,000 × 50%) of wages in computing the wage limit for the QBI deduction but may not consider the $80,000 of wages as QBI, only the $100,000 of income allocated. ♦

11-6e **Special Taxes**

S corporations are not subject to the corporate income tax on their regular taxable income. Under certain circumstances, an S corporation may be liable for tax at the corporate level. An S corporation may be subject to a tax on gains attributable to appreciation in the value of assets held by the corporation prior to the S corporation election, the built-in gains tax. In addition, a tax may be imposed on certain S corporations that have large amounts of passive investment income, such as income from dividends and interest. The rules for the application of these taxes are complex.

Self-Study Problem 11.6

See Appendix E for Solutions to Self-Study Problems

Assume that Aspen Corporation in Self-Study Problem 11.5 is owned by Ava Mendes, who owns all 100 shares outstanding. Ava lives at 1175 Delaware St., Denver, CO 80204 and her Social Security number is 411-41-4141. Also, assume that the corporation has a valid S corporation election in effect for 2022 and is not subject to any special taxes. Assume no wages are included in Aspen's cost of goods sold. Using the relevant information given in Self-Study Problem 11.5 and assuming the corporation's retained earnings are $19,000, instead of $16,060, accounts payable are $24,000, rather than $26,940, and no estimated tax payments are made, complete Form 1120S on Pages 11-25 to 11-29 for Aspen Corporation, and complete Schedule K-1 on Page 11-31 for Ava. Assume there were no cash distributions to Ava during the year.

Learning Objective 11.7

Describe the basic tax rules for the formation of a corporation.

11-7 CORPORATE FORMATION

When a taxpayer incorporates a business and transfers high-value, low-basis property to the corporation in exchange for corporate stock, a substantial gain is realized. This gain is measured at the value of the shares received less the basis of the property transferred. Favorable tax treatment is available in certain cases, which allows many taxpayers to defer the recognition of the realized gain in the year of formation. To defer the gain, the taxpayer must meet certain requirements, including:

1. The taxpayer must transfer property or money to the corporation,
2. The transfer must be solely in exchange for stock of the corporation, and
3. The shareholder(s) qualifying for nonrecognition must own at least 80 percent of the corporation's stock after the transfer.

When the above requirements are met, gains and losses are not recognized on the formation of the corporation.

EXAMPLE Elaine Muskie forms Nikola Corporation by transferring $10,000 cash, equipment valued at $40,000 and a basis of $12,000, and land worth $20,000 with a basis of $1,000 in exchange for all 100 shares of Nikola stock outstanding. Because Elaine meets the requirements to defer the gain, she is not required to recognize the realized gain of $28,000 on the equipment and $19,000 on the land. ♦

The shareholder must transfer property or cash to the corporation; performing services for corporate stock does not qualify for nonrecognition treatment. The shareholder performing services must recognize income in an amount equal to the value of the stock received. If the shareholder receives other property (boot) in addition to stock of the corporation in exchange for the transfer of cash or other property, the transaction may still qualify for partial nonrecognition treatment, provided the control requirement is met. However, realized gain must be recognized to the extent of the boot received.

EXAMPLE Geoff Basil and Jackson Dorsal form Amazitter Corporation. Geoff contributes cash of $60,000 and Jackson contributes a building valued at $70,000 (his basis is $30,000). Geoff and Jackson both receive 50 shares in the exchange and Jackson also receives cash of $10,000. Because Jackson receives $10,000 boot, he must recognize $10,000 of his $40,000 gain realized. Geoff will not recognize any gain. ♦

11-7a Liabilities

As a general rule, the assumption of shareholder liabilities by the corporation is not considered boot. For example, if a shareholder transfers land to the corporation for stock and the land is subject to a liability that is assumed by the corporation, no gain would normally be recognized on the transfer. However, if there is no business purpose for transfer of the liability, or tax avoidance appears to be involved, the recognition of any realized gain is required. Also, when the total liabilities transferred to the corporation by a shareholder exceed the total basis of the property transferred by the shareholder, the excess amount is a gain that must be recognized without regard to whether gain is realized.

EXAMPLE Robusta Corporation is formed by Max, who contributes property with a basis of $12,000 in exchange for 100 percent of the company's stock. On the date of the contribution, the property contributed has a fair market value of $120,000 and is subject to a liability of $20,000. Max must recognize a gain of $8,000 on the transfer of the property to the corporation since the liability transferred to the corporation exceeds his basis in the property transferred. ♦

11-7b Shareholder's Stock Basis

After the transfer, the shareholder's basis in their stock is determined by the following formula:

Basis of the property transferred	$ xxxx
Less: boot received	(xxxx)
Plus: gain recognized	xxxx
Less: liabilities transferred	(xxxx)
Basis in the stock	$ xxxx

TAX BREAK

Two special provisions can apply to taxpayers who are the original owners of small business stocks and sell shares. Section 1202 allows shareholders that sell qualifying stock at a gain to exclude 100 percent of the gain (subject to limitations). Section 1244 allows the loss on qualifying small business stock to be characterized as an ordinary loss up to $50,000 ($100,000 if married filing jointly) and thus avoid capital loss limitations. See IRS Publication 550 for more information on requirements and restrictions.

11-7c Corporation's Basis in Property Contributed

The corporation's basis in the property received from a shareholder in a transaction to which nonrecognition treatment applies is the same as the basis of the property to the shareholder, increased by any gain recognized by the shareholder on the transfer.

EXAMPLE A, B, and C form Hornbeam Corporation. A contributes property with a basis of $25,000 in exchange for 40 shares of stock worth $40,000. B performs services for the corporation in exchange for 10 shares of stock worth $10,000. C contributes property with a basis of $10,000 in exchange for 45 shares of stock worth $45,000 and $5,000 cash. The stock described above is all of the outstanding stock of the corporation. A and C qualify for complete or partial nonrecognition treatment, since together they own 89 percent (85 of 95 shares) of the stock after the transfer. B's stock is not considered because it was received in exchange for services.

1. A has a realized gain of $15,000 ($40,000 − $25,000), but no recognized gain since no boot was received.
2. B's recognized income is $10,000, since she performed services in exchange for the stock, and stock received for services does not fall within the nonrecognition provisions.
3. C's realized gain is $40,000 ($45,000 + $5,000 − $10,000), but only $5,000 of the gain is recognized, the amount of boot received.
4. A's basis in the stock is $25,000 ($25,000 − $0 + $0 − $0), B's basis in the stock is $10,000 ($0 − $0 + $10,000 − $0), and C's basis in the stock is $10,000 ($10,000 − $5,000 + $5,000 − $0).

5. Hornbeam Corporation's basis in the property contributed by A is $25,000 ($25,000 + $0). The corporation's basis in the property contributed by C is $15,000 ($10,000 + $5,000 gain recognized). ♦

Self-Study Problem 11.7 *See Appendix E for Solutions to Self-Study Problems*

Tammy has a business which she decides to incorporate. She transfers to the new corporation, real estate with a basis of $75,000, subject to a $34,000 mortgage, in exchange for all of its stock. The stock is worth $125,000.

a. What is Tammy's realized gain?
b. What is Tammy's recognized gain?
c. What is Tammy's basis in her stock?
d. What is the corporation's basis in the real estate?

The Inflation Reduction Act of 2022 introduced a new tax on the repurchase of stock by a publicly-traded corporation. Starting in 2023, an excise tax of 1 percent of the value of the stock repurchased will apply. The tax applies to any domestic corporation, the stock of which is traded on an established securities market.

Self-Study Problem 11.6

Form **1120-S** | Department of the Treasury Internal Revenue Service

U.S. Income Tax Return for an S Corporation

Do not file this form unless the corporation has filed or is attaching Form 2553 to elect to be an S corporation.
Go to *www.irs.gov/Form1120S* for instructions and the latest information.

OMB No. 1545-0123 | 2022

For calendar year 2022 or tax year beginning , 2022, ending , 20

	TYPE OR PRINT	
A S election effective date	Name	**D Employer identification number**
B Business activity code number (see instructions)	Number, street, and room or suite no. If a P.O. box, see instructions.	**E** Date incorporated
C Check if Sch. M-3 attached ☐	City or town, state or province, country, and ZIP or foreign postal code	**F** Total assets (see instructions) $

G Is the corporation electing to be an S corporation beginning with this tax year? See instructions. ☐ Yes ☐ No

H Check if: **(1)** ☐ Final return **(2)** ☐ Name change **(3)** ☐ Address change **(4)** ☐ Amended return **(5)** ☐ S election termination

I Enter the number of shareholders who were shareholders during any part of the tax year . . . .

J Check if corporation: **(1)** ☐ Aggregated activities for section 465 at-risk purposes **(2)** ☐ Grouped activities for section 469 passive activity purposes

Caution: Include **only** trade or business income and expenses on lines 1a through 21. See the instructions for more information.

Income	1a	Gross receipts or sales	1a			
	b	Returns and allowances	1b			
	c	Balance. Subtract line 1b from line 1a			1c	
	2	Cost of goods sold (attach Form 1125-A)			2	
	3	Gross profit. Subtract line 2 from line 1c			3	
	4	Net gain (loss) from Form 4797, line 17 (attach Form 4797)			4	
	5	Other income (loss) (see instructions—attach statement)			5	
	6	**Total income (loss).** Add lines 3 through 5			6	
Deductions (see instructions for limitations)	7	Compensation of officers (see instructions—attach Form 1125-E)			7	
	8	Salaries and wages (less employment credits)			8	
	9	Repairs and maintenance			9	
	10	Bad debts			10	
	11	Rents			11	
	12	Taxes and licenses			12	
	13	Interest (see instructions)			13	
	14	Depreciation from Form 4562 not claimed on Form 1125-A or elsewhere on return (attach Form 4562)			14	
	15	Depletion **(Do not deduct oil and gas depletion.)**			15	
	16	Advertising			16	
	17	Pension, profit-sharing, etc., plans			17	
	18	Employee benefit programs			18	
	19	Other deductions (attach statement)			19	
	20	**Total deductions.** Add lines 7 through 19			20	
	21	**Ordinary business income (loss).** Subtract line 20 from line 6			21	
Tax and Payments	22a	Excess net passive income or LIFO recapture tax (see instructions)	22a			
	b	Tax from Schedule D (Form 1120-S)	22b			
	c	Add lines 22a and 22b (see instructions for additional taxes)			22c	
	23a	2022 estimated tax payments and 2021 overpayment credited to 2022	23a			
	b	Tax deposited with Form 7004	23b			
	c	Credit for federal tax paid on fuels (attach Form 4136)	23c			
	d	Add lines 23a through 23c			23d	
	24	Estimated tax penalty (see instructions). Check if Form 2220 is attached ☐			24	
	25	**Amount owed.** If line 23d is smaller than the total of lines 22c and 24, enter amount owed			25	
	26	**Overpayment.** If line 23d is larger than the total of lines 22c and 24, enter amount overpaid			26	
	27	Enter amount from line 26: **Credited to 2023 estimated tax**		**Refunded**	27	

Sign Here — Under penalties of perjury, I declare that I have examined this return, including accompanying schedules and statements, and to the best of my knowledge and belief, it is true, correct, and complete. Declaration of preparer (other than taxpayer) is based on all information of which preparer has any knowledge.

Signature of officer | Date | Title | May the IRS discuss this return with the preparer shown below? See instructions. ☐ Yes ☐ No

Paid Preparer Use Only	Print/Type preparer's name	Preparer's signature	Date	Check ☐ if self-employed	PTIN
	Firm's name			Firm's EIN	
	Firm's address			Phone no.	

For Paperwork Reduction Act Notice, see separate instructions. Cat. No. 11510H Form **1120-S** (2022)

Form 1120-S (2022) Page **2**

Schedule B **Other Information** (see instructions)

		Yes	No
1	Check accounting method: **a** ☐ Cash **b** ☐ Accrual **c** ☐ Other (specify) ________		
2	See the instructions and enter the: **a** Business activity ________ **b** Product or service ________		
3	At any time during the tax year, was any shareholder of the corporation a disregarded entity, a trust, an estate, or a nominee or similar person? If "Yes," attach Schedule B-1, Information on Certain Shareholders of an S Corporation . .		
4	At the end of the tax year, did the corporation:		
a	Own directly 20% or more, or own, directly or indirectly, 50% or more of the total stock issued and outstanding of any foreign or domestic corporation? For rules of constructive ownership, see instructions. If "Yes," complete (i) through (v) below		

(i) Name of Corporation	**(ii)** Employer Identification Number (if any)	**(iii)** Country of Incorporation	**(iv)** Percentage of Stock Owned	**(v)** If Percentage in (iv) Is 100%, Enter the Date (if applicable) a Qualified Subchapter S Subsidiary Election Was Made

		Yes	No
b	Own directly an interest of 20% or more, or own, directly or indirectly, an interest of 50% or more in the profit, loss, or capital in any foreign or domestic partnership (including an entity treated as a partnership) or in the beneficial interest of a trust? For rules of constructive ownership, see instructions. If "Yes," complete (i) through (v) below		

(i) Name of Entity	**(ii)** Employer Identification Number (if any)	**(iii)** Type of Entity	**(iv)** Country of Organization	**(v)** Maximum Percentage Owned in Profit, Loss, or Capital

		Yes	No
5a	At the end of the tax year, did the corporation have any outstanding shares of restricted stock?		
	If "Yes," complete lines (i) and (ii) below.		
	(i) Total shares of restricted stock . . . . ________		
	(ii) Total shares of non-restricted stock . . . . ________		
b	At the end of the tax year, did the corporation have any outstanding stock options, warrants, or similar instruments? .		
	If "Yes," complete lines (i) and (ii) below.		
	(i) Total shares of stock outstanding at the end of the tax year . . ________		
	(ii) Total shares of stock outstanding if all instruments were executed ________		
6	Has this corporation filed, or is it required to file, **Form 8918,** Material Advisor Disclosure Statement, to provide information on any reportable transaction?		
7	Check this box if the corporation issued publicly offered debt instruments with original issue discount . . . . . . ☐		
	If checked, the corporation may have to file **Form 8281,** Information Return for Publicly Offered Original Issue Discount Instruments.		
8	If the corporation **(a)** was a C corporation before it elected to be an S corporation **or** the corporation acquired an asset with a basis determined by reference to the basis of the asset (or the basis of any other property) in the hands of a C corporation, **and** **(b)** has net unrealized built-in gain in excess of the net recognized built-in gain from prior years, enter the net unrealized built-in gain reduced by net recognized built-in gain from prior years. See instructions . . . . $ ________		
9	Did the corporation have an election under section 163(j) for any real property trade or business or any farming business in effect during the tax year? See instructions		
10	Does the corporation satisfy one or more of the following? See instructions		
a	The corporation owns a pass-through entity with current, or prior year carryover, excess business interest expense.		
b	The corporation's aggregate average annual gross receipts (determined under section 448(c)) for the 3 tax years preceding the current tax year are more than $27 million and the corporation has business interest expense.		
c	The corporation is a tax shelter and the corporation has business interest expense.		
	If "Yes," complete and attach **Form 8990**, Limitation on Business Interest Expense Under Section 163(j).		
11	Does the corporation satisfy **both** of the following conditions?		
a	The corporation's total receipts (see instructions) for the tax year were less than $250,000.		
b	The corporation's total assets at the end of the tax year were less than $250,000.		
	If "Yes," the corporation is not required to complete Schedules L and M-1.		

Form 1120-S (2022) Page 3

Schedule B	Other Information (see instructions) *(continued)*	Yes	No
12	During the tax year, did the corporation have any non-shareholder debt that was canceled, was forgiven, or had the terms modified so as to reduce the principal amount of the debt?		
	If "Yes," enter the amount of principal reduction . . . $		
13	During the tax year, was a qualified subchapter S subsidiary election terminated or revoked? If "Yes," see instructions		
14a	Did the corporation make any payments in 2022 that would require it to file Form(s) 1099?		
b	If "Yes," did or will the corporation file required Form(s) 1099?		
15	Is the corporation attaching Form 8996 to certify as a Qualified Opportunity Fund?		
	If "Yes," enter the amount from Form 8996, line 15 . . . $		

	Schedule K	Shareholders' Pro Rata Share Items				Total amount
Income (Loss)	1	Ordinary business income (loss) (page 1, line 21)			1	
	2	Net rental real estate income (loss) (attach Form 8825)			2	
	3a	Other gross rental income (loss)	3a			
	b	Expenses from other rental activities (attach statement)	3b			
	c	Other net rental income (loss). Subtract line 3b from line 3a			3c	
	4	Interest income			4	
	5	Dividends: **a** Ordinary dividends			5a	
		b Qualified dividends	5b			
	6	Royalties			6	
	7	Net short-term capital gain (loss) (attach Schedule D (Form 1120-S))			7	
	8a	Net long-term capital gain (loss) (attach Schedule D (Form 1120-S))			8a	
	b	Collectibles (28%) gain (loss)	8b			
	c	Unrecaptured section 1250 gain (attach statement)	8c			
	9	Net section 1231 gain (loss) (attach Form 4797)			9	
	10	Other income (loss) (see instructions) . . . Type:			10	
Deductions	11	Section 179 deduction (attach Form 4562)			11	
	12a	Charitable contributions			12a	
	b	Investment interest expense			12b	
	c	Section 59(e)(2) expenditures . . . Type:			12c	
	d	Other deductions (see instructions) . . . Type:			12d	
Credits	13a	Low-income housing credit (section 42(j)(5))			13a	
	b	Low-income housing credit (other)			13b	
	c	Qualified rehabilitation expenditures (rental real estate) (attach Form 3468, if applicable)			13c	
	d	Other rental real estate credits (see instructions) Type:			13d	
	e	Other rental credits (see instructions) . . . Type:			13e	
	f	Biofuel producer credit (attach Form 6478)			13f	
	g	Other credits (see instructions) . . . Type:			13g	
International	14	Attach Schedule K-2 (Form 1120-S), Shareholders' Pro Rata Share Items—International, and check this box to indicate you are reporting items of international tax relevance . . . ☐				
Alternative Minimum Tax (AMT) Items	15a	Post-1986 depreciation adjustment			15a	
	b	Adjusted gain or loss			15b	
	c	Depletion (other than oil and gas)			15c	
	d	Oil, gas, and geothermal properties—gross income			15d	
	e	Oil, gas, and geothermal properties—deductions			15e	
	f	Other AMT items (attach statement)			15f	
Items Affecting Shareholder Basis	16a	Tax-exempt interest income			16a	
	b	Other tax-exempt income			16b	
	c	Nondeductible expenses			16c	
	d	Distributions (attach statement if required) (see instructions)			16d	
	e	Repayment of loans from shareholders			16e	
	f	Foreign taxes paid or accrued			16f	

Form **1120-S** (2022)

Form 1120-S (2022) Page 4

Schedule K		Shareholders' Pro Rata Share Items *(continued)*		Total amount
Other Information	17a	Investment income	17a	
	b	Investment expenses	17b	
	c	Dividend distributions paid from accumulated earnings and profits	17c	
	d	Other items and amounts (attach statement)		
Reconciliation	18	**Income (loss) reconciliation.** Combine the amounts on lines 1 through 10 in the far right column. From the result, subtract the sum of the amounts on lines 11 through 12d and 16f	18	

Schedule L **Balance Sheets per Books**	Beginning of tax year		End of tax year	
Assets	(a)	(b)	(c)	(d)
1 Cash				
2a Trade notes and accounts receivable				
b Less allowance for bad debts	( )		( )	
3 Inventories				
4 U.S. government obligations				
5 Tax-exempt securities (see instructions)				
6 Other current assets (attach statement)				
7 Loans to shareholders				
8 Mortgage and real estate loans				
9 Other investments (attach statement)				
10a Buildings and other depreciable assets				
b Less accumulated depreciation	( )		( )	
11a Depletable assets				
b Less accumulated depletion	( )		( )	
12 Land (net of any amortization)				
13a Intangible assets (amortizable only)				
b Less accumulated amortization	( )		( )	
14 Other assets (attach statement)				
15 Total assets				
Liabilities and Shareholders' Equity				
16 Accounts payable				
17 Mortgages, notes, bonds payable in less than 1 year				
18 Other current liabilities (attach statement)				
19 Loans from shareholders				
20 Mortgages, notes, bonds payable in 1 year or more				
21 Other liabilities (attach statement)				
22 Capital stock				
23 Additional paid-in capital				
24 Retained earnings				
25 Adjustments to shareholders' equity (attach statement)				
26 Less cost of treasury stock		( )		( )
27 Total liabilities and shareholders' equity				

Form **1120-S** (2022)

Form 1120-S (2022) Page 5

Schedule M-1 **Reconciliation of Income (Loss) per Books With Income (Loss) per Return**
Note: The corporation may be required to file Schedule M-3. See instructions.

1	Net income (loss) per books		5	Income recorded on books this year not included on Schedule K, lines 1 through 10 (itemize):	
2	Income included on Schedule K, lines 1, 2, 3c, 4, 5a, 6, 7, 8a, 9, and 10, not recorded on books this year (itemize)		a	Tax-exempt interest $	
3	Expenses recorded on books this year not included on Schedule K, lines 1 through 12, and 16f (itemize):		6	Deductions included on Schedule K, lines 1 through 12, and 16f, not charged against book income this year (itemize):	
a	Depreciation $		a	Depreciation $	
b	Travel and entertainment $		7	Add lines 5 and 6	
4	Add lines 1 through 3		8	Income (loss) (Schedule K, line 18). Subtract line 7 from line 4	

Schedule M-2 **Analysis of Accumulated Adjustments Account, Shareholders' Undistributed Taxable Income Previously Taxed, Accumulated Earnings and Profits, and Other Adjustments Account** (see instructions)

		(a) Accumulated adjustments account	(b) Shareholders' undistributed taxable income previously taxed	(c) Accumulated earnings and profits	(d) Other adjustments account
1	Balance at beginning of tax year				
2	Ordinary income from page 1, line 21 . . .				
3	Other additions				
4	Loss from page 1, line 21	( )			
5	Other reductions	( )			( )
6	Combine lines 1 through 5				
7	Distributions				
8	Balance at end of tax year. Subtract line 7 from line 6				

Form **1120-S** (2022)

Self-Study Problem 11.6

671121

☐ Final K-1 ☐ Amended K-1 OMB No. 1545-0123

Schedule K-1 (Form 1120-S) **2022**

Department of the Treasury
Internal Revenue Service

For calendar year 2022, or tax year

beginning ___ / ___ / 2022 ending ___ / ___ / ___

Shareholder's Share of Income, Deductions, Credits, etc. **See separate instructions.**

Part I Information About the Corporation

A Corporation's employer identification number

B Corporation's name, address, city, state, and ZIP code

C IRS Center where corporation filed return

D Corporation's total number of shares
Beginning of tax year . . . . . . ______
End of tax year . . . . ______

Part II Information About the Shareholder

E Shareholder's identifying number

F Shareholder's name, address, city, state, and ZIP code

G Current year allocation percentage . . . ______ %

H Shareholder's number of shares
Beginning of tax year . . . . . . ______
End of tax year . . . . ______

I Loans from shareholder
Beginning of tax year . . . . . . $ ______
End of tax year . . . . $ ______

For IRS Use Only

Part III Shareholder's Share of Current Year Income, Deductions, Credits, and Other Items

1	Ordinary business income (loss)	13	Credits
2	Net rental real estate income (loss)		
3	Other net rental income (loss)		
4	Interest income		
5a	Ordinary dividends		
5b	Qualified dividends	14	Schedule K-3 is attached if checked . . . . . ☐
6	Royalties	15	Alternative minimum tax (AMT) items
7	Net short-term capital gain (loss)		
8a	Net long-term capital gain (loss)		
8b	Collectibles (28%) gain (loss)		
8c	Unrecaptured section 1250 gain		
9	Net section 1231 gain (loss)	16	Items affecting shareholder basis
10	Other income (loss)		
		17	Other information
11	Section 179 deduction		
12	Other deductions		

18 ☐ More than one activity for at-risk purposes*
19 ☐ More than one activity for passive activity purposes*

* See attached statement for additional information.

11-8 CORPORATE ACCUMULATIONS

11.8 Learning Objective

Describe the rules for the accumulated earnings tax and the personal holding company tax.

In many cases, taxpayers have established corporations to avoid paying income taxes at the shareholder level by allowing earnings to be accumulated by the corporations, rather than paid out as taxable dividends. To prevent that practice, Congress has enacted two special taxes which may be applied to certain corporations: the accumulated earnings tax and the personal holding company tax.

11-8a Accumulated Earnings Tax

The accumulated earnings tax is designed to prevent the shareholders of a corporation from avoiding tax at the shareholder level by retaining earnings in the corporation. The tax is a penalty tax imposed in addition to the regular corporate income tax. The tax is imposed at a rate of 20 percent on amounts that are deemed to be unreasonable accumulations of earnings. For all corporations except service corporations, such as accounting, law, and health care corporations, the first $250,000 in accumulated earnings is exempt from tax. Service corporations will not be taxed on their first $150,000 of accumulated earnings. Even if the accumulated earnings of a corporation exceed the exemption amount, the tax will not be imposed on accumulations that can be shown to be necessary to meet the reasonable needs of the business.

EXAMPLE Alder Corporation is a manufacturing corporation that has accumulated earnings of $625,000. The corporation can establish reasonable needs for $450,000 of this accumulation. Alder Corporation would be subject to the accumulated earnings tax on $175,000 ($625,000 − $450,000). The amount of the accumulated earnings tax is $35,000 (20% of $175,000). ♦

11-8b Personal Holding Company Tax

Personal holding companies, which are corporations with few shareholders and with income primarily from investments, are subject to a 20-percent tax on their undistributed earnings. The tax is imposed in addition to the regular corporate income tax; however, a corporation cannot be subject to both the accumulated earnings tax and the personal holding company tax in the same year. If both taxes are imposed, the taxpayer pays only the personal holding company tax. The rules for the personal holding company tax are very complex.

Self-Study Problem 11.8 *See Appendix E for Solutions to Self-Study Problems*

Sugarbush Corporation, an accounting corporation, has accumulated earnings of $340,000, and the corporation cannot establish a reasonable need for any of that amount. Calculate the amount of accumulated earnings tax (if any) that will be imposed on Sugarbush Corporation.

KEY TERMS

corporate tax rate, 11-2
personal service corporation, 11-2
corporate gains and losses, 11-2
net operating losses, 11-3
special deductions, 11-4
dividends received deduction, 11-4
organizational expenditures, 11-5
start-up costs, 11-5
corporation charitable contributions deduction, 11-7
Form 1120, 11-8

Schedule M-1, 11-8
book income, 11-8
annualized income method, 11-10
Schedule L (Balance Sheet), 11-11
S Corporation, 11-19
statutorily terminated, 11-19
Form 1120S, 11-19
Schedule K-1, 11-20
pass-through items, 11-20
Qualified business income deduction, 11-21
built-in gains tax, 11-21
nonrecognition treatment, 11-22
boot, 11-22
stock basis, 11-23
corporation's basis, 11-23
accumulated earnings tax, 11-33
personal holding company tax, 11-33

KEY POINTS

Learning Objectives	Key Points
LO 11.1: Employ the corporate tax rates to calculate corporate tax liability.	• The U.S. corporate tax rate is a flat 21 percent regardless of income level. • Qualified personal service corporations (health, law, engineering, architecture, accounting, actuarial science, performing arts, and consulting) are taxed at the same 21-percent tax rate on all taxable income.
LO 11.2: Compute basic gains and losses for corporations.	• Corporate ordinary income and capital gains tax rates are the same, so there is no tax rate benefit to having long-term capital gains in a corporation. • Net short-term capital gains of a corporation are taxed as ordinary income. • Capital losses may be used only to offset capital gains. • If capital losses cannot be used in the year they occur, they may be carried back three years and forward five years, to offset capital gains in those years. • When a long-term capital loss is carried to another year, it is treated as a short-term capital loss and may be offset against either long-term or short-term capital gains. • Net operating losses can be carried forward indefinitely, but are limited to 80 percent of future income.
LO 11.3: Apply special corporate deductions to corporate taxable income.	• Corporations are allowed a dividends received deduction based on their percentage of ownership in the corporation paying the dividend. • The dividends received deduction percentage is 50 percent (for ownership less than 20 percent), 65 percent (for ownership of 20 percent or more, but less than 80 percent), or 100 percent (for ownership of 80 percent or more). • Corporations amortize qualifying organizational costs over 180 months, and there is no upper limit to the amount of qualifying costs that can be amortized. • Corporations can elect to deduct up to $5,000 of organizational costs and $5,000 of start-up costs in the year they begin business. The $5,000 amounts are reduced by each dollar of organizational expenses and start-up costs exceeding $50,000. • A corporation's charitable contribution deduction is limited to 10 percent of taxable income, computed before the deduction for charitable contributions, net operating loss carrybacks, capital loss carrybacks, and the dividends received deduction. • Excess charitable contributions are carried forward to the five succeeding tax years, subject to the (generally) 10-percent annual limitation in the carryover years, with the current year's contributions deducted first.

LO 11.4: Identify the components of Schedule M-1 and how they are reported to the IRS.	• The purpose of Schedule M-1 of the corporate tax return is to reconcile a corporation's accounting "book" income to its taxable income. • On the left side of Schedule M-1 are adjustments that must be added to book income, and on the right side of the schedule are adjustments that must be subtracted from book income to arrive at the amount of taxable income. • The additions to book income include the amount of federal income tax expense, net capital losses deducted for book purposes, income recorded on the tax return but not on the books, and expenses recorded on the books but not deducted on the tax return. • The amounts that must be deducted from book income include income recorded on the books but not included on the tax return, and deductions included on the return but not deducted on the books.
LO 11.5: Describe the corporate tax return filing and estimated tax payment requirements.	• The due date for filing a corporate tax return is the fifteenth day of the fourth month after year-end (fifteenth day of the third month for June 30 year-ends). An extension provides an additional six months; thus a calendar year-end corporation has an initial deadline of April 15 and an extended deadline of October 15. Corporations with a June 30 year-end have a seven-month extended deadline from their initial deadline of September 15 to April 15. • A corporation must pay any tax liability by the original due date of the return. • Corporations must make estimated tax payments similar to those made by self-employed individual taxpayers. The payments are due on the fifteenth day of the fourth, sixth, ninth, and twelfth months of the corporation's tax year.
LO 11.6: Explain how an S corporation operates and is taxed.	• Certain qualified corporations may elect to be taxed under Subchapter S of the Internal Revenue Code in a manner similar to partnerships. • To elect S corporation status, a corporation *must* have the following characteristics: (1) be a domestic corporation; (2) have 100 or fewer shareholders who are either individuals, estates, certain trusts, certain financial institutions, or certain exempt organizations; (3) have only one class of stock; and (4) all shareholders must be U.S. citizens or resident aliens. • Each shareholder of an S corporation reports their share of corporate income based on their stock ownership during the year. • Schedule K-1 of Form 1120S is used to report the allocation of ordinary income or loss, and all separately stated items of income or loss, to each of the shareholders. • Losses from an S corporation pass through to the shareholders, but the loss deduction is limited to the shareholders' adjusted basis in the corporation's stock plus the amount of any loans from the shareholder to the corporation. • S corporation shareholders are eligible for the qualified business income deduction.
LO 11.7: Describe the basic tax rules for the formation of a corporation.	• If property is exchanged for stock in a corporation, the shareholders are in "control" of the corporation after the transfer, and the shareholders receive no boot, gain on the transfer is not recognized. • Realized gain is recognized to the extent that the shareholder receives boot. • The basis of the stock received by the shareholder is equal to the basis of the property transferred plus any gain recognized by the shareholder, less the fair market value of any boot received by the shareholder, less liabilities assumed by the corporation. • The basis of property received by the corporation is equal to the basis in the hands of the transferor plus any gain recognized by the transferor.
LO 11.8: Describe the rules for the accumulated earnings tax and the personal holding company tax.	• The accumulated earnings tax is a penalty tax, imposed in addition to the regular corporate income tax, at a rate of 20 percent on amounts that are deemed to be unreasonable accumulations of earnings. • For all corporations, except personal service corporations, the first $250,000 in accumulated earnings is exempt from tax. The first $150,000 in accumulated earnings is exempt for personal service corporations. • Personal holding companies, which are corporations with few shareholders and income primarily from investments, are subject to a 20 percent tax on undistributed earnings.

QUESTIONS and PROBLEMS

GROUP 1: MULTIPLE CHOICE QUESTIONS

LO 11.1

1. Ironwood Corporation has ordinary taxable income of $25,000 in 2022, and a short-term capital loss of $15,000. What is the corporation's tax liability for 2022?
   a. $2,100
   b. $5,250
   c. $10,500
   d. $13,650
   e. None of the above

LO 11.1

2. Tayla Corporation generated $400,000 of taxable income in the 2022. What is Tayla's corporate tax liability?
   a. $71,400
   b. $84,000
   c. $115,600
   d. $136,000
   e. None of the above

LO 11.2

3. Which of the following statements is *false* regarding corporate capital losses?
   a. Corporations may deduct $3,000 of net capital loss each year until the loss is used up.
   b. Corporations may carry capital losses back 3 years and forward 5 years to offset capital gains in those years.
   c. Corporations are not allowed to deduct capital losses against ordinary income.
   d. A long-term capital loss carried to another year is treated as a short-term capital loss.

LO 11.2

4. Harrison Corporation generates capital gains/(losses) of ($2,000), $4,000, ($14,000) in 2020, 2021, and 2022, respectively. Harrison started operating in 2020. What is Harrison's capital loss carryforward into 2023?
   a. $0
   b. $10,000
   c. $12,000
   d. $14,000
   e. None of the above

LO 11.2

5. Mask Corporation generated a net operating loss of $24,000 in 2022 and taxable income of $10,000 in 2023. How much NOL can Mask use in 2023 to reduce taxable income?
   a. $8,000
   b. $10,000
   c. $19,200
   d. $24,000

LO 11.2

6. Clarion Corporation generated taxable income of $15,000 in 2021 and a net operating loss of $12,000 in 2022. If Clarion generates taxable income of $5,000 in 2023, what is the NOL carryforward into 2024?
   a. $0
   b. $2,000
   c. $7,000
   d. $8,000

LO 11.3

7. Walnut Corporation owns 26 percent of Teak Corporation, a domestic corporation. During the current year, Walnut Corporation received $20,000 in dividends from Teak Corporation. Assuming that Walnut's taxable income for the current year before the

dividends received deduction is $500,000, what is the amount of Walnut's dividends received deduction for the current year?
a. $10,000
b. $13,000
c. $16,000
d. $20,000
e. None of the above

LO 11.3

8. Which of the following is *not* a corporate organizational expenditure that may be amortized?
   a. The cost of organizational meetings
   b. Fees paid to the state for incorporation
   c. Accounting fees incident to organization
   d. Legal fees incident to organization
   e. All of the above are organizational expenditures

LO 11.3

9. In 2022, charitable contributions by a corporation are limited to what percent of taxable income?
   a. 100 percent
   b. 50 percent
   c. 25 percent
   d. 10 percent

LO 11.3

10. Which of the following statements is *true* regarding the dividends received deduction in 2022?
    a. Dividends from an 80 percent-owned corporation are eligible for a 65 percent dividends received deduction
    b. Dividends from a 20 percent-owned corporation are eligible for a 50 percent dividends received deduction
    c. Dividends from a 100 percent-owned corporation are eligible for a 100 percent dividends received deduction
    d. The dividends received deduction is available to individual taxpayers as well as corporations.

LO 11.4

11. The purpose of Schedule M-1 on the corporate tax return is to:
    a. Reconcile accounting (book) income to taxable income.
    b. Summarize the dividends received deduction calculation.
    c. List the officers of the corporation and their compensation.
    d. Calculate the net operating loss deduction.

LO 11.4

12. Which of the following would *not* generally appear on the M-1 reconciliation?
    a. Federal income tax expense per books
    b. Tax-exempt interest income
    c. Excess tax over book depreciation
    d. Dividends received deduction

LO 11.5

13. Which of the following statements is *false* regarding corporate tax return due dates?
    a. Corporate tax returns for 2021 calendar-year corporations are due April 15, 2022.
    b. Corporate tax returns may receive an automatic six-month extension.
    c. Corporate taxes due must be paid no later than the extended due date of the tax return.
    d. When an IRS due date falls on a weekend or holiday, the due date is the next business day.

LO 11.5

14. Mansfield Incorporated, a calendar year corporation, is expecting to have a current year tax liability of $100,000. Which best describes the tax payments Mansfield should make to avoid penalty?
    a. Make payments at the end of June and December of $40,000 each and $20,000 when filing the return on the original due date.
    b. Make no payments during the year but pay the entire balance on the extended due date.

c. Make no payments during the year but pay the entire balance on the original due date.
d. Make quarterly payments totaling $100,000, all during the current year.
e. None of these will avoid penalty.

LO 11.5

15. Which of the following statements is *true* about estimated tax payments?
    a. The annualized income method uses four quarters of estimated income to determine required estimated payments.
    b. A large corporation (for purposes of estimated payments) is permitted to use the prior year tax liability only when determining the first quarter estimated payment.
    c. Estimated payments of corporate federal income tax are due on the fifteenth of the third, sixth, ninth, and twelfth month of the tax year.
    d. Corporations with an expected tax liability of less than $1,000 are not required to make estimated payments.

LO 11.6

16. Which of the following is *not* required for a corporation to be eligible to make an S corporation election?
    a. The corporation must have 100 or fewer shareholders.
    b. The corporation must be a domestic corporation.
    c. The corporation must have both common and preferred stock.
    d. The shareholders of the corporation must not be nonresident aliens.
    e. All shareholders must be either individuals, estates, certain trusts, or financial institutions.

LO 11.6

17. Which of the following items are passed through and separately stated on Schedule K-1 to shareholders of an S corporation?
    a. Wages paid
    b. Typical MACRS depreciation
    c. Net long-term capital gains
    d. Advertising expense
    e. All of the above retain their character when passed through

LO 11.6

18. Which of the following is *true* about S corporations?
    a. S corporations pay corporate taxes like other corporations.
    b. S corporations pay the alternative minimum tax for all income.
    c. S corporations cannot issue corporate stock.
    d. The S corporation status may be elected by stockholders only for corporations that meet certain qualifications.
    e. None of the above.

LO 11.6

19. The allocated non-passive loss of an S corporation is deductible:
    a. If the shareholder has adequate sources of other income
    b. Only if the S corporation is engaged in a residential rental business
    c. If the loss does not exceed the shareholder's basis
    d. If the S corporation makes a loss passthrough election

LO 11.6

20. Wages paid by an S corporation to its shareholder:
    a. are not deductible by the S corporation.
    b. are considered part of qualified business income.
    c. are not considered part of qualified business income but are wages for purposes of the wage limitation.
    d. are reported as income to the shareholder on Schedule K-1.

LO 11.7

21. Travis transfers land with a fair market value of $125,000 and basis of $25,000, to a corporation in exchange for 100 percent of the corporation's stock. What amount of gain must Travis recognize as a result of this transaction?
    a. $0
    b. $25,000
    c. $100,000
    d. $125,000
    e. None of the above

LO 11.7

22. Carl transfers land with a fair market value of $120,000 and basis of $30,000, to a new corporation in exchange for 85 percent of the corporation's stock. The land is subject to a $45,000 liability, which the corporation assumes. What amount of gain must Carl recognize as a result of this transaction?
    a. $0
    b. $15,000
    c. $30,000
    d. $45,000
    e. None of the above

LO 11.7

23. What is the shareholder's basis in stock of a corporation received as a result of the transfer of property to the corporation and as a result of which gain was recognized by the stockholder?
    a. The shareholder's basis is equal to the basis of the property transferred less the gain.
    b. The shareholder's basis is equal to the fair market value of the stock received, less any liabilities transferred by the stockholder.
    c. The shareholder's basis is equal to the basis of the property transferred to the corporation, minus any liabilities transferred by the shareholder, plus the gain.
    d. The shareholder's basis is equal to the basis of the property transferred to the corporation, plus any liabilities transferred by the shareholder.
    e. None of the above.

LO 11.8

24. Which of the following statements regarding personal holding companies is *false*?
    a. A personal holding company is one which has few shareholders.
    b. A personal holding company is generally taxed at a 21 percent rate.
    c. A personal holding company operates a business which is a hobby for its owners.
    d. Personal holding companies are subject to a 20 percent tax on income that is left undistributed.

LO 11.8

25. Boyce Industries, a manufacturing corporation, has accumulated earnings of $325,000 and cannot show any reasonable need for the accumulated earnings. What is Boyce's accumulated earnings tax?
    a. $15,000
    b. $0
    c. $13,750
    d. $75,000

GROUP 2:
PROBLEMS

LO 11.1

1. Quince Corporation has taxable income of $300,000 for its calendar tax year. Calculate the corporation's income tax liability for 2022 before tax credits.

LO 11.1

2. Ulmus Corporation is an engineering consulting firm and has $1,275,000 in taxable income for 2022. Calculate the corporation's income tax liability for 2022.

LO 11.1
LO 11.2

3. For the 2022 tax year, Ilex Corporation has ordinary income of $200,000, a short-term capital loss of $30,000 and a long-term capital gain of $10,000. Calculate Ilex Corporation's tax liability for 2022.

LO 11.2

4. DeMaria Corporation, a calendar year corporation, generates the following taxable income (net operating losses) since its inception in 2020:

Year	*Taxable result*
2020	$40,000
2021	(15,000)
2022	5,000

Assuming DeMaria makes no special elections with regard to NOLs, what is DeMaria's net operating loss carryforward into 2023?

LO 11.3

5. Fisafolia Corporation has gross income from operations of $210,000 and operating expenses of $150,000 for 2022. The corporation also has $30,000 in dividends from publicly-traded domestic corporations in which the ownership percentage was 45 percent.
   a. Calculate the corporation's dividends received deduction for 2022.
   b. Assume that instead of $210,000, Fisafolia Corporation has gross income from operations of $135,000. Calculate the corporation's dividends received deduction for 2022.
   c. Assume that instead of $210,000, Fisafolia Corporation has gross income from operations of $148,000. Calculate the corporation's dividends received deduction for 2022.

LO 11.3

6. Beech Corporation, an accrual-basis, calendar-year taxpayer, was organized and began business in May of the current calendar tax year. During the current year, the corporation incurred the following expenses:

State fees for incorporation	$ 800
Legal and accounting fees incident to organization	5,500
Expenses for the sale of stock	2,500
Organizational meeting expenses	1,000

Assuming that Beech Corporation wishes to deduct organizational expenses as quickly as possible, calculate the corporation's deduction for its current calendar tax year.

LO 11.3

7. Katsura Corporation incurred pre-operating costs:
   - Investigatory expenses of $17,000
   - New employee training $25,000
   - Advertising $10,000
   - Land and building for use as a retail store when opened $150,000

Katsura wishes to maximize its deduction for start-up costs. Assuming they open for business on February 27th of the current year, what the deduction for start-up costs?

LO 11.3

8. Explain the difference in the tax deduction treatment of exploratory or expansion costs and that of start-up costs.

LO 11.3

9. In 2022, Citradoria Corporation is a corporation that contributes $35,000 cash to qualified charitable organizations during the current tax year. The corporation has net operating income of $91,000, before deducting the contributions, and adding dividends received from domestic corporations (ownership in all corporations is less than 20 percent) in the amount of $25,000.
   a. What is the amount of Citradoria Corporation's allowable deduction for charitable contributions for 2022?
   b. In 2023, Citradoria contributes $4,000 to charitable organizations. The corporation has net operating income of $250,000 before deducting the contributions, and no dividend income. What is the amount of Citradoria's allowable deduction for charitable contributions in 2023?
   c. If there is any carryover of the charitable contribution deduction from 2023, what year will it expire?

LO 11.4

10. The Loquat Corporation has book net income of $50,000 for the current year. Included in this figure are the following items, which are reported on the corporation's Schedule M-1, Reconciliation of Income (Loss) per Books with Income per Return.

Federal income tax expense	$ 7,500
Depreciation deducted on the books which is not deductible for tax purposes	10,000
Deduction for 50 percent of meals expense which is not allowed for tax purposes	5,500
Deduction for entertainment not allowed for tax purposes	2,000
Tax-exempt interest income included in book income but not in tax income	4,200

Calculate Loquat Corporation's taxable income for the current year based on the information given. Show your calculations.

LO 11.4

11. Caloundra Corporation has book income of $40,000. Included in the book income is $3,000 of tax-exempt interest, $7,000 of book income tax expense, and a $2,000 non-deductible fine. Also included in book income are $10,000 of dividends Caloundra received from a 30-percent-owned corporation. Using this information and Form 1120, provide the amounts that go on each line on the form listed below.
   a. Form 1120, Schedule M-1 Line 1
   b. Form 1120, Schedule M-1, Line 10
   c. Form 1120, page 1, Line 28
   d. Form 1120, Schedule C, Line 2(a) and 2(c)
   e. Form 1120, Schedule C, Line 24
   f. Form 1120, page 1, Line 29b
   g. Form 1120, page 1, Line 30

LO 11.5

12. Mallory Corporation has a calendar year-end. The corporation has paid estimated taxes of $10,000 during 2022 but still owes an additional $5,000 for its 2022 tax year.
   a. When is the 2022 tax return due?
   b. If an automatic extension of time to file is requested, when is the 2022 tax return due?
   c. If an extension of time to file is requested, when is the additional $5,000 of tax for 2022 due?

LO 11.5

13. Cosplay Costumes Corporation (CCC) is an October 31 year-end taxpayer. CCC's prior year tax liability was $42,000. The current year tax liability is $44,000. CCC prepared estimated payments using the annualized income method of $43,000 (four equal payments of $10,750). Using this information, answer the following questions on the required payments necessary to avoid penalties associated with underpayment of estimated taxes.
   a. What are the month and day due dates of CCC's four estimated tax payments?
   b. If CCC is not considered a large corporation, what is the smallest amount of tax that could have been paid for the year?
   c. If CCC is a large corporation, what is the smallest amount of tax that could have been paid for the year?
   d. If CCC is a large corporation, what is the smallest amount of tax that could have been paid only for the first quarter?

LO 11.6

14. Cedar Corporation has an S corporation election in effect. During the 2022 calendar tax year, the corporation had ordinary taxable income of $200,000, and on January 15, 2022, the corporation paid dividends to shareholders in the amount of $120,000. How

much taxable income, in total, must the shareholders of the corporation report on their 2022 tax returns? Explain your answer.

LO 11.6

15. Bill and Guilda each own 50 percent of the stock of Radiata Corporation, an S corporation. Guilda's basis in her stock is $21,000. On May 26, 2022, Bill sells his stock, with a basis of $40,000, to Loraine for $50,000. For the 2022 tax year, Radiata Corporation has a loss of $104,000.
    a. Calculate the amount of the corporation's loss that may be deducted by Bill on his 2022 tax return.
    b. Calculate the amount of the corporation's loss that may be deducted by Guilda on her 2022 tax return.
    c. Calculate the amount of the corporation's loss that may be deducted by Loraine on her 2022 tax return.

LO 11.6

16. Starlord Corporation is a calendar year-end taxpayer with an S corporation election. Quill is the sole shareholder of Starlord for the entire tax year. The year-end financial statements of Starlord report the following (on a tax basis):

Operating revenues	$ 200,000
Cost of sales	(135,000)
Gross margin	65,000
SG&A expenses	(13,500)
Operating income	51,500
Other income/(loss):	
Capital gains	2,000
Section 1231 losses	(3,000)
Interest income	300
Taxable income	$ 50,800
Distributions to owners	$ 30,000

Included in SG&A expenses are wages to the Starlord's sole shareholder of $8,000 and charitable contributions of $500 cash. The capital gains are short-term. Quill has basis in excess of his distributions. Use this information to determine:
    a. The amount of ordinary business income
    b. Each of the separately stated items
    c. The amount and individual income tax form for the income Quill will report on individual tax return.

LO 11.6

17. Helly holds a 100-percent stake in Macro Data Incorporated (MDI), an S corporation operating a qualified trade or business. In the current year, MDI reports $20,000 of ordinary business income (before deducting any wages paid to Helly). Helly can exert influence over the amount of wages she is paid by MDI and although she recognizes that MDI can only deduct a reasonable wage, she is considering some extreme alternatives to judge the possible effects. Determine the following items below, considering Helly could pay herself wages of $1,000 versus wages of $20,000.
    a. The amount of total employment taxes paid by Helly and MDI on the wages (assume Helly's total wages and self-employment income are below the current year FICA cap)?

b. Assuming Helly has a 25-percent marginal tax rate, the amount of income taxes on her wages?
c. Assuming Helly has a 25-percent marginal tax rate, the amount of income taxes on her allocation of ordinary business income from MDI (Ignore the deduction MDI can take for employment taxes)?
d. Explain the primary difference in the tax burden borne jointly by MDI and Helly in the two wage scenarios Helly is considering.

LO 11.7

18. Dylan, Devon, and Ricken form Lemon Corporation in the current year. Dylan contributes $30,000 cash in exchange for 30 shares of Lemon. Devon contributes land with a market value of $50,000 (basis of $15,000) in exchange for 40 shares and $10,000 cash. Ricken provides services to Lemon valued at $30,000 in exchange for 30 shares.
    a. Determine the realized gain or loss on the exchange for each shareholder.
    b. Determine the recognized gain or loss (or income) on the exchange for each shareholder.
    c. Determine the basis of each shareholder's stock
    d. Determine Lemon's basis in the land.

LO 11.7

19. Dylan, Devon, and Ricken form Lemon Corporation in the current year. Dylan contributes $50,000 cash in exchange for 50 shares of Lemon. Devon contributes land with a market value of $50,000 (basis of $15,000) in exchange for 40 shares and $10,000 cash. Ricken provides services to Lemon valued at $10,000 in exchange for 10 shares.
    a. Determine the realized gain or loss on the exchange for each shareholder.
    b. Determine the recognized gain or loss (or income) on the exchange for each shareholder.
    c. Determine the basis of each shareholder's stock
    d. Determine Lemon's basis in the land.

LO 11.7

20. Karen, in forming a new corporation, transfers land to the corporation in exchange for 100 percent of the stock of the corporation. Karen's basis in the land is $280,000, and the corporation assumes a liability on the property in the amount of $300,000. The stock received by Karen has a fair market value of $550,000.
    a. What is the amount of gain or loss that must be recognized by Karen on this transfer?
    b. What is the amount of Karen's basis in the corporation's stock?
    c. What is the amount of the corporation's basis in the land?

LO 11.8

21. Grevilla Corporation is a manufacturing company. The corporation has accumulated earnings of $950,000, and it can establish reasonable needs for $400,000 of that amount. Calculate the amount of the accumulated earnings tax (if any) that Grevilla Corporation is subject to for this year.

GROUP 3:
COMPREHENSIVE PROBLEMS

1. Floyd Corporation was formed and began operations on January 1, 2022. The corporation is located at 210 N. Main St., Pearisburg, VA 24134 and the EIN is 91-1111111. The corporation's income statement for the year and the balance sheet at year-end are presented below.

The Floyd Corporation Income Statement
for the Year Ended December 31, 2022

Gross income from operations		$ 320,000
Qualified dividends received from a 15-percent-owned domestic corporation		20,000
Total gross income		340,000
Cost of goods sold		(70,000)
Total income		270,000
Other expenses:		
Compensation of officers	$80,000	
Salaries and wages	20,000	
Bad debts (direct charge-offs)	9,000	
Repairs	3,000	
Depreciation for book (tax depreciation = $90,000)	10,000	
Advertising	3,000	
Payroll taxes	15,000	
Total other expenses		(140,000)
Pretax book income		130,000
Income tax expense		25,200
Net income		$ 104,800

The Floyd Corporation Balance Sheet
as of December 31, 2022

Assets:		
Cash	$ 140,600	
Accounts receivable	20,000	
Inventory (at cost)	70,000	
Equipment	90,000	
Less: accumulated depreciation	(10,000)	
Total assets		$310,600
Liabilities and owners' equity:		
Accounts payable	$ 24,000	
Other liabilities	16,800	
Note payable (due in 10 years)	85,000	
Common stock	80,000	
Retained earnings	104,800	
Total liabilities and owners' equity		$310,600

The corporation made estimated tax payments of $9,000. Complete Form 1120 for Floyd Corporation.

2. George Corporation is an S corporation started on January 1, 2022, with 50 shares owned by Trey Martin and 50 shares owned by Brianna Tabor. The corporation is located at 15620 McMullen Hwy SW, Cumberland, MD 21502 and has EIN 94–8888888. The corporation is not subject to any special taxes and no wages are included in cost of goods sold. The corporation's income statement for the year and the balance sheet at year-end are presented below.

The George Corporation Income Statement for the Year Ended December 31, 2022

Gross income from operations		$ 320,000
Qualified dividends received from a 15-percent-owned domestic corporation		20,000
Total gross income		340,000
Cost of goods sold		(70,000)
Total income		270,000
Other expenses:		
Compensation of officers	$ 80,000	
Salaries and wages	20,000	
Bad debts (direct charge-offs)	9,000	
Repairs	3,000	
Depreciation for book (tax depreciation = $90,000)	10,000	
Advertising	3,000	
Payroll taxes	15,000	
Total other expenses		(140,000)
Net income		$ 130,000

The George Corporation Balance Sheet as of December 31, 2022

Assets:		
Cash	$ 109,000	
Accounts receivable	20,000	
Inventory (at cost)	70,000	
Other assets	40,000	
Equipment	90,000	
Less: accumulated depreciation	(10,000)	
Total assets		$319,000
Liabilities and owners' equity:		
Accounts payable	$ 24,000	
Note payable (due in 10 years)	85,000	
Common stock	80,000	
Retained earnings	130,000	
Total liabilities and owners' equity		$319,000

Using this information, complete Form 1120–S for George Corporation and Schedule K–1 for Brianna (who lives at 12 Bowery St., Frostburg, MD 21532 and has SSN 444-11–5555). Assume there are no cash distributions during the year.

CHAPTER 12

Tax Administration and Tax Planning

Tada Images/Shutterstock.com

LEARNING OBJECTIVES

After completing this chapter, you should be able to:

LO 12.1 Identify the organizational structure of the Internal Revenue Service (IRS).

LO 12.2 Describe the IRS audit process.

LO 12.3 Define the common penalties for taxpayers and apply them to specific situations.

LO 12.4 Apply the general rule for the statute of limitations on tax returns and the important exceptions to the general rule.

LO 12.5 Describe the rules and penalties that apply to tax practitioners.

LO 12.6 Describe the Taxpayer Bill of Rights.

LO 12.7 Explain the basic concepts of tax planning.

OVERVIEW

Knowing how the Internal Revenue Service (IRS) operates, and how and why the IRS audits certain tax returns, is extremely important to tax practitioners. This chapter covers these topics as well as tax penalties that apply to taxpayers and tax preparers, the statute of limitations on tax liabilities and refund claims, and rules applicable to tax practitioners (i.e., Circular 230). The Taxpayer Bill of Rights, also covered in this chapter, provides taxpayers with significant rights when dealing with the IRS, such as the ability to record an IRS interview.

Arranging one's financial affairs in order to maximize after-tax cash flows is referred to as tax planning. This chapter includes a discussion of basic tax-planning techniques that may be used by individual taxpayers. This final chapter is intended to give an appreciation for the process of dealing with the IRS and several of the many issues involved in conducting a tax practice.

Learning Objective 12.1

Identify the organizational structure of the Internal Revenue Service (IRS).

12-1 THE INTERNAL REVENUE SERVICE

The tax laws of the United States are administered by the IRS. In administering the tax law, the IRS has the responsibility for determining, assessing, and collecting internal revenue taxes and enforcing other provisions of the tax law. The IRS is a bureau of the Treasury Department. The mission of the IRS is to provide America's taxpayers quality service by helping them understand and meet their tax responsibilities, and enforce the law with integrity and fairness. Congress passes tax laws and requires taxpayers to comply. A taxpayer is expected to understand and meet their tax obligations. The role of the IRS is to help the majority of compliant taxpayers with the tax law, while ensuring that the minority who are unwilling to comply pay their fair share.

The IRS organization currently consists of a national office in Washington, D.C., IRS Campus Processing Sites, and various operational offices throughout the United States. The national office is the headquarters of the commissioner of internal revenue and various deputy and associate commissioners. The commissioner of internal revenue is appointed by the president of the United States with the advice and consent of the Senate. The responsibilities of the commissioner are to establish policy, to supervise the activities of the organization, and to act in an advisory capacity to the Treasury Department on legislative matters. In addition, the commissioner is responsible for the collection of income tax, auditing of tax returns, intelligence operations, and appellate procedures.

The Inflation Reduction Act of 2022 set aside considerable funding for the IRS over the next ten years including $45 billion for enforcement such as legal and litigation support and criminal investigation, including investigative technology, $25 billion for operations support, almost $5 billion for business systems modernization, and $3 billion for taxpayer services.

12-1a IRS Campus Processing Sites

In addition to the various operational offices discussed below, the IRS currently maintains IRS Campus Processing Sites. At these processing sites, the IRS computers process the information from tax documents such as tax returns, payroll tax forms, Forms 1099, and withholding forms.

Paper returns for individuals are processed at the Austin, Kansas City, and Ogden offices while e-filings are processed at many sites. The IRS also maintains a national computer center in Martinsburg, West Virginia, where information from various processing sites is matched with records from other processing sites. This cross-matching of records helps to assure that taxpayers report all their income and do not file multiple refund claims.

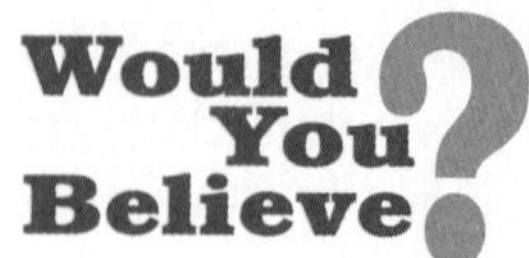

"Tax day is the day that ordinary Americans send their money to Washington, D.C., and wealthy Americans send their money to the Cayman Islands." — Jimmy Kimmel

12-1b The IRS Organizational Structure

The Internal Revenue Service was completely reorganized under the 1998 IRS Restructuring Act (RRA 98), which provided the foundation for the current structure as shown in Figure 12.1.

FIGURE 12.1

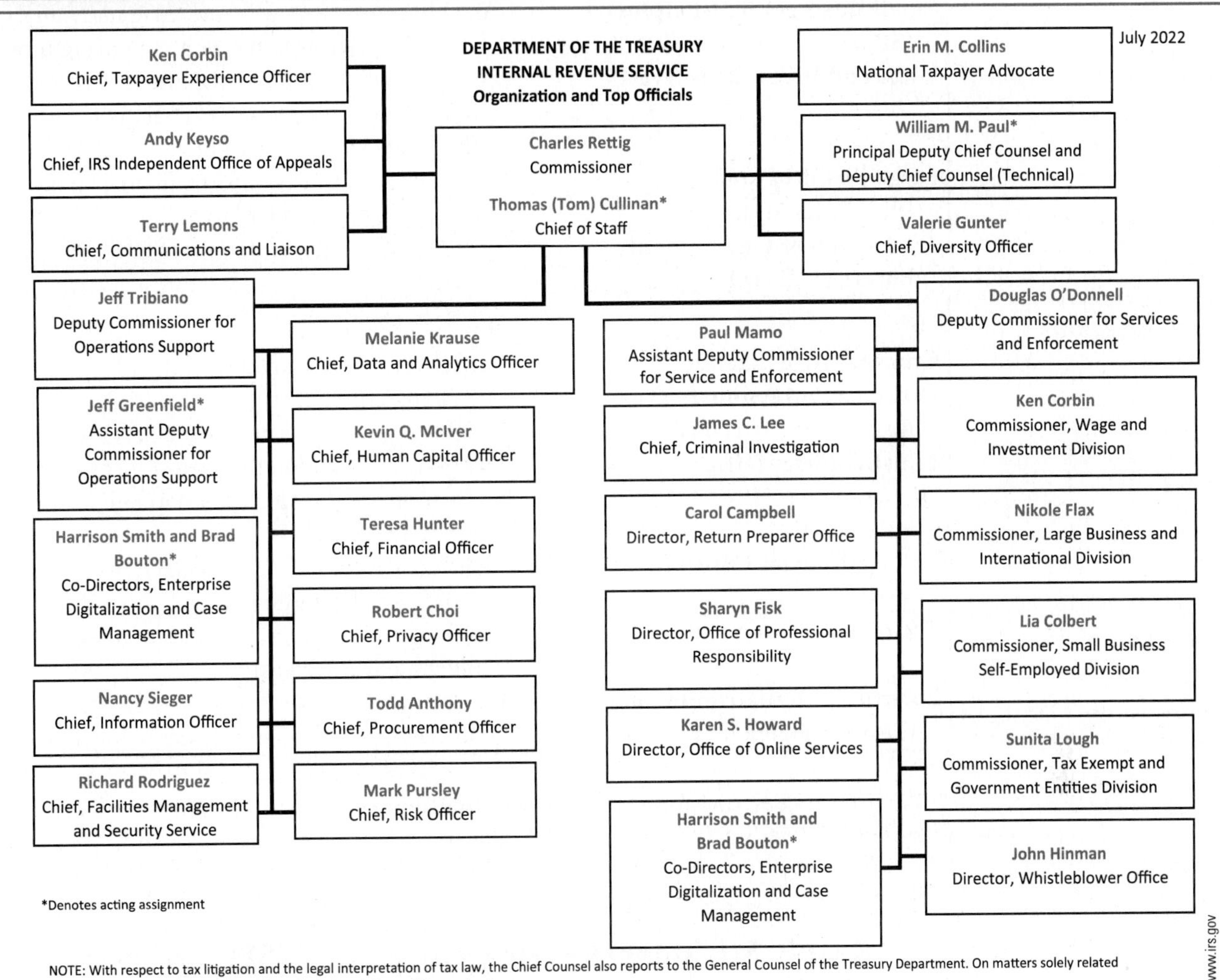

Note: In addition to Figure 12.1 above, more extensive information about the IRS organizational structure is available to the public at **www.irs.gov.**

The Services and Enforcement arm of the IRS, as shown in Figure 12.1, is now responsible for the collection of taxes and the auditing of tax returns, which is done through the following offices:

INTERNAL REVENUE SERVICE DIVISIONS AND PRINCIPAL OFFICES	
Division	*Responsibility*
Small Business/Self-Employed (SB/SE)	Small business taxpayers including individuals who file business forms with their tax returns
Wage and Investment (W&I)	Taxpayers whose primary income is derived from wages and investments and who do not file business forms with their tax returns
Large Business and International (LB&I)	Taxpayers with assets of $10 million or more and the International Program
Tax Exempt & Government Entities (TE/GE)	Tax exempt and government entities
Office	*Responsibility*
Criminal Investigation	Law enforcement activities
Office of Professional Responsibility (OPR)	Regulating enrolled agents, attorneys, and CPAs who practice before the Service
Whistleblower Office (WO)	Handling information that helps uncover tax cheating and providing appropriate rewards to whistleblowers
Return Preparer Office	Registers and promotes a qualified tax professional community
Office of Online Services	Develops and executes strategies to update and integrate IRS Web services
Enterprise Digitalization and Case Management	Enhance the taxpayer experience by improving business processes and modernizing systems

Of these IRS divisions, the most significant to individual and small business taxpayers are the Small Business/Self-Employed (SB/SE) and the Wage and Investment (W&I) offices.

12-1c **Small Business/Self-Employed (SB/SE) Division**

The SB/SE headquarters are located in Lanham, Maryland, with a mission to serve SB/SE customers by educating and informing them of their tax obligations. The division develops educational products and services and helps the public to understand and comply with applicable laws. The SB/SE Division serves the following taxpayers:

- Individuals filing Forms 1040 and 1040-SR (U.S. Individual Income Tax Return), Schedules C, E, or F, and
- All other businesses with assets under $10 million.

The SB/SE Division serves this taxpayer segment through three organizations:

- Collection (specializing in delinquent taxes and tax returns)
- Examination (specializing in correspondence, office, and field audits)
- Operations Support (provides support to other segments to ensure they are properly equipped)

12-1d Wage and Investment (W&I) Division

The mission of the W&I Division is to help taxpayers understand and comply with applicable tax laws and to protect the public interest by applying the tax law with integrity and fairness. The headquarters of the W&I office is in Atlanta, Georgia. The taxpayer profile of W&I is as follows:

- Most pay taxes through withholdings,
- More than half prepare their own returns,
- Most interact with the IRS once a year, and
- Most receive refunds.

Organizationally, the W&I Division is broken down into several operational administrative centers (offices). The key functional operations of the W&I offices include:

- Customer Assistance, Relationships, and Education (CARE)
- Customer Account Services (CAS)
- Return Integrity and Compliance Services (RICS)

12-1e Examination of Records

Federal tax law gives the IRS authority to examine a taxpayer's books and records to determine the correct amount of tax due. The IRS also has the right to summon taxpayers and to make them appear before the IRS and produce necessary accounting records. Taxpayers are required by law to maintain accounting records to facilitate an IRS audit.

The IRS may also issue a summons for taxpayer records from third parties such as banks, brokers, and CPAs. A third party may not have the same incentives to protect the privacy of the taxpayers, and thus, the tax rules generally require that a taxpayer be notified prior to the summons being sent to the third party.

Enforcement of summonses is one of the most litigated areas of tax compliance and has been for almost 15 years. An analysis prepared by the Taxpayer Advocates Office shows that the IRS is extremely successful in these cases, winning over 90 percent.

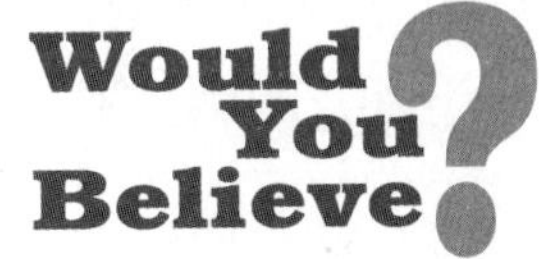

12-1f Collections

Taxpayers have several options when they are unable to pay the money they owe to the IRS as outlined in Publication 594. The IRS wants to help taxpayers move their issues toward resolution, and it has tools to help delinquent taxpayers pay the taxes they owe. Taxpayers may ask the IRS for a short-term administrative extension of time and then borrow money or sell assets to pay their tax debt. They may also enter into an installment agreement with the IRS, if their debt is below certain limits, and pay the debt within a two- or three-year time frame. Another option for certain taxpayers is an *offer in compromise* where the IRS accepts a settlement less than the total amount of tax due. Generally, taxpayers who qualify for an offer in compromise are unlikely to ever be able to pay the amount they owe. Alternatively, sometimes the IRS will accept an offer in compromise when the tax liability is disputed, or to avert a costly and time-consuming legal battle.

If a taxpayer does not pay taxes that are due, ignores notices and demands for payment, and fails to make arrangements to pay the amount owed, the IRS will generally start a collection process. This process may include a tax levy that allows the IRS to take a portion of a taxpayer's wages or to seize property such as the taxpayer's house, car, bank account, or other financial accounts. The IRS may also put a tax lien on the taxpayer's property, which is a legal claim to the property. Liens will not be filed unless a taxpayer owes more than $10,000 in taxes. The IRS also has the power to assess significant penalties, some of which are covered later in this chapter.

Self-Study Problem 12.1 *See Appendix E for Solutions to Self-Study Problems*

Determine whether the following statements are true or false in the current year.

1. The Wage and Investment Division focuses on individuals that receive a Form W-2.
2. Tax returns are processed at IRS Campus Processing Sites.
3. The commissioner of internal revenue is an elected position.
4. The IRS is part of the Justice Department.
5. The IRS has the right to summon a taxpayer's tax records.

Learning Objective 12.2

Describe the IRS audit process.

12-2 THE AUDIT PROCESS

A primary function of the IRS is to audit taxpayers' tax returns. After the service centers have checked the returns for accuracy, some returns are selected for audit. When a return is selected for examination, it may be subject to an "office audit" or a "field audit." An audit may also be conducted through the mail in what is called a "correspondence audit."

Correspondence audits now account for about 75 percent of the IRS examinations of individual returns each year. Correspondence audits are generally handled entirely by mail. The audit begins when the IRS sends a letter to a taxpayer requesting specific information about their tax return. Usually, the areas covered in correspondence audits relate to questions about Forms W-2 and 1099 that do not agree with the tax return, requests for information supporting charitable contributions, and information related to eligibility for claimed earned income credits.

The office audit is conducted in an IRS office and is typically used for individual taxpayers with little or no business activities. In an office audit, the taxpayer takes their records to the IRS office where they are reviewed by a revenue agent. The taxpayer is simply required to substantiate deductions, credits, or income items that appear on their tax return.

In a field audit, the IRS agent reviews a taxpayer's books and records at the taxpayer's place of business or at the office of the taxpayer's accountant. This type of audit is generally used when the accounting records are too extensive to take to the IRS office. Field audits are usually used for taxpayers with substantial trade or business activities. If a taxpayer can present a valid reason, they may have an office audit changed to a field audit.

12-2a Selection of Returns for Audits

The IRS selects returns for audit through a number of different methods:

- Identification of participants in abusive tax avoidance transactions
- Computer scoring (DIF)
- Large corporations
- Information matching
- Related examinations
- Other means

The level of returns being audited is reaching record lows. In 2010, about 1 percent of all individual tax returns were examined. By 2019, individual returns examined had dropped to 0.2 percent of all individual returns. Although coverage is better for high-income taxpayers, for individual taxpayers with income over $10 million, over 21 percent were examined in 2010 versus only about 2 percent of 2019 returns were examined. At the time the data was released, the IRS still had time to examine 2019 returns.

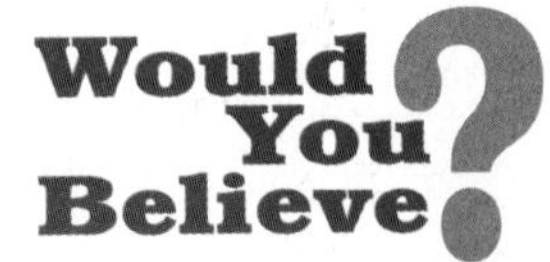

The IRS uses information gleaned from other sources to identify taxpayers involved in abusive tax avoidance transactions. For example, the IRS may identify a promoter of abusive transactions and then use the promoter's records to identify taxpayers that may have engaged in the abusive planning. The IRS also may select a tax return for audit through a related examination. For example, if the IRS selects an entity or taxpayer for examination, they may also select business partners or other investors.

Most large corporations are involved with an IRS audit on a continuous basis and many have set aside permanent office space to house the IRS agents.

For computer scoring, the IRS uses the DIF (Discriminant Function System) and UIDIF (Unreported Income DIF) to select taxpayers for audit. Under the DIF system, the IRS uses mathematical formulas to assign a DIF score to each return. The DIF score represents the potential for discovery of improper treatment of items on the tax return. The higher the DIF score, the more likely the tax return is to be audited. The DIF score is designed to identify tax returns likely to contain errors because they contain amounts of income, deductions, or tax credits that fall outside "normal" ranges. For example, a tax return that contains unusually large charitable contributions claimed as a deduction will be assigned a high DIF score, and the chances of it being selected for audit are greater. The UIDIF scores returns for the likelihood of unreported income.

The IRS has operated a random audit selection process for many years under different program names such as the Taxpayer Compliance Measurement Program (TCMP) or, as currently more benignly named, the National Research Program (NRP). These programs are used to assist the IRS in determining which types of taxpayers should be audited and gather data to update the DIF system. These programs have not been without controversy and remain a sensitive issue for the IRS. The National Taxpayer Advocate has suggested providing compensation to taxpayers that are subjected to an NRP audit that results in no change to tax liability.

The old TCMP audits were sometimes so time-consuming and intrusive that one taxpayer referred to them as "an autopsy without the benefit of dying," according to a *Wall Street Journal*'s "Tax Report" column.

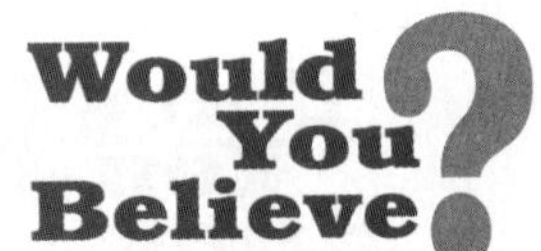

Other tax returns that are audited are selected due to matching problems between the information forms such as Forms W-2 and 1099 and the related taxpayer's return. As more returns are filed electronically and the IRS information systems have improved, the number of matching notices has increased. For the 2020 tax year, the number of automated underreporting and matching notices dwarfs the number of correspondence and field audits by a wide margin. From time to time, the IRS will also target special projects at a local or industry segment. For example, a "random" audit might reveal a tax issue with small auto repair shops. After required approvals from higher positions within the IRS, a number of small auto repair shops may be selected for audit to see if the issue is pervasive within the industry segment.

Lastly, the IRS can also select returns based on information obtained from other taxing jurisdictions, news sources, or whistleblowers. For example, the IRS and many state departments of revenue share tax information to assist in the identification of returns for examination. Although the IRS has procedures in place to ensure that audits are not targeted at certain groups for political or other motivations, the history of such reported behavior continues to haunt the organization.

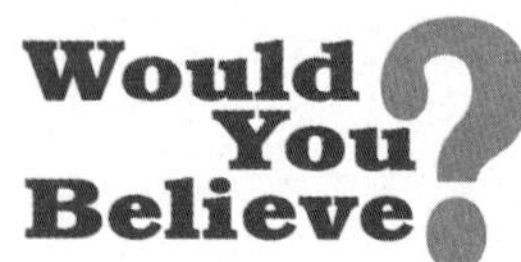

According to the IRS, the cost to process an e-filed Form 1040 individual tax return in 2020 was $0.36 per return. The cost to process a paper-filed return of the same type was $15.21. The error rate for paper-filed returns was over 43 percent in 2020, while the error rate for e-filed returns was below 5 percent. Over 93 percent of individual tax returns were e-filed in 2020 and the IRS is seeking to push that number even higher.

12-2b **The Appeals Process**

After a return is selected for examination, an agent is assigned to perform the audit. There are three possible results arising from the agent's audit. First, the tax return may be found to require no adjustment, in which case the findings are reviewed and the tax return is sent to storage. A second possible outcome of the audit is an agreement between the agent and the taxpayer on a needed change in the tax liability on the tax return. Then, the tax is collected or the refund is paid, and after a review, the return is stored.

The final possible outcome of the audit is a disagreement between the agent and the taxpayer on the amount of the required adjustment to the tax return. In this situation, the appeals procedure begins with the IRS inviting the taxpayer to an informal conference with an appellate agent. If an agreement cannot be reached at the appeals level, then the matter is taken into the federal court system. The Federal Tax Court is open to the public. For tax professionals and tax students, watching the Tax Court in action can be an educational experience. Any group planning a court visit should contact the judge's chambers in advance since the courts are often small and cannot accommodate many spectators. During and subsequent to the COVID-19 pandemic, a selected number of Tax Court proceedings are held virtually and open to the public. See the Tax Court website for more information and a calendar of virtual proceedings. Figures 12.2 and 12.3 on Pages 12-9 and 12-10, respectively, illustrate the audit process, beginning with the selection of a tax return for audit and ending with a decision of the federal courts.

The IRS considers the appeals function to be highly successful, negotiating and settling 85 to 90 percent of the cases with taxpayers. If this high rate of settlement were not achieved, the number of disputed cases would soon overwhelm the courts hearing tax cases.

FIGURE 12.2

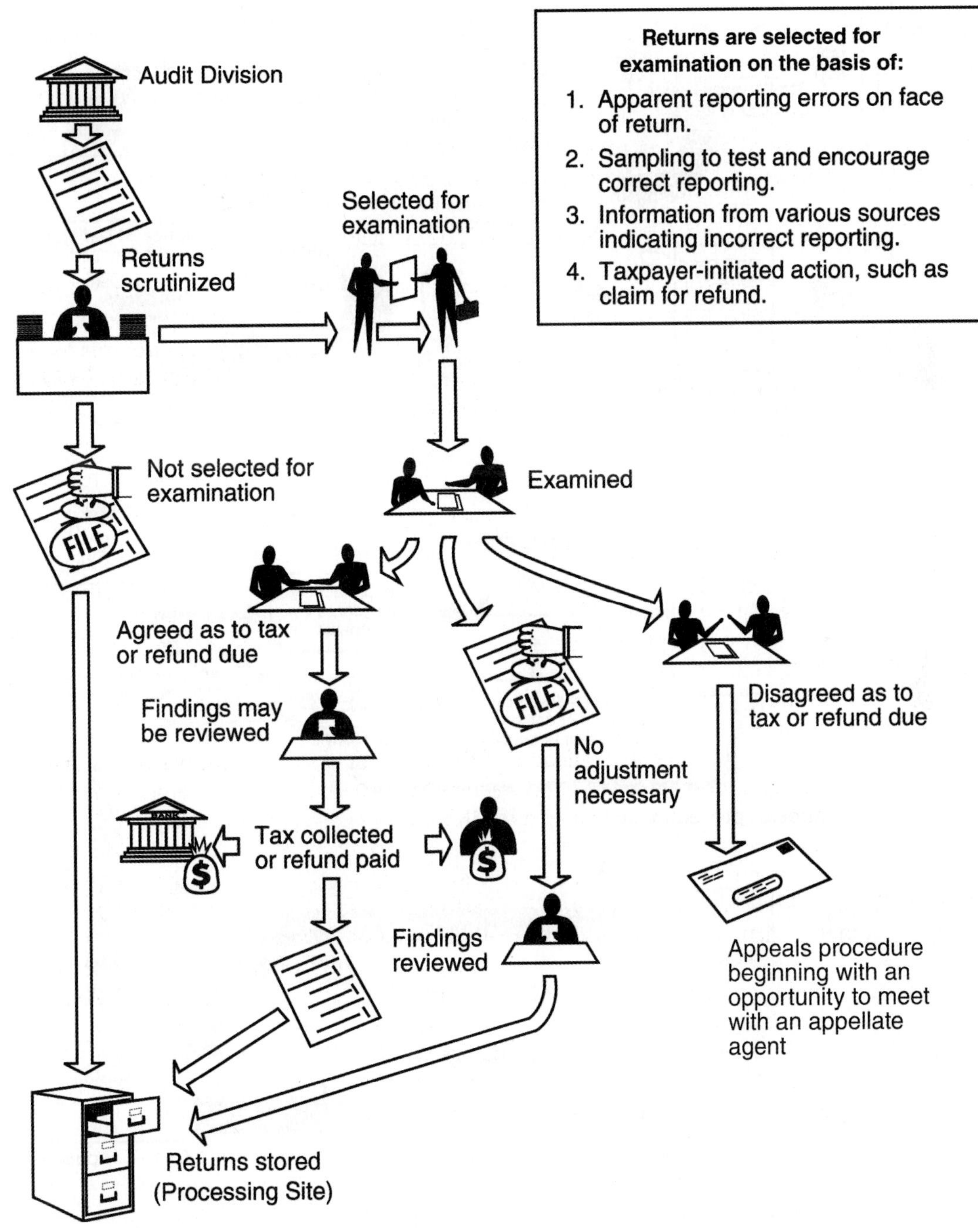
INCOME TAX AUDIT PROCEDURE
OF THE INTERNAL REVENUE SERVICE
Returns are selected for examination on the basis of:
1. Apparent reporting errors on face of return.
2. Sampling to test and encourage correct reporting.
3. Information from various sources indicating incorrect reporting.
4. Taxpayer-initiated action, such as claim for refund.
Audit Division
Returns scrutinized
Selected for examination
Not selected for examination
FILE
Examined
Agreed as to tax or refund due
Findings may be reviewed
Tax collected or refund paid
$
FILE
No adjustment necessary
Disagreed as to tax or refund due
Findings reviewed
Appeals procedure beginning with an opportunity to meet with an appellate agent
Returns stored (Processing Site)

FIGURE 12.3

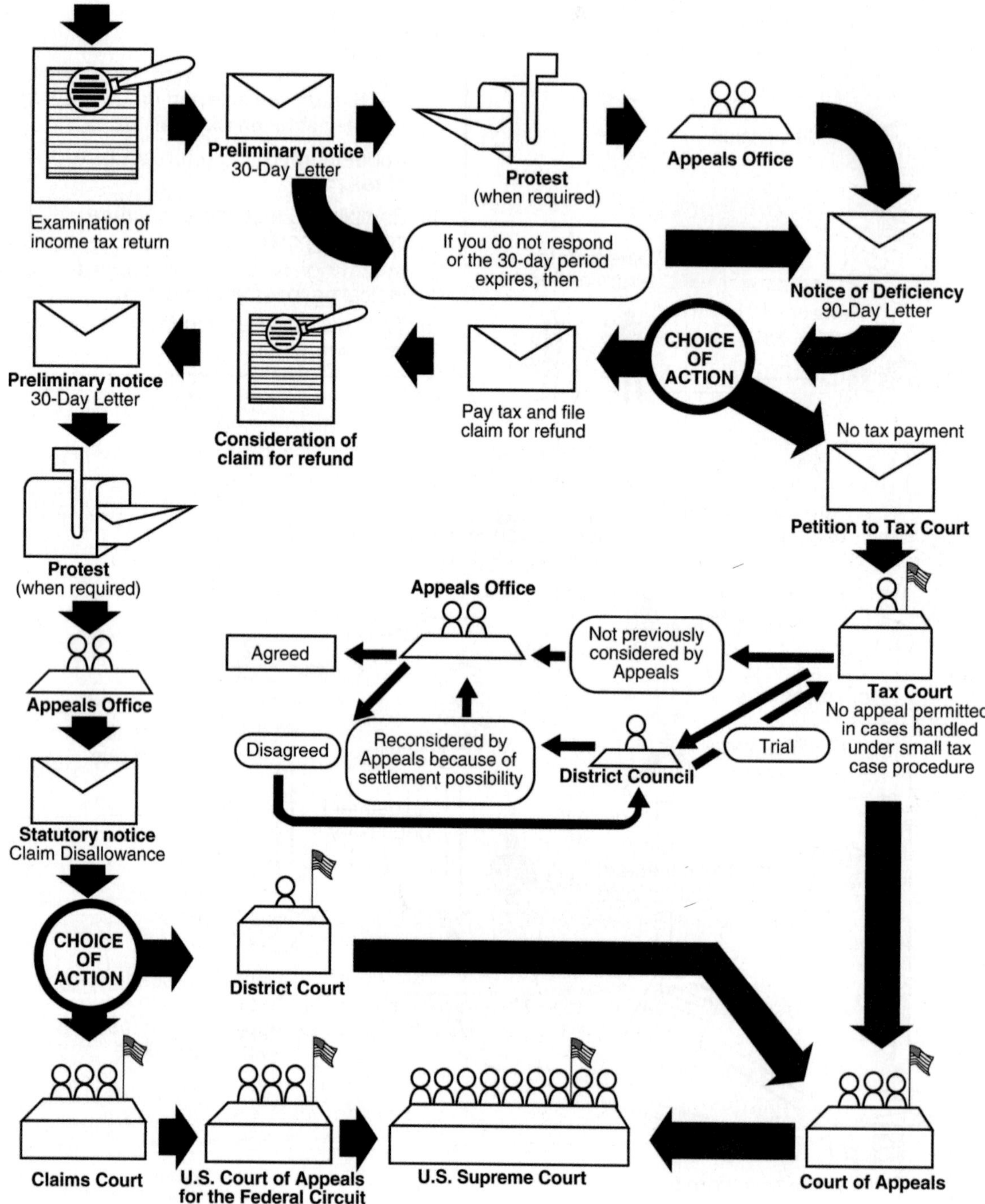

At any stage of procedure:

- You can agree and arrange to pay.
- You can ask the IRS to issue you a notice of deficiency so you can file a petition with the Tax Court.
- You can pay the tax and file a claim for a refund.

Self-Study Problem 12.2 *See Appendix E for Solutions to Self-Study Problems*

Determine whether the following statements are true or false.

1. The IRS uses computers to select tax returns for audit.
2. An office audit is done at the taxpayer's office.
3. NRP audits are selected randomly.
4. An audit may result in a refund.
5. A taxpayer cannot appeal the results of an IRS audit.

12-3 INTEREST AND PENALTIES

12.3 Learning Objective

Define the common penalties for taxpayers and apply them to specific situations.

Taxpayers are charged interest on underpayments of taxes, and in some cases the IRS pays interest to taxpayers when they overpay their taxes. Usually, these interest charges or payments result from the settlement of a tax liability for a prior year's tax return. For example, when an IRS audit results in the taxpayer paying additional taxes for a prior tax year, the IRS will charge the taxpayer interest on the amount of additional taxes from the original due date to the date of payment of the tax. If the audit results in a refund, interest will be paid to the taxpayer based on the amount of the refund. The IRS also imposes a nondeductible penalty based on amounts of underpayments of estimated taxes for the current tax year (see Chapter 9), but a taxpayer is not paid interest on a refund arising from an overpayment of estimated taxes during the current tax year.

The interest rate applicable to underpayments and overpayments of taxes is adjusted each quarter based on the short-term federal rate. The rate is equal to the federal short-term rate plus 3 percentage points. Interest is compounded daily except when calculating the penalty for underpayment of estimated taxes by individuals and corporations. In calculating the penalty for underpayment of estimated taxes, the penalty is calculated as simple interest.

The rate of interest for under and overpayments for noncorporate taxpayers for selected recent periods is as follows:

2022	*Rate*
1st quarter	3%
2nd quarter	4%
3rd quarter	5%
4th quarter	6%

Tables are available from the IRS for performing the actual calculation of interest owed from or due to taxpayers. Interest paid on an underpayment of tax is considered consumer interest; therefore, no deduction is allowed (see Chapter 5). The penalty for underpayment of estimated tax is calculated as interest but is a nondeductible penalty. Interest received on an overpayment is income in the year the payment is received. No interest is paid on a current year overpayment, unless the IRS takes more than 45 days to process the return.

EXAMPLE James pays $2,000 of interest in 2022 for an underpayment of taxes on his 2019 tax return. The $2,000 is not deductible since no deduction is allowed for consumer interest. ♦

EXAMPLE John receives $700 of interest income on the overpayment of his taxes resulting from an IRS audit on his 2019 tax return. The $700 interest is income in the year it is received by John. ♦

The tax law contains various penalties to ensure taxpayers accurately report and pay their taxes. Penalty payments are considered an addition to the amount of the taxes and, therefore, are not deductible. Several of the major taxpayer penalties are described in the following paragraphs.

12-3a The Failure-to-Pay and Failure-to-File Penalties

Taxpayers are subject to a penalty for failure to pay the amount of the taxes due on the due date of their tax return. The penalty for failure to pay is ½ of 1 percent of the amount of taxes due for every month or portion of a month that the payment is late, up to a maximum of 25 percent of the amount of taxes due. The penalty increases to 1 percent per month beginning 10 days after a notice of levy has been given to the taxpayer.

If a taxpayer does not file a tax return on the due date (including extensions), he or she is subject to a penalty equal to 5 percent of the tax due with the return for every month or portion of a month the return is late. The amount of the penalty for failure to file, however, is limited to a maximum of 25 percent of the amount of taxes due with the tax return. In the event the failure to file is fraudulent, the penalty is increased from 5 percent for each month or portion thereof to 15 percent, and the maximum penalty is increased from 25 percent to 75 percent. Also, if the taxpayer fails to file their tax return within 60 days of its due date, the minimum failure-to-file penalty is the lesser of $450 (in 2022) or the total amount of the taxes due with the tax return.

If both the failure-to-file and the failure-to-pay penalties apply, the failure-to-file penalty (5 percent) is reduced by the amount of the failure-to-pay penalty (½ of 1 percent) to 4.5 percent so the total combined penalty stays at 5 percent. The maximum combined penalty is 25 percent for the first 5 months. After 5 months, the failure-to-pay penalty continues at ½ of 1 percent per month for up to an additional 45 months. Thus, the maximum combined penalty could reach 47.5 percent.

Both the failure-to-file and the failure-to-pay penalties are zero if there is no tax due or if a refund is due from the IRS on the late tax return. The failure-to-file and the failure-to-pay penalty will not be assessed if the taxpayer can demonstrate that they had "reasonable cause" for failing to pay or file the tax return on time.

EXAMPLE Nancy filed her 2022 tax return 3½ months after the due date, and she had not requested an extension of time to file. The failure to file was not due to fraud. She included with her late return a check for $2,000, which was the balance of the tax she owed. Disregarding interest, her penalties are calculated as follows:

Failure-to-pay penalty (0.5% × $2,000) × 4 months		$ 40
Plus:		
Failure-to-file penalty (5% × $2,000) × 4 months	$400	
Less: Failure-to-pay penalty	(40)	
Net failure-to-file penalty	360	
Minimum failure-to-file after 60 days	$450	450
Total penalties		$490 ♦

TAX BREAK The IRS has a first-time penalty abatement program which was meant to allow taxpayers who were assessed penalties for the first time to request a one-time penalty amnesty. The program applies to the failure-to-file and failure-to-pay penalties as well as several others, and can save taxpayers significant amounts of money in certain cases. The penalty abatement waiver must be requested by the taxpayer, but few taxpayers who qualify for the waiver request it or even know the program exists.

12-3b Accuracy-Related Penalty

The tax law imposes a penalty of 20 percent of the applicable underpayment due to (1) negligence of or disregard for rules or regulations, (2) a substantial understatement of income tax, or (3) a substantial valuation overstatement, as well as certain other understatements of income tax. Negligence includes the failure to make a reasonable attempt to comply with the tax law. For example, the penalty could be imposed on a taxpayer who deducts a personal expenditure as a business expense. A substantial understatement of income tax occurs where the required amount of tax exceeds the tax shown on the taxpayer's return by the greater of 10 percent (5 percent if claiming a qualified business income deduction) of the amount of tax that should be shown on the return or $5,000 ($10,000 for corporate taxpayers other than S corporations). A substantial valuation overstatement occurs when the value of property is 150 percent or more of the correct valuation. For example, a taxpayer who inflates the value of depreciable property to generate additional depreciation deductions may be subject to this penalty. The accuracy-related penalty applies only if the taxpayer has filed a return. The tax law also imposes a 20-percent penalty for an "excessive" claim for refund or a credit claim. If the taxpayer can demonstrate that he or she has reasonable cause for the understatement of tax or claim for refund or credit and that he or she acted in good faith, the penalty will not be assessed.

EXAMPLE Kim underpaid her taxes for the current year by $15,000 due to negligence. Kim's penalty for negligence under the accuracy-related penalty is calculated as follows:

Accuracy-related penalty (20% × $15,000)	$3,000 ♦

12-3c Fraud Penalty

The tax law also contains provisions for penalties for filing fraudulent tax returns. The fraud penalty is equal to 75 percent of the amount of underpayment of taxes attributable to fraud.

For the IRS to impose the fraud penalty, it must be shown by a "preponderance of evidence" that the taxpayer had an intent to evade taxes; however, once the IRS establishes that any portion of an underpayment of taxes is due to fraud, the entire underpayment is assumed to be attributable to fraud unless the taxpayer establishes otherwise. The tax law does not provide clear rules for what constitutes fraud; however, what is clearly mere negligence by a taxpayer will not cause this penalty to be imposed. When the fraud penalty is applicable, the accuracy-related penalty cannot be imposed. The fraud penalty will be applied only where the taxpayer has actually filed a return. Like the accuracy-related penalty, the fraud penalty will not be assessed if the taxpayer can demonstrate reasonable cause for the underpayment of tax and the taxpayer acted in good faith.

EXAMPLE Jeff has a $20,000 tax deficiency because of civil fraud. Interest on this underpayment amounts to $8,000. Jeff's total amount due on this underpayment is calculated as follows:

Tax deficiency	$20,000
Fraud penalty (75% × $20,000)	15,000
Interest	8,000
Total due	$43,000

The interest is not deductible due to the disallowance of deductions for consumer interest. The fraud penalty is also not deductible. ♦

According to IRS data, 10 percent of Americans feel cheating on taxes is acceptable. Experts agree that tax cheating is a significant problem for the IRS, which must enforce the laws, and for honest taxpayers who pay more in taxes than they would otherwise have to. It is generally believed that tax evasion and noncompliance are costing the government more than $630 billion dollars in lost revenue each year.

ILYA AKINSHIN/Shutterstock.com; Zhukov Oleg/Shutterstock.com.

Sign Here

Under penalties of perjury, I declare that I have examined this return and accompanying schedules and statements, and to the best of my knowledge and belief, they are true, correct, and complete. Declaration of preparer (other than taxpayer) is based on all information of which preparer has any knowledge.

Joint return? See instructions. Keep a copy for your records.

Your signature	Date	Your occupation	If the IRS sent you an Identity Protection PIN, enter it here (see inst.) ▶
Spouse's signature. If a joint return, **both** must sign.	Date	Spouse's occupation	If the IRS sent your spouse an Identity Protection PIN, enter it here (see inst.) ▶
Phone no.	Email address		

Paid Preparer Use Only

Preparer's name	Preparer's signature	Date	PTIN	Check if: ☐ Self-employed
Firm's name ▶			Phone no.	
Firm's address ▶			Firm's EIN ▶	

Would You Sign This Tax Return?

Tim Trying, who is single, purchased a house on the beach in sunny Southern California 35 years ago. He is now retiring and moving to Hawaii for his golden years. Tim sold his house for $1,200,000 this year. Tim has been a client of yours for the past decade. He became a client when he was referred to you by your parents, who lived two houses away from Tim. When asked what his tax basis is in the house, Tim says it is $975,000. Your parents bought their house at about the same time, and you know they paid $100,000 for it. You have seen Tim's house many times and, although the house is well-maintained, you know it does not have any major improvements or betterments. You are reasonably certain that Tim is overstating his tax basis by hundreds of thousands of dollars in order to avoid reporting a taxable gain on the sale. Would you sign the Paid Preparer's declaration (see example above) on this return? Why or why not?

12-3d **Miscellaneous Penalties**

The tax law contains many other penalties applicable to taxpayers. The following are examples of such penalties:

- A civil penalty of $500 and a criminal penalty of up to $1,000 are imposed for filing false withholding information.
- An immediate $5,000 penalty can be assessed against a taxpayer who files a "frivolous" tax return (or document) as a tax protest.
- A tiered penalty system dependent on the timeliness of correction and filing of information returns (including payee information returns) is imposed for failing to file correct information returns. The penalties for information returns filed in 2022 are up to $290 per return, with an annual maximum of $3,532,500 ($1,177,500 for small businesses). If the failure to file is corrected or the information returns are filed closer to the due date, the penalties may be reduced. Exceptions to the information return penalties may be made for reasonable cause.
- Employers are subject to a penalty of 2, 5, or 10 percent of the amount of payroll taxes not deposited on time, depending on the number of days the taxes remain undeposited. A 15-percent penalty may apply where taxes remain undeposited after a delinquency notice has been presented to the taxpayer.
- Taxpayers are subject to a penalty for failure to pay estimated taxes. The penalty is calculated using the interest rates for the period of underpayment (but it is not deductible as interest). See Chapter 9 for more information.
- Taxpayers are subject to a penalty for issuing a "bad" check, unless the taxpayer can demonstrate that the check was issued in good faith. The penalty is equal to 2 percent of the amount of the check. If the check is less than $1,250, then the penalty is the lesser of $25 or the amount of the check.

Self-Study Problem 12.3 *See Appendix E for Solutions to Self-Study Problems*

a. Linda filed her tax return 43 days late. The tax paid with the return amounts to $3,000. What is Linda's total penalty for failure to file and failure to pay, assuming the failure to file is not fraudulent?
b. Using the same information as above in part a, what is Linda's total penalty if the tax return is 63 days late?
c. Kim underpaid her taxes by $10,000 due to negligence. What is Kim's penalty for negligence?

12-4 STATUTE OF LIMITATIONS

12.4 Learning Objective

Apply the general rule for the statute of limitations on tax returns and the important exceptions to the general rule.

The statute of limitations is the time period within which an action may be taken by the IRS and the taxpayer on a tax return. After the statute of limitations has run out on a given tax return, the government cannot assess additional taxes and the taxpayer cannot amend the return to request a refund. In general, the statute of limitations for a tax return runs for three years from the date the tax return was filed or the return due date (without extensions), whichever is later. For taxpayers seeking a refund, the statute of limitations is the later of three years from the time of filing or two years from the date that the taxes were actually paid.

EXAMPLE Norm files his 2022 tax return on March 19, 2023. Unless an exception discussed below applies, the IRS has until April 18, 2026, to assess any additional taxes (recall that the 2022 filing deadline is April 18, 2023 due to the weekend and holidays). ♦

12-4a Exceptions

The tax law contains several exceptions to the general rule of a three-year statute of limitations. Several of these special rules are summarized below:

- If a fraudulent tax return is filed or no return is filed, there is no statute of limitations. The IRS may assess a tax deficiency at any time in the future.
- If a taxpayer omits an amount of gross income in excess of 25 percent of the gross income shown on the return, then the statute of limitations is increased to six years. For example, if a tax return with gross income of $40,000 contains an omission of over $10,000 (25 percent of $40,000) of gross income, the statute of limitations is increased to six years.
- The statute of limitations for the deduction of a bad debt or worthless securities is seven years. This limitation applies only to the bad debt deduction or the worthless security deduction; all other items on the tax return would normally close out after three years.

Besides these exceptions, the statute of limitations may be extended by mutual consent of the IRS and the taxpayer. This extension is for a specific time period and is made by signing the appropriate form in the Form 872 series. An extension is generally used when the statute of limitations is about to lapse and an audit has not been completed.

If a tax deficiency has been assessed by the IRS within the period of the statute of limitations, then the government has 10 years from the date of assessment to collect the tax due.

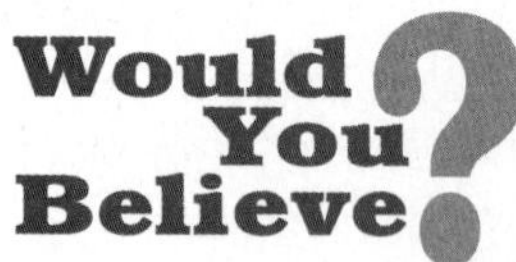

An IRS study shows that many taxpayers miss out on refunds because they fail to file their returns within the statute of limitations for claiming a refund, which can be either two or three years, depending on the circumstances. The IRS denies millions of dollars in refunds each year which were claimed in delinquent returns.

Self-Study Problem 12.4

See Appendix E for Solutions to Self-Study Problems

Determine whether the following statements are true or false.

1. The general statute of limitations for a tax return is three years.
2. The statute of limitations for a bad debt deduction on a tax return is six years.
3. The statute of limitations for a fraudulent tax return is seven years.
4. The special statute of limitations for a tax return that omits income greater than 25 percent of gross income is six years.
5. For the deduction of worthless securities, the statute of limitations is seven years.

12-5 PREPARERS, PROOF, AND PRIVILEGE

12.5 Learning Objective

Describe the rules and penalties that apply to tax practitioners.

12-5a Tax Practitioners

Many taxpayers find it desirable or necessary to have their tax returns prepared by a tax practitioner. Tax practitioners include commercial preparers, enrolled agents, attorneys, and certified public accountants (CPAs). Commercial preparers generally prepare non-complex returns of individuals, small corporations, and partnerships. Enrolled agents are individuals who have passed an IRS exam and are allowed to represent clients at IRS proceedings, as well as prepare tax returns. Attorneys and CPAs are individuals who have met education, examination, and experience requirements and are licensed to practice in their respective professions. CPAs and attorneys normally work with complex tax returns of individuals, corporations, partnerships, estates, and trusts. They also provide tax-planning advice to aid their clients in minimizing the amount of their taxes. Preparers that are enrolled agents, CPAs, and attorneys are sometimes referred to as enrolled preparers while other non-credentialed preparers are known as unenrolled preparers.

Tax preparers are regulated in several different ways. For federal income tax returns, the primary regulation comes from Circular 230, which is a Treasury Department regulation. Circular 230 describes the rules for "practice before the IRS," a tax professional's duties and obligations while practicing before the IRS; authorizes specific sanctions for violations of the duties and obligations; and describes the procedures that apply to administrative proceedings for discipline. Circular 230 can be found on the IRS website (**www.irs.gov/tax-professionals/circular-230-tax-professionals**). A number of key elements of Circular 230 are:

- Any individual who for compensation prepares or assists with the preparation of all or substantially all of a tax return or claim for refund must have a preparer tax identification number (PTIN). PTINs can be obtained and renewed online from the IRS website for a cost of about $36.
- A practitioner must, on a proper and lawful request by the IRS, promptly submit records or information in any matter before the IRS unless the practitioner believes in good faith and on reasonable grounds that the records or information are privileged.
- Where the requested records or information are not in the possession of the practitioner or the practitioner's client, the practitioner must promptly notify the IRS and the practitioner must provide any information regarding the identity of any person who the practitioner believes may have possession or control of the requested information.
- A practitioner who knows that a client has not complied with the tax law or has made an error in or omission from any return, must advise the client promptly of the fact of such noncompliance, error, or omission. The practitioner must advise the client of the consequences of such noncompliance, error, or omission.

EXAMPLE Becca prepared Juno's tax return in the prior year. While preparing the current year's tax return, Becca noted an error in the prior year return. Becca has a responsibility to report the error to Juno and explain the consequences if the error is not corrected. Note that Becca is not responsible to report Juno's failure to comply. ♦

- A practitioner must exercise due diligence: (1) in preparing or assisting in the preparation of, approving, and filing tax returns; (2) in determining the correctness of oral or written representations made by the practitioner to the IRS; and (3) in determining the correctness of oral or written representations made by the practitioner to clients.
- A practitioner may not charge an unconscionable fee or contingent fee (except for contingent fees on audits, challenges to interest and penalty assessments, and judicial proceedings).
- A practitioner may not negotiate any refund check by any means into an account owned or controlled by the practitioner.

Circular 230 also provides some best practices for practitioners to follow:

- A practitioner may not willfully, recklessly, or through gross incompetence sign a tax return or claim for refund, or advise a client to take a position on a tax return or claim for refund, or prepare a portion of a tax return or claim for refund containing a position that the practitioner reasonably should know contains a position that (A) lacks a reasonable basis; (B) is an unreasonable position as described in §6694(a)(2); or (C) is a willful attempt by the practitioner to understate the liability for tax or a reckless or intentional disregard of rules or regulations.
- A practitioner may not advise a client to take a position on a document, affidavit or other paper submitted to the IRS unless the position is not frivolous.
- A practitioner must possess the necessary competence to engage in practice before the IRS. Competent practice requires the appropriate level of knowledge, skill, thoroughness, and preparation necessary for the matter for which the practitioner is engaged.

Circular 230 addresses different types of practitioners such as attorneys, CPAs, enrolled agents, registered tax return preparers (RTRPs), (note that the RTRP program is no longer operative), and participants in the Annual Filing Season Program. The different practitioners have differing degrees of authority to practice under Circular 230:

Responsibility	**Attorney CPA Enrolled Agent**	**Annual Filing Season Program (AFSP)**	**Unenrolled Preparers (non AFSP)**
Practice before IRS	Unlimited	Limited	Limited
Tax preparation	Sign when completed all or substantially all of the return	Sign when completed all or substantially all of the return	Sign when completed all or substantially all of the return
Representation	Before the IRS, during examination and appeals, and for any return or refund	Before IRS revenue agents, customer service, and employees during examination only on returns that were signed by that preparer	Before IRS revenue agents, customer service, and employees during examination only on returns that were signed by that preparer
Advising	Unlimited	Limited to return or refund preparation	Limited to return or refund preparation

Several states also regulate the preparation of income taxes including California, Maryland, Oregon, New York, and Connecticut. Each state has varying requirements. Iowa has a continuing education requirement but does not require registration.

12-5b Annual Filing Season Program

All paid tax return preparers must sign up with the IRS and obtain a preparer tax identification number (PTIN). Every year, paid tax preparers must sign up or renew their PTIN online.

The IRS operates the Annual Filing Season Program (AFSP), a voluntary tax return preparer program designed to encourage preparers to participate in continuing education courses to help stay abreast of changes in tax law and help reduce the risk of using a preparer without professional credentials. The AFSP requires unenrolled preparers to obtain 18 hours of continuing education from an approved provider, including at least 6 hours of an Annual Federal Tax Refresher (AFTR) course focused on filing season issues and tax updates and two hours of ethics. The AFTR must include a knowledge-based exam administered at the end of the course by the course provider.

In addition to being better prepared for the upcoming filing season, a list of tax preparers meeting the AFSP requirements is published at **www.irs.gov** to permit taxpayers to search for qualified tax return preparers. For additional information on the Annual Filing Season Program requirements, see the IRS website **(www.irs.gov)**.

12-5c **Preparer Penalties**

Under the tax law, any person who prepares a tax return, including non-income tax returns (e.g., excise tax returns), for compensation is a "tax return preparer." The tax law has various penalty provisions applicable to tax return preparers. These penalties are designed to help the IRS regulate the preparation of tax returns. The more significant penalties are described below:

- $55 for failing to sign a tax return or failing to furnish the preparer's identifying number, $28,000 annual maximum
- $55 for each failure to keep a copy of the prepared return or include the return on a list of taxpayers for whom returns have been prepared, $28,000 annual maximum
- $55 for failing to provide a taxpayer a copy of the tax return prepared, $28,000 annual maximum
- $560 for endorsing or cashing a refund check issued to a taxpayer, or failing in due diligence for a taxpayer claiming the earned income credit
- $560 for failure to be diligent in the preparation of eligibility to file as head of household, child tax credit, American Opportunities credit, and earned income credit (Form 8867)
- Greater of $1,000 or 50 percent of the income derived (or to be derived) by the tax return preparer for an undisclosed unrealistic position on a return which does not meet a "substantial authority" standard, and which the preparer knew or reasonably should have known about
- Greater of $5,000 or 75 percent of the income derived (or to be derived) by the tax return preparer for each return in which the preparer willfully attempts to understate the amount of the taxpayer's tax liability, or each return in which an understatement is due to the preparer's reckless or intentional disregard of rules or regulations, reduced by the amount of the $1,000 (or 50 percent) penalty for unrealistic positions (discussed above)
- $1,000 ($10,000 for corporate returns) for each return or document filed in aiding or abetting a taxpayer in understating a tax liability
- For each separate activity (sale of an interest, organization of an entity, etc.), the lesser of $1,000 or 100 percent of the gross income derived by the promoter from promoting an "abusive tax shelter"

The tax preparer penalty rules introduce two very important terms: (1) substantial authority and (2) reasonable basis. The understatement penalty can potentially be avoided by the tax preparer if they have substantial authority for the tax position taken or if substantial authority does not exist, a reasonable basis (which is considered a lower standard to meet) for the position exists and such position is disclosed. The substantial authority standard is an objective standard involving an analysis of the law and application of the law to relevant facts and requires that the tax preparer establish that support for the tax position within a set of authoritative guidance:

1. Applicable provisions of the Internal Revenue Code and other federal tax law;
2. Proposed, temporary, and final regulations;

3. Revenue rulings and revenue procedures;
4. Tax treaties and regulations thereunder, and Treasury Department and other official explanations of such treaties;
5. Court cases;
6. Congressional intent as reflected in committee reports, joint explanatory statements of managers included in conference committee reports, and floor statements made prior to enactment by one of a bill's managers;
7. General Explanations of tax legislation prepared by the Joint Committee on Taxation (the Blue Book);
8. Private letter rulings and technical advice memoranda issued after October 31, 1976;
9. Actions on decisions and general counsel memoranda issued after March 12, 1981 (as well as general counsel memoranda published in pre-1955 volumes of the Cumulative Bulletin);
10. Internal Revenue Service information or press releases; and
11. Notices, announcements and other administrative pronouncements published by the Service in the Internal Revenue Bulletin.

Conclusions reached in treatises, periodicals, newspapers, and textbooks are not considered substantial authority.

A reasonable basis for a position is one that is significantly higher than frivolous or not patently improper. It must be more than merely arguable or a colorable claim. The position is considered reasonable if based on one or more of the authorities that are part of substantial authority. The required disclosure is made on Form 8275.

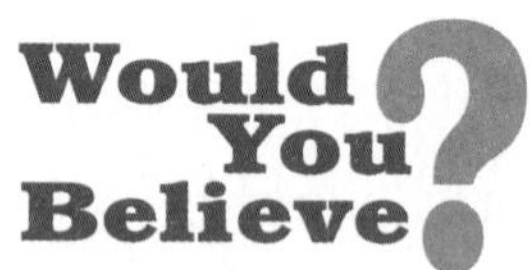

The longstanding position that erroneous instructions from an IRS employee that result in additional tax do not represent an excuse for taxpayers was tested in the Tax Court again in 2021 and unsurprisingly, maintained. As the Tax Court has stated many times, "the authoritative sources of Federal tax law are in the statutes, regulations, and judicial decisions', not in informal advice or publications."

12-5d **Burden of Proof**

In most litigation, the party initiating the case has the burden of convincing the court that he or she is correct with respect to the issue. Historically, however, in most civil tax cases, the Internal Revenue Code (the Code) placed the burden of proof on the taxpayer, whether or not he or she initiated the case, except in cases involving such items as hobby losses, fraud with intent to evade tax, and the accumulated earnings tax.

In the IRS Restructuring and Reform Act of 1998, the tax law was changed to shift the burden of proof to the IRS in many situations. The IRS now has the burden of proof in any court proceeding on an income, gift, estate, or generation-skipping tax liability with respect to factual issues, provided the taxpayer (1) introduces credible evidence of the factual issue, (2) maintains records and substantiates items as presently required under the Code and Regulations, and (3) cooperates with reasonable IRS requests for meetings, interviews, witnesses, information, and documents. For corporations, trusts, and partnerships with net worth exceeding $7 million, the burden of proof remains on the taxpayer.

The burden of proof also automatically shifts to the IRS in two situations:

1. If the IRS uses statistics to reconstruct an individual's income, or
2. If the court proceeding against an individual taxpayer involves a penalty or addition to tax.

12-5e **Tax Confidentiality Privilege**

The 1998 Act also extended the existing attorney-client privilege of confidentiality in tax matters to nonattorneys authorized to practice before the IRS (e.g., CPAs and enrolled agents). The nonattorney-client privilege may be asserted only in a *noncriminal tax* proceeding before the IRS or federal courts. Also, the nonattorney-client privilege does not extend to written communications between a tax practitioner and a corporation in connection with the promotion of any tax shelter.

CPAs and enrolled agents need to understand the rules regarding tax confidentiality as they have been applied to lawyers to be aware of the tax privilege limits. For example, tax privileged communication usually does not apply to the preparation of tax returns, the giving of accounting or business advice, or to tax accrual workpapers. Also, unlike the general attorney-client privilege, the nonattorney-client privilege does not automatically apply to state tax situations.

In 2021, the IRS released guidance reconfirming that Frequently Asked Questions (FAQs) responses posted on their website do not represent tax law and should not be relied upon by taxpayers; however, a taxpayer's reasonable reliance on an FAQ (even one that is subsequently updated or modified) is relevant and will be considered in determining whether certain penalties apply. Taxpayers who show that they relied in good faith on an FAQ and that their reliance was reasonable based on all the facts and circumstances will not be subject to a penalty, to the extent that reliance results in an underpayment of tax.

Self-Study Problem 12.5

See Appendix E for Solutions to Self-Study Problems

Determine whether the following statements are true or false.

1. Only certified public accountants may represent taxpayers before the IRS.
2. A college degree is required to prepare tax returns for compensation.
3. Only attorneys may prepare corporate tax returns.
4. The tax preparer penalty for filing a document aiding and abetting an individual taxpayer in the understatement of a tax liability is $1,000.
5. The tax preparer penalty for endorsing a taxpayer's refund check is $545.
6. The tax preparer penalty for failing to provide a copy of a tax return to a taxpayer is $55.
7. For audits after 1998, if the IRS uses statistics to reconstruct an individual taxpayer's income, the burden of proof is on the taxpayer.
8. For corporations, trusts, and partnerships with net worth over $7 million, the burden of proof is on the IRS in civil tax matters.
9. CPAs and enrolled agents have tax privileged communication only in noncriminal proceedings before the IRS or federal courts.
10. If an individual taxpayer does not cooperate with reasonable IRS requests for meetings, interviews, witnesses, information, and documents, the burden of proof in a tax matter is on the taxpayer.
11. Commercial tax preparers must have a PTIN.
12. A *Wall Street Journal* article on taxes is substantial authority for purposes of tax preparer penalties.
13. A tax preparer has a reasonable basis for a tax position but lacks substantial authority. If the position is disclosed, the tax preparer can avoid penalty.
14. Circular 230 provides guidance for those that wish to practice before the IRS.

Learning Objective 12.6

Describe the Taxpayer Bill of Rights.

12-6 THE TAXPAYER BILL OF RIGHTS

Over the years, the news media carried many horror stories about taxpayers who claimed they had been abused by the IRS. As a result of this publicity, in 1988 Congress passed a set of provisions referred to as the Taxpayer Bill of Rights. The Taxpayer Bill of Rights has been amended several times since it was originally passed by Congress. This set of provisions requires the IRS to inform taxpayers of their rights in dealing with the IRS, and expands taxpayers' rights and remedies when they are involved in disputes with the IRS. The provisions of the Taxpayer Bill of Rights are summarized in IRS Publication 1, which is reproduced on Pages 12-23 and 12-24. Also note, Publication 1 directs taxpayers to other IRS publications with more details on specific taxpayer rights.

The first part of this publication explains some of the most important rights as a taxpayer. The second part explains the examination, appeal, collection, and refund processes.

Self-Study Problem 12.6

See Appendix E for Solutions to Self-Study Problems

Determine whether the following statements are true or false.

1. Taxpayers have the right to represent themselves or, with proper written authorization, have someone else represent them.
2. The IRS may contact a taxpayer's neighbor or employer to verify information.
3. IRS Publication 594 explains a taxpayer's rights and responsibilities regarding payment of federal taxes.
4. If a taxpayer is audited in the current year for an item that was audited in either of the two previous years and the IRS proposed no change to the tax liability, the taxpayer should contact the IRS as soon as possible to attempt to stop the repeat audit.
5. Generally, both a taxpayer and their spouse are responsible, jointly and individually, for the tax and any interest or penalty due on a joint return.
6. Taxpayers must file a claim for refund within three years of the date they filed their return or two years from the date they paid the tax if they think they paid too much tax.

Learning Objective 12.7

Explain the basic concepts of tax planning.

12-7 TAX PLANNING

The process of arranging one's financial affairs to maximize one's after-tax wealth is often referred to as tax planning. There is nothing wrong with tax planning to avoid tax, provided legal methods are used. Judge Learned Hand best stated the doctrine of tax planning in 1947 when he wrote:

"Over and over again, courts have said there is nothing sinister in so arranging one's affairs as to keep taxes as low as possible. Everybody does so, rich or poor, and all do right, for nobody owes any public duty to pay more than the law demands: taxes are enforced extractions, not voluntary contributions." *Commissioner v. Newman*, 159 F.2d 848 (CA-2, 1947).

Your Rights as a Taxpayer

Publication 1

This publication explains your rights as a taxpayer and the processes for examination, appeal, collection, and refunds. Also available in Spanish.

The Taxpayer Bill of Rights

1. The Right to Be Informed

Taxpayers have the right to know what they need to do to comply with the tax laws. They are entitled to clear explanations of the laws and IRS procedures in all tax forms, instructions, publications, notices, and correspondence. They have the right to be informed of IRS decisions about their tax accounts and to receive clear explanations of the outcomes.

2. The Right to Quality Service

Taxpayers have the right to receive prompt, courteous, and professional assistance in their dealings with the IRS, to be spoken to in a way they can easily understand, to receive clear and easily understandable communications from the IRS, and to speak to a supervisor about inadequate service.

3. The Right to Pay No More than the Correct Amount of Tax

Taxpayers have the right to pay only the amount of tax legally due, including interest and penalties, and to have the IRS apply all tax payments properly.

4. The Right to Challenge the IRS's Position and Be Heard

Taxpayers have the right to raise objections and provide additional documentation in response to formal IRS actions or proposed actions, to expect that the IRS will consider their timely objections and documentation promptly and fairly, and to receive a response if the IRS does not agree with their position.

5. The Right to Appeal an IRS Decision in an Independent Forum

Taxpayers are entitled to a fair and impartial administrative appeal of most IRS decisions, including many penalties, and have the right to receive a written response regarding the Office of Appeals' decision. Taxpayers generally have the right to take their cases to court.

6. The Right to Finality

Taxpayers have the right to know the maximum amount of time they have to challenge the IRS's position as well as the maximum amount of time the IRS has to audit a particular tax year or collect a tax debt. Taxpayers have the right to know when the IRS has finished an audit.

7. The Right to Privacy

Taxpayers have the right to expect that any IRS inquiry, examination, or enforcement action will comply with the law and be no more intrusive than necessary, and will respect all due process rights, including search and seizure protections, and will provide, where applicable, a collection due process hearing.

8. The Right to Confidentiality

Taxpayers have the right to expect that any information they provide to the IRS will not be disclosed unless authorized by the taxpayer or by law. Taxpayers have the right to expect appropriate action will be taken against employees, return preparers, and others who wrongfully use or disclose taxpayer return information.

9. The Right to Retain Representation

Taxpayers have the right to retain an authorized representative of their choice to represent them in their dealings with the IRS. Taxpayers have the right to seek assistance from a Low Income Taxpayer Clinic if they cannot afford representation.

10. The Right to a Fair and Just Tax System

Taxpayers have the right to expect the tax system to consider facts and circumstances that might affect their underlying liabilities, ability to pay, or ability to provide information timely. Taxpayers have the right to receive assistance from the Taxpayer Advocate Service if they are experiencing financial difficulty or if the IRS has not resolved their tax issues properly and timely through its normal channels.

The IRS Mission | Provide America's taxpayers top-quality service by helping them understand and meet their tax responsibilities and enforce the law with integrity and fairness to all.

Publication 1 (Rev. 9-2017) Catalog Number 64731W Department of the Treasury **Internal Revenue Service** www.irs.gov

Source: Internal Revenue Service (IRS)

Examinations, Appeals, Collections, and Refunds

Examinations (Audits)

We accept most taxpayers' returns as filed. If we inquire about your return or select it for examination, it does not suggest that you are dishonest. The inquiry or examination may or may not result in more tax. We may close your case without change; or, you may receive a refund.

The process of selecting a return for examination usually begins in one of two ways. First, we use computer programs to identify returns that may have incorrect amounts. These programs may be based on information returns, such as Forms 1099 and W-2, on studies of past examinations, or on certain issues identified by compliance projects. Second, we use information from outside sources that indicates that a return may have incorrect amounts. These sources may include newspapers, public records, and individuals. If we determine that the information is accurate and reliable, we may use it to select a return for examination.

Publication 556, Examination of Returns, Appeal Rights, and Claims for Refund, explains the rules and procedures that we follow in examinations. The following sections give an overview of how we conduct examinations.

By Mail

We handle many examinations and inquiries by mail. We will send you a letter with either a request for more information or a reason why we believe a change to your return may be needed. You can respond by mail or you can request a personal interview with an examiner. If you mail us the requested information or provide an explanation, we may or may not agree with you, and we will explain the reasons for any changes. Please do not hesitate to write to us about anything you do not understand.

By Interview

If we notify you that we will conduct your examination through a personal interview, or you request such an interview, you have the right to ask that the examination take place at a reasonable time and place that is convenient for both you and the IRS. If our examiner proposes any changes to your return, he or she will explain the reasons for the changes. If you do not agree with these changes, you can meet with the examiner's supervisor.

Repeat Examinations

If we examined your return for the same items in either of the 2 previous years and proposed no change to your tax liability, please contact us as soon as possible so we can see if we should discontinue the examination.

Appeals

If you do not agree with the examiner's proposed changes, you can appeal them to the Appeals Office of the IRS. Most differences can be settled without expensive and time-consuming court trials. Your appeal rights are explained in detail in both Publication 5, Your Appeal Rights and How To Prepare a Protest If You Don't Agree, and Publication 556, Examination of Returns, Appeal Rights, and Claims for Refund.

If you do not wish to use the Appeals Office or disagree with its findings, you may be able to take your case to the U.S. Tax Court, U.S. Court of Federal Claims, or the U.S. District Court where you live. If you take your case to court, the IRS will have the burden of proving certain facts if you kept adequate records to show your tax liability, cooperated with the IRS, and meet certain other conditions. If the court agrees with you on most issues in your case and finds that our position was largely unjustified, you may be able to recover some of your administrative and litigation costs. You will not be eligible to recover these costs unless you tried to resolve your case administratively, including going through the appeals system, and you gave us the information necessary to resolve the case.

Collections

Publication 594, The IRS Collection Process, explains your rights and responsibilities regarding payment of federal taxes. It describes:

- What to do when you owe taxes. It describes what to do if you get a tax bill and what to do if you think your bill is wrong. It also covers making installment payments, delaying collection action, and submitting an offer in compromise.
- IRS collection actions. It covers liens, releasing a lien, levies, releasing a levy, seizures and sales, and release of property.
- IRS certification to the State Department of a seriously delinquent tax debt, which will generally result in denial of a passport application and may lead to revocation of a passport.

Your collection appeal rights are explained in detail in Publication 1660, Collection Appeal Rights.

Innocent Spouse Relief

Generally, both you and your spouse are each responsible for paying the full amount of tax, interest, and penalties due on your joint return. However, if you qualify for innocent spouse relief, you may be relieved of part or all of the joint liability. To request relief, you must file Form 8857, Request for Innocent Spouse Relief. For more information on innocent spouse relief, see Publication 971, Innocent Spouse Relief, and Form 8857.

Potential Third Party Contacts

Generally, the IRS will deal directly with you or your duly authorized representative. However, we sometimes talk with other persons if we need information that you have been unable to provide, or to verify information we have received. If we do contact other persons, such as a neighbor, bank, employer, or employees, we will generally need to tell them limited information, such as your name. The law prohibits us from disclosing any more information than is necessary to obtain or verify the information we are seeking. Our need to contact other persons may continue as long as there is activity in your case. If we do contact other persons, you have a right to request a list of those contacted. Your request can be made by telephone, in writing, or during a personal interview.

Refunds

You may file a claim for refund if you think you paid too much tax. You must generally file the claim within 3 years from the date you filed your original return or 2 years from the date you paid the tax, whichever is later. The law generally provides for interest on your refund if it is not paid within 45 days of the date you filed your return or claim for refund. Publication 556, Examination of Returns, Appeal Rights, and Claims for Refund, has more information on refunds.

If you were due a refund but you did not file a return, you generally must file your return within 3 years from the date the return was due (including extensions) to get that refund.

Taxpayer Advocate Service

TAS is an ***independent*** organization within the IRS that can help protect your taxpayer rights. We can offer you help if your tax problem is causing a hardship, or you've tried but haven't been able to resolve your problem with the IRS. If you qualify for our assistance, which is always free, we will do everything possible to help you. Visit *www.taxpayeradvocate.irs.gov* or call 1-877-777-4778.

Tax Information

The IRS provides the following sources for forms, publications, and additional information.

- ***Tax Questions:*** 1-800-829-1040 (1-800-829-4059 for TTY/TDD)
- ***Forms and Publications:*** 1-800-829-3676 (1-800-829-4059 for TTY/TDD)
- ***Internet:*** *www.irs.gov*
- ***Small Business Ombudsman:*** A small business entity can participate in the regulatory process and comment on enforcement actions of the IRS by calling 1-888-REG-FAIR.
- ***Treasury Inspector General for Tax Administration:*** You can confidentially report misconduct, waste, fraud, or abuse by an IRS employee by calling 1-800-366-4484 (1-800-877-8339 for TTY/TDD). You can remain anonymous.

Internal Revenue Service (IRS)

When illegal methods are used to reduce tax liability, the process can no longer be considered tax planning, but instead becomes tax evasion. Tax evasion can subject the taxpayer and tax practitioner to fines, penalties, and incarceration. Illegal acts are outside the realm of tax-planning services offered by a professional tax practitioner.

Tax planning covers two basic categories of transactions: the "open transaction" and the "closed transaction." In an open transaction, all the events have not yet been completed; therefore, the taxpayer has some degree of control over the tax consequences. In a closed transaction, all material parts of the transaction have been completed. As a result, tax planning involving a closed transaction is limited to presentation of the facts to the IRS in the most favorable, legally acceptable manner possible.

EXAMPLE Annie enters into an agreement with Erik to exchange real estate held as an investment. Escrow has not closed and the title of the property has not passed between the parties. Since all significant events (title passing) are not complete, the transaction is considered an open transaction. Once the title to the real estate passes, the tax planning involves a closed transaction. ♦

Tax planning cannot be considered in a void. Any tax-planning advice must consider the business goals of the taxpayer. Tax planning for a transaction should not override sound business judgment.

12-7a Tax Rate Terminology

Important to any tax-planning situation is an evaluation of the tax savings arising from increasing deductions or the tax cost of generating additional income. The tax consequences are dependent on the taxpayer's tax rate. The taxpayer's tax rate may be defined in several ways. For tax-planning purposes, the taxpayer needs to understand the difference between the "average" tax rate and the "marginal" tax rate. The average tax rate merely represents the average rate of tax applicable to the taxpayer's income and is calculated as the total tax paid divided by the total income (or sometimes taxable income) of the taxpayer. The marginal tax rate represents the rate at which tax is imposed on the "next" dollar of income.

EXAMPLE Becky, a single taxpayer, has income of $43,000 during the current year on which she pays tax of $5,077. Her average tax rate is 11.81 percent ($5,077 ÷ $43,000). If Becky's income increases to $53,000, her tax liability will be $7,277. Thus, Becky's marginal rate is 22 percent [($7,277 − $5,077) ÷ ($53,000 − $43,000)]. ♦

When making tax-planning decisions, the taxpayer's marginal tax rate is the most important tax rate. For example, Jason has a 30 percent marginal tax rate and a 20 percent average tax rate and is considering making a tax-deductible expenditure of $2,000. His after-tax cost of the expenditure is calculated using his marginal tax rate, not his average tax rate. Jason's after-tax cost of the expenditure would be $1,400, calculated as follows: [$2,000 − ($2,000 × 30%)]. On the other hand, if Jason is to receive any additional income, he knows that he will pay tax at a rate of 30 percent on the next dollar of income.

12-7b Examples of Tax Planning

Tax planning opportunities can be classified into four categories: (1) timing, (2) jurisdiction, (3) entity, and (4) character. Most tax-planning techniques employ at least one of these characteristics in an attempt to save taxpayers money.

12-7c Timing

In its simplest form, timing implies deferring the payment of taxes to a future year and is generally achieved by either deferring income recognition or accelerating expense deduction.

EXAMPLE Karen operates a small cash-basis, calendar year-end business. In order to lower her current year's income, Karen may prepay January's rent in December. She could also delay invoicing her customers in an attempt to defer the recognition of income. ♦

Most simple timing techniques work best when tax rates are not expected to change. If tax rates are expected to change across the periods in which the timing is being changed, a more thorough analysis is going to be required.

EXAMPLE If in the previous example Karen expects her tax rate to increase from 24 percent in the current year to 37 percent next year, she may want to consider accelerating the recognition of income into the current year at the lower rate and deferring the deduction of expenses until next year, increasing the value of the deduction. ♦

One disadvantage of using the timing technique is that tax recognition frequently occurs simultaneously with cash transactions. For example, one way to defer income recognition might be to earn no income; however, that generally involves fairly disastrous non-tax consequences.

12-7d **Jurisdiction**

Using jurisdiction for tax planning involves exploiting differences in tax rates or tax systems to lower tax liabilities.

EXAMPLE Mark worked for the Lake Tahoe office of the state of California Department of Motor Vehicles for thirty-five years. In the current year, he starts his well-deserved retirement. Realizing that the individual tax rate in California can be over 10 percent, he moves to nearby Reno, Nevada, knowing that Nevada has no state income tax on individuals. He continues to collect his pension without paying state income tax. ♦

Jurisdiction, although simple in concept, can be difficult to implement for many taxpayers. Most individuals do not have the luxury to simply move to a new state to lower the state income tax rate. Larger businesses may have more flexibility than individuals or small businesses to implement a jurisdictional tax plan.

12-7e **Entity**

Entity-based tax planning involves making a choice about the type of entity a taxpayer chooses to operate as.

EXAMPLE Raquel is starting a new small business and expects to operate at a loss for the first few years. In an attempt to take advantage of using the losses to offset her other forms of income, she establishes her new business as a flow-through entity such as an LLC in hopes of passing those losses through to her individual tax return. Perhaps later in the life of her business when it becomes profitable, she will convert to a different entity such as a corporation. ♦

12-7f **Character**

Using character for tax planning often requires a deeper understanding of tax law than the other tax-planning techniques. Using character means the transaction will be designed to take advantage of the tax law or a taxpayer's current situation.

EXAMPLE Axel owns stock purchased eleven months ago which has now doubled in value. Although Axel thinks the stock's value has peaked, he wishes to wait one additional month before selling to convert the short-term capital gain taxed at ordinary tax rates into a long-term capital gain taxed at preferential rates. Although this might also feel like a timing-based plan, the one-month deferral of taxes is not likely to be significant but changing the tax rate from Axel's ordinary rate (as high as 37 percent) to the long-term capital gains rate (as low as 0 percent) is a substantial tax savings. ♦

EXAMPLE Beck is a single taxpayer with a 24 percent marginal tax rate. Beck is debating between an investment in a taxable bond that pays 5 percent or a tax-exempt bond that pays 4.5 percent. Although the pre-tax return on the taxable bond of 5 percent is higher than the 4.5 percent tax-exempt bond, the after-tax return of the taxable bond is only 3.8 percent [5% × (1 − 0.24 tax rate)]. ♦

Self-Study Problem 12.7 *See Appendix E for Solutions to Self-Study Problems*

During the current year, K's taxable income is $89,000 and he pays income tax of $15,197. K is single, has no dependents, and does not itemize his deductions. J, who files in *exactly* the same manner as K, has taxable income of $90,000 and pays income tax of $15,435.50.

1. What is K's average tax rate?
2. What is J's average tax rate?
3. If K's income increased to the same amount as J, what would K's marginal tax rate be?

KEY TERMS

Internal Revenue Service (IRS), 12-2
commissioner of internal revenue, 12-2
IRS Campus Processing Sites, 12-2
IRS organizational structure, 12-3
Small Business/Self-Employed (SB/SE) Division, 12-4
Wage and Investment (W&I) Division, 12-5
offer in compromise, 12-5
tax levy, 12-6
tax lien, 12-6
office audit, 12-6
field audit, 12-6
correspondence audit, 12-6
Discriminant Function System (DIF), 12-7
Unreported Income DIF (UIDIF), 12-7
appeals process, 12-8
Federal Tax Court, 12-8
audit procedure of IRS, 12-9
appeal procedure of IRS, 12-10
interest, 12-11
nondeductible penalty, 12-11
interest rate, 12-11
failure-to-pay penalty, 12-12
failure-to-file penalty, 12-12
penalty abatement waiver, 12-12
accuracy-related penalty, 12-13
fraud penalty, 12-13
statute of limitations, 12-15
tax practitioners, 12-17
enrolled agents, 12-17
enrolled preparers, 12-17
unenrolled preparers, 12-17
Circular 230, 12-17
preparer tax identification number (PTIN), 12-17
Annual Filing Season Program (AFSP), 12-18
Annual Federal Tax Refresher (AFTR), 12-19
tax return preparer, 12-19
substantial authority standard, 12-19
reasonable basis, 12-19
burden of proof, 12-20
nonattorney-client privilege, 12-20
Taxpayer Bill of Rights, 12-22
tax planning, 12-22
tax evasion, 12-25
open transaction, 12-25
closed transaction, 12-25
average tax rate, 12-25
marginal tax rate, 12-25

KEY POINTS

Learning Objectives	Key Points
LO 12.1: Identify the organizational structure of the Internal Revenue Service (IRS).	• The IRS is a bureau of the Treasury Department, tasked with administering the tax laws of the United States. • The national IRS office is the headquarters of the commissioner of internal revenue. The commissioner of internal revenue is appointed by the president of the United States with the advice and consent of the Senate. • The IRS maintains Campus Processing Sites where the IRS computers process the information from tax documents such as tax returns, payroll tax forms, Forms 1099, and withholding forms. • The IRS maintains a national computer center in Martinsburg, West Virginia, where information from various processing sites is matched with records from other processing sites. • The IRS has the authority to examine a taxpayer's books and records to determine the correct amount of tax due. The IRS also has the right to summon taxpayers to appear before the IRS and produce necessary accounting records.
LO 12.2: Describe the IRS audit process.	• A primary function of the IRS is to audit taxpayers' tax returns. • Correspondence audits are generally handled entirely by mail and account for the majority of the individual tax returns examined each year. • The office audit is conducted in an IRS office and is typically used for individual taxpayers with little or no business activities. • In a field audit, the IRS agent reviews a taxpayer's books and records at the taxpayer's place of business or at the office of the taxpayer's accountant. • The IRS uses a computerized statistical sampling technique called the Discriminant Function System (DIF) to select tax returns for audits of individuals. • Under the DIF system, the IRS uses mathematical formulas to assign a DIF score to each return, which represents the potential for discovery of improper treatment of items on the tax return. • The IRS also selects returns for audit through different methods such as identification of participants in abusive tax avoidance transactions, selection of large corporations, information matching, related examinations, and other means. • If an audit results in a disagreement between the agent and the taxpayer, the appeals procedure begins with the IRS inviting the taxpayer to an informal conference with an appellate agent.
LO 12.3: Define the common penalties for taxpayers and apply them to specific situations.	• Taxpayers are charged interest on underpayments of taxes, and in some cases, the IRS pays interest to taxpayers when they overpay their taxes. • The interest rate applicable to underpayments and overpayments of taxes is adjusted each quarter and is equal to the federal short-term rate plus 3 percentage points. • The penalty for failure to pay is ½ of 1 percent of the amount of taxes due for every month or portion of a month that the payment is late (up to a maximum of 25 percent of the total taxes due). • The failure to file a tax return is subject to a penalty equal to 5 percent of the tax due with the return, for every month or portion of a month the return is late (up to a maximum of 25 percent). If filed more than sixty days from the due date, the minimum failure to file is the lesser of the tax due or $450. • The accuracy-related penalty is 20 percent of the applicable underpayment due to (1) negligence of or disregard for rules or regulations, (2) a substantial understatement of income tax, or (3) a substantial valuation overstatement, as well as certain other understatements of income tax. • When a taxpayer files a fraudulent tax return, there is a fraud penalty equal to 75 percent of the amount of underpayment of taxes attributable to fraud. • The tax law contains many other penalties applicable to taxpayers, including but not limited to a civil penalty of $500 and a criminal penalty of up to $1,000 imposed for filing false withholding information, and there is an immediate $5,000 penalty for filing a "frivolous" tax return (or document) as a tax protest.

LO 12.4: Apply the general rule for the statute of limitations on tax returns and the important exceptions to the general rule.	• In general, the statute of limitations for a tax return runs for three years from the date the tax return was filed or the return due date (without extensions), whichever is later. • If a fraudulent tax return is filed or no return is filed, there is no statute of limitations. • If a taxpayer omits an amount of gross income in excess of 25 percent of the gross income shown on the return, then the statute of limitations is increased to six years. • The statute of limitations for the deduction of a bad debt or worthless securities is seven years (all other items on the tax return would normally be considered closed out after three years). • The statute of limitations may be extended by mutual consent of the IRS and the taxpayer. • Amended individual income tax returns are filed on Form 1040-X.
LO 12.5: Describe the rules and penalties that apply to tax practitioners.	• Tax practitioners include commercial preparers, enrolled agents, attorneys, and certified public accountants (CPAs). • Circular 230 describes the rules for practice before the IRS. • Unenrolled preparers can currently participate in the Annual Filing Season Program, a voluntary program created to encourage preparers to participate in continuing education. • Tax return preparer penalties include, but are not limited to, (1) $55 for failing to sign a tax return or failing to furnish the preparer's identifying number, (2) $55 for each failure to keep a copy of the prepared return or include the return on a list of taxpayers for whom returns have been prepared, or (3) $55 for failing to provide a taxpayer with a copy of the tax return prepared. • Tax preparers can avoid penalties by ensuring that tax positions have substantially authority or if no such authority exists, a reasonable basis for the position exists and is disclosed to the IRS. • The IRS has the burden of proof in any court proceeding with respect to factual issues, provided the taxpayer (1) introduces credible evidence of the factual issue, (2) maintains records and substantiates items, and (3) cooperates with reasonable IRS requests for meetings, interviews, witnesses, information, and documents. • The tax law extends the attorney-client privilege of confidentiality in noncriminal tax matters to nonattorneys authorized to practice before the IRS (e.g., CPAs and enrolled agents).
LO 12.6: Describe the Taxpayer Bill of Rights.	• The Taxpayer Bill of Rights (IRS Publication 1) requires the IRS to inform taxpayers of their rights in dealing with the IRS, and expands taxpayers' rights and remedies when they are involved in disputes with the IRS.
LO 12.7: Explain the basic concepts of tax planning.	• Tax planning is the process of arranging one's financial affairs to minimize one's overall tax liability. • When illegal methods are used to reduce tax liability, the process can no longer be considered tax planning, but instead becomes tax evasion. • For making tax-planning decisions, the taxpayer's marginal tax rate is the most important tax rate to consider.

QUESTIONS and PROBLEMS

GROUP 1:
MULTIPLE CHOICE QUESTIONS

LO 12.1

1. Which of the following is a responsibility of a local office of the IRS?
   a. Advising the Treasury Department on legislation
   b. Intelligence operations
   c. Appellate procedures
   d. Developing IRS rules and regulations
   e. None of the above

LO 12.1

2. The IRS does *not* have the authority to:
   a. Examine a taxpayer's books and records
   b. Summon taxpayers to make them appear before the IRS
   c. Summon third parties for taxpayer records
   d. Place a lien on taxpayer property
   e. None of the above—the IRS has the authority to do all these

LO 12.2

3. Which of the following is the most common type of audit for an individual taxpayer?
   a. Office audit
   b. Correspondence audit
   c. Telephone audit
   d. Field audit
   e. Service center audit

LO 12.2

4. In which of the following ways are tax returns selected for audits?
   a. Through the Discriminant Function System
   b. Through informants
   c. Through news sources
   d. Through information matching
   e. All of the above

LO 12.2

5. When the IRS has completed their examination and the result is an assessment of additional tax, which of the following is *not* a viable option for the taxpayer?
   a. Disagree with the assessment and request an appeal
   b. Agree to the assessment and pay the additional tax
   c. Fail to act and wait for the 90-day letter and either pay the tax and file a claim for a refund or petition the Tax Court
   d. Do not pay the tax and request a District Court hearing

LO 12.2

6. Which of the following is *not* a source of information from which the IRS identifies possible audit targets?
   a. A computer scoring system that identifies possible errors on tax returns
   b. The client records of a particularly abusive tax scheme promoter
   c. News sources
   d. Whistleblowers
   e. All of these items could be sources for IRS audit selection

LO 12.3

7. Which of the following is *not* a penalty that may be imposed by the IRS?
   a. Failure-to-file penalty
   b. Failure-to-pay penalty
   c. Penalty for negligence
   d. Early filing penalty
   e. All of the above may be imposed by the IRS

LO 12.3

8. Martha inadvertently failed to file her tax return for eleven months. The tax due on the return was $1,000. Her failure to file penalty will be:
   a. 55 percent of the tax due
   b. 25 percent of the tax due
   c. $450
   d. $5,000

LO 12.3

9. Which of the following best describes the interest and interest rates for under and overpayments of income tax liability?
   a. The underpayment rate is higher than the overpayment rate.
   b. The interest charged on underpayments is deductible.
   c. The interest paid on overpayments is tax-exempt income.
   d. The overpayment rate and underpayment rate are generally equal and underpayment interest is not deductible and overpayment interest is taxable.

LO 12.3

10. A taxpayer incorrectly reports income and has a substantial understatement of income tax in the amount of $20,000 (but no fraud). The accuracy-related penalty for this error is:
    a. $20,000
    b. $1,000 (5 percent)
    c. $4,000 (20 percent)
    d. $15,000 (75 percent)

LO 12.3

11. The taxpayer penalty for writing a check to pay for taxes that has insufficient funds is:
    a. The same amount the bank charges the IRS for a returned check
    b. 5 percent of the amount of the total tax liability of the taxpayer
    c. 2 percent of the amount of the check unless the check is for $1,250 or less
    d. Double the check amount

LO 12.4

12. If a taxpayer's 2022 individual income tax return is due on April 18, 2023 and was filed on March 3, 2023, the statute of limitations would normally run out on:
    a. April 18, 2025
    b. March 3, 2024
    c. April 18, 2026
    d. March 3, 2026
    e. None of the above

LO 12.4

13. If a taxpayer's 2022 individual income tax return is due on April 18, 2023 and was filed on June 3, 2023, the statute of limitations would normally run out on:
    a. April 18, 2025
    b. June 3, 2024
    c. April 18, 2026
    d. June 3, 2026
    e. None of the above

LO 12.4

14. Which of the following has a six-year statute of limitations?
    a. Depreciation
    b. Salaries
    c. Travel and entertainment
    d. A return in which the taxpayer omitted gross income in excess of 25 percent of the gross income shown on the return
    e. Worthless securities

LO 12.5

15. Which of the following tax preparers may *not* represent their clients in all IRS proceedings?
    a. An enrolled agent
    b. A certified public accountant
    c. An attorney
    d. All of the above may represent their clients in IRS proceedings

LO 12.5

16. If a tax preparer notes an error on a client's tax return, under Circular 230, the tax preparer should:
    a. Report the mistake to the IRS immediately
    b. Prepare an amended tax return and file such return immediately
    c. Notify the client of the error and the consequences of not correcting it
    d. Contact local authorities and consider whistleblower rewards

LO 12.5

17. Which of the following does *not* result in a minimum $55 fine for an income tax preparer?
    a. Failure to provide a tax preparer identification number
    b. Cashing a refund check for a customer
    c. Failing to keep any record of the returns prepared
    d. Failing to provide a copy of their prepared return to a customer

LO 12.5

18. In which of the following situations does the burden of proof in a tax matter *not* automatically shift to the IRS?
    a. The IRS uses statistics to reconstruct an individual's income.
    b. A court proceeding against an individual taxpayer involves a penalty or addition to tax.
    c. A taxpayer who did not maintain records.
    d. a and b are correct.
    e. a, b, and c are correct.

LO 12.5

19. Which of the following have privileged communication with a client in a noncriminal tax matter?
    a. CPAs
    b. Enrolled agents
    c. Attorneys
    d. a and c
    e. a, b, and c

LO 12.5

20. The burden of proof remains on the taxpayer for corporations, trusts, and partnerships with net worth exceeding:
    a. $1 million
    b. $3 million
    c. $5 million
    d. $7 million
    e. Some other amount

LO 12.6

21. The IRS does *not* have to furnish the taxpayer with information concerning which of the following items?
    a. The way the taxpayer's return was selected for audit
    b. The procedures for appealing an IRS ruling
    c. The refund claims process
    d. The IRS collection process
    e. All of the above must be provided to the taxpayer

LO 12.6

22. Both spouses are responsible, jointly and individually, for paying the full amount of any tax, interest, or penalties due on a joint return. Which of the following is correct in reference to the preceding statement?
    a. This does not apply to spouses who have divorced after the return was filed.
    b. Spouses are responsible jointly but not individually.
    c. Spouses are responsible individually but not jointly.
    d. Innocent spouses may be relieved of the liability for tax, interest, and penalties.
    e. None of the above.

LO 12.6

23. A taxpayer's rights are explained in:
    a. Publication 5
    b. Publication 17
    c. Publication 556
    d. Publication 1
    e. None of the above

LO 12.6

24. Taxpayers have the right to have an IRS examination take place at:
    a. The IRS office
    b. Any city of the taxpayer's choosing
    c. A neutral site
    d. A reasonable time and place
    e. None of the above

LO 12.6

25. If a U.S. Tax Court agrees with the taxpayer on appeal that the IRS position was largely unjustified, which of the following is correct?
    a. The taxpayer must still pay administrative and litigation costs.
    b. The taxpayer may recover administrative but not litigation costs.
    c. The taxpayer may recover litigation but not administrative costs.
    d. To be eligible to recover some of the administrative and litigation costs, the taxpayer must have tried to resolve the case administratively, including going through the appeals process, and must have given the IRS the information necessary to resolve the case.
    e. None of the above.

LO 12.6

26. If the IRS owes a taxpayer a refund, the law generally provides that the IRS must pay interest on the refund if it is not paid within ____________ days of the date the taxpayer filed his or her tax return or claim for refund.
    a. 30
    b. 45
    c. 60
    d. 90
    e. None of the above

LO 12.7

27. Glen's taxable income is $50,000 and he pays income tax of $6,617. If his income were $60,000, he would pay taxes of $8,817. What is Glen's marginal tax rate?
    a. 18.23%
    b. 22.00%
    c. 12.00%
    d. 25.00%
    e. Some other amount

LO 12.7

28. Melodie's taxable income is $39,000 and she pays income tax of $4,475. If Melodie's taxable income increases to $43,000, she would pay income taxes of $5,077. What is Melodie's marginal tax rate?
    a. 17.00%
    b. 22.00%
    c. 18.25%
    d. 15.05%
    e. Some other amount

LO 12.7

29. Jim has a house payment of $2,000 per month of which $1,700 is deductible interest and real estate taxes with the remaining $300 representing a repayment of the principal balance of the note. Jim's marginal tax rate is 30 percent. What is Jim's after-tax cost of his house payment?
    a. $510
    b. $600
    c. $900
    d. $1,490
    e. Some other amount

GROUP 2: PROBLEMS

LO 12.1
LO 12.2

1. Indicate whether the following statements are true or false:
    a. ______ The IRS is a division of the Treasury Department.
    b. ______ The IRS has three major divisions.
    c. ______ The IRS local offices process most individual tax returns.
    d. ______ IRS Campus Processing Sites are the locations that taxpayers should call to obtain tax information.
    e. ______ Taxpayers should have their CPAs keep their tax records to prevent the IRS from being able to summon their records.
    f. ______ Most IRS audits are conducted through the mail.

LO 12.2
LO 12.3

2. Indicate whether the following statements are true or false:
   a. ____ A field audit by the IRS is an audit conducted at the IRS field office.
   b. ____ A low Discriminant Function System score for a tax return increases the possibility that the return will be selected for audit.
   c. ____ The IRS charges interest on underpayments of taxes, but never pays interest on amounts of overpayments of taxes.
   d. ____ If a taxpayer fails to file a tax return on its due date, he or she may be subject to a failure-to-file penalty.
   e. ____ The tax law includes a penalty for preparing a tax return in a negligent manner.
   f. ____ If a taxpayer fails to file a tax return, the IRS may impose both the failure-to-file penalty and the fraud penalty.

LO 12.3

3. a. Wilson filed his individual tax return on the original due date, but failed to pay $700 in taxes that were due with the return. If Wilson pays the taxes exactly two months (not over sixty days) late, calculate the amount of his failure-to-pay penalty.
   b. Joan filed her individual income tax return 4½ months after it was due. She did not request an extension of time for filing. Along with her return, Joan remitted a check for $750, which was the balance of the taxes she owed with her return. Disregarding interest, calculate the total penalty that Joan will be required to pay, assuming the failure to file was not fraudulent.
   c. Jack filed his tax return two months and three days late and did not request an extension of time for filing. Jack's return indicated that he is to receive a $50 refund in taxes. Calculate the amount of Jack's penalty for failure to file his tax return on time, assuming the failure to file was not fraudulent.

LO 12.3

4. In the 2022 tax year, Michelle paid the following amounts relating to her 2020 tax return:

Tax deficiency	$5,000
Negligence penalty	1,000
Interest	500
Underpayment of estimated tax penalty	350

   Explain which of the above items may be deducted on Michelle's 2022 individual income tax return.

LO 12.3

5. Linda underpaid her taxes for the current year by $4,000 due to negligence.
   a. Calculate Linda's accuracy-related penalty for negligence.
   b. Assume that the underpayment of taxes by Linda was determined to be fraudulent, and calculate the total amount of Linda's fraud penalty.

LO 12.3

6. For each of the following situations, indicate the nature of the penalty and amount of the penalty that could be imposed, if any.
   a. Larry is a tax protester and files his tax return in the name of "Mickey Mouse."
   b. Anne writes a check for $900 in payment of her taxes that she knows will not clear the bank due to insufficient funds in her account.
   c. Gerald understated his tax liability by $10,000. The total amount of tax that should have been shown on his return was $70,000.

LO 12.3
LO 12.4
LO 12.5
LO 12.6

7. Indicate whether the following statements are true or false:
   a. The tax law includes a penalty for writing a "bad" check in payment of the taxpayer's tax liability.
   b. The statute of limitations for a tax return is normally four years.
   c. If a fraudulent tax return is filed, the IRS may assess a deficiency at any time in the future.
   d. Enrolled agents work for the IRS.
   e. A commercial tax preparer may represent tax clients in any proceeding with the IRS.
   f. The IRS is entitled to choose a place and time for an audit, without regard to the inconvenience to the taxpayer or the reasonableness of the request.

LO 12.4

8. Indicate the date that the statute of limitations would run out on each of the following 2022 individual tax returns with an original due date of April 18, 2023:

   a. A fraudulent tax return that was filed April 18, 2023
   b. A tax return that was filed May 19, 2023
   c. A tax return that was filed February 12, 2023
   d. A tax return that was filed March 1, 2023, and omitted $15,000 in income. The total gross income shown on the tax return was $50,000

LO 12.5

9. For each of the following situations, indicate the amount of the penalty that could be imposed on the tax return preparer:

   a. A tax return preparer understates the taxpayer's tax liability with a frivolous position and does not disclose the position.
   b. A tax return preparer fails to furnish his identifying number.
   c. A tax return preparer aids a taxpayer in understating a tax liability.
   d. A tax return preparer endorses and cashes a client's tax refund check.

LO 12.5

10. Classify each of the following as an enrolled or unenrolled preparer:
    a. Certified public accountant
    b. Enrolled agent
    c. A preparer that has completed the annual filing season program
    d. An attorney

LO 12.6

11. The Taxpayer Bill of Rights lists ten different rights. Name four of those rights.

LO 12.7

12. Indicate whether the following statements are true or false:
    a. _____ Decreasing one's tax liability through legal methods is called tax planning, while illegally reducing taxes is called tax evasion.
    b. _____ In a "closed" transaction, all tax-significant events have been completed.
    c. _____ The marginal tax rate is computed as the total tax paid divided by the total income of the taxpayer.
    d. _____ The marginal tax rate is the most important rate for decision making in tax planning situations.
    e. _____ The timing tax planning technique usually has the objective of deferring the payment of tax until a later year.

APPENDIX A

Tax Rate Schedules and Tax Table

CONTENTS

2022 Tax Rate Schedules

The Tax Rate Schedules are shown so you can see the tax rate that applies to all levels of taxable income. Don't use them to figure your tax. Instead, see the instructions for line 16.

Schedule X—If your filing status is **Single**

If your taxable income is: Over—	But not over—	The tax is:	of the amount over—
$0	$10,275	--------- 10%	$0
10,275	41,775	$1,027.50 + 12%	10,275
41,775	89,075	4,807.50 + 22%	41,775
89,075	170,050	15,213.50 + 24%	89,075
170,050	215,950	34,647.50 + 32%	170,050
215,950	539,900	49,335.50 + 35%	215,950
539,900	---------	162,718.00 + 37%	539,900

Schedule Y-1—If your filing status is **Married filing jointly** or **Qualifying widow(er)**

If your taxable income is: Over—	But not over—	The tax is:	of the amount over—
$0	$20,550	--------- 10%	$0
20,550	83,550	$2,055.00 + 12%	20,550
83,550	178,150	9,615.00 + 22%	83,550
178,150	340,100	30,427.00 + 24%	178,150
340,100	431,900	69,295.00 + 32%	340,100
431,900	647,850	98,671.00 + 35%	431,900
647,850	---------	174,253.50 + 37%	647,850

Schedule Y-2—If your filing status is **Married filing separately**

If your taxable income is: Over—	But not over—	The tax is:	of the amount over—
$0	$10,275	--------- 10%	$0
10,275	41,775	$1,027.50 + 12%	10,275
41,775	89,075	4,807.50 + 22%	41,775
89,075	170,050	15,213.50 + 24%	89,075
170,050	215,950	34,647.50 + 32%	170,050
215,950	323,925	49,335.50 + 35%	215,950
323,925	---------	87,126.75 + 37%	323,925

Schedule Z—If your filing status is **Head of household**

If your taxable income is: Over—	But not over—	The tax is:	of the amount over—
$0	$14,650	--------- 10%	$0
14,650	55,900	$1,465.00 + 12%	14,650
55,900	89,050	6,415.00 + 22%	55,900
89,050	170,050	13,708.00 + 24%	89,050
170,050	215,950	33,148.00 + 32%	170,050
215,950	539,900	47,836.00 + 35%	215,950
539,900	---------	161,218.50 + 37%	539,900

Note: The tax rate schedules for income of at least $100,000 are presented in the traditional "additive" format on this page and in the somewhat lesser used "deductive" style on Page A-3. Both formats will compute the same tax amounts for taxable income of at least $100,000.

2022 Tax Computation Worksheet

Section A—Use if your filing status is **Single.** Complete the row below that applies to you.

Taxable income. If line 15 is—	**(a)** Enter the amount from line 15	**(b)** Multiplication amount	**(c)** Multiply (a) by (b)	**(d)** Subtraction amount	**Tax.** Subtract (d) from (c). Enter the result here and on the entry space on line 16.
At least $100,000 but not over $170,050	$	× 24% (0.24)	$	$ 6,164.50	$
Over $170,050 but not over $215,950	$	× 32% (0.32)	$	$ 19,768.50	$
Over $215,950 but not over $539,900	$	× 35% (0.35)	$	$ 26,247.00	$
Over $539,900	$	× 37% (0.37)	$	$ 37,045.00	$

Section B—Use if your filing status is **Married filing jointly** or **Qualifying surviving spouse.** Complete the row below that applies to you.

Taxable income. If line 15 is—	**(a)** Enter the amount from line 15	**(b)** Multiplication amount	**(c)** Multiply (a) by (b)	**(d)** Subtraction amount	**Tax.** Subtract (d) from (c). Enter the result here and on the entry space on line 16.
At least $100,000 but not over $178,150	$	× 22% (0.22)	$	$ 8,766.00	$
Over $178,150 but not over $340,100	$	× 24% (0.24)	$	$ 12,329.00	$
Over $340,100 but not over $431,900	$	× 32% (0.32)	$	$ 39,537.00	$
Over $431,900 but not over $647,850	$	× 35% (0.35)	$	$ 52,494.00	$
Over $647,850	$	× 37% (0.37)	$	$ 65,451.00	$

Section C—Use if your filing status is **Married filing separately.** Complete the row below that applies to you.

Taxable income. If line 15 is—	**(a)** Enter the amount from line 15	**(b)** Multiplication amount	**(c)** Multiply (a) by (b)	**(d)** Subtraction amount	**Tax.** Subtract (d) from (c). Enter the result here and on the entry space on line 16.
At least $100,000 but not over $170,050	$	× 24% (0.24)	$	$ 6,164.50	$
Over $170,050 but not over $215,950	$	× 32% (0.32)	$	$ 19,768.50	$
Over $215,950 but not over $323,925	$	× 35% (0.35)	$	$ 26,247.00	$
Over $323,925	$	× 37% (0.37)	$	$ 32,725.50	$

Section D—Use if your filing status is **Head of household.** Complete the row below that applies to you.

Taxable income. If line 15 is—	**(a)** Enter the amount from line 15	**(b)** Multiplication amount	**(c)** Multiply (a) by (b)	**(d)** Subtraction amount	**Tax.** Subtract (d) from (c). Enter the result here and on the entry space on line 16.
At least $100,000 but not over $170,050	$	× 24% (0.24)	$	$ 7,664.00	$
Over $170,050 but not over $215,950	$	× 32% (0.32)	$	$ 21,268.00	$
Over $215,950 but not over $539,900	$	× 35% (0.35)	$	$ 27,746.50	$
Over $539,900	$	× 37% (0.37)	$	$ 38,544.50	$

2022 Tax Table

See the instructions for line 16 to see if you must use the Tax Table below to figure your tax.

Example. A married couple are filing a joint return. Their taxable income on Form 1040, line 15, is $25,300. First, they find the $25,300-25,350 taxable income line. Next, they find the column for married filing jointly and read down the column. The amount shown where the taxable income line and filing status column meet is $2,628. This is the tax amount they should enter in the entry space on Form 1040, line 16.

Sample Table

At Least	But Less Than	Single	Married filing jointly*	Married filing sepa-rately	Head of a house-hold
		Your tax is—			
25,200	**25,250**	2,822	2,616	2,822	2,734
25,250	**25,300**	2,828	2,622	2,828	2,740
25,300	**25,350**	2,834	(2,628)	2,834	2,746
25,350	**25,400**	2,840	2,634	2,840	2,752

If line 15 (taxable income) is—		And you are—			
At least	But less than	Single	Married filing jointly *	Married filing sepa-rately	Head of a house-hold
		Your tax is—			
0	5	0	0	0	0
5	15	1	1	1	1
15	25	2	2	2	2
25	50	4	4	4	4
50	75	6	6	6	6
75	100	9	9	9	9
100	125	11	11	11	11
125	150	14	14	14	14
150	175	16	16	16	16
175	200	19	19	19	19
200	225	21	21	21	21
225	250	24	24	24	24
250	275	26	26	26	26
275	300	29	29	29	29
300	325	31	31	31	31
325	350	34	34	34	34
350	375	36	36	36	36
375	400	39	39	39	39
400	425	41	41	41	41
425	450	44	44	44	44
450	475	46	46	46	46
475	500	49	49	49	49
500	525	51	51	51	51
525	550	54	54	54	54
550	575	56	56	56	56
575	600	59	59	59	59
600	625	61	61	61	61
625	650	64	64	64	64
650	675	66	66	66	66
675	700	69	69	69	69
700	725	71	71	71	71
725	750	74	74	74	74
750	775	76	76	76	76
775	800	79	79	79	79
800	825	81	81	81	81
825	850	84	84	84	84
850	875	86	86	86	86
875	900	89	89	89	89
900	925	91	91	91	91
925	950	94	94	94	94
950	975	96	96	96	96
975	1,000	99	99	99	99

If line 15 (taxable income) is—		And you are—			
At least	But less than	Single	Married filing jointly *	Married filing sepa-rately	Head of a house-hold
		Your tax is—			
1,000					
1,000	1,025	101	101	101	101
1,025	1,050	104	104	104	104
1,050	1,075	106	106	106	106
1,075	1,100	109	109	109	109
1,100	1,125	111	111	111	111
1,125	1,150	114	114	114	114
1,150	1,175	116	116	116	116
1,175	1,200	119	119	119	119
1,200	1,225	121	121	121	121
1,225	1,250	124	124	124	124
1,250	1,275	126	126	126	126
1,275	1,300	129	129	129	129
1,300	1,325	131	131	131	131
1,325	1,350	134	134	134	134
1,350	1,375	136	136	136	136
1,375	1,400	139	139	139	139
1,400	1,425	141	141	141	141
1,425	1,450	144	144	144	144
1,450	1,475	146	146	146	146
1,475	1,500	149	149	149	149
1,500	1,525	151	151	151	151
1,525	1,550	154	154	154	154
1,550	1,575	156	156	156	156
1,575	1,600	159	159	159	159
1,600	1,625	161	161	161	161
1,625	1,650	164	164	164	164
1,650	1,675	166	166	166	166
1,675	1,700	169	169	169	169
1,700	1,725	171	171	171	171
1,725	1,750	174	174	174	174
1,750	1,775	176	176	176	176
1,775	1,800	179	179	179	179
1,800	1,825	181	181	181	181
1,825	1,850	184	184	184	184
1,850	1,875	186	186	186	186
1,875	1,900	189	189	189	189
1,900	1,925	191	191	191	191
1,925	1,950	194	194	194	194
1,950	1,975	196	196	196	196
1,975	2,000	199	199	199	199

If line 15 (taxable income) is—		And you are—			
At least	But less than	Single	Married filing jointly *	Married filing sepa-rately	Head of a house-hold
		Your tax is—			
2,000					
2,000	2,025	201	201	201	201
2,025	2,050	204	204	204	204
2,050	2,075	206	206	206	206
2,075	2,100	209	209	209	209
2,100	2,125	211	211	211	211
2,125	2,150	214	214	214	214
2,150	2,175	216	216	216	216
2,175	2,200	219	219	219	219
2,200	2,225	221	221	221	221
2,225	2,250	224	224	224	224
2,250	2,275	226	226	226	226
2,275	2,300	229	229	229	229
2,300	2,325	231	231	231	231
2,325	2,350	234	234	234	234
2,350	2,375	236	236	236	236
2,375	2,400	239	239	239	239
2,400	2,425	241	241	241	241
2,425	2,450	244	244	244	244
2,450	2,475	246	246	246	246
2,475	2,500	249	249	249	249
2,500	2,525	251	251	251	251
2,525	2,550	254	254	254	254
2,550	2,575	256	256	256	256
2,575	2,600	259	259	259	259
2,600	2,625	261	261	261	261
2,625	2,650	264	264	264	264
2,650	2,675	266	266	266	266
2,675	2,700	269	269	269	269
2,700	2,725	271	271	271	271
2,725	2,750	274	274	274	274
2,750	2,775	276	276	276	276
2,775	2,800	279	279	279	279
2,800	2,825	281	281	281	281
2,825	2,850	284	284	284	284
2,850	2,875	286	286	286	286
2,875	2,900	289	289	289	289
2,900	2,925	291	291	291	291
2,925	2,950	294	294	294	294
2,950	2,975	296	296	296	296
2,975	3,000	299	299	299	299

(Continued)

* This column must also be used by a qualifying surviving spouse.

2022 Tax Table — *Continued*

If line 15 (taxable income) is—		And you are—			
At least	But less than	Single	Married filing jointly *	Married filing separately	Head of a household
		Your tax is—			
3,000					
3,000	3,050	303	303	303	303
3,050	3,100	308	308	308	308
3,100	3,150	313	313	313	313
3,150	3,200	318	318	318	318
3,200	3,250	323	323	323	323
3,250	3,300	328	328	328	328
3,300	3,350	333	333	333	333
3,350	3,400	338	338	338	338
3,400	3,450	343	343	343	343
3,450	3,500	348	348	348	348
3,500	3,550	353	353	353	353
3,550	3,600	358	358	358	358
3,600	3,650	363	363	363	363
3,650	3,700	368	368	368	368
3,700	3,750	373	373	373	373
3,750	3,800	378	378	378	378
3,800	3,850	383	383	383	383
3,850	3,900	388	388	388	388
3,900	3,950	393	393	393	393
3,950	4,000	398	398	398	398
4,000					
4,000	4,050	403	403	403	403
4,050	4,100	408	408	408	408
4,100	4,150	413	413	413	413
4,150	4,200	418	418	418	418
4,200	4,250	423	423	423	423
4,250	4,300	428	428	428	428
4,300	4,350	433	433	433	433
4,350	4,400	438	438	438	438
4,400	4,450	443	443	443	443
4,450	4,500	448	448	448	448
4,500	4,550	453	453	453	453
4,550	4,600	458	458	458	458
4,600	4,650	463	463	463	463
4,650	4,700	468	468	468	468
4,700	4,750	473	473	473	473
4,750	4,800	478	478	478	478
4,800	4,850	483	483	483	483
4,850	4,900	488	488	488	488
4,900	4,950	493	493	493	493
4,950	5,000	498	498	498	498
5,000					
5,000	5,050	503	503	503	503
5,050	5,100	508	508	508	508
5,100	5,150	513	513	513	513
5,150	5,200	518	518	518	518
5,200	5,250	523	523	523	523
5,250	5,300	528	528	528	528
5,300	5,350	533	533	533	533
5,350	5,400	538	538	538	538
5,400	5,450	543	543	543	543
5,450	5,500	548	548	548	548
5,500	5,550	553	553	553	553
5,550	5,600	558	558	558	558
5,600	5,650	563	563	563	563
5,650	5,700	568	568	568	568
5,700	5,750	573	573	573	573
5,750	5,800	578	578	578	578
5,800	5,850	583	583	583	583
5,850	5,900	588	588	588	588
5,900	5,950	593	593	593	593
5,950	6,000	598	598	598	598
6,000					
6,000	6,050	603	603	603	603
6,050	6,100	608	608	608	608
6,100	6,150	613	613	613	613
6,150	6,200	618	618	618	618
6,200	6,250	623	623	623	623
6,250	6,300	628	628	628	628
6,300	6,350	633	633	633	633
6,350	6,400	638	638	638	638
6,400	6,450	643	643	643	643
6,450	6,500	648	648	648	648
6,500	6,550	653	653	653	653
6,550	6,600	658	658	658	658
6,600	6,650	663	663	663	663
6,650	6,700	668	668	668	668
6,700	6,750	673	673	673	673
6,750	6,800	678	678	678	678
6,800	6,850	683	683	683	683
6,850	6,900	688	688	688	688
6,900	6,950	693	693	693	693
6,950	7,000	698	698	698	698
7,000					
7,000	7,050	703	703	703	703
7,050	7,100	708	708	708	708
7,100	7,150	713	713	713	713
7,150	7,200	718	718	718	718
7,200	7,250	723	723	723	723
7,250	7,300	728	728	728	728
7,300	7,350	733	733	733	733
7,350	7,400	738	738	738	738
7,400	7,450	743	743	743	743
7,450	7,500	748	748	748	748
7,500	7,550	753	753	753	753
7,550	7,600	758	758	758	758
7,600	7,650	763	763	763	763
7,650	7,700	768	768	768	768
7,700	7,750	773	773	773	773
7,750	7,800	778	778	778	778
7,800	7,850	783	783	783	783
7,850	7,900	788	788	788	788
7,900	7,950	793	793	793	793
7,950	8,000	798	798	798	798
8,000					
8,000	8,050	803	803	803	803
8,050	8,100	808	808	808	808
8,100	8,150	813	813	813	813
8,150	8,200	818	818	818	818
8,200	8,250	823	823	823	823
8,250	8,300	828	828	828	828
8,300	8,350	833	833	833	833
8,350	8,400	838	838	838	838
8,400	8,450	843	843	843	843
8,450	8,500	848	848	848	848
8,500	8,550	853	853	853	853
8,550	8,600	858	858	858	858
8,600	8,650	863	863	863	863
8,650	8,700	868	868	868	868
8,700	8,750	873	873	873	873
8,750	8,800	878	878	878	878
8,800	8,850	883	883	883	883
8,850	8,900	888	888	888	888
8,900	8,950	893	893	893	893
8,950	9,000	898	898	898	898
9,000					
9,000	9,050	903	903	903	903
9,050	9,100	908	908	908	908
9,100	9,150	913	913	913	913
9,150	9,200	918	918	918	918
9,200	9,250	923	923	923	923
9,250	9,300	928	928	928	928
9,300	9,350	933	933	933	933
9,350	9,400	938	938	938	938
9,400	9,450	943	943	943	943
9,450	9,500	948	948	948	948
9,500	9,550	953	953	953	953
9,550	9,600	958	958	958	958
9,600	9,650	963	963	963	963
9,650	9,700	968	968	968	968
9,700	9,750	973	973	973	973
9,750	9,800	978	978	978	978
9,800	9,850	983	983	983	983
9,850	9,900	988	988	988	988
9,900	9,950	993	993	993	993
9,950	10,000	998	998	998	998
10,000					
10,000	10,050	1,003	1,003	1,003	1,003
10,050	10,100	1,008	1,008	1,008	1,008
10,100	10,150	1,013	1,013	1,013	1,013
10,150	10,200	1,018	1,018	1,018	1,018
10,200	10,250	1,023	1,023	1,023	1,023
10,250	10,300	1,028	1,028	1,028	1,028
10,300	10,350	1,034	1,033	1,034	1,033
10,350	10,400	1,040	1,038	1,040	1,038
10,400	10,450	1,046	1,043	1,046	1,043
10,450	10,500	1,052	1,048	1,052	1,048
10,500	10,550	1,058	1,053	1,058	1,053
10,550	10,600	1,064	1,058	1,064	1,058
10,600	10,650	1,070	1,063	1,070	1,063
10,650	10,700	1,076	1,068	1,076	1,068
10,700	10,750	1,082	1,073	1,082	1,073
10,750	10,800	1,088	1,078	1,088	1,078
10,800	10,850	1,094	1,083	1,094	1,083
10,850	10,900	1,100	1,088	1,100	1,088
10,900	10,950	1,106	1,093	1,106	1,093
10,950	11,000	1,112	1,098	1,112	1,098
11,000					
11,000	11,050	1,118	1,103	1,118	1,103
11,050	11,100	1,124	1,108	1,124	1,108
11,100	11,150	1,130	1,113	1,130	1,113
11,150	11,200	1,136	1,118	1,136	1,118
11,200	11,250	1,142	1,123	1,142	1,123
11,250	11,300	1,148	1,128	1,148	1,128
11,300	11,350	1,154	1,133	1,154	1,133
11,350	11,400	1,160	1,138	1,160	1,138
11,400	11,450	1,166	1,143	1,166	1,143
11,450	11,500	1,172	1,148	1,172	1,148
11,500	11,550	1,178	1,153	1,178	1,153
11,550	11,600	1,184	1,158	1,184	1,158
11,600	11,650	1,190	1,163	1,190	1,163
11,650	11,700	1,196	1,168	1,196	1,168
11,700	11,750	1,202	1,173	1,202	1,173
11,750	11,800	1,208	1,178	1,208	1,178
11,800	11,850	1,214	1,183	1,214	1,183
11,850	11,900	1,220	1,188	1,220	1,188
11,900	11,950	1,226	1,193	1,226	1,193
11,950	12,000	1,232	1,198	1,232	1,198

(Continued)

* This column must also be used by a qualifying surviving spouse.

2022 Tax Table — *Continued*

If line 15 (taxable income) is— At least	But less than	And you are— Single	Married filing jointly *	Married filing separately	Head of a household
		Your tax is—			
12,000					
12,000	12,050	1,238	1,203	1,238	1,203
12,050	12,100	1,244	1,208	1,244	1,208
12,100	12,150	1,250	1,213	1,250	1,213
12,150	12,200	1,256	1,218	1,256	1,218
12,200	12,250	1,262	1,223	1,262	1,223
12,250	12,300	1,268	1,228	1,268	1,228
12,300	12,350	1,274	1,233	1,274	1,233
12,350	12,400	1,280	1,238	1,280	1,238
12,400	12,450	1,286	1,243	1,286	1,243
12,450	12,500	1,292	1,248	1,292	1,248
12,500	12,550	1,298	1,253	1,298	1,253
12,550	12,600	1,304	1,258	1,304	1,258
12,600	12,650	1,310	1,263	1,310	1,263
12,650	12,700	1,316	1,268	1,316	1,268
12,700	12,750	1,322	1,273	1,322	1,273
12,750	12,800	1,328	1,278	1,328	1,278
12,800	12,850	1,334	1,283	1,334	1,283
12,850	12,900	1,340	1,288	1,340	1,288
12,900	12,950	1,346	1,293	1,346	1,293
12,950	13,000	1,352	1,298	1,352	1,298
13,000					
13,000	13,050	1,358	1,303	1,358	1,303
13,050	13,100	1,364	1,308	1,364	1,308
13,100	13,150	1,370	1,313	1,370	1,313
13,150	13,200	1,376	1,318	1,376	1,318
13,200	13,250	1,382	1,323	1,382	1,323
13,250	13,300	1,388	1,328	1,388	1,328
13,300	13,350	1,394	1,333	1,394	1,333
13,350	13,400	1,400	1,338	1,400	1,338
13,400	13,450	1,406	1,343	1,406	1,343
13,450	13,500	1,412	1,348	1,412	1,348
13,500	13,550	1,418	1,353	1,418	1,353
13,550	13,600	1,424	1,358	1,424	1,358
13,600	13,650	1,430	1,363	1,430	1,363
13,650	13,700	1,436	1,368	1,436	1,368
13,700	13,750	1,442	1,373	1,442	1,373
13,750	13,800	1,448	1,378	1,448	1,378
13,800	13,850	1,454	1,383	1,454	1,383
13,850	13,900	1,460	1,388	1,460	1,388
13,900	13,950	1,466	1,393	1,466	1,393
13,950	14,000	1,472	1,398	1,472	1,398
14,000					
14,000	14,050	1,478	1,403	1,478	1,403
14,050	14,100	1,484	1,408	1,484	1,408
14,100	14,150	1,490	1,413	1,490	1,413
14,150	14,200	1,496	1,418	1,496	1,418
14,200	14,250	1,502	1,423	1,502	1,423
14,250	14,300	1,508	1,428	1,508	1,428
14,300	14,350	1,514	1,433	1,514	1,433
14,350	14,400	1,520	1,438	1,520	1,438
14,400	14,450	1,526	1,443	1,526	1,443
14,450	14,500	1,532	1,448	1,532	1,448
14,500	14,550	1,538	1,453	1,538	1,453
14,550	14,600	1,544	1,458	1,544	1,458
14,600	14,650	1,550	1,463	1,550	1,463
14,650	14,700	1,556	1,468	1,556	1,468
14,700	14,750	1,562	1,473	1,562	1,474
14,750	14,800	1,568	1,478	1,568	1,480
14,800	14,850	1,574	1,483	1,574	1,486
14,850	14,900	1,580	1,488	1,580	1,492
14,900	14,950	1,586	1,493	1,586	1,498
14,950	15,000	1,592	1,498	1,592	1,504

If line 15 (taxable income) is— At least	But less than	And you are— Single	Married filing jointly *	Married filing separately	Head of a household
		Your tax is—			
15,000					
15,000	15,050	1,598	1,503	1,598	1,510
15,050	15,100	1,604	1,508	1,604	1,516
15,100	15,150	1,610	1,513	1,610	1,522
15,150	15,200	1,616	1,518	1,616	1,528
15,200	15,250	1,622	1,523	1,622	1,534
15,250	15,300	1,628	1,528	1,628	1,540
15,300	15,350	1,634	1,533	1,634	1,546
15,350	15,400	1,640	1,538	1,640	1,552
15,400	15,450	1,646	1,543	1,646	1,558
15,450	15,500	1,652	1,548	1,652	1,564
15,500	15,550	1,658	1,553	1,658	1,570
15,550	15,600	1,664	1,558	1,664	1,576
15,600	15,650	1,670	1,563	1,670	1,582
15,650	15,700	1,676	1,568	1,676	1,588
15,700	15,750	1,682	1,573	1,682	1,594
15,750	15,800	1,688	1,578	1,688	1,600
15,800	15,850	1,694	1,583	1,694	1,606
15,850	15,900	1,700	1,588	1,700	1,612
15,900	15,950	1,706	1,593	1,706	1,618
15,950	16,000	1,712	1,598	1,712	1,624
16,000					
16,000	16,050	1,718	1,603	1,718	1,630
16,050	16,100	1,724	1,608	1,724	1,636
16,100	16,150	1,730	1,613	1,730	1,642
16,150	16,200	1,736	1,618	1,736	1,648
16,200	16,250	1,742	1,623	1,742	1,654
16,250	16,300	1,748	1,628	1,748	1,660
16,300	16,350	1,754	1,633	1,754	1,666
16,350	16,400	1,760	1,638	1,760	1,672
16,400	16,450	1,766	1,643	1,766	1,678
16,450	16,500	1,772	1,648	1,772	1,684
16,500	16,550	1,778	1,653	1,778	1,690
16,550	16,600	1,784	1,658	1,784	1,696
16,600	16,650	1,790	1,663	1,790	1,702
16,650	16,700	1,796	1,668	1,796	1,708
16,700	16,750	1,802	1,673	1,802	1,714
16,750	16,800	1,808	1,678	1,808	1,720
16,800	16,850	1,814	1,683	1,814	1,726
16,850	16,900	1,820	1,688	1,820	1,732
16,900	16,950	1,826	1,693	1,826	1,738
16,950	17,000	1,832	1,698	1,832	1,744
17,000					
17,000	17,050	1,838	1,703	1,838	1,750
17,050	17,100	1,844	1,708	1,844	1,756
17,100	17,150	1,850	1,713	1,850	1,762
17,150	17,200	1,856	1,718	1,856	1,768
17,200	17,250	1,862	1,723	1,862	1,774
17,250	17,300	1,868	1,728	1,868	1,780
17,300	17,350	1,874	1,733	1,874	1,786
17,350	17,400	1,880	1,738	1,880	1,792
17,400	17,450	1,886	1,743	1,886	1,798
17,450	17,500	1,892	1,748	1,892	1,804
17,500	17,550	1,898	1,753	1,898	1,810
17,550	17,600	1,904	1,758	1,904	1,816
17,600	17,650	1,910	1,763	1,910	1,822
17,650	17,700	1,916	1,768	1,916	1,828
17,700	17,750	1,922	1,773	1,922	1,834
17,750	17,800	1,928	1,778	1,928	1,840
17,800	17,850	1,934	1,783	1,934	1,846
17,850	17,900	1,940	1,788	1,940	1,852
17,900	17,950	1,946	1,793	1,946	1,858
17,950	18,000	1,952	1,798	1,952	1,864

If line 15 (taxable income) is— At least	But less than	And you are— Single	Married filing jointly *	Married filing separately	Head of a household
		Your tax is—			
18,000					
18,000	18,050	1,958	1,803	1,958	1,870
18,050	18,100	1,964	1,808	1,964	1,876
18,100	18,150	1,970	1,813	1,970	1,882
18,150	18,200	1,976	1,818	1,976	1,888
18,200	18,250	1,982	1,823	1,982	1,894
18,250	18,300	1,988	1,828	1,988	1,900
18,300	18,350	1,994	1,833	1,994	1,906
18,350	18,400	2,000	1,838	2,000	1,912
18,400	18,450	2,006	1,843	2,006	1,918
18,450	18,500	2,012	1,848	2,012	1,924
18,500	18,550	2,018	1,853	2,018	1,930
18,550	18,600	2,024	1,858	2,024	1,936
18,600	18,650	2,030	1,863	2,030	1,942
18,650	18,700	2,036	1,868	2,036	1,948
18,700	18,750	2,042	1,873	2,042	1,954
18,750	18,800	2,048	1,878	2,048	1,960
18,800	18,850	2,054	1,883	2,054	1,966
18,850	18,900	2,060	1,888	2,060	1,972
18,900	18,950	2,066	1,893	2,066	1,978
18,950	19,000	2,072	1,898	2,072	1,984
19,000					
19,000	19,050	2,078	1,903	2,078	1,990
19,050	19,100	2,084	1,908	2,084	1,996
19,100	19,150	2,090	1,913	2,090	2,002
19,150	19,200	2,096	1,918	2,096	2,008
19,200	19,250	2,102	1,923	2,102	2,014
19,250	19,300	2,108	1,928	2,108	2,020
19,300	19,350	2,114	1,933	2,114	2,026
19,350	19,400	2,120	1,938	2,120	2,032
19,400	19,450	2,126	1,943	2,126	2,038
19,450	19,500	2,132	1,948	2,132	2,044
19,500	19,550	2,138	1,953	2,138	2,050
19,550	19,600	2,144	1,958	2,144	2,056
19,600	19,650	2,150	1,963	2,150	2,062
19,650	19,700	2,156	1,968	2,156	2,068
19,700	19,750	2,162	1,973	2,162	2,074
19,750	19,800	2,168	1,978	2,168	2,080
19,800	19,850	2,174	1,983	2,174	2,086
19,850	19,900	2,180	1,988	2,180	2,092
19,900	19,950	2,186	1,993	2,186	2,098
19,950	20,000	2,192	1,998	2,192	2,104
20,000					
20,000	20,050	2,198	2,003	2,198	2,110
20,050	20,100	2,204	2,008	2,204	2,116
20,100	20,150	2,210	2,013	2,210	2,122
20,150	20,200	2,216	2,018	2,216	2,128
20,200	20,250	2,222	2,023	2,222	2,134
20,250	20,300	2,228	2,028	2,228	2,140
20,300	20,350	2,234	2,033	2,234	2,146
20,350	20,400	2,240	2,038	2,240	2,152
20,400	20,450	2,246	2,043	2,246	2,158
20,450	20,500	2,252	2,048	2,252	2,164
20,500	20,550	2,258	2,053	2,258	2,170
20,550	20,600	2,264	2,058	2,264	2,176
20,600	20,650	2,270	2,064	2,270	2,182
20,650	20,700	2,276	2,070	2,276	2,188
20,700	20,750	2,282	2,076	2,282	2,194
20,750	20,800	2,288	2,082	2,288	2,200
20,800	20,850	2,294	2,088	2,294	2,206
20,850	20,900	2,300	2,094	2,300	2,212
20,900	20,950	2,306	2,100	2,306	2,218
20,950	21,000	2,312	2,106	2,312	2,224

(Continued)

* This column must also be used by a qualifying surviving spouse.

2022 Tax Table — *Continued*

If line 15 (taxable income) is—		And you are—			
At least	But less than	Single	Married filing jointly *	Married filing separately	Head of a household
		Your tax is—			
21,000					
21,000	21,050	2,318	2,112	2,318	2,230
21,050	21,100	2,324	2,118	2,324	2,236
21,100	21,150	2,330	2,124	2,330	2,242
21,150	21,200	2,336	2,130	2,336	2,248
21,200	21,250	2,342	2,136	2,342	2,254
21,250	21,300	2,348	2,142	2,348	2,260
21,300	21,350	2,354	2,148	2,354	2,266
21,350	21,400	2,360	2,154	2,360	2,272
21,400	21,450	2,366	2,160	2,366	2,278
21,450	21,500	2,372	2,166	2,372	2,284
21,500	21,550	2,378	2,172	2,378	2,290
21,550	21,600	2,384	2,178	2,384	2,296
21,600	21,650	2,390	2,184	2,390	2,302
21,650	21,700	2,396	2,190	2,396	2,308
21,700	21,750	2,402	2,196	2,402	2,314
21,750	21,800	2,408	2,202	2,408	2,320
21,800	21,850	2,414	2,208	2,414	2,326
21,850	21,900	2,420	2,214	2,420	2,332
21,900	21,950	2,426	2,220	2,426	2,338
21,950	22,000	2,432	2,226	2,432	2,344
22,000					
22,000	22,050	2,438	2,232	2,438	2,350
22,050	22,100	2,444	2,238	2,444	2,356
22,100	22,150	2,450	2,244	2,450	2,362
22,150	22,200	2,456	2,250	2,456	2,368
22,200	22,250	2,462	2,256	2,462	2,374
22,250	22,300	2,468	2,262	2,468	2,380
22,300	22,350	2,474	2,268	2,474	2,386
22,350	22,400	2,480	2,274	2,480	2,392
22,400	22,450	2,486	2,280	2,486	2,398
22,450	22,500	2,492	2,286	2,492	2,404
22,500	22,550	2,498	2,292	2,498	2,410
22,550	22,600	2,504	2,298	2,504	2,416
22,600	22,650	2,510	2,304	2,510	2,422
22,650	22,700	2,516	2,310	2,516	2,428
22,700	22,750	2,522	2,316	2,522	2,434
22,750	22,800	2,528	2,322	2,528	2,440
22,800	22,850	2,534	2,328	2,534	2,446
22,850	22,900	2,540	2,334	2,540	2,452
22,900	22,950	2,546	2,340	2,546	2,458
22,950	23,000	2,552	2,346	2,552	2,464
23,000					
23,000	23,050	2,558	2,352	2,558	2,470
23,050	23,100	2,564	2,358	2,564	2,476
23,100	23,150	2,570	2,364	2,570	2,482
23,150	23,200	2,576	2,370	2,576	2,488
23,200	23,250	2,582	2,376	2,582	2,494
23,250	23,300	2,588	2,382	2,588	2,500
23,300	23,350	2,594	2,388	2,594	2,506
23,350	23,400	2,600	2,394	2,600	2,512
23,400	23,450	2,606	2,400	2,606	2,518
23,450	23,500	2,612	2,406	2,612	2,524
23,500	23,550	2,618	2,412	2,618	2,530
23,550	23,600	2,624	2,418	2,624	2,536
23,600	23,650	2,630	2,424	2,630	2,542
23,650	23,700	2,636	2,430	2,636	2,548
23,700	23,750	2,642	2,436	2,642	2,554
23,750	23,800	2,648	2,442	2,648	2,560
23,800	23,850	2,654	2,448	2,654	2,566
23,850	23,900	2,660	2,454	2,660	2,572
23,900	23,950	2,666	2,460	2,666	2,578
23,950	24,000	2,672	2,466	2,672	2,584
24,000					
24,000	24,050	2,678	2,472	2,678	2,590
24,050	24,100	2,684	2,478	2,684	2,596
24,100	24,150	2,690	2,484	2,690	2,602
24,150	24,200	2,696	2,490	2,696	2,608
24,200	24,250	2,702	2,496	2,702	2,614
24,250	24,300	2,708	2,502	2,708	2,620
24,300	24,350	2,714	2,508	2,714	2,626
24,350	24,400	2,720	2,514	2,720	2,632
24,400	24,450	2,726	2,520	2,726	2,638
24,450	24,500	2,732	2,526	2,732	2,644
24,500	24,550	2,738	2,532	2,738	2,650
24,550	24,600	2,744	2,538	2,744	2,656
24,600	24,650	2,750	2,544	2,750	2,662
24,650	24,700	2,756	2,550	2,756	2,668
24,700	24,750	2,762	2,556	2,762	2,674
24,750	24,800	2,768	2,562	2,768	2,680
24,800	24,850	2,774	2,568	2,774	2,686
24,850	24,900	2,780	2,574	2,780	2,692
24,900	24,950	2,786	2,580	2,786	2,698
24,950	25,000	2,792	2,586	2,792	2,704
25,000					
25,000	25,050	2,798	2,592	2,798	2,710
25,050	25,100	2,804	2,598	2,804	2,716
25,100	25,150	2,810	2,604	2,810	2,722
25,150	25,200	2,816	2,610	2,816	2,728
25,200	25,250	2,822	2,616	2,822	2,734
25,250	25,300	2,828	2,622	2,828	2,740
25,300	25,350	2,834	2,628	2,834	2,746
25,350	25,400	2,840	2,634	2,840	2,752
25,400	25,450	2,846	2,640	2,846	2,758
25,450	25,500	2,852	2,646	2,852	2,764
25,500	25,550	2,858	2,652	2,858	2,770
25,550	25,600	2,864	2,658	2,864	2,776
25,600	25,650	2,870	2,664	2,870	2,782
25,650	25,700	2,876	2,670	2,876	2,788
25,700	25,750	2,882	2,676	2,882	2,794
25,750	25,800	2,888	2,682	2,888	2,800
25,800	25,850	2,894	2,688	2,894	2,806
25,850	25,900	2,900	2,694	2,900	2,812
25,900	25,950	2,906	2,700	2,906	2,818
25,950	26,000	2,912	2,706	2,912	2,824
26,000					
26,000	26,050	2,918	2,712	2,918	2,830
26,050	26,100	2,924	2,718	2,924	2,836
26,100	26,150	2,930	2,724	2,930	2,842
26,150	26,200	2,936	2,730	2,936	2,848
26,200	26,250	2,942	2,736	2,942	2,854
26,250	26,300	2,948	2,742	2,948	2,860
26,300	26,350	2,954	2,748	2,954	2,866
26,350	26,400	2,960	2,754	2,960	2,872
26,400	26,450	2,966	2,760	2,966	2,878
26,450	26,500	2,972	2,766	2,972	2,884
26,500	26,550	2,978	2,772	2,978	2,890
26,550	26,600	2,984	2,778	2,984	2,896
26,600	26,650	2,990	2,784	2,990	2,902
26,650	26,700	2,996	2,790	2,996	2,908
26,700	26,750	3,002	2,796	3,002	2,914
26,750	26,800	3,008	2,802	3,008	2,920
26,800	26,850	3,014	2,808	3,014	2,926
26,850	26,900	3,020	2,814	3,020	2,932
26,900	26,950	3,026	2,820	3,026	2,938
26,950	27,000	3,032	2,826	3,032	2,944
27,000					
27,000	27,050	3,038	2,832	3,038	2,950
27,050	27,100	3,044	2,838	3,044	2,956
27,100	27,150	3,050	2,844	3,050	2,962
27,150	27,200	3,056	2,850	3,056	2,968
27,200	27,250	3,062	2,856	3,062	2,974
27,250	27,300	3,068	2,862	3,068	2,980
27,300	27,350	3,074	2,868	3,074	2,986
27,350	27,400	3,080	2,874	3,080	2,992
27,400	27,450	3,086	2,880	3,086	2,998
27,450	27,500	3,092	2,886	3,092	3,004
27,500	27,550	3,098	2,892	3,098	3,010
27,550	27,600	3,104	2,898	3,104	3,016
27,600	27,650	3,110	2,904	3,110	3,022
27,650	27,700	3,116	2,910	3,116	3,028
27,700	27,750	3,122	2,916	3,122	3,034
27,750	27,800	3,128	2,922	3,128	3,040
27,800	27,850	3,134	2,928	3,134	3,046
27,850	27,900	3,140	2,934	3,140	3,052
27,900	27,950	3,146	2,940	3,146	3,058
27,950	28,000	3,152	2,946	3,152	3,064
28,000					
28,000	28,050	3,158	2,952	3,158	3,070
28,050	28,100	3,164	2,958	3,164	3,076
28,100	28,150	3,170	2,964	3,170	3,082
28,150	28,200	3,176	2,970	3,176	3,088
28,200	28,250	3,182	2,976	3,182	3,094
28,250	28,300	3,188	2,982	3,188	3,100
28,300	28,350	3,194	2,988	3,194	3,106
28,350	28,400	3,200	2,994	3,200	3,112
28,400	28,450	3,206	3,000	3,206	3,118
28,450	28,500	3,212	3,006	3,212	3,124
28,500	28,550	3,218	3,012	3,218	3,130
28,550	28,600	3,224	3,018	3,224	3,136
28,600	28,650	3,230	3,024	3,230	3,142
28,650	28,700	3,236	3,030	3,236	3,148
28,700	28,750	3,242	3,036	3,242	3,154
28,750	28,800	3,248	3,042	3,248	3,160
28,800	28,850	3,254	3,048	3,254	3,166
28,850	28,900	3,260	3,054	3,260	3,172
28,900	28,950	3,266	3,060	3,266	3,178
28,950	29,000	3,272	3,066	3,272	3,184
29,000					
29,000	29,050	3,278	3,072	3,278	3,190
29,050	29,100	3,284	3,078	3,284	3,196
29,100	29,150	3,290	3,084	3,290	3,202
29,150	29,200	3,296	3,090	3,296	3,208
29,200	29,250	3,302	3,096	3,302	3,214
29,250	29,300	3,308	3,102	3,308	3,220
29,300	29,350	3,314	3,108	3,314	3,226
29,350	29,400	3,320	3,114	3,320	3,232
29,400	29,450	3,326	3,120	3,326	3,238
29,450	29,500	3,332	3,126	3,332	3,244
29,500	29,550	3,338	3,132	3,338	3,250
29,550	29,600	3,344	3,138	3,344	3,256
29,600	29,650	3,350	3,144	3,350	3,262
29,650	29,700	3,356	3,150	3,356	3,268
29,700	29,750	3,362	3,156	3,362	3,274
29,750	29,800	3,368	3,162	3,368	3,280
29,800	29,850	3,374	3,168	3,374	3,286
29,850	29,900	3,380	3,174	3,380	3,292
29,900	29,950	3,386	3,180	3,386	3,298
29,950	30,000	3,392	3,186	3,392	3,304

(Continued)

* This column must also be used by a qualifying surviving spouse.

2022 Tax Table — *Continued*

If line 15 (taxable income) is—		And you are—			
At least	But less than	Single	Married filing jointly *	Married filing separately	Head of a household
		Your tax is—			
30,000					
30,000	30,050	3,398	3,192	3,398	3,310
30,050	30,100	3,404	3,198	3,404	3,316
30,100	30,150	3,410	3,204	3,410	3,322
30,150	30,200	3,416	3,210	3,416	3,328
30,200	30,250	3,422	3,216	3,422	3,334
30,250	30,300	3,428	3,222	3,428	3,340
30,300	30,350	3,434	3,228	3,434	3,346
30,350	30,400	3,440	3,234	3,440	3,352
30,400	30,450	3,446	3,240	3,446	3,358
30,450	30,500	3,452	3,246	3,452	3,364
30,500	30,550	3,458	3,252	3,458	3,370
30,550	30,600	3,464	3,258	3,464	3,376
30,600	30,650	3,470	3,264	3,470	3,382
30,650	30,700	3,476	3,270	3,476	3,388
30,700	30,750	3,482	3,276	3,482	3,394
30,750	30,800	3,488	3,282	3,488	3,400
30,800	30,850	3,494	3,288	3,494	3,406
30,850	30,900	3,500	3,294	3,500	3,412
30,900	30,950	3,506	3,300	3,506	3,418
30,950	31,000	3,512	3,306	3,512	3,424
31,000					
31,000	31,050	3,518	3,312	3,518	3,430
31,050	31,100	3,524	3,318	3,524	3,436
31,100	31,150	3,530	3,324	3,530	3,442
31,150	31,200	3,536	3,330	3,536	3,448
31,200	31,250	3,542	3,336	3,542	3,454
31,250	31,300	3,548	3,342	3,548	3,460
31,300	31,350	3,554	3,348	3,554	3,466
31,350	31,400	3,560	3,354	3,560	3,472
31,400	31,450	3,566	3,360	3,566	3,478
31,450	31,500	3,572	3,366	3,572	3,484
31,500	31,550	3,578	3,372	3,578	3,490
31,550	31,600	3,584	3,378	3,584	3,496
31,600	31,650	3,590	3,384	3,590	3,502
31,650	31,700	3,596	3,390	3,596	3,508
31,700	31,750	3,602	3,396	3,602	3,514
31,750	31,800	3,608	3,402	3,608	3,520
31,800	31,850	3,614	3,408	3,614	3,526
31,850	31,900	3,620	3,414	3,620	3,532
31,900	31,950	3,626	3,420	3,626	3,538
31,950	32,000	3,632	3,426	3,632	3,544
32,000					
32,000	32,050	3,638	3,432	3,638	3,550
32,050	32,100	3,644	3,438	3,644	3,556
32,100	32,150	3,650	3,444	3,650	3,562
32,150	32,200	3,656	3,450	3,656	3,568
32,200	32,250	3,662	3,456	3,662	3,574
32,250	32,300	3,668	3,462	3,668	3,580
32,300	32,350	3,674	3,468	3,674	3,586
32,350	32,400	3,680	3,474	3,680	3,592
32,400	32,450	3,686	3,480	3,686	3,598
32,450	32,500	3,692	3,486	3,692	3,604
32,500	32,550	3,698	3,492	3,698	3,610
32,550	32,600	3,704	3,498	3,704	3,616
32,600	32,650	3,710	3,504	3,710	3,622
32,650	32,700	3,716	3,510	3,716	3,628
32,700	32,750	3,722	3,516	3,722	3,634
32,750	32,800	3,728	3,522	3,728	3,640
32,800	32,850	3,734	3,528	3,734	3,646
32,850	32,900	3,740	3,534	3,740	3,652
32,900	32,950	3,746	3,540	3,746	3,658
32,950	33,000	3,752	3,546	3,752	3,664
33,000					
33,000	33,050	3,758	3,552	3,758	3,670
33,050	33,100	3,764	3,558	3,764	3,676
33,100	33,150	3,770	3,564	3,770	3,682
33,150	33,200	3,776	3,570	3,776	3,688
33,200	33,250	3,782	3,576	3,782	3,694
33,250	33,300	3,788	3,582	3,788	3,700
33,300	33,350	3,794	3,588	3,794	3,706
33,350	33,400	3,800	3,594	3,800	3,712
33,400	33,450	3,806	3,600	3,806	3,718
33,450	33,500	3,812	3,606	3,812	3,724
33,500	33,550	3,818	3,612	3,818	3,730
33,550	33,600	3,824	3,618	3,824	3,736
33,600	33,650	3,830	3,624	3,830	3,742
33,650	33,700	3,836	3,630	3,836	3,748
33,700	33,750	3,842	3,636	3,842	3,754
33,750	33,800	3,848	3,642	3,848	3,760
33,800	33,850	3,854	3,648	3,854	3,766
33,850	33,900	3,860	3,654	3,860	3,772
33,900	33,950	3,866	3,660	3,866	3,778
33,950	34,000	3,872	3,666	3,872	3,784
34,000					
34,000	34,050	3,878	3,672	3,878	3,790
34,050	34,100	3,884	3,678	3,884	3,796
34,100	34,150	3,890	3,684	3,890	3,802
34,150	34,200	3,896	3,690	3,896	3,808
34,200	34,250	3,902	3,696	3,902	3,814
34,250	34,300	3,908	3,702	3,908	3,820
34,300	34,350	3,914	3,708	3,914	3,826
34,350	34,400	3,920	3,714	3,920	3,832
34,400	34,450	3,926	3,720	3,926	3,838
34,450	34,500	3,932	3,726	3,932	3,844
34,500	34,550	3,938	3,732	3,938	3,850
34,550	34,600	3,944	3,738	3,944	3,856
34,600	34,650	3,950	3,744	3,950	3,862
34,650	34,700	3,956	3,750	3,956	3,868
34,700	34,750	3,962	3,756	3,962	3,874
34,750	34,800	3,968	3,762	3,968	3,880
34,800	34,850	3,974	3,768	3,974	3,886
34,850	34,900	3,980	3,774	3,980	3,892
34,900	34,950	3,986	3,780	3,986	3,898
34,950	35,000	3,992	3,786	3,992	3,904
35,000					
35,000	35,050	3,998	3,792	3,998	3,910
35,050	35,100	4,004	3,798	4,004	3,916
35,100	35,150	4,010	3,804	4,010	3,922
35,150	35,200	4,016	3,810	4,016	3,928
35,200	35,250	4,022	3,816	4,022	3,934
35,250	35,300	4,028	3,822	4,028	3,940
35,300	35,350	4,034	3,828	4,034	3,946
35,350	35,400	4,040	3,834	4,040	3,952
35,400	35,450	4,046	3,840	4,046	3,958
35,450	35,500	4,052	3,846	4,052	3,964
35,500	35,550	4,058	3,852	4,058	3,970
35,550	35,600	4,064	3,858	4,064	3,976
35,600	35,650	4,070	3,864	4,070	3,982
35,650	35,700	4,076	3,870	4,076	3,988
35,700	35,750	4,082	3,876	4,082	3,994
35,750	35,800	4,088	3,882	4,088	4,000
35,800	35,850	4,094	3,888	4,094	4,006
35,850	35,900	4,100	3,894	4,100	4,012
35,900	35,950	4,106	3,900	4,106	4,018
35,950	36,000	4,112	3,906	4,112	4,024
36,000					
36,000	36,050	4,118	3,912	4,118	4,030
36,050	36,100	4,124	3,918	4,124	4,036
36,100	36,150	4,130	3,924	4,130	4,042
36,150	36,200	4,136	3,930	4,136	4,048
36,200	36,250	4,142	3,936	4,142	4,054
36,250	36,300	4,148	3,942	4,148	4,060
36,300	36,350	4,154	3,948	4,154	4,066
36,350	36,400	4,160	3,954	4,160	4,072
36,400	36,450	4,166	3,960	4,166	4,078
36,450	36,500	4,172	3,966	4,172	4,084
36,500	36,550	4,178	3,972	4,178	4,090
36,550	36,600	4,184	3,978	4,184	4,096
36,600	36,650	4,190	3,984	4,190	4,102
36,650	36,700	4,196	3,990	4,196	4,108
36,700	36,750	4,202	3,996	4,202	4,114
36,750	36,800	4,208	4,002	4,208	4,120
36,800	36,850	4,214	4,008	4,214	4,126
36,850	36,900	4,220	4,014	4,220	4,132
36,900	36,950	4,226	4,020	4,226	4,138
36,950	37,000	4,232	4,026	4,232	4,144
37,000					
37,000	37,050	4,238	4,032	4,238	4,150
37,050	37,100	4,244	4,038	4,244	4,156
37,100	37,150	4,250	4,044	4,250	4,162
37,150	37,200	4,256	4,050	4,256	4,168
37,200	37,250	4,262	4,056	4,262	4,174
37,250	37,300	4,268	4,062	4,268	4,180
37,300	37,350	4,274	4,068	4,274	4,186
37,350	37,400	4,280	4,074	4,280	4,192
37,400	37,450	4,286	4,080	4,286	4,198
37,450	37,500	4,292	4,086	4,292	4,204
37,500	37,550	4,298	4,092	4,298	4,210
37,550	37,600	4,304	4,098	4,304	4,216
37,600	37,650	4,310	4,104	4,310	4,222
37,650	37,700	4,316	4,110	4,316	4,228
37,700	37,750	4,322	4,116	4,322	4,234
37,750	37,800	4,328	4,122	4,328	4,240
37,800	37,850	4,334	4,128	4,334	4,246
37,850	37,900	4,340	4,134	4,340	4,252
37,900	37,950	4,346	4,140	4,346	4,258
37,950	38,000	4,352	4,146	4,352	4,264
38,000					
38,000	38,050	4,358	4,152	4,358	4,270
38,050	38,100	4,364	4,158	4,364	4,276
38,100	38,150	4,370	4,164	4,370	4,282
38,150	38,200	4,376	4,170	4,376	4,288
38,200	38,250	4,382	4,176	4,382	4,294
38,250	38,300	4,388	4,182	4,388	4,300
38,300	38,350	4,394	4,188	4,394	4,306
38,350	38,400	4,400	4,194	4,400	4,312
38,400	38,450	4,406	4,200	4,406	4,318
38,450	38,500	4,412	4,206	4,412	4,324
38,500	38,550	4,418	4,212	4,418	4,330
38,550	38,600	4,424	4,218	4,424	4,336
38,600	38,650	4,430	4,224	4,430	4,342
38,650	38,700	4,436	4,230	4,436	4,348
38,700	38,750	4,442	4,236	4,442	4,354
38,750	38,800	4,448	4,242	4,448	4,360
38,800	38,850	4,454	4,248	4,454	4,366
38,850	38,900	4,460	4,254	4,460	4,372
38,900	38,950	4,466	4,260	4,466	4,378
38,950	39,000	4,472	4,266	4,472	4,384

(Continued)

* This column must also be used by a qualifying surviving spouse.

2022 Tax Table — *Continued*

If line 15 (taxable income) is— At least	But less than	And you are— Single	Married filing jointly *	Married filing separately	Head of a household
		Your tax is—			
39,000					
39,000	39,050	4,478	4,272	4,478	4,390
39,050	39,100	4,484	4,278	4,484	4,396
39,100	39,150	4,490	4,284	4,490	4,402
39,150	39,200	4,496	4,290	4,496	4,408
39,200	39,250	4,502	4,296	4,502	4,414
39,250	39,300	4,508	4,302	4,508	4,420
39,300	39,350	4,514	4,308	4,514	4,426
39,350	39,400	4,520	4,314	4,520	4,432
39,400	39,450	4,526	4,320	4,526	4,438
39,450	39,500	4,532	4,326	4,532	4,444
39,500	39,550	4,538	4,332	4,538	4,450
39,550	39,600	4,544	4,338	4,544	4,456
39,600	39,650	4,550	4,344	4,550	4,462
39,650	39,700	4,556	4,350	4,556	4,468
39,700	39,750	4,562	4,356	4,562	4,474
39,750	39,800	4,568	4,362	4,568	4,480
39,800	39,850	4,574	4,368	4,574	4,486
39,850	39,900	4,580	4,374	4,580	4,492
39,900	39,950	4,586	4,380	4,586	4,498
39,950	40,000	4,592	4,386	4,592	4,504
40,000					
40,000	40,050	4,598	4,392	4,598	4,510
40,050	40,100	4,604	4,398	4,604	4,516
40,100	40,150	4,610	4,404	4,610	4,522
40,150	40,200	4,616	4,410	4,616	4,528
40,200	40,250	4,622	4,416	4,622	4,534
40,250	40,300	4,628	4,422	4,628	4,540
40,300	40,350	4,634	4,428	4,634	4,546
40,350	40,400	4,640	4,434	4,640	4,552
40,400	40,450	4,646	4,440	4,646	4,558
40,450	40,500	4,652	4,446	4,652	4,564
40,500	40,550	4,658	4,452	4,658	4,570
40,550	40,600	4,664	4,458	4,664	4,576
40,600	40,650	4,670	4,464	4,670	4,582
40,650	40,700	4,676	4,470	4,676	4,588
40,700	40,750	4,682	4,476	4,682	4,594
40,750	40,800	4,688	4,482	4,688	4,600
40,800	40,850	4,694	4,488	4,694	4,606
40,850	40,900	4,700	4,494	4,700	4,612
40,900	40,950	4,706	4,500	4,706	4,618
40,950	41,000	4,712	4,506	4,712	4,624
41,000					
41,000	41,050	4,718	4,512	4,718	4,630
41,050	41,100	4,724	4,518	4,724	4,636
41,100	41,150	4,730	4,524	4,730	4,642
41,150	41,200	4,736	4,530	4,736	4,648
41,200	41,250	4,742	4,536	4,742	4,654
41,250	41,300	4,748	4,542	4,748	4,660
41,300	41,350	4,754	4,548	4,754	4,666
41,350	41,400	4,760	4,554	4,760	4,672
41,400	41,450	4,766	4,560	4,766	4,678
41,450	41,500	4,772	4,566	4,772	4,684
41,500	41,550	4,778	4,572	4,778	4,690
41,550	41,600	4,784	4,578	4,784	4,696
41,600	41,650	4,790	4,584	4,790	4,702
41,650	41,700	4,796	4,590	4,796	4,708
41,700	41,750	4,802	4,596	4,802	4,714
41,750	41,800	4,808	4,602	4,808	4,720
41,800	41,850	4,819	4,608	4,819	4,726
41,850	41,900	4,830	4,614	4,830	4,732
41,900	41,950	4,841	4,620	4,841	4,738
41,950	42,000	4,852	4,626	4,852	4,744

If line 15 (taxable income) is— At least	But less than	And you are— Single	Married filing jointly *	Married filing separately	Head of a household
		Your tax is—			
42,000					
42,000	42,050	4,863	4,632	4,863	4,750
42,050	42,100	4,874	4,638	4,874	4,756
42,100	42,150	4,885	4,644	4,885	4,762
42,150	42,200	4,896	4,650	4,896	4,768
42,200	42,250	4,907	4,656	4,907	4,774
42,250	42,300	4,918	4,662	4,918	4,780
42,300	42,350	4,929	4,668	4,929	4,786
42,350	42,400	4,940	4,674	4,940	4,792
42,400	42,450	4,951	4,680	4,951	4,798
42,450	42,500	4,962	4,686	4,962	4,804
42,500	42,550	4,973	4,692	4,973	4,810
42,550	42,600	4,984	4,698	4,984	4,816
42,600	42,650	4,995	4,704	4,995	4,822
42,650	42,700	5,006	4,710	5,006	4,828
42,700	42,750	5,017	4,716	5,017	4,834
42,750	42,800	5,028	4,722	5,020	4,840
42,800	42,850	5,039	4,728	5,039	4,846
42,850	42,900	5,050	4,734	5,050	4,852
42,900	42,950	5,061	4,740	5,061	4,858
42,950	43,000	5,072	4,746	5,072	4,864
43,000					
43,000	43,050	5,083	4,752	5,083	4,870
43,050	43,100	5,094	4,758	5,094	4,876
43,100	43,150	5,105	4,764	5,105	4,882
43,150	43,200	5,116	4,770	5,116	4,888
43,200	43,250	5,127	4,776	5,127	4,894
43,250	43,300	5,138	4,782	5,138	4,900
43,300	43,350	5,149	4,788	5,149	4,906
43,350	43,400	5,160	4,794	5,160	4,912
43,400	43,450	5,171	4,800	5,171	4,918
43,450	43,500	5,182	4,806	5,182	4,924
43,500	43,550	5,193	4,812	5,193	4,930
43,550	43,600	5,204	4,818	5,204	4,936
43,600	43,650	5,215	4,824	5,215	4,942
43,650	43,700	5,226	4,830	5,226	4,948
43,700	43,750	5,237	4,836	5,237	4,954
43,750	43,800	5,248	4,842	5,248	4,960
43,800	43,850	5,259	4,848	5,259	4,966
43,850	43,900	5,270	4,854	5,270	4,972
43,900	43,950	5,281	4,860	5,281	4,978
43,950	44,000	5,292	4,866	5,292	4,984
44,000					
44,000	44,050	5,303	4,872	5,303	4,990
44,050	44,100	5,314	4,878	5,314	4,996
44,100	44,150	5,325	4,884	5,325	5,002
44,150	44,200	5,336	4,890	5,336	5,008
44,200	44,250	5,347	4,896	5,347	5,014
44,250	44,300	5,358	4,902	5,358	5,020
44,300	44,350	5,369	4,908	5,369	5,026
44,350	44,400	5,380	4,914	5,380	5,032
44,400	44,450	5,391	4,920	5,391	5,038
44,450	44,500	5,402	4,926	5,402	5,044
44,500	44,550	5,413	4,932	5,413	5,050
44,550	44,600	5,424	4,938	5,424	5,056
44,600	44,650	5,435	4,944	5,435	5,062
44,650	44,700	5,446	4,950	5,446	5,068
44,700	44,750	5,457	4,956	5,457	5,074
44,750	44,800	5,468	4,962	5,468	5,080
44,800	44,850	5,479	4,968	5,479	5,086
44,850	44,900	5,490	4,974	5,490	5,092
44,900	44,950	5,501	4,980	5,501	5,098
44,950	45,000	5,512	4,986	5,512	5,104

If line 15 (taxable income) is— At least	But less than	And you are— Single	Married filing jointly *	Married filing separately	Head of a household
		Your tax is—			
45,000					
45,000	45,050	5,523	4,992	5,523	5,110
45,050	45,100	5,534	4,998	5,534	5,116
45,100	45,150	5,545	5,004	5,545	5,122
45,150	45,200	5,556	5,010	5,556	5,128
45,200	45,250	5,567	5,016	5,567	5,134
45,250	45,300	5,578	5,022	5,578	5,140
45,300	45,350	5,589	5,028	5,589	5,146
45,350	45,400	5,600	5,034	5,600	5,152
45,400	45,450	5,611	5,040	5,611	5,158
45,450	45,500	5,622	5,046	5,622	5,164
45,500	45,550	5,633	5,052	5,633	5,170
45,550	45,600	5,644	5,058	5,644	5,176
45,600	45,650	5,655	5,064	5,655	5,182
45,650	45,700	5,666	5,070	5,666	5,188
45,700	45,750	5,677	5,076	5,677	5,194
45,750	45,800	5,688	5,082	5,688	5,200
45,800	45,850	5,699	5,088	5,699	5,206
45,850	45,900	5,710	5,094	5,710	5,212
45,900	45,950	5,721	5,100	5,721	5,218
45,950	46,000	5,732	5,106	5,732	5,224
46,000					
46,000	46,050	5,743	5,112	5,743	5,230
46,050	46,100	5,754	5,118	5,754	5,236
46,100	46,150	5,765	5,124	5,765	5,242
46,150	46,200	5,776	5,130	5,776	5,248
46,200	46,250	5,787	5,136	5,787	5,254
46,250	46,300	5,798	5,142	5,798	5,260
46,300	46,350	5,809	5,148	5,809	5,266
46,350	46,400	5,820	5,154	5,820	5,272
46,400	46,450	5,831	5,160	5,831	5,278
46,450	46,500	5,842	5,166	5,842	5,284
46,500	46,550	5,853	5,172	5,853	5,290
46,550	46,600	5,864	5,178	5,864	5,296
46,600	46,650	5,875	5,184	5,875	5,302
46,650	46,700	5,886	5,190	5,886	5,308
46,700	46,750	5,897	5,196	5,897	5,314
46,750	46,800	5,908	5,202	5,908	5,320
46,800	46,850	5,919	5,208	5,919	5,326
46,850	46,900	5,930	5,214	5,930	5,332
46,900	46,950	5,941	5,220	5,941	5,338
46,950	47,000	5,952	5,226	5,952	5,344
47,000					
47,000	47,050	5,963	5,232	5,963	5,350
47,050	47,100	5,974	5,238	5,974	5,356
47,100	47,150	5,985	5,244	5,985	5,362
47,150	47,200	5,996	5,250	5,996	5,368
47,200	47,250	6,007	5,256	6,007	5,374
47,250	47,300	6,018	5,262	6,018	5,380
47,300	47,350	6,029	5,268	6,029	5,386
47,350	47,400	6,040	5,274	6,040	5,392
47,400	47,450	6,051	5,280	6,051	5,398
47,450	47,500	6,062	5,286	6,062	5,404
47,500	47,550	6,073	5,292	6,073	5,410
47,550	47,600	6,084	5,298	6,084	5,416
47,600	47,650	6,095	5,304	6,095	5,422
47,650	47,700	6,106	5,310	6,106	5,428
47,700	47,750	6,117	5,316	6,117	5,434
47,750	47,800	6,128	5,322	6,128	5,440
47,800	47,850	6,139	5,328	6,139	5,446
47,850	47,900	6,150	5,334	6,150	5,452
47,900	47,950	6,161	5,340	6,161	5,458
47,950	48,000	6,172	5,346	6,172	5,464

(Continued)

* This column must also be used by a qualifying surviving spouse.

2022 Tax Table — *Continued*

If line 15 (taxable income) is—		And you are—			
At least	But less than	Single	Married filing jointly *	Married filing sepa-rately	Head of a house-hold
		Your tax is—			
48,000					
48,000	48,050	6,183	5,352	6,183	5,470
48,050	48,100	6,194	5,358	6,194	5,476
48,100	48,150	6,205	5,364	6,205	5,482
48,150	48,200	6,216	5,370	6,216	5,488
48,200	48,250	6,227	5,376	6,227	5,494
48,250	48,300	6,238	5,382	6,238	5,500
48,300	48,350	6,249	5,388	6,249	5,506
48,350	48,400	6,260	5,394	6,260	5,512
48,400	48,450	6,271	5,400	6,271	5,518
48,450	48,500	6,282	5,406	6,282	5,524
48,500	48,550	6,293	5,412	6,293	5,530
48,550	48,600	6,304	5,418	6,304	5,536
48,600	48,650	6,315	5,424	6,315	5,542
48,650	48,700	6,326	5,430	6,326	5,548
48,700	48,750	6,337	5,436	6,337	5,554
48,750	48,800	6,348	5,442	6,348	5,560
48,800	48,850	6,359	5,448	6,359	5,566
48,850	48,900	6,370	5,454	6,370	5,572
48,900	48,950	6,381	5,460	6,381	5,578
48,950	49,000	6,392	5,466	6,392	5,584
49,000					
49,000	49,050	6,403	5,472	6,403	5,590
49,050	49,100	6,414	5,478	6,414	5,596
49,100	49,150	6,425	5,484	6,425	5,602
49,150	49,200	6,436	5,490	6,436	5,608
49,200	49,250	6,447	5,496	6,447	5,614
49,250	49,300	6,458	5,502	6,458	5,620
49,300	49,350	6,469	5,508	6,469	5,626
49,350	49,400	6,480	5,514	6,480	5,632
49,400	49,450	6,491	5,520	6,491	5,638
49,450	49,500	6,502	5,526	6,502	5,644
49,500	49,550	6,513	5,532	6,513	5,650
49,550	49,600	6,524	5,538	6,524	5,656
49,600	49,650	6,535	5,544	6,535	5,662
49,650	49,700	6,546	5,550	6,546	5,668
49,700	49,750	6,557	5,556	6,557	5,674
49,750	49,800	6,568	5,562	6,568	5,680
49,800	49,850	6,579	5,568	6,579	5,686
49,850	49,900	6,590	5,574	6,590	5,692
49,900	49,950	6,601	5,580	6,601	5,698
49,950	50,000	6,612	5,586	6,612	5,704
50,000					
50,000	50,050	6,623	5,592	6,623	5,710
50,050	50,100	6,634	5,598	6,634	5,716
50,100	50,150	6,645	5,604	6,645	5,722
50,150	50,200	6,656	5,610	6,656	5,728
50,200	50,250	6,667	5,616	6,667	5,734
50,250	50,300	6,678	5,622	6,678	5,740
50,300	50,350	6,689	5,628	6,689	5,746
50,350	50,400	6,700	5,634	6,700	5,752
50,400	50,450	6,711	5,640	6,711	5,758
50,450	50,500	6,722	5,646	6,722	5,764
50,500	50,550	6,733	5,652	6,733	5,770
50,550	50,600	6,744	5,658	6,744	5,776
50,600	50,650	6,755	5,664	6,755	5,782
50,650	50,700	6,766	5,670	6,766	5,788
50,700	50,750	6,777	5,676	6,777	5,794
50,750	50,800	6,788	5,682	6,788	5,800
50,800	50,850	6,799	5,688	6,799	5,806
50,850	50,900	6,810	5,694	6,810	5,812
50,900	50,950	6,821	5,700	6,821	5,818
50,950	51,000	6,832	5,706	6,832	5,824

If line 15 (taxable income) is—		And you are—			
At least	But less than	Single	Married filing jointly *	Married filing sepa-rately	Head of a house-hold
		Your tax is—			
51,000					
51,000	51,050	6,843	5,712	6,843	5,830
51,050	51,100	6,854	5,718	6,854	5,836
51,100	51,150	6,865	5,724	6,865	5,842
51,150	51,200	6,876	5,730	6,876	5,848
51,200	51,250	6,887	5,736	6,887	5,854
51,250	51,300	6,898	5,742	6,898	5,860
51,300	51,350	6,909	5,748	6,909	5,866
51,350	51,400	6,920	5,754	6,920	5,872
51,400	51,450	6,931	5,760	6,931	5,878
51,450	51,500	6,942	5,766	6,942	5,884
51,500	51,550	6,953	5,772	6,953	5,890
51,550	51,600	6,964	5,778	6,964	5,896
51,600	51,650	6,975	5,784	6,975	5,902
51,650	51,700	6,986	5,790	6,986	5,908
51,700	51,750	6,997	5,796	6,997	5,914
51,750	51,800	7,008	5,802	7,008	5,920
51,800	51,850	7,019	5,808	7,019	5,926
51,850	51,900	7,030	5,814	7,030	5,932
51,900	51,950	7,041	5,820	7,041	5,938
51,950	52,000	7,052	5,826	7,052	5,944
52,000					
52,000	52,050	7,063	5,832	7,063	5,950
52,050	52,100	7,074	5,838	7,074	5,956
52,100	52,150	7,085	5,844	7,085	5,962
52,150	52,200	7,096	5,850	7,096	5,968
52,200	52,250	7,107	5,856	7,107	5,974
52,250	52,300	7,118	5,862	7,118	5,980
52,300	52,350	7,129	5,868	7,129	5,986
52,350	52,400	7,140	5,874	7,140	5,992
52,400	52,450	7,151	5,880	7,151	5,998
52,450	52,500	7,162	5,886	7,162	6,004
52,500	52,550	7,173	5,892	7,173	6,010
52,550	52,600	7,184	5,898	7,184	6,016
52,600	52,650	7,195	5,904	7,195	6,022
52,650	52,700	7,206	5,910	7,206	6,028
52,700	52,750	7,217	5,916	7,217	6,034
52,750	52,800	7,228	5,922	7,228	6,040
52,800	52,850	7,239	5,928	7,239	6,046
52,850	52,900	7,250	5,934	7,250	6,052
52,900	52,950	7,261	5,940	7,261	6,058
52,950	53,000	7,272	5,946	7,272	6,064
53,000					
53,000	53,050	7,283	5,952	7,283	6,070
53,050	53,100	7,294	5,958	7,294	6,076
53,100	53,150	7,305	5,964	7,305	6,082
53,150	53,200	7,316	5,970	7,316	6,088
53,200	53,250	7,327	5,976	7,327	6,094
53,250	53,300	7,338	5,982	7,338	6,100
53,300	53,350	7,349	5,988	7,349	6,106
53,350	53,400	7,360	5,994	7,360	6,112
53,400	53,450	7,371	6,000	7,371	6,118
53,450	53,500	7,382	6,006	7,382	6,124
53,500	53,550	7,393	6,012	7,393	6,130
53,550	53,600	7,404	6,018	7,404	6,136
53,600	53,650	7,415	6,024	7,415	6,142
53,650	53,700	7,426	6,030	7,426	6,148
53,700	53,750	7,437	6,036	7,437	6,154
53,750	53,800	7,448	6,042	7,448	6,160
53,800	53,850	7,459	6,048	7,459	6,166
53,850	53,900	7,470	6,054	7,470	6,172
53,900	53,950	7,481	6,060	7,481	6,178
53,950	54,000	7,492	6,066	7,492	6,184

If line 15 (taxable income) is—		And you are—			
At least	But less than	Single	Married filing jointly *	Married filing sepa-rately	Head of a house-hold
		Your tax is—			
54,000					
54,000	54,050	7,503	6,072	7,503	6,190
54,050	54,100	7,514	6,078	7,514	6,196
54,100	54,150	7,525	6,084	7,525	6,202
54,150	54,200	7,536	6,090	7,536	6,208
54,200	54,250	7,547	6,096	7,547	6,214
54,250	54,300	7,558	6,102	7,558	6,220
54,300	54,350	7,569	6,108	7,569	6,226
54,350	54,400	7,580	6,114	7,580	6,232
54,400	54,450	7,591	6,120	7,591	6,238
54,450	54,500	7,602	6,126	7,602	6,244
54,500	54,550	7,613	6,132	7,613	6,250
54,550	54,600	7,624	6,138	7,624	6,256
54,600	54,650	7,635	6,144	7,635	6,262
54,650	54,700	7,646	6,150	7,646	6,268
54,700	54,750	7,657	6,156	7,657	6,274
54,750	54,800	7,668	6,162	7,668	6,280
54,800	54,850	7,679	6,168	7,679	6,286
54,850	54,900	7,690	6,174	7,690	6,292
54,900	54,950	7,701	6,180	7,701	6,298
54,950	55,000	7,712	6,186	7,712	6,304
55,000					
55,000	55,050	7,723	6,192	7,723	6,310
55,050	55,100	7,734	6,198	7,734	6,316
55,100	55,150	7,745	6,204	7,745	6,322
55,150	55,200	7,756	6,210	7,756	6,328
55,200	55,250	7,767	6,216	7,767	6,334
55,250	55,300	7,778	6,222	7,778	6,340
55,300	55,350	7,789	6,228	7,789	6,346
55,350	55,400	7,800	6,234	7,800	6,352
55,400	55,450	7,811	6,240	7,811	6,358
55,450	55,500	7,822	6,246	7,822	6,364
55,500	55,550	7,833	6,252	7,833	6,370
55,550	55,600	7,844	6,258	7,844	6,376
55,600	55,650	7,855	6,264	7,855	6,382
55,650	55,700	7,866	6,270	7,866	6,388
55,700	55,750	7,877	6,276	7,877	6,394
55,750	55,800	7,888	6,282	7,888	6,400
55,800	55,850	7,899	6,288	7,899	6,406
55,850	55,900	7,910	6,294	7,910	6,412
55,900	55,950	7,921	6,300	7,921	6,421
55,950	56,000	7,932	6,306	7,932	6,432
56,000					
56,000	56,050	7,943	6,312	7,943	6,443
56,050	56,100	7,954	6,318	7,954	6,454
56,100	56,150	7,965	6,324	7,965	6,465
56,150	56,200	7,976	6,330	7,976	6,476
56,200	56,250	7,987	6,336	7,987	6,487
56,250	56,300	7,998	6,342	7,998	6,498
56,300	56,350	8,009	6,348	8,009	6,509
56,350	56,400	8,020	6,354	8,020	6,520
56,400	56,450	8,031	6,360	8,031	6,531
56,450	56,500	8,042	6,366	8,042	6,542
56,500	56,550	8,053	6,372	8,053	6,553
56,550	56,600	8,064	6,378	8,064	6,564
56,600	56,650	8,075	6,384	8,075	6,575
56,650	56,700	8,086	6,390	8,086	6,586
56,700	56,750	8,097	6,396	8,097	6,597
56,750	56,800	8,108	6,402	8,108	6,608
56,800	56,850	8,119	6,408	8,119	6,619
56,850	56,900	8,130	6,414	8,130	6,630
56,900	56,950	8,141	6,420	8,141	6,641
56,950	57,000	8,152	6,426	8,152	6,652

(Continued)

* This column must also be used by a qualifying surviving spouse.

2022 Tax Table — *Continued*

57,000

If line 15 (taxable income) is— At least	But less than	And you are— Single	Married filing jointly *	Married filing separately	Head of a household
		Your tax is—			
57,000	57,050	8,163	6,432	8,163	6,663
57,050	57,100	8,174	6,438	8,174	6,674
57,100	57,150	8,185	6,444	8,185	6,685
57,150	57,200	8,196	6,450	8,196	6,696
57,200	57,250	8,207	6,456	8,207	6,707
57,250	57,300	8,218	6,462	8,218	6,718
57,300	57,350	8,229	6,468	8,229	6,729
57,350	57,400	8,240	6,474	8,240	6,740
57,400	57,450	8,251	6,480	8,251	6,751
57,450	57,500	8,262	6,486	8,262	6,762
57,500	57,550	8,273	6,492	8,273	6,773
57,550	57,600	8,284	6,498	8,284	6,784
57,600	57,650	8,295	6,504	8,295	6,795
57,650	57,700	8,306	6,510	8,306	6,806
57,700	57,750	8,317	6,516	8,317	6,817
57,750	57,800	8,328	6,522	8,328	6,828
57,800	57,850	8,339	6,528	8,339	6,839
57,850	57,900	8,350	6,534	8,350	6,850
57,900	57,950	8,361	6,540	8,361	6,861
57,950	58,000	8,372	6,546	8,372	6,872

58,000

At least	But less than	Single	Married filing jointly *	Married filing separately	Head of a household
58,000	58,050	8,383	6,552	8,383	6,883
58,050	58,100	8,394	6,558	8,394	6,894
58,100	58,150	8,405	6,564	8,405	6,905
58,150	58,200	8,416	6,570	8,416	6,916
58,200	58,250	8,427	6,576	8,427	6,927
58,250	58,300	8,438	6,582	8,438	6,938
58,300	58,350	8,449	6,588	8,449	6,949
58,350	58,400	8,460	6,594	8,460	6,960
58,400	58,450	8,471	6,600	8,471	6,971
58,450	58,500	8,482	6,606	8,482	6,982
58,500	58,550	8,493	6,612	8,493	6,993
58,550	58,600	8,504	6,618	8,504	7,004
58,600	58,650	8,515	6,624	8,515	7,015
58,650	58,700	8,526	6,630	8,526	7,026
58,700	58,750	8,537	6,636	8,537	7,037
58,750	58,800	8,548	6,642	8,548	7,048
58,800	58,850	8,559	6,648	8,559	7,059
58,850	58,900	8,570	6,654	8,570	7,070
58,900	58,950	8,581	6,660	8,581	7,081
58,950	59,000	8,592	6,666	8,592	7,092

59,000

At least	But less than	Single	Married filing jointly *	Married filing separately	Head of a household
59,000	59,050	8,603	6,672	8,603	7,103
59,050	59,100	8,614	6,678	8,614	7,114
59,100	59,150	8,625	6,684	8,625	7,125
59,150	59,200	8,636	6,690	8,636	7,136
59,200	59,250	8,647	6,696	8,647	7,147
59,250	59,300	8,658	6,702	8,658	7,158
59,300	59,350	8,669	6,708	8,669	7,169
59,350	59,400	8,680	6,714	8,680	7,180
59,400	59,450	8,691	6,720	8,691	7,191
59,450	59,500	8,702	6,726	8,702	7,202
59,500	59,550	8,713	6,732	8,713	7,213
59,550	59,600	8,724	6,738	8,724	7,224
59,600	59,650	8,735	6,744	8,735	7,235
59,650	59,700	8,746	6,750	8,746	7,246
59,700	59,750	8,757	6,756	8,757	7,257
59,750	59,800	8,768	6,762	8,768	7,268
59,800	59,850	8,779	6,768	8,779	7,279
59,850	59,900	8,790	6,774	8,790	7,290
59,900	59,950	8,801	6,780	8,801	7,301
59,950	60,000	8,812	6,786	8,812	7,312

60,000

If line 15 (taxable income) is— At least	But less than	And you are— Single	Married filing jointly *	Married filing separately	Head of a household
		Your tax is—			
60,000	60,050	8,823	6,792	8,823	7,323
60,050	60,100	8,834	6,798	8,834	7,334
60,100	60,150	8,845	6,804	8,845	7,345
60,150	60,200	8,856	6,810	8,856	7,356
60,200	60,250	8,867	6,816	8,867	7,367
60,250	60,300	8,878	6,822	8,878	7,378
60,300	60,350	8,889	6,828	8,889	7,389
60,350	60,400	8,900	6,834	8,900	7,400
60,400	60,450	8,911	6,840	8,911	7,411
60,450	60,500	8,922	6,846	8,922	7,422
60,500	60,550	8,933	6,852	8,933	7,433
60,550	60,600	8,944	6,858	8,944	7,444
60,600	60,650	8,955	6,864	8,955	7,455
60,650	60,700	8,966	6,870	8,966	7,466
60,700	60,750	8,977	6,876	8,977	7,477
60,750	60,800	8,988	6,882	8,988	7,488
60,800	60,850	8,999	6,888	8,999	7,499
60,850	60,900	9,010	6,894	9,010	7,510
60,900	60,950	9,021	6,900	9,021	7,521
60,950	61,000	9,032	6,906	9,032	7,532

61,000

At least	But less than	Single	Married filing jointly *	Married filing separately	Head of a household
61,000	61,050	9,043	6,912	9,043	7,543
61,050	61,100	9,054	6,918	9,054	7,554
61,100	61,150	9,065	6,924	9,065	7,565
61,150	61,200	9,076	6,930	9,076	7,576
61,200	61,250	9,087	6,936	9,087	7,587
61,250	61,300	9,098	6,942	9,098	7,598
61,300	61,350	9,109	6,948	9,109	7,609
61,350	61,400	9,120	6,954	9,120	7,620
61,400	61,450	9,131	6,960	9,131	7,631
61,450	61,500	9,142	6,966	9,142	7,642
61,500	61,550	9,153	6,972	9,153	7,653
61,550	61,600	9,164	6,978	9,164	7,664
61,600	61,650	9,175	6,984	9,175	7,675
61,650	61,700	9,186	6,990	9,186	7,686
61,700	61,750	9,197	6,996	9,197	7,697
61,750	61,800	9,208	7,002	9,208	7,708
61,800	61,850	9,219	7,008	9,219	7,719
61,850	61,900	9,230	7,014	9,230	7,730
61,900	61,950	9,241	7,020	9,241	7,741
61,950	62,000	9,252	7,026	9,252	7,752

62,000

At least	But less than	Single	Married filing jointly *	Married filing separately	Head of a household
62,000	62,050	9,263	7,032	9,263	7,763
62,050	62,100	9,274	7,038	9,274	7,774
62,100	62,150	9,285	7,044	9,285	7,785
62,150	62,200	9,296	7,050	9,296	7,796
62,200	62,250	9,307	7,056	9,307	7,807
62,250	62,300	9,318	7,062	9,318	7,818
62,300	62,350	9,329	7,068	9,329	7,829
62,350	62,400	9,340	7,074	9,340	7,840
62,400	62,450	9,351	7,080	9,351	7,851
62,450	62,500	9,362	7,086	9,362	7,862
62,500	62,550	9,373	7,092	9,373	7,873
62,550	62,600	9,384	7,098	9,384	7,884
62,600	62,650	9,395	7,104	9,395	7,895
62,650	62,700	9,406	7,110	9,406	7,906
62,700	62,750	9,417	7,116	9,417	7,917
62,750	62,800	9,428	7,122	9,428	7,928
62,800	62,850	9,439	7,128	9,439	7,939
62,850	62,900	9,450	7,134	9,450	7,950
62,900	62,950	9,461	7,140	9,461	7,961
62,950	63,000	9,472	7,146	9,472	7,972

63,000

If line 15 (taxable income) is— At least	But less than	And you are— Single	Married filing jointly *	Married filing separately	Head of a household
		Your tax is—			
63,000	63,050	9,483	7,152	9,483	7,983
63,050	63,100	9,494	7,158	9,494	7,994
63,100	63,150	9,505	7,164	9,505	8,005
63,150	63,200	9,516	7,170	9,516	8,016
63,200	63,250	9,527	7,176	9,527	8,027
63,250	63,300	9,538	7,182	9,538	8,038
63,300	63,350	9,549	7,188	9,549	8,049
63,350	63,400	9,560	7,194	9,560	8,060
63,400	63,450	9,571	7,200	9,571	8,071
63,450	63,500	9,582	7,206	9,582	8,082
63,500	63,550	9,593	7,212	9,593	8,093
63,550	63,600	9,604	7,218	9,604	8,104
63,600	63,650	9,615	7,224	9,615	8,115
63,650	63,700	9,626	7,230	9,626	8,126
63,700	63,750	9,637	7,236	9,637	8,137
63,750	63,800	9,648	7,242	9,648	8,148
63,800	63,850	9,659	7,248	9,659	8,159
63,850	63,900	9,670	7,254	9,670	8,170
63,900	63,950	9,681	7,260	9,681	8,181
63,950	64,000	9,692	7,266	9,692	8,192

64,000

At least	But less than	Single	Married filing jointly *	Married filing separately	Head of a household
64,000	64,050	9,703	7,272	9,703	8,203
64,050	64,100	9,714	7,278	9,714	8,214
64,100	64,150	9,725	7,284	9,725	8,225
64,150	64,200	9,736	7,290	9,736	8,236
64,200	64,250	9,747	7,296	9,747	8,247
64,250	64,300	9,758	7,302	9,758	8,258
64,300	64,350	9,769	7,308	9,769	8,269
64,350	64,400	9,780	7,314	9,780	8,280
64,400	64,450	9,791	7,320	9,791	8,291
64,450	64,500	9,802	7,326	9,802	8,302
64,500	64,550	9,813	7,332	9,813	8,313
64,550	64,600	9,824	7,338	9,824	8,324
64,600	64,650	9,835	7,344	9,835	8,335
64,650	64,700	9,846	7,350	9,846	8,346
64,700	64,750	9,857	7,356	9,857	8,357
64,750	64,800	9,868	7,362	9,868	8,368
64,800	64,850	9,879	7,368	9,879	8,379
64,850	64,900	9,890	7,374	9,890	8,390
64,900	64,950	9,901	7,380	9,901	8,401
64,950	65,000	9,912	7,386	9,912	8,412

65,000

At least	But less than	Single	Married filing jointly *	Married filing separately	Head of a household
65,000	65,050	9,923	7,392	9,923	8,423
65,050	65,100	9,934	7,398	9,934	8,434
65,100	65,150	9,945	7,404	9,945	8,445
65,150	65,200	9,956	7,410	9,956	8,456
65,200	65,250	9,967	7,416	9,967	8,467
65,250	65,300	9,978	7,422	9,978	8,478
65,300	65,350	9,989	7,428	9,989	8,489
65,350	65,400	10,000	7,434	10,000	8,500
65,400	65,450	10,011	7,440	10,011	8,511
65,450	65,500	10,022	7,446	10,022	8,522
65,500	65,550	10,033	7,452	10,033	8,533
65,550	65,600	10,044	7,458	10,044	8,544
65,600	65,650	10,055	7,464	10,055	8,555
65,650	65,700	10,066	7,470	10,066	8,566
65,700	65,750	10,077	7,476	10,077	8,577
65,750	65,800	10,088	7,482	10,088	8,588
65,800	65,850	10,099	7,488	10,099	8,599
65,850	65,900	10,110	7,494	10,110	8,610
65,900	65,950	10,121	7,500	10,121	8,621
65,950	66,000	10,132	7,506	10,132	8,632

(Continued)

* This column must also be used by a qualifying surviving spouse.

2022 Tax Table — *Continued*

If line 15 (taxable income) is— At least	But less than	Single	Married filing jointly *	Married filing separately	Head of a household
		Your tax is—			
66,000					
66,000	66,050	10,143	7,512	10,143	8,643
66,050	66,100	10,154	7,518	10,154	8,654
66,100	66,150	10,165	7,524	10,165	8,665
66,150	66,200	10,176	7,530	10,176	8,676
66,200	66,250	10,187	7,536	10,187	8,687
66,250	66,300	10,198	7,542	10,198	8,698
66,300	66,350	10,209	7,548	10,209	8,709
66,350	66,400	10,220	7,554	10,220	8,720
66,400	66,450	10,231	7,560	10,231	8,731
66,450	66,500	10,242	7,566	10,242	8,742
66,500	66,550	10,253	7,572	10,253	8,753
66,550	66,600	10,264	7,578	10,264	8,764
66,600	66,650	10,275	7,584	10,275	8,775
66,650	66,700	10,286	7,590	10,286	8,786
66,700	66,750	10,297	7,596	10,297	8,797
66,750	66,800	10,308	7,602	10,308	8,808
66,800	66,850	10,319	7,608	10,319	8,819
66,850	66,900	10,330	7,614	10,330	8,830
66,900	66,950	10,341	7,620	10,341	8,841
66,950	67,000	10,352	7,626	10,352	8,852
67,000					
67,000	67,050	10,363	7,632	10,363	8,863
67,050	67,100	10,374	7,638	10,374	8,874
67,100	67,150	10,385	7,644	10,385	8,885
67,150	67,200	10,396	7,650	10,396	8,896
67,200	67,250	10,407	7,656	10,407	8,907
67,250	67,300	10,418	7,662	10,418	8,918
67,300	67,350	10,429	7,668	10,429	8,929
67,350	67,400	10,440	7,674	10,440	8,940
67,400	67,450	10,451	7,680	10,451	8,951
67,450	67,500	10,462	7,686	10,462	8,962
67,500	67,550	10,473	7,692	10,473	8,973
67,550	67,600	10,484	7,698	10,484	8,984
67,600	67,650	10,495	7,704	10,495	8,995
67,650	67,700	10,506	7,710	10,506	9,006
67,700	67,750	10,517	7,716	10,517	9,017
67,750	67,800	10,528	7,722	10,528	9,028
67,800	67,850	10,539	7,728	10,539	9,039
67,850	67,900	10,550	7,734	10,550	9,050
67,900	67,950	10,561	7,740	10,561	9,061
67,950	68,000	10,572	7,746	10,572	9,072
68,000					
68,000	68,050	10,583	7,752	10,583	9,083
68,050	68,100	10,594	7,758	10,594	9,094
68,100	68,150	10,605	7,764	10,605	9,105
68,150	68,200	10,616	7,770	10,616	9,116
68,200	68,250	10,627	7,776	10,627	9,127
68,250	68,300	10,638	7,782	10,638	9,138
68,300	68,350	10,649	7,788	10,649	9,149
68,350	68,400	10,660	7,794	10,660	9,160
68,400	68,450	10,671	7,800	10,671	9,171
68,450	68,500	10,682	7,806	10,682	9,182
68,500	68,550	10,693	7,812	10,693	9,193
68,550	68,600	10,704	7,818	10,704	9,204
68,600	68,650	10,715	7,824	10,715	9,215
68,650	68,700	10,726	7,830	10,726	9,226
68,700	68,750	10,737	7,836	10,737	9,237
68,750	68,800	10,748	7,842	10,748	9,248
68,800	68,850	10,759	7,848	10,759	9,259
68,850	68,900	10,770	7,854	10,770	9,270
68,900	68,950	10,781	7,860	10,781	9,281
68,950	69,000	10,792	7,866	10,792	9,292

If line 15 (taxable income) is— At least	But less than	Single	Married filing jointly *	Married filing separately	Head of a household
		Your tax is—			
69,000					
69,000	69,050	10,803	7,872	10,803	9,303
69,050	69,100	10,814	7,878	10,814	9,314
69,100	69,150	10,825	7,884	10,825	9,325
69,150	69,200	10,836	7,890	10,836	9,336
69,200	69,250	10,847	7,896	10,847	9,347
69,250	69,300	10,858	7,902	10,858	9,358
69,300	69,350	10,869	7,908	10,869	9,369
69,350	69,400	10,880	7,914	10,880	9,380
69,400	69,450	10,891	7,920	10,891	9,391
69,450	69,500	10,902	7,926	10,902	9,402
69,500	69,550	10,913	7,932	10,913	9,413
69,550	69,600	10,924	7,938	10,924	9,424
69,600	69,650	10,935	7,944	10,935	9,435
69,650	69,700	10,946	7,950	10,946	9,446
69,700	69,750	10,957	7,956	10,957	9,457
69,750	69,800	10,968	7,962	10,968	9,468
69,800	69,850	10,979	7,968	10,979	9,479
69,850	69,900	10,990	7,974	10,990	9,490
69,900	69,950	11,001	7,980	11,001	9,501
69,950	70,000	11,012	7,986	11,012	9,512
70,000					
70,000	70,050	11,023	7,992	11,023	9,523
70,050	70,100	11,034	7,998	11,034	9,534
70,100	70,150	11,045	8,004	11,045	9,545
70,150	70,200	11,056	8,010	11,056	9,556
70,200	70,250	11,067	8,016	11,067	9,567
70,250	70,300	11,078	8,022	11,078	9,578
70,300	70,350	11,089	8,028	11,089	9,589
70,350	70,400	11,100	8,034	11,100	9,600
70,400	70,450	11,111	8,040	11,111	9,611
70,450	70,500	11,122	8,046	11,122	9,622
70,500	70,550	11,133	8,052	11,133	9,633
70,550	70,600	11,144	8,058	11,144	9,644
70,600	70,650	11,155	8,064	11,155	9,655
70,650	70,700	11,166	8,070	11,166	9,666
70,700	70,750	11,177	8,076	11,177	9,677
70,750	70,800	11,188	8,082	11,188	9,688
70,800	70,850	11,199	8,088	11,199	9,699
70,850	70,900	11,210	8,094	11,210	9,710
70,900	70,950	11,221	8,100	11,221	9,721
70,950	71,000	11,232	8,106	11,232	9,732
71,000					
71,000	71,050	11,243	8,112	11,243	9,743
71,050	71,100	11,254	8,118	11,254	9,754
71,100	71,150	11,265	8,124	11,265	9,765
71,150	71,200	11,276	8,130	11,276	9,776
71,200	71,250	11,287	8,136	11,287	9,787
71,250	71,300	11,298	8,142	11,298	9,798
71,300	71,350	11,309	8,148	11,309	9,809
71,350	71,400	11,320	8,154	11,320	9,820
71,400	71,450	11,331	8,160	11,331	9,831
71,450	71,500	11,342	8,166	11,342	9,842
71,500	71,550	11,353	8,172	11,353	9,853
71,550	71,600	11,364	8,178	11,364	9,864
71,600	71,650	11,375	8,184	11,375	9,875
71,650	71,700	11,386	8,190	11,386	9,886
71,700	71,750	11,397	8,196	11,397	9,897
71,750	71,800	11,408	8,202	11,408	9,908
71,800	71,850	11,419	8,208	11,419	9,919
71,850	71,900	11,430	8,214	11,430	9,930
71,900	71,950	11,441	8,220	11,441	9,941
71,950	72,000	11,452	8,226	11,452	9,952

If line 15 (taxable income) is— At least	But less than	Single	Married filing jointly *	Married filing separately	Head of a household
		Your tax is—			
72,000					
72,000	72,050	11,463	8,232	11,463	9,963
72,050	72,100	11,474	8,238	11,474	9,974
72,100	72,150	11,485	8,244	11,485	9,985
72,150	72,200	11,496	8,250	11,496	9,996
72,200	72,250	11,507	8,256	11,507	10,007
72,250	72,300	11,518	8,262	11,518	10,018
72,300	72,350	11,529	8,268	11,529	10,029
72,350	72,400	11,540	8,274	11,540	10,040
72,400	72,450	11,551	8,280	11,551	10,051
72,450	72,500	11,562	8,286	11,562	10,062
72,500	72,550	11,573	8,292	11,573	10,073
72,550	72,600	11,584	8,298	11,584	10,084
72,600	72,650	11,595	8,304	11,595	10,095
72,650	72,700	11,606	8,310	11,606	10,106
72,700	72,750	11,617	8,316	11,617	10,117
72,750	72,800	11,628	8,322	11,628	10,128
72,800	72,850	11,639	8,328	11,639	10,139
72,850	72,900	11,650	8,334	11,650	10,150
72,900	72,950	11,661	8,340	11,661	10,161
72,950	73,000	11,672	8,346	11,672	10,172
73,000					
73,000	73,050	11,683	8,352	11,683	10,183
73,050	73,100	11,694	8,358	11,694	10,194
73,100	73,150	11,705	8,364	11,705	10,205
73,150	73,200	11,716	8,370	11,716	10,216
73,200	73,250	11,727	8,376	11,727	10,227
73,250	73,300	11,738	8,382	11,738	10,238
73,300	73,350	11,749	8,388	11,749	10,249
73,350	73,400	11,760	8,394	11,760	10,260
73,400	73,450	11,771	8,400	11,771	10,271
73,450	73,500	11,782	8,406	11,782	10,282
73,500	73,550	11,793	8,412	11,793	10,293
73,550	73,600	11,804	8,418	11,804	10,304
73,600	73,650	11,815	8,424	11,815	10,315
73,650	73,700	11,826	8,430	11,826	10,326
73,700	73,750	11,837	8,436	11,837	10,337
73,750	73,800	11,848	8,442	11,848	10,348
73,800	73,850	11,859	8,448	11,859	10,359
73,850	73,900	11,870	8,454	11,870	10,370
73,900	73,950	11,881	8,460	11,881	10,381
73,950	74,000	11,892	8,466	11,892	10,392
74,000					
74,000	74,050	11,903	8,472	11,903	10,403
74,050	74,100	11,914	8,478	11,914	10,414
74,100	74,150	11,925	8,484	11,925	10,425
74,150	74,200	11,936	8,490	11,936	10,436
74,200	74,250	11,947	8,496	11,947	10,447
74,250	74,300	11,958	8,502	11,958	10,458
74,300	74,350	11,969	8,508	11,969	10,469
74,350	74,400	11,980	8,514	11,980	10,480
74,400	74,450	11,991	8,520	11,991	10,491
74,450	74,500	12,002	8,526	12,002	10,502
74,500	74,550	12,013	8,532	12,013	10,513
74,550	74,600	12,024	8,538	12,024	10,524
74,600	74,650	12,035	8,544	12,035	10,535
74,650	74,700	12,046	8,550	12,046	10,546
74,700	74,750	12,057	8,556	12,057	10,557
74,750	74,800	12,068	8,562	12,068	10,568
74,800	74,850	12,079	8,568	12,079	10,579
74,850	74,900	12,090	8,574	12,090	10,590
74,900	74,950	12,101	8,580	12,101	10,601
74,950	75,000	12,112	8,586	12,112	10,612

(Continued)

* This column must also be used by a qualifying surviving spouse.

2022 Tax Table — *Continued*

If line 15 (taxable income) is—		And you are—			
At least	But less than	Single	Married filing jointly *	Married filing separately	Head of a household
		Your tax is—			
75,000					
75,000	75,050	12,123	8,592	12,123	10,623
75,050	75,100	12,134	8,598	12,134	10,634
75,100	75,150	12,145	8,604	12,145	10,645
75,150	75,200	12,156	8,610	12,156	10,656
75,200	75,250	12,167	8,616	12,167	10,667
75,250	75,300	12,178	8,622	12,178	10,678
75,300	75,350	12,189	8,628	12,189	10,689
75,350	75,400	12,200	8,634	12,200	10,700
75,400	75,450	12,211	8,640	12,211	10,711
75,450	75,500	12,222	8,646	12,222	10,722
75,500	75,550	12,233	8,652	12,233	10,733
75,550	75,600	12,244	8,658	12,244	10,744
75,600	75,650	12,255	8,664	12,255	10,755
75,650	75,700	12,266	8,670	12,266	10,766
75,700	75,750	12,277	8,676	12,277	10,777
75,750	75,800	12,288	8,682	12,288	10,788
75,800	75,850	12,299	8,688	12,299	10,799
75,850	75,900	12,310	8,694	12,310	10,810
75,900	75,950	12,321	8,700	12,321	10,821
75,950	76,000	12,332	8,706	12,332	10,832
76,000					
76,000	76,050	12,343	8,712	12,343	10,843
76,050	76,100	12,354	8,718	12,354	10,854
76,100	76,150	12,365	8,724	12,365	10,865
76,150	76,200	12,376	8,730	12,376	10,876
76,200	76,250	12,387	8,736	12,387	10,887
76,250	76,300	12,398	8,742	12,398	10,898
76,300	76,350	12,409	8,748	12,409	10,909
76,350	76,400	12,420	8,754	12,420	10,920
76,400	76,450	12,431	8,760	12,431	10,931
76,450	76,500	12,442	8,766	12,442	10,942
76,500	76,550	12,453	8,772	12,453	10,953
76,550	76,600	12,464	8,778	12,464	10,964
76,600	76,650	12,475	8,784	12,475	10,975
76,650	76,700	12,486	8,790	12,486	10,986
76,700	76,750	12,497	8,796	12,497	10,997
76,750	76,800	12,508	8,802	12,508	11,008
76,800	76,850	12,519	8,808	12,519	11,019
76,850	76,900	12,530	8,814	12,530	11,030
76,900	76,950	12,541	8,820	12,541	11,041
76,950	77,000	12,552	8,826	12,552	11,052
77,000					
77,000	77,050	12,563	8,832	12,563	11,063
77,050	77,100	12,574	8,838	12,574	11,074
77,100	77,150	12,585	8,844	12,585	11,085
77,150	77,200	12,596	8,850	12,596	11,096
77,200	77,250	12,607	8,856	12,607	11,107
77,250	77,300	12,618	8,862	12,618	11,118
77,300	77,350	12,629	8,868	12,629	11,129
77,350	77,400	12,640	8,874	12,640	11,140
77,400	77,450	12,651	8,880	12,651	11,151
77,450	77,500	12,662	8,886	12,662	11,162
77,500	77,550	12,673	8,892	12,673	11,173
77,550	77,600	12,684	8,898	12,684	11,184
77,600	77,650	12,695	8,904	12,695	11,195
77,650	77,700	12,706	8,910	12,706	11,206
77,700	77,750	12,717	8,916	12,717	11,217
77,750	77,800	12,728	8,922	12,728	11,228
77,800	77,850	12,739	8,928	12,739	11,239
77,850	77,900	12,750	8,934	12,750	11,250
77,900	77,950	12,761	8,940	12,761	11,261
77,950	78,000	12,772	8,946	12,772	11,272
78,000					
78,000	78,050	12,783	8,952	12,783	11,283
78,050	78,100	12,794	8,958	12,794	11,294
78,100	78,150	12,805	8,964	12,805	11,305
78,150	78,200	12,816	8,970	12,816	11,316
78,200	78,250	12,827	8,976	12,827	11,327
78,250	78,300	12,838	8,982	12,838	11,338
78,300	78,350	12,849	8,988	12,849	11,349
78,350	78,400	12,860	8,994	12,860	11,360
78,400	78,450	12,871	9,000	12,871	11,371
78,450	78,500	12,882	9,006	12,882	11,382
78,500	78,550	12,893	9,012	12,893	11,393
78,550	78,600	12,904	9,018	12,904	11,404
78,600	78,650	12,915	9,024	12,915	11,415
78,650	78,700	12,926	9,030	12,926	11,426
78,700	78,750	12,937	9,036	12,937	11,437
78,750	78,800	12,948	9,042	12,948	11,448
78,800	78,850	12,959	9,048	12,959	11,459
78,850	78,900	12,970	9,054	12,970	11,470
78,900	78,950	12,981	9,060	12,981	11,481
78,950	79,000	12,992	9,066	12,992	11,492
79,000					
79,000	79,050	13,003	9,072	13,003	11,503
79,050	79,100	13,014	9,078	13,014	11,514
79,100	79,150	13,025	9,084	13,025	11,525
79,150	79,200	13,036	9,090	13,036	11,536
79,200	79,250	13,047	9,096	13,047	11,547
79,250	79,300	13,058	9,102	13,058	11,558
79,300	79,350	13,069	9,108	13,069	11,569
79,350	79,400	13,080	9,114	13,080	11,580
79,400	79,450	13,091	9,120	13,091	11,591
79,450	79,500	13,102	9,126	13,102	11,602
79,500	79,550	13,113	9,132	13,113	11,613
79,550	79,600	13,124	9,138	13,124	11,624
79,600	79,650	13,135	9,144	13,135	11,635
79,650	79,700	13,146	9,150	13,146	11,646
79,700	79,750	13,157	9,156	13,157	11,657
79,750	79,800	13,168	9,162	13,168	11,668
79,800	79,850	13,179	9,168	13,179	11,679
79,850	79,900	13,190	9,174	13,190	11,690
79,900	79,950	13,201	9,180	13,201	11,701
79,950	80,000	13,212	9,186	13,212	11,712
80,000					
80,000	80,050	13,223	9,192	13,223	11,723
80,050	80,100	13,234	9,198	13,234	11,734
80,100	80,150	13,245	9,204	13,245	11,745
80,150	80,200	13,256	9,210	13,256	11,756
80,200	80,250	13,267	9,216	13,267	11,767
80,250	80,300	13,278	9,222	13,278	11,778
80,300	80,350	13,289	9,228	13,289	11,789
80,350	80,400	13,300	9,234	13,300	11,800
80,400	80,450	13,311	9,240	13,311	11,811
80,450	80,500	13,322	9,246	13,322	11,822
80,500	80,550	13,333	9,252	13,333	11,833
80,550	80,600	13,344	9,258	13,344	11,844
80,600	80,650	13,355	9,264	13,355	11,855
80,650	80,700	13,366	9,270	13,366	11,866
80,700	80,750	13,377	9,276	13,377	11,877
80,750	80,800	13,388	9,282	13,388	11,888
80,800	80,850	13,399	9,288	13,399	11,899
80,850	80,900	13,410	9,294	13,410	11,910
80,900	80,950	13,421	9,300	13,421	11,921
80,950	81,000	13,432	9,306	13,432	11,932
81,000					
81,000	81,050	13,443	9,312	13,443	11,943
81,050	81,100	13,454	9,318	13,454	11,954
81,100	81,150	13,465	9,324	13,465	11,965
81,150	81,200	13,476	9,330	13,476	11,976
81,200	81,250	13,487	9,336	13,487	11,987
81,250	81,300	13,498	9,342	13,498	11,998
81,300	81,350	13,509	9,348	13,509	12,009
81,350	81,400	13,520	9,354	13,520	12,020
81,400	81,450	13,531	9,360	13,531	12,031
81,450	81,500	13,542	9,366	13,542	12,042
81,500	81,550	13,553	9,372	13,553	12,053
81,550	81,600	13,564	9,378	13,564	12,064
81,600	81,650	13,575	9,384	13,575	12,075
81,650	81,700	13,586	9,390	13,586	12,086
81,700	81,750	13,597	9,396	13,597	12,097
81,750	81,800	13,608	9,402	13,608	12,108
81,800	81,850	13,619	9,408	13,619	12,119
81,850	81,900	13,630	9,414	13,630	12,130
81,900	81,950	13,641	9,420	13,641	12,141
81,950	82,000	13,652	9,426	13,652	12,152
82,000					
82,000	82,050	13,663	9,432	13,663	12,163
82,050	82,100	13,674	9,438	13,674	12,174
82,100	82,150	13,685	9,444	13,685	12,185
82,150	82,200	13,696	9,450	13,696	12,196
82,200	82,250	13,707	9,456	13,707	12,207
82,250	82,300	13,718	9,462	13,718	12,218
82,300	82,350	13,729	9,468	13,729	12,229
82,350	82,400	13,740	9,474	13,740	12,240
82,400	82,450	13,751	9,480	13,751	12,251
82,450	82,500	13,762	9,486	13,762	12,262
82,500	82,550	13,773	9,492	13,773	12,273
82,550	82,600	13,784	9,498	13,784	12,284
82,600	82,650	13,795	9,504	13,795	12,295
82,650	82,700	13,806	9,510	13,806	12,306
82,700	82,750	13,817	9,516	13,817	12,317
82,750	82,800	13,828	9,522	13,828	12,328
82,800	82,850	13,839	9,528	13,839	12,339
82,850	82,900	13,850	9,534	13,850	12,350
82,900	82,950	13,861	9,540	13,861	12,361
82,950	83,000	13,872	9,546	13,872	12,372
83,000					
83,000	83,050	13,883	9,552	13,883	12,383
83,050	83,100	13,894	9,558	13,894	12,394
83,100	83,150	13,905	9,564	13,905	12,405
83,150	83,200	13,916	9,570	13,916	12,416
83,200	83,250	13,927	9,576	13,927	12,427
83,250	83,300	13,938	9,582	13,938	12,438
83,300	83,350	13,949	9,588	13,949	12,449
83,350	83,400	13,960	9,594	13,960	12,460
83,400	83,450	13,971	9,600	13,971	12,471
83,450	83,500	13,982	9,606	13,982	12,482
83,500	83,550	13,993	9,612	13,993	12,493
83,550	83,600	14,004	9,621	14,004	12,504
83,600	83,650	14,015	9,632	14,015	12,515
83,650	83,700	14,026	9,643	14,026	12,526
83,700	83,750	14,037	9,654	14,037	12,537
83,750	83,800	14,048	9,665	14,048	12,548
83,800	83,850	14,059	9,676	14,059	12,559
83,850	83,900	14,070	9,687	14,070	12,570
83,900	83,950	14,081	9,698	14,081	12,581
83,950	84,000	14,092	9,709	14,092	12,592

(Continued)

* This column must also be used by a qualifying surviving spouse.

2022 Tax Table — *Continued*

If line 15 (taxable income) is—		And you are—			
At least	But less than	Single	Married filing jointly *	Married filing separately	Head of a household
		Your tax is—			
84,000					
84,000	84,050	14,103	9,720	14,103	12,603
84,050	84,100	14,114	9,731	14,114	12,614
84,100	84,150	14,125	9,742	14,125	12,625
84,150	84,200	14,136	9,753	14,136	12,636
84,200	84,250	14,147	9,764	14,147	12,647
84,250	84,300	14,158	9,775	14,158	12,658
84,300	84,350	14,169	9,786	14,169	12,669
84,350	84,400	14,180	9,797	14,180	12,680
84,400	84,450	14,191	9,808	14,191	12,691
84,450	84,500	14,202	9,819	14,202	12,702
84,500	84,550	14,213	9,830	14,213	12,713
84,550	84,600	14,224	9,841	14,224	12,724
84,600	84,650	14,235	9,852	14,235	12,735
84,650	84,700	14,246	9,863	14,246	12,746
84,700	84,750	14,257	9,874	14,257	12,757
84,750	84,800	14,268	9,885	14,268	12,768
84,800	84,850	14,279	9,896	14,279	12,779
84,850	84,900	14,290	9,907	14,290	12,790
84,900	84,950	14,301	9,918	14,301	12,801
84,950	85,000	14,312	9,929	14,312	12,812
85,000					
85,000	85,050	14,323	9,940	14,323	12,823
85,050	85,100	14,334	9,951	14,334	12,834
85,100	85,150	14,345	9,962	14,345	12,845
85,150	85,200	14,356	9,973	14,356	12,856
85,200	85,250	14,367	9,984	14,367	12,867
85,250	85,300	14,378	9,995	14,378	12,878
85,300	85,350	14,389	10,006	14,389	12,889
85,350	85,400	14,400	10,017	14,400	12,900
85,400	85,450	14,411	10,028	14,411	12,911
85,450	85,500	14,422	10,039	14,422	12,922
85,500	85,550	14,433	10,050	14,433	12,933
85,550	85,600	14,444	10,061	14,444	12,944
85,600	85,650	14,455	10,072	14,455	12,955
85,650	85,700	14,466	10,083	14,466	12,966
85,700	85,750	14,477	10,094	14,477	12,977
85,750	85,800	14,488	10,105	14,488	12,988
85,800	85,850	14,499	10,116	14,499	12,999
85,850	85,900	14,510	10,127	14,510	13,010
85,900	85,950	14,521	10,138	14,521	13,021
85,950	86,000	14,532	10,149	14,532	13,032
86,000					
86,000	86,050	14,543	10,160	14,543	13,043
86,050	86,100	14,554	10,171	14,554	13,054
86,100	86,150	14,565	10,182	14,565	13,065
86,150	86,200	14,576	10,193	14,576	13,076
86,200	86,250	14,587	10,204	14,587	13,087
86,250	86,300	14,598	10,215	14,598	13,098
86,300	86,350	14,609	10,226	14,609	13,109
86,350	86,400	14,620	10,237	14,620	13,120
86,400	86,450	14,631	10,248	14,631	13,131
86,450	86,500	14,642	10,259	14,642	13,142
86,500	86,550	14,653	10,270	14,653	13,153
86,550	86,600	14,664	10,281	14,664	13,164
86,600	86,650	14,675	10,292	14,675	13,175
86,650	86,700	14,686	10,303	14,686	13,186
86,700	86,750	14,697	10,314	14,697	13,197
86,750	86,800	14,708	10,325	14,708	13,208
86,800	86,850	14,719	10,336	14,719	13,219
86,850	86,900	14,730	10,347	14,730	13,230
86,900	86,950	14,741	10,358	14,741	13,241
86,950	87,000	14,752	10,369	14,752	13,252
87,000					
87,000	87,050	14,763	10,380	14,763	13,263
87,050	87,100	14,774	10,391	14,774	13,274
87,100	87,150	14,785	10,402	14,785	13,285
87,150	87,200	14,796	10,413	14,796	13,296
87,200	87,250	14,807	10,424	14,807	13,307
87,250	87,300	14,818	10,435	14,818	13,318
87,300	87,350	14,829	10,446	14,829	13,329
87,350	87,400	14,840	10,457	14,840	13,340
87,400	87,450	14,851	10,468	14,851	13,351
87,450	87,500	14,862	10,479	14,862	13,362
87,500	87,550	14,873	10,490	14,873	13,373
87,550	87,600	14,884	10,501	14,884	13,384
87,600	87,650	14,895	10,512	14,895	13,395
87,650	87,700	14,906	10,523	14,906	13,406
87,700	87,750	14,917	10,534	14,917	13,417
87,750	87,800	14,928	10,545	14,928	13,428
87,800	87,850	14,939	10,556	14,939	13,439
87,850	87,900	14,950	10,567	14,950	13,450
87,900	87,950	14,961	10,578	14,961	13,461
87,950	88,000	14,972	10,589	14,972	13,472
88,000					
88,000	88,050	14,983	10,600	14,983	13,483
88,050	88,100	14,994	10,611	14,994	13,494
88,100	88,150	15,005	10,622	15,005	13,505
88,150	88,200	15,016	10,633	15,016	13,516
88,200	88,250	15,027	10,644	15,027	13,527
88,250	88,300	15,038	10,655	15,038	13,538
88,300	88,350	15,049	10,666	15,049	13,549
88,350	88,400	15,060	10,677	15,060	13,560
88,400	88,450	15,071	10,688	15,071	13,571
88,450	88,500	15,082	10,699	15,082	13,582
88,500	88,550	15,093	10,710	15,093	13,593
88,550	88,600	15,104	10,721	15,104	13,604
88,600	88,650	15,115	10,732	15,115	13,615
88,650	88,700	15,126	10,743	15,126	13,626
88,700	88,750	15,137	10,754	15,137	13,637
88,750	88,800	15,148	10,765	15,148	13,648
88,800	88,850	15,159	10,776	15,159	13,659
88,850	88,900	15,170	10,787	15,170	13,670
88,900	88,950	15,181	10,798	15,181	13,681
88,950	89,000	15,192	10,809	15,192	13,692
89,000					
89,000	89,050	15,203	10,820	15,203	13,703
89,050	89,100	15,214	10,831	15,214	13,714
89,100	89,150	15,226	10,842	15,226	13,726
89,150	89,200	15,238	10,853	15,238	13,738
89,200	89,250	15,250	10,864	15,250	13,750
89,250	89,300	15,262	10,875	15,262	13,762
89,300	89,350	15,274	10,886	15,274	13,774
89,350	89,400	15,286	10,897	15,286	13,786
89,400	89,450	15,298	10,908	15,298	13,798
89,450	89,500	15,310	10,919	15,310	13,810
89,500	89,550	15,322	10,930	15,322	13,822
89,550	89,600	15,334	10,941	15,334	13,834
89,600	89,650	15,346	10,952	15,346	13,846
89,650	89,700	15,358	10,963	15,358	13,858
89,700	89,750	15,370	10,974	15,370	13,870
89,750	89,800	15,382	10,985	15,382	13,882
89,800	89,850	15,394	10,996	15,394	13,894
89,850	89,900	15,406	11,007	15,406	13,906
89,900	89,950	15,418	11,018	15,418	13,918
89,950	90,000	15,430	11,029	15,430	13,930
90,000					
90,000	90,050	15,442	11,040	15,442	13,942
90,050	90,100	15,454	11,051	15,454	13,954
90,100	90,150	15,466	11,062	15,466	13,966
90,150	90,200	15,478	11,073	15,478	13,978
90,200	90,250	15,490	11,084	15,490	13,990
90,250	90,300	15,502	11,095	15,502	14,002
90,300	90,350	15,514	11,106	15,514	14,014
90,350	90,400	15,526	11,117	15,526	14,026
90,400	90,450	15,538	11,128	15,538	14,038
90,450	90,500	15,550	11,139	15,550	14,050
90,500	90,550	15,562	11,150	15,562	14,062
90,550	90,600	15,574	11,161	15,574	14,074
90,600	90,650	15,586	11,172	15,586	14,086
90,650	90,700	15,598	11,183	15,598	14,098
90,700	90,750	15,610	11,194	15,610	14,110
90,750	90,800	15,622	11,205	15,622	14,122
90,800	90,850	15,634	11,216	15,634	14,134
90,850	90,900	15,646	11,227	15,646	14,146
90,900	90,950	15,658	11,238	15,658	14,158
90,950	91,000	15,670	11,249	15,670	14,170
91,000					
91,000	91,050	15,682	11,260	15,682	14,182
91,050	91,100	15,694	11,271	15,694	14,194
91,100	91,150	15,706	11,282	15,706	14,206
91,150	91,200	15,718	11,293	15,718	14,218
91,200	91,250	15,730	11,304	15,730	14,230
91,250	91,300	15,742	11,315	15,742	14,242
91,300	91,350	15,754	11,326	15,754	14,254
91,350	91,400	15,766	11,337	15,766	14,266
91,400	91,450	15,778	11,348	15,778	14,278
91,450	91,500	15,790	11,359	15,790	14,290
91,500	91,550	15,802	11,370	15,802	14,302
91,550	91,600	15,814	11,381	15,814	14,314
91,600	91,650	15,826	11,392	15,826	14,326
91,650	91,700	15,838	11,403	15,838	14,338
91,700	91,750	15,850	11,414	15,850	14,350
91,750	91,800	15,862	11,425	15,862	14,362
91,800	91,850	15,874	11,436	15,874	14,374
91,850	91,900	15,886	11,447	15,886	14,386
91,900	91,950	15,898	11,458	15,898	14,398
91,950	92,000	15,910	11,469	15,910	14,410
92,000					
92,000	92,050	15,922	11,480	15,922	14,422
92,050	92,100	15,934	11,491	15,934	14,434
92,100	92,150	15,946	11,502	15,946	14,446
92,150	92,200	15,958	11,513	15,958	14,458
92,200	92,250	15,970	11,524	15,970	14,470
92,250	92,300	15,982	11,535	15,982	14,482
92,300	92,350	15,994	11,546	15,994	14,494
92,350	92,400	16,006	11,557	16,006	14,506
92,400	92,450	16,018	11,568	16,018	14,518
92,450	92,500	16,030	11,579	16,030	14,530
92,500	92,550	16,042	11,590	16,042	14,542
92,550	92,600	16,054	11,601	16,054	14,554
92,600	92,650	16,066	11,612	16,066	14,566
92,650	92,700	16,078	11,623	16,078	14,578
92,700	92,750	16,090	11,634	16,090	14,590
92,750	92,800	16,102	11,645	16,102	14,602
92,800	92,850	16,114	11,656	16,114	14,614
92,850	92,900	16,126	11,667	16,126	14,626
92,900	92,950	16,138	11,678	16,138	14,638
92,950	93,000	16,150	11,689	16,150	14,650

(Continued)

* This column must also be used by a qualifying surviving spouse.

2022 Tax Table — *Continued*

If line 15 (taxable income) is—		And you are—			
At least	But less than	Single	Married filing jointly *	Married filing separately	Head of a household
		Your tax is—			
93,000					
93,000	93,050	16,162	11,700	16,162	14,662
93,050	93,100	16,174	11,711	16,174	14,674
93,100	93,150	16,186	11,722	16,186	14,686
93,150	93,200	16,198	11,733	16,198	14,698
93,200	93,250	16,210	11,744	16,210	14,710
93,250	93,300	16,222	11,755	16,222	14,722
93,300	93,350	16,234	11,766	16,234	14,734
93,350	93,400	16,246	11,777	16,246	14,746
93,400	93,450	16,258	11,788	16,258	14,758
93,450	93,500	16,270	11,799	16,270	14,770
93,500	93,550	16,282	11,810	16,282	14,782
93,550	93,600	16,294	11,821	16,294	14,794
93,600	93,650	16,306	11,832	16,306	14,806
93,650	93,700	16,318	11,843	16,318	14,818
93,700	93,750	16,330	11,854	16,330	14,830
93,750	93,800	16,342	11,865	16,342	14,842
93,800	93,850	16,354	11,876	16,354	14,854
93,850	93,900	16,366	11,887	16,366	14,866
93,900	93,950	16,378	11,898	16,378	14,878
93,950	94,000	16,390	11,909	16,390	14,890
94,000					
94,000	94,050	16,402	11,920	16,402	14,902
94,050	94,100	16,414	11,931	16,414	14,914
94,100	94,150	16,426	11,942	16,426	14,926
94,150	94,200	16,438	11,953	16,438	14,938
94,200	94,250	16,450	11,964	16,450	14,950
94,250	94,300	16,462	11,975	16,462	14,962
94,300	94,350	16,474	11,986	16,474	14,974
94,350	94,400	16,486	11,997	16,486	14,986
94,400	94,450	16,498	12,008	16,498	14,998
94,450	94,500	16,510	12,019	16,510	15,010
94,500	94,550	16,522	12,030	16,522	15,022
94,550	94,600	16,534	12,041	16,534	15,034
94,600	94,650	16,546	12,052	16,546	15,046
94,650	94,700	16,558	12,063	16,558	15,058
94,700	94,750	16,570	12,074	16,570	15,070
94,750	94,800	16,582	12,085	16,582	15,082
94,800	94,850	16,594	12,096	16,594	15,094
94,850	94,900	16,606	12,107	16,606	15,106
94,900	94,950	16,618	12,118	16,618	15,118
94,950	95,000	16,630	12,129	16,630	15,130
95,000					
95,000	95,050	16,642	12,140	16,642	15,142
95,050	95,100	16,654	12,151	16,654	15,154
95,100	95,150	16,666	12,162	16,666	15,166
95,150	95,200	16,678	12,173	16,678	15,178
95,200	95,250	16,690	12,184	16,690	15,190
95,250	95,300	16,702	12,195	16,702	15,202
95,300	95,350	16,714	12,206	16,714	15,214
95,350	95,400	16,726	12,217	16,726	15,226
95,400	95,450	16,738	12,228	16,738	15,238
95,450	95,500	16,750	12,239	16,750	15,250
95,500	95,550	16,762	12,250	16,762	15,262
95,550	95,600	16,774	12,261	16,774	15,274
95,600	95,650	16,786	12,272	16,786	15,286
95,650	95,700	16,798	12,283	16,798	15,298
95,700	95,750	16,810	12,294	16,810	15,310
95,750	95,800	16,822	12,305	16,822	15,322
95,800	95,850	16,834	12,316	16,834	15,334
95,850	95,900	16,846	12,327	16,846	15,346
95,900	95,950	16,858	12,338	16,858	15,358
95,950	96,000	16,870	12,349	16,870	15,370
96,000					
96,000	96,050	16,882	12,360	16,882	15,382
96,050	96,100	16,894	12,371	16,894	15,394
96,100	96,150	16,906	12,382	16,906	15,406
96,150	96,200	16,918	12,393	16,918	15,418
96,200	96,250	16,930	12,404	16,930	15,430
96,250	96,300	16,942	12,415	16,942	15,442
96,300	96,350	16,954	12,426	16,954	15,454
96,350	96,400	16,966	12,437	16,966	15,466
96,400	96,450	16,978	12,448	16,978	15,478
96,450	96,500	16,990	12,459	16,990	15,490
96,500	96,550	17,002	12,470	17,002	15,502
96,550	96,600	17,014	12,481	17,014	15,514
96,600	96,650	17,026	12,492	17,026	15,526
96,650	96,700	17,038	12,503	17,038	15,538
96,700	96,750	17,050	12,514	17,050	15,550
96,750	96,800	17,062	12,525	17,062	15,562
96,800	96,850	17,074	12,536	17,074	15,574
96,850	96,900	17,086	12,547	17,086	15,586
96,900	96,950	17,098	12,558	17,098	15,598
96,950	97,000	17,110	12,569	17,110	15,610
97,000					
97,000	97,050	17,122	12,580	17,122	15,622
97,050	97,100	17,134	12,591	17,134	15,634
97,100	97,150	17,146	12,602	17,146	15,646
97,150	97,200	17,158	12,613	17,158	15,658
97,200	97,250	17,170	12,624	17,170	15,670
97,250	97,300	17,182	12,635	17,182	15,682
97,300	97,350	17,194	12,646	17,194	15,694
97,350	97,400	17,206	12,657	17,206	15,706
97,400	97,450	17,218	12,668	17,218	15,718
97,450	97,500	17,230	12,679	17,230	15,730
97,500	97,550	17,242	12,690	17,242	15,742
97,550	97,600	17,254	12,701	17,254	15,754
97,600	97,650	17,266	12,712	17,266	15,766
97,650	97,700	17,278	12,723	17,278	15,778
97,700	97,750	17,290	12,734	17,290	15,790
97,750	97,800	17,302	12,745	17,302	15,802
97,800	97,850	17,314	12,756	17,314	15,814
97,850	97,900	17,326	12,767	17,326	15,826
97,900	97,950	17,338	12,778	17,338	15,838
97,950	98,000	17,350	12,789	17,350	15,850
98,000					
98,000	98,050	17,362	12,800	17,362	15,862
98,050	98,100	17,374	12,811	17,374	15,874
98,100	98,150	17,386	12,822	17,386	15,886
98,150	98,200	17,398	12,833	17,398	15,898
98,200	98,250	17,410	12,844	17,410	15,910
98,250	98,300	17,422	12,855	17,422	15,922
98,300	98,350	17,434	12,866	17,434	15,934
98,350	98,400	17,446	12,877	17,446	15,946
98,400	98,450	17,458	12,888	17,458	15,958
98,450	98,500	17,470	12,899	17,470	15,970
98,500	98,550	17,482	12,910	17,482	15,982
98,550	98,600	17,494	12,921	17,494	15,994
98,600	98,650	17,506	12,932	17,506	16,006
98,650	98,700	17,518	12,943	17,518	16,018
98,700	98,750	17,530	12,954	17,530	16,030
98,750	98,800	17,542	12,965	17,542	16,042
98,800	98,850	17,554	12,976	17,554	16,054
98,850	98,900	17,566	12,987	17,566	16,066
98,900	98,950	17,578	12,998	17,578	16,078
98,950	99,000	17,590	13,009	17,590	16,090
99,000					
99,000	99,050	17,602	13,020	17,602	16,102
99,050	99,100	17,614	13,031	17,614	16,114
99,100	99,150	17,626	13,042	17,626	16,126
99,150	99,200	17,638	13,053	17,638	16,138
99,200	99,250	17,650	13,064	17,650	16,150
99,250	99,300	17,662	13,075	17,662	16,162
99,300	99,350	17,674	13,086	17,674	16,174
99,350	99,400	17,686	13,097	17,686	16,186
99,400	99,450	17,698	13,108	17,698	16,198
99,450	99,500	17,710	13,119	17,710	16,210
99,500	99,550	17,722	13,130	17,722	16,222
99,550	99,600	17,734	13,141	17,734	16,234
99,600	99,650	17,746	13,152	17,746	16,246
99,650	99,700	17,758	13,163	17,758	16,258
99,700	99,750	17,770	13,174	17,770	16,270
99,750	99,800	17,782	13,185	17,782	16,282
99,800	99,850	17,794	13,196	17,794	16,294
99,850	99,900	17,806	13,207	17,806	16,306
99,900	99,950	17,818	13,218	17,818	16,318
99,950	100,000	17,830	13,229	17,830	16,330

$100,000 or over use the Tax Computation Worksheet

* This column must also be used by a qualifying surviving spouse.

Earned Income Credit Table

CONTENTS

Worksheet A—2022 EIC—Line 27*

Keep for Your Records 

Before you begin: √ Be sure you are using the correct worksheet. Use this worksheet only if you answered "No" to Step 5, question 2. Otherwise, use Worksheet B.

Part 1

All Filers Using Worksheet A

1. Enter your earned income from Step 5. [1 ____]

2. Look up the amount on line 1 above in the EIC Table (right after Worksheet B) to find the credit. Be sure you use the correct column for your filing status and the number of children you have. Enter the credit here. [2 ____]

   If line 2 is zero, STOP You can't take the credit. Enter "No" on the dotted line next to Form 1040 or 1040-SR, line 27.

3. Enter the amount from Form 1040 or 1040-SR, line 11. [3 ____]

4. Are the amounts on lines 3 and 1 the same?

   ☐ **Yes.** Skip line 5; enter the amount from line 2 on line 6.

   ☐ **No.** Go to line 5.

Part 2

Filers Who Answered "No" on Line 4

5. If you have:
   - No qualifying children, is the amount on line 3 less than $9,200 ($15,300 if married filing jointly)?
   - 1 or more qualifying children, is the amount on line 3 less than $20,150 ($26,300 if married filing jointly)?

   ☐ **Yes.** Leave line 5 blank; enter the amount from line 2 on line 6.

   ☐ **No.** Look up the amount on line 3 in the EIC Table to find the credit. Be sure you use the correct column for your filing status and the number of children you have. Enter the credit here. [5 ____]
   Look at the amounts on lines 5 and 2.
   Then, enter the **smaller** amount on line 6.

Part 3

Your Earned Income Credit

6. **This is your earned income credit.** [6 ____]

   Enter this amount on Form 1040 or 1040-SR, line 27.

Reminder—

√ If you have a qualifying child, complete and attach Schedule EIC.

1040 or 1040-SR | EIC | 1040 or 1040-SR

CAUTION *If your EIC for a year after 1996 was reduced or disallowed, see* Form 8862, who must file, *earlier, to find out if you must file Form 8862 to take the credit for 2022.*

*Download the latest version of this worksheet from the Form 1040 Instructions available at www.irs.gov. The 2022 worksheet was not available as we went to print. This worksheet is adapted from the 2021 version.

2022 Earned Income Credit (EIC) Table

Caution. This is **not** a tax table.

1. To find your credit, read down the "At least - But less than" columns and find the line that includes the amount you were told to look up from your EIC Worksheet.

2. Then, go to the column that includes your filing status and the number of qualifying children you have who have valid SSNs as defined earlier. Enter the credit from that column on your EIC Worksheet.

Example. If your filing status is single, you have one qualifying child who has a valid SSN, and the amount you are looking up from your EIC Worksheet is $2,455, you would enter $842.

If the amount you are looking up from the worksheet is–		And your filing status is– Single, head of household, or qualifying surviving spouse and the number of children you have is–			
		0	1	2	3
At least	But less than	Your credit is–			
2,400	2,450	186	825	970	1,091
2,450	2,500	189	842	990	1,114

If the amount you are looking up from the worksheet is–		And your filing status is– Single, head of household, or qualifying surviving spouse★ and you have–				Married filing jointly and you have–			
		0	1	2	3	0	1	2	3
At least	But less than	Your credit is–				Your credit is–			
1	50	2	9	10	11	2	9	10	11
50	100	6	26	30	34	6	26	30	34
100	150	10	43	50	56	10	43	50	56
150	200	13	60	70	79	13	60	70	79
200	250	17	77	90	101	17	77	90	101
250	300	21	94	110	124	21	94	110	124
300	350	25	111	130	146	25	111	130	146
350	400	29	128	150	169	29	128	150	169
400	450	33	145	170	191	33	145	170	191
450	500	36	162	190	214	36	162	190	214
500	550	40	179	210	236	40	179	210	236
550	600	44	196	230	259	44	196	230	259
600	650	48	213	250	281	48	213	250	281
650	700	52	230	270	304	52	230	270	304
700	750	55	247	290	326	55	247	290	326
750	800	59	264	310	349	59	264	310	349
800	850	63	281	330	371	63	281	330	371
850	900	67	298	350	394	67	298	350	394
900	950	71	315	370	416	71	315	370	416
950	1,000	75	332	390	439	75	332	390	439
1,000	1,050	78	349	410	461	78	349	410	461
1,050	1,100	82	366	430	484	82	366	430	484
1,100	1,150	86	383	450	506	86	383	450	506
1,150	1,200	90	400	470	529	90	400	470	529
1,200	1,250	94	417	490	551	94	417	490	551
1,250	1,300	98	434	510	574	98	434	510	574
1,300	1,350	101	451	530	596	101	451	530	596
1,350	1,400	105	468	550	619	105	468	550	619
1,400	1,450	109	485	570	641	109	485	570	641
1,450	1,500	113	502	590	664	113	502	590	664
1,500	1,550	117	519	610	686	117	519	610	686
1,550	1,600	120	536	630	709	120	536	630	709
1,600	1,650	124	553	650	731	124	553	650	731
1,650	1,700	128	570	670	754	128	570	670	754
1,700	1,750	132	587	690	776	132	587	690	776
1,750	1,800	136	604	710	799	136	604	710	799
1,800	1,850	140	621	730	821	140	621	730	821
1,850	1,900	143	638	750	844	143	638	750	844
1,900	1,950	147	655	770	866	147	655	770	866
1,950	2,000	151	672	790	889	151	672	790	889
2,000	2,050	155	689	810	911	155	689	810	911
2,050	2,100	159	706	830	934	159	706	830	934
2,100	2,150	163	723	850	956	163	723	850	956
2,150	2,200	166	740	870	979	166	740	870	979
2,200	2,250	170	757	890	1,001	170	757	890	1,001
2,250	2,300	174	774	910	1,024	174	774	910	1,024
2,300	2,350	178	791	930	1,046	178	791	930	1,046
2,350	2,400	182	808	950	1,069	182	808	950	1,069
2,400	2,450	186	825	970	1,091	186	825	970	1,091
2,450	2,500	189	842	990	1,114	189	842	990	1,114
2,500	2,550	193	859	1,010	1,136	193	859	1,010	1,136
2,550	2,600	197	876	1,030	1,159	197	876	1,030	1,159
2,600	2,650	201	893	1,050	1,181	201	893	1,050	1,181
2,650	2,700	205	910	1,070	1,204	205	910	1,070	1,204
2,700	2,750	208	927	1,090	1,226	208	927	1,090	1,226
2,750	2,800	212	944	1,110	1,249	212	944	1,110	1,249

If the amount you are looking up from the worksheet is–		And your filing status is– Single, head of household, or qualifying surviving spouse★ and you have–				Married filing jointly and you have–			
		0	1	2	3	0	1	2	3
At least	But less than	Your credit is–				Your credit is–			
2,800	2,850	216	961	1,130	1,271	216	961	1,130	1,271
2,850	2,900	220	978	1,150	1,294	220	978	1,150	1,294
2,900	2,950	224	995	1,170	1,316	224	995	1,170	1,316
2,950	3,000	228	1,012	1,190	1,339	228	1,012	1,190	1,339
3,000	3,050	231	1,029	1,210	1,361	231	1,029	1,210	1,361
3,050	3,100	235	1,046	1,230	1,384	235	1,046	1,230	1,384
3,100	3,150	239	1,063	1,250	1,406	239	1,063	1,250	1,406
3,150	3,200	243	1,080	1,270	1,429	243	1,080	1,270	1,429
3,200	3,250	247	1,097	1,290	1,451	247	1,097	1,290	1,451
3,250	3,300	251	1,114	1,310	1,474	251	1,114	1,310	1,474
3,300	3,350	254	1,131	1,330	1,496	254	1,131	1,330	1,496
3,350	3,400	258	1,148	1,350	1,519	258	1,148	1,350	1,519
3,400	3,450	262	1,165	1,370	1,541	262	1,165	1,370	1,541
3,450	3,500	266	1,182	1,390	1,564	266	1,182	1,390	1,564
3,500	3,550	270	1,199	1,410	1,586	270	1,199	1,410	1,586
3,550	3,600	273	1,216	1,430	1,609	273	1,216	1,430	1,609
3,600	3,650	277	1,233	1,450	1,631	277	1,233	1,450	1,631
3,650	3,700	281	1,250	1,470	1,654	281	1,250	1,470	1,654
3,700	3,750	285	1,267	1,490	1,676	285	1,267	1,490	1,676
3,750	3,800	289	1,284	1,510	1,699	289	1,284	1,510	1,699
3,800	3,850	293	1,301	1,530	1,721	293	1,301	1,530	1,721
3,850	3,900	296	1,318	1,550	1,744	296	1,318	1,550	1,744
3,900	3,950	300	1,335	1,570	1,766	300	1,335	1,570	1,766
3,950	4,000	304	1,352	1,590	1,789	304	1,352	1,590	1,789
4,000	4,050	308	1,369	1,610	1,811	308	1,369	1,610	1,811
4,050	4,100	312	1,386	1,630	1,834	312	1,386	1,630	1,834
4,100	4,150	316	1,403	1,650	1,856	316	1,403	1,650	1,856
4,150	4,200	319	1,420	1,670	1,879	319	1,420	1,670	1,879
4,200	4,250	323	1,437	1,690	1,901	323	1,437	1,690	1,901
4,250	4,300	327	1,454	1,710	1,924	327	1,454	1,710	1,924
4,300	4,350	331	1,471	1,730	1,946	331	1,471	1,730	1,946
4,350	4,400	335	1,488	1,750	1,969	335	1,488	1,750	1,969
4,400	4,450	339	1,505	1,770	1,991	339	1,505	1,770	1,991
4,450	4,500	342	1,522	1,790	2,014	342	1,522	1,790	2,014
4,500	4,550	346	1,539	1,810	2,036	346	1,539	1,810	2,036
4,550	4,600	350	1,556	1,830	2,059	350	1,556	1,830	2,059
4,600	4,650	354	1,573	1,850	2,081	354	1,573	1,850	2,081
4,650	4,700	358	1,590	1,870	2,104	358	1,590	1,870	2,104
4,700	4,750	361	1,607	1,890	2,126	361	1,607	1,890	2,126
4,750	4,800	365	1,624	1,910	2,149	365	1,624	1,910	2,149
4,800	4,850	369	1,641	1,930	2,171	369	1,641	1,930	2,171
4,850	4,900	373	1,658	1,950	2,194	373	1,658	1,950	2,194
4,900	4,950	377	1,675	1,970	2,216	377	1,675	1,970	2,216
4,950	5,000	381	1,692	1,990	2,239	381	1,692	1,990	2,239
5,000	5,050	384	1,709	2,010	2,261	384	1,709	2,010	2,261
5,050	5,100	388	1,726	2,030	2,284	388	1,726	2,030	2,284
5,100	5,150	392	1,743	2,050	2,306	392	1,743	2,050	2,306
5,150	5,200	396	1,760	2,070	2,329	396	1,760	2,070	2,329
5,200	5,250	400	1,777	2,090	2,351	400	1,777	2,090	2,351
5,250	5,300	404	1,794	2,110	2,374	404	1,794	2,110	2,374
5,300	5,350	407	1,811	2,130	2,396	407	1,811	2,130	2,396
5,350	5,400	411	1,828	2,150	2,419	411	1,828	2,150	2,419
5,400	5,450	415	1,845	2,170	2,441	415	1,845	2,170	2,441
5,450	5,500	419	1,862	2,190	2,464	419	1,862	2,190	2,464
5,500	5,550	423	1,879	2,210	2,486	423	1,879	2,210	2,486
5,550	5,600	426	1,896	2,230	2,509	426	1,896	2,230	2,509

★ Use this column if your filing status is married filing separately and you qualify to claim the EIC. See the instructions for line 27.

(Continued)

Earned Income Credit (EIC) Table - *Continued* (**Caution.** This is **not** a tax table.)

If the amount you are looking up from the worksheet is–		And your filing status is– Single, head of household, or qualifying surviving spouse★ and you have–				Married filing jointly and you have–			
		0	1	2	3	0	1	2	3
At least	But less than	Your credit is–				Your credit is–			
5,600	5,650	430	1,913	2,250	2,531	430	1,913	2,250	2,531
5,650	5,700	434	1,930	2,270	2,554	434	1,930	2,270	2,554
5,700	5,750	438	1,947	2,290	2,576	438	1,947	2,290	2,576
5,750	5,800	442	1,964	2,310	2,599	442	1,964	2,310	2,599
5,800	5,850	446	1,981	2,330	2,621	446	1,981	2,330	2,621
5,850	5,900	449	1,998	2,350	2,644	449	1,998	2,350	2,644
5,900	5,950	453	2,015	2,370	2,666	453	2,015	2,370	2,666
5,950	6,000	457	2,032	2,390	2,689	457	2,032	2,390	2,689
6,000	6,050	461	2,049	2,410	2,711	461	2,049	2,410	2,711
6,050	6,100	465	2,066	2,430	2,734	465	2,066	2,430	2,734
6,100	6,150	469	2,083	2,450	2,756	469	2,083	2,450	2,756
6,150	6,200	472	2,100	2,470	2,779	472	2,100	2,470	2,779
6,200	6,250	476	2,117	2,490	2,801	476	2,117	2,490	2,801
6,250	6,300	480	2,134	2,510	2,824	480	2,134	2,510	2,824
6,300	6,350	484	2,151	2,530	2,846	484	2,151	2,530	2,846
6,350	6,400	488	2,168	2,550	2,869	488	2,168	2,550	2,869
6,400	6,450	492	2,185	2,570	2,891	492	2,185	2,570	2,891
6,450	6,500	495	2,202	2,590	2,914	495	2,202	2,590	2,914
6,500	6,550	499	2,210	2,010	2,936	499	2,219	2,610	2,936
6,550	6,600	503	2,236	2,630	2,959	503	2,236	2,630	2,959
6,600	6,650	507	2,253	2,650	2,981	507	2,253	2,650	2,981
6,650	6,700	511	2,270	2,670	3,004	511	2,270	2,670	3,004
6,700	6,750	514	2,287	2,690	3,026	514	2,287	2,690	3,026
6,750	6,800	518	2,304	2,710	3,049	518	2,304	2,710	3,049
6,800	6,850	522	2,321	2,730	3,071	522	2,321	2,730	3,071
6,850	6,900	526	2,338	2,750	3,094	526	2,338	2,750	3,094
6,900	6,950	530	2,355	2,770	3,116	530	2,355	2,770	3,116
6,950	7,000	534	2,372	2,790	3,139	534	2,372	2,790	3,139
7,000	7,050	537	2,389	2,810	3,161	537	2,389	2,810	3,161
7,050	7,100	541	2,406	2,830	3,184	541	2,406	2,830	3,184
7,100	7,150	545	2,423	2,850	3,206	545	2,423	2,850	3,206
7,150	7,200	549	2,440	2,870	3,229	549	2,440	2,870	3,229
7,200	7,250	553	2,457	2,890	3,251	553	2,457	2,890	3,251
7,250	7,300	557	2,474	2,910	3,274	557	2,474	2,910	3,274
7,300	7,350	560	2,491	2,930	3,296	560	2,491	2,930	3,296
7,350	7,400	560	2,508	2,950	3,319	560	2,508	2,950	3,319
7,400	7,450	560	2,525	2,970	3,341	560	2,525	2,970	3,341
7,450	7,500	560	2,542	2,990	3,364	560	2,542	2,990	3,364
7,500	7,550	560	2,559	3,010	3,386	560	2,559	3,010	3,386
7,550	7,600	560	2,576	3,030	3,409	560	2,576	3,030	3,409
7,600	7,650	560	2,593	3,050	3,431	560	2,593	3,050	3,431
7,650	7,700	560	2,610	3,070	3,454	560	2,610	3,070	3,454
7,700	7,750	560	2,627	3,090	3,476	560	2,627	3,090	3,476
7,750	7,800	560	2,644	3,110	3,499	560	2,644	3,110	3,499
7,800	7,850	560	2,661	3,130	3,521	560	2,661	3,130	3,521
7,850	7,900	560	2,678	3,150	3,544	560	2,678	3,150	3,544
7,900	7,950	560	2,695	3,170	3,566	560	2,695	3,170	3,566
7,950	8,000	560	2,712	3,190	3,589	560	2,712	3,190	3,589
8,000	8,050	560	2,729	3,210	3,611	560	2,729	3,210	3,611
8,050	8,100	560	2,746	3,230	3,634	560	2,746	3,230	3,634
8,100	8,150	560	2,763	3,250	3,656	560	2,763	3,250	3,656
8,150	8,200	560	2,780	3,270	3,679	560	2,780	3,270	3,679
8,200	8,250	560	2,797	3,290	3,701	560	2,797	3,290	3,701
8,250	8,300	560	2,814	3,310	3,724	560	2,814	3,310	3,724
8,300	8,350	560	2,831	3,330	3,746	560	2,831	3,330	3,746
8,350	8,400	560	2,848	3,350	3,769	560	2,848	3,350	3,769
8,400	8,450	560	2,865	3,370	3,791	560	2,865	3,370	3,791
8,450	8,500	560	2,882	3,390	3,814	560	2,882	3,390	3,814
8,500	8,550	560	2,899	3,410	3,836	560	2,899	3,410	3,836
8,550	8,600	560	2,916	3,430	3,859	560	2,916	3,430	3,859
8,600	8,650	560	2,933	3,450	3,881	560	2,933	3,450	3,881
8,650	8,700	560	2,950	3,470	3,904	560	2,950	3,470	3,904
8,700	8,750	560	2,967	3,490	3,926	560	2,967	3,490	3,926
8,750	8,800	560	2,984	3,510	3,949	560	2,984	3,510	3,949

If the amount you are looking up from the worksheet is–		And your filing status is– Single, head of household, or qualifying surviving spouse★ and you have–				Married filing jointly and you have–			
		0	1	2	3	0	1	2	3
At least	But less than	Your credit is–				Your credit is–			
8,800	8,850	560	3,001	3,530	3,971	560	3,001	3,530	3,971
8,850	8,900	560	3,018	3,550	3,994	560	3,018	3,550	3,994
8,900	8,950	560	3,035	3,570	4,016	560	3,035	3,570	4,016
8,950	9,000	560	3,052	3,590	4,039	560	3,052	3,590	4,039
9,000	9,050	560	3,069	3,610	4,061	560	3,069	3,610	4,061
9,050	9,100	560	3,086	3,630	4,084	560	3,086	3,630	4,084
9,100	9,150	560	3,103	3,650	4,106	560	3,103	3,650	4,106
9,150	9,200	560	3,120	3,670	4,129	560	3,120	3,670	4,129
9,200	9,250	555	3,137	3,690	4,151	560	3,137	3,690	4,151
9,250	9,300	551	3,154	3,710	4,174	560	3,154	3,710	4,174
9,300	9,350	547	3,171	3,730	4,196	560	3,171	3,730	4,196
9,350	9,400	544	3,188	3,750	4,219	560	3,188	3,750	4,219
9,400	9,450	540	3,205	3,770	4,241	560	3,205	3,770	4,241
9,450	9,500	536	3,222	3,790	4,264	560	3,222	3,790	4,264
9,500	9,550	532	3,239	3,810	4,286	560	3,239	3,810	4,286
9,550	9,600	528	3,256	3,830	4,309	560	3,256	3,030	4,309
9,600	9,650	524	3,273	3,850	4,331	560	3,273	3,850	4,331
9,650	9,700	521	3,290	3,870	4,354	560	3,290	3,870	4,354
9,700	9,750	517	3,307	3,890	4,376	560	3,307	3,890	4,376
9,750	9,800	513	3,324	3,910	4,399	560	3,324	3,910	4,399
9,800	9,850	509	3,341	3,930	4,421	560	3,341	3,930	4,421
9,850	9,900	505	3,358	3,950	4,444	560	3,358	3,950	4,444
9,900	9,950	501	3,375	3,970	4,466	560	3,375	3,970	4,466
9,950	10,000	498	3,392	3,990	4,489	560	3,392	3,990	4,489
10,000	10,050	494	3,409	4,010	4,511	560	3,409	4,010	4,511
10,050	10,100	490	3,426	4,030	4,534	560	3,426	4,030	4,534
10,100	10,150	486	3,443	4,050	4,556	560	3,443	4,050	4,556
10,150	10,200	482	3,460	4,070	4,579	560	3,460	4,070	4,579
10,200	10,250	479	3,477	4,090	4,601	560	3,477	4,090	4,601
10,250	10,300	475	3,494	4,110	4,624	560	3,494	4,110	4,624
10,300	10,350	471	3,511	4,130	4,646	560	3,511	4,130	4,646
10,350	10,400	467	3,528	4,150	4,669	560	3,528	4,150	4,669
10,400	10,450	463	3,545	4,170	4,691	560	3,545	4,170	4,691
10,450	10,500	459	3,562	4,190	4,714	560	3,562	4,190	4,714
10,500	10,550	456	3,579	4,210	4,736	560	3,579	4,210	4,736
10,550	10,600	452	3,596	4,230	4,759	560	3,596	4,230	4,759
10,600	10,650	448	3,613	4,250	4,781	560	3,613	4,250	4,781
10,650	10,700	444	3,630	4,270	4,804	560	3,630	4,270	4,804
10,700	10,750	440	3,647	4,290	4,826	560	3,647	4,290	4,826
10,750	10,800	436	3,664	4,310	4,849	560	3,664	4,310	4,849
10,800	10,850	433	3,681	4,330	4,871	560	3,681	4,330	4,871
10,850	10,900	429	3,698	4,350	4,894	560	3,698	4,350	4,894
10,900	10,950	425	3,715	4,370	4,916	560	3,715	4,370	4,916
10,950	11,000	421	3,733	4,390	4,939	560	3,733	4,390	4,939
11,000	11,050	417	3,733	4,410	4,961	560	3,733	4,410	4,961
11,050	11,100	413	3,733	4,430	4,984	560	3,733	4,430	4,984
11,100	11,150	410	3,733	4,450	5,006	560	3,733	4,450	5,006
11,150	11,200	406	3,733	4,470	5,029	560	3,733	4,470	5,029
11,200	11,250	402	3,733	4,490	5,051	560	3,733	4,490	5,051
11,250	11,300	398	3,733	4,510	5,074	560	3,733	4,510	5,074
11,300	11,350	394	3,733	4,530	5,096	560	3,733	4,530	5,096
11,350	11,400	391	3,733	4,550	5,119	560	3,733	4,550	5,119
11,400	11,450	387	3,733	4,570	5,141	560	3,733	4,570	5,141
11,450	11,500	383	3,733	4,590	5,164	560	3,733	4,590	5,164
11,500	11,550	379	3,733	4,610	5,186	560	3,733	4,610	5,186
11,550	11,600	375	3,733	4,630	5,209	560	3,733	4,630	5,209
11,600	11,650	371	3,733	4,650	5,231	560	3,733	4,650	5,231
11,650	11,700	368	3,733	4,670	5,254	560	3,733	4,670	5,254
11,700	11,750	364	3,733	4,690	5,276	560	3,733	4,690	5,276
11,750	11,800	360	3,733	4,710	5,299	560	3,733	4,710	5,299
11,800	11,850	356	3,733	4,730	5,321	560	3,733	4,730	5,321
11,850	11,900	352	3,733	4,750	5,344	560	3,733	4,750	5,344
11,900	11,950	348	3,733	4,770	5,366	560	3,733	4,770	5,366
11,950	12,000	345	3,733	4,790	5,389	560	3,733	4,790	5,389

★ Use this column if your filing status is married filing separately and you qualify to claim the EIC. See the instructions for line 27.

(Continued)

Earned Income Credit (EIC) Table - *Continued* (**Caution.** This is **not** a tax table.)

If the amount you are looking up from the worksheet is–		And your filing status is– Single, head of household, or qualifying surviving spouse★ and you have–				Married filing jointly and you have–			
		0	1	2	3	0	1	2	3
At least	But less than	Your credit is–				Your credit is–			
12,000	12,050	341	3,733	4,810	5,411	560	3,733	4,810	5,411
12,050	12,100	337	3,733	4,830	5,434	560	3,733	4,830	5,434
12,100	12,150	333	3,733	4,850	5,456	560	3,733	4,850	5,456
12,150	12,200	329	3,733	4,870	5,479	560	3,733	4,870	5,479
12,200	12,250	326	3,733	4,890	5,501	560	3,733	4,890	5,501
12,250	12,300	322	3,733	4,910	5,524	560	3,733	4,910	5,524
12,300	12,350	318	3,733	4,930	5,546	560	3,733	4,930	5,546
12,350	12,400	314	3,733	4,950	5,569	560	3,733	4,950	5,569
12,400	12,450	310	3,733	4,970	5,591	560	3,733	4,970	5,591
12,450	12,500	306	3,733	4,990	5,614	560	3,733	4,990	5,614
12,500	12,550	303	3,733	5,010	5,636	560	3,733	5,010	5,636
12,550	12,600	299	3,733	5,030	5,659	560	3,733	5,030	5,659
12,600	12,650	295	3,733	5,050	5,681	560	3,733	5,050	5,681
12,650	12,700	291	3,733	5,070	5,704	560	3,733	5,070	5,704
12,700	12,750	287	3,733	5,090	5,726	560	3,733	5,090	5,726
12,750	12,800	283	3,733	5,110	5,749	560	3,733	5,110	5,749
12,800	12,850	280	3,733	5,130	5,771	560	3,733	5,130	5,771
12,850	12,900	276	3,733	5,150	5,794	560	3,733	5,150	5,794
12,900	12,950	272	3,733	5,170	5,816	560	3,733	5,170	5,816
12,950	13,000	268	3,733	5,190	5,839	560	3,733	5,190	5,839
13,000	13,050	264	3,733	5,210	5,861	560	3,733	5,210	5,861
13,050	13,100	260	3,733	5,230	5,884	560	3,733	5,230	5,884
13,100	13,150	257	3,733	5,250	5,906	560	3,733	5,250	5,906
13,150	13,200	253	3,733	5,270	5,929	560	3,733	5,270	5,929
13,200	13,250	249	3,733	5,290	5,951	560	3,733	5,290	5,951
13,250	13,300	245	3,733	5,310	5,974	560	3,733	5,310	5,974
13,300	13,350	241	3,733	5,330	5,996	560	3,733	5,330	5,996
13,350	13,400	238	3,733	5,350	6,019	560	3,733	5,350	6,019
13,400	13,450	234	3,733	5,370	6,041	560	3,733	5,370	6,041
13,450	13,500	230	3,733	5,390	6,064	560	3,733	5,390	6,064
13,500	13,550	226	3,733	5,410	6,086	560	3,733	5,410	6,086
13,550	13,600	222	3,733	5,430	6,109	560	3,733	5,430	6,109
13,600	13,650	218	3,733	5,450	6,131	560	3,733	5,450	6,131
13,650	13,700	215	3,733	5,470	6,154	560	3,733	5,470	6,154
13,700	13,750	211	3,733	5,490	6,176	560	3,733	5,490	6,176
13,750	13,800	207	3,733	5,510	6,199	560	3,733	5,510	6,199
13,800	13,850	203	3,733	5,530	6,221	560	3,733	5,530	6,221
13,850	13,900	199	3,733	5,550	6,244	560	3,733	5,550	6,244
13,900	13,950	195	3,733	5,570	6,266	560	3,733	5,570	6,266
13,950	14,000	192	3,733	5,590	6,289	560	3,733	5,590	6,289
14,000	14,050	188	3,733	5,610	6,311	560	3,733	5,610	6,311
14,050	14,100	184	3,733	5,630	6,334	560	3,733	5,630	6,334
14,100	14,150	180	3,733	5,650	6,356	560	3,733	5,650	6,356
14,150	14,200	176	3,733	5,670	6,379	560	3,733	5,670	6,379
14,200	14,250	173	3,733	5,690	6,401	560	3,733	5,690	6,401
14,250	14,300	169	3,733	5,710	6,424	560	3,733	5,710	6,424
14,300	14,350	165	3,733	5,730	6,446	560	3,733	5,730	6,446
14,350	14,400	161	3,733	5,750	6,469	560	3,733	5,750	6,469
14,400	14,450	157	3,733	5,770	6,491	560	3,733	5,770	6,491
14,450	14,500	153	3,733	5,790	6,514	560	3,733	5,790	6,514
14,500	14,550	150	3,733	5,810	6,536	560	3,733	5,810	6,536
14,550	14,600	146	3,733	5,830	6,559	560	3,733	5,830	6,559
14,600	14,650	142	3,733	5,850	6,581	560	3,733	5,850	6,581
14,650	14,700	138	3,733	5,870	6,604	560	3,733	5,870	6,604
14,700	14,750	134	3,733	5,890	6,626	560	3,733	5,890	6,626
14,750	14,800	130	3,733	5,910	6,649	560	3,733	5,910	6,649
14,800	14,850	127	3,733	5,930	6,671	560	3,733	5,930	6,671
14,850	14,900	123	3,733	5,950	6,694	560	3,733	5,950	6,694
14,900	14,950	119	3,733	5,970	6,716	560	3,733	5,970	6,716
14,950	15,000	115	3,733	5,990	6,739	560	3,733	5,990	6,739
15,000	15,050	111	3,733	6,010	6,761	560	3,733	6,010	6,761
15,050	15,100	107	3,733	6,030	6,784	560	3,733	6,030	6,784
15,100	15,150	104	3,733	6,050	6,806	560	3,733	6,050	6,806
15,150	15,200	100	3,733	6,070	6,829	560	3,733	6,070	6,829
15,200	15,250	96	3,733	6,090	6,851	560	3,733	6,090	6,851
15,250	15,300	92	3,733	6,110	6,874	560	3,733	6,110	6,874
15,300	15,350	88	3,733	6,130	6,896	557	3,733	6,130	6,896
15,350	15,400	85	3,733	6,150	6,919	553	3,733	6,150	6,919
15,400	15,450	81	3,733	6,164	6,935	550	3,733	6,164	6,935
15,450	15,500	77	3,733	6,164	6,935	546	3,733	6,164	6,935
15,500	15,550	73	3,733	6,164	6,935	542	3,733	6,164	6,935
15,550	15,600	69	3,733	6,164	6,935	538	3,733	6,164	6,935
15,600	15,650	65	3,733	6,164	6,935	534	3,733	6,164	6,935
15,650	15,700	62	3,733	6,164	6,935	531	3,733	6,164	6,935
15,700	15,750	58	3,733	6,164	6,935	527	3,733	6,164	6,935
15,750	15,800	54	3,733	6,164	6,935	523	3,733	6,164	6,935
15,800	15,850	50	3,733	6,164	6,935	519	3,733	6,164	6,935
15,850	15,900	46	3,733	6,164	6,935	515	3,733	6,164	6,935
15,900	15,950	42	3,733	6,164	6,935	511	3,733	6,164	6,935
15,950	16,000	39	3,733	6,164	6,935	508	3,733	6,164	6,935
16,000	16,050	35	3,733	6,164	6,935	504	3,733	6,164	6,935
16,050	16,100	31	3,733	6,164	6,935	500	3,733	6,164	6,935
16,100	16,150	27	3,733	6,164	6,935	496	3,733	6,164	6,935
16,150	16,200	23	3,733	6,164	6,935	492	3,733	6,164	6,935
16,200	16,250	20	3,733	6,164	6,935	488	3,733	6,164	6,935
16,250	16,300	16	3,733	6,164	6,935	485	3,733	6,164	6,935
16,300	16,350	12	3,733	6,164	6,935	481	3,733	6,164	6,935
16,350	16,400	8	3,733	6,164	6,935	477	3,733	6,164	6,935
16,400	16,450	4	3,733	6,164	6,935	473	3,733	6,164	6,935
16,450	16,500	•	3,733	6,164	6,935	469	3,733	6,164	6,935
16,500	16,550	0	3,733	6,164	6,935	466	3,733	6,164	6,935
16,550	16,600	0	3,733	6,164	6,935	462	3,733	6,164	6,935
16,600	16,650	0	3,733	6,164	6,935	458	3,733	6,164	6,935
16,650	16,700	0	3,733	6,164	6,935	454	3,733	6,164	6,935
16,700	16,750	0	3,733	6,164	6,935	450	3,733	6,164	6,935
16,750	16,800	0	3,733	6,164	6,935	446	3,733	6,164	6,935
16,800	16,850	0	3,733	6,164	6,935	443	3,733	6,164	6,935
16,850	16,900	0	3,733	6,164	6,935	439	3,733	6,164	6,935
16,900	16,950	0	3,733	6,164	6,935	435	3,733	6,164	6,935
16,950	17,000	0	3,733	6,164	6,935	431	3,733	6,164	6,935
17,000	17,050	0	3,733	6,164	6,935	427	3,733	6,164	6,935
17,050	17,100	0	3,733	6,164	6,935	423	3,733	6,164	6,935
17,100	17,150	0	3,733	6,164	6,935	420	3,733	6,164	6,935
17,150	17,200	0	3,733	6,164	6,935	416	3,733	6,164	6,935
17,200	17,250	0	3,733	6,164	6,935	412	3,733	6,164	6,935
17,250	17,300	0	3,733	6,164	6,935	408	3,733	6,164	6,935
17,300	17,350	0	3,733	6,164	6,935	404	3,733	6,164	6,935
17,350	17,400	0	3,733	6,164	6,935	400	3,733	6,164	6,935
17,400	17,450	0	3,733	6,164	6,935	397	3,733	6,164	6,935
17,450	17,500	0	3,733	6,164	6,935	393	3,733	6,164	6,935
17,500	17,550	0	3,733	6,164	6,935	389	3,733	6,164	6,935
17,550	17,600	0	3,733	6,164	6,935	385	3,733	6,164	6,935
17,600	17,650	0	3,733	6,164	6,935	381	3,733	6,164	6,935
17,650	17,700	0	3,733	6,164	6,935	378	3,733	6,164	6,935
17,700	17,750	0	3,733	6,164	6,935	374	3,733	6,164	6,935
17,750	17,800	0	3,733	6,164	6,935	370	3,733	6,164	6,935
17,800	17,850	0	3,733	6,164	6,935	366	3,733	6,164	6,935
17,850	17,900	0	3,733	6,164	6,935	362	3,733	6,164	6,935
17,900	17,950	0	3,733	6,164	6,935	358	3,733	6,164	6,935
17,950	18,000	0	3,733	6,164	6,935	355	3,733	6,164	6,935
18,000	18,050	0	3,733	6,164	6,935	351	3,733	6,164	6,935
18,050	18,100	0	3,733	6,164	6,935	347	3,733	6,164	6,935
18,100	18,150	0	3,733	6,164	6,935	343	3,733	6,164	6,935
18,150	18,200	0	3,733	6,164	6,935	339	3,733	6,164	6,935
18,200	18,250	0	3,733	6,164	6,935	335	3,733	6,164	6,935
18,250	18,300	0	3,733	6,164	6,935	332	3,733	6,164	6,935
18,300	18,350	0	3,733	6,164	6,935	328	3,733	6,164	6,935
18,350	18,400	0	3,733	6,164	6,935	324	3,733	6,164	6,935

★ Use this column if your filing status is married filing separately and you qualify to claim the EIC. See the instructions for line 27.

• If the amount you are looking up from the worksheet is at least $16,450 but less than $16,480, and you have no qualifying children who have valid SSNs, your credit is $1.

If the amount you are looking up from the worksheet is $16,480 or more, and you have no qualifying children who have valid SSNs, you can't take the credit.

(Continued)

Earned Income Credit (EIC) Table - *Continued* (**Caution.** This is **not** a tax table.)

If the amount you are looking up from the worksheet is–		And your filing status is– Single, head of household, or qualifying surviving spouse★ and you have–				Married filing jointly and you have–			
		0	1	2	3	0	1	2	3
At least	But less than	Your credit is–				Your credit is–			
18,400	18,450	0	3,733	6,164	6,935	320	3,733	6,164	6,935
18,450	18,500	0	3,733	6,164	6,935	316	3,733	6,164	6,935
18,500	18,550	0	3,733	6,164	6,935	313	3,733	6,164	6,935
18,550	18,600	0	3,733	6,164	6,935	309	3,733	6,164	6,935
18,600	18,650	0	3,733	6,164	6,935	305	3,733	6,164	6,935
18,650	18,700	0	3,733	6,164	6,935	301	3,733	6,164	6,935
18,700	18,750	0	3,733	6,164	6,935	297	3,733	6,164	6,935
18,750	18,800	0	3,733	6,164	6,935	293	3,733	6,164	6,935
18,800	18,850	0	3,733	6,164	6,935	290	3,733	6,164	6,935
18,850	18,900	0	3,733	6,164	6,935	286	3,733	6,164	6,935
18,900	18,950	0	3,733	6,164	6,935	282	3,733	6,164	6,935
18,950	19,000	0	3,733	6,164	6,935	278	3,733	6,164	6,935
19,000	19,050	0	3,733	6,164	6,935	274	3,733	6,164	6,935
19,050	19,100	0	3,733	6,164	6,935	270	3,733	6,164	6,935
19,100	19,150	0	3,733	6,164	6,935	267	3,733	6,164	6,935
19,150	19,200	0	3,733	6,164	6,935	263	3,733	6,164	6,935
19,200	19,250	0	3,733	6,164	6,935	259	3,733	6,164	6,935
19,250	19,300	0	3,733	6,164	6,935	255	3,733	6,161	0,935
19,300	19,350	0	3,733	6,164	6,935	251	3,733	6,164	6,935
19,350	19,400	0	3,733	6,164	6,935	247	3,733	6,164	6,935
19,400	19,450	0	3,733	6,164	6,935	244	3,733	6,164	6,935
19,450	19,500	0	3,733	6,164	6,935	240	3,733	6,164	6,935
19,500	19,550	0	3,733	6,164	6,935	236	3,733	6,164	6,935
19,550	19,600	0	3,733	6,164	6,935	232	3,733	6,164	6,935
19,600	19,650	0	3,733	6,164	6,935	228	3,733	6,164	6,935
19,650	19,700	0	3,733	6,164	6,935	225	3,733	6,164	6,935
19,700	19,750	0	3,733	6,164	6,935	221	3,733	6,164	6,935
19,750	19,800	0	3,733	6,164	6,935	217	3,733	6,164	6,935
19,800	19,850	0	3,733	6,164	6,935	213	3,733	6,164	6,935
19,850	19,900	0	3,733	6,164	6,935	209	3,733	6,164	6,935
19,900	19,950	0	3,733	6,164	6,935	205	3,733	6,164	6,935
19,950	20,000	0	3,733	6,164	6,935	202	3,733	6,164	6,935
20,000	20,050	0	3,733	6,164	6,935	198	3,733	6,164	6,935
20,050	20,100	0	3,733	6,164	6,935	194	3,733	6,164	6,935
20,100	20,150	0	3,733	6,164	6,935	190	3,733	6,164	6,935
20,150	20,200	0	3,726	6,155	6,925	186	3,733	6,164	6,935
20,200	20,250	0	3,718	6,144	6,914	182	3,733	6,164	6,935
20,250	20,300	0	3,710	6,133	6,904	179	3,733	6,164	6,935
20,300	20,350	0	3,702	6,123	6,893	175	3,733	6,164	6,935
20,350	20,400	0	3,694	6,112	6,883	171	3,733	6,164	6,935
20,400	20,450	0	3,686	6,102	6,872	167	3,733	6,164	6,935
20,450	20,500	0	3,678	6,091	6,862	163	3,733	6,164	6,935
20,500	20,550	0	3,670	6,081	6,851	160	3,733	6,164	6,935
20,550	20,600	0	3,662	6,070	6,841	156	3,733	6,164	6,935
20,600	20,650	0	3,654	6,060	6,830	152	3,733	6,164	6,935
20,650	20,700	0	3,646	6,049	6,820	148	3,733	6,164	6,935
20,700	20,750	0	3,638	6,039	6,809	144	3,733	6,164	6,935
20,750	20,800	0	3,630	6,028	6,799	140	3,733	6,164	6,935
20,800	20,850	0	3,622	6,018	6,788	137	3,733	6,164	6,935
20,850	20,900	0	3,614	6,007	6,778	133	3,733	6,164	6,935
20,900	20,950	0	3,606	5,997	6,767	129	3,733	6,164	6,935
20,950	21,000	0	3,598	5,986	6,757	125	3,733	6,164	6,935
21,000	21,050	0	3,590	5,976	6,746	121	3,733	6,164	6,935
21,050	21,100	0	3,582	5,965	6,735	117	3,733	6,164	6,935
21,100	21,150	0	3,574	5,954	6,725	114	3,733	6,164	6,935
21,150	21,200	0	3,566	5,944	6,714	110	3,733	6,164	6,935
21,200	21,250	0	3,558	5,933	6,704	106	3,733	6,164	6,935
21,250	21,300	0	3,550	5,923	6,693	102	3,733	6,164	6,935
21,300	21,350	0	3,542	5,912	6,683	98	3,733	6,164	6,935
21,350	21,400	0	3,534	5,902	6,672	94	3,733	6,164	6,935
21,400	21,450	0	3,526	5,891	6,662	91	3,733	6,164	6,935
21,450	21,500	0	3,518	5,881	6,651	87	3,733	6,164	6,935
21,500	21,550	0	3,510	5,870	6,641	83	3,733	6,164	6,935
21,550	21,600	0	3,502	5,860	6,630	79	3,733	6,164	6,935
21,600	21,650	0	3,494	5,849	6,620	75	3,733	6,164	6,935
21,650	21,700	0	3,486	5,839	6,609	72	3,733	6,164	6,935
21,700	21,750	0	3,478	5,828	6,599	68	3,733	6,164	6,935
21,750	21,800	0	3,470	5,818	6,588	64	3,733	6,164	6,935
21,800	21,850	0	3,462	5,807	6,578	60	3,733	6,164	6,935
21,850	21,900	0	3,454	5,797	6,567	56	3,733	6,164	6,935
21,900	21,950	0	3,446	5,786	6,556	52	3,733	6,164	6,935
21,950	22,000	0	3,438	5,775	6,546	49	3,733	6,164	6,935
22,000	22,050	0	3,430	5,765	6,535	45	3,733	6,164	6,935
22,050	22,100	0	3,422	5,754	6,525	41	3,733	6,164	6,935
22,100	22,150	0	3,414	5,744	6,514	37	3,733	6,164	6,935
22,150	22,200	0	3,406	5,733	6,504	33	3,733	6,164	6,935
22,200	22,250	0	3,398	5,723	6,493	29	3,733	6,164	6,935
22,250	22,300	0	3,390	5,712	6,483	26	3,733	6,164	6,935
22,300	22,350	0	3,382	5,702	6,472	22	3,733	6,164	6,935
22,350	22,400	0	3,374	5,691	6,462	18	3,733	6,164	6,935
22,400	22,450	0	3,366	5,001	6,451	14	3,733	6,164	6,935
22,450	22,500	0	3,358	5,670	6,441	10	3,733	6,164	6,935
22,500	22,550	0	3,350	5,660	6,430	7	3,733	6,164	6,935
22,550	22,600	0	3,342	5,649	6,420	3	3,733	6,164	6,935
22,600	22,650	0	3,334	5,639	6,409	*	3,733	6,164	6,935
22,650	22,700	0	3,327	5,628	6,399	0	3,733	6,164	6,935
22,700	22,750	0	3,319	5,617	6,388	0	3,733	6,164	6,935
22,750	22,800	0	3,311	5,607	6,377	0	3,733	6,164	6,935
22,800	22,850	0	3,303	5,596	6,367	0	3,733	6,164	6,935
22,850	22,900	0	3,295	5,586	6,356	0	3,733	6,164	6,935
22,900	22,950	0	3,287	5,575	6,346	0	3,733	6,164	6,935
22,950	23,000	0	3,279	5,565	6,335	0	3,733	6,164	6,935
23,000	23,050	0	3,271	5,554	6,325	0	3,733	6,164	6,935
23,050	23,100	0	3,263	5,544	6,314	0	3,733	6,164	6,935
23,100	23,150	0	3,255	5,533	6,304	0	3,733	6,164	6,935
23,150	23,200	0	3,247	5,523	6,293	0	3,733	6,164	6,935
23,200	23,250	0	3,239	5,512	6,283	0	3,733	6,164	6,935
23,250	23,300	0	3,231	5,502	6,272	0	3,733	6,164	6,935
23,300	23,350	0	3,223	5,491	6,262	0	3,733	6,164	6,935
23,350	23,400	0	3,215	5,481	6,251	0	3,733	6,164	6,935
23,400	23,450	0	3,207	5,470	6,241	0	3,733	6,164	6,935
23,450	23,500	0	3,199	5,460	6,230	0	3,733	6,164	6,935
23,500	23,550	0	3,191	5,449	6,220	0	3,733	6,164	6,935
23,550	23,600	0	3,183	5,438	6,209	0	3,733	6,164	6,935
23,600	23,650	0	3,175	5,428	6,198	0	3,733	6,164	6,935
23,650	23,700	0	3,167	5,417	6,188	0	3,733	6,164	6,935
23,700	23,750	0	3,159	5,407	6,177	0	3,733	6,164	6,935
23,750	23,800	0	3,151	5,396	6,167	0	3,733	6,164	6,935
23,800	23,850	0	3,143	5,386	6,156	0	3,733	6,164	6,935
23,850	23,900	0	3,135	5,375	6,146	0	3,733	6,164	6,935
23,900	23,950	0	3,127	5,365	6,135	0	3,733	6,164	6,935
23,950	24,000	0	3,119	5,354	6,125	0	3,733	6,164	6,935
24,000	24,050	0	3,111	5,344	6,114	0	3,733	6,164	6,935
24,050	24,100	0	3,103	5,333	6,104	0	3,733	6,164	6,935
24,100	24,150	0	3,095	5,323	6,093	0	3,733	6,164	6,935
24,150	24,200	0	3,087	5,312	6,083	0	3,733	6,164	6,935
24,200	24,250	0	3,079	5,302	6,072	0	3,733	6,164	6,935
24,250	24,300	0	3,071	5,291	6,062	0	3,733	6,164	6,935
24,300	24,350	0	3,063	5,281	6,051	0	3,733	6,164	6,935
24,350	24,400	0	3,055	5,270	6,041	0	3,733	6,164	6,935
24,400	24,450	0	3,047	5,259	6,030	0	3,733	6,164	6,935
24,450	24,500	0	3,039	5,249	6,019	0	3,733	6,164	6,935
24,500	24,550	0	3,031	5,238	6,009	0	3,733	6,164	6,935
24,550	24,600	0	3,023	5,228	5,998	0	3,733	6,164	6,935
24,600	24,650	0	3,015	5,217	5,988	0	3,733	6,164	6,935
24,650	24,700	0	3,007	5,207	5,977	0	3,733	6,164	6,935
24,700	24,750	0	2,999	5,196	5,967	0	3,733	6,164	6,935
24,750	24,800	0	2,991	5,186	5,956	0	3,733	6,164	6,935

★ Use this column if your filing status is married filing separately and you qualify to claim the EIC. See the instructions for line 27.

* If the amount you are looking up from the worksheet is at least $22,600 but less than $22,610, and you have no qualifying children who have valid SSNs, your credit is $0.

If the amount you are looking up from the worksheet is $22,610 or more, and you have no qualifying children who have valid SSNs, you can't take the credit.

(Continued)

Earned Income Credit (EIC) Table - *Continued* (**Caution.** This is **not** a tax table.)

If the amount you are looking up from the worksheet is–		And your filing status is– Single, head of household, or qualifying surviving spouse★ and you have–				Married filing jointly and you have–			
		0	1	2	3	0	1	2	3
At least	But less than	Your credit is–				Your credit is–			
24,800	24,850	0	2,983	5,175	5,946	0	3,733	6,164	6,935
24,850	24,900	0	2,975	5,165	5,935	0	3,733	6,164	6,935
24,900	24,950	0	2,967	5,154	5,925	0	3,733	6,164	6,935
24,950	25,000	0	2,959	5,144	5,914	0	3,733	6,164	6,935
25,000	25,050	0	2,951	5,133	5,904	0	3,733	6,164	6,935
25,050	25,100	0	2,943	5,123	5,893	0	3,733	6,164	6,935
25,100	25,150	0	2,935	5,112	5,883	0	3,733	6,164	6,935
25,150	25,200	0	2,927	5,102	5,872	0	3,733	6,164	6,935
25,200	25,250	0	2,919	5,091	5,861	0	3,733	6,164	6,935
25,250	25,300	0	2,911	5,080	5,851	0	3,733	6,164	6,935
25,300	25,350	0	2,903	5,070	5,840	0	3,733	6,164	6,935
25,350	25,400	0	2,895	5,059	5,830	0	3,733	6,164	6,935
25,400	25,450	0	2,887	5,049	5,819	0	3,733	6,164	6,935
25,450	25,500	0	2,879	5,038	5,809	0	3,733	6,164	6,935
25,500	25,550	0	2,871	5,028	5,798	0	3,733	6,164	6,935
25,550	25,600	0	2,863	5,017	5,788	0	3,733	6,164	6,935
25,600	25,650	0	2,855	5,007	5,777	0	3,733	6,164	6,935
25,650	25,700	0	2,847	4,996	5,767	0	3,733	6,164	6,935
25,700	25,750	0	2,839	4,986	5,756	0	3,733	6,164	6,935
25,750	25,800	0	2,831	4,975	5,746	0	3,733	6,164	6,935
25,800	25,850	0	2,823	4,965	5,735	0	3,733	6,164	6,935
25,850	25,900	0	2,815	4,954	5,725	0	3,733	6,164	6,935
25,900	25,950	0	2,807	4,944	5,714	0	3,733	6,164	6,935
25,950	26,000	0	2,799	4,933	5,704	0	3,733	6,164	6,935
26,000	26,050	0	2,791	4,923	5,693	0	3,733	6,164	6,935
26,050	26,100	0	2,783	4,912	5,682	0	3,733	6,164	6,935
26,100	26,150	0	2,775	4,901	5,672	0	3,733	6,164	6,935
26,150	26,200	0	2,767	4,891	5,661	0	3,733	6,164	6,935
26,200	26,250	0	2,759	4,880	5,651	0	3,733	6,164	6,935
26,250	26,300	0	2,751	4,870	5,640	0	3,733	6,164	6,935
26,300	26,350	0	2,743	4,859	5,630	0	3,723	6,150	6,921
26,350	26,400	0	2,735	4,849	5,619	0	3,715	6,140	6,910
26,400	26,450	0	2,727	4,838	5,609	0	3,707	6,129	6,900
26,450	26,500	0	2,719	4,828	5,598	0	3,699	6,119	6,889
26,500	26,550	0	2,711	4,817	5,588	0	3,691	6,108	6,879
26,550	26,600	0	2,703	4,807	5,577	0	3,683	6,098	6,868
26,600	26,650	0	2,695	4,796	5,567	0	3,675	6,087	6,858
26,650	26,700	0	2,687	4,786	5,556	0	3,667	6,077	6,847
26,700	26,750	0	2,679	4,775	5,546	0	3,659	6,066	6,837
26,750	26,800	0	2,671	4,765	5,535	0	3,651	6,056	6,826
26,800	26,850	0	2,663	4,754	5,525	0	3,643	6,045	6,816
26,850	26,900	0	2,655	4,744	5,514	0	3,635	6,034	6,805
26,900	26,950	0	2,647	4,733	5,503	0	3,627	6,024	6,794
26,950	27,000	0	2,639	4,722	5,493	0	3,619	6,013	6,784
27,000	27,050	0	2,631	4,712	5,482	0	3,611	6,003	6,773
27,050	27,100	0	2,623	4,701	5,472	0	3,603	5,992	6,763
27,100	27,150	0	2,615	4,691	5,461	0	3,595	5,982	6,752
27,150	27,200	0	2,607	4,680	5,451	0	3,587	5,971	6,742
27,200	27,250	0	2,599	4,670	5,440	0	3,579	5,961	6,731
27,250	27,300	0	2,591	4,659	5,430	0	3,571	5,950	6,721
27,300	27,350	0	2,583	4,649	5,419	0	3,563	5,940	6,710
27,350	27,400	0	2,575	4,638	5,409	0	3,555	5,929	6,700
27,400	27,450	0	2,567	4,628	5,398	0	3,547	5,919	6,689
27,450	27,500	0	2,559	4,617	5,388	0	3,539	5,908	6,679
27,500	27,550	0	2,551	4,607	5,377	0	3,531	5,898	6,668
27,550	27,600	0	2,543	4,596	5,367	0	3,523	5,887	6,658
27,600	27,650	0	2,535	4,586	5,356	0	3,515	5,877	6,647
27,650	27,700	0	2,528	4,575	5,346	0	3,507	5,866	6,637
27,700	27,750	0	2,520	4,564	5,335	0	3,499	5,855	6,626
27,750	27,800	0	2,512	4,554	5,324	0	3,491	5,845	6,615
27,800	27,850	0	2,504	4,543	5,314	0	3,483	5,834	6,605
27,850	27,900	0	2,496	4,533	5,303	0	3,475	5,824	6,594
27,900	27,950	0	2,488	4,522	5,293	0	3,467	5,813	6,584
27,950	28,000	0	2,480	4,512	5,282	0	3,459	5,803	6,573
28,000	28,050	0	2,472	4,501	5,272	0	3,451	5,792	6,563
28,050	28,100	0	2,464	4,491	5,261	0	3,443	5,782	6,552
28,100	28,150	0	2,456	4,480	5,251	0	3,435	5,771	6,542
28,150	28,200	0	2,448	4,470	5,240	0	3,427	5,761	6,531
28,200	28,250	0	2,440	4,459	5,230	0	3,419	5,750	6,521
28,250	28,300	0	2,432	4,449	5,219	0	3,411	5,740	6,510
28,300	28,350	0	2,424	4,438	5,209	0	3,403	5,729	6,500
28,350	28,400	0	2,416	4,428	5,198	0	3,395	5,719	6,489
28,400	28,450	0	2,408	4,417	5,188	0	3,387	5,708	6,479
28,450	28,500	0	2,400	4,407	5,177	0	3,379	5,698	6,468
28,500	28,550	0	2,392	4,396	5,167	0	3,371	5,687	6,457
28,550	28,600	0	2,384	4,385	5,156	0	3,363	5,676	6,447
28,600	28,650	0	2,376	4,375	5,145	0	3,355	5,666	6,436
28,650	28,700	0	2,368	4,364	5,135	0	3,347	5,655	6,426
28,700	28,750	0	2,360	4,354	5,124	0	3,339	5,645	6,415
28,750	28,800	0	2,352	4,343	5,114	0	3,331	5,634	6,405
28,800	28,850	0	2,344	4,333	5,103	0	3,323	5,624	6,394
28,850	28,900	0	2,336	4,322	5,093	0	3,315	5,613	6,384
28,900	28,950	0	2,328	4,312	5,082	0	3,307	5,603	6,373
28,950	29,000	0	2,320	4,301	5,072	0	3,299	5,592	6,363
29,000	29,050	0	2,312	4,291	5,061	0	3,291	5,582	6,352
29,050	29,100	0	2,304	4,280	5,051	0	3,283	5,571	6,342
29,100	29,150	0	2,296	4,270	5,040	0	3,275	5,561	6,331
29,150	29,200	0	2,288	4,259	5,030	0	3,267	5,550	6,321
29,200	29,250	0	2,280	4,249	5,019	0	3,259	5,540	6,310
29,250	29,300	0	2,272	4,238	5,009	0	3,251	5,529	6,300
29,300	29,350	0	2,264	4,228	4,998	0	3,243	5,519	6,289
29,350	29,400	0	2,256	4,217	4,988	0	3,235	5,508	6,278
29,400	29,450	0	2,248	4,206	4,977	0	3,227	5,497	6,268
29,450	29,500	0	2,240	4,196	4,966	0	3,219	5,487	6,257
29,500	29,550	0	2,232	4,185	4,956	0	3,211	5,476	6,247
29,550	29,600	0	2,224	4,175	4,945	0	3,203	5,466	6,236
29,600	29,650	0	2,216	4,164	4,935	0	3,195	5,455	6,226
29,650	29,700	0	2,208	4,154	4,924	0	3,187	5,445	6,215
29,700	29,750	0	2,200	4,143	4,914	0	3,179	5,434	6,205
29,750	29,800	0	2,192	4,133	4,903	0	3,172	5,424	6,194
29,800	29,850	0	2,184	4,122	4,893	0	3,164	5,413	6,184
29,850	29,900	0	2,176	4,112	4,882	0	3,156	5,403	6,173
29,900	29,950	0	2,168	4,101	4,872	0	3,148	5,392	6,163
29,950	30,000	0	2,160	4,091	4,861	0	3,140	5,382	6,152
30,000	30,050	0	2,152	4,080	4,851	0	3,132	5,371	6,142
30,050	30,100	0	2,144	4,070	4,840	0	3,124	5,361	6,131
30,100	30,150	0	2,136	4,059	4,830	0	3,116	5,350	6,121
30,150	30,200	0	2,128	4,049	4,819	0	3,108	5,340	6,110
30,200	30,250	0	2,120	4,038	4,808	0	3,100	5,329	6,099
30,250	30,300	0	2,112	4,027	4,798	0	3,092	5,318	6,089
30,300	30,350	0	2,104	4,017	4,787	0	3,084	5,308	6,078
30,350	30,400	0	2,096	4,006	4,777	0	3,076	5,297	6,068
30,400	30,450	0	2,088	3,996	4,766	0	3,068	5,287	6,057
30,450	30,500	0	2,080	3,985	4,756	0	3,060	5,276	6,047
30,500	30,550	0	2,072	3,975	4,745	0	3,052	5,266	6,036
30,550	30,600	0	2,064	3,964	4,735	0	3,044	5,255	6,026
30,600	30,650	0	2,056	3,954	4,724	0	3,036	5,245	6,015
30,650	30,700	0	2,048	3,943	4,714	0	3,028	5,234	6,005
30,700	30,750	0	2,040	3,933	4,703	0	3,020	5,224	5,994
30,750	30,800	0	2,032	3,922	4,693	0	3,012	5,213	5,984
30,800	30,850	0	2,024	3,912	4,682	0	3,004	5,203	5,973
30,850	30,900	0	2,016	3,901	4,672	0	2,996	5,192	5,963
30,900	30,950	0	2,008	3,891	4,661	0	2,988	5,182	5,952
30,950	31,000	0	2,000	3,880	4,651	0	2,980	5,171	5,942
31,000	31,050	0	1,992	3,870	4,640	0	2,972	5,160	5,931
31,050	31,100	0	1,984	3,859	4,629	0	2,964	5,150	5,920
31,100	31,150	0	1,976	3,848	4,619	0	2,956	5,139	5,910
31,150	31,200	0	1,968	3,838	4,608	0	2,948	5,129	5,899

★ Use this column if your filing status is married filing separately and you qualify to claim the EIC. See the instructions for line 27.

(Continued)

Earned Income Credit (EIC) Table - *Continued*

(**Caution.** This is **not** a tax table.)

If the amount you are looking up from the worksheet is–		And your filing status is– Single, head of household, or qualifying surviving spouse★ and you have–				Married filing jointly and you have–			
		0	1	2	3	0	1	2	3
At least	**But less than**	Your credit is–				Your credit is–			
31,200	**31,250**	0	1,960	3,827	4,598	0	2,940	5,118	5,889
31,250	**31,300**	0	1,952	3,817	4,587	0	2,932	5,108	5,878
31,300	**31,350**	0	1,944	3,806	4,577	0	2,924	5,097	5,868
31,350	**31,400**	0	1,936	3,796	4,566	0	2,916	5,087	5,857
31,400	**31,450**	0	1,928	3,785	4,556	0	2,908	5,076	5,847
31,450	**31,500**	0	1,920	3,775	4,545	0	2,900	5,066	5,836
31,500	**31,550**	0	1,912	3,764	4,535	0	2,892	5,055	5,826
31,550	**31,600**	0	1,904	3,754	4,524	0	2,884	5,045	5,815
31,600	**31,650**	0	1,896	3,743	4,514	0	2,876	5,034	5,805
31,650	**31,700**	0	1,888	3,733	4,503	0	2,868	5,024	5,794
31,700	**31,750**	0	1,880	3,722	4,493	0	2,860	5,013	5,784
31,750	**31,800**	0	1,872	3,712	4,482	0	2,852	5,003	5,773
31,800	**31,850**	0	1,864	3,701	4,472	0	2,844	4,992	5,763
31,850	**31,900**	0	1,856	3,691	4,461	0	2,836	4,981	5,752
31,900	**31,950**	0	1,848	3,680	4,450	0	2,828	4,971	5,741
31,950	**32,000**	0	1,840	3,669	4,440	0	2,820	4,960	5,731
32,000	**32,050**	0	1,832	3,659	4,429	0	2,812	4,950	5,720
32,050	**32,100**	0	1,824	3,648	4,419	0	2,804	4,939	5,710
32,100	**32,150**	0	1,816	3,638	4,408	0	2,796	4,929	5,699
32,150	**32,200**	0	1,808	3,627	4,398	0	2,788	4,918	5,689
32,200	**32,250**	0	1,800	3,617	4,387	0	2,780	4,908	5,678
32,250	**32,300**	0	1,792	3,606	4,377	0	2,772	4,897	5,668
32,300	**32,350**	0	1,784	3,596	4,366	0	2,764	4,887	5,657
32,350	**32,400**	0	1,776	3,585	4,356	0	2,756	4,876	5,647
32,400	**32,450**	0	1,768	3,575	4,345	0	2,748	4,866	5,636
32,450	**32,500**	0	1,760	3,564	4,335	0	2,740	4,855	5,626
32,500	**32,550**	0	1,752	3,554	4,324	0	2,732	4,845	5,615
32,550	**32,600**	0	1,744	3,543	4,314	0	2,724	4,834	5,605
32,600	**32,650**	0	1,736	3,533	4,303	0	2,716	4,824	5,594
32,650	**32,700**	0	1,729	3,522	4,293	0	2,708	4,813	5,584
32,700	**32,750**	0	1,721	3,511	4,282	0	2,700	4,802	5,573
32,750	**32,800**	0	1,713	3,501	4,271	0	2,692	4,792	5,562
32,800	**32,850**	0	1,705	3,490	4,261	0	2,684	4,781	5,552
32,850	**32,900**	0	1,697	3,480	4,250	0	2,676	4,771	5,541
32,900	**32,950**	0	1,689	3,469	4,240	0	2,668	4,760	5,531
32,950	**33,000**	0	1,681	3,459	4,229	0	2,660	4,750	5,520
33,000	**33,050**	0	1,673	3,448	4,219	0	2,652	4,739	5,510
33,050	**33,100**	0	1,665	3,438	4,208	0	2,644	4,729	5,499
33,100	**33,150**	0	1,657	3,427	4,198	0	2,636	4,718	5,489
33,150	**33,200**	0	1,649	3,417	4,187	0	2,628	4,708	5,478
33,200	**33,250**	0	1,641	3,406	4,177	0	2,620	4,697	5,468
33,250	**33,300**	0	1,633	3,396	4,166	0	2,612	4,687	5,457
33,300	**33,350**	0	1,625	3,385	4,156	0	2,604	4,676	5,447
33,350	**33,400**	0	1,617	3,375	4,145	0	2,596	4,666	5,436
33,400	**33,450**	0	1,609	3,364	4,135	0	2,588	4,655	5,426
33,450	**33,500**	0	1,601	3,354	4,124	0	2,580	4,645	5,415
33,500	**33,550**	0	1,593	3,343	4,114	0	2,572	4,634	5,404
33,550	**33,600**	0	1,585	3,332	4,103	0	2,564	4,623	5,394
33,600	**33,650**	0	1,577	3,322	4,092	0	2,556	4,613	5,383
33,650	**33,700**	0	1,569	3,311	4,082	0	2,548	4,602	5,373
33,700	**33,750**	0	1,561	3,301	4,071	0	2,540	4,592	5,362
33,750	**33,800**	0	1,553	3,290	4,061	0	2,532	4,581	5,352
33,800	**33,850**	0	1,545	3,280	4,050	0	2,524	4,571	5,341
33,850	**33,900**	0	1,537	3,269	4,040	0	2,516	4,560	5,331
33,900	**33,950**	0	1,529	3,259	4,029	0	2,508	4,550	5,320
33,950	**34,000**	0	1,521	3,248	4,019	0	2,500	4,539	5,310
34,000	**34,050**	0	1,513	3,238	4,008	0	2,492	4,529	5,299
34,050	**34,100**	0	1,505	3,227	3,998	0	2,484	4,518	5,289
34,100	**34,150**	0	1,497	3,217	3,987	0	2,476	4,508	5,278
34,150	**34,200**	0	1,489	3,206	3,977	0	2,468	4,497	5,268
34,200	**34,250**	0	1,481	3,196	3,966	0	2,460	4,487	5,257
34,250	**34,300**	0	1,473	3,185	3,956	0	2,452	4,476	5,247
34,300	**34,350**	0	1,465	3,175	3,945	0	2,444	4,466	5,236
34,350	**34,400**	0	1,457	3,164	3,935	0	2,436	4,455	5,225
34,400	**34,450**	0	1,449	3,153	3,924	0	2,428	4,444	5,215
34,450	**34,500**	0	1,441	3,143	3,913	0	2,420	4,434	5,204
34,500	**34,550**	0	1,433	3,132	3,903	0	2,412	4,423	5,194
34,550	**34,600**	0	1,425	3,122	3,892	0	2,404	4,413	5,183
34,600	**34,650**	0	1,417	3,111	3,882	0	2,396	4,402	5,173
34,650	**34,700**	0	1,409	3,101	3,871	0	2,388	4,392	5,162
34,700	**34,750**	0	1,401	3,090	3,861	0	2,380	4,381	5,152
34,750	**34,800**	0	1,393	3,080	3,850	0	2,373	4,371	5,141
34,800	**34,850**	0	1,385	3,069	3,840	0	2,365	4,360	5,131
34,850	**34,900**	0	1,377	3,059	3,829	0	2,357	4,350	5,120
34,900	**34,950**	0	1,369	3,048	3,819	0	2,349	4,339	5,110
34,950	**35,000**	0	1,361	3,038	3,808	0	2,341	4,329	5,099
35,000	**35,050**	0	1,353	3,027	3,798	0	2,333	4,318	5,089
35,050	**35,100**	0	1,345	3,017	3,787	0	2,325	4,308	5,078
35,100	**35,150**	0	1,337	3,006	3,777	0	2,317	4,297	5,068
35,150	**35,200**	0	1,329	2,996	3,766	0	2,309	4,287	5,057
35,200	**35,250**	0	1,321	2,985	3,755	0	2,301	4,276	5,046
35,250	**35,300**	0	1,313	2,974	3,745	0	2,293	4,265	5,036
35,300	**35,350**	0	1,305	2,964	3,734	0	2,285	4,255	5,025
35,350	**35,400**	0	1,297	2,953	3,724	0	2,277	4,244	5,015
35,400	**35,450**	0	1,289	2,943	3,713	0	2,269	4,234	5,004
35,450	**35,500**	0	1,281	2,932	3,703	0	2,261	4,223	4,994
35,500	**35,550**	0	1,273	2,922	3,692	0	2,253	4,213	4,983
35,550	**35,600**	0	1,265	2,911	3,682	0	2,245	4,202	4,973
35,600	**35,650**	0	1,257	2,901	3,671	0	2,237	4,192	4,962
35,650	**35,700**	0	1,249	2,890	3,661	0	2,229	4,181	4,952
35,700	**35,750**	0	1,241	2,880	3,650	0	2,221	4,171	4,941
35,750	**35,800**	0	1,233	2,869	3,640	0	2,213	4,160	4,931
35,800	**35,850**	0	1,225	2,859	3,629	0	2,205	4,150	4,920
35,850	**35,900**	0	1,217	2,848	3,619	0	2,197	4,139	4,910
35,900	**35,950**	0	1,209	2,838	3,608	0	2,189	4,129	4,899
35,950	**36,000**	0	1,201	2,827	3,598	0	2,181	4,118	4,889
36,000	**36,050**	0	1,193	2,817	3,587	0	2,173	4,107	4,878
36,050	**36,100**	0	1,185	2,806	3,576	0	2,165	4,097	4,867
36,100	**36,150**	0	1,177	2,795	3,566	0	2,157	4,086	4,857
36,150	**36,200**	0	1,169	2,785	3,555	0	2,149	4,076	4,846
36,200	**36,250**	0	1,161	2,774	3,545	0	2,141	4,065	4,836
36,250	**36,300**	0	1,153	2,764	3,534	0	2,133	4,055	4,825
36,300	**36,350**	0	1,145	2,753	3,524	0	2,125	4,044	4,815
36,350	**36,400**	0	1,137	2,743	3,513	0	2,117	4,034	4,804
36,400	**36,450**	0	1,129	2,732	3,503	0	2,109	4,023	4,794
36,450	**36,500**	0	1,121	2,722	3,492	0	2,101	4,013	4,783
36,500	**36,550**	0	1,113	2,711	3,482	0	2,093	4,002	4,773
36,550	**36,600**	0	1,105	2,701	3,471	0	2,085	3,992	4,762
36,600	**36,650**	0	1,097	2,690	3,461	0	2,077	3,981	4,752
36,650	**36,700**	0	1,089	2,680	3,450	0	2,069	3,971	4,741
36,700	**36,750**	0	1,081	2,669	3,440	0	2,061	3,960	4,731
36,750	**36,800**	0	1,073	2,659	3,429	0	2,053	3,950	4,720
36,800	**36,850**	0	1,065	2,648	3,419	0	2,045	3,939	4,710
36,850	**36,900**	0	1,057	2,638	3,408	0	2,037	3,928	4,699
36,900	**36,950**	0	1,049	2,627	3,397	0	2,029	3,918	4,688
36,950	**37,000**	0	1,041	2,616	3,387	0	2,021	3,907	4,678
37,000	**37,050**	0	1,033	2,606	3,376	0	2,013	3,897	4,667
37,050	**37,100**	0	1,025	2,595	3,366	0	2,005	3,886	4,657
37,100	**37,150**	0	1,017	2,585	3,355	0	1,997	3,876	4,646
37,150	**37,200**	0	1,009	2,574	3,345	0	1,989	3,865	4,636
37,200	**37,250**	0	1,001	2,564	3,334	0	1,981	3,855	4,625
37,250	**37,300**	0	993	2,553	3,324	0	1,973	3,844	4,615
37,300	**37,350**	0	985	2,543	3,313	0	1,965	3,834	4,604
37,350	**37,400**	0	977	2,532	3,303	0	1,957	3,823	4,594
37,400	**37,450**	0	969	2,522	3,292	0	1,949	3,813	4,583
37,450	**37,500**	0	961	2,511	3,282	0	1,941	3,802	4,573
37,500	**37,550**	0	953	2,501	3,271	0	1,933	3,792	4,562
37,550	**37,600**	0	945	2,490	3,261	0	1,925	3,781	4,552

★ Use this column if your filing status is married filing separately and you qualify to claim the EIC. See the instructions for line 27.

(Continued)

Earned Income Credit (EIC) Table - *Continued*

(**Caution.** This is **not** a tax table.)

If the amount you are looking up from the worksheet is–		And your filing status is– Single, head of household, or qualifying surviving spouse★ and you have–				Married filing jointly and you have–			
		0	1	2	3	0	1	2	3
At least	But less than	Your credit is–				Your credit is–			
37,600	37,650	0	937	2,480	3,250	0	1,917	3,771	4,541
37,650	37,700	0	930	2,469	3,240	0	1,909	3,760	4,531
37,700	37,750	0	922	2,458	3,229	0	1,901	3,749	4,520
37,750	37,800	0	914	2,448	3,218	0	1,893	3,739	4,509
37,800	37,850	0	906	2,437	3,208	0	1,885	3,728	4,499
37,850	37,900	0	898	2,427	3,197	0	1,877	3,718	4,488
37,900	37,950	0	890	2,416	3,187	0	1,869	3,707	4,478
37,950	38,000	0	882	2,406	3,176	0	1,861	3,697	4,467
38,000	38,050	0	874	2,395	3,166	0	1,853	3,686	4,457
38,050	38,100	0	866	2,385	3,155	0	1,845	3,676	4,446
38,100	38,150	0	858	2,374	3,145	0	1,837	3,665	4,436
38,150	38,200	0	850	2,364	3,134	0	1,829	3,655	4,425
38,200	38,250	0	842	2,353	3,124	0	1,821	3,644	4,415
38,250	38,300	0	834	2,343	3,113	0	1,813	3,634	4,404
38,300	38,350	0	826	2,332	3,103	0	1,805	3,623	4,394
38,350	38,400	0	818	2,322	3,092	0	1,797	3,613	4,383
38,400	38,450	0	810	2,311	3,082	0	1,789	3,602	4,373
38,450	38,500	0	802	2,301	3,071	0	1,781	3,592	4,362
38,500	38,550	0	794	2,290	3,061	0	1,773	3,581	4,351
38,550	38,600	0	786	2,279	3,050	0	1,765	3,570	4,341
38,600	38,650	0	778	2,269	3,039	0	1,757	3,560	4,330
38,650	38,700	0	770	2,258	3,029	0	1,749	3,549	4,320
38,700	38,750	0	762	2,248	3,018	0	1,741	3,539	4,309
38,750	38,800	0	754	2,237	3,008	0	1,733	3,528	4,299
38,800	38,850	0	746	2,227	2,997	0	1,725	3,518	4,288
38,850	38,900	0	738	2,216	2,987	0	1,717	3,507	4,278
38,900	38,950	0	730	2,206	2,976	0	1,709	3,497	4,267
38,950	39,000	0	722	2,195	2,966	0	1,701	3,486	4,257
39,000	39,050	0	714	2,185	2,955	0	1,693	3,476	4,246
39,050	39,100	0	706	2,174	2,945	0	1,685	3,465	4,236
39,100	39,150	0	698	2,164	2,934	0	1,677	3,455	4,225
39,150	39,200	0	690	2,153	2,924	0	1,669	3,444	4,215
39,200	39,250	0	682	2,143	2,913	0	1,661	3,434	4,204
39,250	39,300	0	674	2,132	2,903	0	1,653	3,423	4,194
39,300	39,350	0	666	2,122	2,892	0	1,645	3,413	4,183
39,350	39,400	0	658	2,111	2,882	0	1,637	3,402	4,172
39,400	39,450	0	650	2,100	2,871	0	1,629	3,391	4,162
39,450	39,500	0	642	2,090	2,860	0	1,621	3,381	4,151
39,500	39,550	0	634	2,079	2,850	0	1,613	3,370	4,141
39,550	39,600	0	626	2,069	2,839	0	1,605	3,360	4,130
39,600	39,650	0	618	2,058	2,829	0	1,597	3,349	4,120
39,650	39,700	0	610	2,048	2,818	0	1,589	3,339	4,109
39,700	39,750	0	602	2,037	2,808	0	1,581	3,328	4,099
39,750	39,800	0	594	2,027	2,797	0	1,574	3,318	4,088
39,800	39,850	0	586	2,016	2,787	0	1,566	3,307	4,078
39,850	39,900	0	578	2,006	2,776	0	1,558	3,297	4,067
39,900	39,950	0	570	1,995	2,766	0	1,550	3,286	4,057
39,950	40,000	0	562	1,985	2,755	0	1,542	3,276	4,046
40,000	40,050	0	554	1,974	2,745	0	1,534	3,265	4,036
40,050	40,100	0	546	1,964	2,734	0	1,526	3,255	4,025
40,100	40,150	0	538	1,953	2,724	0	1,518	3,244	4,015
40,150	40,200	0	530	1,943	2,713	0	1,510	3,234	4,004
40,200	40,250	0	522	1,932	2,702	0	1,502	3,223	3,993
40,250	40,300	0	514	1,921	2,692	0	1,494	3,212	3,983
40,300	40,350	0	506	1,911	2,681	0	1,486	3,202	3,972
40,350	40,400	0	498	1,900	2,671	0	1,478	3,191	3,962
40,400	40,450	0	490	1,890	2,660	0	1,470	3,181	3,951
40,450	40,500	0	482	1,879	2,650	0	1,462	3,170	3,941
40,500	40,550	0	474	1,869	2,639	0	1,454	3,160	3,930
40,550	40,600	0	466	1,858	2,629	0	1,446	3,149	3,920
40,600	40,650	0	458	1,848	2,618	0	1,438	3,139	3,909
40,650	40,700	0	450	1,837	2,608	0	1,430	3,128	3,899
40,700	40,750	0	442	1,827	2,597	0	1,422	3,118	3,888
40,750	40,800	0	434	1,816	2,587	0	1,414	3,107	3,878

If the amount you are looking up from the worksheet is–		And your filing status is– Single, head of household, or qualifying surviving spouse★ and you have–				Married filing jointly and you have–			
		0	1	2	3	0	1	2	3
At least	But less than	Your credit is–				Your credit is–			
40,800	40,850	0	426	1,806	2,576	0	1,406	3,097	3,867
40,850	40,900	0	418	1,795	2,566	0	1,398	3,086	3,857
40,900	40,950	0	410	1,785	2,555	0	1,390	3,076	3,846
40,950	41,000	0	402	1,774	2,545	0	1,382	3,065	3,836
41,000	41,050	0	394	1,764	2,534	0	1,374	3,054	3,825
41,050	41,100	0	386	1,753	2,523	0	1,366	3,044	3,814
41,100	41,150	0	378	1,742	2,513	0	1,358	3,033	3,804
41,150	41,200	0	370	1,732	2,502	0	1,350	3,023	3,793
41,200	41,250	0	362	1,721	2,492	0	1,342	3,012	3,783
41,250	41,300	0	354	1,711	2,481	0	1,334	3,002	3,772
41,300	41,350	0	346	1,700	2,471	0	1,326	2,991	3,762
41,350	41,400	0	338	1,690	2,460	0	1,318	2,981	3,751
41,400	41,450	0	330	1,679	2,450	0	1,310	2,970	3,741
41,450	41,500	0	322	1,669	2,439	0	1,302	2,960	3,730
41,500	41,550	0	314	1,658	2,429	0	1,294	2,949	3,720
41,550	41,600	0	306	1,648	2,418	0	1,286	2,939	3,709
41,600	41,650	0	298	1,637	2,408	0	1,278	2,928	3,699
41,650	41,700	0	290	1,627	2,397	0	1,270	2,918	3,688
41,700	41,750	0	282	1,616	2,387	0	1,262	2,907	3,678
41,750	41,800	0	274	1,606	2,376	0	1,254	2,897	3,667
41,800	41,850	0	266	1,595	2,366	0	1,246	2,886	3,657
41,850	41,900	0	258	1,585	2,355	0	1,238	2,875	3,646
41,900	41,950	0	250	1,574	2,344	0	1,230	2,865	3,635
41,950	42,000	0	242	1,563	2,334	0	1,222	2,854	3,625
42,000	42,050	0	234	1,553	2,323	0	1,214	2,844	3,614
42,050	42,100	0	226	1,542	2,313	0	1,206	2,833	3,604
42,100	42,150	0	218	1,532	2,302	0	1,198	2,823	3,593
42,150	42,200	0	210	1,521	2,292	0	1,190	2,812	3,583
42,200	42,250	0	202	1,511	2,281	0	1,182	2,802	3,572
42,250	42,300	0	194	1,500	2,271	0	1,174	2,791	3,562
42,300	42,350	0	186	1,490	2,260	0	1,166	2,781	3,551
42,350	42,400	0	178	1,479	2,250	0	1,158	2,770	3,541
42,400	42,450	0	170	1,469	2,239	0	1,150	2,760	3,530
42,450	42,500	0	162	1,458	2,229	0	1,142	2,749	3,520
42,500	42,550	0	154	1,448	2,218	0	1,134	2,739	3,509
42,550	42,600	0	146	1,437	2,208	0	1,126	2,728	3,499
42,600	42,650	0	138	1,427	2,197	0	1,118	2,718	3,488
42,650	42,700	0	131	1,416	2,187	0	1,110	2,707	3,478
42,700	42,750	0	123	1,405	2,176	0	1,102	2,696	3,467
42,750	42,800	0	115	1,395	2,165	0	1,094	2,686	3,456
42,800	42,850	0	107	1,384	2,155	0	1,086	2,675	3,446
42,850	42,900	0	99	1,374	2,144	0	1,078	2,665	3,435
42,900	42,950	0	91	1,363	2,134	0	1,070	2,654	3,425
42,950	43,000	0	83	1,353	2,123	0	1,062	2,644	3,414
43,000	43,050	0	75	1,342	2,113	0	1,054	2,633	3,404
43,050	43,100	0	67	1,332	2,102	0	1,046	2,623	3,393
43,100	43,150	0	59	1,321	2,092	0	1,038	2,612	3,383
43,150	43,200	0	51	1,311	2,081	0	1,030	2,602	3,372
43,200	43,250	0	43	1,300	2,071	0	1,022	2,591	3,362
43,250	43,300	0	35	1,290	2,060	0	1,014	2,581	3,351
43,300	43,350	0	27	1,279	2,050	0	1,006	2,570	3,341
43,350	43,400	0	19	1,269	2,039	0	998	2,560	3,330
43,400	43,450	0	11	1,258	2,029	0	990	2,549	3,320
43,450	43,500	0	*	1,248	2,018	0	982	2,539	3,309
43,500	43,550	0	0	1,237	2,008	0	974	2,528	3,298
43,550	43,600	0	0	1,226	1,997	0	966	2,517	3,288
43,600	43,650	0	0	1,216	1,986	0	958	2,507	3,277
43,650	43,700	0	0	1,205	1,976	0	950	2,496	3,267
43,700	43,750	0	0	1,195	1,965	0	942	2,486	3,256
43,750	43,800	0	0	1,184	1,955	0	934	2,475	3,246
43,800	43,850	0	0	1,174	1,944	0	926	2,465	3,235
43,850	43,900	0	0	1,163	1,934	0	918	2,454	3,225
43,900	43,950	0	0	1,153	1,923	0	910	2,444	3,214
43,950	44,000	0	0	1,142	1,913	0	902	2,433	3,204

★ Use this column if your filing status is married filing separately and you qualify to claim the EIC. See the instructions for line 27.

* If the amount you are looking up from the worksheet is at least $43,450 but less than $43,492, and you have one qualifying child who has a valid SSN, your credit is $3.

If the amount you are looking up from the worksheet is $43,492 or more, and you have one qualifying child who has a valid SSN, you can't take the credit.

(Continued)

Earned Income Credit (EIC) Table - *Continued* **(Caution.** This is **not** a tax table.)

If the amount you are looking up from the worksheet is–		And your filing status is– Single, head of household, or qualifying surviving spouse★ and you have–				Married filing jointly and you have–			
		0	1	2	3	0	1	2	3
At least	But less than	Your credit is–				Your credit is–			
44,000	44,050	0	0	1,132	1,902	0	894	2,423	3,193
44,050	44,100	0	0	1,121	1,892	0	886	2,412	3,183
44,100	44,150	0	0	1,111	1,881	0	878	2,402	3,172
44,150	44,200	0	0	1,100	1,871	0	870	2,391	3,162
44,200	44,250	0	0	1,090	1,860	0	862	2,381	3,151
44,250	44,300	0	0	1,079	1,850	0	854	2,370	3,141
44,300	44,350	0	0	1,069	1,839	0	846	2,360	3,130
44,350	44,400	0	0	1,058	1,829	0	838	2,349	3,119
44,400	44,450	0	0	1,047	1,818	0	830	2,338	3,109
44,450	44,500	0	0	1,037	1,807	0	822	2,328	3,098
44,500	44,550	0	0	1,026	1,797	0	814	2,317	3,088
44,550	44,600	0	0	1,016	1,786	0	806	2,307	3,077
44,600	44,650	0	0	1,005	1,776	0	798	2,296	3,067
44,650	44,700	0	0	995	1,765	0	790	2,286	3,056
44,700	44,750	0	0	984	1,755	0	782	2,275	3,046
44,750	44,800	0	0	974	1,744	0	775	2,265	3,035
44,800	44,850	0	0	963	1,734	0	767	2,254	3,025
44,850	44,900	0	0	953	1,723	0	759	2,244	3,014
44,900	44,950	0	0	042	1,/13	0	751	2,233	3,004
44,950	45,000	0	0	932	1,702	0	743	2,223	2,993
45,000	45,050	0	0	921	1,692	0	735	2,212	2,983
45,050	45,100	0	0	911	1,681	0	727	2,202	2,972
45,100	45,150	0	0	900	1,671	0	719	2,191	2,962
45,150	45,200	0	0	890	1,660	0	711	2,181	2,951
45,200	45,250	0	0	879	1,649	0	703	2,170	2,940
45,250	45,300	0	0	868	1,639	0	695	2,159	2,930
45,300	45,350	0	0	858	1,628	0	687	2,149	2,919
45,350	45,400	0	0	847	1,618	0	679	2,138	2,909
45,400	45,450	0	0	837	1,607	0	671	2,128	2,898
45,450	45,500	0	0	826	1,597	0	663	2,117	2,888
45,500	45,550	0	0	816	1,586	0	655	2,107	2,877
45,550	45,600	0	0	805	1,576	0	647	2,096	2,867
45,600	45,650	0	0	795	1,565	0	639	2,086	2,856
45,650	45,700	0	0	784	1,555	0	631	2,075	2,846
45,700	45,750	0	0	774	1,544	0	623	2,065	2,835
45,750	45,800	0	0	763	1,534	0	615	2,054	2,825
45,800	45,850	0	0	753	1,523	0	607	2,044	2,814
45,850	45,900	0	0	742	1,513	0	599	2,033	2,804
45,900	45,950	0	0	732	1,502	0	591	2,023	2,793
45,950	46,000	0	0	721	1,492	0	583	2,012	2,783
46,000	46,050	0	0	711	1,481	0	575	2,001	2,772
46,050	46,100	0	0	700	1,470	0	567	1,991	2,761
46,100	46,150	0	0	689	1,460	0	559	1,980	2,751
46,150	46,200	0	0	679	1,449	0	551	1,970	2,740
46,200	46,250	0	0	668	1,439	0	543	1,959	2,730
46,250	46,300	0	0	658	1,428	0	535	1,949	2,719
46,300	46,350	0	0	647	1,418	0	527	1,938	2,709
46,350	46,400	0	0	637	1,407	0	519	1,928	2,698
46,400	46,450	0	0	626	1,397	0	511	1,917	2,688
46,450	46,500	0	0	616	1,386	0	503	1,907	2,677
46,500	46,550	0	0	605	1,376	0	495	1,896	2,667
46,550	46,600	0	0	595	1,365	0	487	1,886	2,656
46,600	46,650	0	0	584	1,355	0	479	1,875	2,646
46,650	46,700	0	0	574	1,344	0	471	1,865	2,635
46,700	46,750	0	0	563	1,334	0	463	1,854	2,625
46,750	46,800	0	0	553	1,323	0	455	1,844	2,614
46,800	46,850	0	0	542	1,313	0	447	1,833	2,604
46,850	46,900	0	0	532	1,302	0	439	1,822	2,593
46,900	46,950	0	0	521	1,291	0	431	1,812	2,582
46,950	47,000	0	0	510	1,281	0	423	1,801	2,572
47,000	47,050	0	0	500	1,270	0	415	1,791	2,561
47,050	47,100	0	0	489	1,260	0	407	1,780	2,551
47,100	47,150	0	0	479	1,249	0	399	1,770	2,540
47,150	47,200	0	0	468	1,239	0	391	1,759	2,530
47,200	47,250	0	0	458	1,228	0	383	1,749	2,519
47,250	47,300	0	0	447	1,218	0	375	1,738	2,509
47,300	47,350	0	0	437	1,207	0	367	1,728	2,498
47,350	47,400	0	0	426	1,197	0	359	1,717	2,488
47,400	47,450	0	0	416	1,186	0	351	1,707	2,477
47,450	47,500	0	0	405	1,176	0	343	1,600	2,467
47,500	47,550	0	0	395	1,165	0	335	1,686	2,456
47,550	47,600	0	0	384	1,155	0	327	1,675	2,446
47,600	47,650	0	0	374	1,144	0	319	1,665	2,435
47,650	47,700	0	0	363	1,134	0	311	1,654	2,425
47,700	47,750	0	0	352	1,123	0	303	1,643	2,414
47,750	47,800	0	0	342	1,112	0	295	1,633	2,403
47,800	47,850	0	0	331	1,102	0	287	1,622	2,393
47,850	47,900	0	0	321	1,091	0	279	1,612	2,382
47,900	47,950	0	0	310	1,081	0	271	1,601	2,372
47,950	48,000	0	0	300	1,070	0	263	1,591	2,361
48,000	48,050	0	0	289	1,060	0	255	1,580	2,351
48,050	48,100	0	0	279	1,049	0	247	1,570	2,340
48,100	48,150	0	0	268	1,039	0	239	1,559	2,330
48,150	48,200	0	0	258	1,028	0	231	1,549	2,319
48,200	48,250	0	0	247	1,018	0	223	1,538	2,309
48,250	48,300	0	0	237	1,007	0	215	1,528	2,298
48,300	48,350	0	0	226	997	0	207	1,517	2,288
48,350	48,400	0	0	216	986	0	199	1,507	2,277
48,400	48,450	0	0	205	976	0	191	1,496	2,267
48,450	48,500	0	0	195	965	0	183	1,486	2,256
48,500	48,550	0	0	184	955	0	175	1,475	2,245
48,550	48,600	0	0	173	944	0	167	1,464	2,235
48,600	48,650	0	0	163	933	0	159	1,454	2,224
48,650	48,700	0	0	152	923	0	151	1,443	2,214
48,700	48,750	0	0	142	912	0	143	1,433	2,203
48,750	48,800	0	0	131	902	0	135	1,422	2,193
48,800	48,850	0	0	121	891	0	127	1,412	2,182
48,850	48,900	0	0	110	881	0	119	1,401	2,172
48,900	48,950	0	0	100	870	0	111	1,391	2,161
48,950	49,000	0	0	89	860	0	103	1,380	2,151
49,000	49,050	0	0	79	849	0	95	1,370	2,140
49,050	49,100	0	0	68	839	0	87	1,359	2,130
49,100	49,150	0	0	58	828	0	79	1,349	2,119
49,150	49,200	0	0	47	818	0	71	1,338	2,109
49,200	49,250	0	0	37	807	0	63	1,328	2,098
49,250	49,300	0	0	26	797	0	55	1,317	2,088
49,300	49,350	0	0	16	786	0	47	1,307	2,077
49,350	49,400	0	0	*	776	0	39	1,296	2,066
49,400	49,450	0	0	0	765	0	31	1,285	2,056
49,450	49,500	0	0	0	754	0	23	1,275	2,045
49,500	49,550	0	0	0	744	0	15	1,264	2,035
49,550	49,600	0	0	0	733	0	7	1,254	2,024

★ Use this column if your filing status is married filing separately and you qualify to claim the EIC. See the instructions for line 27.

* If the amount you are looking up from the worksheet is at least $49,350 but less than $49,399, and you have two qualifying children who have valid SSNs, your credit is $5.

If the amount you are looking up from the worksheet is $49,399 or more, and you have two qualifying children who have valid SSNs, you can't take the credit.

(Continued)

Earned Income Credit (EIC) Table - *Continued* (**Caution.** This is **not** a tax table.)

If the amount you are looking up from the worksheet is–		And your filing status is– Single, head of household, or qualifying surviving spouse★ and you have–				Married filing jointly and you have–			
		0	1	2	3	0	1	2	3
At least	But less than	Your credit is–				Your credit is–			
49,600	49,650	0	0	0	723	0	*	1,243	2,014
49,650	49,700	0	0	0	712	0	0	1,233	2,003
49,700	49,750	0	0	0	702	0	0	1,222	1,993
49,750	49,800	0	0	0	691	0	0	1,212	1,982
49,800	49,850	0	0	0	681	0	0	1,201	1,972
49,850	49,900	0	0	0	670	0	0	1,191	1,961
49,900	49,950	0	0	0	660	0	0	1,180	1,951
49,950	50,000	0	0	0	649	0	0	1,170	1,940
50,000	50,050	0	0	0	639	0	0	1,159	1,930
50,050	50,100	0	0	0	628	0	0	1,149	1,919
50,100	50,150	0	0	0	618	0	0	1,138	1,909
50,150	50,200	0	0	0	607	0	0	1,128	1,898
50,200	50,250	0	0	0	596	0	0	1,117	1,887
50,250	50,300	0	0	0	586	0	0	1,106	1,877
50,300	50,350	0	0	0	575	0	0	1,096	1,866
50,350	50,400	0	0	0	565	0	0	1,085	1,856
50,400	50,450	0	0	0	554	0	0	1,075	1,845
50,450	50,500	0	0	0	544	0	0	1,064	1,835
50,500	50,550	0	0	0	533	0	0	1,054	1,824
50,550	50,600	0	0	0	523	0	0	1,043	1,814
50,600	50,650	0	0	0	512	0	0	1,033	1,803
50,650	50,700	0	0	0	502	0	0	1,022	1,793
50,700	50,750	0	0	0	491	0	0	1,012	1,782
50,750	50,800	0	0	0	481	0	0	1,001	1,772
50,800	50,850	0	0	0	470	0	0	991	1,761
50,850	50,900	0	0	0	460	0	0	980	1,751
50,900	50,950	0	0	0	449	0	0	970	1,740
50,950	51,000	0	0	0	439	0	0	959	1,730
51,000	51,050	0	0	0	428	0	0	948	1,719
51,050	51,100	0	0	0	417	0	0	938	1,708
51,100	51,150	0	0	0	407	0	0	927	1,698
51,150	51,200	0	0	0	396	0	0	917	1,687
51,200	51,250	0	0	0	386	0	0	906	1,677
51,250	51,300	0	0	0	375	0	0	896	1,666
51,300	51,350	0	0	0	365	0	0	885	1,656
51,350	51,400	0	0	0	354	0	0	875	1,645
51,400	51,450	0	0	0	344	0	0	864	1,635
51,450	51,500	0	0	0	333	0	0	854	1,624
51,500	51,550	0	0	0	323	0	0	843	1,614
51,550	51,600	0	0	0	312	0	0	833	1,603
51,600	51,650	0	0	0	302	0	0	822	1,593
51,650	51,700	0	0	0	291	0	0	812	1,582
51,700	51,750	0	0	0	281	0	0	801	1,572
51,750	51,800	0	0	0	270	0	0	791	1,561
51,800	51,850	0	0	0	260	0	0	780	1,551
51,850	51,900	0	0	0	249	0	0	769	1,540
51,900	51,950	0	0	0	238	0	0	759	1,529
51,950	52,000	0	0	0	228	0	0	748	1,519

If the amount you are looking up from the worksheet is–		And your filing status is– Single, head of household, or qualifying surviving spouse★ and you have–				Married filing jointly and you have–			
		0	1	2	3	0	1	2	3
At least	But less than	Your credit is–				Your credit is–			
52,000	52,050	0	0	0	217	0	0	738	1,508
52,050	52,100	0	0	0	207	0	0	727	1,498
52,100	52,150	0	0	0	196	0	0	717	1,487
52,150	52,200	0	0	0	186	0	0	706	1,477
52,200	52,250	0	0	0	175	0	0	696	1,466
52,250	52,300	0	0	0	165	0	0	685	1,456
52,300	52,350	0	0	0	154	0	0	675	1,445
52,350	52,400	0	0	0	144	0	0	664	1,435
52,400	52,450	0	0	0	133	0	0	654	1,424
52,450	52,500	0	0	0	123	0	0	643	1,414
52,500	52,550	0	0	0	112	0	0	633	1,403
52,550	52,600	0	0	0	102	0	0	622	1,393
52,600	52,650	0	0	0	91	0	0	612	1,382
52,650	52,700	0	0	0	81	0	0	601	1,372
52,700	52,750	0	0	0	70	0	0	590	1,361
52,750	52,800	0	0	0	59	0	0	580	1,350
52,800	52,850	0	0	0	49	0	0	569	1,340
52,850	52,900	0	0	0	38	0	0	559	1,329
52,900	52,950	0	0	0	28	0	0	548	1,319
52,950	53,000	0	0	0	17	0	0	538	1,308
53,000	53,050	0	0	0	7	0	0	527	1,298
53,050	53,100	0	0	0	**	0	0	517	1,287
53,100	53,150	0	0	0	0	0	0	506	1,277
53,150	53,200	0	0	0	0	0	0	496	1,266
53,200	53,250	0	0	0	0	0	0	485	1,256
53,250	53,300	0	0	0	0	0	0	475	1,245
53,300	53,350	0	0	0	0	0	0	464	1,235
53,350	53,400	0	0	0	0	0	0	454	1,224
53,400	53,450	0	0	0	0	0	0	443	1,214
53,450	53,500	0	0	0	0	0	0	433	1,203
53,500	53,550	0	0	0	0	0	0	422	1,192
53,550	53,600	0	0	0	0	0	0	411	1,182
53,600	53,650	0	0	0	0	0	0	401	1,171
53,650	53,700	0	0	0	0	0	0	390	1,161
53,700	53,750	0	0	0	0	0	0	380	1,150
53,750	53,800	0	0	0	0	0	0	369	1,140
53,800	53,850	0	0	0	0	0	0	359	1,129
53,850	53,900	0	0	0	0	0	0	348	1,119
53,900	53,950	0	0	0	0	0	0	338	1,108
53,950	54,000	0	0	0	0	0	0	327	1,098
54,000	54,050	0	0	0	0	0	0	317	1,087
54,050	54,100	0	0	0	0	0	0	306	1,077
54,100	54,150	0	0	0	0	0	0	296	1,066
54,150	54,200	0	0	0	0	0	0	285	1,056
54,200	54,250	0	0	0	0	0	0	275	1,045
54,250	54,300	0	0	0	0	0	0	264	1,035
54,300	54,350	0	0	0	0	0	0	254	1,024
54,350	54,400	0	0	0	0	0	0	243	1,013

★ Use this column if your filing status is married filing separately and you qualify to claim the EIC. See the instructions for line 27.

* If the amount you are looking up from the worksheet is at least $49,600 but less than $49,622, and you have one qualifying child who has a valid SSN, your credit is $2.

If the amount you are looking up from the worksheet is $49,622 or more, and you have one qualifying child who has a valid SSN, you can't take the credit.

** If the amount you are looking up from the worksheet is at least $53,050 but less than $53,057, and you have three qualifying children who have valid SSNs, your credit is $1.

If the amount you are looking up from the worksheet is $53,057 or more, and you have three qualifying children who have valid SSNs, you can't take the credit.

(Continued)

Earned Income Credit (EIC) Table - *Continued*

(**Caution.** This is **not** a tax table.)

If the amount you are looking up from the worksheet is–		And your filing status is–							
		Single, head of household, or qualifying surviving spouse★ and you have–				Married filing jointly and you have–			
		0	1	2	3	0	1	2	3
At least	But less than	Your credit is–				Your credit is–			
54,400	54,450	0	0	0	0	0	0	232	1,003
54,450	54,500	0	0	0	0	0	0	222	992
54,500	54,550	0	0	0	0	0	0	211	982
54,550	54,600	0	0	0	0	0	0	201	971
54,600	54,650	0	0	0	0	0	0	190	961
54,650	54,700	0	0	0	0	0	0	180	950
54,700	54,750	0	0	0	0	0	0	169	940
54,750	54,800	0	0	0	0	0	0	159	929
54,800	54,850	0	0	0	0	0	0	148	919
54,850	54,900	0	0	0	0	0	0	138	908
54,900	54,950	0	0	0	0	0	0	127	898
54,950	55,000	0	0	0	0	0	0	117	887
55,000	55,050	0	0	0	0	0	0	106	877
55,050	55,100	0	0	0	0	0	0	96	866
55,100	55,150	0	0	0	0	0	0	85	856
55,150	55,200	0	0	0	0	0	0	75	845
55,200	55,250	0	0	0	0	0	0	64	834
55,250	55,300	0	0	0	0	0	0	53	824
55,300	55,350	0	0	0	0	0	0	43	813
55,350	55,400	0	0	0	0	0	0	32	803
55,400	55,450	0	0	0	0	0	0	22	792
55,450	55,500	0	0	0	0	0	0	11	782
55,500	55,550	0	0	0	0	0	0	*	771
55,550	55,600	0	0	0	0	0	0	0	761
55,600	55,650	0	0	0	0	0	0	0	750
55,650	55,700	0	0	0	0	0	0	0	740
55,700	55,750	0	0	0	0	0	0	0	729
55,750	55,800	0	0	0	0	0	0	0	719
55,800	55,850	0	0	0	0	0	0	0	708
55,850	55,900	0	0	0	0	0	0	0	698
55,900	55,950	0	0	0	0	0	0	0	687
55,950	56,000	0	0	0	0	0	0	0	677
56,000	56,050	0	0	0	0	0	0	0	666
56,050	56,100	0	0	0	0	0	0	0	655
56,100	56,150	0	0	0	0	0	0	0	645
56,150	56,200	0	0	0	0	0	0	0	634
56,200	56,250	0	0	0	0	0	0	0	624
56,250	56,300	0	0	0	0	0	0	0	613
56,300	56,350	0	0	0	0	0	0	0	603
56,350	56,400	0	0	0	0	0	0	0	592
56,400	56,450	0	0	0	0	0	0	0	582
56,450	56,500	0	0	0	0	0	0	0	571
56,500	56,550	0	0	0	0	0	0	0	561
56,550	56,600	0	0	0	0	0	0	0	550
56,600	56,650	0	0	0	0	0	0	0	540
56,650	56,700	0	0	0	0	0	0	0	529
56,700	56,750	0	0	0	0	0	0	0	519
56,750	56,800	0	0	0	0	0	0	0	508
56,800	56,850	0	0	0	0	0	0	0	498
56,850	56,900	0	0	0	0	0	0	0	487
56,900	56,950	0	0	0	0	0	0	0	476
56,950	57,000	0	0	0	0	0	0	0	466
57,000	57,050	0	0	0	0	0	0	0	455
57,050	57,100	0	0	0	0	0	0	0	445
57,100	57,150	0	0	0	0	0	0	0	434
57,150	57,200	0	0	0	0	0	0	0	424
57,200	57,250	0	0	0	0	0	0	0	413
57,250	57,300	0	0	0	0	0	0	0	403
57,300	57,350	0	0	0	0	0	0	0	392
57,350	57,400	0	0	0	0	0	0	0	382
57,400	57,450	0	0	0	0	0	0	0	371
57,450	57,500	0	0	0	0	0	0	0	361
57,500	57,550	0	0	0	0	0	0	0	350
57,550	57,600	0	0	0	0	0	0	0	340
57,600	57,650	0	0	0	0	0	0	0	329
57,650	57,700	0	0	0	0	0	0	0	319
57,700	57,750	0	0	0	0	0	0	0	308
57,750	57,800	0	0	0	0	0	0	0	297
57,800	57,850	0	0	0	0	0	0	0	287
57,850	57,900	0	0	0	0	0	0	0	276
57,900	57,950	0	0	0	0	0	0	0	266
57,950	58,000	0	0	0	0	0	0	0	255
58,000	58,050	0	0	0	0	0	0	0	245
58,050	58,100	0	0	0	0	0	0	0	234
58,100	58,150	0	0	0	0	0	0	0	224
58,150	58,200	0	0	0	0	0	0	0	213
58,200	58,250	0	0	0	0	0	0	0	203
58,250	58,300	0	0	0	0	0	0	0	192
58,300	58,350	0	0	0	0	0	0	0	182
58,350	58,400	0	0	0	0	0	0	0	171
58,400	58,450	0	0	0	0	0	0	0	161
58,450	58,500	0	0	0	0	0	0	0	150
58,500	58,550	0	0	0	0	0	0	0	139
58,550	58,600	0	0	0	0	0	0	0	129
58,600	58,650	0	0	0	0	0	0	0	118
58,650	58,700	0	0	0	0	0	0	0	108
58,700	58,750	0	0	0	0	0	0	0	97
58,750	58,800	0	0	0	0	0	0	0	87
58,800	58,850	0	0	0	0	0	0	0	76
58,850	58,900	0	0	0	0	0	0	0	66
58,900	58,950	0	0	0	0	0	0	0	55
58,950	59,000	0	0	0	0	0	0	0	45
59,000	59,050	0	0	0	0	0	0	0	34
59,050	59,100	0	0	0	0	0	0	0	24
59,100	59,150	0	0	0	0	0	0	0	13
59,150	59,187	0	0	0	0	0	0	0	**

★ Use this column if your filing status is married filing separately and you qualify to claim the EIC. See the instructions for line 27.

* If the amount you are looking up from the worksheet is at least $55,500 but less than $55,529, and you have two qualifying children who have valid SSNs, your credit is $3.

If the amount you are looking up from the worksheet is $55,529 or more, and you have two qualifying children who have valid SSNs, you can't take the credit.

** If the amount you are looking up from the worksheet is at least $59,150 but less than $59,187, and you have three qualifying children who have valid SSNs, your credit is $4.

If the amount you are looking up from the worksheet is $59,187 or more, and you have three qualifying children who have valid SSNs, you can't take the credit.

Withholding Tables

CONTENTS

2. Wage Bracket Method Tables for Manual Payroll Systems With Forms W-4 From 2020 or Later

If you compute payroll manually, your employee has submitted a Form W-4 for 2020 or later, and you prefer to use the Wage Bracket method, use the worksheet below and the Wage Bracket Method tables that follow to figure federal income tax withholding.

These Wage Bracket Method tables cover a limited amount of annual wages (generally, less than $100,000). If you can't use the Wage Bracket Method tables because taxable wages exceed the amount from the last bracket of the table (based on filing status and pay period), use the Percentage Method tables in section 4.

Worksheet 2. Employer's Withholding Worksheet for Wage Bracket Method Tables for Manual Payroll Systems With Forms W-4 From 2020 or Later

Keep for Your Records 

Table 5	Monthly	Semimonthly	Biweekly	Weekly	Daily
	12	24	26	52	260

Step 1.	**Adjust the employee's wage amount**		
	1a Enter the employee's total taxable wages this payroll period	1a	$
	1b Enter the number of pay periods you have per year (see Table 5)	1b	
	1c Enter the amount from Step 4(a) of the employee's Form W-4	1c	$
	1d Divide the amount on line 1c by the number of pay periods on line 1b	1d	$
	1e Add lines 1a and 1d	1e	$
	1f Enter the amount from Step 4(b) of the employee's Form W-4	1f	$
	1g Divide the amount on line 1f by the number of pay periods on line 1b	1g	$
	1h Subtract line 1g from line 1e. If zero or less, enter -0-. This is the **Adjusted Wage Amount**	1h	$
Step 2.	**Figure the Tentative Withholding Amount**		
	2a Use the amount on line 1h to look up the tentative amount to withhold in the appropriate Wage Bracket Method table in this section for your pay frequency, given the employee's filing status and whether the employee has checked the box in Step 2 of Form W-4. This is the **Tentative Withholding Amount**	2a	$
Step 3.	**Account for tax credits**		
	3a Enter the amount from Step 3 of the employee's Form W-4	3a	$
	3b Divide the amount on line 3a by the number of pay periods on line 1b	3b	$
	3c Subtract line 3b from line 2a. If zero or less, enter -0-	3c	$
Step 4.	**Figure the final amount to withhold**		
	4a Enter the additional amount to withhold from Step 4(c) of the employee's Form W-4	4a	$
	4b Add lines 3c and 4a. **This is the amount to withhold from the employee's wages this pay period**	4b	$

2022 Wage Bracket Method Tables for Manual Payroll Systems with Forms W-4 From 2020 or Later

SEMIMONTHLY Payroll Period

If the **Adjusted Wage Amount** (line 1h) is		Married Filing Jointly		Head of Household		Single or Married Filing Separately	
At least	But less than	Standard withholding	Form W-4, Step 2, Checkbox withholding	Standard withholding	Form W-4, Step 2, Checkbox withholding	Standard withholding	Form W-4, Step 2, Checkbox withholding
		The Tentative Withholding Amount is:					
$0	$270	$0	$0	$0	$0	$0	$0
$270	$280	$0	$0	$0	$0	$0	$1
$280	$290	$0	$0	$0	$0	$0	$2
$290	$300	$0	$0	$0	$0	$0	$3
$300	$310	$0	$0	$0	$0	$0	$4
$310	$320	$0	$0	$0	$0	$0	$5
$320	$330	$0	$0	$0	$0	$0	$6
$330	$340	$0	$0	$0	$0	$0	$7
$340	$350	$0	$0	$0	$0	$0	$8
$350	$360	$0	$0	$0	$0	$0	$9
$360	$370	$0	$0	$0	$0	$0	$10
$370	$380	$0	$0	$0	$0	$0	$11
$380	$390	$0	$0	$0	$0	$0	$12
$390	$400	$0	$0	$0	$0	$0	$13
$400	$410	$0	$0	$0	$0	$0	$14
$410	$420	$0	$0	$0	$1	$0	$15
$420	$430	$0	$0	$0	$2	$0	$16
$430	$440	$0	$0	$0	$3	$0	$17
$440	$450	$0	$0	$0	$4	$0	$18
$450	$460	$0	$0	$0	$5	$0	$19
$460	$470	$0	$0	$0	$6	$0	$20
$470	$480	$0	$0	$0	$7	$0	$21
$480	$495	$0	$0	$0	$8	$0	$22
$495	$510	$0	$0	$0	$10	$0	$24
$510	$525	$0	$0	$0	$11	$0	$25
$525	$540	$0	$0	$0	$13	$0	$27
$540	$555	$0	$1	$0	$14	$1	$29
$555	$570	$0	$2	$0	$16	$2	$31
$570	$585	$0	$4	$0	$17	$4	$33
$585	$600	$0	$5	$0	$19	$5	$34
$600	$615	$0	$7	$0	$20	$7	$36
$615	$630	$0	$8	$0	$22	$8	$38
$630	$645	$0	$10	$0	$23	$10	$40
$645	$660	$0	$11	$0	$25	$11	$42
$660	$675	$0	$13	$0	$26	$13	$43
$675	$690	$0	$14	$0	$28	$14	$45
$690	$705	$0	$16	$0	$29	$16	$47
$705	$720	$0	$17	$0	$31	$17	$49
$720	$735	$0	$19	$0	$33	$19	$51
$735	$750	$0	$20	$0	$34	$20	$52
$750	$765	$0	$22	$0	$36	$22	$54
$765	$780	$0	$23	$0	$38	$23	$56
$780	$795	$0	$25	$0	$40	$25	$58
$795	$810	$0	$26	$0	$42	$26	$60
$810	$825	$0	$28	$1	$43	$28	$61
$825	$840	$0	$29	$2	$45	$29	$63
$840	$855	$0	$31	$4	$47	$31	$65
$855	$870	$0	$32	$5	$49	$32	$67
$870	$885	$0	$34	$7	$51	$34	$69
$885	$900	$0	$35	$8	$52	$35	$70
$900	$915	$0	$37	$10	$54	$37	$72
$915	$930	$0	$38	$11	$56	$38	$74
$930	$945	$0	$40	$13	$58	$40	$76
$945	$960	$0	$41	$14	$60	$41	$78
$960	$975	$0	$43	$16	$61	$43	$79
$975	$990	$0	$45	$17	$63	$45	$81
$990	$1,005	$0	$46	$19	$65	$46	$83
$1,005	$1,020	$0	$48	$20	$67	$48	$85
$1,020	$1,035	$0	$50	$22	$69	$50	$87
$1,035	$1,050	$0	$52	$23	$70	$52	$88
$1,050	$1,065	$0	$54	$25	$72	$54	$90
$1,065	$1,080	$0	$55	$26	$74	$55	$92
$1,080	$1,095	$1	$57	$28	$76	$57	$94
$1,095	$1,110	$2	$59	$29	$78	$59	$96
$1,110	$1,125	$4	$61	$31	$79	$61	$97

2022 Wage Bracket Method Tables for Manual Payroll Systems with Forms W-4 From 2020 or Later

SEMIMONTHLY Payroll Period

If the **Adjusted Wage Amount** (line 1h) is		Married Filing Jointly		Head of Household		Single or Married Filing Separately	
At least	But less than	Standard withholding	Form W-4, Step 2, Checkbox withholding	Standard withholding	Form W-4, Step 2, Checkbox withholding	Standard withholding	Form W-4, Step 2, Checkbox withholding
		The Tentative Withholding Amount is:					
$1,125	$1,140	$5	$63	$32	$81	$63	$99
$1,140	$1,160	$7	$65	$34	$83	$65	$102
$1,160	$1,180	$9	$67	$36	$86	$67	$107
$1,180	$1,200	$11	$69	$38	$88	$69	$111
$1,200	$1,220	$13	$72	$40	$91	$72	$116
$1,220	$1,240	$15	$74	$42	$93	$74	$120
$1,240	$1,260	$17	$77	$44	$95	$77	$124
$1,260	$1,280	$19	$79	$46	$98	$79	$129
$1,280	$1,300	$21	$81	$48	$100	$81	$133
$1,300	$1,320	$23	$84	$50	$103	$84	$138
$1,320	$1,340	$25	$86	$52	$105	$86	$142
$1,340	$1,360	$27	$89	$54	$107	$89	$146
$1,360	$1,380	$29	$91	$56	$110	$91	$151
$1,380	$1,400	$31	$93	$58	$112	$93	$155
$1,400	$1,420	$33	$96	$60	$115	$96	$160
$1,420	$1,440	$35	$98	$62	$117	$98	$164
$1,440	$1,460	$37	$101	$65	$119	$101	$168
$1,460	$1,480	$39	$103	$67	$122	$103	$173
$1,480	$1,500	$41	$105	$70	$124	$105	$177
$1,500	$1,520	$43	$108	$72	$127	$108	$182
$1,520	$1,540	$45	$110	$74	$129	$110	$186
$1,540	$1,560	$47	$113	$77	$131	$113	$190
$1,560	$1,580	$49	$115	$79	$134	$115	$195
$1,580	$1,600	$51	$117	$82	$138	$117	$199
$1,600	$1,620	$53	$120	$84	$143	$120	$204
$1,620	$1,640	$55	$122	$86	$147	$122	$208
$1,640	$1,660	$57	$125	$89	$152	$125	$212
$1,660	$1,680	$59	$127	$91	$156	$127	$217
$1,680	$1,700	$61	$129	$94	$160	$129	$221
$1,700	$1,720	$63	$132	$96	$165	$132	$226
$1,720	$1,740	$65	$134	$98	$169	$134	$230
$1,740	$1,760	$67	$137	$101	$174	$137	$234
$1,760	$1,780	$69	$139	$103	$178	$139	$239
$1,780	$1,800	$71	$141	$106	$182	$141	$243
$1,800	$1,820	$73	$144	$108	$187	$144	$248
$1,820	$1,840	$75	$146	$110	$191	$146	$252
$1,840	$1,860	$77	$149	$113	$196	$149	$256
$1,860	$1,880	$79	$151	$115	$200	$151	$261
$1,880	$1,900	$81	$153	$118	$204	$153	$265
$1,900	$1,920	$83	$156	$120	$209	$156	$270
$1,920	$1,940	$85	$158	$122	$213	$158	$274
$1,940	$1,960	$87	$161	$125	$218	$161	$278
$1,960	$1,980	$90	$163	$127	$222	$163	$283
$1,980	$2,000	$92	$165	$130	$226	$165	$287
$2,000	$2,020	$95	$168	$132	$231	$168	$292
$2,020	$2,040	$97	$170	$134	$235	$170	$296
$2,040	$2,060	$99	$173	$137	$240	$173	$300
$2,060	$2,080	$102	$175	$139	$244	$175	$305
$2,080	$2,100	$104	$177	$142	$248	$177	$309
$2,100	$2,120	$107	$180	$144	$253	$180	$314
$2,120	$2,140	$109	$182	$146	$257	$182	$318
$2,140	$2,170	$112	$185	$149	$263	$185	$324
$2,170	$2,200	$116	$189	$153	$269	$189	$331
$2,200	$2,230	$119	$192	$157	$276	$192	$338
$2,230	$2,260	$123	$196	$160	$282	$196	$346
$2,260	$2,290	$126	$200	$164	$289	$200	$353
$2,290	$2,320	$130	$206	$167	$297	$206	$360
$2,320	$2,350	$134	$212	$171	$304	$212	$367
$2,350	$2,380	$137	$219	$175	$311	$219	$374
$2,380	$2,410	$141	$226	$178	$318	$226	$382
$2,410	$2,440	$144	$232	$182	$325	$232	$389
$2,440	$2,470	$148	$239	$185	$333	$239	$396
$2,470	$2,500	$152	$245	$189	$340	$245	$403
$2,500	$2,530	$155	$252	$193	$347	$252	$410
$2,530	$2,560	$159	$259	$196	$354	$259	$418

2022 Wage Bracket Method Tables for Manual Payroll Systems with Forms W-4 From 2020 or Later

SEMIMONTHLY Payroll Period

If the **Adjusted Wage Amount** (line 1h) is		**Married Filing Jointly**		**Head of Household**		**Single or Married Filing Separately**	
At least	But less than	Standard withholding	Form W-4, Step 2, Checkbox withholding	Standard withholding	Form W-4, Step 2, Checkbox withholding	Standard withholding	Form W-4, Step 2, Checkbox withholding
		The Tentative Withholding Amount is:					
$2,560	**$2,590**	$162	$265	$200	$361	$265	$425
$2,590	**$2,620**	$166	$272	$203	$369	$272	$432
$2,620	**$2,650**	$170	$278	$207	$376	$278	$439
$2,650	**$2,680**	$173	$285	$211	$383	$285	$446
$2,680	**$2,710**	$177	$292	$214	$390	$292	$454
$2,710	**$2,740**	$180	$298	$218	$397	$298	$461
$2,740	**$2,770**	$184	$305	$221	$405	$305	$468
$2,770	**$2,800**	$188	$311	$225	$412	$311	$475
$2,800	**$2,830**	$191	$318	$229	$419	$318	$482
$2,830	**$2,860**	$195	$325	$232	$426	$325	$490
$2,860	**$2,890**	$198	$331	$236	$433	$331	$497
$2,890	**$2,920**	$202	$338	$239	$441	$338	$504
$2,920	**$2,950**	$206	$344	$243	$448	$344	$511
$2,950	**$2,980**	$209	$351	$247	$455	$351	$518
$2,980	**$3,010**	$213	$358	$250	$462	$358	$526
$3,010	**$3,040**	$216	$364	$254	$469	$364	$533
$3,040	**$3,070**	$220	$371	$257	$477	$371	$540
$3,070	**$3,100**	$224	$377	$261	$484	$377	$547
$3,100	**$3,130**	$227	$384	$265	$491	$384	$554
$3,130	**$3,160**	$231	$391	$269	$498	$391	$562
$3,160	**$3,190**	$234	$397	$276	$505	$397	$569
$3,190	**$3,220**	$238	$404	$282	$513	$404	$576
$3,220	**$3,250**	$242	$410	$289	$520	$410	$583
$3,250	**$3,280**	$245	$417	$295	$527	$417	$590
$3,280	**$3,310**	$249	$424	$302	$534	$424	$598
$3,310	**$3,340**	$252	$430	$309	$541	$430	$605
$3,340	**$3,370**	$256	$437	$315	$549	$437	$612
$3,370	**$3,400**	$260	$443	$322	$556	$443	$619
$3,400	**$3,430**	$263	$450	$328	$563	$450	$626
$3,430	**$3,460**	$267	$457	$335	$570	$457	$634
$3,460	**$3,490**	$270	$463	$342	$577	$463	$641
$3,490	**$3,520**	$274	$470	$348	$585	$470	$648
$3,520	**$3,550**	$278	$476	$355	$592	$476	$655
$3,550	**$3,580**	$281	$483	$361	$599	$483	$662
$3,580	**$3,610**	$285	$490	$368	$606	$490	$670
$3,610	**$3,640**	$288	$496	$375	$613	$496	$677
$3,640	**$3,670**	$292	$503	$381	$621	$503	$684
$3,670	**$3,700**	$296	$509	$388	$628	$509	$691
$3,700	**$3,730**	$299	$516	$394	$635	$516	$698
$3,730	**$3,760**	$303	$523	$401	$642	$523	$706
$3,760	**$3,790**	$306	$529	$408	$649	$529	$713
$3,790	**$3,820**	$310	$536	$414	$657	$536	$720
$3,820	**$3,850**	$314	$542	$421	$664	$542	$729
$3,850	**$3,880**	$317	$549	$427	$671	$549	$739
$3,880	**$3,910**	$321	$556	$434	$678	$556	$748
$3,910	**$3,940**	$324	$562	$441	$685	$562	$758
$3,940	**$3,970**	$328	$569	$447	$693	$569	$767
$3,970	**$4,000**	$332	$575	$454	$703	$575	$777
$4,000	**$4,030**	$335	$582	$460	$712	$582	$787
$4,030	**$4,060**	$339	$589	$467	$722	$589	$796
$4,060	**$4,090**	$342	$595	$474	$732	$595	$806
$4,090	**$4,120**	$346	$602	$480	$741	$602	$815

3. Wage Bracket Method Tables for Manual Payroll Systems With Forms W-4 From 2019 or Earlier

If you compute payroll manually and your employee **has not** submitted a Form W-4 for 2020 or later, use the worksheet below and the Wage Bracket Method tables that follow to figure federal income tax withholding.

These Wage Bracket Method tables cover a limited amount of annual wages (generally, less than $100,000) and up to 10 allowances. If you can't use the Wage Bracket Method tables because taxable wages exceed the amount from the last bracket of the table (based on marital status and pay period) or the employee claimed more than 10 allowances, use the Percentage Method tables in section 5.

Periodic payments of pensions or annuities with a 2021 or earlier Form W-4P. In lieu of Worksheet 1B and the Percentage Method tables in section 1, you may use Worksheet 3 and the Wage Bracket Method tables in this section to figure federal income tax withholding on periodic payments of pensions or annuities with a 2021 or earlier Form W-4P. As an alternative, if you prefer to use the Percentage Method of withholding, you may use Worksheet 5 and the Percentage Method tables in section 5 to figure federal income tax withholding on periodic payments of pensions or annuities with a 2021 or earlier Form W-4P.

Worksheet 3. Employer's Withholding Worksheet for Wage Bracket Method Tables for Manual Payroll Systems With Forms W-4 From 2019 or Earlier

Keep for Your Records 

Step 1.		**Figure the tentative withholding amount**		
	1a	Enter the employee's total taxable wages this payroll period	1a	$
	1b	Use the amount on line 1a to look up the tentative amount to withhold in the appropriate Wage Bracket Method table in this section for your pay frequency, given the employee's marital status (line 3 of Form W-4) and number of allowances claimed. This is the **Tentative Withholding Amount**	1b	$
Step 2.		**Figure the final amount to withhold**		
	2a	Enter the additional amount to withhold from line 6 of the employee's Form W-4	2a	$
	2b	Add lines 1b and 2a. **This is the amount to withhold from the employee's wages this pay period**	2b	$

2022 Wage Bracket Method Tables for Manual Payroll Systems With Forms W-4 From 2019 or Earlier

SEMIMONTHLY Payroll Period

If the **Wage Amount** (line 1a) is		**MARRIED** Persons										
		And the number of allowances is:										
At least	But less than	0	1	2	3	4	5	6	7	8	9	10
		The Tentative Withholding Amount is:										
$0	**$545**	$0	$0	$0	$0	$0	$0	$0	$0	$0	$0	$0
$545	**$555**	$1	$0	$0	$0	$0	$0	$0	$0	$0	$0	$0
$555	**$565**	$2	$0	$0	$0	$0	$0	$0	$0	$0	$0	$0
$565	**$575**	$3	$0	$0	$0	$0	$0	$0	$0	$0	$0	$0
$575	**$585**	$4	$0	$0	$0	$0	$0	$0	$0	$0	$0	$0
$585	**$595**	$5	$0	$0	$0	$0	$0	$0	$0	$0	$0	$0
$595	**$605**	$6	$0	$0	$0	$0	$0	$0	$0	$0	$0	$0
$605	**$615**	$7	$0	$0	$0	$0	$0	$0	$0	$0	$0	$0
$615	**$625**	$8	$0	$0	$0	$0	$0	$0	$0	$0	$0	$0
$625	**$635**	$9	$0	$0	$0	$0	$0	$0	$0	$0	$0	$0
$635	**$645**	$10	$0	$0	$0	$0	$0	$0	$0	$0	$0	$0
$645	**$655**	$11	$0	$0	$0	$0	$0	$0	$0	$0	$0	$0
$655	**$665**	$12	$0	$0	$0	$0	$0	$0	$0	$0	$0	$0
$665	**$675**	$13	$0	$0	$0	$0	$0	$0	$0	$0	$0	$0
$675	**$685**	$14	$0	$0	$0	$0	$0	$0	$0	$0	$0	$0
$685	**$695**	$15	$0	$0	$0	$0	$0	$0	$0	$0	$0	$0
$695	**$705**	$16	$0	$0	$0	$0	$0	$0	$0	$0	$0	$0
$705	**$715**	$17	$0	$0	$0	$0	$0	$0	$0	$0	$0	$0
$715	**$725**	$18	$0	$0	$0	$0	$0	$0	$0	$0	$0	$0
$725	**$735**	$19	$1	$0	$0	$0	$0	$0	$0	$0	$0	$0
$735	**$745**	$20	$2	$0	$0	$0	$0	$0	$0	$0	$0	$0
$745	**$755**	$21	$3	$0	$0	$0	$0	$0	$0	$0	$0	$0
$755	**$765**	$22	$4	$0	$0	$0	$0	$0	$0	$0	$0	$0
$765	**$775**	$23	$5	$0	$0	$0	$0	$0	$0	$0	$0	$0
$775	**$785**	$24	$6	$0	$0	$0	$0	$0	$0	$0	$0	$0
$785	**$795**	$25	$7	$0	$0	$0	$0	$0	$0	$0	$0	$0
$795	**$805**	$26	$8	$0	$0	$0	$0	$0	$0	$0	$0	$0
$805	**$815**	$27	$9	$0	$0	$0	$0	$0	$0	$0	$0	$0
$815	**$825**	$28	$10	$0	$0	$0	$0	$0	$0	$0	$0	$0
$825	**$835**	$29	$11	$0	$0	$0	$0	$0	$0	$0	$0	$0
$835	**$845**	$30	$12	$0	$0	$0	$0	$0	$0	$0	$0	$0
$845	**$855**	$31	$13	$0	$0	$0	$0	$0	$0	$0	$0	$0
$855	**$865**	$32	$14	$0	$0	$0	$0	$0	$0	$0	$0	$0
$865	**$875**	$33	$15	$0	$0	$0	$0	$0	$0	$0	$0	$0
$875	**$885**	$34	$16	$0	$0	$0	$0	$0	$0	$0	$0	$0
$885	**$895**	$35	$17	$0	$0	$0	$0	$0	$0	$0	$0	$0
$895	**$905**	$36	$18	$0	$0	$0	$0	$0	$0	$0	$0	$0
$905	**$915**	$37	$19	$1	$0	$0	$0	$0	$0	$0	$0	$0
$915	**$925**	$38	$20	$2	$0	$0	$0	$0	$0	$0	$0	$0
$925	**$935**	$39	$21	$3	$0	$0	$0	$0	$0	$0	$0	$0
$935	**$945**	$40	$22	$4	$0	$0	$0	$0	$0	$0	$0	$0
$945	**$955**	$41	$23	$5	$0	$0	$0	$0	$0	$0	$0	$0
$955	**$965**	$42	$24	$6	$0	$0	$0	$0	$0	$0	$0	$0
$965	**$975**	$43	$25	$7	$0	$0	$0	$0	$0	$0	$0	$0
$975	**$985**	$44	$26	$8	$0	$0	$0	$0	$0	$0	$0	$0
$985	**$995**	$45	$27	$9	$0	$0	$0	$0	$0	$0	$0	$0
$995	**$1,005**	$46	$28	$10	$0	$0	$0	$0	$0	$0	$0	$0
$1,005	**$1,015**	$47	$29	$11	$0	$0	$0	$0	$0	$0	$0	$0
$1,015	**$1,025**	$48	$30	$12	$0	$0	$0	$0	$0	$0	$0	$0
$1,025	**$1,035**	$49	$31	$13	$0	$0	$0	$0	$0	$0	$0	$0
$1,035	**$1,045**	$50	$32	$14	$0	$0	$0	$0	$0	$0	$0	$0

2022 Wage Bracket Method Tables for Manual Payroll Systems With Forms W-4 From 2019 or Earlier

SEMIMONTHLY Payroll Period

If the **Wage Amount** (line 1a) is		**MARRIED** Persons										
		And the number of allowances is:										
At least	But less than	0	1	2	3	4	5	6	7	8	9	10
		The Tentative Withholding Amount is:										
$1,045	**$1,055**	$51	$33	$15	$0	$0	$0	$0	$0	$0	$0	$0
$1,055	**$1,065**	$52	$34	$16	$0	$0	$0	$0	$0	$0	$0	$0
$1,065	**$1,075**	$53	$35	$17	$0	$0	$0	$0	$0	$0	$0	$0
$1,075	**$1,085**	$54	$36	$18	$0	$0	$0	$0	$0	$0	$0	$0
$1,085	**$1,095**	$55	$37	$19	$1	$0	$0	$0	$0	$0	$0	$0
$1,095	**$1,105**	$56	$38	$20	$2	$0	$0	$0	$0	$0	$0	$0
$1,105	**$1,115**	$57	$39	$21	$3	$0	$0	$0	$0	$0	$0	$0
$1,115	**$1,125**	$58	$40	$22	$4	$0	$0	$0	$0	$0	$0	$0
$1,125	**$1,135**	$59	$41	$23	$5	$0	$0	$0	$0	$0	$0	$0
$1,135	**$1,145**	$60	$42	$24	$6	$0	$0	$0	$0	$0	$0	$0
$1,145	**$1,155**	$61	$43	$25	$7	$0	$0	$0	$0	$0	$0	$0
$1,155	**$1,165**	$62	$44	$26	$8	$0	$0	$0	$0	$0	$0	$0
$1,165	**$1,175**	$63	$45	$27	$9	$0	$0	$0	$0	$0	$0	$0
$1,175	**$1,185**	$64	$46	$28	$10	$0	$0	$0	$0	$0	$0	$0
$1,185	**$1,195**	$65	$47	$20	$11	$0	$0	$0	$0	$0	$0	$0
$1,195	**$1,205**	$66	$48	$30	$12	$0	$0	$0	$0	$0	$0	$0
$1,205	**$1,215**	$67	$49	$31	$13	$0	$0	$0	$0	$0	$0	$0
$1,215	**$1,225**	$68	$50	$32	$14	$0	$0	$0	$0	$0	$0	$0
$1,225	**$1,235**	$69	$51	$33	$15	$0	$0	$0	$0	$0	$0	$0
$1,235	**$1,245**	$70	$52	$34	$16	$0	$0	$0	$0	$0	$0	$0
$1,245	**$1,255**	$71	$53	$35	$17	$0	$0	$0	$0	$0	$0	$0
$1,255	**$1,265**	$72	$54	$36	$18	$0	$0	$0	$0	$0	$0	$0
$1,265	**$1,275**	$73	$55	$37	$19	$1	$0	$0	$0	$0	$0	$0
$1,275	**$1,285**	$74	$56	$38	$20	$2	$0	$0	$0	$0	$0	$0
$1,285	**$1,295**	$75	$57	$39	$21	$3	$0	$0	$0	$0	$0	$0
$1,295	**$1,305**	$76	$58	$40	$22	$4	$0	$0	$0	$0	$0	$0
$1,305	**$1,315**	$77	$59	$41	$23	$5	$0	$0	$0	$0	$0	$0
$1,315	**$1,325**	$78	$60	$42	$24	$6	$0	$0	$0	$0	$0	$0
$1,325	**$1,335**	$79	$61	$43	$25	$7	$0	$0	$0	$0	$0	$0
$1,335	**$1,345**	$80	$62	$44	$26	$8	$0	$0	$0	$0	$0	$0
$1,345	**$1,355**	$81	$63	$45	$27	$9	$0	$0	$0	$0	$0	$0
$1,355	**$1,365**	$82	$64	$46	$28	$10	$0	$0	$0	$0	$0	$0
$1,365	**$1,375**	$83	$65	$47	$29	$11	$0	$0	$0	$0	$0	$0
$1,375	**$1,385**	$84	$66	$48	$30	$12	$0	$0	$0	$0	$0	$0
$1,385	**$1,395**	$85	$67	$49	$31	$13	$0	$0	$0	$0	$0	$0
$1,395	**$1,405**	$86	$68	$50	$32	$14	$0	$0	$0	$0	$0	$0
$1,405	**$1,445**	$89	$70	$53	$35	$17	$0	$0	$0	$0	$0	$0
$1,445	**$1,485**	$94	$74	$57	$39	$21	$3	$0	$0	$0	$0	$0
$1,485	**$1,525**	$98	$78	$61	$43	$25	$7	$0	$0	$0	$0	$0
$1,525	**$1,565**	$103	$82	$65	$47	$29	$11	$0	$0	$0	$0	$0
$1,565	**$1,605**	$108	$87	$69	$51	$33	$15	$0	$0	$0	$0	$0
$1,605	**$1,645**	$113	$91	$73	$55	$37	$19	$1	$0	$0	$0	$0
$1,645	**$1,685**	$118	$96	$77	$59	$41	$23	$5	$0	$0	$0	$0
$1,685	**$1,725**	$122	$101	$81	$63	$45	$27	$9	$0	$0	$0	$0
$1,725	**$1,765**	$127	$106	$85	$67	$49	$31	$13	$0	$0	$0	$0
$1,765	**$1,805**	$132	$111	$89	$71	$53	$35	$17	$0	$0	$0	$0
$1,805	**$1,845**	$137	$115	$94	$75	$57	$39	$21	$3	$0	$0	$0
$1,845	**$1,885**	$142	$120	$99	$79	$61	$43	$25	$7	$0	$0	$0
$1,885	**$1,925**	$146	$125	$103	$83	$65	$47	$29	$11	$0	$0	$0
$1,925	**$1,965**	$151	$130	$108	$87	$69	$51	$33	$15	$0	$0	$0
$1,965	**$2,005**	$156	$135	$113	$92	$73	$55	$37	$19	$1	$0	$0

2022 Wage Bracket Method Tables for Manual Payroll Systems With Forms W-4 From 2019 or Earlier

SEMIMONTHLY Payroll Period

If the **Wage Amount** (line 1a) is		**MARRIED** Persons										
		And the number of allowances is:										
At least	But less than	0	1	2	3	4	5	6	7	8	9	10
		The Tentative Withholding Amount is:										
$2,005	**$2,045**	$161	$139	$118	$96	$77	$59	$41	$23	$5	$0	$0
$2,045	**$2,085**	$166	$144	$123	$101	$81	$63	$45	$27	$9	$0	$0
$2,085	**$2,125**	$170	$149	$127	$106	$85	$67	$49	$31	$13	$0	$0
$2,125	**$2,165**	$175	$154	$132	$111	$89	$71	$53	$35	$17	$0	$0
$2,165	**$2,205**	$180	$159	$137	$116	$94	$75	$57	$39	$21	$3	$0
$2,205	**$2,245**	$185	$163	$142	$120	$99	$79	$61	$43	$25	$7	$0
$2,245	**$2,285**	$190	$168	$147	$125	$104	$83	$65	$47	$29	$11	$0
$2,285	**$2,325**	$194	$173	$151	$130	$108	$87	$69	$51	$33	$15	$0
$2,325	**$2,365**	$199	$178	$156	$135	$113	$92	$73	$55	$37	$19	$1
$2,365	**$2,405**	$204	$183	$161	$140	$118	$97	$77	$59	$41	$23	$5
$2,405	**$2,445**	$209	$187	$166	$144	$123	$101	$81	$63	$45	$27	$9
$2,445	**$2,485**	$214	$192	$171	$149	$128	$106	$85	$67	$49	$31	$13
$2,485	**$2,525**	$218	$197	$175	$154	$132	$111	$89	$71	$53	$35	$17
$2,525	**$2,565**	$223	$202	$180	$159	$137	$116	$94	$75	$57	$39	$21
$2,565	**$2,605**	$228	$207	$185	$164	$142	$121	$99	$79	$61	$43	$25
$2,605	**$2,645**	$233	$211	$190	$168	$147	$125	$104	$83	$65	$47	$29
$2,645	**$2,685**	$238	$216	$195	$173	$152	$130	$109	$87	$69	$51	$33
$2,685	**$2,725**	$242	$221	$199	$178	$156	$135	$113	$92	$73	$55	$37
$2,725	**$2,765**	$247	$226	$204	$183	$161	$140	$118	$97	$77	$59	$41
$2,765	**$2,805**	$252	$231	$209	$188	$166	$145	$123	$102	$81	$63	$45
$2,805	**$2,845**	$257	$235	$214	$192	$171	$149	$128	$106	$85	$67	$49
$2,845	**$2,885**	$262	$240	$219	$197	$176	$154	$133	$111	$90	$71	$53
$2,885	**$2,925**	$266	$245	$223	$202	$180	$159	$137	$116	$94	$75	$57
$2,925	**$2,965**	$271	$250	$228	$207	$185	$164	$142	$121	$99	$79	$61
$2,965	**$3,005**	$276	$255	$233	$212	$190	$169	$147	$126	$104	$83	$65
$3,005	**$3,045**	$281	$259	$238	$216	$195	$173	$152	$130	$109	$87	$69
$3,045	**$3,085**	$286	$264	$243	$221	$200	$178	$157	$135	$114	$92	$73
$3,085	**$3,125**	$290	$269	$247	$226	$204	$183	$161	$140	$118	$97	$77
$3,125	**$3,165**	$295	$274	$252	$231	$209	$188	$166	$145	$123	$102	$81
$3,165	**$3,205**	$300	$279	$257	$236	$214	$193	$171	$150	$128	$107	$85
$3,205	**$3,245**	$305	$283	$262	$240	$219	$197	$176	$154	$133	$111	$90
$3,245	**$3,285**	$310	$288	$267	$245	$224	$202	$181	$159	$138	$116	$95

2022 Wage Bracket Method Tables for Manual Payroll Systems With Forms W-4 From 2019 or Earlier

SEMIMONTHLY Payroll Period

If the **Wage Amount** (line 1a) is		**SINGLE** Persons										
		And the number of allowances is:										
At least	But less than	0	1	2	3	4	5	6	7	8	9	10
		The Tentative Withholding Amount is:										
$0	$185	$0	$0	$0	$0	$0	$0	$0	$0	$0	$0	$0
$185	$195	$1	$0	$0	$0	$0	$0	$0	$0	$0	$0	$0
$195	$205	$2	$0	$0	$0	$0	$0	$0	$0	$0	$0	$0
$205	$215	$3	$0	$0	$0	$0	$0	$0	$0	$0	$0	$0
$215	$225	$4	$0	$0	$0	$0	$0	$0	$0	$0	$0	$0
$225	$235	$5	$0	$0	$0	$0	$0	$0	$0	$0	$0	$0
$235	$245	$6	$0	$0	$0	$0	$0	$0	$0	$0	$0	$0
$245	$255	$7	$0	$0	$0	$0	$0	$0	$0	$0	$0	$0
$255	$265	$8	$0	$0	$0	$0	$0	$0	$0	$0	$0	$0
$265	$275	$9	$0	$0	$0	$0	$0	$0	$0	$0	$0	$0
$275	$285	$10	$0	$0	$0	$0	$0	$0	$0	$0	$0	$0
$285	$295	$11	$0	$0	$0	$0	$0	$0	$0	$0	$0	$0
$295	$305	$12	$0	$0	$0	$0	$0	$0	$0	$0	$0	$0
$305	$315	$13	$0	$0	$0	$0	$0	$0	$0	$0	$0	$0
$315	$325	$14	$0	$0	$0	$0	$0	$0	$0	$0	$0	$0
$325	$335	$15	$0	$0	$0	$0	$0	$0	$0	$0	$0	$0
$335	$345	$16	$0	$0	$0	$0	$0	$0	$0	$0	$0	$0
$345	$355	$17	$0	$0	$0	$0	$0	$0	$0	$0	$0	$0
$355	$365	$18	$0	$0	$0	$0	$0	$0	$0	$0	$0	$0
$365	$375	$19	$1	$0	$0	$0	$0	$0	$0	$0	$0	$0
$375	$385	$20	$2	$0	$0	$0	$0	$0	$0	$0	$0	$0
$385	$395	$21	$3	$0	$0	$0	$0	$0	$0	$0	$0	$0
$395	$405	$22	$4	$0	$0	$0	$0	$0	$0	$0	$0	$0
$405	$415	$23	$5	$0	$0	$0	$0	$0	$0	$0	$0	$0
$415	$425	$24	$6	$0	$0	$0	$0	$0	$0	$0	$0	$0
$425	$435	$25	$7	$0	$0	$0	$0	$0	$0	$0	$0	$0
$435	$445	$26	$8	$0	$0	$0	$0	$0	$0	$0	$0	$0
$445	$455	$27	$9	$0	$0	$0	$0	$0	$0	$0	$0	$0
$455	$465	$28	$10	$0	$0	$0	$0	$0	$0	$0	$0	$0
$465	$475	$29	$11	$0	$0	$0	$0	$0	$0	$0	$0	$0
$475	$485	$30	$12	$0	$0	$0	$0	$0	$0	$0	$0	$0
$485	$495	$31	$13	$0	$0	$0	$0	$0	$0	$0	$0	$0
$495	$505	$32	$14	$0	$0	$0	$0	$0	$0	$0	$0	$0
$505	$515	$33	$15	$0	$0	$0	$0	$0	$0	$0	$0	$0
$515	$525	$34	$16	$0	$0	$0	$0	$0	$0	$0	$0	$0
$525	$535	$35	$17	$0	$0	$0	$0	$0	$0	$0	$0	$0
$535	$545	$36	$18	$0	$0	$0	$0	$0	$0	$0	$0	$0
$545	$555	$37	$19	$1	$0	$0	$0	$0	$0	$0	$0	$0
$555	$565	$38	$20	$2	$0	$0	$0	$0	$0	$0	$0	$0
$565	$575	$39	$21	$3	$0	$0	$0	$0	$0	$0	$0	$0
$575	$585	$40	$22	$4	$0	$0	$0	$0	$0	$0	$0	$0
$585	$595	$41	$23	$5	$0	$0	$0	$0	$0	$0	$0	$0
$595	$605	$42	$24	$6	$0	$0	$0	$0	$0	$0	$0	$0
$605	$615	$43	$25	$7	$0	$0	$0	$0	$0	$0	$0	$0
$615	$655	$46	$27	$10	$0	$0	$0	$0	$0	$0	$0	$0
$655	$695	$51	$31	$14	$0	$0	$0	$0	$0	$0	$0	$0
$695	$735	$55	$35	$18	$0	$0	$0	$0	$0	$0	$0	$0
$735	$775	$60	$39	$22	$4	$0	$0	$0	$0	$0	$0	$0
$775	$815	$65	$44	$26	$8	$0	$0	$0	$0	$0	$0	$0
$815	$855	$70	$48	$30	$12	$0	$0	$0	$0	$0	$0	$0
$855	$895	$75	$53	$34	$16	$0	$0	$0	$0	$0	$0	$0

2022 Wage Bracket Method Tables for Manual Payroll Systems With Forms W-4 From 2019 or Earlier

SEMIMONTHLY Payroll Period

If the **Wage Amount** (line 1a) is		**SINGLE** Persons										
		And the number of allowances is:										
At least	But less than	0	1	2	3	4	5	6	7	8	9	10
		The Tentative Withholding Amount is:										
$895	**$935**	$79	$58	$38	$20	$2	$0	$0	$0	$0	$0	$0
$935	**$975**	$84	$63	$42	$24	$6	$0	$0	$0	$0	$0	$0
$975	**$1,015**	$89	$68	$46	$28	$10	$0	$0	$0	$0	$0	$0
$1,015	**$1,055**	$94	$72	$51	$32	$14	$0	$0	$0	$0	$0	$0
$1,055	**$1,095**	$99	$77	$56	$36	$18	$0	$0	$0	$0	$0	$0
$1,095	**$1,135**	$103	$82	$60	$40	$22	$4	$0	$0	$0	$0	$0
$1,135	**$1,175**	$108	$87	$65	$44	$26	$8	$0	$0	$0	$0	$0
$1,175	**$1,215**	$113	$92	$70	$49	$30	$12	$0	$0	$0	$0	$0
$1,215	**$1,255**	$118	$96	$75	$53	$34	$16	$0	$0	$0	$0	$0
$1,255	**$1,295**	$123	$101	$80	$58	$38	$20	$2	$0	$0	$0	$0
$1,295	**$1,335**	$127	$106	$84	$63	$42	$24	$6	$0	$0	$0	$0
$1,335	**$1,375**	$132	$111	$89	$68	$46	$28	$10	$0	$0	$0	$0
$1,375	**$1,415**	$137	$116	$94	$73	$51	$32	$14	$0	$0	$0	$0
$1,415	**$1,455**	$142	$120	$99	$77	$56	$36	$18	$0	$0	$0	$0
$1,455	**$1,495**	$147	$125	$104	$82	$61	$40	$22	$4	$0	$0	$0
$1,495	**$1,535**	$151	$130	$108	$87	$65	$44	$26	$8	$0	$0	$0
$1,535	**$1,575**	$156	$135	$113	$92	$70	$49	$30	$12	$0	$0	$0
$1,575	**$1,615**	$161	$140	$118	$97	$75	$54	$34	$16	$0	$0	$0
$1,615	**$1,655**	$166	$144	$123	$101	$80	$58	$38	$20	$2	$0	$0
$1,655	**$1,695**	$171	$149	$128	$106	$85	$63	$42	$24	$6	$0	$0
$1,695	**$1,735**	$175	$154	$132	$111	$89	$68	$46	$28	$10	$0	$0
$1,735	**$1,775**	$180	$159	$137	$116	$94	$73	$51	$32	$14	$0	$0
$1,775	**$1,815**	$185	$164	$142	$121	$99	$78	$56	$36	$18	$0	$0
$1,815	**$1,855**	$190	$168	$147	$125	$104	$82	$61	$40	$22	$4	$0
$1,855	**$1,895**	$195	$173	$152	$130	$109	$87	$66	$44	$26	$8	$0
$1,895	**$1,935**	$199	$178	$156	$135	$113	$92	$70	$49	$30	$12	$0
$1,935	**$1,975**	$208	$183	$161	$140	$118	$97	$75	$54	$34	$16	$0
$1,975	**$2,015**	$216	$188	$166	$145	$123	$102	$80	$59	$38	$20	$2
$2,015	**$2,055**	$225	$192	$171	$149	$128	$106	$85	$63	$42	$24	$6
$2,055	**$2,095**	$234	$197	$176	$154	$133	$111	$90	$68	$47	$28	$10
$2,095	**$2,135**	$243	$203	$180	$159	$137	$116	$94	$73	$51	$32	$14
$2,135	**$2,175**	$252	$212	$185	$164	$142	$121	$99	$78	$56	$36	$18
$2,175	**$2,215**	$260	$221	$190	$169	$147	$126	$104	$83	$61	$40	$22
$2,215	**$2,255**	$269	$230	$195	$173	$152	$130	$109	$87	$66	$44	$26
$2,255	**$2,295**	$278	$239	$200	$178	$157	$135	$114	$92	$71	$49	$30
$2,295	**$2,335**	$287	$247	$208	$183	$161	$140	$118	$97	$75	$54	$34
$2,335	**$2,375**	$296	$256	$217	$188	$166	$145	$123	$102	$80	$59	$38
$2,375	**$2,415**	$304	$265	$226	$193	$171	$150	$128	$107	$85	$64	$42
$2,415	**$2,455**	$313	$274	$234	$197	$176	$154	$133	$111	$90	$68	$47
$2,455	**$2,495**	$322	$283	$243	$204	$181	$159	$138	$116	$95	$73	$52
$2,495	**$2,535**	$331	$291	$252	$213	$185	$164	$142	$121	$99	$78	$56
$2,535	**$2,575**	$340	$300	$261	$221	$190	$169	$147	$126	$104	$83	$61
$2,575	**$2,615**	$348	$309	$270	$230	$195	$174	$152	$131	$109	$88	$66
$2,615	**$2,655**	$357	$318	$278	$239	$200	$178	$157	$135	$114	$92	$71
$2,655	**$2,695**	$366	$327	$287	$248	$208	$183	$162	$140	$119	$97	$76
$2,695	**$2,735**	$375	$335	$296	$257	$217	$188	$166	$145	$123	$102	$80
$2,735	**$2,775**	$384	$344	$305	$265	$226	$193	$171	$150	$128	$107	$85
$2,775	**$2,815**	$392	$353	$314	$274	$235	$198	$176	$155	$133	$112	$90
$2,815	**$2,855**	$401	$362	$322	$283	$244	$204	$181	$159	$138	$116	$95
$2,855	**$2,895**	$410	$371	$331	$292	$252	$213	$186	$164	$143	$121	$100
$2,895	**$2,935**	$419	$379	$340	$301	$261	$222	$190	$169	$147	$126	$104

2022 Wage Bracket Method Tables for Manual Payroll Systems With Forms W-4 From 2019 or Earlier

SEMIMONTHLY Payroll Period

If the **Wage Amount** (line 1a) is		**SINGLE** Persons — And the number of allowances is:										
At least	But less than	0	1	2	3	4	5	6	7	8	9	10
		The Tentative Withholding Amount is:										
$2,935	**$2,975**	$428	$388	$349	$309	$270	$231	$195	$174	$152	$131	$109
$2,975	**$3,015**	$436	$397	$358	$318	$279	$239	$200	$179	$157	$136	$114
$3,015	**$3,055**	$445	$406	$366	$327	$288	$248	$209	$183	$162	$140	$119
$3,055	**$3,095**	$454	$415	$375	$336	$296	$257	$218	$188	$167	$145	$124
$3,095	**$3,135**	$463	$423	$384	$345	$305	$266	$226	$193	$171	$150	$128
$3,135	**$3,175**	$472	$432	$393	$353	$314	$275	$235	$198	$176	$155	$133
$3,175	**$3,215**	$480	$441	$402	$362	$323	$283	$244	$204	$181	$160	$138
$3,215	**$3,255**	$489	$450	$410	$371	$332	$292	$253	$213	$186	$164	$143
$3,255	**$3,295**	$498	$459	$419	$380	$340	$301	$262	$222	$191	$169	$148
$3,295	**$3,335**	$507	$467	$428	$389	$349	$310	$270	$231	$195	$174	$152
$3,335	**$3,375**	$516	$476	$437	$397	$358	$319	$279	$240	$200	$179	$157
$3,375	**$3,415**	$524	$485	$446	$406	$367	$327	$288	$248	$209	$184	$162
$3,415	**$3,455**	$533	$494	$454	$415	$376	$336	$297	$257	$218	$188	$167
$3,455	**$3,495**	$542	$503	$463	$424	$384	$345	$306	$266	$227	$193	$172
$3,495	**$3,535**	$551	$511	$472	$433	$393	$354	$314	$275	$235	$198	$176
$3,535	**$3,575**	$560	$520	$481	$441	$402	$363	$323	$284	$244	$205	$181
$3,575	**$3,615**	$568	$529	$490	$450	$411	$371	$332	$292	$253	$214	$186
$3,615	**$3,655**	$577	$538	$498	$459	$420	$380	$341	$301	$262	$222	$191
$3,655	**$3,695**	$586	$547	$507	$468	$428	$389	$350	$310	$271	$231	$196
$3,695	**$3,735**	$595	$555	$516	$477	$437	$398	$358	$319	$279	$240	$201
$3,735	**$3,775**	$604	$564	$525	$485	$446	$407	$367	$328	$288	$249	$209
$3,775	**$3,815**	$612	$573	$534	$494	$455	$415	$376	$336	$297	$258	$218
$3,815	**$3,855**	$621	$582	$542	$503	$464	$424	$385	$345	$306	$266	$227
$3,855	**$3,895**	$630	$591	$551	$512	$472	$433	$394	$354	$315	$275	$236
$3,895	**$3,935**	$639	$599	$560	$521	$481	$442	$402	$363	$323	$284	$245
$3,935	**$3,975**	$649	$608	$569	$529	$490	$451	$411	$372	$332	$293	$253
$3,975	**$4,015**	$658	$617	$578	$538	$499	$459	$420	$380	$341	$302	$262
$4,015	**$4,055**	$668	$626	$586	$547	$508	$468	$429	$389	$350	$310	$271

4. Percentage Method Tables for Manual Payroll Systems With Forms W-4 From 2020 or Later

If you compute payroll manually, your employee has submitted a Form W-4 for 2020 or later, and you prefer to use the Percentage Method or you can't use the Wage Bracket Method tables because the employee's annual wages exceed the amount from the last bracket of the table (based on marital status and pay period), use the worksheet below and the Percentage Method tables that follow to figure federal income tax withholding. This method works for any amount of wages.

Worksheet 4. Employer's Withholding Worksheet for Percentage Method Tables for Manual Payroll Systems With Forms W-4 From 2020 or Later

Keep for Your Records 

Table 6	Monthly	Semimonthly	Biweekly	Weekly	Daily
	12	24	26	52	260

Step 1. **Adjust the employee's wage amount**

1a Enter the employee's total taxable wages this payroll period . . . . . 1a $______

1b Enter the number of pay periods you have per year (see Table 6) . . . . . 1b ______

1c Enter the amount from Step 4(a) of the employee's Form W-4 . . . . . 1c $______

1d Divide line 1c by the number on line 1b . . . . . 1d $______

1e Add lines 1a and 1d . . . . . 1e $______

1f Enter the amount from Step 4(b) of the employee's Form W-4 . . . . . 1f $______

1g Divide line 1f by the number on line 1b . . . . . 1g $______

1h Subtract line 1g from line 1e. If zero or less, enter -0-. This is the **Adjusted Wage Amount** . . . . . 1h $______

Step 2. **Figure the Tentative Withholding Amount**

based on your pay frequency, the employee's Adjusted Wage Amount, filing status (Step 1(c) of Form W-4), and whether the box in Step 2 of Form W-4 is checked.

2a Find the row in the STANDARD Withholding Rate Schedules (if the box in Step 2 of Form W-4 is NOT checked) or the Form W-4, Step 2, Checkbox, Withholding Rate Schedules (if it HAS been checked) of the Percentage Method tables in this section in which the amount on line 1h is at least the amount in column A but less than the amount in column B, and then enter here the amount from column A of that row . . . . . 2a $______

2b Enter the amount from column C of that row . . . . . 2b $______

2c Enter the percentage from column D of that row . . . . . 2c ______%

2d Subtract line 2a from line 1h . . . . . 2d $______

2e Multiply the amount on line 2d by the percentage on line 2c . . . . . 2e $______

2f Add lines 2b and 2e. This is the **Tentative Withholding Amount** . . . . . 2f $______

Step 3. **Account for tax credits**

3a Enter the amount from Step 3 of the employee's Form W-4 . . . . . 3a $______

3b Divide the amount on line 3a by the number of pay periods on line 1b . . . . . 3b $______

3c Subtract line 3b from line 2f. If zero or less, enter -0- . . . . . 3c $______

Step 4. **Figure the final amount to withhold**

4a Enter the additional amount to withhold from Step 4(c) of the employee's Form W-4 . . . . . 4a $______

4b Add lines 3c and 4a. **This is the amount to withhold from the employee's wages this pay period** . . . . . 4b $______

2022 Percentage Method Tables for Manual Payroll Systems With Forms W-4 from 2020 or Later

SEMIMONTHLY Payroll Period

STANDARD Withholding Rate Schedules (Use these if the box in Step 2 of Form W-4 is **NOT** checked)					**Form W-4, Step 2, Checkbox, Withholding Rate Schedules** (Use these if the box in Step 2 of Form W-4 **IS** checked)				
If the Adjusted Wage Amount (line 1h) is:					**If the Adjusted Wage Amount (line 1h) is:**				
At least—	**But less than—**	**The tentative amount to withhold is:**	**Plus this percentage—**	**of the amount that the Adjusted Wage exceeds—**	**At least—**	**But less than—**	**The tentative amount to withhold is:**	**Plus this percentage—**	**of the amount that the Adjusted Wage exceeds—**
A	**B**	**C**	**D**	**E**	**A**	**B**	**C**	**D**	**E**
Married Filing Jointly					**Married Filing Jointly**				
$0	$1,079	$0.00	0%	$0	$0	$540	$0.00	0%	$0
$1,079	$1,935	$0.00	10%	$1,079	$540	$968	$0.00	10%	$540
$1,935	$4,560	$85.60	12%	$1,935	$968	$2,280	$42.80	12%	$968
$4,560	$8,502	$400.60	22%	$4,560	$2,280	$4,251	$200.24	22%	$2,280
$8,502	$15,250	$1,267.84	24%	$8,502	$4,251	$7,625	$633.86	24%	$4,251
$15,250	$19,075	$2,887.36	32%	$15,250	$7,625	$9,538	$1,443.62	32%	$7,625
$19,075	$28,073	$4,111.36	35%	$19,075	$9,538	$14,036	$2,055.78	35%	$9,538
$28,073		$7,260.66	37%	$28,073	$14,036		$3,630.08	37%	$14,036
Single or Married Filing Separately					**Single or Married Filing Separately**				
$0	$540	$0.00	0%	$0	$0	$270	$0.00	0%	$0
$540	$968	$0.00	10%	$540	$270	$484	$0.00	10%	$270
$968	$2,280	$42.80	12%	$968	$484	$1,140	$21.40	12%	$484
$2,280	$4,251	$200.24	22%	$2,280	$1,140	$2,126	$100.12	22%	$1,140
$4,251	$7,625	$633.86	24%	$4,251	$2,126	$3,813	$317.04	24%	$2,126
$7,625	$9,538	$1,443.62	32%	$7,625	$3,813	$4,769	$721.92	32%	$3,813
$9,538	$23,035	$2,055.78	35%	$9,538	$4,769	$11,518	$1,027.84	35%	$4,769
$23,035		$6,779.73	37%	$23,035	$11,518		$3,389.99	37%	$11,518
Head of Household					**Head of Household**				
$0	$808	$0.00	0%	$0	$0	$404	$0.00	0%	$0
$808	$1,419	$0.00	10%	$808	$404	$709	$0.00	10%	$404
$1,419	$3,138	$61.10	12%	$1,419	$709	$1,569	$30.50	12%	$709
$3,138	$4,519	$267.38	22%	$3,138	$1,569	$2,259	$133.70	22%	$1,569
$4,519	$7,894	$571.20	24%	$4,519	$2,259	$3,947	$285.50	24%	$2,259
$7,894	$9,806	$1,381.20	32%	$7,894	$3,947	$4,903	$690.62	32%	$3,947
$9,806	$23,304	$1,993.04	35%	$9,806	$4,903	$11,652	$996.54	35%	$4,903
$23,304		$6,717.34	37%	$23,304	$11,652		$3,358.69	37%	$11,652

5. Percentage Method Tables for Manual Payroll Systems With Forms W-4 From 2019 or Earlier

If you compute payroll manually and your employee **has not** submitted a Form W-4 for 2020 or later, and you prefer to use the Percentage Method or you can't use the Wage Bracket Method tables because the employee's annual wages exceed the amount from the last bracket of the table (based on marital status and pay period) or the employee claimed more than 10 allowances, use the worksheet below and the Percentage Method tables that follow to figure federal income tax withholding. This method works for any number of withholding allowances claimed and any amount of wages.

Periodic payments of pensions or annuities with a 2021 or earlier Form W-4P. In lieu of Worksheet 1B and the Percentage Method tables in section 1, you may use Worksheet 5 and the Percentage Method tables in this section to figure federal income tax withholding on periodic payments of pensions or annuities with a 2021 or earlier Form W-4P. As an alternative, if you prefer to use the Wage Bracket Method of withholding, you may use Worksheet 3 and the Wage Bracket Method tables in section 3 to figure federal income tax withholding on periodic payments of pensions or annuities with a 2021 or earlier Form W-4P.

Worksheet 5. Employer's Withholding Worksheet for Percentage Method Tables for Manual Payroll Systems With Forms W-4 From 2019 or Earlier

Keep for Your Records 

Table 7	Annually	Semiannually	Quarterly	Monthly	Semimonthly	Biweekly	Weekly	Daily
	$4,300	$2,150	$1,075	$358	$179	$165	$83	$17

Step 1. Adjust the employee's wage amount

1a Enter the employee's total taxable wages this payroll period . . . . . 1a $_____

1b Enter the number of allowances claimed on the employee's most recent Form W-4 . . . . . 1b _____

1c Multiply line 1b by the amount in Table 7 for your pay frequency . . . . . 1c $_____

1d Subtract line 1c from line 1a. If zero or less, enter -0-. This is the **Adjusted Wage Amount** . . . . . 1d $_____

Step 2. Figure the Tentative Withholding Amount

based on your pay frequency, the employee's Adjusted Wage Amount, and marital status (line 3 of Form W-4).

2a Find the row in the Percentage Method table in this section in which the amount on line 1d is at least the amount in column A but less than the amount in column B, and then enter here the amount from column A of that row . . . . . 2a $_____

2b Enter the amount from column C of that row . . . . . 2b $_____

2c Enter the percentage from column D of that row . . . . . 2c _____%

2d Subtract line 2a from line 1d . . . . . 2d $_____

2e Multiply the amount on line 2d by the percentage on line 2c . . . . . 2e $_____

2f Add lines 2b and 2e. This is the **Tentative Withholding Amount** . . . . . 2f $_____

Step 3. Figure the final amount to withhold

3a Enter the additional amount to withhold from line 6 of the employee's Form W-4 . . . . . 3a $_____

3b Add lines 2f and 3a. **This is the amount to withhold from the employee's wages this pay period** . . . . . 3b $_____

2022 Percentage Method Tables for Manual Payroll Systems With Forms W-4 From 2019 or Earlier

WEEKLY Payroll Period

MARRIED Persons					SINGLE Persons				
If the Adjusted Wage Amount (line 1d) is at least...	But less than...	The tentative amount to withhold is...	Plus this percentage ...	of the amount that the wage exceeds...	If the Adjusted Wage Amount (line 1d) is at least...	But less than...	The tentative amount to withhold is...	Plus this percentage ...	of the amount that the wage exceeds...
A	B	C	D	E	A	B	C	D	E
$0	$250	$0.00	0%	$0	$0	$84	$0.00	0%	$0
$250	$645	$0.00	10%	$250	$84	$281	$0.00	10%	$84
$645	$1,857	$39.50	12%	$645	$281	$887	$19.70	12%	$281
$1,857	$3,676	$184.94	22%	$1,857	$887	$1,797	$92.42	22%	$887
$3,676	$6,790	$585.12	24%	$3,676	$1,797	$3,354	$292.62	24%	$1,797
$6,790	$8,556	$1,332.48	32%	$6,790	$3,354	$4,237	$666.30	32%	$3,354
$8,556	$12,709	$1,897.60	35%	$8,556	$4,237	$10,466	$948.86	35%	$4,237
$12,709		$3,351.15	37%	$12,709	$10,466		$3,129.01	37%	$10,466

BIWEEKLY Payroll Period

MARRIED Persons					SINGLE Persons				
If the Adjusted Wage Amount (line 1d) is at least...	But less than...	The tentative amount to withhold is...	Plus this percentage ...	of the amount that the wage exceeds...	If the Adjusted Wage Amount (line 1d) is at least...	But less than...	The tentative amount to withhold is...	Plus this percentage ...	of the amount that the wage exceeds...
A	B	C	D	E	A	B	C	D	E
$0	$500	$0.00	0%	$0	$0	$167	$0.00	0%	$0
$500	$1,290	$0.00	10%	$500	$167	$563	$0.00	10%	$167
$1,290	$3,713	$79.00	12%	$1,290	$563	$1,774	$39.60	12%	$563
$3,713	$7,352	$369.76	22%	$3,713	$1,774	$3,593	$184.92	22%	$1,774
$7,352	$13,581	$1,170.34	24%	$7,352	$3,593	$6,708	$585.10	24%	$3,593
$13,581	$17,112	$2,665.30	32%	$13,581	$6,708	$8,473	$1,332.70	32%	$6,708
$17,112	$25,417	$3,795.22	35%	$17,112	$8,473	$20,933	$1,897.50	35%	$8,473
$25,417		$6,701.97	37%	$25,417	$20,933		$6,258.50	37%	$20,933

SEMIMONTHLY Payroll Period

MARRIED Persons					SINGLE Persons				
If the Adjusted Wage Amount (line 1d) is at least...	But less than...	The tentative amount to withhold is...	Plus this percentage ...	of the amount that the wage exceeds...	If the Adjusted Wage Amount (line 1d) is at least...	But less than...	The tentative amount to withhold is...	Plus this percentage ...	of the amount that the wage exceeds...
A	B	C	D	E	A	B	C	D	E
$0	$542	$0.00	0%	$0	$0	$181	$0.00	0%	$0
$542	$1,398	$0.00	10%	$542	$181	$609	$0.00	10%	$181
$1,398	$4,023	$85.60	12%	$1,398	$609	$1,922	$42.80	12%	$609
$4,023	$7,965	$400.60	22%	$4,023	$1,922	$3,893	$200.36	22%	$1,922
$7,965	$14,713	$1,267.84	24%	$7,965	$3,893	$7,267	$633.98	24%	$3,893
$14,713	$18,538	$2,887.36	32%	$14,713	$7,267	$9,179	$1,443.74	32%	$7,267
$18,538	$27,535	$4,111.36	35%	$18,538	$9,179	$22,677	$2,055.58	35%	$9,179
$27,535		$7,260.31	37%	$27,535	$22,677		$6,779.88	37%	$22,677

MONTHLY Payroll Period

MARRIED Persons					SINGLE Persons				
If the Adjusted Wage Amount (line 1d) is at least...	But less than...	The tentative amount to withhold is...	Plus this percentage ...	of the amount that the wage exceeds...	If the Adjusted Wage Amount (line 1d) is at least...	But less than...	The tentative amount to withhold is...	Plus this percentage ...	of the amount that the wage exceeds...
A	B	C	D	E	A	B	C	D	E
$0	$1,083	$0.00	0%	$0	$0	$363	$0.00	0%	$0
$1,083	$2,796	$0.00	10%	$1,083	$363	$1,219	$0.00	10%	$363
$2,796	$8,046	$171.30	12%	$2,796	$1,219	$3,844	$85.60	12%	$1,219
$8,046	$15,929	$801.30	22%	$8,046	$3,844	$7,785	$400.60	22%	$3,844
$15,929	$29,425	$2,535.56	24%	$15,929	$7,785	$14,533	$1,267.62	24%	$7,785
$29,425	$37,075	$5,774.60	32%	$29,425	$14,533	$18,358	$2,887.14	32%	$14,533
$37,075	$55,071	$8,222.60	35%	$37,075	$18,358	$45,354	$4,111.14	35%	$18,358
$55,071		$14,521.20	37%	$55,071	$45,354		$13,559.74	37%	$45,354

Additional Comprehensive Tax Return Problems

CONTENTS

Comprehensive Problem One

Noah and Joan Arc's Tax Return

Noah and Joan Arc live with their family in Dayton, OH. Noah's Social Security number is 434-11-3311. Noah was born on February 22, 1987, and Joan was born on July 1, 1988. Both enjoy good health and eyesight. Noah owns and operates a pet store, and Joan is a firefighter for the city of Dayton.

1. The Arcs have two children, a son named Shem (Social Security number 598-01-2345), born on March 21, 2015, and a daughter named Nora (Social Security number 554-33-2411), born on December 3, 2018.
2. Joan and Noah brought a folder of tax documents located on Pages D-3 to D-5.
3. Noah's pet store is located at 1415 S. Patterson Blvd, Dayton, OH 45409. The name of the store is "The Arc" and its taxpayer identification number is 95-9876556. Since you handle Noah's bookkeeping, you have printed the income statement from your Quickbooks software, shown on Page D-5.
4. Details of The Arc's meals and entertainment:

Restaurant meals associated with business travel	$ 500
Arc employee holiday party	300
Restaurant overtime meals for employees	200
Sports tickets for entertaining large customers	600
	$ 1,600

5. Travel costs are business related and do not include meals. Miscellaneous expense is a $300 contribution to Re-elect Goldie Wilson, Mayor of Dayton.
6. Noah and Joan paid the following amounts during the year:

Contributions to Re-elect Goldie Wilson, Mayor of Dayton	$ 250
Church donations (for which a written acknowledgment was received)	5,000
Real estate taxes on their home	2,400
Medical co-pays for doctor visits	700
Mortgage interest for purchase of home	See Form 1098 (Page D-4)
Tax return preparation fees	350
Credit card interest	220
Automobile insurance premiums	600
Uniforms for Joan	125
Contribution to Noah's individual retirement account (made on April 1, 2023)	5,000

7. Noah has a long-term capital loss carryover from last year of $1,300.
8. Noah and Joan own a condo and use it as a rental property. The condo is located at 16 Oakwood Ave, Unit A, Dayton, OH 45409. Noah provides the management services for the rental including selection of tenants, maintenance, repairs, rent collection, and other services as needed. On average, Noah spends about two hours per week on the rental activity. The revenue and expenses for the year are as follows:

Rental income received	$16,200
Insurance	800
Interest expense	5,800
Property taxes	1,500
Miscellaneous expenses	500

Rental income includes $1,150 per month for two months under the previous lease (which ended February 28, 2022). The new lease is $1,300 per month for ten months under the new lease but the tenant paid only $900 in May 2022 because the tenant paid $400 for repairs to the apartment, and with the Arc's permission, reduced May's rent by $400. The new lease also required the tenant to pay last month's $1,300 rent in February 2022. The home was acquired for $85,000 in 2006. On May 12, 2022, the Arcs installed new fixtures (7-year recovery period) at a cost of $3,500. They wish to maximize the cost recovery on the new fixtures but make no elections.

9. The Arcs paid Ohio general sales tax of $1,076 during the year.

Required: You are to prepare the Arcs' federal income tax return in good form, signing the return as the preparer. Do not complete an Ohio state income tax return. Make realistic assumptions about any missing data that you may need. The following forms and schedules are required:

Form 1040	Schedule E
Schedule 1	Schedule SE
Schedule 2	Form 2441
Schedule 3	Form 4562
Schedule A	Schedule 8812
Schedule B	Form 8995
Schedule C	Qualified Dividends and Capital Gain Tax Worksheet
Schedule D	

a Employee's social security number 456-87-5432	OMB No. 1545-0008	Safe, accurate, FAST! Use IRS e-file. Visit the IRS website at www.irs.gov/efile
b Employer identification number (EIN) 33-4382966	1 Wages, tips, other compensation 31,000.00	2 Federal income tax withheld 5,100.00
c Employer's name, address, and ZIP code City of Dayton Fire and Rescue, 123 Warren Street, Dayton, OH 45402	3 Social security wages 31,000.00	4 Social security tax withheld 1,922.00
	5 Medicare wages and tips 31,000.00	6 Medicare tax withheld 449.50
	7 Social security tips	8 Allocated tips
d Control number	9	10 Dependent care benefits
e Employee's first name and initial / Last name / Suff. Joan Arc, 1265 W. Riverview Avenue, Dayton, OH 45402	11 Nonqualified plans	12a See instructions for box 12: DD 10,100.00
	13 Statutory employee ☐ Retirement plan ☒ Third-party sick pay ☐	12b
	14 Other	12c
f Employee's address and ZIP code		12d

15 State	Employer's state ID number	16 State wages, tips, etc.	17 State income tax	18 Local wages, tips, etc.	19 Local income tax	20 Locality name
OH	1126-87021	31,000.00	1,950.00	31,000.00	770.45	DAYTN

Form **W-2** Wage and Tax Statement 2022 Department of the Treasury—Internal Revenue Service

Copy B—To Be Filed With Employee's FEDERAL Tax Return.
This information is being furnished to the Internal Revenue Service.

Substitute 1099 Statement

Charlotte Squab Financial Services

123 Wall Street
New York, NY 10005

Joan and Noah Arc
1265 W. Riverview Avenue
Dayton, OH 45402
SSN: 456-87-5432

Date
December 31, 2022

Dividends						
Payor	*Box 1a Ordinary Dividends*	*Box 1b Qualified Dividends*	*Box 2a Cap Gain Distrib*	*Box 4 Federal Income Tax withheld*	*Box 7 Foreign Tax Paid*	*Box 11 Tax-exempt Dividends*
ExxonMobil	350.00	350.00	0.00	0.00	0.00	0.00
Texas Util.	1,200.00	1,200.00	0.00	0.00	0.00	0.00
CS Growth Fund	395.00	380.00	250.00	0.00	30.00	0.00

Stock Transactions Box 1a	Box 1b	Box 1c	Box 1d	Box 1e	Box 2
Description	*Date Acq.*	*Date Sold*	*Net Proceeds*	*Basis (reported to IRS)*	*Character*
100 shs. Blue Corp.	02/11/2012	08/15/2022	4,700.00	2,700.00	LT
50 shs.Yellow Corp.	01/13/2022	06/05/2022	6,000.00	5,500.00	ST
25 shs. Red Co.	10/02/2013	10/07/2022	12,000.00	2,000.00	LT

☐ CORRECTED (if checked)

Mortgage Interest Statement

OMB No. 1545-1380
Form **1098**
(Rev. January 2022)
For calendar year 20 22

RECIPIENT'S/LENDER'S name, street address, city or town, state or province, country, ZIP or foreign postal code, and telephone no.
Chase Mortgage
100 Park Avenue
New York, NY 10017

***Caution:** The amount shown may not be fully deductible by you. Limits based on the loan amount and the cost and value of the secured property may apply. Also, you may only deduct interest to the extent it was incurred by you, actually paid by you, and not reimbursed by another person.

RECIPIENT'S/LENDER'S TIN: 13-4296127

PAYER'S/BORROWER'S TIN: 434-11-3311

1 Mortgage interest received from payer(s)/borrower(s)*: $ 10,056.32

2 Outstanding mortgage principal: $ 275,873.55

3 Mortgage origination date: 03/13/2013

4 Refund of overpaid interest: $

5 Mortgage insurance premiums: $

6 Points paid on purchase of principal residence: $

7 ☒ If address of property securing mortgage is the same as PAYER'S/BORROWER'S address, the box is checked, or the address or description is entered in box 8.

8 Address or description of property securing mortgage

PAYER'S/BORROWER'S name: Noah and Joan Arc

Street address (including apt. no.): 1265 W. Riverview Avenue

City or town, state or province, country, and ZIP or foreign postal code: Dayton, OH 45402

9 Number of properties securing the mortgage: 1

10 Other

Account number (see instructions)

Copy B
For Payer/Borrower

The information in boxes 1 through 9 and 11 is important tax information and is being furnished to the IRS. If you are required to file a return, a negligence penalty or other sanction may be imposed on you if the IRS determines that an underpayment of tax results because you overstated a deduction for this mortgage interest or for these points, reported in boxes 1 and 6; or because you didn't report the refund of interest (box 4); or because you claimed a nondeductible item.

11 Mortgage acquisition date

Form **1098** (Rev. 1-2022) (Keep for your records) www.irs.gov/Form1098 Department of the Treasury - Internal Revenue Service

ROUNDUP DAY CARE CENTER
245 N. WILKINSON STREET
DAYTON, OH 45402

January 12, 2023

Joan and Noah Arc
1265 W. Riverview Avenue
Dayton, OH 45402

Dear Joan and Noah,

Thank you for a great 2022 at Roundup! We appreciate your patronage during the year and hope to continue to provide excellent service for Nora in 2023. We have provided the tax information for calendar year 2022 below. Please let us know if you need any additional information.

Sincerely,

Charles F. Burgundian

Charles F. Burgundian
Executive Director, Roundup Day Care
EIN 54-0983456

Date of service	Amount Paid	Child
January 1, 2022 – December 31, 2022	$7,000.00	Nora Arc

The Arc
95-9876556
Income Statement
For the Year Ended December 31, 2022

Revenue:		
Gross Sales		$ 150,000.00
Less: Sales Returns and Allowances		-
Net Sales		150,000.00
Cost of Goods Sold:		
Beginning Inventory	11,000.00	
Add: Purchases	66,000.00	
	77,000.00	
Less: Ending Inventory	10,000.00	
Cost of Goods Sold		67,000.00
Gross Profit (Loss)		83,000.00
Expenses:		
Dues and Subscriptions	-	
Estimated Federal Tax Payments	4,000.00	
Estimated State Tax Payments	3,800.00	
Insurance	4,000.00	
Meals and Entertainment	1,600.00	
Miscellaneous	300.00	
Payroll Taxes	4,000.00	
Professional Fees	1,800.00	
Rent	8,500.00	
Travel	1,300.00	
Utilities	1,500.00	
Vehicle Expenses	-	
Wages	25,000.00	
Total Expenses		55,800.00
Net Operating Income		$ 27,200.00

Comprehensive Problem Two

Michael and Jeanette Boyd's Tax Return

Michael D. and Jeanette S. Boyd live with their family at the Rock Glen House Bed & Breakfast, which Michael operates. The Bed & Breakfast (B&B) is located at 33333 Fume Blanc Way, Temecula, CA 92591. Michael (born May 4, 1979) and Jeanette (born June 12, 1980) enjoy good health and eyesight.

1. The Boyds have three sons. Maxwell was born April 16, 2003, Seve was born December 2, 2010, and Denzel was born January 13, 2012. All three boys live at home, and the Boyds provide more than 50 percent of their support.
2. The Rock Glen House B&B is operated as a sole proprietorship and had the following income and expenses for the year:

Room rental income	$138,137
Vending machine income	2,167
Advertising expense	4,945
Depreciation for book and tax purposes	18,000
Mortgage interest on the B&B	22,900
Wages of custodial services	17,800
Taxes and licenses	6,400
Supplies consumed	19,185
Business insurance	6,233
Laundry expenses	4,200
Accounting fees	1,800
Office expenses	2,281
Utilities	6,283

All of the above amounts relate to the business portion of the Bed & Breakfast; the personal portion is accounted for separately. The Rock Glen House B&B uses the cash method of accounting and has no inventory. The employer tax ID number is 95-1234567.

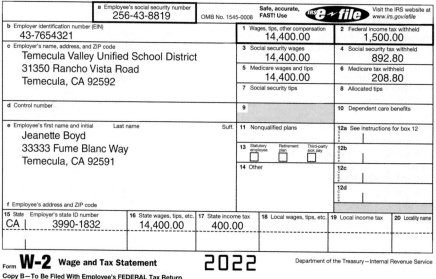

a Employee's social security number: 256-43-8819	OMB No. 1545-0008	Safe, accurate, FAST! Use IRS e-file	Visit the IRS website at www.irs.gov/efile
b Employer identification number (EIN): 43-7654321		1 Wages, tips, other compensation: 14,400.00	2 Federal income tax withheld: 1,500.00
c Employer's name, address, and ZIP code: Temecula Valley Unified School District, 31350 Rancho Vista Road, Temecula, CA 92592		3 Social security wages: 14,400.00	4 Social security tax withheld: 892.80
		5 Medicare wages and tips: 14,400.00	6 Medicare tax withheld: 208.80
		7 Social security tips	8 Allocated tips
d Control number		9	10 Dependent care benefits
e Employee's first name and initial / Last name / Suff.: Jeanette Boyd, 33333 Fume Blanc Way, Temecula, CA 92591		11 Nonqualified plans	12a See instructions for box 12
		13 Statutory employee / Retirement plan / Third-party sick pay	12b
		14 Other	12c
f Employee's address and ZIP code			12d

15 State	Employer's state ID number	16 State wages, tips, etc.	17 State income tax	18 Local wages, tips, etc.	19 Local income tax	20 Locality name
CA	3990-1832	14,400.00	400.00			

Form **W-2** Wage and Tax Statement 2022 — Department of the Treasury—Internal Revenue Service

Copy B—To Be Filed With Employee's FEDERAL Tax Return.
This information is being furnished to the Internal Revenue Service.

3. The Boyds made estimated state income tax payments of $3,000 (all made during 2022).
4. Jeanette worked about 1,000 hours as a substitute schoolteacher with the local school district. She also spent $306 out-of-pocket for various supplies for her classroom. For the current year, Jeanette's Form W-2 from the school district is presented on the previous page.
5. Michael is retired from the U.S. Navy. His annual statement from the Navy, Form 1099-R, is shown on Page D-12.
6. Michael and Jeanette paid (and can substantiate) the following amounts during the year:

Mastercard interest	$1,480
Dental expenses (orthodontics for Maxwell)	5,400
California state income tax (for 2021)	2,100
Charitable contributions	900
Life insurance premiums	845
Automobile registration fees (deductible portion)	50
Tax return preparation fee	475
Contributions to the president's re-election campaign	1,000

The Boyds are taking the standard deduction in 2022.

7. During the year, Michael and Jeanette received the following qualifying dividends and interest:

Interest:	
Bob's Big Bank	$ 411
Bank of California	289
City of Temecula Tax-Exempt Bonds	1,500
Vintage Bank	See 1099-INT (Page D-12)
Qualified dividends:	
Southwest Airlines	$ 312
Heinz Foods	579

Also, Jeanette owns Series EE U.S. savings bonds. During the year, the bond redemption value increased by $1,300. Jeanette has not elected the accrual method for these bonds. All the above stocks, bonds, and bank accounts are community property.

8. Jeanette has a stock portfolio. During the year, she sold the following stock, shown on her Forms 1099-B as follows (basis was provided to the IRS in all cases):

	Orange Co.	*Gold Co.*	*Green Co.*
Sales price	$8,000	See	$1,555
Basis	3,600	Form	2,417
Date acquired	02/11/22	1099-B	10/31/20
Date sold	06/19/22	(Page D-12)	10/23/22

9. Michael does all the significant work in the Bed & Breakfast and therefore he pays self-employment tax on 100 percent of the earnings from the B&B.
10. During the year, Michael's Uncle Boris died. Boris had a $50,000 life insurance policy that named Michael as the beneficiary. Michael received the check for the benefits payable under the policy on November 30 of the current year. Boris also left Michael a parcel of land with an appraised value of $120,000.

11. Michael is a general partner in a partnership that owns a boutique hotel in northern California and leases the property to a hotel management company. Michael does not materially participate in the partnership activity but the partnership activity does rise to the level of a trade or business. The Schedule K-1 from the partnership is shown on Page D-9.
12. Jeanette was not eligible for health care benefits due to the part-time nature of her job, thus health insurance for the Boyd household was purchased through the Covered California program and the Boyds received the Form 1095-A shown on Page D-11. They had no other health insurance during 2022. Assume that the self-employed health insurance deduction is $0. The Boyds were not paid an advance premium tax credit.

Required: Michael and Jeanette have come to you to prepare their 2022 federal income tax return. Do not complete a California state income tax return. Michael and Jeanette have given you several IRS forms (see Pages D-9 to D-12). Make realistic assumptions about any missing data that you need. Do not file a federal Form 4952. The following is a list of the forms and schedules that you will need to complete the tax return:

Form 1040	Schedule E
Schedule 1	Schedule SE
Schedule 2	Schedule 8812
Schedule 3	Form 8962
Schedule B	Form 8995
Schedule C	Qualified Dividends and Capital Gain Tax Worksheet
Schedule D	

651121

☐ Final K-1 ☐ Amended K-1 OMB No. 1545-0123

Schedule K-1 (Form 1065) 2022
Department of the Treasury
Internal Revenue Service

For calendar year 2022, or tax year
beginning / / 2022 ending / /

Partner's Share of Income, Deductions, Credits, etc. See separate instructions.

Part I Information About the Partnership

A Partnership's employer identification number
11-2343212

B Partnership's name, address, city, state, and ZIP code
Wine Acres Partners
581 Coombs Street
Napa, CA 94559

C IRS center where partnership filed return: Ogden, UT

D ☐ Check if this is a publicly traded partnership (PTP)

Part II Information About the Partner

E Partner's SSN or TIN (Do not use TIN of a disregarded entity. See instructions.)
543-88-9756

F Name, address, city, state, and ZIP code for partner entered in E. See instructions.
Michael Boyd
33333 Fume Blanc Way
Temecula, CA 92591

G ☒ General partner or LLC member-manager ☐ Limited partner or other LLC member

H1 ☒ Domestic partner ☐ Foreign partner

H2 ☐ If the partner is a disregarded entity (DE), enter the partner's:
TIN ______ Name ______

I1 What type of entity is this partner? ______

I2 If this partner is a retirement plan (IRA/SEP/Keogh/etc.), check here ☐

J Partner's share of profit, loss, and capital (see instructions):

	Beginning	Ending
Profit	2 %	2 %
Loss	2 %	2 %
Capital	2 %	2 %

Check if decrease is due to sale or exchange of partnership interest ☐

K Partner's share of liabilities:

	Beginning	Ending
Nonrecourse	$ 4,679	$ 4,679
Qualified nonrecourse financing	$	$
Recourse	$	$

Check this box if item K includes liability amounts from lower-tier partnerships ☐

L Partner's Capital Account Analysis

Beginning capital account	$ 13,256
Capital contributed during the year	$
Current year net income (loss)	$ 710
Other increase (decrease) (attach explanation)	$
Withdrawals and distributions	$ (350)
Ending capital account	$ 13,616

M Did the partner contribute property with a built-in gain (loss)?
☐ Yes ☒ No If "Yes," attach statement. See instructions.

N Partner's Share of Net Unrecognized Section 704(c) Gain or (Loss)
Beginning $ ______
Ending $ ______

Part III Partner's Share of Current Year Income, Deductions, Credits, and Other Items

1	Ordinary business income (loss)	
2	Net rental real estate income (loss)	1,600
3	Other net rental income (loss)	
4a	Guaranteed payments for services	
4b	Guaranteed payments for capital	
4c	Total guaranteed payments	
5	Interest income	
6a	Ordinary dividends	10
6b	Qualified dividends	10
6c	Dividend equivalents	
7	Royalties	
8	Net short-term capital gain (loss)	
9a	Net long-term capital gain (loss)	(900)
9b	Collectibles (28%) gain (loss)	
9c	Unrecaptured section 1250 gain	
10	Net section 1231 gain (loss)	
11	Other income (loss)	
12	Section 179 deduction	
13	Other deductions	
14	Self-employment earnings (loss)	A 1,600
15	Credits	
16	Schedule K-3 is attached if checked ☐	
17	Alternative minimum tax (AMT) items	
18	Tax-exempt income and nondeductible expenses	
19	Distributions	A 350
20	Other information	Z 1,600
21	Foreign taxes paid or accrued	

22 ☐ More than one activity for at-risk purposes*
23 ☐ More than one activity for passive activity purposes*
*See attached statement for additional information.

For IRS Use Only

Form **1095-A** Department of the Treasury Internal Revenue Service

Health Insurance Marketplace Statement

☐ VOID ☐ CORRECTED

OMB No. 1545-2232 **2022**

Do not attach to your tax return. Keep for your records.
Go to *www.irs.gov/Form1095A* for instructions and the latest information.

Part I Recipient Information

1 Marketplace identifier 31-1234567	2 Marketplace-assigned policy number A1000HT	3 Policy issuer's name Covered California
4 Recipient's name Michael Boyd	5 Recipient's SSN 543-88-9756	6 Recipient's date of birth 05/04/1979
7 Recipient's spouse's name Jeanette Boyd	8 Recipient's spouse's SSN 256-43-8819	9 Recipient's spouse's date of birth 06/12/1980
10 Policy start date 05/01/2022	11 Policy termination date 12/31/2022	12 Street address (including apartment no.) 33333 Fume Blanc Way
13 City or town Temecula	14 State or province CA	15 Country and ZIP or foreign postal code 92591

Part II Covered Individuals

	A. Covered individual name	B. Covered individual SSN	C. Covered individual date of birth	D. Coverage start date	E. Coverage termination date
16	Michael Boyd	543-88-9756	05/04/1979	05/01/2022	12/31/2022
17	Jeanette Boyd	256-43-8819	06/12/1980	05/01/2022	12/31/2022
18	Maxwell Boyd	466-74-1131	04/16/2003	05/01/2022	12/31/2022
19	Seve Boyd	465-76-8375	12/02/2010	05/01/2022	12/31/2022
20	Denzel Boyd	475-23-1426	01/13/2012	05/01/2022	12/31/2022

Part III Coverage Information

Month	A. Monthly enrollment premiums	B. Monthly second lowest cost silver plan (SLCSP) premium	C. Monthly advance payment of premium tax credit
21 January			
22 February			
23 March			
24 April			
25 May	1,450	1,610	
26 June	1,450	1,610	
27 July	1,450	1,610	
28 August	1,450	1,610	
29 September	1,450	1,610	
30 October	1,450	1,610	
31 November	1,450	1,610	
32 December	1,450	1,610	
33 **Annual Totals**	11,600	12,880	

For Privacy Act and Paperwork Reduction Act Notice, see separate instructions. Cat. No. 60703Q Form **1095-A** (2022)

☐ CORRECTED (if checked)

Distributions From Pensions, Annuities, Retirement or Profit-Sharing Plans, IRAs, Insurance Contracts, etc.

OMB No. 1545-0119 | 2022 | Form 1099-R

PAYER'S name, street address, city or town, state or province, country, ZIP or foreign postal code, and telephone no.	United States Navy Retired Benefits Center Cleveland, OH 43267
1 Gross distribution	$ 14,800.00
2a Taxable amount	$ 14,800.00
2b Taxable amount not determined	☐
Total distribution	☐
PAYER'S TIN	11-4662891
RECIPIENT'S TIN	543-88-9756
3 Capital gain (included in box 2a)	$
4 Federal income tax withheld	$ 1,300.00
RECIPIENT'S name	Michael D. Boyd
5 Employee contributions/ Designated Roth contributions or insurance premiums	$
6 Net unrealized appreciation in employer's securities	$
Street address (including apt. no.)	33333 Fume Blanc Way
7 Distribution code(s)	7
IRA/ SEP/ SIMPLE	☐
8 Other	$ %
City or town, state or province, country, and ZIP or foreign postal code	Temecula, CA 92591
9a Your percentage of total distribution	%
9b Total employee contributions	$
10 Amount allocable to IRR within 5 years	$
11 1st year of desig. Roth contrib.	
12 FATCA filing requirement	☐
14 State tax withheld	$ 370.00 $
15 State/Payer's state no.	CA
16 State distribution	$ $
Account number (see instructions)	
13 Date of payment	
17 Local tax withheld	$ $
18 Name of locality	
19 Local distribution	$ $

Copy B

Report this income on your federal tax return. If this form shows federal income tax withheld in box 4, attach this copy to your return.

This information is being furnished to the IRS.

Form **1099-R** www.irs.gov/Form1099R Department of the Treasury - Internal Revenue Service

☐ CORRECTED (if checked)

Proceeds From Broker and Barter Exchange Transactions

OMB No. 1545-0715 | 2022 | Form 1099-B

PAYER'S name, street address, city or town, state or province, country, ZIP or foreign postal code, and telephone no.	Bear Stearns 269 Wall Street New York, NY 10001
Applicable checkbox on Form 8949	A
1a Description of property (Example: 100 sh. XYZ Co.)	100 shs Gold Company
1b Date acquired	03/27/2022
1c Date sold or disposed	09/18/2022
PAYER'S TIN	11-4396782
RECIPIENT'S TIN	256-43-8819
1d Proceeds	$ 12,100.00
1e Cost or other basis	$ 14,250.00
1f Accrued market discount	$
1g Wash sale loss disallowed	$
RECIPIENT'S name	Jeanette Boyd
2 Short-term gain or loss	☒
Long-term gain or loss	☐
Ordinary	☐
3 If checked, proceeds from: Collectibles	☐
QOF	☐
Street address (including apt. no.)	33333 Fume Blanc Way
4 Federal income tax withheld	$
5 If checked, noncovered security	☐
City or town, state or province, country, and ZIP or foreign postal code	Temecula, CA 92591
6 Reported to IRS: Gross proceeds	☐
Net proceeds	☒
7 If checked, loss is not allowed based on amount in 1d	☐
Account number (see instructions)	
8 Profit or (loss) realized in 2022 on closed contracts	$
9 Unrealized profit or (loss) on open contracts—12/31/2021	$
CUSIP number	
FATCA filing requirement	☐
10 Unrealized profit or (loss) on open contracts—12/31/2022	$
11 Aggregate profit or (loss) on contracts	$
14 State name	
15 State identification no.	
16 State tax withheld	$ $
12 If checked, basis reported to IRS	☒
13 Bartering	$

Copy B
For Recipient

This is important tax information and is being furnished to the IRS. If you are required to file a return, a negligence penalty or other sanction may be imposed on you if this income is taxable and the IRS determines that it has not been reported.

Form **1099-B** (Keep for your records) www.irs.gov/Form1099B Department of the Treasury - Internal Revenue Service

☐ CORRECTED (if checked)

Interest Income

OMB No. 1545-0112 | Form 1099-INT | (Rev. January 2022) | For calendar year 20 22

PAYER'S name, street address, city or town, state or province, country, ZIP or foreign postal code, and telephone no.	Vintage Bank 6792 Main Street Temecula, CA 92591
Payer's RTN (optional)	
1 Interest income	$ 1,413.78
2 Early withdrawal penalty	$
PAYER'S TIN	96-8724390
RECIPIENT'S TIN	543-88-9756
3 Interest on U.S. Savings Bonds and Treasury obligations	$
RECIPIENT'S name	Michael Boyd
4 Federal income tax withheld	$
5 Investment expenses	$
6 Foreign tax paid	$
7 Foreign country or U.S. possession	
Street address (including apt. no.)	33333 Fume Blanc Way
8 Tax-exempt interest	$
9 Specified private activity bond interest	$
City or town, state or province, country, and ZIP or foreign postal code	Temecula, CA 92591
10 Market discount	$
11 Bond premium	$
FATCA filing requirement	☐
12 Bond premium on Treasury obligations	$
13 Bond premium on tax-exempt bond	$
Account number (see instructions)	
14 Tax-exempt and tax credit bond CUSIP no.	
15 State	
16 State identification no.	
17 State tax withheld	$ $

Copy B

For Recipient

This is important tax information and is being furnished to the IRS. If you are required to file a return, a negligence penalty or other sanction may be imposed on you if this income is taxable and the IRS determines that it has not been reported.

Form **1099-INT** (Rev. 1-2022) (keep for your records) www.irs.gov/Form1099INT Department of the Treasury - Internal Revenue Service

Solutions to Self-Study Problems

CHAPTER 1 THE INDIVIDUAL INCOME TAX RETURN

Self-Study Problem 1.1

Answer is d. Answers a, b, and c are goals of the U.S. income tax system.

Self-Study Problem 1.2

1. Schedule B, Forms 1040 and 1040-SR.
2. Schedule D, Forms 1040 and 1040-SR.
3. Schedule 1 and Schedule F, Forms 1040 and 1040-SR.
4. Form 1041 is used to report the income of estates and trusts.
5. Schedule K-1, Form 1065.
6. Form 1040.
7. Schedule 1 and Schedule C, Forms 1040 and 1040-SR.
8. Schedule 1 and Schedule E, Forms 1040 and 1040-SR.
9. Schedule B, Forms 1040 and 1040-SR.
10. Form 1120 or Form 1120S if making an S election.
11. Form 1065.
12. Schedule A, Forms 1040 and 1040-SR.
13. Form 1040-SR (may also use Form 1040).

Self-Study Problem 1.3

1. Gross income = $31,000 + $1,400 = $32,400
2. Adjusted gross income = $32,400 − $2,000 = $30,400
3. Standard deduction = $12,950 (exceeds his itemized deduction amount of $6,500)
4. Taxable income = $30,400 − $12,950 = $17,450

Self-Study Problem 1.4

Refer to Figures 1.1, 1.2, and 1.3 in Chapter 1.

1. No Income is below single under 65 threshold. See Figure 1.1.
2. No Income is below MFJ with one spouse 65 or older limit. See Figure 1.1.
3. No Standard deduction is earned income plus $400 up to $12,950 for single dependent. See Figure 1.2.

4. Yes Self-employment income is greater than $400. See Figure 1.3.
5. No Income is below MFJ threshold; however, the taxpayers should file to obtain a refund. See Figure 1.1.
6. Yes Social Security taxes are due on the tip income. See Figure 1.3.
7. No Income is below surviving spouse threshold under 65. See Figure 1.1.

Self-Study Problem 1.5

1. B or C
2. D
3. A
4. C
5. D
6. E

Self-Study Problem 1.6

1. Yes A baby born on or before December 31 qualifies as a dependent for that tax year.
2. No The brother is not a qualifying child (he is older than Charlie) and fails the gross income test for qualifying relative.
3. Yes The mother is a qualifying relative under the multiple support agreement rules.
4. Yes The son qualifies as a qualifying child and the daughter-in-law is a qualifying relative. The joint return was only filed to claim a refund.
5. Yes The daughter is a full-time student under the age of 24 and Gary provides more than 50 percent of her support. Scholarships are excluded and do not count toward support.
6. Yes The mother is a qualifying relative. Non-taxable Social Security benefits are not counted toward the gross income test.

Self-Study Problem 1.7

1. $12,950
2. $27,300 = $25,900 + $1,400
3. $16,450 = $12,950 + $1,750 + $1,750
4. $19,400
5. $1,150
6. $25,900

Self-Study Problem 1.8

1. $12,600 = $12,800 − $200
2. $8,750
3. $3,850 = $12,600 − $8,750
4. $3,850 = $12,600 − $8,750
5. Because the stock has been held for more than a year, the gain is a long-term capital gain. The long-term capital gain will be taxed at 0, 15, or 20 percent, depending on the taxpayer's income. A net investment income tax of 3.8 percent may also apply to certain high-income taxpayers.

Self-Study Problem 1.9

1. True
2. True
3. True

Self-Study Problem 1.10

1. True
2. True
3. True
4. False Taxpayers who e-file may have their refund returned through direct deposit or by check.

CHAPTER 2 GROSS INCOME AND EXCLUSIONS

Self-Study Problem 2.1

1. Included
2. Included
3. Excluded
4. Excluded
5. Included
6. Excluded
7. Excluded
8. Excluded
9. Included
10. Included
11. Excluded
12. Included
13. Excluded
14. Included
15. Excluded
16. Excluded
17. Included
18. Included
19. Excluded

Self-Study Problem 2.2

a. Box 1: $56,500
b. Box 3: $3,509
c. Box 12a: $5,000
d. Box 17: $1,165

Self-Study Problem 2.3

None. Neither the premiums nor the reimbursement are included in gross income.

Self-Study Problem 2.4

1. Excluded
2. Included
3. Excluded
4. Included
5. Excluded

Self-Study Problem 2.5

1. Excluded
2. Included (the excess discount over 15%)
3. Excluded
4. Excluded
5. Included
6. Excluded (up to $5,000 in 2022)
7. Excluded

Self-Study Problem 2.6

1. $2,000
2. $10,000 The award was not transferred directly to a charitable organization.
3. $2,500
4. $5,000
5. $0 A service award less than $400 may be excluded from income.

Self-Study Problem 2.7

a. $14,645 The amount excluded from income will be $16,500 × [$42,500 ÷ ($1,500 × 12 months × 21 years)] = $1,855. Therefore, Phil will have taxable income of $14,645 ($16,500 − $1,855).

b. **SIMPLIFIED METHOD WORKSHEET**

1. Enter total amount received this year.		1. $ 16,500.00
2. Enter cost in the plan at the annuity starting date.		2. $ 42,500.00
3. Age at annuity starting date:	***Enter***	
55 or under	360	
56–60	310	
61–65	260	3. 260
66–70	210	
71 or older	160	
4. Divide line 2 by line 3.		4. $ 163.46
5. Multiply line 4 by the number of monthly payments this year. If the annuity starting date was before 1987, also enter this amount on line 8; and skip lines 6 and 7. Otherwise, go to line 6.		5. $ 1,798.06
6. Enter the amount, if any, recovered tax free in prior years.		6. 0.00
7. Subtract line 6 from line 2.		7. $ 42,500.00
8. Enter the smaller of line 5 or 7.		8. $ 1,798.06
9. Taxable amount this year: Subtract line 8 from line 1. Do not enter less than 0.		9. $ 14,701.94

Self-Study Problem 2.8

Amount received	$ 11,250
Less: 1/10 of $100,000	(10,000)
Taxable interest	$ 1,250

Self-Study Problem 2.9

See Schedule B on Page E-5.

Self-Study Problem 2.10

See Schedule B and the Qualifying Dividends and Capital Gain Tax Worksheet on Pages E-5 and E-6.

Self-Study Problem 2.11

$40,000 Gifts in a business setting are taxable income, even if there was no obligation to make the payment. This problem is similar to the facts of a court case (*Duberstein*) in which the Supreme Court held that the value of the automobile was income, even where there was no legal obligation to make the gift.

Self-Study Problems 2.9 and 2.10

SCHEDULE B (Form 1040)
Department of the Treasury
Internal Revenue Service

Interest and Ordinary Dividends

Go to *www.irs.gov/ScheduleB* for instructions and the latest information.
Attach to Form 1040 or 1040-SR.

OMB No. 1545-0074
2022
Attachment Sequence No. 08

Name(s) shown on return: Christy and John Harris-Thomas
Your social security number: 313-44-5454

Part I Interest

(See instructions and the Instructions for Form 1040, line 2b.)

Note: If you received a Form 1099-INT, Form 1099-OID, or substitute statement from a brokerage firm, list the firm's name as the payer and enter the total interest shown on that form.

			Amount
1	List name of payer. If any interest is from a seller-financed mortgage and the buyer used the property as a personal residence, see the instructions and list this interest first. Also, show that buyer's social security number and address:		
	Lake Osbourne Savings and Loan	1	1,356
	Friar Tuck Investments		358
	Friar Tuck Investments US T Bills		800
	Accured interest		(107)
2	Add the amounts on line 1	2	2,407
3	Excludable interest on series EE and I U.S. savings bonds issued after 1989. Attach Form 8815	3	
4	Subtract line 3 from line 2. Enter the result here and on Form 1040 or 1040-SR, line 2b	4	2,407

Note: If line 4 is over $1,500, you must complete Part III.

Part II Ordinary Dividends

(See instructions and the Instructions for Form 1040, line 3b.)

Note: If you received a Form 1099-DIV or substitute statement from a brokerage firm, list the firm's name as the payer and enter the ordinary dividends shown on that form.

			Amount
5	List name of payer:		
	Tangerine Equity Fund	5	980
	Friar Tuck Investments		1700
6	Add the amounts on line 5. Enter the total here and on Form 1040 or 1040-SR, line 3b	6	2,680

Note: If line 6 is over $1,500, you must complete Part III.

Part III Foreign Accounts and Trusts

Caution: If required, failure to file FinCEN Form 114 may result in substantial penalties. Additionally, you may be required to file Form 8938, Statement of Specified Foreign Financial Assets. See instructions.

You must complete this part if you **(a)** had over $1,500 of taxable interest or ordinary dividends; **(b)** had a foreign account; or **(c)** received a distribution from, or were a grantor of, or a transferor to, a foreign trust.

		Yes	No
7a	At any time during 2022, did you have a financial interest in or signature authority over a financial account (such as a bank account, securities account, or brokerage account) located in a foreign country? See instructions		✓
	If "Yes," are you required to file FinCEN Form 114, Report of Foreign Bank and Financial Accounts (FBAR), to report that financial interest or signature authority? See FinCEN Form 114 and its instructions for filing requirements and exceptions to those requirements		
b	If you are required to file FinCEN Form 114, list the name(s) of the foreign country(-ies) where the financial account(s) are located:		
8	During 2022, did you receive a distribution from, or were you the grantor of, or transferor to, a foreign trust? If "Yes," you may have to file Form 3520. See instructions		✓

For Paperwork Reduction Act Notice, see your tax return instructions. Cat. No. 17146N **Schedule B (Form 1040) 2022**

Self-Study Problem 2.10

Qualified Dividends and Capital Gain Tax Worksheet—Line 16

Keep for Your Records 

Before you begin:
√ See the earlier instructions for line 16 to see if you can use this worksheet to figure your tax.
√ Before completing this worksheet, complete Form 1040 or 1040-SR through line 15.
√ If you don't have to file Schedule D and you received capital gain distributions, be sure you checked the box on Form 1040 or 1040-SR, line 7.

1.	Enter the amount from Form 1040 or 1040-SR, line 15. However, if you are filing Form 2555 (relating to foreign earned income), enter the amount from line 3 of the Foreign Earned Income Tax Worksheet			1.	85,000		
2.	Enter the amount from Form 1040 or 1040-SR, line 3a*	2.	2,600 a				
3.	Are you filing Schedule D?* ☐ **Yes.** Enter the **smaller** of line 15 or 16 of Schedule D. If either line 15 or 16 is blank or a loss, enter -0-. ☒ **No.** Enter the amount from Form 1040 or 1040-SR, line 7.	3.	120				
4.	Add lines 2 and 3	4.	2,720				
5.	Subtract line 4 from line 1. If zero or less, enter -0-			5.	82,280		
6.	Enter: $41,675 if single or married filing separately, $83,350 if married filing jointly or qualifying widow(er), $55,800 if head of household.			6.	83,350		
7.	Enter the smaller of line 1 or line 6			7.	83,350		
8.	Enter the smaller of line 5 or line 7			8.	82,280		
9.	Subtract line 8 from line 7. This amount is taxed at 0%			9.	1,070		
10.	Enter the smaller of line 1 or line 4			10.	2,720		
11.	Enter the amount from line 9			11.	1,070		
12.	Subtract line 11 from line 10			12.	1,650		
13.	Enter: $459,750 if single, $258,600 if married filing separately, $517,200 if married filing jointly or qualifying widow(er), $488,500 if head of household.			13.	517,200		
14.	Enter the smaller of line 1 or line 13			14.	85,000		
15.	Add lines 5 and 9			15.	83,350		
16.	Subtract line 15 from line 14. If zero or less, enter -0-			16.	1,650		
17.	Enter the smaller of line 12 or line 16			17.	1,650		
18.	Multiply line 17 by 15% (0.15)					18.	248
19.	Add lines 9 and 17			19.	2,720		
20.	Subtract line 19 from line 10			20.	0		
21.	Multiply line 20 by 20% (0.20)					21.	0
22.	Figure the tax on the amount on line 5. If the amount on line 5 is less than $100,000, use the Tax Table to figure the tax. If the amount on line 5 is $100,000 or more, use the Tax Computation Worksheet					22.	9,462
23.	Add lines 18, 21, and 22					23.	9,710
24.	Figure the tax on the amount on line 1. If the amount on line 1 is less than $100,000, use the Tax Table to figure the tax. If the amount on line 1 is $100,000 or more, use the Tax Computation Worksheet					24.	9,940
25.	**Tax on all taxable income.** Enter the **smaller** of line 23 or 24. Also include this amount on the entry space on Form 1040 or 1040-SR, line 16. If you are filing Form 2555, don't enter this amount on the entry space on Form 1040 or 1040-SR, line 16. Instead, enter it on line 4 of the Foreign Earned Income Tax Worksheet					25.	9,710

* *If you are filing Form 2555, see the footnote in the Foreign Earned Income Tax Worksheet before completing this line.*

This worksheet adapted from the 2021 worksheet.

a. $980 from Tangerine + $1,620 from Friar Tuck

Self-Study Problem 2.12

1. Excluded
2. Included
3. Included
4. Included
5. Included and Excluded. The $7,600 used for qualifying expenses is excluded but the excess scholarship of $2,400 in included in taxable income.
6. Included

Self-Study Problem 2.13

	Deductible by payer	Includable by recipient
a.	$ 0	$ 0
b.	12,000	12,000
c.	0	0

Self-Study Problem 2.14

a. $0. Used for qualified higher education costs.
b. $2,000. Henry's AGI is under $95,000, so there is no phase-out.

Self-Study Problem 2.15

$3,200 Unemployment compensation is fully taxable.

Self-Study Problem 2.16

Simplified Taxable Social Security Worksheet (for most people)

1. Enter the total amount of Social Security income.	1. $13,000
2. Enter one-half of line 1.	2. 6,500
3. Enter the total of taxable income items on Form 1040 except Social Security income.	3. 20,000
4. Enter the amount of tax-exempt interest income.	4. 30,000
5. Add lines 2, 3, and 4.	5. 56,500
6. Enter all adjustments for AGI except for student loan interest deduction.	6. 0
7. Subtract line 6 from line 5. If 0 or less, stop here, none of the Social Security benefits are taxable.	7. 56,500
8. Enter $25,000 ($32,000 if married filing jointly; $0 if married filing separately and living with spouse at any time during the year).	8. 32,000
9. Subtract line 8 from line 7. If 0 or less, enter -0-.	9. 24,500
Note: *If line 9 is 0 or less, stop here; none of your benefits are taxable. Otherwise, go on to line 10.*	
10. Enter $9,000 ($12,000 if married filing jointly; $0 if married filing separately and living with spouse at any time during the year).	10. 12,000
11. Subtract line 10 from line 9. If 0 or less, enter -0-.	11. 12,500
12. Enter the **smaller of line 9 or line 10.**	12. 12,000
13. Enter one-half of line 12.	13. 6,000
14. Enter the **smaller of line 2 or line 13.**	14. 6,000
15. Multiply line 11 by 85% (.85). If line 11 is 0, enter -0-.	15. 10,625
16. Add lines 14 and 15.	16. 16,625
17. Multiply line 1 by 85% (.85).	17. 11,050
18. **Taxable benefits. Enter the smaller of line 16 or line 17.**	18. $11,050

Self-Study Problem 2.17

a. Tom's salary (50 percent)	$20,000
Rachel's salary (50 percent)	15,000
Dividends, Rachel's property (100 percent)	3,000
Interest (50 percent)	2,000
Total	$40,000

b. Tom's salary (50 percent) $20,000
Rachel's salary (50 percent) 15,000
Dividends, Tom's property (50 percent) 2,500
Dividends, Rachel's property (50 percent) 1,500
Interest (50 percent) 2,000
Total $41,000

Self-Study Problem 2.18

a. $0. Stuart may exclude the cancellation of debt income on the mortgage and student loan.
b. $160,000. The original basis of $200,000 is reduced by the excluded cancellation of debt income of $40,000.

CHAPTER 3 BUSINESS INCOME AND EXPENSES

Self-Study Problem 3.1

See Schedule C on Pages E-9 and E-10.

Self-Study Problem 3.2

Part III **Cost of Goods Sold** (see instructions)

33 Method(s) used to value closing inventory: a ☑ Cost b ☐ Lower of cost or market c ☐ Other (attach explanation)

34 Was there any change in determining quantities, costs, or valuations between opening and closing inventory? If "Yes," attach explanation . . . ☐ Yes ☑ No

35	Inventory at beginning of year. If different from last year's closing inventory, attach explanation	35	62,500
36	Purchases less cost of items withdrawn for personal use	36	178,750
37	Cost of labor. Do not include any amounts paid to yourself	37	
38	Materials and supplies	38	
39	Other costs	39	
40	Add lines 35 through 39	40	241,250
41	Inventory at end of year	41	68,400
42	**Cost of goods sold.** Subtract line 41 from line 40. Enter the result here and on line 4	42	172,850

Self-Study Problem 3.3

Marc's transportation deduction is the greater of his actual costs or his deduction using the standard mileage method.

Actual Cost Calculation:

Cash Outlays	$ 4,028
Depreciation	4,000
	8,028
Business percentage (13,000/16,000)	×81.25%
Subtotal	6,523
Tolls & Fees	327
Actual Costs	$ 6,850

Standard Mileage Calculation:

6,000 miles at 58.5¢	$3,510
7,000 miles at 62.5¢	4,375
Tolls and fees	327
Mark's deduction for 2022	$8,212

Self-Study Problem 3.1

SCHEDULE C (Form 1040) Department of the Treasury Internal Revenue Service	**Profit or Loss From Business** (Sole Proprietorship) Go to *www.irs.gov/ScheduleC* for instructions and the latest information. Attach to Form 1040, 1040-SR, 1040-NR, or 1041; partnerships must generally file Form 1065.	OMB No. 1545-0074 2022 Attachment Sequence No. 09

Name of proprietor: Teri Kataoka — **Social security number (SSN)** 466-47-8833

A Principal business or profession, including product or service (see instructions): Golf Instructor — **B** Enter code from instructions: 812990

C Business name. If no separate business name, leave blank. — **D** Employer ID number (EIN) (see instr.)

E Business address (including suite or room no.) 4300 Diamond Head Road
City, town or post office, state, and ZIP code Honolulu, HI 96816

F Accounting method: (1) ☑ Cash (2) ☐ Accrual (3) ☐ Other (specify)

G Did you "materially participate" in the operation of this business during 2022? If "No," see instructions for limit on losses ☑ Yes ☐ No

H If you started or acquired this business during 2022, check here ☐

I Did you make any payments in 2022 that would require you to file Form(s) 1099? See instructions ☐ Yes ☑ No

J If "Yes," did you or will you file required Form(s) 1099? ☐ Yes ☐ No

Part I Income

1	Gross receipts or sales. See instructions for line 1 and check the box if this income was reported to you on Form W-2 and the "Statutory employee" box on that form was checked ☐	1	40,125
2	Returns and allowances	2	
3	Subtract line 2 from line 1	3	40,125
4	Cost of goods sold (from line 42)	4	
5	**Gross profit.** Subtract line 4 from line 3	5	40,125
6	Other income, including federal and state gasoline or fuel tax credit or refund (see instructions)	6	
7	**Gross income.** Add lines 5 and 6	7	40,125

Part II Expenses. Enter expenses for business use of your home **only** on line 30.

		Line	Amount			Line	Amount
8	Advertising	8		18	Office expense (see instructions)	18	660
9	Car and truck expenses (see instructions)	9	3,025	19	Pension and profit-sharing plans	19	
				20	Rent or lease (see instructions):		
10	Commissions and fees	10		a	Vehicles, machinery, and equipment	20a	
11	Contract labor (see instructions)	11		b	Other business property	20b	2,700
12	Depletion	12		21	Repairs and maintenance	21	
13	Depreciation and section 179 expense deduction (not included in Part III) (see instructions)	13		22	Supplies (not included in Part III)	22	
				23	Taxes and licenses	23	250
				24	Travel and meals:		
14	Employee benefit programs (other than on line 19)	14		a	Travel	24a	3,000
15	Insurance (other than health)	15	475	b	Deductible meals (see instructions)	24b	985
16	Interest (see instructions):			25	Utilities	25	515
a	Mortgage (paid to banks, etc.)	16a		26	Wages (less employment credits)	26	
b	Other	16b		27a	Other expenses (from line 48)	27a	500
17	Legal and professional services	17		b	**Reserved for future use**	27b	

28	**Total expenses** before expenses for business use of home. Add lines 8 through 27a	28	12,110
29	Tentative profit or (loss). Subtract line 28 from line 7	29	28,015
30	Expenses for business use of your home. Do not report these expenses elsewhere. Attach Form 8829 unless using the simplified method. See instructions. **Simplified method filers only:** Enter the total square footage of (a) your home: ______ and (b) the part of your home used for business: ______. Use the Simplified Method Worksheet in the instructions to figure the amount to enter on line 30	30	
31	**Net profit or (loss).** Subtract line 30 from line 29. • If a profit, enter on both **Schedule 1 (Form 1040), line 3,** and on **Schedule SE, line 2.** (If you checked the box on line 1, see instructions.) Estates and trusts, enter on **Form 1041, line 3.** • If a loss, you **must** go to line 32.	31	28,015

32 If you have a loss, check the box that describes your investment in this activity. See instructions.
• If you checked 32a, enter the loss on both **Schedule 1 (Form 1040), line 3,** and on **Schedule SE, line 2.** (If you checked the box on line 1, see the line 31 instructions.) Estates and trusts, enter on **Form 1041, line 3.**
• If you checked 32b, you **must** attach **Form 6198.** Your loss may be limited.

32a ☐ All investment is at risk.
32b ☐ Some investment is not at risk.

For Paperwork Reduction Act Notice, see the separate instructions. Cat. No. 11334P **Schedule C (Form 1040) 2022**

a. $(2{,}500 \times \$0.585) + (2{,}500 \times \$0.625)$

Self-Study Problem 3.1

Schedule C (Form 1040) 2022 Page **2**

Part III **Cost of Goods Sold** (see instructions)

33 Method(s) used to value closing inventory: **a** ☐ Cost **b** ☐ Lower of cost or market **c** ☐ Other (attach explanation)

34 Was there any change in determining quantities, costs, or valuations between opening and closing inventory? If "Yes," attach explanation . . . ☐ **Yes** ☐ **No**

35	Inventory at beginning of year. If different from last year's closing inventory, attach explanation	35	
36	Purchases less cost of items withdrawn for personal use	36	
37	Cost of labor. Do not include any amounts paid to yourself	37	
38	Materials and supplies	38	
39	Other costs	39	
40	Add lines 35 through 39	40	
41	Inventory at end of year	41	
42	**Cost of goods sold.** Subtract line 41 from line 40. Enter the result here and on line 4	42	

Part IV **Information on Your Vehicle.** Complete this part **only** if you are claiming car or truck expenses on line 9 and are not required to file Form 4562 for this business. See the instructions for line 13 to find out if you must file Form 4562.

43 When did you place your vehicle in service for business purposes? (month/day/year) 01 / 01 / 2022

44 Of the total number of miles you drove your vehicle during 2022, enter the number of miles you used your vehicle for:

a Business 5,000 **b** Commuting (see instructions) 1,200 **c** Other 4,500

45 Was your vehicle available for personal use during off-duty hours? . . . ☑ **Yes** ☐ **No**

46 Do you (or your spouse) have another vehicle available for personal use?. . . ☐ **Yes** ☑ **No**

47a Do you have evidence to support your deduction? . . . ☑ **Yes** ☐ **No**

b If "Yes," is the evidence written? . . . ☑ **Yes** ☐ **No**

Part V **Other Expenses.** List below business expenses not included on lines 8–26 or line 30.

Memberships	500
48 Total other expenses. Enter here and on line 27a . . . 48	500

Schedule C (Form 1040) 2022

Self-Study Problem 3.4

Deductible expenses:

Airfare	$ 480
Hotel while working on the audit	825
Meals while working on the audit	168
Laundry	22
Taxi	72
Total travel deduction	$1,567

Self-Study Problem 3.5

Business meals ($500 + $600) × 100% = $1,100. Entertainment, dues, and personal expenses are not generally deductible.

Self-Study Problem 3.6

Lodging	$1,200
Transportation	350
Snacks and drinks (50% of $30)	15
Restaurant meals	170
Books	175
Tuition	550
Total Deduction	$2,460

The cost of the weekend trip to the Grand Canyon is not deductible.

Self-Study Problem 3.7

1. Deductible
2. Not Deductible
3. Not Deductible
4. Not Deductible
5. Not Deductible

Self-Study Problem 3.8

Safety shoes and orange vest	$ 650
Climbing equipment, etc.	275
Total special clothing deduction	$ 925

Self-Study Problem 3.9

1. Mr. Jones	$ 20
2. Mr. Brown	25
3. Mrs. and Mr. Green	25
4. Ms. Gray	0
5. Mr. Edwards	75
6. Various customers	140
Total business gift deduction	$ 285

Self-Study Problem 3.10

1. Business
2. Nonbusiness
3. Nonbusiness
4. Business
5. Nonbusiness

Self-Study Problem 3.11

Gross income	$ 3,900
Less: interest and taxes	(2,100)
Balance	$ 1,800
Less: maintenance, utilities, and cleaning	(1,400)
Balance	$ 400
Depreciation (limited)	(400)
Net income	$ 0

Note: The excess depreciation of $3,600 may be carried forward.

Self-Study Problem 3.12

Income $250. The hobby income must be recognized.
Deduction $0. No deduction is permitted.

CHAPTER 4 ADDITIONAL INCOME AND THE QUALIFIED BUSINESS INCOME DEDUCTION

Self-Study Problem 4.1

1. No — Inventory is specifically excluded from the definition of a capital asset.
2. Yes
3. No — Property held by the creator is specifically excluded from the definition of a capital asset.
4. No — Accounts receivable are specifically excluded from the definition of a capital asset.
5. Yes — The copyright is not held by the creator.
6. No — Section 1231 assets (depreciable property and real estate used in a trade or business) are specifically excluded from the definition of a capital asset.
7. Yes
8. Yes
9. Yes
10. Yes
11. No — Inventory is specifically excluded from the definition of a capital asset.
12. Yes

Self-Study Problem 4.2

1. Short-term
2. Long-term
3. Short-term
4. Long-term

Self-Study Problem 4.3

1. Adjusted basis = $11,000
2. Capital improvements = $2,000
3. Accumulated depreciation = $15,000
4. Original cost = $23,000

Self-Study Problem 4.4

Net long-term ($12,000 – $4,000) + ($14,000 – $17,500) =	$ 4,500
Net short-term	(1,800)
Net capital gains	2,700
Capital gains rate	× 15%
Tax	$ 405

Self-Study Problem 4.5

See Schedule D, Form 8949, and the Qualified Dividends and Capital Gain Tax Worksheet on Pages E-14 through E-18.

Self-Study Problem 4.6

a.

Sales price	$350,000
Basis	(30,000)
Realized gain	320,000
Exclusion	(250,000)
Recognized gain	$ 70,000

b. $0. The $500,000 exclusion for joint filers exceeds the $320,000 realized gain.

c. $25,000 = ($350,000 – $200,000) – (½ × $250,000)

Self-Study Problem 4.7

See Schedule E on Page E-19.

Self-Study Problem 4.8

See Form 8582 on Page E-20.

Self-Study Problem 4.9

1. F NOLs for the year 2022 can be carried forward indefinitely.
2. F Generally, NOLs are only from the operation of a trade or business or casualty and theft losses.
3. F Individual NOLs require an analysis of business and nonbusiness income and deductions to determine the business portion that compose the NOL.
4. T Although temporarily suspended through 2020, the excess business loss provisions apply for 2021–2028 and serve to limit the net business loss an individual taxpayer can deduct.
5. F NOLs generated after 2020 can only offset 80 percent of the taxable income.

Self-Study Problem 4.10

See Schedule SE of Form 1040 on Page E-21.

Self-Study Problem 4.5

SCHEDULE D (Form 1040)

Department of the Treasury
Internal Revenue Service

Capital Gains and Losses

Attach to Form 1040, 1040-SR, or 1040-NR.
Go to *www.irs.gov/ScheduleD* for instructions and the latest information.
Use Form 8949 to list your transactions for lines 1b, 2, 3, 8b, 9, and 10.

OMB No. 1545-0074
2022
Attachment Sequence No. **12**

Name(s) shown on return: Louis Winthorpe

Your social security number: 123-44-3214

Did you dispose of any investment(s) in a qualified opportunity fund during the tax year? ☐ **Yes** ☑ **No**
If "Yes," attach Form 8949 and see its instructions for additional requirements for reporting your gain or loss.

Part I **Short-Term Capital Gains and Losses—Generally Assets Held One Year or Less** (see instructions)

See instructions for how to figure the amounts to enter on the lines below. This form may be easier to complete if you round off cents to whole dollars.	(d) Proceeds (sales price)	(e) Cost (or other basis)	(g) Adjustments to gain or loss from Form(s) 8949, Part I, line 2, column (g)	(h) Gain or (loss) Subtract column (e) from column (d) and combine the result with column (g)
1a Totals for all short-term transactions reported on Form 1099-B for which basis was reported to the IRS and for which you have no adjustments (see instructions). However, if you choose to report all these transactions on Form 8949, leave this line blank and go to line 1b .				
1b Totals for all transactions reported on Form(s) 8949 with **Box A** checked	12,000	19,200		(7,200)
2 Totals for all transactions reported on Form(s) 8949 with **Box B** checked				
3 Totals for all transactions reported on Form(s) 8949 with **Box C** checked				

4 Short-term gain from Form 6252 and short-term gain or (loss) from Forms 4684, 6781, and 8824 . .	4	
5 Net short-term gain or (loss) from partnerships, S corporations, estates, and trusts from Schedule(s) K-1	5	
6 Short-term capital loss carryover. Enter the amount, if any, from line 8 of your **Capital Loss Carryover Worksheet** in the instructions	6	( )
7 **Net short-term capital gain or (loss).** Combine lines 1a through 6 in column (h). If you have any long-term capital gains or losses, go to Part II below. Otherwise, go to Part III on the back	7	(7,200)

Part II **Long-Term Capital Gains and Losses—Generally Assets Held More Than One Year** (see instructions)

See instructions for how to figure the amounts to enter on the lines below. This form may be easier to complete if you round off cents to whole dollars.	(d) Proceeds (sales price)	(e) Cost (or other basis)	(g) Adjustments to gain or loss from Form(s) 8949, Part II, line 2, column (g)	(h) Gain or (loss) Subtract column (e) from column (d) and combine the result with column (g)
8a Totals for all long-term transactions reported on Form 1099-B for which basis was reported to the IRS and for which you have no adjustments (see instructions). However, if you choose to report all these transactions on Form 8949, leave this line blank and go to line 8b .				
8b Totals for all transactions reported on Form(s) 8949 with **Box D** checked	43,000	33,500		9,500
9 Totals for all transactions reported on Form(s) 8949 with **Box E** checked				
10 Totals for all transactions reported on Form(s) 8949 with **Box F** checked.				

11 Gain from Form 4797, Part I; long-term gain from Forms 2439 and 6252; and long-term gain or (loss) from Forms 4684, 6781, and 8824	11	
12 Net long-term gain or (loss) from partnerships, S corporations, estates, and trusts from Schedule(s) K-1	12	
13 Capital gain distributions. See the instructions	13	
14 Long-term capital loss carryover. Enter the amount, if any, from line 13 of your **Capital Loss Carryover Worksheet** in the instructions	14	( )
15 **Net long-term capital gain or (loss).** Combine lines 8a through 14 in column (h). Then, go to Part III on the back	15	9,500

Self-Study Problem 4.5

Schedule D (Form 1040) 2022 Page **2**

Part III **Summary**

16	Combine lines 7 and 15 and enter the result	**16**	2,300
	• If line 16 is a **gain**, enter the amount from line 16 on Form 1040, 1040-SR, or 1040-NR, line 7. Then, go to line 17 below. • If line 16 is a **loss**, skip lines 17 through 20 below. Then, go to line 21. Also be sure to complete line 22. • If line 16 is **zero**, skip lines 17 through 21 below and enter -0- on Form 1040, 1040-SR, or 1040-NR, line 7. Then, go to line 22.		
17	Are lines 15 and 16 **both** gains? ☑ **Yes.** Go to line 18. ☐ **No.** Skip lines 18 through 21, and go to line 22.		
18	If you are required to complete the **28% Rate Gain Worksheet** (see instructions), enter the amount, if any, from line 7 of that worksheet	**18**	0
19	If you are required to complete the **Unrecaptured Section 1250 Gain Worksheet** (see instructions), enter the amount, if any, from line 18 of that worksheet	**19**	0
20	Are lines 18 and 19 both zero or blank and you are not filing Form 4952? ☑ **Yes.** Complete the **Qualified Dividends and Capital Gain Tax Worksheet** in the instructions for Form 1040, line 16. **Don't** complete lines 21 and 22 below. ☐ **No.** Complete the **Schedule D Tax Worksheet** in the instructions. **Don't** complete lines 21 and 22 below.		
21	If line 16 is a loss, enter here and on Form 1040, 1040-SR, or 1040-NR, line 7, the **smaller** of: • The loss on line 16; or • ($3,000), or if married filing separately, ($1,500) . . . . **Note:** When figuring which amount is smaller, treat both amounts as positive numbers.	**21**	( )
22	Do you have qualified dividends on Form 1040, 1040-SR, or 1040-NR, line 3a? ☐ **Yes.** Complete the **Qualified Dividends and Capital Gain Tax Worksheet** in the instructions for Form 1040, line 16. ☐ **No.** Complete the rest of Form 1040, 1040-SR, or 1040-NR.		

Schedule D (Form 1040) 2022

Self-Study Problem 4.5

Form **8949**

Department of the Treasury
Internal Revenue Service

Sales and Other Dispositions of Capital Assets

Go to *www.irs.gov/Form8949* for instructions and the latest information.

File with your Schedule D to list your transactions for lines 1b, 2, 3, 8b, 9, and 10 of Schedule D.

OMB No. 1545-0074

2022

Attachment Sequence No. **12A**

Name(s) shown on return: Louis Winthorpe

Social security number or taxpayer identification number: 123-44-3214

Before you check Box A, B, or C below, see whether you received any Form(s) 1099-B or substitute statement(s) from your broker. A substitute statement will have the same information as Form 1099-B. Either will show whether your basis (usually your cost) was reported to the IRS by your broker and may even tell you which box to check.

Part I **Short-Term.** Transactions involving capital assets you held 1 year or less are generally short-term (see instructions). For long-term transactions, see page 2.

Note: You may aggregate all short-term transactions reported on Form(s) 1099-B showing basis was reported to the IRS and for which no adjustments or codes are required. Enter the totals directly on Schedule D, line 1a; you aren't required to report these transactions on Form 8949 (see instructions).

You *must* check Box A, B, *or* C below. Check only one box. If more than one box applies for your short-term transactions, complete a separate Form 8949, page 1, for each applicable box. If you have more short-term transactions than will fit on this page for one or more of the boxes, complete as many forms with the same box checked as you need.

☑ **(A)** Short-term transactions reported on Form(s) 1099-B showing basis was reported to the IRS (see **Note** above)
☐ **(B)** Short-term transactions reported on Form(s) 1099-B showing basis **wasn't** reported to the IRS
☐ **(C)** Short-term transactions not reported to you on Form 1099-B

1 (a) Description of property (Example: 100 sh. XYZ Co.)	(b) Date acquired (Mo., day, yr.)	(c) Date sold or disposed of (Mo., day, yr.)	(d) Proceeds (sales price) (see instructions)	(e) Cost or other basis See the **Note** below and see *Column (e)* in the separate instructions.	Adjustment, if any, to gain or loss. If you enter an amount in column (g), enter a code in column (f). See the separate instructions. (f) Code(s) from instructions	(g) Amount of adjustment	(h) Gain or (loss) Subtract column (e) from column (d) and combine the result with column (g).
100 shs. Sargent Corp	04/18/2022	12/07/2022	12,000	19,200			(7,200)
2 Totals. Add the amounts in columns (d), (e), (g), and (h) (subtract negative amounts). Enter each total here and include on your Schedule D, **line 1b** (if **Box A** above is checked), **line 2** (if **Box B** above is checked), or **line 3** (if **Box C** above is checked) . .			12,000	19,200			(7,200)

Note: If you checked Box A above but the basis reported to the IRS was incorrect, enter in column (e) the basis as reported to the IRS, and enter an adjustment in column (g) to correct the basis. See *Column (g)* in the separate instructions for how to figure the amount of the adjustment.

Self-Study Problem 4.5

Form 8949 (2022) Attachment Sequence No. **12A** Page **2**

Name(s) shown on return. Name and SSN or taxpayer identification no. not required if shown on other side	**Social security number or taxpayer identification number**

Before you check Box D, E, or F below, see whether you received any Form(s) 1099-B or substitute statement(s) from your broker. A substitute statement will have the same information as Form 1099-B. Either will show whether your basis (usually your cost) was reported to the IRS by your broker and may even tell you which box to check.

Part II **Long-Term.** Transactions involving capital assets you held more than 1 year are generally long-term (see instructions). For short-term transactions, see page 1.

Note: You may aggregate all long-term transactions reported on Form(s) 1099-B showing basis was reported to the IRS and for which no adjustments or codes are required. Enter the totals directly on Schedule D, line 8a; you aren't required to report these transactions on Form 8949 (see instructions).

You *must* check Box D, E, *or* F below. Check only one box. If more than one box applies for your long-term transactions, complete a separate Form 8949, page 2, for each applicable box. If you have more long-term transactions than will fit on this page for one or more of the boxes, complete as many forms with the same box checked as you need.

☑ **(D)** Long-term transactions reported on Form(s) 1099-B showing basis was reported to the IRS (see **Note** above)
☐ **(E)** Long-term transactions reported on Form(s) 1099-B showing basis **wasn't** reported to the IRS
☐ **(F)** Long-term transactions not reported to you on Form 1099-B

1 (a) Description of property (Example: 100 sh. XYZ Co.)	(b) Date acquired (Mo., day, yr.)	(c) Date sold or disposed of (Mo., day, yr.)	(d) Proceeds (sales price) (see instructions)	(e) Cost or other basis See the **Note** below and see *Column (e)* in the separate instructions.	Adjustment, if any, to gain or loss If you enter an amount in column (g), enter a code in column (f). **See the separate instructions.** (f) Code(s) from instructions	(g) Amount of adjustment	(h) **Gain or (loss)** Subtract column (e) from column (d) and combine the result with column (g).
50 shs Reynolds Corp	12/18/2013	10/02/2022	25,000	21,000			4,000
100 shs Second Maid Juice	06/12/2013	08/15/2022	18,000	12,500			5,500
2 Totals. Add the amounts in columns (d), (e), (g), and (h) (subtract negative amounts). Enter each total here and include on your Schedule D, **line 8b** (if **Box D** above is checked), **line 9** (if **Box E** above is checked), or **line 10** (if **Box F** above is checked) . .			43,000	33,500			9,500

Note: If you checked Box D above but the basis reported to the IRS was incorrect, enter in column (e) the basis as reported to the IRS, and enter an adjustment in column (g) to correct the basis. See *Column (g)* in the separate instructions for how to figure the amount of the adjustment.

Self-Study Problem 4.5

Qualified Dividends and Capital Gain Tax Worksheet—Line 16

Keep for Your Records 

Before you begin:
- ✓ See the earlier instructions for line 16 to see if you can use this worksheet to figure your tax.
- ✓ Before completing this worksheet, complete Form 1040 or 1040-SR through line 15.
- ✓ If you don't have to file Schedule D and you received capital gain distributions, be sure you checked the box on Form 1040 or 1040-SR, line 7.

1.	Enter the amount from Form 1040 or 1040-SR, line 15. However, if you are filing Form 2555 (relating to foreign earned income), enter the amount from line 3 of the Foreign Earned Income Tax Worksheet			1.	59,000	
2.	Enter the amount from Form 1040 or 1040-SR, line 3a*	2.				
3.	Are you filing Schedule D?* ☒ **Yes.** Enter the **smaller** of line 15 or 16 of Schedule D. If either line 15 or 16 is blank or a loss, enter -0-. ☐ **No.** Enter the amount from Form 1040 or 1040-SR, line 7.	3.	2,300			
4.	Add lines 2 and 3	4.	2,300			
5.	Subtract line 4 from line 1. If zero or less, enter -0-			5.	56,700	
6.	Enter: $41,675 if single or married filing separately, $83,350 if married filing jointly or qualifying widow(er), $55,800 if head of household.			6.	41,675	
7.	Enter the smaller of line 1 or line 6			7.	41,675	
8.	Enter the smaller of line 5 or line 7			8.	41,675	
9.	Subtract line 8 from line 7. This amount is taxed at 0%			9.	0	
10.	Enter the smaller of line 1 or line 4			10.	2,300	
11.	Enter the amount from line 9			11.	0	
12.	Subtract line 11 from line 10			12.	2,300	
13.	Enter: $459,750 if single, $258,600 if married filing separately, $517,200 if married filing jointly or qualifying widow(er), $488,500 if head of household.			13.	459,750	
14.	Enter the smaller of line 1 or line 13			14.	59,000	
15.	Add lines 5 and 9			15.	56,700	
16.	Subtract line 15 from line 14. If zero or less, enter -0-			16.	2,300	
17.	Enter the smaller of line 12 or line 16			17.	2,300	
18.	Multiply line 17 by 15% (0.15)					18. 345
19.	Add lines 9 and 17			19.	2,300	
20.	Subtract line 19 from line 10			20.	0	
21.	Multiply line 20 by 20% (0.20)					21. 0
22.	Figure the tax on the amount on line 5. If the amount on line 5 is less than $100,000, use the Tax Table to figure the tax. If the amount on line 5 is $100,000 or more, use the Tax Computation Worksheet					22. 8,097
23.	Add lines 18, 21, and 22					23. 8,442
24.	Figure the tax on the amount on line 1. If the amount on line 1 is less than $100,000, use the Tax Table to figure the tax. If the amount on line 1 is $100,000 or more, use the Tax Computation Worksheet					24. 8,603
25.	**Tax on all taxable income.** Enter the **smaller** of line 23 or 24. Also include this amount on the entry space on Form 1040 or 1040-SR, line 16. If you are filing Form 2555, don't enter this amount on the entry space on Form 1040 or 1040-SR, line 16. Instead, enter it on line 4 of the Foreign Earned Income Tax Worksheet					25. 8,442

* *If you are filing Form 2555, see the footnote in the Foreign Earned Income Tax Worksheet before completing this line.*

This worksheet adapted from the 2021 worksheet.

Self-Study Problem 4.7

SCHEDULE E (Form 1040)

Department of the Treasury Internal Revenue Service

Supplemental Income and Loss

(From rental real estate, royalties, partnerships, S corporations, estates, trusts, REMICs, etc.)

Attach to Form 1040, 1040-SR, 1040-NR, or 1041.

Go to *www.irs.gov/ScheduleE* for instructions and the latest information.

OMB No. 1545-0074

2022

Attachment Sequence No. 13

Name(s) shown on return: Nancy Kapiolani | **Your social security number**

Part I Income or Loss From Rental Real Estate and Royalties

Note: If you are in the business of renting personal property, use **Schedule C**. See instructions. If you are an individual, report farm rental income or loss from **Form 4835** on page 2, line 40.

A Did you make any payments in 2022 that would require you to file Form(s) 1099? See instructions . . . . ☐ Yes ☑ No

B If "Yes," did you or will you file required Form(s) 1099? . . . . ☐ Yes ☐ No

1a	Physical address of each property (street, city, state, ZIP code)
A	1218 Park Avenue S., Tacoma, WA 98447
B	
C	

1b	Type of Property (from list below)	2 For each rental real estate property listed above, report the number of fair rental and personal use days. Check the QJV box only if you meet the requirements to file as a qualified joint venture. See instructions.		Fair Rental Days	Personal Use Days	QJV
A	2		A	365		☐
B			B			☐
C			C			☐

Type of Property:

1 Single Family Residence 3 Vacation/Short-Term Rental 5 Land 7 Self-Rental
2 Multi-Family Residence 4 Commercial 6 Royalties 8 Other (describe)

			Properties: A	B	C
Income:					
3	Rents received	3	9,700	(a)	
4	Royalties received	4			
Expenses:					
5	Advertising	5			
6	Auto and travel (see instructions)	6			
7	Cleaning and maintenance	7			
8	Commissions	8			
9	Insurance	9	225		
10	Legal and other professional fees	10			
11	Management fees	11			
12	Mortgage interest paid to banks, etc. (see instructions)	12	1,700		
13	Other interest	13			
14	Repairs	14	400		
15	Supplies	15			
16	Taxes	16	1,100		
17	Utilities	17	900		
18	Depreciation expense or depletion	18	4,364		
19	Other (list)	19			
20	Total expenses. Add lines 5 through 19	20	8,689		
21	Subtract line 20 from line 3 (rents) and/or 4 (royalties). If result is a (loss), see instructions to find out if you must file **Form 6198**	21	1,011		
22	Deductible rental real estate loss after limitation, if any, on **Form 8582** (see instructions)	22	( )	( )	( )

23a	Total of all amounts reported on line 3 for all rental properties	23a	9,700
b	Total of all amounts reported on line 4 for all royalty properties	23b	
c	Total of all amounts reported on line 12 for all properties	23c	1,700
d	Total of all amounts reported on line 18 for all properties	23d	4,364
e	Total of all amounts reported on line 20 for all properties	23e	8,689
24	**Income.** Add positive amounts shown on line 21. **Do not** include any losses	24	1,011
25	**Losses.** Add royalty losses from line 21 and rental real estate losses from line 22. Enter total losses here	25	( )
26	**Total rental real estate and royalty income or (loss).** Combine lines 24 and 25. Enter the result here. If Parts II, III, IV, and line 40 on page 2 do not apply to you, also enter this amount on Schedule 1 (Form 1040), line 5. Otherwise, include this amount in the total on line 41 on page 2	26	1,011

For Paperwork Reduction Act Notice, see the separate instructions. Cat. No. 11344L **Schedule E (Form 1040) 2022**

(a) $2,500 in rent collected from the old tenant + $200 security deposit kept + $6,000 monthly rent collected from new tenant plus last month's rent of $1,000.

Self-Study Problem 4.8

Form **8582**

Department of the Treasury
Internal Revenue Service

Passive Activity Loss Limitations

See separate instructions.
Attach to Form 1040, 1040-SR, or 1041.
Go to *www.irs.gov/Form8582* for instructions and the latest information.

OMB No. 1545-1008
2022
Attachment Sequence No. **858**

Name(s) shown on return: Sherry Lockey | **Identifying number**

Part I **2022 Passive Activity Loss**
Caution: Complete Parts IV and V before completing Part I.

Rental Real Estate Activities With Active Participation (For the definition of active participation, see ***Special Allowance for Rental Real Estate Activities*** in the instructions.)

1a	Activities with net income (enter the amount from Part IV, column (a))	**1a**			
b	Activities with net loss (enter the amount from Part IV, column (b))	**1b**	(9,000)		
c	Prior years' unallowed losses (enter the amount from Part IV, column (c))	**1c**	( )		
d	Combine lines 1a, 1b, and 1c			**1d**	(9,000)

All Other Passive Activities

2a	Activities with net income (enter the amount from Part V, column (a))	**2a**			
b	Activities with net loss (enter the amount from Part V, column (b))	**2b**	(15,000)		
c	Prior years' unallowed losses (enter the amount from Part V, column (c))	**2c**	( )		
d	Combine lines 2a, 2b, and 2c			**2d**	(15,000)
3	Combine lines 1d and 2d. If this line is zero or more, stop here and include this form with your return; all losses are allowed, including any prior year unallowed losses entered on line 1c or 2c. Report the losses on the forms and schedules normally used			**3**	(24,000)

If line 3 is a loss and:
- Line 1d is a loss, go to Part II.
- Line 2d is a loss (and line 1d is zero or more), skip Part II and go to line 10.

Caution: If your filing status is married filing separately and you lived with your spouse at any time during the year, **do not** complete Part II. Instead, go to line 10.

Part II **Special Allowance for Rental Real Estate Activities With Active Participation**
Note: Enter all numbers in Part II as positive amounts. See instructions for an example.

4	Enter the **smaller** of the loss on line 1d or the loss on line 3			**4**	9,000
5	Enter $150,000. If married filing separately, see instructions	**5**	150,000		
6	Enter modified adjusted gross income, but not less than zero. See instructions	**6**	138,000		
	Note: If line 6 is greater than or equal to line 5, skip lines 7 and 8 and enter -0- on line 9. Otherwise, go to line 7.				
7	Subtract line 6 from line 5	**7**	12,000		
8	Multiply line 7 by 50% (0.50). **Do not** enter more than $25,000. If married filing separately, see instructions			**8**	6,000
9	Enter the **smaller** of line 4 or line 8			**9**	6,000

Part III **Total Losses Allowed**

10	Add the income, if any, on lines 1a and 2a and enter the total	**10**	
11	**Total losses allowed from all passive activities for 2022.** Add lines 9 and 10. See instructions to find out how to report the losses on your tax return	**11**	6,000

Part IV **Complete This Part Before Part I, Lines 1a, 1b, and 1c.** See instructions.

Name of activity	Current year		Prior years	Overall gain or loss	
	(a) Net income (line 1a)	**(b)** Net loss (line 1b)	**(c)** Unallowed loss (line 1c)	**(d)** Gain	**(e)** Loss
Rental house		9,000			9,000
Total. Enter on Part I, lines 1a, 1b, and 1c		9,000			

For Paperwork Reduction Act Notice, see instructions. Cat. No. 63704F Form **8582** (2022)

Self-Study Problem 4.10

SCHEDULE SE (Form 1040)
Department of the Treasury Internal Revenue Service

Self-Employment Tax

Go to *www.irs.gov/ScheduleSE* for instructions and the latest information.
Attach to Form 1040, 1040-SR, or 1040-NR.

OMB No. 1545-0074
2022
Attachment Sequence No. **17**

Name of person with self-employment income (as shown on Form 1040, 1040-SR, or 1040-NR): Joanne Plummer

Social security number of person with **self-employment** income:

Part I Self-Employment Tax

Note: If your only income subject to self-employment tax is **church employee income**, see instructions for how to report your income and the definition of church employee income.

A If you are a minister, member of a religious order, or Christian Science practitioner **and** you filed Form 4361, but you had $400 or more of **other** net earnings from self-employment, check here and continue with Part I . . . . ☐

Skip lines 1a and 1b if you use the farm optional method in Part II. See instructions.

1a	Net farm profit or (loss) from Schedule F, line 34, and farm partnerships, Schedule K-1 (Form 1065), box 14, code A			1a	
b	If you received social security retirement or disability benefits, enter the amount of Conservation Reserve Program payments included on Schedule F, line 4b, or listed on Schedule K-1 (Form 1065), box 20, code AH			1b	( )
	Skip line 2 if you use the nonfarm optional method in Part II. See instructions.				
2	Net profit or (loss) from Schedule C, line 31; and Schedule K-1 (Form 1065), box 14, code A (other than farming). See instructions for other income to report or if you are a minister or member of a religious order			2	36,600
3	Combine lines 1a, 1b, and 2			3	36,600
4a	If line 3 is more than zero, multiply line 3 by 92.35% (0.9235). Otherwise, enter amount from line 3. **Note:** If line 4a is less than $400 due to Conservation Reserve Program payments on line 1b, see instructions.			4a	33,800
b	If you elect one or both of the optional methods, enter the total of lines 15 and 17 here			4b	
c	Combine lines 4a and 4b. If less than $400, **stop**; you don't owe self-employment tax. **Exception:** If less than $400 and you had **church employee income**, enter -0- and continue			4c	33,800
5a	Enter your **church employee income** from Form W-2. See instructions for definition of church employee income	5a			
b	Multiply line 5a by 92.35% (0.9235). If less than $100, enter -0-			5b	
6	Add lines 4c and 5b			6	33,800
7	Maximum amount of combined wages and self-employment earnings subject to social security tax or the 6.2% portion of the 7.65% railroad retirement (tier 1) tax for 2022			7	147,000
8a	Total social security wages and tips (total of boxes 3 and 7 on Form(s) W-2) and railroad retirement (tier 1) compensation. If $147,000 or more, skip lines 8b through 10, and go to line 11	8a	4,400		
b	Unreported tips subject to social security tax from Form 4137, line 10	8b			
c	Wages subject to social security tax from Form 8919, line 10	8c			
d	Add lines 8a, 8b, and 8c			8d	4,400
9	Subtract line 8d from line 7. If zero or less, enter -0- here and on line 10 and go to line 11			9	142,600
10	Multiply the **smaller** of line 6 or line 9 by 12.4% (0.124)			10	4,191
11	Multiply line 6 by 2.9% (0.029)			11	980
12	**Self-employment tax.** Add lines 10 and 11. Enter here and on **Schedule 2 (Form 1040), line 4**			12	5,171
13	**Deduction for one-half of self-employment tax.** Multiply line 12 by 50% (0.50). Enter here and on **Schedule 1 (Form 1040), line 15**	13	2,586		

Part II Optional Methods To Figure Net Earnings (see instructions)

Farm Optional Method. You may use this method **only** if **(a)** your gross farm income[1] wasn't more than $9,060, **or (b)** your net farm profits[2] were less than $6,540.

14	Maximum income for optional methods	14	6,040
15	Enter the **smaller** of: two-thirds (2/3) of gross farm income[1] (not less than zero) **or** $6,040. Also, include this amount on line 4b above	15	

Nonfarm Optional Method. You may use this method **only** if **(a)** your net nonfarm profits[3] were less than $6,540 and also less than 72.189% of your gross nonfarm income,[4] **and (b)** you had net earnings from self-employment of at least $400 in 2 of the prior 3 years. **Caution:** You may use this method no more than five times.

16	Subtract line 15 from line 14	16	
17	Enter the **smaller** of: two-thirds (2/3) of gross nonfarm income[4] (not less than zero) **or** the amount on line 16. Also, include this amount on line 4b above	17	

[1] From Sch. F, line 9; and Sch. K-1 (Form 1065), box 14, code B.
[2] From Sch. F, line 34; and Sch. K-1 (Form 1065), box 14, code A—minus the amount you would have entered on line 1b had you not used the optional method.
[3] From Sch. C, line 31; and Sch. K-1 (Form 1065), box 14, code A.
[4] From Sch. C, line 7; and Sch. K-1 (Form 1065), box 14, code C.

Self-Study Problem 4.11

Taxpayer	Eligible for QBI deduction (Y/N)?
a.	Aretha is not eligible for the QBI deduction. Corporations are not eligible for the QBI deduction and Aretha's dividend income from the corporation is not considered QBI income.
b.	Terri is eligible for a $24,000 QBI deduction. Terri's business likely falls into the special services category that would subject her to the wage limitation; however, Terri is not subject to the wage or special service limits because her taxable income is below the $170,050 threshold. See Form 8995 below.
c.	Alice is eligible for a $19,482 QBI deduction. Alice's restaurant business is not subject to the special service limitation; however, her joint taxable income exceeds the $340,100 threshold. As a result, her QBI deduction is subject to the wage limitation. See Form 8995-A on Pages E-23 and E-24.

Self-Study Problem 4.11b

Form **8995**

Department of the Treasury
Internal Revenue Service

Qualified Business Income Deduction Simplified Computation

▶ Attach to your tax return.

▶ Go to *www.irs.gov/Form8995* for instructions and the latest information.

OMB No. 1545-2294

2021

Attachment Sequence No. **55**

Name(s) shown on return: Terri Jones

Your taxpayer identification number: 317-65-4321

Note. *You can claim the qualified business income deduction* ***only*** *if you have qualified business income from a qualified trade or business, real estate investment trust dividends, publicly traded partnership income, or a domestic production activities deduction passed through from an agricultural or horticultural cooperative. See instructions.*

Use this form if your taxable income, before your qualified business income deduction, is at or below $164,900 ($164,925 if married filing separately; $329,800 if married filing jointly), and you aren't a patron of an agricultural or horticultural cooperative.

1	(a) Trade, business, or aggregation name	(b) Taxpayer identification number	(c) Qualified business income or (loss)
i	The Bee Hive	317-65-4321	120,000
ii			
iii			
iv			
v			

2	Total qualified business income or (loss). Combine lines 1i through 1v, column (c)	2	120,000		
3	Qualified business net (loss) carryforward from the prior year	3	( )		
4	Total qualified business income. Combine lines 2 and 3. If zero or less, enter -0-	4	120,000		
5	Qualified business income component. Multiply line 4 by 20% (0.20)			5	24,000
6	Qualified REIT dividends and publicly traded partnership (PTP) income or (loss) (see instructions)	6			
7	Qualified REIT dividends and qualified PTP (loss) carryforward from the prior year	7	( )		
8	Total qualified REIT dividends and PTP income. Combine lines 6 and 7. If zero or less, enter -0-	8			
9	REIT and PTP component. Multiply line 8 by 20% (0.20)			9	
10	Qualified business income deduction before the income limitation. Add lines 5 and 9			10	24,000
11	Taxable income before qualified business income deduction (see instructions)	11	133,000		
12	Net capital gain (see instructions)	12			
13	Subtract line 12 from line 11. If zero or less, enter -0-	13	133,000		
14	Income limitation. Multiply line 13 by 20% (0.20)			14	26,600
15	Qualified business income deduction. Enter the smaller of line 10 or line 14. Also enter this amount on the applicable line of your return (see instructions) ▶			15	24,000
16	Total qualified business (loss) carryforward. Combine lines 2 and 3. If greater than zero, enter -0-			16	( )
17	Total qualified REIT dividends and PTP (loss) carryforward. Combine lines 6 and 7. If greater than zero, enter -0-			17	( )

For Privacy Act and Paperwork Reduction Act Notice, see instructions. Cat. No. 37806C Form **8995** (2021)

Please go to **www.irs.gov** to download the latest Form 8995. The 2022 version of Form 8995 was not available as we went to print.

Self-Study Problem 4.11c

Form **8995-A** | **Qualified Business Income Deduction** | OMB No. 1545-2294

Department of the Treasury Internal Revenue Service

► Attach to your tax return.

► Go to *www.irs.gov/Form8995A* for instructions and the latest information.

2021 Attachment Sequence No. **55A**

Name(s) shown on return: Alice Delvecchio

Your taxpayer identification number: 565-22-4321

Note: *You can claim the qualified business income deduction **only** if you have qualified business income from a qualified trade or business, real estate investment trust dividends, publicly traded partnership income, or a domestic production activities deduction passed through from an agricultural or horticultural cooperative. See instructions. Use this form if your taxable income, before your qualified business income deduction, is above $164,900 ($164,925 if married filing separately; $329,800 if married filing jointly), or you're a patron of an agricultural or horticultural cooperative.*

Part I Trade, Business, or Aggregation Information

Complete Schedules A, B, and/or C (Form 8995-A), as applicable, before starting Part I. Attach additional worksheets when needed. See instructions.

1	(a) Trade, business, or aggregation name	(b) Check if specified service	(c) Check if aggregation	(d) Taxpayer identification number	(e) Check if patron
A	D's Pizza	☐	☐	565-22-4321	☐
B		☐	☐		☐
C		☐	☐		☐

Part II Determine Your Adjusted Qualified Business Income

			A	B	C
2	Qualified business income from the trade, business, or aggregation. See instructions	2	100,000		
3	Multiply line 2 by 20% (0.20). If your taxable income is $164,900 or less ($164,925 if married filing separately; $329,800 if married filing jointly), skip lines 4 through 12 and enter the amount from line 3 on line 13	3	20,000		
4	Allocable share of W-2 wages from the trade, business, or aggregation	4	36,000		
5	Multiply line 4 by 50% (0.50)	5	18,000		
6	Multiply line 4 by 25% (0.25)	6	9,000		
7	Allocable share of the unadjusted basis immediately after acquisition (UBIA) of all qualified property	7	67,000		
8	Multiply line 7 by 2.5% (0.025)	8	1,675		
9	Add lines 6 and 8	9	10,675		
10	Enter the greater of line 5 or line 9	10	18,000		
11	W-2 wage and UBIA of qualified property limitation. Enter the smaller of line 3 or line 10	11	18,000		
12	Phased-in reduction. Enter the amount from line 26, if any. See instructions	12	19,482		
13	Qualified business income deduction before patron reduction. Enter the greater of line 11 or line 12	13	19,482		
14	Patron reduction. Enter the amount from Schedule D (Form 8995-A), line 6, if any. See instructions	14			
15	Qualified business income component. Subtract line 14 from line 13	15	19,482		
16	Total qualified business income component. Add all amounts reported on line 15 ►	16	19,482		

For Privacy Act and Paperwork Reduction Act Notice, see separate instructions. Cat. No. 71661B Form **8995-A** (2021)

*Please go to **www.irs.gov** to download the latest Form 8995-A. The 2022 version of Form 8995-A was not available as we went to print. If using the prior year form included in the textbook, be sure and use updated income limits on Line 3 and Line 21 ($340,100 for married filing joint returns, $170,050 for all other returns).

Form 8995-A (2021) Page **2**

Part III Phased-in Reduction

Complete Part III only if your taxable income is more than $164,900 but not $214,900 ($164,925 and $214,925 if married filing separately; $329,800 and $429,800 if married filing jointly) and line 10 is less than line 3. Otherwise, skip Part III.

					A	B	C
17	Enter the amounts from line 3			17	20,000		
18	Enter the amounts from line 10			18	18,000		
19	Subtract line 18 from line 17			19	2,000		
20	Taxable income before qualified business income deduction	20	366,000				
21	Threshold. Enter $164,900 ($164,925 if married filing separately; $329,800 if married filing jointly)	21	340,100				
22	Subtract line 21 from line 20	22	25,900				
23	Phase-in range. Enter $50,000 ($100,000 if married filing jointly)	23	100,000				
24	Phase-in percentage. Divide line 22 by line 23	24	25.9 %				
25	Total phase-in reduction. Multiply line 19 by line 24			25	518		
26	Qualified business income after phase-in reduction. Subtract line 25 from line 17. Enter this amount here and on line 12, for the corresponding trade or business			26	19,482		

Part IV Determine Your Qualified Business Income Deduction

27	Total qualified business income component from all qualified trades, businesses, or aggregations. Enter the amount from line 16	27	19,482		
28	Qualified REIT dividends and publicly traded partnership (PTP) income or (loss). See instructions	28			
29	Qualified REIT dividends and PTP (loss) carryforward from prior years	29	( )		
30	Total qualified REIT dividends and PTP income. Combine lines 28 and 29. If less than zero, enter -0-	30			
31	REIT and PTP component. Multiply line 30 by 20% (0.20)	31			
32	Qualified business income deduction before the income limitation. Add lines 27 and 31 ▶			32	19,482
33	Taxable income before qualified business income deduction	33	366,000		
34	Net capital gain. See instructions	34	12,000		
35	Subtract line 34 from line 33. If zero or less, enter -0-			35	354,000
36	Income limitation. Multiply line 35 by 20% (0.20)			36	70,800
37	Qualified business income deduction before the domestic production activities deduction (DPAD) under section 199A(g). Enter the smaller of line 32 or line 36 ▶			37	19,482
38	DPAD under section 199A(g) allocated from an agricultural or horticultural cooperative. Don't enter more than line 33 minus line 37			38	
39	Total qualified business income deduction. Add lines 37 and 38 ▶			39	19,482
40	Total qualified REIT dividends and PTP (loss) carryforward. Combine lines 28 and 29. If zero or greater, enter -0-			40	( )

Form **8995-A** (2021)

*Please go to **www.irs.gov** to download the latest Form 8995-A. The 2022 version of Form 8995-A was not available as we went to print. If using the prior year form included in the textbook, be sure and use updated income limits on Line 3 and Line 21 ($340,100 for married filing joint returns, $170,050 for all other returns).

CHAPTER 5 DEDUCTIONS FOR AND FROM AGI

Self-Study Problem 5.1

a. 1. $7,300
   2. $0 A plan with no deductible does not qualify.
   3. $2,000 (the limit is $3,650)
   4. $0 Individuals are not allowed to make contributions to an HSA after age 65 since they qualify for Medicare.

b. HSA Deduction is $3,000 and taxable distribution is $0. See Form 8889 on Page E-25.

Self-Study Problem 5.1b

Form **8889** Department of the Treasury Internal Revenue Service

Health Savings Accounts (HSAs)

Attach to Form 1040, 1040-SR, or 1040-NR.

Go to *www.irs.gov/Form8889* for instructions and the latest information.

OMB No. 1545-0074 | 2022 | Attachment Sequence No. 52

Name(s) shown on Form 1040, 1040-SR, or 1040-NR: Alex Morton

Social security number of HSA beneficiary. If both spouses have HSAs, see instructions.: 213-21-3121

Before you begin: Complete Form 8853, Archer MSAs and Long-Term Care Insurance Contracts, if required.

Part I **HSA Contributions and Deduction.** See the instructions before completing this part. If you are filing jointly and both you and your spouse each have separate HSAs, complete a separate Part I for each spouse.

1	Check the box to indicate your coverage under a high-deductible health plan (HDHP) during 2022. See instructions . . . ☑ Self-only ☐ Family		
2	HSA contributions you made for 2022 (or those made on your behalf), including those made in 2023 by the unextended due date of your tax return that were for 2022. **Do not** include employer contributions, contributions through a cafeteria plan, or rollovers. See instructions	2	3,000
3	If you were under age 55 at the end of 2022 and, on the first day of **every** month during 2022, you were, or were considered, an eligible individual with the **same** coverage, enter $3,650 ($7,300 for family coverage). **All others**, see the instructions for the amount to enter	3	3,650
4	Enter the amount you and your employer contributed to your Archer MSAs for 2022 from Form 8853, lines 1 and 2. If you or your spouse had family coverage under an HDHP at any time during 2022, also include any amount contributed to your spouse's Archer MSAs	4	
5	Subtract line 4 from line 3. If zero or less, enter -0-	5	3,650
6	Enter the amount from line 5. But if you and your spouse each have separate HSAs and had family coverage under an HDHP at any time during 2022, see the instructions for the amount to enter	6	3,650
7	If you were age 55 or older at the end of 2022, married, and you or your spouse had family coverage under an HDHP at any time during 2022, enter your additional contribution amount. See instructions	7	
8	Add lines 6 and 7	8	3,650
9	Employer contributions made to your HSAs for 2022 . . . 9 . . . 240		
10	Qualified HSA funding distributions . . . 10		
11	Add lines 9 and 10	11	240
12	Subtract line 11 from line 8. If zero or less, enter -0-	12	3,410
13	**HSA deduction.** Enter the **smaller** of line 2 or line 12 here and on Schedule 1 (Form 1040), Part II, line 13 **Caution:** If line 2 is more than line 13, you may have to pay an additional tax. See instructions.	13	3,000

Part II **HSA Distributions.** If you are filing jointly and both you and your spouse each have separate HSAs, complete a separate Part II for each spouse.

14a	Total distributions you received in 2022 from all HSAs (see instructions)	14a	1,925
b	Distributions included on line 14a that you rolled over to another HSA. Also include any excess contributions (and the earnings on those excess contributions) included on line 14a that were withdrawn by the due date of your return. See instructions	14b	
c	Subtract line 14b from line 14a	14c	1,925
15	Qualified medical expenses paid using HSA distributions (see instructions)	15	2,000
16	**Taxable HSA distributions.** Subtract line 15 from line 14c. If zero or less, enter -0-. Also, include this amount in the total on Schedule 1 (Form 1040), Part I, line 8f	16	0
17a	If any of the distributions included on line 16 meet any of the **Exceptions to the Additional 20% Tax** (see instructions), check here ☐		
b	**Additional 20% tax** (see instructions). Enter 20% (0.20) of the distributions included on line 16 that are subject to the additional 20% tax. Also, include this amount in the total on Schedule 2 (Form 1040), Part II, line 17c	17b	

Part III **Income and Additional Tax for Failure To Maintain HDHP Coverage.** See the instructions before completing this part. If you are filing jointly and both you and your spouse each have separate HSAs, complete a separate Part III for each spouse.

18	Last-month rule	18	
19	Qualified HSA funding distribution	19	
20	**Total income.** Add lines 18 and 19. Include this amount on Schedule 1 (Form 1040), Part I, line 8f	20	
21	**Additional tax.** Multiply line 20 by 10% (0.10). Include this amount in the total on Schedule 2 (Form 1040), Part II, line 17d	21	

For Paperwork Reduction Act Notice, see your tax return instructions. Cat. No. 37621P Form **8889** (2022)

Self-Study Problem 5.2

$20,850 = $15,000 + $2,000 + $3,000 + $850 (limited by age)

Self-Study Problem 5.3

a. $\$4{,}200 = \$6{,}000 \times \dfrac{\$78{,}000 - \$71{,}000}{\$10{,}000}$

b. $\$5{,}200 = \$6{,}000 \times \dfrac{\$144{,}000 - \$131{,}000}{\$15{,}000}$

c. $10,000

d. $0

Self-Study Problem 5.4

a. $10,000, the lesser of (0.25/1.25) × $50,000 or $61,000

b. i. $10,000, lesser of 25% × $40,000 or $20,500 (annual dollar limit effective for 2022)

   ii. $20,500 (annual dollar limit effective for 2022)

c. $25,000. Laura has no basis in her contributions as they were all pre-tax. The entire distribution is taxable.

Self-Study Problem 5.5

a. $0 Professor Hill is not a K-12 educator.

b. $1,100 Jackie worked for two employers, both of which paid her more than $200; her expenses exceeded 10 percent of the gross income from performing artist work ($1,100 > $8,000 × 10%); and her AGI was below $16,000.

c. $4,500

Self-Study Problems 5.6 through 5.10

See Schedule A, worksheet, and Form 4684 on Pages E-27 to E-29.
Line 1 of Schedule A is computed as follows:

Medical insurance	$ 425
Prescription medicines and drugs	364
Hospital bills	2,424
Eyeglasses for Frank's dependent mother	75
Doctor bills for Betty's sister, who is claimed as a dependent by Frank and Betty	220
Medical transportation in personal vehicle (700 miles * $0.22)	154
Total	3,662
Less reimbursement	(1,400)
Medical and dental expenses	$2,262

Line 5 of Schedule A—The $225 refund is included on Line 1 of Schedule 1 of Form 1040 as gross income.
Line 11 of Schedule A—See worksheet on Page E-28. The Guayaquil Soup Kitchen is not a qualified organization (non-U.S.) and there is no deduction for sporting tickets.

Continued on Page E-30

Self-Study Problems 5.6, 5.7, 5.8, 5.9, and 5.10

SCHEDULE A (Form 1040)
Department of the Treasury Internal Revenue Service

Itemized Deductions

Go to *www.irs.gov/ScheduleA* for instructions and the latest information.
Attach to Form 1040 or 1040-SR.
Caution: If you are claiming a net qualified disaster loss on Form 4684, see the instructions for line 16.

OMB No. 1545-0074
2022
Attachment Sequence No. **07**

Name(s) shown on Form 1040 or 1040-SR | **Your social security number**

Medical and Dental Expenses		**Caution:** Do not include expenses reimbursed or paid by others.				
	1	Medical and dental expenses (see instructions)	1	2,262		
	2	Enter amount from Form 1040 or 1040-SR, line 11 [2] 25,000				
	3	Multiply line 2 by 7.5% (0.075)	3	1,875		
	4	Subtract line 3 from line 1. If line 3 is more than line 1, enter -0-			4	387
Taxes You Paid	5	State and local taxes.				
	a	State and local income taxes or general sales taxes. You may include either income taxes or general sales taxes on line 5a, but not both. If you elect to include general sales taxes instead of income taxes, check this box ☐	5a	6,600		
	b	State and local real estate taxes (see instructions)	5b	3,300		
	c	State and local personal property taxes	5c	120		
	d	Add lines 5a through 5c	5d	10,020		
	e	Enter the smaller of line 5d or $10,000 ($5,000 if married filing separately)	5e	10,000		
	6	Other taxes. List type and amount:	6			
	7	Add lines 5e and 6			7	10,000
Interest You Paid Caution: Your mortgage interest deduction may be limited. See instructions.	8	Home mortgage interest and points. If you didn't use all of your home mortgage loan(s) to buy, build, or improve your home, see instructions and check this box ☐				
	a	Home mortgage interest and points reported to you on Form 1098. See instructions if limited	8a	9,250		
	b	Home mortgage interest not reported to you on Form 1098. See instructions if limited. If paid to the person from whom you bought the home, see instructions and show that person's name, identifying no., and address	8b			
	c	Points not reported to you on Form 1098. See instructions for special rules	8c			
	d	Reserved for future use	8d			
	e	Add lines 8a through 8c	8e	9,250		
	9	Investment interest. Attach Form 4952 if required. See instructions	9	1,000		
	10	Add lines 8e and 9			10	10,250
Gifts to Charity Caution: If you made a gift and got a benefit for it, see instructions.	11	Gifts by cash or check. If you made any gift of $250 or more, see instructions	11	10,500		
	12	Other than by cash or check. If you made any gift of $250 or more, see instructions. You **must** attach Form 8283 if over $500	12	12,000		
	13	Carryover from prior year	13			
	14	Add lines 11 through 13			14	22,500
Casualty and Theft Losses	15	Casualty and theft loss(es) from a federally declared disaster (other than net qualified disaster losses). Attach Form 4684 and enter the amount from line 18 of that form. See instructions			15	5,400
Other Itemized Deductions	16	Other—from list in instructions. List type and amount: Gambling losses (limited to winnings)			16	1,400
Total Itemized Deductions	17	Add the amounts in the far right column for lines 4 through 16. Also, enter this amount on Form 1040 or 1040-SR, line 12			17	
	18	If you elect to itemize deductions even though they are less than your standard deduction, check this box ☐				

For Paperwork Reduction Act Notice, see the Instructions for Form 1040. Cat. No. 17145C **Schedule A (Form 1040) 2022**

Self-Study Problem 5.9

	Step 1. Enter charitable contributions made during the year.		
1	Enter contributions of capital gain property to non-50 percent qualified organizations		1,500
2	Enter other contributions to qualified organizations that are non-50 percent organizations. Do not include any contributions entered on the previous line		3,200
3	Enter contributions of capital gain property to 50% limit organizations deducted at fair market value. Do not include any contributions entered on a previous line		11,000
4	Enter noncash contributions to 50% limit organizations other than capital gain property deducted at fair market value. Be sure to include contributions of capital gain property to 50% limit organizations if electing to deduct at basis. Do not include any contributions entered on a previous line		1,000
5	Enter cash contributions to 50% limit organizations. Do not include any contributions entered on a previous line		8,000
	Step 2. Figure the deduction for the year (if any result is zero or less, enter -0-)		
6	Enter adjusted gross income (AGI)		45,000
	Cash contributions subject to the limit based on 60% of AGI (If line 5 is zero, enter -0- on lines 7 through 9)		
7	Multiply line 6 by 0.6	27,000	
8	Deductible amount. Enter the smaller of line 5 or line 7	8,000	
9	Carryover. Subtract line 8 from line 5		-
	Noncash contributions subject to the limit based on 50% of AGI (If line 4 is zero, enter -0- on lines 10 through 13)		
10	Multiply line 6 by 0.5	22,500	
11	Subtract line 8 from line 10	14,500	
12	Deductible amount. Enter the smaller of line 4 or line 11	1,000	
13	Carryover. Subtract line 12 from line 4		-
	Contributions (other than capital gain property) subject to limit based on 30% of AGI (If line 2 is zero, enter -0- on lines 14		
14	Multiply line 6 by 0.5	22,500	
15	Add lines 3, 4, and 5	20,000	
16	Subtract line 15 from line 14	2,500	
17	Multiply line 6 by 0.3	13,500	
18	Enter line 2	3,200	
19	Deductible amount. Enter the smallest of line 16, 17, or 18	2,500	
20	Carryover. Subtract line 19 from line 18		700
	Contributions of capital gain property subject to limit based on 30% of AGI (If line 3 is zero, enter -0- on lines 21 through 26.)		
21	Multiply line 6 by 0.5	22,500	
22	Add lines 4 and 5	9,000	
23	Subtract line 22 from line 21	13,500	
24	Multiply line 6 by 0.3	13,500	
25	Deductible amount. Enter the smallest of line 3, 23, or 24	11,000	
26	Carryover. Subtract line 25 from line 3		-
	Contributions subject to the limit based on 20% of AGI (If line 1 is zero, enter -0- on lines 27 through 36)		
27	Multiply line 6 by 0.5	22,500	
28	Add lines 8, 12, 19, and 25	22,500	
29	Subtract line 28 from line 27	-	
30	Multiply line 6 by 0.3	13,500	
31	Subtract line 19 from line 30	11,000	
32	Subtract line 25 from line 30	2,500	
33	Multiply line 6 by 0.2	9,000	
34	Enter line 1	1,500	
35	Deductible amount. Enter the smallest of line 29, 31, 32, 33, or 34	-	
36	Carryover. Subtract line 35 from line 34		1,500
37	Deduction for the year. Add lines 8, 12, 19, 25, and 35	22,500	

This worksheet has been adapted from Worksheet 2 of IRS Publication 526.

Self-Study Problem 5.10

Form **4684** | **Casualties and Thefts** | OMB No. 1545-0177

Go to *www.irs.gov/Form4684* for instructions and the latest information.
Attach to your tax return.
Use a separate Form 4684 for each casualty or theft.

2022 Attachment Sequence No. **26**

Department of the Treasury Internal Revenue Service

Name(s) shown on tax return: Robert | **Identifying number**

SECTION A—Personal Use Property (Use this section to report casualties and thefts of property **not** used in a trade or business or for income-producing purposes. For tax years 2018 through 2025, if you are an individual, casualty or theft losses of personal-use property are deductible only if the loss is attributable to a federally declared disaster. You must use a separate Form 4684 (through line 12) for each casualty or theft event involving personal-use property. **If reporting a qualified disaster loss, see the instructions for special rules that apply before completing this section.)**

If the casualty or theft loss is attributable to a federally declared disaster, check here ☑ and enter the DR- 4657 or EM-_______ declaration number assigned by FEMA. (See instructions.)

1 Description of properties (show type, location (city, state, and ZIP code), and date acquired for each property). Use a separate line for each property lost or damaged from the same casualty or theft. If you checked the box and entered the FEMA disaster declaration number above, enter the ZIP code for the property most affected on the line for Property **A**.

	Type of Property	City and State	ZIP Code	Date Acquired
Property **A**	Automobile	Tulsa, OK	74119	July 2019
Property **B**				
Property **C**				
Property **D**				

			A	B	C	D
2	Cost or other basis of each property	2	18,500			
3	Insurance or other reimbursement (whether or not you filed a claim) (see instructions)	3	5,000			
	Note: If line 2 is **more** than line 3, skip line 4.					
4	Gain from casualty or theft. If line 3 is **more** than line 2, enter the difference here and skip lines 5 through 9 for that column. See instructions if line 3 includes insurance or other reimbursement you did not claim, or you received payment for your loss in a later tax year	4				
5	Fair market value **before** casualty or theft	5	14,000			
6	Fair market value **after** casualty or theft	6	0			
7	Subtract line 6 from line 5	7	14,000			
8	Enter the **smaller** of line 2 or line 7	8	14,000			
9	Subtract line 3 from line 8. If zero or less, enter -0-	9	9,000			

Line	Description		Amount
10	Casualty or theft loss. Add the amounts on line 9 in columns A through D	10	9,000
11	Enter $100 ($500 if qualified disaster loss rules apply; see instructions)	11	100
12	Subtract line 11 from line 10. If zero or less, enter -0-	12	8,900
	Caution: Use only one Form 4684 for lines 13 through 18.		
13	Add the amounts on line 4 of all Forms 4684	13	
14	Add the amounts on line 12 of all Forms 4684. If you have losses not attributable to a federally declared disaster, see the instructions	14	8,900
	Caution: See instructions before completing line 15.		
15	• If line 13 is **more** than line 14, enter the difference here and on Schedule D. **Do not** complete the rest of this section. • If line 13 is **equal** to line 14, enter -0- here. **Do not** complete the rest of this section. • If line 13 is **less** than line 14, and you have no qualified disaster losses subject to the $500 reduction on line 11 on any Form(s) 4684, enter -0- here and go to line 16. If you have qualified disaster losses subject to the $500 reduction, subtract line 13 from line 14 and enter the smaller of this difference or the amount on line 12 of the Form(s) 4684 reporting those losses. Enter that result here and on Schedule A (Form 1040), line 16; or Schedule A (Form 1040-NR), line 7. If you claim the standard deduction, also include on Schedule A (Form 1040), line 16, the amount of your standard deduction (see the Instructions for Form 1040). Do not complete the rest of this section if all of your casualty or theft losses are subject to the $500 reduction.	15	0
16	Add lines 13 and 15. Subtract the result from line 14	16	8,900
17	Enter 10% of your adjusted gross income from Form 1040, 1040-SR, or 1040-NR, line 11. Estates and trusts, see instructions	17	3,500
18	Subtract line 17 from line 16. If zero or less, enter -0-. Also, enter the result on Schedule A (Form 1040), line 15; or Schedule A (Form 1040-NR), line 6. Estates and trusts, enter the result on the "Other deductions" line of your tax return	18	5,400

Self-Study Problems 5.6 through 5.10 *(Continued)*

See Schedule A of Page E-27 for reporting of interest on Lines 8 through 10 under Problem 5.8.

	Total	***Part a.***	***Part b.***	***Part c.***
Interest on her home mortgage	$9,250	$ 9,250	$ 9,250	$ 9,250
Service charges on her checking account	48	0	0	0
Credit card interest	168	0	0	0
Auto loan interest	675	0	0	0
Interest from a home equity line of credit (HELOC)	2,300	0	2,300	0
Interest from a loan used to purchase stock	1,600	1,000	1,000	1,000
Credit investigation fee for loan	75	0	0	0
Deductible amount		$10,250	$12,550	$10,250

Dorothie's mortgage interest is from qualified mortgage debt (secured by residence, less than $1,000,000) and is deductible in parts a–c. Because Dorothie's mortgage originated prior to December 16, 2017, the $1 million threshold continues to apply in 2022. The home equity interest is not deductible in part a in 2022 as generally home equity interest is not deductible under TCJA. In part b, the home equity debt is treated as acquisition debt which continues to qualify as deductible post-TCJA (subject to the $1 million limitation for grandfathered debt). The investment interest remains deductible after TCJA but also remains limited to net investment income ($1,000 in this example). The other forms of interest are nondeductible personal interest.

Line 11 and 12 of Schedule A—See worksheet on Page E-28. The Guayaquil Soup Kitchen is not a qualified organization (non-U.S.) and there is no deduction for sporting tickets.

Line 11: $8,000 + $3,200 − $700 carryover

Line 12: $11,000 + $1,000 + $1,500 − $1,500 carryover

Line 15—See Form 4684 on Page E-29.

Line 16 of Schedule A—Gambling losses are deductible subject to the limit of gambling winnings. Miscellaneous deductions subject to the 2 percent of AGI rule are suspended through 2025.

CHAPTER 6 ACCOUNTING PERIODS AND OTHER TAXES

Self-Study Problem 6.1

Taxpayer	Calendar year-end	Fiscal year-end	Fiscal year-end but some restrictions
1. Individual with no separate books and records	X		
2. Partnership for which all the partners are calendar year-end individuals	X		X
3. A corporation that keeps its book and records on a fiscal year ending June 30		X	
4. An S corporation for which all shareholders are calendar year-end individuals	X		X

Self-Study Problem 6.2

a.

Business income	$ 63,000
Less: business expenses	(42,000)
Operating income	21,000
Add: rent received	9,000
Add: prepaid interest received	12,000
Less: rent expense for one month ($7,200/6)	(1,200)
Net income	$ 40,800

b. 1. Yes, The corporation is involved in farming.
   2. Yes
   3. No, annual receipts exceed $27 million
   4. Yes, assuming this is a personal service corporation.

Self-Study Problem 6.3

1. 56%; 40% owned directly and 16% (80% × 20%) through X Corporation.
2. 40%; 20% owned directly plus 20% as Gene's brother.
3. 40%; 20% owned directly plus 20% as Frank's brother.
4. $0; since they are related parties, the loss would be disallowed.

Self-Study Problem 6.4

a. See Form 8615 on Page E-32.
b. See Form 8814 on Page E-33.

Self-Study Problem 6.5

See Form 6251 on Page E-34.

Self-Study Problem 6.6

See Schedule H on Pages E-35 and E-36.

Self-Study Problem 6.7

A. See Form 8960 on Page E-37.
B. See Form 8959 on Page E-38.

Self-Study Problem 6.8

1. F The first step is to contact the employer or payer and request a copy.
2. F An amended return is filed on Form 1040-X.
3. F A trial separation does not typically rise to the level of a legal separation and thus the taxpayers remain married.
4. T A qualified domestic relations order is used to divide qualified plan assets.
5. F Mary should file for equitable relief.
6. F Taxpayer are generally required to file a final income tax return.
7. F Chamu should request a correction from her employer and if unable to get one, file Form 843.
8. F If the individual meets the threshold for both foreign account reporting types, both must be filed.
9. T Farmers use Schedule F as part of Form 1040.

Self-Study Problem 6.4a

Form **8615** — Department of the Treasury, Internal Revenue Service

Tax for Certain Children Who Have Unearned Income

Attach only to the child's Form 1040 or 1040-NR.
Go to *www.irs.gov/Form8615* for instructions and the latest information.

OMB No. 1545-0074 — 2022 — Attachment Sequence No. **33**

Child's name shown on return: Robert — **Child's social security number**

A Parent's name (first, initial, and last). **Caution:** See instructions before completing. Bill and Janet — **B Parent's social security number**

C Parent's filing status (check one):
☐ Single ☑ Married filing jointly ☐ Married filing separately ☐ Head of household ☐ Qualifying widow(er)

Part I Child's Net Unearned Income

1	Enter the child's unearned income. See instructions	1	3,000	
2	If the child **did not** itemize deductions on **Schedule A** (Form 1040) or **Schedule A** (Form 1040-NR), enter $2,300. Otherwise, see instructions	2	2,300	
3	Subtract line 2 from line 1. If zero or less, **stop**; do not complete the rest of this form but **do** attach it to the child's return	3	700	
4	Enter the child's **taxable income** from Form 1040 or 1040-NR, line 15. If the child files Form 2555, see the instructions	4	1,850	(a)
5	Enter the **smaller** of line 3 or line 4. If zero, **stop**; do not complete the rest of this form but **do** attach it to the child's return	5	700	

Part II Tentative Tax Based on the Tax Rate of the Parent

6	Enter the parent's **taxable income** from Form 1040 or 1040-NR, line 15. If zero or less, enter -0-. If the parent files Form 2555, see the instructions	6	45,600	(b)
7	Enter the total, if any, from Forms 8615, line 5, of **all other** children of the parent named above. **Do not** include the amount from line 5 above	7		
8	Add lines 5, 6, and 7. See instructions	8	46,300	
9	Enter the tax on the amount on line 8 based on the **parent's** filing status above. See instructions. If the Qualified Dividends and Capital Gain Tax Worksheet, Schedule D Tax Worksheet, or Schedule J (Form 1040) is used to figure the tax, check here ☐	9	5,148	(c)
10	Enter the parent's tax from Form 1040 or 1040-NR, line 16, minus any alternative minimum tax. **Do not** include any tax from **Form 4972** or **Form 8814**, or any tax from the recapture of an education credit. If the parent files Form 2555, see the instructions. If the Qualified Dividends and Capital Gain Tax Worksheet, Schedule D Tax Worksheet, or Schedule J (Form 1040) was used to figure the tax, check here ☐	10	5,064	
11	Subtract line 10 from line 9 and enter the result. If line 7 is blank, also enter this amount on line 13 and go to **Part III**	11	84	
12a	Add lines 5 and 7 — 12a			
b	Divide line 5 by line 12a. Enter the result as a decimal (rounded to at least three places)	12b	× .	
13	Multiply line 11 by line 12b	13	84	

Part III Child's Tax—If lines 4 and 5 above are the same, enter -0- on line 15 and go to line 16.

Line	Description		Amount
14	Subtract line 5 from line 4 — 14: 1,150		
15	Enter the tax on the amount on line 14 based on the **child's** filing status. See instructions. If the Qualified Dividends and Capital Gain Tax Worksheet, Schedule D Tax Worksheet, or Schedule J (Form 1040) is used to figure the tax, check here ☐	15	116
16	Add lines 13 and 15	16	200
17	Enter the tax on the amount on line 4 based on the **child's** filing status. See instructions. If the Qualified Dividends and Capital Gain Tax Worksheet, Schedule D Tax Worksheet, or Schedule J (Form 1040) is used to figure the tax, check here ☐	17	186
18	Enter the **larger** of line 16 or line 17 here and on the **child's** Form 1040 or 1040-NR, line 16. If the child files Form 2555, see the instructions	18	200

For Paperwork Reduction Act Notice, see your tax return instructions. Cat. No. 64113U Form **8615** (2022)

a. $3,000 less standard deduction $1,150.
b. $71,500 less $25,900 standard deduction.
c. Tax is from tax tables for income less than $100,000 in Appendix A.

Self-Study Problem 6.4b

Form **8814** | **Parents' Election To Report Child's Interest and Dividends** | OMB No. 1545-0074
Department of the Treasury Internal Revenue Service
Go to *www.irs.gov/Form8814* for the latest information.
Attach to parents' Form 1040, 1040-SR, or 1040-NR.
2022 Attachment Sequence No. **40**

Name(s) shown on your return	Your social security number
Bill and Janet	

Caution: The federal income tax on your child's income, including qualified dividends and capital gain distributions, may be less if you file a separate tax return for the child instead of making this election. This is because you cannot take certain tax benefits that your child could take on his or her own return. For details, see *Tax benefits you cannot take* in the instructions.

A Child's name (first, initial, and last)	B Child's social security number
Robert	

C If more than one Form 8814 is attached, check here . . . ☐

Part I Child's Interest and Dividends To Report on Your Return

1a	Enter your child's **taxable** interest. If this amount is different from the amounts shown on the child's Forms 1099-INT and 1099-OID, see the instructions			1a	3,000
b	Enter your child's **tax-exempt** interest. **Do not** include this amount on line 1a	1b			
2a	Enter your child's ordinary dividends, including any Alaska Permanent Fund dividends. If your child received any ordinary dividends as a nominee, see the instructions			2a	
b	Enter your child's qualified dividends included on line 2a. See the instructions	2b			
3	Enter your child's capital gain distributions. If your child received any capital gain distributions as a nominee, see the instructions			3	
4	Add lines 1a, 2a, and 3. If the total is $2,300 or less, skip lines 5 through 12 and go to line 13. If the total is $11,500 or more, **do not** file this form. Your child **must** file his or her own return to report the income			4	3,000
5	Base amount. Enter 2,300			5	2,300
6	Subtract line 5 from line 4			6	700
	If both lines 2b and 3 are zero or blank, skip lines 7 through 10, enter -0- on line 11, and go to line 12. Otherwise, go to line 7.				
7	Divide line 2b by line 4. Enter the result as a decimal (rounded to at least three places)	7	.		
8	Divide line 3 by line 4. Enter the result as a decimal (rounded to at least three places)	8	.		
9	Multiply line 6 by line 7. Enter the result here. See the instructions for where to report this amount on your return	9			
10	Multiply line 6 by line 8. Enter the result here. See the instructions for where to report this amount on your return	10			
11	Add lines 9 and 10			11	0
12	Subtract line 11 from line 6. Include this amount in the total on Schedule 1 (Form 1040), line 8z. In the space next to that line, enter "Form 8814" and show the amount. If you checked the box on line C above, see the instructions. Go to line 13 below			12	700

Part II Tax on the First $2,300 of Child's Interest and Dividends

13	Amount not taxed. Enter 1,150	13	1,150
14	Subtract line 13 from line 4. If the result is zero or less, enter -0-	14	1,850
15	**Tax.** Is the amount on line 14 less than $1,150? ☑ **No.** Enter $115 here and see the **Note** below. ☐ **Yes.** Multiply line 14 by 10% (0.10). Enter the result here and see the **Note** below.	15	115

Note: If you checked the box on line C above, see the instructions. Otherwise, include the amount from line 15 in the tax you enter on Form 1040,1040-SR, or 1040-NR, line 16. Be sure to check box 1 on Form 1040, 1040-SR, or 1040-NR, line 16.

Self-Study Problem 6.5

Form **6251** | **Alternative Minimum Tax—Individuals** | OMB No. 1545-0074

Department of the Treasury
Internal Revenue Service

Go to *www.irs.gov/Form6251* for instructions and the latest information.
Attach to Form 1040, 1040-SR, or 1040-NR.

2022
Attachment Sequence No. **32**

Name(s) shown on Form 1040, 1040-SR, or 1040-NR: Harold Brown | **Your social security number**

Part I Alternative Minimum Taxable Income (See instructions for how to complete each line.)

1	Enter the amount from Form 1040 or 1040-SR, line 15, if more than zero. If Form 1040 or 1040-SR, line 15, is zero, subtract line 14 of Form 1040 or 1040-SR from line 11 of Form 1040 or 1040-SR and enter the result here. (If less than zero, enter as a negative amount.)	1	556,000
2a	If filing Schedule A (Form 1040), enter the taxes from Schedule A, line 7; otherwise, enter the amount from Form 1040 or 1040-SR, line 12	2a	10,000
b	Tax refund from Schedule 1 (Form 1040), line 1 or line 8z	2b	( )
c	Investment interest expense (difference between regular tax and AMT)	2c	
d	Depletion (difference between regular tax and AMT)	2d	
e	Net operating loss deduction from Schedule 1 (Form 1040), line 8a. Enter as a positive amount	2e	
f	Alternative tax net operating loss deduction	2f	( )
g	Interest from specified private activity bonds exempt from the regular tax	2g	100,000
h	Qualified small business stock, see instructions	2h	
i	Exercise of incentive stock options (excess of AMT income over regular tax income)	2i	
j	Estates and trusts (amount from Schedule K-1 (Form 1041), box 12, code A)	2j	
k	Disposition of property (difference between AMT and regular tax gain or loss)	2k	
l	Depreciation on assets placed in service after 1986 (difference between regular tax and AMT)	2l	
m	Passive activities (difference between AMT and regular tax income or loss)	2m	
n	Loss limitations (difference between AMT and regular tax income or loss)	2n	
o	Circulation costs (difference between regular tax and AMT)	2o	
p	Long-term contracts (difference between AMT and regular tax income)	2p	
q	Mining costs (difference between regular tax and AMT)	2q	
r	Research and experimental costs (difference between regular tax and AMT)	2r	
s	Income from certain installment sales before January 1, 1987	2s	( )
t	Intangible drilling costs preference	2t	
3	Other adjustments, including income-based related adjustments	3	
4	**Alternative minimum taxable income.** Combine lines 1 through 3. (If married filing separately and line 4 is more than $776,100, see instructions.)	4	666,000

Part II Alternative Minimum Tax (AMT)

5 Exemption.

IF your filing status is...	AND line 4 is not over...	THEN enter on line 5...
Single or head of household	$ 539,900	$ 75,900
Married filing jointly or qualifying widow(er)	1,079,800	118,100
Married filing separately	539,900	59,050

If line 4 is **over** the amount shown above for your filing status, see instructions. — **5** 44,375 (a)

6	Subtract line 5 from line 4. If more than zero, go to line 7. If zero or less, enter -0- here and on lines 7, 9, and 11, and go to line 10	6	621,625
7	• If you are filing Form 2555, see instructions for the amount to enter. • If you reported capital gain distributions directly on Form 1040 or 1040-SR, line 7; you reported qualified dividends on Form 1040 or 1040-SR, line 3a; **or** you had a gain on both lines 15 and 16 of Schedule D (Form 1040) (as refigured for the AMT, if necessary), complete Part III on the back and enter the amount from line 40 here. • **All others:** If line 6 is $206,100 or less ($103,050 or less if married filing separately), multiply line 6 by 26% (0.26). Otherwise, multiply line 6 by 28% (0.28) and subtract $4,122 ($2,061 if married filing separately) from the result.	7	169,933
8	Alternative minimum tax foreign tax credit (see instructions)	8	
9	Tentative minimum tax. Subtract line 8 from line 7	9	169,933
10	Add Form 1040 or 1040-SR, line 16 (minus any tax from Form 4972), and Schedule 2 (Form 1040), line 2. Subtract from the result Schedule 3 (Form 1040), line 1 and any negative amount reported on Form 8978, line 14 (treated as a positive number). If zero or less, enter -0-. If you used Schedule J to figure your tax on Form 1040 or 1040-SR, line 16, refigure that tax without using Schedule J before completing this line. See instructions	10	168,675
11	**AMT.** Subtract line 10 from line 9. If zero or less, enter -0-. Enter here and on Schedule 2 (Form 1040), line 1	11	1,258

For Paperwork Reduction Act Notice, see your tax return instructions. Cat. No. 13600G Form **6251** (2022)

(a) $44,375 = $75,900 − [($666,000 − $539,900) × 25%]

Self-Study Problem 6.6

SCHEDULE H (Form 1040)
Department of the Treasury
Internal Revenue Service

Household Employment Taxes

(For Social Security, Medicare, Withheld Income, and Federal Unemployment (FUTA) Taxes)
Attach to Form 1040, 1040-SR, 1040-NR, 1040-SS, or 1041.
Go to *www.irs.gov/ScheduleH* for instructions and the latest information.

OMB No. 1545-0074
2022
Attachment Sequence No. **44**

Name of employer
Susan Green

Social security number

Employer identification number

Calendar year taxpayers having no household employees in 2022 don't have to complete this form for 2022.

A Did you pay **any one** household employee cash wages of $2,400 or more in 2022? (If any household employee was your spouse, your child under age 21, your parent, or anyone under age 18, see the line A instructions before you answer this question.)
- ☑ **Yes.** Skip lines B and C and go to line 1a.
- ☐ **No.** Go to line B.

B Did you withhold federal income tax during 2022 for any household employee?
- ☐ **Yes.** Skip line C and go to line 7.
- ☐ **No.** Go to line C.

C Did you pay **total** cash wages of $1,000 or more in **any** calendar **quarter** of 2021 or 2022 to **all** household employees? (**Don't** count cash wages paid in 2021 or 2022 to your spouse, your child under age 21, or your parent.)
- ☐ **No. Stop.** Don't file this schedule.
- ☐ **Yes.** Skip lines 1a–9 and go to line 10.

Part I Social Security, Medicare, and Federal Income Taxes

1a	Total cash wages subject to social security tax	1a	3,600		
b	Qualified sick and family leave wages paid in 2022 for leave taken after March 31, 2020, and before April 1, 2021, included on line 1a	1b			
2a	Social security tax. Multiply line 1a by 12.4% (0.124)			2a	446
b	Employer share of social security tax on qualified sick and family leave wages paid in 2022 for leave taken after March 31, 2020, and before April 1, 2021. Multiply line 1b by 6.2% (0.062)			2b	
c	Total social security tax. Subtract line 2b from line 2a			2c	446
3	Total cash wages subject to Medicare tax	3	3,600		
4	Medicare tax. Multiply line 3 by 2.9% (0.029)			4	104
5	Total cash wages subject to Additional Medicare Tax withholding	5			
6	Additional Medicare Tax withholding. Multiply line 5 by 0.9% (0.009)			6	
7	Federal income tax withheld, if any			7	
8a	Total social security, Medicare, and federal income taxes. Add lines 2c, 4, 6, and 7			8a	550
b	Nonrefundable portion of credit for qualified sick and family leave wages for leave taken before April 1, 2021			8b	
c	Nonrefundable portion of credit for qualified sick and family leave wages for leave taken after March 31, 2021, and before October 1, 2021			8c	
d	Total social security, Medicare, and federal income taxes after nonrefundable credits. Add lines 8b and 8c and then subtract that total from line 8a			8d	550
e	Refundable portion of credit for qualified sick and family leave wages for leave taken before April 1, 2021			8e	
f	Refundable portion of credit for qualified sick and family leave wages for leave taken after March 31, 2021, and before October 1, 2021			8f	
g	Qualified sick leave wages for leave taken before April 1, 2021			8g	
h	Qualified health plan expenses allocable to qualified sick leave wages reported on line 8g			8h	
i	Qualified family leave wages for leave taken before April 1, 2021			8i	
j	Qualified health plan expenses allocable to qualified family leave wages reported on line 8i			8j	
k	Qualified sick leave wages for leave taken after March 31, 2021, and before October 1, 2021			8k	
l	Qualified health plan expenses allocable to qualified sick leave wages reported on line 8k			8l	
m	Qualified family leave wages for leave taken after March 31, 2021, and before October 1, 2021			8m	
n	Qualified health plan expenses allocable to qualified family leave wages reported on line 8m			8n	

9 Did you pay **total** cash wages of $1,000 or more in **any** calendar **quarter** of 2021 or 2022 to **all** household employees? (**Don't** count cash wages paid in 2021 or 2022 to your spouse, your child under age 21, or your parent.)
- ☐ **No. Stop.** Include the amount from line 8d above on Schedule 2 (Form 1040), line 9. Include the amounts, if any, from line 8e on Schedule 3 (Form 1040), line 13b, and line 8f on Schedule 3 (Form 1040), line 13h. If you're not required to file Form 1040, see the line 9 instructions.
- ☑ **Yes.** Go to line 10.

Self-Study Problem 6.6

Schedule H (Form 1040) 2022 Page **2**

Part II Federal Unemployment (FUTA) Tax

			Yes	No
10	Did you pay unemployment contributions to only one state? If you paid contributions to a credit reduction state, see instructions and check "**No**"	10	✓	
11	Did you pay all state unemployment contributions for 2022 by April 18, 2023? Fiscal year filers, see instructions	11	✓	
12	Were all wages that are taxable for FUTA tax also taxable for your state's unemployment tax?	12	✓	

Next: If you checked the "**Yes**" box on **all** the lines above, complete Section A.
If you checked the "**No**" box on **any** of the lines above, skip Section A and complete Section B.

Section A

13 Name of the state where you paid unemployment contributions Virginia

14 Contributions paid to your state unemployment fund . . . 14 194

15 Total cash wages subject to FUTA tax . . . 15 3,600

16 **FUTA tax.** Multiply line 15 by 0.6% (0.006). Enter the result here, skip Section B, and go to line 25 . 16 22

Section B

17 Complete all columns below that apply (if you need more space, see instructions):

(a) Name of state	(b) Taxable wages (as defined in state act)	(c) State experience rate period From	(c) To	(d) State experience rate	(e) Multiply col. (b) by 0.054	(f) Multiply col. (b) by col. (d)	(g) Subtract col. (f) from col. (e). If zero or less, enter -0-.	(h) Contributions paid to state unemployment fund

18 Totals . . . 18

19 Add columns (g) and (h) of line 18 . . . 19

20 Total cash wages subject to FUTA tax (see the line 15 instructions) . . . 20

21 Multiply line 20 by 6.0% (0.06) . . . 21

22 Multiply line 20 by 5.4% (0.054) . . . 22

23 Enter the **smaller** of line 19 or line 22.
(If you paid state unemployment contributions late or you're in a credit reduction state, see instructions and check here) . . . ☐ 23

24 **FUTA tax.** Subtract line 23 from line 21. Enter the result here and go to line 25 . . . 24

Part III Total Household Employment Taxes

25 Enter the amount from line 8d. If you checked the "**Yes**" box on line C of page 1, enter -0- . . . 25 550

26 Add line 16 (or line 24) and line 25 . . . 26 572

27 Are you required to file Form 1040?

☑ **Yes. Stop.** Include the amount from line 26 above on Schedule 2 (Form 1040), line 9. Include the amounts, if any, from line 8e on Schedule 3 (Form 1040), line 13b, and line 8f on Schedule 3 (Form 1040), line 13h. **Don't** complete Part IV below.

☐ **No.** You may have to complete Part IV. See instructions for details.

Part IV Address and Signature — Complete this part **only** if required. See the line 27 instructions.

Address (number and street) or P.O. box if mail isn't delivered to street address | Apt., room, or suite no.

City, town or post office, state, and ZIP code

Under penalties of perjury, I declare that I have examined this schedule, including accompanying statements, and to the best of my knowledge and belief, it is true, correct, and complete. No part of any payment made to a state unemployment fund claimed as a credit was, or is to be, deducted from the payments to employees. Declaration of preparer (other than taxpayer) is based on all information of which preparer has any knowledge.

Employer's signature | Date

Paid Preparer Use Only	Print/Type preparer's name	Preparer's signature	Date	Check ☐ if self-employed	PTIN
	Firm's name			Firm's EIN	
	Firm's address			Phone no.	

Schedule H (Form 1040) 2022

Self-Study Problem 6.7A

Form **8960**

Department of the Treasury
Internal Revenue Service

Net Investment Income Tax— Individuals, Estates, and Trusts

Attach to your tax return.

Go to *www.irs.gov/Form8960* for instructions and the latest information.

OMB No. 1545-2227

2022

Attachment Sequence No. **72**

Name(s) shown on your tax return: Ronald Trunk

Your social security number or EIN

Part I Investment Income
☐ Section 6013(g) election (see instructions)
☐ Section 6013(h) election (see instructions)
☐ Regulations section 1.1411-10(g) election (see instructions)

1	Taxable interest (see instructions)			1	53,000
2	Ordinary dividends (see instructions)			2	45,000
3	Annuities (see instructions)			3	
4a	Rental real estate, royalties, partnerships, S corporations, trusts, etc. (see instructions)	4a			
b	Adjustment for net income or loss derived in the ordinary course of a non-section 1411 trade or business (see instructions)	4b			
c	Combine lines 4a and 4b			4c	
5a	Net gain or loss from disposition of property (see instructions)	5a	23,000		
b	Net gain or loss from disposition of property that is not subject to net investment income tax (see instructions)	5b			
c	Adjustment from disposition of partnership interest or S corporation stock (see instructions)	5c			
d	Combine lines 5a through 5c			5d	23,000
6	Adjustments to investment income for certain CFCs and PFICs (see instructions)			6	
7	Other modifications to investment income (see instructions)			7	
8	Total investment income. Combine lines 1, 2, 3, 4c, 5d, 6, and 7			8	121,000
Part II	**Investment Expenses Allocable to Investment Income and Modifications**				
9a	Investment interest expenses (see instructions)	9a			
b	State, local, and foreign income tax (see instructions)	9b			
c	Miscellaneous investment expenses (see instructions)	9c			
d	Add lines 9a, 9b, and 9c			9d	
10	Additional modifications (see instructions)			10	
11	Total deductions and modifications. Add lines 9d and 10			11	
Part III	**Tax Computation**				
12	Net investment income. Subtract Part II, line 11, from Part I, line 8. Individuals, complete lines 13–17. Estates and trusts, complete lines 18a–21. If zero or less, enter -0-			12	121,000
	Individuals:				
13	Modified adjusted gross income (see instructions)	13	333,000		
14	Threshold based on filing status (see instructions)	14	200,000		
15	Subtract line 14 from line 13. If zero or less, enter -0-	15	133,000		
16	Enter the smaller of line 12 or line 15			16	121,000
17	Net investment income tax for individuals. Multiply line 16 by 3.8% (0.038). **Enter here and include on your tax return** (see instructions)			17	4,598
	Estates and Trusts:				
18a	Net investment income (line 12 above)	18a			
b	Deductions for distributions of net investment income and deductions under section 642(c) (see instructions)	18b			
c	Undistributed net investment income. Subtract line 18b from line 18a (see instructions). If zero or less, enter -0-	18c			
19a	Adjusted gross income (see instructions)	19a			
b	Highest tax bracket for estates and trusts for the year (see instructions)	19b			
c	Subtract line 19b from line 19a. If zero or less, enter -0-	19c			
20	Enter the smaller of line 18c or line 19c			20	
21	Net investment income tax for estates and trusts. Multiply line 20 by 3.8% (0.038). **Enter here and include on your tax return** (see instructions)			21	

For Paperwork Reduction Act Notice, see your tax return instructions. Cat. No. 59474M Form **8960** (2022)

Self-Study Problem 6.7B

Form **8959**

Department of the Treasury
Internal Revenue Service

Additional Medicare Tax

If any line does not apply to you, leave it blank. See separate instructions.
Attach to Form 1040, 1040-SR, 1040-NR, 1040-PR, or 1040-SS.
Go to *www.irs.gov/Form8959* for instructions and the latest information.

OMB No. 1545-0074
2022
Attachment Sequence No. **71**

Name(s) shown on return: Meng and Eang Ung | **Your social security number**

Part I Additional Medicare Tax on Medicare Wages

Line	Description		Amount		Amount
1	Medicare wages and tips from Form W-2, box 5. If you have more than one Form W-2, enter the total of the amounts from box 5	1	265,000		
2	Unreported tips from Form 4137, line 6	2			
3	Wages from Form 8919, line 6	3			
4	Add lines 1 through 3	4	265,000		
5	Enter the following amount for your filing status: Married filing jointly $250,000; Married filing separately $125,000; Single, Head of household, or Qualifying widow(er) $200,000	5	250,000		
6	Subtract line 5 from line 4. If zero or less, enter -0-			6	15,000
7	Additional Medicare Tax on Medicare wages. Multiply line 6 by 0.9% (0.009). Enter here and go to Part II			7	135

Part II Additional Medicare Tax on Self-Employment Income

Line	Description		Amount		Amount
8	Self-employment income from Schedule SE (Form 1040), Part I, line 6. If you had a loss, enter -0- (Form 1040-PR or 1040-SS filers, see instructions.)	8	130,000		
9	Enter the following amount for your filing status: Married filing jointly $250,000; Married filing separately $125,000; Single, Head of household, or Qualifying widow(er) $200,000	9	250,000		
10	Enter the amount from line 4	10	265,000		
11	Subtract line 10 from line 9. If zero or less, enter -0-	11	0		
12	Subtract line 11 from line 8. If zero or less, enter -0-			12	130,000
13	Additional Medicare Tax on self-employment income. Multiply line 12 by 0.9% (0.009). Enter here and go to Part III			13	1,170

Part III Additional Medicare Tax on Railroad Retirement Tax Act (RRTA) Compensation

Line	Description		Amount		Amount
14	Railroad retirement (RRTA) compensation and tips from Form(s) W-2, box 14 (see instructions)	14			
15	Enter the following amount for your filing status: Married filing jointly $250,000; Married filing separately $125,000; Single, Head of household, or Qualifying widow(er) $200,000	15			
16	Subtract line 15 from line 14. If zero or less, enter -0-			16	
17	Additional Medicare Tax on railroad retirement (RRTA) compensation. Multiply line 16 by 0.9% (0.009). Enter here and go to Part IV			17	

Part IV Total Additional Medicare Tax

18	Add lines 7, 13, and 17. Also include this amount on Schedule 2 (Form 1040), line 11 (Form 1040-PR or 1040-SS filers, see instructions), and go to Part V	18	1,305

Part V Withholding Reconciliation

Line	Description		Amount		Amount
19	Medicare tax withheld from Form W-2, box 6. If you have more than one Form W-2, enter the total of the amounts from box 6	19	4,428		
20	Enter the amount from line 1	20	265,000		
21	Multiply line 20 by 1.45% (0.0145). This is your regular Medicare tax withholding on Medicare wages	21	3,843		
22	Subtract line 21 from line 19. If zero or less, enter -0-. This is your Additional Medicare Tax withholding on Medicare wages			22	585
23	Additional Medicare Tax withholding on railroad retirement (RRTA) compensation from Form W-2, box 14 (see instructions)			23	
24	**Total Additional Medicare Tax withholding.** Add lines 22 and 23. Also include this amount with federal income tax withholding on Form 1040, 1040-SR, or 1040-NR, line 25c (Form 1040-PR or 1040-SS filers, see instructions)			24	585

For Paperwork Reduction Act Notice, see your tax return instructions. Cat. No. 59475X Form **8959** (2022)

CHAPTER 7 TAX CREDITS

Self-Study Problem 7.1

a. 4,500. $2,000 for the children under 17 and $500 for the other dependent child.

b. $4,200. Total possible credit is $4,500. Income of $405,600 exceeds $400,000 threshold by $5,600 which is rounded up to $6,000. $6,000/$1,000 = 6. 6 × $50 = phase out of $300. $4,500 less $300 = $4,200

c. See Schedule 8812 on Pages E-40 and E-41.

Self-Study Problem 7.2

$3,773. See Worksheet A—EIC Worksheet on Page E-42.

Self-Study Problem 7.3

$200. See Form 2441 on Pages E-43 and E-44.

Self-Study Problem 7.4

1. $2,385.
2. Excess advance credit of $3,495.
3. Repayment of $2,800.

See Form 8962 on Page E-45.

Self-Study Problem 7.5

a. $500. Refundable American Opportunity tax credit, Line 8 of Form 8863. $750. Nonrefundable American Opportunity tax credit, Line 19 of Form 8863. See Form 8863 on Pages E-46 and E-47.

b. $1,040 = 20% × $5,200 ($10,000 maximum)

Self-Study Problem 7.6

Overall limitation:

$$\frac{\$1{,}500}{\$58{,}000} \times \$8{,}383 = \$217$$

The foreign tax credit is limited to $217. The remaining balance of $215 can be carried back one year or carried forward 10 years.

Self-Study Problem 7.7

See Form 8839 on Pages E-48 and E-49.

Self-Study Problem 7.8

a. $7,500.

b. $3,000 (30% × $10,000). The solar system for the hot tub is not an allowed cost for the credit.

Self-Study Problem 7.1c

SCHEDULE 8812 (Form 1040) Department of the Treasury Internal Revenue Service	**Credits for Qualifying Children and Other Dependents** Attach to Form 1040, 1040-SR, or 1040-NR. Go to *www.irs.gov/Schedule8812* for instructions and the latest information.	OMB No. 1545-0074 2022 Attachment Sequence No. 47

Name(s) shown on return: Marie and Pierre Curry | Your social security number

Part I Child Tax Credit and Credit for Other Dependents

1	Enter the amount from line 11 of your Form 1040, 1040-SR, or 1040-NR			1	26,400
2a	Enter income from Puerto Rico that you excluded	2a			
b	Enter the amounts from lines 45 and 50 of your Form 2555	2b			
c	Enter the amount from line 15 of your Form 4563	2c			
d	Add lines 2a through 2c			2d	
3	Add lines 1 and 2d			3	26,400
4	Number of qualifying children under age 17 with the required social security number	4	3		
5	Multiply line 4 by $2,000			5	6,000
6	Number of other dependents, including any qualifying children who are not under age 17 or who do not have the required social security number	6			
	Caution: Do not include yourself, your spouse, or anyone who is not a U.S. citizen, U.S. national, or U.S. resident alien. Also, do not include anyone you included on line 4.				
7	Multiply line 6 by $500			7	
8	Add lines 5 and 7			8	6,000
9	Enter the amount shown below for your filing status. • Married filing jointly—$400,000 • All other filing statuses—$200,000			9	400,000
10	Subtract line 9 from line 3. • If zero or less, enter -0-. • If more than zero and not a multiple of $1,000, enter the next multiple of $1,000. For example, if the result is $425, enter $1,000; if the result is $1,025, enter $2,000, etc.			10	0
11	Multiply line 10 by 5% (0.05)			11	0
12	Is the amount on line 8 more than the amount on line 11?			12	6,000
	☐ **No. STOP.** You cannot take the child tax credit, credit for other dependents, or additional child tax credit. Skip Parts II-A and II-B. Enter -0- on lines 14 and 27. ☑ **Yes.** Subtract line 11 from line 8. Enter the result.				
13	Enter the amount from the **Credit Limit Worksheet A**			13	50
14	Enter the smaller of line 12 or 13. **This is your child tax credit and credit for other dependents** **Enter this amount on Form 1040, 1040-SR, or 1040-NR, line 19.**			14	50

If the amount on line 12 is more than the amount on line 14, you may be able to take the **additional child tax credit** on Form 1040, 1040-SR, or 1040-NR, line 28. Complete your Form 1040, 1040-SR, or 1040-NR through line 27 (also complete Schedule 3, line 11) before completing Part II-A.

For Paperwork Reduction Act Notice, see your tax return instructions. Cat. No. 59761M **Schedule 8812 (Form 1040) 2022**

Self-Study Problem 7.1c

Schedule 8812 (Form 1040) 2022 — Page **2**

Part II-A Additional Child Tax Credit for All Filers

Caution: If you file Form 2555, you cannot claim the additional child tax credit.

15	Check this box if you **do not** want to claim the additional child tax credit. Skip Parts II-A and II-B. Enter -0- on line 27 ☐				
16a	Subtract line 14 from line 12. If zero, **stop here**; you cannot take the additional child tax credit. Skip Parts II-A and II-B. Enter -0- on line 27			16a	5,950
b	Number of qualifying children under 17 with the required social security number: 3 x $1,500. Enter the result. If zero, **stop here**; you cannot claim the additional child tax credit. Skip Parts II-A and II-B. Enter -0- on line 27			16b	4,500
	TIP: The number of children you use for this line is the same as the number of children you used for line 4.				
17	Enter the **smaller** of line 16a or line 16b			17	4,500
18a	Earned income (see instructions)	18a	26,400		
b	Nontaxable combat pay (see instructions) — 18b				
19	Is the amount on line 18a more than $2,500? ☐ **No.** Leave line 19 blank and enter -0- on line 20. ☑ **Yes.** Subtract $2,500 from the amount on line 18a. Enter the result	19	23,900		
20	Multiply the amount on line 19 by 15% (0.15) and enter the result			20	3,585
	Next. On line 16b, is the amount $4,500 or more? ☐ **No.** If you are a bona fide resident of Puerto Rico, go to line 21. Otherwise, skip Part II-B and enter the **smaller** of line 17 or line 20 on line 27. ☑ **Yes.** If line 20 is equal to or more than line 17, skip Part II-B and enter the amount from line 17 on line 27. Otherwise, go to line 21.				

Part II-B Certain Filers Who Have Three or More Qualifying Children and Bona Fide Residents of Puerto Rico

21	Withheld social security, Medicare, and Additional Medicare taxes from Form(s) W-2, boxes 4 and 6. If married filing jointly, include your spouse's amounts with yours. If your employer withheld or you paid Additional Medicare Tax or tier 1 RRTA taxes, see instructions	21	2,020		
22	Enter the total of the amounts from Schedule 1 (Form 1040), line 15; Schedule 2 (Form 1040), line 5; Schedule 2 (Form 1040), line 6; and Schedule 2 (Form 1040), line 13	22			
23	Add lines 21 and 22	23	2,020		
24	**1040 and 1040-SR filers:** Enter the total of the amounts from Form 1040 or 1040-SR, line 27, and Schedule 3 (Form 1040), line 11. **1040-NR filers:** Enter the amount from Schedule 3 (Form 1040), line 11.	24			
25	Subtract line 24 from line 23. If zero or less, enter -0-			25	2,020
26	Enter the **larger** of line 20 or line 25			26	3,585
	Next, enter the **smaller** of line 17 or line 26 on line 27.				

Part II-C Additional Child Tax Credit

27	**This is your additional child tax credit. Enter this amount on Form 1040, 1040-SR, or 1040-NR, line 28**	27	3,585

Schedule 8812 (Form 1040) 2022

Self-Study Problem 7.2

Worksheet A—2022 EIC—Line 27a

Keep for Your Records 

Before you begin: √ Be sure you are using the correct worksheet. Use this worksheet only if you answered "No" to Step 5, question 2. Otherwise, use Worksheet B.

Part 1

All Filers Using Worksheet A

1. Enter your earned income from Step 5. | **1** | 15,800 |

2. Look up the amount on line 1 above in the EIC Table (right after Worksheet B) to find the credit. Be sure you use the correct column for your filing status and the number of qualifying children you have who have a valid SSN as defined earlier. Enter the credit here. | **2** | 3,733 |

   If line 2 is zero, STOP You can't take the credit.
   Enter "No" on the dotted line next to Form 1040 or 1040-SR, line 27.

3. Enter the amount from Form 1040 or 1040-SR, line 11. | **3** | 15,900 |

4. Are the amounts on lines 3 and 1 the same?

   ☐ **Yes.** Skip line 5; enter the amount from line 2 on line 6.

   ☒ **No.** Go to line 5.

Part 2

Filers Who Answered "No" on Line 4

5. If you have:
   - No qualifying children who have a valid SSN, is the amount on line 3 less than $9,200 ($15,300 if married filing jointly)?
   - 1 or more qualifying children who have a valid SSN, is the amount on line 3 less than $20,150 ($26,300 if married filing jointly)?

   ☒ **Yes.** Leave line 5 blank; enter the amount from line 2 on line 6.

   ☐ **No.** Look up the amount on line 3 in the EIC Table to find the credit. Be sure you use the correct column for your filing status and the number of qualifying children you have who have a valid SSN. Enter the credit here. | **5** | |
   Look at the amounts on lines 5 and 2.
   Then, enter the **smaller** amount on line 6.

Part 3

Your Earned Income Credit

6. **This is your earned income credit.** | **6** | 3,733 |

   Enter this amount on Form 1040 or 1040-SR, line 27.

Reminder—

√ If you have a qualifying child, complete and attach Schedule EIC.

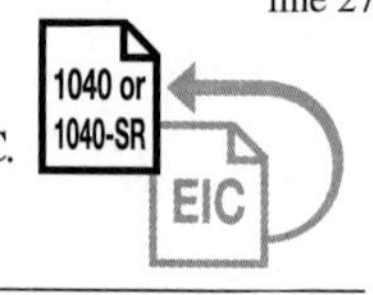

If your EIC for a year after 1996 was reduced or disallowed, see Form 8862, who must file, *earlier, to find out if you must file Form 8862 to take the credit for 2022.*

The 2022 Worksheet A was not available when we went to print. Be sure and download the most current version from the Form 1040 Instructions at www.irs.gov.

Self-Study Problem 7.3

Form **2441** | Department of the Treasury Internal Revenue Service

Child and Dependent Care Expenses

Attach to Form 1040, 1040-SR, or 1040-NR.
Go to *www.irs.gov/Form2441* for instructions and the latest information.

OMB No. 1545-0074 | 2022 | Attachment Sequence No. 21

Name(s) shown on return: Julie Brown | Your social security number: 456-23-6543

A You can't claim a credit for child and dependent care expenses if your filing status is married filing separately unless you meet the requirements listed in the instructions under *Married Persons Filing Separately*. If you meet these requirements, check this box . . ☐

B If you or your spouse was a student or was disabled during 2022 and you're entering deemed income of $250 or $500 a month on Form 2441 based on the income rules listed in the instructions under *If You or Your Spouse Was a Student or Disabled*, check this box . ☐

Part I Persons or Organizations Who Provided the Care—You **must** complete this part.
If you have more than three care providers, see the instructions and check this box . . . . ☐

1 (a) Care provider's name	(b) Address (number, street, apt. no., city, state, and ZIP code)	(c) Identifying number (SSN or EIN)	(d) Was the care provider your household employee in 2022? For example, this generally includes nannies but not daycare centers. (see instructions)	(e) Amount paid (see instructions)
Ivy Childcare	1 Sunflower Street Terre Haute, IN 47803	56-7654321	☐ Yes ☑ No	3,500
De Anza Adult Care	13 Fort Harrison Rd. Dewey, IN 47805	43-1234567	☐ Yes ☑ No	3,400
			☐ Yes ☐ No	

Did you receive **dependent care benefits**?
- **No** — Complete only Part II below.
- **Yes** — Complete Part III on page 2 next.

Caution: If the care provider is your household employee, you may owe employment taxes. For details, see the Instructions for Schedule H (Form 1040). If you incurred care expenses in 2022 but didn't pay them until 2023, or if you prepaid in 2022 for care to be provided in 2023, don't include these expenses in column (d) of line 2 for 2022. See the instructions.

Part II Credit for Child and Dependent Care Expenses

2 Information about your **qualifying person(s)**. If you have more than three qualifying persons, see the instructions and check this box ☐

(a) Qualifying person's name — First	Last	(b) Qualifying person's social security number	(c) Check here if the qualifying person was over age 12 and was disabled. (see instructions)	(d) Qualified expenses you incurred and paid in 2022 for the person listed in column (a)
Chuck	Brown	123-33-4444	☐	3,500
Devona	Neuporte	214-55-6666	☑	3,400
			☐	

3	Add the amounts in column (d) of line 2. **Don't** enter more than $3,000 if you had one qualifying person or $6,000 if you had two or more persons. If you completed Part III, enter the amount from line 31	3	1,000
4	Enter your **earned income**. See instructions	4	90,000
5	If married filing jointly, enter your spouse's earned income (if you or your spouse was a student or was disabled, see the instructions); **all others**, enter the amount from line 4	5	90,000
6	Enter the **smallest** of line 3, 4, or 5	6	1,000
7	Enter the amount from Form 1040, 1040-SR, or 1040-NR, line 11 . . . 7 — 44,450		
8	Enter on line 8 the decimal amount shown below that applies to the amount on line 7.	8	X. 20

If line 7 is: Over — But not over	Decimal amount is	If line 7 is: Over — But not over	Decimal amount is	If line 7 is: Over — But not over	Decimal amount is
$0—15,000	.35	$25,000—27,000	.29	$37,000—39,000	.23
15,000—17,000	.34	27,000—29,000	.28	39,000—41,000	.22
17,000—19,000	.33	29,000—31,000	.27	41,000—43,000	.21
19,000—21,000	.32	31,000—33,000	.26	43,000—No limit	.20
21,000—23,000	.31	33,000—35,000	.25		
23,000—25,000	.30	35,000—37,000	.24		

9a	Multiply line 6 by the decimal amount on line 8	9a	200
b	If you paid 2021 expenses in 2022, complete Worksheet A in the instructions. Enter the amount from line 13 of the worksheet here. Otherwise, enter -0- on line 9b and go to line 9c	9b	
c	Add lines 9a and 9b and enter the result	9c	200
10	Tax liability limit. Enter the amount from the Credit Limit Worksheet in the instructions 10 — 5,044		
11	**Credit for child and dependent care expenses.** Enter the **smaller** of line 9c or line 10 here and on Schedule 3 (Form 1040), line 2	11	200

For Paperwork Reduction Act Notice, see your tax return instructions. Cat. No. 11862M Form **2441** (2022)

Self-Study Problem 7.3

Form 2441 (2022) Page 2

Part III Dependent Care Benefits

12	Enter the total amount of **dependent care benefits** you received in 2022. Amounts you received as an employee should be shown in box 10 of your Form(s) W-2. **Don't** include amounts reported as wages in box 1 of Form(s) W-2. If you were self-employed or a partner, include amounts you received under a dependent care assistance program from your sole proprietorship or partnership	12	5,000
13	Enter the amount, if any, you carried over from 2020 and/or 2021 and used in 2022. See instructions	13	
14	If you forfeited or carried over to 2023 any of the amounts reported on line 12 or 13, enter the amount. See instructions	14	( )
15	Combine lines 12 through 14. See instructions	15	5,000
16	Enter the total amount of **qualified expenses** incurred in 2022 for the care of the **qualifying person(s)** — 16: 11,900		
17	Enter the **smaller** of line 15 or 16 — 17: 5,000		
18	Enter your **earned income**. See instructions — 18: 90,000		
19	Enter the amount shown below that applies to you. • If married filing jointly, enter your spouse's earned income (if you or your spouse was a student or was disabled, see the instructions for line 5). • If married filing separately, see instructions. • All others, enter the amount from line 18. — 19: 90,000		
20	Enter the **smallest** of line 17, 18, or 19 — 20: 5,000		
21	Enter $5,000 ($2,500 if married filing separately **and** you were required to enter your spouse's earned income on line 19). If you entered an amount on line 13, add it to the $5,000 or $2,500 amount you enter on line 21. However, don't enter more than the maximum amount allowed under your dependent care plan. If your dependent care plan uses a non-calendar plan year, see instructions — 21: 5,000		
22	Is any amount on line 12 or 13 from your sole proprietorship or partnership? ☑ **No.** Enter -0-. ☐ **Yes.** Enter the amount here	22	0
23	Subtract line 22 from line 15 — 23: 5,000		
24	**Deductible benefits.** Enter the **smallest** of line 20, 21, or 22. Also, include this amount on the appropriate line(s) of your return. See instructions	24	0
25	**Excluded benefits.** If you checked "No" on line 22, enter the smaller of line 20 or 21. Otherwise, subtract line 24 from the smaller of line 20 or line 21. If zero or less, enter -0-	25	5,000
26	**Taxable benefits.** Subtract line 25 from line 23. If zero or less, enter -0-. Also, enter this amount on Form 1040, 1040-SR, or 1040-NR, line 1e	26	0

To claim the child and dependent care credit, complete lines 27 through 31 below.

27	Enter $3,000 ($6,000 if two or more qualifying persons)	27	6,000
28	Add lines 24 and 25	28	5,000
29	Subtract line 28 from line 27. If zero or less, **stop.** You can't take the credit. **Exception.** If you paid 2021 expenses in 2022, see the instructions for line 9b	29	1,000
30	Complete line 2 on page 1 of this form. **Don't** include in column (d) any benefits shown on line 28 above. Then, add the amounts in column (d) and enter the total here	30	6,900
31	Enter the **smaller** of line 29 or 30. Also, enter this amount on line 3 on page 1 of this form and complete lines 4 through 11	31	1,000

Form **2441** (2022)

Self-Study Problem 7.4

Form **8962** | **Premium Tax Credit (PTC)** | OMB No. 1545-0074 | 2022

Department of the Treasury Internal Revenue Service

Attach to Form 1040, 1040-SR, or 1040-NR.
Go to *www.irs.gov/Form8962* for instructions and the latest information.

Attachment Sequence No. **73**

Name shown on your return: Tracy and Marco Brigantine | Your social security number: 123-44-5555

A. You cannot take the PTC if your filing status is married filing separately unless you qualify for an exception. See instructions. If you qualify, check the box ☐

Part I Annual and Monthly Contribution Amount

1	Tax family size. Enter your tax family size. See instructions	1	4
2a	Modified AGI. Enter your modified AGI. See instructions	2a	98,050 (a)
b	Enter the total of your dependents' modified AGI. See instructions	2b	
3	Household income. Add the amounts on lines 2a and 2b. See instructions	3	98,050
4	Federal poverty line. Enter the federal poverty line amount from Table 1-1, 1-2, or 1-3. See instructions. Check the appropriate box for the federal poverty table used. a ☐ Alaska b ☐ Hawaii c ☑ Other 48 states and DC	4	26,500
5	Household income as a percentage of federal poverty line (see instructions)	5	370 %
6	Reserved for future use		
7	Applicable figure. Using your line 5 percentage, locate your "applicable figure" on the table in the instructions	7	.0775
8a	Annual contribution amount. Multiply line 3 by line 7. Round to nearest whole dollar amount	8a	7,599
b	Monthly contribution amount. Divide line 8a by 12. Round to nearest whole dollar amount	8b	633

Part II Premium Tax Credit Claim and Reconciliation of Advance Payment of Premium Tax Credit

9 Are you allocating policy amounts with another taxpayer or do you want to use the alternative calculation for year of marriage? See instructions.
☐ **Yes.** Skip to Part IV, Allocation of Policy Amounts, or Part V, Alternative Calculation for Year of Marriage. ☑ **No.** Continue to line 10.

10 See the instructions to determine if you can use line 11 or must complete lines 12 through 23.
☑ **Yes.** Continue to line 11. Compute your annual PTC. Then skip lines 12–23 and continue to line 24.
☐ **No.** Continue to lines 12–23. Compute your monthly PTC and continue to line 24.

Annual Calculation	(a) Annual enrollment premiums (Form(s) 1095-A, line 33A)	(b) Annual applicable SLCSP premium (Form(s) 1095-A, line 33B)	(c) Annual contribution amount (line 8a)	(d) Annual maximum premium assistance (subtract (c) from (b); if zero or less, enter -0-)	(e) Annual premium tax credit allowed (smaller of (a) or (d))	(f) Annual advance payment of PTC (Form(s) 1095-A, line 33C)
11 Annual Totals	11,580	9,984	7,599	2,385	2,385	5,880
Monthly Calculation	**(a)** Monthly enrollment premiums (Form(s) 1095-A, lines 21–32, column A)	**(b)** Monthly applicable SLCSP premium (Form(s) 1095-A, lines 21–32, column B)	**(c)** Monthly contribution amount (amount from line 8b or alternative marriage monthly calculation)	**(d)** Monthly maximum premium assistance (subtract (c) from (b); if zero or less, enter -0-)	**(e)** Monthly premium tax credit allowed (smaller of (a) or (d))	**(f)** Monthly advance payment of PTC (Form(s) 1095-A, lines 21–32, column C)
12 January						
13 February						
14 March						
15 April						
16 May						
17 June						
18 July						
19 August						
20 September						
21 October						
22 November						
23 December						

24	Total premium tax credit. Enter the amount from line 11(e) or add lines 12(e) through 23(e) and enter the total here	24	2,385
25	Advance payment of PTC. Enter the amount from line 11(f) or add lines 12(f) through 23(f) and enter the total here	25	5,880
26	Net premium tax credit. If line 24 is greater than line 25, subtract line 25 from line 24. Enter the difference here and on Schedule 3 (Form 1040), line 9. If line 24 equals line 25, enter -0-. Stop here. If line 25 is greater than line 24, leave this line blank and continue to line 27	26	

Part III Repayment of Excess Advance Payment of the Premium Tax Credit

27	Excess advance payment of PTC. If line 25 is greater than line 24, subtract line 24 from line 25. Enter the difference here	27	3,495
28	Repayment limitation (see instructions)	28	2,800
29	Excess advance premium tax credit repayment. Enter the smaller of line 27 or line 28 here and on Schedule 2 (Form 1040), line 2	29	2,800

For Paperwork Reduction Act Notice, see your tax return instructions. Cat. No. 37784Z Form **8962** (2022)

a. \$46,490 + \$49,560 + \$2,000

Self-Study Problem 7.5a

Form **8863** — Department of the Treasury, Internal Revenue Service

Education Credits
(American Opportunity and Lifetime Learning Credits)
Attach to Form 1040 or 1040-SR.
Go to *www.irs.gov/Form8863* for instructions and the latest information.

OMB No. 1545-0074 — 2022 — Attachment Sequence No. **50**

Name(s) shown on return: Santiago and Sophia Estudiante — Your social security number:

CAUTION *Complete a separate Part III on page 2 for each student for whom you're claiming either credit before you complete Parts I and II.*

Part I Refundable American Opportunity Credit

1	After completing Part III for each student, enter the total of all amounts from all Parts III, line 30			1	2,500
2	Enter: $180,000 if married filing jointly; $90,000 if single, head of household, or qualifying widow(er)	2	180,000		
3	Enter the amount from Form 1040 or 1040-SR, line 11. If you're filing Form 2555 or 4563, or you're excluding income from Puerto Rico, see Pub. 970 for the amount to enter	3	170,000		
4	Subtract line 3 from line 2. If zero or less, **stop**; you can't take any education credit	4	10,000		
5	Enter: $20,000 if married filing jointly; $10,000 if single, head of household, or qualifying widow(er)	5	20,000		
6	If line 4 is: • Equal to or more than line 5, enter 1.000 on line 6 • Less than line 5, divide line 4 by line 5. Enter the result as a decimal (rounded to at least three places)			6	.500
7	Multiply line 1 by line 6. **Caution:** If you were under age 24 at the end of the year **and** meet the conditions described in the instructions, you **can't** take the refundable American opportunity credit; skip line 8, enter the amount from line 7 on line 9, and check this box ☐			7	1,250
8	**Refundable American opportunity credit.** Multiply line 7 by 40% (0.40). Enter the amount here and on Form 1040 or 1040-SR, line 29. Then go to line 9 below			8	500

Part II Nonrefundable Education Credits

9	Subtract line 8 from line 7. Enter here and on line 2 of the Credit Limit Worksheet (see instructions)			9	750
10	After completing Part III for each student, enter the total of all amounts from all Parts III, line 31. If zero, skip lines 11 through 17, enter -0- on line 18, and go to line 19			10	
11	Enter the smaller of line 10 or $10,000			11	
12	Multiply line 11 by 20% (0.20)			12	
13	Enter: $180,000 if married filing jointly; $90,000 if single, head of household, or qualifying widow(er)	13			
14	Enter the amount from Form 1040 or 1040-SR, line 11. If you're filing Form 2555 or 4563, or you're excluding income from Puerto Rico, see Pub. 970 for the amount to enter	14			
15	Subtract line 14 from line 13. If zero or less, skip lines 16 and 17, enter -0- on line 18, and go to line 19	15			
16	Enter: $20,000 if married filing jointly; $10,000 if single, head of household, or qualifying widow(er)	16			
17	If line 15 is: • Equal to or more than line 16, enter 1.000 on line 17 and go to line 18 • Less than line 16, divide line 15 by line 16. Enter the result as a decimal (rounded to at least three places)			17	.
18	Multiply line 12 by line 17. Enter here and on line 1 of the Credit Limit Worksheet (see instructions)			18	0
19	**Nonrefundable education credits.** Enter the amount from line 7 of the Credit Limit Worksheet (see instructions) here and on Schedule 3 (Form 1040), line 3			19	750

For Paperwork Reduction Act Notice, see your tax return instructions. Cat. No. 25379M Form **8863** (2022)

Note: The taxpayers have a large tax liability relative to the AOTC. As a result, the nonrefundable AOTC will not be limited.

Self-Study Problem 7.5a

Form 8863 (2022) Page **2**

Name(s) shown on return	Your social security number
Santiago and Sophia Estudiante	

CAUTION ***Complete Part III for each student for whom you're claiming either the American opportunity credit or lifetime learning credit. Use additional copies of page 2 as needed for each student.***

Part III **Student and Educational Institution Information.** See instructions.

20 Student name (as shown on page 1 of your tax return) Judy Estudiante	**21** Student social security number (as shown on page 1 of your tax return) 434 | 11 | 7812

22 Educational institution information (see instructions)

a. Name of first educational institution Southwest University	**b.** Name of second educational institution (if any)
(1) Address. Number and street (or P.O. box). City, town or post office, state, and ZIP code. If a foreign address, see instructions. 1234 Cleveland Avenue El Paso, TX 79925	**(1)** Address. Number and street (or P.O. box). City, town or post office, state, and ZIP code. If a foreign address, see instructions.
(2) Did the student receive Form 1098-T from this institution for 2022? ☑ Yes ☐ No	**(2)** Did the student receive Form 1098-T from this institution for 2022? ☐ Yes ☐ No
(3) Did the student receive Form 1098-T from this institution for 2021 with box 7 checked? ☐ Yes ☑ No	**(3)** Did the student receive Form 1098-T from this institution for 2021 with box 7 checked? ☐ Yes ☐ No
(4) Enter the institution's employer identification number (EIN) if you're claiming the American opportunity credit or if you checked "Yes" in **(2)** or **(3).** You can get the EIN from Form 1098-T or from the institution. 1 2 - 7 6 5 2 3 1 1	**(4)** Enter the institution's employer identification number (EIN) if you're claiming the American opportunity credit or if you checked "Yes" in **(2)** or **(3).** You can get the EIN from Form 1098-T or from the institution. __ __ - __ __ __ __ __ __ __

23 Has the American opportunity credit been claimed for this student for any 4 tax years before 2022? ☐ Yes — **Stop!** Go to line 31 for this student. ☑ No — Go to line 24.

24 Was the student enrolled at least half-time for at least one academic period that began or is treated as having begun in 2022 at an eligible educational institution in a program leading towards a postsecondary degree, certificate, or other recognized postsecondary educational credential? See instructions. ☑ Yes — Go to line 25. ☐ No — **Stop!** Go to line 31 for this student.

25 Did the student complete the first 4 years of postsecondary education before 2022? See instructions. ☐ Yes — **Stop!** Go to line 31 for this student. ☑ No — Go to line 26.

26 Was the student convicted, before the end of 2022, of a felony for possession or distribution of a controlled substance? ☐ Yes — **Stop!** Go to line 31 for this student. ☑ No — Complete lines 27 through 30 for this student.

CAUTION *You* ***can't*** *take the American opportunity credit and the lifetime learning credit for the* ***same student*** *in the same year. If you complete lines 27 through 30 for this student, don't complete line 31.*

American Opportunity Credit

27	Adjusted qualified education expenses (see instructions). **Don't enter more than $4,000**	**27**	4,000 (a)
28	Subtract $2,000 from line 27. If zero or less, enter -0-	**28**	2,000
29	Multiply line 28 by 25% (0.25)	**29**	500
30	If line 28 is zero, enter the amount from line 27. Otherwise, add $2,000 to the amount on line 29 and enter the result. Skip line 31. Include the total of all amounts from all Parts III, line 30, on Part I, line 1	**30**	2,500

Lifetime Learning Credit

31	Adjusted qualified education expenses (see instructions). Include the total of all amounts from all Parts III, line 31, on Part II, line 10	**31**	

Form **8863** (2022)

a. $3,950 from 1098-T plus $275 for books

Self-Study Problem 7.7

Form **8839** | **Qualified Adoption Expenses** | OMB No. 1545-0074

Department of the Treasury Internal Revenue Service

Attach to Form 1040, 1040-SR, or 1040-NR.

Go to *www.irs.gov/Form8839* for instructions and the latest information.

2022 Attachment Sequence No. **38**

Name(s) shown on return: James and Michael Bass | **Your social security number**

Part I **Information About Your Eligible Child or Children—**You **must** complete this part. See instructions for details, including what to do if you need more space.

1	(a) Child's name First	(a) Child's name Last	(b) Child's year of birth	(c) born **before 2005** and disabled	(d) a child with special needs	(e) a foreign child	(f) Child's identifying number	(g) Check if adoption became final in 2022 or earlier
Child 1	Allison	Bass	2022	☐	☐	☐	466-47-3311	☑
Child 2				☐	☐	☐		☐
Child 3				☐	☐	☐		☐

(Columns (c)–(e): Check if child was—)

Caution: If the child was a foreign child, see **Special rules** in the instructions for line 1, column (e), before you complete Part II or Part III. If you received **employer-provided adoption benefits**, complete Part III on the back next.

Part II **Adoption Credit**

			Child 1	Child 2	Child 3		
2	Maximum adoption credit per child. Enter $14,890 (see instructions)	2	14,890				
3	Did you file Form 8839 for a prior year for the same child? ☑ **No.** Enter -0-. ☐ **Yes.** See instructions for the amount to enter.	3	0				
4	Subtract line 3 from line 2	4	14,890				
5	**Qualified adoption expenses** (see instructions)	5	17,000				
	Caution: Your qualified adoption expenses may not be equal to the adoption expenses you paid in 2022.						
6	Enter the **smaller** of line 4 or line 5	6	14,890				
7	Enter modified adjusted gross income (see instructions)			7	231,410		
8	Is line 7 more than $223,410? ☐ **No.** Skip lines 8 and 9, and enter -0- on line 10. ☑ **Yes.** Subtract $223,410 from line 7			8	8,000		
9	Divide line 8 by $40,000. Enter the result as a decimal (rounded to at least three places). Do not enter more than 1.000					9	× .20
10	Multiply each amount on line 6 by line 9	10	2,978				
11	Subtract line 10 from line 6	11	11,912				
12	Add the amounts on line 11					12	11,912
13	Credit carryforward, if any, from prior years. See your Adoption Credit Carryforward Worksheet in the 2021 Form 8839 instructions					13	
14	Add lines 12 and 13					14	11,912
15	Enter the amount from line 5 of the Credit Limit Worksheet in the instructions					15	28,300
16	**Adoption Credit.** Enter the smaller of line 14 or line 15 here and on Schedule 3 (Form 1040), line 6c. If line 15 is smaller than line 14, you may have a credit carryforward (see instructions)					16	11,912

For Paperwork Reduction Act Notice, see your tax return instructions. Cat. No. 22843L Form **8839** (2022)

Self-Study Problem 7.7

Form 8839 (2022) Page **2**

Part III Employer-Provided Adoption Benefits

			Child 1	Child 2	Child 3		
17	Maximum exclusion per child. Enter $14,890 (see instructions)	**17**	14,890				
18	Did you receive employer-provided adoption benefits for a prior year for the same child? ☐ **No.** Enter -0-. ☑ **Yes.** See instructions for the amount to enter.	**18**	0				
19	Subtract line 18 from line 17	**19**	14,890				
20	Employer-provided adoption benefits you received in 2022. This amount should be shown in box 12 of your 2022 Form(s) W-2 with code **T**	**20**	4,000				
21	Add the amounts on line 20					**21**	4,000
22	Enter the **smaller** of line 19 or line 20. But if the child was a child with special needs and the adoption became final in 2022, enter the amount from line 19	**22**	4,000				
23	Enter modified adjusted gross income (from the worksheet in the instructions)	**23**	231,410				
24	Is line 23 more than $223,410? ☐ **No.** Skip lines 24 and 25, and enter -0- on line 26. ☑ **Yes.** Subtract $223,410 from line 23	**24**	8,000				
25	Divide line 24 by $40,000. Enter the result as a decimal (rounded to at least three places). Do not enter more than 1.000	**25**	× . 20				
26	Multiply each amount on line 22 by line 25	**26**	800				
27	**Excluded benefits.** Subtract line 26 from line 22	**27**	3,200				
28	Add the amounts on line 27					**28**	3,200
29	**Taxable benefits.** Is line 28 more than line 21? ☑ **No.** Subtract line 28 from line 21. Also, include this amount, if more than zero, on line 1f of Form 1040, 1040-SR, or 1040-NR. ☐ **Yes.** Subtract line 21 from line 28. Enter the result as a negative number. Also, enter the result on line 1f of Form 1040, 1040-SR, or 1040-NR.					**29**	800

You may be able to claim the adoption credit in Part II on the front of this form if any of the following apply.

- You paid adoption expenses in 2021, those expenses were not fully reimbursed by your employer or otherwise, and the adoption was not final by the end of 2021.
- The total adoption expenses you paid in 2022 were not fully reimbursed by your employer or otherwise, and the adoption became final in 2022 or earlier.
- You adopted a child with special needs and the adoption became final in 2022.

Form **8839** (2022)

Self-Study Problem 7.9

See Form 8880 below.

Form **8880** — Department of the Treasury, Internal Revenue Service

Credit for Qualified Retirement Savings Contributions

Attach to Form 1040, 1040-SR, or 1040-NR.

Go to *www.irs.gov/Form8880* for the latest information.

OMB No. 1545-0074 — 2022 — Attachment Sequence No. **54**

Name(s) shown on return: Robin and Steve Harrington — Your social security number

*You **cannot** take this credit if **either** of the following applies.*

- *The amount on Form 1040, 1040-SR, or 1040-NR, line 11, is more than $34,000 ($51,000 if head of household; $68,000 if married filing jointly).*
- *The person(s) who made the qualified contribution or elective deferral **(a)** was born after January 1, 2005; **(b)** is claimed as a dependent on someone else's 2022 tax return; or **(c)** was a **student** (see instructions).*

			(a) You	(b) Your spouse
1	Traditional and Roth IRA contributions, and ABLE account contributions by the designated beneficiary for 2022. **Do not** include rollover contributions	1	6,000	6,000
2	Elective deferrals to a 401(k) or other qualified employer plan, voluntary employee contributions, and 501(c)(18)(D) plan contributions for 2022 (see instructions)	2		
3	Add lines 1 and 2	3	6,000	6,000
4	Certain distributions received **after** 2019 and **before** the due date (including extensions) of your 2022 tax return (see instructions). If married filing jointly, include **both** spouses' amounts in **both** columns. See instructions for an exception	4		
5	Subtract line 4 from line 3. If zero or less, enter -0-	5	6,000	6,000
6	In each column, enter the **smaller** of line 5 or $2,000	6	2,000	2,000

7 Add the amounts on line 6. If zero, **stop**; you can't take this credit . . . **7** 4,000

8 Enter the amount from Form 1040, 1040-SR, or 1040-NR, line 11* . . . **8** 39,500

9 Enter the applicable decimal amount from the table below.

If line 8 is—		And your filing status is—		
Over—	But not over—	Married filing jointly	Head of household	Single, Married filing separately, or Qualifying widow(er)
		Enter on line 9—		
---	$20,500	0.5	0.5	0.5
$20,500	$22,000	0.5	0.5	0.2
$22,000	$30,750	0.5	0.5	0.1
$30,750	$33,000	0.5	0.2	0.1
$33,000	$34,000	0.5	0.1	0.1
$34,000	$41,000	0.5	0.1	0.0
$41,000	$44,000	0.2	0.1	0.0
$44,000	$51,000	0.1	0.1	0.0
$51,000	$68,000	0.1	0.0	0.0
$68,000	---	0.0	0.0	0.0

9 x 0. 50

Note: If line 9 is zero, **stop**; you can't take this credit.

10 Multiply line 7 by line 9 . . . **10** 2,000

11 Limitation based on tax liability. Enter the amount from the Credit Limit Worksheet in the instructions **11** 1,363

12 **Credit for qualified retirement savings contributions.** Enter the **smaller** of line 10 or line 11 here and on Schedule 3 (Form 1040), line 4 . . . **12** 1,363

* See Pub. 590-A for the amount to enter if you claim any exclusion or deduction for foreign earned income, foreign housing, or income from Puerto Rico or for bona fide residents of American Samoa.

CHAPTER 8 DEPRECIATION AND SALE OF BUSINESS PROPERTY

Self-Study Problem 8.1

a. Capitalize. New property does not meet any safe harbors.
b. Capitalize. Restoration does not meet any safe harbors.
c. Capitalize. Betterment not eligible for safe harbor.
d. Deduct. Acquisition meets safe harbor for company with AFS and a written policy.
e. Capitalize. Betterment is not eligible for safe harbor.

Self-Study Problem 8.2

a. $20,274. Bonus on 7-year property: $17,000 ($11,000 + $6,000)
Real estate: $180,000 × 0.01819 = $3,274
See Form 4562 on Page E-52.
b. $5,703. MACRS: $11,000 × 0.1429 = $1,572
MACRS: $6,000 × 0.1429 = $857
Total 7-year property = $2,429
Real estate: $180,000 × 0.01819 = $3,274
c. $4,615. 7-year property: $0 (cost fully recovered through bonus depreciation in year 1)
Real estate: $180,000 × 0.02564 = $4,615

Self-Study Problem 8.3

a. $405,407. $2,837,000 × 0.1429 (MACRS depreciation factor for the first year for 7-year property using the half-year convention).
b. $1,213,653. Chang's eligible §179 property exceeds the $2,700,000 threshold by $137,000; thus, she must reduce the 2022 Section 179 $1,080,000 annual limit to $943,000. The $1,894,000 remaining balance of the property ($2,837,000 − $943,000) is depreciated using the MACRS: $1,894,000 × 0.1429 = $270,653. The total cost recovery is $943,000 + $270,653 = $1,213,653.
c. $2,837,000. Chang is eligible for 100% bonus depreciation on the equipment and there are no taxable income limits or thresholds associated with bonus depreciation. Chang will generate a $337,000 net operating loss.

Self-Study Problem 8.4

1. Yes — Qualified business use is 50 percent or less; therefore, Alvarez must use the straight-line method of depreciation for the auto.
2. No — Qualified business use is more than 50 percent; therefore, Laura may use the accelerated method of depreciation.

Self-Study Problem 8.5

	2022	2023	2024
Original cost	$58,000	$58,000	$58,000
Business use percentage	0.90	0.90	0.90
Basis for depreciation	$ 52,200	$ 52,200	$ 52,200
Depreciation factor	20%	32%	19.2%
MACRS depreciation	$ 10,440	$ 16,704	$ 10,022
Annual depreciation limit × 90%	$10,080	$ 16,200	$ 9,720

Self-Study Problem 8.2a

Form **4562** Department of the Treasury Internal Revenue Service

Depreciation and Amortization
(Including Information on Listed Property)
Attach to your tax return.
Go to *www.irs.gov/Form4562* for instructions and the latest information.

OMB No. 1545-0172 **2022** Attachment Sequence No. **179**

Name(s) shown on return	Business or activity to which this form relates	Identifying number
Mary Moser		

Part I Election To Expense Certain Property Under Section 179
Note: If you have any listed property, complete Part V before you complete Part I.

1	Maximum amount (see instructions)	1	
2	Total cost of section 179 property placed in service (see instructions)	2	
3	Threshold cost of section 179 property before reduction in limitation (see instructions)	3	
4	Reduction in limitation. Subtract line 3 from line 2. If zero or less, enter -0-	4	
5	Dollar limitation for tax year. Subtract line 4 from line 1. If zero or less, enter -0-. If married filing separately, see instructions	5	

6 (a) Description of property	(b) Cost (business use only)	(c) Elected cost
7 Listed property. Enter the amount from line 29	7	

8	Total elected cost of section 179 property. Add amounts in column (c), lines 6 and 7	8	
9	Tentative deduction. Enter the **smaller** of line 5 or line 8	9	
10	Carryover of disallowed deduction from line 13 of your 2021 Form 4562	10	
11	Business income limitation. Enter the smaller of business income (not less than zero) or line 5. See instructions	11	
12	Section 179 expense deduction. Add lines 9 and 10, but don't enter more than line 11	12	
13	Carryover of disallowed deduction to 2023. Add lines 9 and 10, less line 12	13	

Note: Don't use Part II or Part III below for listed property. Instead, use Part V.

Part II Special Depreciation Allowance and Other Depreciation (Don't include listed property. See instructions.**)**

14	Special depreciation allowance for qualified property (other than listed property) placed in service during the tax year. See instructions	14	17,000
15	Property subject to section 168(f)(1) election	15	
16	Other depreciation (including ACRS)	16	

Part III MACRS Depreciation (Don't include listed property. See instructions.**)**

Section A

17	MACRS deductions for assets placed in service in tax years beginning before 2022	17	
18	If you are electing to group any assets placed in service during the tax year into one or more general asset accounts, check here ☐		

Section B—Assets Placed in Service During 2022 Tax Year Using the General Depreciation System

(a) Classification of property	(b) Month and year placed in service	(c) Basis for depreciation (business/investment use only—see instructions)	(d) Recovery period	(e) Convention	(f) Method	(g) Depreciation deduction
19a 3-year property						
b 5-year property						
c 7-year property						
d 10-year property						
e 15-year property						
f 20-year property						
g 25-year property			25 yrs.		S/L	
h Residential rental			27.5 yrs.	MM	S/L	
property			27.5 yrs.	MM	S/L	
i Nonresidential real	4/2022	180,000	39 yrs.	MM	S/L	3,274
property				MM	S/L	

Section C—Assets Placed in Service During 2022 Tax Year Using the Alternative Depreciation System

20a Class life					S/L	
b 12-year			12 yrs.		S/L	
c 30-year			30 yrs.	MM	S/L	
d 40-year			40 yrs.	MM	S/L	

Part IV Summary (See instructions.)

21	Listed property. Enter amount from line 28	21	
22	**Total.** Add amounts from line 12, lines 14 through 17, lines 19 and 20 in column (g), and line 21. Enter here and on the appropriate lines of your return. Partnerships and S corporations—see instructions	22	20,274
23	For assets shown above and placed in service during the current year, enter the portion of the basis attributable to section 263A costs	23	

For Paperwork Reduction Act Notice, see separate instructions. Cat. No. 12906N Form **4562** (2022)

Self-Study Problem 8.6

1. 15-year Amortization.
2. Useful Life.
3. Useful Life.
4. 15-year Amortization.
5. 15-year Amortization.
6. Not Amortizable.
7. 15-year Amortization.
8. Not Amortizable.

Self-Study Problem 8.7

	Land	***Computer***	***Equipment***
Proceeds	$37,000	$14,000	$16,000
Selling Costs	500	0	1,600
Amount Realized	36,500	14,000	14,400
Adjusted Basis:			
Cost	$24,000	$53,906	$28,177
Cost Recovery	0	33,206	7,477
Adjusted Basis	24,000	20,700	20,700
Gain/(Loss)	$12,500	$ (6,700)	$ (6,300)

The land and the computer are both Section 1231 properties and thus, the gain and loss is netted resulting in a $5,800 net Section 1231 gain. As a result, both the gain on the land and the loss on the computer will be treated as long-term capital gains. The equipment was not held for more than one year and thus, is an ordinary asset (depreciable business property is not a capital asset—see Chapter 4) and the loss will be treated as an ordinary loss.

Self-Study Problem 8.8

See Form 4797 on Pages E-54 and E-55.

Self-Study Problem 8.9

	Furniture (completely destroyed)	***Machinery (partially destroyed)***
Insurance proceeds	$ 0	$10,000
Adjusted basis	5,000	**14,000**
Decrease in FMV	n/a	15,000
Loss	$(5,000)	$ (4,000)

Since both result in a casualty loss, the losses are excluded from Section 1231 treatment and are treated as ordinary losses. The gain on the sale of the land would be treated as a Section 1231 long-term capital gain.

Self-Study Problem 8.8

Form **4797** Department of the Treasury Internal Revenue Service

Sales of Business Property
(Also Involuntary Conversions and Recapture Amounts Under Sections 179 and 280F(b)(2))
Attach to your tax return.
Go to *www.irs.gov/Form4797* for instructions and the latest information.

OMB No. 1545-0184 | 2022 | Attachment Sequence No. **27**

Name(s) shown on return: Serena | **Identifying number**: 74-8976432

1a	Enter the gross proceeds from sales or exchanges reported to you for 2022 on Form(s) 1099-B or 1099-S (or substitute statement) that you are including on line 2, 10, or 20. See instructions	1a	
b	Enter the total amount of gain that you are including on lines 2, 10, and 24 due to the partial dispositions of MACRS assets	1b	
c	Enter the total amount of loss that you are including on lines 2 and 10 due to the partial dispositions of MACRS assets	1c	

Part I Sales or Exchanges of Property Used in a Trade or Business and Involuntary Conversions From Other Than Casualty or Theft—Most Property Held More Than 1 Year (see instructions)

2 (a) Description of property	(b) Date acquired (mo., day, yr.)	(c) Date sold (mo., day, yr.)	(d) Gross sales price	(e) Depreciation allowed or allowable since acquisition	(f) Cost or other basis, plus improvements and expense of sale	(g) Gain or (loss) Subtract (f) from the sum of (d) and (e)
Land	12/03/2010	01/05/2022	37,000	0	24,500	12,500
Computer	04/05/2020	05/02/2022	14,000	33,206	53,906	(6,700)

3	Gain, if any, from Form 4684, line 39	3	
4	Section 1231 gain from installment sales from Form 6252, line 26 or 37	4	
5	Section 1231 gain or (loss) from like-kind exchanges from Form 8824	5	
6	Gain, if any, from line 32, from other than casualty or theft	6	146,050
7	Combine lines 2 through 6. Enter the gain or (loss) here and on the appropriate line as follows	7	151,850

Partnerships and S corporations. Report the gain or (loss) following the instructions for Form 1065, Schedule K, line 10, or Form 1120-S, Schedule K, line 9. Skip lines 8, 9, 11, and 12 below.

Individuals, partners, S corporation shareholders, and all others. If line 7 is zero or a loss, enter the amount from line 7 on line 11 below and skip lines 8 and 9. If line 7 is a gain and you didn't have any prior year section 1231 losses, or they were recaptured in an earlier year, enter the gain from line 7 as a long-term capital gain on the Schedule D filed with your return and skip lines 8, 9, 11, and 12 below.

8	Nonrecaptured net section 1231 losses from prior years. See instructions	8	
9	Subtract line 8 from line 7. If zero or less, enter -0-. If line 9 is zero, enter the gain from line 7 on line 12 below. If line 9 is more than zero, enter the amount from line 8 on line 12 below and enter the gain from line 9 as a long-term capital gain on the Schedule D filed with your return. See instructions	9	

Part II Ordinary Gains and Losses (see instructions)

10 Ordinary gains and losses not included on lines 11 through 16 (include property held 1 year or less):

(a)	(b)	(c)	(d)	(e)	(f)	(g)
Equipment	10/21/2021	07/22/2022	16,000	7,477	29,777	(6,300)

11	Loss, if any, from line 7	11	( )
12	Gain, if any, from line 7 or amount from line 8, if applicable	12	
13	Gain, if any, from line 31	13	7,600
14	Net gain or (loss) from Form 4684, lines 31 and 38a	14	
15	Ordinary gain from installment sales from Form 6252, line 25 or 36	15	
16	Ordinary gain or (loss) from like-kind exchanges from Form 8824	16	
17	Combine lines 10 through 16	17	1,300
18	For all except individual returns, enter the amount from line 17 on the appropriate line of your return and skip lines a and b below. For individual returns, complete lines a and b below.		
a	If the loss on line 11 includes a loss from Form 4684, line 35, column (b)(ii), enter that part of the loss here. Enter the loss from income-producing property on Schedule A (Form 1040), line 16. (Do not include any loss on property used as an employee.) Identify as from "Form 4797, line 18a." See instructions	18a	
b	Redetermine the gain or (loss) on line 17 excluding the loss, if any, on line 18a. Enter here and on Schedule 1 (Form 1040), Part I, line 4	18b	1,300

Self-Study Problem 8.8

Form 4797 (2022) Page **2**

Part III Gain From Disposition of Property Under Sections 1245, 1250, 1252, 1254, and 1255 (see instructions)

19	(a) Description of section 1245, 1250, 1252, 1254, or 1255 property:	(b) Date acquired (mo., day, yr.)	(c) Date sold (mo., day, yr.)
A	Building	12/03/2010	10/07/2022
B	Furniture	12/03/2010	10/07/2022
C			
D			

	These columns relate to the properties on lines 19A through 19D.		Property A	Property B	Property C	Property D
20	Gross sales price (**Note:** *See line 1a before completing.*)	20	355,000	7,600		
21	Cost or other basis plus expense of sale	21	335,000	15,000		
22	Depreciation (or depletion) allowed or allowable	22	126,050	15,000		
23	Adjusted basis. Subtract line 22 from line 21	23	208,950	0		
24	Total gain. Subtract line 23 from line 20	24	146,050	7,600		
25	**If section 1245 property:**					
a	Depreciation allowed or allowable from line 22	25a		15,000		
b	Enter the **smaller** of line 24 or 25a	25b		7,600		
26	**If section 1250 property:** If straight line depreciation was used, enter -0- on line 26g, except for a corporation subject to section 291.					
a	Additional depreciation after 1975. See instructions	26a				
b	Applicable percentage multiplied by the **smaller** of line 24 or line 26a. See instructions	26b				
c	Subtract line 26a from line 24. If residential rental property **or** line 24 isn't more than line 26a, skip lines 26d and 26e	26c				
d	Additional depreciation after 1969 and before 1976	26d				
e	Enter the **smaller** of line 26c or 26d	26e				
f	Section 291 amount (corporations only)	26f				
g	Add lines 26b, 26e, and 26f	26g	0			
27	**If section 1252 property:** Skip this section if you didn't dispose of farmland or if this form is being completed for a partnership.					
a	Soil, water, and land clearing expenses	27a				
b	Line 27a multiplied by applicable percentage. See instructions	27b				
c	Enter the **smaller** of line 24 or 27b	27c				
28	**If section 1254 property:**					
a	Intangible drilling and development costs, expenditures for development of mines and other natural deposits, mining exploration costs, and depletion. See instructions	28a				
b	Enter the **smaller** of line 24 or 28a	28b				
29	**If section 1255 property:**					
a	Applicable percentage of payments excluded from income under section 126. See instructions	29a				
b	Enter the **smaller** of line 24 or 29a. See instructions	29b				

Summary of Part III Gains. Complete property columns A through D through line 29b before going to line 30.

30	Total gains for all properties. Add property columns A through D, line 24	30	153,650
31	Add property columns A through D, lines 25b, 26g, 27c, 28b, and 29b. Enter here and on line 13	31	7,600
32	Subtract line 31 from line 30. Enter the portion from casualty or theft on Form 4684, line 33. Enter the portion from other than casualty or theft on Form 4797, line 6	32	146,050

Part IV Recapture Amounts Under Sections 179 and 280F(b)(2) When Business Use Drops to 50% or Less (see instructions)

			(a) Section 179	(b) Section 280F(b)(2)
33	Section 179 expense deduction or depreciation allowable in prior years	33		
34	Recomputed depreciation. See instructions	34		
35	Recapture amount. Subtract line 34 from line 33. See the instructions for where to report	35		

Form **4797** (2022)

Self-Study Problem 8.10

See Form 6252 on Page E-57.

Self-Study Problem 8.11

See Form 8824 on Pages E-58 and E-59.

Self-Study Problem 8.12

1. Insurance proceeds	$150,000
Less: the adjusted basis of the property	(70,000)
Gain realized	$ 80,000
Insurance proceeds	$150,000
Less: the cost of the replacement store	(135,000)
Proceeds not reinvested	$ 15,000
Gain recognized (the lesser of the gain realized or the proceeds not reinvested)	$ 15,000
2. Cost of the new store	$135,000
Less: the gain deferred ($80,000 – $15,000)	(65,000)
Basis of the new store	$ 70,000

Self-Study Problem 8.10

Form **6252** — Department of the Treasury, Internal Revenue Service

Installment Sale Income

Attach to your tax return.
Use a separate form for each sale or other disposition of property on the installment method.
Go to *www.irs.gov/Form6252* for the latest information.

OMB No. 1545-0228 — 2022 — Attachment Sequence No. 67

Name(s) shown on return: Brian — **Identifying number**

1 Description of property: Rental House
2a Date acquired (mm/dd/yyyy): 01/01/2006 **b** Date sold (mm/dd/yyyy): 1/15/2022
3 Was the property sold to a related party? See instructions. If "Yes," complete Part III for the year of sale and 2 years after the year of the sale unless you received the final payment during the tax year. If "No," skip line 4 ☐ Yes ☑ No
4 Did you sell the property to an intermediary? If "Yes," provide the name and address of the intermediary on line 27 ☐ Yes ☑ No

Part I — Gross Profit and Contract Price. Complete this part for all years of the installment agreement.

5	Selling price including mortgages and other debts. **Don't** include interest, whether stated or unstated			5	120,000
6	Mortgages, debts, and other liabilities the buyer assumed or took the property subject to (see instructions)	6	12,000		
7	Subtract line 6 from line 5	7	108,000		
8	Cost or other basis of property sold	8	80,000		
9	Depreciation allowed or allowable	9	26,000		
10	Adjusted basis. Subtract line 9 from line 8	10	54,000		
11	Commissions and other expenses of sale	11			
12	Income recapture from Form 4797, Part III (see instructions)	12			
13	Add lines 10, 11, and 12			13	54,000
14	Subtract line 13 from line 5. If zero or less, **don't** complete the rest of this form. See instructions			14	66,000
15	If the property described on line 1 above was your main home, enter the amount of your excluded gain. See instructions. Otherwise, enter -0-			15	
16	**Gross profit.** Subtract line 15 from line 14			16	66,000
17	Subtract line 13 from line 6. If zero or less, enter -0-			17	0
18	**Contract price.** Add line 7 and line 17			18	108,000

Part II — Installment Sale Income. Complete this part for all years of the installment agreement.

19	Gross profit percentage (expressed as a decimal amount). Divide line 16 by line 18. (For years after the year of sale, see instructions.)			19	61.111
20	If this is the year of sale, enter the amount from line 17. Otherwise, enter -0-			20	0
21	Payments received during year (see instructions). **Don't** include interest, whether stated or unstated			21	8,000
22	Add lines 20 and 21			22	8,000
23	Payments received in prior years (see instructions). **Don't** include interest, whether stated or unstated	23			
24	**Installment sale income.** Multiply line 22 by line 19			24	4,889
25	Enter the part of line 24 that is ordinary income under the recapture rules. See instructions			25	0
26	Subtract line 25 from line 24. Enter here and on Schedule D or Form 4797. See instructions			26	4,889

Part III — Related Party Installment Sale Income. Don't complete if you received the final payment this tax year.

27 Name, address, and taxpayer identifying number of related party
28 Did the related party resell or dispose of the property ("second disposition") during this tax year? ☐ Yes ☐ No
29 **If the answer to question 28 is "Yes," complete lines 30 through 37 below unless one of the following conditions is met. Check the box that applies.**
a ☐ The second disposition was more than 2 years after the first disposition (other than dispositions of marketable securities). If this box is checked, enter the date of disposition (mm/dd/yyyy)
b ☐ The first disposition was a sale or exchange of stock to the issuing corporation.
c ☐ The second disposition was an involuntary conversion and the threat of conversion occurred after the first disposition.
d ☐ The second disposition occurred after the death of the original seller or buyer.
e ☐ It can be established to the satisfaction of the IRS that tax avoidance wasn't a principal purpose for either of the dispositions. If this box is checked, attach an explanation. See instructions.

30	Selling price of property sold by related party (see instructions)	30	
31	Enter contract price from line 18 for year of first sale	31	
32	Enter the **smaller** of line 30 or line 31	32	
33	Total payments received by the end of your 2022 tax year (see instructions)	33	
34	Subtract line 33 from line 32. If zero or less, enter -0-	34	
35	Multiply line 34 by the gross profit percentage on line 19 for year of first sale	35	
36	Enter the part of line 35 that is ordinary income under the recapture rules. See instructions	36	
37	Subtract line 36 from line 35. Enter here and on Schedule D or Form 4797. See instructions	37	

For Paperwork Reduction Act Notice, see page 4. Cat. No. 13601R Form **6252** (2022)

Self-Study Problem 8.11

Form **8824**
Department of the Treasury
Internal Revenue Service

Like-Kind Exchanges
(and section 1043 conflict-of-interest sales)
Attach to your tax return.
Go to *www.irs.gov/Form8824* for instructions and the latest information.

OMB No. 1545-1190
2022
Attachment Sequence No. **109**

Name(s) shown on tax return: Daniel James
Identifying number

Part I Information on the Like-Kind Exchange

Note: Only real property should be described on lines 1 and 2. If the property described on line 1 or line 2 is real property located outside the United States, indicate the country.

1 Description of like-kind property given up:
Land

2 Description of like-kind property received:
Land

3	Date like-kind property given up was originally acquired (month, day, year)	3	02/14/2015
4	Date you actually transferred your property to the other party (month, day, year)	4	05/12/2022
5	Date like-kind property you received was identified by written notice to another party (month, day, year). See instructions for 45-day written identification requirement	5	05/12/2022
6	Date you actually received the like-kind property from other party (month, day, year). See instructions	6	05/12/2022

7 Was the exchange of the property given up or received made with a related party, either directly or indirectly (such as through an intermediary)? See instructions. If "Yes," complete Part II. If "No," go to Part III . . . ☐ **Yes** ☑ **No**

Note: Do not file this form if a related party sold property into the exchange, directly or indirectly (such as through an intermediary); that property became your replacement property; and none of the exceptions on line 11 applies to the exchange. Instead, report the disposition of the property as if the exchange had been a sale. If one of the exceptions on line 11 applies to the exchange, complete Part II.

Part II Related Party Exchange Information

8 Name of related party	Relationship to you	Related party's identifying number

Address (no., street, and apt., room, or suite no.; city or town; state; and ZIP code)

9 During this tax year (and before the date that is 2 years after the last transfer of property that was part of the exchange), did the related party sell or dispose of any part of the like-kind property received from you (or an intermediary) in the exchange? ☐ **Yes** ☐ **No**

10 During this tax year (and before the date that is 2 years after the last transfer of property that was part of the exchange), did you sell or dispose of any part of the like-kind property you received? ☐ **Yes** ☐ **No**

*If both lines 9 and 10 are "No" and this is the year of the exchange, go to Part III. If both lines 9 and 10 are "No" and this is **not** the year of the exchange, stop here. If either line 9 or line 10 is "Yes," complete Part III and report on this year's tax return the deferred gain or (loss) from line 24 **unless** one of the exceptions on line 11 applies.*

11 If one of the exceptions below applies to the disposition, check the applicable box.

a ☐ The disposition was after the death of either of the related parties.

b ☐ The disposition was an involuntary conversion, and the threat of conversion occurred after the exchange.

c ☐ You can establish to the satisfaction of the IRS that neither the exchange nor the disposition had tax avoidance as one of its principal purposes. If this box is checked, attach an explanation. See instructions.

Self-Study Problem 8.11

Form 8824 (2022) Page **2**

Name(s) shown on tax return. Do not enter name and social security number if shown on other side. | **Your social security number**

Part III Realized Gain or (Loss), Recognized Gain, and Basis of Like-Kind Property Received

Caution: If you transferred **and** received (**a**) more than one group of like-kind properties, or (**b**) cash or other (not like-kind) property, see ***Reporting of multi-asset exchanges*** in the instructions.

Note: Complete lines 12 through 14 **only** if you gave up property that was not like-kind. Otherwise, go to line 15.

12	Fair market value (FMV) of other property given up. See instructions . . . **12**		
13	Adjusted basis of other property given up **13**		
14	Gain or (loss) recognized on other property given up. Subtract line 13 from line 12. Report the gain or (loss) in the same manner as if the exchange had been a sale	14	
	Caution: If the property given up was used previously or partly as a home, see ***Property used as home*** in the instructions.		
15	Cash received, FMV of other property received, plus net liabilities assumed by other party, reduced (but not below zero) by any exchange expenses you incurred. See instructions	15	8,000
16	FMV of like-kind property you received	16	22,000
17	Add lines 15 and 16	17	30,000
18	Adjusted basis of like-kind property you gave up, net amounts paid to other party, plus any exchange expenses **not** used on line 15. See instructions	18	18,000
19	**Realized gain or (loss).** Subtract line 18 from line 17	19	12,000
20	Enter the smaller of line 15 or line 19, but not less than zero	20	8,000
21	Ordinary income under recapture rules. Enter here and on Form 4797, line 16. See instructions . .	21	
22	Subtract line 21 from line 20. If zero or less, enter -0-. If more than zero, enter here and on Schedule D or Form 4797, unless the installment method applies. See instructions	22	8,000
23	**Recognized gain.** Add lines 21 and 22	23	8,000
24	Deferred gain or (loss). Subtract line 23 from line 19. If a related party exchange, see instructions . .	24	4,000
25	**Basis of like-kind property received.** Subtract line 15 from the sum of lines 18 and 23. See instructions	25	18,000

Part IV Deferral of Gain From Section 1043 Conflict-of-Interest Sales

Note: This part is to be used **only** by officers or employees of the executive branch of the federal government or judicial officers of the federal government (including certain spouses, minor or dependent children, and trustees as described in section 1043) for reporting nonrecognition of gain under section 1043 on the sale of property to comply with the conflict-of-interest requirements. This part can be used **only** if the cost of the replacement property is more than the basis of the divested property.

26	Enter the number from the upper right corner of your certificate of divestiture. (**Do not** attach a copy of your certificate. Keep the certificate with your records.)		–
27	Description of divested property		
28	Description of replacement property		
29	Date divested property was sold (month, day, year)	29	MM/DD/YYYY
30	Sales price of divested property. See instructions **30**		
31	Basis of divested property **31**		
32	**Realized gain.** Subtract line 31 from line 30	32	
33	Cost of replacement property purchased within 60 days after date of sale . **33**		
34	Subtract line 33 from line 30. If zero or less, enter -0-	34	
35	Ordinary income under recapture rules. Enter here and on Form 4797, line 10. See instructions . .	35	
36	Subtract line 35 from line 34. If zero or less, enter -0-. If more than zero, enter here and on Schedule D or Form 4797. See instructions	36	
37	**Deferred gain.** Subtract the sum of lines 35 and 36 from line 32	37	
38	**Basis of replacement property.** Subtract line 37 from line 33	38	

Form **8824** (2022)

CHAPTER 9 EMPLOYMENT TAXES, ESTIMATED PAYMENTS, AND RETIREMENT PLANS

Self-Study Problem 9.1

1. See Form W-4 on Pages E-61 and E-62.
2. a. Percentage Method: $30.47. See Worksheet 4 on Page E-63.
   b. Wage Bracket Method: $29.83. See Worksheet 2 on Page E-64.

Self-Study Problem 9.2

1. a. Employee's portion: Social Security tax $9,052.00 [$150,000 – ($151,000 – $147,000)] × 6.2%. Note that Juliette's year-to-date pay exceeds the 2022 FICA cap of $147,000.
   b. Employer's portion: Social Security tax $9,052.00 [$150,000 – ($151,000 – $147,000)] × 6.2%
   c. Employee's portion: Medicare tax $2,175.00 ($150,000 × 1.45%)
   d. Employer's portion: Medicare tax $2,175.00 ($150,000 × 1.45%)

Self-Study Problem 9.3

a. The required annual payment is $21,000. See 2022 Estimated Tax Worksheet on Page E-65.
b. See Form 1040-ES voucher on Page E-66.
c. $5,023. Since Ray's prior year AGI exceeds $150,000, the annual required payment is the lesser of 90% of the current year or 110% of the prior year. 110% of the prior year tax of $21,000 is $23,100. 90% of his current year tax is $21,991, as calculated in part a. Thus Ray's annual required payment is $21,991. One-quarter of the required payment less the $475 prior year overpayment is $5,023.

Self-Study Problem 9.4

See pages 1 and 2 of Form 941 on Pages E-67 and E-68.

Self-Study Problem 9.1, part 1

Form **W-4**

Department of the Treasury
Internal Revenue Service

Employee's Withholding Certificate

► Complete Form W-4 so that your employer can withhold the correct federal income tax from your pay.
► Give Form W-4 to your employer.
► Your withholding is subject to review by the IRS.

OMB No. 1545-0074

2022

Step 1: Enter Personal Information

(a) First name and middle initial: Lillian
Last name: Miles
(b) Social security number

Address: 456 Peachtree Court

City or town, state, and ZIP code: Atlanta, GA 30310

► **Does your name match the name on your social security card?** If not, to ensure you get credit for your earnings, contact SSA at 800-772-1213 or go to *www.ssa.gov.*

(c) ☐ **Single** or **Married filing separately**
☑ **Married filing jointly** or **Qualifying widow(er)**
☐ **Head of household** (Check only if you're unmarried and pay more than half the costs of keeping up a home for yourself and a qualifying individual.)

Complete Steps 2–4 ONLY if they apply to you; otherwise, skip to Step 5. See page 2 for more information on each step, who can claim exemption from withholding, when to use the estimator at *www.irs.gov/W4App*, and privacy.

Step 2: Multiple Jobs or Spouse Works

Complete this step if you (1) hold more than one job at a time, or (2) are married filing jointly and your spouse also works. The correct amount of withholding depends on income earned from all of these jobs.

Do **only one** of the following.

(a) Use the estimator at *www.irs.gov/W4App* for most accurate withholding for this step (and Steps 3–4); **or**

(b) Use the Multiple Jobs Worksheet on page 3 and enter the result in Step 4(c) below for roughly accurate withholding; **or**

(c) If there are only two jobs total, you may check this box. Do the same on Form W-4 for the other job. This option is accurate for jobs with similar pay; otherwise, more tax than necessary may be withheld . . ► ☑

TIP: To be accurate, submit a 2022 Form W-4 for all other jobs. If you (or your spouse) have self-employment income, including as an independent contractor, use the estimator.

Complete Steps 3–4(b) on Form W-4 for only ONE of these jobs. Leave those steps blank for the other jobs. (Your withholding will be most accurate if you complete Steps 3–4(b) on the Form W-4 for the highest paying job.)

Step 3: Claim Dependents

If your total income will be $200,000 or less ($400,000 or less if married filing jointly):

Multiply the number of qualifying children under age 17 by $2,000 ► $ 2,000

Multiply the number of other dependents by $500 . . . . ► $ 500

Add the amounts above and enter the total here . . . . **3** $ 2,500

Step 4 (optional): Other Adjustments

(a) Other income (not from jobs). If you want tax withheld for other income you expect this year that won't have withholding, enter the amount of other income here. This may include interest, dividends, and retirement income . . . . **4(a)** $ 6,500

(b) Deductions. If you expect to claim deductions other than the standard deduction and want to reduce your withholding, use the Deductions Worksheet on page 3 and enter the result here . . . . **4(b)** $ 5,300

(c) Extra withholding. Enter any additional tax you want withheld each **pay period** . . **4(c)** $

Step 5: Sign Here

Under penalties of perjury, I declare that this certificate, to the best of my knowledge and belief, is true, correct, and complete.

► **Employee's signature** (This form is not valid unless you sign it.) ► **Date**

Employers Only

Employer's name and address	First date of employment	Employer identification number (EIN)

For Privacy Act and Paperwork Reduction Act Notice, see page 3. Cat. No. 10220Q Form **W-4** (2022)

Self-Study Problem 9.1, part 1

Note: Lillian will not complete the Multiple Jobs Worksheet because her wages and John's wages are similar. Instead, she will check the box at Step 2(c) on page 1 of the Form W-4.

Form W-4 (2022) Page **3**

Step 2(b)—Multiple Jobs Worksheet *(Keep for your records.)*

If you choose the option in Step 2(b) on Form W-4, complete this worksheet (which calculates the total extra tax for all jobs) on **only ONE** Form W-4. Withholding will be most accurate if you complete the worksheet and enter the result on the Form W-4 for the highest paying job.

Note: If more than one job has annual wages of more than $120,000 or there are more than three jobs, see Pub. 505 for additional tables; or, you can use the online withholding estimator at *www.irs.gov/W4App*.

1	**Two jobs.** If you have two jobs or you're married filing jointly and you and your spouse each have one job, find the amount from the appropriate table on page 4. Using the "Higher Paying Job" row and the "Lower Paying Job" column, find the value at the intersection of the two household salaries and enter that value on line 1. Then, **skip** to line 3	**1**	$
2	**Three jobs.** If you and/or your spouse have three jobs at the same time, complete lines 2a, 2b, and 2c below. Otherwise, skip to line 3.		
	a Find the amount from the appropriate table on page 4 using the annual wages from the highest paying job in the "Higher Paying Job" row and the annual wages for your next highest paying job in the "Lower Paying Job" column. Find the value at the intersection of the two household salaries and enter that value on line 2a	**2a**	$
	b Add the annual wages of the two highest paying jobs from line 2a together and use the total as the wages in the "Higher Paying Job" row and use the annual wages for your third job in the "Lower Paying Job" column to find the amount from the appropriate table on page 4 and enter this amount on line 2b	**2b**	$
	c Add the amounts from lines 2a and 2b and enter the result on line 2c	**2c**	$
3	Enter the number of pay periods per year for the highest paying job. For example, if that job pays weekly, enter 52; if it pays every other week, enter 26; if it pays monthly, enter 12, etc.	**3**	
4	**Divide** the annual amount on line 1 or line 2c by the number of pay periods on line 3. Enter this amount here and in **Step 4(c)** of Form W-4 for the highest paying job (along with any other additional amount you want withheld)	**4**	$

Step 4(b)—Deductions Worksheet *(Keep for your records.)*

1	Enter an estimate of your 2022 itemized deductions (from Schedule A (Form 1040)). Such deductions may include qualifying home mortgage interest, charitable contributions, state and local taxes (up to $10,000), and medical expenses in excess of 7.5% of your income	**1**	$
2	Enter: • $25,900 if you're married filing jointly or qualifying widow(er) • $19,400 if you're head of household • $12,950 if you're single or married filing separately	**2**	$
3	If line 1 is greater than line 2, subtract line 2 from line 1 and enter the result here. If line 2 is greater than line 1, enter "-0-"	**3**	$
4	Enter an estimate of your student loan interest, deductible IRA contributions, and certain other adjustments (from Part II of Schedule 1 (Form 1040)). See Pub. 505 for more information	**4**	$ 5,300 (a)
5	**Add** lines 3 and 4. Enter the result here and in **Step 4(b)** of Form W-4	**5**	$ 5,300

Privacy Act and Paperwork Reduction Act Notice. We ask for the information on this form to carry out the Internal Revenue laws of the United States. Internal Revenue Code sections 3402(f)(2) and 6109 and their regulations require you to provide this information; your employer uses it to determine your federal income tax withholding. Failure to provide a properly completed form will result in your being treated as a single person with no other entries on the form; providing fraudulent information may subject you to penalties. Routine uses of this information include giving it to the Department of Justice for civil and criminal litigation; to cities, states, the District of Columbia, and U.S. commonwealths and possessions for use in administering their tax laws; and to the Department of Health and Human Services for use in the National Directory of New Hires. We may also disclose this information to other countries under a tax treaty, to federal and state agencies to enforce federal nontax criminal laws, or to federal law enforcement and intelligence agencies to combat terrorism.

You are not required to provide the information requested on a form that is subject to the Paperwork Reduction Act unless the form displays a valid OMB control number. Books or records relating to a form or its instructions must be retained as long as their contents may become material in the administration of any Internal Revenue law. Generally, tax returns and return information are confidential, as required by Code section 6103.

The average time and expenses required to complete and file this form will vary depending on individual circumstances. For estimated averages, see the instructions for your income tax return.

If you have suggestions for making this form simpler, we would be happy to hear from you. See the instructions for your income tax return.

(a) $4,000 IRA deduction + $1,300 ($6,500 × 20%) QBI deduction

Self-Study Problem 9.1, part 2 a.

4. Percentage Method Tables for Manual Payroll Systems With Forms W-4 From 2020 or Later

If you compute payroll manually, your employee has submitted a Form W-4 for 2020 or later, and you prefer to use the Percentage Method or you can't use the Wage Bracket Method tables because the employee's annual wages exceed the amount from the last bracket of the table (based on marital status and pay period), use the worksheet below and the Percentage Method tables that follow to figure federal income tax withholding. This method works for any amount of wages.

Worksheet 4. Employer's Withholding Worksheet for Percentage Method Tables for Manual Payroll Systems With Forms W-4 From 2020 or Later

Keep for Your Records 

Table 6	Monthly	Semimonthly	Biweekly	Weekly	Daily
	12	24	26	52	260

Step 1. Adjust the employee's wage amount

1a	Enter the employee's total taxable wages this payroll period	1a	$ 1,683.33
1b	Enter the number of pay periods you have per year (see Table 6)	1b	24
1c	Enter the amount from Step 4(a) of the employee's Form W-4	1c	$ 6,500.00
1d	Divide line 1c by the number on line 1b	1d	$ 270.83
1e	Add lines 1a and 1d	1e	$ 1,954.16
1f	Enter the amount from Step 4(b) of the employee's Form W-4	1f	$ 5,300.00
1g	Divide line 1f by the number on line 1b	1g	$ 220.83
1h	Subtract line 1g from line 1e. If zero or less, enter -0-. This is the **Adjusted Wage Amount**	1h	$ 1,733.33

Step 2. Figure the Tentative Withholding Amount

based on your pay frequency, the employee's Adjusted Wage Amount, filing status (Step 1(c) of Form W-4), and whether the box in Step 2 of Form W-4 is checked.

2a	Find the row in the STANDARD Withholding Rate Schedules (if the box in Step 2 of Form W-4 is NOT checked) or the Form W-4, Step 2, Checkbox, Withholding Rate Schedules (if it HAS been checked) of the Percentage Method tables in this section in which the amount on line 1h is at least the amount in column A but less than the amount in column B, and then enter here the amount from column A of that row	2a	$ 968.00
2b	Enter the amount from column C of that row	2b	$ 42.80
2c	Enter the percentage from column D of that row	2c	12%
2d	Subtract line 2a from line 1h	2d	$ 765.33
2e	Multiply the amount on line 2d by the percentage on line 2c	2e	$ 91.84
2f	Add lines 2b and 2e. This is the **Tentative Withholding Amount**	2f	$ 134.64

Step 3. Account for tax credits

3a	Enter the amount from Step 3 of the employee's Form W-4	3a	$ 2,500.00
3b	Divide the amount on line 3a by the number of pay periods on line 1b	3b	$ 104.17
3c	Subtract line 3b from line 2f. If zero or less, enter -0-	3c	$ 30.47

Step 4. Figure the final amount to withhold

4a	Enter the additional amount to withhold from Step 4(c) of the employee's Form W-4	4a	$ 0.00
4b	Add lines 3c and 4a. **This is the amount to withhold from the employee's wages this pay period**	4b	$ 30.47

Self-Study Problem 9.1, part 2 b.

2. Wage Bracket Method Tables for Manual Payroll Systems With Forms W-4 From 2020 or Later

If you compute payroll manually, your employee has submitted a Form W-4 for 2020 or later, and you prefer to use the Wage Bracket method, use the worksheet below and the Wage Bracket Method tables that follow to figure federal income tax withholding.

These Wage Bracket Method tables cover a limited amount of annual wages (generally, less than $100,000). If you can't use the Wage Bracket Method tables because taxable wages exceed the amount from the last bracket of the table (based on filing status and pay period), use the Percentage Method tables in section 4.

Worksheet 2. Employer's Withholding Worksheet for Wage Bracket Method Tables for Manual Payroll Systems With Forms W-4 From 2020 or Later

Keep for Your Records 

Table 5	Monthly	Semimonthly	Biweekly	Weekly	Daily
	12	24	26	52	260

Step 1. Adjust the employee's wage amount

1a	Enter the employee's total taxable wages this payroll period	1a	$ 1,683.33
1b	Enter the number of pay periods you have per year (see Table 5)	1b	24
1c	Enter the amount from Step 4(a) of the employee's Form W-4	1c	$ 6,500.00
1d	Divide the amount on line 1c by the number of pay periods on line 1b	1d	$ 270.83
1e	Add lines 1a and 1d	1e	$ 1,954.16
1f	Enter the amount from Step 4(b) of the employee's Form W-4	1f	$ 5,300.00
1g	Divide the amount on line 1f by the number of pay periods on line 1b	1g	$ 220.83
1h	Subtract line 1g from line 1e. If zero or less, enter -0-. This is the **Adjusted Wage Amount**	1h	$ 1,733.33

Step 2. Figure the Tentative Withholding Amount

2a	Use the amount on line 1h to look up the tentative amount to withhold in the appropriate Wage Bracket Method table in this section for your pay frequency, given the employee's filing status and whether the employee has checked the box in Step 2 of Form W-4. This is the **Tentative Withholding Amount**	2a	$ 134.00

Step 3. Account for tax credits

3a	Enter the amount from Step 3 of the employee's Form W-4	3a	$ 2,500.00
3b	Divide the amount on line 3a by the number of pay periods on line 1b	3b	$ 104.17
3c	Subtract line 3b from line 2a. If zero or less, enter -0-	3c	$ 29.83

Step 4. Figure the final amount to withhold

4a	Enter the additional amount to withhold from Step 4(c) of the employee's Form W-4	4a	$ 0.00
4b	Add lines 3c and 4a. **This is the amount to withhold from the employee's wages this pay period**	4b	$ 29.83

Self-Study Problem 9.3, part a

2022 Estimated Tax Worksheet

Keep for Your Records

1	Adjusted gross income you expect in 2022 (see instructions)			1	94,794
2a	Deductions • If you plan to itemize deductions, enter the estimated total of your itemized deductions. • If you don't plan to itemize deductions, enter your standard deduction.			2a	12,950
b	If you can take the qualified business income deduction, enter the estimated amount of the deduction			2b	16,369
c	Add lines 2a and 2b ▶			2c	29,319
3	Subtract line 2c from line 1			3	65,475
4	**Tax.** Figure your tax on the amount on line 3 by using the **2022 Tax Rate Schedules.** **Caution:** *If you will have qualified dividends or a net capital gain, or expect to exclude or deduct foreign earned income or housing, see Worksheets 2-5 and 2-6 in Pub. 505 to figure the tax.*			4	10,022
5	Alternative minimum tax from **Form 6251**			5	0
6	Add lines 4 and 5. Add to this amount any other taxes you expect to include in the total on Form 1040 or 1040-SR, line 16			6	10,022
7	Credits (see instructions). **Do not** include any income tax withholding on this line			7	0
8	Subtract line 7 from line 6. If zero or less, enter -0-			8	10,022
9	Self-employment tax (see instructions)			9	14,412
10	Other taxes (see instructions)			10	0
11a	Add lines 8 through 10			11a	24,434
b	Earned income credit, refundable child tax credit* or additional child tax credit, fuel tax credit, net premium tax credit, refundable American opportunity credit, section 1341 credit, and refundable credit from Form 8885*			11b	0
c	**Total 2022 estimated tax.** Subtract line 11b from line 11a. If zero or less, enter -0- ▶			11c	24,434
12a	Multiply line 11c by 90% (66⅔% for farmers and fishermen)	12a	21,991		
b	Required annual payment based on prior year's tax (see instructions)	12b	21,000		
c	**Required annual payment to avoid a penalty.** Enter the **smaller** of line 12a or 12b ▶ **Caution:** *Generally, if you do not prepay (through income tax withholding and estimated tax payments) at least the amount on line 12c, you may owe a penalty for not paying enough estimated tax. To avoid a penalty, make sure your estimate on line 11c is as accurate as possible. Even if you pay the required annual payment, you may still owe tax when you file your return. If you prefer, you can pay the amount shown on line 11c. For details, see chapter 2 of Pub. 505.*			12c	21,000
13	Income tax withheld and estimated to be withheld during 2022 (including income tax withholding on pensions, annuities, certain deferred income, etc.)			13	0
14a	Subtract line 13 from line 12c Is the result zero or less? ☐ **Yes.** Stop here. You are not required to make estimated tax payments. ☑ **No.** Go to line 14b.	14a	21,000		
b	Subtract line 13 from line 11c Is the result less than $1,000? ☐ **Yes.** Stop here. You are not required to make estimated tax payments. ☑ **No.** Go to line 15 to figure your required payment.	14b	24,434		
15	If the first payment you are required to make is due April 18, 2022, enter ¼ of line 14a (minus any 2021 overpayment that you are applying to this installment) here, and on your estimated tax payment voucher(s) if you are paying by check or money order			15	5,250

* If applicable.

Self-Study Problem 9.3, part b

Form **1040-ES** Department of the Treasury Internal Revenue Service	**2022 Estimated Tax**	**Payment Voucher 1**	OMB No. 1545-0074

File only if you are making a payment of estimated tax by check or money order. Mail this voucher with your check or money order payable to **"United States Treasury."** Write your social security number and "2022 Form 1040-ES" on your check or money order. Do not send cash. Enclose, but do not staple or attach, your payment with this voucher.

Calendar year—Due April 18, 2022

Amount of estimated tax you are paying by check or money order. 4,775.00

Pay online at *www.irs.gov/etpay*

Simple. Fast. Secure.

Print or type

Your first name and middle initial	Your last name	Your social security number
Ray	Adams	321-45-9876
If joint payment, complete for spouse		
Spouse's first name and middle initial	Spouse's last name	Spouse's social security number
Address (number, street, and apt. no.) 1905 Hardin Valley Road		
City, town, or post office. If you have a foreign address, also complete spaces below. Knoxville	State TN	ZIP code 37932
Foreign country name	Foreign province/county	Foreign postal code

For Privacy Act and Paperwork Reduction Act Notice, see instructions. **Form 1040-ES (2022)**

Self-Study Problem 9.4

950122

Form **941 for 2022: Employer's QUARTERLY Federal Tax Return** OMB No. 1545-0029
(Rev. June 2022) Department of the Treasury — Internal Revenue Service

Employer identification number (EIN) 3 3 – 4 4 3 4 4 3 2

Name (not your trade name) Hills Scientific Corporation

Trade name (if any)

Address
Number Street Suite or room number
City State ZIP code
Foreign country name Foreign province/county Foreign postal code

Report for this Quarter of 2022
(Check one.)

- [ ] 1: January, February, March
- [X] 2: April, May, June
- [ ] 3: July, August, September
- [ ] 4: October, November, December

Go to *www.irs.gov/Form941* for instructions and the latest information.

Read the separate instructions before you complete Form 941. Type or print within the boxes.

Part 1: Answer these questions for this quarter.

1	**Number of employees who received wages, tips, or other compensation for the pay period including:** ***June 12*** **(Quarter 2),** ***Sept. 12*** **(Quarter 3), or** ***Dec. 12*** **(Quarter 4)**		1	6
2	**Wages, tips, and other compensation**		2	150,000 . 00
3	**Federal income tax withheld from wages, tips, and other compensation**		3	37,630 . 00
4	**If no wages, tips, and other compensation are subject to social security or Medicare tax**		☐	**Check and go to line 6.**

		Column 1		Column 2
5a	**Taxable social security wages***	146,000 . 00	× 0.124 =	18,104 . 00
5a	**(i) Qualified sick leave wages***	.	× 0.062 =	.
5a	**(ii) Qualified family leave wages***	.	× 0.062 =	.
5b	**Taxable social security tips**	.	× 0.124 =	.
5c	**Taxable Medicare wages & tips**	150,000 . 00	× 0.029 =	4,350 . 00
5d	**Taxable wages & tips subject to Additional Medicare Tax withholding**	.	× 0.009 =	.

Include taxable qualified sick and family leave wages paid in this quarter of 2022 for leave taken after March 31, 2021, and before October 1, 2021, on line 5a. Use lines 5a(i) and 5a(ii)* ***only* *for taxable qualified sick and family leave wages paid in this quarter of 2022 for leave taken after March 31, 2020, and before April 1, 2021.*

5e	**Total social security and Medicare taxes.** Add Column 2 from lines 5a, 5a(i), 5a(ii), 5b, 5c, and 5d	5e	22,454 . 00
5f	**Section 3121(q) Notice and Demand—Tax due on unreported tips** (see instructions)	5f	.
6	**Total taxes before adjustments.** Add lines 3, 5e, and 5f	6	60,084 . 00
7	**Current quarter's adjustment for fractions of cents**	7	.
8	**Current quarter's adjustment for sick pay**	8	.
9	**Current quarter's adjustments for tips and group-term life insurance**	9	.
10	**Total taxes after adjustments.** Combine lines 6 through 9	10	60,084 . 00
11a	**Qualified small business payroll tax credit for increasing research activities.** Attach Form 8974	11a	.
11b	**Nonrefundable portion of credit for qualified sick and family leave wages for leave taken before April 1, 2021**	11b	.
11c	**Reserved for future use**	11c	.

▶ **You MUST complete all three pages of Form 941 and SIGN it.** Next ▶

For Privacy Act and Paperwork Reduction Act Notice, see the back of the Payment Voucher. Cat. No. 17001Z Form **941** (Rev. 6-2022)

Self-Study Problem 9.4

951222

Name *(not your trade name)*: Hills Scientific Corporation

Employer identification number (EIN): 33 – 4434432

Part 1: Answer these questions for this quarter. *(continued)*

11d	**Nonrefundable portion of credit for qualified sick and family leave wages for leave taken after March 31, 2021, and before October 1, 2021**	11d	.
11e	**Reserved for future use**	11e	.
11f	**Reserved for future use**		
11g	**Total nonrefundable credits.** Add lines 11a, 11b, and 11d	11g	.
12	**Total taxes after adjustments and nonrefundable credits.** Subtract line 11g from line 10	12	60,084 . 00
13a	**Total deposits for this quarter, including overpayment applied from a prior quarter and overpayments applied from Form 941-X, 941-X (PR), 944-X, or 944-X (SP) filed in the current quarter**	13a	60,000 . 00
13b	**Reserved for future use**	13b	.
13c	**Refundable portion of credit for qualified sick and family leave wages for leave taken before April 1, 2021**	13c	.
13d	**Reserved for future use**	13d	.
13e	**Refundable portion of credit for qualified sick and family leave wages for leave taken after March 31, 2021, and before October 1, 2021**	13e	.
13f	**Reserved for future use**	13f	.
13g	**Total deposits and refundable credits.** Add lines 13a, 13c, and 13e	13g	60,000 . 00
13h	**Reserved for future use**	13h	.
13i	**Reserved for future use**	13i	.
14	**Balance due.** If line 12 is more than line 13g, enter the difference and see instructions	14	84 . 00

15 **Overpayment.** If line 13g is more than line 12, enter the difference [.] Check one: ☐ Apply to next return. ☐ Send a refund.

Part 2: Tell us about your deposit schedule and tax liability for this quarter.

If you're unsure about whether you're a monthly schedule depositor or a semiweekly schedule depositor, see section 11 of Pub. 15.

16 **Check one:**

☐ **Line 12 on this return is less than $2,500 or line 12 on the return for the prior quarter was less than $2,500, and you didn't incur a $100,000 next-day deposit obligation during the current quarter.** If line 12 for the prior quarter was less than $2,500 but line 12 on this return is $100,000 or more, you must provide a record of your federal tax liability. If you're a monthly schedule depositor, complete the deposit schedule below; if you're a semiweekly schedule depositor, attach Schedule B (Form 941). Go to Part 3.

☐ **You were a monthly schedule depositor for the entire quarter.** Enter your tax liability for each month and total liability for the quarter, then go to Part 3.

Tax liability:	**Month 1**	.
	Month 2	.
	Month 3	.
Total liability for quarter		. **Total must equal line 12.**

☐ **You were a semiweekly schedule depositor for any part of this quarter.** Complete Schedule B (Form 941), Report of Tax Liability for Semiweekly Schedule Depositors, and attach it to Form 941. Go to Part 3.

► **You MUST complete all three pages of Form 941 and SIGN it.** Next ►

Self-Study Problem 9.5

a.

	a Employee's social security number 398-22-4212	OMB No. 1545-0008	Safe, accurate, FAST! Use IRS e-file	Visit the IRS website at www.irs.gov/efile
b Employer identification number (EIN) 95-1234567			1 Wages, tips, other compensation 17,523.12	2 Federal income tax withheld 610.00
c Employer's name, address, and ZIP code David Flock PO Box 12344 Melbourne, FL 32901			3 Social security wages 17,523.12	4 Social security tax withheld 1,086.43
			5 Medicare wages and tips 17,523.12	6 Medicare tax withheld 254.09
			7 Social security tips	8 Allocated tips
d Control number			9	10 Dependent care benefits
e Employee's first name and initial Last name Suff. China Jones 2702 Carlson Circle, Apt 2K Melbourne, FL 32901			11 Nonqualified plans	12a See instructions for box 12
			13 Statutory employee ☐ Retirement plan ☐ Third-party sick pay ☐	12b
			14 Other	12c
f Employee's address and ZIP code				12d

15 State	Employer's state ID number	16 State wages, tips, etc.	17 State income tax	18 Local wages, tips, etc.	19 Local income tax	20 Locality name
FL						

Form **W-2** Wage and Tax Statement 2022 Department of the Treasury—Internal Revenue Service

Copy B—To Be Filed With Employee's FEDERAL Tax Return.
This information is being furnished to the Internal Revenue Service.

b.

DO NOT STAPLE

33333	a Control number	For Official Use Only ▶ OMB No. 1545-0008	
b Kind of Payer (Check one): 941 ☒ Military ☐ 943 ☐ 944 ☐ CT-1 ☐ Hshld. emp. ☐ Medicare govt. emp. ☐		Kind of Employer (Check one): None apply ☒ 501c non-govt. ☐ State/local non-501c ☐ State/local 501c ☐ Federal govt. ☐	Third-party sick pay (Check if applicable) ☐
c Total number of Forms W-2 2	d Establishment number	1 Wages, tips, other compensation 31,523.12	2 Federal income tax withheld 845.00
e Employer identification number (EIN) 95-1234567		3 Social security wages 31,523.12	4 Social security tax withheld 1,954.43
f Employer's name David Flock		5 Medicare wages and tips 31,523.12	6 Medicare tax withheld 457.09
PO Box 12344 Melbourne, FL 32901		7 Social security tips	8 Allocated tips
		9	10 Dependent care benefits
g Employer's address and ZIP code		11 Nonqualified plans	12a Deferred compensation
h Other EIN used this year		13 For third-party sick pay use only	12b
15 State FL	Employer's state ID number	14 Income tax withheld by payer of third-party sick pay	
16 State wages, tips, etc.	17 State income tax	18 Local wages, tips, etc.	19 Local income tax
Employer's contact person David Flock		Employer's telephone number 800-555-1212	For Official Use Only
Employer's fax number		Employer's email address	

Under penalties of perjury, I declare that I have examined this return and accompanying documents, and, to the best of my knowledge and belief, they are true, correct, and complete.

Signature ▶ Title ▶ Date ▶

Form **W-3** Transmittal of Wage and Tax Statements 2022 Department of the Treasury Internal Revenue Service

Self-Study Problem 9.5, part c

☐ CORRECTED (if checked)

PAYER'S name, street address, city or town, state or province, country, ZIP or foreign postal code, and telephone no. David Flock PO Box 12344 Melbourne, FL 32901	OMB No. 1545-0116 Form **1099-NEC** (Rev. January 2022) For calendar year 20 22	**Nonemployee Compensation**
PAYER'S TIN 95-1234567 — RECIPIENT'S TIN 566-29-9819	1 Nonemployee compensation $ 878.78	**Copy B** **For Recipient** This is important tax information and is being furnished to the IRS. If you are required to file a return, a negligence penalty or other sanction may be imposed on you if this income is taxable and the IRS determines that it has not been reported.
RECIPIENT'S name Cielle Harris	2 Payer made direct sales totaling $5,000 or more of consumer products to recipient for resale ☐	
Street address (including apt. no.) 224 Deland Ave.	3	
City or town, state or province, country, and ZIP or foreign postal code Indialantic, FL 32903	**4 Federal income tax withheld** $	
Account number (see instructions)	5 State tax withheld $ / $ — 6 State/Payer's state no.	7 State income $ / $

Form **1099-NEC** (Rev. 1-2022) (keep for your records) www.irs.gov/Form1099NEC Department of the Treasury - Internal Revenue Service

Self-Study Problem 9.6

See Form 940 on Pages E-71 and E-72.

Self-Study Problem 9.6

Form **940 for 2022: Employer's Annual Federal Unemployment (FUTA) Tax Return** 850113

Department of the Treasury — Internal Revenue Service OMB No. 1545-0028

Employer identification number (EIN) 9 4 – 0 0 0 1 1 1 2

Name *(not your trade name)* Anatolian Corporation

Trade name *(if any)*

Address 400 8th Street N

Number Street Suite or room number

La Crosse WI 54601

City State ZIP code

Foreign country name Foreign province/county Foreign postal code

Type of Return
(Check all that apply.)

☐ **a.** Amended

☐ **b.** Successor employer

☐ **c.** No payments to employees in 2022

☐ **d.** Final: Business closed or stopped paying wages

Go to *www.irs.gov/Form940* for instructions and the latest information.

Read the separate instructions before you complete this form. Please type or print within the boxes.

Part 1: Tell us about your return. If any line does NOT apply, leave it blank. See instructions before completing Part 1.

1a	If you had to pay state unemployment tax in one state only, enter the state abbreviation	1a	W I
1b	If you had to pay state unemployment tax in more than one state, you are a multi-state employer	1b	☐ Check here. Complete Schedule A (Form 940).
2	If you paid wages in a state that is subject to CREDIT REDUCTION	2	☐ Check here. Complete Schedule A (Form 940).

Part 2: Determine your FUTA tax before adjustments. If any line does NOT apply, leave it blank.

3	Total payments to all employees	3	318,040.00
4	Payments exempt from FUTA tax	4	.
	Check all that apply: 4a ☐ Fringe benefits; 4b ☐ Group-term life insurance; 4c ☐ Retirement/Pension; 4d ☐ Dependent care; 4e ☐ Other		
5	Total of payments made to each employee in excess of $7,000	5	234,690.00
6	Subtotal (line 4 + line 5 = line 6)	6	234,690.00
7	Total taxable FUTA wages (line 3 – line 6 = line 7). See instructions.	7	83,350.00
8	FUTA tax before adjustments (line 7 x 0.006 = line 8)	8	500.10

Part 3: Determine your adjustments. If any line does NOT apply, leave it blank.

9	If ALL of the taxable FUTA wages you paid were excluded from state unemployment tax, multiply line 7 by 0.054 (line 7 × 0.054 = line 9). Go to line 12	9	.
10	If SOME of the taxable FUTA wages you paid were excluded from state unemployment tax, OR you paid ANY state unemployment tax late (after the due date for filing Form 940), complete the worksheet in the instructions. Enter the amount from line 7 of the worksheet	10	.
11	If credit reduction applies, enter the total from Schedule A (Form 940)	11	.

Part 4: Determine your FUTA tax and balance due or overpayment. If any line does NOT apply, leave it blank.

12	Total FUTA tax after adjustments (lines 8 + 9 + 10 + 11 = line 12)	12	500.10
13	FUTA tax deposited for the year, including any overpayment applied from a prior year	13	0.00
14	Balance due. If line 12 is more than line 13, enter the excess on line 14. • If line 14 is more than $500, you must deposit your tax. • If line 14 is $500 or less, you may pay with this return. See instructions	14	500.10
15	Overpayment. If line 13 is more than line 12, enter the excess on line 15 and check a box below	15	.

You **MUST** complete both pages of this form and **SIGN** it. Check one: ☐ Apply to next return. ☐ Send a refund.

For Privacy Act and Paperwork Reduction Act Notice, see the back of the Payment Voucher. Cat. No. 11234O Form **940** (2022)

Self-Study Problem 9.6

850212

Name (not your trade name)	Employer identification number (EIN)
Anatolian Corporation	94 – 0001112

Part 5: Report your FUTA tax liability by quarter only if line 12 is more than $500. If not, go to Part 6.

16 Report the amount of your FUTA tax liability for each quarter; do NOT enter the amount you deposited. If you had no liability for a quarter, leave the line blank.

16a 1st quarter (January 1 – March 31)	**16a**	298 . 80
16b 2nd quarter (April 1 – June 30)	**16b**	135 . 00
16c 3rd quarter (July 1 – September 30)	**16c**	45 . 90
16d 4th quarter (October 1 – December 31)	**16d**	20 . 40
17 Total tax liability for the year (lines 16a + 16b + 16c + 16d = line 17)	**17**	500 . 10 **Total must equal line 12.**

Part 6: May we speak with your third-party designee?

Do you want to allow an employee, a paid tax preparer, or another person to discuss this return with the IRS? See the instructions for details.

☐ **Yes.** Designee's name and phone number

Select a 5-digit personal identification number (PIN) to use when talking to the IRS.

☐ **No.**

Part 7: Sign here. You MUST complete both pages of this form and SIGN it.

Under penalties of perjury, I declare that I have examined this return, including accompanying schedules and statements, and to the best of my knowledge and belief, it is true, correct, and complete, and that no part of any payment made to a state unemployment fund claimed as a credit was, or is to be, deducted from the payments made to employees. Declaration of preparer (other than taxpayer) is based on all information of which preparer has any knowledge.

Sign your name here

Print your name here

Print your title here

Date / /

Best daytime phone

Paid Preparer Use Only

Check if you are self-employed ☐

Preparer's name

PTIN

Preparer's signature

Date / /

Firm's name (or yours if self-employed)

EIN

Address

Phone

City

State

ZIP code

Self-Study Problem 9.7

a. $50,000, lesser of 100% × $50,000 or $61,000 (annual limit for 2022)
b. $61,000, lesser of 100% of $270,000 or $61,000 (annual limit for 2022)

Self-Study Problem 9.8

a. $150,000
b. $120,000, [$150,000 − (20% × $150,000)]
c. August 30, 20XX, which is the 60th day after the day the distribution was received, unless the hardship waiver provisions apply.
d. $150,000, the full balance from the Blue Mutual Fund.

CHAPTER 10 PARTNERSHIP TAXATION

Self-Study Problem 10.1

1. False	The mere joint ownership of property does not constitute a partnership; the owners must engage in some type of business activity.
2. True	A trade or business with more than one owner has been formed as a partnership.
3. False	Although generally very useful, a written partnership agreement is not required to form a partnership for tax purposes.
4. False	Luis will recognize $7,000 ($14,000 × his 50% interest). A cash distribution does not generally increase or decrease income recognized.
5. False	It would appear that Luis and Bheem are both general partners and thus are liable for any partnership liabilities even in excess of their investment.

Self-Study Problem 10.2

1. $0	
2. $36,000	The amount of cash contributed.
3. $0	
4. $17,500	The same as Linda's basis in the equipment contributed to the partnership.
5. $17,500	The same as Linda's basis in the equipment contributed.

Self-Study Problem 10.3

See Form 1065 and Schedule K-1 on Pages E-75 to E-81.

Self-Study Problem 10.4

Year 1: Jiang and Jackson both recognize ordinary business income of $3,000. The tax-exempt income and non-deductible expenses do not affect taxable income (although the tax-exempt income will be reported by each partner). Each partner has a basis of $13,100 calculated as follows:

Beginning balance	$10,000
Income allocated	3,000
Tax-exempt income allocated	150
Non-deductible expenses	(50)
Ending balance	$13,100

Year 2: Each partner has an outside basis of $0 at year end:

Beginning balance	$13,100
Cash distribution	(7,100)
Basis prior to loss	6,000
Loss allocated and deducted	(6,000)
Ending balance	$ 0

A loss of $10,000 is allocated to each partner; however, the deductible loss amount is limited to basis of $6,000. Each partner has a suspended loss of $4,000. Jiang will also report income of $2,000 from guaranteed payments. Note that guaranteed payments do not directly affect outside basis.

Year 3: Each partner has an outside basis of $0 at year end:

Beginning balance	$ 0
Income allocated	2,000
LT capital gain allocated	500
Basis prior to loss	2,500
Suspended loss deducted	(2,500)
Ending balance	$ 0

Both partners will be able to deduct $2,500 of the loss suspended in the previous year and will have remaining suspended losses of $1,500. Jiang will also report income of $2,000 from guaranteed payments.

Self-Study Problem 10.3

Form **1065** U.S. Return of Partnership Income — OMB No. 1545-0123 — **2022**

Department of the Treasury, Internal Revenue Service

For calendar year 2022, or tax year beginning ________, 2022, ending ________, 20__.

Go to *www.irs.gov/Form1065* for instructions and the latest information.

A Principal business activity	Advertising Services
B Principal product or service	Advertising
C Business code number	541800
Name of partnership	Cahokia Partnership
Number, street, and room or suite no. If a P.O. box, see instructions.	40 Rainy Street
City or town, state or province, country, and ZIP or foreign postal code	Collinsville, IL 62234
D Employer identification number	44-4444444
E Date business started	01/01/2022
F Total assets (see instructions)	$ 257,750

G Check applicable boxes: (1) ☑ Initial return (2) ☐ Final return (3) ☐ Name change (4) ☐ Address change (5) ☐ Amended return

H Check accounting method: (1) ☐ Cash (2) ☑ Accrual (3) ☐ Other (specify):

I Number of Schedules K-1. Attach one for each person who was a partner at any time during the tax year: 2

J Check if Schedules C and M-3 are attached ☐

K Check if partnership: (1) ☐ Aggregated activities for section 465 at-risk purposes (2) ☐ Grouped activities for section 469 passive activity purposes

Caution: Include **only** trade or business income and expenses on lines 1a through 22 below. See instructions for more information.

Income	1a	Gross receipts or sales	1a	255,600		
	b	Returns and allowances	1b			
	c	Balance. Subtract line 1b from line 1a			1c	255,600
	2	Cost of goods sold (attach Form 1125-A)			2	
	3	Gross profit. Subtract line 2 from line 1c			3	255,600
	4	Ordinary income (loss) from other partnerships, estates, and trusts (attach statement)			4	
	5	Net farm profit (loss) (attach Schedule F (Form 1040))			5	
	6	Net gain (loss) from Form 4797, Part II, line 17 (attach Form 4797)			6	
	7	Other income (loss) (attach statement)			7	
	8	**Total income (loss).** Combine lines 3 through 7			8	255,600
Deductions (see instructions for limitations)	9	Salaries and wages (other than to partners) (less employment credits)			9	148,000
	10	Guaranteed payments to partners			10	20,000
	11	Repairs and maintenance			11	
	12	Bad debts			12	
	13	Rent			13	12,000
	14	Taxes and licenses			14	6,100
	15	Interest (see instructions)			15	
	16a	Depreciation (if required, attach Form 4562)	16a	9,250		
	b	Less depreciation reported on Form 1125-A and elsewhere on return	16b		16c	9,250
	17	Depletion **(Do not deduct oil and gas depletion.)**			17	
	18	Retirement plans, etc.			18	
	19	Employee benefit programs			19	
	20	Other deductions (attach statement)			20	
	21	**Total deductions.** Add the amounts shown in the far right column for lines 9 through 20			21	195,350
	22	**Ordinary business income (loss).** Subtract line 21 from line 8			22	60,250
Tax and Payment	23	Interest due under the look-back method—completed long-term contracts (attach Form 8697)			23	
	24	Interest due under the look-back method—income forecast method (attach Form 8866)			24	
	25	BBA AAR imputed underpayment (see instructions)			25	
	26	Other taxes (see instructions)			26	
	27	**Total balance due.** Add lines 23 through 26			27	
	28	Payment (see instructions)			28	
	29	**Amount owed.** If line 28 is smaller than line 27, enter amount owed			29	
	30	**Overpayment.** If line 28 is larger than line 27, enter overpayment			30	

Sign Here

Under penalties of perjury, I declare that I have examined this return, including accompanying schedules and statements, and to the best of my knowledge and belief, it is true, correct, and complete. Declaration of preparer (other than partner or limited liability company member) is based on all information of which preparer has any knowledge.

Signature of partner or limited liability company member — Date

May the IRS discuss this return with the preparer shown below? See instructions. ☐ Yes ☐ No

Paid Preparer Use Only

Print/Type preparer's name	Preparer's signature	Date	Check ☐ if self-employed	PTIN
Firm's name			Firm's EIN	
Firm's address			Phone no.	

Self-Study Problem 10.3

Form 1065 (2022) Page **2**

Schedule B **Other Information**

		Yes	No
1	What type of entity is filing this return? Check the applicable box: **a** ☑ Domestic general partnership **b** ☐ Domestic limited partnership **c** ☐ Domestic limited liability company **d** ☐ Domestic limited liability partnership **e** ☐ Foreign partnership **f** ☐ Other:		
2	At the end of the tax year:		
a	Did any foreign or domestic corporation, partnership (including any entity treated as a partnership), trust, or tax-exempt organization, or any foreign government own, directly or indirectly, an interest of 50% or more in the profit, loss, or capital of the partnership? For rules of constructive ownership, see instructions. If "Yes," attach Schedule B-1, Information on Partners Owning 50% or More of the Partnership		✓
b	Did any individual or estate own, directly or indirectly, an interest of 50% or more in the profit, loss, or capital of the partnership? For rules of constructive ownership, see instructions. If "Yes," attach Schedule B-1, Information on Partners Owning 50% or More of the Partnership	✓	
3	At the end of the tax year, did the partnership:		
a	Own directly 20% or more, or own, directly or indirectly, 50% or more of the total voting power of all classes of stock entitled to vote of any foreign or domestic corporation? For rules of constructive ownership, see instructions. If "Yes," complete (i) through (iv) below		✓

(i) Name of Corporation	(ii) Employer Identification Number (if any)	(iii) Country of Incorporation	(iv) Percentage Owned in Voting Stock

		Yes	No
b	Own directly an interest of 20% or more, or own, directly or indirectly, an interest of 50% or more in the profit, loss, or capital in any foreign or domestic partnership (including an entity treated as a partnership) or in the beneficial interest of a trust? For rules of constructive ownership, see instructions. If "Yes," complete (i) through (v) below		✓

(i) Name of Entity	(ii) Employer Identification Number (if any)	(iii) Type of Entity	(iv) Country of Organization	(v) Maximum Percentage Owned in Profit, Loss, or Capital

		Yes	No
4	Does the partnership satisfy **all four** of the following conditions?		
a	The partnership's total receipts for the tax year were less than $250,000.		
b	The partnership's total assets at the end of the tax year were less than $1 million.		
c	Schedules K-1 are filed with the return and furnished to the partners on or before the due date (including extensions) for the partnership return.		
d	The partnership is not filing and is not required to file Schedule M-3		✓
	If "Yes," the partnership is not required to complete Schedules L, M-1, and M-2; item F on page 1 of Form 1065; or item L on Schedule K-1.		
5	Is this partnership a publicly traded partnership, as defined in section 469(k)(2)?		✓
6	During the tax year, did the partnership have any debt that was canceled, was forgiven, or had the terms modified so as to reduce the principal amount of the debt?		✓
7	Has this partnership filed, or is it required to file, Form 8918, Material Advisor Disclosure Statement, to provide information on any reportable transaction?		✓
8	At any time during calendar year 2022, did the partnership have an interest in or a signature or other authority over a financial account in a foreign country (such as a bank account, securities account, or other financial account)? See instructions for exceptions and filing requirements for FinCEN Form 114, Report of Foreign Bank and Financial Accounts (FBAR). If "Yes," enter the name of the foreign country		✓
9	At any time during the tax year, did the partnership receive a distribution from, or was it the grantor of, or transferor to, a foreign trust? If "Yes," the partnership may have to file Form 3520, Annual Return To Report Transactions With Foreign Trusts and Receipt of Certain Foreign Gifts. See instructions		✓
10a	Is the partnership making, or had it previously made (and not revoked), a section 754 election? See instructions for details regarding a section 754 election.		✓
b	Did the partnership make for this tax year an optional basis adjustment under section 743(b) or 734(b)? If "Yes," attach a statement showing the computation and allocation of the basis adjustment. See instructions		✓
c	Is the partnership required to adjust the basis of partnership assets under section 743(b) or 734(b) because of a substantial built-in loss (as defined under section 743(d)) or substantial basis reduction (as defined under section 734(d))? If "Yes," attach a statement showing the computation and allocation of the basis adjustment. See instructions		✓

Form **1065** (2022)

Self-Study Problem 10.3

Form 1065 (2022) Page **3**

Schedule B **Other Information** *(continued)*

		Yes	No
11	Check this box if, during the current or prior tax year, the partnership distributed any property received in a like-kind exchange or contributed such property to another entity (other than disregarded entities wholly owned by the partnership throughout the tax year) . . . ☐		
12	At any time during the tax year, did the partnership distribute to any partner a tenancy-in-common or other undivided interest in partnership property?		✓
13	If the partnership is required to file Form 8858, Information Return of U.S. Persons With Respect to Foreign Disregarded Entities (FDEs) and Foreign Branches (FBs), enter the number of Forms 8858 attached. See instructions ______		
14	Does the partnership have any foreign partners? If "Yes," enter the number of Forms 8805, Foreign Partner's Information Statement of Section 1446 Withholding Tax, filed for this partnership ______		✓
15	Enter the number of Forms 8865, Return of U.S. Persons With Respect to Certain Foreign Partnerships, attached to this return ______		
16a	Did you make any payments in 2022 that would require you to file Form(s) 1099? See instructions	✓	
b	If "Yes," did you or will you file required Form(s) 1099?	✓	
17	Enter the number of Forms 5471, Information Return of U.S. Persons With Respect to Certain Foreign Corporations, attached to this return ______		
18	Enter the number of partners that are foreign governments under section 892 ______		
19	During the partnership's tax year, did the partnership make any payments that would require it to file Forms 1042 and 1042-S under chapter 3 (sections 1441 through 1464) or chapter 4 (sections 1471 through 1474)?		✓
20	Was the partnership a specified domestic entity required to file Form 8938 for the tax year? See the Instructions for Form 8938		✓
21	Is the partnership a section 721(c) partnership, as defined in Regulations section 1.721(c)-1(b)(14)?		✓
22	During the tax year, did the partnership pay or accrue any interest or royalty for which one or more partners are not allowed a deduction under section 267A? See instructions		✓
	If "Yes," enter the total amount of the disallowed deductions . . . $______		
23	Did the partnership have an election under section 163(j) for any real property trade or business or any farming business in effect during the tax year? See instructions		✓
24	Does the partnership satisfy one or more of the following? See instructions		✓
a	The partnership owns a pass-through entity with current, or prior year carryover, excess business interest expense.		
b	The partnership's aggregate average annual gross receipts (determined under section 448(c)) for the 3 tax years preceding the current tax year are more than $27 million and the partnership has business interest.		
c	The partnership is a tax shelter (see instructions) and the partnership has business interest expense. If "Yes" to any, complete and attach Form 8990.		
25	Is the partnership attaching Form 8996 to certify as a Qualified Opportunity Fund?		✓
	If "Yes," enter the amount from Form 8996, line 15 . . . $______		
26	Enter the number of foreign partners subject to section 864(c)(8) as a result of transferring all or a portion of an interest in the partnership or of receiving a distribution from the partnership ______ Complete Schedule K-3 (Form 1065), Part XIII, for each foreign partner subject to section 864(c)(8) on a transfer or distribution.		
27	At any time during the tax year, were there any transfers between the partnership and its partners subject to the disclosure requirements of Regulations section 1.707-8?		✓
28	Since December 22, 2017, did a foreign corporation directly or indirectly acquire substantially all of the properties constituting a trade or business of your partnership, and was the ownership percentage (by vote or value) for purposes of section 7874 greater than 50% (for example, the partners held more than 50% of the stock of the foreign corporation)? If "Yes," list the ownership percentage by vote and by value. See instructions. Percentage: By vote: ______ By value: ______		✓
29	How many Schedules K-1 and Schedules K-3 were not furnished or will not be furnished timely? ______		
30	Is the partnership electing out of the centralized partnership audit regime under section 6221(b)? See instructions. If "Yes," the partnership must complete Schedule B-2 (Form 1065). Enter the total from Schedule B-2, Part III, line 3 ______ If "No," complete Designation of Partnership Representative below.		✓

Designation of Partnership Representative (see instructions)

Enter below the information for the partnership representative (PR) for the tax year covered by this return.

Name of PR

U.S. address of PR ______	U.S. phone number of PR

If the PR is an entity, name of the designated individual for the PR

U.S. address of designated individual ______	U.S. phone number of designated individual

Form **1065** (2022)

Self-Study Problem 10.3

Form 1065 (2022) Page **4**

Schedule K **Partners' Distributive Share Items**

Section	Line	Description		Total amount
Income (Loss)	1	Ordinary business income (loss) (page 1, line 22)	1	60,250
	2	Net rental real estate income (loss) (attach Form 8825)	2	
	3a	Other gross rental income (loss) — 3a		
	b	Expenses from other rental activities (attach statement) — 3b		
	c	Other net rental income (loss). Subtract line 3b from line 3a	3c	
	4	Guaranteed payments: a Services 4a 20,000 b Capital 4b		
		c Total. Add lines 4a and 4b	4c	20,000
	5	Interest income	5	
	6	Dividends and dividend equivalents: a Ordinary dividends	6a	
		b Qualified dividends 6b c Dividend equivalents 6c		
	7	Royalties	7	
	8	Net short-term capital gain (loss) (attach Schedule D (Form 1065))	8	
	9a	Net long-term capital gain (loss) (attach Schedule D (Form 1065))	9a	
	b	Collectibles (28%) gain (loss) — 9b		
	c	Unrecaptured section 1250 gain (attach statement) — 9c		
	10	Net section 1231 gain (loss) (attach Form 4797)	10	
	11	Other income (loss) (see instructions) Type:	11	
Deductions	12	Section 179 deduction (attach Form 4562)	12	
	13a	Contributions	13a	1,500
	b	Investment interest expense	13b	
	c	Section 59(e)(2) expenditures: (1) Type: (2) Amount:	13c(2)	
	d	Other deductions (see instructions) Type:	13d	
Self-Employment	14a	Net earnings (loss) from self-employment	14a	80,250 (a)
	b	Gross farming or fishing income	14b	
	c	Gross nonfarm income	14c	
Credits	15a	Low-income housing credit (section 42(j)(5))	15a	
	b	Low-income housing credit (other)	15b	
	c	Qualified rehabilitation expenditures (rental real estate) (attach Form 3468, if applicable)	15c	
	d	Other rental real estate credits (see instructions) Type:	15d	
	e	Other rental credits (see instructions) Type:	15e	
	f	Other credits (see instructions) Type:	15f	
International	16	Attach Schedule K-2 (Form 1065), Partners' Distributive Share Items—International, and check this box to indicate that you are reporting items of international tax relevance ☐		
Alternative Minimum Tax (AMT) Items	17a	Post-1986 depreciation adjustment	17a	
	b	Adjusted gain or loss	17b	
	c	Depletion (other than oil and gas)	17c	
	d	Oil, gas, and geothermal properties—gross income	17d	
	e	Oil, gas, and geothermal properties—deductions	17e	
	f	Other AMT items (attach statement)	17f	
Other Information	18a	Tax-exempt interest income	18a	
	b	Other tax-exempt income	18b	
	c	Nondeductible expenses	18c	
	19a	Distributions of cash and marketable securities	19a	50,000
	b	Distributions of other property	19b	
	20a	Investment income	20a	
	b	Investment expenses	20b	
	c	Other items and amounts (attach statement)		
	21	Total foreign taxes paid or accrued	21	

Form **1065** (2022)

(a) Ordinary business income ($60,250) plus guaranteed payments ($20,000).

Self-Study Problem 10.3

Form 1065 (2022) Page **5**

Analysis of Net Income (Loss) per Return

1	Net income (loss). Combine Schedule K, lines 1 through 11. From the result, subtract the sum of Schedule K, lines 12 through 13d, and 21					1	78,750
2	Analysis by partner type:	(i) Corporate	(ii) Individual (active)	(iii) Individual (passive)	(iv) Partnership	(v) Exempt Organization	(vi) Nominee/Other
a	General partners		78,750				
b	Limited partners						

Schedule L Balance Sheets per Books

	Assets	Beginning of tax year (a)	(b)	End of tax year (c)	(d)
1	Cash		Initial Return		27,000
2a	Trade notes and accounts receivable			10,000	
b	Less allowance for bad debts				10,000
3	Inventories				
4	U.S. Government obligations				
5	Tax-exempt securities				
6	Other current assets (attach statement)				
7a	Loans to partners (or persons related to partners)				
b	Mortgage and real estate loans				
8	Other investments (attach statement)				
9a	Buildings and other depreciable assets			115,000	
b	Less accumulated depreciation			9,250	105,750
10a	Depletable assets				
b	Less accumulated depletion				
11	Land (net of any amortization)				115,000
12a	Intangible assets (amortizable only)				
b	Less accumulated amortization				
13	Other assets (attach statement)				
14	Total assets				257,750
	Liabilities and Capital				
15	Accounts payable		Initial Return		29,750
16	Mortgages, notes, bonds payable in less than 1 year				
17	Other current liabilities (attach statement)				
18	All nonrecourse loans				
19a	Loans from partners (or persons related to partners)				
b	Mortgages, notes, bonds payable in 1 year or more				187,750
20	Other liabilities (attach statement)				
21	Partners' capital accounts				40,250
22	Total liabilities and capital				257,750

Schedule M-1 Reconciliation of Income (Loss) per Books With Analysis of Net Income (Loss) per Return

Note: The partnership may be required to file Schedule M-3. See instructions.

1	Net income (loss) per books	58,750	6	Income recorded on books this year not included on Schedule K, lines 1 through 11 (itemize):	
2	Income included on Schedule K, lines 1, 2, 3c, 5, 6a, 7, 8, 9a, 10, and 11, not recorded on books this year (itemize):		a	Tax-exempt interest $	
3	Guaranteed payments (other than health insurance)	20,000	7	Deductions included on Schedule K, lines 1 through 13d, and 21, not charged against book income this year (itemize):	
4	Expenses recorded on books this year not included on Schedule K, lines 1 through 13d, and 21 (itemize):		a	Depreciation $	
a	Depreciation $		8	Add lines 6 and 7	
b	Travel and entertainment $		9	Income (loss) (Analysis of Net Income (Loss), line 1). Subtract line 8 from line 5	78,750
5	Add lines 1 through 4	78,750			

Schedule M-2 Analysis of Partners' Capital Accounts

1	Balance at beginning of year	0	6	Distributions: **a** Cash	50,000
2	Capital contributed: **a** Cash	31,500		**b** Property	
	b Property		7	Other decreases (itemize):	
3	Net income (loss) (see instructions)	78,750		Guaranteed Payment	20,000
4	Other increases (itemize):		8	Add lines 6 and 7	70,000
5	Add lines 1 through 4	110,250	9	Balance at end of year. Subtract line 8 from line 5	40,250

Form **1065** (2022)

Self-Study Problem 10.3

651121

☐ Final K-1 ☐ Amended K-1 OMB No. 1545-0123

Schedule K-1 (Form 1065) **2022**

Department of the Treasury
Internal Revenue Service

For calendar year 2022, or tax year

beginning / / 2022 ending / /

Partner's Share of Income, Deductions, Credits, etc. **See separate instructions.**

Part I Information About the Partnership

A Partnership's employer identification number
44-4444444

B Partnership's name, address, city, state, and ZIP code
Cahokia Partnership
40 Rainy Street
Collinsville, IL 62234

C IRS center where partnership filed return: Ogden, UT

D ☐ Check if this is a publicly traded partnership (PTP)

Part II Information About the Partner

E Partner's SSN or TIN (Do not use TIN of a disregarded entity. See instructions.)
444-14-1414

F Name, address, city, state, and ZIP code for partner entered in E. See instructions.
Sapat Illiniwek

G ☒ General partner or LLC member-manager ☐ Limited partner or other LLC member

H1 ☒ Domestic partner ☐ Foreign partner

H2 ☐ If the partner is a disregarded entity (DE), enter the partner's:
TIN ________ Name ________

I1 What type of entity is this partner? Individual

I2 If this partner is a retirement plan (IRA/SEP/Keogh/etc.), check here ☐

J Partner's share of profit, loss, and capital (see instructions):

	Beginning	Ending
Profit	%	50 %
Loss	%	50 %
Capital	%	50 %

Check if decrease is due to sale or exchange of partnership interest ☐

K Partner's share of liabilities:

	Beginning	Ending
Nonrecourse	$	$
Qualified nonrecourse financing	$	$
Recourse	$	$ 108,750

Check this box if item K includes liability amounts from lower-tier partnerships ☐

L **Partner's Capital Account Analysis**

Beginning capital account	$ 0
Capital contributed during the year	$ 15,750
Current year net income (loss)	$ 29,375
Other increase (decrease) (attach explanation)	$
Withdrawals and distributions	$ (25,000)
Ending capital account	$ 20,125

M Did the partner contribute property with a built-in gain (loss)?
☐ **Yes** ☒ **No** If "Yes," attach statement. See instructions.

N **Partner's Share of Net Unrecognized Section 704(c) Gain or (Loss)**
Beginning $
Ending $

Part III Partner's Share of Current Year Income, Deductions, Credits, and Other Items

1	Ordinary business income (loss)	30,125	14	Self-employment earnings (loss)	50,125
2	Net rental real estate income (loss)				
3	Other net rental income (loss)		15	Credits	
4a	Guaranteed payments for services	20,000			
4b	Guaranteed payments for capital		16	Schedule K-3 is attached if checked ☐	
4c	Total guaranteed payments	20,000	17	Alternative minimum tax (AMT) items	
5	Interest income				
6a	Ordinary dividends				
6b	Qualified dividends		18	Tax-exempt income and nondeductible expenses	
6c	Dividend equivalents				
7	Royalties				
8	Net short-term capital gain (loss)		19	Distributions	
9a	Net long-term capital gain (loss)		A		25,000
9b	Collectibles (28%) gain (loss)		20	Other information	
9c	Unrecaptured section 1250 gain		Z*		30,125
10	Net section 1231 gain (loss)		Z**		84,000
11	Other income (loss)		Z***		57,500
12	Section 179 deduction		21	Foreign taxes paid or accrued	
13	Other deductions				
A		750			

22 ☐ More than one activity for at-risk purposes*
23 ☐ More than one activity for passive activity purposes*
*See attached statement for additional information.

For IRS Use Only

For Paperwork Reduction Act Notice, see the Instructions for Form 1065. www.irs.gov/Form1065 Cat. No. 11394R **Schedule K-1 (Form 1065) 2022**

* The IRS uses code Z for QBI deduction reporting and recommends Statement A from the Form 1065 instructions. Use of Intuit ProConnect software will create Statement A. A version of Statement A is presented on the next page.

Statement A—QBI Pass-Through Entity Reporting

Partnership's name: Cahokia Partnership		Partnership's EIN: 44-4444444	
Partner's name: Sapat Illiniwek	Partner's identifying number: 444-14-1414		
Partner's share of:	Trade or Business 1 ☐ PTP ☐ Aggregated ☐ SSTB	Trade or Business 2 ☐ PTP ☐ Aggregated ☐ SSTB	Trade or Business 3 ☐ PTP ☐ Aggregated ☐ SSTB
QBI or qualified PTP items subject to partner-specific determinations:			
Ordinary business income (loss)	30,125		
Rental income (loss)			
Royalty income (loss)			
Section 1231 gain (loss)			
Other income (loss)			
Section 179 deduction			
Other deductions			
W-2 wages	84,000		
UBIA of qualified property	57,500		
Section 199A dividends			

Self-Study Problem 10.5

12 months × $1,000 per month guaranteed payment	$12,000
Add: Robert's distributive share of income	21,000
Total income	$33,000

The $1,500 per month received in September, October, November, and December of 2022 will be reported on Robert's 2023 income tax return. The guaranteed payments received are reported for the partnership tax year that ends with or within the partner's tax year, in the same manner as a distributive share of the partnership income.

Self-Study Problem 10.6

1. Maxwell has a $5,000 realized loss ($70,000 – $75,000), but the loss is not recognized since he is a more-than-50 percent partner, 50 percent directly and 50 percent indirectly from his daughter.
2. The daughter has a $15,000 gain ($40,000 – $25,000). Since she is a more-than-50 percent partner (50 percent directly and 50 percent indirectly), and the car is not a capital asset to the partnership, the gain is ordinary income. If the car was a capital asset to the partnership, the gain would still be considered ordinary since Pam is a more-than-50 percent partner.

Self-Study Problem 10.7

a. Marla's QBI deduction with no limitation is $200,000 × 20% = $40,000. The guaranteed payments and the capital gains are not part of QBI income. Because Marla's income exceeds the phase-out range for taxable income (starts at $170,050 and is completely phased out by $220,050 in 2022), the W-2 wage limitation applies.

   W-2 Wages allocated to Marla are $46,000 ($230,000 × 20% interest). Qualified property allocated to Marla is $240,000 ($1,200,000 × 20%). The limit is the greater of:

   i. $46,000 × 50% = $23,000
   ii. ($46,000 × 25%) + ($240,000 × 2.5%) = $17,500

   The W-2 wages limit of $23,000 is less than $40,000; thus the QBI deduction is $23,000 (note that the taxable income limit of $155,200 ($776,000 × 20%) exceeds the QBI deduction).

b. If Salem is a service business, because Marla's income exceeds the phase-out range for taxable income (starts at $170,050 and completely phased out by $220,050 in 2022), she is not eligible for any QBI deduction.

Self-Study Problem 10.8

1. $45,000, his amount at risk in the activity.
2. Profit

2. Profit	$ 31,000
Less: carryover of disallowed loss from the prior year ($60,000 – $45,000)	(15,000)
Taxable income for next year	$ 16,000

Self-Study Problem 10.9

1. False	An election must be made to be treated like a corporation for tax purposes.
2. False	LLCs are not required to have a general partner. Also, the owners of LLCs are members, not partners.
3. True	
4. True	

5. False Debt of an LLC is generally treated as non-recourse debt due to the limited liability of the LLC members.

CHAPTER 11 THE CORPORATE INCOME TAX

Self-Study Problem 11.1

$335,000 × 21% = $70,350

Self-Study Problem 11.2

a. $110,000 × 21% = $23,100

Neither of the capital losses may be used to offset current year ordinary income. The capital losses may be carried back 3 years and forward 5 years to offset capital gains, if any, recognized during those years.

b. The 2020 loss of $40,000 can be used to offset a maximum of $36,000 of 2021 income (80 percent × $45,000). The remaining $4,000 2020 NOL is carried forward into 2022 and added to the $20,000 loss, resulting in a $24,000 NOL carryforward to 2023.

Self-Study Problem 11.3

a. The dividends received deduction is equal to the lesser of $45,500 = 65% × $70,000; or $39,000 = 65% × $60,000 ($90,000 + $70,000 − $100,000). $39,000 is the amount of the deduction.

b. Organization costs of $5,222.22 can be deducted in 2022. Boyce is eligible to expense $5,000 organization costs. The balance of $8,000 ($13,000 − $5,000) is amortized over 180 months for 5 months of 2022 for a deduction of $222.22 ($8,000 ÷ 180 × 5 months). In 2023, Boyce will deduct $533.33 ($8,000 ÷ 180 × 12 months).

Start-up costs exceed $50,000, thus Boyce is not eligible to deduct the entire $5,000 of start-up costs. The $5,000 is reduced by $2,000 (the start-up costs in excess of $50,000) to $3,000. The remaining balance of $49,000 ($52,000 − $3,000) is amortized over 180 months × 5 months in 2022 or $1,361.11 for a total 2022 deduction of $4,361.11. In 2023, Boyce will deduct $3,266.67 ($49,000 ÷ 180 × 12).

c. Gant's modified taxable income for purposes of the charitable contribution deduction limit of 10% is $95,000 ($65,000 + $5,000 + $25,000). Thus the charitable contribution limit is $9,500 ($95,000 × 10%). The remaining $15,500 can be carried forward for up to 5 years.

Self-Study Problem 11.4

Schedule M-1 Reconciliation of Income (Loss) per Books With Income per Return

Note: The corporation may be required to file Schedule M-3. See instructions.

1	Net income (loss) per books	115,600	7	Income recorded on books this year not included on this return (itemize): Tax-exempt interest $ 4,700	4,700
2	Federal income tax per books	29,400			
3	Excess of capital losses over capital gains	9,100			
4	Income subject to tax not recorded on books this year (itemize):		8	Deductions on this return not charged against book income this year (itemize): a Depreciation $; b Charitable contributions $	4,000
5	Expenses recorded on books this year not deducted on this return (itemize): a Depreciation $; b Charitable contributions $; c Travel and entertainment $		9	Add lines 7 and 8	8,700
6	Add lines 1 through 5	154,100	10	Income (page 1, line 28)—line 6 less line 9	145,400

Self-Study Problem 11.5

1.

Quarter	YTD Estimate	Annualization Factor	Annualized	Tax Rate	Annual Taxes	Portion Due	Estimated Amount
Q1	$225,000	4	$900,000	21%	$189,000	25%	$47,250
Q2	225,000	4	900,000	21%	189,000	50%	94,500
Q3	475,000	2	950,000	21%	199,500	75%	149,625
Q4	660,000	12/9	880,000	21%	184,800	100%	184,800

Since taxable income in one of the three preceding years exceeds $1 million, Alberta is considered a large corporation and thus may use the prior year liability only during the first quarter.

Q1: $42,750. Prior year liability was $194,250 × 25% = $48,562.50 which is greater than the estimated Q1 payment above; thus Alberta's Q1 payment will be $42,750 ($47,250 less prior year overpayment applied of $4,500)
Q2: $47,250 ($94,500 less amounts previously paid of $42,750 + $4,500)
Q3: $55,125 ($149,625 less amounts previously paid of $94,500)
Q4: $35,175 ($184,800 less amounts previously paid of $149,625)

2. See Form 1120 on Pages E-85 to E-90. The calculation of tax for Aspen Corporation is as follows: 21% × $14,000 = $2,940. Net income per the books is equal to $16,060 ($19,000 net income before income tax expense − $2,940 income tax expense).

Self-Study Problem 11.6

See Form 1120S and Schedule K-1 on Pages E-91 to E-97.

Self-Study Problem 11.7

a. Tammy's realized gain is $125,000 + $34,000 − $75,000 = $84,000.
b. Tammy's recognized gain is $0.
c. Tammy's basis in her stock is $75,000 − $0 + $0 − $34,000 = $41,000.
d. The corporation's basis in the real estate is $75,000 + $0 = $75,000.

Self-Study Problem 11.5

Form **1120** Department of the Treasury Internal Revenue Service

U.S. Corporation Income Tax Return

For calendar year 2022 or tax year beginning ____, 2022, ending ____, 20 ___

Go to *www.irs.gov/Form1120* for instructions and the latest information.

OMB No. 1545-0123 **2022**

A Check if:	TYPE OR PRINT		
1a Consolidated return (attach Form 851) ☐		Name: Aspen Corporation	B Employer identification number: 92-2222222
b Life/nonlife consolidated return ☐		Number, street, and room or suite no. If a P.O. box, see instructions.: 470 Rio Grande Place	C Date incorporated: 01/01/22
2 Personal holding co. (attach Sch. PH) ☐		City or town, state or province, country, and ZIP or foreign postal code: Aspen, CO 81611	D Total assets (see instructions): $ 183,000
3 Personal service corp. (see instructions) ☐			
4 Schedule M-3 attached ☐			

E Check if: (1) ☑ Initial return (2) ☐ Final return (3) ☐ Name change (4) ☐ Address change

DRAFT AS OF October 3, 2022 DO NOT FILE

Income	1a	Gross receipts or sales	1a	285,000		
	b	Returns and allowances	1b			
	c	Balance. Subtract line 1b from line 1a			1c	285,000
	2	Cost of goods sold (attach Form 1125-A)			2	80,000
	3	Gross profit. Subtract line 2 from line 1c			3	205,000
	4	Dividends and inclusions (Schedule C, line 23)			4	10,000
	5	Interest			5	
	6	Gross rents			6	
	7	Gross royalties			7	
	8	Capital gain net income (attach Schedule D (Form 1120))			8	
	9	Net gain or (loss) from Form 4797, Part II, line 17 (attach Form 4797)			9	
	10	Other income (see instructions—attach statement)			10	
	11	**Total income.** Add lines 3 through 10			11	215,000
Deductions (See instructions for limitations on deductions.)	12	Compensation of officers (see instructions—attach Form 1125-E)			12	90,000
	13	Salaries and wages (less employment credits)			13	82,000
	14	Repairs and maintenance			14	8,000
	15	Bad debts			15	
	16	Rents			16	
	17	Taxes and licenses			17	11,000
	18	Interest (see instructions)			18	
	19	Charitable contributions			19	
	20	Depreciation from Form 4562 not claimed on Form 1125-A or elsewhere on return (attach Form 4562)			20	5,000
	21	Depletion			21	
	22	Advertising			22	
	23	Pension, profit-sharing, etc., plans			23	
	24	Employee benefit programs			24	
	25	Reserved for future use			25	
	26	Other deductions (attach statement)			26	
	27	**Total deductions.** Add lines 12 through 26			27	196,000
	28	Taxable income before net operating loss deduction and special deductions. Subtract line 27 from line 11.			28	19,000
	29a	Net operating loss deduction (see instructions)	29a			
	b	Special deductions (Schedule C, line 24)	29b	5,000		
	c	Add lines 29a and 29b			29c	5,000
Tax, Refundable Credits, and Payments	30	**Taxable income.** Subtract line 29c from line 28. See instructions			30	14,000
	31	Total tax (Schedule J, Part I, line 11)			31	2,940
	32	Reserved for future use			32	
	33	Total payments and credits (Schedule J, Part III, line 23)			33	3,000
	34	Estimated tax penalty. See instructions. Check if Form 2220 is attached ☐			34	
	35	**Amount owed.** If line 33 is smaller than the total of lines 31 and 34, enter amount owed			35	
	36	**Overpayment.** If line 33 is larger than the total of lines 31 and 34, enter amount overpaid			36	60
	37	Enter amount from line 36 you want: **Credited to 2023 estimated tax**	60	**Refunded**	37	0

Sign Here

Under penalties of perjury, I declare that I have examined this return, including accompanying schedules and statements, and to the best of my knowledge and belief, it is true, correct, and complete. Declaration of preparer (other than taxpayer) is based on all information of which preparer has any knowledge.

Signature of officer | Date | Title

May the IRS discuss this return with the preparer shown below? See instructions. ☑ Yes ☐ No

Paid Preparer Use Only

Print/Type preparer's name	Preparer's signature	Date	Check ☐ if self-employed	PTIN
Firm's name			Firm's EIN	
Firm's address			Phone no.	

Self-Study Problem 11.5

Form 1120 (2022) Aspen Corporation Page **2**

Schedule C **Dividends, Inclusions, and Special Deductions** (see instructions)	**(a)** Dividends and inclusions	**(b)** %	**(c)** Special deductions **(a)** × **(b)**
1 Dividends from less-than-20%-owned domestic corporations (other than debt-financed stock)	10,000	50	5,000
2 Dividends from 20%-or-more-owned domestic corporations (other than debt-financed stock)		65	
3 Dividends on certain debt-financed stock of domestic and foreign corporations		See instructions	
4 Dividends on certain preferred stock of less-than-20%-owned public utilities		23.3	
5 Dividends on certain preferred stock of 20%-or-more-owned public utilities		26.7	
6 Dividends from less-than-20%-owned foreign corporations and certain FSCs		50	
7 Dividends from 20%-or-more-owned foreign corporations and certain FSCs		65	
8 Dividends from wholly owned foreign subsidiaries		100	
9 **Subtotal.** Add lines 1 through 8. See instructions for limitations	10,000	See instructions	5,000
10 Dividends from domestic corporations received by a small business investment company operating under the Small Business Investment Act of 1958		100	
11 Dividends from affiliated group members		100	
12 Dividends from certain FSCs		100	
13 Foreign-source portion of dividends received from a specified 10%-owned foreign corporation (excluding hybrid dividends) (see instructions)		100	
14 Dividends from foreign corporations not included on line 3, 6, 7, 8, 11, 12, or 13 (including any hybrid dividends)			
15 Reserved for future use			
16a Subpart F inclusions derived from the sale by a controlled foreign corporation (CFC) of the stock of a lower-tier foreign corporation treated as a dividend (attach Form(s) 5471) (see instructions)		100	
b Subpart F inclusions derived from hybrid dividends of tiered corporations (attach Form(s) 5471) (see instructions)			
c Other inclusions from CFCs under subpart F not included on line 16a, 16b, or 17 (attach Form(s) 5471) (see instructions)			
17 Global Intangible Low-Taxed Income (GILTI) (attach Form(s) 5471 and Form 8992)			
18 Gross-up for foreign taxes deemed paid			
19 IC-DISC and former DISC dividends not included on line 1, 2, or 3			
20 Other dividends			
21 Deduction for dividends paid on certain preferred stock of public utilities			
22 Section 250 deduction (attach Form 8993)			
23 **Total dividends and inclusions.** Add column (a), lines 9 through 20. Enter here and on page 1, line 4	10,000		
24 **Total special deductions.** Add column (c), lines 9 through 22. Enter here and on page 1, line 29b			5,000

Form **1120** (2022)

Self-Study Problem 11.5

Form 1120 (2022) Aspen Corporation Page 3

Schedule J Tax Computation and Payment (see instructions)

Part I—Tax Computation

1	Check if the corporation is a member of a controlled group (attach Schedule O (Form 1120)). See instructions ☐				
2	Income tax. See instructions			2	2,940
3	Base erosion minimum tax amount (attach Form 8991)			3	
4	Add lines 2 and 3			4	2,940
5a	Foreign tax credit (attach Form 1118)	5a			
b	Credit from Form 8834 (see instructions)	5b			
c	General business credit (attach Form 3800)	5c			
d	Credit for prior year minimum tax (attach Form 8827)	5d			
e	Bond credits from Form 8912	5e			
6	**Total credits.** Add lines 5a through 5e			6	
7	Subtract line 6 from line 4			7	2,940
8	Personal holding company tax (attach Schedule PH (Form 1120))			8	
9a	Recapture of investment credit (attach Form 4255)	9a			
b	Recapture of low-income housing credit (attach Form 8611)	9b			
c	Interest due under the look-back method—completed long-term contracts (attach Form 8697)	9c			
d	Interest due under the look-back method—income forecast method (attach Form 8866)	9d			
e	Alternative tax on qualifying shipping activities (attach Form 8902)	9e			
f	Interest/tax due under section 453A(c) and/or section 453(l)	9f			
g	Other (see instructions—attach statement)	9g			
10	**Total.** Add lines 9a through 9g			10	
11	**Total tax.** Add lines 7, 8, and 10. Enter here and on page 1, line 31			11	2,940

Part II—Reserved For Future Use

12	Reserved for future use	12	

Part III—Payments and Refundable Credits

13	2021 overpayment credited to 2022			13	
14	2022 estimated tax payments			14	3,000
15	2022 refund applied for on Form 4466			15	( )
16	Combine lines 13, 14, and 15			16	3,000
17	Tax deposited with Form 7004			17	
18	Withholding (see instructions)			18	
19	**Total payments.** Add lines 16, 17, and 18			19	3,000
20	Refundable credits from:				
a	Form 2439	20a			
b	Form 4136	20b			
c	Reserved for future use	20c			
d	Other (attach statement—see instructions)	20d			
21	**Total credits.** Add lines 20a through 20d			21	
22	Reserved for future use			22	
23	**Total payments and credits.** Add lines 19 and 21. Enter here and on page 1, line 33			23	3,000

Form **1120** (2022)

Self-Study Problem 11.5

Form 1120 (2022) Aspen Corporation Page **4**

Schedule K **Other Information** (see instructions)

		Yes	No
1	Check accounting method: **a** ☐ Cash **b** ☑ Accrual **c** ☐ Other (specify)		
2	See the instructions and enter the:		
a	Business activity code no.		
b	Business activity		
c	Product or service		
3	Is the corporation a subsidiary in an affiliated group or a parent–subsidiary controlled group? If "Yes," enter name and EIN of the parent corporation		✓
4	At the end of the tax year:		
a	Did any foreign or domestic corporation, partnership (including any entity treated as a partnership), trust, or tax-exempt organization own directly 20% or more, or own, directly or indirectly, 50% or more of the total voting power of all classes of the corporation's stock entitled to vote? If "Yes," complete Part I of Schedule G (Form 1120) (attach Schedule G)		✓
b	Did any individual or estate own directly 20% or more, or own, directly or indirectly, 50% or more of the total voting power of all classes of the corporation's stock entitled to vote? If "Yes," complete Part II of Schedule G (Form 1120) (attach Schedule G)		✓
5	At the end of the tax year, did the corporation:		
a	Own directly 20% or more, or own, directly or indirectly, 50% or more of the total voting power of all classes of stock entitled to vote of any foreign or domestic corporation not included on **Form 851,** Affiliations Schedule? For rules of constructive ownership, see instructions. If "Yes," complete (i) through (iv) below.		✓

(i) Name of Corporation	**(ii)** Employer Identification Number (if any)	**(iii)** Country of Incorporation	**(iv)** Percentage Owned in Voting Stock

		Yes	No
b	Own directly an interest of 20% or more, or own, directly or indirectly, an interest of 50% or more in any foreign or domestic partnership (including an entity treated as a partnership) or in the beneficial interest of a trust? For rules of constructive ownership, see instructions. If "Yes," complete (i) through (iv) below.		✓

(i) Name of Entity	**(ii)** Employer Identification Number (if any)	**(iii)** Country of Organization	**(iv)** Maximum Percentage Owned in Profit, Loss, or Capital

		Yes	No
6	During this tax year, did the corporation pay dividends (other than stock dividends and distributions in exchange for stock) in excess of the corporation's current and accumulated earnings and profits? See sections 301 and 316. If "Yes," file **Form 5452,** Corporate Report of Nondividend Distributions. See the instructions for Form 5452. If this is a consolidated return, answer here for the parent corporation and on Form 851 for each subsidiary.		✓
7	At any time during the tax year, did one foreign person own, directly or indirectly, at least 25% of the total voting power of all classes of the corporation's stock entitled to vote or at least 25% of the total value of all classes of the corporation's stock? For rules of attribution, see section 318. If "Yes," enter: **(a)** Percentage owned ______ and **(b)** Owner's country ______ **(c)** The corporation may have to file **Form 5472,** Information Return of a 25% Foreign-Owned U.S. Corporation or a Foreign Corporation Engaged in a U.S. Trade or Business. Enter the number of Forms 5472 attached ______		✓
8	Check this box if the corporation issued publicly offered debt instruments with original issue discount ☐ If checked, the corporation may have to file **Form 8281,** Information Return for Publicly Offered Original Issue Discount Instruments.		
9	Enter the amount of tax-exempt interest received or accrued during the tax year $ ______		
10	Enter the number of shareholders at the end of the tax year (if 100 or fewer) ______		
11	If the corporation has an NOL for the tax year and is electing to forego the carryback period, check here (see instructions) ☐ If the corporation is filing a consolidated return, the statement required by Regulations section 1.1502-21(b)(3) must be attached or the election will not be valid.		
12	Enter the available NOL carryover from prior tax years (do not reduce it by any deduction reported on page 1, line 29a.) $		

Form **1120** (2022)

Self-Study Problem 11.5

Form 1120 (2022) Aspen Corporation Page **5**

Schedule K **Other Information** *(continued from page 4)*

		Yes	No
13	Are the corporation's total receipts (page 1, line 1a, plus lines 4 through 10) for the tax year **and** its total assets at the end of the tax year less than $250,000?		✓
	If "Yes," the corporation is not required to complete Schedules L, M-1, and M-2. Instead, enter the total amount of cash distributions and the book value of property distributions (other than cash) made during the tax year $		
14	Is the corporation required to file Schedule UTP (Form 1120), Uncertain Tax Position Statement? See instructions		✓
	If "Yes," complete and attach Schedule UTP.		
15a	Did the corporation make any payments in 2022 that would require it to file Form(s) 1099?	✓	
b	If "Yes," did or will the corporation file required Form(s) 1099?	✓	
16	During this tax year, did the corporation have an 80%-or-more change in ownership, including a change due to redemption of its own stock?		✓
17	During or subsequent to this tax year, but before the filing of this return, did the corporation dispose of more than 65% (by value) of its assets in a taxable, non-taxable, or tax deferred transaction?		✓
18	Did the corporation receive assets in a section 351 transfer in which any of the transferred assets had a fair market basis or fair market value of more than $1 million?		✓
19	During the corporation's tax year, did the corporation make any payments that would require it to file Forms 1042 and 1042-S under chapter 3 (sections 1441 through 1464) or chapter 4 (sections 1471 through 1474) of the Code?		✓
20	Is the corporation operating on a cooperative basis?		✓
21	During the tax year, did the corporation pay or accrue any interest or royalty for which the deduction is not allowed under section 267A? See instructions		✓
	If "Yes," enter the total amount of the disallowed deductions $		
22	Does the corporation have gross receipts of at least $500 million in any of the 3 preceding tax years? (See sections 59A(e)(2) and (3))		✓
	If "Yes," complete and attach Form 8991.		
23	Did the corporation have an election under section 163(j) for any real property trade or business or any farming business in effect during the tax year? See instructions		✓
24	Does the corporation satisfy one or more of the following? See instructions		✓
a	The corporation owns a pass-through entity with current, or prior year carryover, excess business interest expense.		
b	The corporation's aggregate average annual gross receipts (determined under section 448(c)) for the 3 tax years preceding the current tax year are more than $27 million and the corporation has business interest expense.		
c	The corporation is a tax shelter and the corporation has business interest expense.		
	If "Yes," complete and attach Form 8990.		
25	Is the corporation attaching Form 8996 to certify as a Qualified Opportunity Fund?		✓
	If "Yes," enter amount from Form 8996, line 15 $		
26	Since December 22, 2017, did a foreign corporation directly or indirectly acquire substantially all of the properties held directly or indirectly by the corporation, and was the ownership percentage (by vote or value) for purposes of section 7874 greater than 50% (for example, the shareholders held more than 50% of the stock of the foreign corporation)? If "Yes," list the ownership percentage by vote and by value. See instructions		✓
	Percentage: By Vote By Value		

Form **1120** (2022)

Self-Study Problem 11.5

Form 1120 (2022) Aspen Corporation Page **6**

Schedule L **Balance Sheets per Books**

Assets		Beginning of tax year (a)	(b)	End of tax year (c)	(d)
1	Cash		Initial Return		35,000
2a	Trade notes and accounts receivable			10,000	
b	Less allowance for bad debts	( )		( )	10,000
3	Inventories				
4	U.S. government obligations				
5	Tax-exempt securities (see instructions)				
6	Other current assets (attach statement)				
7	Loans to shareholders				
8	Mortgage and real estate loans				
9	Other investments (attach statement)				
10a	Buildings and other depreciable assets			125,000	
b	Less accumulated depreciation	( )		(5,000)	120,000
11a	Depletable assets				
b	Less accumulated depletion	( )		( )	
12	Land (net of any amortization)				18,000
13a	Intangible assets (amortizable only)				
b	Less accumulated amortization	( )		( )	
14	Other assets (attach statement)				
15	Total assets				183,000
	Liabilities and Shareholders' Equity				
16	Accounts payable				26,940
17	Mortgages, notes, bonds payable in less than 1 year				
18	Other current liabilities (attach statement)				
19	Loans from shareholders				
20	Mortgages, notes, bonds payable in 1 year or more				
21	Other liabilities (attach statement)				
22	Capital stock: **a** Preferred stock				
	b Common stock			140,000	140,000
23	Additional paid-in capital				
24	Retained earnings—Appropriated (attach statement)				
25	Retained earnings—Unappropriated				16,060
26	Adjustments to shareholders' equity (attach statement)				
27	Less cost of treasury stock		( )		( )
28	Total liabilities and shareholders' equity				183,000

Schedule M-1 **Reconciliation of Income (Loss) per Books With Income per Return**

Note: The corporation may be required to file Schedule M-3. See instructions.

1	Net income (loss) per books	16,060	7	Income recorded on books this year not included on this return (itemize): Tax-exempt interest $	
2	Federal income tax per books	2,940			
3	Excess of capital losses over capital gains				
4	Income subject to tax not recorded on books this year (itemize):				
5	Expenses recorded on books this year not deducted on this return (itemize):		8	Deductions on this return not charged against book income this year (itemize):	
a	Depreciation $		a	Depreciation $	
b	Charitable contributions $		b	Charitable contributions $	
c	Travel and entertainment $				
			9	Add lines 7 and 8	0
6	Add lines 1 through 5	19,000	10	Income (page 1, line 28)—line 6 less line 9	19,000

Schedule M-2 **Analysis of Unappropriated Retained Earnings per Books (Schedule L, Line 25)**

1	Balance at beginning of year	0	5	Distributions: **a** Cash	
2	Net income (loss) per books	16,060		**b** Stock	
3	Other increases (itemize):			**c** Property	
			6	Other decreases (itemize):	
			7	Add lines 5 and 6	0
4	Add lines 1, 2, and 3	16,060	8	Balance at end of year (line 4 less line 7)	16,060

Self-Study Problem 11.6

Form **1120-S** | Department of the Treasury Internal Revenue Service

U.S. Income Tax Return for an S Corporation

Do not file this form unless the corporation has filed or is attaching Form 2553 to elect to be an S corporation.
Go to *www.irs.gov/Form1120S* for instructions and the latest information.

OMB No. 1545-0123 | **2022**

For calendar year 2022 or tax year beginning , 2022, ending , 20

A S election effective date: 01/01/2022	Name: Aspen Corporation	D Employer identification number: 92-2222222
B Business activity code number (see instructions)	TYPE OR PRINT — Number, street, and room or suite no. If a P.O. box, see instructions.: 470 Rio Grande Place	E Date incorporated: 01/01/2022
C Check if Sch. M-3 attached ☐	City or town, state or province, country, and ZIP or foreign postal code: Aspen, CO 81611	F Total assets (see instructions): $ 183,000

G Is the corporation electing to be an S corporation beginning with this tax year? See instructions. ☑ Yes ☐ No

H Check if: (1) ☐ Final return (2) ☐ Name change (3) ☐ Address change (4) ☐ Amended return (5) ☐ S election termination

I Enter the number of shareholders who were shareholders during any part of the tax year . . . 1

J Check if corporation: (1) ☐ Aggregated activities for section 465 at-risk purposes (2) ☐ Grouped activities for section 469 passive activity purposes

Caution: Include **only** trade or business income and expenses on lines 1a through 21. See the instructions for more information.

Income	1a	Gross receipts or sales	1a	285,000		
	b	Returns and allowances	1b			
	c	Balance. Subtract line 1b from line 1a			1c	285,000
	2	Cost of goods sold (attach Form 1125-A)			2	80,000
	3	Gross profit. Subtract line 2 from line 1c			3	205,000
	4	Net gain (loss) from Form 4797, line 17 (attach Form 4797)			4	
	5	Other income (loss) (see instructions—attach statement)			5	
	6	**Total income (loss).** Add lines 3 through 5			6	205,000
Deductions (see instructions for limitations)	7	Compensation of officers (see instructions—attach Form 1125-E)			7	90,000
	8	Salaries and wages (less employment credits)			8	82,000
	9	Repairs and maintenance			9	8,000
	10	Bad debts			10	
	11	Rents			11	
	12	Taxes and licenses			12	11,000
	13	Interest (see instructions)			13	
	14	Depreciation from Form 4562 not claimed on Form 1125-A or elsewhere on return (attach Form 4562)			14	5,000
	15	Depletion **(Do not deduct oil and gas depletion.)**			15	
	16	Advertising			16	
	17	Pension, profit-sharing, etc., plans			17	
	18	Employee benefit programs			18	
	19	Other deductions (attach statement)			19	
	20	**Total deductions.** Add lines 7 through 19			20	196,000
	21	**Ordinary business income (loss).** Subtract line 20 from line 6			21	9,000
Tax and Payments	22a	Excess net passive income or LIFO recapture tax (see instructions)	22a			
	b	Tax from Schedule D (Form 1120-S)	22b			
	c	Add lines 22a and 22b (see instructions for additional taxes)			22c	0
	23a	2022 estimated tax payments and 2021 overpayment credited to 2022	23a			
	b	Tax deposited with Form 7004	23b			
	c	Credit for federal tax paid on fuels (attach Form 4136)	23c			
	d	Add lines 23a through 23c			23d	0
	24	Estimated tax penalty (see instructions). Check if Form 2220 is attached ☐			24	
	25	**Amount owed.** If line 23d is smaller than the total of lines 22c and 24, enter amount owed			25	
	26	**Overpayment.** If line 23d is larger than the total of lines 22c and 24, enter amount overpaid			26	0
	27	Enter amount from line 26: **Credited to 2023 estimated tax** — **Refunded**			27	

Sign Here

Under penalties of perjury, I declare that I have examined this return, including accompanying schedules and statements, and to the best of my knowledge and belief, it is true, correct, and complete. Declaration of preparer (other than taxpayer) is based on all information of which preparer has any knowledge.

Signature of officer | Date | Title

May the IRS discuss this return with the preparer shown below? See instructions. ☑ Yes ☐ No

Paid Preparer Use Only

Print/Type preparer's name	Preparer's signature	Date	Check ☐ if self-employed	PTIN
Firm's name			Firm's EIN	
Firm's address			Phone no.	

Self-Study Problem 11.6

Form 1120-S (2022) Aspen Corporation Page **2**

Schedule B **Other Information** (see instructions)

		Yes	No
1	Check accounting method: **a** ☐ Cash **b** ☑ Accrual **c** ☐ Other (specify)		
2	See the instructions and enter the: **a** Business activity **b** Product or service		
3	At any time during the tax year, was any shareholder of the corporation a disregarded entity, a trust, an estate, or a nominee or similar person? If "Yes," attach Schedule B-1, Information on Certain Shareholders of an S Corporation		✓
4	At the end of the tax year, did the corporation:		
a	Own directly 20% or more, or own, directly or indirectly, 50% or more of the total stock issued and outstanding of any foreign or domestic corporation? For rules of constructive ownership, see instructions. If "Yes," complete (i) through (v) below		✓

(i) Name of Corporation	**(ii)** Employer Identification Number (if any)	**(iii)** Country of Incorporation	**(iv)** Percentage of Stock Owned	**(v)** If Percentage in (iv) Is 100%, Enter the Date (if applicable) a Qualified Subchapter S Subsidiary Election Was Made

		Yes	No
b	Own directly an interest of 20% or more, or own, directly or indirectly, an interest of 50% or more in the profit, loss, or capital in any foreign or domestic partnership (including an entity treated as a partnership) or in the beneficial interest of a trust? For rules of constructive ownership, see instructions. If "Yes," complete (i) through (v) below		✓

(i) Name of Entity	**(ii)** Employer Identification Number (if any)	**(iii)** Type of Entity	**(iv)** Country of Organization	**(v)** Maximum Percentage Owned in Profit, Loss, or Capital

		Yes	No
5a	At the end of the tax year, did the corporation have any outstanding shares of restricted stock? If "Yes," complete lines (i) and (ii) below.		✓
	(i) Total shares of restricted stock		
	(ii) Total shares of non-restricted stock		
b	At the end of the tax year, did the corporation have any outstanding stock options, warrants, or similar instruments? If "Yes," complete lines (i) and (ii) below.		✓
	(i) Total shares of stock outstanding at the end of the tax year		
	(ii) Total shares of stock outstanding if all instruments were executed		
6	Has this corporation filed, or is it required to file, **Form 8918,** Material Advisor Disclosure Statement, to provide information on any reportable transaction?		✓
7	Check this box if the corporation issued publicly offered debt instruments with original issue discount ☐ If checked, the corporation may have to file **Form 8281,** Information Return for Publicly Offered Original Issue Discount Instruments.		
8	If the corporation **(a)** was a C corporation before it elected to be an S corporation **or** the corporation acquired an asset with a basis determined by reference to the basis of the asset (or the basis of any other property) in the hands of a C corporation, **and (b)** has net unrealized built-in gain in excess of the net recognized built-in gain from prior years, enter the net unrealized built-in gain reduced by net recognized built-in gain from prior years. See instructions $		
9	Did the corporation have an election under section 163(j) for any real property trade or business or any farming business in effect during the tax year? See instructions		✓
10	Does the corporation satisfy one or more of the following? See instructions		✓
a	The corporation owns a pass-through entity with current, or prior year carryover, excess business interest expense.		
b	The corporation's aggregate average annual gross receipts (determined under section 448(c)) for the 3 tax years preceding the current tax year are more than $27 million and the corporation has business interest expense.		
c	The corporation is a tax shelter and the corporation has business interest expense. If "Yes," complete and attach **Form 8990,** Limitation on Business Interest Expense Under Section 163(j).		
11	Does the corporation satisfy **both** of the following conditions?		✓
a	The corporation's total receipts (see instructions) for the tax year were less than $250,000.		
b	The corporation's total assets at the end of the tax year were less than $250,000. If "Yes," the corporation is not required to complete Schedules L and M-1.		

Form **1120-S** (2022)

Self-Study Problem 11.6

Form 1120-S (2022) Aspen Corporation Page 3

Schedule B Other Information (see instructions) *(continued)*

		Yes	No
12	During the tax year, did the corporation have any non-shareholder debt that was canceled, was forgiven, or had the terms modified so as to reduce the principal amount of the debt?		✓
	If "Yes," enter the amount of principal reduction . . . $		
13	During the tax year, was a qualified subchapter S subsidiary election terminated or revoked? If "Yes," see instructions		✓
14a	Did the corporation make any payments in 2022 that would require it to file Form(s) 1099?	✓	
b	If "Yes," did or will the corporation file required Form(s) 1099?	✓	
15	Is the corporation attaching Form 8996 to certify as a Qualified Opportunity Fund?		✓
	If "Yes," enter the amount from Form 8996, line 15 . . . $		

Schedule K Shareholders' Pro Rata Share Items

						Total amount
Income (Loss)	1	Ordinary business income (loss) (page 1, line 21)			1	9,000
	2	Net rental real estate income (loss) (attach Form 8825)			2	
	3a	Other gross rental income (loss)	3a			
	b	Expenses from other rental activities (attach statement)	3b			
	c	Other net rental income (loss). Subtract line 3b from line 3a			3c	
	4	Interest income			4	
	5	Dividends: a Ordinary dividends			5a	10,000
		b Qualified dividends	5b	10,000		
	6	Royalties			6	
	7	Net short-term capital gain (loss) (attach Schedule D (Form 1120-S))			7	
	8a	Net long-term capital gain (loss) (attach Schedule D (Form 1120-S))			8a	
	b	Collectibles (28%) gain (loss)	8b			
	c	Unrecaptured section 1250 gain (attach statement)	8c			
	9	Net section 1231 gain (loss) (attach Form 4797)			9	
	10	Other income (loss) (see instructions) Type:			10	
Deductions	11	Section 179 deduction (attach Form 4562)			11	
	12a	Charitable contributions			12a	
	b	Investment interest expense			12b	
	c	Section 59(e)(2) expenditures Type:			12c	
	d	Other deductions (see instructions) Type:			12d	
Credits	13a	Low-income housing credit (section 42(j)(5))			13a	
	b	Low-income housing credit (other)			13b	
	c	Qualified rehabilitation expenditures (rental real estate) (attach Form 3468, if applicable)			13c	
	d	Other rental real estate credits (see instructions) Type:			13d	
	e	Other rental credits (see instructions) Type:			13e	
	f	Biofuel producer credit (attach Form 6478)			13f	
	g	Other credits (see instructions) Type:			13g	
International	14	Attach Schedule K-2 (Form 1120-S), Shareholders' Pro Rata Share Items—International, and check this box to indicate you are reporting items of international tax relevance ☐				
Alternative Minimum Tax (AMT) Items	15a	Post-1986 depreciation adjustment			15a	
	b	Adjusted gain or loss			15b	
	c	Depletion (other than oil and gas)			15c	
	d	Oil, gas, and geothermal properties—gross income			15d	
	e	Oil, gas, and geothermal properties—deductions			15e	
	f	Other AMT items (attach statement)			15f	
Items Affecting Shareholder Basis	16a	Tax-exempt interest income			16a	
	b	Other tax-exempt income			16b	
	c	Nondeductible expenses			16c	
	d	Distributions (attach statement if required) (see instructions)			16d	
	e	Repayment of loans from shareholders			16e	
	f	Foreign taxes paid or accrued			16f	

Form **1120-S** (2022)

Self-Study Problem 11.6

Form 1120-S (2022) Aspen Corporation Page **4**

Schedule K	**Shareholders' Pro Rata Share Items** *(continued)*		**Total amount**
Other Information	17a Investment income	17a	
	b Investment expenses	17b	
	c Dividend distributions paid from accumulated earnings and profits	17c	
	d Other items and amounts (attach statement)		
Reconciliation	18 **Income (loss) reconciliation.** Combine the amounts on lines 1 through 10 in the far right column. From the result, subtract the sum of the amounts on lines 11 through 12d and 16f	18	19,000

Schedule L **Balance Sheets per Books**	Beginning of tax year (a)	(b)	End of tax year (c)	(d)
Assets				
1 Cash		Initial Return		35,000
2a Trade notes and accounts receivable			10,000	
b Less allowance for bad debts	( )		(0)	10,000
3 Inventories				
4 U.S. government obligations				
5 Tax-exempt securities (see instructions)				
6 Other current assets (attach statement)				
7 Loans to shareholders				
8 Mortgage and real estate loans				
9 Other investments (attach statement)				
10a Buildings and other depreciable assets			125,000	
b Less accumulated depreciation	( )		(5,000)	120,000
11a Depletable assets				
b Less accumulated depletion	( )		( )	
12 Land (net of any amortization)				18,000
13a Intangible assets (amortizable only)				
b Less accumulated amortization	( )		( )	
14 Other assets (attach statement)				
15 Total assets				183,000
Liabilities and Shareholders' Equity				
16 Accounts payable				24,000
17 Mortgages, notes, bonds payable in less than 1 year				
18 Other current liabilities (attach statement)				
19 Loans from shareholders				
20 Mortgages, notes, bonds payable in 1 year or more				
21 Other liabilities (attach statement)				
22 Capital stock				140,000
23 Additional paid-in capital				
24 Retained earnings				19,000
25 Adjustments to shareholders' equity (attach statement)				
26 Less cost of treasury stock		( )		( )
27 Total liabilities and shareholders' equity				183,000

Form **1120-S** (2022)

Self-Study Problem 11.6

Form 1120-S (2022) Aspen Corporation Page **5**

Schedule M-1 Reconciliation of Income (Loss) per Books With Income (Loss) per Return

Note: The corporation may be required to file Schedule M-3. See instructions.

1	Net income (loss) per books	19,000	5	Income recorded on books this year not included on Schedule K, lines 1 through 10 (itemize):	
2	Income included on Schedule K, lines 1, 2, 3c, 4, 5a, 6, 7, 8a, 9, and 10, not recorded on books this year (itemize)		a	Tax-exempt interest $	
3	Expenses recorded on books this year not included on Schedule K, lines 1 through 12, and 16f (itemize):		6	Deductions included on Schedule K, lines 1 through 12, and 16f, not charged against book income this year (itemize):	
a	Depreciation $		a	Depreciation $	
b	Travel and entertainment $		7	Add lines 5 and 6	0
4	Add lines 1 through 3	19,000	8	Income (loss) (Schedule K, line 18). Subtract line 7 from line 4	19,000

Schedule M-2 Analysis of Accumulated Adjustments Account, Shareholders' Undistributed Taxable Income Previously Taxed, Accumulated Earnings and Profits, and Other Adjustments Account (see instructions)

		(a) Accumulated adjustments account	(b) Shareholders' undistributed taxable income previously taxed	(c) Accumulated earnings and profits	(d) Other adjustments account
1	Balance at beginning of tax year	0			
2	Ordinary income from page 1, line 21	9,000			
3	Other additions	10,000			
4	Loss from page 1, line 21	( )			
5	Other reductions	( )			( )
6	Combine lines 1 through 5	19,000			
7	Distributions				
8	Balance at end of tax year. Subtract line 7 from line 6	19,000			

Form **1120-S** (2022)

Self-Study Problem 11.6

671121

☐ Final K-1 ☐ Amended K-1 OMB No. 1545-0123

Schedule K-1 (Form 1120-S) **2022**

Department of the Treasury
Internal Revenue Service

For calendar year 2022, or tax year

beginning / / 2022 ending / /

Shareholder's Share of Income, Deductions, Credits, etc. See separate instructions.

Part I Information About the Corporation

A Corporation's employer identification number
92-2222222

B Corporation's name, address, city, state, and ZIP code
Aspen Corporation
470 Rio Grande Place
Aspen, CO 81611

C IRS Center where corporation filed return
Ogden, UT

D Corporation's total number of shares
Beginning of tax year . . . . . .
End of tax year 100

Part II Information About the Shareholder

E Shareholder's identifying number
411-41-4141

F Shareholder's name, address, city, state, and ZIP code
Ava Mendes
1175 Delaware Street
Denver, CO 80204

G Current year allocation percentage . . . 100 %

H Shareholder's number of shares
Beginning of tax year . . . . . .
End of tax year 100

I Loans from shareholder
Beginning of tax year . . . . . . $
End of tax year . . . . $

For IRS Use Only

Part III Shareholder's Share of Current Year Income, Deductions, Credits, and Other Items

1	Ordinary business income (loss)	9,000
2	Net rental real estate income (loss)	
3	Other net rental income (loss)	
4	Interest income	
5a	Ordinary dividends	10,000
5b	Qualified dividends	10,000
6	Royalties	
7	Net short-term capital gain (loss)	
8a	Net long-term capital gain (loss)	
8b	Collectibles (28%) gain (loss)	
8c	Unrecaptured section 1250 gain	
9	Net section 1231 gain (loss)	
10	Other income (loss)	
11	Section 179 deduction	
12	Other deductions	
13	Credits	
14	Schedule K-3 is attached if checked . . . . . . ☐	
15	Alternative minimum tax (AMT) items	
16	Items affecting shareholder basis	
17	Other information	
	A	10,000
	V*	9,000
	V**	172,000
	V***	125,000
	AC	295,000

18 ☐ More than one activity for at-risk purposes*
19 ☐ More than one activity for passive activity purposes*

* See attached statement for additional information.

For Paperwork Reduction Act Notice, see the Instructions for Form 1120-S. www.irs.gov/Form1120S Cat. No. 11520D **Schedule K-1 (Form 1120-S) 2022**

* The IRS uses code V for QBI deduction reporting and recommends Statement A from the Form 1120S instructions. Use of Intuit ProConnect software will create Statement A. A version of Statement A is presented on the next page.

Statement A—QBI Pass-Through Entity Reporting

Pass-through entity's name: Aspen Corporation		Pass-through entity's EIN: 92-2222222	
Shareholder's name: Ava Mendes	Shareholder's identifying number: 411-41-4141		
Shareholder's share of:	Trade or Business 1 ☐ PTP ☐ Aggregated ☐ SSTB	Trade or Business 2 ☐ PTP ☐ Aggregated ☐ SSTB	Trade or Business 3 ☐ PTP ☐ Aggregated ☐ SSTB
QBI or qualified PTP items subject to shareholder-specific determinations:			
Ordinary business income (loss)	9,000		
Rental income (loss)			
Royalty income (loss)			
Section 1231 gain (loss)			
Other income (loss)			
Section 179 deduction			
Other deductions			
W-2 wages	172,000		
UBIA of qualified property	125,000		
Section 199A dividends			

Self-Study Problem 11.8

Only \$190,000 (\$340,000 − \$150,000) is subject to the accumulated earnings tax.
20% × \$190,000 = \$38,000

CHAPTER 12 TAX ADMINISTRATION AND TAX PLANNING

Self-Study Problem 12.1

1. True
2. True
3. False — The commissioner of internal revenue is appointed by the president of the United States.
4. False — The IRS is part of the Treasury Department.
5. True

Self-Study Problem 12.2

1. True
2. False — An office audit is conducted at the IRS office.
3. True
4. True
5. False — Audits can be appealed to an appellate agent.

Self-Study Problem 12.3

Part a. Failure-to-pay penalty:

\$3,000 × 0.5% × 2 months		\$ 30
Failure-to-file penalty:		
\$3,000 × 5% × 2 months	\$ 300	
Less: failure-to-pay penalty	(30)	
		270
Total		\$300

The minimum failure-to-file penalty does not apply since the return was filed within 60 days of the due date.

Part b. Failure-to-pay penalty:

\$3,000 × 0.5% × 3 months		\$ 45
Failure-to-file penalty:		
\$3,000 × 5% × 3 months	\$ 450	
Less: failure-to-pay penalty	(45)	
	405	
Minimum failure-to-file penalty		450
Total		\$495

Part c. 20% × \$10,000 — \$2,000

Self-Study Problem 12.4

1. True
2. False — For bad debts, the statute of limitations is 7 years.
3. False — There is no statute of limitations for fraudulent returns.
4. True
5. True

Self-Study Problem 12.5

1. False — Lawyers and enrolled agents may also represent taxpayers before the IRS.
2. False — A college degree is not required.
3. False — Anyone may prepare corporate tax returns.
4. True
5. False — The penalty is $560 for tax returns filed in 2021.
6. True
7. False — The burden of proof is on the IRS.
8. False — The burden of proof remains on the taxpayer.
9. True
10. True
11. True
12. False. — Periodicals and newspapers are not substantial authority.
13. True
14. True

Self-Study Problem 12.6

1. True
2. True
3. True — Publication 1 directs the reader to Publication 594.
4. True
5. True
6. True

Self-Study Problem 12.7

1. 17.08% = $15,197 / $89,000
2. 17.15% = $15,435.50 / $90,000
3. 23.85% = ($15,435.50 − $15,197) / ($90,000 − $89,000)

K's $1,000 increase in income is subject to tax in two different single taxpayer rate brackets. The first $75 ($89,075 − $89,000) is taxed at 22% while the remaining $925 is taxed at 24%.

GLOSSARY OF TAX TERMS

NOTE: The words and phrases appearing below have been defined to reflect their conventional use in the field of taxation. Such definitions may therefore, be incomplete for other purposes.

20-percent limitation

Taxpayers may not deduct donations of capital gain property in excess of 20 percent of the taxpayer's adjusted gross income (AGI) to a non-50-percent charitable organization.

30-percent limitation

The 30-percent limit of AGI applies to capital gain property donated to a 50-percent organization and also to cash donations made to a non-50-percent organization.

50-percent limitation

Taxpayers may not deduct certain charitable contributions in excess of 50 percent of the taxpayer's gross income.

50-percent organization

Defined by the Internal Revenue Service (IRS) as specific organizations such as public charities, churches, most educational institutions, hospitals, the United States or any state or local government, all private operating foundations, and private nonoperating foundations if they distribute their contributions to public charities within a specific time period. All other qualified organizations are non-50-percent organizations.

60-percent limitation

Taxpayers may not deduct donations for cash contributions to 50-percent organizations in excess of 60 percent of the taxpayer's AGI for tax years 2022 to 2025.

Abandoned spouse

In order to qualify to file as an abandoned spouse, a person must file a separate tax return; must pay more than half the costs of maintaining a home in a year, and must not have a spouse living with them at any time in the last 6 months of the year.

Accelerated death benefits

Early payouts of life insurance, also called accelerated death benefits or viatical settlements, are excluded from gross income for certain terminally or chronically ill taxpayers. The taxpayer may either collect an early payout from the insurance company or sell or assign the policy to a viatical settlement provider. See *Viatical settlements.*

Accelerated depreciation

The depreciation of fixed assets at a faster rate early in their useful lives.

Accident and health benefits

Employee fringe benefits provided by employers through the payment of health and accident insurance premiums, or the establishment of employer-funded medical reimbursement plans. Employers generally are entitled to a deduction for such payments, whereas employees generally exclude the fringe benefits from gross income.

Accounting methods

The two main accounting methods are cash and accrual-basis accounting.

Accounting periods

The timeframe reflected in a business's financial statements and reports to stakeholders.

Accrual method

A method of accounting that reflects expenses incurred and income earned for any one tax year. In contrast to the cash basis of accounting, expenses do not have to be paid to be deductible, nor does income have to be received to be taxable.

Accumulated earnings tax

A tax imposed by the federal government on companies with retained earnings determined to be in excess of what is considered ordinary and necessary.

Accuracy-related penalty

A penalty imposed by the Internal Revenue Service on a taxpayer when a significant amount of taxable income is not reported on a return.

Actual cost method

The IRS-approved method for calculating and claiming expenses related to automobile use for business.

Adaptation

An amount paid to allow the property or facility to be used in a new or different use.

Adjusted basis

The cost or other basis of property reduced by depreciation allowed or allowable and increased by capital improvements. See *Basis.*

Adjusted gross income (AGI)

A determination unique to individual taxpayers used as the basis to calculate limitations on the amount of certain expenses which may be deductible, including medical expenses, charitable contributions, certain personal casualty losses, and certain other itemized deductions. Generally, AGI represents gross income minus specific deductions such as certain trade or business expenses (deductions *for* AGI) but before itemized deductions or the standard deduction (deductions *from* AGI).

Adoption credit

The nonrefundable income tax credit allowed for qualified adoption expenses of an individual.

Adoption expenses

Adoption fees, court costs, attorney fees, and other expenses directly related to the legal adoption of an eligible child.

Affordable Care Act (ACA)

Also referred to as Obamacare, ACA is a federal law providing for a fundamental reform of the U.S. healthcare and health insurance system, signed by President Barack Obama in 2010.

Alimony payments

Payments from one spouse or former spouse, to the other, required as a result of a divorce or separation agreement, which meet certain statutory requirements. Alimony and separate maintenance payments, but not child support payments, are included in the gross income of the recipient and are deducted by the payor for divorces occurring before 2019. The Tax Cuts and Jobs Act (TCJA) has repealed both the deduction of and inclusion of alimony for tax years beginning in 2019. See also *Child support payments.*

Alternative minimum tax (AMT)

The AMT is a tax calculation that ensures that wealthy taxpayers cannot take advantage of special tax write-offs to avoid paying tax.

American Opportunity tax credit (AOTC)

Previously referred to as the Hope credit, the AOTC is a tax credit available for the first 4 years of postsecondary education expenses for students who meet specific requirements.

Amortization

The allocation (and charge to expense) of the cost or other basis of an intangible asset over its estimated useful life. Examples of amortizable intangibles include patents and copyrights.

Amount realized

The amount received by a taxpayer on the sale or exchange of property less the cost incurred to transfer the property. The measure of the amount received is the sum of the cash and the fair market value of any property or services plus any relieved liability of the taxpayer. Determining the amount realized is the starting point for arriving at a realized gain or loss.

AMT adjustments

Timing differences that arise when there are differences between regular and AMT tax calculations (e.g., depreciation timing differences).

AMT exemption allowance

Statutory deduction reducing AMT income for taxpayers based on their filing status.

AMT preferences

Items excluded from the computation of regular taxable income but required to be added to compute alternative minimum taxable income.

Annual contribution limits

The cap on total contributions individuals may make to traditional IRAs and Roth IRAs in a given tax year.

Annual Federal Tax Refresher (AFTR)

The continuing education course required to be taken by all paid tax return preparers; focusing on the upcoming tax filing season issues and tax updates.

Annual Filing Season Program (AFSP)

A voluntary program that encourages paid tax return preparers to participate in continuing education on tax law changes.

Annualized period

A given period that is less than one year but is computed as if the period was for a full year.

Annuity

A fixed sum payable at specified intervals for a specific period of time or for life. Payments represent a partial return of capital and a return (e.g., interest income) on the capital investment. An exclusion ratio is generally used to compute the amounts of nontaxable and taxable income.

Appeals process of IRS

When a disagreement arises between a taxpayer and the IRS over the outcome of a tax audit, an appeals process is available. If agreement cannot be reached at an informal appeals conference, the process moves to a formal appeals process in the Federal Tax Court.

Asset depreciation range (ADR)

An accounting method established by the IRS to determine the useful life of specific classes of depreciable assets.

At-risk rule

Prevents taxpayers from deducting losses from activities in excess of the investment in the activities. Most commonly related to investments in partnerships.

Audit procedure of IRS

A primary function of the IRS, the process involves selecting some returns for examination in a correspondence audit, an office audit, or a field audit.

Automobile expenses

Automobile expenses are generally deductible only to the extent the automobile is used in business or for the production of income. Personal commuting expenses are not deductible. When calculating the deductible automobile expenses, the taxpayer may deduct actual expenses (including depreciation and insurance), or choose to use the standard mileage rate.

Average tax rate

The tax rate representing the average rate of tax applicable to the taxpayer's income; calculated as the total tax paid divided by the total income of the taxpayer.

Backup withholding

Certain situations in which the issuer of payments such as dividends or interest is required to withhold income tax at the time of payment. Designed to ensure that income tax is collected on income from certain taxpayers (generally, non-U.S. tax residents).

Bad debts

An ordinary deduction is permitted if a business debt, such as an account receivable, subsequently becomes worthless (uncollectible), provided the income arising from the debt was previously included in taxable income. The deduction is allowed only in the year of worthlessness. A nonbusiness bad debt deduction is allowed as a short-term capital loss when a debt which did not arise in connection with the creditor's trade or business activities becomes worthless.

Barter

An exchange of goods or services for other goods or services without using money. The fair market value of bartered goods must be included in reporting gross income for taxation.

Basis

The amount assigned to an asset for income tax purposes. For assets acquired by purchase, the basis would be the cost of the asset plus any direct costs incidental to the purchase. Special rules govern the basis of property received as a result of another's death or by gift. See also *Adjusted basis.*

Betterment

An amount paid to improve and increase the productivity, efficiency, strength, quality, or output of the property or facility.

Bona fide

Authentic and genuine. In the context of tax law, serving a specific business purpose.

Bonus depreciation

The immediate deduction of all or some of the cost of otherwise depreciated property.

Book income

Another term for a corporation's financial accounting income. Schedule M-1 of the Form 1120 reconciles a corporation's book income to its taxable income, computed before any net operating loss and dividends are deducted.

Boot

Cash or property of a type other than that permitted to be received tax-free in a nontaxable like-kind exchange. The receipt of boot will cause an otherwise tax-free transfer to become taxable to the extent of the lesser of the fair market value of such boot or the realized gain on the transfer.

Built-in gains tax

An S corporation may be subject to a tax on gains attributable to appreciation in the value of assets held by the corporation prior to the S corporation election, referred to as the built-in gains tax.

Business and nonbusiness bad debts

When a taxpayer sells goods or services on credit and the accounts receivable become uncollectible, a bad debt is incurred. Similarly, when a taxpayer makes a personal loan that becomes uncollectible, a nonbusiness bad debt is incurred.

Business gifts

Business gifts are deductible only to the extent that each gift does not exceed $25 per person per year. Exceptions are made for promotional gifts and for certain employee awards.

Cancellation of debt income

Also referred to as forgiveness of debt income. When a lender forgives or cancels all or some of the taxpayer's outstanding loans or other credit account. In general, the amount of debt that has been forgiven is considered taxable income unless specifically excluded.

Capital asset

All assets are capital assets except those specifically excluded by the tax law. Major categories of noncapital assets include property held for sale in the normal course of business (i.e., inventory), trade accounts and notes receivable, depreciable property, and real estate used in a trade or business.

Capital expenditure

An expenditure, the amount of which should be added to the basis of the property improved. For income tax purposes, this generally precludes a deduction for the full amount of the expenditure in the year paid or incurred. Any tax deduction has to come in the form of cost recovery or depreciation.

Capital gain

The gain from the sale or exchange of a capital asset. Gain from property held 12 months or less is deemed to be a short-term capital gain. If the property is held more than 12 months, the gain is deemed to be long-term. See *Capital asset* and *Holding period.*

Capital improvements

Major expenditures for permanent improvements to or restoration of a taxpayer's property.

Capital loss

The loss from the sale or exchange of a capital asset. A loss from property held 12 months or less is deemed to be a short-term capital loss. If the property is held more than 12 months, the loss is deemed to be long-term. See *Capital asset* and *Holding period.*

Capital loss carryovers

A net capital loss that is not deducted in the current tax year but is eligible to be carried forward into future taxable years.

Cash basis

A method of accounting under which income is reported when received and expenses are deductible when paid by the taxpayer. Prepaid rent and prepaid interest must be deducted using the accrual method.

Cash method

The cash method utilizes the cash-basis of accounting whereby income is not counted until payment is actually received, and expenses are not counted until they are actually paid. The cash method is the more commonly used method of accounting by small businesses.

Casualty loss

A casualty is defined as the complete or partial destruction of property resulting from an identifiable event of a sudden, unexpected or unusual nature (e.g., floods, shipwrecks, storms, fires, automobile accidents). Beginning in 2018, personal casualty losses are only eligible for deduction when resulting from a federally declared disaster area. Personal casualty losses are deductible as itemized deductions subject to a $100 nondeductible floor and only to the extent that the taxpayer's total losses from personal-use property (net of the $100 floor) exceed 10 percent of adjusted gross income. Special rules are provided for the combining (netting) of certain casualty gains and losses.

"Catch-up" contribution

A type of retirement savings contribution that allows people 50 or older to make additional contributions to 401(k) accounts and individual retirement accounts (IRAs).

Certified Public Accountant (CPA)

A designation provided by a state's Board of Accounting to an individual who has passed the Uniform Certified Public Accountant Examination and met the required amount of accounting-related experience.

Charitable contributions

Contributions may be deductible (subject to various restrictions and ceiling limitations) if made to qualified charitable organizations. A cash-basis taxpayer is entitled to a deduction in the year of payment. Accrual-basis corporations may accrue contributions at year-end under certain circumstances.

Child and dependent care credit

This credit is available to individuals who are employed on a full-time basis and maintain a household for a dependent child or disabled spouse or dependent. The amount of the credit is equal to a percentage of the cost of employment-related child and dependent care expenses, up to a stated maximum amount.

Child support payments

Payments for child support do not constitute alimony, and are, therefore, not included in gross income by the recipient or deducted as alimony by the payor to the extent permitted otherwise. See also *Alimony payments.*

Child tax credit

Certain individual taxpayers may take a tax credit based on the number of their dependent children, subject to limitations.

Closed transaction

A transaction in which all material parts of the transaction have been completed.

Community property

Community property is all property, other than separate property, owned by a married couple. The income from community property is generally split equally between spouses. The classification of property as community property is important in determining the separate taxable income of married taxpayers.

Constructive ownership

A close relationship with an owner, e.g., a spouse; the person in question is treated as an owner.

Consumer interest

Not deductible for tax purposes, consumer interest is interest expense generated from personal loans, credit cards, or other debt used for personal purposes.

Corporate alternative minimum tax

The corporate AMT was repealed for tax years after 2017 by the TCJA.

Corporate tax rate

Since 2018, corporations have been subject to a flat income tax rate of 21 percent.

Correspondence audit

A tax audit conducted by the IRS via written or electronic correspondence without in-person meetings.

Cost of goods sold

The amount equal to the cost of inventory sold during the period. Generally computed as beginning inventory plus purchases of inventory (or the cost to create inventory) less ending inventory. Cost of goods sold is deducted from gross receipts on Schedule C.

Coverdell Education Savings Accounts

Educational savings accounts that allow taxpayers to pay for qualified education expenses, with a maximum contribution allowed of $2,000 annually.

De minimis fringe benefits

A de minimis fringe benefit is one which, considering its value and the frequency with which it is provided, is so small as to make accounting for it unreasonable or impractical. De minimis fringe benefits are excluded under Internal Revenue Code section 132(a)(4) and include items which are not specifically excluded under other sections of the Code.

Deferred compensation

Compensation which will be taxed when received or upon the removal of certain restrictions, not when earned. An example would be contributions by an employer to a qualified pension or profit-sharing plan on behalf of an employee. Such contributions will not be taxed to the employee until the funds are made available or distributed to the employee (e.g., upon retirement). See *Qualified pension or profit-sharing plan.*

Defined benefit plan

A type of pension plan in which the plan specifies the pension payment amounts payable to an employee upon retirement, based on the employee's earnings' history, tenure of service, and age.

Defined contribution plan

A type of pension plan in which the plan specifies the regular contributions made by the employer and employee in which the pension benefits are based on the contribution amounts and the returns of the plan's investments.

Dependent

A child or relative whose characteristics and relationship to a taxpayer allow the taxpayer to claim certain tax deductions and credits, such as from the head of household filing status, the Child Tax Credit, the Earned Income Tax Credit, or the Child and Dependent Care Credit.

Dependent care flexible spending account

A pre-tax benefit account used to pay for eligible dependent care services, such as preschool, summer day camp, before or after school programs, and child or adult daycare.

Depreciation

The reduction in the value of an asset or assets, depreciation decreases the amount of taxes a company or business pays via tax deductions.

Depreciation recapture

The recharacterizing of gain on the sale of certain property used in a trade or business to ordinary income to the extent of depreciation previously allowed.

Discriminant Function System (DIF)

One process by which the IRS selects tax returns for audits. The DIF is a computerized statistical sampling technique.

Dividends received deduction

A special deduction for corporations that receive dividend income distributions from a domestic corporation of which it has an ownership interest. Generally designed to prevent double taxation of corporate dividends paid by a corporate subsidiary to its corporate owner(s).

Earned income

Income from personal services as distinguished from income generated by property.

Earned income credit

The earned income credit is a refundable credit available to qualifying individuals with income and AGI below certain levels.

Economic performance

All activities related to the incurrence of a liability have been performed.

Education assistance plans

Under an educational assistance plan, employers may provide up to $5,250 of excludable annual tuition assistance.

Education expenses

Employees may deduct education expenses if such items are incurred either (1) to maintain or improve existing job-related skills or (2) to meet the express requirements of the employer or the requirements imposed by law to retain employment status. Such expenses are not deductible if the education is required to meet the minimum educational requirements for the taxpayer's job or the education qualifies the individual for a new trade or business.

Educational savings account

See Coverdell Education Savings Accounts.

E-filing

The process of transmitting federal income tax return information to the IRS Service Center using a device with Internet access.

EFTPS

The Electronic Federal Tax Payment System, a free service of the U.S. Department of the Treasury.

Election to expense (Section 179)

The tax code Section 179 allows a taxpayer to elect to immediately expense and deduct the cost of certain property when placed in service, up to a certain limit, rather than capitalizing and depreciating such property.

Employee annuities

Retirement plans organized by employers, who make periodic payments into the plans on behalf of the employees.

Employee fringe benefits

Non-wage benefits or perquisites (perks) provided to employees in addition to their normal wages and salaries. Most fringe benefits are required to be included in the employee's gross income; however, certain *qualified* fringe benefits such as employee-paid health insurance premiums may be excluded from the employee's gross income but remain deductible by the business.

Employee Stock Ownership Plan (ESOP)

A type of defined contribution pension plan in which employers provide their employees with ownership in the employer's stock.

Encumbered property

Also known as collateral, this is property pledged for a liability in the amount of the liability.

Energy credit

Tax law in the past decade included personal tax credits associated with energy-efficient products. Many have been extended or expired but the IRS website maintains updated information.

Entertainment expenses

Starting in 2018, the TCJA has disallowed the deductibility of entertainment expenses.

Estimated payments

Self-employed taxpayers are not subject to income tax withholding but must make quarterly estimated tax payments in four installments in a tax year.

Exclusions—gross income

Certain types of income are specifically excluded from gross income. These may be referred to as exempt income, exclusions, or tax exemptions.

Exclusion ratio

The percentage of an investor's return that is not subject to taxes.

Failure-to-file penalty

A penalty charged on tax returns filed after the due date or extended due date, absent a reasonable cause for filing late. The failure-to-file penalty is 5 percent of the unpaid taxes for each month or part of a month that a tax return is late; not to exceed 25 percent of unpaid taxes.

Failure-to-pay penalty

A penalty charged for failing to pay tax by its due date. The late payment penalty is 0.5 percent of the tax owed after the due date, for each month or part of a month the tax remains unpaid, up to 25 percent.

Fair market value

The amount at which property would change hands between a willing buyer and a willing seller, neither being under any compulsion to buy or sell, and both having reasonable knowledge of the relevant facts.

Federal Insurance Contributions Act (FICA)

FICA imposes social taxes on forms of earned income to provide benefits for retired and disabled workers. Referred to as FICA taxes, Social Security and Medicare taxes are withheld using a specific percentage from an employee's wages. The employer, the employee, and the self-employed are responsible for the payment of FICA taxes.

Federal poverty level (FPL)

A measure of income issued annually by the Department of Health and Human Services (HHS). Federal poverty levels are used to determine eligibility for certain programs and benefits.

Federal Tax Court

A federal trial court of record established by the U.S. Congress which specializes in adjudicating disputes over federal income tax, generally prior to the time at which formal tax assessments are made by the Internal Revenue Service.

Field audit

One of three types of tax return audits conducted by the IRS; this audit is conducted at either a taxpayer's home, place of business, or accountant's office.

First in, first out (FIFO)

An accounting method for determining the cost of inventories. Under this method, the first merchandise acquired is the first to be sold. Thus, the cost of inventory on hand is deemed to be the cost of the most recently acquired merchandise (goods).

Fiscal year

A fiscal year is a one-year (12-month) period that companies and governments use for financial reporting and budgeting that ends on a month-end other than December.

Fiscal year-end

An annual accounting period which does not end on December 31, a calendar year-end. An example of a fiscal year is July 1 through June 30.

Flexible spending account

A pre-tax benefit account used to pay for eligible out-of-pocket healthcare costs.

Foreign income exclusion

The foreign earned income exclusion is intended to prevent double taxation by excluding income from U.S. taxation that has been earned in another country.

Foreign tax credit or deduction

Both U.S. individual taxpayers and U.S. corporations may claim a foreign tax credit on income earned and subject to tax in a foreign country or U.S. possession. As an alternative to the credit, a deduction may be taken for the foreign taxes paid. The purpose of this credit is to eliminate double taxation on income earned in a foreign country.

Forgiveness of debt

See *Cancellation of debt income.*

Fraud penalty

Under the IRS Code, "if any part of an underpayment of tax required to be shown on a return is due to fraud, there shall be added to the tax an amount equal to 75 percent of the portion of the underpayment which is attributable to fraud." Criminal charges are also possible in some cases.

FUTA

The Federal Unemployment Tax Act (FUTA) along with state unemployment systems provides for payments of unemployment compensation to workers who have lost their jobs. Most employers pay both a federal and a state unemployment tax.

General (ordinary) partnerships

A basic form of partnership that is a business arrangement between two or more parties and may be formed by a simple verbal agreement The partners agree to unlimited liability and share in all assets, profits and financial and legal liabilities.

Gift

A transfer of property for less than adequate consideration. Gifts usually occur in a personal setting (such as between members of the same family) and are generally excluded from taxable income. Business gifts are subject to dollar limitations in order to be tax deductible. See *qualified plan award.*

Goodwill

The ability of a business to generate income in excess of a normal rate on assets due to superior managerial skills, market position, new product technology, etc. In the purchase of a business, goodwill is the difference between the purchase price and the value of the net assets. Goodwill is an intangible asset which possesses an indefinite life; however, it is amortized over a 15-year period for federal income tax purposes.

Gross income

All income from whatever source derived except that which is specifically excluded by tax law. Gross income does not include income such as interest on municipal bonds. In the case of a manufacturing or merchandising business, gross income means gross profit (i.e., gross sales or gross receipts less cost of goods sold).

Guaranteed payments

Payments made to a partner for services rendered or for use of the partner's capital, that are made without regard to the income of the partnership (similar to wages). The payments are generally ordinary income to the partner and deductible by the partnership.

Half-year convention

The half-year convention is a depreciation tax rule that assumes the asset is obtained and disposed of halfway through the acquisition and disposal year.

Head of household

An unmarried individual who maintains a household for another and satisfies certain conditions. Such status enables the taxpayer to use income tax rates lower than those applicable to other unmarried individuals (single) but higher than those applicable to surviving spouses [widow(er)] and married persons filing a joint return.

Health savings accounts (HSA)

A type of savings account established by an employer to pay unreimbursed medical expenses by taxpayers with certain high-deductible medical insurance. Contributions to HSAs are deductible for AGI and are subject to limitations.

Healthcare flexible spending accounts

(*see Flexible Spending Account*).

High-low method

A simplified way of computing the federal per diem rate for travel within the United States.

Hobby loss

A nondeductible loss arising from a personal hobby as contrasted with an activity engaged in for profit. Generally, the law provides a presumption that an activity is engaged in for profit if profits are earned during any 3 or more years in a 5-year period.

Household workers

Employees hired to work at specific tasks within a household, including child care, cleaning, meal preparation, and household administration. The payment of household workers generally subjects the taxpayer to a requirement to withhold or pay related payroll taxes. See *Nanny tax.*

Holding period

The period of time that property has been held by a taxpayer. The holding period is of significance in determining whether gains or losses from the sale or exchange of capital assets are classified as long-term or short-term. See *Capital asset, Capital gain,* and *Capital loss.*

Hybrid method

A method of accounting that involves the use of both the cash and accrual methods of accounting. The tax law permits the use of a hybrid method, provided the taxpayer's income is clearly reflected by the method.

Independent contractor

Classification of a worker that provides goods or services via a written contract or verbal agreement. Independent contractors differ from employees based on a number of criteria and are classified by law not by choice of the worker or the employer. The distinguishment between an independent contractor and an employee is important as the costs for business owners to maintain employees are often significantly higher due to federal and state requirements for employers to pay employment taxes and other employee benefits.

Inflation Reduction Act

Signed into law in 2022, its tax provisions impacted energy-related tax credits and brought back a form of the corporate alternative minimum tax to a limited number of very large corporations.

Installment method

A method of accounting enabling a taxpayer to spread the recognition of gain on the sale of property over the payment period. Under this procedure, the seller computes the gross profit percentage from the sale (i.e., the gain divided by the contract price) and applies the percentage to each payment received to arrive at the gain recognized for each accounting period.

Installment sales

A sale in which part of the proceeds will be received in a tax year or years following the year of sale resulting in the partial deferral of gain to future tax years. See *Installment method.*

Intangible assets

An asset that does not have a physical presence but has value. Some examples of intangible assets include copyrights, goodwill, patents, trademarks, etc.

Interest

The amount paid for the use of borrowed funds.

Internal Revenue Code

Sometimes referred to as the Tax Code or the Code, the comprehensive set of tax laws enacted as Title 26 of the United States Code of Congress. The Code is organized according to topic, and covers all relevant rules pertaining to income, gift, estate sales, payroll, and excise taxes. The IRS is the implementing agency of the Internal Revenue Code.

Internal Revenue Service (IRS)

A United States government agency that is responsible for the enforcement of the Internal Revenue Code and collection of taxes. The IRS was established in 1862 by President Lincoln and operates under the authority of the United States Department of the Treasury.

Inventory

The goods and raw materials used to produce goods, held for sale by a business, to be sold to produce a profit.

Involuntary conversion

The loss or destruction of property through theft, casualty, or condemnation. If the owner reinvests any proceeds received within a prescribed period of time in property that is similar or related in service or use, any gain realized on an involuntary conversion can, at the taxpayer's election, be deferred for federal income tax purposes.

IRS Campus Processing Sites

Sites at which IRS computers process information from tax documents such as tax returns, payroll tax forms, Forms 1099, and withholding forms.

IRS online withholding estimator

An online estimator that uses information from recent paystubs of a taxpayer and spouse, details from other sources of income, and a previous tax return to estimate additional withholding needs.

Itemized deductions

Tax deductions taken for various personal expenses incurred during the tax year that decrease taxable income. Itemized deductions are generally used by the taxpayer when the total exceeds the standard deduction. See *Standard deduction.*

Kiddie tax

The amount of tax on the unearned income of certain dependent children.

Last in, first out (LIFO)

An accounting method for determining the cost of inventories. Under this method, the most recently acquired goods are sold first and the cost of inventory on hand is deemed to consist of the earliest purchased merchandise (goods).

Life insurance proceeds

Generally, life insurance proceeds paid to a beneficiary upon the death of the insured are exempt from federal income tax. An exception exists when a life insurance contract has been transferred for valuable consideration to another individual who assumes ownership rights. In such a case, the proceeds are income to the assignee to the extent that the proceeds exceed the amount paid for the policy (cash surrender value at the time of transfer) plus any subsequent premiums paid.

Lifetime learning credit

The lifetime learning credit may be used in any tax year the American Opportunity tax credit is not used for expenses paid for education. Unlike the American Opportunity tax credit, the lifetime learning credit may be claimed for an unlimited number of tax years.

Like-kind exchange

An exchange of property held for productive use in a trade or business or for investment (except inventory and stocks and bonds) for property of the same type. Unless different property is received (i.e., "boot"), the exchange will be nontaxable.

Like-kind property

See *Like-kind exchange.*

Limited Liability Company (LLC)

Business organizations usually treated as partnerships for tax purposes but offering the limited liability of a corporate stockholder to all members.

Limited liability partnerships (LLPs)

A partnership structure where each partner's liability is limited to the amount contributed to the business.

Low-income Retirement Plan Contribution Credit

Certain low-income taxpayers may claim a nonrefundable "Low-Income Retirement Plan Contribution Credit," also called the "Saver's Credit," to encourage participation in tax-saving retirement plans, including IRAs.

Marginal tax rate

The amount of additional tax paid for every additional dollar earned as income.

Market discount

The excess of an bond's stated redemption price over its lower trading price in the secondary market.

Market premium

The excess of a bond's trading price on the secondary market over its lower stated redemption price.

Married filing jointly

A filing status for married couples that have wed before the end of the tax year.

Married filing separately

A tax status used by married couples who choose to record their incomes, exemptions, and deductions on separate tax returns.

Medical expenses

Medical expenses of an individual, spouse, and dependents may be allowed as an itemized deduction to the extent that total medical expenses, less insurance reimbursements, exceed limitations based on the taxpayer's AGI.

Medical flexible spending account (FSA)

A medical flexible spending account is a fringe benefit that allows employees to be reimbursed for medical expenses tax-free up to a certain dollar limit when incurred and claimed within a specific time period. FSAs are usually funded through an employee's voluntary salary reduction agreement with their employer.

Medicare tax

After 2012, the Affordable Care Act (ACA) imposed an additional Medicare tax on high-income taxpayers, at a rate of 0.9 percent applicable to wages, compensation, and self-employment income above an annual threshold amount.

Mid-month convention

The mid-month convention states that all fixed asset acquisitions are assumed to have been purchased in the middle of the month for depreciation purposes.

Mid-quarter convention

The mid-quarter convention states that a business acquiring fixed assets in a reporting quarter should account for them as though they were acquired at the mid-point of the quarter.

Medicare

Federal health insurance provided by the government for persons 65 and over in the United States.

Modified Accelerated Cost Recovery System (MACRS)

The current tax depreciation system in the United States.

Modified adjusted gross income (MAGI)

A household's adjusted gross income with any tax-exempt interest income and certain deductions added back.

Moving expenses

A deduction in arriving at adjusted gross income available to employees and self-employed individuals provided certain tests are met (e.g., the taxpayer's new job must be at least 50 miles farther from the former residence than the former residence was from the former place of work). However, the TCJA has suspended the deduction of moving expenses for all taxpayers except members of the U.S. Armed Services beginning in the 2018 tax year and ending in 2025.

Municipal bond interest

Interest income that is generally exempt from federal tax.

Nanny tax

Payroll taxes paid by a taxpayer that employs certain household workers. See *Household workers.*

Necessary

Appropriate and helpful in furthering the taxpayer's business or income-producing activity. See *Ordinary.*

Net capital gains

The amount by which net long-term capital gains are more than net short-term capital losses.

Net capital losses

The amount that total capital losses exceed total capital gains.

Net investment income

Income such as dividends and interest from investment assets such as stocks, bonds, mutual funds and other investment assets, less investment expenses other than interest expense.

Net investment income tax

The ACA imposed a 3.8 percent Medicare tax on certain net investment income of individuals that have net investment income or modified adjusted gross income above the annual statutory threshold amounts.

Net operating loss (NOL)

When a business's allowable deductions exceed its taxable income within a tax period, a NOL is generated. The NOL can generally be used to offset a business's taxable income subject to annual limitations.

Non-50-percent organization

See *50-percent organization.*

Nonattorney-client privilege

The extension of attorney-client privilege of confidentiality in tax matters to nonattorneys authorized to practice before the IRS. This privilege may be asserted only in noncriminal tax proceedings before the IRS or federal courts.

Nonbusiness bad debts

A bad debt loss not incurred in connection with a taxpayer's trade or business. Such loss is deductible subject to annual limitations, as a short-term capital loss, and will only be allowed in the year the debt becomes entirely worthless. Many investor losses fall into the classification of nonbusiness bad debts.

Nondeductible penalty

Taxpayers are not allowed to deduct penalties assessed by the IRS.

Nondeductible traditional IRA

A retirement plan funded with after-tax dollars.

Nonqualified recipients

Charitable contributions made to nonqualified recipients are not tax deductible. These include needy individuals, social clubs, labor unions, international organizations, and political parties.

Nonrecourse debt

An obligation for which the endorser is not personally liable. An example of a nonrecourse debt is a mortgage on real estate acquired by a partnership without the assumption of any liability on the mortgage by the partnership or any of the partners. The acquired property generally is pledged as collateral for the loan.

OASDI

Old age, survivors, and disability insurance tax; the money that an employer collects goes to the federal government in order to fund the Social Security program. A component of the FICA tax. See *Federal Insurance Contributions Act (FICA)* and *Social security tax.*

Offer in compromise

The IRS may make an offer in compromise that allows a taxpayer to settle tax debt for less than the full amount owed. It may be a legitimate option if someone can't pay their full tax liability, or if doing so creates a financial hardship.

Office audit

A type of tax return audit conducted by the IRS at one of their offices.

Open transaction

Transaction in which not all of the tax events have been completed, therefore providing an opportunity to make modifications and influence the tax result.

Ordinary

Common, accepted, and legitimate in the general industry or type of activity in which the taxpayer is engaged. It comprises one of the tests for the deductibility of expenses incurred or paid in connection with a trade or business: for the production or collection of income; for the management, conservation, or maintenance of property held for the production of income; or in connection with the determination, collection, or refund of any tax. See *Necessary.*

Ordinary gains and losses

Gains and losses that are realized in the course of doing business and from the sale of noncapital assets are typically ordinary.

Organizational expenses/expenditures

Organizational expenses (also known as organizational costs) are associated with the formation of a business prior to the beginning of operation. A corporation may amortize organizational expenses over a period of 180 months. Certain expenses related to starting a company do not qualify for amortization (e.g., expenses connected with issuing or selling stock or other securities).

Original Issue Discount (OID)

The difference between a bond's original redemption value and the lower issuance price of the bond.

Partnerships

Partnerships are conduit, reporting entities that engage in some type of business or financial activity, and are not subject to taxation. Various items of partnership income, expenses, gains, and losses flow through to the partners and are reported on the partners' respective individual income tax returns.

Passive activity

A trade or business in which the taxpayer does not materially participate. Passive activities include most rental real estate activity.

Passive losses

Passive losses are deductible only to the extent of passive income. Losses from actively managed rental real estate may be deducted up to $25,000 annually. Unused passive losses carry forward indefinitely (or until the activity which generated the losses is disposed of) and can be used by taxpayers to offset passive income in future years.

Patents

A patent is an intangible asset which may be amortized over its life. The sale of a patent usually results in long-term capital gain treatment.

Payroll Deduction IRA

Under a Payroll Deduction IRA, employees establish an IRA (either a Traditional or Roth IRA) with a financial institution and authorize a payroll deduction amount for it.

Pension plans

A pension plan is a type of retirement plan where employers promise to pay a defined benefit to employees for life after they retire.

Per diem

An alternative to reporting actual expenses, a per diem allows for a daily allowance for travel expenses including lodging, meals, and incidentals to be reimbursed to employees. Per diem reporting is designed to eliminate the record keeping usually associated with travel expenses.

Percentage method of withholding

A method of calculating employees' federal tax withholdings; this method has no wage or allowance limits and can be used if the employee's wages exceed the wage bracket's limit.

Personal expenses

Expenses of an individual incurred for personal reasons which are not deductible unless specifically allowed under the tax law.

Personal holding company tax

Personal holding companies are subject to a 20-percent tax on their undistributed earnings.

Personal property

Generally, all property other than real estate. Personal property is sometimes designated as "personalty" while real estate is termed "realty." Personal property can also refer to property not used in a taxpayer's trade or business or held for the production or collection of income. When used in this sense, personal property could include both realty (e.g., a personal residence) and personalty (e.g., personal effects such as clothing and furniture).

Personal residence

The sale of a personal residence may result in the recognition of capital gain (but not loss). Taxpayers may permanently exclude $250,000 ($500,000 if married) of gain on the sale of their personal residence from income provided certain requirements are met, but generally not more than once every two years.

Points

Loan origination fees paid that are generally deductible as interest expense by a buyer of property.

Portfolio income

Portfolio income includes dividends, interest, royalties, annuities, and realized gains or losses on the sale of assets producing portfolio income.

Premium tax credit

Lower income individuals who obtain health insurance coverage may be eligible for the premium tax credit to assist in covering the cost of health care premiums. Eligible individuals can choose to receive the credit paid in advance or claim the total credit when filing their tax return. If an individual chooses to have the credit paid in advance, the individual will reconcile the amount paid in advance with the actual credit computed when filing their tax return.

Prepaid interest

Prepaid interest is the interest a borrower pays on a loan before the first scheduled debt repayment.

Preparer tax identification number (PTIN)

A PTIN is a number issued by the IRS to paid tax return preparers. It is used as the tax return preparer's identification number and, when applicable, must be placed in the Paid Preparer section of a tax return that the tax return preparer prepared for compensation.

Private mortgage insurance (PMI)

Mortgage insurance is an additional expense charged to a borrower that is often required when the borrower makes only a small investment (down payment) on their home at time of purchase.

Prizes and awards

The fair market value of a prize or award generally is included in gross income.

Property transfers

A property transfer occurs when money or the ownership title on a piece of property, such as a house or parcel of land, changes hands. The majority of property transfers occur on someone's death, where the will stipulates who will inherit the deceased's property.

Qualified business income (QBI)

The income attributed to individual taxpayers by a pass-through entity such as a sole proprietorship, partnership, or S corporation that excludes capital gains, most dividends, interest, and other nonbusiness income.

Qualified business income (QBI) deduction

A deduction in the amount of 20 percent of the qualified business income, subject to certain limitations such as the taxable income limit, the wage limitation, and the specified service business limitation. The limitations are computed before considering the QBI deduction.

Qualified business property

Tangible property subject to depreciation (i.e., not inventory or land) for which the depreciable period has not ended before the close of the taxable year, held by the business at year-end, and used at any point during the year in the production of QBI. Qualified business property is an element of the wage and capital limitation, which is a component of the wage limitation.

"Qualified" federal disasters

Disasters such as hurricanes and wildfires, which may be termed "qualified" by the U.S. government and eligible for federal relief.

Qualified higher education expenses

These include tuition, fees, books, supplies, and equipment required for the enrollment or attendance at an eligible educational institution.

Qualified improvement property (QIP)

Any improvement to a building's interior with the exception of improvements relating to enlarging the building, any elevator or escalator, or the internal structural framework of the building.

Qualified nonrecourse financing

Debt secured by real estate and loaned or guaranteed by a governmental agency or borrowed from any person who actively and regularly engages in the lending of money (bank, insurance company).

Qualified pension or profit-sharing plan

An employer-sponsored plan that meets certain requirements. If these requirements are met, none of the employer's contributions to the plan will be taxed to the employee until distributed to him or her. The employer will be allowed a deduction in the year the contributions are made.

Qualified plan

A retirement plan that meets requirements that allow tax benefits to be extended to it.

Qualified plan award

An employee achievement award in the form of tangible personal property; it has a maximum exclusion of $1,600.

Qualified recipient

An individual, group, or organization eligible for tax deductible charitable contributions, having met appropriate tax law criteria.

Qualified replacement property

Replacement property that must be "similar or related in service or use," as defined by tax law.

Qualified residence acquisition debt

Debt secured by the taxpayer's primary or secondary residence in acquiring, constructing, or substantially improving that residence.

Qualified tuition program

See *Section 529 tuition plan*.

Qualified trade or business

Any trade or business other than a specified service trade or business, or the trade or business of performing services as an employee.

Qualifying child

A dependent child who has met the tests set forth by the IRS: relationship, domicile, age, joint return, citizenship, and self-support.

Qualifying widow(er)

See *Surviving spouse*.

Realized gain or loss

The difference between the amount realized upon the sale or other disposition of property and the adjusted basis of such property.

Recognized gain or loss

The portion of realized gain or loss that is subject to income taxation. See *Realized gain or loss*.

Recovery period

The amount of time in which a business asset is depreciated and thereby creating a tax deduction, under the useful life requirements established by the IRS.

Related parties

IRS rules define related parties for disallowance purposes. Common related parties include defined family members; a corporation or individual who owns more than 50 percent of the corporation; two corporations that are members of the same controlled group; and trust, corporations, and certain charitable organizations.

Required minimum distributions (RMDs)

The minimum amount of money that must be withdrawn each year from a traditional IRA, SEP, or SIMPLE IRA by owners and qualified retirement plan participants of retirement age. The retiree must withdraw the RMD amount annually, starting in the year the retiree turns age 72 (70½years old before January 1, 2021). Roth IRAs do not require withdrawals until after the death of the owner.

Rollover

Transfer of pension funds from one plan or trustee to another. The transfer may be a direct transfer or a rollover distribution.

Roth 401(k)

A Roth 401(k) is an employer-sponsored investment savings account that is funded with after-tax dollars up to the plan's contribution limit.

Roth IRA

The Roth individual retirement account (IRA) allows nondeductible contributions. Although the contributions to a Roth IRA are not deductible, earnings accumulate tax-free, and qualified distributions are generally not included in income when received.

Roth IRA conversion

A transfer of retirement assets from a Traditional, SEP, or SIMPLE IRA into a Roth IRA, which creates a taxable event.

S corporation

A small business corporation whose shareholders have filed an election permitting the corporation to be treated in a manner similar to partnerships for income tax purposes. Of major significance are the facts that S corporations usually avoid the corporate income tax and that corporate losses can be claimed by the shareholders, limited to individual shareholder's adjusted basis.

Safe harbor 401(k)

A type of tax-deductible 401(k) plan that ensures all employees at a company have some set of minimum contributions made to their individual 401(k) plans, regardless of their title, compensation, or length of service. It is not subject to the complex annual nondiscrimination tests that apply to traditional 401(k) plans.

Sale or exchange

A sale generally requires the receipt of money or the relief from liabilities in exchange for property; an exchange is the transfer of ownership of one property for another property.

Saver's Credit

A tax credit designed to give low-to-moderate-income taxpayers a tax credit for part of a contribution to a qualified retirement plan.

Scholarships

Scholarships are generally taxable income to the recipient except for amounts received for tuition, fees, books, and course-required supplies and equipment.

Section 179

See *Election to expense (Section 179)*.

Section 197 intangibles

The category of intangibles that consists of those acquired by a taxpayer as part of the acquisition of a trade or business. They are amortized over a 15-year period, beginning with the month of acquisition.

Section 401(k) plan

A Section 401(k) plan is a qualified retirement plan which grants employee participants a deferral of income for employer contributions to the plan. The plan allows taxpayers to elect to contribute compensation or to have the employer make a contribution to the retirement plan. The plan may be structured as a salary reduction plan. There is a maximum annual dollar limitation, as well as a limitation based on the employee's compensation. Some employers match employee contributions up to a certain limit in order to encourage participation.

Section 529 tuition plan

Also known as a Qualified Tuition Program; allows taxpayers to buy in–kind tuition credits or certificates for qualified higher education expenses (a prepaid plan); or to contribute to an account established to meet qualified higher education expenses (a savings plan).

Section 1231 assets

Section 1231 assets include depreciable assets and real estate used in a trade or business, held for the long-term holding period. Under certain circumstances, the classification also includes timber, coal, domestic iron ore, livestock (held for draft, breeding, dairy, or sporting purposes), and unharvested crops. Gains may be treated as long-term capital gains while losses in some cases may be deducted as ordinary losses.

Section 1245 recapture

See *Depreciation recapture*.

Section 1250 recapture

See *Depreciation recapture*.

Self-employment income

Self-employment income is the taxpayer's net earnings from self-employment, which includes gross income from a taxpayer's trade or business, less trade or business deductions. Self-employment income also includes the taxpayer's share of income from a partnership trade or business.

Self-employment tax

Tax required to be paid by self-employed taxpayers, sole proprietors, and independent contractors with net earnings of $400 or more annually.

Simplified Employee Pension (SEP)

A retirement plan that any employer or self-employed individual can establish. SEPs are simple to establish and have flexible funding arrangements with contributions that are limited on an annual basis.

Separate property

Separate property is property, other than community property, acquired by a spouse before marriage or after marriage as a gift or inheritance.

Short-period taxable income

When taxpayers have a short year other than their first or last year of operations, they are required to annualize their taxable income to calculate the tax for the short period.

SIMPLE IRA

A form of qualified retirement plan for small businesses with 100 or fewer employees. Unlike a SEP, employers are required to make certain contributions.

Simplified Employee Pension (SEP) IRA

A form of qualified retirement plan for certain small businesses. See *SEP*.

Simplified method

A specific calculation used by individual taxpayers to calculate the taxable amount of a payment from an annuity after November 18, 1996.

Single filing status

A taxpayer who does not meet the definition of married, surviving spouse, or head of household status must file as single.

Social Security

The U.S. social insurance program consisting of retirement, disability, and survivor benefits.

Social Security number

A unique 9-digit number provided by the U.S. Social Security Administration to identify each person and track Social Security benefits. Most taxpayers use the Social Security number as their taxpayer identification number. See *Taxpayer identification number*.

Social Security tax

A component of FICA (see *Federal Insurance Contributions Act [FICA]*), Social Security taxes refer to Old Age, Survivors, and Disability Insurance (OASDI) and is applied to all wages, up to an annual limitation. See *OASDI*.

Specified service trade or business

Used in the context of qualified business income as being excluded from a qualified trade or business, it involves the performance of services where the principal asset of such trade or business is based on the reputation or skill of one or more of its employees, such as accounting, actuarial science, consulting, financial and brokerage services, health, law, performing arts, and professional athletes.

Standard deduction

Taxpayers can deduct the larger of the standard deduction or their itemized deductions in calculating taxable income. An extra standard deduction amount is allowed for elderly and blind taxpayers. The standard deduction amounts are set by the IRS and may change annually. See *"Catch up" contribution* and *Itemized deductions*.

Standard mileage method

Using a rate determined annually by the IRS, some taxpayers are entitled to calculate deductions for transportation costs.

Standard mileage rate

The rate announced annually by the IRS for use in calculating a standard mileage deduction.

Start-up costs

New business start-up costs include investigatory and preopening costs.

Statute of limitations

A time period within which an action may be taken by the IRS or a taxpayer on a tax return. In general, the statute of limitations for a tax return runs for 3 years from the date the tax return was filed or the return extended due date, whichever is later.

Stock bonus plan

Under tax law, a stock bonus plan is one of several qualified retirement plans. Employer contributions on behalf of an employee consisted of stock of the employer company.

Straight-line depreciation

The simplest method of depreciation, it results in an equal portion of cost being deducted in each period of an asset's life.

Surviving spouse

Also referred to as a qualifying widow(er), a tax filing status available to widows or widowers for two years after their spouse's death. To claim this status, the taxpayer must also have a dependent child who lives in the household for whom the taxpayer pays over half the cost of maintaining the household.

Tangible personal property

Property that can be moved or touched, and commonly includes items such as business equipment, furniture, and automobiles. This is contrasted with intangible personal property, which includes stocks, bonds, and intellectual property like copyrights and patents.

Tax

A tax is imposed by a government to raise revenue for general public purposes.

Tax credit

An amount of money that can be offset directly against a tax liability. Tax credits can be refundable (may exceed the tax liability) or nonrefundable (limited to the tax liability and any excess is lost).

Tax Cuts and Jobs Act (TCJA)

The TCJA was signed into law in 2017 representing the most dramatic change to the tax code since 1986. Significant changes include reforms to the itemized deductions and alternative minimum tax, an expanded standard deduction and child tax credit, and lower marginal tax rates across brackets. Some of the individual income tax changes are scheduled to expire after December 31, 2025.

Tax evasion

Failing to pay taxes, failing to file taxes, inaccurate information on taxes, and fraud are all considered part of tax evasion and noncompliance, which may cost the government $1 trillion annually.

Tax Exempt Organization Search

An online search tool of the IRS that provides information about the deductibility of a charitable contribution to a specific organization.

Tax home

Since travel expenses of a taxpayer are deductible only if the taxpayer is away from home, the deductibility of such expenses rests upon the definition of "tax home." The IRS position is that the "tax home" is the business location, post, or station of the taxpayer. If the taxpayer is temporarily reassigned to a new post for a period of one year or less, the taxpayer's home should be his or her personal residence and the travel expenses should be deductible.

Tax planning

The process of arranging one's financial affairs to maximize one's after-tax wealth.

Tax practitioner

Commercial tax preparers, enrolled agents, attorneys, and CPAs are all considered to be tax practitioners.

Tax return preparer

Any person who prepares a tax return for compensation.

Taxpayer Bill of Rights

Passed by Congress in 1988 and amended several times, this set of provisions requires that the IRS informs taxpayers of their rights when dealing with the IRS and it expands taxpayers' rights and remedies when involved in disputes with the IRS. The provisions of the Taxpayer Bill of Rights are summarized in IRS Publication 1.

Taxpayer identification number

A unique number of a taxpayer used by the IRS in the administration of tax laws. For individuals, it is generally a Social Security number, but can also be an Individual Taxpayer Identification Number (ITIN) which is issued by the IRS to individuals who are not eligible to receive a Social Security number. For employers, it is an IRS-issued number known as an Employer Identification Number (EIN). See *Social Security number.*

Trade or business expenses

Deductions for AGI which are attributable to a taxpayer's business or profession. The expenses must be ordinary and necessary to that business. See *Ordinary* and *Necessary*.

Traditional IRA

An individual retirement account (IRA) for taxpayers. The traditional IRA often permits a deduction for contributions and deferred taxation of earnings until withdrawals.

Transportation expenses

Transportation expenses for a taxpayer include only the costs of transportation (taxi fares, automobile expenses, etc.) in the course of employment where the taxpayer is not "away from home" in a travel status. Commuting expenses are not deductible.

Travel expenses

Travel expenses include restaurant meals (100 percent deductible in 2021 and 2022), lodging, and transportation expenses while away from home in the pursuit of a trade or business (including that as an employee).

Trustee-to-trustee transfer

When a trustee of a retirement plan transfers assets to the trustee of a different retirement plan, upon instruction from the taxpayer. There are no tax implications nor are there any restrictions on amounts or number of transfer occurrences in a given year.

Unearned income

For tax purposes, unearned income (e.g., rent) is taxable in the year of receipt. In certain cases involving advance payments for goods and services, income may be deferred.

U.S. savings bond

The U.S. government issues the following basic types of savings bonds to individuals: Series EE and Series I, which do not pay interest until maturity.

Unreported Income DIF (UIDIF)

One of two systems used by the IRS to select taxpayers for audit.

Vacation home

The Internal Revenue Code places restrictions upon taxpayers who rent their residence or vacation home for part of the tax year. The restrictions may result in the limitation of certain expenses related to the vacation home.

Viatical settlements

An early payout resulting from the sale of a life insurance policy often due to the insured being terminally or chronically ill. A viatical settlement is a way to extract value from the policy while the policy holder is still alive. See *Accelerated death benefits.*

Wage and capital limitation

A limitation on the qualified business income deduction of 25 percent of wages and 2.5 percent of qualified business property.

Wage and Investment (W&I) Division

A division of the IRS that helps taxpayers understand and comply with applicable tax laws and to protect the public interest by applying the tax law with integrity and fairness.

Wage bracket method

A method for determining tax withholding in which wage bracket tables are provided each year by the IRS for weekly, biweekly, semi-monthly, monthly, and daily payroll periods.

Wage limitation

A limitation on the qualified business income deduction of 50 percent of wages.

Withholding

The amount of tax deducted (withheld) by a payer and ultimately remitted to the tax authority as a tax payment on behalf of the payment recipient. For example, income taxes are often withheld from an employee's wages and then remitted on behalf of the employee as a tax payment to the IRS.

INDEX

D

G

H

I

J

K

L

T

W

Y